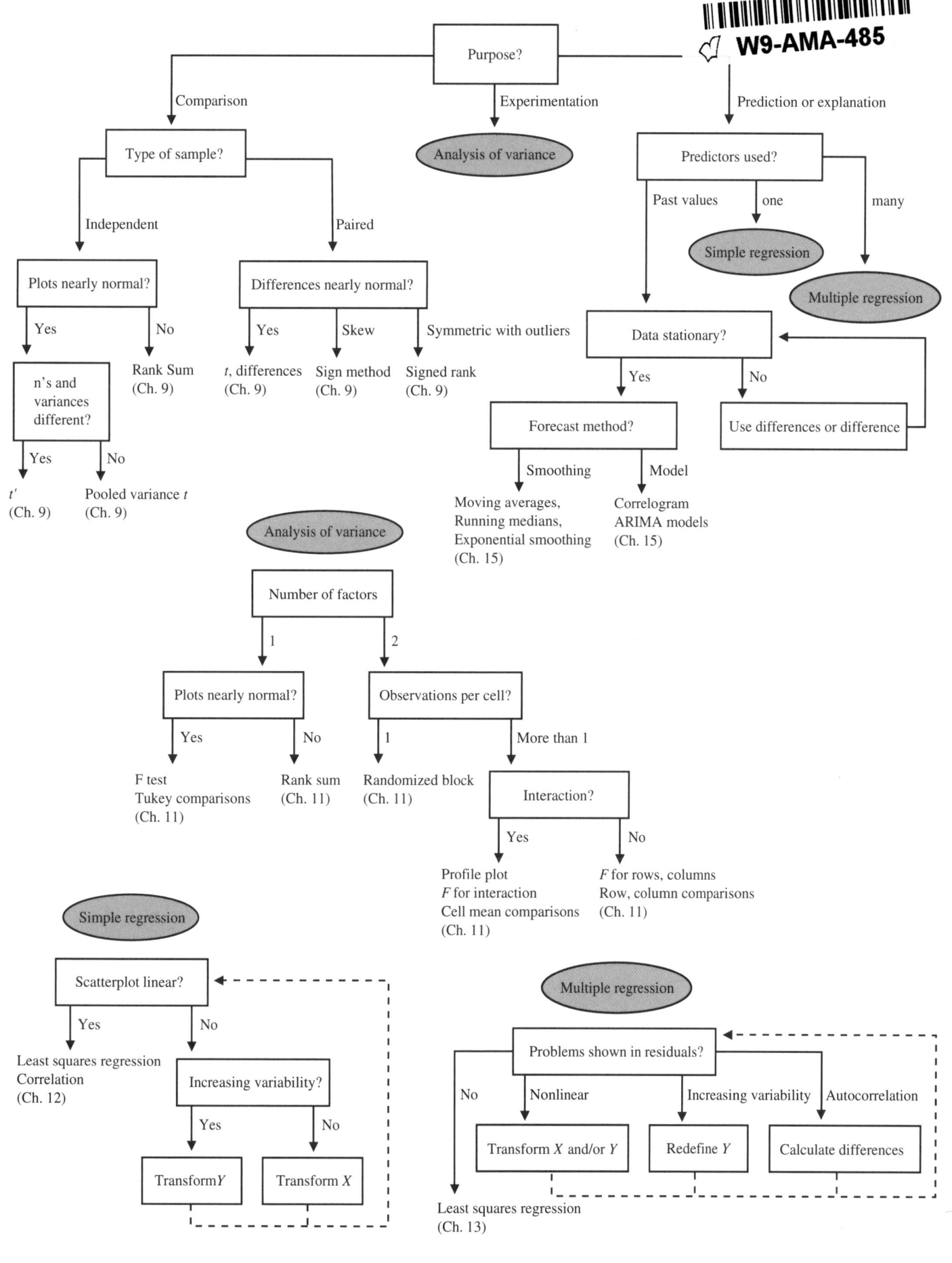

W9-AMA-485

STATISTICAL THINKING

FOR MANAGERS

Fourth Edition

STATISTICAL THINKING
FOR MANAGERS

Fourth Edition

David K. Hildebrand

University of Pennsylvania

R. Lyman Ott

Hoechst Marion Roussel

THOMSON

SOUTH-WESTERN

Australia · Brazil · Canada · Mexico · Singapore · Spain · United Kingdom · United States

THOMSON

SOUTH-WESTERN

Statistical Thinking for Managers, 4th Editon
David K. Hildebrand and R. Lyman Ott

VP/Editorial Director:
Jack W. Calhoun

Sponsoring Editor:
Curt Hinrichs

Assistant Editor:
Cynthia Mazow

Marketing:
Marcy Perman

Editorial Assistant:
Rita Jaramillo

Production Editor:
Tessa McGlasson

Manuscript Editor:
Carol Dondrea

Typesetting:
SuperScript

Printer:
Courier-Kendallville
Kendallville, IN

Interior Design:
Cloyce Wall

Cover Design:
Lisa Henry

Cover Illustration:
Pat Scott

Cover Printing:
Phoenix Color Corp.

Library of Congress Cataloging-in-Publication
Data

Hildebrand, David K., [date] –
  Statistical thinking for managers / David K.
 Hildebrand, R. Lyman Ott.—4th ed.
    p.   cm
    Includes bibliographical references and
    Index.
    ISBN 0-534-20406-6
    1. Industrial Management—Statistical
methods.   2. Industrial management—
Statistical methods—Data processing.   3.
Economics—Statisical methods.   4.
Statistics—Data processing.   I. Ott, Lyman.
II. Title.
HD30.215.H54 1998
519.5'024658—DC21

For more information about our products,
contact us at:

Thomson Learning Academic Resource
Center

1-800-423-0563

Thomson Higher Education
5191 Natorp Boulevard
Mason, OH 45040
USA

About the Authors

DAVID HILDEBRAND arrived at the University of Pennsylvania somewhat later than Ben Franklin. He has remained there since, teaching uncounted numbers of Wharton School and Penn students in all classifications from beginning undergraduate to Ph.D. student. He has served as department chair and faculty senate chair at Penn without causing noticeable damage, and has a long affiliation with the Making Statistics More Effective in Schools of Business conferences. He has not been shy about publishing his ideas. Besides the four editions of this text, he has written *Statistical Thinking for Behavioral Scientists* and *Basic Statistical Ideas for Managers* (Duxbury, 1996) *Prediction Analysis of Cross Classifications* (John Wiley) *Analysis of Ordinal Data* (Sage Publications), and numerous articles in professional journals. He also has been known to compose a limerick on occasion (and he's not too fussy about the occasions).

R. LYMAN OTT is Senior Vice President, Hoechst Marion Roussel, responsible for Business Process Improvement, Global Development Information Systems, and Biometrics and Data Management. Previously, Dr. Ott was Vice President of Systems and Quality Improvement, at Marion Merrell Dow. At Merrell Dow Research Institute he was responsible for biostatistics, computer services, clinical data processing, laboratory automation and scientific information services and an Adjunct Professor in the Division of Biostatistics at the University of Cincinnati. Prior to his career in the pharmaceutical industry, he was a faculty member in the Department of Statistics at the University of Florida, where he taught service courses and courses for statistics majors at both the undergraduate and graduate levels.

He has published many research articles in various statistical journals and several textbooks, including *An Introduction and Statistical Methods and Data Analysis*, Fourth Edition (Duxbury, 1993), *Basic Statistical Ideas for Managers* (Duxbury, 1996) with D. Hildebrand, *Understanding Statistics*, Sixth Edition (Duxbury 1994) with W. Mendenhall, and *Elementary Survey Sampling*, Fifth Edition (Duxbury, 1996) with R. Schaeffer and W. Mendenhall. He is a Fellow of the American Statistical Association and has served on the ASA Board of Directors. He holds a Ph.D. in statistics from the Virginia Polytechnic Institute and an undergraduate degree in mathematics and education from Bucknell University. In his spare time, he enjoys tennis and golf. He has served as the voice of reason and moderation for this revision.

To Pat, Marty, and Jeff
  Sally, Curtis, and Kathy
who all helped

Brief Contents

Contents

Preface

From the first attempt at a first draft of the first edition of this book, we have held to a basic premise: **Students should think, computers should calculate.** This edition continues our effort to show students the benefits of thinking carefully with and about data. We believe our approach is especially meaningful today. A manager can easily be overwhelmed by the masses of data that modern business and computer technology accumulate about customers, products, and markets. To use this data to understand customers and markets and to improve products and services, a manager must become literate in the practice of data analysis.

Our title wasn't chosen casually. Effective use of data requires a manager to consider how to obtain data, what forms of analysis are most relevant, what assumptions are being made (and how to check those assumptions), and what the results mean and don't mean. Questions of how to calculate particular results, which never should have been a central issue, can now be delegated to any of hundreds of computer programs.

Audience and Prerequisites

This book is intended for a one or two-term introduction to business and economic statistics for undergraduates and MBAs. The book assumes the student will have access to the computer and a statistical package or spreadsheets. We do not emphasize one package over another and include computer output from a variety of sources. As stated earlier, the emphasis is on problem solving, not calculation. However, to effectively understand statistical concepts, one must learn how these methods work and we employ the computer and mathematical means to do so. With the exception of the calculus used in the Continuous Probability Distributions sections in Chapter 4, the book assumes only knowledge of algebra.

Changes to the Fourth Edition

Much has changed in the use of statistics and technology in business since the last edition was published and we've tried to reflect these changes in the many revisions we've made. We have also made revisions to the text to enhance its value in teaching students about statistical thinking.

- A new introductory chapter, "Data," considers issues of when and how to recognize the need for data. In addition, the chapter offers some suggestions for evaluating statistical studies done by others.

- Executive Summaries begin each chapter, giving a quick overview of the contents of the chapter.

- "Summing Up" sections end each chapter, giving some suggestions for ways to use the ideas in the chapter and to avoid some common errors and confusions.

- The large majority of exercises are accompanied by output from one or another statistical packages. Others have results from Microsoft Excel spreadsheets, from the Maple symbolic processing program, or (for simulation results) from the Resampling Statistics program.

- Hundreds of new exercises are included; many others have been updated and revised.

- Additional less-structured exercises, akin to guided case studies, have been included at the end of each chapter.

- Data sets are available on the accompanying disk in several formats including Excel, JMP IN, Minitab, and ASCII. In addition, data sets may be downloaded in these and other formats from the publisher's Data Library web site at www.duxbury.com.

- Some material has been deleted in the interest of weight loss. Previously separate chapters on point estimation and interval estimation have been combined. The decision theory chapter has been omitted, because this topic typically has moved to a management science course.

- Discussion of some relatively recent graphical methods such as LOWESS and spline scatterplot matrices has been added.

- Just for fun, we've added limericks at the end of each chapter. Students have enjoyed these when they've seen them.

Other features of the third edition have been retained.

- A case concludes each chapter. The cases ask the student to deal with a relatively unstructured situation, and to explain the statistical reasoning in non-technical language.

- Review exercises follow every two or three chapters. These exercises follow no particular order, so that students can't rely on the artificial cue of where the exercise is placed.

- Regression and correlation methods have three full chapters. This is an important topic for every management student.

- There is an emphasis on quality control and improvement throughout the book.

Organization and Coverage

Much of the organization has been retained from the third edition. We have expanded, merged, or deleted material as needed to reflect what we think should be taught in an introductory business statistics course. All concepts are developed with the computer allowing instructors to cover more (and more important) material in the course.

While statistics requires some sequential development of topics, we tried to make the last half of the text modular; allowing for maximum ßexibility for courses that need to pick and choose selected topics. We hope that many one-term courses welcome this feature. Chapter 17, Data Management and Report Preparation, should be useful to students who are required to complete a project in the course.

Supplements

To accommodate the many teaching and learning activities that exist in the modern business statistics course, a complete array of useful ancillary material is available to faculty and students. Some of the following items will be useful to faculty while others were speciÞcally developed for students and are available at a discount when packaged with the text. For example, for an instructor using Excel in the course and wanting students to have a guide book that teaches them how to analyze data with Excel, we suggest the Berk & Carey or the Middleton books.

- **Instructors Resource Manual** contains complete worked-out solutions to every exercise and case study.

- **Student Solutions Manual** contains complete, worked-out solutions to selected exercises.

- **Powerpoint slides** accompany the Instructors Resource Manual and contain lecture outlines, key defenitions, and points of interest.

- **Data Disk** contains data for appropriate exercises in Excel, Minitab, JMP IN and ASCII formats and accompanies every new copy of the text.

- **World Wide Web** site may be accessed through www.swlearning.com under the *Online Book Companions* heading. The web page contains additional information about the book and updates on technology.

- **JMP IN 3.2** (for Windows or Macintosh), by SAS Institute, is state-of-the-art statistical software for data visualization and analysis. Simply the most powerful software available to students, its dynamically linked graphics allow students to discover relationships in data in ways never before possible. Its easy-to-use menus and limitless data-handling capability make the software useful throughout a student's academic career.

- **JMP IN Companion**, by Al Best, provides step-by-step instructions keyed to examples in the text.

- **Data Analysis with Microsoft Excel**, by Berk & Carey, provides step-by-step instructions and software add-ins for Excel that address Excel's statistical limitations. The book is available at a discount when packaged with the text.

- **Data Analysis Using Microsoft Excel**, by Michael Middleton, contains step-by-step instructions on using Excel's built-in capabilities throughout the course. This book is available at a discount when purchased with the text.

- **StatConcepts: A Visual Tour of Statistical Ideas**, by Joe Newton and Jane Harvill, is an interactive, visual introduction to statistical concepts. Twenty-eight simulations with accompanying labs provide students with immediate access to the dynamic visual nature of statistical concepts.

Acknowledgments

Much of the evolution of this book through its editions has been influenced by the annual Making Statistics More Effective in Schools of Business conferences. Although we haven't adopted every idea presented at these meetings, the MSMESB faithful will certainly recognize the source of many of the ideas and examples in the text. We are indebted to the many hard-working organizers of these conferences.

We thank Kathy Szabat of La Salle University for many of the new real-data exercises. Drafts of this edition have benefited from some careful reviews. In particular, we thank Jerry May of the University of Pittsburgh for an extraordinarily thoughtful, thorough, and constructive commentary. In addition, we have received helpful comments from Bruce K. Cooil, Vanderbilt University; Thomas E. Love, Case Western Reserve University; Michael Parzen, University of Chicago; Lawrence A. Sherr, University of Kansas; Robert A. Stine, University of Pennsylvania; Nancy Weida, Bucknell University; and Reginald Worthley, University of Hawaii. Though we have not been able to adopt every suggestion these reviewers have made, their work has certainly improved the book. Thanks.

David Hildebrand
R. Lyman Ott

Data

1

"In God we trust. All others bring data."

This slogan, a takeoff on the familiar sentence on U.S. currency, is a watchword in many organizations. Why?

Well-managed organizations use data intelligently; poorly managed ones don't. Virtually every manager—corporate president, cabinet member, hospital director, junior assistant to the associate deputy vice comptroller—has the need and opportunity to deal with data. The need may be obvious, as it is to loan officers who check the performance of thousands of consumer loans or to hospital managers who track the daily occupancy of beds and operating rooms. The opportunity may be less obvious (and therefore even more valuable) to hotel managers, for example, who might not realize they could experiment with advance check-in to reduce lines at the registration desk, or to owners of a chain of sound equipment stores, who might not think to combine sales and inventory data to see that the rush to meet quarterly sales quotas is causing avoidable quarterly inventory problems. Statistical thinking is important for every manager in every organization, both in dealing with day-to-day operations and in finding opportunities for improvement.

This is a book about making sense of data. To begin it, we need to consider what we mean by data, where and how data should be collected, what to do with the collected data, and how to assess other people's data. That's the agenda for this chapter in particular, and really for the whole book. ■

1.1   What Do We Mean by "Data"?

Statistical thinking deals with *numerical* data. Certainly there are other kinds of data. Anecdotal data, for example—specific results that happen in particular situations—can also be useful in pointing out problems or a need for change. But casual and anecdotal information is not systematic and may well emphasize extremes or odd cases. Thinking about numerical data usually provides a more complete picture.

Numbers by themselves don't constitute data. There's a great line from an old movie, along the lines of: "Today's baseball scores are 7 to 2, 6 to 3, and 8 to 1." We need more than numbers to have data. We need to know what is being measured or counted. If a test of the acidity of various brands of orange juice yields an average of 5.7, we need to know the scale. Is it chemical pH, where 7 is neutral and where the lower the score, the more intense the acidity? Is it a concentration measure? Or is it a rating by veteran orange juice drinkers? To have data, we must have a description of the variable that's being measured or counted, together with the numerical results of the measurement or count.

A full description of data requires answers to two questions: How are the quantities defined, and how are the measured entities chosen? Some variables, such as acidity, have well-defined measurement scales, such as pH. Other variables are not so clearly defined.

As any accountant can tell you, for example, the yearly net profit of a corporation can be measured in several ways. How is inventory valued? Are special one-time costs taken into account? Is the income from subsidiaries included? That's why there are notes to financial statements. As another example, customer satisfaction with repair work done under warranty by a car dealer might be measured by customer answers to a questionnaire, percentage of second attempts at repair, or number of complaints received by the manufacturer.

operational definition

Understanding data well requires knowledge of the **operational definition** of the variables. An operational definition specifies just how a variable is measured or counted. For example, the weekly hours worked by clerical staff is likely to be measured by the hours during which employees are expected to be present at the office, possibly excepting a lunch break. Note that this definition does not directly measure the time during which employees are actually performing tasks, because it includes whatever time is spent in breaks, tending to personal business, and so on. The daily number of customers in a supermarket is likely to be measured by the number of transactions made at checkout stands; this definition excludes those who enter the store but make no purchases and counts as one person those who shop—and pay—together. Understanding the operational definition of a variable can help you understand the uses and limitations of the data.

Understanding data well also requires information about the entities that were actually measured. For example, a magazine tests automobiles. Were those tested obtained from the manufacturers especially for that purpose (and therefore likely to be the best the manufacturer can provide) or were they purchased randomly from dealers? Were the participants in a taste test of two brands of cola selected from people who were in the act of purchasing brand A, or were they chosen on a more neutral basis? Asking how the individual measurements were obtained can sometimes uncover "loaded" data, designed for propaganda, not information.

There is a danger of becoming too cynical. If you think long enough, you can almost always come up with objections, however farfetched, to almost any data-gathering method. Data that have been collected in obviously biased ways can be, and should be, discounted; that doesn't mean that data collected honestly but imperfectly should be ignored.

In summary, data are numerical results of measurements on specified variables. To begin to understand the data, learn the operational definitions of how the measurements or counts were made and how the entities in the data-gathering process were selected.

1.2 Data About What?

In order to use data, you first have to realize that you need them. How can a manager decide what data may be important?

Most business and management courses deal with data needs specific to that field. Accounting classes deal with several kinds of data: financial (how much money was taken in and spent in this month, for example), physical (how much product is for sale on the shelves, for example), and operating (how many worker hours were expended on this product this month, for example). Marketing courses work with the kinds of data that are needed to see if a business is providing desired products or services to customers, making customers aware of the products and services, and introducing new or better products and services. Finance courses deal with data on yields and interest rates and risks. Much of business training and education has to do with gathering and using various kinds of data.

There are methods to help you think systematically about what data may be needed. A useful way to think about an organization is as a set of **processes**—systematic, repetitive actions whose purpose is to create something of value. These processes link to one another, as well as to the external customers and environment of the organization. For example, think about a college or university. Every college routinely carries out many different processes. Scheduling classes, securing instructors, enrolling students, providing textbooks, securing payments, and paying creditors are all repeated actions taken by someone at that college. Each of these actions requires a systematic process to make sure it's done—preferably done well. The processes must be connected. The student-enrollment process at our college had better obtain information from the course scheduling process, or else students will be enrolled for nonexistent courses or courses that meet at unpredictable times. It would be better if there were a link from the enrollment process to the scheduling process, so additional sections could be scheduled for courses with high demand, and courses with low demand could be reduced.

Thinking in terms of processes and the links among processes is one good way to discover what data will be useful. For a specific process, good questions are: "Where in the process are decisions made?" and "What parts of the problem are most frustrating to the people in the process?" A flowchart helps to pinpoint answers to these questions. In ordering textbooks, for example, the key decisions are what text to use and how many copies to order. The decision about which book to use is made by the instructor or the department teaching the course, and is really basic input to the process. For a bookstore, the decision about the number of copies to order requires data. In the past, how many students have bought texts for this course through this bookstore? The answer will not be the same as enrollment in the course because students in the course may buy the book through other stores or (as used copies) from previous students. Typical frustrations for a bookstore manager are either having large numbers of copies unsold or having to reorder and deal with unhappy customers until the new shipment arrives. By collecting data comparing past enrollments and past number of purchases, the bookstore's manager might well improve forecasts about demand. Or, a manager might just find a professor's handwriting illegible. (Unlikely, of course, but possible.) In this case, a little data about how often illegibility is a problem might lead to redesigning the order form with individual letter boxes, thus encouraging printing rather than handwriting.

A flowchart can also help to identify steps in the process that cause **rework**, undoing and redoing actions taken previously, and **scrap**, complete abandonment of a partly completed task. For example, if the bookstore orders a text but is told that a new edition is available, the textbook manager must rework the order, going back to the department and finding out which edition is desired. If the book is out of print and unavailable, the order must be scrapped and the process begun all over again. Rework and scrap are often the causes of major costs. Obtaining data on where these costs occur may pinpoint where improvements in the process could be made most readily.

One of the important ideas of modern quality-improvement methods is that the people who actually operate the processes of an organization should have a large say in how to improve those processes. The person in charge of actually obtaining textbooks for a bookstore is likely to know a great deal more about how that process works than is the Executive Vice President of Everything and Director of University Business Services. Furthermore, most processes involve several people at different points. Therefore, a good way to find out where problems are occurring and where data are needed is to form teams that include people who work "in the trenches." Such teams are often a great help in getting started on data collection and on making improvements to processes in an organization.

processes

rework
scrap

How Do You Gather Data?

O nce a manager or a team decides to gather data, how should it be done? What are good and bad ways to obtain data? There are too many data-gathering situations to provide a simple recipe, but we can provide some useful general ideas.

Good data gathering takes planning. A little time spent considering what to measure (or count) and how to do it will pay off.

As was indicated in the first section of this chapter, it's important to have a clear operational definition of what's being measured. Even such a simple variable as the number of items purchased by a customer at a supermarket needs to be defined. If the customer buys a pack of six cola bottles, is that one item or six? If the customer buys three boxes of the same cereal, is that one item or three? If the customer takes some items from a cart and pays for them and then takes the remaining items and pays for them separately, is that one purchase or two? In this example, it is likely that the data will be obtained from scanner records and will be defined the way the scanner program is written. It's worth taking a moment to be clear on exactly how the measurement is defined.

Many studies suffer from vague definitions. Consider the familiar opinion survey that asks whether you strongly favor, favor, oppose, or strongly oppose something, or are neutral. Many such surveys give no information about what "strongly" means. Does it mean that you have a clear, immediate opinion? Does it mean that this matter is very important to you and you will be seriously affected by the result? Because respondents will differ in their interpretation, there is some vagueness in the response categories. Even a simple question such as "How many doors are there in your apartment?" needs an operational definition. What is a door? One that leads outside? One between rooms? The refrigerator door? The little door in the coffee maker? Unless the definition is clear, the results can be badly contaminated.

Once an operational definition of the variables to be measured is agreed upon, the next issue is when and where to measure these variables. How the data are measured is another critical part of an operational definition. Unless we think about it, we can easily measure data in biased, systematically distorting ways. Certainly, we shouldn't measure the waiting times at airport check-in stations by waiting until there are at least 100 people in line, then measuring the time for the next person in line. When comparing two methods for evaluating new employees, we should not have the people who proposed the methods also evaluate the results; they're committed to a method. Part of the problem in getting good data is deciding how and when to make the measurements. Think about whether the data collection method will distort what you're trying to find out.

What Should You Do with the Data?

G athering good data is hard work. Once data are gathered, they should be treated with respect and analyzed with care. Most of this book deals with methods for analyzing data. We don't mean to imply that the data-gathering process isn't important—far from it. But the technical part of statistics deals with analyzing data that have already been gathered.

The most basic idea of statistical reasoning is that almost all data are a sample from a much larger underlying population or process. No sample is exactly, perfectly representative. We must always allow for error, if only from randomness. Newspapers reporting on political polls are careful to note an allowance for error. Much of this book indicates what those allowances for error should be, in various situations. One of the questions you, as a consumer of statistical analysis, should routinely ask is what is the appropriate allowance for error. Instinctively, you already have some idea of what's important in allowing for error; in particular, you know that the allowance for error in a small sample is more than the allowance in a big one. Any sample is imperfectly representative of the underlying reality; small samples are more imperfect than big ones.

To go beyond these obvious ideas, we need some technical machinery. First, any summary information based on sample data is subject to random variation from sample to sample. The language and technical basis of random variation is probability theory. We will introduce basic probability ideas (though not the deepest theory) in Chapters 3 through 6.

Given the language and concepts of probability, we can then introduce the basic question of statistical inference: What can one say from a limited sample about the underlying population or process? That's the core question for Chapters 7 and 8.

Once we have the basic principles, we can talk about specific methods for specific questions. There are many statistical methods—just look at the manual for any statistical computer package. We can't explain all the methods, but we can explain some of the most important ones. That's what we plan to do for the rest of the book.

What should you do with the data? Understand that they represent only a sample, summarize them in ways that help illuminate the underlying management question, and allow for a sensible amount of random error and systematic bias. Do that, and you won't be fooled very often. All the technical ideas that follow in this book really elaborate on this basic theme.

1.5 How Can You Evaluate Other People's Data?

Most managers, especially as they progress to senior positions, spend less time analyzing data themselves and more time evaluating others' analyses. Therefore, it's important to think about assessing statistical analyses. There are some key questions to ask.

First, how were the entities selected to be in the sample? Think about possible biases. Are there evident, clear distortions in the way the data were gathered? Particularly when sampling people, it's almost impossible to have a perfectly unbiased sample. Are the biases—distortions—minor or serious?

Second, exactly what is being measured? A statement that the study measures "customer satisfaction" isn't very meaningful. A statement that the study measures responses to the question "Will you recommend this product/service to your friends and relatives?" is much better defined, and more helpful. An experiment that is said to measure "product quality" is very vague; an experiment that is said to measure "variation in fat content of individual potato chips" is much better defined. It's worth a manager's time to understand the actual, operational definition of what's being measured.

Third, what does the conclusion mean, and what does it not mean? We will spend a lot of time and effort talking about the concept of statistical significance, beginning in Chapter 8. To say that a result is statistically significant sounds like it means "this is important." As we will see, that's not what it really means. In Chapter 7, we will encounter statements such as "A 95% confidence interval for the true mean answer ranges from 3.9 to 4.6." It turns out that that does not mean that 95% of the individuals in the sample gave answers in that range; it means that we are 95% sure that the average value in the whole population falls in that range. How widely the individual responses vary is a completely different issue. One of the most important things that a manager-to-be should learn from a statistics book like this one is what the technical language really means.

Fourth, are the assumptions underlying the analysis reasonable? We will consistently look at assumptions as we consider various statistical methods. We will also consider "diagnostics"—methods for checking the reasonableness of these assumptions. A good statistical analysis should be backed up by consideration of the assumptions and diagnostics. If the person presenting the analysis hasn't checked the assumptions, that's a bad sign; the analysis may well be casual or thoughtless. Some assumptions are more important than others; as we consider various statistical methods, we will try to indicate which assumptions are most crucial and which less so.

We can't guarantee that obtaining answers to these four questions will always protect a manager from being fooled by a bad statistical analysis, but we can say that getting answers to these questions will go a long way toward giving the manager a good idea of the value (or lack thereof) of such an analysis.

1.6 The Role of the Computer

Making sense of data has become a great deal easier with the advent of modern computers. Computer programs have been written to do even the most tedious calculations described in this book. Some of the methods require so much calculation that they would be utterly impossible without a computer. Perhaps even more important, computers can plot the data easily and clearly. Therefore, managers can explore data rather than rely on cut-and-dried formulas. The results can be communicated effectively and clearly using plots and graphics. In addition, any statistical method involves assumptions; with a decent computer program, it's possible to check the reasonableness of these assumptions. Computers both reduce the tedium of data analysis and make better analyses possible.

The mere fact that data analysis has been done by computer, however, doesn't guarantee that it's any good. The data may be bad, in that the variables aren't really relevant, the data collection is biased, or the assumptions are grossly violated. The choice of the data analysis method may have been a bad one. The results may be correctly calculated but wrongly interpreted. A human being must still decide what data to use, choose the method of analysis, check the assumptions, and interpret the results reasonably. Until artificial intelligence improves greatly, human intelligence will still be required.

Literally hundreds of computer software packages are available to analyze data. Some, such as Minitab, SAS, SPSS, and BMDP, were originally developed for mainframe computers and later adapted for personal computers. Others, such as StatGraphics (for IBM compatibles), DataDesk (for Apple Macintosh), Systat, and JMP (for either platform), were originally developed for personal computers. It isn't necessary to know computer programming to use these packages. Most of them can be learned fairly readily, though there are always frustrations from minor errors and misinterpretations. These packages are so useful, both in doing computations and in plotting data, that the investment in learning to use one is most amply repaid.

One needn't learn everything about a package to use it effectively. To begin, you need only learn the steps necessary to obtain the particular results you need. Typically, you'll need to enter the data, assign labels so the output is readable, select those variables and observations you want to use in a particular analysis, and call the correct part of the program to carry out the desired step. Depending on the program, the results may be printed or displayed on a monitor.

We will use output from several widely available packages throughout this book. Most of the methods we describe can be carried out with any of these packages. There are so many packages, and they change so quickly, that trying to describe how to use them all is futile. Instead, we'll concentrate on interpreting the output. *Don't try to interpret every number in the outputs.* The designers of most packages, particularly the older, mainframe-based packages, had to include in the output almost everything that a user could conceivably want to know. As a result, in any particular situation, some of the output is likely to be irrelevant. *Look for the specific results you need; don't worry about the rest.* As you learn more about statistical methods, you'll understand more of the output. In the meantime, select only the specific output you need.

1.7

Summary

T his chapter sets the agenda for the book. The essential steps in making sense of data are gathering the data, summarizing the data, using pictures and summary numbers, and making inferences and predictions from the limited available data to other data or to the future. The logical structure of the book involves two separate bases—methods for summarizing data (Chapter 2) and concepts of probability (Chapters 3 through 6). These bases are combined to produce the basic theoretical structure of statistical inference (Chapters 7 and 8). Once the basic theory is in place, we will apply it (Chapters 9 through 16) using many methods in many specific situations.

Have pity on young Joe McCooter,
Who hired an expensive stat tutor.
His money he burned,
And all that he learned
Was how to screw up by computer.

2

Summarizing Data About One Variable

This chapter describes some of the important ideas for summarizing data. The key ideas are these:

1   Distinguish between qualitative variables, where numbers are merely codes, and quantitative variables, where numbers are actual measurements.

2   Plotting data is the most important step in understanding basic patterns. There are several convenient plots. Histograms indicate the general shape of the data distribution. Using a smoother can sometimes clarify a histogram by smoothing off the arbitrary corners. Stem-and-leaf diagrams are a convenient way to get histogram-like plots.

3   In these plots, look for the average value, the amount of variability, any skewness, any outliers, and any possible multiple peaks. Boxplots are particularly convenient to check for outliers.

4   The most widely used measures of the typical, average value of a variable are: the mode, the most common value, for qualitative variables; the median, the middle value, for quantitative and ordinal variables; and the mean, for quantitative variables. Skewness can pull the mean away from the median, in the direction of the long tail of the data.

5   The most common measure of variability is the standard deviation. It is the square root of the average squared deviation from the mean. Because it is based on squared deviations, it can be seriously distorted by skewness or outliers. Interpret the numerical value of the standard deviation using the Empirical Rule.

6   The Empirical Rule assumes that a bell-shaped normal curve is a good approximation. For many, but not all, distributions, a normal curve is a reasonable approximation. To check this assumption, a normal probability plot is useful; normally distributed data appear as a straight line in this plot.

7   For data taken over time, a sequence plot of the data against time will reveal trends or cycles in the data. An especially important plot is a control chart. An x-bar chart plots means for each time period, and can show any drift in the average value. R charts of the ranges or S charts of standard deviations can show any problem of increasing variability.

8   Control charts are a key tool for quality management. They can reveal when a process goes out of statistical control. When a process is in control—statistically stable—a manager can consider special causes of large variability and common causes of normal variability. In most cases, improving quality implies reducing variability.

9   A process is statistically capable if it produces items that meet specifications. A process can be in statistical control, yet not capable. This will happen if the average value is wrong or if variation is too large.

An unorganized mass of numbers is virtually useless in understanding anything. The first task in making sense of a data set is to summarize it. In this chapter we focus on three aspects of the data-summarization problem: finding and displaying the frequencies of various data values, calculating a typical value, and indicating the degree of variability around that typical value.

Summarizing data is one important part of the fundamental management problem of controlling and improving quality. Many of the ideas in this chapter are central to modern quality methods. The computations aren't hard, and a computer can do them; the major issue is understanding what the results mean.

Most statistical problems encountered in practice involve several key variables. But an important first step in making sense of such data is to summarize the variables one by one; methods for doing so are described in this chapter. ∎

2.1

The Distribution of Values of a Variable

The single best summary of a set of data is a picture. Not only does a plot of the data help the manager who's analyzing the results, it also helps in communicating the results to others. This section explains some standard, useful methods for plotting data on a single variable.

Many plots are based on simple counts, called *frequencies*, of how many times each possible data value occurs in a set of data. Either by hand or by computer, start by finding the frequencies with which all the various values occur and displaying them in a **frequency table**. Such a table specifies the **distribution** of the data. A simple variation displays the **relative frequency** of each value, which is the frequency of that value divided by the total number of measurements.

frequency table
distribution
relative frequency

E X A M P L E 2 . 1

A small printing firm has a total of 20 salespeople working in four offices. The downtown office is numbered 1, the western suburban office is 2, the northern office is 3, and the southern suburban office is 4. The firm's records show that the respective offices of the salespeople (when the names were listed in alphabetical order) are

$$1 \quad 4 \quad 1 \quad 3 \quad 3 \quad 2 \quad 1 \quad 1 \quad 1 \quad 3 \quad 4 \quad 4 \quad 2 \quad 2 \quad 1 \quad 1 \quad 2 \quad 4 \quad 4 \quad 1$$

Summarize the data by displaying the frequencies associated with the values 1, 2, 3, and 4 in a frequency table. Calculate the relative frequencies as well.

Solution

The easiest way to obtain the frequencies is to list the values and count the frequencies. Then the frequency table is as follows:

Value (office number):	1	2	3	4
Frequency (number of salespeople):	8	4	3	5
Relative frequency:	$\frac{8}{20} = .40$	.20	.15	.25 ∎

qualitative

bar chart

Office number in Example 2.1 is a **qualitative** variable—a variable that merely defines categories, with no true numerical meaning. We could just as well have listed the names of the offices rather than the code numbers. A very simple, useful plot of qualitative, categorical data is a **bar chart**. Bar charts use rectangles to portray the data. The base of each rectangle indicates a value or a group (class) of values. The height of each rectangle represents the frequency or the relative frequency of each value or class. To create a bar chart, label the horizontal axis with values or categories of the variable, label the vertical axis with frequencies, and construct separate rectangles for each value, with height corresponding to the frequency or relative frequency of that value. Figure 2.1 shows a bar chart (without spaces between rectangles) of the data from Example 2.1.

Sometimes the axes are reversed, with values along the vertical axis and frequencies along the horizontal axis. With a bit of practice, it's easy enough to read either form.

A bar chart is an easy way to see whether the data are spread out more or less evenly among the possibilities, or whether the data are concentrated at one or a few values.

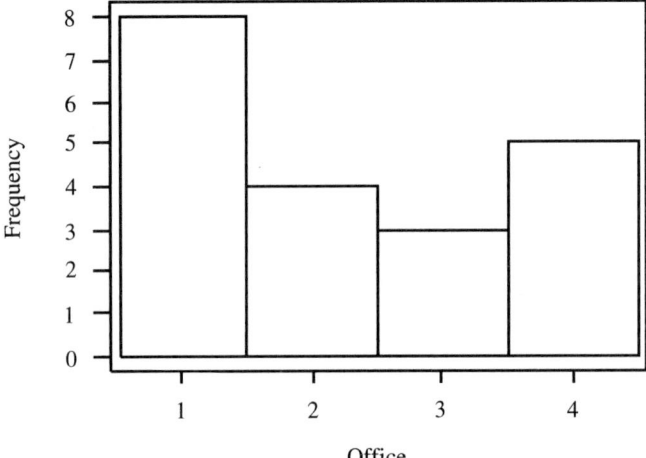

Pareto chart

An important use of bar charts in statistical quality control is the **Pareto** (pronounced "pah-RAY-toe") **chart**. In such a chart, alternative reasons for inadequate quality are specified, the number of occurrences are counted, and the frequencies are displayed. Usually, the reasons are displayed in order of frequency from highest to lowest. A Pareto chart is an effective way to highlight quality problems. For example, a mail-order firm analyzing reasons for returns of men's sport coats might find that, among the 54 returned coats in the most recent month, 4 returns were for poor fit, 22 for dislike of color, 30 for dislike of fabric, 1 for poorly finished sleeves, 2 for improper installation of buttons, and 1 for poor attachment of the lining. Note that there are 60 reasons for 54 returned coats, implying that some coats were returned for multiple reasons; because we're more interested in quality issues than in accounting, we'll count each reason separately. A Pareto chart for these returns is shown in Figure 2.2. That figure illustrates the point that we should look for the relevant parts of computer output and ignore what is not needed. The line at the top of the plot (which happens to be based on the cumulative total frequency) is not important for our purposes, so we ignore it. The chart makes it clear that color and fabric are major quality concerns *and* that finish (aspects of sewing the sport coats) is *not* such a major concern until the color and fabric problems are resolved.

quantitative

grouped data

Bar charts are used for qualitative (categorical) variables, where any numbers are arbitrary codes. Typically, such variables have only a few possible values. **Quantitative** variables, however, are actual numerical measurements and typically have many possible values. With a variable that has many possible values, it's usually better to combine values into groups. The resulting data are referred to as **grouped data**. Suppose you had a list of the amounts paid by 850 customers at a supermarket's checkout counters in one day. If you listed the amounts to the penny and counted frequencies, you would probably list over 800 values with a frequency of 1 and a few values with frequencies of 2 or 3. That wouldn't be a very useful summary! In such a case you might want to round off the amounts to the nearest dollar or the nearest 5 dollars. This rounding-off process creates groups of similar checkout amounts.

classes

The choice of groups (often called **classes**) for summarizing data from a single variable is somewhat arbitrary, but the selection of classes should conform to the requirement that each measurement falls into one and only one class. In addition, it is desirable to choose the classes so that (1) no gaps appear between the classes and (2) the classes have a common width. Typically, we want somewhere between 5 and 20 classes—relatively fewer

FIGURE 2.2 **Pareto Chart of Reasons for Returning Sport Coats**

Pareto Chart for: Reason

Reason for Return

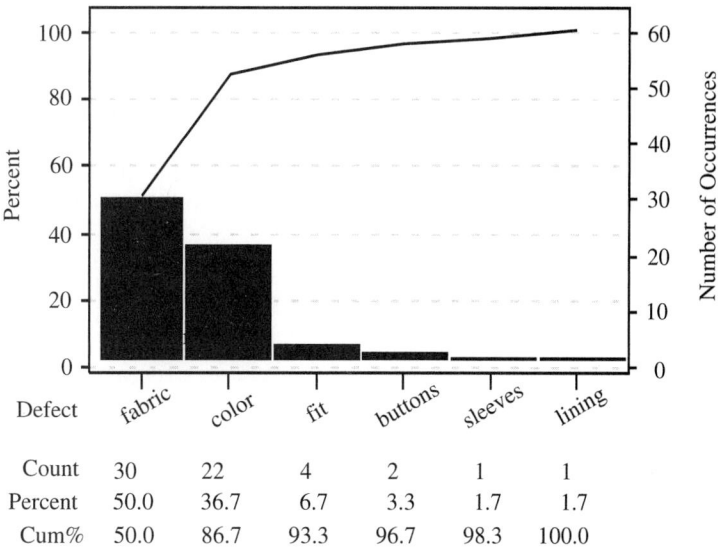

Defect	fabric	color	fit	buttons	sleeves	lining
Count	30	22	4	2	1	1
Percent	50.0	36.7	6.7	3.3	1.7	1.7
Cum%	50.0	86.7	93.3	96.7	98.3	100.0

for small data sets, relatively more for large ones. The midpoints of the classes should be convenient numbers. Most statistical computer programs do this reasonably well, so we needn't worry about specific rules for grouping.

EXAMPLE 2.2

Suppose that the 20 salespeople in Example 2.1 had the following commission incomes (excluding salaries) in a certain month:

$850	$1265	$895	$575	$2410	$470	$660	$1820	$1510	$1100
$620	$425	$751	$965	$840	$1505	$1375	$695	$1125	$1475

Use these data to construct a frequency table with suitable class intervals.

Solution

With only 20 observations, we want a small number of classes, such as 5. The incomes range from $425 to $2410; one convenient choice of classes takes incomes to the nearest $500. The results of one such grouping of the data are displayed here in a frequency table. We took the class midpoints at $500, $1000, and so on.

Class:	$250 to $749	$750 to $1249	$1250 to $1749	$1750 to $2249	$2250 to $2749
Frequency:	6	7	5	1	1
Relative frequency:	.30	.35	.25	.05	.05

Note that each measurement (recorded in dollars) falls into exactly one class; that's why we stated the first interval (for example) as $250 to $749 rather than as $250 to $750.

There are no gaps between the intervals, and the classes have a common interval width of 500. ∎

histograms

Histograms are constructed in the same way as bar charts. A minor difference is that the rectangles in a bar chart are usually separated by space, whereas the rectangles in a histogram are directly adjacent to each other. A histogram is often used with grouped data. Figure 2.3 shows a histogram of commission income data, grouped as in Example 2.2.

Bar charts are used with qualitative variables; the usual separation of rectangles suggests that each value of the variable represents a distinct category. Histograms are used with quantitative variables. The fact that rectangles in a histogram are adjacent (for intervals with nonzero frequencies) suggests that the variable's values are measured along a scale.

FIGURE 2.3 **Histogram of Grouped Commission Income Data**

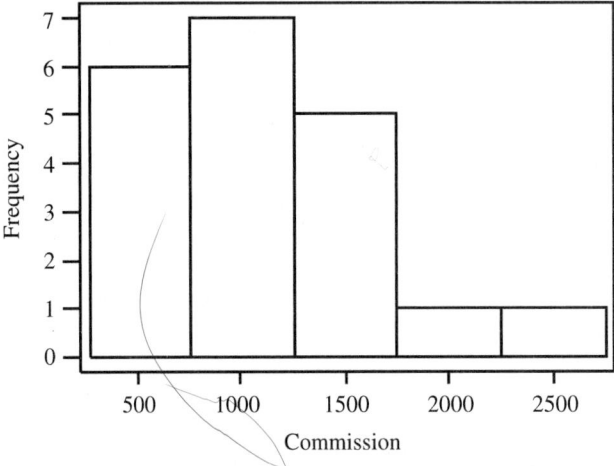

EXAMPLE 2.3

Data from the Bureau of Labor Statistics gave monthly changes in the Consumer Price Index (CPI) from February 1970 through May 1996. A histogram of the data was constructed by the JMP computer package. Does the histogram have a reasonable number of classes?

	A	B	C	D	E	F	G	H	I	J	K	L	M	N	O
2	1970		1.02	0.75	0.25	0.75	0.25	0.25	0.49	1.22	0.72	0.48	0.24		
3	1971	0	0.48	0.24	0.24	0.71	0.7	-0.5	0	0.7	0.46	-0.2	0.23		
4	1972	-0.2	0.23	0.46	0.23	0	0.46	0.46	0.23	0.68	0.23	0.45	-0.2		
5	1973	0.22	1.12	1.55	0.65	0.43	0.43	0.21	1.71	0.63	1.05	0.62	0.62		
6	1974	1.02	1.62	1.39	0.79	0.78	0.97	0.57	1.14	1.51	0.93	0.92	0.36		
7	1975	0.18	0.54	0.54	0	0.54	0.89	0.88	0.35	0.87	0.69	0.17	0		
8	1976	0.34	0.34	0	0.34	0.51	0.51	0.5	0.17	0.83	0.33	0.33	-0.2		
9	1977	0.82	1.14	0.81	0.96	0.63	0.32	0.63	0	0.94	0.15	0.31	-0.3		
10	1978	0.31	0.31	0.77	0.61	0.61	1.05	1.19	0.15	0.74	0.29	0.58	0.72		
11	1979	0.57	0.86	0.42	1.41	1.39	1.51	1.08	0.8	0.8	0.26	1.05	0.52		
12	1980	1.55	1.78	1.5	1.23	0.85	1.21	0.72	0.83	0.47	0.23	0.58	0.46		
13	1981	1.04	1.14	0.9	1.01	0.44	1.32	0.87	0.97	1.5	0.11	-0.2	0.32		
14	1982	0.21	0	-0.3	0.11	0	1.68	0.52	0.1	0.62	-0.5	0.41	-0.4		
15	1983	0.1	0	0.41	0.1	0.31	0.61	0.81	0.5	0.6	0	0.2	0		
16	1984	0.89	0.69	0.1	0.49	0.19	0.39	0.48	0.48	0.38	0	0.76	-0.3		
17	1985	0.38	0.94	0.37	0.65	0.65	0	0.37	0.09	0.27	0.27	0.45	0.27		
18	1986	0.18	0	-0.3	-0.5	0.36	0.91	0.36	0	0.89	-0.4	-0.2	0.36		
19	1987	0.71	0.44	0.09	1.32	0.78	0.86	0	0.85	0.25	0.34	-0.4	0.25		
20	1988	0.34	0	0.25	0.33	0.75	0.83	1.07	0.57	1.05	-0.5	0.56	0.24		
21	1989	0.08	-0.2	0.48	0.56	0.95	0.7	0.39	-0.2	0.85	0.23	-0.3	-0.2		
22	1990	1	0.76	1.06	0.52	0.22	0.37	0.89	0.73	0.66	0.43	0.22	0.22		
23	1991	0.72	0.14	0.28	-0.1	0.36	0.35	0.42	0.63	0.35	-0.5	0.14	0.77		
24	1992	0	-0.1	0.83	0	0.21	1.24	-0.1	0.48	0.07	0	-0.3	0		
25	1993	0	0.68	0.54	0.2	-0.1	0.74	0.13	0	0.33	0.73	0	-0.5		
26	1994	0.79	0.26	0.39	-0.3	0.07	0.91	0.45	0.26	0.32	0.26	0.06	-0.8		
27	1995	0.77	0.77	0.13	-0.1	0	0.38	0.32	0.44	0.44	0.06	-0.5	-0.3		
28	1996	0.75	0.56	0.5	0.06	-0.2									

Solution

The data range from roughly −1 to 2. If we define classes by rounding to the nearest unit (midpoints 0.00, 1.00, and so on), we will have only 3 classes, which would not be acceptable. We might round to the nearest quarter unit (endpoints 0.00, 0.25, 0.50, and so on) to see somewhat more detail. A JMP histogram based on the latter choice is shown in Figure 2.4.

FIGURE 2.4   **Histogram of CPI Change Data**

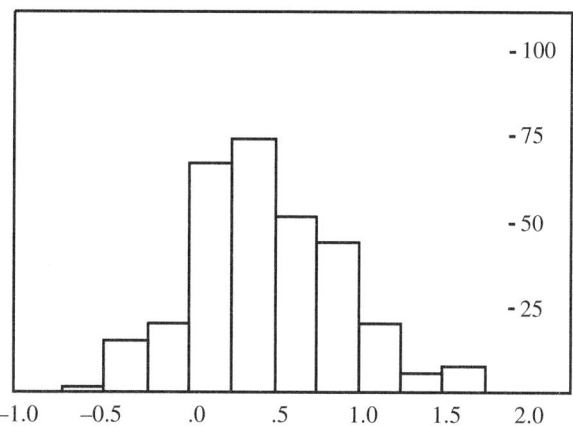

There are some minor variations in the presentation of histograms. The horizontal axis can be labeled with either class midpoints, as in Figure 2.3, or class endpoints, as in Figure 2.4. Thus, in Figure 2.3, we could have labeled the edges of the rectangles as $250, $750, . . . , rather than labeling the midpoints.

One axis of a histogram is labeled with frequencies or with relative frequencies. Because relative frequencies are proportional to frequencies, the frequency histogram and the relative frequency histogram have the same shape. The specific choice is mostly a matter of taste.

Recently, statisticians and computer programmers have developed improved versions of histograms by "smoothing off the corners." Smoothed histograms, also called *density estimates* or *kernel estimates*, avoid the arbitrary choice of class intervals in regular histograms, and tend to show the important features of the distribution without the distraction of corners. To oversimplify, a smoothed histogram is constructed by selecting a point on the horizontal axis, finding the height of a rectangle centered at that point, moving right or left a little bit to another point, doing the same thing for that point, and so on. Then the heights are connected in a smooth curve. The width of the rectangle is called the *bandwidth*, and can often be varied in a computer program. Wide bandwidths give very smooth curves at the cost of missing details; narrow bandwidths reveal detail at the cost of a "wiggly" plot. Trial and error is the best way to pick a bandwidth. There are a number of variations, depending on the computer program used. The details aren't crucial. A smoothed histogram of the CPI change data of Example 2.3 drawn by JMP is shown in Figure 2.5.

A histogram will reveal most of the important features of the distribution of data for a quantitative variable.

1   What is a typical, average value?

2   How much variability is there around the typical value? Are the data values all close to the same point, or do they spread out widely?

FIGURE 2.5   Smoothed Histogram of CPI Change Data

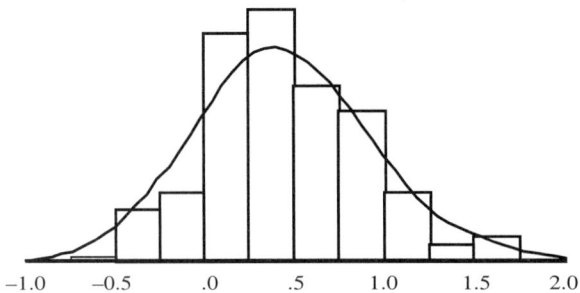

3   What is the general shape of the data? Are the data values distributed symmetrically around the middle or are they **skewed**, with a long tail in one direction or the other?

skewed

4   Are there **outliers**—"wild" values that are far from the bulk of the data?

outliers

5   Does the distribution have a single peak or is it clearly **bimodal**, with two separate peaks separated by a pronounced valley?

bimodal

In the histogram of commission income, shown in Figure 2.3, an average value appears to be slightly above 1000. But there is substantial variability, with many values around 500 or so and a few around 2500. The data are skewed, with a long tail to the right. There don't seem to be any "wild" values, nor are there separate peaks.

stem-and-leaf diagram

A clever device that constructs a histogram-like picture is the **stem-and-leaf diagram**. It is best explained by an example.

E X A M P L E   2 . 4

Suppose that the grades of 40 job applicants on an aptitude test are as follows. Construct a stem-and-leaf diagram for these data.

	A	B	C	D	E	F	G	H	I	J
1	42	21	46	69	87	29	34	59	81	97
2	64	60	87	81	69	77	75	47	73	82
3	91	74	70	65	86	87	67	69	49	57
4	55	68	74	66	81	90	75	82	37	94

Solution

The scores range from 21 to 97 The first digits, 2 through 9, are placed in a column—the stem—on the left of the diagram. The respective second digits are recorded in the appropriate rows—the leaves. The first three scores, 42, 21, and 46, would be represented as

	A	B	C
1	2	1	
2	3		
3	4	2	6

The full stem-and-leaf diagram is shown next.

	A	B	C	D	E	F	G	H	I	J
1	2	1	9							
2	3	4	7							
3	4	2	6	7	9					
4	5	5	7	9						
5	6	0	4	5	6	7	8	9	9	9
6	7	0	3	4	4	5	5	7		
7	8	1	1	1	2	2	6	7	7	7
8	9	0	1	4	7					

In general, the first digit of each data value is placed in the stem, and the second digit in the leaf. Sometimes it's necessary to put the first two digits in the stem. If the data ranged between 170 and 245, we wouldn't want the stem to consist just of the numbers 1 and 2; we would want stem values 17, 18, up to 24. To get a reasonable number of groups, we sometimes split up the stem. If the data values ranged between 20 and 43, we wouldn't want the stem to consist just of the numbers 2, 3, and 4; we could split the values in the 20s into low 20s (20 through 24) and high 20s (25 through 29) and the values in the 30s into low 30s and high 30s. If there were lots of values, we could even split the 20s into five groups (20 and 21, 22 and 23, 24 and 25, 26 and 27, 28 and 29) and similarly for the 30s and 40s. The aim is to have a reasonable number of categories, somewhere between 5 and 20.

The diagram can be made a bit neater by ordering the data within a row, from lowest to highest score, but this process is time-consuming if done by hand. The end result of a stem-and-leaf diagram looks much like a histogram turned sideways. The advantage of such a diagram is that it not only reflects frequencies but also contains the first digits of the actual values. Little or no information is lost.

There are many possible variations. A display (using Minitab) of the data from Example 2.4 with more classes is shown here.

```
MTB > Stem-and-Leaf 'Grades';
SUBC>    Trim.

Stem-and-leaf of Grades    N = 40
Leaf Unit = 1.0

         LO  21,

     2    2 9
     3    3 4
     4    3 7
     5    4 2
     8    4 679
     8    5
    11    5 579
    13    6 04
    20    6 5678999
    20    7 0344
    16    7 557
    13    8 11122
     8    8 6777
     4    9 014
     1    9 7
```

This Minitab stem-and-leaf diagram divides each interval in half by placing observations from the 90–94 range, for example, in the first 9 row, and observations in the 95–99 range in the second 9 row. Similar subdivisions are made in the other rows. Note also the ordering of observations within a row. The LO 21 entry is a Minitab suggestion that 21 may be an outlier—a wild, extreme value. We would not agree. The mysterious column of numbers on the left of the stem-and-leaf is another example of why we want to be selective in interpreting computer output. This column (which happens to be keeping cumulative totals added from both ends toward the middle) is not relevant to the main issues we're concerned with, so we can ignore it.

The stem-and-leaf diagram, and many other data-summarization ideas, are discussed in Tukey (1977).

EXERCISES

2.1 An automobile manufacturer routinely keeps records on the number of finished (passing all inspections) cars produced per 8-hour shift. The data for the last 28 shifts are

366 390 324 385 380 375 384 383 375 339 360 386 387 384
379 386 374 366 377 385 381 359 363 371 379 385 367 364

a Construct a histogram using convenient class intervals. Can you think of an explanation for the apparent shape of the histogram?

b Construct a stem-and-leaf diagram of the data and compare it to the histogram. The left-hand "stem" should have an initial 3 in each value.

2.2 A city manager receives 17 bids for supplying new memory typewriters. The dollar costs per typewriter are

	A	B	C	D	E	F	G	H	I	J
1										
2	847	849	838	841	852	846	812	838	850	836
3	871	849	824	846	864	843	839			

A histogram of the data was constructed using Statistix and is shown in Figure 2.6. A smoothed histogram drawn using Systat is shown in Figure 2.7.

FIGURE 2.6 **Histogram of Bid Data**

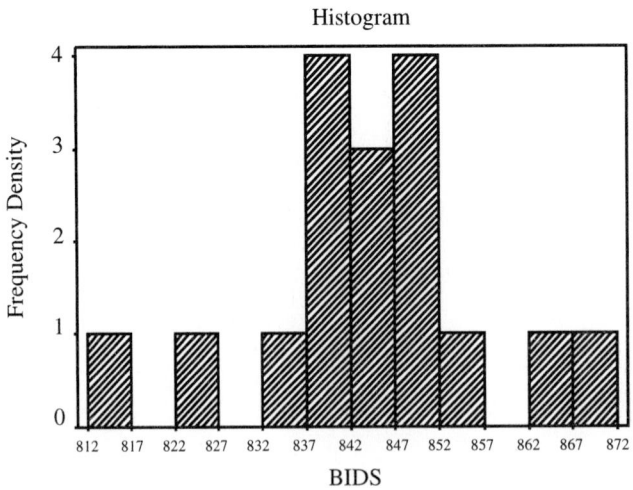

FIGURE 2.7 **Smoothed Histogram of Bid Data**

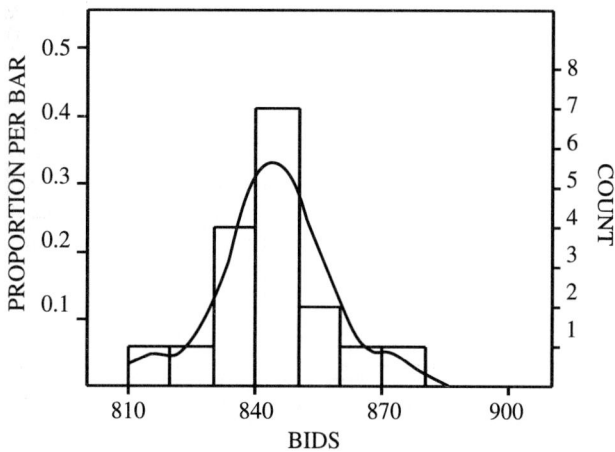

a According to the histogram, approximately what is the average bid? Is there little variability around that average? Is the histogram roughly symmetric or seriously skewed?

b Does the smoothed histogram indicate skewness?

2.3 A stem-and-leaf diagram for the data in Exercise 2.2, also constructed by the Statistix package, is as follows:

STEM AND LEAF PLOT OF BIDS

LEAF DIGIT UNIT = 1
1 2 REPRESENTS 12.

	STEM	LEAVES
1	81	2
2	82	4
6	83	6889
(7)	84	1366799
4	85	02
2	86	4
1	87	1

Are the classes defined by the stem-and-leaf display identical to those in the histogram? Do the two plots give the same general sense of the data?

2.4 A purchasing agent tests samples of 10 batteries for hand calculators from each of two manufacturers. Each battery is tested in a calculator that is programmed to do a continuous "loop" of typical calculations; the time in hours to failure of each battery is recorded in the following table:

Manufacturer	Time				
E	11.80	11.91	11.95	12.00	12.02
	12.03	12.04	12.07	12.13	12.20
S	12.06	12.14	12.18	12.19	12.20
	12.20	12.21	12.23	12.27	12.33

A combined histogram of all 20 times is shown in Figure 2.8. What is the approximate average value? Can you think of an explanation for the slight dip in the histogram?

FIGURE 2.8 **Histogram for Battery Data**

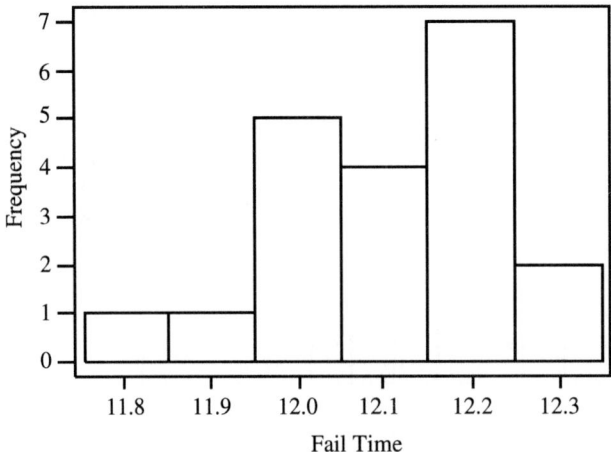

2.5 Separate histograms for each manufacturer in Exercise 2.4 are shown in Figure 2.9. Do the two together explain the dip in the histogram?

2.6 Price–earnings ratios for a sample of 24 publicly owned companies involved in the sale of computer software used in manufacturing operations are as follows:

	C	D	E	F	G	H	I	J	K	L
1	9.6	10.3	13.6	14.5	19.5	10.1	9.7	11.4	17.8	15.9
2	20.7	22.1	25.9	29.1	32.6	36.7	32.4	35.9	40.1	45.9

  a What sort of skewness is shown in the stem-and-leaf display of Figure 2.10?

  b Use the same data to construct a histogram. Compare the histogram to the stem-and-leaf plot. Which one do you find more informative?

2.7 A large state university obtained information on class size for all the courses it offered in a particular year. A histogram constructed by JMP is shown in Figure 2.11.

  a Roughly what is a typical, average class size?

  b Is the distribution of sizes essentially symmetric around the average value, or is it skewed?

FIGURE 2.9 **Histograms for Battery Data by Supplier**

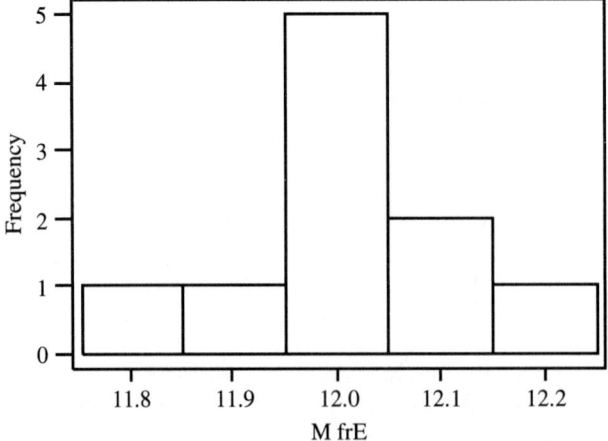

FIGURE 2.9 (continued) Histograms for Battery Data by Supplier

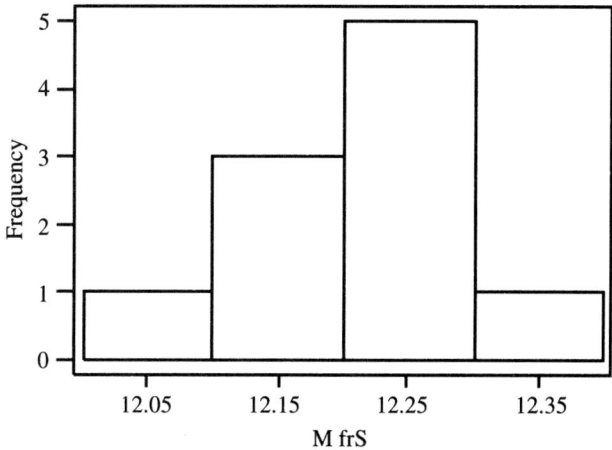

M frS

FIGURE 2.10   Stem-and-Leaf Display of Price–Earnings Ratios

	A	B	C	D	E	F	G	H
1	0	7	8	9	9			
2	1	0	0	1	3	3	4	4
3	1	5	7	9				
4	2	0	2					
5	2	5	9					
6	3	2	2					
7	3	5	6					
8	4	0						
9	4	5						

FIGURE 2.11   Class Sizes

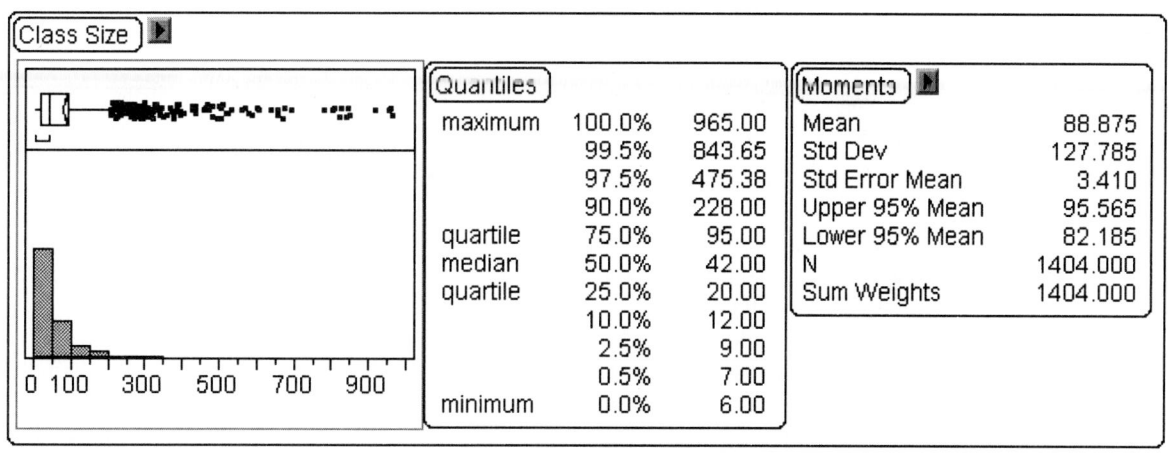

2.8   A hotel kept records over time of the reasons why guests requested room changes. The frequencies were as follows:

Reason	Frequency
Room not cleaned	2
Plumbing not working	1
Wrong type of bed	13
Noisy location	4
Wanted nonsmoking room	18
Didn't like view	1
Room not properly equipped	8
Other, not coded	6

a Construct a Pareto chart.

b The hotel management had expected that the primary problems would be connected with maintenance and housekeeping. Does the chart confirm that such reasons were the primary complaints? ■

2.2

On the Average: Typical Values

Frequency tables, bar charts, histograms, and stem-and-leaf displays all give a general sense of the pattern or distribution of values in a data set. They do not indicate a typical, middle, or average value explicitly. A great many management decisions are based on what a typical result is. For example, the formulation of a particular frozen dinner may well be based on comparing the typical favorability ratings of three possible formulations. The choice of an investment adviser for a pension fund will be based largely on comparing the typical performance over time (relative to market averages) of each of several candidates. Many quality-improvement measures attempt to reduce the typical number of improperly made items per thousand. In this section we define some standard measures of the typical or average value.

The word *average* has at least three meanings. It can mean the most common value, the mode; it can mean the middle value, the median; or it can mean the arithmetic average, the mean. This section contains more careful definitions of these three basic concepts of typical values.

Definition 2.1   Mode

The mode of a variable is the value or category with the highest frequency in the data. It is most commonly used with qualitative data.   ■

In Example 2.1, the frequencies (counts) for offices 1, 2, 3, and 4 were 8, 4, 3, and 5, respectively. Therefore, the modal category for the qualitative variable "office number" is 1, because that office has the largest number of salespeople.

Because we do not usually have the original measurements that were used to form a frequency table, the mode for grouped data is defined as the midpoint of the class with the highest frequency. This value approximates the mode of the actual (ungrouped) data.

In Example 2.2 the modal commission income is $1000, the midpoint of the class with endpoints of $750 to $1249. Unfortunately, the modal value is very sensitive to small changes in data values or class definitions. Had we defined the classes as $252 to $751, $752 to $1251, and so on in Example 2.2, the frequency table would change slightly, as shown here:

Class	Frequency
252–751	7
752–1251	6
1252–1751	5
1752–2251	1
2252–2751	1

The mode for these grouped data would be 501, the midpoint of the first interval, rather than 1000, as we found previously.

As was just illustrated, a mode calculated from a small amount of data or based on arbitrary class definitions is not too reliable and shouldn't be taken too seriously.

Definition 2.2   Median

The median of a set of data is the middle value when the data are arranged from lowest to highest. It is meaningful only if there is a natural ordering of the values from lowest to highest. If n, the sample size, is odd, the median is the $(n+1)/2$th value; if n is even, the median is the average of the $n/2$th and $(n+2)/2$th values.   ■

E X A M P L E   2 . 5

Suppose that the number of units per day of whole blood used in transfusions at a hospital over the previous 11 days is

| 25 | 16 | 61 | 12 | 18 | 15 | 20 | 24 | 17 | 19 | 28 |

Find the median.

Solution

Arranged in increasing order, the values are

| 12 | 15 | 16 | 17 | 18 | 19 | 20 | 24 | 25 | 28 | 61 |

The sample size, n, is 11, so the median value is the $(11+1)/2$th, or sixth, value, 19.   ■

If n, the number of measurements, is odd, there is no problem in finding the middle value. However, where n is even, no value is exactly in the middle; for this situation, the median is conventionally defined as the average of the middle two values when the data are ordered from smallest to largest. If, in Example 2.5, there had been a twelfth value of 72, the median would be the average of the sixth and seventh values $(19+20)/2 = 19.5$. Whether n is odd or even, there are equal numbers of observations above and below the median.

Definition 2.3   Mean

The mean of a variable is the sum of the measurements taken on that variable divided by the number of measurements. It is meaningful only for quantitative data.   ■

The mean is simply the average of all the data values. It is the point at which a histogram of the data balances. Think of each point as a weight along a line. If a fulcrum (like the pivot point on a child's seesaw) is placed at the mean, the weights below the mean will exactly balance those above the mean. This is a good way to visualize the mean in a histogram or stem-and-leaf diagram.

In Example 2.2 the mean commission income was ($850 + $1265 + \cdots + $1475)/20, or $1066.55. We use two different symbols for the mean, depending on whether we want to regard the data as the entire population of interest or as a sample of measurements from the population of interest.

As we indicated in Chapter 1, a population of measurements is the complete set of measurements of interest to a manager; a sample of measurements is a subset of measurements selected from the population of interest. If we let $y_1, y_2, \ldots, y_n$ represent a sample of n measurements selected from a population, the sample mean is denoted by the symbol $\bar{y}$:

$$\bar{y} = \frac{\sum_i y_i}{n}$$

The corresponding mean of the population from which the sample was drawn is denoted by the Greek letter μ (mu).

In most situations we do not know the population mean; the sample mean is used to make inferences about the corresponding unknown population mean. This is discussed in greater detail beginning in Chapter 7.

The mean is the most useful and convenient measure of the average value; however, any user of statistics should be alert to the possibility of distortions due to skewness or outliers. An extreme value can pull the mean in its direction and cause the mean to appear atypical of the values in the set. For this reason, statisticians have developed the idea of **trimmed means**. To find a 40% trimmed mean, for instance, drop the highest 20% and lowest 20% of the values and average the remaining values. This trimming process eliminates the effect of outliers, data values that lie far above or below the preponderance of the data. Trimmed means are particularly useful in estimating a population mean based on sample data, because they reduce the impact of possible "freak" values.

The mode, median, mean, and trimmed means are called **measures of location** or **measures of central tendency**; they indicate the center or general location of data values. The relation among these measures depends on the skewness of the data. If the distribution is mound-shaped—symmetric around a single peak—the mode, median, mean, and trimmed means are all equal. For a skewed distribution, one having a long tail in one direction and a single peak, the mean is pulled out toward the long tail; usually the median falls between the mode and the mean, and a trimmed mean falls between the median and the mean (see Figure 2.12).

The mean is the most widely used measure of central tendency; one reason for this popularity is its utility in statistical inference problems. Another reason is that it is possible to combine subgroup means into an overall mean. This property does not hold for the other measures of central tendency. For example, if the means for three equal-sized subgroups are 23, 25, and 30, the mean for the combined group must be $(23 + 25 + 30)/3 = 26$.

trimmed means

measures of location
measures of central tendency

FIGURE 2.12 **Measures of Location for Skewed Distribution**

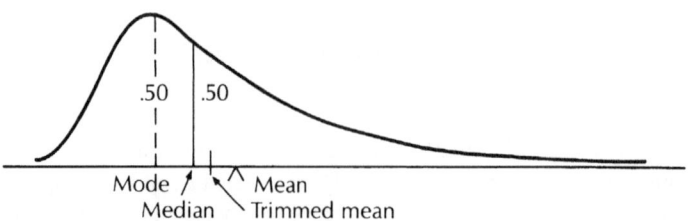

However, for the same data, if we know that the subgroup medians are 23, 25, and 30, we know only that the combined group median is somewhere between 23 and 30. Subgroup modes are even less informative.

weighted average

When subgroup sizes are not equal, the overall mean is a **weighted average** of the subgroup means, with weights equal to the subgroup sizes. To construct a weighted average, multiply each value by its weight, sum, and divide by the sum of the weights. The values that are given relatively large weights will contribute more heavily to the weighted average. For example, if the values with large weights happen to be relatively small numbers, the weighted average will be pulled down by the weighting. For the case of subgroup means, if $\bar{y}_j$ denotes the mean in subgroup $j, j = 1, \ldots, k$, and n_j is the number in subgroup j, then multiplying means by weights, summing, and dividing by the sum of the weights yields the following expression:

$$\bar{y} = \frac{\sum_j n_j \bar{y}_j}{\sum_j n_j}$$

E X A M P L E   2 . 6

Find $\bar{y}$ for the following 10 measurements, using the subgroup means:

Subgroup	Values	Total	$\bar{y}_j$	n_j
1	21, 21, 23, 24, 26	115	23	5
2	23, 26, 26	75	25	3
3	29, 31	60	30	2
		Grand total = 250		$n = 10$

Solution

Substituting into the calculation for $\bar{y}$ using subgroup means, we obtain

$$\bar{y} = \frac{5(23) + 3(25) + 2(30)}{5 + 3 + 2} = \frac{250}{10} = 25.0$$

Note that when we multiply each subgroup mean by its sample size, we get back to the total in the subgroup. Then we add the totals to get the overall total, and divide by the overall sample size to get the mean. Note also that the larger weight given to $\bar{y}_1$ causes the overall mean to fall below the simple average of the three means $(23 + 25 + 30)/3 = 26$. ■

Statistical thinking focuses very heavily on typical, average values. In many situations, inferences related to average or typical values will suffice, but there is a limit to such thinking. Sometimes the average value isn't important. A single, dramatically effective drug can propel a small pharmaceutical firm's ledger from the red to the black very quickly; a single disaster can propel an insurance firm into bankruptcy court. But it would be foolish to ignore statistical thinking on these grounds. Most products will not be overwhelming successes; most accidents will not be bankruptcy-causing disasters. Managers who assume that their results will always be better than average are in grave danger of becoming ex-managers. Measures of variability provide another dimension to our thinking; they are discussed in the next section.

means chart

In statistical quality control, a remarkably simple, remarkably useful device is a **means chart**, often called an *x-bar chart*. (Because we usually use y to denote the variable of interest, we'd call it a y-bar chart—but someone else got there first.) A simplified means chart is simply a plot of times (hours, days, weeks, or months) versus means of observations taken at those times. A process that is operating consistently will be in **statistical control**. The means will vary randomly, but won't show any systematic changes. A careful look will show any patterns that indicate a process that is out of statistical control—a slow increasing or decreasing trend in the means, a sudden jump or drop, or a cyclic pattern.

A critical aspect of automatic transmissions for cars is the internal fluid pressure of the transmission. The ideal value is 35, in appropriate units. Too low a pressure results in sluggish performance; anything under 32 can be detected and any pressure under 30 results in bad performance. Too high a pressure results in jumpy overperformance; 38 is detectable and 40 is bad. A manufacturer of transmissions randomly samples five units from each day's production and measures the internal pressure on each. A list of the pressures for 40 days and an x-bar plot of means versus day is shown here. The initial 3 has been dropped, so 6.01 represents 36.01.

Day	item1	item2	item3	item4	item5	mean
1	6.01	4.46	4.90	3.83	4.61	4.762
2	6.06	6.26	5.44	3.86	5.88	5.500
3	4.46	6.17	4.07	4.29	4.29	4.656
4	5.08	4.68	4.37	4.50	4.40	4.606
5	4.11	5.84	5.67	4.55	5.62	5.158
6	4.58	5.90	4.35	5.25	4.18	4.852
7	6.04	4.45	4.22	5.09	4.68	4.896
8	4.98	5.19	5.70	4.91	2.97	4.750
9	6.48	5.95	4.53	6.25	6.08	5.858
10	5.30	5.98	5.36	3.83	4.56	5.006
11	3.56	3.95	6.38	4.90	4.86	4.730
12	4.96	6.78	6.56	4.32	5.25	5.574
13	4.39	3.16	4.31	4.43	6.33	4.524
14	2.88	4.62	5.70	5.77	3.83	4.560
15	2.81	4.27	3.19	6.02	5.94	4.446
16	2.77	3.20	3.60	5.75	4.57	3.978
17	4.88	3.37	4.69	4.02	3.30	4.052
18	6.06	4.49	3.40	5.03	6.63	5.122
19	6.17	2.64	5.90	4.75	5.22	4.936
20	5.85	5.00	3.31	4.58	7.37	5.222
21	5.10	5.39	5.37	4.33	7.28	5.494
22	7.29	2.77	3.54	7.45	5.14	5.238
23	4.44	5.87	5.52	5.03	4.13	4.998
24	4.94	5.97	6.30	8.22	4.72	6.030
25	5.56	5.59	4.63	3.56	6.84	5.236
26	5.48	4.74	6.51	6.76	4.13	5.524
27	5.31	6.87	2.82	3.55	3.47	4.404
28	3.69	4.01	5.16	3.87	4.93	4.332
29	3.32	6.22	2.12	6.01	5.60	4.654
30	5.14	6.57	6.37	6.98	6.66	6.344
31	4.93	6.02	5.10	5.58	6.62	5.650
32	4.93	5.45	2.16	6.25	5.05	4.768
33	6.64	7.00	5.39	4.87	6.76	6.132
34	7.85	4.97	4.68	5.48	4.07	5.410
35	4.02	6.64	7.62	5.91	4.15	5.668

36	4.51	5.42	4.81	5.00	3.74	4.696
37	3.62	5.41	4.78	1.78	3.88	3.894
38	3.06	5.90	6.96	4.96	2.72	4.720
39	2.04	3.22	3.76	3.44	6.76	3.844
40	4.99	6.20	4.73	3.87	3.79	4.716

A simplifed *x*-bar chart is shown in Figure 2.13. There are no obvious trends up or down, nor are there jumps to new plateaus. The means mostly stay in the 4.00 to 6.00 range, corresponding to mean pressures of 34 to 36 units. Perhaps there are some cycles of a few days' length, but nothing huge. One troubling feature is that the mean in days 31–40 seem to "jump around" a little more. Several of the largest and smallest means occur during these days. We will need to consider this more when we measure variability in the next section.

FIGURE 2.13 **Simplified Means Chart for Transmission Data**

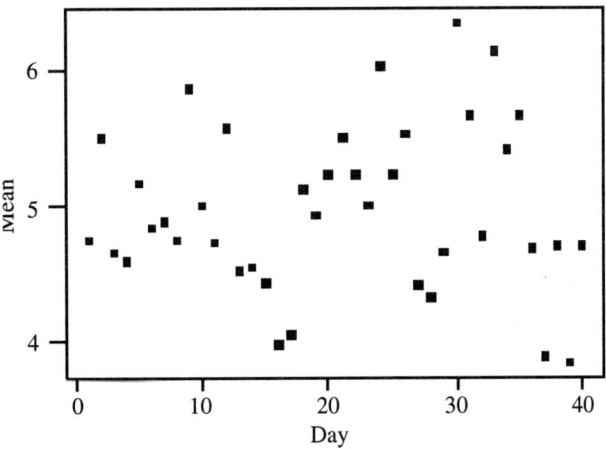

EXAMPLE 2.7

A nationwide chain of motels has a national reservation center. Customers phone in reservations to an 800 number. One key measure of the quality of the center's service is the amount of "dead time"—waiting for the phone to be answered, being on hold, waiting for a response once a request has been made—endured by a customer. The chain's four regular inspectors record the dead time (in units of minutes) for their one reservation call each day. The results are averaged over each 5-day workweek. A separate analysis is done for weekends and holiday weeks. Means are shown next. A simplified *x*-bar chart is shown in Figure 2.14. Is there any clear evidence of a problem?

mean
0.765	0.775	1.025	0.910	0.665	0.825	0.720	0.720	0.795
0.845	0.645	0.905	0.845	0.790	0.950	0.735	0.765	0.710
1.045	1.215	1.085	0.925	1.075	1.100	1.330	1.215	0.996
1.185	1.115	1.110						

FIGURE 2.14   **Simplified Means Plot for Dead Time Data**

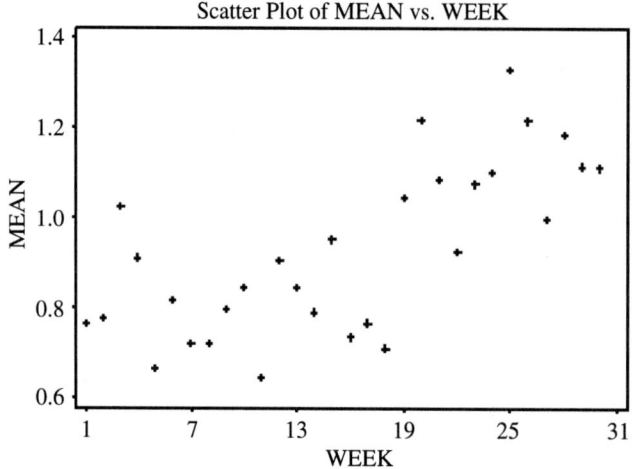

Solution

For the first 18 weeks, except for week 3, the means are relatively low. Beginning at week 19, the means suddenly increase. The chart clearly signals that we should look for a cause for an increase in dead time around week 19.   ■

In these control charts, means vary from one time period to another. Our next task is to measure and summarize variability. That's the topic of the next section.

EXERCISES

2.9   Compute the mean, median, and mode for the following data:

11   17   18   10   22   23   15   17   14   13   10   12   18   18   11   14

2.10   The Insurance Institute for Highway Safety published data on the total damage suffered by compact automobiles in a series of controlled, low-speed collisions. The data, in dollars, with brand names removed, are

361	393	430	543	566	610	763	851	886
887	976	1039	1124	1267	1328	1415	1425	1444
1476	1542	1544	2048	2197				

A histogram is shown in Figure 2.15. A summary (from the Excel spreadsheet) follows.

Damage

Mean	1090.6522
Standard Error	105.83343
Median	1039
Mode	#N/A
Standard Deviation	507.55928
Sample Variance	257616.42
Kurtosis	-0.363327
Skewness	0.4189689
Range	1836

FIGURE 2.15   **Histogram for Auto Damage Data**

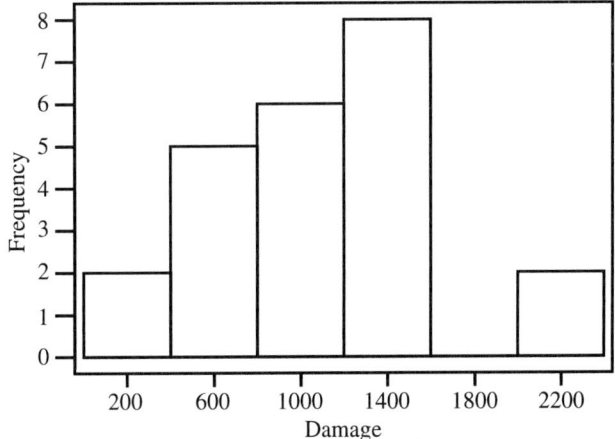

Minimum	361
Maximum	2197
Sum	25085
Count	23

What does the relation between the mean and median indicate about the shape of the data?

2.11   Production records for an automobile manufacturer show the following figures for production per shift (maximum production is 720 cars per shift):

688   711   625   701   688   667   694   630   547   703   688   697   703
656   677   700   702   688   691   664   688   679   708   699   667   703

a Would the mode be a useful summary statistic for these data? Why?

b Find the median.

c Find the mean.

d What does the relation between the mean and median indicate about the shape of the data?

2.12   Draw a stem-and-leaf plot of the data in Exercise 2.11. The "stem" should include (from highest to lowest) 71, 70, 69, ... Does the shape of the stem-and-leaf display confirm your judgment in part d of Exercise 2.11?   ■

2.3

Measuring Variability

O ne of the most important unifying ideas in statistics is the notion of variability. Customers vary in the time it takes them to pay bills. Caplets of a particular drug vary in their potency—but had better not vary too much. Overtime payments to a city police force vary sharply from week to week. Variability in return on investment is the key to the idea of risk in finance. Variability is an absolutely fundamental idea in quality control; in many situations, such as caplets that vary in potency, variability is a major enemy of quality. One of the major themes of statistical quality control (and of this book, as well) is accounting for sources of variability.

The first task in dealing with variability is summarizing it. In this section, we'll define several measures of variability and discuss the strengths and weaknesses of each.

The simplest measure of variability is the **range**—the difference between the largest and smallest values. It's easy to compute, so it is widely used in quality control to measure variability. When data are taken over time and the range is plotted against time, the result is an **R chart**. For example, in the automatic transmission example from Section 2.2, ranges were computed as follows:

Day	Range	Day	Range	Day	Range	Day	Range
1	2.18	11	2.82	21	2.95	31	1.69
2	2.40	12	2.46	22	4.68	32	4.09
3	2.10	13	3.17	23	1.74	33	2.13
4	0.71	14	2.89	24	3.50	34	3.78
5	1.73	15	3.21	25	3.28	35	3.60
6	1.72	16	2.98	26	2.63	36	1.68
7	1.82	17	1.58	27	4.05	37	3.63
8	2.73	18	3.23	28	1.47	38	4.24
9	1.95	19	3.53	29	4.10	39	4.72
10	2.15	20	4.06	30	1.84	40	2.41

The automatic transmission data shown in Section 2.2 indicate that the largest value in day 1 is 6.01 (item 1) and the smallest value in day 1 is 3.83 (item 4). The range for day 1 is therefore $6.01 - 3.83 = 2.18$, as shown. Note that the actual pressures were 36.01 and 33.83; adding 30 to all the data doesn't change the range, because the 30s cancel. An R chart of range plotted against day is shown in Figure 2.16.

F I G U R E   2 . 1 6   Range Chart of Automatic Transmission Data

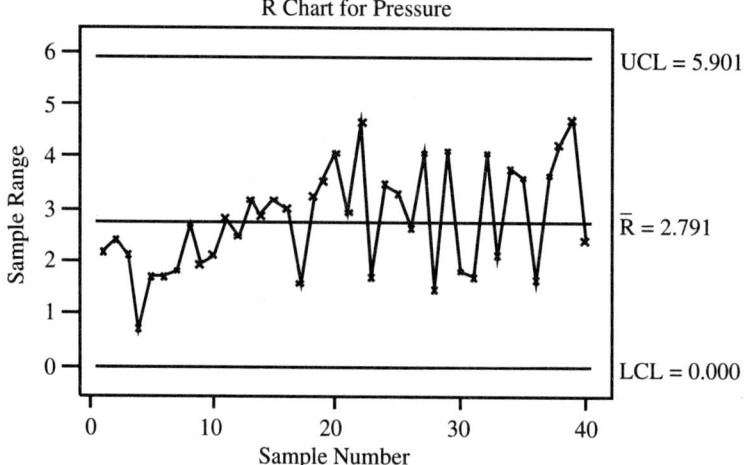

This chart shows that a problem is developing over time. Notice that in the first 10 days or so, the ranges are always lower than the average range for the entire period, shown as the center line of the graph. In the last 10 days, the ranges sometimes (not always) are above average. It appears that the ranges generally are increasing over time, so there's more and more variability as time goes by. The process is not in statistical control, not stable. Higher variability means that more transmissions will be either too high or too low in pressure. In seeking the cause, we should notice that there's no sudden jump upward but rather a gradual increase; we should look for a gradual factor such as machine wearout or worker complacency.

EXAMPLE 2.8

Ranges were calculated and an R chart was prepared for the "dead time" data of Example 2.7. They're shown in Figure 2.17. Is there an indication that variability is changing over time?

FIGURE 2.17 **Range Chart for Dead Time Data**

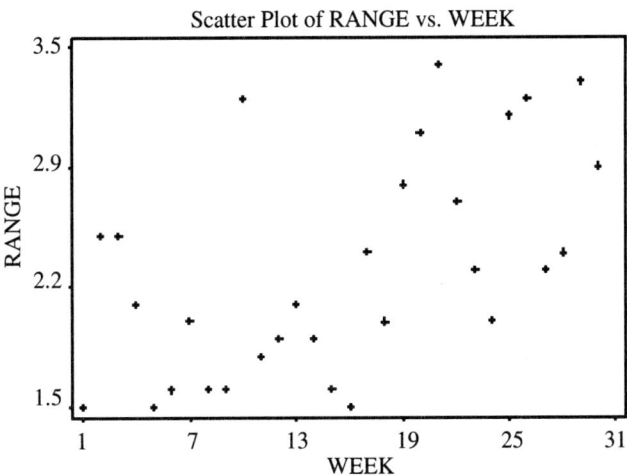

Solution

It appears that the ranges are increasing with week number. In Example 2.7, we found that the means jumped at about week 19. It's not so obvious, but the ranges may have jumped at about that time as well. ■

There are at least two problems with using the range as a measure of variability. First, the range is very sensitive to outliers. Second, as the sample size increases, the range tends to increase as well; in the automatic transmission data, adding another 10 measurements to the original 5 per week couldn't decrease the range, and probably would increase it.

deviations from the mean

More useful measures of variability are based on **deviations from the mean**. The deviation of a sample measurement y_i from its mean $\bar{y}$ is defined as $(y_i - \bar{y})$. Some of these deviations are positive, others negative; their algebraic sum is always zero. Thus the positive and negative deviations balance exactly. To measure variability, we must look at the magnitudes (ignoring the positive or negative sign) of the deviations; large positive and negative deviations indicate large variability.

average absolute deviation

The simplest measure of the magnitudes of the deviations is the **average absolute deviation** (AD), defined as the average of the absolute values of the deviations:

$$AD = \frac{\sum_i |y_i - \bar{y}|}{n}$$

Regard the data values 11, 12, 13, 14, and 30 as a sample of five measurements selected from a population of interest. Compute the average absolute deviation for the sample data. It is easy to show that $\bar{y} = 80/5 = 16$, so

$$AD = \frac{|11 - 16| + |12 - 16| + |13 - 16| + |14 - 16| + |30 - 16|}{5}$$

$$= \frac{5 + 4 + 3 + 2 + 14}{5} = 5.6$$

Thus, on the average, an individual measurement deviates 5.6 units from the mean.

The average absolute deviation is easy to compute and to interpret. However, it is difficult to deal mathematically with absolute values. Most statistical methods deal with squared deviations instead.

The most useful statistical measures of variability are the *variance* and the *standard deviation*. The variance of a sample of n measurements $y_1, y_2, \ldots, y_n$ is often called the *mean squared error*. It is the average squared deviation, defined as the sum of the squared deviations divided by $(n - 1)$. We denote the sample variance by s^2.

The sample standard deviation s of the measurements is the (positive) square root of the variance. The corresponding population variance and standard deviation are denoted by σ^2 and σ, respectively.

<table>
<tr><td>variance</td></tr>
<tr><td>standard deviation</td></tr>
</table>

Definition 2.4   Variance and Standard Deviation

$$s^2 = \frac{\sum_i (y_i - \bar{y})^2}{n - 1}$$

$$s = \sqrt{s^2} \qquad \blacksquare$$

E X A M P L E   2 . 9

Compute the sample variance and sample standard deviation for the values 11, 12, 13, 14, and 30 (which have a mean of 16).

Solution

With $\bar{y} = 16$, we can substitute into the formula for s^2 to obtain

$$s^2 = \frac{(11 - 16)^2 + (12 - 16)^2 + (13 - 16)^2 + (14 - 16)^2 + (30 - 16)^2}{5 - 1}$$

$$= \frac{250}{4} = 62.5$$

and thus

$$s = \sqrt{62.5} = 7.906 \qquad \blacksquare$$

The use of $n - 1$ as the denominator of s^2 is not arbitrary. This definition of the sample variance makes it an "unbiased estimator" of the population variance σ^2. This roughly means that if we were to draw a very large number of samples, each of size n, from the population and if we computed s^2 for each sample, the average sample variance would equal the population variance σ^2. Had we divided by n in the definition of s^2, the average sample variance would be slightly less than the population variance, and hence s^2 would tend to slightly underestimate σ^2. The use of $n - 1$ rather than n is standard in most computer packages. Unless the sample size is very small, the effect of using $n - 1$ instead of n is numerically quite small, and not crucial.

The definitions of variance and standard deviation depend on whether the data are regarded as a population or as a sample. In practice, the available data are almost always a sample. Unless specifically indicated otherwise, we regard all data sets as samples and consider population means and variances as conceptual quantities to be estimated from the samples. Virtually all statistical computer programs also make this assumption.[1]

We have defined the variance and standard deviation but have not yet indicated how to interpret them. What does a standard deviation of, say, $552.51 mean? One reasonably good approximation assumes that the measurements have roughly a mound-shaped histogram—that is, a symmetric, single-peaked histogram that tapers off smoothly from the peak toward the tails. We call the approximation the Empirical Rule.

Definition 2.5   Empirical Rule

For a set of measurements having a mound-shaped histogram, the interval

$\bar{y} \pm 1s$ contains approximately 68% of the measurements.

$\bar{y} \pm 2s$ contains approximately 95% of the measurements.

$\bar{y} \pm 3s$ contains approximately all of the measurements.

The approximation may be poor if the data are severely skewed, bimodal, or contain outliers.   ■

EXAMPLE 2.10

A sample of 20 days from throughout the previous year indicates that the average wholesale price per pound for steers at a particular stockyard was $.61 and that the standard deviation was $.07. If the histogram for the measurements is mound-shaped, describe the variability of the data using the Empirical Rule.

Solution

Applying the Empirical Rule, we conclude that:

The interval .61 ± .07, or $.54 to $.68, contains approximately 68% of the measurements.

The interval .61 ± .14, or $.47 to $.75, contains approximately 95% of the measurements.

The interval .61 ± .21, or $.40 to $.82, contains approximately all of the measurements.   ■

Because the standard deviation is based on *squared* deviations from the mean, it is more sensitive to outliers than the mean is, for instance. For example, suppose that the 10 salespeople at a new car dealership have monthly sales of 16, 18, 19, 20, 20, 22, 24, 26, 28, and 80 vehicles. (The "80" figure includes a very large fleet sale.) Taking all 10 scores into account, the mean is 27.30 and the standard deviation is 18.88. If the 80 score is omitted because it was obtained under different conditions—a fleet sale rather than individual sales—the mean drops to 21.44, but the standard deviation falls way down to only 3.91. Squaring the extremely large deviation yielded by an outlier blows up the variance; even taking the square root to get the standard deviation still results in a very large standard deviation.

---

[1] When a set of data is regarded as a population, the population variance is defined as the sum of squared deviations from the population mean μ, all divided by N, the population size—not by $N - 1$.

However, the standard deviation is less outlier-sensitive than the range. Thus an **S chart**, a plot of standard deviations against time, is also a useful quality-control tool in assessing whether there has been a change in variability.

EXAMPLE 2.11

Standard deviations for the automatic transmission data of Section 2.2 were plotted in Figure 2.18 against week number to make an S chart. Is there evidence of a trend?

FIGURE 2.18   **S Chart of Transmission Pressure Data**

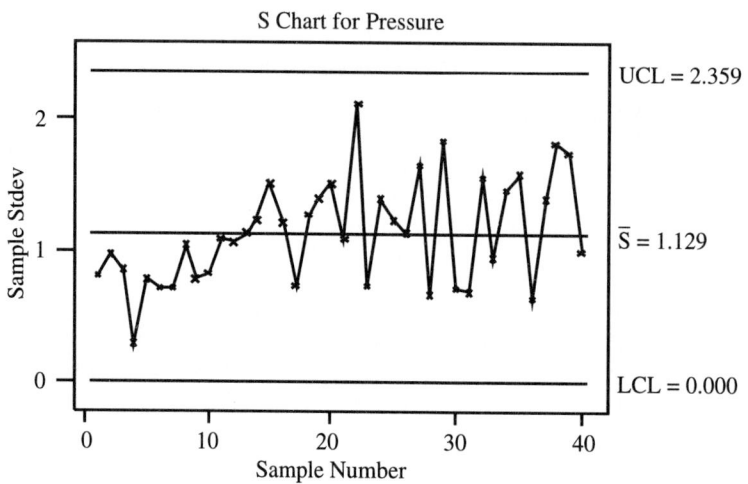

Solution

There is somewhat of an increasing trend in the standard deviations. Notice that the standard deviations up through week 10 are all lower than the average standard deviation, shown as the center line on the S chart. In later periods, the standard deviations often—though not always—are larger, indicating that variability is increasing with time.   ■

The standard deviation is also useful in x-bar quality-control charts. From data taken when a process is in control, one can calculate the standard deviation of the means. In a complete x-bar chart, upper and lower **control limits** are drawn at the desired mean plus 3 standard deviations (of the mean) and at the desired mean minus 3 standard deviations. Any mean that falls outside these limits is taken as evidence that the process is out of control. According to the Empirical Rule, if the process is in control, very few means should fall outside the control limits, so "false alarms" should be rare. If and when the process goes seriously out of control, the means should go outside one control limit or the other. Control limits are very useful in reducing the tendency of managers to go chasing after every minor variation; only deviations that are very likely more than random will fall outside the control limits.

EXAMPLE 2.12

A control chart for the transmission data of Section 2.2 is shown in Figure 2.19. How, if at all, does it indicate that trouble is brewing?

FIGURE 2.19   **Control Chart for Automatic Transmission Data**

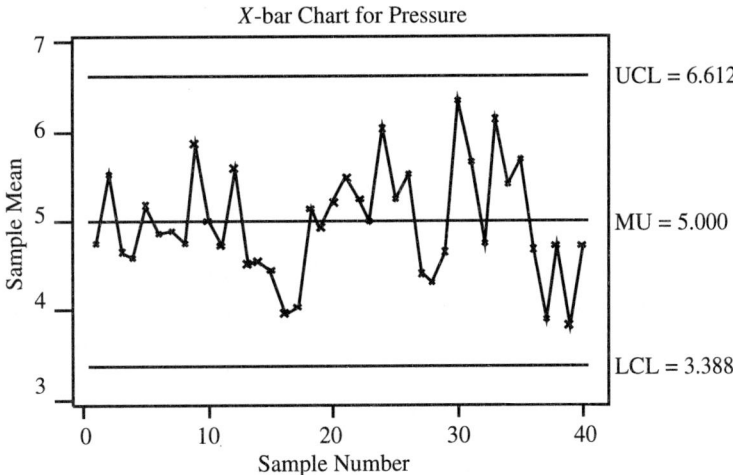

Solution

At first glance, the chart doesn't indicate trouble. Every mean is within the control limits. Therefore, there don't seem to be any problems with the average value. The next thing to consider is variability. The best way to do that would be to look at an R or S chart. We can get some indirect evidence from the x-bar chart. Near the right-hand side of the chart, the means seem to jump around, suggesting that the process is not under control. Because there is no pattern of consistently high or consistently low readings, it seems reasonable to think that the problem is excessive variability. To confirm that variability is the problem, we should check an R or S chart. Results from previous examples confirm our idea. Management's task seems to be to find out why there is such variation in the transmission data.   ■

interquartile range

 An alternative way to approach variability is to use the **interquartile range** (IQR). The quartiles of a data distribution are the 25th and 75th percentiles—the values that mark the bottom one-fourth and top one-fourth of the data. Tukey (1977) calls these values "hinges" and notes that they can be found by taking medians of each half of the data. The median of the bottom half of the data is the 25th percentile, simply because half of one-half is one-fourth; similarly, the median of the top half of the data is the 75th percentile. The interquartile range is the difference between the two quartiles.

Definition 2.6   Interquartile Range

To find the quartiles of a set of data on a variable,

1 Sort the data and find the median.

2 Divide the data into top and bottom halves (above and below the median). If the sample size n is odd, arbitrarily include the median in both halves.

3 Find the medians of both halves. These are the 25th and 75th percentiles, or "hinges."

4 IQR = 75th percentile − 25th percentile ◼

EXAMPLE 2.13

Find the interquartile range for the following data:

24	26	26	28	29	29	29	30	30	31	32	33	33	34	35
35	35	36	36	37	37	38	39	40	40	41	42	44	45	49

Solution

The data are already sorted, lowest to highest. Because $n = 30$, the median is the average of the fifteenth and sixteenth values (both of which are 35)—namely, 35. The bottom half of the data is the lowest 15 values; the top half is the highest 15 values. The median of the bottom half (that is, the 25th percentile) is the eighth value, 30. The 75th percentile is the eighth value from the top, 39. The IQR is $39 - 30 = 9$. ◼

The IQR is most commonly used in checking for outliers. Tukey (1977) defines the inner fences as follows:

$$\text{lower inner fence} = \text{25th percentile} - 1.5 \text{ IQR}$$

$$\text{upper inner fence} = \text{75th percentile} + 1.5 \text{ IQR}$$

Any value outside the inner fences is an outlier candidate. The choice of the number 1.5 is arbitrary, but it seems to work decently. Similarly, the outer fences are defined as three times the IQR from the "hinges."

$$\text{lower outer fence} = \text{25th percentile} - 3.0 \text{ IQR}$$

$$\text{upper outer fence} = \text{75th percentile} + 3.0 \text{ IQR}$$

Any data value outside the outer fences is a serious outlier.

EXAMPLE 2.14

Calculate the various fences for the data of Example 2.13. Does the fence test identify any outliers? Do there appear to be outliers on visual inspection?

Solution

A plot of the data, or merely a scan by eye, does not indicate that any value should be regarded as an outlier. The closest thing to an outlier is the value 49, but it is close to several other values. The 25th percentile and 75th percentile were found in Example 2.13 to be 30 and 39, so the IQR is 9. The inner fences are $30 - 1.5(9) = 16.5$ and $39 + 1.5(9) = 52.5$. No data value even comes close to the inner fences, so the fence test identifies no outliers. ◼

The interquartile range is the basis for still another Tukey (1977) idea, the boxplot, sometimes called the "box-and-whiskers plot."

Definition 2.7   Boxplot

1   Draw the edges of a box at the 25th and 75th percentiles. Draw a vertical bar through the box at the median.

2   Draw lines ("whiskers") from the edges of the box to the adjacent values—the smallest and largest nonoutliers.

3   Plot each outlier candidate separately, by convention using a $*$ symbol. Plot each serious outlier, by convention using a 0 symbol.   ■

EXAMPLE 2.15

Suppose that the return on investments for 21 companies in a certain industry for a certain year is

$$-24.6 \quad -2.6 \quad 2.4 \quad 2.7 \quad 3.8 \quad 5.6 \quad 5.9 \quad 6.7 \quad 7.0 \quad 7.2 \quad 7.5$$
$$8.0 \quad 8.2 \quad 8.5 \quad 8.6 \quad 8.8 \quad 9.0 \quad 9.2 \quad 9.7 \quad 10.0 \quad 20.5$$

Draw a boxplot of these data.

Solution

With $n = 21$, the median is the eleventh score, 7.5. The 25th percentile is the median of the bottom 11 scores—namely, 5.6. (Note that because n is an odd number, we include the median in both halves of the data. Thus, the bottom half of the data comprises 11 scores, not 10.) The 75th percentile is the median of the top 11 scores—namely, 8.8. Thus, IQR = $8.8 - 5.6 = 3.2$. The fences are

$$\text{lower outer fence} = 5.6 - 3.0(3.2) = -4.0$$

$$\text{lower inner fence} = 5.6 - 1.5(3.2) = 0.8$$

$$\text{upper inner fence} = 8.8 + 1.5(3.2) = 13.6$$

$$\text{upper outer fence} = 8.8 + 3.0(3.2) = 18.4$$

The fence test identifies two serious outliers, -24.6 and 20.5, and one outlier candidate, -2.6. (A plot of the data indicates that the serious outliers are obviously extreme and that the outlier candidate is debatably out.) The adjacent values are the smallest and largest nonoutliers, 2.4 and 10.0. The resulting boxplot is shown in Figure 2.20.

FIGURE 2.20   **Boxplot Example**

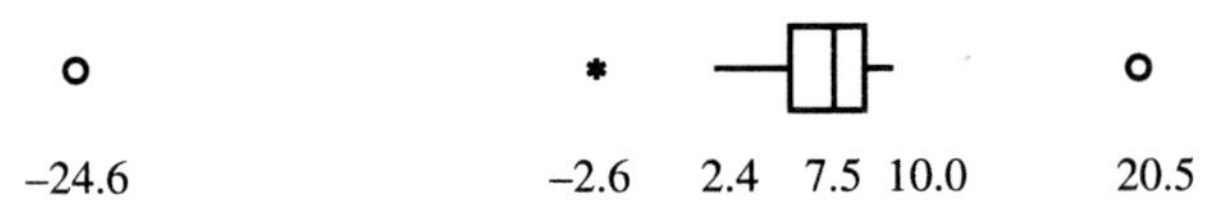

Apart from its use in boxplots, the IQR is not as widely reported as the standard deviation. For most of our purposes, the standard deviation will be the most important measure of variability.

2.13 Suppose that the data from two samples are

Sample 1:   15   19   21   25
Sample 2:   14   17   18   19   19   20   20   20   21   21   22   23   26

  a Find the range for each sample.

  b Find the standard deviation for each sample.

  c Which sample shows more variability? Construct histograms or boxplots to support your opinion.

2.14 Data for car production per shift, given in Exercise 2.11, are reproduced here, along with selected Excel output:

688   711   625   701   688   667   694   630   547   703   688   697   703
656   677   700   702   688   691   664   688   679   708   699   667   703

Production	
Mean	679.38
Median	688
Mode	688
Standard Deviation	34.83
Sample Variance	1213.13
Range	164
Minimum	547
Maximum	711
Count	26

  a Find the mean and standard deviation.

  b How well does the Empirical Rule work for the fraction of data falling within 1 standard deviation of the mean?

2.15   **a** Find the median and IQR for the data in Exercise 2.14.

  b Find the inner and outer fences. Are there outliers?

  c Draw a boxplot of the data.

2.16 Directory assistance (information) operators receive requests for telephone numbers from customers. The procedure for obtaining and reporting numbers is highly computerized, so each operator should be able to handle a large number of calls in a workday. At one office, the minimum standard is regarded as 780 calls cleared per day—roughly 2 calls cleared per minute. Data were collected for a day on 60 day-shift operators. What sources of variability among operators might be present?

2.17 Data on the 60 operators of Exercise 2.16 were analyzed using Minitab.

MTB > describe ´Cleared´

	N	MEAN	MEDIAN	TRMEAN	STDEV	SEMEAN
Cleared	60	794.23	799.00	797.91	34.25	4.42

	MIN	MAX	Q1	Q3
Cleared	601.00	844.00	789.00	807.75

MTB > Print ´Cleared´

Cleared
797   794   817   813   817   793   762   719   804   811   837   804   790   796
807   801   805   811   835   787   800   771   794   805   797   724   820   601
817   801   798   797   788   802   792   779   803   807   789   787   794   792
786   808   808   844   790   763   784   739   805   817   804   807   800   785
796   789   842   829

  a Calculate the "mean plus-or-minus 1 standard deviation" interval used in the Empirical Rule.

b Of the 60 scores in Cleared, 51 fall within the 1 standard deviation interval. How does this result compare with the theoretical value of the Empirical Rule? What might explain the discrepancy?

2.18 A boxplot of the data in Exercise 2.17 is shown in Figure 2.21. How does the plot explain the failure of the Empirical Rule?

FIGURE 2.21 **Boxplot of Calls Cleared Data**

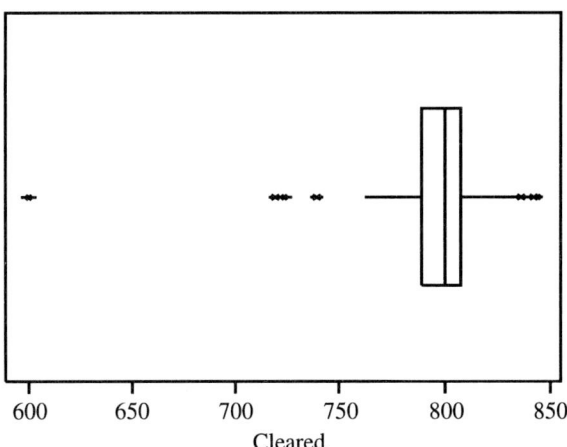

Cleared

2.19 Operator 28 (the one with the 601 score in the data for Exercise 2.17) was a trainee who wasn't expected to perform to the standard of long-term operators. The data were reanalyzed omitting this operator.

a How would you expect omitting the 601 score to affect the mean? The standard deviation?

b Minitab output is as follows. How much were the mean and standard deviation affected?

```
MTB > describe 'Longterm'

              N     MEAN    MEDIAN   TRMEAN   STDEV   SEMEAN
Longterm     59    797.51   800.00   799.02   23.21    3.02

             MIN     MAX      Q1       Q3
Longterm   719.00  844.00   789.00   808.00
```

2.20 An automobile dealership maintains a service department. Customers state their needs to one of two service advisers, who determine the needed work and assign the work to mechanics and then explain the result to the customer. As a continuing check on service quality, the dealer randomly samples one job per adviser per day and calls the customer about the customer's satisfaction with the job. The customer rates the service on a scale of 1 to 5, with 5 being best. What does the control chart in Figure 2.22 indicate about the average satisfaction level of the dealer's customers?

2.21 Is there a clear indication in the control charts of Figure 2.22 that the variability in ratings is changing over time?

2.22 Scheduling the duration of airplane flights is critical to an airline's service, particularly at "hub" centers. At such centers, flights arrive in groups, passengers transfer to other flights, and these flights depart. If incoming flights take longer than scheduled, passengers may miss connecting flights, or the outgoing flights may have to be delayed. If, however, most flights take less time than scheduled, passengers will have to wait for their connecting flights. An operations manager routinely records the actual times taken by 38 flights scheduled to arrive between 4:30 and 5:00 P.M. at a hub. The times are converted to percentage of scheduled

FIGURE 2.22 **Control Charts for Customer Satisfaction**

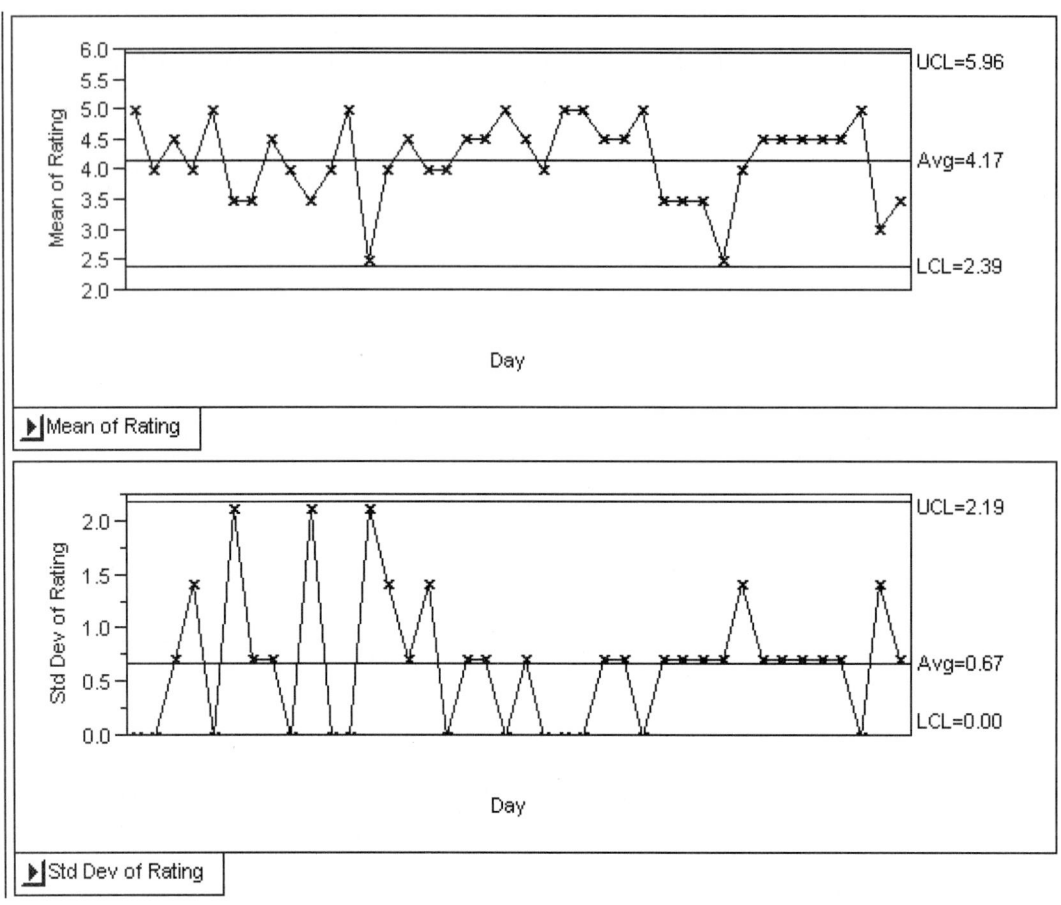

time, so a "late percentage" of 100 indicates that a flight is exactly on time. Systat computer output of the 38 percentages is shown here.

```
TOTAL OBSERVATIONS:     38

                    LATEPERC

    N OF CASES             38
    MINIMUM           91.000
    MAXIMUM          125.000
    MEAN             101.579
    STANDARD DEV       6.479
```

a On average, how well did the flights do in meeting their schedules?

b What sources of variability can you think of?

c Find Empirical Rule limits that should include 95% of the flights.

2.23 A stem-and-leaf display of the data for Exercise 2.22, created by Systat, is shown in Figure 2.23.

a Do the data appear bell-shaped, so that the Empirical Rule should work reasonably well?

b What percentage of the 38 scores fall within the limits calculated in part c of Exercise 2.22?

FIGURE 2.23 **Stem-and-Leaf Display for Flight Time Data**

```
 9    1
 9    23
 9    55
 9H   67777
 9    8999
10M   000000
10    22222333
10H   455
10    67
10    89
11    1
      ***OUTSIDE VALUES***
11    6
12    5
```

2.24 The late percentage data of Exercise 2.22 were plotted in Figure 2.24, in order of scheduled arrival, by Systat. Is there any indication of a trend?

FIGURE 2.24 **Sequence Plot of Lateness Data**

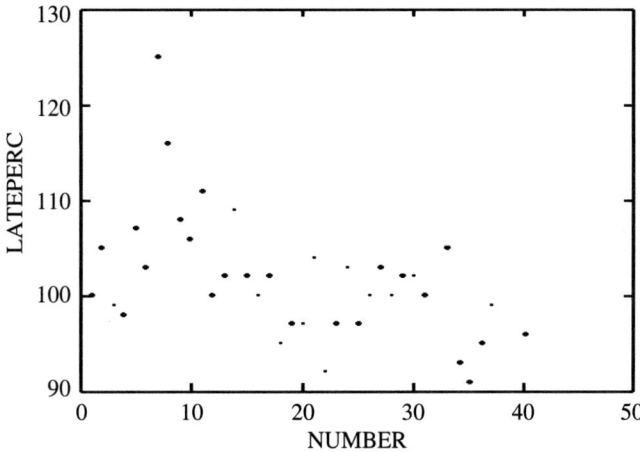

2.25 The operations manager of Exercise 2.22 also kept track of the lateness percentage of each flight over time. The results for flight 483 for 40 consecutive weekdays were analyzed by Minitab, as follows:

```
MTB > print 'Lateperc'

LatePerc
100 107  97 101 103 101  95  92  96  93 104 109 106 107 112 102 101  99  99
 98 104 109 116 118 104 106  99 105 104 107  97  94 100 101 102 105 109  99
105  99

MTB > describe 'Lateperc'

               N    MEAN  MEDIAN  TRMEAN  STDEV  SEMEAN
LatePerc      40  102.62  102.00  102.39   5.75    0.91


             MIN     MAX      Q1      Q3
LatePerc   92.00  118.00   99.00  106.00
```

a Should we expect essentially the same variability in these time-series numbers as we found for the cross-sectional data of Exercise 2.22?

b Which standard deviation turned out smaller?

2.26 The lateness percentage data of Exercise 2.25 were plotted against day number, as shown in Figure 2.25.

a Is there any evidence of a time trend?

b The target percentage is 100. Use the standard deviation from Exercise 2.25 to construct control limits. Did any days qualify as out of control?

FIGURE 2.25 **Sequence Plot for Lateness Data**

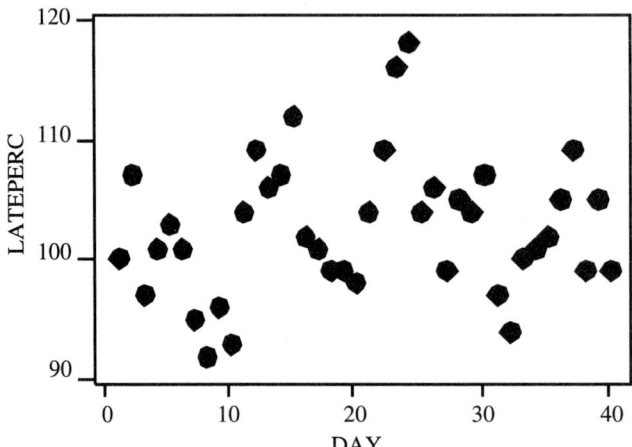

2.27 A manufacturer of tools for homeowners and contractors produces a line of masonry bits for drills. One of the critical qualities of these bits is hardness, measured on a standard scale. If the bits are not hard enough, they wear out rapidly. If the bits are too hard, they may be brittle and break; because the bits are used to drill holes in concrete and brick, it can be extremely dangerous to have a bit break. The scale used to measure hardness is quite sensitive; what would seem to an outsider to be small changes in hardness lead to fairly large changes on the scale. The target value on this scale is 16.0. Even when the production process is working well, there is some variability in bit hardness, mostly because of imperfect mixing of metals in the alloy and variation in heating during the tempering process. The target standard deviation is 0.5.

The tool manufacturer instituted a quality-improvement approach, involving, among many other actions, use of control charts. Each production day, a sample of five bits is selected randomly from the day's production. The hardness of each bit is measured carefully (by a destructive process, which necessitates using a sample) and recorded. Data for the first 30 days following overhaul of the production process were used in control charts for the mean and the range, shown in Figure 2.26.

a Do the charts indicate there is a problem with the mean? If so, does it appear there was a sudden jump or a gradual trend?

b Do the charts indicate there is a problem of excessive variability? If so, was there a jump or a trend?

2.28 The tool manufacturer in Exercise 2.27 believed there were two major explanations for unsatisfactory bit hardness. One potential problem was bad lots of metal. Each lot is used for about six days of production, and each lot is completely used up before another lot is begun. A second potential problem was the heating system used to temper the bits. Over time, this system can drift to higher or lower temperatures. Based on the control charts in Figure 2.26, which seems to be the more plausible culprit for any problems you identified in Exercise 2.27? ■

FIGURE 2.28 **Control Charts for Bit Hardness Data**

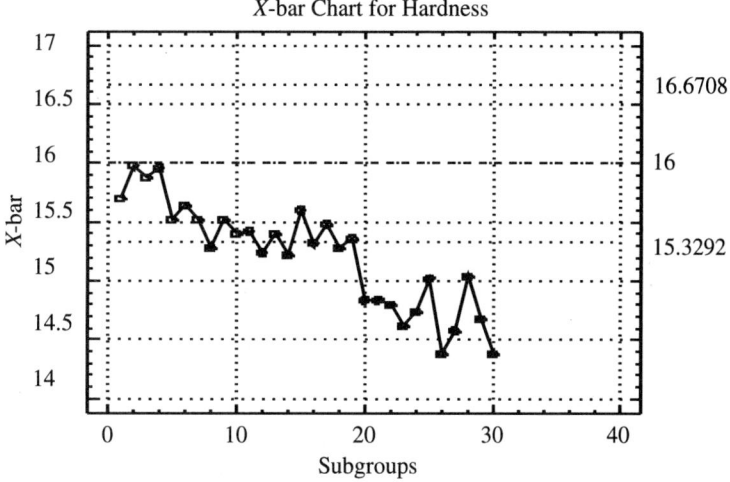

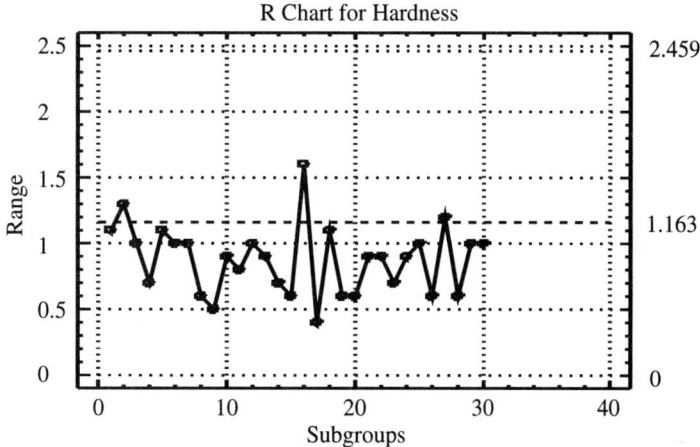

The Normal Distribution: A Preview

e have mentioned the bell-shaped normal distribution several times. In particular, this distribution of data is the basis for the Empirical Rule. Here we briefly discuss the nature of this distribution, how to evaluate whether actual data are a reasonable approximation to this distribution, and how this distribution helps to evaluate whether a manufacturing process is capable of meeting desired specifications. This section is only a brief preview. We will have a "feature length" discussion in Chapter 5.

The normal distribution of data occurs quite frequently. There are theoretical reasons for this occurrence, including the Central Limit Theorem, which will be explained in Chapter 6. Sometimes, data just happen to fit this distribution well. It certainly is *not* true that every distribution should look normal, or that other distributions are somehow "abnormal." But the distribution occurs often enough—and is the basis for enough statistical methods—that special tools have been developed to assess whether data fit a normal distribution.

Many statistical packages superimpose a plot of a normal curve over a histogram. For example, a manufacturer of plastic sheeting used as a protective cover while painting walls and ceilings sells one grade that is stated to be 2 mils thick. If the sheeting is not thick enough, it is likely to tear and fail in its job of protection. If it's too thick, the manufacturer is wasting money on the extra material. The manufacturer can measure the thickness quite closely using material trimmed off in the process of cutting the material for packaging. Suppose that a sample of 400 measurements is obtained. A histogram and normal curve, produced by the JMP IN package, are shown in Figure 2.27.

FIGURE 2.27   **Histogram and Normal Curve for Thickness Data**

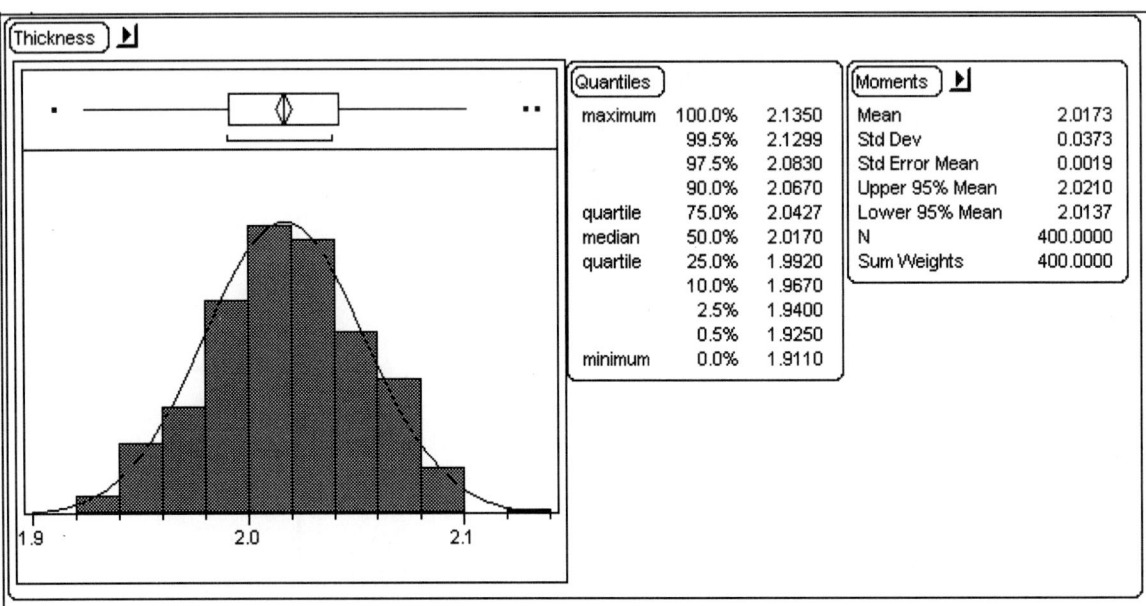

The data appear to be quite close to a normal distribution. The normal curve appears to be a good approximation to the histogram. Notice that the mean is 2.0173, just above the stated value of 2 mils; the standard deviation is 0.0373. Because the data appear quite close to normally distributed, we can expect that the Empirical Rule will be a good approximation for these data. In fact, it is excellent; 266 of the 400 values (66.5%) are within 1 standard deviation of the mean and 382 of the 400 values (95.5%) are within 2 standard deviations of the mean. Incidentally, rather than counting by hand, we had the program create a new variable that equaled 1 for each value within 1 standard deviation of the mean, and 0 for all other values. The sum of these 1s and 0s is simply the number of values within 1 standard deviation of the mean. A similar process gave us the count of values within 2 standard deviations of the mean.

EXAMPLE 2.16

A manufacturer of telephone cable cuts the cable into lengths that are sent to field engineers. The engineers use the cable to connect new installations to phone lines and to replace broken or defective cable. The cutting process is done at high speed, and the production manager was concerned that the cuts were not accurate. A sample of 84 sections of wire, each supposedly 100 meters long, was measured for actual length. The data were plotted by JMP IN, with a normal curve superimposed on the histogram, as shown in Figure 2.28. Does it appear that the Empirical Rule will work well for the length data?

FIGURE 2.28   **Plots for Cable Data**

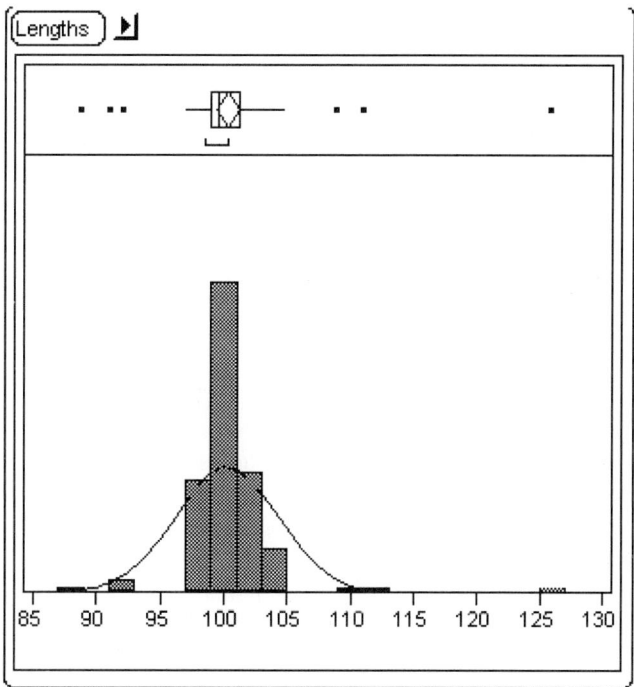

Solution

The histogram does not match the normal curve at all well. The sharp peak in the middle is much higher than the curve, and several values in the histogram are beyond the range shown for the normal curve. These values appear to be outliers. Notice that there are several outliers. In fact, we counted 77 of the 84 values within 1 standard deviation of the mean; that's more than 90%, a very bad approximation to 68%. ∎

normal probability plot

Another graphical method that is useful in checking whether data follow a normal distribution is a **normal probability plot**, sometimes called a *normal quantile plot*. We don't yet have all the ideas needed to describe how such a plot is constructed. For now, we simply state that (nearly) normally distributed data should appear as a (nearly) straight line in this plot. For example, we noted that the data on thickness of plastic sheeting appeared nearly normal. A normal probability plot of the data, constructed by JMP IN, is shown in Figure 2.29. The points in the plot are, indeed, quite close to a line, confirming that the data are nearly normally distributed.

FIGURE 2.29   Normal Probability Plot for Thickness Data

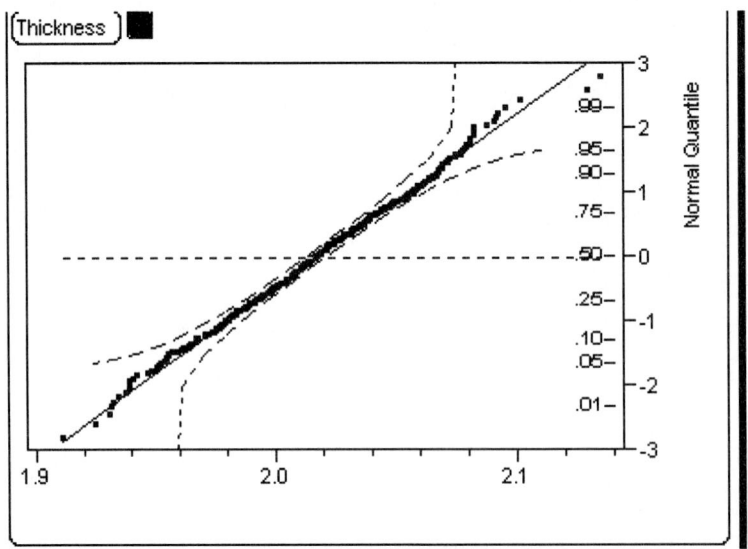

EXAMPLE 2.17

A normal probability plot for the cable length data of the previous example is shown in Figure 2.30. How does the plot indicate that the data are not normally distributed?

Solution

The plot doesn't look like a straight line. Instead, it has something of an S shape. Note the point in the upper right corner, which is far away from the reference line.

FIGURE 2.30   Normal Probability Plot for Cable Lengths

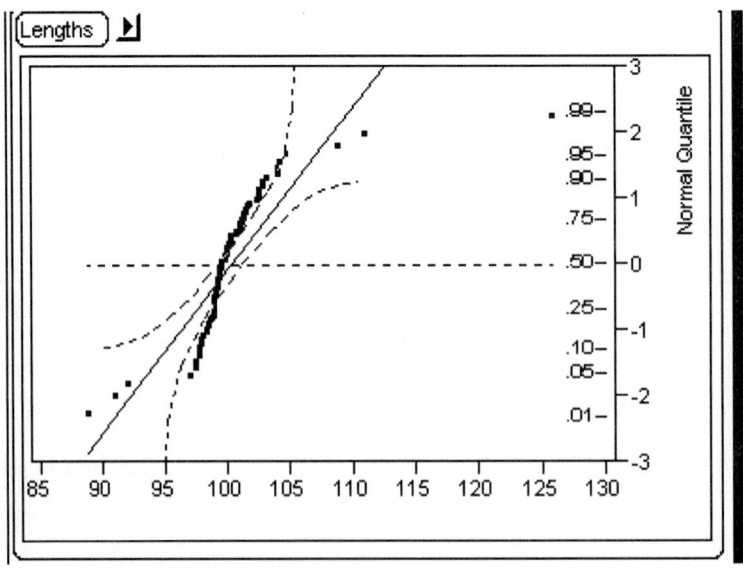

The normal distribution and Empirical Rule are useful tools in assessing the **capability** of a manufacturing process. Capability refers to the ability of a process to produce products that meet specifications. For example, suppose that external specifications for the thickness of 2-mil plastic sheeting call for actual thicknesses between 1.85 and 2.15 mils. Our sample of 400 thicknesses had a mean of 2.0173 and a standard deviation of 0.0373. If we assume that these values represent the actual mean and standard deviation of all the sheeting that's produced, we can calculate that virtually all the values will be within 3 standard deviations of the mean. The range $2.0173 \pm 3(0.0373)$ is from 1.9054 to 2.1292, so practically all thicknesses should be in the specified range: 1.85 to 2.15.

A process can be incapable—fail to meet specifications—for several reasons. The process may be "off target," having a seriously incorrect average value. Or it may yield too much variation, having too large a standard deviation. Or it may produce outlying values that prevent application of the Empirical Rule. There are a number of special indices of process capability; we won't go into them here, except to note that several of them assume a roughly normal distribution of measurements.

E X A M P L E   2 . 1 8

The cable-cutting process in the previous two examples is intended to produce cables that are between 97 and 103 meters long. Based on the sample data, is the process capable?

Solution

No. Assuming that 97 to 103 is intended to be the mean ± 3 standard deviations, we would need a mean of 100 and a standard deviation of 1. The standard deviation in the data is much larger than 1, so there is too much variability. Also, we saw that the data contained several outlying values; these values are well outside the desired range. ■

E X E R C I S E S

2.29 In the previous section's exercises, we considered the number of calls cleared by operators in a directory assistance center. The data were somewhat skewed, with an outlier. A normal probability plot, produced using Minitab, is shown in Figure 2.31.

  a How does the normal probability plot reveal the skewness?

  b How does the plot show the outlier?

2.30 In the calls cleared data, how will the outlier affect the standard deviation and the quality of the Empirical Rule approximation?

2.31 In Section 2.1, we considered changes in the Consumer Price Index (CPI) for the Philadelphia region. A Minitab normal probability plot is shown in Figure 2.32. What does the plot indicate about the shape of the distribution?

2.32 A supplier of lumber for home building sells construction grade 2-by-4 lumber in 8-foot lengths. Because of irregularities in the wood and shrinkage caused by drying, there is some variation in actual length. Lumber is acceptable if it is between 95.5 and 96.5 inches. The current process produces lengths that are normally distributed with a mean of 96.04 inches and a standard deviation of 0.52 inch. Is this process capable of meeting standards of acceptability?

2.33 Lumber that is too long (over 96.5 inches) can be cut by the home builder. Lumber that is too short must be discarded. The supplier can increase the mean length to 96.54 inches without changing the standard deviation. What would this change do to the proportion of lumber that is too short?

FIGURE 2.31 **Normal Probability Plot for Calls Cleared Data**

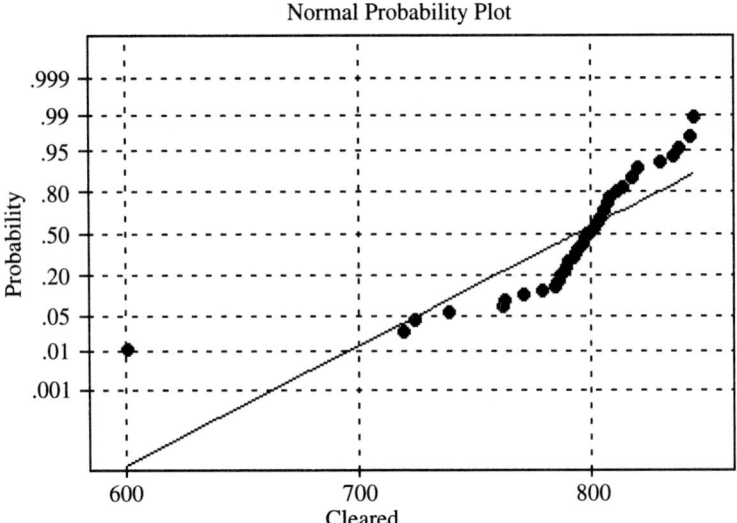

Calculators and Computer Software Systems

2.5

Inexpensive hand calculators can be quite useful in performing many of the calculations in this chapter, especially for relatively small amounts of data. For example, many calculators have keys for obtaining the mean and standard deviation directly once the data have been entered. Some have special keys or programmable routines that will do more elaborate computations as well. When using a hand calculator, one must be very careful to enter data correctly because the entries are usually unavailable for later review. It's a good idea to check answers for reasonableness. The mean should be in the middle of the data; if the calculated result is near one end or the other of the data, a data-entry error should be suspected. The Empirical Rule provides a useful check on the size of a standard deviation. If the 1 standard deviation interval around the mean includes virtually all the data rather than about 68%, one should again suspect a data-entry error.

For larger amounts of data, a computer is extremely useful. There are literally hundreds of programs available for doing statistical analyses by computer. Many are special-purpose programs for statistical analysis. Some spreadsheet programs, such as Excel, have limited statistical capabilities. Naturally, the special-purpose programs have more capability, but if you already are familiar with a spreadsheet, you may wish to try that first. Most of the programs will carry out virtually all the computations in this book and many more besides. Even more important, the good ones will do data plots very quickly and conveniently.

In general, these packages carry out several steps. First, data must be entered into the program, either from a keyboard or by importing a data file from a disk or tape. To make eventual output more readable, a package will usually have some ability to name variables in a data set. There should be a facility to review the data set and edit it to remove errors. Once the data set is ready for analysis, any package can do plots and computations very quickly and make the results available in a variety of ways.

E notation

Some computer outputs state results in **E notation**. Rather than reporting a mean as 15,326, for example, a particular package may report the mean as 1.5326E04. The E

FIGURE 2.32   **Normal Plot for Change in CPI Data**

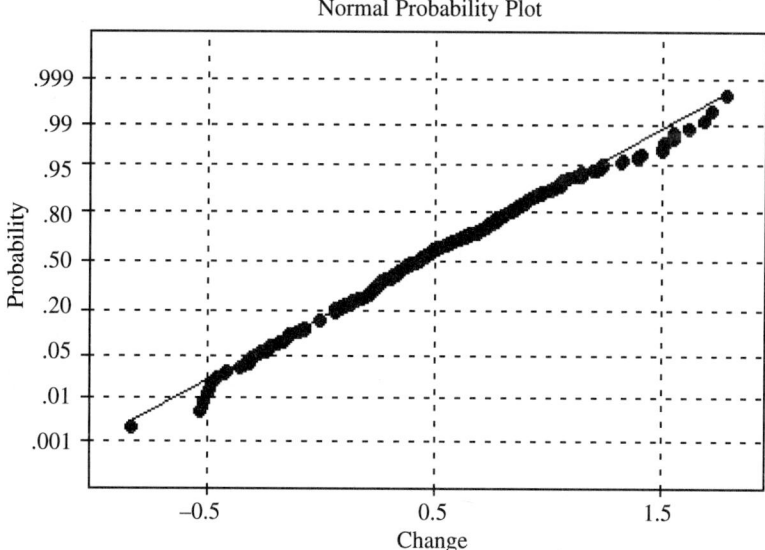

(exponent) part of the expression tells you how many places to the right to move the decimal point. For instance, E04 indicates that the decimal point should be moved four places to the right, so $1.5326E04 = 15,326$. Similarly, a negative exponent corresponds to moving the decimal place to the left: $1.5326E - 04 = 0.00015326$.

We think that the data-plotting ability of computer packages, especially the ones developed specially for statistical analysis, is their most crucial feature. It's so easy to obtain histograms, stem-and-leaf displays, boxplots, and other data displays discussed in later chapters that there's little excuse for doing computations before looking at the data. Any good display should alert you to skewness, outliers, or bimodality—characteristics that distort the meaning of a mean or standard deviation.

It is perfectly possible to use any computer package badly. If you insist on entering "continent" as a numerical variable, with 1 meaning Africa; 2, Asia; 3, Australia; 4, Europe; 5, North America; and 6, South America; and if you ask for the mean continent, any package we know of will calculate it, to lots of decimal places. A good package will have a method for distinguishing qualitative from quantitative variables, but you have to use it. Further, if you ask for a standard deviation from wildly outlier-prone data, any package we know of will give it to you. You must take responsibility for looking at the data and doing sensible things with it.

We will use output from many statistical packages in this book. Remember that not all the output provided by a package will be relevant to a particular problem; rather than trying to interpret every number, find the relevant numbers. Used with thought, these packages can be immensely convenient and useful.

If you use data consisting of very large numbers with very little variability, you may get round-off errors because of the limited storage capacity of a computer word. For example, consider the Excel output in Figure 2.33. If you compute the sample variance for the original data by hand, you'll find that it comes out 1.50, yet Excel shows it as 1.00. The same error occurred in other packages as well. Eliminating all the lead digits (subtracting 53127500 from each value) doesn't change the variability and the sample variance at all; it's still 1.50. With the recoded data, the computer gets it right.

FIGURE 2.33   Excel Output for Original and Recoded Data

	A	B	C	D
1	Original Data	Recoded Data		
2	53127501	1		
3	53127502	2		
4	53127502	2		
5	53127503	3		
6	53127503	3		
7	53127503	3		
8	53127504	4		
9	53127504	4		
10	53127505	5		
11				
12	*Original Data*		*Recoded Data*	
13				
14	Mean	53127503	Mean	3
15	Median	53127503	Median	3
16	Standard Deviation	1	Standard Deviation	1.225
17	Sample Variance	1	Sample Variance	1.50

2.6   Statistical Methods and Quality Improvement

Statistical tools are a major contributor to quality control and process improvement. We have introduced control charts in this chapter and will describe other statistical quality methods in later chapters. Thinking statistically about averages, and especially about variability, is crucially important in thinking about quality and its improvement.

There are several kinds of control charts. We have described the most common ones: means (*x*-bar) charts, range (R) charts, and standard deviation (S) charts. These charts apply to measured, quantitative characteristics such as the strength of seat belt materials, the time required for a telephone to be answered, or the internal pressure of an automatic transmission. Another form of chart that is useful for quantitative characteristics is the

cusum chart

cusum chart, which keeps track of the cumulative sum of a series of measurements. It is best suited for detecting a drift upward or downward in average level; it's not intended to detect a change in variability.

There are also control charts for tracking qualitative characteristics. The simplest chart applies to counting the number of defective items in a sample, where each item is categorized as either good or defective. For this situation, *p* charts and *np* charts are useful.

The same basic ideas apply with all control charts. The first concern is whether an

statistical control

ongoing process is in **statistical control**. A process is said to be in statistical control if it is statistically stable—that is, if both the mean value and the amount of variability are staying constant over time. Sudden jumps or clear trends in either average values or amount of variability are indications that the process is changing and that the process needs to be corrected.

Just because a process is in statistical control does not mean that it's working well. Previously, we discussed the idea of statistical capability—the ability of a process to meet specified standards. If a coating process for computer chips consistently produces thicknesses with a mean of 18 and a standard deviation of 2, with no trends in mean or in variability, then it is in statistical control. But if the coating process should be giving thicknesses between 14.5 and 15.5, the process is not capable. The average value is wrong and the degree of variability is too large to meet the desired standard.

Assuming that the process is in control and has the proper average value, the next concern is the degree of variability. In many cases, variability is an enemy of quality. There are exceptions—we wouldn't want all sports events to come out exactly the same or every diamond ring to be identical to every other one. But in most cases, the less variability there is, the better. A useful way to think about causes of variability is to divide them into **common causes** and **special causes**.

common causes
special causes

Common causes are the continuing sources of variability that affect a process. For example, a bakery tries to control the height of loaves of bread. Common causes of variation would include the amounts of flour, shortening, salt, and water put into the bread dough; the length of time allowed for the loaves to rise; and the temperature of the baking oven. Typically, common causes are small and yield results that stay within control limits; they are the reasons why the process varies within control limits. Special causes, in contrast, are large, one-time causes that often take the process beyond control limits, temporarily. For a bread bakery, special causes of variation might include a contaminated batch of yeast that didn't allow the dough to rise, or an accidental loss of heat in an oven.

Special causes are usually evident to the people running the process; common causes require systematic searching. When a control chart indicates a sudden failure in the process, typically the reason is obvious or relatively easy to figure out. If somebody left the oven partly open during the bread-baking process (which we would hope was a special situation, not a common one), one look at the oven door would tell us why the bread didn't come out well. However, if the amount of flour measured for a loaf varies somewhat because of humidity variation or moisture differences in the flour, that problem wouldn't be so easy to detect. As long as the people running the process are committed to quality, they should be able to deal with special causes. Managers can be more helpful by investigating the subtler, common causes of variation, and finding ways to reduce them.

Statistical methods alone aren't enough. Control charts have been known in American industry for 60 years. If they cured all quality problems by themselves, American products would universally be the highest quality in the world; however, some individuals assert that American quality is not absolutely the best.

Almost all the people who have studied good-quality and poor-quality operations agree that improving quality requires sustained, long-term, patient commitment by managers and workers at all levels. The best-known quality expert was probably W. Edwards Deming, a professional statistician who introduced statistical quality control and improvement methods in postwar Japan. Deming (1986) formulated a 14-point program for quality improvement. An interesting outsider's view is given in Walton (1986). Deming insisted on the absolute necessity of *sustained* management commitment; he abhorred short-term sloganeering ("zero defects") as a substitute for real effort.

Almost all quality experts concentrate on improving processes, as opposed to exhorting people. At bottom, most of the fundamental tasks of organizations are repetitive processes conducted under similar conditions. Most people tend to think of processes and quality control in the context of manufacturing, but the same ideas apply just as well to granting loans, servicing automobiles, handling airline reservations, and many other service sector activities. One of the key messages to managers from modern quality-improvement experts is to think more about long-run improvements in processes and less about short-run "fire fighting." If managers modify a process in response to every short-term, random variation, that just adds another source of variation, without accomplishing anything systematic. Managers should identify the goals of the process, consider what aspects of the process can be varied, and carry out well-considered experiments to find the best possible design for the process.

Rarely does quality leap upward. Instead, quality inches upward in small increments. An improved product design here, a modification of a service process there, improved cooperation with a supplier, a tailoring of a product to better fit customers' needs—all are small steps that must be taken repeatedly to improve quality. These common, small gains usually have a greater cumulative effect than the large dramatic ones. It takes a patient, persevering management to press on for quality improvement without immediate, dramatic payoffs.

One key to improving process quality is intelligent experimentation. Almost any task can be accomplished in many ways—some good, some bad. A remarkably effective method for avoiding quality improvement is to insist on doing a task one way "because we've always done it that way." A not much better approach to quality improvement is casual, unplanned experimentation—manipulating one aspect of a process, then another, without pattern or planning. A far more productive approach is planned experimentation—that is, systematically thinking about all the key aspects of a process and deliberately, systematically seeking improvements in all of them. Here's one place where statistical thinking becomes vital. One of the great success stories of recent years in quality improvement has been the effective use of statistically controlled experiments.

Statistical thinking is crucial in considering processes, particularly in dealing with variation within a process. Most accounting systems are designed to deal with averages and totals. Statistical thinking adds the key idea of variability. Any manufacturing or service process will have some degree of natural variability in results. The proverbial widgets will vary from one another because of differences in raw materials, wear on machine parts, changes in temperature and humidity, and many other reasons. Adjustable-rate mortgage loans will sometimes be in default because of a mortgage holder's losing a job, a sharp decline in value of the property, or a change in interest rates. The key question is whether recent variations in process results are within the normal range (and therefore not worth worrying much about) or into the "out-of-control" range (and therefore a cause for concern). One of the important functions of control charts is to indicate what is *not* worth management attention.

The statistical ideas of variation and experimentation often come together. In many quality-improvement problems, reducing variability is at least as important as improving average quality. A motel chain might institute a change in its reservations process that cuts the average time per reservation by 10%, but if that change increased variability in times by 100%, the chain could expect to reduce the demand for its reservations considerably. An airline that reduced the average duration of a Kansas City to Philadelphia flight by 2 minutes (98% of the flights arrive 3 minutes earlier, 2% arrive 47 minutes later) would not make either of the authors happy. A manager who uses statistical experiments and thinks about both averages and variability should be able to make a real difference in quality, given patience and sustained effort.

2.7

Summing Up

H ere are some suggestions for dealing with summarizing data.

1   Decide whether the variable being summarized should be regarded as quantitative (so that means and standard deviations make sense) or qualitative.

2   Decide whether the data are a cross section or a time series.

3   The first step in summarizing a time series is to plot the data in time order. If the data show a trend in either average or variability, overall summary figures that ignore the trend can be misleading.

4   Control charts are a form of time order plot. An x-bar chart for means and either an S chart or an R chart for variability will indicate whether the process is in statistical control (statistically stable) or not.

5   For cross sections or stable time series, obtain one or more plots of the distribution of the variable. Histograms, stem-and-leaf displays, boxplots, and normal probability plots all help to indicate typical values, the degree of variability, the amount of skewness, and the presence of any outliers.

6   The mean and median are the most common measures of the typical average value. A large difference between these two numbers suggests severe skewness or outliers.

7   The standard deviation is the most useful measure of variability. Its numerical value may be interpreted by the Empirical Rule, provided that the distribution is not grossly skewed or outlier-prone.

In addition, you may want to reread the summary of key ideas at the beginning of the chapter.

EXAMPLE 2.19

Data were collected state by state on the average 1995–1996 tuition and fees for in-state residents at 4-year public colleges (tuition), median 1994 household income (income), tuition as a percent of household income (tuit%), and geographic region in the United States (region: 1 = Northeast, 2 = South, 3 = Midwest, 4 = West). The data are as follows:

Code	State	Tuition	Income	Tuit%	Region
01	Alabama	2234	27196	08.21	2
02	Alaska	2502	45367	05.52	4
03	Arizona	1943	31293	06.21	4
04	Arkansas	2062	25565	08.07	2
05	California	2918	35331	08.26	4
06	Colorado	2458	37833	06.50	4
07	Connecticut	3828	41097	09.31	1
08	Delaware	3962	35873	11.04	2
09	Florida	1790	29294	06.11	2
10	Georgia	2076	31457	06.60	2
11	Hawaii	1524	42255	03.61	4
12	Idaho	1714	31536	05.44	4
13	Illinois	3388	35081	09.66	3
14	Indiana	3040	27858	10.91	3
15	Iowa	2565	33079	07.75	3
16	Kansas	2110	28322	07.45	3
17	Kentucky	2160	25595	08.12	2
18	Louisiana	2139	25676	08.33	2
19	Maine	3582	30316	11.75	1
20	Maryland	3572	39198	09.11	2
21	Massachusetts	4178	40500	10.31	1
22	Michigan	3789	35284	10.74	3

23	Minnesota	3108	33644	09.24	3
24	Mississippi	2443	25400	09.62	2
25	Missouri	3007	30190	09.96	2
26	Montana	2346	27631	08.49	3
27	Nebraska	2294	31794	07.22	3
28	Nevada	1830	35871	05.10	4
29	N Hampshire	4537	35245	12.87	1
30	N Jersey	3649	42280	09.10	1
31	N Mexico	1938	26905	07.20	4
32	N York	3697	31899	11.59	1
33	N Carolina	1622	30114	05.39	2
34	North Dakota	2211	32278	07.82	3
35	Ohio	3664	31855	11.50	3
36	Oklahoma	1741	25991	06.45	2
37	Oregon	3241	31456	10.30	4
38	Pennsylvania	4693	32066	14.64	1
39	Rhode Island	3619	31298	11.33	1
40	S Carolina	3103	29846	10.40	2
41	South Dakota	2549	29733	08.57	3
42	Tennessee	2001	28639	06.99	2
43	Texas	1832	30755	05.96	2
44	Utah	2007	35716	05.62	4
45	Vermont	5521	35802	15.42	1
46	Virginia	3965	37647	10.53	2
47	Washington	2726	33533	08.13	4
48	West Virginia	1997	23564	08.45	2
49	Wisconsin	2555	35389	07.22	3
50	Wyoming	2005	33140	06.05	4

Source: USA Today/General Accounting Office

Summary results, calculated using JMP IN, are shown in Figure 2.34. Note that the data have not been weighted by population, so, for example, the tuition results do not necessarily describe the costs for a typical student. Summarize the results, including the shape of the data, average values, and variability. What notable differences are there among the four regions?

Solution

First of all, the data are cross-sectional at a given time, so we need not be concerned about time trends. Next, we look at the graphical displays of the data. The histograms for tuition and income are clearly right skewed (with the long tail toward the larger values). The data for tuition percentage are less skewed, though there is still some slight right skewness. We can confirm the skewness by noting that in each case the mean is greater than the median.

The overall summary numbers show that there is considerable state-to-state variation. For tuition, the standard deviation is almost $975, with a mean of almost $2800. For income, the standard deviation is over $4900, with a mean of almost $34,500. Note that the mean and, especially, the standard deviation are inflated by the modest outlier shown in the boxplot; a look through the data shows that Alaska has an exceptionally high household income. For tuition percentage, the mean is 8.60 and the standard deviation is 2.46. The Empirical Rule should work decently for these data; thus, about 95% of states should have a tuition percentage in the range $8.60 \pm 2(2.46)$, or 2.68 to 14.52. In fact, 2 of the 50 states (Pennsylvania and Vermont) fall outside this range, so 48 of 50 (96%) fall within it.

FIGURE 2.34

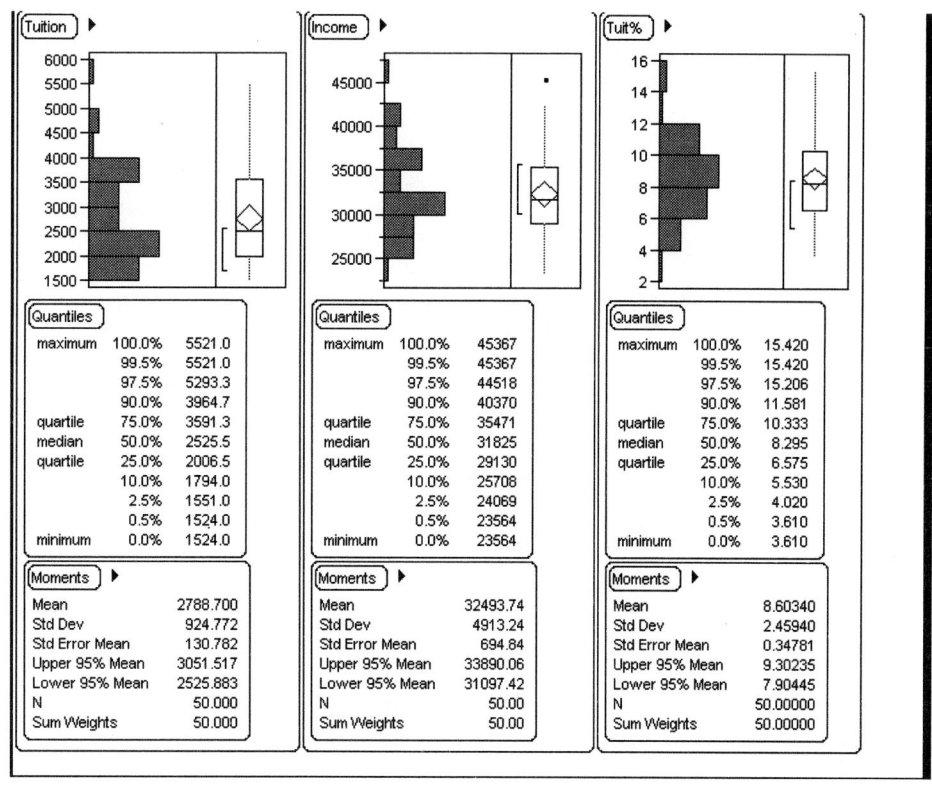

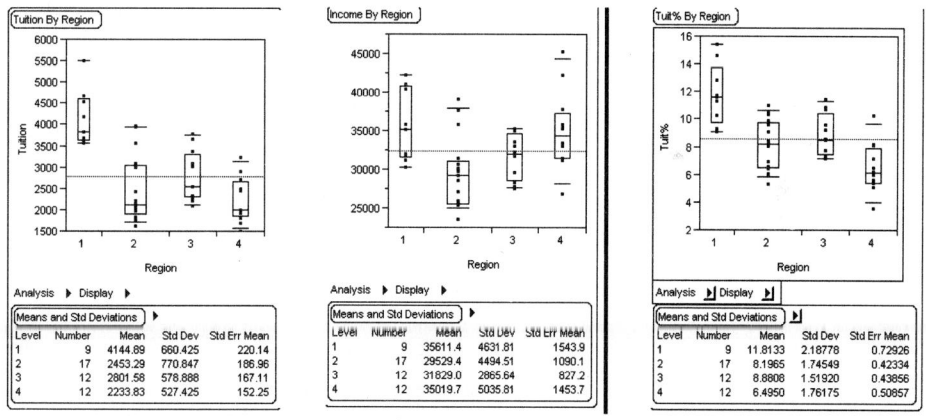

It's worth reiterating that we look only for what we need in the output—and don't worry about the rest. Such mysterious (for now) entries as "Std Error Mean" and "Upper 95% Mean" can be ignored.

Turning to the analysis by region, we see that region 1 has the highest average tuition, both in dollar terms and as a percentage of income. The other three regions have similar averages on these scales. Region 2 is noticeably more variable in dollar tuition, but region 1 is more variable in tuition percentage. For income, regions 1 and 4 have notably higher averages; region 4 is somewhat more variable (there's Alaska again), and region 3 is noticeably less variable than the others. ■

2.34 A study of sick leave days over one year for a sample of 20 workers in a company yields the following numbers, arranged in increasing order:

0 0 0 0 0 0 1 1 1 1 2 2 2 3 3 4 6 9 14 31

a Verify that the sample mean is 4.0 and the sample standard deviation is 7.27.

b What fraction of the observations actually falls within 1 standard deviation of the mean? What aspect of the data explains the discrepancy between this fraction and the Empirical Rule approximation?

2.35 If a computer package is available to you, use it to find the mean, median, and standard deviation for the data of Exercise 2.34. Is the standard deviation calculated with a denominator of $n - 1$ or n? Compare your results with these results from Excel:

	A	B
1	mean	4
2	standard error	1.6255
3	median	1.5
4	mode	0
5	standard deviation	7.2693
6	sample variance	52.842

2.36 Consider the following artificial data:

8 9 10 10 10 10 10 10 11 12 19 20 20
20 21 28 29 30 30 30 30 30 30 31 32

a Plot the data using 5 classes. What pattern of skewness and modality do you see?

b The mean of these values is 20. How can this result be obtained without computation? How about the median?

c Calculate the standard deviation.

d What fraction of the values falls within 1 standard deviation of the mean? How does this compare with the Empirical Rule fraction? Explain the discrepancy.

e What fraction of the values falls within 2 standard deviations of the mean? How does this fraction compare with the Empirical Rule fraction?

2.37 Here is another artificial data set:

−36 −1 −1 −1 −1 0 0 1 1 2 3 4 6 9 14

a Verify that the mean is 0 and that the standard deviation is 10.84.

b Calculate the skewness coefficient $(\bar{y} - \text{median})/s$.

c Plot the data. Can you identify an obvious skewness?

2.38 Assembling a circuit board requires several dozen soldering connections. The main soldering operation is automated. However, the process can yield defective connections, usually caused by poor penetration of a flux material used to prepare the connections. Each soldered board must be inspected visually and each defective soldering connection repaired by a relatively expensive hand touch-up. The number of defects on each board is recorded. Twenty boards are produced each hour; an average of 2 defects per board is considered in control. The following means were obtained for a 30-hour production week. From the numbers, is there indication of an upward or downward trend?

```
MTB > print 'mean'

mean
    1.45   1.65   1.50   2.25   1.65   1.60   2.30   2.20   2.70
```

1.70	2.35	1.70	1.90	1.45	1.40	2.60	2.05	1.70
1.05	2.35	1.90	1.55	1.95	1.60	2.05	2.05	1.70
2.30	1.30	2.35						

2.39 A simplified x-bar chart of the means in the previous exercise is shown in Figure 2.35. Does the chart indicate a trend?

FIGURE 2.35 **Simplified x-bar Chart**

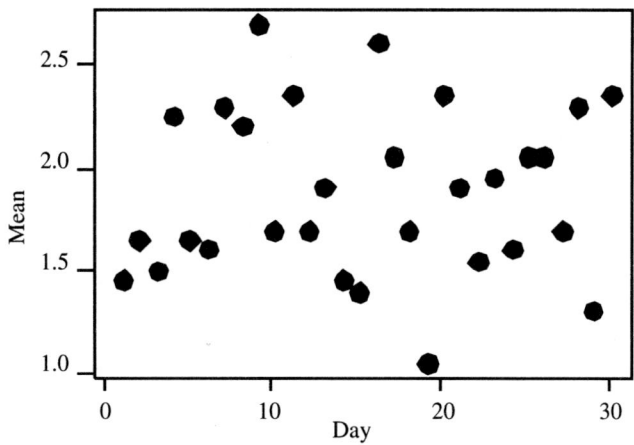

2.40 Experience with the soldering process indicates that the standard deviation applicable to the average number of defectives among 20 boards is 0.38. Recall that the in-control mean is regarded as 2.0.

   a Calculate upper and lower control limits. Do any means fall outside these limits?

   b If a mean fell below the lower control limit, would this indicate a problem?

2.41 The individual board data underlying the mean number of soldering defects was not shown. Obviously, there can't be a negative number of defects; theoretically, there might be dozens of defects on a single board. Assuming that the process is in control (mean number of defects equals 2), what might be expected regarding the shape of the data? In particular, what kind of skewness might be expected?

2.42 A regional public transit agency runs a fleet of buses from suburban areas to the western terminal of a subway line. One important measure of service quality is how late buses are in arriving at the terminal; typically, riders are not concerned about a minute or two of lateness, but longer delays indicate a deterioration in service. Each weekday morning, a dispatcher records the number of minutes late for a random sample of eight buses scheduled to arrive at the terminal between 7:30 and 8:30 A.M. The means over a 58-day period are shown here:

	A	B	C	D	E	F	G	H	I	J
4	Mean									
5	1.125	1.3125	1.5	1.6875	1.625	1.9375	1.625	1.6875	1.9375	1.875
6	2.0625	1.5	1.4375	1.375	1.5	1.5625	2.25	1.1875	1.125	1.8125
7	2	2.625	1.5	1.8125	1.1875	1.75	2.375	2	2	2.4375
8	1.1825	2.4375	1.75	1.5625	1.75	2.25	1.4375	1.625	2.0625	2.375
9	1.75	1.6875	2.125	1.5625	1.875	1.6875	1.375	1.625	1.6875	1.5
10	1.375	4	4	2.0625	4.75	3.125				

By looking at the numbers, is it possible to detect where a lateness problem has occurred?

2.43 A simplified x-bar chart for the means in Exercise 2.42 is shown in Figure 2.36. Where were there lateness problems?

FIGURE 2.36   Simplified *x*-bar Chart for Bus Lateness

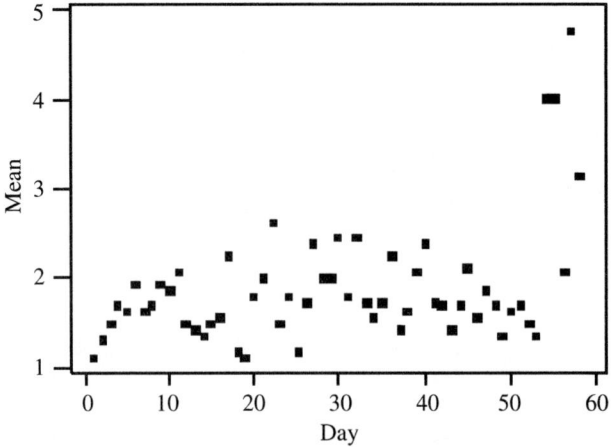

2.44 The standard deviation for the mean lateness of the eight buses in Exercise 2.42 is about 0.30 minute.

    a Construct control limits assuming that the target mean is 1.5 minutes.

    b On which days did the arrival process appear out of control?

2.45 An S chart for the bus arrival process is shown in Figure 2.37. Do the high variability days essentially coincide with the high mean days?

FIGURE 2.37   **Simplified S Chart for Bus Lateness**

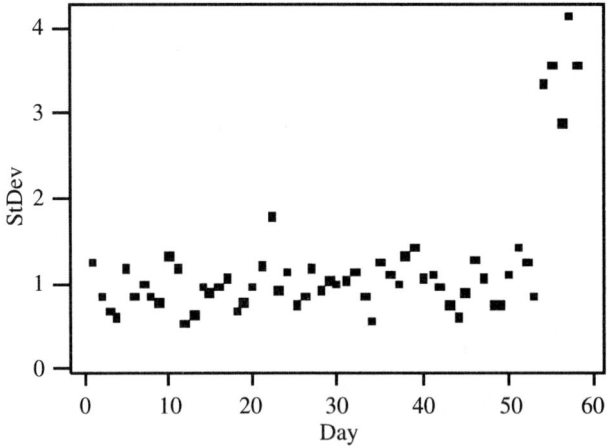

2.46 A major food products company uses sales representatives to work with wholesalers and supermarket chains. The representatives' chief tasks are to sell new products, secure adequate display space in stores, and coordinate promotions. Each representative is solely responsible for a district. Yearly volume of sales in the district is the primary measure of the representative's effectiveness. The results for the last year (in thousands of dollars) are analyzed in the following computer output:

```
MTB > describe 'Volume'
```

	N	MEAN	MEDIAN	TRMEAN	STDEV	SEMEAN
Volume	118	4336.2	4334.0	4350.1	401.4	37.0

	MIN	MAX	Q1	Q3
Volume	3058.0	5301.0	4154.2	4551.8

a The company had attempted, with only partial success, to set up the districts to have equal sales volume potential. What other sources of variability can you think of?

b What does the boxplot in Figure 2.38 indicate about the overall shape of the data—in particular, the skewness and outlier-proneness?

FIGURE 2.38 **Boxplot of Sales Volume Data**

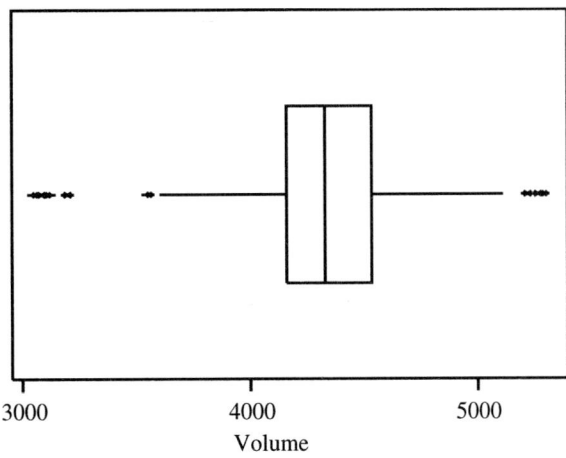

2.47 The data underlying Exercise 2.46 were plotted against the identification number of each sales representative in Figure 2.39. The numbers are in order of seniority, with 1 being the most senior representative. Is there an evident trend in the plot?

2.48 A junior manager, examining the data of Exercise 2.46, noticed that half the sales representatives were performing below average. The manager felt that this fact indicated deficiencies in the company's training or in the representatives' motivation. Is the manager's reasoning valid?

2.49 A publisher of computer science books needs fast action in handling page proofs of forthcoming books. These proofs must be delivered to the authors for a final check of layout, typographical errors, and other features. Because speed is essential in tight publication schedules, the publisher is considering using express delivery services. The last 90 sets of proofs have been randomly allocated to three different services. The number of hours required for the delivery of each set has been recorded.

a Which would be more desirable to the publisher: a smaller mean or a larger one?

b Which would be more desirable to the publisher: a smaller standard deviation or a larger one?

c Judging from the boxplots in Figure 2.40, which server has the smaller mean? The smallest standard deviation?

FIGURE 2.39 **Sequence Plot of Sales Volume Data**

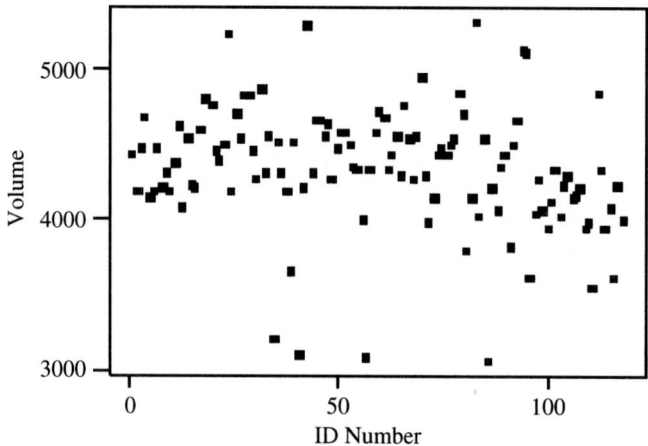

FIGURE 2.40   **Boxplots of Delivery Time Data**

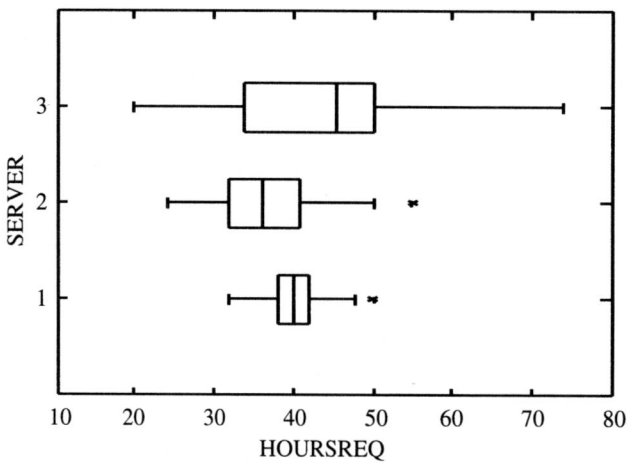

2.50 Do the following computed results from Systat confirm your opinions from part c of Exercise 2.49?

```
THE FOLLOWING RESULTS ARE FOR:
         SERVER    =        1.000

TOTAL OBSERVATIONS:     30


                     HOURSREQ

    N OF CASES             30
    MINIMUM            32.000
    MAXIMUM            50.000
    MEAN               40.067
    STANDARD DEV        4.533
    MEDIAN             40.000
```

```
THE FOLLOWING RESULTS ARE FOR:
        SERVER    =       2.000

TOTAL OBSERVATIONS:    30


                  HOURSREQ

    N OF CASES            30
    MINIMUM          24.000
    MAXIMUM          55.000
    MEAN             37.167
    STANDARD DEV      7.254
    MEDIAN           36.000



THE FOLLOWING RESULTS ARE FOR:
        SERVER    =       3.000

TOTAL OBSERVATIONS:    30


                  HOURSREQ

    N OF CASES            30
    MINIMUM          20.000
    MAXIMUM          74.000
    MEAN             44.600
    STANDARD DEV     13.553
    MEDIAN           45.500
```

2.51 A bank with a large number of credit card accounts in five different divisions records the balance due as a fraction of the credit limit for each account. Each division reports the average value of this fraction weekly. The data are used to obtain the JMP control charts in Figure 2.41.

   a Does the means chart indicate that the average value is not in statistical control?

   b Does the means chart indicate any cases of special-cause variation?

   c Do the control charts indicate increasing or decreasing variability?

2.52 In assessing the fraction of credit limits for each account, the bank in the previous exercise found unusually large values (beyond control limits) for the last two weeks in December. Can you think of a potential special cause?

2.53 Most fast-food restaurants have a continuing problem with employee turnover. As a result, they must expend a great deal of time and effort hiring and training new workers. The franchise owner of 13 outlets of a hamburger chain conducted exit interviews with all employees who left any outlet voluntarily, as opposed to being fired. The interviewer found that the primary reasons for leaving fell into 12 categories:

   a Don't like the type of work

   b Don't like the hours of work

   c Don't like the work environment

   d Conflict with other employees

   e Conflict with managers

   f Better pay elsewhere in the food industry

   g Better pay elsewhere in a different industry

   h More responsible job elsewhere

   i Pay not enough for loss of free time

FIGURE 2.41 Control Charts for Credit Balance Data

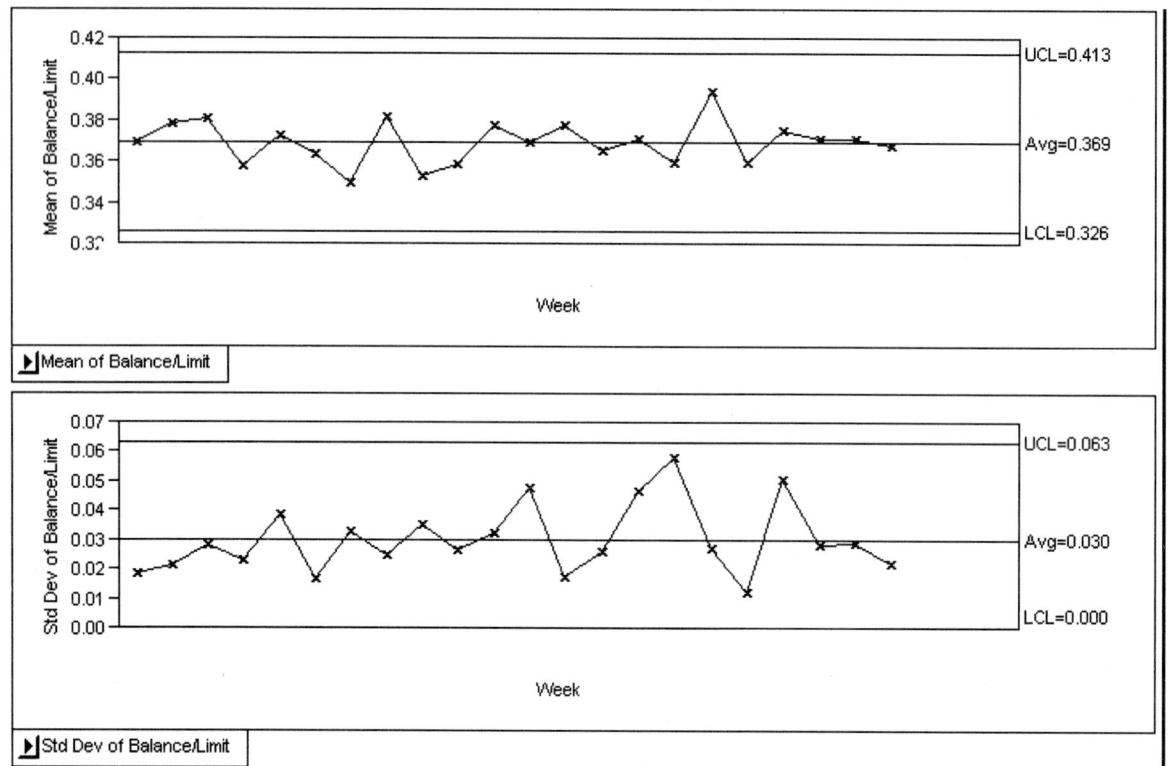

j Leaving to enter college

k Moving to different geographical area

l Promotion within the franchise outlets

The interviewer placed summary statistics in the following spreadsheet:

	B	C	D	E	F
2	DESCRIPTIVE STATISTICS				
3					
4					
5	VARIABLE	N	MEAN	SD	MEDIAN
6	REASON	101	6.9703	2.3767	6.0000

The interviewer noted that the mean (average) was quite a bit larger than the median. What does this fact indicate about the data?

2.54 A Pareto chart of the reasons for leaving the hamburger outlet of Exercise 2.53, generated by Statistix according to the exit interview codes of that exercise, is shown in Figure 2.42.

    a Which codes account for the great majority of the reasons for leaving? Exactly what constitutes the "great majority" is up to you.

    b Are these codes related in any way?

2.55 The manager combined codes from Exercise 2.53 into four basic categories: Conditions (codes 1, 2, 3, 4, and 5); Improvement (codes 8 and 12); Pay (codes 6, 7, and 9); and

FIGURE 2.42 **Reasons for Leaving Employment—Interview Codes**

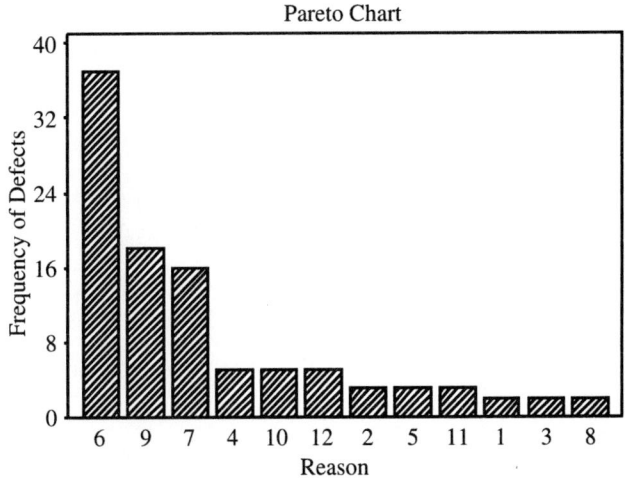

Personal (codes 10 and 11). A Pareto chart by categories is shown in Figure 2.43. Does the combining process reveal the essential reason for turnover more clearly, in your opinion?

FIGURE 2.43   **Reasons for Leaving Employment—Combined Categories**

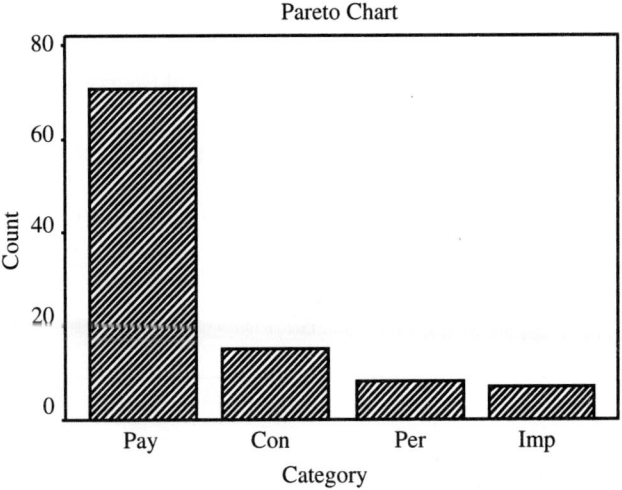

2.56 One of the important factors in a customer's perception of food quality is the age of the product. Even with good, airtight packaging, a food product loses some of its appeal as it gets older. This problem is particularly acute for snack products, such as chips and crackers intended for casual munching. A local manufacturer of one such snack visited 63 convenience stores that were outlets for the product. In each store, the age of the frontmost package was determined from the data code stamped on the package. The data were stored as follows:

	A	B	C	D	E	F	G	H
1	View Data							
2								
3								
4								
5	Case							
6	Snackage							
7								
8								
9	1	29.000		22	12.000		43	21.000
10	2	16.000		23	24.000		44	29.000
11	3	47.000		24	25.000		45	41.000
12	4	49.000		25	25.000		46	20.000
13	5	26.000		26	45.000		47	53.000
14	6	18.000		27	19.000		48	19.000
15	7	17.000		28	15.000		49	28.000
16	8	27.000		29	14.000		50	57.000
17	9	16.000		30	46.000		51	11.000
18	10	19.000		31	25.000		52	21.000
19	11	22.000		32	18.000		53	35.000
20	12	16.000		33	37.000		54	56.000
21	13	19.000		34	17.000		55	20.000
22	14	25.000		35	14.000		56	12.000
23	15	27.000		36	10.000		57	13.000
24	16	12.000		37	20.000		58	27.000
25	17	18.000		38	14.000		59	19.000
26	18	10.000		39	13.000		60	40.000
27	19	25.000		40	20.000		61	15.000
28	20	40.000		41	12.000		62	17.000
29	21	16.000		42	11.000		63	28.000

a Construct a stem-and-leaf display of the data using intervals with a width of 10 days.

b Redo the stem-and-leaf using intervals with a width of 5 days.

c Describe the general shape of the data. How much difference does it make which stem-and-leaf you look at?

2.57 A smoothed histogram of the snack age data of Exercise 2.56 was constructed using Systat, as shown in Figure 2.44.

a Does the histogram indicate the same general shape as the stem-and-leaf displays constructed in Exercise 2.56?

b Why isn't the histogram shape exactly like either stem-and-leaf shape?

FIGURE 2.44 **Smoothed Histogram of Snack Age Data**

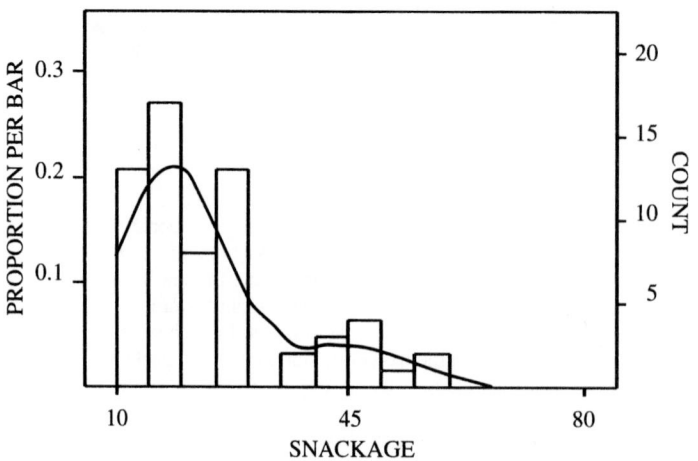

2.58   Summary statistics for the data of Exercise 2.56 were obtained using Excel, as follows:

	A	B
1	Mean	24
2		
3	Standard Error	1.516
4		
5	Median	20
6		
7	Mode	19
8		
9	Standard Deviation	12.031
10		
11	Sample Variance	144.742
12		
13	Kurtosis	0.769
14		
15	Skewness	1.237
16		
17	Range	47
18		
19	Minimum	10
20		
21	Maximum	57
22		
23	Sum	1512
24		
25	Count	63

How is the right skewness of the data reflected in the mean (average) and median?

2.59   A manufacturer of seat belts must be concerned about the breaking strengths of the belts. If a particular belt strength is lower than the design specification, the belt can give way too easily in a crash, causing injury to the wearer. As one part of its quality-control program, the manufacturer finds the breaking strength of five belts each day. (The test involves literally tearing the belt apart, so the manufacturer is less than eager to test all belts.) Design specifications are for a mean strength of 30.0 (in the appropriate units) and a standard deviation of 0.2 units. A control chart for the sample mean and standard deviation for each of the most recent 30 days is shown in Figure 2.45.

FIGURE 2.45   **Control Chart for Seat Belt Strength**

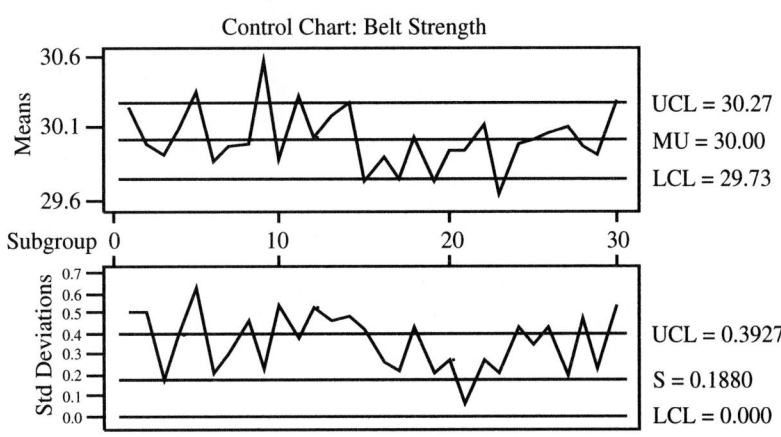

X-bar and S Chart for: Strength

a Is the mean strength consistently within the control limits?

b Does there appear to be a trend in the means or a sudden jump to a new level?

2.60 Refer to the standard deviation portion of the control chart in Figure 2.45.

a Does it appear that the sample standard deviations are consistently within control limits? If not, are they generally too big or too small?

b What appears to be the primary quality problem for the manufacturer—average level or variability around the average?

2.61 An office supply company does a third of its business supplying local governments and school districts. This business is done by competitive bids. Each potential sale requires that a clerk prepare a bid form. The firm had no real idea of how much effort the bid preparation required, so the bid clerk was asked to record the start and stop times for a sample of 65 bids. The data were recorded in two ways: minutes spent per bid (MINPRBID in the following Systat output) and bids per hour (BIDPERHR = 60/MINPRBID).

	B	C	D	E	F	G
3	CASE	MINPERBID	BIDPERHR	CASE	MINPERBID	BIDPERHR
4	1	155.000	0.387	33	30.000	2.000
5	2	66.000	0.909	34	76.000	0.789
6	3	134.000	0.448	35	103.000	0.583
7	4	39.000	1.538	36	48.000	1.250
8	5	61.000	0.984	37	29.000	2.069
9	6	46.000	1.304	38	29.000	2.069
10	7	23.000	2.609	39	46.000	1.304
11	8	21.000	2.857	40	26.000	2.308
12	9	54.000	1.111	41	27.000	2.222
13	10	31.000	1.935	42	24.000	2.500
14	11	30.000	2.000	43	41.000	1.463
15	12	149.000	0.403	44	50.000	1.200
16	13	51.000	1.176	45	82.000	0.732
17	14	120.000	0.500	46	114.000	0.526
18	15	23.000	2.609	47	23.000	2.609
19	16	41.000	1.463	48	49.000	1.224
20	17	56.000	1.071	49	65.000	0.923
21	18	38.000	1.579	50	20.000	3.000
22	19	25.000	2.400	51	22.000	2.727
23	20	42.000	1.429	52	100.000	0.600
24	21	35.000	1.714	53	62.000	0.968
25	22	28.000	2.143	54	24.000	2.500
26	23	80.000	0.750	55	200.000	0.300
27	24	46.000	1.304	56	65.000	0.923
28	25	24.000	2.500	57	50.000	1.200
29	26	46.000	1.304	58	42.000	1.429
30	27	47.000	1.277	59	29.000	2.069
31	28	73.000	0.822	60	145.000	0.414
32	29	220.000	0.273	61	110.000	0.545
33	30	80.000	0.750	62	43.000	1.395
34	31	25.000	2.400	63	40.000	1.500
35	32	20.000	3.000	64	191.000	0.314
36				65	126.000	0.476

a Scan the MINPRBID columns and give a rough guess as to the mean.

b Do the same for the BIDPERHR columns.

2.62 Systat constructed histograms for the data of Exercise 2.61; they're shown in Figure 2.46.

FIGURE 2.46   **Histograms for Exercise 2.61**

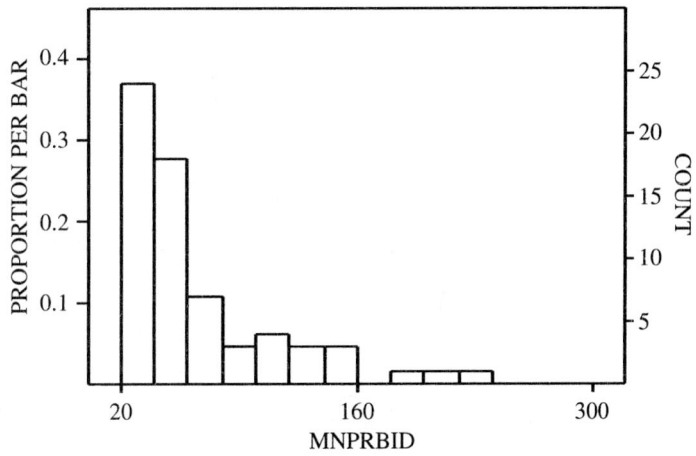

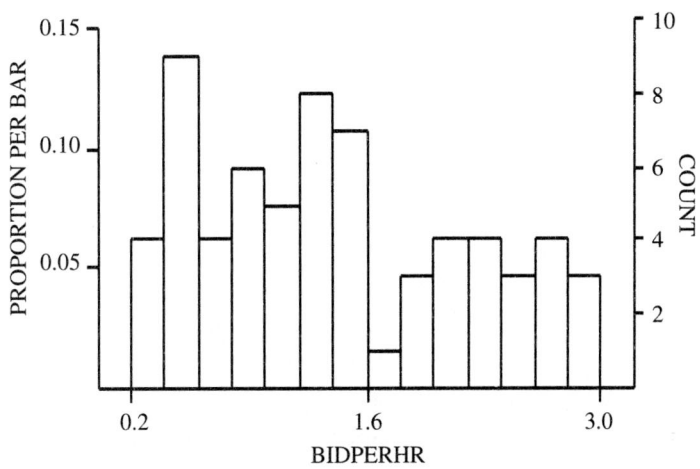

a Use these histograms to check the guess you made in Exercise 2.61 as to the mean.

b Are the two variables skewed in about the same way?

2.63 Systat actually computed summary figures for the data of Exercise 2.61.

```
TOTAL OBSERVATIONS:     65
```

	MINPRBID	BIDPERHR
N OF CASES	65	65
MINIMUM	20.000	0.273
MAXIMUM	220.000	3.000
MEAN	62.462	1.432
VARIANCE	2199.971	0.610
STANDARD DEV	46.904	0.781
SKEWNESS(G1)	1.618	0.356

a Locate the means.

b Is it true that the mean for BIDPERHR is 60 divided by the mean for MINPRBID?

2.64 An automobile insurance company was considering expanding its sales effort in a midwestern city. As one part of its study, the claims department collected data on the size of claims for collision damage over the past year. Would you expect the data to be roughly symmetric around the mean?

2.65 The collision claims data in Exercise 2.64 were analyzed by the Statistix package. A stem-and-leaf display of the data is as follows:

```
STEM AND LEAF PLOT OF CLAIMSIZE

    LEAF DIGIT UNIT = 0.1
    1  2  REPRESENTS 1.2

          STEM  LEAVES
      27    0  7777777777778888888899999999
      61    1  001111111222223333344666678888899999
      79    2  000112335556677799
     (21)   3  0000123334555555666778
      87    4  0122223344466666777899
      65    5  023377889
      56    6  0112557
      49    7  11123344467779
      35    8  2335567889
      25    9  7
      24   10  11
      22   11  0345
      18   12  99
      16   13  123
      13   14  24
      11   15  2
HI     16.8,17.4,19.0,19.4,20.5,20.7,20.9,22.6,26.6,33.7
```

Note that Statistix, like most packages, doesn't round off numbers for a stem-and-leaf display; instead, it simply uses the first two digits of a number.

a Does the stem-and-leaf display appear roughly symmetric?

b Can you guess why some of the numbers are displayed in the HI leaf?

2.66 The data on collision insurance claims (in thousands of dollars) from Exercise 2.65 were summarized by Statistix and displayed in the following spreadsheet:

	A	B
1	**Descriptive Statistics**	
2		
3		
4		
5		Claimsize
6	N	187
7	Mean	5.1775
8	SD	5.2838
9	Minimum	0.7000
10	Median	3.5000
11	Maximum	33.7000
12	Skew	2.2158
13	Kurtosis	6.2068

a One standard deviation below the mean is about −0.1, which is an impossible value for an insurance claim. The Empirical Rule doesn't seem to work at all for these data. Why?

b The mean (average) value is quite a bit larger than the median. Why did that happen?

2.67 A Statistix boxplot of the claim size data for Exercise 2.65 is shown in Figure 2.47. What does this plot indicate about the shape of the claim size data?

FIGURE 2.47 **Boxplot of Collision Claims Data**

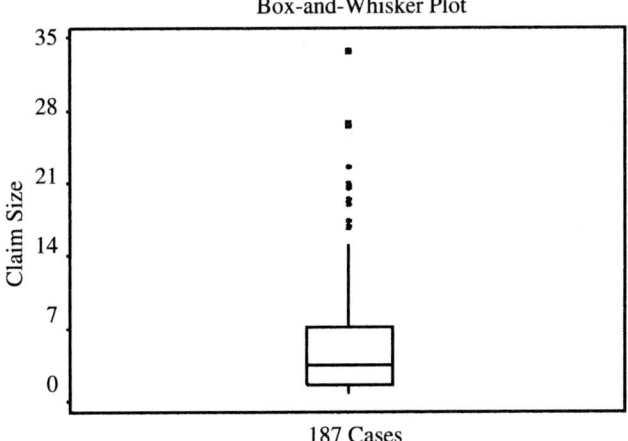

2.68 The customer support service of a word-processing software company must call a customer back if it can't provide a problem-solving suggestion immediately. Callbacks are expensive and less satisfactory for the customer. A set of codes was developed to indicate the reason for each callback. The frequencies for a period of time were as follows:

Code	Explanation	Frequency
01	Problem not covered in manuals	27
02	Operator could not find correct section	56
03	Manual incorrect	3
04	Manual ambiguous	5
11	Customer's problem misstated	42
12	Customer's equipment inadequate	19
13	Task not achievable in customer's version	5
21	Operator's suggestion failed	11
22	Operator answered for wrong version	8
99	All others	17

a According to the Pareto chart in Figure 2.48, what are the most commonly occurring problems?

b The company could do little about customer-related errors (codes 11–13). What do the results for other codes suggest about the most important possible improvements to the service?

2.69 The customer service manager for the software company in Exercise 2.68 asked what the average reason for a callback was. How would you answer this question?

2.70 The editor of a metropolitan newspaper's food section constructed a market basket of 30 items to reflect the "typical" family of four's basic food needs for a week. The editor also put together another list of nonfood items, such as cleaning supplies and paper goods, typically purchased at supermarkets. Reporters obtained prices for all items on both lists at 53 markets in the metropolitan area. The total cost of the food basket at each market is stored in column 1 of the EX0270.DAT file on the data disk that accompanies this book. The total cost of the nonfood list is stored in column 2. (Check with your instructor as to how to obtain this disk.)

a Use any computer package that is available to you to load the data. Technically, the data are stored as an ASCII (text) file, delimited by blanks, without titles for the columns.

b Obtain a histogram of the food cost data. How would you describe the general shape of the data?

c From the histogram, make a rough guess of what the mean is.

FIGURE 2.48   Pareto Chart for Service Problems

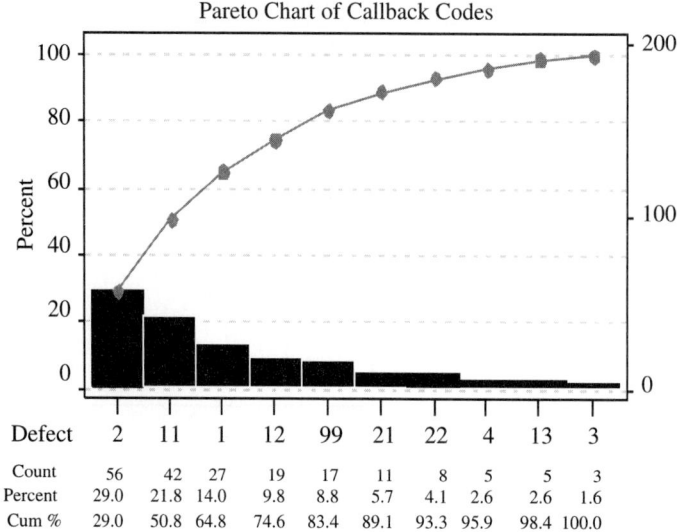

Pareto Chart of Callback Codes

Defect	2	11	1	12	99	21	22	4	13	3
Count	56	42	27	19	17	11	8	5	5	3
Percent	29.0	21.8	14.0	9.8	8.8	5.7	4.1	2.6	2.6	1.6
Cum %	29.0	50.8	64.8	74.6	83.4	89.1	93.3	95.9	98.4	100.0

  d Use the Empirical Rule idea that about 95% of the data should be within 2 standard deviations of the mean to guess the value of the standard deviation.

  e Have the computer package calculate the mean and standard deviation.

2.71 **a** Obtain a stem-and-leaf display of the nonfood cost data from Exercise 2.70. Describe the general shape.

  b Obtain the mean, median, and standard deviation of the nonfood cost.

2.72 **a** Have your computer package calculate the ratio of food cost to the sum of food and nonfood costs for the data set of Exercise 2.70. Obtain a boxplot of the ratio data.

  b Does the boxplot show any outliers?

  c Is the mean of the ratio data the same as the ratio of the mean food cost to the sum of the means of the two costs?

2.73 A copy center located near a university campus offers self-service copying. The daily number of copies made on self-service machines varies, depending on weather, number of assignments due at the university, number of machines under repair, and many other factors. The copy center recorded the number of copies made each day for 44 days. The data are stored in the EX0273.DAT file on the data disk; column 1 is number of copies, column 2 is day number. Like all files on this disk, this is an ASCII (text) file, delimited by spaces, without variable labels.

  a Use a computer package to read in the data. Obtain a boxplot of the number of copies made each day for this period.

  b Identify any days that yielded outlier values.

  c Obtain the mean and standard deviation of the number of copies.

  d Delete all outliers from the data and recompute the mean and standard deviation. Which number changes more?

2.74 **a** Have a computer package plot the number of copies data of Exercise 2.73 against day number. The package should have a "plot" or "scatterplot" capability; if it has a special capability for plotting time-series data, that would be handy here.

  b Can you see an evident upward or downward trend in the plot?

  c Are there evident cycles in the data?

2.75 An office-cleaning service has developed a numerical scale to assess the general cleanliness of an area. The scale ranges from 0 (worst) to 100 (best). The target value is 80 or higher.

(The service managers believe that shooting for a perfect 100 score would require excessive labor costs.) Supervisors calculated scores for each of four randomly chosen areas on each of 60 days. The data are stored in the EX0275.DAT file on the data disk, with scores in column 1 and day number in column 2.

a Read the data into a computer package and obtain a stem-and-leaf display of the cleanliness scores.

b Identify any evident departures from a normal distribution.

c The president of the service suspected that supervisors might make a fast guess at the cleanliness score, rather than go through the details. If so, many scores would be likely to end in 0 or 5. Is there evidence of that phenomenon in the stem-and-leaf display?

2.76 **a** Obtain the mean and standard deviation of the cleanliness scores from Exercise 2.75.

b Have the computer package obtain the mean score for each day and compute the standard deviation of those means.

c If your computer package has the capability, obtain a control chart of the daily means. Use a target mean of 80 and the standard deviation of the means found in part b of this exercise.

d Were there any days when the cleanliness was "out of control"?

2.77 A mutual fund receives a large number of telephone calls daily from investors who wish to take action on their accounts—add funds, withdraw them, obtain statements of current status, open new accounts, or close out accounts. Each call is handled by a fund representative who has been trained to carry out all but the most complex actions. It is expensive and time-consuming for the fund to train new representatives, but turnover rates are quite high. Therefore, the fund manager is eager to find ways to reduce turnover.

One possible change involves *telecommuting*, in which employees work primarily from their homes. Telecommuting representatives are equipped with telephones, computers, and modems to communicate from home with callers and the fund office. The representatives work at home except for one day every second week, during which they go into the office for ongoing training and for communication with the fund office staff.

The fund manager arranged a 2-month trial of the telecommuting concept. One set of 54 representatives was chosen to work at home; another set of 54 worked at the fund office. The manager was able to obtain records of the daily average number of calls handled by each of the 108 representatives, for each of the two months of the trial. A simple Minitab analysis yielded summary figures and stem- and-leaf displays. The 1 and 2 codes refer to the months.

```
MTB > describe 'telecom1' 'telecom2'

              N      MEAN    MEDIAN   TRMEAN   STDEV   SEMEAN
telecom1     54     55.88     56.55    56.68    8.45    1.15
telecom2     54     59.443    59.650   59.881   4.973   0.677

             MIN      MAX       Q1       Q3
telecom1    22.10    69.10    52.47    61.53
telecom2    40.100   67.400   57.700   62.850

MTB > describe 'office1' 'office2'

              N      MEAN    MEDIAN   TRMEAN   STDEV   SEMEAN
office1      54     55.21     56.50    55.77    7.91    1.08
office2      54     54.68     55.65    55.12    8.44    1.15

             MIN      MAX       Q1       Q3
office1     27.80    66.70    52.10    60.38
office2     26.00    69.30    48.58    59.78

MTB > name c5 'chgtelec' c6 'chgoffic'
MTB > let 'chgtelec'='telecom2'-'telecom1'
MTB > let 'chgoffic'='office2'-'office1'
```

```
MTB > describe 'chgtelec' 'chgoffic'

                N      MEAN    MEDIAN    TRMEAN     STDEV    SEMEAN
chgtelec       54     3.563     3.200     3.183     3.614     0.492
chgoffic       54    -0.535    -0.750    -0.537     5.014     0.682

              MIN       MAX        Q1        Q3
chgtelec   -1.700    18.000     1.000     4.675
chgoffic  -13.100    11.400    -3.600     2.325

MTB > stem 'telecom1'

Stem-and-leaf of telecom1   N  = 54
Leaf Unit = 1.0


      1     2 2
      1     2
      2     3 3
      3     3 9
      5     4 24
      7     4 99
     20     5 0022223334444
    (15)    5 555666777788899
     19     6 111111223333444
      4     6 6789



MTB > stem 'telecom2'

Stem-and-leaf of telecom2   N  = 54
Leaf Unit = 1.0


      1     4 0
      1     4
      1     4
      2     4 7
      3     4 8
      3     5
      5     5 23
      8     5 455
     11     5 777
     25     5 88888888889999
    (10)    6 0000011111
     19     6 2233333333
      9     6 444555
      3     6 677

MTB > stem 'office1'

Stem-and-leaf of office1    N  = 54
Leaf Unit = 1.0


      1     2 8
      1     3
      3     3 88
      5     4 14
     11     4 577888
     22     5 12223444444
    (14)    5 55666777889999
     18     6 00000112223344
```

```
    4    6 6777
```

MTB > stem 'office2'

```
Stem-and-leaf of office2   N = 54
Leaf Unit = 1.0

     1    2 6
     1    3
     3    3 69
     4    4 3
    15    4 55667788899
    22    5 0123334
   (16)   5 5555666667779999
    16    6 00002223344
     5    6 58889
```

MTB > stem 'chgtelec'

```
Stem-and-leaf of chgtelec  N = 54
Leaf Unit = 1.0


     4   -0 1000
    17    0 0000111111111
   (12)   0 222222333333
    25    0 44444444445555
    11    0 666777
     5    0 89
     3    1 0
     2    1
     2    1 5
     1    1
     1    1 8
```

MTB > stem 'chgoffic'

```
Stem-and-leaf of chgoffic  N = 54
Leaf Unit = 1.0


     1   -1 2
     2   -1 0
     4   -0 88
     6   -0 76
    10   -0 5554
    15   -0 33332
   (14)  -0 11111111100000
    25    0 0111111
    18    0 22222223
    10    0 445
     7    0 6677
     3    0 9
     2    1 01
```

You have been asked to explain the output to the manager. In particular, the manager wants to know if there is any indication that the typical telecommuter did better or worse on average than the typical office-based representative. In addition, the manager should be alerted to any difference in variability and any other notable features of the data. Write a brief report to the manager, who understands means and standard deviations fairly well. ∎

Summarizing Data

A meat packer sells portion-controlled sirloin steaks to restaurant chains. The meat is cut, frozen, and packaged on two production lines called (not too imaginatively) the *Left* and *Right lines*. The target size for each steak is 12 ounces, but there is variability because of differences in meat density, slight differences in cut, slight differences in fat content, and several other factors. Each steak is visually inspected and also weighed by a rough scale along the production line; the scale is supposed to reject any steak that weighs less than 11.5 ounces and set aside any steak that weighs more than 12.6 ounces.

The production managers have noticed an increase in the number of 24-steak packages being rejected by customers for inadequate average weight. The managers traced the source of each rejected package and found that most had come from the Right line. They have written to you for help. "As you know, quality control picks 10 steaks each week from each line for careful testing. Before they're cooked, they're all weighed carefully. We've got weights for each line for the last 25 weeks. During the first 10 weeks, we were running at speeds well below capacity to make sure that our cutting was OK. During the last 15 weeks, we've been running at nearly full capacity. What we can't figure out is that the average weights from the two lines are practically identical; if anything, the Right line averages a little heavier. So why are so many more of the Right line packages coming up short?" They enclosed the weights for each week's sample of 10 steaks.

Left Line

Week											Average
1	12.32	12.16	12.34	12.03	11.95	12.05	11.78	12.01	11.95	12.39	12.098
2	12.04	11.98	12.06	11.95	12.12	11.84	12.29	12.10	11.92	12.07	12.037
3	11.78	12.07	12.11	11.71	11.87	11.88	11.61	11.93	12.08	12.01	11.905
4	12.37	11.98	11.94	12.06	11.88	12.24	12.05	12.10	12.32	11.82	12.076
5	12.08	11.95	11.82	11.86	12.51	12.07	12.07	12.25	11.98	12.28	12.087
6	12.12	11.62	12.01	12.04	11.86	12.05	11.80	12.05	12.17	12.20	11.992
7	12.49	12.12	11.92	11.76	11.97	11.78	11.80	11.69	12.04	12.01	11.958
8	11.78	12.29	12.52	12.23	12.32	12.14	11.64	12.12	12.24	12.08	12.136
9	12.00	11.95	12.05	12.15	11.89	12.27	12.23	12.00	12.01	12.22	12.077
10	11.95	11.81	11.99	12.00	11.93	12.01	12.01	11.74	12.50	11.77	11.971
11	11.85	12.13	12.55	12.09	12.28	12.43	11.92	11.96	11.95	12.19	12.135
12	11.81	11.86	11.75	11.86	12.13	12.43	12.14	11.81	12.21	12.19	12.019
13	12.15	11.87	12.36	12.29	12.13	11.82	12.30	11.76	11.88	11.90	12.046
14	12.10	11.82	11.94	12.22	11.61	12.15	11.92	12.06	12.08	12.06	11.996
15	12.19	11.77	11.89	11.96	11.97	11.93	12.18	12.12	12.37	12.27	12.065
16	11.84	12.03	12.07	11.91	11.90	11.86	11.98	12.25	11.96	12.05	11.985
17	12.24	11.80	12.03	12.13	11.88	12.52	12.06	11.90	12.01	11.91	12.048
18	12.08	12.02	11.87	11.89	12.06	12.19	11.91	12.06	11.91	11.85	11.984
19	12.18	12.17	12.03	11.74	11.65	12.01	12.45	11.84	11.88	12.00	11.995
20	12.42	12.00	11.89	11.92	12.06	12.00	11.63	12.12	12.02	12.28	12.034
21	11.60	11.85	12.08	11.68	12.28	12.12	11.96	12.16	11.81	11.93	11.947
22	12.01	11.68	11.96	11.88	11.62	11.82	11.77	12.17	11.78	12.07	11.876
23	12.54	12.35	11.96	12.11	11.94	12.11	11.98	12.16	12.28	11.80	12.123
24	12.25	11.97	12.21	12.03	12.01	11.94	11.76	12.15	11.71	12.07	12.010
25	11.63	12.10	12.14	12.19	11.74	12.19	11.88	12.11	11.76	11.88	11.962

Right Line

Week											Average
1	12.07	11.88	11.89	12.21	11.93	11.94	11.99	12.21	11.90	12.20	12.022
2	11.82	11.83	12.22	12.06	11.96	12.11	11.52	11.96	12.11	11.93	11.952
3	12.34	12.02	12.08	12.33	12.07	12.38	12.06	11.97	11.81	11.97	12.103
4	11.87	12.17	12.01	12.02	12.21	12.33	11.98	12.04	11.80	12.33	12.076
5	12.17	11.60	12.22	12.06	11.70	12.12	11.90	12.13	12.08	11.83	11.981
6	12.00	12.05	11.91	12.24	11.99	12.00	12.21	12.15	11.98	11.73	12.026
7	12.40	11.90	11.72	12.57	11.60	12.20	12.02	12.31	11.82	12.25	12.079
8	11.99	11.95	12.19	12.24	12.19	12.08	12.27	12.15	12.43	12.14	12.163
9	11.83	12.19	11.40	11.69	11.99	11.85	12.14	12.17	12.10	12.04	11.940
10	11.82	12.00	11.89	12.07	11.70	11.67	12.07	11.95	12.06	11.86	11.909
11	11.83	12.04	12.35	12.40	11.82	12.28	11.94	12.21	12.34	12.23	12.144
12	11.81	11.71	11.60	12.03	11.91	11.93	12.10	12.51	12.09	11.86	11.955
13	11.99	12.12	11.67	11.88	12.27	11.50	12.18	12.25	11.71	12.23	11.980
14	12.78	11.34	11.58	12.82	11.40	13.10	11.55	12.70	12.44	12.22	12.193
15	11.59	12.13	11.94	12.45	12.55	11.23	11.52	12.48	12.74	11.07	11.970
16	12.20	12.36	12.00	12.30	11.08	12.21	12.16	12.04	12.50	11.65	12.050
17	12.18	11.70	11.96	12.71	12.07	12.06	11.64	12.78	12.03	11.57	12.070
18	11.96	12.43	11.37	12.54	12.32	12.67	12.21	12.32	12.64	11.90	12.236
19	12.31	12.37	11.74	11.56	11.94	12.24	11.93	11.93	12.74	12.06	12.082
20	11.58	12.06	12.13	12.16	11.94	11.90	11.89	12.33	12.28	12.46	12.073
21	11.90	12.27	11.94	12.37	12.13	11.47	12.26	11.33	11.49	11.63	11.879
22	11.64	11.41	11.90	12.24	11.66	12.23	12.34	12.43	11.57	11.41	11.883
23	11.73	11.34	11.81	12.62	11.43	12.14	12.41	12.46	12.57	11.64	12.015
24	12.15	12.29	12.64	12.40	12.62	12.43	12.47	12.50	11.28	12.08	12.286
25	12.25	12.28	11.94	11.88	12.09	12.24	11.91	11.80	11.62	10.98	11.899

Can you identify any difference between the Left and Right data that might explain the problem? Does the difference show up after the initial 10 weeks or during that period? You may want to use a computer program to do the arithmetic. Write a memorandum to the managers; they don't know any technical terms, so try to use ordinary English as much as possible. ■

Beginner at stat Charley Heft
Of good common sense was bereft.
The numbers he'd grind
No pictures, no mind
Which skewed all the grades to the left.

3

A First Look at Probability

Probability is the basic mathematical language of uncertainty. It gives us a way to deal with variability. This chapter presents a very basic introduction to that language. The key ideas are:

1 Probability may be interpreted as classical probability if we can count equally likely outcomes, as long-run relative frequency probability if we can conceptually repeat the experiment many times, or as subjective probability if we are stating a personal opinion.

2 There are three basic principles of probability: (1) the addition law for finding the probability of one event *or* another; (2) the complements law for calculating the probability that an event does *not* happen; and (3) the multiplication law for finding the probability of one event *and* another.

3 Probabilities may be conditional (given that another event has happened) or unconditional. The conditional probability of one event given another is the unconditional probability of both events, divided by the probability of the given event.

4 Statistical independence of two events means that the occurrence of one event does not change the probability of the other. Sometimes, statistical independence is an empirical question. Often, independence is assumed in solving probability problems. Because it *is* an assumption, it should be checked for reasonableness.

5 Probability tables and trees are useful devices for clarifying probability reasoning. To make these devices work properly, we must define mutually exclusive categories—for the rows and columns of a table or for the branches of a tree.

6 Addition (for mutually exclusive events), complements, and multiplication laws are all used to complete probability tables and trees. Conditional probabilities may be calculated by using the definition.

Probability theory is the basis of statistical inference; it is also fundamental in analyzing variability. In this chapter we sketch the basic concepts and principles of probability theory, beginning with some alternative interpretations of probability statements. Then we introduce the basic mathematical principles that underlie the more complex computations, and the important idea of statistical independence. Finally, we describe some techniques that can be used to combine the basic mathematical principles in the solution of more complicated problems.

This is an important foundation chapter for our later discussion of statistical inference. Probability theory is a major branch of pure and applied mathematics, and this chapter barely skims the surface. The illustrations and examples that we use are relatively simple, but they will suggest the wide variety of managerial applications possible. ■

3.1 Basic Principles of Probability

The theory of probability is the basic language of uncertainty. It is also the basis for statistical inference. If 20% of the work force at a textile company have signed union election cards, and if 8 randomly chosen workers are to be fired, then the probability of choosing 8 workers who have signed the cards is very small. Thus, if it turns out that all

8 workers fired by the company had signed union election cards, then we can make the inference that the firings were related to union activity.

The first step in the study of probability is understanding the possible interpretations of probability statements. The earliest mathematics, and the first interpretation, of probability theory arose from various games of chance. "The probability that a flip of a balanced coin will show heads is 1/2" and "the probability that a card selected at random from a standard deck of 52 cards will be a king is 4/52" are typical examples of this kind of probability statement. The numerical probability values arise from the physical nature of the experiment. A coin flip has only two possible outcomes: heads or tails. The probability that a head occurs is therefore 1 out of 2. In a standard deck of 52 cards, 4 are kings, so the probability of drawing a king should be 4 out of 52.

classical interpretation
outcome
event These probability calculations are based on the **classical interpretation** of probability. In this interpretation, each distinct possible result of an experiment is called an **outcome**; an **event** is identified with certain of these outcomes. In the card-drawing illustration, there are 52 possible outcomes, 4 of which are identified with the event, drawing a king. According to the classical interpretation, the probability of an event E is taken to be the ratio of the number of outcomes favorable to an event N_E to the total number of possible outcomes N, or symbolically,

$$P(\text{event } E) = \frac{N_E}{N}$$

The usefulness of this interpretation depends completely on the assumption that all possible outcomes are *equally likely*. If that assumption is false—if the coin is loaded or the deck marked, for instance—the classical interpretation does not apply.

EXAMPLE 3.1

An ordinary thumbtack is dropped on a hard surface. It can come to rest point up or on its side. Are the two outcomes equally likely?

Solution

There is no reason to assume so. There is no symmetry to the two possibilities. ∎

random sample The classical interpretation has many uses, even outside the gambling casino. A **random sample**, by definition, is taken in such a way that any possible sample (of a specific size) has the same probability as any other of being selected. Therefore the outcomes (possible samples) are equally likely, and probabilities can be found by counting favorable outcomes. We use this idea extensively throughout this book.

long-run relative frequency Situations that do not readily allow a classical interpretation sometimes can be given a **long-run relative frequency** interpretation. If an experiment has been repeated over a huge number of trials, and if 24% of these trials have resulted in a particular event E, then the probability of the event E should be .24, at least to a very good approximation. Symbolically, if an experiment is repeated over n trials and the event E occurs in n_E trials, the probability of an event E is approximately n_E divided by n:

$$P(\text{event } E) \approx \frac{n_E}{n}$$

This definition looks very much like the definition of classical probability, but the meaning is different. In the relative frequency interpretation, n is the (very large) number of trials and n_E is the number of trials where event E occurs. In the classical interpretation, N is the number of possible, equally likely, outcomes and N_E is the number of outcomes in event E.

EXAMPLE 3.2

Suppose that in the thumbtack-tossing experiment of Example 3.1, it is claimed that the probability of the tack landing point up is .70. Give a long-run relative frequency interpretation that would justify the claim.

Solution

The claim could be justified on grounds of long-run relative frequency if a tack had been tossed many times, with 70% of the results being point up. ■

computer simulation

The relative frequency interpretation is often convenient. We use it whenever it seems sensible to imagine a large number of repeated trials of an experiment. This interpretation is also the basis for **computer simulation** of probabilities. As we will see, it is possible to program a computer to imitate a random, probabilistic situation a large number of times. Assuming that the program accurately reflects the reality of the situation, we can use computer simulation to find probabilities that are difficult to calculate mathematically.

Sometimes, neither the classical nor the relative frequency interpretation is sensible. Many applications of probability, particularly in management problems, seem to be "one-shot" situations—those in which it's hard to imagine repeated trials. A product manager who estimates the probability that a new item will receive adequate shelf space is not imagining a long series of trials with this item; it can be introduced as a new product only once. The director of a state welfare agency who estimates the probability that a proposed revision in eligibility rules will pass the state legislature is not imagining a long series of identical proposals; the proposal will be considered only once in the particular legislative session. What then is the meaning of, say, a .6 probability of adequate shelf space or a .3 probability of legislative approval? Such probabilities are **subjective** or **personal** probabilities. One interpretation of such probabilities is that they represent willingness to make certain bets. If someone states that the probability of a certain event is .5, that person regards an even-money bet on the occurrence of that event as a fair bet (and is willing to take either side of the gamble). A subjective probability of .6 for an event means that "lose $6 if the event doesn't occur, win $4 if it does" is regarded as a fair bet. This subjective, betting interpretation of probability is natural in describing the risk-taking questions that confront most managers.

subjective/personal probability

The mathematical laws of probability can help one make logically consistent probability estimates, but they cannot guarantee that those estimates are correct. A good manager will take better risks than a bad one and should do better in the long run. But there is no way to guarantee that one assessment of a particular subjective probability is correct and another incorrect. That, as they say, is what makes horse races!

EXAMPLE 3.3

Give a subjective probability interpretation of the statement "The probability that a thumbtack will land point up is .5."

Solution

If you made such a statement, you would be saying that you would take either side of a bet of $1 that the tack would land point up against $1 that it would not. As we suggested in Example 3.1, we would not agree with you. We believe that the tack is more likely to land point up and would prefer that side of the "even-money" bet. ■

The classical interpretation of probability gives us a good way to think about basic probability principles. All the basic probability ideas may be derived from the random drawing of individuals from a population. For example, suppose that a tasting panel of 200 men, who vary in marital status, tests a potential new frozen dinner. The following table shows their opinions, broken down by marital status. For now, we'll regard the panelists as the entire population; in practice, we'd want to regard them as a sample from the much larger pool of potential male customers.

| | | Opinion | | | | |
		Poor	Fair	Good	Excellent	Total
Marital Status	Never married	5	9	26	10	50
	Divorced	1	4	16	9	30
	Married	12	23	37	32	104
	Widowed	2	8	5	1	16
	Total	20	44	84	52	200

Suppose that a panelist is drawn at random. What is the probability that he rates the dinner as poor? Using the classical interpretation, we have 20 poor opinion outcomes and 200 possible outcomes; the probability of poor opinion is $20/200 = .1$. Other probabilities can be found the same way.

EXAMPLE 3.4

The following program uses the Resampling Stats package to carry out a simple computer simulation, using the panelist data. Give a relative frequency interpretation of the result. (The lines in the program that begin with ' are comments, and don't affect the results.)

```
 1: 'SET AN INITIAL VALUE FOR GENERATING RANDOM NUMBERS.
 2: 'IF OMITTED, THE PROGRAM USES ITS OWN VALUE.
 3: SEED 13579123
 4: 'HAVE THE PROGRAM DRAW 1000 INDIVIDUALS.
 5: REPEAT 1000
 6: 'DRAW A NUMBER BETWEEN 1 AND 200 AND PUT THE RESULT IN RAND.
 7: GENERATE 1 1,200 RAND
 8: 'IF RAND IS BETWEEN 1 AND 20, COUNT 1 POORRATE, ELSE 0 POORRATE
 9: COUNT RAND BETWEEN 1 20 POORRATE
10: 'SAVE THE RESULT AS POORS
11: SCORE POORRATE POORS
12: 'GO BACK TO DRAW THE NEXT NUMBER
13: END
14: 'CALCULATE AND PRINT THE FRACTION OF POORS
15: SUM POORS TOTPOOR
16: DIVIDE TOTPOOR 1000 FRACPOOR
17: PRINT FRACPOOR
```

FRACPOOR =   0.103

Solution

In 1000 trials the computer program obtained a proportion .103 of "poor" ratings, corresponding closely to the .100 probability. ■

The first probability principle is the **addition law**. It has two forms, depending on whether or not events are **mutually exclusive**. Events are mutually exclusive if they have no outcomes in common. The events "poor opinion" and "fair opinion" are mutually exclusive in drawing a panelist at random; the events "poor opinion" and "widowed" are not mutually exclusive. The addition law applies to finding "or" probabilities. What is the probability that a randomly chosen panelist has a poor opinion or a fair opinion? There are $20 + 44 = 64$ such panelists, so $P(\text{poor opinion or fair opinion}) = 64/200 = .32$. $P(\text{poor opinion}) = 20/200 = .10$ and $P(\text{fair opinion}) = 44/200 = .22$, so $P(\text{poor opinion or fair opinion}) = P(\text{poor opinion}) + P(\text{fair opinion})$.

Definition 3.1   Addition Law for Mutually Exclusive Events

If events A and B are mutually exclusive, then

$$P(A \text{ or } B) = P(A) + P(B) \qquad \blacksquare$$

If events are not mutually exclusive, then adding probabilities double-counts the outcomes that belong to both events. If we pick a panelist at random, the events "poor opinion" and "widowed" are not mutually exclusive; there are two panelists who are both. To find $P(\text{poor opinion or widowed})$, we must correct for the double counting. $P(\text{poor opinion or widowed}) = P(\text{poor opinion}) + P(\text{widowed}) - P(\text{poor opinion and widowed}) = 20/200 + 16/200 - 2/200 = .10 + .08 - .01 = .17$. Alternatively, we can count the panelists who either have a poor opinion or are widowed, or both; there are $5 + 1 + 12 + 2 + 8 + 5 + 1 = 34$ such panelists. So $P(\text{poor opinion or widowed}) = 34/200 = .17$, once again.

Definition 3.2   General Addition Law

For any events A and B, not necessarily mutually exclusive,

$$P(A \text{ or } B) = P(A) + P(B) - P(A \text{ and } B) \qquad \blacksquare$$

We will sometimes use the symbol $\cup$ for "or" and the symbol $\cap$ for "and." If you happen to know some set theory, you'll recognize these as the symbols for union and intersection of sets. However, we needn't use formal set theory. Just read $\cup$ as "or" and $\cap$ as "and." In this notation, the general addition law is

$$P(A \cup B) = P(A) + P(B) - P(A \cap B)$$

E X A M P L E   3 . 5

A direct retailer receives orders from the order forms in its catalog, from the order forms sent to repeat customers, and by phone. The orders are classified as small (under $25.00), medium ($25.00–$99.99), large ($100.00–$299.99), or major ($300.00 and up). An analysis of the retailer's last 4000 orders yields the following table.

	Size				
	Small	**Medium**	**Large**	**Major**	**Total**
Catalog	1021	216	109	14	1360
Repeat	86	371	308	49	814
Phone	1497	230	86	13	1826
Total	2604	817	503	76	4000

a Catalog and repeat-customer forms must go through an initial entry step. What is the probability that a randomly chosen order went through this step? That is, what is the probability that an order is either a catalog or a repeat-customer order?

b Major orders and phone orders are held for verification of credit. What is the probability that a randomly chosen order is held?

Solution

a
$$P(\text{entry step}) = P(\text{catalog or repeat})$$

$$= P(\text{catalog}) + P(\text{repeat}) = \frac{1360}{4000} + \frac{814}{4000}$$

$$= .3400 + .2035 = .5435$$

We needn't worry about double counting because catalog and repeat are mutually exclusive categories.

b Some orders are both major and phone orders. For these, we must use the general addition principle:

$$P(\text{held}) = P(\text{major or phone})$$

$$= P(\text{major}) + P(\text{phone}) - P(\text{major and phone})$$

$$= \frac{76}{4000} + \frac{1826}{4000} - \frac{13}{4000}$$

$$= .01900 + .45650 - .00325 = .47225 \quad \blacksquare$$

complements law

A second probability principle is the **complements law**. It is often easier to find the probability that an event *doesn't* happen than the probability that it does. Because the total probability must equal 1, the complements principle is easy.

Definition 3.3   Complements Law

If $\overline{A}$ is the event "not A,"

$$P(A) = 1 - P(\overline{A}) \quad \blacksquare$$

The tasting panel results can be used to illustrate the complements law. To find the probability that a randomly chosen rater gives a poor opinion or fair opinion or good opinion rating, we could note that the complementary event is excellent. So

$$P(\text{poor opinion or fair opinion or good opinion}) = 1 - P(\text{excellent})$$

$$= 1 - \frac{52}{200} = .74$$

Of course, we could also have used the addition law and added the probabilities of poor opinion, fair opinion, and good opinion. Very often, there are several ways to solve a probability problem.

EXAMPLE 3.6

As a quality-control measure, the direct retailer in Example 3.5 does an order verification check on all large and major orders, as well as on all catalog and repeat orders. Use the complements law to find the probability that a randomly chosen order will be checked.

Solution

The only orders that are *not* checked are small or medium phone orders.

$$P(\text{checked}) = 1 - P(\text{small or medium phone order})$$

$$= 1 - [P(\text{small and phone}) + P(\text{medium and phone})]$$

$$= 1 - \left(\frac{1497}{4000} + \frac{230}{4000} \right) = .56825$$

Without the complements law, we would have had to add up 10 different probabilities, corresponding to the 10 types of orders that are checked. ■

conditional probability

The concept of **conditional probability** is important in its own right, and it is also the key to another probability principle, the multiplication law. Many probability questions involve some restriction or condition on randomness. For example, in the tasting panel results, we might ask for the probability that a randomly chosen married man would rate the product excellent. The condition—that the panelist be married—restricts the random choice to a subgroup, the 104 married men, of the population. Of this group, 32 rated the product excellent, so we should have $P(\text{excellent opinion} \mid \text{married}) = 32/104 = .308$. In this notation $P(B \mid A)$, the conditioning event is placed after the vertical bar. The bar should be read as "given," so $P(\text{excellent opinion} \mid \text{married})$ should be read as "the probability that a panelist will rate the product excellent given that the panelist is married."

A conditional probability such as $P(\text{excellent opinion} \mid \text{married})$ differs from a *joint* ("and" type) probability such as $P(\text{excellent opinion and married}) = 32/200$ in that the conditioning event has already occurred, or is assumed to occur. In the joint probability, the event (such as married) is random, and might or might not occur. The following definition of conditional probability indicates that there is a close relationship between conditional and joint probabilities.

Definition 3.4   Conditional Probability $P(B \mid A)$

$$P(B \mid A) = \frac{P(A \text{ and } B)}{P(A)} \qquad ■$$

According to this definition,

$$P(\text{excellent opinion} \mid \text{married}) = \frac{P(\text{married and exellent opinion})}{P(\text{married})}$$

$$= \frac{32/200}{104/200} = \frac{32}{104}$$

as we found before.

E X A M P L E   3 . 7

For the direct retailer of Example 3.5, what is the probability that a written (nonphone) order is a repeat order?

Solution

First of all, we're looking for a conditional probability. We're assuming that the order is written. There are $1360 + 814 = 2174$ written orders, of which 814 are repeat. So $P(\text{repeat} \mid \text{written}) = 814/2174 = .374$. Alternatively, we may use the definition of conditional probability. Note that all repeat orders are written orders, so $P(\text{written and repeat}) = P(\text{repeat}) = 814/4000$.

$$P(\text{repeat} \mid \text{written}) = \frac{P(\text{written and repeat})}{P(\text{written})} = \frac{814/4000}{2174/4000}$$

$$= \frac{814}{2174} = .374 \quad \text{once again} \quad \blacksquare$$

multiplication law

The **multiplication law** of probability is simply a rewrite of the definition of conditional probability. The multiplication law is used to evaluate "and" probabilities, just as the addition law is used to evaluate "or" probabilities.

Definition 3.5 Multiplication Law for Joint Probabilities

$$\text{For any events } A \text{ and } B, P(A \text{ and } B) = P(A)P(B \mid A)$$

$$= P(B)P(A \mid B) \quad \blacksquare$$

In the tasting panelists example, we could find $P(\text{married and excellent opinion}) = 32/200 = .160$ directly. Alternatively, we could use the multiplication principle. We previously found that $P(\text{excellent opinion} \mid \text{married}) = 32/104 = .308$ and that $P(\text{married}) = 104/200 = .520$. Therefore $P(\text{married and excellent opinion}) = P(\text{married})P(\text{excellent opinion} \mid \text{married}) = (.520)(.308) = .160$, once again.

E X A M P L E   3 . 8

The table in Example 3.5 can be converted to conditional and unconditional probabilities by appropriate division, as shown in the next table.

Type of Order	Size				
	Small	**Medium**	**Large**	**Major**	**Total**
Catalog	.751	.159	.080	.010	1.000
Repeat	.106	.456	.378	.060	1.000
Phone	.820	.126	.047	.007	1.000

	Type of Order			
	Catalog	**Repeat**	**Phone**	**Total**
Unconditional probability	.3400	.2035	.4565	1.000

a How were the .751 and .3400 probabilities obtained?

b Use the multiplication law to find $P(\text{catalog and small})$.

Solution

a The .751 probability is $P(\text{small} \mid \text{catalog})$. It was obtained by dividing the number of small catalog orders (1021) by the total number of catalog orders (1360): $1021/1360 = .751$. The .3400 is the unconditional probability of a catalog order. It is the number of catalog orders divided by the total number of all orders (4000): $1360/4000 = .3400$.

b
$$P(\text{catalog and small}) = P(\text{catalog})P(\text{small} \mid \text{catalog})$$
$$= (.3400)(.751) = .255$$

This could also have been obtained by dividing the 1021 small catalog orders by the 4000 total orders: $1021/4000 = .255$. ∎

EXAMPLE 3.9

A Resampling Stats program performed a computer simulation to find the probability of an order that is both small and catalog. How does the result compare to the probability found in the preceding example?

```
 1: 'SET INITIAL VALUE FOR RANDOM NUMBERS. TRY OMITTING THIS LINE.
 2: SEED 13579123
 3: 'TRY THE EXPERIMENT 1000 TIMES
 4: REPEAT 1000
 5: 'IF A RANDOM NUMBER BETWEEN 1 AND 4000 IS
 6: 'BETWEEN 1 AND 1360, COUNT 1 CATORDER
 7: GENERATE 1 1,4000 RAND
 8: COUNT RAND <= 1360 CATORDER
 9: 'PICK A NUMBER BETWEEN 1 AND 1360; IF <=1021, COUNT A SMALL ORDER
10: GENERATE 1 1,1360 RAND2
11: COUNT RAND2 <= 1021 SMALL
12: 'MULTIPLY; RESULT IS 1 ONLY IF BOTH CATALOG AND SMALL
13: MULTIPLY CATORDER SMALL BOTH
14: 'SAVE THE RESULT
15: SCORE BOTH RESULT
16: 'END OF TRIAL; GO BACK AND DO IT AGAIN
17: END
18: 'TOTAL NUMBER OF BOTH, FIND FRACTION, PRINT
19: SUM RESULT TOTBOTH
20: DIVIDE TOTBOTH 1000 FRACBOTH
21: PRINT FRACBOTH

FRACBOTH =     0.252
```

Solution

The simulation probability .252 is virtually the same as the calculated probability .255. ∎

These basic principles—addition, complements, and multiplication laws and the definition of conditional probability—form the basis for all probability calculations.

EXERCISES

3.1 For each of the following situations, indicate which interpretation of the probability statement seems most appropriate. (In many situations, it is debatable which is the best interpretation.)

a A new statistics textbook for managers is about to be published. The editor states that the probability that at least enough copies will sell to break even is .8.

b A small manufacturing firm produces a certain kind of dial for various electrical devices. A critical component of the dial assembly is a certain gear. The probability that a particular gear fails to satisfy tolerances is .002.

c A random sample of 100 employees is to be taken from the 13,000 employees of a firm. It is known that 55% of the employees are men. As a check on the sampling process, the number of men in the sample will be counted. The probability that there will be 42 or fewer men in the sample is .0061.

d The probability that the German inflation rate next year will exceed 6% is .3.

e The probability that on a given day the demand for coronary-care beds at a local hospital exceeds the normal capacity is .004.

3.2 Give your own subjective probability for each of the following statements. If an entire class does this problem, it might be interesting to tabulate the various probabilities.

a Russia will purchase wheat from the United States next year.

b The next elected president of the United States will be a Democrat.

c The increase in tuition costs for the major state university in your state will exceed 5% next year.

d It will rain at some time next week.

3.3 An automobile dealer sells two brands of new cars. One, C, is primarily American in origin; the other, G, is primarily Japanese. The dealer performs repair work under warranty for both brands. Each warranty job is classified according to the primary problem to be fixed. If there is more than one problem in a given job, all problems are listed separately. Records for the past year indicate the following numbers of problems:

		Problem Area					
		Engine	Transmission	Exhaust	Fit/Finish	Other	Total
Brand	C	106	211	67	133	24	541
	G	21	115	16	24	6	182
	Total	127	326	83	157	30	723

a What is the probability that a randomly chosen problem comes from brand C?

b Serious problems are those involving the engine or transmission. What is the probability that a randomly chosen problem is serious?

c The dealer is fully reimbursed for all brand C problems and all brand G engine, transmission, and fit/finish problems. What is the probability that a randomly chosen problem is *not* fully reimbursed?

3.4 **a** For the automobile dealer's data in Exercise 3.3, what is the probability that a randomly chosen problem is an engine problem, given that it comes from brand C?

b Construct a table of conditional probabilities of problem areas, given the brand. Are the probability distributions similar for the two brands?

3.5 The automobile dealer's warranty repair data from Exercise 3.3 were reanalyzed to take into account multiple problems on a particular repair job.

		Number of Problems			
		1	2	3	Total
Brand	C	382	54	17	453
	G	135	16	5	156
	Total	517	70	22	609

a What is the probability that a randomly chosen job involves more than one problem?

b What is the probability that a randomly chosen brand C job involves more than one problem?

3.6 Use the data of Exercise 3.5 to construct a table of the conditional probabilities of the number of problems, given the brand. Would you say that the conditional probabilities are similar?

3.7 In both Exercises 3.3 and 3.5, the number of brand C entries is much higher than the number for brand G. Does this fact indicate that brand C is of poorer quality than brand G?

3.8 On a typical day a convenience store recorded 186 sales of gas, 207 sales of dairy products, 188 sales of sodas, 339 sales of packaged foods, and 316 sales of nonfood products, for a total of 1236 sales.

   a What is the probability that a randomly chosen sale is gas?

   b What is the probability that a randomly chosen sale is of some food product (including dairy and, by courtesy, soda)?

3.9 In Exercise 3.8, what is the probability that a randomly chosen food sale is a dairy product sale?

3.10 A market research firm regularly assembles panels of consumers to test new television commercials for effectiveness. The consumers are told that they are evaluating a pilot TV program. After viewing the hour-long program, complete with commercials, they are asked many questions about the program and some about the commercial—the actual object of research. A tabulation of results from one panel counted the number of panelists who recalled the product incorrectly, the number who recalled the product correctly and had a favorable opinion, and the number who recalled the product correctly and had an unfavorable opinion.

	Incorrect	Favorable	Unfavorable	Total
Men	42	38	20	100
Women	63	57	30	150
Total	105	95	50	250

   a Use the addition law to find the probability that a randomly chosen consumer recalled the commercial.

   b Use the complements principle to find the same probability.

3.11 In Exercise 3.10, what is the probability that a randomly chosen consumer is either a man or someone who recalled the product favorably?

3.12 **a** Use the data of Exercise 3.10 to calculate the conditional probabilities of incorrect, favorable, and unfavorable responses among men. Do the same for women.

   b Are there gender differences in response to the commercial? ■

Statistical Independence

The concept of statistical independence is fundamental in probability theory and particularly in its statistical applications. Suppose that an auditor is auditing the receivables of a small company. There are 216 accounts, of which 24 contain errors; 36 of the 216 accounts are "foreign" and 4 of the 36 foreign accounts are in error. Does the probability of error given a foreign account differ from the overall (unconditional) probability of error? There were 24 erroneous accounts in the group of 216, so $P(error) = 24/216 = 1/9$. The conditional probability of error given a foreign account is $P(error \mid foreign) = P(foreign\ and\ error)/P(foreign) = (4/216)/(36/216) = 4/36 = 1/9$ also. Because the conditional probability of error is exactly the same as the unconditional probability, the events—observing a foreign account and observing an account in error—are said to be **statistically independent**.

statistically independent

The idea of statistical independence is that the occurrence of event A does not change the probability that event B occurs. For the auditing example, the probability of error is the same when dealing with a foreign account as it is in the whole population, so it doesn't matter whether we're talking about a foreign account, an account generally, or a nonforeign account. In other words, the conditional probability $P(B|A)$ is the same as the unconditional probability $P(B)$.

Definition 3.6   Definition of Independent Events

Events A and B are statistically independent if and only if $P(B|A) = P(B)$. Otherwise they are dependent. *Note:* If A and B are independent, it also follows that $P(A|B) = P(A)$.   ∎

Hereafter, we simply say *independent events* and omit the word *statistically*.

E X A M P L E   3 . 1 0

Suppose two different accounts are drawn at random (the first is not replaced before the second is drawn) in the receivables auditing situation. Determine whether the events "first account erroneous" and "second account erroneous" are independent.

Solution

Because the receivables sampling is done without replacement, the occurrence of an erroneous account on the first draw (slightly) reduces the probability of an erroneous account on the second. Therefore the events are not independent. If the first account drawn is erroneous, there are 215 accounts remaining, of which 23 are erroneous. Therefore, P(second is erroneous | first is erroneous) $= 23/215 = .107$. If we are not given the result of the first account, there is no difference between the first and second draws, so the unconditional probability P(second is erroneous) $= 24/216 = .111$. The numerical difference in probabilities is very small, so the events are nearly—but not quite—independent.   ∎

E X A M P L E   3 . 1 1

Suppose that in a university computing center 192 of 960 jobs are high-priority jobs: 128 of these are submitted by students and 64 by faculty. Of all the jobs, 640 are from students and 320 from faculty. If one job is selected at random, are the events "high-priority job" and "student job" independent?

Solution

Let A be the event that the job is submitted by a student and B the event that the job is a high-priority job. In order for events A and B to be independent, we must show

$$P(A \mid B) = P(A)$$

or

$$P(B \mid A) = P(B)$$

For this example, we can compute $P(B|A)$ using the definition of conditional probability:

$$P(B \mid A) = \frac{P(A \cap B)}{P(A)}$$

$$= \frac{128/960}{640/960} = \frac{128}{640} = .200$$

Also, $P(B) = 192/960 = .200$, so the events A and B are independent.   ∎

The concepts of mutually exclusive events and independent events are *not* the same. "Mutually exclusive" is a logical concept; two events are mutually exclusive if one event logically can't happen when the other one does. "Statistically independent" is a probability concept; two events are independent if the occurrence of one doesn't change the probability of the other. Mutually exclusive events can't be independent. For mutually exclusive events, the occurrence of one event changes the probability of the other—to zero!

The definition of independent events leads to a special case of the multiplication law that applies to independent events.

Definition 3.7   Multiplication Law for Independent Events

If events A and B are independent,

$$P(A \cap B) = P(A \text{ and } B) = P(A)P(B) \qquad \blacksquare$$

This result is an alternate definition of independence.

E X A M P L E   3 . 1 2

Use the multiplication law for independent events to verify that the two events of Example 3.11 are independent.

Solution

We showed previously that $P(A \cap B) = 128/960 = .133$. Similarly, $P(A)P(B) = (640/960) \times (192/960) = .133$. Because $P(A \cap B) = P(A)P(B)$, events A and B are independent. $\blacksquare$

The definition of independence suggests that we should find $P(A \text{ and } B)$, $P(A)$, and $P(B)$ and then check to determine if the events are independent. Sometimes this is in fact the procedure. More often, independence is a natural *assumption*. For example, sampling with replacement leads naturally to assumed independence. The multiplication principle is then used to calculate joint probabilities such as $P(A \text{ and } B)$.

E X A M P L E   3 . 1 3

Suppose that 70% of the teachers in a school district are rated as satisfactory, that 59% are age 40 or more, and that rating and age are assumed to be independent. What is the probability that a randomly chosen teacher is (a) rated satisfactory and over 40; (b) not rated satisfactory and not over 40; (c) not rated satisfactory, given under 40?

Solution

a   Because the events "rated satisfactory" and "over 40 years of age" are independent, it follows that

$$P(\text{satisfactory and over 40}) = P(\text{satisfactory})P(\text{over 40})$$

$$= (.70)(.59) = .413$$

b   Because the events "rated satisfactory" and "over 40 years of age" are independent, their complements ("not rated satisfactory" and "not over 40") are also independent.

Hence,

$$P(\text{not satisfactory and not over 40}) = (1 - .70)(1 - .59)$$

$$= .123$$

c
$$P(\text{not satisfactory} \mid \text{not over 40}) = \frac{P(\text{not satisfactory and not over 40})}{P(\text{not over 40})}$$

$$= \frac{.123}{.41} = .30$$

This is exactly the probability of the event "not rated satisfactory." ■

The multiplication law can be extended to more than two independent events, but to do so, we need the idea of independent processes. Processes are independent if *any* event from one process is independent of events from all other processes. If, for instance, there are four independent processes and events A, B, C, and D, then the probability of all four events occurring is

$$P(A \text{ and } B \text{ and } C \text{ and } D) = P(A)P(B)P(C)P(D)$$

E X A M P L E   3 . 1 4

Assume that the probability that a buyer of a new automobile orders factory-installed air-conditioning is .6 and that the decisions of buyers are independent processes. What is the probability that the next five buyers all order factory air-conditioning?

Solution

Let A_1, A_2, A_3, A_4, A_5 be the events that buyers 1, 2, 3, 4, 5 order factory air-conditioning. Then

$$P(\text{all five order factory air-conditioning}) = P(A_1 \cap A_2 \cap A_3 \cap A_4 \cap A_5)$$

$$= P(A_1)P(A_2)P(A_3)P(A_4)P(A_5)$$

$$= (.6)(.6)(.6)(.6)(.6)$$

$$= .07776$$

Remember that the $\cap$ sign should be read as "and." ■

E X E R C I S E S

3.13 A personnel officer for a firm that employs many part-time salespeople tries out a sales-aptitude test on several hundred applicants. Because the test is unproven, results are not used in hiring. Forty percent of applicants show high aptitude on the test and 12% of those hired both show high aptitude and achieve good sales records. The firm's experience shows that 30% of all salespeople achieve good sales. Let A be the event "shows high aptitude" and let B be the event "achieves good sales."

a Find $P(A)$, $P(A \text{ and } B)$, and $P(B|A)$.

b Are A and B independent?

c How useful is the test in predicting good sales achievement?

d Find $P(A \text{ and not } B)$ and $P(\text{not } B|A)$.

e Are A and not B independent?

3.14 A survey of workers in two plants of a manufacturing firm includes the question: "How effective is management in responding to legitimate grievances of workers?" In plant 1, 48 of 192 workers respond "poor"; in plant 2, 80 of 248 workers respond "poor." An employee of the manufacturing firm is to be selected randomly. Let A be the event "worker comes from plant 1" and let B be the event "response is poor."

    a Find $P(A)$, $P(B)$, and $P(A \text{ and } B)$.

    b Are the events A and B independent?

    c Find $P(B|A)$ and $P(B| \text{ not } A)$. Are they equal?

3.15 Show that if A and B are independent, $P(B|A) = P(B| \text{ not } A)$. (*Hint:* B and not A are also independent.)

3.16 A school district must staff two primary schools and one high school. On any particular day, the probability that no substitute for an absent teacher is needed at primary school 1 is .60; the same probability holds for primary school 2. At the high school, the probability that no substitute is needed is .50. Assume that absenteeism at the three schools defines three independent processes. Find the probability that no substitute is needed at any of the schools on a particular day.

3.17 Do you believe that the assumption of independent processes in Exercise 3.16 is realistic?

3.18 A computer manufacturer's sales data indicated that the probability that a randomly chosen computer had standard memory was .84, and the probability that it had both a floppy disk drive and a CD-ROM reader was .40. The probability that it had both types of input devices (floppy and CD-ROM) and also had standard memory was .24.

    a Find the probability that a computer has both input devices, given that it has standard memory.

    b Find the probability that a computer has standard memory, given that it has both types of input devices.

    c Are the events "standard memory" and "both types of input devices" independent?

3.19 In addition to the probabilities given in the previous exercise, the probability that a computer has an extra-capacity hard disk is .45. The probability that a computer has both types of input devices and also an extra-capacity hard disk is .18. Are the events "both types of input devices" and "extra-capacity hard disk" independent?

3.20 An airline keeps track of adjustment problems faced by airport attendants. It finds that 40% of all problems involve a missed connection; 10% of all problems involve mishandled baggage. Is it plausible to assume that 4% of all problems will involve both mishandled baggage and a missed connection?

3.21 A direct-order retailer finds that 40% of all orders arrive by telephone (and the remainder by mail). A partial or complete merchandise return is made in 10% of all orders. Is it reasonable to assume that 4% of all orders will arrive by telephone and involve a merchandise return?

3.22 Some people who use control charts say that 8 or more consecutive values on the same side of the target mean indicate an out-of-control process. The following Resampling Stats program simulates 60-day periods, where the day-to-day results are independent processes. The simulated process is in control; there is a 50–50 chance that a value will fall above the target. What do the program results indicate about the probability of obtaining a "run" of at least 8 consecutive values on the same side of the target, under these conditions?

```
 1: 'SET INITIAL VALUE.  YOU MAY WISH TO OMIT THIS STEP.
 2: SEED 13579123
 3: 'REPEAT 10000 TIMES
 4: MAXSIZE DEFAULT 10000
 5: REPEAT 10000
 6: 'DRAW 60 INDEPENDENT DAYS; 0 MEANS BELOW TARGET, 1, ABOVE.
 7: GENERATE 60 0,1 RANDOM
 8: 'COUNT NUMBER OF RUNS AT LEAST 8 DAYS LONG
 9: RUNS RANDOM >=8 NUMRUNS
10: 'SAVE RESULT
11: SCORE NUMRUNS RUNS8
12: 'END OF THIS TIME
13: END
14: 'PRINT RESULT
```

Vector no. 1: RUNS8

Bin Center	Freq	Pct	Cum Pct
0	8082	80.8	80.8
1	1774	17.7	98.6
2	139	1.4	99.9
3	5	0.1	100.0

3.23 How would you find the probability of the preceding problem mathematically? ∎

3.3

Probability Tables, Trees, and Simulations

Many probability problems require the successive use of several of the basic principles to obtain a solution. These problems can be solved algebraically, but it is helpful to be familiar with some devices that can help you keep the logic straight.

EXAMPLE 3.15

A firm has found that 46% of its junior executives have two-career marriages, 37% have single-career marriages, and 17% are unmarried. The firm estimates that 40% of the two-career marriage executives would refuse a transfer to another office, as would 15% of the single-career marriage executives and 10% of the unmarried executives. If a transfer offer is made to a randomly selected executive, what is the probability that it will be refused?

Solution

First, the event "refused" can be thought of as "(refused and two-career) or (refused and single-career) or (refused and unmarried)." The three possibilities are mutually exclusive, so the addition law yields

$$P(\text{refused}) = P(\text{refused and two-career}) + P(\text{refused and single-career})$$
$$+ P(\text{refused and unmarried})$$

Second, each of the three joint probabilities can be evaluated by the multiplication law. For instance,

$$P(\text{refused and two-career}) = P(\text{two-career})P(\text{refused} \mid \text{two-career})$$
$$= (.46)(.40)$$

Putting the two ideas together, we have

$$P(\text{refused}) = P(\text{two-career})P(\text{refused} \mid \text{two-career})$$
$$+ P(\text{single-career})P(\text{refused} \mid \text{single-career})$$
$$+ P(\text{unmarried})P(\text{refused} \mid \text{unmarried})$$
$$= (.46)(.40) + (.37)(.15) + (.17)(.10) = .2565 \quad ∎$$

EXAMPLE 3.16

Investments of $100 each are made in two projects. Project A is assumed to yield a net return of $8, $10, or $12, with respective probabilities .2, .6, and .2. Project B is assumed to yield a net return of $8, $10, or $12, with respective probabilities .3, .4, and .3. The returns from the two projects are assumed to be independent. What is the probability that the total of the two returns is exactly $20?

Solution

By the addition law,

$$P(\text{total} = \$20) = P(\text{A yields } \$8 \text{ and B yields } \$12)$$
$$+ P(\text{A yields } \$10 \text{ and B yields } \$10)$$
$$+ P(\text{A yields } \$12 \text{ and B yields } \$8)$$

The multiplication law for independent events may be applied to each joint probability to obtain

$$P(\text{total} = \$20) = P(\text{A yields } \$8)P(\text{B yields } \$12)$$
$$+ P(\text{A yields } \$10)P(\text{B yields } \$10)$$
$$+ P(\text{A yields } \$12)P(\text{B yields } \$8)$$
$$= (.2)(.3) + (.6)(.4) + (.2)(.3) = .36 \quad \blacksquare$$

No new ideas are involved in the solution of such problems, but it is sometimes tricky to find the right order in which to apply the basic principles. With larger, more complicated problems, the difficulty is increased. Several methods have been invented to help clarify the reasoning involved in solving a problem.

One useful approach is to construct a table of joint probabilities. The desired answer can sometimes be found by adding the appropriate table entries.

EXAMPLE 3.17

Construct a joint probability table for marital status versus action on transfer offers for the data of Example 3.15. Use it to find P(refused).

Solution

First, put any known marginal probabilities on the appropriate margins of the table.

	Two-career	Single-career	Unmarried
Refused			
Accepted			
	.46	.37	.17

Now the body of the table can be filled in using the multiplication law. The remaining marginals can be found by addition.

	Two-career	Single-career	Unmarried	
Refused	$(.46)(.40) = .1840$	$(.37)(.15) = .0555$	$(.17)(.10) = .0170$	.2565
Accepted	$(.46)(.60) = .2760$	$(.37)(.85) = .3145$	$(.17)(.90) = .1530$	.7435
	.46	.37	.17	

P(refused) is shown, in the right margin, to be .2565, as in Example 3.15. ∎

EXAMPLE 3.18

Construct a joint probability table and find P(total return = $20) for the data of Example 3.16.

Solution

In this case, both sets of marginal probabilities have been specified.

		Return from A			
		$8	$10	$12	
Return	$8				.3
from	$10				.4
B	$12				.3
		.2	.6	.2	

The multiplication law for independent events can be used to fill in the body of the table.

		Return from A			
		$8	$10	$12	
Return	$8	.06	.18	.06*	.3
from	$10	.08	.24*	.08	.4
B	$12	.06*	.18	.06	.3
		.2	.6	.2	

The entries that correspond to a total return of $20 are marked with an asterisk. The addition law yields

$$P(\text{total return} = \$20) = .06 + .24 + .06 = .36$$

as in Example 3.16. ∎

Probability tables are a convenient, compact way of solving many problems. As a by-product, they often yield the solution to related problems as well. You should have no difficulty, for instance, in finding P(total return = $22) or P(total return = $16) using the table in Example 3.18. For problems involving more than two categories of events, probability tables are at best awkward to use. If there had also been a project C in Example 3.16, some sort of three-dimensional table would have been necessary.

probability tree

Another device that often can be used is a **probability tree**. This method is best introduced by an illustration.

EXAMPLE 3.19

Use a probability tree to solve Example 3.15.

Solution

First, construct branches for a set of events with known marginal probabilities. In this example, we start with type of marriage, as in Figure 3.1.

Then, at the tip of each of these branches, construct branches for another set of events, using conditional probabilities (given the appropriate first branch). In this case, the second set of branches is based on whether the transfer offer is refused or accepted, as in Figure 3.2.

FIGURE 3.1   **Beginning of a Probability Tree**

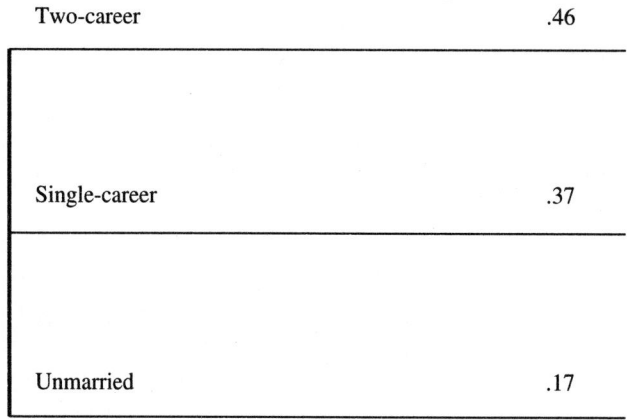

FIGURE 3.2   **Completion of a Probability Tree**

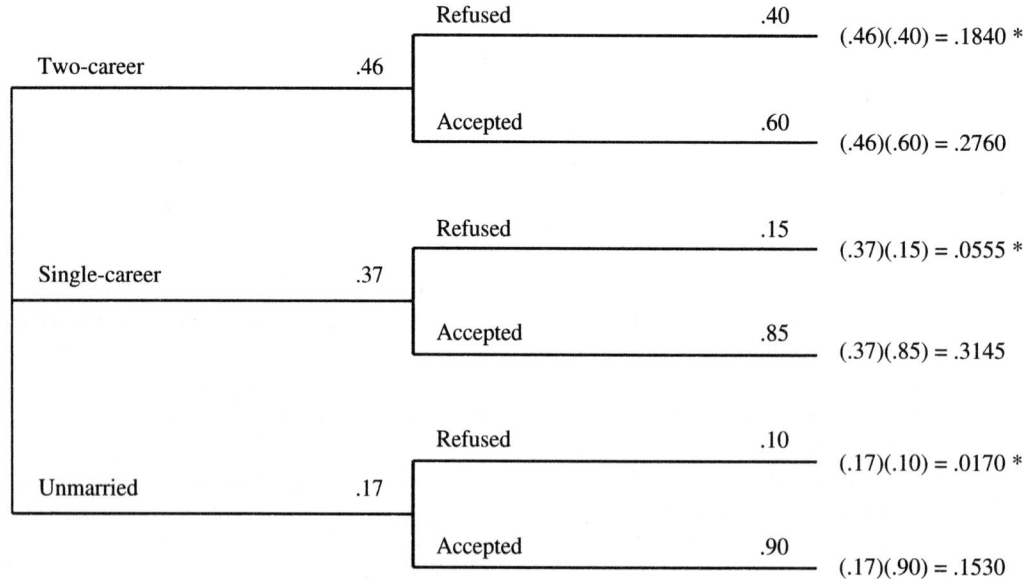

Had there been another set of relevant events, we would have added another set of branches. The probability for each specific path (sequence of branches) is found by multiplying the probabilities along that path, as shown in Figure 3.2. The probability of an event can be found by adding the probabilities of all paths that satisfy that event. The paths corresponding to "refused" are marked with an asterisk: P(refused) $= .1840 + .0555 + .0170 = .2565$, once again. ■

EXAMPLE 3.20

Use a probability tree to solve Example 3.16.

Solution

Marginal probabilities are specified for both project A and project B, so we may use the returns to either project for the first set of branches. Out of sheer perversity, we begin by branching on project B in Figure 3.3.

In this case, because of assumed independence, the conditional probabilities of A returns given particular B returns are unnecessary. The path probabilities for a total return of $20 are marked with an asterisk: P(total return $= \$20) = .06 + .24 + .06 = .36$.

FIGURE 3.3 **Probability Tree for Investments**

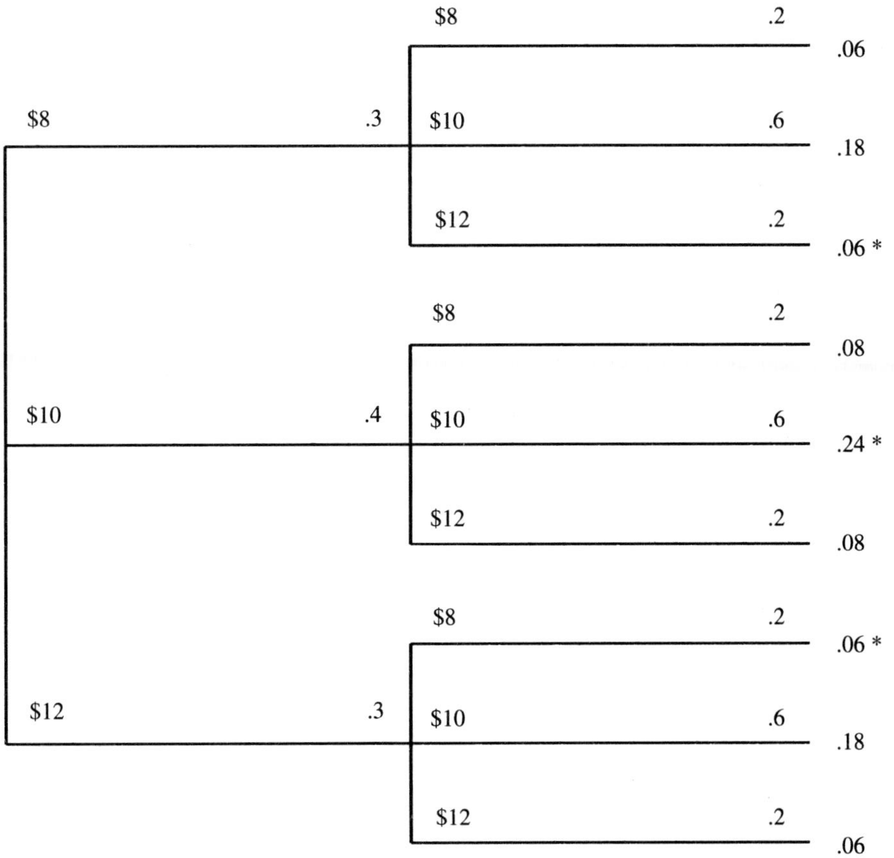

To give correct answers, a probability tree must be constructed according to some simple rules.

Definition 3.8   Rules for Constructing a Probability Tree

1   Events forming the first set of branches must have known marginal probabilities, must be mutually exclusive, and should exhaust all possibilities (so that the sum of the branch probabilities is 1).

2   Events forming the second set of branches must be entered at the tip of each of the sets of first branches. Conditional probabilities, given the relevant first branch, must be entered, unless assumed independence allows the use of unconditional probabilities. Again, the branches must be mutually exclusive and exhaustive (so that the sum of the probabilities branching from any one tip is 1).

3   If there are additional sets of branches, the probabilities must be conditional on all preceding events. As always, the branches must be mutually exclusive and exhaustive.

4   The sum of path probabilities must be taken over all paths included in the relevant event.   ■

With a little practice, most people find probability trees quite easy to use. Trees and tables are both very useful in clarifying the logic of a solution. Both methods in effect construct a set of outcomes; a particular outcome corresponds to a path in a probability tree or to an entry in a probability table. Trees can be used in a wider variety of problems. The only difficulty with using a tree for a large, complicated problem is that the tree can become impractically large. As long as one is willing to use a lot of paper, it is possible to solve some rather nasty problems surprisingly quickly.

EXAMPLE 3.21

In a certain television game show, a valuable prize is hidden behind one of three doors. You, the contestant, pick one of the three doors. Before opening it, the announcer opens one of the other two doors and you see that the prize isn't behind that door. The announcer offers you the chance to switch to the remaining door. Should you switch, or does it matter?

Solution

Let's make a tree.

Call the door that you select A, the others B and C. Assuming that the prize is distributed randomly among the doors, the probability that it's behind each of the doors is 1/3. If you picked a wrong door in door A, the announcer has no choice. If B contains the prize, the announcer must open C; if C has the prize, he must open B. But if you picked correctly and A has the prize, the announcer does have a choice. Let's assume that the announcer picks B or C randomly, each with probability 1/2 in this situation. We can construct the tree in Figure 3.4.

Suppose that the announcer has chosen B (and you chose A initially). What is the probability that the prize is behind door C?

$$P(\text{behind C} \mid \text{chose B}) = \frac{P(\text{behind C and chose B})}{P(\text{chose B})}$$

$$= \frac{1/3}{1/6 + 1/3} = \frac{1/3}{1/2} = \frac{2}{3}$$

FIGURE 3.4 **Probability Tree for Three Doors**

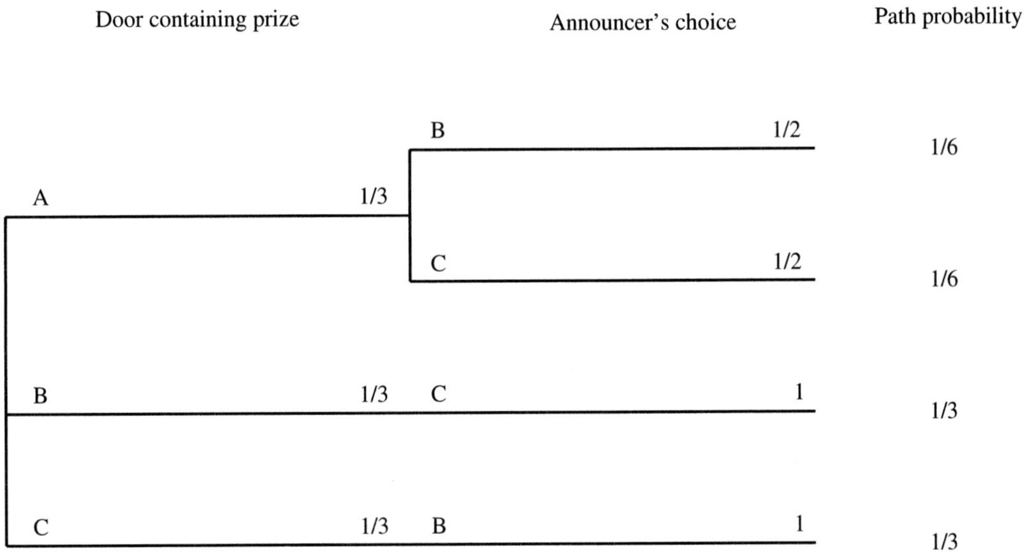

Door containing prize   Announcer's choice   Path probability

so $P(\text{behind A} \mid \text{chose B}) = 1 - 2/3 = 1/3$. You have a better chance of winning if you switch to door C! ∎

EXAMPLE 3.22

Suppose that 40% of all theoretically plausible pharmaceutical drug concepts are biologically active. Of the active drugs, 70% show serious side effects. Of those drugs that prove to be inactive, 20% can be reformulated to be active, and among these reformulated drugs, 80% show serious side effects. All drugs that are to be marketed must be approved by a government agency. The probability that a drug will be approved, given that it is biologically active and shows no side effects, is .90. Of drugs that are biologically active but show side effects, 5% will be approved. If a drug is not biologically active, it will not be approved.

a   What is the probability that a new drug concept will result in an approved drug?

b   What is the probability that a new drug concept will lead to a drug with side effects?

c   If a drug is approved, what is the probability that it will show side effects?

Solution

We can construct a moderately large probability tree, something like Figure 3.5. In this case, as often happens, the natural sequence of branches is chronological. The natural first branch reflects whether or not the drug is active. Whether the drug can be reformulated, whether it shows side effects, and finally whether it is approved are then considered.

a   To find the probability that a drug is approved, simply add the probabilities for all paths corresponding to a "yes" branch on the "approved" question:

$$P(\text{approved}) = .0140 + .1080 + .0048 + .0216 = .1484$$

FIGURE 3.5   **Probability Tree for New Drug Example**

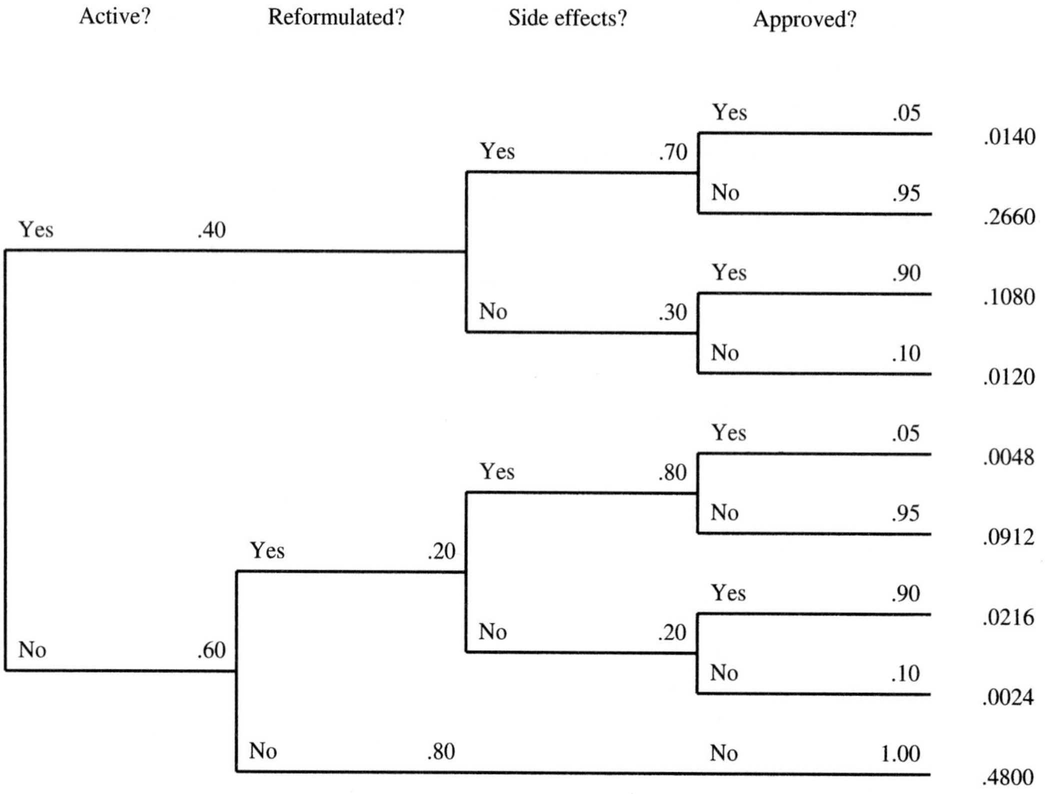

Active?	Reformulated?	Side effects?	Approved?

Yes .40
Yes .70
Yes .05 — .0140
No .95 — .2660
No .30
Yes .90 — .1080
No .10 — .0120
No .60
Yes .20
Yes .80
Yes .05 — .0048
No .95 — .0912
No .20
Yes .90 — .0216
No .10 — .0024
No .80
No 1.00 — .4800

b   Again, we must add the appropriate path probabilities. The paths corresponding to existence of side effects are the first, second, fifth, and sixth paths:

$$P(\text{side effects}) = .0140 + .2660 + .0048 + .0912 = .3760$$

Alternatively, we can draw the tree without the "approved" branches and obtain

$$P(\text{side effects}) = .40(.70) + .60(.20)(.80) = .280 + .096 = .376$$

once again.

c   To find a conditional probability like this one, we use the definition of conditional probability:

$$P(\text{side effects} \mid \text{approved}) = \frac{P(\text{side effects and approved})}{P(\text{approved})}$$

In part a, we found $P(\text{approved}) = .1484$. Note that the first and fifth branches, with respective probabilities .0140 and .0048, are the only ones corresponding to "side effects and approved." Thus

$$P(\text{side effects} \mid \text{approved}) = (.0140 + .0048)/(.1484) \qquad ∎$$

There is one large class of probability problems, readily solved by a probability tree or table, that occurs frequently enough to be given a name. In this section, we introduce Bayes' Theorem, which indicates how to revise probabilities in light of new information. This theorem is not a new concept—it is simply a sometimes-convenient combination of ideas we already know.

Suppose that in a certain population, one-tenth of 1% of all individuals are infected with the HIV virus that causes AIDS. Tests for the presence of the virus are imperfect: Suppose that 95% of those who are infected test positive, 2% of those who really are *not* infected also test positive. If a randomly chosen person tests positive, what is the probability that the person really has AIDS? We could carry out a probability tree calculation as shown in Figure 3.6.

FIGURE 3.6 **Probability Tree for AIDS Example**

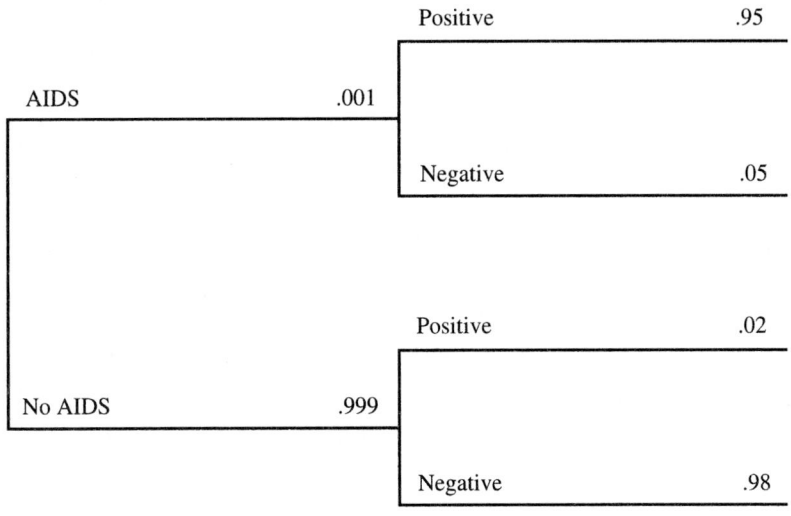

From the tree,

$$P(\text{AIDS} \mid \text{positive}) = \frac{P(\text{AIDS and positive})}{P(\text{positive})}$$

$$= \frac{.00095}{.00095 + .01998} = .045$$

This example has all the elements of Bayes' Theorem. We begin with **prior probabilities** of an event or "state of nature." In this case, the prior probabilities (prior, that is, before we obtain new information) apply to whether or not a randomly chosen person has AIDS. The information—in our case, the test results—is an imperfect indication of the true state; the probabilities of various information outcomes, such as positive or negative diagnoses, are called **likelihoods**. These probabilities are combined to yield **posterior probabilities** (that is, after obtaining information) of the various states of nature.

prior probabilities

likelihoods
posterior probabilities

Definition 3.9 Bayes' Theorem

If $A_1, \ldots, A_k$ are mutually exclusive states of nature and if $B_1, \ldots, B_m$ are m possible mutually exclusive observable events, then

$$P(A_i \mid B_j) = \frac{P(B_j \mid A_i)P(A_i)}{P(B_j \mid A_1)P(A_1) + P(B_j \mid A_2)P(A_2) + \cdots + P(B_j \mid A_k)P(A_k)}$$

$$= \frac{P(B_j \mid A_i)P(A_i)}{\sum_i P(B_j \mid A_j)P(A_i)} \quad \blacksquare$$

Bayes' Theorem summarizes tree-type calculations. In the AIDS example, the states of nature are A_1 = has AIDS, and A_2 = doesn't have AIDS; the observable events are B_1 = positive, and B_2 = negative. The numerator of Bayes' Theorem is $P(A_i \text{ and } B_j)$ and is found by multiplying probabilities along one particular path of the tree; for example, $P(\text{AIDS and positive}) = P(A_1 \text{ and } B_1) = 001(.95) = .00095$. The denominator is found by adding probabilities for all paths corresponding to B_j; for example, $P(\text{positive}) = P(B_1) = .00095 + .01998$. When it applies, Bayes' Theorem is a shortcut for a tree calculation.

Sometimes the results are surprising. In the AIDS example, the posterior probability of having AIDS given a positive test result is only .045. Therefore, of all the people who got a positive result (and were terribly frightened as a result), only 4.5% actually have the disease. The positive result did increase the probability of having AIDS, as it should; but the prior probability was so low that even an increased probability is still quite small. Massive screening programs for diseases like AIDS are sometimes proposed; apart from the high cost of such programs, the "false positive" phenomenon illustrated by our example is a strong argument against such programs.

There is another approach to finding approximate answers to probability problems. We can simulate the events using a computer program. Applying the long-run relative frequency idea of probability, if we run a large number of trials and find the fraction of cases in which an event occurs, we have a close approximation to the correct probability. We can't get an exact answer without an infinite number of trials, but usually we can get close enough for most purposes.

For example, a computer database program "freezes" with probability .1 in a particular application. The database is backed up less often than it should be. There is only a .8 probability that the current database is backed up at any time. The program works acceptably if it does not "freeze" or if the current database is backed up. What is the probability that the program will work acceptably?

This is a simple enough problem that we can solve it directly. We can assume that "freezing" and whether the database is backed up are independent events (unless you believe that the program knows when the database hasn't been backed up and tries to freeze then).

So

$$P(\text{does not freeze or backed up}) = P(\text{does not freeze}) + P(\text{backed up}) - P(\text{both})$$

$$= .9 + .8 - (.9)(.8) = .98$$

To simulate this situation, we had Excel generate two columns of 1000 random 1s and 0s. In the first column, simulating the database program's freezing, there was a 10% chance of having a 1 in a given cell and a 90% chance of a 0. In the second column, simulating the backing up of the database, there was an 80% chance of a 1 and a 20% chance of a 0 in a given cell. In a third column called "OK?" we used a formula that came out 1 if either column 1 was a 0 or column 2 was a 1, or both. Then Excel counted the number of 1s and 0s in this column. Results:

OK?	Frequency
0	21
1	979

The simulation probability is $979/1000 = .979$, virtually identical to the exact answer: .980.

E X A M P L E   3 . 2 3

A 10-year-old girl collects baseball cards of major league players. Having taste and judgment, she prefers National League players, who constitute only half the cards sold. Her father suggests a strategy for improving the number of National Leaguers she gets. He tells her that each time she goes to buy cards, she should stop as soon as she gets one National League player. Her mother thinks that this suggestion is not a winner. To avoid serious allowance depletion, they agree to simulate this on a computer. The computer draws a series of 1s and 0s with equal probability, and prints them out in sequence. Then the girl draws a line each time a 1 appears, indicating stopping when a National Leaguer is found. In a long series of numbers, what fraction will be 1s? (This example is a modification of a suggestion by Peter Bruce of the Resampling Stats project.)

Solution

Really, we don't need any computer output for this. Where the lines are drawn in the sequence doesn't matter. In the long run, half the values will be 1 and the other half 0. Sorry, Dad. ∎

EXERCISES

3.24 The experience of a data-processing firm has shown that the first time a new program is tested there is a .6 probability of finding one or more major "bugs"—flaws in the program that cause the program to fail completely. There is a .3 chance of detecting minor bugs—flaws that allow the program to run but produce erroneous results in certain situations—and a .1 chance that no bugs are detected. In each case, an attempt is made to correct all detected programming errors. Then the program is retested on a more extensive basis. The likely results of the retest are summarized in the following table of conditional probabilities:

		Retest		
		Major	Minor	None
	Major	.3	.5	.2
First test	Minor	.1	.3	.6
	None	0	.2	.8

   a Construct a table giving the joint probabilities of all the possible combinations of first test and retest results.

   b Find the probability that major bugs are still found at the retest.

   c Find the probabilities of minor bugs at retest and of no bugs at retest.

3.25 Construct a probability tree to answer Exercise 3.24.

3.26 In the data-processing firm of Exercise 3.24, programs that still show major or minor bugs on retesting are sent through one more round of correction. Programs that had major bugs in retest have a .1 probability of retaining major bugs in the third test (regardless of the result of the initial test) and a .2 probability of showing minor bugs. Those that showed only minor bugs at retesting have essentially no chance of showing major bugs at third test but a .1 chance of showing minor bugs (again regardless of the result of the first test). It is assumed that programs showing no bugs at retesting need not go through a third round.

   a Construct a probability tree for this situation.

   b Find the probability that a program will show major bugs at all three tests.

   c Find the probability that a program will show major bugs at the third test. Why is this answer different from that of part b?

   d Find the probability that a program will achieve no-bug status (whether after two or three tests).

3.27 A purchasing unit for a state government has found that 60% of the winning bids for office-cleaning contracts come from regular bidders, 30% from occasional bidders, and 10% from first-time bidders. The services provided by successful bidders are rated satisfactory or unsatisfactory after one year on the job. Experience indicates that 90% of the jobs done by regular bidders are satisfactory, as are 80% of the jobs done by occasional bidders and 60% of the jobs done by first-time bidders.

a What is the probability that a job will be done by a first-time bidder and will be satisfactory?

b What is the probability that a job will be satisfactory?

c Given that a job is satisfactory, what is the probability that it was done by a first-time bidder?

3.28 A manufacturer of snack crackers introduces several new products each year. About 60% of the introductions are failures, 30% are moderate successes, and 10% are major successes. To try to improve the odds, the manufacturer tests new products in a customer tasting panel. Of the failures, 50% receive a poor rating in the panel, 30% a fair rating, and 20% a good rating. For the moderate successes, 20% receive a poor rating, 40% a fair rating, and 40% a good rating. For major successes, the percentages are 10% poor, 30% fair, and 60% good.

a Find the joint probability of a new product being a failure and receiving a poor rating.

b Construct a probability table of all possible joint probabilities of new product results and panel ratings.

c If a new product receives a good rating, what is the probability that the product will be a failure?

3.29 Create a probability tree using the probabilities in Exercise 3.28. Use the tree to find the probability that a new product will be a major success, given that it gets a poor rating.

3.30 A trucking company specializing in bulk cargos has contract customers and occasional customers. Company policy dictates that contract customers' calls receive priority; contract calls are 40% of the total. The first four calls each day are assigned immediately to trucks; if at least three of these calls are from contract customers, the dispatcher must decline any further calls that day from occasional customers.

a Construct a probability tree for the first four calls. The first branch should be for a contract or occasional customer on the first call.

b What is the probability that the dispatcher must decline any further calls from occasional customers?

3.31 In Exercise 3.30, suppose that the dispatcher must decline further calls from occasional customers. What is the probability that all four of the first four calls were from contract customers?

3.32 Screening people for the presence of a disease is not perfectly exact. One test has a 5% chance of a "false positive"—saying that someone has the disease who in fact doesn't. It also has a 2% chance of a "false negative"—saying that someone doesn't have the disease who in fact does. Suppose that one-tenth of 1% of the people in the screened population have the disease. According to the following Resampling Stats program, if a randomly chosen person is tested to have the disease, what is the probability that the person actually does have it?

```
 1: MAXSIZE DEFAULT 5000
 2: REPEAT 5000
 3: 'DRAW RANDOM PATIENT; ANY VALUE OF EXACTLY 1  OUT OF 1000 MEANS
    'HAS DISEASE
 4:   GENERATE 1 1,1000 PATIENT
 5:   COUNT PATIENT <=1 DISEASE
 6: 'DRAW ANOTHER RANDOM NUMBER TO DETERMINE TEST RESULT
 7:   GENERATE 1 1,100   TEST
 8: 'IF DISEASE IS 1, ANY NUMBER 95 OR LESS MEANS TESTS POSITIVE
 9:   IF DISEASE =1
10:     COUNT TEST <=95 POSDIAG
11:   END
12: 'IF DISEASE IS 0, ANY NUMBER 2 OR LESS MEANS TESTS POSITIVE
13:   IF DISEASE =0
14:     COUNT TEST <=2 POSDIAG
15:   END
16: 'KEEP TRACK OF WHETHER OR NOT POSITIVE DIAGNOSIS
17:   SCORE POSDIAG POSRSLT
18: 'FIND IF BOTH DISEASE AND DIAGNOSIS ARE 1 BY MULTIPLYING THEM
```

```
19:   MULTIPLY DISEASE POSDIAG BOTH
20: 'KEEP TRACK OF WHETHER BOTH THINGS HAPPENED
21:   SCORE BOTH BOTHRSLT
22: 'END OF A TRIAL
23: CLEAR POSDIAG
24: CLEAR DISEASE
25: CLEAR BOTH
26: END
27: 'HOW MANY POSITIVE DIAGNOSES?
28: SUM POSRSLT TOTPOS
29: 'HOW MANY BOTH POSITIVE DIAGNOSIS AND HAVING DISEASE?
30: SUM BOTHRSLT TOTBOTH
31: 'FIND THE FRACTION--THE APPROXIMATE PROBABILITY--AND PRINT
32: DIVIDE TOTBOTH TOTPOS FRACTION
33: PRINT TOTBOTH TOTPOS FRACTION


TOTBOTH  =        3
TOTPOS   =      100
FRACTION =     0.03
```

3.33   Construct a probability table to find the probability of having the disease, given a positive diagnosis, as in the previous exercise.   ■

3.4 Summing Up

Here are some suggestions for dealing with basic probability problems.

1   First, determine what probabilities are specified. In each case, is the probability conditional on something else or unconditional?

2   Next, determine what probabilities must be calculated. Are we trying to find a conditional or an unconditional probability?

3   Try using one of the reasoning devices—tables or trees—to help you work through the logic. Tables are often helpful if joint ("and" type) probabilities are specified; trees are often helpful if conditional probabilities have been specified.

4   Be alert to any assumption of statistical independence of events. To assume that the probability of one event does not change when another event occurs *is* an assumption; is it reasonable?

In addition, you may want to reread the summary of key ideas at the beginning of the chapter.

EXAMPLE 3.24

A review of the Home Mortgage Disclosure Act reports of 1990 indicates that in one particular city, 70% of all home mortgage loan applications were filed with banks (including the few remaining savings and loan associations), whereas 30% were filed with mortgage companies. Loan applications were categorized by requested loan amount (at most $30,000 versus more than $30,000) as well as by family income (less than $33,000 versus at least $33,000).

Of the loan applications filed with banks, 33% were requests for loan amounts of at most $30,000; of the loan applications filed with mortgage companies, 5% were requests for loan amounts of at most $30,000. Eighty percent of the bank applications for loan amounts of at most $30,000 were filed by families with an income of less than $33,000; 85% of the bank applications for loan amounts of more than $30,000 were filed by families with an income of at least $33,000; 75% of the mortgage company loans for loan amounts of at most $30,000 were filed by families with incomes of less than $33,000; and 90% of the mortgage company loans for loan amounts of more than $30,000 were filed by families with incomes of at least $33,000.

Would you expect that the events "income at least $33,000" and "loan amount more than $30,000" should be dependent? For these probabilities, are they? Also, if a randomly chosen application is from a family with an income of at least $33,000 and is for a loan amount of more than $30,000, what is the probability that it was filed with a bank?

Solution

The first step is to translate the information into probability terms. We have that P(bank) = .70 and P(mortgage company) = .30. The information about loan amounts is stated in terms of where the application was filed or, in other words, conditionally. So P(amount at most $30K | bank) = .33 and P(amount at most $30K | mortgage company) = .05. The information about incomes is conditional on both the filing place and the loan amount. That is, P(income less than $33K | bank and amount at most $30K) = .80, P(income at least $33K | bank and amount more than $30K) = .85, P(income less than $33K | mortgage company and amount at most $30K) = .75, and P(income at least $33K | mortgage company and amount more than $30K) = .90. Note that the income event sometimes is stated as "less than $33K" and other times as "at least $33K," so we need to be careful in translation.

In this example, there is no need to make any assumption of independence because we have all the relevant conditional probabilities. Indeed, one of the questions has to do with whether independence is a fact.

Now, what questions are asked? First, are the income and loan amount events independent? We definitely would expect dependence; families with higher incomes certainly should be more likely to ask for larger mortgages. One way to check is to see if P(income at least $33K and amount more than $30K) = P(income at least $33K)$P$(amount more than $30K). We are also asked to find P(bank | income at least $33K and amount greater than $30K).

Next, what is a reasonable way to arrange the calculations? We could draw a probability tree, with place of application as the first branch, loan amount the second branch, and income the final branch. Alternatively, we could work out a probability table. An Excel spreadsheet that looks somewhat like a probability tree is shown in Figure 3.7, first showing the formulas used and then showing the results.

Now we can answer the questions. To check for independence (or, as we would expect, dependence), we must see whether P(income at least $33K and amount more than $30K) = P(income at least $33K)$P$(amount more than $30K). The two paths in the table corresponding to income at least $33K and amount more than $30K have probabilities that add to $.39865 + .25650 = .65515$. Similarly, P(income at least $33K) = .70510, and P(amount more than $30K)= .75400. P(income at least $33K)$P$(amount more than $30K) = $(.70510)(.75400) = .53165$. Because the product of the two probabilities is not equal to the joint probability of both events, the events are not independent.

To find P(bank | income at least $33K and amount greater than $30K), we may use the definition of conditional probability:

$$P(\text{bank} \mid \text{income at least \$33K and amount greater than \$30K})$$

$$= \frac{P(\text{bank and income at least \$33K and amount greater than \$30K})}{P(\text{income at least \$33K and amount greater than \$30K})}$$

$$= .39865/.65515 = .60849$$

FIGURE 3.7   Excel Spreadsheets for Mortgage Example

	A	B	C	D	E	F	G
1	Application	Probability	Amount	Prob.	Income	Prob.	Path prob.
2							
3					less than $33K	0.8	=B5*D4*F3
4			at most $30K	0.33	at least $33k	=1-F3	=B5*D4*F4
5	Bank	0.7			less than $33K	=1-F6	=B5*D6*F5
6			more than $30K	=1-D4	at least $33k	0.85	=B5*D6*F6
7					less than $33K	0.75	=B9*D8*F7
8			at most $30K	0.05	at least $33k	=1-F7	=B9*D8*F8
9		0.3			less than $33K	=1-F10	=B9*D10*F9
10			more than $30K	=1-D8	at least $33k	0.9	=B9*D10*F10

	A	B	C	D	E	F	G
1	Application	Probability	Amount	Prob.	Income	Prob.	Path prob.
2							
3					less than $33K	0.80	0.1848
4			at most $30K	0.33	at least $33k	0.20	0.0462
5	Bank	0.70			less than $33K	0.15	0.07035
6			more than $30K	0.67	at least $33k	0.85	0.39865
7					less than $33K	0.75	0.01125
8			at most $30K	0.05	at least $33k	0.25	0.00375
9	Mtge. co.	0.30			less than $33K	0.10	0.02850
10			more than $30K	0.95	at least $33k	0.90	0.25650

SUPPLEMENTARY EXERCISES

3.34 Airlines often accept tickets bought for other airlines' flights to the same destination. Suppose that final accounting and settlement of all such tickets is made yearly, and that approximate monthly settlements are made on the basis of random samples of the month's accumulated tickets. Airline A draws a monthly sample of 60 tickets, which may have been bought from airlines B, C, or D. Indicate what a typical outcome of this experiment would be. Should all the outcomes be regarded as equally likely?

3.35 Suppose that in the packaged cereals industry, 29% of all vice presidents hold MBA degrees, 24% hold undergraduate business degrees, and 8% hold both. A vice president is to be selected at random.

a What is the probability that the vice president holds either an MBA or an undergraduate business degree (or both)?

b What is the probability that the vice president holds neither degree?

3.36 In Exercise 3.35, what is the probability that the vice president holds one degree or the other, but not both?

3.37 Suppose that the records of an automobile maker show that, for a certain compact car model, 50% of all customers order air-conditioning, 49% order power steering, and 26% order both. An order is selected randomly.

a Construct a probability table.

b What is the probability that air-conditioning is ordered but power steering is not?

c What is the probability that neither option is ordered?

3.38 In Exercise 3.37, suppose that 68% of all customers order automatic transmissions, 19% order automatic transmissions and power steering without air-conditioning, 13% order automatic transmissions and air-conditioning without power steering, and 21% order all three options.

a Construct a probability table for this situation. Use the results of the previous exercise to construct four rows of the table, respectively both air-conditioning and power steering, air-conditioning but not power steering, power steering but not air-conditioning, neither air-conditioning nor power steering.

b What is the probability that at least one of the options is ordered?

c What is the probability that exactly one option is ordered?

3.39 Use the data of Exercises 3.37 and 3.38 to find P(automatic transmission and air-conditioning). Are these events independent?

3.40 Proponents of the random walk theory of stock prices hold that predictions of whether a particular stock will do better or worse than the market in the short run (say, over a 1-month period) are no better than what could be obtained by flipping a fair coin. Suppose that a securities analyst selects eight stocks that are predicted to beat the market in the next month.

a What is the probability that all eight stocks do beat the market, assuming the validity of the random walk theory?

b State the assumptions you made in answering part a.

3.41 Refer to Exercise 3.40 and assume that the random walk theory of stock behavior is valid. Suppose that each of 100 different analysts selects eight stocks.

a What is the probability that no analyst gets eight winners?

b What is the probability that at least one analyst gets eight winners?

3.42 A paperback book seller estimates the following probabilities for the weekly sales of a particular historical romance:

Sales:	10	20	30	40
Probability:	.40	.30	.20	.10

Assume independence of sales from week to week.

a Construct a probability table for the joint probabilities of various sales levels in week 1 and week 2.

b Find the probability that the average sales level per week (over a 2-week period) is 25.

3.43 Do you believe that the independence assumption made in Exercise 3.42 is reasonable?

3.44 A purchasing department finds that 75% of its special orders are received on time. Of those orders that are on time, 80% meet specifications completely; of those orders that are late, 60% meet specifications.

a Find the probability that an order is on time and meets specifications.

b Construct a probability table or tree for this situation.

c Find the probability that an order meets specifications.

3.45 For the situation of Exercise 3.44, suppose that four orders are placed.

a Find the probability that all four orders meet specifications.

b State what assumptions you made in answering part a.

3.46 A large credit card company finds that 50% of all cardholders pay a given monthly bill in full.

a Suppose two cardholders are chosen at random. What is the probability that both pay a monthly bill in full? (The number of cardholders is so large that you need not worry about whether the choice is made with replacement or without.)

b Suppose a cardholder is chosen at random. What is the probability that the holder pays both of two consecutive monthly bills in full?

c What did you assume in answering parts a and b? Does the assumption seem unreasonable in either case?

3.47 A more detailed examination of the records of the credit card company in Exercise 3.46 shows that 90% of the customers who pay one monthly bill in full also pay the next monthly bill in full; only 10% of the customers who pay less than the full amount of one monthly bill pay the next monthly bill in full.

a Find the probability that a randomly chosen customer pays two consecutive monthly bills in full.

b Find the probability that a randomly chosen customer pays neither of two consecutive monthly bills in full.

c Find the probability that a randomly chosen customer pays exactly one of two consecutive monthly bills in full.

3.48 In the previous exercise, if a randomly chosen customer pays the second monthly bill in full, what is the probability that that customer also pays the first monthly bill in full?

3.49 Records of a men's clothing shop show that alterations are required for 40% of the suit jackets that are bought and for 30% of the suit trousers. Alterations are required for both jacket and trousers in 22% of the purchases.

a Find the probability that no alterations are required in a randomly chosen purchase. You may want to construct a table.

b Find the probability that alterations are required for either the jacket or the trousers, but not for both.

3.50 Are the events in Exercise 3.49, "alteration to jacket" and "alteration to trousers," independent?

3.51 Suppose that in Exercise 3.49 a customer purchases two suits made by different manufacturers.

a What is the probability that both suit jackets require alterations?

b What did you assume in answering part a? Is the assumption reasonable?

3.52 A computer-supply retailer selected one batch of 10,000 disks and attempted to format them all for a particular machine. There were 8847 perfect disks, 1128 disks that were usable but had bad sectors, and 25 disks that couldn't be used at all.

a What is the probability that a randomly chosen disk is not perfect?

b If the disk is not perfect, what is the probability that it is not usable at all?

3.53 New MBA graduates from a certain business school hunger for jobs with a certain consulting company. Half the MBA graduates major in finance. The company interviews 20% of the finance majors who request interviews and 10% of other majors. The company actually hires 10% of all those it interviews, regardless of major.

a If a student (assumed to be randomly chosen from the class of graduates) requests an interview, what is the chance that the student will be hired?

b If a randomly chosen student is hired, what is the probability that the student did not major in finance?

3.54 Suppose that two students, the first a finance major and the second not, both request interviews with the same company. Assuming that the company can make interviewing and hiring decisions independently from one student to another, what is the probability that both students will be hired?

3.55 A simple piece of electronic equipment has 50 components. Each component must work for the equipment to work properly. Component quality isn't perfect; 99% of the components work, but 1% fail. The following Minitab output simulates the working of the equipment. What does it indicate about the probability that a randomly chosen item will work properly?

```
MTB > note Generate 1000 trials.  Each trial is 50 components (c1-c50)
MTB > note A 1 means that the component works; 0 means it fails.
MTB > Random 1000 c1-c50;
SUBC>   Bernoulli .99.
MTB > note If the minimum across a row is 1, the equipment works.
MTB > note If the minimum is 0, the equipment contains a failing component.
MTB > rmin c1-c50 put in c51
MTB > table c51


Tabulated Statistics

 ROWS: C51

        COUNT

   0     390
```

```
      1      610
    ALL     1000
```

3.56 Calculate the probability of the previous exercise. You might start a probability tree with the first component (work or fail), then the second (work or fail), and so on, until you see a pattern.

3.57 Suppose that the piece of equipment contains 100 components, each with probability .995 of failing. Is the probability that the equipment works much different from what was found in the two previous exercises?

```
MTB > note 100 components each with prob .995 of working
MTB > note C101 contains the minimum of 100 components
MTB > table c101


Tabulated Statistics

ROWS: C101

          COUNT

    0      396
    1      604
  ALL     1000
```

3.58 A famous problem in the history of probability theory (which started with the analysis of games of chance) goes like this: In one game, a player rolls 6 fair six-sided dice, and wins if one or more 6s appear. In a second game, the player rolls 12 fair dice and wins if at least two 6s appear. In a third game, the player rolls 18 fair dice and wins if at least three 6s appear. It was argued that a 6 would appear, on average, one-sixth of the time, so the three games should have an equal chance of winning. According to the following Resampling Stats simulation, is this argument correct?

```
 1: 'PLAY GAME 1000 TIMES
 2: REPEAT 1000
 3: 'ROLL 6 DICE, LISTING FACE SHOWING FOR EACH
 4:    GENERATE 6 1,6 ROLL6
 5: 'COUNT HOW MANY 6'S SHOW
 6:    COUNT ROLL6 =6 NUMBER6S
 7: 'KEEP TRACK OF THIS NUMBER
 8:    SCORE NUMBER6S RESULT
 9: 'END OF GAME
10: END
11: 'COUNT HOW MANY GAMES YIELDED AT LEAST ONE 6
12: COUNT RESULT >=1 DIDWIN
13: 'FIND AVERAGE NUMBER OF 6'S
14: MEAN RESULT AVG6S
15: PRINT DIDWIN  AVG6S

DIDWIN  =        635

AVG6S   =      0.966

 1: 'PLAY GAME 1000 TIMES
 2: REPEAT 1000
 3: 'ROLL 12 DICE, LISTING FACE SHOWING FOR EACH
 4:    GENERATE 12 1,6 ROLL12
 5: 'COUNT HOW MANY 6'S SHOW
 6:    COUNT ROLL12 =6 NUMBER6S
 7: 'KEEP TRACK OF THIS NUMBER
 8:    SCORE NUMBER6S RESULT
 9: 'END OF GAME
10: END
11: 'COUNT HOW MANY GAMES YIELDED AT LEAST TWO 6'S
```

```
12: COUNT RESULT >=2 DIDWIN
13: 'FIND AVERAGE NUMBER OF 6'S
14: MEAN RESULT AVG6S
15: PRINT DIDWIN  AVG6S
```

```
DIDWIN  =        627

AVG6S   =       2.015
```

```
 1: 'PLAY GAME 1000 TIMES
 2: REPEAT 1000
 3: 'ROLL 18 DICE, LISTING FACE SHOWING FOR EACH
 4:    GENERATE 18 1,6 ROLL18
 5: 'COUNT HOW MANY 6'S SHOW
 6:    COUNT ROLL18 =6 NUMBER6S
 7: 'KEEP TRACK OF THIS NUMBER
 8:    SCORE NUMBER6S RESULT
 9: 'END OF GAME
10: END
11: 'COUNT HOW MANY GAMES YIELDED AT LEAST THREE 6'S
12: COUNT RESULT >=3 DIDWIN
13: 'FIND AVERAGE NUMBER OF 6'S
14: MEAN RESULT AVG6S
15: PRINT DIDWIN  AVG6S
```

```
DIDWIN  =        601

AVG6S   =        3.05
```

3.59 A remodeling contractor specializes in renovating and converting former factory buildings into apartments and condominiums. The buildings typically are located near the fringes of the business district of a city and were acquired by submitting bids. One of the important problems for the company is to acquire enough properties to keep its crews at work, but not so many that it must hold them as empty buildings, paying maintenance and taxes while earning nothing on the investment. Typically, the contractor would like to have two active projects and no idle ones at a given time.

Currently, the contractor is nearing the end of current jobs and would like to acquire two properties to renovate. Four potential sites are available for bid; decisions on what to bid must be made on all four before the results of any are known. For each of the properties separately, the contractor may make a high bid, a conservative bid, or no bid at all.

The contractor has one primary competitor. This competitor typically offers high bids on 20% of all properties, conservative bids on 70%, and no bid on the remaining 10%. If both the contractor and the competitor make high bids on a property, one or the other will win; as to which one wins, each has just about a 50–50 chance. If one submits a high bid and the other a conservative bid or no bid, the high bid will, of course, be the winner. If both submit conservative bids, each has a 40% chance of winning because occasionally some third party bids on a building. If one submits a conservative bid and the other no bid, the bidder has about an 80% chance of winning.

The contractor is trying to decide between two strategies: either bidding high on three properties and not at all on the fourth, or bidding high on two properties and conservatively on the other two. You've been asked to indicate what the chances are, under each of the two strategies, of winning two of the bids and also what the risks are of winning more than two. As a first approximation, assume that the competitor's bidding decision on any one property is independent of the decision on others, although this may not be fully realistic. Write a brief report, showing your reasoning. The contractor doesn't know much about probability. A probability tree might be useful. ∎

CASE STUDY

Probability Principles

The president of a small market research firm faced a problem with the data from a recent survey ordered by a major bank. The bank was considering a shift to consolidated billing of its revolving credit accounts (typically credit cards and equity loans). The change would have the most impact on customers who had multiple accounts with the bank, so the bank was most interested in the opinions of multiple-account customers.

The bank had provided the market research firm with random samples of essentially equal size from three lists of customers. The "pink" list (provided on pink index cards) was a sample from 190,878 customers and supposedly contained customers with no revolving accounts; the "yellow" list, a sample from 48,328 customers supposedly with exactly one such account; and the "blue" list, a sample from 21,539 customers supposedly with two or more accounts. The market researchers conducted phone interviews with all the customers; they asked each customer for an opinion on the proposed billing change and they also asked how many accounts the customer had. Tabulation of the responses showed that the customers disagreed with the bank on how many accounts they had.

		Reported Number of Accounts			
		0	1	2+	Total
	Pink	66	56	28	150
Sample	Yellow	24	90	36	150
	Blue	46	16	89	151
	Total	136	162	153	451

A check with the bank indicated that the lists were several months old, so many customers had, since then, changed the number of accounts they had with the bank. The market researchers also tabulated opinions on the proposed consolidated billing method.

Pink Sample

		Reported Number of Accounts		
		0	1	2+
	Favor	31	32	16
Opinion	Neutral	20	18	8
	Oppose	15	6	4

Yellow Sample

		Reported Number of Accounts		
		0	1	2+
	Favor	9	41	19
Opinion	Neutral	7	30	9
	Oppose	8	19	8

Blue Sample

		Reported Number of Accounts		
		0	1	2+
	Favor	18	6	44
Opinion	Neutral	21	5	20
	Oppose	7	5	25

The president has asked you for help in estimating the proportions of people in each account group having each opinion. For example, what proportion of those who have two or more accounts favors the change? The president understands that the data are subject to sampling variation, but mostly wants help in obtaining logical estimates of these proportions. In addition, the president is concerned whether these estimates would depend heavily on the numbers of customers from which the lists were drawn; everyone was suspicious of the accuracy of those numbers. Prepare a report. The justification for your answer will be an important part of the firm's report to the bank, so you should explain your logic as clearly as possible. ■

Old widower Chance's wife Nance
Had willed him the family manse.
But she'd played roulette
And lost a big bet,
And therefore left nothing to Chance.

REVIEW EXERCISES—CHAPTERS 2–3

These exercises are intended to help you check your understanding of the topics in the chapters just completed. The problems are *not* in any particular order, so you can't tell how to do a problem by its location.

R1 Samples of car door locks from four different suppliers are tested under high-stress conditions to determine the number of times that the locks can be operated before they fail. The data, in thousands, are

Supplier	Operations Before Failure									
A	24.7	19.8	22.0	37.6	21.8	25.4	20.6	48.7	23.9	22.6
B	26.8	25.7	39.7	25.8	28.0	52.4	29.4	31.1	26.0	28.4
C	15.3	35.7	18.2	15.3	21.0	19.9	42.6	21.1	18.9	19.7
D	31.4	21.2	24.5	22.0	26.7	61.0	22.6	23.5	25.0	22.6

The following results are obtained from Systat:

```
                     A          B          C          D
N OF CASES          10         10         10         10
MINIMUM         19.800     25.700     15.300     21.200
MAXIMUM         48.700     52.400     42.600     61.000
MEAN            26.710     31.330     22.770     28.050
VARIANCE        84.897     72.073     81.273    142.698
STANDARD DEV     9.214      8.490      9.015     11.946
MEDIAN          23.250     28.200     19.800     24.000
```

a Summarize the data separately for each supplier. Be sure to discuss average, variability, and skewness.

b Can the Empirical Rule be expected to work well for these data? Why or why not? You may want to construct stem-and-leaf displays for each supplier.

R2 Find the mean and variance of the combined data in Exercise R1. Can the mean be found directly from the supplier means in that exercise? Can the variance be found directly from the separate variances?

R3 Prices posted on the shelves of a supermarket do not always match the correct current price of the item because of errors in posting price changes. Suppose that over time 60% of the price changes are increases and 40% are decreases. Also suppose that 93% of the price increases are posted correctly, as are 98% of the price decreases. If a price change is not posted correctly, what is the probability that the change is a decrease?

R4 A study of small savings and loan associations yielded the following financial information:

Deposits ($000,000)	Capital ($000,000)	Reserves ($000,000)	Bad Debts (Percent of Portfolio)	Type of Bank (1 = Savings, 2 = Joint S & L, 3 = Stocks S & L)
3.68	1.14	0.97	1.62	2
11.64	4.03	3.28	0.97	1
31.62	10.63	9.22	2.00	3
2.62	0.85	0.53	3.97	2
1.97	0.61	0.79	0.75	1
15.21	5.21	3.77	1.11	3
3.88	0.65	1.10	1.77	2
5.01	1.00	1.15	0.32	1
7.53	1.16	3.02	4.31	3
3.67	0.89	0.92	1.12	2

Minitab output:

```
Stem-and-leaf of Deposits   N  = 10
Leaf Unit = 1.0

    1    0 1
    5    0 2333
    5    0 5
    4    0 7
    3    0
    3    1 1
    2    1
    2    1 5

         HI  31,


Stem-and-leaf of Capital   N  = 10
Leaf Unit = 0.10

    4    0 6688
   (3)   1 011
    3    1
    3    2
    3    2
    3    3
    3    3
    3    4 0
    2    4
    2    5 2

         HI  106,


Stem-and-leaf of Reserves  N  = 10
Leaf Unit = 0.10

    4    0 5799
   (2)   1 11
    4    1
    4    2
    4    2
    4    3 02
    2    3 7

         HI  92,


Stem-and-leaf of BadDebts  N  = 10
Leaf Unit = 0.10

    1    0 3
    1    0
    2    0 7
    3    0 9
    5    1 11
    5    1
    5    1
    5    1 67
    3    1
    3    2 0

         HI  39, 43,
```

```
Stem-and-leaf of TypeBank   N = 10
Leaf Unit = 0.10

    3    1 000
   (4)   2 0000
    3    3 000
```

a Calculate the mean and standard deviation for the Bad Debts variable. Assuming that this sample is representative of all S & L's, within what range should most of the bad debt values fall for the general population of S & L's?

b Are there any outliers in any of the variables?

R5 A coal-burning electric generator occasionally is improperly stoked and emits unacceptable amounts of various gases. In the long run, this problem occurs in 1% of the generator's operating time. An air sample is taken and analyzed every hour. The analysis is not a perfect indicator of gas emissions. Calibration tests indicate that if the generator is emitting acceptable levels of the gases, the test shows excess emissions 4% of the time, borderline emissions 5% of the time, and acceptable emissions 91% of the time. If the generator is emitting excessive amounts of the gases, the test shows excess emissions 92% of the time, borderline emissions 5% of the time, and acceptable emissions 3% of the time. If the test indicates excess emissions, what is the probability that the generator is in fact emitting unacceptable amounts of the gases?

R6 Show that "borderline emissions in the test" and "unacceptable emissions by the generator" are independent events in the preceding exercise.

R7 A supermarket chain does a study of the effectiveness of its own coupons in inducing additional sales in the meat department. The data from the preliminary pilot study were

X_1 Cents Off	X_2 Current Price (Cents)	X_3 Type of Meat	X_4 Normal Sales	X_5 Sales in Coupon Week
29	379	1	37,000	42,000
19	109	2	67,200	79,900
50	399	1	21,200	32,500
25	199	5	11,600	12,900
59	209	4	18,800	22,800
100	379	1	37,000	51,300
20	109	2	67,200	83,100
40	229	3	12,000	13,200
79	399	1	21,200	36,000
50	209	4	18,800	20,100
29	109	2	67,200	83,900
30	379	1	37,000	40,900
50	229	3	12,000	14,100

One part of the Execustat output for these data is as follows:

	CentsOff	Price	Type
Sample size	13	13	13
Mean	44.6154	256.692	2.30769
Median	40	229	2
Std. deviation	24.0019	115.553	1.37747

a Locate the mean and standard deviation of X_3.

b What is the interpretation of the numbers determined in part a?

R8 Calculate means, medians, and standard deviations of X_4, X_5, and $Y = X_5 - X_4$ in the preceding exercise. Is there a simple relation among the means? Does the same relation hold for the medians? For the standard deviations?

R9 Is there reason to think that the price data are skewed? If so, which way?

R10 Experience indicates that about 10% of new television shows place in the top third of all shows in audience ratings during the first year. About 40% place in the middle third and about 50% place in the bottom third. Of new shows placing in the top third, only 2% are canceled; 40% of shows placing in the middle third are canceled, as are 85% of shows placing in the bottom third. What fraction of new shows are in the bottom third and are not canceled?

R11 In the previous exercise, are rating and cancellation assumed to be independent? What would independence mean in this context?

R12 Junior managers in a firm are rated by their bosses in terms of current performance and managerial potential. The current performance ratings are 18% excellent, 71% satisfactory, and 11% unsatisfactory. The managerial potential ratings are 24% definite, 40% possible, and 36% unlikely.

   a Using this information and any additional assumptions you must make, find the probability that a randomly selected junior manager will be rated "excellent" on the performance scale and "definite" on the potential scale.

   b What did you assume in answering part a? Are the assumptions reasonable? If not, is the probability you calculated likely to be too low or too high?

R13 Records for a sample of employees in a large firm indicate the following distribution of claimed deductions on W-4 tax withholding forms:

Deductions:	0	1	2	3	4	5	6
Frequency:	201	287	364	332	151	97	52
Deductions:	7	8	9	10	11	12	
Frequency:	28	11	5	2	0	3	

   a Find the mean number of deductions.

   b Find the standard deviation. Does it make much difference if the data are regarded as a sample rather than a population?

   c How well does the Empirical Rule work for data within 1 standard deviation of the mean?

R14 A W-4 form is drawn at random from the data of the previous exercise.

   a What is the probability that it claims at least one deduction?

   b If the form claims at least one deduction, what is the probability that it claims at most three?

R15 Data are collected on the total compensation (salary plus bonuses) of samples of men and women junior managers in a firm. The data (in thousands of dollars per year) were

Men:	39.6	28.9	35.4	36.8	33.7	32.8	35.1	36.7	38.4	35.7	33.1
	31.6	34.7	33.8	36.2	34.9	35.7	40.2	36.5	37.4	35.2	36.6
Women:	34.2	31.8	32.7	27.6	33.0	38.1	33.0	31.5	29.8	31.8	44.7
	22.5	30.0	34.3	31.0	32.5	.	.	.	.	.	.

Excel output included the following:

	A	B	C	D	E
1	Men:			Women:	
2					
3	Mean	35.41		Mean	32.41
4					
5	Median	35.55		Median	32.15
6					
7	Mode	35.7		Mode	31.8
8					
9	Standard Deviation	2.54		Standard Deviation	4.68
10					
11	Sample Variance	6.469		Sample Variance	21.901

a From the looks of the data, should the mean and median compensation for men be similar? Verify your answer from the Excel output.

b Show that the smaller group (women) has a larger range than the other group (men). Explain what causes this phenomenon.

R16 Construct boxplots for both sets of data in the previous exercise. Include a check for outliers.

R17 Calculate the mean and median compensation for the combined sample of managers in Exercise R15. How do these values relate to the means and medians of the two groups separately?

R18 Data from an automobile manufacturer indicate that, of all cars repaired under warranty, 57% require engine work, 47% require interior work, and 30% require exterior work. Also, 23% require both engine and interior work, 7% both engine and exterior work, and 13% both interior and exterior work; 5% require all three types of work. Some cars require other types of work.

a Find the probability that a car repaired under warranty requires engine work but no interior or exterior work.

b Find the probability that a car requires exactly one of the three types of work.

c Are the events "engine work" and "interior work" independent?

R19 A cereal manufacturer collects samples of the time required for workers to clean out the manufacturing line when switching from production of one cereal to production of another. The data, in actual worker-hours expended, were

Previous Flour Base	Time									
Corn	10.0	11.0	11.5	9.5	10.0	12.5	8.5	9.0	10.0	10.5
	11.5	13.0	9.5	16.5	14.5	11.0	10.5	10.0	11.0	15.0
Oats	13.5	11.0	10.0	11.5	12.0	10.5	11.0	16.5	13.0	19.0
	12.5	17.0	11.0	13.5	12.0	11.0	13.5	15.0	.	.
Wheat	28.0	31.0	33.0	35.0	30.0	28.5	27.5	26.5	32.0	24.0
	30.5	32.0	31.5	40.5	31.0	33.0	30.5	33.0	28.5	47.5
	31.0	33.5	35.0	33.5	30.0	36.5	39.5	29.0	30.5	.

Minitab output included boxplots and histograms, shown in Figures 3.8 and 3.9, and summary statistics:

```
MTB > Describe 'Time';
SUBC>   By 'Code'.

          Descriptive Statistics

Variable   Code     N     Mean   Median   TrMean    StDev  SEMean
Time          1    20   11.250   10.750   11.111    2.093   0.468
              2    18   12.972   12.250   12.781    2.482   0.585
              3    29   32.138   31.000   31.870    4.613   0.857

Variable   Code    Min      Max       Q1       Q3
Time          1   8.500   16.500   10.000   12.250
              2  10.000   19.000   11.000   13.875
              3  24.000   47.500   29.500   33.500
```

a Based on the boxplots, what is the general shape of the data?

b Locate the means and medians for the three sets of times. Does the relation between the resulting means and medians confirm your judgment about the shapes?

R20 Calculate the mean and median for the combined samples in the previous exercise. Is either of them a reasonable summary figure for a typical cleaning time?

R21 Administrators at a rural regional hospital tracked the occupancy of beds in the surgical ward. Keeping these beds reasonably full was important to the financial stability of the hospital, but it was always preferable to have a few beds available for emergency cases. Careful scheduling of elective surgery was useful in reducing variability in bed usage.

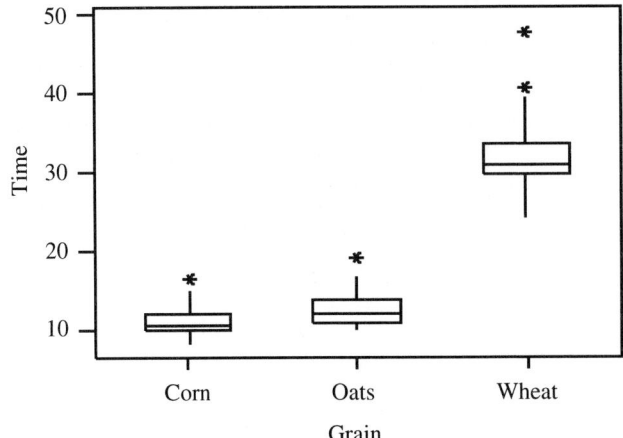

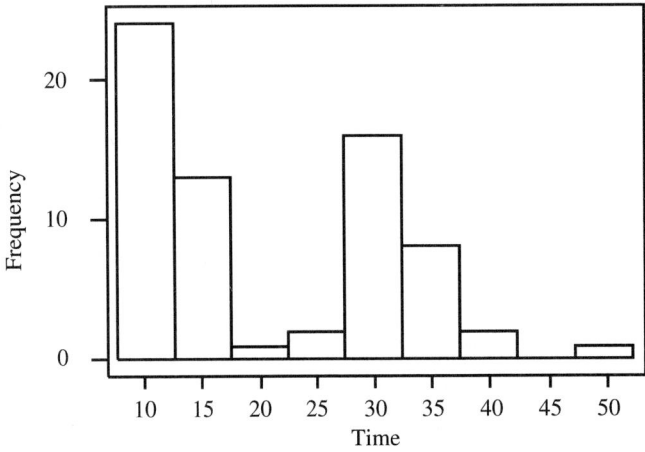

Occupancy had been fairly stable around 78%, but administrators were concerned about a possible trend downward. The number of beds occupied at 6 o'clock each evening was recorded. Occupancy was always lower on weekends, so the weekly average was recorded on a control chart. X-bar and S charts are shown in Figure 3.10.

a Is there any indication of a trend in means?

b Is there any indication of a trend in variability?

c Would you consider the process under statistical control?

R22 Hospital administrators from the preceding exercise investigated the unusually high occupancy number in week 16. They found that the number of patients hadn't changed much. The head nurse in the surgical unit reminded them that several beds had been removed from service to allow for renovations. Should this result be regarded as a common cause or a special cause of variation? Does the value at week 16 indicate an improvement in performance?

FIGURE 3.10 Control Charts for Bed Occupancy Data

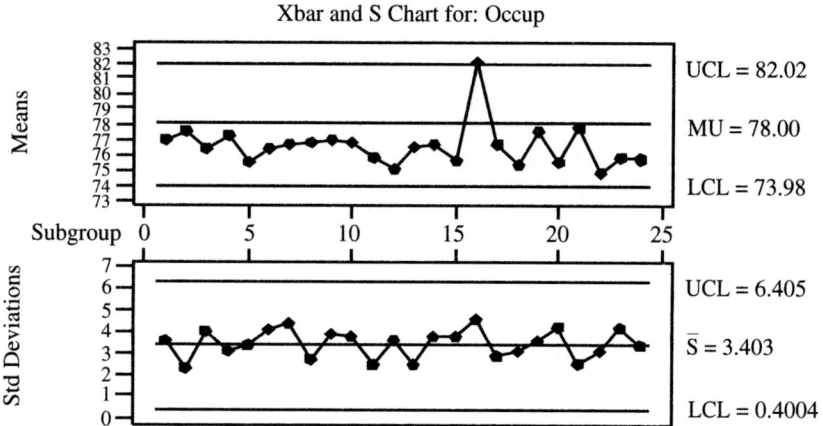

Random Variables and Probability Distributions

Random variables and probability distributions provide the language for quantitative variables that have a random component. They give us a way to tie together data summarization ideas like histograms, means, and standard deviations with probability ideas like addition and multiplication principles and independence. The fundamental concepts of this chapter are:

1   A probability distribution is specified by stating the possible values for the random quantity and calculating the probability of each value. The probability principles of the previous chapter apply here as well. Probabilities may be specified directly as a probability distribution or in terms of the cumulative distribution function.

2   The expected value (mean) of a random variable is the probability-weighted average of its possible values. It is the point at which a probability histogram balances. It is the long-run average value of the random quantity averaged over many repetitions of the experiment.

3   The standard deviation of a random variable is the square root of the variance, which in turn is the probability-weighted average of squared deviations from the mean. The standard deviation may be interpreted according to the Empirical Rule, but this rule doesn't work very well for discrete random variables with very few possible values.

4   Two random variables may be treated together by specifying the joint probability distribution of each pair of possible values. From the joint distribution, the marginal probability distribution of each random variable may be found by addition.

5   Two random variables are (statistically) independent if the probabilities for one random variable do not change, regardless of the value taken by the other one. Independence is often an assumption, which should be checked for reasonableness.

6   The correlation of two random variables measures the strength of the linear relation between the two. It is calculated using the standard deviations of both random variables and their covariance, the probability-weighted product of deviations from the respective means.

7   An important application of the ideas of correlation and covariance is the assessment of the overall riskiness of an investment portfolio. Risk, as measured by variance, can be reduced by selecting investments that have low—or even better, negative—covariances.

The probability concepts and laws developed in Chapter 3 apply to any kind of experiment, whether it yields qualitative or quantitative results. The most important uses of these ideas for managers lead to numerical, quantitative results. Ideas such as averaging apply only to numerical results. To connect probability concepts with ideas such as mean and standard deviation (from Chapter 2), we need some additional probability concepts. The main ones are random variable (Section 4.1) and probability distribution (Sections 4.2 and 4.3). Once we understand these, we can link probability concepts such as independence with the concepts of mean and standard deviation in the following sections of this chapter. In Sections A and B, at the end of the chapter, we derive some of the relevant mathematics. ■

Random Variable: Basic Ideas

M any of the probability issues most relevant to managers involve random, numerical outcomes. For example, the number of no-shows on a particular flight (people holding reservations for the flight who don't actually take it) is critically important in establishing an airline's reservation policy. The number of no-shows is random, varying from one flight to another and also from day to day on the same flight. Certainly, the number of no-shows is a numerical variable. It makes perfectly good sense to talk about the average number of no-shows. The concept of *random variable* is the basis for understanding random, numerical outcomes.

random variable

Informally, a **random variable** is a quantitative (numerical) result from a random experiment. For instance, consider the experiment of selecting a manager randomly from the middle management of an automobile manufacturer. Define the random variable Y to be number of years of formal schooling the manager has had. First of all, Y is numerical; the result will be a number such as 12 or 16, not a category such as "private college." Second, Y is subject to random variation. If the experiment is repeated with a new random selection, the result very likely will change. These two features—numerical result, subject to randomness—are the key aspects of the definition of a random variable.

To specify a random variable, we need to know its possible values and their respective probabilities. For the years of formal schooling example, the possible values could be 0, 1, 2, . . . , up to some maximum number—perhaps 20. Probabilities could be obtained from company personnel records; for example, if 284 of the 500 managers had completed exactly 4 years of college (after 12 years of elementary and high school), the probability that $Y = 16$ would be 284/500 = .568. Probabilities for other values could be filled in similarly.

> **Definition 4.1   Random Variable: Informal Definition**
>
> A random variable is any quantitative result from an experiment that is subject to random variability. It is determined by specifying its possible values and the probability associated with each value. This specification states the *probability distribution* of the random variable.   ■

The probability associated with each value of a random variable is found by adding the probabilities for all outcomes that are assigned that value. Suppose that a plant produces portable telephones in equal numbers on two production lines. Three phones are selected at random each day for destructive testing. Call the lines H and T; this experiment is just like flipping a fair coin three times. Find the probability distribution of Y, the number of sampled phones produced on line H. There are eight possibilities:

Outcome	HHH	HHT	HTH	THH	HTT	THT	TTH	TTT
Probability	1/8	1/8	1/8	1/8	1/8	1/8	1/8	1/8
Value Assigned by Y	3	2	2	2	1	1	1	0

Then, for instance,

$$P(Y = 2) = P(\text{HHT}) + P(\text{HTH}) + P(\text{THH}) = \frac{1}{8} + \frac{1}{8} + \frac{1}{8} = \frac{3}{8}$$

The custom is to denote random variables by capital letters at the end of the alphabet; thus we might define X = number of heads observed in three flips of a coin and Y = number of Theater Guild subscribers in a random sample of 200 persons. Possible values of a random variable are usually denoted by the corresponding lowercase letter; we would say that x could be 0, 1, 2, or 3 and y could be 0, 1, 2, ..., 200. The subtle distinction between Y, the random variable itself, and y, one of its possible values, is the distinction between a process and one particular result of that process; it becomes clear with practice.

EXAMPLE 4.1

Suppose that a random sample of two persons is to be selected from a large population consisting of 30% Theater Guild subscribers and 70% nonsubscribers.

a List the possible outcomes.

b Assign probabilities.

c Define the quantitative random variable Y as the number of Theater Guild subscribers in the sample. Specify the possible values that the random variable may assume and determine the probability of each.

Solution

a If we let S designate a subscriber and N a nonsubscriber, then the possible outcomes for the two persons sampled are

$$S = \{(S, S); (S, N); (N, S); \text{ and } (N, N)\}$$

b From the statement of the problem, we know that $P(S) = .3$ and $P(N) = .7$. Under the assumption that the outcomes for the two persons sampled are independent, we have the following probabilities associated with the four outcomes:

$$P(S, S) = (.3)^2 = .09$$
$$P(S, N) = (.3)(.7) = .21$$
$$P(N, S) = (.7)(.3) = .21$$
$$P(N, N) = (.7)^2 = .49$$
$$\overline{1.00}$$

c If the random variable Y is the number of subscribers in a sample of two from the population of interest, then the possible values for Y are 0, 1, and 2. The probabilities associated with these values can be determined from probabilities for the outcomes that make up each numerical event.

Outcome	Probability	y	$P(y)$
(N, N)	.49	0	.49
(N, S)	.21	1	.42
(S, N)	.21	1	
(S, S)	.09	2	.09

■

discrete

continuous

The random variables we have considered so far have been **discrete**; their possible values have been distinct and separate, like 0 or 1 or 2 or 3. Other random variables are most useful when they are considered to be **continuous**; their possible values form a whole interval (or range or continuum). For instance, the 1-year return per dollar invested in a common stock could range from 0 to something quite large. In practice, virtually all random variables assume a discrete set of values; the return per dollar of a million-dollar common stock investment could be 1.06219423 or 1.06219424 or 1.06219425 or .... But, when there are many, many possible values for a random variable, it is sometimes mathematically useful to treat that random variable as continuous. In fact, one of the most important theoretical probability specifications—the bell-shaped normal distribution—formally applies only to continuous random variables. Every probability concept for discrete random variables has a parallel for continuous random variables. (Technically, there can be other types of random variables, but the discrete and continuous cases cover all the important situations.) Because the ideas for continuous random variables require a knowledge of calculus, we will treat them in separate sections.

4.2 Probability Distributions: Discrete Random Variables

probability distribution

The **probability distribution** $P_Y(y)$ for a discrete random variable Y assigns a probability to each value y of the random variable Y. The probability distribution for Y can be expressed as a formula, a graph, or a table.

Definition 4.2   Properties of a Discrete Probability Distribution

1   The probability $P_Y(y)$ associated with each value of Y must lie in the interval

$$0 \leq P_Y(y) \leq 1$$

2   The sum of the probabilities for all values of Y equals 1.

$$\sum_{\text{all } y} P_Y(y) = 1$$

3   Because different values of Y are mutually exclusive events, their probabilities are additive. Thus

$$P(Y = a \text{ or } Y = b) = P_Y(a) + P_Y(b) \quad \blacksquare$$

For the random variable $Y =$ number of line H phones in a sample of three, we might define $P_Y(y)$ by a table, as follows:

y	0	1	2	3
$P_Y(y)$	1/8	3/8	3/8	1/8

Or we might use the formula

$$P_Y(y) = \frac{3!}{y!(3-y)!} \left(\frac{1}{8}\right)$$

where, in general, $k! = k(k-1)(k-2)\cdots(1)$ and $0! = 1$ by convention. Substituting $y = 0$, 1, 2, and 3 into the formula yields the same probabilities as those listed in the previous table:

y	0	1	2	3
$P_Y(y)$	$\dfrac{3\cdot2\cdot1}{(1)(3\cdot2\cdot1)}\dfrac{1}{8} = \dfrac{1}{8}$	$\dfrac{3\cdot2\cdot1}{(1)(2\cdot1)}\dfrac{1}{8} = \dfrac{3}{8}$	$\dfrac{3\cdot2\cdot1}{(2\cdot1)(1)}\dfrac{1}{8} = \dfrac{3}{8}$	$\dfrac{3\cdot2\cdot1}{(3\cdot2\cdot1)(1)}\dfrac{1}{8} = \dfrac{1}{8}$

probability histogram

A graph of this probability distribution, called a **probability histogram**, is shown in Figure 4.1. The discrete random variable Y is the number of line H phones in a sample of three.

FIGURE 4.1 Graph of $P_Y(y)$ for the Phone-Sampling Experiment

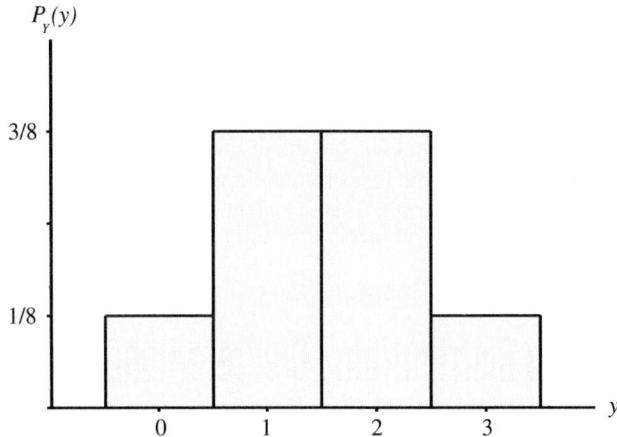

A spreadsheet program can be used to give a plot of a probability distribution. Figure 4.2 shows an Excel plot of the distribution of X = number of checkout lanes open at 8 P.M. weekdays at a supermarket. Each point indicates a probability; the graph could be modified to be a probability histogram.

FIGURE 4.2 Graph of $P_X(x)$ for Checkout Lane Probabilities

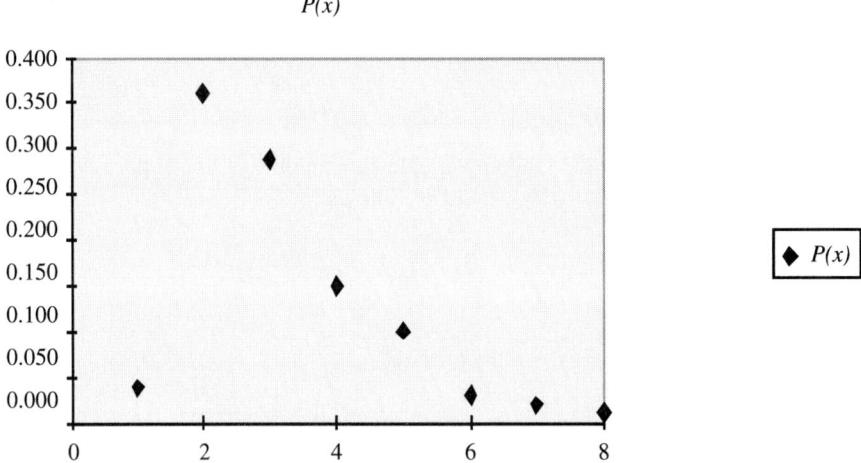

cumulative distribution function

The **cumulative distribution function** (cdf) is another way to specify probabilities that is particularly useful in calculating probabilities from tables. This cdf also has applications in computer simulation methods. In general, the cumulative distribution function $F_Y(y)$ for a discrete random variable Y is a function that specifies the probability that $Y \leq y$ for all values of y. By the addition law for probabilities, all we must do is add (cumulate) the individual probabilities for values less than or equal to the specified y. Thus

$$F_Y(y) = P(Y \leq y) = P_Y(0) + P_Y(1) + \cdots + P_Y(y)$$

This can be illustrated for the phone-sampling example discussed previously:

y	0	1	2	3
$P_Y(y)$	1/8	3/8	3/8	1/8
$F_Y(y)$	1/8	4/8	7/8	8/8

As the name suggests and the example illustrates, the cumulative distribution function at a particular value y sums all probabilities for $Y \leq y$. For example,

$$F_Y(2) = P(Y \leq 2) = \frac{1}{8} + \frac{3}{8} + \frac{3}{8} = \frac{7}{8}$$

and

$$F_Y(3) = P(Y \leq 3) = 1$$

The cumulative distribution function (cdf) is often used in constructing probability tables so the table user does not have to add up many table entries to find a certain probability. As an illustration, suppose that a large metropolitan teaching hospital has data on the number of acute coronary cases Y arriving at the hospital in a given day. The cdf is tabulated as follows:

y	0	1	2	3	4	5	6	7	8
$F_Y(y)$	.001	.003	.006	.011	.024	.061	.139	.224	.336

y	9	10	11	12	13	14	15	16	17
$F_Y(y)$	.510	.672	.782	.870	.925	.964	.988	.997	1.000

Suppose that the hospital has 14 coronary-care beds available at the beginning of a particular day. The probability that the number of new cases Y is less than or equal to 14 can be read directly from the table as .964. It's almost as easy to find the probability that Y is 15 or more: $P(Y \geq 15) = 1 - P(Y \leq 14) = 1 - .964 = .036$. Had the table been stated in terms of individual probabilities $P(y)$, it would have been necessary to add up many entries to find these probabilities.

General use of cdf tables is easy enough if you draw a probability histogram. A probability histogram for the coronary-care illustration is shown in Figure 4.3; the probability

FIGURE 4.3 **Probability Histogram for the Coronary-Care Illustration**

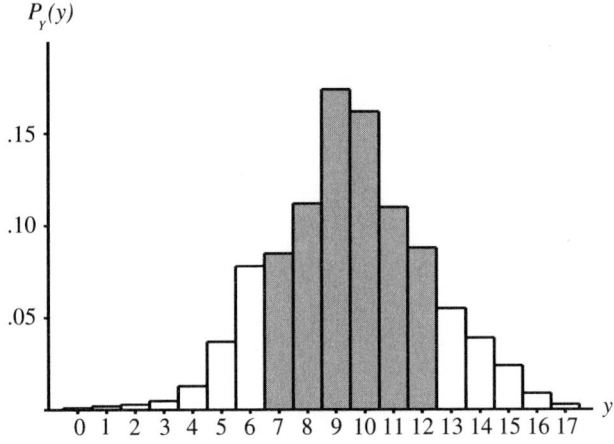

$P_Y(y)$ of each particular value y is indicated by the height of the rectangle erected atop that y value.

For example, suppose we want $P(7 \leq Y \leq 12)$. We want the total area of the rectangles above $y = 7, 8, 9, 10, 11$, and 12, which are shaded in Figure 4.3. $F_Y(12)$ is the total area of all the rectangles above $y = 0, 1, \ldots, 12$. To find $P(7 \leq Y \leq 12)$, we must subtract the combined probabilities for $y = 0, 1, \ldots, 6$—namely, $F_Y(6)$—from $F_Y(12)$:

$$P(7 \leq Y \leq 12) = F_Y(12) - F_Y(6) = .870 - .139 = .731$$

Generally, it's useful to draw a probability histogram whenever you want to use tables to calculate probabilities.

E X A M P L E   4 . 2

Suppose that a cosmetic company plans to market a new perfume. The product manager has assessed the following subjective probabilities for the first-year sales (denoted by X) in millions of bottles:

x	0	1	2	3	4	5	6	7	8
$F_X(x)$	.05	.20	.40	.60	.75	.85	.90	.95	1.00

Find the following probabilities, as assessed by the product manager:

a $P(X \geq 5)$ **b** $P(2 \leq X \leq 4)$ **c** $P(X \leq 1)$

Solution

A probability histogram for this example is shown in Figure 4.4. Areas relevant to each problem are indicated by a, b, or c.

FIGURE 4.4 **Probability Histogram**

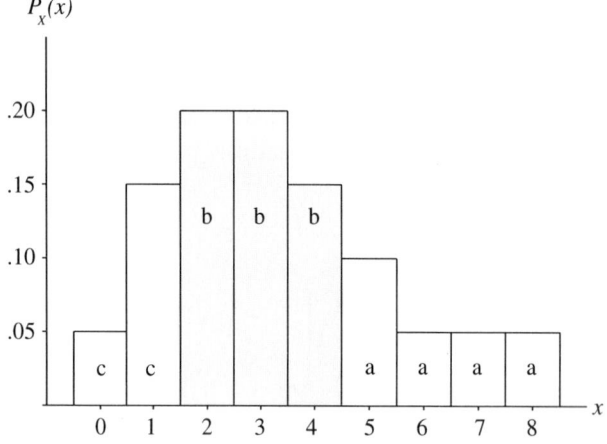

a $P(X \geq 5) = 1 - P(X \leq 4) = 1.00 - .75 = .25$
The area of all the rectangles is 1.00. We must subtract the areas of all rectangles through $x = 4$.

b Subtract the areas for $x = 0, 1$ from the areas for $x = 0, 1, 2, 3, 4$ to get $P(2 \leq X \leq 4)$:

$$P(2 \leq X \leq 4) = F_X(4) - F_X(1) = .75 - .20 = .55$$

c By definition, $P(X \leq 1) = F_X(1) = .20$; no subtraction is needed. ■

EXERCISES

4.1 Among its various routes, a transit agency operates a trolley line. The line has a total of 18 trolley cars. Some of these cars are unavailable because they are being maintained or repaired. The probability distribution of $Y = $ number of cars out of service on a randomly chosen day is given by the following Excel spreadsheet result:

	A	B
1	y	P(y)
2	0	0.28
3	1	0.16
4	2	0.11
5	3	0.1
6	4	0.08
7	5	0.07
8	6	0.05
9	7	0.04
10	8	0.04
11	9	0.03
12	10	0.02
13	11	0.01
14	12	0.01

a What is the probability that all the trolleys are operating?

b The agency needs at least 14 cars available for normal operation of the line. What is the probability that the operation will not be normal?

4.2 Calculate the cdf for Y in the previous exercise. Use it to recalculate the probabilities for that exercise.

4.3 The personnel department of a large firm employs five men and three women as college recruiters. For visits to certain large campuses, a team of two people is sent. Suppose that two of the eight recruiters are chosen at random. Let $Y = $ number of women selected.

a Construct a list of possible outcomes (a sample space); call the recruiters A, B, ..., H.

b Find the value of Y for each outcome in the sample space.

4.4 In Exercise 4.3, find $P_Y(y)$ by counting. Construct a probability histogram.

4.5 Find the cdf of Y in Exercise 4.3. Plot $F_Y(y)$ against y.

4.6 An appliance store has the following probabilities for $Y = $ number of major appliances sold on a given day:

y	0	1	2	3	4	5	6	7	8	9	10
$P_Y(y)$	.100	.150	.250	.140	.090	.080	.060	.050	.040	.025	.015

a Construct a probability histogram.

b Find $P(Y \leq 2)$.

c Find $P(Y \geq 7)$.

d Find $P(1 \leq Y \leq 5)$.

4.7 Calculate the cdf corresponding to $P_Y(y)$ in Exercise 4.6. Use this cdf to find $P(Y \leq 2)$, $P(Y \geq 7)$, and $P(1 \leq Y \leq 5)$. Part of an Excel spreadsheet showing the formulas used to calculate the cdf is shown on the next page:

	A	B	C	D	E
1	y	0	1	2	3
2	P(y)	0.1	0.15	0.25	0.14
3	F(y)	0.1	0.25	0.5	0.64

4.8   The weekly demand X for copies of a popular word-processing program at a computer store has the following probability distribution:

x	0	1	2	3	4	5	6	7	8	9	10
$P_X(x)$	.06	.14	.16	.14	.12	.10	.08	.07	.06	.04	.03

  a What is the probability that three or more copies of the program will be demanded in a particular week?

  b What is the probability that the demand will be for at least two but no more than six?

  c The store policy is to have eight copies of the program available at the beginning of every week. What is the probability that the demand will exceed the supply in a particular week?

  d If demand does not exceed supply in a particular week, what is the probability that exactly eight copies are sold?

4.9   **a** Find the cumulative distribution function (cdf) $F_X(x)$ for the probability distribution shown in Exercise 4.8.

  b Use the cdf to recalculate the probabilities in Exercise 4.8.   ■

4.3

Probability Distributions:
Continuous Random Variables $(\partial, \int)$

I n Section 4.1 we distinguished between discrete random variables, which can assume only distinct, separate values, and continuous random variables, which can assume (for all practical purposes) a complete range of values along some interval. In this section we develop the basic concepts and notation that apply to continuous random variables.

To illustrate, suppose that a U.S. resident is to be chosen at random according to that person's nine-digit Social Security number. Define $Y =$ the Social Security number chosen. Literally speaking, Y is a discrete random variable that can take on any one of the billion possible values 000–00–0000 to 999–99–9999. We are not overly eager to specify one billion different probabilities, so for practical reasons we regard Y as a continuous random variable that can assume all possible values between 0 and 1 billion.

It seems plausible to assume that Y probabilities are uniform; no one value is more likely than any other. Suppose we construct a probability histogram. First we consider only the first digit of the Social Security number drawn. Based on the assumption of uniform probability, the histogram should assign equal probabilities to all rectangles, as in Figure 4.5. If we had considered the first two digits, we would have a 100-rectangle histogram, as shown in Figure 4.6.

As we refine this process—considering the first three digits, then the first four, and so on—we get more and more, thinner and thinner rectangles. Very soon (and in the limit, mathematically) the rectangles disappear into a continuous blur.

FIGURE 4.5   Uniform Probabilities: First Digit

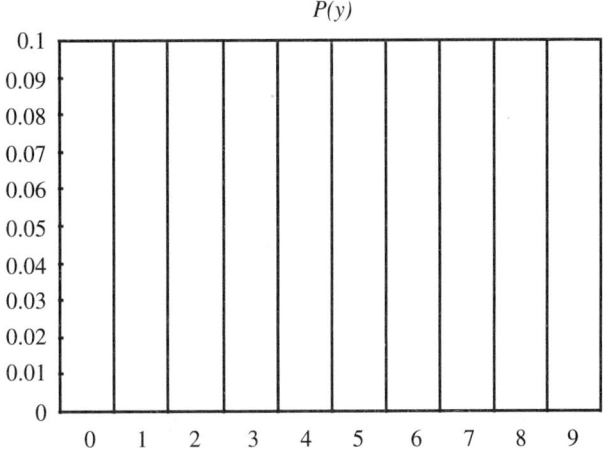

FIGURE 4.6   Uniform Probabilities: First Two Digits

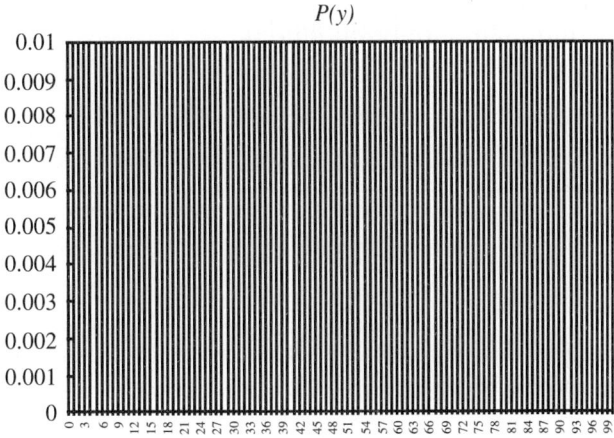

EXAMPLE 4.3

Suppose that a personnel manager measures Y, the actual weekly work time of supermarket employees. Construct histograms that indicate the probability distribution of Y when measurements are made (a) to the nearest hour; (b) to the nearest 10 minutes; and (c) to the nearest second.

Solution

a   Assume a nominal 40-hour week with modest overtime. The nearest-hour histogram might look like the top histogram in Figure 4.7.

b   The nearest 10-minutes histogram might look like the bottom histogram in Figure 4.7.

FIGURE 4.7 **Histograms for Weekly Work Time**

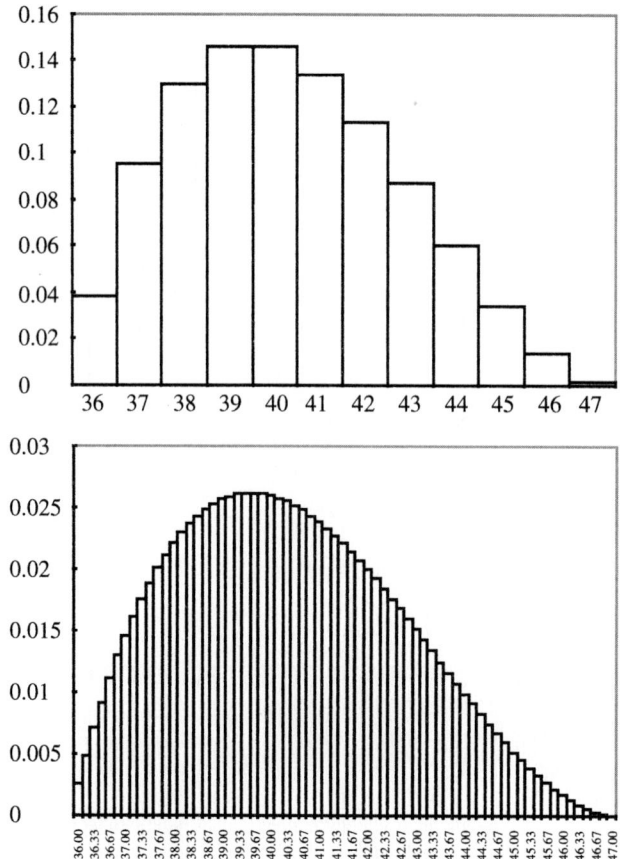

c For all practical purposes, the nearest-second histogram would look like the smooth curve in Figure 4.8.

FIGURE 4.8 **Limiting Curve of Work-Time Histograms**

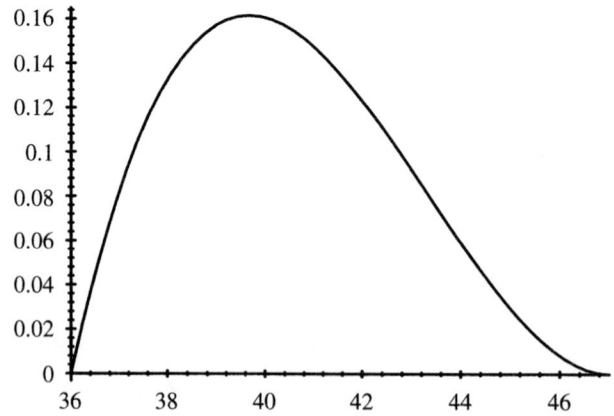

Probability histograms were introduced in Section 4.2 when we defined the cumulative distribution function (cdf) F. The cdf concept works just as well with continuous random variables. For a continuous random variable Y, the **cumulative distribution function** is defined as before:

cumulative distribution function

$$F_Y(y) = P(Y \le y)$$

For any particular example of a continuous random variable, the cdf is almost inevitably defined by a formula. For example, suppose that a file-transfer computer program sends lines of a program across a noisy transmission device. One important variable is $X =$ the proportion of lines correctly transmitted. Suppose that, as a model, the cdf is assumed to be

$$F_X(x) = 21x^{20} - 20x^{21} \qquad \text{for } 0 < x < 1$$

Then the probability that the proportion of correctly transmitted lines is less than .9 is

$$F_X(.9) = 21(.9)^{20} - 20(.9)^{21} = .3647$$

and the probability that the proportion is greater than .9 is

$$1 - F_X(.9) = 1 - .3647 = .6353$$

Furthermore, the probability that the proportion X is between .7 and .9 is

$$F_X(.9) - F_X(.7) = .3647 - .0056 = .3591$$

Recalling the calculations made for discrete random variables, you might expect that in computing $P(.7 \le X \le .9)$ we would subtract $F_X(.6)$ or perhaps $F_X(.69)$ rather than $F_X(.7)$. But the probability that the continuous random variable X equals exactly .7000 . . . is negligibly small; as a mathematical idealization, we may take the probability to be zero. Thus, in the continuous case, we may ignore the probability that the random variable is "right on the boundary."

E X A M P L E   4 . 4

Suppose that the reservations manager for a large airline assumes that the time T (measured in minutes) between successive phone calls to the reservation center is a continuous random variable with cdf

$$F_T(t) = 1 - e^{-2t} \qquad \text{for } t \ge 0$$

where

$$e \approx 2.7183, \text{ the base of the natural logarithm}$$

Find

a $P(T \ge 5)$ b $P(2 \le T \le 4)$ c $P(T \le 1)$

Solution

The three parts of this example seem to be identical to those of Example 4.2. Because T is continuous, however, the solution procedure differs from that of Example 4.2.

a $P(T \ge 5) = 1 - P(T < 5)$
But, because T is a continuous random variable, $P(T = 5.000000 \ldots)$ is assumed to be zero and $P(T < 5) = P(T \le 5)$.

$$P(T \ge 5) = 1 - P(T \le 5) = 1 - F_T(5)$$

$$= 1 - (1 - e^{-2(5)}) = .0000454$$

(Values of e^x can be calculated by most calculators or obtained from tables.)

b $P(2 \leq T \leq 4) = P(T \leq 4) - P(T < 2)$
The event $T = 2.000\ldots$ has probability zero, so

$$P(2 \leq T \leq 4) = P(T \leq 4) - P(T \leq 2)$$
$$= F_T(4) - F_T(2)$$
$$= (1 - e^{-2(4)}) - (1 - e^{-2(2)})$$
$$= .0180$$

c $P(T \leq 1) = F_T(1)$ by definition equals $1 - e^{-2(1)} = .865.$ ∎

The cumulative distribution function F means the same thing for discrete and continuous random variables. For any random variable Y, $F_Y(y) = P(Y \leq y)$. For continuous random variables, another function, the probability density function (pdf), is widely used. For a random variable Y, the probability density function is denoted $f_Y(y)$. The probability density function is the limiting smooth curve obtained by taking narrower and narrower intervals, as in our previous examples. It is analogous to the probability distribution $P_X(x)$ defined for discrete random variables in that it measures how the probability is spread out—distributed—over the range of possible values of the random variable. But for a continuous random variable Y, the probability that Y exactly equals a particular number is zero. The probability density function does not yield probabilities directly. Instead, this function defines a smooth curve; probability is calculated, using integral calculus, as the area under the curve. If both the cdf $F_Y(y)$ and the pdf $f_y(y)$ are known, we can compute the probability that Y is between numbers a and b in two ways:

$$P(a \leq Y \leq b) = F_Y(b) - F_Y(a)$$

or

$$P(a \leq Y \leq b) = \int_a^b f_Y(y)dy$$

In the example in which $X =$ the proportion of lines correctly transmitted, it can be shown that

$$f_X(x) = 21(20)x^{19}(1 - x) \qquad 0 < x < 1$$

The probability that X is larger than .9 can be computed by integrating the probability density over the region $.9 < x < 1$ because X cannot be larger than 1.

$$P(.9 < X) = \int_{.9}^1 21(20)x^{19}(1 - x)\, dx$$
$$= \int_{.9}^1 21(20)(x^{19} - x^{20})\, dx$$
$$= (21x^{20} - 20x^{21})\Big|_{.9}^1$$
$$= 1 - .3647 = .6353$$

as we found previously.

E X A M P L E   4 . 5

The random variable T of Example 4.4 can be shown to have probability density

$$f_T(t) = 2e^{-2t} \qquad t \geq 0$$

Calculate the probability that T is between 2 and 4 using this probability density.

Solution

To solve this problem, we need the elementary calculus result that the indefinite integral of ce^{-ct} is $-e^{-ct}$. Then

$$P(2 \leq T \leq 4) = \int_2^4 2e^{-2t} \, dt = -e^{-2t} \Big|_2^4$$

$$= -.000335 - (-.018316) = .0180$$

as in Example 4.4. The calculation is shown in Figure 4.9.

FIGURE 4.9 **Area (Probability) Between 2 and 4 Hours**

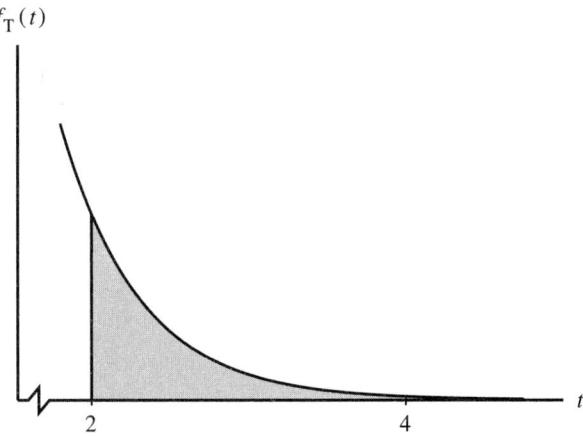

Sometimes, finding the integral of a specified density function can be difficult or very tedious. In such cases, a mathematical computer program such as Maple or Mathematica can help. For example, assume that the probability density for X = market share achieved six months after introduction by a new cereal product is

$$f_X(x) = 506x(1-x)^{21} \qquad 0 < x < 1$$

The following Maple output shows the density; verifies that the integral of the density from $x = 0$ to $x = 1$ really equals 1, as it should; and calculates the probability that X will be between .05 and .10, as approximately .364.

```
density:=506*x*(1-x)^21;
                              21
           density = 506 x (1 - x)

int(density,x=0..1);
                      1

int(density,x=0.05..0.10);
                    .3642937554
```

A probability histogram generated by Maple is shown in Figure 4.10. Because the density is much higher near $x = 0$ than near $x = 1$, most of the probability will be associated with small values of X. Note also that the numerical value of the probability density can be greater than 1.0; the density does not give probabilities directly, but must be integrated to find probabilities.

FIGURE 4.10 **Probability Density for Market Share of New Product**

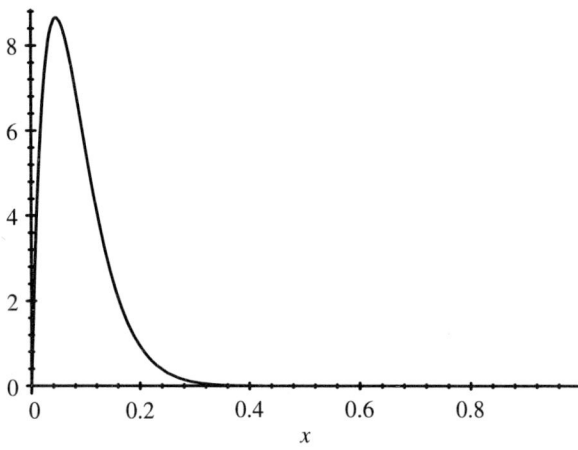

EXAMPLE 4.6

A bank's trust department conducts a daily "sweep" of the cash balances of trust funds into a money market fund. One of the considerations that went into pricing this service was the amount of computer time needed to sweep an account. The data-processing group of the bank obtained data for a large number of sweeps. The time Y (in seconds) required per sweep seemed to be modeled quite well by the following probability density:

$$f_Y(y) = 62.5y^2 e^{-5y} \qquad 0 < y < \infty$$

A histogram of the density, drawn by Maple, is shown in Figure 4.11.

FIGURE 4.11 **Density of Sweep Times**

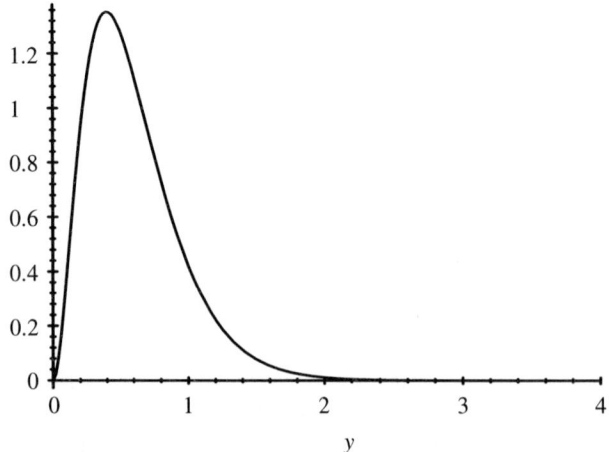

The following Maple results were obtained. Note that "int" means "integral," with the limits of integration shown as the second argument.

```
int(density,y=0..0.5);
                    .4561868840
```

```
int(density,y=0.5..1.5);
                    .5235564009
```

What is the probability that the sweep of an account requires less than half a second? Less than 1.5 seconds? More than 1.5 seconds?

Solution

The Maple output shows that the integral of the probability density between 0 and 0.5, which is exactly the probability that the sweep time is less than half a second, is .456. The probability of a sweep time between 0.5 and 1.5 seconds (the integral of the density between these limits) is .524. Therefore, the probability of a sweep time between 0 and 1.5 seconds is .456 + .524 = .980. (Remember that the probability of a value that is either between 0 and 0.5 or between 0.5 and 1.5 is the sum of the respective probabilities. Also, recall from calculus that the integral of a function from a to c is the integral from a to b plus the integral from b to c.) By the complements principle, the probability that a sweep requires more than 1.5 seconds is $1 - P(\text{less than } 1.5) = 1 - .980 = .020$. ∎

The probability density function (pdf) $f_Y(y)$ of a continuous random variable Y may be either specified directly or derived from the cdf $F_Y(y)$. Because the calculus operation of integration is the opposite of the operation of differentiation, it follows that

$$f_Y(y) = \frac{d}{dy} F_Y(y)$$

For example, we initially specified the cdf of X = the proportion of correctly transmitted lines as

$$F_X(x) = 21x^{20} - 20x^{21} \qquad 0 < x < 1$$

Differentiation yields the expression that we used for the pdf:

$$f_X(x) = \frac{d}{dx}(21x^{20} - 20x^{21}) = 21(20)x^{19} - 21(20)x^{20}$$

$$= 21(20)x^{19}(1 - x)$$

The process of finding the density function from the cdf may be reversed. Just as in the discrete case, where

$$F_X(x) = \sum_{x' \le x} P_X(x')$$

in the continuous case

$$F_X(x) = \int_{-\infty}^{x} f_X(x')\, dx'$$

In performing the integration, we must be a bit careful to exclude regions where the random variable cannot occur and thus has a probability density of zero. If a random variable X is by definition nonnegative, the probability that it is less than zero (that is, $\int_{-\infty}^{0} f_X(x)\, dx$) is zero.

EXAMPLE 4.7

Show that the probability density specified in Example 4.4 yields the cdf of Example 4.4.

Solution

We note first that T, as an elapsed time measure, cannot be negative. Therefore, the probability density function of T must be zero for all values $t < 0$. The probability density of T is stated in Example 4.5 to be $f_T(t) = 2e^{-2t}$, for $t > 0$.

Thus

$$F_T(t) = \int_0^t 2e^{-2t'} \, dt' = -e^{-2t'} \Big|_0^t = -e^{-2t} - (-1)$$

$$= 1 - e^{-2t}$$

as stated in Example 4.4. ■

Generally speaking, every calculation of a discrete random variable involving a summation has an analogous calculation of a continuous random variable involving an integration. The technical difficulties in performing a particular summation or integration should not obscure the fact that the operations of summation and integration are direct analogues.

EXERCISES

4.10 A certain charity is planning a direct-mail campaign. The fraction Y of nonrespondents is taken to be a continuous random variable with the following cdf:

$$F_Y(y) = 5y^4 - 4y^5 \qquad 0 \le y \le 1$$

  a Calculate $F_Y(y)$ for various values of y between 0 and 1. Sketch the function $F_Y(y)$.

  b Use the graph of $F_Y(y)$ to calculate $P(Y \le .8)$, $P(Y \ge .6)$, and $P(.5 \le Y \le .9)$.

4.11   **a** Show that the probability density of Y in Exercise 4.10 is

$$f_Y(y) = 20(y^3 - y^4) \qquad 0 \le y \le 1$$

  b Use this density to calculate $P(.2 \le Y \le .7)$, $P(Y \le .6)$, and $P(Y \ge .5)$.

  c Use the cdf $F_Y(y)$ to find the probabilities indicated in part b.

4.12 A data-processing company owns a large computer. Access to the computer is gained via a large number of remote terminals. A reasonable probability model for the time Y (in minutes) between successive job submissions to the computer assumes that

$$F_Y(y) = 1 - e^{-.5y} \qquad 0 \le y < \infty$$

  a Calculate numerical values of $F_Y(y)$ for $y = 1.0, 2.0, \ldots$, until $F_Y(y)$ exceeds .98 or so. Graph $F_Y(y)$ versus y.

  b Use the graph of $F_Y(y)$ to find $P(Y \le .75)$, $P(Y \ge 4.0)$, and $P(2.0 \le Y \le 3.5)$.

4.13 A securities analyst summarizes some subjective probability estimates for the after-tax profit per share Y of a particular stock in the following continuous probability density:

$$f_Y(y) = \frac{4}{27}(9y - 6y^2 + y^3) \qquad 0 \le y \le 3$$

  a Calculate $f_Y(y)$ for several y values (such as 0, .25, .50, ...), and graph $f_Y(y)$ against y.

  b Find $P(Y \le 1.50)$, $P(Y \ge 2.00)$, and $P(1 \le Y \le 2.50)$.

  c Find $F_Y(y)$ and sketch it.

4.14 Find the mode (y value where the density is at its maximum) for Y in the previous exercise.

4.15 A city streets department must deal with the mundane problem of replacing light bulbs in traffic signals. The bulbs wear out or break at random times. The probability density of $X =$ the life in thousands of hours of a randomly chosen bulb is shown in the following Maple output:

```
density;
                              3           2
                .0008000000000 x  exp( - .02 x )

int(density,x=0..10);
                          .5939941504

int(density,x=10..20);
                          .4029866860


cdf:=1+int(density,x);
                            2                        2
          cdf := 1 - .02000000000 x  exp( - .02000000000 x )



                                   2
              - 1. exp( - .02000000000 x )
```

a Find the probability that X will be greater than 10.

b Find the probability that X will be less than 20.

4.16 The part of the output labeled "cdf" in the preceding exercise is indeed the cumulative distribution function of X. Use the cdf to find the probability that X will be between 10 and 20.

4.17 A plot, drawn by Maple, of the density of bulb lifetimes is shown in Figure 4.12. From the figure, approximately where is the mode?

FIGURE 4.12 **Bulb Lifetime Density**

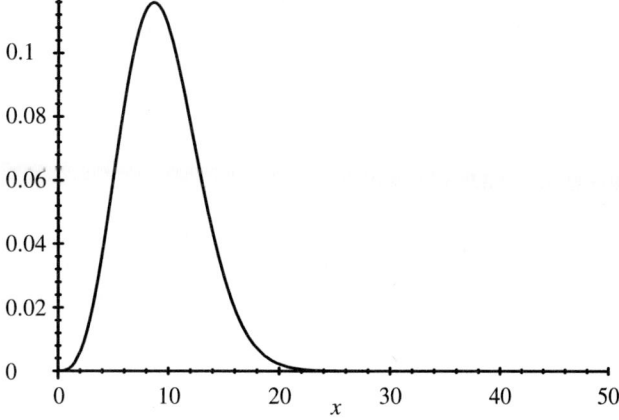

4.18 The "back office" of a brokerage house owns a powerful computer network on which it processes all records of transactions. Excess computer time is sold to other companies. To determine how much time to sell, the firm has studied the distribution of $Y =$ computer time (in minutes) needed daily to process its own transactions. To a good approximation, the density of Y is

$$f_Y(y) = .0009375[40 - .1(y - 100)^2] \qquad \text{for } 80 < y < 120$$

$$= 0 \qquad \text{outside } 80 < y < 120$$

If the firm reserves 115 minutes of time daily, what is the probability that the actual required time will be longer?

4.19 Calculate the cdf $F_Y(y)$ for the density in Exercise 4.18. Use the cdf to recalculate the probability in that exercise.

4.20 The time in worker-hours required to assemble a complex manufactured item is random, with probability density

$$f_Y(y) = 3y^{-4} \qquad \text{for } 1 < y < \infty$$

    a Find the probability that an item will require between 2 and 4 worker-hours to assemble. How important is it whether 2.00 and 4.00 hours are included or excluded from the interval?

    b Find the probability that an item will require between 0.5 and 1.5 worker-hours. (Think before integrating.)

4.21   **a** Find the cdf $F_Y(y)$ corresponding to the density in Exercise 4.20.

    b Find the 99th percentile of times; that is, solve $F_Y(y) = .99$. ■

Expected Value and Standard Deviation: Discrete Random Variables

I n the previous sections, we introduced the language of random variables. Because random variables have numerical values, it makes sense to talk about averages and variability. In the next two sections, we'll define the mean (or expected value) and variance of a random quantity. This section discusses discrete random variables that take on distinct, separate values; the next section considers the parallel case of continuous random variables.

    The average value of a random variable must take into account not only the possible values of that variable, but also the respective probabilities. The **expected value** of a discrete random variable Y with probability distribution $P_Y(y)$ is the probability-weighted average of its possible values.

expected value

    Recall that a weighted average is the sum of weights times values, divided by the sum of the weights. If the relatively heavy weights are toward one end of the range of values, a weighted average is pulled in that direction, as compared to an unweighted average. The expected value is also called the mean of Y and is denoted by $E(Y)$ or μ_Y.

Definition 4.3   Expected Value of a Discrete Random Variable

For a discrete random variable Y with probability distribution $P_Y(y)$, the expected value of Y is

$$E(Y) = \sum_{\text{all } y} y P_Y(y)$$

To find $E(Y)$, take each possible value y, multiply (weight) it by the associated probability $P_Y(y)$, and add the results. ■

E X A M P L E   4 . 8

A firm is considering two possible investments. As a rough approximation, the firm assigns to each project (subjective) probabilities of losing 20% per dollar invested, losing 10%, breaking even, gaining 10%, and gaining 20%. Let Y be the return per dollar invested in the first project and Z the return per dollar invested in the second. The firm's probabilities are

y	$-.20$	$-.10$	0	$+.10$	$+.20$
$P_Y(y)$	.1	.2	.4	.2	.1

z	$-.20$	$-.10$	0	$+.10$	$+.20$
$P_Z(z)$	.01	.04	.10	.50	.35

Calculate expected returns per dollar invested in each project. Which project appears to be the more attractive investment?

Solution

Project Y, by any reasonable standard, appears less attractive. It is thought to be as likely to lose 20% as to gain 20%, and as likely to lose 10% as to gain 10%. Project Z is thought to be very likely to gain 10% or 20% and relatively unlikely to lose.

Calculations are as follows:

y	$P_Y(y)$	$yP_Y(y)$	z	$P_Z(z)$	$zP_Z(z)$
$-.20$	.1	$-.02$	$-.20$	.01	$-.002$
$-.10$	.2	$-.02$	$-.10$	.04	$-.004$
0	.4	0	0	.10	0
$+.10$	.2	$+.02$	$+.10$	.50	$+.050$
$+.20$	.1	$+.02$	$+.20$	.35	$+.070$
		$E(Y) = 0$			$E(Z) = .114$

The expected Y return is (as anticipated) less than the expected Z return. ∎

These calculations can be done easily with a spreadsheet or a statistical package. List the possible values in one row or column and the corresponding probabilities in another row or column, multiply the corresponding values, and sum.

The expected value (mean) of a random variable Y can be interpreted in several useful ways. First, it is simply a probability-weighted average, a summary figure that takes into account the relative probabilities of different values of Y. Second, it can be thought of as a **long-run average** of Y. For example, suppose that the firm of Example 4.8 could invest in a very large number of projects with the same return probabilities as project Z. The average return per dollar invested would be .114 or 11.4%. (This fact follows because about 1 of 100 such projects would lose 20%, 4 of 100 would lose 10%, 10 of 100 would break even, 50 of 100 would earn 10%, and 35 of 100 would earn 20%.) Third, the expected value defines, in a certain sense,[1] the **fair value** of a gamble. Suppose that a casino gambling game pays $3 with probability 12/38 and nothing with probability 26/38. If we let $Y =$ return on one play of the game, $E(Y) = 3(12/38) + 0(26/38) = 36/38$, or about .947. In a fair game, the casino ought to charge the player 36/38 of a dollar, or about 94.7 cents, to play. (Devotees of the American form of the game of roulette will recognize the nature of the game, the fact that the actual charge is $1, and the long-run effect of the 2/38 increment on casino profitability.) Fourth, the expected value is a **balance point** for a probability histogram. Think of probabilities as weights along a line. A fulcrum (like the pivot point on a child's seesaw) placed at the expected value will make these probabilities

long-run average

fair value

balance point

[1]This interpretation ignores the risk factor.

balance exactly. In particular, if the probabilities are exactly symmetric around a particular value, that value must be the expected value. Notice that the probability distribution for the Y investment return was symmetric around a value of 0, and the expected value was, therefore, 0. And finally, the expected value of Y represents a generalization of the concept of a population mean μ. If Y is a discrete random variable corresponding to a value drawn at random from a discrete population of values, then $E(Y) = \mu$, the mean of the population.

EXAMPLE 4.9

Suppose that a population consists of the following values and associated frequencies:

Value:	1000	2000	3000	4000
Frequency:	80	60	40	20

($N = 200$)

The population mean is 2000. Let Y denote a single value drawn at random from the population. Find $P_Y(y)$ and $E(Y)$.

Solution

The possible values and their probabilities are

y	1000	2000	3000	4000
$P_Y(y)$	$80/200 = .4$	$60/200 = .3$	$40/200 = .2$	$20/200 = .1$

The expected value is

$$E(Y) = 1000(.4) + 2000(.3) + 3000(.2) + 4000(.1)$$
$$= 400 + 600 + 600 + 400 = 2000$$

$E(Y)$ is exactly equal to the population mean. ∎

EXAMPLE 4.10

Another way to approximate an expected value is by computer simulation. We took the values and probabilities for the random variable Z of Example 4.8 and entered them into the Excel spreadsheet package. Using Excel's random number generator and LOOKUP function (with cumulative probabilities), we drew 1000 observations (which is a reasonably long run) from the Z distribution. We obtained the following results:

```
Z Value Frequency
   -0.2      11
   -0.1      44
      0      91
    0.1     501
    0.2     353

        ZValue

Mean              0.1141
Median               0.1
```

```
Mode              0.1
Standard Deviation    0.0837
Sample Variance    0.006998
```

How do the simulation approximations compare to the exact frequencies and expected value?

Solution

The frequencies in the simulation are very close to correct. For example, $Z = -.2$ occurred in $11/1000 = .011$ of the trials, compared to the correct .010. The mean of the 1000 trials should be, and is, very close to the expected value (long-run average), 0.114. ∎

We have discussed the different interpretations associated with the expected value of a discrete random variable. Equally important characteristics of a discrete random variable are the **variance** and standard deviation, which measure the probability dispersion or variability of a random variable. Recall from Chapter 2 that the variance of a set of data is the average squared deviation from the mean. Similarly, the variance of a random variable Y, Var(Y), is the probability-weighted average of squared deviations from the mean (expected value).

variance

Definition 4.4   Variance and Standard Deviation: Discrete Random Variable

If Y is a discrete random variable, then

$$\sigma_Y^2 = \text{Var}(Y) = \sum_{\text{all } y} (y - \mu_Y)^2 P_Y(y) \qquad \text{where } \mu_Y = E(Y)$$

The standard deviation of Y, denoted σ_Y, is (as for other standard deviations) the positive square root of the variance

$$\sigma_Y = \sqrt{\text{Var}(Y)}$$

To calculate Var(Y), take each value y, subtract the expected value $\mu_Y = E(Y)$, square the result, multiply by the probability $P_Y(y)$, and sum. ∎

E X A M P L E   4 . 1 1

Find the variance and standard deviation for Y and Z in Example 4.8.

Solution

In Example 4.8, we found $\mu_Y = E(Y) = 0$ and $\mu_Z = E(Z) = .114$. A worksheet shows the computations required.

y	$P_Y(y)$	$(y - \mu_Y)$	$(y - \mu_Y)^2$	$(y - \mu_Y)^2 P_Y(y)$
$-.20$	.1	$-.20$	.04	.004
$-.10$	.2	$-.10$	.01	.002
0	.4	0	0	0
.10	.2	.10	.01	.002
.20	.1	.20	.04	.004

$$\sigma_Y^2 = .012$$

$$\sigma_Y = \sqrt{.012} = .110$$

z	$P_Z(z)$	$(z - \mu_Z)$	$(z - \mu_Z)^2$	$(z - \mu_Z)^2 P_Z(z)$
$-.20$	.01	$-.314$	.098596	.00098596
$-.10$	.04	$-.214$	.045796	.00183184
0	.10	$-.114$	.012996	.00129960
.10	.50	$-.014$	.000196	.00009800
.20	.35	.086	.007396	.00258860

$$\sigma_Z^2 = .00680400$$

$$\sigma_Z = .082$$

The Y distribution has greater variability. The bulk of the Z distribution is concentrated on the larger values .10 and .20, whereas the Y probabilities are somewhat more spread out over all possible values. The variance for a return on investment is often taken as a measure of risk, with larger variances indicating greater risk. In this example, the Z investment has both a higher expected return and a lower risk. ∎

Variance and standard deviation computations are easy with a spreadsheet or statistical package. List values and probabilities in two rows (or two columns), as we did to compute the expected value. Calculate a new row or column by subtracting the mean from each value and squaring the result. Multiply the values in the new row or column by the corresponding probabilities and sum to get the variance. Then take the square root to get the standard deviation. Using a feature such as Excel's "array" calculation (check the manual or help files) makes the computation even easier. The following Excel output shows the array formulas needed to calculate the expected value, variance, and standard deviation for $Y = $ number of checkout lanes open at a supermarket at 8 P.M.; the last part of the output is the result of the array calculations.

	A	B	C	D	E	L
1	y	0	1	2	...	10
2	P(y)	0.1	0.15	0.25	...	0.015
3						
4	Exp. Value	=SUM(B1:L1*B2:L2)				
5	Variance	=SUM((B1:L1-B4)^2*B2:L2)				
6	Std. Dev.	=SQRT(B5)				
7						
8	Exp. Value	3.235				
9						
10	Variance	6.079775				
11						
12	Std. Dev.	2.46572				

The variance and standard deviation of a random variable can't be negative. They are 0 only if all the probability is concentrated at one value. The more the probability is spread out toward the extremes of the possible values, the larger the variance and standard deviation will be. This fact follows because the variance is a probability-weighted average of squared deviations. If the large squared deviations, corresponding to values at the extremes, have large probabilities, the variance and standard deviation will be large.

Computing a variance by hand can be clumsy and can involve lots of many-digit numbers, as in Var(Z) in the previous example. Most statistical computer packages can be used to do the arithmetic, as can a spreadsheet. If you must do the computations by hand, the following shortcut formula for variance computations can be of help.

If Y is a discrete random variable,

$$\text{Var}(Y) = \sum_{\text{all } y} y^2 P_Y(y) - \mu_Y^2 \qquad \text{where } \mu_Y = E(Y)$$

We square the original values, weight by $P_Y(y)$, and add. At the end of that computation, we subtract the square of the mean (expected value) to get the variance. ■

E X A M P L E   4 . 1 2

Use the shortcut formula to repeat the variance calculations of Example 4.11.

Solution

For Y, it is the same calculation because $\mu_Y = E(Y) = 0$. It doesn't matter when we subtract 0, or even 0^2. For Z, with $\mu_Z = E(Z) = .114$,

z	$P_Z(z)$	z^2	$z^2 P_Z(z)$
−.20	.01	.04	.0004
−.10	.04	.01	.0004
0	.10	0	0
.10	.50	.01	.0050
.20	.35	.04	.0140
			.0198

So $\text{Var}(Z) = .0198 - (.114)^2 = .006804$, as in Example 4.11. ■

E X A M P L E   4 . 1 3

Computer simulation can also be used to approximate the variance and standard deviation of a random variable. The Excel output of Example 4.10 yielded these results:

	A	B	C
1		Z Value	
2			
3	Mean		0.1141
4			
5	Median		0.1
6			
7	Mode		0.1
8			
9	Standard Deviation		0.0837
10			
11	Sample Variance		0.006998

How closely does the simulation variance compare to the correct variance of Z, .006804?

Solution

The variance is shown as .006998, only slightly larger than the correct value. ■

The Empirical Rule, introduced for samples and populations in Chapter 2, applies to random variables as well. It works less well when there are very few possible values for the random variable.

Definition 4.6 Empirical Rule for Random Variables

If the random variable Y has roughly a mound-shaped probability histogram,

$$P(Y \text{ falls within one } \sigma_Y \text{ of its mean } \mu_Y) \approx .68$$

and

$$P(Y \text{ falls within two } \sigma_Y \text{ of its mean } \mu_y) \approx .95 \quad \blacksquare$$

For the random variable Y of Example 4.8, $E(Y) = 0$ and $\sigma_Y = .110$. The actual probabilities are

$$P(Y \text{ falls within } \sigma_Y \text{ of its mean}) = P(-.110 \leq Y \leq .110)$$
$$= P(Y = -.10) + P(Y = 0) + P(Y = .10)$$
$$= .80$$

and

$$P(Y \text{ falls within two } \sigma_Y \text{ of its mean}) = P(-.220 \leq Y \leq .220) = 1.00$$

The Empirical Rule approximation is mediocre in this case, in part because Y takes on a small number of values. Had the firm assessed subjective probabilities for returns of, say, $-.25, -.20, -.15, \ldots, +.15, +.20, +.25$, the Empirical Rule would most likely have been a somewhat better approximation, although the distribution might not be exactly mound-shaped.

Just as the mean of a random variable is a generalization of the idea of a population mean, so the variance of a random variable Y is a generalization of a population variance. If Y is a random variable corresponding to a value drawn randomly from a population, $\sigma_Y^2 =$ population variance.

We have defined the expected value, variance, and standard deviation for discrete random variables. The mathematical definitions of their counterparts for continuous random variables necessarily involve calculus. The next section discusses the same topics, for the continuous case.

EXERCISES

4.22 The product-development laboratory of a paint manufacturer is asked to develop a modified paint for automobiles. The director of the laboratory estimates the following probabilities for the required development time (in months):

y	2	3	4	5	6	7	8	9	10	11	12
$P(y)$	.20	.30	.15	.10	.08	.06	.04	.03	.02	.01	.01

    a Construct a probability histogram.

    b Calculate the expected value of Y.

    c Mark $E(Y)$ on the histogram. How does the shape of the histogram affect $E(Y)$?

4.23 Refer to Exercise 4.22.

    a Calculate the standard deviation of Y. Use the definition.

    b Use the shortcut method to calculate σ_Y.

4.24 Refer to Exercise 4.22. What is the actual probability that Y differs from μ_Y by less than 1 standard deviation? Why does this probability differ from the Empirical Rule estimate?

4.25 An investment syndicate is trying to decide which of two $200,000 apartment houses to buy. An adviser estimates the following probabilities for the 5-year net returns (in thousands of dollars):

Return:	−50	0	50	100	150	200	250
Probability for house 1:	.02	.03	.20	.50	.20	.03	.02
Probability for house 2:	.15	.10	.10	.10	.30	.20	.05

The following Excel output was obtained:

	A	B	C
1	Return	House 1 probs.	House 2 probs.
2	-50	0.02	0.15
3	0	0.03	0.1
4	50	0.2	0.1
5	100	0.5	0.1
6	150	0.2	0.3
7	200	0.03	0.2
8	250	0.02	0.05
9			
10 Exp. Value		100	105
11 Variance		2500	8475
12 St. Dev.		50.00	92.06

    The expected value and variance were calculated using Excel's "array" calculation method and the formulas

```
=SUM(A2:A8*B2:B8)
```

and

```
=SUM((A2:A8)^2*B2:B8)-(B9)^2
```

Similar array calculations yielded the expected value and variance for the second house.

    a Locate the expected net return for house 1 and for house 2.

    b Locate the respective variances and standard deviations.

    c Is one investment better than the other in terms of both expected return and risk?

    d If you had a spare $200,000 to invest, which investment would you prefer?

4.26 Suppose that the probabilities for house 1 returns are changed to the following:

Return:	−50	0	50	100	150	200	250
Probability for house 1:	.04	.05	.20	.46	.20	.05	.04

Without calculation, should the expected return increase or decrease as a result of the change? Should the variance increase or decrease?

4.27 In Exercise 4.8 we considered the probability distribution

x	0	1	2	3	4	5	6	7	8	9	10
$P_X(x)$	.06	.14	.16	.14	.12	.10	.08	.07	.06	.04	.03

a Find the mean of X.

b Use the definition to calculate the variance of X.

c Use the shortcut method to recalculate the variance of X.

4.28 Calculate the probability that X in Exercise 4.27 is within 2 standard deviations of its mean. How does this probability compare to the theoretical values given by the Empirical Rule?

4.29 A transit agency runs a trolley line, among its services. The line has 18 cars, but some of the cars are unavailable at a given time because they are being renovated or repaired. The probability distribution of $Y =$ the number of cars being repaired is given by the following Excel output:

	A	B
1	y	P(y)
2		
3	0	0.28
4	1	0.16
5	2	0.11
6	3	0.10
7	4	0.08
8	5	0.07
9	6	0.05
10	7	0.04
11	8	0.04
12	9	0.03
13	10	0.02
14	11	0.01
15	12	0.01

a Find the expected value and standard deviation of Y.

b The agency needs to have at least 14 cars available to run full service on the line. Can the Empirical Rule give a reasonable approximation to this probability?

4.30 In the previous exercise, if the agency is running full service, what is the probability that it has exactly 14 cars available?

4.31 Sketch a probability histogram of the distribution of Y in the previous two exercises. Is the histogram basically symmetric or clearly skewed?

4.32 A manufacturer of disk controllers subjects each new controller to rigorous testing. Of newly assembled controllers, 84% pass the test with no rework. Controllers that fail the initial test are reworked once; 75% of these machines pass a second test. Those controllers that fail the second test are reworked a second time and retested; 90% of them pass and the rest are scrapped. Define Y to be the number of rework cycles for a randomly chosen controller.

a Specify the possible values of y.

b Calculate the probability distribution of Y. A small probability tree may be helpful.

4.33 **a** Find the expected value of Y in Exercise 4.32. What is the interpretation of this number?

b Find the variance and standard deviation of Y.

4.34 The manufacturer in Exercise 4.32 could reallocate resources so that 92% of all controllers pass the first test with no rework. However, of those that don't pass, only 60% would pass after one rework cycle. Of those controllers that fail the second cycle, 80% would pass after a second cycle (and the rest would be scrapped).

a How would these changes alter the probability distribution in Exercise 4.32?

b How would the probability that a machine is scrapped change?

c Should these changes increase or decrease the expected value of Y found in Exercise 4.33? Recalculate the expected value to verify your answer.

4.35 A mail-order gift supplier tracks the number of items purchased in each order. Based on extensive records, it finds the distribution of $Y =$ items per order, as shown in the following Excel output:

	A	B	C
7	4	0.084	0.729
8	5	0.065	0.794
9	6	0.053	0.847
10	7	0.032	0.879
11	8	0.025	0.904
12	9	0.016	0.92
13	10	0.013	0.933
14	11	0.012	0.945
15	12	0.011	0.956
16	13	0.01	0.966
17	14	0.009	0.975
18	15	0.008	0.983
19	16	0.006	0.989
20	17	0.005	0.994
21	18	0.003	0.997
22	19	0.002	0.999
23	20	0.001	1
24			
25	Exp. Value		3.726
26			
27	Variance		12.437
28			
29	St. Dev.		3.527

a Find the probability that a randomly chosen order will involve 10 or more items.

b The number of items can't be negative, yet the Empirical Rule range of the expected value, ±2 standard deviations, includes negative numbers. What aspect of the probability distribution explains this oddity?

4.36 In the previous exercise, verify the calculation of the expected value and standard deviation, perhaps using a spreadsheet.

4.37 An office supply company currently holds 30% of the market for supplying suburban governments. This share has been quite stable and there is no reason to think it will change. The company has three bids outstanding, prepared by its standard procedure. Let Y be the number of the company's bids that are accepted.

a Find the probability distribution of Y.

b What assumptions did you make in answering part a? Are any of the assumptions clearly unreasonable?

4.38 Find the expected value and variance of Y in Exercise 4.37.

4.39 It could be argued that if the company in Exercise 4.37 loses on the first bid, that signals that a competitor is cutting prices and the company is more likely to lose the other bids also. Similarly, if the company wins on the first bid, that signals that competitors are trying to improve profit margins and the company is more likely to win the other bids also. If this argument is correct, and the two sides of the argument balance out to a 30% market share for the company, will the expected value of Y be increased or decreased compared to the value found in Exercise 4.38? Will the variance be increased or decreased? That is, will there be more variability in results, or less? ∎

4.5

Expected Value and Standard Deviation: Continuous Random Variables ($\int$)

We have defined the expected value (long-run average) and the measures of variability, the variance and standard deviation, for discrete random variables. The exact same ideas apply when a random variable takes values throughout an interval. The mathematical definitions of expected value, variance, and standard deviation for continuous random variables necessarily involve calculus. However, the basic ideas are the same, with probability densities replacing discrete probability distributions and integration replacing summation.

The definition of expected value for a continuous random variable Y follows this pattern.

Definition 4.7   Expected Value for a Continuous Random Variable

$$E(Y) = \int_{-\infty}^{\infty} y f_Y(y) \, dy \qquad \blacksquare$$

Take each value y, multiply (weight) by the probability density $f_Y(y)$, and integrate (instead of add). The technicalities should not obscure the fact that $E(Y)$ is a probability-weighted average, with the same interpretations as for a discrete random variable. It is a probability-weighted average, a long-run average, the fair value of a gamble, the balance point for a histogram (of a probability density), and a generalization of a population mean, just as for a discrete expected value.

E X A M P L E   4 . 1 4

Find $E(T)$, where T is the time between calls of Example 4.4, and $f_T(t) = 2e^{-2t}$, $t \geq 0$. What is the interpretation of this figure?

Solution

Implicitly, $f_T(t) = 0$ for $t < 0$ because $t < 0$ (a negative time between calls) is impossible in this context. It is necessary to know that

$$\int_0^{\infty} t e^{-ct} \, dt = \frac{1}{c^2}$$

Then it follows that

$$E(T) = \int_{-\infty}^{\infty} t f_T(t) \, dt$$

$$= 2 \int_0^{\infty} t e^{-2t} \, dt$$

(because $f_T(t) = 0$ for $t < 0$ and $f_T(t) = 2e^{-2t}$)

$$= 2 \left(\frac{1}{2^2} \right) = \frac{1}{2}$$

Because T is the time in minutes between successive calls, $E(T) = 1/2$ means that in the long run, calls come, on the average, half a minute apart. $\blacksquare$

The definition and shortcut formula for Var(Y) were stated only for discrete random variables. When speaking of continuous random variables, we substitute a probability density for a discrete probability distribution and an integral for a sum.

If Y is a continuous random variable, then

$$\text{Var}(Y) = \int_{-\infty}^{\infty} (y - \mu_Y)^2 f_Y(y)\, dy$$

and a shortcut formula is

$$\text{Var}(Y) = \int_{-\infty}^{\infty} y^2 f_Y(y)\, dy - \mu_Y^2 \qquad \blacksquare$$

E X A M P L E   4 . 1 5

Find Var(T), where T is defined in Examples 4.4 and 4.14. It is known that $\int_0^{\infty} t^2 e^{-ct}\, dt = 2/c^3$.

Solution

Use the shortcut formula and notice that the integral may be taken from 0 to ∞ because $f_T(t) = 0$ for $t < 0$. In Example 4.14 we found $\mu_T = E(T) = 1/2$.

$$\text{Var}(T) = \int_0^{\infty} t^2 f_T(t)\, dt - \mu_T^2$$

$$= \left(\int_0^{\infty} t^2 e^{-2t}\, dt \right) - \left(\frac{1}{2} \right)^2$$

$$= 2 \int_0^{\infty} t^2 e^{-2t}\, dt - \frac{1}{4}$$

$$= 2 \left(\frac{2}{2^3} \right) - \frac{1}{4} = \frac{1}{2} - \frac{1}{4} = \frac{1}{4} \qquad \blacksquare$$

The Empirical Rule approximation can be used for continuous random variables as well. It works best for mound-shaped histograms.

A program such as Maple or Mathematica can be used to calculate expected values and variances, just as it can be used to calculate probabilities for a continuous random variable.

E X A M P L E   4 . 1 6

In Section 4.3 we considered the probable market share for a new product being introduced. Here is the Maple output:

```
density;
                            21
                  506 x (1 - x)

mean:=int(x*density,x=0..1);
                  mean := 1/12
```

```
variance:=int(x^2*density,x=0..1)-mean^2;
                              11
               variance := ----
                             3600
```

```
stdev:=sqrt(variance);
                                1/2
                stdev := 1/60 11
```

```
stdev:=evalf(sqrt(variance));

                stdev := .05527707984
```

What are the expected value and standard deviation? Will the Empirical Rule work well?

Solution

The expected value is shown as "mean:= 1/12," which is 0.083333. The standard deviation is shown as $(1/60)\sqrt{11}$ and evaluated numerically (using "evalf") as 0.055277. The density was shown to be very skewed in the previous section, so we would not expect the Empirical Rule to be a good approximation. ∎

EXERCISES

4.40 In Exercise 4.20, we defined

$$f_Y(y) = 3y^{-4} \qquad \text{for } 1 < y < \infty$$

  a Calculate the mean. What is the interpretation of the resulting number?

  b Calculate the variance and standard deviation. The shortcut method may be easier.

4.41 **a** Calculate values of the density in Exercise 4.40 for $y = 1.0, 1.5, 2.0, 2.5,$ and 3.0. Sketch the density.

  b Should the Empirical Rule work well for this density? Find the probability that Y will be within 1 standard deviation of its mean. Remember that Y can't be less than 1.

4.42 Specifications call for a metal rod used in an assembly to have a diameter of 10 cm. Rods are inspected, and any rods with diameters less than 9.90 cm or greater than 10.10 cm are discarded. Careful measurements indicate that the density of $Y =$ diameter of a randomly chosen rod (after inspection) is

$$f_Y(y) = 100(y - 9.9) \qquad \text{if } 9.9 < y < 10$$
$$= 100(10.1 - y) \qquad \text{if } 10 < y < 10.1$$

The density is 0 for all other y values.

  a What must the expected value of Y equal?

  b Find the standard deviation of Y.

4.43 A firm renovates historically certified buildings into upscale apartments. The firm invites individual investors to buy shares in particular buildings; the shareholders may sell back their shares after two years. The price of a share at the end of two years depends on several uncertainties, primarily the level of interest rates and the demand for apartments. The firm estimates that the probability distribution of X, the net return of a share after two years, is

$$f_X(x) = 7.8125(x + 1)^2 e^{-2.5(x+1)} \qquad \text{for } -1 < x < \infty$$

a Find the probability that a shareholder will actually lose money—that is, that the net return will be negative. From calculus, it is known that an antiderivative of $f_X(x)$ is

$$1 - e^{-2.5(x+1)} - 2.5(x+1)e^{-2.5(x+1)} - 6.25(x+1)^2 e^{-2.5(x+1)}/2$$

b Currently, an investor can obtain a no-risk Treasury bill investment that will yield a net return of .176 over two years. If the apartment investment is to be attractive, the probability of a yield larger than .176 must be high. Is it, according to the estimated probability distribution?

4.44 **a** Find the expected value of X in Exercise 4.43. What is the economic meaning of this number? The math might be easier if you consider $Y = X + 1$ and remember that the integral from 0 to infinity of $y^k e^{-cy}$ is $k!/c^{k+1}$; the expected value of X can be determined from that of Y.

b Find the variance of X in Exercise 4.43. Again, you may want to work with $Y = X + 1$.

c Suppose an investor has an alternative investment, say W, that has an expected value (over the same time period) of 0.24 and a variance of 0.30. Which investment do you think the investor is likely to choose?

4.45 In the exercises for Section 4.2 we considered X = life of a randomly chosen traffic signal bulb (in thousands of hours). Here is additional Maple output for this situation:

```
density;
                          3              2
        .0008000000000 x   exp( - .02 x )

int(x*density,x=0..infinity);
                    9.399856040

int(x^2*density,x=0..infinity);
                    100.0000000
```

a From the output, what is the expected value of X?

b Use the output results to calculate the variance and standard deviation of X. ■

4.6 Joint Probability Distributions and Independence

We have developed some basic language for dealing with one random variable. In this section we extend that language to deal with joint probability distributions for two random variables, X and Y. For now, we define everything in terms of discrete random variables. In the next section, we extend the ideas to continuous random variables.

To begin, we deal with two random variables, X and Y, and define joint probabilities. The joint probability of events A and B is the probability of both events, $P(A \text{ and } B)$. Let A be the event $X = x$, and B the event $Y = y$. Define the **joint probability distribution** $P_{XY}(x, y)$ to be a function that supplies the joint probability for each pair of values, x and y.

joint probability distribution

EXAMPLE 4.17

Suppose that, in the emergency room of a small hospital, the most serious cases involve coronary attack and trauma (injury by violence or severe accident). Define X = number of coronary cases and Y = number of trauma cases arriving on a particular weekday night. It is assumed that

$$P_{XY}(x, y) = \frac{(x + 1)(y + 2)}{84} \qquad x = 0, 1, 2; y = 0, 1, 2, 3$$

Calculate a numerical table of joint probabilities.

Solution

Simply substitute the desired x and y values to get the joint probabilities: $P_{XY}(0, 3) = P(X = 0 \text{ and } Y = 3) = (0 + 1)(3 + 2)/84 = 5/84$, and so on. A tabular display of the joint probability distribution $P_{XY}(x, y)$ is shown here:

	y			
x	**0**	**1**	**2**	**3**
0	2/84	3/84	4/84	5/84
1	4/84	6/84	8/84	10/84
2	6/84	9/84	12/84	15/84

■

marginal probabilities

Once a joint probability distribution has been specified, **marginal probabilities** can be calculated by summation. In Chapter 3, when we dealt with joint probabilities like $P(A \text{ and } B)$, $P(A \text{ and not } B)$, and so on, the term *marginal probability* referred to the probability of one event alone, like $P(A)$. We calculated marginal probabilities by the addition law. Because the ideas in this section are different only in notation from the basic principles of probability, the same principle can be used here.

E X A M P L E   4 . 1 8

Find the marginal probability distribution of X and the marginal probability distribution of Y in Example 4.17.

Solution

Sum across rows to get X probabilities and down columns to get Y probabilities.

	y				
x	**0**	**1**	**2**	**3**	$P_X(x)$
0	2/84	3/84	4/84	5/84	14/84
1	4/84	6/84	8/84	10/84	28/84
2	6/84	9/84	12/84	15/84	42/84
$P_Y(y)$	12/84	18/84	24/84	30/84	

This idea can be expressed in a formula. To find the probability $P_X(x)$, add up the joint probabilities of that x value and each possible y value:

$$P_X(x) = \sum_{\text{all } y} P_{XY}(x, y)$$

In this example,

$$P(X = 1) = \sum_{\text{all } y} P_{XY}(1, y)$$

$$= P_{XY}(1, 0) + P_{XY}(1, 1) + P_{XY}(1, 2) + P_{XY}(1, 3)$$

$$= \frac{4}{84} + \frac{6}{84} + \frac{8}{84} + \frac{10}{84} = \frac{28}{84}$$

In the same way, the marginal probabilities for Y can be computed as

$$P_Y(y) = \sum_{\text{all } x} P_{XY}(x, y)$$

In this example,

$$P(Y = 1) = \sum_{\text{all } x} P_{XY}(x, 1)$$
$$= P_{XY}(0, 1) + P_{XY}(1, 1) + P_{XY}(2, 1)$$
$$= \frac{3}{84} + \frac{6}{84} + \frac{9}{84} = \frac{18}{84}$$

The formula may look difficult, but the idea is simply a translation of the addition principle.[2] ∎

    A spreadsheet program can do these calculations very easily. For example, suppose that an automobile loan company, as part of its credit scoring system, collects information on $X = $ number of mortgages held and $Y = $ number of unpaid credit card balances outstanding, for a randomly chosen applicant. The following Excel output shows how to calculate marginal probabilities, and the result:

	A	B	C	D	E	F	G
1	Joint probs				y		
2			0	1	2	3	
3		0	0.06	0.11	0.16	0.03	=SUM(C3:F3)
4	x	1	0.13	0.24	0.09	0.02	=SUM(C4:F4)
5		2	0.08	0.04	0.03	0.01	=SUM(C5:F5)
6			=SUM(C3:C5)	=SUM(D3:D5)	=SUM(E3:E5)	=SUM(F3:F5)	=SUM(G3:G5)

	A	B	C	D	E	F	G
1	Joint probs				y		
2			0	1	2	3	
3		0	0.06	0.11	0.16	0.03	0.36
4	x	1	0.13	0.24	0.09	0.02	0.48
5		2	0.08	0.04	0.03	0.01	0.16
6			0.27	0.4	0.28	0.06	1

The "=SUM" formulas calculate the marginal probabilities immediately.

    We can extend basic probability notation to conditional probabilities. Just as we defined the conditional probability of B given A as

$$P(B|A) = \frac{P(A \cap B)}{P(A)}$$

conditional distribution   we can define the **conditional distribution** of Y given $X = x$ as

$$P_{Y|X}(y|x)$$

Thus, for any value of Y,

$$P(Y = y | X = x) = \frac{P(X = x \cap Y = y)}{P(X = x)}$$
$$= \frac{P_{XY}(x, y)}{P_X(x)}$$

---

[2] Now we can explain why we use the apparently redundant notation $P_X(x)$, $P_Y(y)$. If we merely wrote $P(x)$ or $P(y)$, we would not know whether $P(1)$ meant $P(X = 1) = P_X(1)$ or $P(Y = 1) = P_Y(1)$.

One use for this notation arises from the idea of independence. Remember that we had two equivalent definitions of independence for events A and B:

$$P(B|A) = P(B)$$

$$P(A \cap B) = P(A)P(B)$$

equivalent definitions of statistical independence

We also have two **equivalent definitions of statistical independence** for random variables X and Y:

$$P_{Y|X}(y|x) = P_Y(y) \qquad \text{for all } x, y$$

$$P_{XY}(x, y) = P_X(x)P_Y(y) \qquad \text{for all } x, y$$

In this text, we usually use the second form of the independence definition.

EXAMPLE 4.19

Show that X and Y of Examples 4.17 and 4.18 are independent.

Solution

In Example 4.18, we found $P_X(x)$ and $P_Y(y)$. When we multiply appropriate $P_X(x)$ and $P_Y(y)$, we get the following table:

x	y 0	1	2	3	
0	(12/84)(14/84)	(18/84)(14/84)	(24/84)(14/84)	(30/84)(14/84)	14/84
1	(12/84)(28/84)	(18/84)(28/84)	(24/84)(28/84)	(30/84)(28/84)	18/84
2	(12/84)(42/84)	(18/84)(42/84)	(24/84)(42/84)	(30/84)(42/84)	42/84
	12/84	18/84	24/84	30/84	

When we reduce the fractions in this table, we find that every table entry equals the $P_{XY}(x, y)$ entry in Example 4.17. Therefore $P_{XY}(x, y) = P_X(x)P_Y(y)$ for all x and y; that is, X and Y are independent. ∎

The assumption of independence was built into the mathematical form of this particular $P_{XY}(x, y)$. In practice, we often assume that X and Y are independent; once we specify $P_X(x)$ and $P_Y(y)$, this assumption lets us calculate $P_{XY}(x, y)$ as the product $P_X(x)P_Y(y)$. Example 4.17 is one situation in which the independence assumption seems reasonable. The number of coronary cases arriving at an emergency room should have no relevance to predictions of the number of trauma cases.

The calculation of conditional distributions can also be done easily using a spreadsheet. For the credit-scoring example used before in this section, here are Excel instructions to compute the conditional distribution of Y given $X = x$, followed by the results:

	A	B	C	D	E	F	G
1	Joint probs				y		
2			0	1	2	3	
3		0	0.06	0.11	0.16	0.03	=SUM(C3:F3)
4	x	1	0.13	0.24	0.09	0.02	=SUM(C4:F4)
5		2	0.08	0.04	0.03	0.01	=SUM(C5:F5)
6			=SUM(C3:C5)	=SUM(D3:D5)	=SUM(E3:E5)	=SUM(F3:F5)	=SUM(G3:G5)

```
7 Conditional                                    y
8 .                      0         1            2           3
9         0         =C3/$G3   =D3/$G3      =E3/$G3     =F3/$G3
10    x   1         =C4/$G4   =D4/$G4      =E4/$G4     =F4/$G4
11        2         =C5/$G5   =D5/$G5      =E5/$G5     =F5/$G5


7 Conditional                                    y
8                       0         1            2           3
9        0         0.166667   0.305556    0.444444    0.083333
10    x  1         0.270833   0.5         0.1875      0.041667
11       2         0.5        0.25        0.1875      0.0625
```

In this case, X and Y are *not* independent. The conditional distribution of Y given $X = x$ varies with (depends on) the particular number x of mortgages held.

In Chapter 3, we discussed how prior probabilities of various states of nature can be modified by the likelihoods of observable events, using Bayes' Theorem. Sometimes the states of nature and observable events are numerical in nature, so that ideas of average and variability make sense. In such cases, it's useful to write Bayes' Theorem in random variable notation. For example, the agent for an author of best-selling novels wants to estimate the final bid for the paperback book publishing rights of a new novel. Based on past results for the author and recent trends in the paperback industry, the agent thinks that the bid could be $100,000, $150,000, $200,000, or $250,000, with respective probabilities of approximately .4, .3, .2, and .1. The agent keeps track of the order of a "bellwether" bookstore chain whose buyer is a fairly good predictor of commercial success. The bookstore chain orders 10,000, 20,000, or 30,000 copies. The agent thinks that the likelihoods of these order sizes, given the eventual bid price, should be roughly as follows:

	Order Amount		
Bid	10,000	20,000	30,000
$100,000	.60	.30	.10
$150,000	.50	.30	.20
$200,000	.30	.40	.30
$250,000	.20	.40	.40

Based on these prior probabilities, the expected value of the paperback bid is $100,000(.4) + $150,000(.3) + $200,000(.2) + $250,000(.1) = $150,000$. But now suppose that the bookstore chain orders 30,000 copies; this optimistic note leads the agent to revise the prior probabilities. From Bayes' Theorem (or, equivalently, a probability tree calculation):

$$P(\$100,000|30,000) = \frac{P(30,000|\$100,000)P(\$100,000)}{\begin{aligned} &P(30,000|\$100,000)P(\$100,000) \\ &+ P(30,000|\$150,000)P(\$150,000) \\ &+ P(30,000|\$200,000)P(\$200,000) \\ &+ P(30,000|\$250,000)P(\$250,000) \end{aligned}}$$

$$= \frac{(.10)(.4)}{(.10)(.4) + (.20)(.3) + (.30)(.2) + (.40)(.1)}$$

$$= .20$$

Similar calculations show that $P(\$150,000|30,000) = .30$, $P(\$200,000|30,000) = .30$, and $P(\$250,000|30,000) = .20$. Using these posterior probabilities, the expected value of the bid is now $\$100,000(.20) + \$150,000(.30) + \$200,000(.30) + \$250,000(.20) = \$175,000$. The expected value of the bid has indeed increased, given the optimistic order.

The concepts in this section can be extended to any number of random variables. The only problem is understanding tables of probabilities in three (or more) dimensions. A spreadsheet program is helpful in doing the arithmetic. For example, here is Excel output for the joint distribution of three random variables: $W =$ the number of patients arriving at an acute-care facility on a randomly chosen weeknight who require hospitalization, $X =$ the number of arriving patients who require repeat visits, and $Y =$ the number of patients who require only minor treatment. At the bottom of the output is the distribution of X and Y, obtained by summing over the possible w values.

w = 0

		0	1	2	3	4	5
				y			
	0	0.063	0.063	0.042	0.0245	0.014	0.0035
x	1	0.056	0.098	0.056	0.042	0.021	0.007
	2	0.014	0.042	0.028	0.021	0.021	0.014
	3	0.007	0.007	0.014	0.0175	0.014	0.0105

w = 1

		0	1	2	3	4	5
				y			
	0	0.018	0.018	0.012	0.007	0.004	0.001
x	1	0.016	0.028	0.016	0.012	0.006	0.002
	2	0.004	0.012	0.008	0.006	0.006	0.004
	3	0.002	0.002	0.004	0.005	0.004	0.003

w = 2

		0	1	2	3	4	5
				y			
	0	0.009	0.009	0.006	0.0035	0.002	0.0005
x	1	0.008	0.014	0.008	0.006	0.003	0.001
	2	0.002	0.006	0.004	0.003	0.003	0.002
	3	0.001	0.001	0.002	0.0025	0.002	0.0015

		0	1	2	3	4	5	
				y				
	0	0.09	0.09	0.06	0.035	0.02	0.005	0.3
x	1	0.08	0.14	0.08	0.06	0.03	0.01	0.4
	2	0.02	0.06	0.04	0.03	0.03	0.02	0.2
	3	0.01	0.01	0.02	0.025	0.02	0.015	0.1
		0.2	0.3	0.2	0.15	0.1	0.05	1

We can extend the definition of statistical independence to deal with several random variables. A set of random variables is statistically independent if the joint probability is the product of marginal probabilities for all possible sets of values. In the acute-care example, we (or a spreadsheet program) can obtain w probabilities by adding all the probabilities for the block corresponding to that value, x probabilities by adding all probabilities in all the rows with that x value, and y probabilities by adding all the probabilities in the column for that y. The results:

w	0	1	2
P(w)	0.7	0.2	0.1

x	0	1	2	3		
P(x)	0.3	0.4	0.2	0.1		

y	0	1	2	3	4	5
P(y)	0.2	0.3	0.2	0.15	0.1	0.05

To check for independence, note that $P_{WXY}(0, 0, 0) = .063$ but $P_W(0)P_X(0)P_Y(0) = (.7)(.3)(.2) = .042$. Therefore, equality doesn't hold for that set of values and independence does not hold. If we had obtained equality for that set of values, we would still have to check all the other sets before we could claim independence.

Once again, independence is very often an assumption. If we are willing to assume that (say) random variables $W, X, Y,$ and Z are independent, we can obtain joint probabilities by multiplying the four marginal probabilities.

EXERCISES

4.46 A manufacturer of television sets sells two principal models. Define $X =$ sales of model A next December (nearest 100,000) and $Y =$ sales of model B next December. The marketing staff estimates that the joint probabilities $P_{XY}(x, y)$ are

		y		
x	**1**	**2**	**3**	**4**
1	.030	.055	.070	.075
2	.055	.070	.075	.070
3	.070	.075	.070	.055
4	.075	.070	.055	.030

a Find $P(X = 1, Y = 2)$.   **b** Find $P(X \leq 2, Y \leq 2)$.

c Find $P_X(x)$ and $P_Y(y)$.   **d** Are X and Y independent?

4.47 Show that the formula

$$P_{XY}(x, y) = .005(-10 + 10x + 10y - x^2 - y^2 - 2xy)$$

yields the joint probability table of Exercise 4.46. Can you find a formula for $P_X(x)$?

4.48 The owner of a small sound-system store determines the following probabilities for $X =$ number of amplifiers sold during a weekday and for $Y =$ number of speaker systems sold during the same day:

x	0	1	2	3	4	
$P_X(x)$	.10	.40	.25	.20	.05	

y	0	1	2	3	4	5
$P_Y(y)$	.10	.30	.25	.20	.10	.05

a Assuming that X and Y are independent, calculate the joint probability distribution $P_{XY}(x, y)$.

b Check your work by finding the marginal probabilities $P_X(x)$ and $P_Y(y)$.

4.49 Do you believe that independence is a reasonable assumption for Exercise 4.48? Should it be true that the sales of amplifiers will be irrelevant to the sales of speakers?

4.50 A small management consulting firm presents both written and oral proposals in an effort to get new consulting contracts. Records indicate that the probability distribution $P_{XY}(x, y)$ of

X = number of oral proposals in a week and Y = number of written proposals in that week is given by the following table:

	y				
x	0	1	2	3	4
0	.010	.015	.030	.075	.050
1	.020	.030	.045	.060	.040
2	.030	.045	.100	.045	.030
3	.040	.060	.045	.030	.020
4	.050	.075	.030	.015	.010

a Find the probability that there are two oral proposals and two written proposals in a particular week.

b Find the probability that there are exactly two oral proposals and two or fewer written proposals in a particular week.

c Find the probability that there are two or fewer oral proposals and two or fewer written proposals in a particular week.

4.51 **a** Use the probability distribution of Exercise 4.50 to calculate the marginal probability distributions of X and of Y.

b Assuming these probabilities, are X and Y independent?

4.52 Calculate the conditional distribution of Y given each possible value of X, using the probability distribution of Exercise 4.50. Do these conditional probability distributions indicate that X and Y are independent?

4.53 A computer software firm licenses a very complicated database management system to businesses and nonprofit organizations. Payment of the license fee entitles the licensee to designate people to attend each of three types of training session—one for database managers and another for user-training managers. The licensee may choose not to send anyone or may send additional people for an additional fee. The software firm has some experience with attendance at the sessions, and assumes the following probabilities for X = number of persons attending the database managers' session and Y = number attending the training managers' session, from a randomly chosen company. The probabilities are reported via an Excel spreadsheet:

	A	B	C	D
1	X	Y	P(x,y)	
2				
3	0	0	0.014	
4	0	1	0.056	
5	0	2	0.070	
6	1	0	0.036	
7	1	1	0.144	
8	1	2	0.180	
9	2	0	0.050	
10	2	1	0.200	
11	2	2	0.250	
12				
13				
14	x	P(x)	y	P(y)
15				
16	0	0.140	0	0.100
17	1	0.360	1	0.400
18	2	0.500	2	0.500

a Verify the computation of the X marginal probabilities.

b Are X and Y independent in these probabilities?

4.54 Find the conditional distribution of Y given that $X = 0$ for the probabilities in the preceding exercise. How does this distribution compare to the marginal Y distribution? Why?

4.55 The software firm of the previous exercises also offers a training course for system operators, the people who are concerned with the inner workings of the computer. If W = number of people attending this course, and X and Y are defined as before, the following Excel output gives $P_{WXY}(w, x, y)$:

	A	B	C	D
1	w	x	y	P(w,x,y)
2	0	0	0	0.0014
3	0	0	1	0.0056
4	0	0	2	0.007
5	0	1	0	0.0036
6	0	1	1	0.0144
7	0	1	2	0.018
8	0	2	0	0.005
9	0	2	1	0.02
10	0	2	2	0.025
11	1	0	0	0.0035
12	1	0	1	0.014
13	1	0	2	0.0175
14	1	1	0	0.009
15	1	1	1	0.036
16	1	1	2	0.045
17	1	2	0	0.0125
18	1	2	1	0.05
19	1	2	2	0.0625
20	2	0	0	0.0049
21	2	0	1	0.0196
22	2	0	2	0.0245
23	2	1	0	0.0126
24	2	1	1	0.0504
25	2	1	2	0.063
26	2	2	0	0.0175
27	2	2	1	0.07
28	2	2	2	0.0875
29	3	0	0	0.0042
30	3	0	1	0.0168
31	3	0	2	0.021
32	3	1	0	0.0108
33	3	1	1	0.0432
34	3	1	2	0.054
35	3	2	0	0.015
36	3	2	1	0.06
37	3	2	2	0.075

  a Find the marginal probability distribution of W.

  b Are the three random variables independent? ■

4.7 Covariance and Correlation of Random Variables

I n the previous section, we defined the *independence* of two random variables. Now we consider how to measure the degree of *dependence* between two random variables. There are many measures of dependence we might use. Two related measures, covariance and correlation, are particularly important because they are closely related to the concept of variance of a random variable. Correlation, in particular, is a way to measure how closely two random quantities vary together. Covariance may be regarded as an intermediate calculation on the way to finding the correlation of two random variables.

Again we begin with an example. A trust officer of a bank assumes the following (subjective) joint probabilities for the percentage return (interest plus change in market value) of two utility bonds. The returns are labeled X and Y.

X	Y					$P_X(x)$
	8	9	10	11	12	
8	.03	.04	.03	.00	.00	.10
9	.04	.06	.06	.04	.00	.20
10	.02	.08	.20	.08	.02	.40
11	.00	.04	.06	.06	.04	.20
12	.00	.00	.03	.04	.03	.10
$P_Y(y)$	.09	.22	.38	.22	.09	

There is a relation between X and Y. For example, given $x = 8$, the Y probabilities are concentrated on the smaller values $y = 8, 9$, and 10. At the other extreme, given $x = 12$, the Y probabilities are concentrated on the larger values $y = 10, 11$, and 12. In general, there is a tendency for the X and Y outcomes to vary together. The covariance and correlation of two random variables measure the *strength* of that tendency.

The covariance of two random variables is based on products of deviations from means, weighted by joint probabilities. If a particular x value is below μ_X and a y value is below μ_Y, both deviations will be negative numbers, and their product will be positive. Similarly, if both values are above their expected values, both deviations will be positive, and their product will be positive. Negative products result for one value above its mean and the other below its mean. If most of the probability is associated with (low, low) and (high, high) pairs of (x, y) values, as in the bond return example, then most of the weight will go to positive products, and the covariance will be positive. If most of the probability is associated with (low, high) and (high, low) values, the covariance will be negative.

Definition 4.9 Covariance of Random Variables *X* and *Y*

If X and Y are discrete random variables with respective expected values μ_X and μ_Y, and with joint probability distribution $P_{XY}(x, y)$, the covariance of X and Y, denoted by $\text{Cov}(X, Y)$, is defined as

$$\text{Cov}(X, Y) = \sum_x \sum_y (x - \mu_X)(y - \mu_Y)P_{XY}(x, y)$$

A shortcut method for computing the covariance is

$$\text{Cov}(X, Y) = \left[\sum_x \sum_y xy P_{XY}(x, y) \right] - \mu_X \mu_Y \quad \blacksquare$$

E X A M P L E   4 . 2 0

Compute $\text{Cov}(X, Y)$ for the joint distribution of bond yields given in the preceding discussion. Use the definition first and check to see that the shortcut method gives the same answer.

Solution

From the marginal probabilities $P_X(x)$ and $P_Y(y)$, we get the expected values:

$$\mu_X = 8(.10) + 9(.20) + 10(.40) + 11(.20) + 12(.10) = 10$$

$$\mu_Y = 8(.09) + 9(.22) + 10(.38) + 11(.22) + 12(.09) = 10$$

In fact, we could have noted that the marginal probability distribution for X is symmetric around 10, so μ_X must equal 10; the same holds for μ_Y.

The covariance can be computed using the definition as follows:

$$\text{Cov}(X, Y) = \sum_x \sum_y (x - \mu_X)(y - \mu_Y)P_{XY}(x, y)$$

$$= (8 - 10)(8 - 10)(.03) + (8 - 10)(9 - 10)(.04)$$

$$+ (8 - 10)(10 - 10)(.03) + \cdots + (12 - 10)(12 - 10)(.03)$$

$$= .60$$

Similarly, using the shortcut method,

$$\text{Cov}(X, Y) = \sum \sum xyP_{XY}(x, y) - \mu_X\mu_Y$$

$$= 8(8)(.03) + 8(9)(.04) + 8(10)(.03) + \cdots + 12(12)(.03) - 10(10)$$

$$= 100.60 - 100 = .60$$

A spreadsheet program will do the computations readily. In the following Excel output, the bottom part of the table contains computed values of $(x - \mu_X)(y - \mu_Y)P_{XY}(x, y)$ for each (x, y) combination. The total of these values, shown at the bottom right of the output, is the covariance. The computations could also have been done using Excel's "array" method.

	C	D	E	F	G	H	I	J
4	prob		8	9	10	11	12	Total
5		8	0.03	0.04	0.03	0	0	0.1
6		9	0.04	0.06	0.06	0.04	0	0.2
7		10	0.02	0.08	0.2	0.08	0.02	0.4
8		11	0	0.04	0.06	0.06	0.04	0.2
9		12	0	0	0.03	0.04	0.03	0.1
10								
11			0.09	0.22	0.38	0.22	0.09	1
12								
13								
14	(X-10)*(Y-10)*prob							
15								
16		0.12	0.08	0	0	0		
17		0.08	0.06	0	-0.04	0		
18		0	0	0	0	0		
19		0	-0.04	0	0.06	0.08		
20		0	0	0	0.08	0.12		

Note that most of the terms in the bottom part of the table are positive numbers in this example. Also, the positive numbers are larger in magnitude than the negative numbers because of the relatively high probability in the "northwest" and "southeast" parts of the table. That's why the covariance comes out positive in this case. ∎

The covariance of two random variables is closely related to their correlation.

Definition 4.10   Correlation of Random Variables X and Y

If X and Y are discrete random variables with respective standard deviations σ_X and σ_Y, their correlation ρ_{XY} is defined as

$$\rho_{XY} = \frac{\text{Cov}(X, Y)}{\sigma_X\sigma_Y}$$

It follows that

$$\text{Cov}(X, Y) = \rho_{XY}\sigma_X\sigma_Y \qquad ∎$$

The correlation between X and Y ranges between -1.00 and $+1.00$. A value of -1.00 or $+1.00$ indicates perfect *linear* prediction in the population, whereas a value of zero indicates no linear predictive value. Correlation is a symmetric idea; the correlation between X and Y is the same as the correlation between Y and X. The same symmetry holds for covariance.

E X A M P L E   4 . 2 1

Find ρ_{XY} for the bond yield distribution discussed earlier in this section.

Solution

In Example 4.20, we found $\text{Cov}(X, Y) = .60$. To get ρ_{XY}, we need the standard deviations of X and Y, which can be computed from the respective marginal probabilities. The shortcut formula for a variance can be used to compare σ_X^2 and σ_Y^2:

$$\sigma_X^2 = \sum_x x^2 P_X(x) - \mu_X^2$$

$$= 8^2(.10) + 9^2(.20) + 10^2(.40) + 11^2(.20) + 12^2(.10) - (10)^2$$

$$= 101.20 - 100 = 1.20$$

and hence $\sigma_X = \sqrt{1.20} = 1.095$.

Similarly, we have

$$\sigma_Y^2 = \sum_Y y^2 P_Y(y) - \mu_Y^2 = 1.16$$

and $\sigma_Y = \sqrt{1.16} = 1.077$.

Substituting into the definition for ρ_{XY}, we find

$$\rho_{XY} = \frac{\text{Cov}(X, Y)}{\sigma_X \sigma_Y} = \frac{.60}{1.095(1.077)} = .509 \quad \blacksquare$$

E X A M P L E   4 . 2 2

Covariance and correlation may also be approximated by computer simulation. We used Excel's random number generation and LOOKUP function (in a cumulative probability list) to draw 1000 pairs of x and y values in the previous example. Then Excel's built-in covariance and correlation functions were applied to these simulated values, with the following results:

	B	C	D	E	F
3	Variances, Covariances			X	Y
4			X	1.2208	
5			Y	0.5877	1.0974
6					
7					
8	Correlations			X	Y
9			X	1	
10			Y	0.506	1

How closely do the covariance and correlation compare to the exact values, .600 and .509, respectively?

Solution

The covariance is shown as .5877 and the correlation as .5060, both slightly less than the correct values. Presumably, if we had taken some enormous number of pairs, the simulation values would be very close to the correct ones; even with 1000 pairs, the values are close enough for all practical purposes. ∎

Covariance and correlation are immensely important ideas in managing portfolios of investments. The main reason someone invests in a portfolio of several different assets is to reduce risk. Suppose that the returns to two assets are strongly negatively correlated. If one return happens to be low, the other will tend to be high, thus reducing the overall risk of variability in returns. On the other hand, suppose that the returns are highly positively correlated. In this case, if one return happens to be low, the other will also tend to be low; investing in such a portfolio won't reduce the risk much.

Mathematically, return can be measured by expected value and risk can be measured by variance. If we denote the returns per monetary unit (say, per French franc) on two investments as R_1 and R_2, and denote the number of francs invested in each by c_1 and c_2, the random amount earned by the portfolio is $c_1 R_1 + c_2 R_2$.

$$E(c_1 R_1 + c_2 R_2) = c_1 E(R_1) + c_2 E(R_2)$$

$$\text{Var}(c_1 R_1 + c_2 R_2) = c_1^2 \text{Var}(R_1) + c_2^2 \text{Var}(R_2) + 2 c_1 c_2 \text{Cov}(R_1, R_2)$$

The variance property follows from the algebraic fact that $(a + b)^2 = a^2 + b^2 + 2ab$. The expected return depends only on the expected returns of the two investments (and, of course, the amounts invested in each). The risk (variance) of the combined investment depends not only on the risk of each return separately, but also on the covariance between them. All else being equal, if the correlation between the returns is low or, even better, negative, the covariance will also be low or negative, and the variance of the total return will be reduced.

These ideas can be extended to any number of investments. For a portfolio of three investments,

$$E(c_1 R_1 + c_2 R_2 + c_3 R_3) = c_1 E(R_1) + c_2 E(R_2) + c_3 E(R_3)$$

$$\text{Var}(c_1 R_1 + c_2 R_2 + c_3 R_3) = c_1^2 \text{Var}(R_1) + c_2^2 \text{Var}(R_2) + c_3^2 \text{Var}(R_3) + 2 c_1 c_2 \text{Cov}(R_1, R_2)$$
$$+ 2 c_1 c_3 \text{Cov}(R_1, R_3) + 2 c_2 c_3 \text{Cov}(R_2, R_3)$$

Notice that the covariance terms involve only two returns at a time; there is no such thing as a covariance among three investments. The general pattern for many investments should be clear; to write a general equation is best done using matrix notation, which is a bit much for now. The general portfolio analysis idea is elaborated on in most finance books.

If the random variables X and Y are independent, there should be no relation (linear or otherwise) between them. Reasonably enough, when X and Y are independent, $\text{Cov}(X, Y) = 0$ and therefore $\rho_{XY} = 0$ also.

EXAMPLE 4.23

An assembly line can be stopped temporarily to adjust for either bad parts alignment or bad welds. Production records indicate the following joint distribution for X = number of stops in a production shift for bad alignment and Y = number of stops in a production shift for bad welds:

		y				
x	**0**	**1**	**2**	**3**	**4**	
0	.03	.06	.12	.06	.03	.30
1	.04	.08	.16	.08	.04	.40
2	.03	.06	.12	.06	.03	.30
	.10	.20	.40	.20	.10	1.00

a What should Cov(X, Y) equal for these probabilities?

b Verify your answer numerically.

Solution

a In every case $P_{XY}(x, y) = P_X(x)P_Y(y)$. For example, $P_{XY}(2, 4) = .03$ and $P_X(2) \times P_Y(4) = (.30)(.10) = .03$ also. Therefore X and Y are independent, and Cov(X, Y) should equal zero.

b By the symmetry of the marginal probabilities for X and for Y, it follows that $\mu_X = 1$ and $\mu_Y = 2$. So

$$\begin{aligned}\text{Cov}(X, Y) &= [0(0)(.03) + 0(1)(.06) + \cdots + 2(4)(.03)] - 1(2) \\ &= 2.00 - 2 = 0\end{aligned}$$

as it should. ■

It is mathematically possible to have Cov(X, Y) = 0 even though X and Y are independent. The reason is that covariance and correlation measure only the strength of the *linear* relation. If there is a relation between X and Y, but that relation cannot even be approximated by a linear relation, the covariance can be zero.

EXAMPLE 4.24

Suppose that in Example 4.23 the following probabilities are obtained:

		y				
x	**0**	**1**	**2**	**3**	**4**	
0	.01	.05	.18	.05	.01	.30
1	.03	.10	.14	.10	.03	.40
2	.06	.05	.08	.05	.06	.30
	.10	.20	.40	.20	.10	1.00

Are X and Y independent? What is the covariance between X and Y?

Solution

No, there is dependence. For example, $P_{XY}(0, 0) = .01$, but $P_X(0)P_Y(0) = (.10)(.30) = .03$. However,

$$\begin{aligned}\text{Cov}(X, Y) &= [0(0)(.01) + 0(1)(.05) + \cdots + 2(4)(.06)] - 1(2) \\ &= 2.00 - 2 = 0\end{aligned}$$

(Note that $\mu_X = 1$ and $\mu_Y = 2$, as in Example 4.23.) The reason that the covariance is zero is that there is no linear relation. Note that when y is either 0 or 4, the most likely x value is 2; when y is either 1 or 3, the most likely x value is 1; and when y is 2, the most likely x value is 0. Computation of expected X values given each value y also shows a completely nonlinear pattern. Given $y = 0$, the probabilities for $x = 0, 1, 2$ are $1/10, 3/10, 6/10$, respectively, so the expected value of X given $Y = 0$ is $0(1/10) + 1(3/10) + 2(6/10) = 1.5$. Similar computations yield the following table:

y	0	1	2	3	4
$E(X|Y = y)$	1.50	1.00	0.75	1.00	1.50

As y increases from 0 to 2, the expected value of X given $Y = y$ decreases; but then, as y increases from 2 to 4, the expected value of X given $Y = y$ increases right back. There is no straight-line relation at all. ∎

EXERCISES

4.56 In Exercise 4.50, we considered the following joint distribution $P_{XY}(x, y)$ of $X =$ number of oral proposals in a week and $Y =$ number of written proposals in that week, as given by the following table:

			y			
x	**0**	**1**	**2**	**3**	**4**	**Total**
0	.010	.015	.030	.075	.050	.180
1	.020	.030	.045	.060	.040	.195
2	.030	.045	.100	.045	.030	.250
3	.040	.060	.045	.030	.020	.195
4	.050	.075	.030	.015	.010	.180
Total	.150	.225	.250	.225	.150	

   a What are the means of X and Y? (Think, don't calculate.)

   b Calculate the standard deviations of X and Y.

4.57   **a** Find the covariance of X and Y in Exercise 4.56.

   b Find the correlation of X and Y in Exercise 4.56. What does it indicate about the relation between X and Y? In particular, could X and Y be independent?

4.58 Find the conditional expectation of Y, given $X = 0$, for the probability distribution of Exercise 4.56. That is, calculate conditional probabilities given $X = 0$ and use these probabilities to calculate an expected value. Do the same for other x values. Does the conditional expectation change with x?

4.59 Define $T = X + Y$ to be the total number of proposals made by the firm in Exercises 4.50 and 4.56 in a particular week.

   a Calculate the probability distribution of T, using the probability table. Note, for example, that the probability that $T = 2$ is the sum of the probabilities for $(2, 0)$, $(1, 1)$, and $(0, 2)$.

   b Calculate the expected value and variance of T directly from this probability distribution.

   c Use the facts that $E(X + Y) = E(X) + E(Y)$ and $\text{Var}(X + Y) = \text{Var}(X) + \text{Var}(Y) + 2\text{Cov}(X, Y)$ to recalculate the mean and variance of T.

4.60 An auto loan company investigated the relation between $X =$ number of mortgages held by applicants for loans and $Y =$ number of unpaid credit card balances held. The following Excel spreadsheet shows the joint probabilities:

	A	B	C	D	E	F	G	H	I	J
1	Joint probs									
2						y				
3				0	1	2	3	Total	Y mean	Y variance
4			0	0.06	0.11	0.16	0.03	0.36	1.13	0.7731
5		x	1	0.13	0.24	0.09	0.02	0.48		
6			2	0.08	0.04	0.03	0.01	0.16		
7										
8		Total		0.27	0.39	0.28	0.06	1		
9										
10		X mean		0.8						
11		X variance		0.48						

   a Show that X and Y are not independent.

   b The probabilities in the upper left and lower right parts of the joint probability table are smaller than would be true if the two variables were independent. The probabilities in the lower left and upper right parts are larger than the independence probabilities. From this fact, should the covariance of X and Y be positive, negative, or zero?

4.61 Excel was used to calculate the product of deviations from means, weighted by probabilities. These values were summed to obtain the covariance.

	B	C	D	E	F
1					
2					
3					
4					
5		0.05424	0.01144	-0.11136	-0.04488
6		-0.02938	-0.00624	0.01566	0.00748
7		-0.10848	-0.00624	0.03132	0.02244
8					
9	Covariance	-0.164			
10					
11	Correlation	-0.26922			

Locate the covariance and verify the calculation of the correlation. Does the sign agree with your answer in the previous exercise?

4.62 An investor was considering investing 10,000 British pounds in each of two investments chosen from among four possibilities. Historical data suggest that the expected returns, variances, and covariances will be as shown in the following Excel spreadsheet:

	B	C	D	E	F
4	Investment		Expected return		
5					
6		1	0.085		
7		2	0.08		
8		3	0.075		
9		4	0.07		
10					
11					
12	Variances, Covariances				
13					
14		1	2	3	4
15	1	0.005	0.0035	0.0006	0.0031
16	2	0.0035	0.0045	0.0038	0.0028
17	3	0.0006	0.0038	0.004	0.0024
18	4	0.0031	0.0028	0.0024	0.0032

Variances are shown along the main diagonal of the table and covariances in the remaining entries. Thus, the expected returns per pound for investments 1 and 2 are 0.085 and 0.080, respectively. The variances for investments 1 and 2 are 0.0050 and 0.0045, respectively and the covariance between these two is 0.0035.

   a Calculate the expected return and variance if the investor puts 10,000 pounds in investments 1 and 2.

b The investor thought that combining investments 1 and 4 should give a smaller risk than combining investments 1 and 3, because investment 4 has a smaller variance than investment 3. Is this belief correct? Calculate the variance for these two portfolios to find out.

4.63 In the previous exercise, which portfolio of two equal investments yields the highest expected return? The lowest variance?

4.64 A quality issue concerns a manufacturing process in which holes are drilled in blocks. The probability that a hole is defectively drilled is .10. Let X = number of defects in a sample of two blocks (there is only one hole per block).

    a Find the probability distribution of X. You may wish to draw a tree.

    b Find the expected value and variance of X.

    c What have you assumed in answering parts a and b? Under what conditions might the assumption be unreasonable?

4.65 Assume that an inspector in the process of the previous exercise fails to detect a defect with probability .10; implicitly, we assume that the inspector does not "detect" defects when in fact there are none. Let Y = number of detected defects. Use a probability tree to derive the joint distribution of X (from Exercise 4.64) and Y. Note that Y cannot be larger than X.

4.66   **a** Find the mean and standard deviation of Y in Exercise 4.65.

    b Use the joint distribution of X and Y found in Exercise 4.65 to find the correlation of X and Y.

    c Explain why the correlation should naturally be positive. Remember, X is the actual number of defects and Y is the detected number of defects in the same, randomly chosen item. ■

4.8 Joint Probability Densities for Continuous Random Variables ($\int$)

Our discussion of joint probabilities has, up until now, focused on discrete random variables. Now we turn briefly to continuous random variables. As we shall see once again, every discrete summation has a direct analogue in a continuous integration. The technical details of calculus are needed in this section, but they should not obscure the recurring analogy of continuous integration with discrete summation.

When discussing discrete random variables, we considered joint probabilities $P_{XY}(x, y) = P(X = x \text{ and } Y = y)$. Probabilities for X, Y, or both were obtained by appropriate sums. When we turn to continuous random variables X and Y, we consider joint density functions $f_{XY}(x, y)$. In the continuous case, probabilities are obtained by integration (rather than summation) of the joint probability density. For example, suppose that a study of the time T required to prepare a bid in worker-days and the size of the bid U in millions of dollars indicates that the joint probability density is

$$f_{TU}(t, u) = .02(t + 1)(t + 2)(10 - t)u^t(1 - u) \qquad 0 < t < 10, 0 < u < 1$$

In this case, both T and U are continuous random variables, as indicated by the fact that they vary over continuous ranges $0 < t < 10$ and $0 < u < 1$. Thus, instead of finding the probability that T and U lie in specified intervals by summing probabilities, we find such probabilities by integrating densities.

If X and Y are continuous random variables with joint probability density $f_{XY}(x, y)$, then probabilities concerning X and Y are calculated as

$$P(a < X < b, c < Y < d) = \int_{x=a}^{x=b} \int_{y=c}^{y=d} f_{XY}(x, y) \, dy \, dx \quad \blacksquare$$

(Note for those not familiar with double integrals: The integrations are performed "from the inside out." Thus, in the preceding expression, the first integration is performed with respect to y, with x being regarded as a constant. Once the y variable has been integrated out, the single integration with respect to x is carried out. The integration may be performed in either order.)

For example, suppose that continuous random variables X and Y have joint density

$$f_{XY}(x, y) = (6/17)[4 - (x + y)^2] \qquad 0 < x < 1, 0 < y < 1$$

Find the probability that both X and Y are less than .5.

We note first that both X and Y can't be negative, so that we're finding $P(0 < X < .5$ and $0 < Y < .5)$. Thus

$$P(0 < X < .5 \text{ and } 0 < Y < .5) = (6/17) \int_0^{.5} \int_0^{.5} [4 - (x + y)^2] \, dy \, dx$$

$$= (6/17) \int_0^{.5} \left[4y - \frac{(x + y)^3}{3} \right]\Bigg|_{y=0}^{y=.5} dx$$

$$= (6/17) \int_0^{.5} \left\{ \left[2 - \frac{(x + .5)^3}{3} \right] + \frac{x^3}{3} \right\} dx$$

$$= (6/17) \left[2x - \frac{(x + .5)^4}{12} + \frac{x^4}{12} \right]\Bigg|_{x=0}^{x=.5}$$

$$= (6/17) \left[1.0 - \left(\frac{1}{12} - \frac{(.5)^4}{12} \right) + \frac{(.5)^4}{12} \right]$$

$$= .3272$$

A mathematical computer package such as Maple or Mathematica can sometimes be helpful in carrying out the calculations. Here is Maple output for the previous integral. Note that we get the same answer integrating in either order.

```
jointdensity:=(6/17)*(4-(x+y)^2);
```

$$
\text{jointdensity} := \frac{24}{17} - 6/17 \, (x + y)^2
$$

```
int(int(jointdensity,y=0..0.5),x=0..0.5);
```

$$.3272058824$$

```
int(int(jointdensity,x=0..0.5),y=0..0.5);
```

$$.3272058824$$

EXAMPLE 4.25

Histograms of past data on $X =$ time required to cut bolts of cloth to a pattern and $Y =$ time required to sew the same bolts of cloth for military uniforms (both measured in worker-hours) indicate that

$$f_{XY}(x, y) = 72x^2(1 - x)y(1 - y) \qquad \text{for } 0 < x < 1, 0 < y < 1$$

Find the probability that Y will be less than X and X will be between 0 and .5.

Solution

This problem presents some technical difficulties in that the limits for integrating Y depend on the specified x value. We must have $y < x$ and $0 < x < .5$. Thus the region of integration of $f_{XY}(x, y)$ is $0 < x < .5, 0 < y < x$ (because y, by definition, cannot be less than 0). So

$$P(0 < Y < X < .5) = \int_{x=0}^{x=.5} \int_{y=0}^{y=x} 72x^2(1 - x)y(1 - y) \, dy \, dx$$

$$= \int_{x=0}^{x=.5} 72x^2(1 - x) \int_{y=0}^{y=x} y(1 - y) \, dy \, dx$$

$$= \int_{x=0}^{x=.5} 72x^2(1 - x) \left[\frac{y^2}{2} - \frac{y^3}{3} \right] \Big|_{y=0}^{y=x} dx$$

$$= \int_{x=0}^{x=.5} 72x^2(1 - x) \left[\left(\frac{x^2}{2} - \frac{x^3}{3} \right) - (0 - 0) \right] dx$$

$$= 36 \int_{x=0}^{x=.5} x^4(1 - x) \, dx - 24 \int_{x=0}^{x=.5} x^5(1 - x) \, dx$$

$$= 36 \left(\frac{x^5}{5} - \frac{x^6}{6} \right) \Big|_{x=0}^{x=.5} - 24 \left(\frac{x^6}{6} - \frac{x^7}{7} \right) \Big|_{x=0}^{x=.5}$$

$$= 36 \left[\frac{(.5)^5}{5} - \frac{(.5)^6}{6} \right] - 24 \left[\frac{(.5)^6}{6} - \frac{(.5)^7}{7} \right]$$

$$= .0955$$

after some arithmetic. ■

In Section 4.6, we showed that we could find the marginal probability distribution of X by summing over y in the joint probability distribution $P_{XY}(x, y)$. You may not be overwhelmingly surprised to hear that, when dealing with continuous random variables, we substitute an integral over y for a sum over y. In the continuous case,

$$f_X(x) = \int_{\text{all } y} f_{XY}(x, y) \, dy$$

For $T =$ time spent in preparing a bid and $U =$ size of the bid, with joint density

$$f_{TU}(t, u) = .02(t + 1)(t + 2)(10 - t)u^t(1 - u) \qquad 0 < t < 10, 0 < u < 1$$

we can find the marginal density of T by integrating out u:

$$f_T(t) = \int_{u=0}^{u=1} .02(t+1)(t+2)(10-t)u^t(1-u)\,du$$

$$= 0.2(t+1)(t+2)(10-t)\left[\frac{u^{t+1}}{(t+1)} - \frac{u^{t+2}}{(t+2)}\right]\Bigg|_{u=0}^{u=1}$$

$$= .02(t+1)(t+2)(10-t)\left[\frac{1}{(t+1)} - \frac{1}{(t+2)}\right] = .02(10-t)$$

E X A M P L E   4 . 2 6

Find the marginal density of X in Example 4.25.

Solution

$$f_X(x) = \int_{y=0}^{y=1} 72x^2(1-x)y(1-y)\,dy$$

$$= 72x^2(1-x)\int_{y=0}^{y=1} y(1-y)\,dy$$

$$= 72x^2(1-x)\left[\frac{1}{2} - \frac{1}{3}\right] = 12x^2(1-x)$$

The calculation can also be done using Maple. The result looks a bit different, but is algebraically the same.

```
jointdensity;
```

$$72 \text{ x}^2 (1 - \text{x}) \text{ y } (1 - \text{y})$$

```
Xdensity:=int(jointdensity,y=0..1);
```

$$\text{Xdensity} := - 12 \text{ x}^2 (- 1 + \text{x})$$ ∎

    We may extend the definition of conditional probability distribution to the idea of the conditional density of Y given X. Just as we define the conditional probability distribution in the discrete case as the ratio of the joint probability $P_{XY}(x, y)$ to the marginal probability $P_X(x)$, we can define the conditional density as

$$f_{Y|X}(y|x) = \frac{f_{XY}(x, y)}{f_X(x)}$$

In particular, we can extend the definition of independence by saying that a continuous random variable Y is independent of another continuous random variable X if

$$f_{Y|X}(y|x) = f_Y(y)$$

or, equivalently, if $f_{XY}(x, y) = f_X(x)f_Y(y)$ for every x and y. If

$$f_{TU}(t, u) = .02(t+1)(t+2)(10-t)u^t(1-u) \qquad 0 < t < 10, 0 < u < 1$$

we have shown that $f_T(t) = .02(10-t)$, so

$$f_{U|T}(u|t) = \frac{f_{TU}(t, u)}{f_T(t)} = \frac{.02(t + 1)(t + 2)(10 - t)u^t(1 - u)}{.02(10 - t)}$$

$$= (t + 1)(t + 2)u^t(1 - u)$$

Because the conditional density of U given $T = t$ is a function of t as well as u, U is not independent of T.

E X A M P L E   4 . 2 7

Refer to Example 4.25. Are X and Y independent in this case?

Solution

We defined

$$f_{XY}(x, y) = 72x^2(1 - x)y(1 - y) \qquad 0 < x < 1, 0 < y < 1$$

In Example 4.26 we showed that

$$f_X(x) = 12x^2(1 - x)$$

so

$$f_{YX}(y, x) = \frac{72x^2(1 - x)y(1 - y)}{12x^2(1 - x)} = 6y(1 - y)$$

is a function only of y. (We must also be careful to notice that the range of definition of the formula for y is independent of x, as it is here.) Thus X and Y are independent.

Alternatively, we can calculate the marginal probability density of Y as $f_Y(y) = 6y(1 - y)$, for $0 < y < 1$. Thus

$$f_X(x)f_Y(y) = 12x^2(1 - x)6y(1 - y) \qquad 0 < x < 1, 0 < y < 1$$

$$= f_{XY}(x, y)$$

so once again X and Y are independent. ■

The definition of the covariance of two random variables X and Y indicated that we should multiply the deviation of x from the X mean times the deviation of y from the Y mean, multiply by the joint probability, and sum over all values. For the continuous case, replace the joint probability by the joint density and (here we go again) replace summation by integration.

Definition 4.12   Joint Probabilities for Continuous Random Variables

If X and Y are continuous random variables with joint probability density $f_{XY}(x, y)$, then

$$\text{Cov}(X, Y) = \int_{\text{all } x} \int_{\text{all } y} (x - \mu_X)(y - \mu_Y)f_{XY}(x, y)\, dy\, dx$$

A shortcut method is

$$\text{Cov}(X, Y) = \int_{\text{all } x} \int_{\text{all } y} xyf_{XY}(x, y)\, dy\, dx - \mu_X\mu_Y$$

The correlation of X and Y is once again their covariance divided by the product of their standard deviations. ■

We can use Maple to find the covariance and correlation for the joint density

$$f_{XY}(x, y) = (6/17)[4 - (x + y)^2] \qquad 0 < x < 1, 0 < y < 1$$

```
Xdensity:=int(jointdensity,y=0..1);
                              2    22
            Xdensity := - 6/17 x  + ---- - 6/17 x
                                    17

Xmean:=int(x*Xdensity,x=0..1);
                          15
                Xmean := ----
                          34

Xvariance:=int(x^2*Xdensity,x=0..1)-Xmean^2;
                          1351
             Xvariance := -----
                          17340

Ydensity:=int(jointdensity,x=0..1);
                              2    22
            Ydensity := - 6/17 y  + ---- - 6/17 y
                                    17

Ymean:=int(y*Ydensity,y=0..1);
                          15
                Ymean := ----
                          34

Yvariance:=int(y^2*Ydensity,y=0..1)-Ymean^2;
                          1351
             Yvariance := -----
                          17340

Covariance:=int(int(x*y*jointdensity,y=0..1),x=0..1)-Xmean*Ymean;
                            29
             Covariance := - ----
                            3468

Correlation:=Covariance/sqrt(Xvariance*Yvariance);
                            145
             Correlation := - ----
                            1351

evalf(Correlation);
                -.1073279053
```

EXERCISES

4.67 A daily newspaper in a small city keeps records of the column-inches of classified ads in a given weekday's paper. Saturday and Sunday editions have different patterns of ads and are excluded. The probabilities for Y = number of column-inches (in thousands) on a randomly chosen day are approximated by the density function

$$f_Y(y) = 30y^4(1 - y) \qquad 0 < y < 1$$

Note that $f_Y(y) = 0$ for y outside the range $0 < y < 1$.

a Calculate the density for $y = .1, .2, \ldots, .9$ and draw a sketch of the density.

b Find the probability that between 700 and 900 column-inches are used (that is, that $.7 < Y < .9$) in a randomly chosen day.

c Find the probability that $Y > .8$.

4.68 Find the mean and standard deviation of the number of column-inches used in Exercise 4.67 according to the probability density.

4.69 The newspaper in Exercise 4.67 also keeps track of X = number of column-inches of commercial ads (in thousands). The distribution of X appears to be

$$f_X(x) = (6/125)x(5 - x) \qquad 0 < x < 5$$

and zero for all other x.

a Find the cdf of X.

b Find the probability that X is at least 3.

c Find the mean and standard deviation of X.

4.70 The random variables X and Y in Exercises 4.67 and 4.69 appear (according to the records of the newspaper) to be independent of each other. If this is assumed, what is the correlation of X and Y?

4.71 A wholesale appliance dealer receives large lots of refrigerators and freezers from a manufacturer. One concern about each shipment is the proportion of "seconds"—appliances with minor defects (such as scratches) that must be sold at a lower price. The management science analyst for the dealer fit a complicated model for the joint density of X = proportion of seconds among refrigerators in a shipment and Y = proportion of seconds among freezers in the same shipment. Maple was used to carry out integration on the model, with the following results:

```
jointdensity;
            140857405920           17        13        4
            ----------- x y (1 - x)   (1 - y)   (1 - (x - y) )
              1960303

Xdensity:=int(jointdensity,y=0..1);
 Xdensity :=

    173052          17                   2      4        3
    ------- x (- 1 + x)   (- 76 x - 3871 + 513 x  + 3876 x  - 1938 x )
    1960303

Xmean:=int(x*Xdensity,x=0..1);
                               980123
                   Xmean := -------
                             9801515

Xvariance:=int(x^2*Xdensity,x=0..1)-(Xmean)^2;
                                  2879632663209
                  Xvariance := --------------
                               672487874066575

Ydensity:=int(jointdensity,x=0..1);
 Ydensity :=
    46512           13            3       2      4
    ------- y (- 1 + y)   (- 92 y - 3542 y  + 759 y  + 8855 y  - 8850)
    1960303
Ymean:=int(y*Ydensity,y=0..1);
                               244897
                   Ymean := -------
                            1960303

Yvariance:=int(y^2*Ydensity,y=0..1)-(Ymean)^2;
                                 123280262838
                  Yvariance := --------------
                               19213939259045

Covariance:=int(int(x*y*jointdensity,y=0..1),x=0..1)-Xmean*Ymean;
                                67921287
                  Covariance := --------------
                                15371151407236
```

```
Correlation:=Covariance/sqrt(Xvariance*Yvariance);
                              113202145
              Correlation := -----------------------------------
                             2021032414138585842297867476216740
```
                               1/2   1/2
         4382739155522166080582   516845646590379013060036835

```
evalf(Correlation);
                       .0008430136764
```

(Rather obviously, doing the integrals by hand would not be much fun.)

a Are X and Y independent?

b How strong a relation does there appear to be?

4.72 A company offering overseas telephone service believes that the key variable cost factors for a call are $X =$ number of seconds of computer time used in placing the call and $Y =$ number of minutes of operator time used in placing the call. The probability structure can be represented by the following joint density:

$$f_{XY}(x, y) = (.0625)xe^{-.5y-x/y} \qquad 0 < X < \infty, 0 < y < \infty$$

a Find $f_Y(y)$. From calculus, it is known that $\int_0^\infty xe^{-kx} = 1/k^2$.

b Find the conditional density of X given $Y = y$.

c In practice, should X and Y be independent? In this joint density, are they?

4.73 Find the conditional expected value of X, given $Y = y$, for the density given in Exercise 4.72.

4.74 Find the covariance of X and Y for the density in Exercise 4.72. ∎

4.9   Summing Up

Here are some suggestions for dealing with random variables and probability distributions. The ideas in this chapter combine the probability ideas from Chapter 3 and the summarization ideas from Chapter 2.

1 Decide whether the random variables are discrete—with distinct, separate possible values—or continuous—with an entire interval or range of possible values. Discrete random variables require addition; continuous ones, integration.

2 A random variable is determined by its possible values and their probabilities. Probabilities may be specified directly or calculated using the methods of Chapter 3.

3 The cumulative distribution function (cdf) is convenient for tables and is often used in computer packages. Probabilities can be found from cdfs by subtraction (in both discrete and continuous cases).

4 The expected value of a random variable is a generalization of the concept of a mean. It is found by weighting each value by its probability (or probability density) and summing (or integrating) over all possible values.

5 The variance and standard deviation of a random variable also are generalizations of concepts from Chapter 2, and also require the same weighting by probabilities.

6 Joint probabilities may be defined for two (or more) random variables. Marginal probabilities may be found for each variable separately by summing (or integrating) over the other variable or variables.

7 Covariance and correlation measure the extent to which random variables tend to vary together. They only reflect the degree of linear relation; if the relation is nonlinear, they understate the closeness of the relation.

8 Covariances enter the calculation of risk (variance) of a portfolio of investments and consideration of the trade-off of risk and return (expected profit). The smaller the correlation between investments, the more benefit there is in reducing risk.

In addition, you may want to reread the summary of key ideas at the beginning of the chapter.

EXAMPLE 4.28

An examination was undertaken of census tracts in the United States with at most five banks and at most five mortgage companies holding mortgages in the tract. This restriction tended to exclude urban areas with substantial competition among many lenders. The questions to be answered were: How many banks and mortgage companies typically serve these tracts? Is it generally true that such tracts are either largely bank served or largely mortgage company served? The number of banks and the number of mortgage companies has the joint distribution shown in the Excel spreadsheet results in Figure 4.13.

Solution

To see how many banks and mortgage companies "typically" serve such areas, look at the expected values. On average, there are 1.19 banks and 2.09 mortgage companies in these areas. There is considerable variation, as shown by the standard deviations.

If such areas were typically served largely by banks or largely by mortgage companies, there would be a negative correlation between the two: If there were a large number of banks, there would be a small number of mortgage companies, and vice versa. But in fact there is a small positive correlation between the two. Therefore, there is a slight tendency for the numbers of banks and mortgage companies to vary together. ■

SUPPLEMENTARY EXERCISES

4.75 A new car dealer offers three packages of optional equipment for a particular model. There is an automatic transmission package, with a profit of $200 to the dealer; an air-conditioning package, with a profit of $150; and an interior decor package, with a profit of $100. Data indicate that 80% of customers order the automatic transmission package; 60% of these also order the air-conditioning package, as do 50% of those who don't order automatic transmissions. Of those who order both of these packages, 40% order the interior decor package, as do 30% of those who order exactly one of the transmission and air-conditioning packages and 20% of those who order neither of the other packages. Let Y = number of packages ordered on a randomly chosen new car.

    a Find the probability distribution of Y.   **b** Find $P(Y \geq 2)$.

    c Find the cumulative distribution function of Y; use it to recalculate $P(Y \geq 2)$.

4.76 Find the mean and standard deviation of Y in Exercise 4.75.

4.77 Let X = profit from sales of optional packages for the dealer in Exercise 4.75. Note that X is not directly a function of Y because the profit depends not only on how many but also on which packages are sold.

    a Find the probability distribution of X.

    b Find the mean and standard deviation of X.

FIGURE 4.13   **Excel Results for Joint Probabilities**

	A	B	C	D	E	F	G	H	I	J	K	L	
2													
3				0	1	2	3	4	5	Total			
4	Number of banks												
5													
6			0	0.1	0.1	0.07	0.03	0.03	0.06	0.39		Exp. value	1.1900
7			1	0.03	0.09	0.07	0.04	0.01	0.04	0.28		Variance	1.7139
8			2	0.04	0.04	0.05	0.02	0.01	0.02	0.18		St. dev.	1.3092
9			3	0.02	0	0.02	0.01	0.01	0.03	0.09			
10			4	0.01	0	0	0	0.01	0	0.02			
11			5	0	0.02	0	0	0.01	0.01	0.04			
12		Total		0.2	0.25	0.21	0.1	0.08	0.16	1			
13													
14		Esp. value	2.090										
15		Variance	5.182										
16		St. dev.	2.276										
17													
18		Covariance	0.2729										
19		Correlation	0.0699										
20													

4.78 Consider the probability density function $f_Y(y) = 20(y^3 - y^4)$, $0 \leq y \leq 1$.

   a Find $E(y)$ and σ_Y. Use the shortcut formula

$$\sigma_Y^2 = \int_{\text{all } y} y^2 f_Y(y) \, dy - \mu_Y^2$$

   b By finding an area under the $f_Y(y)$ curve, find

$$P(\mu_Y - 2\sigma_Y \leq Y \leq \mu_Y + 2\sigma_Y)$$

4.79 A community college offers a wide variety of courses to a wide variety of students. The registrar of the college obtained information on the total number of credit hours for currently enrolled students. Most courses carry 3 hours of credit; others, such as laboratories, carry other numbers of credit hours. The information was converted into relative frequencies and analyzed by Excel, with the following results:

	A	B	C
1	Credit Hours	Probability	Cumulative
2	x	P(x)	F(x)
3	3	0.14	0.14
4	4	0.03	0.17
5	5	0.02	0.19
6	6	0.13	0.32
7	7	0.04	0.36
8	8	0.03	0.39
9	9	0.12	0.51
10	10	0.04	0.55
11	11	0.02	0.57
12	12	0.28	0.85
13	13	0.03	0.88
14	14	0.02	0.9
15	15	0.07	0.97
16	16	0.01	0.98
17	17	0.01	0.99
18	18	0.01	1
19			
20			
21	Exp. Value	9.23	
22	Variance	15.4971	
23	St. Dev.	3.9366	

   a Find the probability that X = number of credit hours of a randomly chosen student will be at least 9 (the minimum needed to be classified as a full-time student).

b If a student is classifed as full-time, what is the probability that the student receives exactly 9 credit hours?

c What is the actual probability that X is within 1 standard deviation of the mean? How well does the actual probability compare to the Empirical Rule approximation?

4.80 Construct a probability histogram of the distribution of credit hours in the previous exercise. What fact accounts for the rather odd shape?

4.81 As part of the production process of compact disk (CD) players, the assembled reading unit (a laser-based system that receives digital signals from the disk) is given an initial test. Any unit that fails in reading a test disk, usually because of misalignment, must be reworked at considerable expense. If Y is the proportion of passing units on a randomly chosen day, the probability density looks like

$$f_Y(y) = 3990y^{18}(1-y)^2 \qquad 0 < y < 1$$

a Calculate values of the density for $y = .70, .75, .80, .85, .90,$ and $.95$. Draw a rough sketch of the density.

b Find the value y that maximizes the density $f_Y(y)$ (or equivalently, the value y that maximizes the logarithm of the density). In other words, what is the mode of Y?

c Find the probability that at least 90% of the units pass the initial test on a randomly chosen day. Find the probability that no more than 85% pass.

4.82 **a** Find the expected value of Y for the density of Exercise 4.81.

b Find the standard deviation.

c In discussing control charts in Chapter 2, we set one of the control limits at the mean -3 standard deviations. What is the probability that Y will fall below this control limit?

4.83 Stock market analysts watch the "short interest" in the market carefully. An investor sells a stock short by borrowing shares from a broker to sell. The investor hopes that the stock's price will go down, so that the broker can be repaid with lower-priced shares. One analyst said that the distribution of X, the proportion of all sales that are short sales, is

$$f_X(x) = 272x(1-x)^{15} \qquad \text{for } 0 < x < 1$$

a Would you think that X would often be a large proportion like .8? If that happened, what would it mean about the stock market? Calculate a few values of $f_X(x)$. For which x values is the density relatively high?

b Find the probability that X is less than .10. (In doing the integration, you might find it convenient to substitute $w = 1 - x$, so that $dw = -dx$.)

4.84 **a** Find the expected value of X in Exercise 4.83. It is known from calculus that the integral from 0 to 1 of $x^a(1-x)^b$ is $a!b!/(a+b+1)!$

b Interpret the number you calculated in part a. In particular, is this the most likely value for the short-sale proportion, X?

c Find the variance and standard deviation of X. What does the numerical value of the standard deviation tell you about the reasonable range of values for X?

4.85 The analyst of Exercise 4.83 also considered $Y =$ daily proportion of sales to individual, noninstitutional investors. The conventional (and rather cynical) wisdom is that individual investors tend to buy at the worst times, right before declines in the stock market, so that high levels of individual purchases are a signal to sell stocks short. The analyst modeled the conditional density of Y given $X = x$ as

$$f_{Y|X}(y|x) = (x+8)(x+7)\cdots(x)y^{x-1}(1-y)^8 \qquad \text{for } 0 < y < 1$$

a Is the analyst assuming that X and Y are statistically independent? How can you tell?

b It can be shown that the expected value of Y given $X = x$ is an increasing function of x. Is this fact compatible with the conventional wisdom about individual investors and short sales?

4.86 A food delivery route for a chain of fast-food restaurants is scheduled to require 7 hours. Traffic jams and other problems usually extend the actual time to some degree. Records of the required time (in hours), Y, indicate that it may be treated as a continuous random variable with cumulative probability distribution

$$F_Y(y) = 1 - (y-6)^4 \qquad \text{for } y \geq 7$$

a The delivery driver must be paid overtime if the route requires more than 8 hours. What is the probability that overtime must be paid?

b If the route requires more than 9 hours, some of the restaurants run short of product. What is the probability that the route will require overtime, but will not cause restaurants to run short?

4.87 **a** Find the probability density of the random route time, Y, in Exercise 4.86.

b Use this density to find the probability that the route will be completed within 7.0 to 7.5 hours.

4.88 A direct-order retailer keeps track of the fraction of incoming calls each day that are answered within three rings. The quality target is that at least a proportion .80 of calls will be answered promptly. The daily proportion X may be treated as a continuous random variable with density

$$f_X(y) = 30(x^4 - x^5) \qquad \text{for } 0 < x < 1$$

a What is the probability that the quality target is met?

b A "disaster day" occurs when less than half of all calls are answered promptly. What is the probability of that disaster?

4.89 Refer again to X, the proportion of promptly answered calls, in Exercise 4.88. Given that the quality target is met, what is the probability that X will be less than .9?

4.90 The direct-order retailer in Exercise 4.88 also keeps track of the dollar amounts of all telephoned orders. The order size (in hundreds of dollars), Y, of a randomly chosen customer may be regarded as a continuous random variable with cumulative distribution function

$$F_Y(y) = 1 - e^{-2y} - 2ye^{-2y} \qquad \text{for } y > 0$$

a Find the probability that a randomly chosen customer will place an order of somewhere between $200 and $400.

b Special expediting is used for all orders larger than $1000. What is the probability that the next call will require some expediting?

4.91 **a** Find the probability density function $f_Y(y)$ of the order size Y in Exercise 4.90.

b Find the mode of Y—that is, the value y at which the density reaches its maximum.

4.92 A plumbing supply house sells large plumbing items such as tubs and shower stalls to individuals who visit the store, sometimes several times, before purchasing. The supply house keeps track of $X =$ the number of visits and $Y =$ the number of large items purchased. Here is an Excel spreadsheet showing the joint probabilities:

	B	C	D	E	F	G	H	I	J	K	L	M	N
2													
3													
4													
5					y								
6			0	1	2	3	4	5		P(x)			
7		1	0.2	0.05	0.03	0.02	0.05	0.15		0.5		mean(X)	1.7
8	x	2	0.1	0.05	0.02	0.03	0.04	0.06		0.3		var(X)	0.61
9		3	0.02	0.03	0.05	0.05	0.03	0.02		0.2			
10		P(y)	0.32	0.13	0.1	0.1	0.12	0.23					
11													
12			mean(Y)		2.26								
13			var(Y)		3.9924								
14			covar(X<Y)		0.058								

a Find the probability that a randomly chosen individual will make at least two visits and will purchase at least three large items.

b Are X and Y independent?

4.93 In the previous exercise, calculate the correlation of X and Y. Is there any reason why this number may not reflect the strength of the relation between X and Y adequately?

4.94 A state public health agency investigates reported unhealthful practices in restaurants, food stores, and the like. The number of cases varies week to week. The data indicate the following:

Number of cases/week:	0	1	2	3	4	5	6
Probability:	.02	.13	.20	.30	.19	.15	.01

a For Y = number of cases in a specified week, find $F_Y(y)$.

b Find $E(Y)$ and σ_Y.

c Find $P(\mu_Y - \sigma_Y \le Y \le \mu_Y + \sigma_Y)$. Compare to the Empirical Rule approximation.

4.95 A catalog retailer found the probability distribution for Y = the number of different orders placed by a particular customer in a calendar year. The results were analyzed using Excel, with the following results:

	A	B	C
1	Number Purchased	Probability	Cumulative
2	y	P(x)	F(x)
3	1	0.302	0.302
4	2	0.215	0.517
5	3	0.128	0.645
6	4	0.084	0.729
7	5	0.065	0.794
8	6	0.053	0.847
9	7	0.032	0.879
10	8	0.025	0.904
11	9	0.016	0.92
12	10	0.013	0.933
13	11	0.012	0.945
14	12	0.011	0.956
15	13	0.01	0.966
16	14	0.009	0.975
17	15	0.008	0.983
18	16	0.006	0.989
19	17	0.005	0.994
20	18	0.003	0.997
21	19	0.002	0.999
22	20	0.001	1
23			
24	Exp. Val		3.726
25	Variance		12.436924
26	St. dev.		3.5266023

a Find the probability that a randomly chosen customer will order at least 8 times in a year.

b If a customer orders at least 8 times in a year, what is the probability that the customer will order no more than 12 times?

4.96 Would you expect the Empirical Rule to be a good approximation for the probability distribution of number of orders in the previous exercise? What is the actual probability that Y is within 1 standard deviation of the mean?

4.97 An executive search firm (alias "headhunter") kept records on the fraction Y of the contracted time needed to place executives in the pharmaceutical industry. The probability density for Y is, to a very good approximation,

$$f_Y(y) = 72y^7(1-y) \qquad 0 < y < 1$$

a Find the probability that a placement will require somewhere between .6 and .8 of the contracted time. The following Maple output may be useful:

```
int(density,y=0..0.6);
                    .070543872
int(density,y=0..0.8);
                    .436207616
int(y*density,y=0..1);
                    4/5
int(y^2*density,y=0..1)-16/25;
                    4/275
```

b What are the expected value and standard deviation of the required search time?

4.98 For the search firm's probability distribution in the previous exercise, what is the mode (the value where the density is at its maximum)? Is the mode larger or smaller than the mean? What does the relation between mode and mean suggest about the skewness of the distribution?

4.99 The records of a small auto body repair shop indicate the following relative frequencies for the number of customers per day:

Number of customers:	0	1	2	3	4	5	6
Relative frequency:	.21	.38	.20	.11	.06	.03	.01

Let Y = number of customers on one particular day.

a Calculate $F_Y(y)$.

b Find $E(Y)$ and σ_Y.

4.100 Assume that the numbers of customers on successive days in Exercise 4.99 are independent. Let Y_1 and Y_2 be the respective numbers of customers on two consecutive days.

a Construct a table for $P_{Y_1 Y_2}(y_1, y_2)$.

b Define $S = Y_1 + Y_2$, the 2-day total number of customers. Find $P_S(s)$.

c Calculate $E(S)$ and σ_S.

4.101 In Chapter 3, we considered a baseball card collector who preferred cards of National League players—50% of all players. A proposed strategy was to buy cards until she obtained one National League card. Define X to be the total number of cards she obtains before getting the National Leaguer.

a What are the possible values of x? In particular, what does it mean for x to be 1?

b What is $P(X = 1)$?

c What must happen in order to have $x = 2$?

d Find $P(X = 2)$ and then a general expression for $P_X(x)$.

4.102 In the previous exercise, what should be $E(X)$? Remember that in the population there are as many National League cards as American League cards.

4.103 The Excel spreadsheet was programmed to simulate 1000 purchases of baseball cards, as in the two previous exercises. The following frequencies and summary numbers were obtained:

	A	B
1	Bin	Frequency
2	1	501
3	2	255
4	3	131
5	4	53
6	5	32
7	6	15
8	7	4
9	8	3
10	9	1
11		
12	Mean	1.939759
13	Median	1
14	Mode	1
15	Std. Dev.	1.281639

Compare the frequencies (divided by 1000) to the probability distribution of X. What simulation result should be compared to $E(X)$, as found in the previous exercise?

4.104 An automobile manufacturer keeps records on the number of first-year repairs made under warranty for a particular sport utility model. Define X = number of motor/transmission repairs and Y = number of body repairs. The frequencies are as follows:

		y		
x	0	1	2	3
0	.25	.08	.04	.00
1	.22	.15	.05	.01
2	.05	.05	.06	.01
3	.00	.00	.01	.01

   a Calculate marginal probability distributions for X and for Y.

   b Show that X and Y are not independent.

4.105   **a** From the appearance of the joint probabilities in the previous exercise, does it seem that the correlation between X and Y should be positive, negative, or zero?

     b Calculate the means of both random variables and their covariance.

     c Calculate the standard deviations of both random variables and their correlation.

4.106   Users of a computerized database have established that X = number of thousands of lines of instructions and Y = time in minutes required to run the program have joint density

$$f_{XY}(x, y) = (3/320)(16 - 4x^2 - y^2 + 4xy) \qquad 0 < x < 2, 0 < y < 4$$

     a Find the probability that both X and Y will be less than .5.

     b Find the probability that Y will be larger than 1. (X could take any value.)

4.107   **a** Calculate the marginal density of X for the joint density given in Exercise 4.106.

     b Find $f_{Y|X}(y|x)$.

4.108   Considering their nature, should the random variables X and Y in Exercise 4.106 be independent? According to Exercise 4.107, are they?

4.109   Maple output for the joint density follows:

```
Xdensity:=int(jointdensity,y=0..4);
                                    2
                Xdensity := 2/5 - 3/20 x  + 3/10 x

Xmean:=int(x*Xdensity,x=0..2);
                        Xmean := 1

Xvariance:=int(x^2*Xdensity,x=0..2)-Xmean^2;
                                23
                Xvariance := ----
                                75

Ydensity:=int(jointdensity,x=0..2);
                                            2
                Ydensity := 1/5 + 3/40 y - 3/160 y

Ymean:=int(y*Ydensity,y=0..4);
                        Ymean := 2

Yvariance:=int(y^2*Ydensity,y=0..4);
                                392
                Yvariance := ---
                                75

Covariance:=int(int(x*y*jointdensity,y=0..4),x=0..2)-Xmean*Ymean;
                Covariance := 2/15

Correlation:=Covariance/sqrt(Xvariance*Yvariance);
                                1/2
                Correlation := 5/322 46

evalf(Correlation);
                .1053156830
```

Locate the correlation. How does its value correspond to your answer in the previous exercise?

4.110 An insurance firm receives records semiannually from independent agents. From past data, a model for the joint density of X = proportion of records requiring a coverage update and Y = proportion of records requiring an address change is

$$f_{XY}(x, y) = 240xy(1 - x)^2(1 - y)^3 \qquad \text{for } 0 < x < 1, 0 < y < 1$$

a Find the probability that both X and Y are greater than .5.

b Find the probability that Y is between .1 and .3.

4.111 **a** Find the marginal densities of X and Y in Exercise 4.110.

b What does the covariance of X and Y equal?

4.112 An electrical cooperative normally serves customers from its own generating capacity. On some days—typically very hot ones—it must purchase electrical power at high cost from a grid linking to other power companies. The cooperative has kept track of the excess demand and believes that the joint density of X = excess demand for home use and Y = excess demand for business use (both in millions of kW peak) is

$$f_{XY}(x, y) = (3/320)(16 - 4x^2 - y^2 + 4xy) \qquad x > 0, y > 0$$

It can be proven that the expected value of X is .75, the expected value of Y is .1875, and $\int_{\text{all } x} \int_{\text{all } y} xy f_{XY}(x, y) \, dy \, dx = .1875$. Find the covariance of X and Y. Do these variables tend to vary together or in opposite directions?

4.113 An investment analyst must allocate a $1,000,000 fund among three given investments. Historically, each investment has averaged an 8% return. The standard deviations of the investment returns have been 2.5%, 3%, and 3.5%, respectively. The correlations of returns have been .50 (for investments 1 and 2), .60 (for 1 and 3), and $-.20$ (for 2 and 3). The analyst must choose among three possibilities: equal amounts to investments 1 and 2, equal amounts to 1 and 3, or equals amounts to 2 and 3. The investor does not like risk and proposes to invest all the money in the lowest-variation investment. Is this the lowest-variability strategy or does another possibility have lower variability?

4.114 Data are available on the historical performance of most common stocks and of various indexes of stocks. The following summary figures from Execustat refer to four common stocks, the Standard and Poor's 500 index, and five "sector" indexes, corresponding to the smallest one-fifth (S1) of the companies listed on the New York Stock Exchange at the beginning of June 1973, the next smallest one-fifth (S2), and so on. The data are monthly returns. So, for example, the average return on IBM stock is .0099 per month, or just about 1% per month.

One typical stock market strategy is to invest in a set of stocks that mimic an index such as the S&P 500. An investor asks you to use these results (and the assumption that the same patterns will hold in the future) to suggest reasonable choices of investment. The investor is considering investing solely in the S&P index or splitting the investment, half in the S&P index and half in one of the sectors. Alternatively, an investment could be made equally between WalMart and any of the other common stocks.

What are the consequences, in terms of average return and risk, of these alternatives?

Summary Statistics

	IBM	PACGE	VW
Sample size	119	119	119
Mean	0.00992269	0.0127185	0.0137697
Std. deviation	0.0591351	0.0483731	0.0497768

	WALMART	SP500	S1
Sample size	119	119	119
Mean	0.0366529	0.00978487	0.0180916
Std. deviation	0.0885852	0.0485713	0.0643936

```
                    S2              S3              S4

Sample size         119             119             119
Mean                0.0167244       0.0164025       0.0152824
Std. deviation      0.0609979       0.0575515       0.0546376

                    S5

Sample size         119
Mean                0.0137067
Std. deviation      0.0488148
```

Correlation Analysis

	IBM	PACGE	VW	WALMART	SP500
IBM		0.0807	0.6305	0.5000	0.6460
PACGE	0.0807		0.3249	0.2576	0.3116
VW	0.6305	0.3249		0.6963	0.9932
WALMART	0.5000	0.2576	0.6963		0.6823
SP500	0.6460	0.3116	0.9932	0.6823	
S1	0.5498	0.2468	0.8628	0.6829	0.8246
S2	0.5905	0.2819	0.9229	0.7122	0.8907
S3	0.5918	0.2892	0.9439	0.7179	0.9165
S4	0.5937	0.3187	0.9740	0.7200	0.9551
S5	0.6150	0.3431	0.9962	0.6898	0.9939

	S1	S2	S3	S4	S5
IBM	0.5498	0.5905	0.5918	0.5937	0.6150
PACGE	0.2468	0.2819	0.2892	0.3187	0.3431
VW	0.8628	0.9229	0.9439	0.9740	0.9962
WALMART	0.6829	0.7122	0.7179	0.7200	0.6898
SP500	0.8246	0.8907	0.9165	0.9551	0.9939
S1		0.9748	0.9528	0.9106	0.8358
S2	0.9748		0.9861	0.9629	0.9021
S3	0.9528	0.9861		0.9803	0.9264
S4	0.9106	0.9629	0.9803		0.9648
S5	0.8358	0.9021	0.9264	0.9648	

Probability Distributions

A regional bank was interested in new products and services to expand its customer base. One suggested product was a debit card. This card works like a credit card in that a cardholder presents it to a merchant as payment. The difference is that the cardholder keeps a balance in an account, and the debit card payments are deducted from this account directly, rather than the cardholder effectively borrowing from a bank, which is the case with credit cards. The cardholder does not pay interest on a loan when using a debit card, but the holder must have sufficient funds in the bank to use the card. The bank usually does not charge fees for a debit card; it makes its profit on the difference between interest earned on the cardholder's funds and the costs of servicing the account.

A product manager for the bank carried out a survey of 2150 current bank customers. You are assigned to do a careful analysis of three items from the survey: the reported number of cards in active use by the customer, the reported number of cards that usually have some unpaid balance after a payment, and the reported number of debit cards that the customer would like to have. If we call these items X, Y, and Z, respectively, the survey data yield the following frequencies:

x:	0	0	0	1	1	1	1	1	1	2	2	2	2	2	2
y:	0	0	0	0	0	0	1	1	1	0	0	0	1	1	1
z:	0	1	2	0	1	2	0	1	2	0	1	2	0	1	2
Freq.:	98	45	10	125	110	28	171	203	38	96	87	18	150	228	66

x:	2	2	2	3	3	3	3	3	3	3	3	3	3	3	3
y:	2	2	2	0	0	0	1	1	1	2	2	2	3	3	3
z:	0	1	2	0	1	2	0	1	2	0	1	2	0	1	2
Freq.:	43	160	51	11	15	10	37	78	29	13	51	22	10	23	34

The product manager had a hunch that customers with few cards in active use and customers who had few cards with unpaid balances would like to have more debit cards than those with many cards or with many unpaid balances. Use the survey results as if they perfectly represented the entire population of the bank's current customers (thereby ignoring all variation due to sampling) to investigate these hunches. Write a brief report to the product manager explaining your findings; you should prepare a 1-paragraph summary, followed by supporting evidence. The product manager doesn't remember probability theory, so be careful with your use of technical language. ■

Professional parents McHugh
Had children without much ado;
Had triplets and quints
With nary a wince,
Thus giving the data a skew.

Properties of Expected Values and Variances

A

I n this section, we present some simple mathematical results about expected values and variances. The results are stated in the language of random variables. Because the notions of expected value and variance of a random variable are generalizations of the corresponding population concepts, the same results apply to populations.

The first results deal with the effect of adding or subtracting a constant. In analyzing the probable return on an investment, there must be a close relation between the gross return (which does not consider the original investment outlay) and net return (which subtracts that outlay).

Definition 4.13   Effect of Adding a Constant

If a is any constant and Y is any random variable,

$$E(Y + a) = E(Y) + a$$

$$\text{Var}(Y + a) = \text{Var}(Y) \qquad \sigma_{Y+a} = \sigma_Y \qquad \blacksquare$$

If Y is the gross return and l is the investment outlay, then the expected net return $E(Y - l)$ is, reasonably enough, the expected gross return less the investment, $E(Y) - l$. The variances of gross and net return are equal and therefore the standard deviations are also equal. The effect of subtracting l is to shift the whole probability histogram to the left by l units; because that shifting doesn't alter the spread of the histogram, the variance is unchanged. It is fairly easy to prove these two results:

$$E(Y + a) = \sum_{\text{all } y}(y + a)P_Y(y)$$

$$= \sum_{\text{all } y} yP_Y(y) + \sum_{\text{all } y} aP_Y(y)$$

$$= E(Y) + a \sum_{\text{all } y} P_Y(y)$$

$$= E(Y) + a \qquad \text{because } \sum_{\text{all } y} P_Y(y) = 1$$

$$\text{Var}(Y + a) = \sum_{\text{all } y}[(y + a) - E(Y + a)]^2 P_Y(y)$$

$$= \sum_{\text{all } y}[(y + a) - (E(Y) + a)]^2 P_Y(y)$$

$$= \sum_{\text{all } y}[y - E(Y)]^2 P_Y(y)$$

$$= \text{Var}(Y)$$

Another set of results deals with multiplying or dividing by a constant. This mathematical operation is simply a change in the scale of measurement. For instance, multiplying a dollar amount by 100 changes the amounts to units of cents.

Definition 4.14   Effect of Multiplying by a Constant

If c is any constant and Y any random variable,

$$E(cY) = cE(Y)$$

$$\text{Var}(cY) = c^2\text{Var}(Y) \qquad \sigma_{cY} = |c|\sigma_Y$$

If c_1 and c_2 are constants and Y_1 and Y_2 are random variables,

$$\text{Cov}(c_1Y_1, c_2Y_2) = c_1c_2\text{Cov}(Y_1, Y_2) \qquad \blacksquare$$

If $c = 100$ and Y is the cost in dollars, then cY is the cost in cents. The expected cost in cents $E(cY)$ is 100 times the expected cost in dollars, $cE(Y)$. The variance is multiplied by $10,000 = (100)^2$ because variance is average squared error; once we take square roots, the standard deviation of the cost in cents σ_{cY} is 100 times the standard deviation of cost in dollars, $c\sigma_Y$.[3] The proof is a matter of writing down the definitions of expected value, variance, and covariance, and then factoring out c, c^2, and c_1c_2, respectively.

E X A M P L E   4 . 2 9

A U.S. firm has an investment opportunity in France. The initial outlay is 5,000,000 francs. The firm estimates that the gross return Y has an expected value of 6,200,000 francs and a standard deviation of 500,000 francs. Find the expected value and standard deviation of the net return in dollars, assuming an exchange rate of 5 francs to the dollar.

Solution

One way to proceed is to work first with net return in francs, then convert to dollars. The net return is $Y - 5,000,000$, so it has expected value $E(Y) - 5,000,000$, or 1,200,000 francs, and the standard deviation of 500,000 francs is unchanged. To convert to dollars, divide both the expected value and standard deviation of Y by 5. The expected net return is \$240,000 and the standard deviation is \$100,000. $\blacksquare$

The last mathematical results we present involve adding two random variables. This operation arises in a wide variety of situations—the total return on two different investments, the total of cardiac and trauma cases in an emergency room, the total daily output from two automobile assembly lines. Of course, there's nothing magical about adding *two* random variables; the results extend immediately to any number of random variables.

Definition 4.15   Mean and Variance for Sums of Random Variables

For any random variables X and Y,

$$E(X + Y) = E(X) + E(Y)$$

$$\text{Var}(X + Y) = \text{Var}(X) + 2\,\text{Cov}(X, Y) + \text{Var}(Y)$$

If X and Y are independent, then

$$\text{Var}(X + Y) = \text{Var}(X) + \text{Var}(Y) \qquad \sigma_{X+Y} = \sqrt{\text{Var}(X) + \text{Var}(Y)} \qquad \blacksquare$$

---

[3] The absolute value in the standard deviation formula takes care of multiplying by a negative number. Notice that $\sqrt{(-5)^2}$ is +5.

The proof of these results is a bit longer than the other proofs, but not difficult.

$$E(X + Y) = \sum_{\text{all } x} \sum_{\text{all } y} (x + y) P_{XY}(x, y)$$

$$= \sum_{\text{all } x} \sum_{\text{all } y} x P_{XY}(x, y) + \sum_{\text{all } x} \sum_{\text{all } y} y P_{XY}(x, y)$$

In the first double sum, think of summing over y first:

$$\sum_{\text{all } y} x P_{XY}(x, y) = x \sum_{\text{all } y} P_{XY}(x, y) = x P_X(x)$$

by definition of the marginal distribution $P_X(x)$. So the first double sum reduces to $\sum_{\text{all } x} x P_X(x) = E(X)$. A similar argument shows that the second double sum is $E(Y)$, which proves the expected value result.

The variance result proceeds by expanding the square. Recall that $(a + b)^2 = a^2 + 2ab + b^2$.

$$\text{Var}(X + Y) = \sum_{\text{all } x} \sum_{\text{all } y} (x + y - \mu_{X+Y})^2 P_{XY}(x, y)$$

$$= \sum_{\text{all } x} \sum_{\text{all } y} (x - \mu_X + y - \mu_Y)^2 P_{XY}(x, y)$$

because we just proved that $\mu_{X+Y} = \mu_X + \mu_Y$. Now expand the square with $a = x - \mu_X$ and $b = y - \mu_Y$:

$$\text{Var}(X + Y) = \sum_{\text{all } x} \sum_{\text{all } y} (x - \mu_X)^2 P_{XY}(x, y)$$

$$+ 2 \sum_{\text{all } x} \sum_{\text{all } y} (x - \mu_X)(y - \mu_Y) P_{XY}(x, y)$$

$$+ \sum_{\text{all } x} \sum_{\text{all } y} (y - \mu_Y)^2 P_{XY}(x, y)$$

The first double sum is

$$\sum_{\text{all } x} (x - \mu_X)^2 \left[\sum_{\text{all } y} P_{XY}(x, y) \right] = \sum_{\text{all } x} (x - \mu_X)^2 P_X(x)[1] = \text{Var}(X)$$

The same procedure shows that the third double sum is $\text{Var}(Y)$. The second double sum is $2 \, \text{Cov}(X, Y)$ by the definition of covariance given in Section 4.7. Therefore, in general,

$$\text{Var}(X + Y) = \text{Var}(X) + 2 \, \text{Cov}(X, Y) + \text{Var}(Y)$$

In Section 4.7, we showed that $\text{Cov}(X, Y) = 0$ when X and Y are independent (as well as in some other cases). Therefore, if X and Y are independent, the covariance term in $\text{Var}(X + Y)$ drops out, and we have $\text{Var}(X + Y) = \text{Var}(X) + \text{Var}(Y)$.

B

Some Reminders About Calculus

C alculus methods are not critical to understanding the essential ideas of this text, but there are a few occasions when it is convenient to use some basic concepts from calculus. This appendix gives a quick refresher in basic calculus methods; it is not intended as an introduction to calculus.

The first key concept is **function**. Informally, a function assigns an "output" number (say, w) to an "input" number (say, x) according to a specified rule. Because we want to reserve the letters f and F for other uses, we use g or G to indicate a function; we write $w = g(x)$.

The **derivative** of a function g at a point $x = a$ is informally defined as the slope of g when $x = a$. We may think of a line tangent to the curve $w = g(x)$ at $x = a$, as in Figure 4.14. The derivative is the slope of the tangent line. The derivative is denoted

$$\frac{d}{dx}g(x)$$

or $g'(x)$. We have no need to emphasize the particular value $x = a$ that is being considered. A very brief table of derivatives is given in Table 4.1.

F I G U R E 4 . 1 4   **Tangent Line at $x = a$**

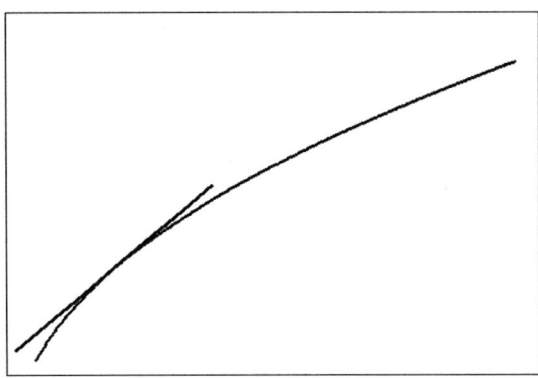

T A B L E 4 . 1   **Elementary Derivatives**

$g(x)$	$\dfrac{d}{dx}g(x)$
c, a constant	0
x^n	nx^{n-1}
e^x	e^x
e^{cx}	ce^{cx}
$\log_e(x)$	$\dfrac{1}{x}$
$ag_1(x) + bg_2(x)$	$a\dfrac{d}{dx}g_1(x) + b\dfrac{d}{dx}g_2(x)$
$g_1(x)g_2(x)$	$g_1(x)\left[\dfrac{d}{dx}g_2(x)\right] + g_2(x)\left[\dfrac{d}{dx}g_1(x)\right]$

We sometimes use the **chain rule** for composite functions—functions that are defined in stages; that is, some functions may be thought of as taking an input x, transforming it to an intermediate value $w = g_1(x)$, and then transforming w to a final value $v = g_2(w)$. We write such a two-stage function as

$$v = g_2[g_1(x)]$$

For example,

$$v = e^{x^2}$$

can be thought of as a two-stage function. Transform x to $w = x^2$; then transform w to

$$v = e^w = e^{x^2}$$

Alternatively, we write $w = g_1(x) = x^2$ and $v = g_2(w) = e^w$, so $v = g_1[g_2(x)]$. For such "stage-wise" functions, the derivative also goes in stages. First, find the derivative of $g_2(w)$, evaluated at $w = g_1(x)$; next multiply by the derivative of $g_1(x)$. Together, the chain rule asserts that

$$\frac{d}{dx}g_2[g_1(x)] = \left\{\frac{d}{dw}g_2[w = g_1(x)]\right\}\left[\frac{d}{dx}g_1(x)\right]$$

For $g(x) = e^{x^2}$, take $w = g_1(x) = x^2$ and $v = g_2(w) = e^2$. Then

$$\frac{d}{dx}g(x) = \left[\frac{d}{dw}e^w\right]\left[\frac{d}{dx}x^2\right]$$

$$= [e^w][2x] = 2xe^{x^2}$$

from elementary derivatives.

One of the important uses of derivatives is in finding relative maxima and minima. In Figure 4.15, notice that at both the peaks and the valleys of the function $g(x)$, the slope (derivative) of $g(x)$ is zero.

Thus, to locate a maximum or minimum of $g(x)$, we must solve the equation $(d/dx)g(x) = 0$ for x. In our problems it is usually obvious whether a particular solution is a minimum or a maximum; more sophisticated analyses (such as second-derivative tests) are not needed.

The characteristics of derivatives discussed so far may be extended to functions of several variables, such as

$$w = g(x_1, x_2, x_3) = x_1^2 e^{3x_2} + \log_e(x_3)$$

partial derivatives

We may take **partial derivatives** with respect to each variable by (temporarily) treating the other variables as constants. Partial derivative notation is, for example,

$$\frac{\partial}{\partial x_2}[x_1^2 e^{3x_2} + \log_e(x_3)]$$

In this example, x_1 (and thus x_1^2) and x_3 [and thus $\log_e(x_3)$] should be taken as constants—say, c_1 and c_3. Thus

$$\frac{\partial}{\partial x_2}(c_1 e^{3x_2} + c_3) = c_1 \frac{\partial}{\partial x_2}(e^{3x_2}) + c_3$$

$$= c_1(e^{3x_2})(3) + 0 = 3x_1^2 e^{3x_2}$$

FIGURE 4.15   **Derivative Is Zero at Minima and Maxima**

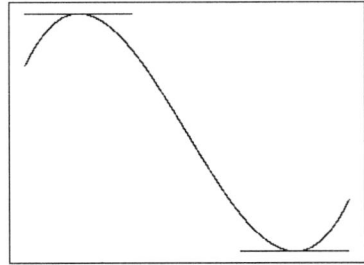

where we have applied the chain rule to get

$$\frac{\partial}{\partial x_2}e^{3x_2} = (e^{3x_2})\frac{\partial}{\partial x_2}(3x_2) = (e^{3x_2})(3)$$

To find a maximum or minimum of a function of several variables, we must equate *all* partial derivatives to zero and solve the resulting set of equations for the values of all the variables. In our problems, it is obvious whether the solution is a minimum or a maximum. To find a minimum or maximum of

$$w = g(x_1, x_2) = (x_1 - 4)^2 + (2x_1 + x_2 - 4)^2$$

we must solve the two equations

$$\frac{\partial}{\partial x_1}[(x_1 - 4)^2 + (2x_1 + x_2 - 4)^2] = 2(x_1 - 4) + 4(2x_1 + x_2 - 4) = 0$$

and

$$\frac{\partial}{\partial x_2}[(x_1 - 4)^2 + (2x_1 + x_2 - 4)^2] = 2(2x_1 + x_2 - 4) = 0$$

and obtain $x_1 = 4$ and $x_2 = -4$. We note that $g(x_1, x_2)$ is never negative and that $g(4, -4) = (4 - 4)^2 + [2(4) + (-4) - 4]^2 = 0$. Therefore, we have clearly found the only minimum of g; because the given solution is the only one, there is no finite maximum of g.

In addition to a need for differential (derivative) calculus, we have some use for integral calculus. In general, we need to evaluate **definite integrals** of the form

definite integrals

$$\int_a^b g(x)dx$$

Recall that a definite integral is the area under the curve defined by $g(x)$ between the points a and b, as shown in Figure 4.16. The standard way to evaluate definite integrals is to appeal to the Fundamental Theorem of Calculus. According to this theorem, we should

antiderivative

1 Find a function $G(x)$ having derivative $g(x)$—called the **antiderivative** of $g(x)$.

2 Evaluate $\int_a^b g(x)\,dx = G(x)\Big|_a^b = G(b) - G(a)$.

A few of the most useful antiderivatives are shown in Table 4.2.

For example, to evaluate $\int_1^4 2e^{-2x}\,dx$, we find the antiderivative of $g(x) = e^{-2x}$ to be $G(x) = e^{-2x}/(-2)$ and note that the antiderivative of $2e^{-2x}$ is $2e^{-2x}/(-2) = -e^{-2x}$. It follows that

$$\int_1^4 2e^{-2x}\,dx = -e^{-2x}\Big|_1^4 = [-e^{-2(4)}] - [-e^{-2(1)}] = e^{-2} - e^{-8}$$

F I G U R E 4 . 1 6   **Integral as Area**

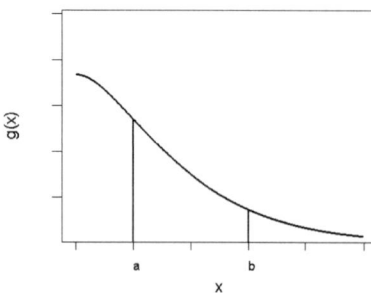

Antiderivatives for Integration

Function, $g(x)$	Antiderivative, $G(x)$
$(x+c)^n, n \neq -1$	$(x+c)^{n+1}/(n+1)$
x^{-1}	$\log_e(x)$
e^{cx}	e^{cx}/c
xe^{cx}	$xe^{cx}/c - e^{cx}/c^2$
$c_1 g_1(x) + c_2 g_2(x)$	$c_1 G_1(x) + c_2 G_2(x)$
$c_n x^n + c_{n-1}x^{n-1} + \cdots + c_0$	$c_n x^{n+1}/(n+1) + c_{n-1}x^n/n + \cdots + c_0 x$

Occasionally, we need to evaluate integrals with infinite endpoints, such as

$$\int_0^\infty g(x)\, dx = \lim_{M \to \infty} \int_0^M g(x)\, dx$$

assuming that the limit exists. The evaluation of the limit is usually clear, but it can sometimes be tricky. Consider the integral (see Table 4.2)

$$\int_0^\infty xe^{-x}\, dx = \int_0^\infty xe^{(-1)x}\, dx = [xe^{-x}/(-1) - e^{-x}/(-1)^2]\Big|_0^\infty$$

The problem is in evaluating $-xe^{-x}|_0^\infty$. As $x \to \infty$, $e^{-x} \to 0$ and $x \to \infty$, so that the limit of xe^{-x} (as $x \to \infty$) is "$0 \cdot \infty$." An application of a theorem of calculus called L'Hôpital's Rule indicates that $e^{-x} \to 0$ faster than $x \to \infty$, so

$$\lim_{x \to \infty} xe^{-x} = 0$$

Thus,

$$\int_0^\infty xe^{-x}\, dx = (0 - 0) - [0 - (-1)] = 1$$

Finally, we need to evaluate double integrals $\int_a^b \int_c^d g(x_1, x_2)\,dx_1\,dx_2$. Under certain technical conditions (which are always met in our situations), double integrals may be evaluated in two steps. First, regard x_2 as a constant c_2 and perform the integral with respect to x_1. Then integrate the result with respect to x_2. The integral may also be done in the reverse order, with respect to x_2 first, then x_1. For example, we may use the fact that the antiderivative of $(x+c)^n$ is $(x+c)^{n+1}/(n+1)$ to evaluate

$$\int_0^1 \int_0^2 (x_1 + 2x_2)^2 dx_1\, dx_2 = \int_0^1 \left[\int_0^2 (x_1 + 2x_2)^2 dx_1 \right] dx_2$$

$$= \int_0^1 \frac{(x_1 + 2x_2)^3}{3} \bigg|_0^2 dx_2$$

$$= \int_0^1 \left[\frac{(2 + 2x_2)^3}{3} - \frac{(0 + 2x_2)^3}{3} \right] dx_2$$

$$= \left[\frac{8(1 + x_2)^4}{12} - \frac{8(x_2)^4}{12} \right] \bigg|_0^1$$

$$= \left[\frac{8(2)^4}{12} - \frac{8(1)^4}{12} \right] - \left[\frac{8(1)^4}{12} - \frac{8(0)^4}{12} \right]$$

$$= 9.3333$$

We can also integrate with respect to x_2 first, then with respect to x_1; the result is once again 9.3333.

5

Some Special Probability Distributions

This chapter introduces some special probability distributions that apply to many managerial situations. There are, of course, many more, but these distributions cover a wide range of such applications. The key concepts are:

1 We have methods for counting the number of sequences (where order matters) and subsets (where order doesn't matter) of a specified number of items chosen from a larger set. These methods allow us to determine probabilities where equally likely outcomes are assumed. In particular, these methods yield hypergeometric probabilities when sampling with replacement.

2 When an experiment consists of a specified number of distinct success/failure trials, binomial probabilities may apply. Two assumptions that must be checked for reasonableness are constant probability of success over trials, and independence of the results from one trial to the next. The independence assumption is numerically most crucial. Positive dependence from one trial to the next yields more variability than that given by the binomial model.

3 If the nature of the experiment specifies a fixed, predetermined number of successes rather than a fixed number of trials, negative binomial (or, as a special case, geometric) probabilities may apply. The same assumptions as in the binomial case must be checked for reasonableness.

4 When an experiment consists of counting the number of randomly occurring events over a specified length of time, Poisson probabilities may apply. Two assumptions that must be checked for reasonableness are "nonclumping"—that events do not occur together—and independence over time. Violation of either assumption tends to yield more variability than that given by the Poisson model.

5 If the question is the time until the next random event, and if the Poisson assumptions are met, exponential probabilities apply.

6 Many measurements yield approximately a bell-shaped, normal probability distribution. This distribution arises whenever the random variable is a sum or average of many measurements, as well as by construction. Whether it, in fact, is a good approximation should be checked by a histogram or other data plot.

7 For all these distributions, probability tables or computer programs may be used to calculate probabilities. For all these probability models, expected values and standard deviations can be found using shortcut formulas.

The ideas, notations, and results of the previous chapter apply to any random variables and any probability distributions. Now we identify and present formulas for particular probability distributions that often arise in practice. In particular, we describe the kind of situation and the critically important assumptions that justify the use of each distribution. ■

Counting Possible Outcomes

A mong the most common probability distributions that apply to several managerial situations is taking a random sample. As we suggested when we discussed the classical interpretation of probability, we have considerable use for the idea that

$$P(\text{event}) = \frac{\text{number of outcomes favoring event}}{\text{total number of outcomes}}$$

To use this idea, we need a method for counting possible outcomes without the labor of actually listing the outcomes. This section contains a brief discussion of counting formulas. These formulas are also needed for the development of the binomial probability distribution discussed in the next section. The counting methods arise as answers to the following two questions:

sequences

1 How many **sequences** of k symbols can be formed from a set of r distinct symbols, using each symbol no more than once?

subsets

2 How many **subsets** of k symbols can be formed from a set of r distinct symbols, using each symbol no more than once?

The only difference between a sequence and a subset is that order matters for sequences and not for subsets. The sequence ABC is not the same as the sequence CAB, but the subset {A, B, C} is the same as the subset {C, A, B}. As an example, consider sequences and subsets consisting of three of the first five letters. There are 60 sequences but only 10 subsets (Table 5.1).

$$\text{number of sequences} = r(r-1)\cdots(r-k+1)$$

For example, to choose a sequence of $k = 3$ letters from $r = 5$ letters, as in Table 5.1, we have 5 choices for the first letter, 4 for the second, and 3 for the third. There are $5 \times 4 \times 3 = 60$ different sequences.

The sequences formula looks like a factorial ($r!$) except that it is truncated at $r - k + 1$ instead of continuing down to 1. The number of sequences is often called the number of

permutations

permutations of r symbols taken k at a time, and we denote it as $_kP_r$ or r_k. It can be expressed via factorials as

$$_kP_r = \frac{r!}{(r-k)!} = r(r-1)\cdots(r-k+1)$$

combinations

The number of subsets is called the number of **combinations** of r symbols taken k at a time and is denoted as $_kC_r$ or $\binom{r}{k}$.

$$\binom{r}{k} = \frac{r!}{k!(r-k)!}$$

For example, to choose a subset of $k = 3$ letters from $r = 5$ letters, as in Table 5.1, we have

$$\binom{5}{3} = \frac{5!}{3!(5-3)!} = \frac{5 \times 4 \times 3 \times 2 \times 1}{(3 \times 2 \times 1)(2 \times 1)} = 10$$

The symbol $\binom{r}{k}$ is read "r choose k," suggesting a choice of a subset of k things from a set of r things.

TABLE 5.1 **Subsets and Sequences of the Five Letters A, B, C, D, and E**

Subsets	Sequences					
{A,B,C}	ABC	ACB	BAC	CAB	BCA	CBA
{A,B,D}	ABD	ADB	BAD	DAB	BDA	DBA
{A,B,E}	ABE	AEB	BAE	EAB	BEA	EBA
{A,C,D}	ACD	ADC	CAD	DAC	CDA	DCA
{A,C,E}	ACE	AEC	CAE	EAC	CEA	ECA
{A,D,E}	ADE	AED	DAE	EAD	DEA	EDA
{B,C,D}	BCD	BDC	CBD	DBC	CDB	DCB
{B,C,E}	BCE	BEC	CBE	EBC	CEB	ECB
{B,D,E}	BDE	BED	DBE	EBD	DEB	EDB
{C,D,E}	CDE	CED	DCE	ECD	DEC	EDC

The combinations formula is particularly useful in random sampling because choosing a sample of size k without replacement from a population of size r is exactly the same as choosing a subset of k things from a set of r things. We do not typically care about the ordering of items during sampling, so the permutation formula is somewhat less central. There are many uses for these ideas in probability theory; games of chance in particular can often be figured out with these formulas. However, we won't go deeply into such applications.

Very often, we must count the number of ways that we can obtain *two* subsets. For example, if we have a total of 920 good items and 80 bad items, how many ways are there to choose 12 good and 4 bad items? Order doesn't matter, so we're considering subsets. We can choose the good items in $\binom{920}{12}$ ways and the bad items in $\binom{80}{4}$ ways. Any choice of good items can be put together with any choice of bad ones; to find the number of ways of choosing 12 good items *and* 4 bad ones, multiply. There are $\binom{920}{12}\binom{80}{4}$ ways of making the choices.

E X A M P L E   5 . 1

In auditing the 87 accounts payable of a small firm, a sample of 10 account balances is checked. How many possible samples are there? If we assume that 13 of the accounts contain errors, how many samples contain exactly 2 erroneous accounts?

Solution

There is no need to consider the sequence (order) in which the 10 accounts are drawn because all 10 are checked. Therefore, we can count the number of combinations. There are $\binom{87}{10} = \frac{87!}{10!77!} \approx 4,000,000,000,000$ possible samples. To obtain all samples with 2 erroneous accounts, we can combine any of the $\binom{13}{2}$ choices of 2 from the 13 erroneous accounts with any of the $\binom{74}{8}$ choices of 8 from the 74 correct accounts. Because any choice of 2 erroneous accounts can be matched with any choice of 8 correct ones, we must multiply these numbers together. There are $\binom{13}{2}\binom{74}{8} \approx 1,200,000,000,000$ samples with 2 erroneous and 8 correct accounts. ∎

E X A M P L E   5 . 2

In a sales contest, the 10 top performers out of 612 salespeople receive prizes ranging from a free vacation for the overall winner to \$50 for the tenth-place finisher. How many different prize lists are possible?

Solution

Here the ordering is certainly relevant, so the permutation formula applies. There are $_{10}P_{612} = 612!/602! \approx 6,800,000,000,000,000,000,000,000,000$ possibilities. ∎

E X E R C I S E S

5.1 In a certain state, an appeals court consists of seven judges. For a routine case, three judges are chosen at random as a panel to hear a case and render a decision. How many distinct panels can be formed?

5.2 Suppose that five of the seven judges on the appeals court in Exercise 5.1 are considered potentially sympathetic to a particular legal argument. How many panels can be formed having exactly two potentially sympathetic judges? How many panels have at least two such judges?

5.3 A grocery chain wants to taste-test a private-label cola drink. A tester is given eight unmarked glasses, four containing the private-label drink and four containing a nationally advertised cola. The tester is asked to identify the four glasses containing the private-label drink. How many different choices of four glasses can the taster make?

5.4 How many of the choices in Exercise 5.3 include three correct glasses and one incorrect glass?   ∎

5.2

Bernoulli Trials and the Binomial Distribution

The simplest data-gathering process is counting the number of times a certain event occurs. When taking a random sample of registered voters, we can count the number who prefer the incumbent to the challenger. When sampling pistons for an auto engine assembly, we can count the number that fail to meet tolerances. When examining hiring practices, we can count the number of minority workers hired by a firm. When examining credit policies, we can count the number of bad-debt accounts. We can reduce an almost endless variety of situations to this simple yes/no process. All these situations can be abstracted as variations on flipping a (possibly unfair) coin.

trials

These examples, and many others, share certain common features. First, the overall process can be thought of as a series of **trials**, each trial yielding exactly one of two possible outcomes. In sampling registered voters, each person constitutes a trial. The incumbent is either preferred or not preferred. In sampling pistons, each trial yields a defective piston or a piston within tolerances. Each person hired is or is not a minority member, and each credit account is or is not a bad debt. The standard language is to call one outcome "success" and the other "failure." Which outcome is called success does not matter; a bad-debt account could be called a success.

Second, in each of these situations, it is reasonable to assume that the probability of success is constant over trials. The probability of finding a registered voter who favors the incumbent does not change in mid-sample (unless the sample is conducted over an extended period of time), nor does the probability of a defective piston, nor does the probability of a bad debt. If relative unemployment rates and the firm's hiring practices do not change, the probability that a given new employee is a minority worker does not change. We denote the probability of success on any one trial as π (not to be confused with $\pi \approx 3.14159$ from geometry).

And finally, in each situation, the results of the various trials can be assumed to be independent. The preference of one voter for the incumbent should not affect the preference of another voter; at least that shouldn't occur in a carefully designed study. If one account happens to be a bad debt, that fact doesn't change the likelihood that the next account sampled will be good.

Bernoulli trials

These three assumptions—each trial results in either a success or failure, constant probability π of success, and independence of trials—define a series of **Bernoulli trials**. The assumptions *are* assumptions; not every counting process can reasonably be modeled as Bernoulli trials. Whether these assumptions are reasonable depends on the situation. Success/failure trials are not always independent and identical. But in many cases these assumptions hold to a good approximation, which makes Bernoulli trials a useful model.

EXAMPLE 5.3

Discuss whether or not a series of Bernoulli trials provides a reasonable model for each of the following situations.

a A telephone researcher involved in a television-viewing survey calls different homes (selected at random), one each 15 minutes between 5:30 P.M. and 10:00 P.M. Each person contacted is asked if anyone in the household is watching the ABC network program. A trial consists of contacting a household to determine whether or not someone in the house is watching an ABC network program.

b A trust officer examines a sample of stock listings from those on the New York Stock Exchange to determine whether or not each stock has risen in price during the past week. Here a trial consists of selecting a stock and determining whether or not the price has risen during the past week.

c Each of 50 newly hired management trainees is rated outstanding, acceptable, or unsatisfactory at the conclusion of a training program. Determining the rating for a newly hired management trainee constitutes a trial.

Solution

a The assumption of constant probability from trial to trial is not plausible in this survey because the level of television watching in general is relatively lower early in the evening. Hence, the probability of finding someone watching the ABC network program may vary depending on the time of the call.

b The independence assumption is very dubious. During any particular time period, there's a moderately strong tendency for stock prices to move up or down together because of interest rate changes, political news, or the herd instinct of investors. So, for the stocks listed in the sample, the outcome on any one trial would depend heavily on price changes for the other stocks.

c For this problem there are three possible outcomes on each trial, not two. However, if we define a success to be a rating of outstanding and a failure to be the complement (not rated outstanding), Bernoulli trials may be a good model. The key question is whether the trial outcomes are independent. If there is an effective ceiling or quota for the number (or proportion) of outstanding ratings (for instance, a restriction that the supervisor can rate no more than 10% of the group as outstanding), then the independence assumption is violated. But if each trainee is rated according to established, reasonably objective criteria, independence of trials (ratings) should be a reasonable assumption. ■

One additional feature is common to all the situations in Example 5.3. We are counting the number of successes that occur in a fixed number n of trials, without regard to the particular order in which successes and failures occur. This would not be true, however, if, for instance, a telephone interviewer called homes at random until 24 television-watching homes had been obtained. In this situation, n is not fixed and the order of successes and failures *is* relevant; the last trial (call) is guaranteed to be a success.

binomial experiment   A collection of a fixed number n of Bernoulli trials in which the researcher is interested in the total number of successes defines a **binomial experiment**. The properties of a binomial experiment are repeated here.

Definition 5.1 Properties of a Binomial Experiment

1 There are n Bernoulli trials; each one results in either a success (S) or a failure (F).

2 The probability of a success, $\pi = P(\text{S})$, remains constant over trials $[P(\text{F}) = 1 - \pi]$.

3 The trials are independent. (Assumptions 1–3 define Bernoulli trials.)

4 The random variable of interest is Y, which is the number of successes in n trials. The ordering of successes is not important. ■

binomial random variable
binomial probability distribution

A **binomial random variable** is a discrete random variable that can assume any one of the values $0, 1, 2, \ldots, n$. The **binomial probability distribution** $P_Y(y)$, which assigns probabilities to each value of Y, is best understood by considering a simple example.

Suppose we take a random sample of three individuals from a population with a proportion π of successes. Figure 5.1 shows a probability tree for calculating the distribution of Y. By adding up the probabilities of appropriate paths, we can find the binomial probability distribution for $n = 3$. For instance, the second, third, and fifth paths (counting from the top) give $y = 2$; each of these paths has probability $\pi^2(1 - \pi)$. We add the path probabilities to get $P(Y = 2)$; $P_Y(2) = \pi^2(1 - \pi) + \pi^2(1 - \pi) + \pi^2(1 - \pi) = 3\pi^2(1 - \pi)$. The complete probability distribution is

y	0	1	2	3
$P_Y(y)$	$(1 - \pi)^3$	$3\pi(1 - \pi)^2$	$3\pi^2(1 - \pi)$	π^3

FIGURE 5.1 **Probability Tree for Binomial Distribution with $n = 3$**

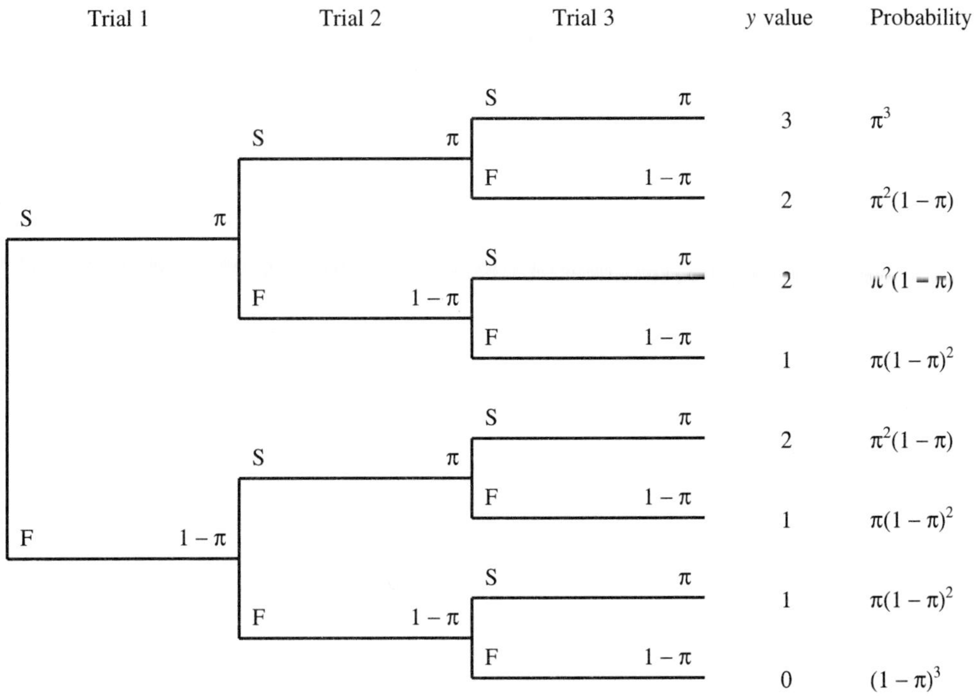

EXAMPLE 5.4

Find the binomial distribution for $n = 4$.

Solution

To save space, we have listed the paths instead of drawing the tree. You may wish to construct the probability tree that gives rise to these paths.

Path Number	Path Sequence	y	Probability
1	SSSS	4	π^4
2	SSSF	3	$\pi^3(1 - \pi)$
3	SSFS	3	$\pi^3(1 - \pi)$
4	SSFF	2	$\pi^2(1 - \pi)^2$
5	SFSS	3	$\pi^3(1 - \pi)$
6	SFSF	2	$\pi^2(1 - \pi)^2$
7	SFFS	2	$\pi^2(1 - \pi)^2$
8	SFFF	1	$\pi(1 - \pi)^3$
9	FSSS	3	$\pi^3(1 - \pi)$
10	FSSF	2	$\pi^2(1 - \pi)^2$
11	FSFS	2	$\pi^2(1 - \pi)^2$
12	FSFF	1	$\pi(1 - \pi)^3$
13	FFSS	2	$\pi^2(1 - \pi)^2$
14	FFSF	1	$\pi(1 - \pi)^3$
15	FFFS	1	$\pi(1 - \pi)^3$
16	FFFF	0	$(1 - \pi)^4$

All the paths corresponding to a particular y value have the same probability; for instance, each of the six paths that yield $y = 2$ has probability $\pi^2(1 - \pi)^2$. So adding up the path probabilities for a particular y value amounts to multiplying the number of paths by the appropriate probability.

y	0	1	2	3	4
$P_Y(y)$	$(1 - \pi)^4$	$4\pi(1 - \pi)^3$	$6\pi^2(1 - \pi)^2$	$4\pi^3(1 - \pi)$	π^4

■

We need a formula to save the labor of actually counting paths. We can use the methods of Section 5.1. One way to specify a path in a binomial experiment is to state the trials on which a success occurs. For example, if $n = 5$, to say that the successes occur only at trials 1 and 4—for short, S at (1,4)—specifies the path SFFSF. The ordering of the trial numbers is irrelevant; S at (4,1) also specifies the path SFFSF. Therefore, in n trials, the number of paths containing y successes is the same as the number of subsets of size y out of the first n integers. From Section 5.1, this number is

$$\binom{n}{y} = \frac{(n!)}{y!(n - y)!}$$

Using this expression for the relevant number of paths in a binomial probability tree, we obtain a general expression for the binomial probability distribution.

Definition 5.2   Binomial Probability Distribution

$$P_Y(y) = \frac{n!}{y!(n - y)!}\pi^y(1 - \pi)^{n-y} \qquad \text{for } y = 0, 1, \ldots, n \qquad ■$$

Appendix Table 1 (at the end of the book) contains numerical values of binomial probabilities. Each value of n determines a block of probabilities. For values of π below .5, values of π are read at the top of the block and values of y are read on the left. For values of π above .5, values of π are read at the bottom and values of y on the right. Many computer programs will also calculate these probabilities. For example, Figure 5.2 shows the formulas defined in Microsoft Excel to calculate binomial probabilities. The formula takes advantage of the fact that, for binomial probabilities,

$$P_Y(y) = \frac{(n - y + 1)}{y} \frac{\pi}{1 - \pi} P_Y(y - 1)$$

Figure 5.3 shows one particular example of the calculation; substituting other values for n and π will give any desired binomial probabilities.

FIGURE 5.2   **Formulas for Binomial Probabilities**

	A	B	C	D	E
1	n	P(Success)	y	P(y)	Cum. prob.
2	25	0.4	0	=(1-$B$2)^$A$2	=$D$2
3			1	=$D2*($A$2+1-$C3)*($B$2)/($C3*(1-$B$2))	=$E2+$D3
4			2	=$D3*($A$2+1-$C4)*($B$2)/($C4*(1-$B$2))	=$E3+$D4
5			3	=$D4*($A$2+1-$C5)*($B$2)/($C5*(1-$B$2))	=$E4+$D5
6			4	=$D5*($A$2+1-$C6)*($B$2)/($C6*(1-$B$2))	=$E5+$D6
7			5	=$D6*($A$2+1-$C7)*($B$2)/($C7*(1-$B$2))	=$E6+$D7
8			6	=$D7*($A$2+1-$C8)*($B$2)/($C8*(1-$B$2))	=$E7+$D8
9			7	=$D8*($A$2+1-$C9)*($B$2)/($C9*(1-$B$2))	=$E8+$D9
10			8	=$D9*($A$2+1-$C10)*($B$2)/($C10*(1-$B$2))	=$E9+$D10
11			9	=$D10*($A$2+1-$C11)*($B$2)/($C11*(1-$B$2))	=$E10+$D11
12			10	=$D11*($A$2+1-$C12)*($B$2)/($C12*(1-$B$2))	=$E11+$D12

FIGURE 5.3   **Binomial Probabilities, $n = 25$, $\pi = .40$**

	A	B	C	D	E
1	n	P(Success)	y	P(y)	Cum. prob.
2	25	0.4	0	0.0000	0.0000
3			1	0.0000	0.0001
4			2	0.0004	0.0004
5			3	0.0019	0.0024
6			4	0.0071	0.0095
7			5	0.0199	0.0294
8			6	0.0442	0.0736
9			7	0.0800	0.1536
10			8	0.1200	0.2735
11			9	0.1511	0.4246
12			10	0.1612	0.5858
13			11	0.1465	0.7323

EXAMPLE 5.5

In Appendix Table 1 of binomial probabilities, find the probability distribution of a binomial random variable for $n = 5$ and (a) $\pi = .2$, (b) $\pi = .5$, and (c) $\pi = .7$.

Solution

We look in the $n = 5$ block of Appendix Table 1. For $\pi = .2$, we read *down* the .20 column; for $\pi = .5$, we use the $\pi = .50$ column; for $\pi = .7$, we read *up* the $\pi = .70$ column. The resulting distribution is

y	0	1	2	3	4	5
$P_Y(y)$ for $\pi=.20$	.3277	.4096	.2048	.0512	.0064	.0003
$P_Y(y)$ for $\pi=.50$	.0313	.1563	.3125	.3125	.1563	.0313
$P_Y(y)$ for $\pi=.70$	.0024	.0284	.1323	.3087	.3602	.1681	∎

EXAMPLE 5.6

In the long run, 20% of all management trainees are rated outstanding, 50% acceptable, and 30% unsatisfactory. In a sample of 20 randomly selected trainees, find the following probabilities:

a Exactly 4 trainees are rated outstanding.

b At least 4 trainees are rated outstanding.

c Exactly 15 trainees are rated outstanding or acceptable.

d At least 15 trainees are rated outstanding or acceptable.

Assume that we have a set of Bernoulli trials.

Solution

a Find the entry for $n = 20$, $\pi = .20$ (on top of the block), and $y = 4$ (to the left). The probability is .2182.

b Add the entries for $n = 20$, $\pi = .20$, $y = 4, 5, 6, \ldots, 20$, and get .5886.

c The probability that a rating is outstanding or acceptable is $.20 + .50 = .70$. Find the entry for $n = 20$, $\pi = .70$ (below the block), and $y = 15$ (to the right): .1789. Alternatively, this probability must equal the probability of exactly five unsatisfactory ratings, which has $\pi = .30$ and $y = 5$. This reasoning yields the same table entry: .1789.

d Add the entries for $n = 20$, $\pi = .70$, $y = 15, 16, \ldots, 20$ to get .4163. Or add the entries for $n = 20$, $\pi = .30$, and $y = 5, 4, \ldots, 0$ to get the equivalent probability of five or fewer unsatisfactory ratings. ∎

EXAMPLE 5.7

Use the following Minitab output to find the probabilities of the preceding example. In the output, PDF is the probability of the specified value and CDF is the cumulative probability up through the specified value.

```
MTB > PDF 4;
SUBC>   Binomial 20 .20.
       K          P( X = K)
     4.00           0.2182
MTB > CDF 3;
```

```
SUBC>   Binomial 20 .20.
      K   P( X LESS OR = K)
    3.00              0.4114
MTB > PDF 15;
SUBC>   Binomial 20 .70.
      K          P( X = K)
   15.00            0.1789
MTB > CDF 14;
SUBC>   Binomial 20 .70.
      K   P( X LESS OR = K)
   14.00            0.5836
```

Solution

a   As in the table, the probability of exactly 4 successes is shown as .2182.

b $P(Y \geq 4) = 1 - P(Y \leq 3) = 1 - .4114 = .5886$.

c   Once again, the probability of exactly 15 successes is shown directly as .1789.

d $P(Y \geq 15) = 1 - P(Y \leq 14) = 1 - .5836 = .4164$. There is a tiny discrepancy from the part d answer of the previous example because of round-off error.   ■

The expected value and variance of a binomial random variable Y depend, of course, on the values of n and π.

Definition 5.3   Mean and Variance of a Binomial Random Variable

$$E(Y) = n\pi$$

$$\mathrm{Var}(Y) = n\pi(1 - \pi) \qquad \sigma_Y = \sqrt{n\pi(1 - \pi)} \qquad ■$$

The resulting expected value for a binomial random variable seems intuitively reasonable. If, on average, 30% of all trainees are rated outstanding, then in a sample of 20 trainees, we would expect to find $20(.3) = 6$ who are rated outstanding. The variance and standard deviation expressions aren't particularly intuitive. Notice that the standard deviation of the *number* of successes increases like the square root of n, the number of trials. The variance and standard deviation are largest (for a specified n) when $\pi = .50$. This makes sense; there is the most random variability in results when there is a 50–50 chance of a success on any trial.

The effect of violation of assumptions can be understood in terms of these formulas. The two assumptions of interest here are constant probability and independence. (If there are more than two outcomes on a given trial, or if the experiment doesn't count the number of successes in a fixed number of trials, then binomial probabilities are simply irrelevant.)

There is a difference between constant probability and independence. The constant probability assumption is violated if the probability of success changes *regardless* of the results of past trials; the independence assumption is violated if the probability of success changes *depending* on the results of past trials. For example, suppose a house inspector checks 20 houses to see whether or not each house's roof is sound. Ten of the houses are in a relatively new subdivision, about 10 years old; the remaining 10 are in a much older subdivision. Whether or not any particular house happens to have a sound roof, the probability that a house in the new subdivision will have a sound roof will be higher than the probability that a house in the older subdivision will have one. The constant probability assumption would almost certainly be violated. For another example, suppose a sales representative checks 20 boxes of snack crackers to see if the boxes have been bent or cut by rough handling. If one box has been marred, the probability that other boxes also are marred will go up, because all the boxes have been handled (or perhaps placekicked) in about the same way. Notice the condition: *If* one box has been marred, the probability for others will go up. Here, the independence assumption would almost certainly be violated.

Violation of the independence assumption usually has more numerical effect on binomial probabilities. In particular, if there is positive dependence (a success tends to be followed by other successes, a failure by other failures), the binomial variance and standard deviation expressions will be too small. There will be more random variation than indicated by those formulas; there will be more cases of very large numbers of successes and of very small numbers of successes. In contrast (and perhaps oddly), if the probability of success changes at a fixed point during the trials, the violation of the constant probability assumption actually reduces the amount of random variation. Consider the extreme case of 20 trials, where the first 10 have probability 0 of success and the last 10 have probability 1 of success. The 20 trials are guaranteed to yield 10 successes, with no random variation at all. In most reasonable situations, the numerical effect of dependence is greater than that of nonconstant probability.

E X A M P L E   5 . 8

A Resampling Stats program took 1000 samples, each of size 100. The first 50 trials had a probability of success equal to .3 and the remaining 50 had a probability of success equal to .7. What binomial assumption is violated? What is the anticipated effect of this violation? Where does the simulation show this effect?

```
 1: 'SET INITIAL VALUE; CHANGE THE NUMBER FOR A NEW SIMULATION.
 2: SEED 13579123
 3: 'CARRY OUT THE RUN 1000 TIMES
 4: REPEAT 1000
 5: 'DO 50 TRIALS WITH PROBABILITY OF SUCCESS .3.
 6: GENERATE 50 1,10 TEMP
 7: COUNT TEMP <=3 SFIRST50
 8: 'DO 50 MORE TRIALS WITH PROBABILITY OF SUCCESS .7.
 9: GENERATE 50 1,10 TEMP
10: COUNT TEMP <=7 SNEXT50
11: 'PUT THE TRIALS TOGETHER.
12: CONCAT SFIRST50 SNEXT50 SALL
13: SUM SALL STOTAL
14: 'SAVE THE RESULT FOR THIS RUN
15: SCORE STOTAL NUMSUCC
16: 'END OF THIS RUN
17: END
18: 'SUMMARIZE THE RESULTS OF THE 1000 RUNS
19: MEAN NUMSUCC EXPVALUE
20: VARIANCE NUMSUCC VAR
21: PRINT EXPVALUE VAR

EXPVALUE =     50.003

VAR      =     20.966
```

Solution

The probability of success is not constant; it changes from .3 to .7 halfway through the series of trials. The "average π" is .5. If binomial assumptions are met, the expected value will be $n\pi = 100(.5) = 50$. The violation of assumptions should reduce the variance (and standard deviation). If the probability of success had been constant at .5, the variance would be $100(.5)(1 - .5) = 25.0$. The simulation shows that the mean value is almost exactly 50.0, but the variance is 20.966, smaller than the binomial value, 25.0. ∎

E X A M P L E   5 . 9

Another Resampling Stats program took 1000 samples, each of size 100. The probability of success on the first trial was .5. If one trial is a success, the probability of success on the next trial is .7. If one trial is a failure, the probability of success on the next trial is .3. What binomial assumption is violated? What is the anticipated effect of this violation? Where does the simulation show this effect? Is the effect larger or smaller than the effect in the previous example?

```
 1: 'SET INITIAL VALUE.  VARY THE NUMBER FOR A NEW SIMULATION.
 2: SEED 13579123
 3: 'DO THE OVERALL RUN 1000 TIMES
 4: REPEAT 1000
 5: 'FIRST TRIAL HAS PROBABILITY OF SUCCESS .5.
 6: GENERATE 1 1,10 TEMP
 7: COUNT TEMP <=5 CURRENT
 8: 'SAVE THE RESULT
 9: COPY CURRENT SORF
10:    'CARRY OUT NEXT 99 TRIALS ONE AT A TIME.
11:    REPEAT 99
12:    GENERATE 1 1,10 TEMP
13:    'PROB OF NEXT SUCCESS DEPENDS ON WHETHER CURRENT IS 1 OR 0.
14:    IF CURRENT =1
15:      COUNT TEMP <=7 NEXT
16:      END
17:    IF CURRENT =0
18:      COUNT TEMP <=3 NEXT
19:      END
20:    'SAVE THE RESULT OF THIS TRIAL
21:    CONCAT SORF NEXT SORF
22:    'MAKE THE RESULT OF THIS TRIAL BE THE CURRENT VALUE
23:    COPY NEXT CURRENT
24:    'END OF THIS TRIAL; GO TO THE NEXT
25:    END
26: 'AFTER 100 TRIALS, ADD NUMBER OF SUCCESSES AND SAVE.
27: SUM SORF TOTALSUC
28: SCORE TOTALSUC NUMSUCC
29: 'END OF THIS RUN
30: END
31: 'SUMMARIZE AND PRINT THE RESULTS
32: MEAN NUMSUCC EXPVALUE
33: VARIANCE NUMSUCC VAR
34: PRINT EXPVALUE VAR
```

EXPVALUE =   50.041

VAR   =   54.029

Solution

Again, the "average π" is .5. (Draw a tree if that's not clear.) This time, the independence assumption is violated. The binomial variance equals 25.0 once again. In this simulation, the variance is much larger than the theoretical value. The simulation variance is 54.029. The discrepancy between the theoretical variance and the simulation variance is much larger in this simulation than in the previous one, indicating that violation of the independence assumption has a greater numerical effect than violation of the constant probability assumption. ∎

E X E R C I S E S

5.5 Let Y be a binomial random variable. Compute $P_Y(y)$ for each of the following situations.

    a $n = 10, \pi = .2, y = 3$ **b** $n = 4, \pi = .4, y = 2$ **c** $n = 16, \pi = .7, y = 12$

5.6 Let Y have a binomial probability distribution with $n = 6$ and $\pi = .25$.

    a Calculate $P_Y(y)$ by hand for $y = 1, 2,$ and 3. Compare your results to those listed in Appendix Table 1.

    b Draw a probability histogram of $P_Y(y)$.

    c Find the mean and standard deviation of Y.

5.7 Let $Y =$ the number of successes in 20 independent trials, where the probability of success on any one trial is .4. Find

    a $P(Y \geq 4)$ **b** $P(Y > 4)$ **c** $P(Y \leq 10)$ **d** $P(Y > 16)$

5.8 Let Y be a binomial random variable with $n = 20$ and $\pi = .6$. Find $P(Y \leq 16)$ and $P(Y < 16)$. Compare these probabilities to the ones found in parts a and b of Exercise 5.7.

5.9 A chain of motels has adopted a policy of giving a 3% discount to customers who pay in cash rather than by credit cards. Its experience is that 30% of all customers take the discount. Let $Y =$ number of discount takers among the next 20 customers.

    a Do you think the binomial assumptions are reasonable in this situation?

    b Assuming that binomial probabilities apply, find the probabilities that exactly 5 of the next 20 customers take the discount.

    c Find $P(5$ or fewer customers take the discount).

    d What is the most probable number of discount takers in the next 20 customers?

5.10 Find the expected value and standard deviation of the number of discount takers in Exercise 5.9.

5.11 Use the Empirical Rule to approximate the probability that Y in Exercise 5.9 falls within 1 standard deviation of its expected value. Use binomial tables to find the exact probability. How good is the Empirical Rule approximation?

5.12 A small company uses a parcel service to ship packages of special cheeses ordered as gifts. The company has found that 90% of all orders are delivered on time. A batch of 100 packages is sent out. Let $Y =$ number of packages delivered on time.

    a Do the binomial assumptions seem reasonable in this situation?

    b Assuming that binomial probabilities apply, find $P(Y \geq 85)$.

5.13 Find $E(Y)$ and σ_Y in Exercise 5.12, assuming binomial probabilities.

5.14 A prescription drug manufacturer claims that only 10% of all new drugs that are shown to be effective in animal tests ever pass through all the additional testing required to be marketed.

The manufacturer currently has 8 new drugs that have been shown to be effective in animal tests, and they await further testing and approval.

a Find the probability that none of the 8 drugs is marketed.

b Find the probability that at least 2 are marketed.

c Find the expected number of marketed drugs among the 8.

5.15 Plot a probability histogram of $P_Y(y)$ in Exercise 5.14.

5.16 A direct-mail advertiser has a continuing problem with mailing lists. Historically, about 18% of the addresses on mailing lists have been bad, so the intended recipient never gets the mail. The advertiser has an opportunity to buy a new list, which claims to have a lower percentage of bad addresses. As a test, the advertiser takes a random sample of 200 addresses and mails catalogs by first-class mail. For this class of mail, undeliverable catalogs are returned to the sender, giving a count of the number of bad addresses in the sample of 200.

The following Resampling Stats program gives a computer simulation of this experiment, assuming that the 18% bad address rate still holds. (Some irrelevant output has been omitted.)

```
 1: 'REPEAT THE EXPERIMENT 1000 TIMES
 2:
 3: REPEAT 1000
 4: 'CHOOSE 200 NUMBERS WITH REPLACEMENT, BETWEEN 1 AND 100
 5: SAMPLE 200 1,100 RANDNUM
 6: 'COUNT NUMBER OF BAD ADDRESSES (VALUES BETWEEN 1 AND 18)
 7: COUNT RANDNUM <=18 HOWMANY
 8: 'KEEP TRACK OF THE RESULT
 9: SCORE HOWMANY BADADDR
10: 'END OF TRIAL
11: END
12: HISTOGRAM BADADDR
13: MEAN BADADDR EXPVALUE
14: STDEV BADADDR SD
15: PRINT EXPVALUE SD
```

Vector no. 1: BADADDR

Bin Center	Freq	Pct	Cum Pct
22	2	0.2	0.2
23	5	0.5	0.7
24	3	0.3	1.0
25	13	1.3	2.3
26	14	1.4	3.7
27	17	1.7	5.4
28	22	2.2	7.6
29	46	4.6	12.2
30	50	5.0	17.2

Note: Each bin covers all values within 0.25 of its center.
EXPVALUE =   35.685

SD   =   5.264

a According to the output, what is the probability of 25 or fewer bad addresses?

b What is the expected number of bad addresses? The standard deviation?

5.17 Calculate the exact binomial probabilities, expected value, and standard deviation for the previous exercise.

5.18 In Chapter 3, we simulated three different dice games. In the first, the player wins if there is at least one 6 rolling six fair dice. In the second, the player wins if there are at least two 6s rolling twelve fair dice. In the third, the player wins if there are at least three 6s rolling eighteen fair dice. The simulation probabilities for winning were .635, .627, and .601, respectively. Assuming that binomial probabilities apply, calculate the exact probabilities. You may want to use a computer program. ■

The Hypergeometric Distribution

The counting formulas of Section 5.1 can be used to define the **hypergeometric probability distribution**. In this section we give a formula for this distribution and relate it to the binomial distribution.

The situation that leads to the hypergeometric distribution is easily described. There must be a population consisting of some number N_S of successes and some number N_F of failures. The total population size is $N = N_S + N_F$.[1] A sample of size n is taken from the population without replacement. The relevant random variable is $Y =$ observed number of successes in the sample. Example 5.1 illustrates one such situation: There are 13 successes (erroneous accounts) and 74 failures in the population, and the sample size is $n = 10$. That example indicates the basic principle of the hypergeometric distribution, which is straight out of the classical interpretation of probability:

$$P(\text{event}) = \frac{\text{number of outcomes favoring the event}}{\text{total number of outcomes}}$$

In this context, outcome means sample. There are $\binom{N}{n}$ possible samples of size n that can be drawn from a population of size N. The samples that favor the event are those that have exactly y successes and exactly $n - y$ failures. As indicated in Example 5.1, there are $\binom{N_S}{y}\binom{N_F}{n-y}$ such samples, which leads to the following hypergeometric distribution.

Definition 5.4   Hypergeometric Probability Distribution

Define $Y =$ the number of S's in a random sample of size n (taken without replacement) from a population consisting of N_S S's and N_F F's.

$$P_Y(y) = \frac{\binom{N_S}{y}\binom{N_F}{n-y}}{\binom{N}{n}} \qquad y = 0, 1, \ldots, n$$

(If $y > N_S$, take $\binom{N_S}{y}$ and $P_Y(y)$ to be 0; if $n - y > N_F$, take $\binom{N_F}{n-y}$ and $P_Y(y)$ to be 0.)   ∎

E X A M P L E   5 . 1 0

In Example 5.1, we considered sampling 10 of the 87 accounts of a small firm. Thirteen of the 87 accounts contain errors. Find $P(2$ erroneous accounts in the sample$)$.

Solution

We have $N = 87$, $N = 10$, $N_S = 13$, and therefore $N_F = 74$; we want $P(Y = 2)$.

$$P_Y(2) = \frac{\binom{13}{2}\binom{74}{10-2}}{\binom{87}{10}} \approx \frac{1,175,600,000,000}{4,000,800,000,000} = .294 \qquad ∎$$

Although we could set out many other illustrations of hypergeometric situations, we want to emphasize the close relation of hypergeometric and binomial probabilities. If the

---

[1] These Ns are not random variables, although we usually use capital letters to denote random variables. The Ns are constants.

population size N is large (relative to the sample size n), the distinction between the binomial and the hypergeometric is negligible. If a random sample of 100 is taken from a population of 100,000,000, it does not matter in any serious way whether hypergeometric or binomial probabilities are used.

EXAMPLE 5.11

Find $P(2$ erroneous accounts$)$ in Example 5.10 using a binomial probability distribution.

Solution

We take $n = 10$ and $\pi = 13/87 \approx .149$. Thus

$$P(2 \text{ erroneous accounts}) = \binom{10}{2}(.149)^2(.851)^8 \approx .275.$$

We calculated this probability using the binomial probability distribution. It is approximately equal to the probability of two erroneous accounts, .30, which we calculated using the hypergeometric probability distribution. As N gets larger, these probabilities become closer. ∎

The close relation between hypergeometric and binomial probabilities extends to expected values and variances. We don't prove it, but the mean and variance for a hypergeometric probability distribution are as follows.

Definition 5.5   Expected Value and Variance for a Hypergeometric Random Variable Y

$$E(Y) = n\frac{N_S}{N}$$

$$\text{Var}(Y) = n\frac{N_S}{N}\left(1 - \frac{N_S}{N}\right)\frac{N-n}{N-1} \quad ∎$$

finite population correction

The ratio N_S/N is exactly π, the probability of success on a single trial. In Example 5.11, we took $\pi = 13/87$. Therefore, the expected value of Y for the hypergeometric is $E(Y) = n\pi$, just like the binomial. By substituting $\pi = N_S/N$, the hypergeometric variance reduces to $n\pi(1 - \pi)[(N - n)/(N - 1)]$, as compared to the binomial variance $n\pi(1 - \pi)$. An extra factor, $(N - n)/(N - 1)$, is called the **finite population correction**. This factor is exactly equal to 1 when $n = 1$; otherwise, it is less than 1. For most practical situations in which the sample is a small fraction of the population (n is much smaller than N), the factor $(N - n)/(N - 1)$ is nearly 1. For example, if $n = 100$ and $N = 100,000,000$, then $(N - n)/(N - 1) \approx .999999$. Therefore, we do not worry about the distinction between the hypergeometric and the binomial probability distributions in most situations; the distinction makes little numerical difference.

EXERCISES

5.19   Let Y be a hypergeometric random variable with $N_S = 3$, $N_F = 4$, and $n = 3$.

    a Compute $P_Y(y)$ for $y = 0, 1, 2, 3$.   **b** Graph this probability distribution.

5.20   Find the mean and standard deviation for the random variable Y defined in Exercise 5.19.

5.21   Compute $P_Y(2)$ for a hypergeometric variable Y in each of the following situations:

    a $N_S = 2, N_F = 3, n = 3$ **b** $N_S = 4, N_F = 4, n = 5$ **c** $N_S = 5, N_F = 1, n = 3$

5.22 Compute the probability that $Y = 0$ in both of the following situations:

    a Y is binomial with $n = 5$ and $\pi = .40$.

    b Y is hypergeometric with $N_S = 2$, $N_F = 3$, and $n = 5$.

5.23 Refer to Exercises 5.3 and 5.4, in which a tester selected four glasses thought to contain a private-label cola, when given four glasses of that cola and four glasses of a national brand.

    a Find the probability that the tester selects the four correct glasses, assuming random selection.

    b Find $P_Y(y)$, where $Y =$ number of correct choices.

5.24 Assume that in the 2500 business accounts of a bank, 125 have been fraudulently altered. The alterations are sufficiently subtle that only a detailed audit can uncover them. Fifty business accounts are chosen at random for detailed auditing. What is the probability that at least one of the alterations is discovered?

5.25 Find the expected value and variance of the number of altered accounts discovered during the audit in Exercise 5.24.

5.26 Use a binomial approximation to answer Exercises 5.24 and 5.25. How close are the numerical answers? ■

5.4

Geometric and Negative Binomial Distributions

Bernoulli trials, yielding success or failure on each trial with constant probabilities and independence from trial to trial, were discussed in Section 5.2. There we were concerned with the case in which the number of trials was fixed and the number of successes was random. In a number of cases, however, the situation is reversed: The number of successes is fixed and the number of trials is random. In this section, we deal with this situation, which leads to the geometric and negative binomial probability distributions.

Many banks supplement their usual teller services with card-operated automatic teller machines. There is some risk of unauthorized use of bank cards at these machines. Suppose that one of every thousand attempted automatic teller transactions is based on unauthorized use of a bank card. Regarding each transaction as a trial (and ignoring the possibility of repeated transactions using the same card), we can assume that transactions are a series of Bernoulli trials. The binomial distribution of Section 5.2 would apply to problems such as finding the probability that there are more than 20 unauthorized uses within the next 10,000 transactions. In such a problem, the number of trials (transactions) would be regarded as fixed, and the number of successes (unauthorized uses) as random. Alternatively, we could ask for the number of transactions that occur before the next unauthorized use, or before the tenth unauthorized use. These questions lead to the geometric and negative binomial probability distributions.

The geometric distribution arises when we consider $Y =$ number of trials required to obtain the next success. The probability tree for a geometric random variable is very simple. To require y trials to obtain a success is to require that there be $y - 1$ consecutive failures followed by a success.

Definition 5.6   Geometric Probability Distribution

In a Bernoulli trials situation, define $Y =$ number of trials required to obtain a success. Then

$$P_Y(y) = \pi(1 - \pi)^{y-1} \qquad y = 1, 2, 3, \ldots$$

where π is the probability of success on any trial. ■

These probabilities form a geometric series. If $\pi = .2$, the probabilities are $.2, .2(.8), .2(.8)^2, \ldots$

EXAMPLE 5.12

The labels on bottles of medication are examined with an optical scanner to see that they are properly affixed to the bottles. Assume that the probability of detecting an improperly affixed label is $\pi = .0001$ and compute the probability that the process will detect an improper label on the very first trial. Also compute the probability that the process will first detect an improper label on exactly the 10,000th bottle.

Solution

The event "improper label at trial 1" is the same as the event "$Y = 1$," where $Y =$ number of trials to find the first improper label. Assuming Bernoulli trials with $P(\text{success}) = \pi = .0001$, the geometric distribution applies. $P(Y = 1) = P_Y(1) = (.0001)(.9999)^{1-1} = .0001$. The event "first improper label at bottle 10,000" is the same as the event "$Y = 10,000$" and has probability

$$P_Y(10,000) = (.0001)(.9999)^{10,000-1} = .0000368.$$

Note that, even though we expect one improper label for every 10,000 bottles, there is a higher probability that the next bad label will occur at the very next bottle than that it will occur at precisely the next 10,000th bottle. ■

The mean (expected value) and variance of a geometric random variable can be computed by another convenient shortcut formula.

Definition 5.7   Mean and Variance for a Geometric Random Variable

$$E(Y) = \frac{1}{\pi}$$

$$\text{Var}(Y) = \frac{1 - \pi}{\pi^2}$$

where π is the probability of success on any given trial. ■

EXAMPLE 5.13

Using the assumptions of Example 5.12, find the expected value and variance of the number of labels examined until the next improper label is found.

Solution

We have $\pi = .0001$, so $E(Y) = 1/(.0001) = 10,000$. It is reasonable that, if 1 out of every 10,000 labels is improper, we will wait an average of 10,000 bottles to find the next improper label. The variance is $(1 - .0001)/(.0001)^2 = 99,990,000$; therefore, the standard deviation of Y is $\sqrt{99,990,000} = 9999.5$. ■

The idea of counting the number of trials to the next success may be extended to counting the number of trials to the kth success. For example, a market research firm that needs to obtain $k = 100$ women who have full-time jobs and also watch a certain local television newscast has to interview a random number of potential candidates. Each interview is a trial; the most relevant random variable is $Y =$ number of interviews needed to obtain 100 qualifying women. If the assumptions of Bernoulli trials (success or failure trials, constant probability of success, independent trials) hold, the probability distribution of $Y =$ number of trials required to obtain k successes is a negative binomial.

Definition 5.8   Negative Binomial Distribution

If $Y =$ number of trials to obtain k successes, then

$$P_Y(y) = \frac{(y-1)!}{(k-1)!(y-k)!} \pi^k (1-\pi)^{y-k} \qquad y = k, k+1, \dots \quad \blacksquare$$

The reason that $y - 1$ and $k - 1$ occur in the expression for the negative binomial distribution is that there must be $k - 1$ successes in the first $y - 1$ trials, followed by one success (at trial y).

E X A M P L E   5 . 1 4

In Example 5.12, we assumed that the probability of an improperly affixed label was .0001. Suppose that 50 improperly affixed labels are needed to study the cause of improper label fixing. Write an expression for the probability that 100,000 or more bottles are needed to obtain 50 improper labels.

Solution

We can regard the number of successes (improperly affixed labels) as fixed, and we can find the probability that $Y =$ number of bottles required is at least 100,000:

$$P(Y \geq 100,000) = \sum_{100,000}^{\infty} \frac{(y-1)!}{(50-1)!(y-50)!}(.0001)^{50}(.9999)^{y-50} \quad \blacksquare$$

Because the negative binomial distribution is simply the extension of the geometric distribution to $k > 1$ successes, it is not surprising that expressions for the mean and variance of the negative binomial distribution are extensions of those for the geometric distribution.

Definition 5.9   Mean and Variance of the Negative Binomial Distribution

Define $Y =$ number of trials required to obtain k successes,

$$E(Y) = \frac{k}{\pi}$$

$$\text{Var}(Y) = \frac{k(1-\pi)}{\pi^2} \quad \blacksquare$$

E X A M P L E   5 . 1 5

Find the expected value and standard deviation of the number of bottles required to find 50 improperly affixed labels, assuming that the probability of an improperly affixed label is .0001.

Solution

$$E(Y) = 50/.0001 = 500,000$$

$$\text{Var}(Y) = 50(.9999)/(.0001)^2 = 4,999,500,000$$

The standard deviation is $\sqrt{4,999,500,000} = 70,707.$ ∎

Not all Bernoulli trials situations can be solved by binomial or negative binomial methods. If Y = number of trials until two consecutive successes occur, then neither the number of trials nor the number of successes is fixed, so neither binomial nor negative binomial probabilities apply. In such cases, one must go back to basic principles to find the relevant probabilities.

5.5 The Poisson Distribution

Poisson probability distribution

A different sort of probability situation occurs when a succession of events seems to happen at random over time. An electrical utility faces occasional thunderstorms that down power lines or damage transformers. Although the long-run probability of the occurrence of such storms can be determined quite accurately, the timing of the next storm is rather unpredictable. A company that insures oil tankers cannot predict the time of the next sinking. The manager of a university computer center faces random variation in the timing of job submissions. It's important to be able to protect against probable variation in such situations.

The **Poisson probability distribution**[2] is the simplest and most widely used model of events occurring randomly in time. This distribution is the mathematical result of certain assumptions. If the assumptions are not correct, at least approximately, for a particular situation, then the Poisson distribution may be a bad model in that situation. The two crucial assumptions can be translated (without doing much violence to the mathematical niceties) as follows:

1   Events occur one at a time. Two or more events do not occur at precisely the same time.

2   The occurrence of the event of interest in a given period is independent of the occurrence of the event in a nonoverlapping period; that is, the occurrence (or nonoccurrence) of an event during one period does not change the probability of an event occurring in some later period.

In many discussions on this topic, a third assumption is added: that the expected number of events in a period of specified length stays constant, so that the expected number of events during any one period is the same as during any other period. This third assumption makes the math easier, but it has been proven to be essentially irrelevant. As long as the first two assumptions hold, the Poisson distribution results.

There are two approaches to assessing whether or not a Poisson distribution is a reasonable model in a given situation. One is to see if the assumptions seem reasonable in a given context; the other is to see if the actual data histogram looks like a Poisson probability histogram. Of course, the ideal is to have both.

---

[2] Named for Simeon Poisson, the mathematician who first derived it.

EXAMPLE 5.16

In the three situations described at the beginning of this section, should the Poisson assumptions hold?

Solution

We would expect that the assumption of independence would be shaky for the electrical utility example. It seems to us that if lightning from one storm knocks out some equipment, it is quite likely that lightning from the same storm or another in the vicinity will knock out other equipment. For the oil tanker example, one could argue that, because one large tanker might collide with another, sinking both, the assumption that events happen one at a time doesn't hold. Although this is certainly possible, we would guess that such flukes are sufficiently rare that the Poisson distribution would be a decent model for the probability of a tanker sinking in a given period. In the computer center, much depends on the situation. If there are only a few terminals, which are tied up during the processing of a job, then the submission of a job now reduces the probability of submission of another job (from the same terminal) a bit later, which violates the assumption of independence. But if there are many terminals or if a terminal is not tied up during processing, the Poisson assumptions look good to us. We would like to see some data! ■

Definition 5.10   Poisson Probability Distribution

$$P_Y(y) = \frac{e^{-\mu}\mu^y}{y!} \qquad y = 0, 1, 2, \ldots$$

where μ is the expected number of events occurring in a given period and $e = 2.71828\ldots$ ■

A Poisson random variable Y is the number of random events that occur in a fixed period; in principle, there's no upper limit to the values of y. In practice, very large values of y are extremely unlikely. Probabilities for the Poisson probability distribution are shown in Appendix Table 2 and can also be calculated by many computer packages. To find μ, it is often necessary to multiply the expected rate for one time unit (for example, one hour) times the number of time units per period (for example, hours per shift).

It is also possible to use a computer package to obtain Poisson probabilities. For example, Figure 5.4 shows Excel calculations for these probabilities; the calculations use the fact that

$$P_Y(y) = \frac{\mu}{y}P_Y(y-1)$$

Figure 5.5 shows the results of the calculation for a particular choice of mean value.

EXAMPLE 5.17

On Saturday mornings, customers enter a boutique at a suburban shopping mall at an average rate of .50 per minute. Let $Y =$ number of customers arriving in a specified 10-minute interval of time. Find the following probabilities:

a $P(Y = 3)$ b $P(Y \leq 3)$

c $P(Y \geq 4)$ d $P(4 \leq Y \leq 10)$

FIGURE 5.4 Formulas for Calculating Poisson Probabilities

	A	B	C	D
1	Mean	y	P(y)	Cum. Probability
2	4.75	0	=EXP(-$A$2)	=$C$2
3		1	=$C2*$A$2/$B3	=$D2+$C3
4		2	=$C3*$A$2/$B4	=$D3+$C4
5		3	=$C4*$A$2/$B5	=$D4+$C5
6		4	=$C5*$A$2/$B6	=$D5+$C6
7		5	=$C6*$A$2/$B7	=$D6+$C7
8		6	=$C7*$A$2/$B8	=$D7+$C8
9		7	=$C8*$A$2/$B9	=$D8+$C9
10		8	=$C9*$A$2/$B10	=$D9+$C10
11		9	=$C10*$A$2/$B11	=$D10+$C11
12		10	=$C11*$A$2/$B12	=$D11+$C12
13		11	=$C12*$A$2/$B13	=$D12+$C13
14		12	=$C13*$A$2/$B14	=$D13+$C14
15		13	=$C14*$A$2/$B15	=$D14+$C15
16		14	=$C15*$A$2/$B16	=$D15+$C16
17		15	=$C16*$A$2/$B17	=$D16+$C17

FIGURE 5.5 Poisson Probabilities

	A	B	C	D
1	Mean	y	P(y)	Cum. Probability
2	4.75	0	0.0087	0.0087
3		1	0.0411	0.0497
4		2	0.0976	0.1473
5		3	0.1545	0.3019
6		4	0.1835	0.4854
7		5	0.1743	0.6597
8		6	0.1380	0.7978
9		7	0.0937	0.8914
10		8	0.0556	0.9470
11		9	0.0293	0.9764
12		10	0.0139	0.9903
13		11	0.0060	0.9963
14		12	0.0024	0.9987
15		13	0.0009	0.9996
16		14	0.0003	0.9999
17		15	0.0001	1.0000

Solution

The Poisson assumptions seem fairly reasonable in this context. We assume that customers don't arrive in groups (or else count the entire group as one arrival) and that the arrival of one customer neither decreases nor increases the probability of other arrivals.

To obtain μ, we note that, at an average rate of .50 per minute over a 10-minute time span, we would expect $\mu = (.50)(10) = 5.0$ arrivals. To find the probabilities, we consult Appendix Table 2.

a $P(Y = 3)$ is read directly from Appendix Table 2 with $\mu = 5$ and $y = 3$: $P(Y = 3) = .1403$.

b $P(Y \leq 3) = P(Y = 0) + P(Y = 1) + P(Y = 2) + P(Y = 3) = .0067 + .0337 + .0843 + .1403 = .2650.$

c $P(Y \geq 4) = 1 - P(Y \leq 3) = 1 - .2650 = .7350$

d $P(4 \leq Y \leq 10) = P(Y = 4) + P(Y = 5) + \cdots + P(Y = 10) = .1755 + .1755 + \cdots + .0181 = .7213$ ∎

E X A M P L E   5 . 1 8

Use the following Minitab output to obtain the probabilities found in the previous example. Once again, PDF is the probability of the indicated value and CDF, the cumulative probability up through the indicated value.

```
MTB > PDF 3;
SUBC>   Poisson 5.
        K          P( X = K)
      3.00           0.1404
MTB > CDF 3;
SUBC>   Poisson 5.
      K  P( X LESS OR = K)
     3.00          0.2650
MTB > CDF 10;
SUBC>   Poisson 5.
      K  P( X LESS OR = K)
    10.00          0.9863
```

Solution

The probability shown for $y = 3$, .1404, differs by .0001 from the answer found previously because of round-off. The cumulative probability $F_Y(3) = .2650$ is the answer to part b of the previous exercise, and its complement, .7350, is the answer to part c. To find $P(4 \leq Y \leq 10)$, take $F_Y(10) - F_Y(3) = .9863 - .2650 = .7213$, as before. ∎

As indicated in the definition of the Poisson probability distribution, the expected value is $E(Y) = \mu$. Coincidentally, the variance of a Poisson random variable is also μ.

Definition 5.11   Mean and Variance for a Poisson Random Variable

If Y has a Poisson distribution, then

$$E(Y) = \mu$$

$$\text{Var}(Y) = \mu$$ ∎

E X A M P L E   5 . 1 9

Find the standard deviation of Y in Example 5.17.

Solution

We noted in Example 5.17 that $\mu = 5.0$. Thus,

$$\sigma_Y = \sqrt{\text{Var}(Y)} = \sqrt{5.0} = 2.24$$ ∎

The most important assumptions underlying the Poisson probability model are "non-clumping" (events don't occur together) and independence (the occurrence of one event doesn't change the probability of another). If events do, in fact, occur together, or if there is positive dependence—that is, if the occurrence of one event increases the probability of another event happening soon—there will be more random variation than the Poisson model states. In this case, the standard deviation of the number of events will be larger than the square root of the mean, which is what the Poisson model specifies.

E X A M P L E   5 . 2 0

The emergency telephone (911) center in a suburban county receives an average of 42 calls per hour during the busiest period, weekend evenings between 7 and 11 o'clock. Each call requires about 2 minutes for a dispatcher to receive the emergency call, determine the nature and location of the problem, and send the required individuals (police, fire, or ambulance) to the scene. The center must have an adequate number of dispatchers on duty; it has asked a consultant to determine the proper staffing level. The consultant assumes that calls come in completely at random over time, so that Poisson probabilities apply. However, the current dispatchers point out that many times, several calls are received at nearly the same time, reporting on the same emergency. What does this fact imply about the use of Poisson probabilities?

Solution

The fact that multiple calls are received at virtually the same time indicates a violation of the "nonclumping" assumption. Therefore, there will be more variability than would occur if Poisson probabilities apply. There will be more time periods with very few calls and more periods with very large numbers of calls. To deal with the bursts of multiple calls will most likely require more dispatchers than would be needed if the Poisson model applies. ■

E X E R C I S E S

5.27 Let Y denote a random variable with a Poisson distribution. Use Appendix Table 2 or a computer package to calculate:

    a $P_Y(1)$ for $\mu = .4$, $\mu = .7$, and $\mu = 4.8$
    b $P(Y \le 3)$ for $\mu = 1.6$ and $\mu = 7.0$
    c $P(Y \le 10)$ for $\mu = 2.1$ and $\mu = 10.0$

5.28 Graph the Poisson probability distribution for $\mu = .5$. Is the distribution roughly symmetric?

5.29 A firm that insures homes against fire assumes that claims arise according to a Poisson distribution at an average rate of 2.25 per week. Let Y be the number of claims arising in a 4-week period. Find

    a $P(Y \le 10)$ **b** $P(Y \ge 7)$ **c** $P(7 \le Y \le 11)$

5.30 Find the expected value and standard deviation of Y in Exercise 5.29.

5.31 Can you think of insurance situations that would make the Poisson assumption in Exercise 5.29 unreasonable?

5.32 Logging trucks have a particular problem with tire failures due to blowouts, cuts, and large punctures; these trucks are driven fast over very rough, temporary roads. Assume that such failures occur according to a Poisson distribution at a mean rate of 4.0 per 10,000 miles.

a If a truck drives 1000 miles in a given week, what is the probability that it does not have any tire failures?

b What is the probability that it has at least two failures?

5.33 What is the expected value and standard deviation of the number of tire failures per 1000 miles driven in Exercise 5.32?

5.34 The Poisson distribution also applies to events occurring randomly over an area or in a volume. Chocolate chips spread through well-mixed cookie dough tend to follow a Poisson distribution. A commercial baker produces cookies with an average of 8 chips per cookie.

a What is the probability of (horrors!) a chipless cookie?

b A cookie is considered acceptable only if it has at least 5 chips. What fraction of the cookies is acceptable? ■

5.6 The Uniform Distribution

The simplest continuous distribution is the uniform distribution. If Y has a uniform distribution, its probability density is spread out evenly over some range a to b. The uniform density is shown in Figure 5.6. The uniform density arises naturally in random number selection. If $Y = $ a number chosen randomly between 0 and 1, then the probability density of Y is flat over the 0 to 1 range; no one number has higher probability (density) than any other.

FIGURE 5.6 Uniform Probability Density

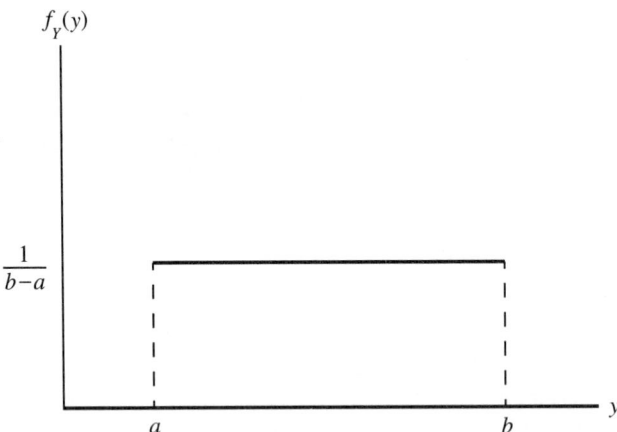

The basic formulas—probability density, expected value, and variance—for a uniform random variable are very simple.

Definition 5.12   Probability Density, Mean, and Variance for a Uniform Random Variable

$$f_Y(y) = \begin{cases} \dfrac{1}{b-a} & \text{if } a < y < b \\ 0, & \text{otherwise} \end{cases}$$

$$E(Y) = \frac{a+b}{2}$$

$$\text{Var}(Y) = \frac{(b-a)^2}{12} \quad \blacksquare$$

Probabilities for uniform random variables may be found by simple geometry. For example, suppose that Y is uniformly distributed between 0 and 50. What is the probability that Y is between 10 and 40? Figure 5.7 describes the situation. The desired probability is the area of a rectangle: the base times the height. Therefore, $P(10 < Y < 40) = 30(1/50) = .6$.

FIGURE 5.7 **Probabilities from a Uniform Distribution**

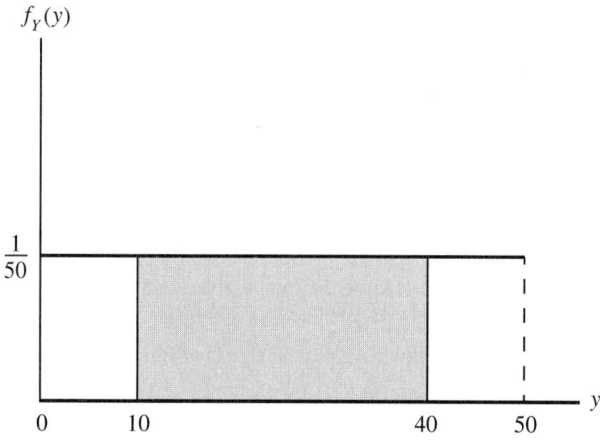

Alternatively, we may find uniform probabilities using elementary calculus. If Y is uniformly distributed between 0 and 50,

$$P(10 < Y < 40) = \int_{10}^{40} \left(\frac{1}{50}\right) dy = \frac{y}{50}\Big|_{10}^{40}$$

$$= \frac{(40-10)}{50} = .6$$

EXAMPLE 5.21

A mail-order company specializing in software programs for microcomputers has found that between 5% and 15% of all orders in a day require special shipping. Suppose that, as a first approximation, we take the distribution of Y = percentage of orders on a randomly chosen day to be uniform over the range 5 to 15. Find the mean and standard deviation of Y and the probability that Y is between 9 and 12.

Solution

We have $a = 5$ and $b = 15$. Therefore,

$$E(Y) = \frac{(5+15)}{2} = 10$$

$$Var(Y) = \frac{(15-5)^2}{12} = 8.3333$$

$$\sigma_Y = \sqrt{8.3333} = 2.89$$

The probability that Y is between 9 and 12 is the area of a rectangle with base $12 - 9 = 3$ and height $1/(15 - 5) = .1$. Therefore,

$$P(9 < Y < 12) = 3(.1) = .3 \qquad \blacksquare$$

E X E R C I S E S

5.35 Suppose Y is a uniformly distributed random variable on the interval $10 < y < 120$. Graph the density of Y and find the probability that Y lies in the interval $60 < y < 85$.

5.36 Find the expected value and standard deviation of Y in Exercise 5.35.

5.37 Calculate the following probabilities for a uniform random variable over the interval $0 < y < 200$:

    a $P(10 < Y < 50)$ **b** $P(Y > 50)$ **c** $P(Y \le 120)$

5.38 A random-number telephone-dialing machine picks the last four digits of telephone numbers randomly between 0000 and 9999 (both included). Treat the random variable $Y = $ number selected as continuous (even though there are 10,000 discrete possibilities) and uniformly distributed.

    a Find $P(0300 < Y \le 1300)$.   **b** Find the variance of Y.

5.39 On summer days, $Y = $ time that a suburban commuter train is late can be modeled as uniformly distributed between 0 and 20 minutes.

    a Find the probability that the train is at least 8 minutes late.

    b Find the standard deviation of the amount of time the train is late. $\blacksquare$

5.7

Exponential Distribution ($\int$)

The Poisson distribution we discussed in Section 5.5 applies to events occurring randomly over time. Specifically, it applies to $Y = $ number of events occurring in a fixed period. If events occur randomly in time, we may also ask about $W = $ waiting time until the next occurrence of an event. Given appropriate assumptions, the probability distribution of W follows an exponential distribution. In contrast to the discrete Poisson random variable, an exponential random variable is continuous.

Recall that the assumptions for a Poisson distribution are that events occur separately and that the occurrence of an event in one period does not change the probability of occurrence in another period. In a waiting-time problem, we must also assume that the expected rate of occurrence is constant over the period. Thus, if there is a rush-hour/off-hour situation in which events occur frequently and then infrequently, exponential probabilities do not apply.

One of the many uses of exponential probabilities is in reliability problems. If a component of a system fails only because of random occurrences (as opposed to wearing out), it's reasonable to assume that nonfailure in previous periods does not change the probability of failure in the next period and also that the rate of failure is constant over time. Of course, there can be no clumping of multiple failures of a single component in a single period. Given these assumptions, the probability density $W =$ time to the next event is exponential.

Definition 5.13 Exponential Density

Assume that events occur randomly over time, with the expected rate of occurrence per unit time denoted λ. If $W =$ time to the next event, then

$$f_W(w) = \lambda e^{-\lambda w} \qquad w > 0$$

$$E(W) = \frac{1}{\lambda}$$

$$\text{Var}(W) = \frac{1}{\lambda^2} \qquad \blacksquare$$

The exponential density is often called a "waiting-time" distribution because it is so often used as a model for the length of time one must wait to obtain the next event.

Probabilities involving the exponential density may be found using elementary integral calculus. It is not hard to show that

$$\int_a^b \lambda e^{-\lambda w} dw = e^{-\lambda a} - e^{-\lambda b}$$

Most calculators and many computer programs evaluate e^x automatically.

EXAMPLE 5.22

The average length of time between submissions of jobs to a mainframe computer during the workday is 2.5 minutes. Assume that jobs arrive randomly over time at a constant expected rate.

a   What is the probability that the waiting time between jobs is between 2 and 5 minutes?

b   Find the mean and standard deviation of the waiting time between jobs.

Solution

a   It is specified that the expected time between arrivals is 2.5 minutes per job; therefore, the expected *rate* of arrivals is $1/2.5 = 0.4$ job per minute.

$$P(2 < W < 5) = \int_2^5 0.4 e^{-0.4w} dw$$

$$= e^{-(0.4)2} - e^{-(0.4)5}$$

$$= .4493 - .1353$$

$$= .3140$$

b   The mean of W was given as 2.5, or it could be computed as $1/\lambda = 1/0.4 = 2.5$. The variance is the square of the expected value for an exponential: $\mu^2 = (2.5)^2 = 6.25$. Alternatively, the variance is $1/\lambda^2 = 1/(0.4)^2 = 6.25$. The standard deviation is, as always, the square root of the variance, $\sqrt{6.25} = 2.5$. Curiously, the standard deviation equals the mean in this distribution. $\blacksquare$

The exponential density is only a model. Accurate use of the model requires that the underlying assumptions hold. The assumption of independence over time is particularly critical for the exponential density to apply. The assumption of a constant average rate is also important.

EXAMPLE 5.23

We assumed in Example 5.22 that jobs are submitted to the computer at a rate of 0.4 job per minute (2.5 minutes per job). Suppose

a There is a tendency for one job submission to be followed immediately by another, related submission.

b There is a tendency for jobs to be submitted "on the hour," when employees arrive from or leave for meetings.

What assumptions are called into question by each tendency?

Solution

a Here there is a dependence. If a job is submitted at one period, there is a higher probability that another job will be submitted shortly thereafter.

b Here there is a nonconstant average rate of occurrence. The rate is higher "on the hour." ∎

EXERCISES

5.40 Use a computer or a calculator that finds e^x to compute the value of the exponential density function $f_Y(y)$ for $\lambda = 0.4$ and $y = 0, 0.5, 1.0, 1.5$, and 2.0. Sketch the density function.

5.41 Compute the following probabilities for an exponential random variable with $\lambda = 0.5$.

    a $P(Y > 2)$ **b** $P(Y > 1)$

    c $P(1 < Y < 2)$ **d** $P(1 \leq Y \leq 2)$

(*Hint:* For part d, use your head, not your calculator.)

5.42 The time between arrivals at a rural emergency treatment center follows an exponential distribution with an average time between arrivals of 1.25 hours. Find the probability that the time between arrivals is more than 1 hour. Find the probability that the time between arrivals is more than 2 hours.

5.43 Rather than focus on the time between arrivals at the treatment center in Exercise 5.42, focus on the arrivals in a given period. Note that the assumptions for the exponential and Poisson distributions are identical; note also that an average time between arrivals of 1.25 hours indicates an average of $1/1.25 = 0.80$ arrival per hour.

    a Using Poisson probabilities, find the probability that there are no arrivals in 1 hour.

    b Find the probability that there are no arrivals in 2 hours.

    c Compare your answers to this exercise with those of Exercise 5.42. Explain your findings.

5.44 The service times for unticketed passengers at an airline ticket counter follow an exponential distribution with a mean of 5 minutes.

    a Find the probability of a service time less than 2.5 minutes.

    b Find the probability of a service time longer than 10 minutes.

5.45 Consider the passenger service situation of Exercise 5.44.

    a What is the expected number of passengers served per minute?

b Find the probability that at least one passenger is served within 2.5 minutes.

c Find the probability that no passenger is served within 10 minutes.

5.46 "Unusual events"—minor operating problems—occur randomly over time at a nuclear power station. The average time between events is 40 days.

    a What is the probability that the time to the next "unusual event" is between 20 and 60 days?

    b Find the standard deviation of the time to the next "unusual event."

5.47 Examination of the records of the power station in Exercise 5.46 shows that "unusual events" occur much more frequently on weekends than on weekdays. What assumption underlying your answers to Exercise 5.46 is called into question?

5.48 A major league baseball team sells individual game tickets at a downtown ticket office during normal working hours. Ticket buyers arrive at the office at the average rate of 12 per hour. Buyers arrive individually and randomly; the average rate stays essentially constant during the day.

    a Find the probability that there are more than 5 arrivals in a 10-minute (1/6-hour) period.

    b Find the probability that the next buyer arrives within 3 minutes.

5.49 Find a number k such that the probability of k or more arrivals in 1/4 hour in Exercise 5.48 is close to .10.

5.50 The time between "crashes" of a certain computer network appears to have an exponential probability distribution. The average time between crashes is 5 days.

    a What is the probability that the time to the next crash will be at least 1 (7-day) week?

    b What is the probability that there will be a 2-week period with no crashes?

    c What is the probability that there will be 4 or more crashes of the computer within a specified 7-day week? ■

5.8   The Normal Distribution

N ow we turn to the most fundamental distribution used in statistical theory: the normal distribution. The normal distribution is a bell-shaped curve that appears in a very wide variety of settings. Standardized test scores are often constructed to yield normal distributions. In fact, a recent and very controversial book on intelligence tests is titled *The Bell Curve* (Herrnstein & Murray, 1994).

Services that rate mutual funds publish data on the yields of various funds that have a specified objective; these yields appear nearly normally distributed. Yields of lumber from trees in a mature forest appear normally distributed. There are theoretical reasons why the normal distribution occurs so often. In particular, the Central Limit Theorem, which we consider in the next chapter, says that any random quantity that is a sum or average of many components will have a nearly normal distribution. Even in situations for which there doesn't seem to be a theoretical reason for a normal distribution, that distribution "just happens" very often.

Many standard statistical procedures that we discuss in later chapters are based on the formal mathematical assumption that the underlying population has a normal distribution. In addition, many methods that are widely used in economics, finance, and marketing are based on an assumption of a normal population. This section is therefore important in understanding many later sections of the text.

A normally distributed random variable is continuous, as opposed to the discrete binomial and Poisson probabilities. Therefore, it has a probability density, a smooth curve that may be thought of as an idealized histogram. Probabilities are not found by simply adding numbers in a table; instead they must be found by calculating areas under the curve. We won't need to do a lot of math with the normal distribution equation, but it's worth presenting.

Definition 5.14   Normal Probability Density

$$f_Y(y) = \frac{1}{\sqrt{2\pi}\,\sigma} e^{-.5((y-\mu)/\sigma)^2} \qquad \blacksquare$$

Notice that the value of y appears in this equation only in the term $((y - \mu)/\sigma)$. The values μ and σ in the normal density function are, in fact, the mean and standard deviation of Y (though we don't prove it). A probability histogram, called the **normal curve**, for a normal random variable is bell-shaped and symmetric around the mean μ, as shown in Figure 5.8.

normal curve

FIGURE 5.8   **Normal Probability Distribution**

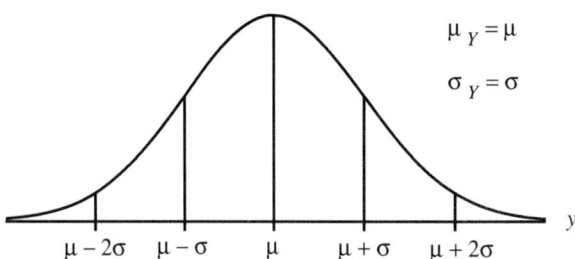

$$\mu_Y = \mu$$
$$\sigma_Y = \sigma$$

Because the math of the normal curve is a little too much like hard work, we will either use computer packages or use normal distribution tables to find normal distribution probabilities. Most statistical packages will calculate cumulative normal distribution probabilities. In Excel, the function

```
=NORMDIST(70,50,10,TRUE)
```

means "find the cumulative probability that Y will be less than or equal to 70, when Y has a normal distribution with mean 50 and standard deviation 10." The result is .9772. Similarly,

```
=NORMDIST(30,50,10,TRUE)
```

results in .0228. To find the probability that Y is between 30 and 70, subtract:

$$P(30 \le Y \le 70) = .9772 - .0228 = .9544$$

Note that we don't need to worry about the probability that Y will exactly equal 70.0000000. For a continuous distribution, that probability is theoretically 0 and practically so small as to be negligible. Note also that this is the Empirical Rule result that the probability of being within 2 standard deviations of the mean is .95.

The "inverse" problem—finding the numerical value corresponding to a given cumulative probability—also can be solved using many statistical packages. In Excel, the function

```
=NORMINV(.9772,50,10)
```

means "find the value y such that $P(Y \le y) = .9772$." The result is 69.99, effectively 70.

If a computer package is not convenient, we can use tables. Tables of normal curve areas (probabilities) are always given for the **standard normal distribution**, which has mean 0 and standard deviation 1. This distribution is universally called the Z distribution. Appendix Table 3 gives areas between 0 and a positive number z. For instance, the entry for $z = 1.00$ is .3413; if Z is the standard normal random variable, then $P(0 \leq Z \leq 1.00) = .3413$, as in Figure 5.9.

FIGURE 5.9 **Standard Normal Probability Distribution**

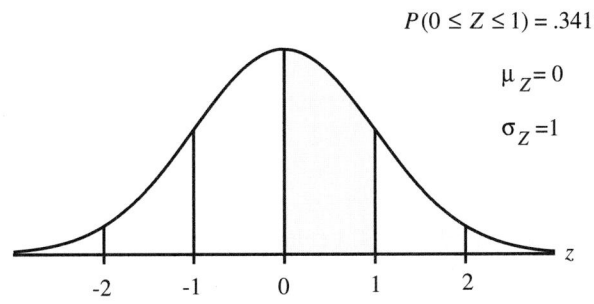

EXAMPLE 5.24

Let Z be a standard normal random variable. Find

a $P(0 \leq Z \leq 1.96)$ b $P(Z > 1.96)$

c $P(-1.96 \leq Z \leq 1.96)$ d $P(-1.00 \leq Z \leq 1.96)$

Solution

An illustration like Figure 5.10 makes it much easier to use normal tables. The entry for $z = 1.96$ (found by looking in the 1.9 row and .06 column) is .4750.

FIGURE 5.10 **Illustration of Normal Probability Calculations**

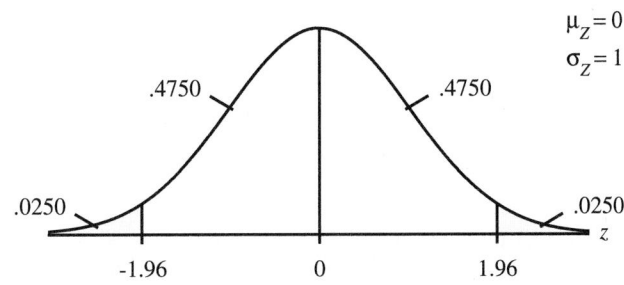

a $P(0 \leq Z \leq 1.96) = .4750$

b   Because the area to the right of 0 must be .5000 (the normal curve is symmetric and the total area beneath the curve is 1), $P(Z > 1.96) = .5000 - .4750 = .0250$.

c By symmetry, the area between -1.96 and 0 must also be .4750. So $P(-1.96 \leq Z \leq 1.96) = .4750 + .4750 = .9500$.

d $P(-1.00 \leq Z \leq 1.96) = .3413 + .4750 = .8163$ (Draw a picture.) ∎

EXAMPLE 5.25

Find k_1 such that $P(0 \leq Z \leq k_1) = .40$ and k_2 such that $P(-k_2 \leq Z \leq k_2) = .60$.

Solution

This problem is the inverse of Example 5.24. In that problem, values are given and probabilities have to be found. Here probabilities are given and values have to be found. Again, a picture is helpful (see Figure 5.11).

FIGURE 5.11 **Inverse Normal Distribution Calculation**

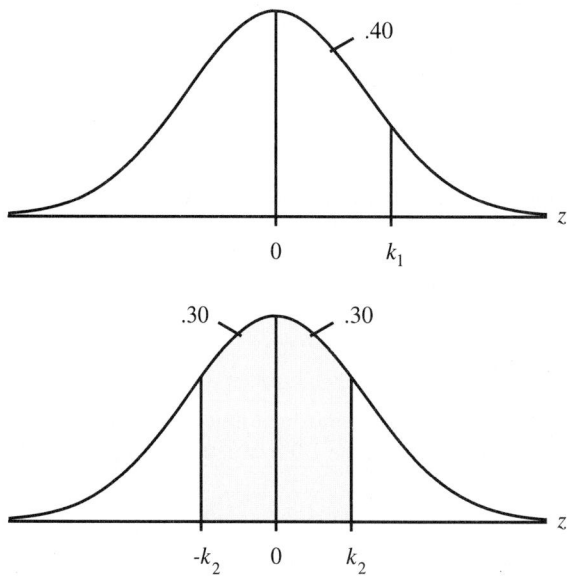

a Looking through Appendix Table 3 for an area of .40, we find that the closest z value is 1.28. Therefore $P(0 \leq Z \leq 1.28) = .40$; that is, $k_1 = 1.28$.

b An area of .30 (half the desired probability, as shown in Figure 5.11) corresponds to $z \approx .84$, so $P(-.84 \leq Z \leq .84) = .60$; that is, $k_2 = .84$. ∎

Any normal random variable Y can be transformed into a standard normal random variable Z by subtracting the expected value μ and dividing the result by the standard deviation σ:

$$Z = \frac{Y - \mu}{\sigma}$$

z-score

For a given value of y, the corresponding value of z, sometimes called a *z*-**score**, is the number of standard deviations that y lies away from μ. If $\mu = 100$ and $\sigma = 20$, a y value of 130 is 1.5 standard deviations above (to the right of) the mean μ and corresponding z-score is $z = (130 - 100)/20 = 1.50$. A y value of 85 is .75 standard deviations below (to the left of) the mean μ and

$$z = \frac{85 - 100}{20} = -.75$$

The relation between specific values of a normal random variable Y and corresponding z-scores is shown in Figure 5.12. [Note that $z = (y - \mu)/\sigma$.]

FIGURE 5.12   **Relation Between Specific Values of Y and z-Scores**

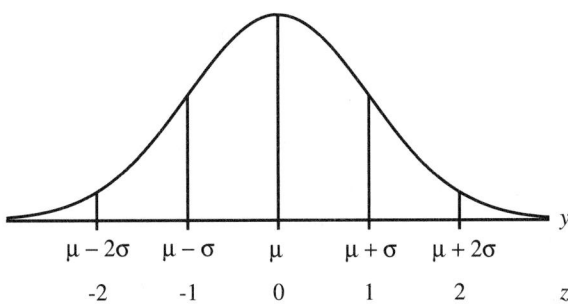

EXAMPLE 5.26

Annual benefits costs for career service employees at a large university are approximately normally distributed with a mean of $18,600 and a standard deviation of $2700. Find the probability that an employee chosen at random has an annual benefits cost less than $15,000; an annual benefits cost greater than $21,000.

Solution

First we draw a figure showing the areas in question (Figure 5.13). Now we must determine the area between 15,000 and 18,600.

$$z = \frac{y - \mu}{\sigma} = \frac{15,000 - 18,600}{2700}$$
$$= \frac{-3600}{2700}$$
$$= -1.33$$

The area between the mean of a normal distribution and a value 1.33 standard deviations to the left of the mean, from Appendix Table 3, is .4082. Hence, the probability of observing an annual benefits cost less than $15,000 is

$$.5 - .4082 = .0918$$

Similarly, to compute the probability of observing a cost over $21,000, we determine the area between 18,600 and 21,000:

$$z = \frac{y - \mu}{\sigma} = \frac{21,000 - 18,600}{2700} = .89$$

The area corresponding to $z = .89$ is .3133. Hence the desired probability is

$$.5 - .3133 = .1867$$

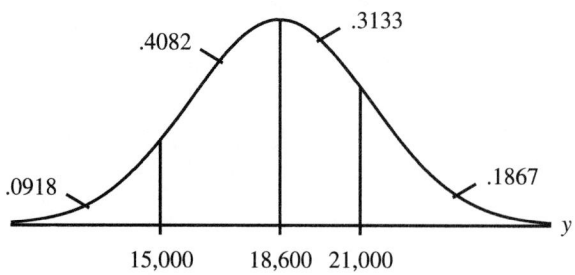

■

EXAMPLE 5.27

If Y has a normal distribution with mean 500 and standard deviation 100, find

a $P(500 \leq Y \leq 696)$ **b** $P(Y \geq 696)$ **c** $P(304 \leq Y \leq 696)$

d k such that $P(500 - k \leq Y \leq 500 + k) = .60$

Solution

a   A y value of 696 is 1.96 standard deviations above the mean; $z = (696 - 500)/100 = 1.96$. Of course, 500 is 0 standard deviations above the mean, so $z = (500 - 500)/100 = 0.00$. Thus $P(500 \leq Y \leq 696) = P(0 \leq Z \leq 1.96) = .4750$.

b $P(Y \geq 696) = P(Z \geq 1.96) = .0250$

c $P(304 \leq Y \leq 696) = P(-1.96 \leq Z \leq 1.96) = .9500$ because 304 corresponds to a z of $(304 - 500)/100 = -.196$.

d   As in Example 5.25, $P(-.84 \leq Z \leq .84) = .60$, so we want a range for Y from .84 standard deviation below the mean $\mu = 500$ to .84 standard deviation above the mean: $P[500 - .84(100) \leq Y \leq 500 + .84(100)] = P(416 \leq Y \leq 584) = .60$ (see Figure 5.14).

FIGURE 5.14   **Normal Distribution Calculations**

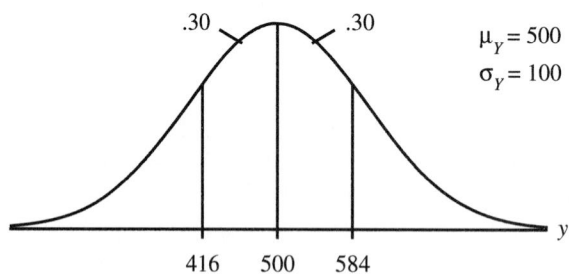

■

A little practice with such problems and a habit of drawing pictures makes normal probability calculations fairly easy.

As we've indicated previously, the concept of a continuous random variable is really an abstraction, because most variables of interest do have a finite number of possible values. But for many situations it is convenient to assume that the random variable of interest has a continuous distribution. In the same way, the normal random variable is an abstraction, because in theory any numerical value, negative as well as positive, is possible, and the probability histogram is a smooth, symmetric, bell-shaped curve. In practice, negative values or positive values such as $612.3142769 may be impossible.

Such issues often don't really matter. If a random variable Y is assumed normal with mean 500 and standard deviation 100, the probability that $Y < 0$ is, by assumption, $P(Z < -5)$, which is effectively zero. Whether or not Y can actually assume negative values hardly matters. Similarly, the errors incurred by rounding $612.3142769 to $612.31 or to $612 are tiny. If a population histogram for a random variable is generally bell-shaped, the normal probability distribution usually provides an excellent model for the actual probability distribution.

EXERCISES

5.51 Suppose that Z represents a standard (tabled) normal random variable. Find the following probabilities, using a computer program if you wish to:

a $P(0 \le Z \le 1.00)$ **b** $P(0 \le Z \le 1.65)$

c $P(-1.00 \le Z \le 0)$ **d** $P(-1.28 \le Z \le 0)$

e $P(-1.65 \le Z \le 1.65)$ **f** $P(-1.28 \le Z \le 1.28)$

g $P(-1.07 \le Z \le 2.33)$ **h** $P(Z \ge 2.65)$

i $P(Z \le -2.42)$ **j** $P(Z \ge 1.39 \text{ or } Z \le -1.39)$

Draw pictures.

5.52 For the standard normal random variable Z, solve the following equations for k, possibly using a computer program:

a $P(Z \ge k) = .01$ **b** $P(-k \le Z \le k) = .98$

c $P(Z \le -k) = .01$ **d** $P(-k \le Z \le k) = .6826$

e $P(-k \le Z \le k) = .9544$ **f** $P(Z \ge k) = .95$

Again, draw pictures.

5.53 Refer to the answers to Exercise 5.52, parts d and e. How do these answers relate to the Empirical Rule?

5.54 Suppose that Y represents a normally distributed random variable with expected value (mean) equal to 100 and standard deviation 15.

a Show that the event $(Y \le 130)$ is equivalent to $(Z \le 2)$.

b Convert the event $(Y \ge 82.5)$ to z-score form.

c Find $P(Y \le 130)$ and $P(Y \ge 82.5)$.

d Find $P(Y > 106)$, $P(Y < 94)$, and $P(94 \le Y \le 106)$.

e Find $P(Y \le 70)$, $P(Y \ge 130)$, and $P(70 < Y < 130)$.

5.55 Consider the random variable Y of Exercise 5.54. Find the value of k satisfying the following:

a $P(100 \le Y \le 100 + k) = .45$ **b** $P(100 - k \le Y \le 100 + k) = .90$

c $P(Y \ge k) = .20$ **d** $P(Y \le k) = .30$

e $P(Y \le k) = .80$ **f** $P(Y \ge k) = .70$

Draw appropriate pictures for each part.

5.56 A financial analyst states that the (subjective probability) price Y of a long-term $1000 government bond one year later is normally distributed with expected value $980 and standard deviation $40.

a Find $P(Y \ge 1000)$. **b** Find $P(Y \le 940)$.

c Find $P(960 \le Y \le 1060)$.

5.57 Refer to the random variable Y of Exercise 5.56.

    a Find the value of k satisfying $P(Y \geq k) = .90$.

    b Find the value k such that the probability that the price of the bond (one year later) exceeds k is .60.

5.58 Assume that the hourly wage rate earned by a worker in a clothing factory (based on a piecework pay system) is normally distributed with expected value \$5.10 and standard deviation \$0.40.

    a Find the probability that a worker's hourly rate exceeds \$5.40.

    b Find the probability that a worker's hourly rate is between \$4.70 and \$5.50.

    c Find the probability that a worker's hourly rate exceeds a contractual minimum of \$3.90. ■

5.9

Summing Up

H ere are some issues to consider when considering whether a particular probability distribution applies to a problem.

1 Binomial, negative binomial, and geometric probabilities apply when there is a series of distinct, separate trials. In contrast, Poisson and exponential probabilities may apply when there is a random process occurring continuously, usually continuously over time.

2 Hypergeometric probabilities apply in the special situation of sampling a success/failure population without replacement. If the population size is large compared to the sample size, hypergeometric and binomial probabilities are numerically very close to the same.

3 One key to choosing which probability model should apply is determining whether the number of trials (or the length of time) is fixed, as opposed to prespecifying the number of successes (or the number of events). Binomial probabilities may apply if the number of trials is fixed, and Poisson probabilities may apply if the length of time is fixed. But if the number of successes is fixed, negative binomial probabilities (or geometric probabilities in the special case of only one success) may apply. If the number of events occurring randomly over time is fixed at one, exponential probabilities may apply.

4 Think about the reasonableness of assumptions. For binomial and negative binomial probabilities, the key assumptions are fixed probability of success and (especially) independent trials. For Poisson and exponential probabilities, the key assumptions are nonclumping and independence; in addition, exponential probabilities require a constant expected rate of occurrence.

5 All these models apply only in special situations. If none of them is applicable, the general methods of Chapter 3 can still be used to find probabilities.

6 The shortcut formulas for expected values and variances also apply only to the special situations. If underlying assumptions aren't reasonable, the shortcut formulas don't apply, and the general definitions in Chapter 4 must be used.

In addition, you may want to reread the summary of key ideas at the beginning of the chapter.

EXAMPLE 5.28

A regional public transportation agency has a problem with injury claims as a result of bus and trolley accidents. Agency managers became convinced that many of the claims were fraudulent when 30 or 40 injury claims were routinely received from an accident with 20 passengers on board. The agency began to contest claims that it believed were fraudulent. After an initial learning period, the agency was successful in about 80% of the actions. There was wide variation in results, however; when the agency contested 30 claims from an accident, it normally succeeded in anywhere from 16 to all 30 of the cases, occasionally fewer.

Is this a reasonable range of variation making standard assumptions? If not, what might explain the extra variation? If an accident resulted in 60 claims rather than 30, is it likely that the agency will succeed in between 32 and 60 contests?

Solution

Each contested claim can be regarded as either a success or a failure, so we might hope that binomial probabilities would apply. The expected number of successes, assuming $n = 30$ and $\pi = .80$, should be 24.0; the standard deviation should be $\sqrt{30(.80)(.20)} = 2.191$. A range from 16 to 30 would be from $(16 - 24)/ = -3.65$ standard deviations below the mean to $(30 - 24)/ = 2.74$ standard deviations above the mean, which seems quite wide. The exact binomial probability of 15 or fewer successes, from tables or a statistical package, is .0002. Therefore, if the binomial assumptions were met, it would be extremely rare for the authority to succeed in 15 or fewer challenges. In this case, it is likely that an assumption has been violated; most likely there is dependence, with some accidents yielding a set of evidently false claims and others yielding much more plausible claims. Dependence increases the variability of results above the binomial value, as seems to be occurring in this case.

Doubling the number of trials from 30 to 60 would *not* double the probable range of results. Variability (as measured by the standard deviation) increases as the square root of n, so doubling n would increase variability by $\sqrt{2} \approx 1.414$ times, not twice. ∎

SUPPLEMENTARY EXERCISES

5.59 A telephone sales firm is considering purchasing a machine that randomly selects and automatically dials telephone numbers. The firm would be using the machine to call residences during the evening; calls to business phones would be wasted. The manufacturer of the machine claims that its programming reduces the business phone rate to 15%. As a test, 100 phone numbers are to be selected at random from a very large set of possible numbers.

    a Are the binomial assumptions satisfied in this situation?

    b Find the probability that at least 24 of the numbers belong to business phones.

    c If, in fact, 24 of the 100 numbers turn out to be business phones, does this cast serious doubt on the manufacturer's claim? Explain.

5.60 Refer to Exercise 5.59. Find the expected value and variance of Y, the number of business phone numbers in the sample.

5.61 It is estimated that 5% of all Medicaid claims in a particular city are fraudulent. A random sample of 50 claims is taken.

    a What is the probability that at most 1 claim in the sample is fraudulent?

    b What is the probability that at least 4 are fraudulent?

5.62 Some people claim that female managers tend to be placed in fringe areas, such as public relations or personnel management, as opposed to the central areas of production, marketing, and finance. Suppose that a firm has 24 male and 6 female managers at the assistant vice president level. Of these positions, 14 are regarded as fringe positions.

    a In how many distinct ways can the 14 fringe managers be selected?

    b In how many ways can the fringe managers be selected such that 5 of the 6 women are included?

    c If the fringe managers had been randomly selected, what is the probability that at least 5 would be women?

5.63 Assume that lost-time industrial accidents occur in a plant according to a Poisson distribution with mean .12 per day. Let $Y =$ number of such accidents in a 10-day period.

    a Find $P(Y = 1)$ and $P(Y \le 1)$.   **b** Find $E(Y)$ and σ_Y.

5.64 The weekly demand for 5-pound sacks of flour at a particular supermarket is assumed to be approximately normal with mean 72.0 cases and standard deviation 1.6 cases. Let $Y =$ demand in a particular week.

    a Find $P(Y \le 72.8)$ and $P(71.2 \le Y \le 72.8)$.

    b Find $P(Y \ge 74.0)$.

    c The ordering policy of the market is that there be a 1% chance of stockout (demand exceeding supply) in any particular week. How much flour must be stocked to achieve this goal?

5.65 Refer to Exercise 5.64.

    a What is the probability that demand exceeds 73.0 cases in a particular week?

    b What is the probability that demand exceeds 73.0 cases in exactly 3 or 4 consecutive weeks? Assume independence from week to week.

5.66 A certain amount of material is wasted in cutting patterns for garments. A producer of army uniforms has found that the wastage is normally distributed with mean 4.1% and standard deviation .6% from lot to lot.

    a In a particular lot, what is the probability that the wastage exceeds 5%?

    b If the actual amount of material required for a lot is 4700 yards, and 5000 yards of material are available, what is the probability that the supply of material is adequate?

5.67 Suppose that in Exercise 5.66 a particular cutter exceeds 5% wastage in 8 of 10 lots.

    a What is the probability of exceeding 5% in at least 8 of 10 lots?

    b Would such a result conclusively indicate that the cutter was inefficient?

5.68 A modem is an electronic device used in communication between computers. The specifications for a particular modem demand that the mean number of errors in transmitting through the device be 1 per 5000 words (or better). A particular modem is to be tested on a 25,000-word transmission. If 8 or more errors occur in transmission, the device will not be accepted. Assume that Poisson probabilities apply and that the modem just meets the 1 per 5000 standard.

    a What is the probability that the device will be accepted?

    b Can you think of a reason why the Poisson assumptions may not hold?

5.69 Assume that the Poisson distribution applies in Exercise 5.68, but also that the modem has a mean error rate of 1 per 2500 words, thus not meeting specifications. What is the probability that the device will be accepted?

5.70 Executives at a soft drink company wish to test a new formulation of their chief product. The new drink is tested in comparison to the current one. Each of 1000 potential customers is given a cup of the current formulation and a cup of the new one. The cups are labeled H and K to avoid bias. Each customer indicates a preference. Assume that, in fact, the customers can't detect a difference and are, in effect, guessing. Define Y to be the number (out of 1000) indicating preference for the new formulation.

    a What probability distribution should apply to Y? Do the assumptions underlying that distribution seem plausible in this context?

b Find the mean and standard deviation of Y.

5.71 A firm is considering using telemarketing techniques to supplement traditional marketing methods. It's estimated that 1 of every 100 calls results in a sale. Suppose that 250 calls are made in a single day.

    a Write an expression for the probability that there are 5 or fewer sales. Don't carry out any arithmetic.

    b What did you assume in answering part a? Are any of these assumptions grossly unreasonable?

5.72 The chief executive officer (CEO) of a medium-size corporation must select 3 individuals to head the firm's annual drive for community charities. There are three divisions (A, B, and C) within the firm and 5, 6, and 4 individuals, respectively, within the divisions who could be chosen.

    a How many combinations of 3 individuals can be chosen such that 1 individual comes from each of the three divisions?

    b Suppose that the CEO chooses the individuals at random. What is the probability that at least 2 of them come from division A?

5.73 Refer to Exercise 5.72, part b. Let Y = number of individuals chosen from division A. Find the expected value and variance of Y.

5.74 Brand managers at a consumer products company regard an introductory advertising campaign for a new product as successful if at least 20% of the target group is made aware of the product. After one such campaign, a market research study finds that 56 of 400 individuals sampled are aware of the product. The target group is all adults who possess driver's licenses in the United States.

    a Write an expression for the exact probability that 56 or fewer people in the sample are aware of the product, assuming that 20% of the target group is aware of the product. What probability distribution applies? What assumptions have you made?

    b Find the expected value and standard deviation for the number of people in the sample who are aware of the product.

    c Use the normal distribution with the mean and standard deviation just found to find a numerical value for this probability.

    d If you were the brand manager, would you believe that the advertising campaign had been successful?

5.75 A certain birth defect occurs with probability .0001; that is, 1 of every 10,000 babies has this defect. If 5000 babies are born at a particular hospital in a given year, what is the probability that there is at least one baby with the defect? If you have access to a computer package that calculates probabilities, use it to find a numerical answer.

5.76 Several states now have a Lotto lottery game. A player chooses 6 distinct integers in the range 1 to 40. If exactly those 6 numbers are selected as the winning numbers, the player receives a very large prize. What is the probability that a particular set of 6 numbers will be drawn? You may wish to think of the 6 numbers drawn as "success" numbers.

5.77 In the Lotto game described in Exercise 5.76, there are smaller prizes for selecting exactly 5 of the 6 winning numbers and even smaller prizes for selecting exactly 4 of the 6 winning numbers.

    a What is the probability of selecting exactly 4 of the 6 winning numbers?

    b What is the probability of selecting at least 4 of the 6 winning numbers?

5.78 Suppose that the Lotto game in Exercise 5.76 is changed such that 6 numbers were chosen in the range 1 to 42, rather than 1 to 40.

    a Without doing any arithmetic, determine if the probability of selecting all 6 winning numbers should be larger or smaller than it was in Exercise 5.76. Will the change be small or large?

    b Now compute the probability of selecting all 6 winning numbers, chosen from the numbers 1 to 42.

    c Compare your answer to part b with the answer to Exercise 5.76. Did the probability change as you expected in part a of this exercise?

5.79 Suppose that, in the Lotto game of Exercise 5.76 (with 40 numbers), 1,000,000 players make independent choices of the 6 numbers.

   a What probability distribution applies to the random variable Y = number of players selecting all 6 numbers?

   b Find an expression for $P(Y = 0)$. Don't carry out the arithmetic.

   c Write an expression for $P(Y \geq 2)$.

5.80 **a** Find the expected value and variance of the random variable Y in Exercise 5.79.

   b If you have a suitable computer program, use it to calculate a numerical value for the exact probability.

5.81 Fires in occupied homes in a particular city occur at a rate of 1 every 2 days.

   a What is the expected number of fires in homes over a 7-day week?

   b Find the probability that there are at least 4 fires in a particular week.

   c What are you assuming about the occurrence of fires in your answer to part b? Do any of the assumptions seem grossly unreasonable?

5.82 The operator of a mainframe computer system receives unscheduled requests to mount tapes. By policy, these requests must be answered as quickly as possible; therefore, they interrupt scheduled work flow. Data indicate that the rate of such requests during the 9 A.M. to 5 P.M. shift is about 1.5 per hour. Let Y = number of requests received in a particular 9 A.M. to 5 P.M. shift.

   a Find the mean and standard deviation of Y.

   b Find $P(Y > 8)$.

5.83 Refer to Exercise 5.82. Find the probability that the time between successive requests is at least 2 hours.

5.84 The computer system manager in Exercise 5.82 notes that the demand for unscheduled tape mounts varies during the typical workday. Between 9 A.M. and 1 P.M. there is an average of 1 request per hour; between 1 P.M. and 5 P.M. there is an average of 2 requests per hour.

   a Does this fact change your answers to part a of Exercise 5.82?

   b Does this fact affect your answer to part b of that exercise?

5.85 Airlines have an ongoing problem with "no-shows," individuals who make reservations for a flight and purchase a ticket, but do not appear at flight time. Almost all no-shows are business travelers holding full-fare tickets. For competitive reasons, airlines feel obligated to honor these tickets for another flight or for a refund. Thus, if an airline makes only as many reservations as it has seats, it is quite likely to have empty seats as a result of the no-shows.

To deal with the problem, airlines overbook flights. This means they deliberately make more reservations than the flight has seats. Of course, the risk of this policy is that more people will appear for the flight than can be accommodated. When this happens, passengers must be bumped to a later flight, at considerable cost in money and good will.

Airlines have adopted specific rules for how much overbooking will be allowed on a flight. Typically, such a rule will say "book no more than 190 reservations on a 184 seat plane." Such rules ignore the difference between full-fare and special-fare reservations. The latter typically do not allow refunds, or require a substantial charge for a reservation change. They are used largely for personal travel and rarely result in no-shows. If a particular flight has a large number of special-fare reservations, overbooking will very likely lead to bumping.

Experience with one particular flight indicates that about 8% of full-fare reservations (and virtually no special-fare reservations) result in no-shows. There is no particular reason to think that one no-show increases or decreases the chance of another. The plane has 156 seats. The airline wants to have no more than a 10% chance of bumping a passenger. Assuming that 80 of the seats have been reserved for special-fare reservations, how many full-fare reservations can the airline accept? This is not a question that can be answered by a simple formula; trial and error may be needed. Write a brief report to the airline's reservations manager, explaining how to carry out the calculations for varying numbers of special-fare reservations. ■

Special Probability Distributions

A copy machine provider is about to undergo a major expansion. The company leases and services copiers for businesses and institutions. It is about to absorb another firm in the same business. One major question facing the company is: How many service technicians are required for the combined load of the two firms?

The company distinguishes two categories of copier. Office-use copiers are typically used for small numbers of copies and are operated by secretaries and casual users. Production-use copiers are typically used for major jobs and are operated by specialists. The company leases different styles of copiers for the two uses. It maintains separate staffs of service technicians for the two. Because the copiers are standard brands, service is the main area of competition with other providers. The company wants to have an adequate staff of technicians, but it doesn't want to have so many that they are idle a large part of the time.

Currently—before it absorbs the other firm—the company has 2105 office-use copiers and 386 production-use copiers under lease. Requests for service are treated basically on a first-called, first-served basis. The service dispatcher logs requests and assigns technicians to them in order of request. Office-use technicians normally can service a maximum of 8 requests per day; production-use technicians typically work on more complex problems and can service a maximum of 4 requests per day. There is relatively little variation in the service time required per job.

Most of the variation in the process occurs on the demand side. If a sudden burst of requests overloads the supply of technicians, jobs are bumped to the next day. The company's president feels that bumped customers are likely to go elsewhere when their contracts expire. The company currently employs 8 technicians for office-use copiers and 7 technicians for production-use copiers. The company uses a guideline that office-use copiers will need service once every 50 workdays (though some think it's once every 40 or once every 60 days) and production-use copiers, once every 20 workdays (possibly once every 16 or once every 24 days).

When the company absorbs the other firm, it will have 3185 office-use copiers and 596 production-use copiers under lease. The company president has heard two arguments about the required number of technicians. First, the absorption represents basically a 50% increase in leases, so an increase of 50% in technicians is necessary. The counterargument is that the company maintains an excess of technicians to protect against exceptionally heavy bursts of requests. The law of averages says that the bigger pool of copiers under lease should tend to even out these bursts, so a proportionate increase in technicians isn't necessary.

The president has asked you to examine the question, particularly the risk of bumping requests to the next workday. You might reasonably assume that service calls occur essentially randomly and that the concern is with variability rather than a time trend in the average number of calls per day. The president is willing to read technical material, but has had no formal training in statistics, so you'll have to explain your ideas clearly. ■

A very bad writer named Nunn
Sent love letters out by the ton.
His prose wasn't deathless—
Left no woman breathless.
His chance of success? .01.

Random Sampling and Sampling Distributions

Any summary statistic will vary from one sample to another and from the true population or process value. We can determine the pattern of that variation. Using probability theory or computer simulation, we can determine the theoretical (sampling) distribution of a statistic, given certain assumptions. Several important concepts in this chapter will be used heavily later on:

1   Any statistical study can be seriously distorted by bias— systematic distortions in the collection of data. There are several sources of bias, including selection bias, in which some subgroups are systematically over- or underrepresented in the data. One of the important steps in evaluating any statistical study is consideration of how serious the bias problem is.

2   If a sample is genuinely random, we can derive the theoretical distribution of any summary statistic, given limited assumptions about the population. This theoretical distribution is different from the population distribution.

3   In particular, the sample mean has expected value equal to the population or process mean. The standard deviation of its theoretical distribution, called the *standard error of the mean*, is the population standard deviation divided by the square root of the sample size.

4   The sample mean (and sample sum) have approximately a normal distribution. The distribution is exactly normal if the population distribution is exactly normal. Otherwise, according to the Central Limit Theorem the distribution is approximately normal for a large enough sample size. The quality of the approximation depends most importantly on the skewness of the population or process distribution.

5   A normal probability plot is useful for checking whether a distribution is nearly normal. It can be applied either to sample data or to a summary statistic such as a mean or median in a simulation study. Normality is indicated by a straight line. Skewness appears as a curve, with the direction of the curve depending on the choice of axes. A heavy-tailed, outlier-prone distribution appears as an S shape in a normal plot.

Now we can combine the ideas on summarizing data from Chapter 2 and the probability concepts from Chapters 3–5 into a central notion of statistics, which is the concept of the sampling distribution of a statistic.

Summary statistics—means, medians, standard deviations, anything—vary from one sample to another. Samples from populations are taken randomly, so the means (for example) of two samples from the same population will differ to some degree. Samples from ongoing processes, such as production or sales, are affected by uncontrolled, random influences, so two sample means from the same process will differ randomly. The sampling distribution of a summary statistic is a way to describe the variability of that statistic from one sample to another.

Probability theory can be used to obtain a sampling distribution, given certain assumptions. Such probability concepts as expected value and standard deviation of a random variable will be used repeatedly in this chapter.

It's useful to distinguish two kinds of samples. **Cross-sectional samples** are taken from an underlying population at a particular time. As the name implies, the idea is to obtain a reasonably accurate cross section of the relevant population at a particular time. **Time-series samples** are taken over time from a random process. A closely related distinction is between **enumerative studies** and **analytic studies**. Enumerative studies involve sampling from a reasonably well-defined population; the purpose is usually to describe the nature of the population. Enumerative studies usually use cross-sectional samples. Analytic studies typically look at the results of a random process; the purpose is often to predict the future behavior of the process. Analytic studies usually involve time-series samples.

In this chapter, we focus on cross-sectional samples and enumerative studies. The basic ideas are easier to grasp in this context. However, the same principles apply to time-series samples and analytic studies. Sample statistics will vary from one sample to another whether the sample is cross-sectional or time series. The reason for the random variation, though, is different in the two kinds of studies. In cross-sectional samples, the variation arises from the random sampling process. In time-series samples, the variation is part of the random process itself—it is not introduced by sampling. Time-series samples require some extra care in analysis. The random variation may be more complicated than simply random sampling. In particular, there may well be statistical dependence in the series over time. This dependence violates one key assumption underlying many statistical procedures.

One way that randomness and probability relate to summary statistics is in random sampling. In Section 6.1, we consider why we want to sample randomly and discuss how to do it. Then, in Section 6.2, we turn to the basic definition of a sampling distribution and the use of expected value and standard deviation in that context. In Section 6.3, we apply the basic ideas to the most important special case—namely, the sample mean. In this section, we first encounter a critical mathematical result, the Central Limit Theorem, which we'll use heavily thereafter. Finally, we discuss a very useful form of data plotting, the normal probability plot, in Section 6.4.

This is necessarily a theoretical chapter. The results of this chapter will be used over and over again in the methods of the following chapters. The uses may not be obvious to you at first reading, but we promise that you'll see them later. Bear with us. ∎

Random Sampling

S ampling to obtain data is an important managerial role. Customers need to be sampled to find out what they like and don't like about the manager's business. The very definition of quality in a service business is customer satisfaction. One of the best ways of finding out if customers are satisfied is to ask them. Also, it's too expensive to check every part in a supplier's shipment to see if it meets the manager's specification; if testing the part is destructive, checking every part is *really* expensive. In addition, auditing records is time-consuming and costly; almost all audits are based on sampling rather than a complete census.

Statistics books, including this one, urge you to use random sampling to collect data. A basic reason for using random sampling is to ensure that the inferences made from the sample data are not distorted by a **selection bias**. A selection bias exists whenever there is a systematic tendency to overrepresent or underrepresent some part of the population. For example, a telephone sample of households in a region, conducted entirely between the hours of 9 A.M. and 5 P.M., would be severely biased toward households with at least one nonworking member. Hence, any inferences made from the sample data would be biased toward the attitudes or opinions of nonworking members and might not be truly representative of households in the region. Similarly, a sample of charge accounts taken by selecting a set of transactions would be biased toward active, many-transaction accounts, and away from inactive ones. Inferences from these data might not reflect the characteristics of the set of all accounts. A random sampling plan, by definition, avoids this kind of bias.

selection bias

There are several other potential sources of bias. In general, a manager evaluating a statistical study should consider what possible systematic distortions there are in the way the data were gathered. Selection bias is one possibility. Another is *nonresponse*, or refusal, bias. Even though potential sample members have been chosen at random, not all of them will be willing to participate. It's a rather heroic assumption to believe that nonrespondents behave and believe the same way as respondents. This bias is a severe problem for market research studies. To the extent that repeated studies are done and sample results are compared to actual outcomes (such as the market share of new products), a manager can get some handle on this problem. It is always a concern.

Still another distortion can arise from the way questions are phrased. Many public opinion polls seem to swing wildly in assessing voters' beliefs about various issues. If you look carefully at the way questions are worded, very often you will see that the question is encouraging a particular response. One of the important steps in any sample survey of people is pretesting the questions to ensure they are neutral and allow the respondent to make a response without artificial pressure.

operational definitions

The bias in phrasing questions is one example of the need for **operational definitions**. Consider, for example, an opinion poll that reports on "attitudes toward unions." If this is defined as the answer to a question such as "Do you agree that unions can cause inconvenience and bad labor–management relations?" you will get one kind of answer. If the finding is defined as the answer to a question such as "Do you agree that unions have been important in securing employee rights and decent pay?" you will very likely get quite a different answer. Before taking a result at face value, ask exactly how the variables have been measured. A little detective work can often reveal which studies are propaganda and which are serious. An excellent question to ask of any statistical study is "Just how did you define what you're measuring?" David Levine of Baruch College has a nice example: "How many doors are there in your home?" Does that include only the doors that people can walk through? The door to your refrigerator? The little trapdoor to pour water into your coffee maker? Obviously, definition matters a lot.

Simple random sampling is a process whereby each possible sample of a given size has the same probability of being selected. Obtaining a truly, or even approximately, random sample requires some thought and effort. A random sample is not a casual or haphazard sample. The **target population** must be identified. In principle, a list of all elements (possible individual values) in the population ought to be constructed, with elements to be included in the sample selected randomly from the list using a table of random numbers.

target population

EXAMPLE 6.1

Suppose that the research staff of a Federal Reserve bank wishes to take a random sample of checks written on individual (nonbusiness) checking accounts to determine average amount, time to clearance, and insufficient-funds rates. How might they do so?

Solution

First, the target population must be defined. Is it all individual checks written in a given period, or is it all checks processed by the Federal Reserve clearinghouse during that time? There's a difference because a check that is cashed at the bank on which it was originally drawn never gets to the clearinghouse. Assume that the clearinghouse definition is chosen. The next step is to establish a random sampling method. One could, in principle, put a numerical tag on every one of the 326,274 (or whatever number) checks processed by the center on a particular day. Then a random sample of 1000 could be drawn by selecting 6-digit random numbers and the checks with corresponding tags (passing over 000000 and anything larger than 326274). Obviously, this would be a very impractical and expensive way to obtain a random sample. Such a method only serves as an idealization against which a more practical method can be measured.

Another possibility is to sample every 326th check processed. This method is not literally random sampling because, for instance, two successive checks couldn't be included in the sample. No doubt we could dream up situations for which sampling every 326th check would introduce some kind of selection bias; however, this process should yield a fairly good approximation to random sampling, at a manageable cost. ■

The applicability of sampling methods is much broader than just the familiar political polls and market research studies. Sampling should be considered whenever information is desired and the cost (in dollars, in labor, or in time) of obtaining complete information is excessive. For example, suppose that a processor of potato chips sells the product through 1943 retail outlets. A critical variable for the success of the product is the average amount of shelf space devoted to the product per outlet. It would be absurd for the processor to visit every outlet and measure the shelf space devoted to that product. Assuming that the potato chip processor had a list of the retail outlets, it would be relatively easy to obtain a random sample of, say, 100 outlets and to measure the average shelf space in that sample.

sampling frame Ideally, one has a list of the elements of the target population. More often, one has a list that almost, but not quite, equals the target population. The almost right list is called the **sampling frame**, to indicate that it is not exactly the same as the target population. A good sampling frame is sometimes fairly easy to obtain, as it would be in the case of the potato chip processor, who most likely knows almost all, but not quite all, retail outlets. When sampling human populations, a good sampling frame is harder to develop. People move; a directory or a mailing list can become outdated quickly. Telephone directories are not a completely reliable source for developing a sampling frame; there are unlisted phone numbers and multiple phone numbers. Perhaps the most serious problem is that people without phones tend strongly to be poor people. This problem was a major cause of one of the most notorious failures in sampling, the *Literary Digest* poll before the 1936 U.S. presidential election. The *Literary Digest*, a popular magazine of the time, took a huge survey (2.4 million responses), based in large part on telephone books. In 1936, during the Great Depression, this procedure introduced a substantial bias. The magazine forecast that the Republican candidate would win the election; he won only two states. Much of the effort in conducting a good sampling study should go into developing the sampling frame.

Given a decent sampling frame, random sampling can be done with a computer program that generates random numbers, or with a table of random numbers. For example, the Resampling Stats program generated random samples of 10 items from a population numbered 1 to 916, as follows:

```
1: SEED 135791
2: 'SELECT 10 NUMBERS AT RANDOM IN THE RANGE 1 TO 916
3: GENERATE 10 1,916 LIST1
4: PRINT LIST1
5: SEED 197531
6: 'SELECT ANOTHER 10 NUMBERS
7: GENERATE 10 1,916 LIST2
8: PRINT LIST1 LIST2
```

```
LIST1   =   58   714   145   18   485   830   259   365   17
750

LIST2   =   501   845   212   72   530   409   749   463   713
694
```

The SEED statements specify a beginning point for the random number sequence. If you used a different SEED number, or omitted it and let the computer pick a seed randomly, you would get a different sequence. Most statistical packages can be used to generate random numbers.

Careful planning and a certain amount of ingenuity are required to have even a decent approximation to a random sample. This is especially true when the elements in the target population are people. People throw away mail questionnaires, they are not home to answer telephone surveys, and they modify answers to conform to social norms. Too often, surveys of people are done in a haphazard way, using a hastily composed questionnaire mailed (often addressed to "occupant") according to a conveniently chosen mailing list, with no provisions for following up on those who do not respond. The result is bad data, riddled with biases that have unknowable effects. Lots of statistical methods can be applied to such data, but the well-known adage applies: Garbage in, garbage out. Getting reasonable samples of human populations is a considerable art (and a fairly substantial industry); we will not try to capture the essence of that art in a couple of pages.

Although there are other valid and useful sampling methods, such as stratified sampling, most uses of probability theory in the remaining chapters are based on simple random sampling. The basic ideas remain the same when other sampling methods are used. The formulas just get a little more complicated.

EXERCISES

6.1 Assume we want to select a random sample of $n = 10$ entities from a population of 800 individuals. Use a computer package to identify the individuals to be sampled.

6.2 City officials sample the opinions of homeowners in a community about the possibility of raising taxes to improve the quality of local schools. A directory of all homes in the city is used; a computer generates random numbers to identify the addresses to be sampled. An interviewer visits each home between the hours of 3 P.M. and 6 P.M. If no one is home, the address is eliminated from the sample and replaced by another randomly chosen address. Does this process approximate random sampling?

6.3 A university bookstore manager is mildly concerned about the number of textbooks that were underordered and thus unavailable two days after the beginning of classes. The manager instructs an employee to pick a random number, go to the place where that number book is shelved, examine the next 50 titles, and record how many titles are unavailable.

    a Technically, this process doesn't yield a random sample of the books in the store. Why not?

    b How could a truly random sample be obtained?

6.4 A professional baseball team has a 20-game ticket plan and a 40-game ticket plan. The sales director wants to assess fan interest in a combination plan that would allow two separate purchasers of 20-game plans to pool their money and buy a 40-game plan at a modest discount. The target population to be sampled is all current 20-game plan purchasers. An up-to-date list of the 4256 current purchasers is available. Explain how to obtain a random sample of the current purchasers.

6.5 One way to sample the purchasers in Exercise 6.4 is to develop a list of the seat numbers held by purchasers and to take a random sample of seat numbers. Most likely this will not yield a random sample of purchasers, however. Explain why not.

6.6 A building manager for a 2526-office complex hires a new cleaning contractor. The manager wants to get a rough idea of how satisfactory the contractor's weekend cleaning efforts are. One possible strategy is to select 3 offices on the first three floors and to examine those offices and the 10 offices on either side. Another strategy, which requires roughly the same amount of time, is to select 15 offices completely at random. It is argued that the first strategy is better because it allows for inspection of more offices. Is the argument valid? ∎

6.2   Sample Statistics and Sampling Distributions

Once a sample has been selected and numerical data obtained, the first task is to summarize the data. In Chapter 2, we defined several summary measures, such as the sample mean and the sample standard deviation. Each of these is an example of a **sample statistic**.

sample statistic

The value of any summary statistic will vary from one sample to another. The numerical value that a sample statistic will have cannot be exactly predicted in advance. Even if we know that a population mean μ is \$216.37 and that the population standard deviation σ is \$32.90—even if we know the complete population distribution—we cannot say that the sample mean $\overline{Y}$ will be exactly \$216.37. A sample statistic is a random variable; it is subject to random variation because it is based on a random sample of measurements selected from the population or process of interest. Like any other random variable, a sample statistic has a probability distribution. We call the theoretical probability distribution of a sample statistic the **sampling distribution** of that statistic.

sampling distribution

One useful way to think of a sampling distribution is to have a computer program draw many random samples from a specified population, compute the statistic for each sample, and construct a histogram of the results. The Resampling Stats program drew 1000 samples, each of size 4, from an exponential population with mean 1.0 and standard deviation 1.0. The exponential distribution is very skewed, as shown in Figure 6.1. The program yielded the following results:

```
 1: SEED 135791
 2: 'DRAW 1000 SAMPLES FROM AN EXPONENTIAL POPULATION.
 3: REPEAT 1000
 4:   EXPONENTIAL 4 1 SAMPLE
 5:   'CALCULATE MEAN FOR THE SAMPLE.
 6:   MEAN SAMPLE AMEAN
 7:   'SAVE THE RESULT
 8:   SCORE AMEAN YBARS
 9: END
10: 'PLOT DATA, FIND AVERAGE, STD. ERROR.
11: HISTOGRAM YBARS
12: MEAN YBARS AVGMEAN
13: STDEV YBARS STDMEANS
14: PRINT AVGMEAN STDMEANS
```

FIGURE 6.1 **Exponential Distribution**

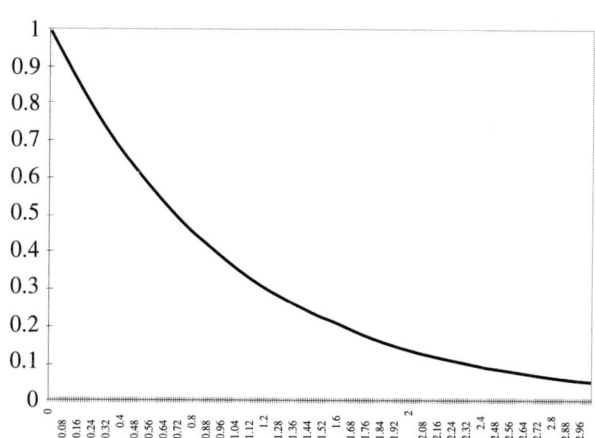

Exponential Distribution

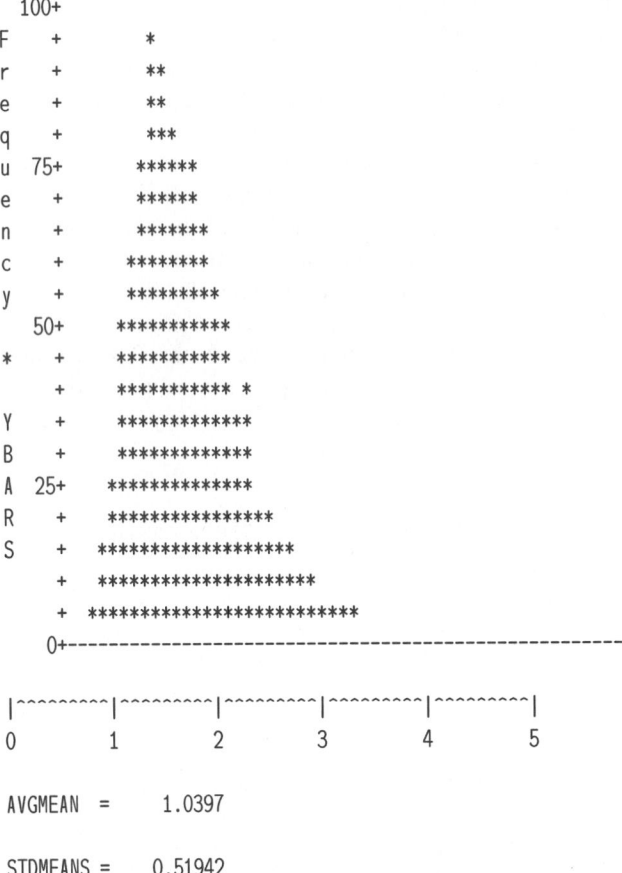

```
    100+
F    +         *
r    +        **
e    +        **
q    +        ***
u   75+       ******
e    +        ******
n    +        *******
c    +        ********
y    +        *********
    50+       **********
*    +        **********
     +        ********** *
Y    +        ************
B    +        ************
A   25+       *************
R    +        ***************
S    +        ******************
     +        ********************
     +        *************************
     0+-------------------------------------------------------

   |∿∿∿∿∿∿∿∿|∿∿∿∿∿∿∿∿|∿∿∿∿∿∿∿∿|∿∿∿∿∿∿∿∿|∿∿∿∿∿∿∿∿|
   0        1        2        3        4        5
```

AVGMEAN =   1.0397

STDMEANS =   0.51942

Notice that the histogram of the sampling distribution of means does *not* have the same shape as the population, although it is also slightly right skewed.

The average of the sample means, printed as AVGMEAN, is (nearly) the same as the population mean $\mu = 1.0$, but the standard deviation of the sample means (STDMEANS) is *not* the same as the population standard deviation $\sigma = 1.0$.

The sampling distribution of a sample statistic is a probability distribution. Its exact form depends on the population distribution being sampled. Fortunately, we can derive the basic properties of the most important sampling distributions—those of sample means—from minimal assumptions about the population. In this section we find expected values and variances for these distributions. In the next section we show that the normal distribution is often a good approximation to the exact shapes of these sampling distributions.

The sample mean is the most widely used of all statistics, so its sampling distribution is most important. The expected value, variance, and standard deviation of this sampling distribution can be found using basic probability theory.

Definition 6.1   Expected Value and Standard Deviation of $\overline{Y}$

If a random sample of size n is drawn from a population, the expected value and standard deviation of $\overline{Y}$ are

$$E(\overline{Y}) = \frac{n\mu}{n} = \mu$$

$$\sigma_{\overline{Y}} = \frac{\sqrt{n}\sigma}{n} = \frac{\sigma}{\sqrt{n}} \qquad \blacksquare$$

EXAMPLE 6.2

Suppose that the long-run average of the number of Medicare claims submitted per week to a regional office is 62,000 and that the standard deviation is 7000. If we assume that the weekly claims submissions during a 4-week period constitute a random sample of size 4, what are the expected value and standard error of the average weekly number of claims over a 4-week period?

Solution

We have $\mu = 62,000$, $\sigma = 7000$, and $n = 4$. If $\overline{Y}$ is the 4-week average of the weekly number of claims, then

$$E(\overline{Y}) = \mu = 62,000$$

$$\sigma_{\overline{Y}} = \frac{\sigma}{\sqrt{n}} = 7000/\sqrt{4} = 3500 \quad \blacksquare$$

The fact that $E(\overline{Y}) = \mu$ means that, on average, the sample mean estimates the population mean correctly. In one particular sample, the sample mean may overestimate the population mean. In another, the sample mean may underestimate. But in the long run there is no *systematic* tendency for a sample mean to overestimate or underestimate the population mean. This is true regardless of the sample size. Remember, when the computer drew 1000 samples of 4 from an exponential population, the mean of the 1000 sample means (an approximation to the expected value, which would be the mean of an infinite number of sample means) was just about equal to the population mean.

At this point, it is very handy to introduce a new name for an existing concept. We specify many sample statistics and many sampling distributions in the next several chapters; it turns out that there are many different formulas for the standard deviations of the sampling distributions of these statistics. Most of the formulas (like the one for the standard deviation of $\overline{Y}$) involve the population standard deviation, and it becomes difficult to distinguish between the different standard deviations. From here on, then, we use the term **standard error** to denote the theoretically derived standard deviation of the sampling distribution of a statistic. The standard error of the sample mean $\overline{Y}$ is the standard deviation of its sampling distribution: $\sigma_{\overline{Y}} = \sigma/\sqrt{n}$.

standard error

The standard deviation of the sampling distribution of the mean (the standard error of the sample mean) is crucial in determining the probable amount of error in an estimate. We just said that there is no systematic tendency to over- or underestimate μ with $\overline{Y}$. This wouldn't be much of a consolation if we knew that half the time we made a huge overestimate, the other half an equally huge underestimate! The standard error of a sample mean $\sigma_{\overline{Y}}$, in conjunction with the Empirical Rule of Chapter 2, can be used to give a good indication of the probable deviation of a particular sample mean from the population mean.

EXAMPLE 6.3

Suppose that a supermarket manager is interested in estimating the mean checkout time for the nonexpress checkout lanes. An assistant manager obtains a random sample of 25 checkout times. If previous data suggest that the population standard deviation is 1.10 minutes, describe the probable deviation of $\overline{Y}$ from the unknown population mean μ.

Solution

The Empirical Rule indicates that approximately 95% of the time $\overline{Y}$ is within 2 standard errors $(2\sigma_{\overline{Y}})$ of the population mean μ. For $n = 25$,

$$2\sigma_{\overline{Y}} = \frac{2\sigma}{\sqrt{n}} = \frac{2(1.10)}{5} = .44$$

The probable error for $\overline{Y}$ is no more than .44 minute. ∎

The probable accuracy of a sample mean, as measured by its standard error, is affected by the sample size. Because the standard error of the sample mean is the population standard deviation divided by the square root of the sample size, the standard error decreases as the sample size increases. For example, if the sample size had been either 50 or 100 instead of 25 in the previous example, the probable errors $(2\sigma_{\overline{Y}})$ would have been, respectively, .31 or .22.

E X A M P L E   6 . 4

The Resampling Stats program also drew 1000 samples of sizes 10, 30, and 60 from an exponential population having mean and standard deviation both 1.0. The averages of the 1000 means in each situation were, respectively, 1.0109, 1.0047, and 1.0025. The standard deviations of the 1000 means were, respectively, 0.31815, 0.17943, and 0.12662. Show that these values are close approximations to the theoretical expected value and standard error.

Solution

The average of the means should and does approximate the expected value, $\mu = 1.0000$. The standard deviation of the means should approximate the standard error of the sample mean, $\sigma/\sqrt{n} = 1.0/\sqrt{n}$. For $n = 10, 30$, and 60, the theoretical standard errors are $1.0/\sqrt{10} = 0.31623$, $1.0/\sqrt{30} = 0.18257$, and $1.0/\sqrt{60} = 0.12910$, respectively. The approximations are quite close in all cases. ∎

As the sample size increases to infinity, the standard error of the sample mean decreases toward zero. For a very large sample size, the standard error of the mean is very small, and the sample mean based on a huge, genuinely unbiased sample is very close to the true population mean with very high probability. The condition that the sample be unbiased would be crucial in such a situation; a huge sample would reduce random variation to near zero but would *not* eliminate any data-gathering bias.

In Chapter 2, we defined control limits by adding and subtracting 3 standard deviations from the desired target value. The standard deviation in question is the standard error of the sample mean, based on the sample size used. For example, we discussed an automatic transmission in which the desired internal pressure was 35. The standard deviation of pressures of individual transmissions was about 1.2, and 5 transmissions were sampled each day. Thus, the standard deviation of the sample mean (standard error) should theoretically be 1.2 divided by the square root of 5, or 0.54.

In quality-control practice, there is an additional source of variability that's not found in sampling from fixed populations. Even if a process is in control, it will vary somewhat over time; for example, the true mean pressure for all transmissions may vary somewhat (over time) around 35, even though the process is basically satisfactory. This additional variation often makes the actual standard deviation of sample means slightly higher than the theoretical value. In the transmission example, the actual standard deviation of the means was 0.60.

6.7 A random sample of size 8 is to be taken with replacement from a population with the following probability distribution:

Value:	4	8	12	16
Probability:	.50	.30	.15	.05

The exact sampling distributions of $\overline{Y}$, the sample mean, can be shown to be (to four decimal places):

$\overline{y}$	4.0	4.5	5.0	5.5	6.0	6.5	7.0	7.5	8.0
$P_{\overline{Y}}(\overline{y})$	.0039	.0188	.0488	.0898	.1293	.1535	.1550	.1359	.1048

$\overline{y}$	8.5	9.0	9.5	10.0	10.5	11.0	11.5	12.0	12.5
$P_{\overline{Y}}(\overline{y})$	.0718	.0439	.0242	.0119	.0053	.0021	.0008	.0002	.0001

$\overline{y}$	13.0	13.5	14.0	14.5	15.0	15.5	16.0
$P_{\overline{Y}}(\overline{y})$	.0000	.0000	.0000	.0000	.0000	.0000	.0000

Find the expected value and standard deviation of the *population* and the expected value and standard deviation of $\overline{Y}$. Show that these results agree with the theoretical results of this section.

6.8 An automobile insurer has found that repair claims have an average of $927 and a standard deviation of $871. Suppose that the next 50 claims can be regarded as a random sample from the long-run claims process. Find the expected value and standard error of the average of the next 50 claims.

6.9 A computer simulation can itself be regarded as a sampling process. Suppose that a simulation study is done concerning the time required to complete a research and development project. There is considerable uncertainty in the times required to complete the various pieces of the project, so the overall completion time has considerable variability. Assume that the time to completion has a mean of 28.2 months and a standard deviation of 6.9 months.

a If the simulation involves 1000 independent trials of the project, find the expected value and standard error of the simulation (sample) mean.

b Find the expected value and standard error if 4000 trials are simulated. ■

6.3 Sampling Distributions for Means and Sums

In the last section we stated the appropriate expected values and standard errors for the sample mean $\overline{Y}$. In this section we show that in most situations a normal distribution provides a good approximation to the sampling distribution for $\overline{Y}$. According to a theorem of mathematical statistics, if a population distribution is (exactly) normal, then the sampling distribution for the sample mean $\overline{Y}$ is also (exactly) normal. The relevant expected value and standard error are given in the previous section.

Suppose that a meat packer provides "12-ounce" steaks that, in fact, have a mean weight of 12.10 ounces and a standard deviation of 0.20 ounce. Also, the individual weights have a normal distribution. Assume that a package of 25 steaks constitutes a random sample from the population (which might also be thought of as a long-run process) of steaks. What is the probability that the mean weight in the package exceeds 12.00 ounces? According to the theorem we just mentioned, if the population distribution is normal, the sampling distribution of sample means is also normal. The expected value for the sample mean will be 12.10, equal to the population mean. The standard deviation for the sample mean will *not* equal the population standard deviation; sample means are less variable than individual scores. The relevant standard deviation for the sample mean is the standard error: $\sigma_{\bar{Y}} = \sigma/\sqrt{n} = 0.20/\sqrt{25} = 0.040$. To find the probability that the sample mean will exceed 12.00 ounces, we go through the familiar z calculation, and we make sure that we use the standard error of the sample mean, not the population standard deviation.

$$P(\bar{Y} > 12.00) = P(z > (12.00 - 12.10)/0.040) = P(z > -2.50)$$

$$= .5000 + .4938 = .9938 \qquad \text{(from Appendix Table 3)}$$

E X A M P L E   6 . 5

A timber company is planning to harvest 400 trees from a very large 50-year-old stand. The yield of lumber from each tree is largely determined by its diameter. Assume that the distribution of diameters in the stand is normal with mean 44 inches and standard deviation 4 inches. Also assume (perhaps unrealistically) that the selection of the 400 trees is effectively random. Find the probability that the average diameter of the harvested trees is between 43.5 and 44.5 inches.

Solution

The population distribution (of the diameters of all trees in the stand) is assumed to be normal. It follows from the previous result that the sampling distribution of $\bar{Y}$ is also normal. The appropriate expected value and standard error are

$$\mu_{\bar{Y}} = \mu = 44$$

$$\sigma_{\bar{Y}} = \frac{\sigma}{\sqrt{n}} = \frac{4}{\sqrt{400}} = .20$$

As usual, we calculate normal probabilities by calculating z-scores (see Figure 6.2):

$$P(43.5 \leq \bar{Y} \leq 44.5) = P\left(\frac{43.5 - 44}{.20} \leq Z \leq \frac{44.5 - 44}{.20}\right)$$

$$= P(-2.50 \leq Z \leq 2.50)$$

$$= 2(.4938) = .9876$$

FIGURE 6.2   Probability Calculation for Sampling Distribution

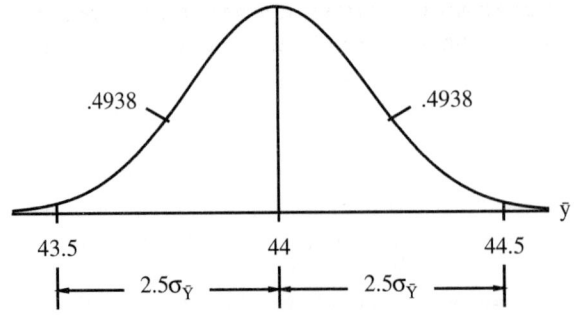

Use of this theorem, as stated, requires the assumption that the population distribution is exactly normal. In practice, no distribution is exactly normal. Another theorem, called the **Central Limit Theorem**, implies that the assumption of a normal population is not crucial.

Definition 6.2   Central Limit Theorem for Means

For *any* population (with finite mean μ and standard deviation σ), the sampling distribution of the sample mean is approximately normal if the sample size n is sufficiently large.   ■

This is a rather remarkable theorem. Regardless of the nature of the population distribution—discrete or continuous, symmetric or skewed, unimodal or multimodal—the sampling distribution $\overline{Y}$ is always nearly normal as long as the sample size is large enough. This is illustrated in Figure 6.3 for the sample mean. The condition that the population mean and standard deviation must be finite is almost always satisfied.[1]

An obvious question is: How large a sample is sufficiently large? The Central Limit Theorem is a mathematical theorem—"n sufficiently large" is translated into "as n goes to infinity"—so it does not contain the answer to this question. An enormous number of studies have tried to answer the question, using other mathematical theorems and computer simulations. Many textbooks give a blanket rule: Use the normal approximation anytime n exceeds 30.

FIGURE 6.3   **An Illustration of the Central Limit Theorem**

Population

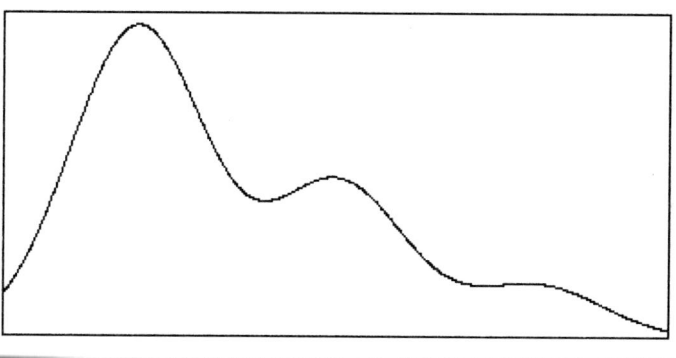

Sample Mean

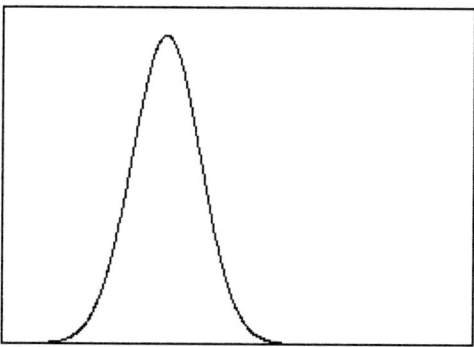

[1]The only exception we know of is the case of so-called stable laws, which are sometimes used as models in finance.

This rule is a good basic guide for using the Central Limit Theorem. A better rule would consider the effect of skewness. If the population distribution is very skewed, the actual sampling distribution for $n = 20$ or for $n = 40$ is also somewhat skewed—less so than the population distribution but enough to make the normal approximation mediocre. If the population distribution is symmetric, the sampling distribution, even with $n = 10$ or so, is remarkably close to normal. A better rule would be based on a plot of the sample data (and drawing a picture of the data is always a good idea). If a histogram of the sample data shows obvious skewness (and hence suggests skewness for the population distribution), a normal approximation should be used skeptically unless n is up around 100. If the histogram has little skewness, the normal approximation may be used confidently, even with an n of 15 or 20.[2]

EXAMPLE 6.6

A computer program was used to draw 1000 samples each, with sample sizes 4, 10, 30, and 60, from an exponential population having mean and standard deviation both equal to 1. Histograms of the sample means are shown in Figure 6.4. As the sample size increases, how does the shape of the theoretical (sampling) distribution of means change? How does the variability of sample means change?

Solution

For $n = 4$, the distribution of means is clearly right skewed, although not as skewed as the exponential distribution itself. As the sample size increases, the skewness decreases. For a sample of size 60, the distribution of means appears to be very close to normal. The Central Limit Theorem indicates that the theoretical distribution of sample means should, indeed, approach a normal distribution as the sample size increases.

FIGURE 6.4   **Histogram of Sample Means: (a) Sample of Size 4; (b) Sample of Size 10; (c) Sample of Size 30; (d) Sample of Size 60**

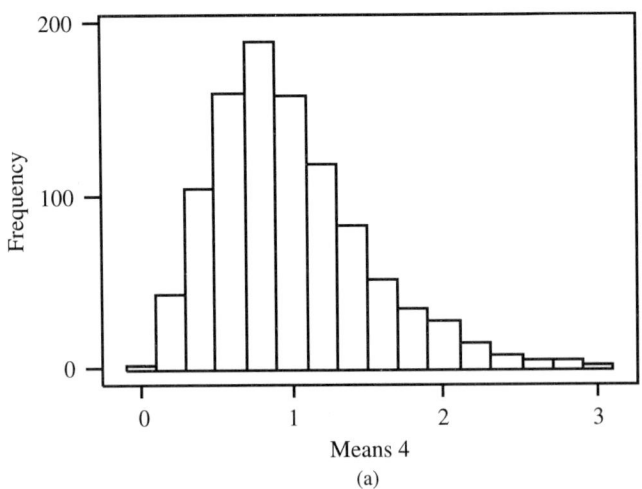

Means 4
(a)

[2]The quality of a normal approximation is also slightly affected by how heavy the tails are in the population. Even if a population is nearly symmetric, it may contain many more extremely large and extremely small values than would a near-normal distribution. A heavy-tailed population in a sample is suggested by the presence of outliers—a few individual values that fall very far from the bulk of the data. We discuss the treatment of outliers in later chapters.

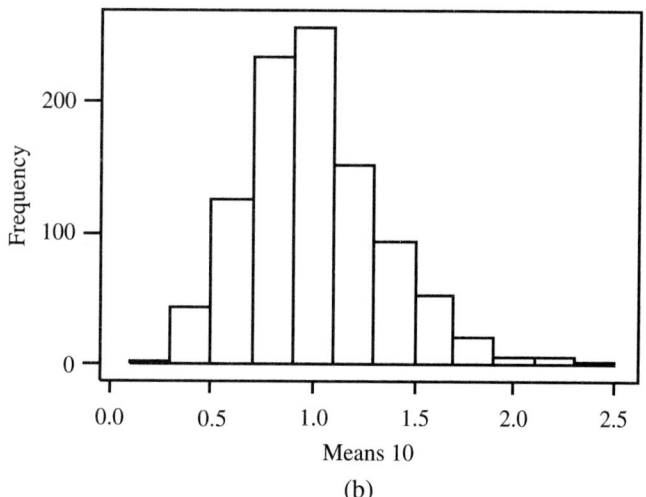

(b)

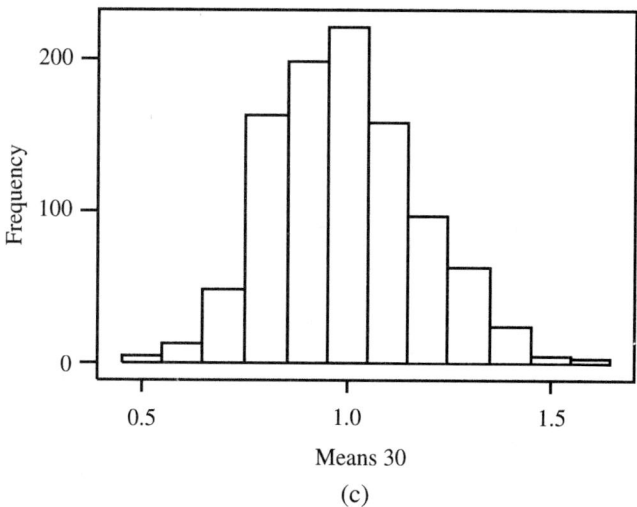

(c)

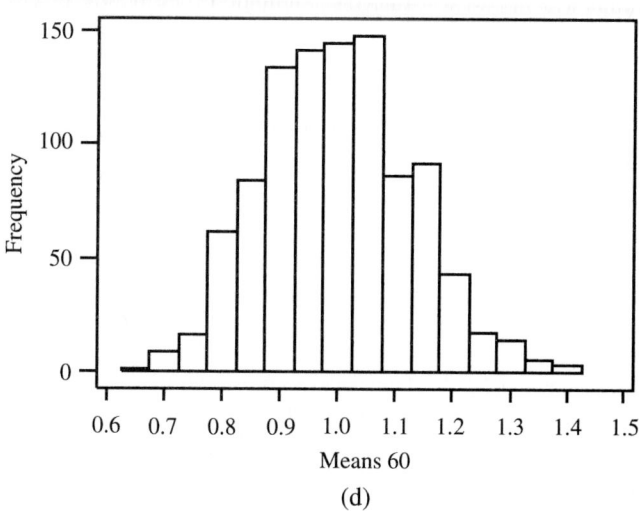

(d)

From the scale at the bottom of each histogram, we can assess the variability of sample means. As n increases, the range of sample means decreases, indicating that variability decreases. The fact that the standard error of the sample mean decreases as n increases indicates that the variability of sample means should decrease as n increases. ■

Remember that you usually can't plot the sampling distribution itself—that is, the theoretical, long-run distribution arising from repeated sampling. In practice, you take only one sample. The data plot that we refer to is the sample histogram. The sample histogram is useful as a rough indicator of the population shape, which is known to have an effect on the quality of the Central Limit Theorem normal approximation.

E X A M P L E   6 . 7

In the supermarket checkout time situation of Example 6.3, the following actual times in minutes were observed ($n = 25$): 0.4, 0.4, 0.5, 0.5, 0.5, 0.6, 0.6, 0.7, 0.8, 0.9, 1.1, 1.2, 1.4, 1.5, 1.8, 2.0, 2.3, 2.6, 2.9, 3.4, 4.2, 5.0, 6.6, 9.2, 16.3 ($\bar{y} = 2.70$). Does it appear that a normal approximation to the sampling distribution of $\overline{Y}$ (for future samples of size $n = 25$, for instance) would be satisfactory?

```
MTB > print 'Checkout'

Checkout
   0.4    0.4    0.5    0.5    0.5    0.6    0.6    0.7    0.8    0.9    1.1
   1.2    1.4    1.5    1.8    2.0    2.3    2.6    2.9    3.4    4.2    5.0
   6.6    9.2   16.3

MTB > Describe 'Checkout'

                 N    MEAN   MEDIAN   TRMEAN   STDEV   SEMEAN
Checkout        25   2.696    1.400    2.204   3.563    0.713
```

Solution

The sample data suggest that the population distribution of checkout times is likely to be highly skewed. See the histogram in Figure 6.5. Most times are quite brief, but there are a few people who really slow things up. A sample of 25 is not enough to *deskew* the sampling distribution. Even a sample of 50 isn't really enough in this situation. Therefore, the Empirical Rule probabilities (which are based on the normal distribution) in Example 6.3 are most likely inaccurate for $n = 25$ and perhaps for $n = 50$. For $n = 100$, the probabilities should be fairly close. ■

E X A M P L E   6 . 8

A firm that sells frozen 9-ounce steaks to restaurants is concerned about the fat content of individual steaks. It has claimed that the fat content has mean 8.1% and standard deviation 1.0%. Use a normal approximation to find the probability that the mean fat content in a random sample of 25 steaks exceeds 8.5%. Would you expect the normal approximation to be accurate?

FIGURE 6.5 **Histogram for Checkout Time Data**

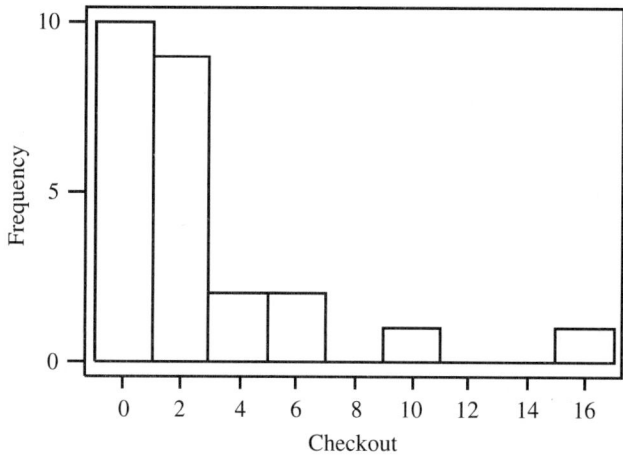

Solution

The appropriate expected value and standard error are

$$\mu_{\overline{Y}} = \mu = 8.1\%$$

$$\sigma\overline{Y} = \frac{\sigma}{\sqrt{n}} = \frac{1.0}{\sqrt{25}} = .2\%$$

The normal approximation yields

$$P(\overline{Y} > 8.5) = P(Z > \frac{8.5 - 8.1}{.2}) = P(Z > 2.00) \approx .0228$$

In this situation we would expect the distribution to be fairly symmetric; we would not expect to see fat contents of (say) 15% or more (at least for a firm that stays in business) nor fat contents of practically 0%. (Of course, a plot of actual data would be useful in checking our guesses.) If our expectation is correct, the normal approximation should be quite good for $n = 25$. ∎

EXERCISES

6.10 The number of column-inches of classified advertisements appearing on Mondays in a certain daily newspaper is roughly normally distributed with mean 327 inches and standard deviation 34 inches. Assume that the results for 10 consecutive Mondays can be regarded as a random sample.

a Find the expected value and standard error of the total number of column-inches of classified advertisements for 10 Mondays.

b Find the probability that the total is between 3150 and 3390 column-inches.

c Find the probability that the average number of column-inches per Monday is between 314 and 339.

6.11 Refer to Exercise 6.10. Find a range of the form $327 - k$ to $327 + k$ such that

$$P(327 - k \leq \overline{Y} \leq 327 + k) \approx .95$$

6.12 Suppose that a certain population has the following distribution:

Value:	200	300	400	500	600
Relative frequency:	.60	.20	.12	.06	.02

The population mean is 270, and the population standard deviation is 102.470. Exact probability computations show the following:

n	$\sigma_{\overline{Y}}$	$P(\overline{Y} > \mu - 2\sigma_{\overline{Y}})$	$P(\overline{Y} > \mu - \sigma_{\overline{Y}})$	$P(\overline{Y} < \mu + \sigma_{\overline{Y}})$	$P(\overline{Y} < \mu + 2\sigma_{\overline{Y}})$
2	72.46	0	0	.2160	.0336
4	51.23	0	.1296	.1965	.0521
8	36.23	0	.1460	.1594	.0319
16	25.62	.0173	.1876	.1486	.0295
32	18.11	.0127	.1543	.1473	.0340

a Draw a histogram of the population distribution. What is the obvious feature of this histogram?

b For each sample size, compute the exact probability that $\overline{Y}$ falls within 2 standard errors of μ. How good is the normal approximation for various values of n?

c Repeat part b for $\overline{Y}$ within 1 standard error of μ.

6.13 In Exercise 6.8 we considered an automobile insurer whose repair claims averaged $927 over the past with a standard deviation of $871. A random sample of 50 new claims is taken.

a Describe the sampling distribution for $\overline{Y}$.

b Use a normal approximation to calculate $P(\overline{Y} > 1100)$.

6.14 How good would you expect the normal approximation in Exercise 6.13 to be? (Would you expect individual claims data to be something close to bell-shaped?)

6.15 Refer to Exercise 6.13. Suppose $\overline{y} = \$1100$ is observed for the 50 new claims. What do you conclude about repair claims for this year? Would your conclusions change if $\overline{y} = \$1000$?

6.16 The average demand for rental skis on winter Saturdays at a particular area is 148 pairs, which has been quite stable over time. There is variation due to weather conditions and competing areas; the standard deviation is 21 pairs. The demand distribution seems to be roughly normal.

a The rental shop stocks 170 pairs of skis. What is the probability that demand will exceed this supply on any one winter Saturday?

b The shop manager will change the stock of skis for the next year if the average demand over the 12 winter Saturdays in a season (considered as a random sample) is over 155 or under 135. These limits aren't equidistant from the long-run process mean of 148 because the costs of oversupply and undersupply are different. If the population mean stays at 148, what is the probability that the manager will change the stock?

6.17 In Exercise 6.16, one could argue that the demand will not be normal. Instead, most Saturdays' demand will be around the mean, but on those few days when skiing conditions are poor, the demand will fall well below the mean.

a According to this argument, what will be the shape (skewness) of the demand distribution?

b Will the two answers in Exercise 6.16 be made equally wrong if this argument is correct? Why?

6.18 Computer chips have pins to connect them into sockets on computer boards. The thickness of the pins is important in determining the quality of the connection to the board. When the production process is running properly, the mean diameter of pins (relative to the design specification) is 1.000. There is some inevitable variation in diameters; the standard deviation is 0.006 unit. The distribution of diameters is normal.

a A pin will make a highest-quality connection only if its diameter is between 0.997 and 1.003 units. What is the probability that an individual pin will make such a connection?

b As part of its ongoing quality monitoring, the chip manufacturer takes samples of 20 pins from each lot of 25,000 pins. Assuming that the process is running properly, what is the probability that the mean diameter in the sample will be between 0.997 and 1.003 units?

c Suppose that the process mean remains at 1.000 unit, but the variability increases greatly so that the standard deviation is 0.020 unit. Without doing any arithmetic, what should this change do to the probability that an individual pin will make a highest-quality connection? Verify your answer by computing a revised probability and comparing it to your answer in part a.

d If the standard deviation is 0.020, what is the probability that a mean of a sample of 20 pins will be between 0.997 and 1.003 units?

6.19 In Exercise 6.18, suppose that the mean diameter of the population of pins is 1.000 but that the distribution is not normal. Instead, the standard deviation of 0.006 is the result of most pin diameters being extremely close to 1.000 and a few pin diameters being extremely far from that value. Does this mean that your answer to part b of Exercise 6.18 is seriously incorrect? Explain why or why not.

6.20 A downtown hotel runs a special promotion to try to fill rooms that aren't usually occupied on weekends. The long-run average response is 71 rooms per weekend. There is considerable variation due to weather, competing attractions, and other unknown causes. The standard deviation of responses is about 15 rooms. Suppose that the distribution of responses is normal.

a The hotel schedules adequate staff to handle a response of 80 rooms. If more guests arrive, additional staff must be brought in at overtime rates. What is the probability that additional staff will be needed on one particular weekend?

b The promotion manager reviews response rates for blocks of 10 weekends, which is regarded as a random sample. If the average demand over the 10-week sample exceeds 80, the manager will increase the scheduled staff. If the long-run mean stays at 71, what is the probability that a 10-week sample mean will exceed 80?

6.21 In Exercise 6.20, we assumed a normal distribution of responses. In fact, the distribution is skewed by a few weekends with extremely heavy demand. Can you assume that your answer to part b of that exercise is still correct because of the Central Limit Theorem effect?   ■

6.4 Checking Normality

In this book, we present the results of many data analyses and computer simulations. We are concerned with the correctness not only of expected value and standard error formulas, but especially with that of theoretical results about the shape of the sampling distribution. If the sampling distribution of a certain statistic theoretically should be normal, but simulation results indicate that the actual distribution is clearly nonnormal, that indicates that statistical inferences based on the statistic could be seriously wrong.

normal probability plot

normal scores

A **normal probability plot** is an excellent way to assess whether data (or means in a computer simulation) are close to normally distributed. This plot is based on **normal scores**: the predicted values of data, assuming a normal distribution. A computer program that carries out a normal probability plot calculates these normal scores automatically.

A normal plot is a plot of the actual data (or simulation means) against the normal scores. Data that are (essentially) normally distributed yield (essentially) a straight line in a normal plot. It turns out that skewed data from a plot as an S shape. The direction of the curve depends on which axis contains the actual data and which axis, the normal scores.

Definition 6.3 Normal Probability Plots

A normal probability plot is a plot of the actual data against their theoretical values, assuming a normal distribution. Nearly normally distributed data form a plot that is nearly a straight line.

1 If the actual data are on the vertical axis and the theoretical values are on the horizontal axis, right-skewed data appear as a curve with the slope getting steeper as one moves to the right. Left-skewed data appear as a curve with the slope getting flatter as one moves to the right. Symmetric but outlier-prone data appear as an S shape, with the slope steepest at both sides.

2   If the actual data are on the horizontal axis and the theoretical values are on the vertical axis, right-skewed data appear as a curve with the slope getting flatter as one moves to the right. Left-skewed data appear as a curve with the slope getting steeper as one moves to the right. Symmetric but outlier-prone data appear as an S shape, with the slope flattest at both sides.   ■

In looking at a computer-generated normal plot, look for the basic, overall pattern rather than the "wiggles and jiggles and bumps." A normal plot is particularly helpful in assessing whether data are outlier-prone; the S shape in a normal plot is often easier to see than the long tails in a histogram. Figure 6.6 shows Minitab-generated normal plots for, respectively, normally distributed, right-skewed, and outlier-prone data. In this figure, the data are plotted on the vertical axis. You should be able to see the basic straight-line, single-curve, and S-shape patterns in the three plots; hold a ruler or other straightedge up to the plot to help you see the patterns.

F I G U R E   6 . 6   **Normal Plots for (a) Normally Distributed; (b) Skewed; and (c) Outlier-Prone Data**

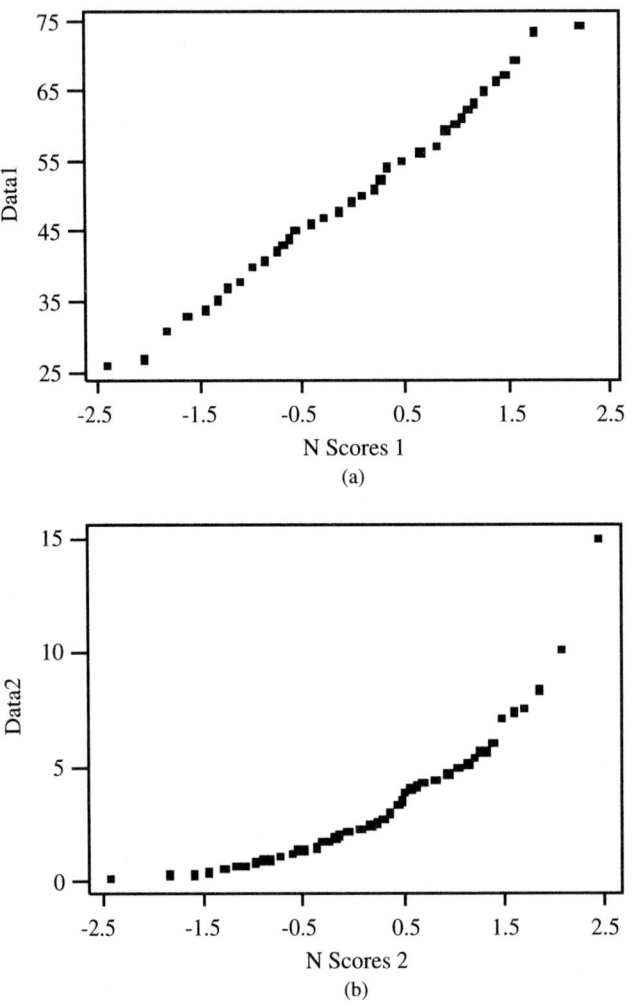

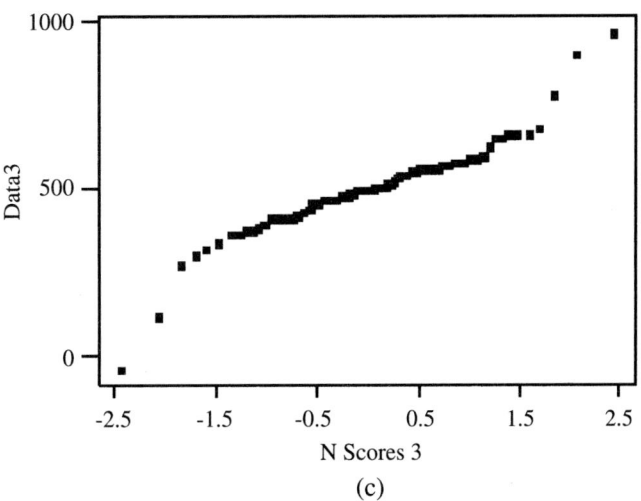

N Scores 3

(c)

EXAMPLE 6.9

A normal plot (Systat) of 1000 means, each based on a sample of size 10 taken from a skewed population is shown in Figure 6.7. The data are plotted along the horizontal axis, the reverse of the previous figure. Does the normal plot indicate that the sampling distribution of means is approximately normal in this situation?

FIGURE 6.7 Normal Plot of Means: Sample Size 10

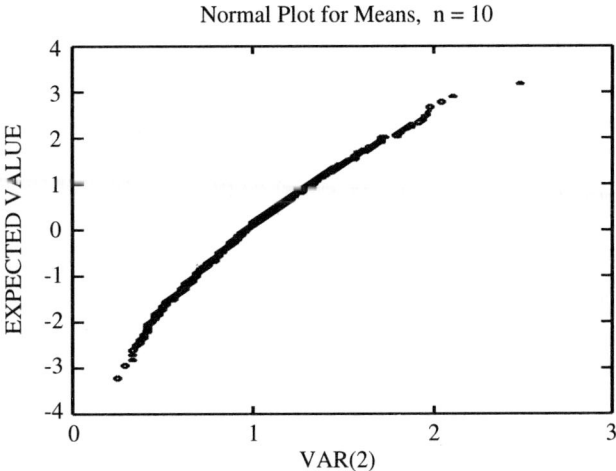

Normal Plot for Means, n = 10

VAR(2)

Solution

No. There is a moderate but clear curve in the plot, indicating that the sampling distribution of the sample means is clearly somewhat skewed in this situation. ■

EXAMPLE 6.10

Normal plots (Systat) of 1000 means, based on samples of size 30 and 60 from the same distribution as in the preceding example, are shown in Figure 6.8. The data are along the horizontal axis. What is the effect of increasing sample size?

Solution

As the sample size increases, the normal plot comes closer to a straight line, which indicates that the theoretical (sampling) distribution of the sample mean approaches the normal distribution as the sample size increases. This is precisely what the Central Limit Theorem states.

FIGURE 6.8 **Normal Plot of Means: (a) Sample of Size 30; (b) Sample Size 60**

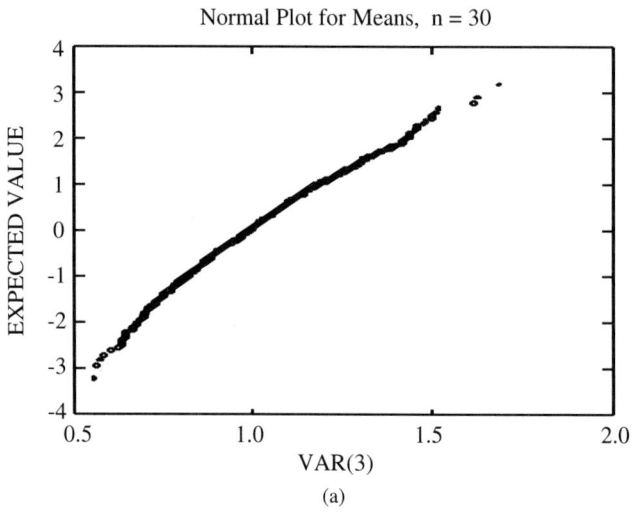

(a)

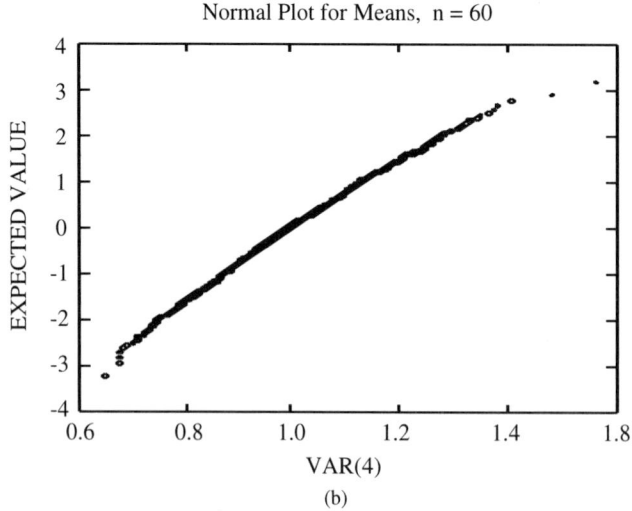

(b)

6.22   In Chapter 2, we considered the number of calls cleared by directory assistance operators over a full shift. A normal plot and a histogram, created using Minitab, are shown in Figure 6.9.

  a What skewness, if any, is shown in the histogram?

  b What skewness, if any, is shown in the normal plot? Recall that the first step in interpreting this plot is to check which axis is which.

FIGURE 6.9   **Histogram and Normal Plot for Call Data**

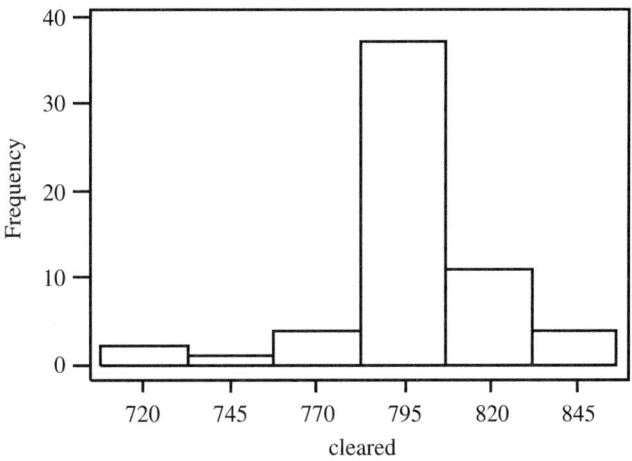

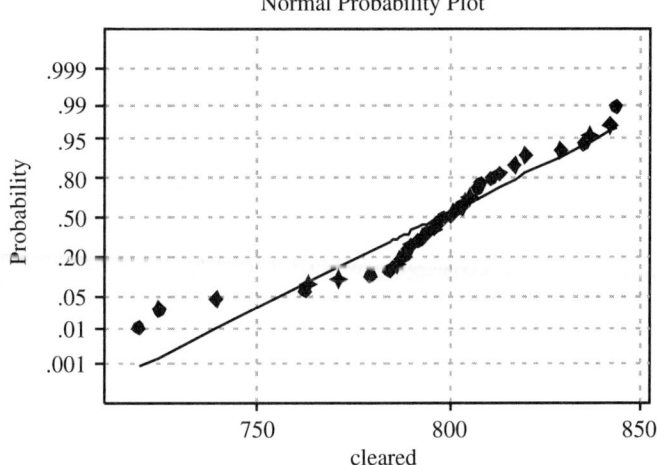

Average: 797.508   Anderson-Darling Normality Test
Std Dev: 23.2122   A-Squared: 1.965
N of data: 59   p-value: 0.000

6.23   In Chapter 2, we also considered sizes of automobile collision insurance claims. A normal probability plot, created using Statistix, is shown in Figure 6.10. Are the data nearly normal, right-skewed, left-skewed, or symmetric but outlier-prone?

FIGURE 6.10   **Normal Plot of Claim Size Data**

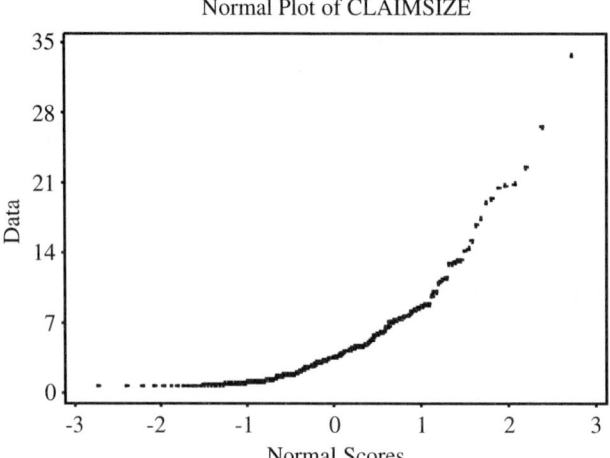

Normal Plot of CLAIMSIZE

6.24   In Chapter 2, we also considered the lateness percentage of a particular flight daily over several weeks. A normal plot of the data, created using StatGraphics Plus, is shown in Figure 6.11. Are the data nearly normal, right-skewed, left-skewed, or symmetric but outlier-prone?

FIGURE 6.11   **Normal Plot of Lateness Percentage**

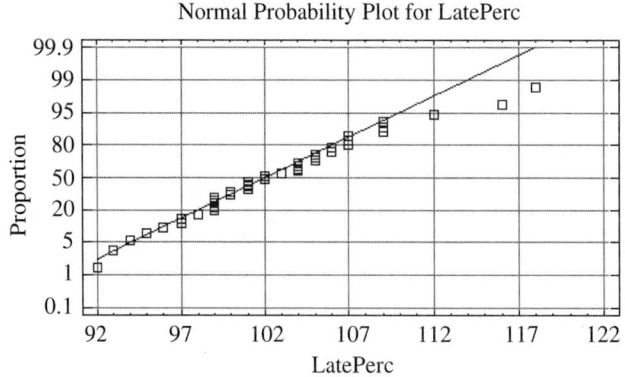

Normal Probability Plot for LatePerc

6.25   Sample medians are found for 1000 samples of size 30 taken from a Laplace population (a symmetric, moderately outlier-prone population). The average of the medians is .0082 and the standard deviation is .2070. What do these results indicate about the theoretical (sampling) distribution of the median?

6.26   A normal plot of the medians calculated in Exercise 6.25 looks basically like a straight line. What does this fact indicate about the theoretical distribution of the median in this case?

6.27   Sample maxima are found for 1000 samples of size 10 taken from the same Laplace distribution. A Minitab normal plot is shown in Figure 6.12. Does it indicate that the distribution of this statistic is nearly normal?

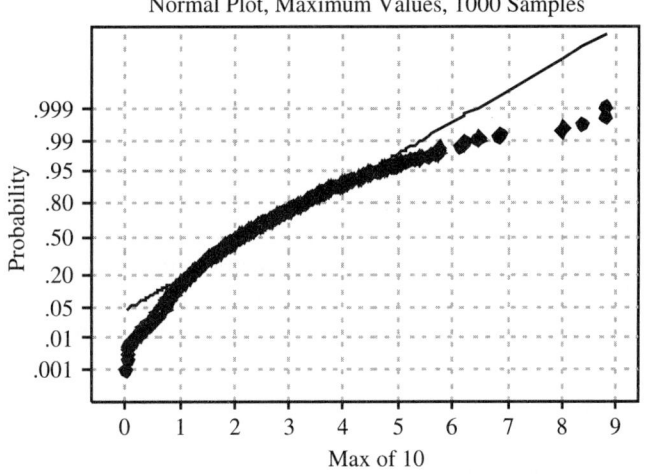

Average: 2.27351

Std Dev: 1.27762

N of data: 1000

Anderson-Darling Normality Test

A-Squared: 14.223

p-value: 0.000

6.28   Another Minitab normal plot of sample maxima, this time for sample size 30, from the Laplace distribution is shown in Figure 6.13.

a Does the plot indicate that the distribution of this statistic is nearly normal?

b Comparing this plot to the previous one, does it appear that the Central Limit Theorem works for sample maxima?

F I G U R E   6 . 1 3   **Normal Probability Plot for Sample Maxima, $n = 30$**

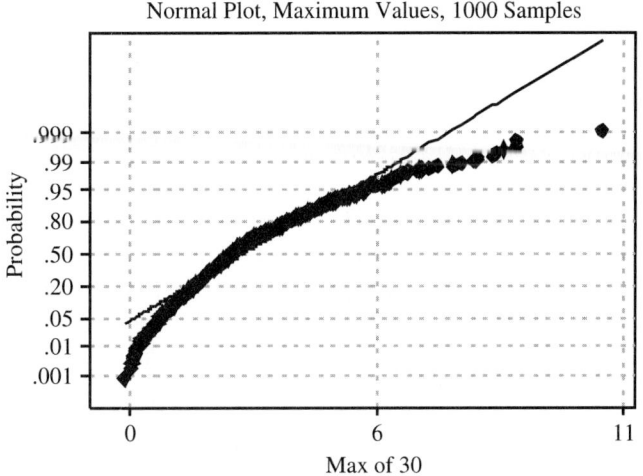

Average: 3.27198

Std Dev: 1.28437

N of data: 1000

Anderson-Darling Normality Test

A-Squared: 16.539

p-value: 0.000

Summing Up

H ere are some of the important ideas for thinking about sampling and about the random variation in a summary statistic.

1 The first thing to consider about a data-gathering process is possible bias. Bias is any systematic distortion in the way the data are collected. In general, statistical methods can't compensate for biases. Biases may occur in the selection of individual items because of refusal to participate or because the measurement process doesn't yield correct answers. The ideal is that every individual item in the population or process has the same chance of being measured, and measured accurately.

2 A sampling distribution measures how a summary statistic varies from sample to sample (and therefore from the true population or process value). It is different from the pattern of variation of data within a sample.

3 A sampling distribution is a theoretical concept. It cannot be seen directly in a particular sample of data, although computer simulations that draw many samples can illustrate sampling distributions.

4 Two key theoretical results for any sample statistic are the expected value (the long-run average over many samples) and the standard error (the standard deviation of the statistic over many samples). The mathematical form of these quantities depends on which statistic is being considered and on the sampling method.

5 The Central Limit Theorem says that sample means (and sums) will follow approximately a normal distribution. The approximation gets better and better as the sample size gets larger. This theorem, as stated, applies only to sample means and sums; without further evidence, we can't assume that other statistics also follow a normal distribution.

6 The distribution of data within a sample, insofar as it indicates the distribution in the whole population, gives some idea as to whether key assumptions hold. In particular, extreme skewness in a sample indicates population skewness, which in turn indicates that the Central Limit Theorem effect will require a relatively large sample size.

In addition, you may want to reread the summary of key ideas at the beginning of the chapter.

EXAMPLE 6.11

A catalog-order retailer sometimes must place items on "back order," which means that they are not shipped until the required items are received by the retailer from manufacturers. The retailer gives an estimated delivery date for each back-ordered item, so the customer can decide whether to wait or to cancel the order. Getting the delivery date reasonably close to accurate is important. If the stated delivery date is too optimistic, the customer will be angered by failure to meet the date. If the stated delivery date is too pessimistic, customers will cancel orders unnecessarily.

A team of junior managers for the retailer wanted to take a sample of back-ordered items and find the average difference between the actual and estimated delivery dates. They proposed to take every hundredth back-ordered item that the customer agreed to wait for, beginning with a randomly chosen number like order 57. They would determine the difference between actual and estimated delivery dates; if the customer chose in the meantime to cancel the order, the difference would be set to 0.

One question that arose was how large a sample should be taken. The managers wanted be reasonably sure to estimate the average difference accurately to about 1 day. They had a rough idea that most back-ordered items were delivered within about 6 days before or after the estimated date, but a few were even farther off than that. In addition, there was some concern that the data would be somewhat skewed by a few very late deliveries.

Comment on these issues.

Solution

The first concern is possible bias in the sample. Ideally, the back orders should be sampled completely randomly. Taking every hundredth item might conceivably match some sort of cycle; however, this seems to be a minor quibble. Much more serious is the bias in setting differences to 0. Clearly, this will underestimate the variability of the differences. If, as seems likely, customers tend to cancel orders that are taking a long time to arrive, this procedure will also underestimate the average difference. To minimize the bias, it would be much better to continue to track the cancelled orders, note when the back order could have been shipped, add normal delivery time, and find what the difference would have been.

The question of sample size can be assessed using the standard error of the sample mean. By the Empirical Rule, the sample mean will be within ± 2 standard errors about 95% of the time. If we take 95% as a translation of "reasonably sure," and the desired $\pm$ value to be 1 day, we want the standard error to be 1/2 day. The standard error of the sample mean is $\sigma/\sqrt{n}$, so we need some idea of what σ, the standard deviation of individual differences, may be. If "most" (presumably roughly 95%, more or less) of the differences are within ± 6 days, then the standard deviation should be roughly 3 days. If we guess that σ is about 3, and we want $\sigma/\sqrt{n}$ to be 0.5, then we must take n to be 36: $3/\sqrt{36} = 3/6 = 0.5$.

Skewness should not be the biggest concern unless it is very severe. A sample size of 36 will allow the Central Limit Theorem to work fairly well. The claimed 95% probability may not be highly accurate, but given the other uncertainties in the study, this is not the biggest concern. The major problem is the bias in sampling. ∎

EXERCISES

6.29 While demonstrating the role of variability in statistical quality control, the statistician W. Edwards Deming had seminar participants dip a wooden paddle with 50 holes into a bowl containing 20% red beads and 80% white beads. The beads had been thoroughly mixed.

    a What would you think the expected number of red beads would be in the "paddle sample" of 50 beads?

    b In answering part a, you made an assumption about the sampling method. What was it, and how might it be wrong?

6.30 In thousands of repetitions of the bead experiment of Exercise 6.29, Deming reported that the average number of red beads is approximately 9.4. What does this fact indicate about the assumption you made in answering Exercise 6.29?

6.31 One important application of sampling ideas in quality control is the inspection of incoming components from suppliers. In the assembly of an automobile door, suppliers must provide window glass, window-lowering mechanisms, door handles, door-lock mechanisms, and trim parts. All of these components can be tested to see if they meet initial fitness and long-term reliability specifications. In particular, suppose that the auto manufacturer specifies that door-lock mechanisms should work smoothly through 50,000 lock-unlock cycles.

    a Why would it be absolutely necessary to use sampling in testing the door-lock mechanisms?

b One possible sampling method would be to test the first 5 door-lock mechanisms in each 1000-item shipment. Why would this method be unwise?

6.32 One way to specify inspection sampling of the auto door parts in Exercise 6.31 would be to demand that half of 1% of each shipment of each component be randomly sampled and tested. Shipment sizes range from 1000 door handles (from a new supplier of unknown quality) to 50,000 trim parts (from a long-time supplier with an established reputation for high quality). Would the "half a percent" rule yield a reasonable inspection approach?

6.33 Suppose that a random sample of 20 power window mechanisms is taken from each lot of 5000 supplied to the auto manufacturer in Exercise 6.31. Each sampled mechanism is tested by putting it through continuous up-down cycles until it fails. Suppose that in the entire lot, the mean time to failure (under these high-stress conditions) is 4200 cycles and that the standard deviation is 3400. The mean failure time for the sample is recorded.

    a What is the expected value of the sample mean?

    b What is the standard deviation of the sample mean? How much would it matter if the sample of 20 had been taken from a lot of 10,000 rather than from a lot of 5000 mechanisms?

    c Would it be reasonable to assume that the distribution of individual failure times should be roughly normal? Should the Empirical Rule apply?

    d Would it be reasonable to assume that the distribution of the sample mean should be roughly normal?

6.34 Assume that the testing method of Exercise 6.33 is modified by testing 40 mechanisms per lot rather than 20. Would this modification result in doubling the accuracy of estimation of the mean failure time?

6.35 Bad sectors on a microcomputer floppy disk cannot be used for data storage. Suppose that in a very large supply of floppy disks the mean bad-sector volume is 2.13K (kilobytes) per disk and that the standard deviation is 0.83K. A retailer assembles packs of 100 floppy disks from the supply.

    a What is the expected average bad-sector volume in a pack?

    b What is the standard deviation of average bad-sector volume in a pack?

6.36 What did you assume about the assembly process of the retailer in Exercise 6.35? If the assumption is wrong, which part of your answer would be affected?

6.37 A purchaser of floppy disks assembles many 100-disk packs, laboriously finds the average bad-sector volume in each pack, and draws a histogram of the data. What would you expect the shape of the histogram to be? Why?

6.38 A newspaper columnist asserts that directors of Fortune 1000 firms paid, on the average, only 19.1% of their gross income in federal income tax the previous year. From the published column, it can be inferred that the claimed standard deviation is 6.8%. Suppose that you, as an Internal Revenue Service officer, are charged with taking a sample of 200 such executives to test this claim.

    a The names of all Fortune 1000 firm directors are publicly available. How can you use such a list to select a random sample? What problems might you encounter?

    b Can you assume that, because $n = 200$ is a fairly large sample, the distribution of percentage of gross income paid by individuals in income tax in the sample is approximately normal? Explain.

6.39 In Exercise 5.64 we assumed that the weekly demand for 5-pound sacks of flour at a particular supermarket is normally distributed with mean 72.0 cases and standard deviation 1.6 cases.

    a Do you think that a normal distribution might be a decent model?

    b How could you take a reasonable random sample of size 15 from this population?

6.40 Assume that a random sample of size 15 has been taken in Exercise 6.39.

    a What is $P(\overline{Y} \geq 73.0)$?

    b Find a 95% range for $\overline{Y}$; that is, find a value k such that $P(72.0 - k \leq \overline{Y} \leq 72.0 + k) = .95$.

6.41 A department store expects the average "inventory shrinkage" (a euphemism for theft by employees and customers) to be 2.2%. The standard deviation from one sale category to another is assumed to be 1.6%. The store has 2571 sales categories, from which a sample of 100 categories is to be selected for detailed inventory checking.

    a How would you select such a random sample?

    b Is a simple random sample desirable here? Granted that you don't know about fancier sampling methods, can you think of other considerations for sampling?

6.42 Suppose that a random sample of 100 categories is chosen in Exercise 6.41.

    a Find the expected value and standard error of the sample average shrinkage.

    b How much difference does it make in part a whether you use sampling without replacement or sampling with replacement?

    c Use a normal approximation to calculate $P(\overline{Y} \geq 2.4\%)$.

6.43 How good do you expect the normal approximation in Exercise 6.42 to be? How would you use the sample data to help indicate how much faith you have in the approximation?

6.44 Suppose that a population has the following distribution:

Values:	10	80	90	100	110	120	190
Relative frequency:	.02	.10	.20	.36	.20	.10	.02

    a Verify that the population mean is 100 and the population standard deviation is 21.07.

    b Draw a histogram of this distribution. What is the obvious feature?

6.45 Refer to Exercise 6.44. The exact sampling distribution of the sample mean (for sample sizes 2, 4, and 8) has the following properties:

Sample Size	Standard Error	$P(\overline{Y} < \mu - 2\sigma_{\overline{Y}})$	$P(\overline{Y} < \mu - \sigma_{\overline{Y}})$	$P(\overline{Y} > \mu + \sigma_{\overline{Y}})$	$P(\overline{Y} > \mu + 2\sigma_{\overline{Y}})$
2	14.90	.0388	.0888	.0888	.0388
4	10.54	.0488	.0899	.0899	.0488
8	7.45	.0333	.1456	.1456	.0333

    a For each sample size, compute the exact probability that $\overline{Y}$ is within 1 standard error of μ.

    b How good is the normal approximation for each n?

    c Repeat parts a and b for $\overline{Y}$ within 2 standard errors of μ.

6.46 The personnel records of an insurance firm's main office contain data on the number of leave days (for illness or personal reasons) taken in a year by each of 533 employees. The numbers are stored in column 1 of the EX0646.DAT data set on the data disk for this book.

    a Obtain a histogram or stem-and-leaf display of the data. Would you say that the population data were roughly normally distributed?

    b Obtain the mean and standard deviation. A computer program will probably regard the data as a sample, not a population. What difference will that make in the calculations? How important, numerically, will the difference be?

    c Have the computer program draw 25 random samples from the population, each of size 20, and compute the mean for each sample.

    d Obtain a histogram or stem-and-leaf display of the 25 sample means. Does this picture have the same shape as the population distribution? What explains the difference?

6.47 Have a computer program calculate the standard deviation of the sample means obtained in Exercise 6.46. What theoretical quantity is being approximated by this standard deviation? Does the numerical value you obtained come close to the theoretical value?

6.48 Many computer programs will choose random numbers that are uniformly distributed between 0 and 1. This distribution has a flat histogram over the range 0 to 1 and no probability outside this range.

a Have the program take 100 such samples, each of size 12. Obtain the means of the 100 samples. Have the program draw a histogram of these means.

b Should the histogram of means be approximately uniformly distributed between 0 and 1? Theoretically, why? Does the histogram you obtained roughly correspond to the theoretical result?

c The variance of a uniform distribution (between 0 and 1) is $1/12 = 0.0833333$. What is the theoretical standard deviation of the means obtained in part a? Have the program compute this standard deviation. How well does it approximate the theoretical value?

d What should be the mean (expected value) for a uniform distribution between 0 and 1? How does the average of the 100 sample means compare to this theoretical value?

6.49 A chain of about 1200 full-service motels (ones that include restaurants) plans to survey a sample of its customers to get their opinions on the quality of each motel. A questionnaire has been developed and pretested to ensure that it is clear and unambiguous. The headquarters staff is trying to decide how to carry out the sample.

There are three proposed methods for sampling:

a Specify a sampling day for each motel. Each day, four motels will be selected. The manager of each motel will be notified a few days in advance to forward a list of the names and addresses of everyone who registers on the selected day. Questionnaires will be sent by mail to each of these people. Typically 100 to 150 people register each day, and the chain hopes that 40% will respond.

b Select motels each day as in the preceding method, but give the questionnaires to the people as they check out.

c Each day, take a sample of 500 people from the lists of those who have registered at all motels in the country; the information is available through the chain's management information system. Mail questionnaires to the selected people.

The major objective in sampling is to obtain an average satisfaction rating for each motel. The rating is on a 1 to 5 scale, with 5 being best. Limited experience with the rating system suggests that the vast majority of ratings will be within one point of the average. No one claims that the sample will give exact values for average ratings; it's not feasible to send questionnaires to every single guest, let alone hope that all guests will fill them out. The chain would like to be able to distinguish those motels with an average rating of about 4 from those with an average rating of about 3.

Write a brief memo to the headquarters staff discussing the pros and cons of each method. Any of the methods is expected to yield a sample of about 50 responses for each motel. The cost of obtaining the data should be quite similar for all three methods. ■

Sampling and Sampling Distributions

Y our employer, a long-distance telephone company, issues charge cards to any customers who request them. Most customers are sales employees and executives of small or medium-sized firms. For such firms, telephone bill payments do not take highest priority and your employer has difficulty collecting payment on about 8% of its charge cards. Therefore, the company is considering a credit-worthiness scoring system (available from a consulting firm) to decide whether or not to issue charge cards to employees of a particular firm. To try and decide whether to use the system in the future, the company plans to sample its current card users to estimate the average score on the system. Some of the variables in the scoring system are not available on the company's computer, so each firm in the sample requires about an hour of a clerk's time to find and enter the required information. The company can't decide how to take the sample: Some people want to sample individual card users, others want to sample the firms responsible for paying the phone bills. Some people want to sample about 200 accounts; others argue that such a sample would be too small a fraction of the (approximately) 80,000 accounts the company currently has. No one seems to have thought much about how to take the sample, though the information systems group has available an up-to-date listing of all accounts, classified virtually in any desired way. The consultants aren't willing to specify what the average should be, though they have said that, in other applications of the system, a clear majority of firms tend to score between 75 and 85, and scores between 65 and 75 or between 85 and 95 aren't terribly unusual.

Write a brief position paper on these problems, and focus on how the sample might be taken. Give your recommendations on choosing a sample size of 200 or some other sample size. You can assume that your readers will know what an average is, but don't assume that they know much more about technicial statistical issues. You can also figure that your readers have a one-page attention span. ■

A

Standard Error of a Mean

S ome students want to understand *why* the formula for the standard error of $\overline{Y}$ comes out as it does. For their benefit, this appendix contains a sketchy proof. There are two key ideas; each is stated in terms of variance. First, multiplying a random variable by a constant multiplies its variance by the *square* of the constant. Second, the variance of a sum of *independent* random variables is the sum of the component variances. Therefore,

$$\text{Var}(\overline{Y}) = \text{Var}\left(\frac{\sum Y_i}{n}\right)$$

$$= 1/n^2 \text{Var}\left(\sum Y_i\right) \qquad \text{because dividing by } n \text{ is equivalent to multilplying by } 1/n$$

$$= 1/n^2 \sum \text{Var}(Y_i) \qquad \text{because the individual variables are, by assumption, independent}$$

$$= \frac{1}{n^2}(\sigma^2 + \sigma^2 + \cdots + \sigma^2) \qquad \text{because the variables are drawn} \atop \text{from a population with variance } \sigma^2$$

$$= \frac{n\sigma^2}{n^2} = \frac{\sigma^2}{n}$$

Taking a square root yields the standard error of $\overline{Y}$:

$$\sigma_{\overline{Y}} = \sqrt{\text{Var}(\overline{Y})}$$

$$= \frac{\sigma}{\sqrt{n}}$$

Two minor-league studs named Tobias
Cried "Hey, little girls, come and try us!
We'll knock you all dead!
We're super in bed!"
They got quite a nonresponse bias.

REVIEW EXERCISES—CHAPTERS 4–6

R23 Scores on an aptitude test for assembly workers are roughly normally distributed with a mean of 200 and a standard deviation of 40.

a Find the probability that a randomly chosen individual score is above 210.

b Find the probability that the mean of a random sample of 25 individuals is larger than 210.

R24 If the distribution of scores in Exercise R23 is not exactly normal, which answer is a poorer approximation? Why?

R25 A supermarket makes errors in posting 5% of the price changes it makes in the long run. Suppose that a random sample of 50 price changes is selected. The number of changes made during the period is so large that it doesn't matter whether the sample is taken with or without replacement.

a Write an expression for the probability that three or fewer changes are posted incorrectly.

b Find a numerical value for the probability in part a.

c What assumptions were made in answering part a? From what you know about supermarkets, under what conditions might any of these assumptions be in error?

R26 A certain part is kept in inventory at an automobile dealership; the parts manager wants a maximum of 10 on hand. The number in stock at a given time follows the probability distribution

$$P_X(x) = \frac{(x+1)}{66} \qquad x = 0, 1, \ldots, 10$$

a Write out a table of numerical probabilities.

b Find the mean and standard deviation of the number in stock at a given time.

c If the dealer requires 3 of this part on a given day, what is the probability that there is enough in stock?

R27 Suppose that the auto dealer in the previous exercise has 4 separate parts in stock and that the probability distribution for the number of each in stock is the distribution specified there.

a Find the mean and variance of the average stock of the 4 parts.

b What additional assumptions, if any, did you make in answering part a? For each assumption, is the assumption more critical in determining the mean or in determining the variance?

R28 Now suppose that the dealer in the preceding exercises has 200 separate parts and that the availability of each part is given by the same probability distribution. Find the approximate probability that the average number in stock (averaged over the 200 parts) is greater than 7. Should the approximation be a good one?

R29 The manufacturing process for glass wire used in fiber-optic transmission cables introduces impurities at an average rate of .0002 impurities per foot of wire. The wire is cut into 1000-foot sections; if any impurity is found in a section, that section is recycled. What is the probability that a randomly chosen section contains no impurities?

R30 What additional assumptions beyond the stated ones did you make in answering the previous exercise?

R31 A certain radio show has a catalog from which fans of the show may order records or tapes, as well as souvenir items. Suppose that 40% of the orders involve no records or tapes, 30% involve 1 record or tape, 15% involve 2, 10% involve 3, and 5% involve 4. For each possible number of records or tapes ordered, the percentage of orders of 0, 1, 2, 3, 4, or 5 souvenir items is given in the following table:

Records/Tapes Ordered	Souvenirs Ordered (%)					
	0	1	2	3	4	5
0	0	60	30	5	3	2
1	10	40	25	15	5	5
2	5	30	40	10	8	7
3	3	15	22	30	20	10
4	1	4	15	30	40	10

Calculate, in table form, the joint probability distribution of X = number of records or tapes ordered and Y = number of souvenirs ordered. Are the two types of orders independent?

R32 Find the expected number of souvenirs ordered, assuming the probabilities shown in the previous exercise. Also find the standard deviation of the number of souvenirs ordered.

R33 A manufacturing process that is working properly produces 5% defective items because of impurities in materials or other random factors. Suppose that 20 items are selected from the output of the process and inspected. Assume that the process is working properly.

   a Find the probability that 2 or more of the selected items are defective.

   b What did you assume in answering part a?

R34 An alternative inspection method for the process in the previous exercise is to inspect every item and stop the process whenever 2 defectives have been found within the most recent 10 inspected. Does this inspection method satisfy the assumptions of a binomial random variable?

R35 Suppose it has been established that the number of program lines per week produced by computer programmers using a commercially available toolbox has a mean of 250 and a standard deviation of 70. Suppose that a random sample of 40 programmers is taken. What is the approximate probability that the average lines produced is greater than 265?

R36 What did you assume in answering the previous exercise? Under what circumstances might the answer to that exercise be a poor approximation?

R37 A realtor believes that, under current conditions, 45% of walk-in customers eventually purchase a home through that realtor. In a random sample of 16 walk-in customers, what is the probability that 3 or fewer eventually purchase a home through the realtor? Provide a numerical answer.

R38 Specify all assumptions you made in answering the previous exercise. Do any assumptions appear grossly unreasonable to you?

R39 A bond broker occasionally calls clients to try to place tax-exempt bonds. Define X = number of calls made to a particular client in a 3-month period and Y = number of orders made in that period by the client. Assume that

$$P_{XY}(x, y) = \frac{(4 - x)(xy + 1)}{30(1 + 2x)} \qquad x = 1, 2, 3, y = 0, 1, 2, 3, 4$$

The Excel spreadsheet program was used to create the following table of probabilities:

	A	B	C	D	E	F	G	H
3					y			
4			0	1	2	3	4	Total
5								
6		1	0.0333	0.0667	0.1	0.1333	0.1667	0.5
7	x	2	0.0133	0.04	0.0667	0.0933	0.12	0.3333
8		3	0.0048	0.0190	0.0333	0.0476	0.0619	0.1667
9								
10		Total	0.0514	0.1257	0.2	0.2743	0.3486	1

a Verify the calculation for $x = 1, y = 0$.

b Find the conditional distribution of Y given X, in either mathematical or tabular form.

c Are X and Y independent? In context, should they be?

R40 Find the mean and variance of Y in the previous exercise.

R41 In the preceding exercises, would the bond broker expect a positive or a negative correlation between X, the number of calls made, and Y, the number of orders received?

R42 The Excel program calculated each value of $(x - \mu_X)(y - \mu_Y)P_{XY}(x, y)$, as shown in the following output. The sum of these values is shown in the lower right, followed by this sum divided by the product of the X and Y standard deviations.

	B	C	D	E	F	G	H	I
2					y			
3			0	1	2	3	4	
4								
5		1	0.0609	0.0775	0.0495	-0.0229	-0.1397	
6	x	2	-0.0122	-0.0232	-0.0165	0.008	0.0503	
7		3	-0.0174	-0.0443	-0.033	0.0163	0.1038	
8								
9								0.0571
10								
11								0.0637

a What is the technical name for the sum 0.0571?

b Does the output show the sign (positive or negative) of the correlation that you would expect in this situation? Does the correlation seem strong, moderate, or weak?

R43 A computer software wholesaler occasionally gets special-handling orders that must be shipped by air. Such orders are expensive and unprofitable. Records indicate that such orders occur at an average rate of 1.6 per workday. In a week with five workdays, what is the probability that there are 10 or more special-handling orders? Provide a numerical answer.

R44 Carefully specify the assumptions you made in answering the previous exercise. Are any of these assumptions obviously wrong? ■

Estimation

The basic problem of statistical theory is how to infer a population or process value given only sample data. Because any sample statistic will vary from the population value, we must consider random error in estimation. This chapter presents methods that make an explicit allowance for random error—but not systematic bias—in summary numbers. The key ideas in the chapter are the following:

1   The first issue in making an inference from a sample is the choice of summary statistic. It's desirable to have an estimator be correct on average over many samples, technically called being *unbiased*. Among many possible unbiased estimators, the preferred method has the smallest possible standard error, technically called being *efficient*.

2   A minimal requirement for an estimation method is that it be consistent—that it approach the correct population value as the sample size becomes huge. An estimator will be inconsistent if it is very unreasonable or if an important assumption is violated.

3   A confidence interval is a process that has a specified chance of including the true population or process value over the long run of multiple samples. Often, this interval can be constructed as the sample estimate plus or minus a table value times a standard error. If the population/process standard deviation is somehow known, the standard error is the population standard deviation divided by the square root of n, and the table value comes from the z table.

4   As a related method, a confidence interval for the proportion of "successes" can be calculated as the sample proportion plus or minus a z table value times a standard error. The standard error is the square root of the proportion times 1 minus the proportion divided by the sample size. This interval follows by regarding successes as 1s in data and failures as 0s. The same principles and interpretations apply.

5   Confidence interval methods provide a method for deciding how large a sample is needed. Given a desired confidence level and allowance for error, the confidence interval may be solved to find how large n must be. In the case of a proportion, an additional step is necessary: indicating whether the population proportion is assumed to be near .5 (the worst case) or can be bounded away from that value.

6   In the realistic case that the population/process standard deviation is not known, the sample standard deviation must be used. When the sample standard deviation and estimated standard error are used, t tables rather than z tables must be used. In such a case, one must specify the degrees of freedom, which are equal to the sample size minus 1 in a random sample. Otherwise, the same confidence interval method applies.

7   The key assumptions underlying confidence interval methods are lack of bias and independence of sample observations. Violation of either assumption can distort results seriously. Further, standard methods assume that the underlying population/process distribution is nearly normal. Violation of this assumption can make standard methods incorrect or, more likely with large n, inefficient. ∎

7.1   Point Estimators

point estimation

T he simplest statistical inference is **point estimation**, where we compute a single value (statistic) from the sample data to estimate a population parameter. How do we decide which sample statistic to compute to give a single, numerical estimate for a population parameter? Suppose we are trying to estimate a population mean and we are willing to assume that the population distribution is normal. One natural summary statistic that can be used to estimate the population mean is the sample mean. Because the population mean for a normal distribution is also the population median, the sample median is also a plausible estimating statistic. So is a 20% trimmed mean, the average of the middle 80% of the values. Even if the population is symmetric, the sample is almost sure to be somewhat asymmetric because of random variation. Thus, for any particular sample, the three methods yield somewhat different estimates. The mean is heavily influenced by outliers. A trimmed mean is less influenced by outliers, but it wastes data by ignoring (for instance) 20% of the data. We can think of the median as an extremely trimmed mean, where one discards all but the middle one or two data points. Which method should we use?

To begin the discussion, we need a technical definition. We use θ as the generic symbol for a population parameter. We use $\hat{\theta}$ to indicate an estimate of θ based on sample data.

Definition 7.1   Estimator

An estimator of a population or process parameter is a function of random sample values $Y_1, Y_2, \ldots, Y_n$ that yields a numerical estimate of the parameter. Because the sample data will vary randomly from sample to sample, an estimator is itself a random variable and therefore has a theoretical (sampling) distribution.   ■

There is a technical distinction between an *estimator* as a function of random variables and an *estimate* as a single number. It is the distinction between a process (the estimator) and the result of that process (the estimate). The important aspect of this definition is that we can only define good processes (estimators), not guarantee good results (estimates). We will show, for example, that when one samples from a normal population, the sample mean is the best estimator. However, we cannot guarantee that the result will always be optimal—that is, we cannot guarantee that, in every single sample, the sample mean will always be closer to the population mean than, say, the sample median. The best we can do is to find estimators that give good results in the long run.

E X A M P L E   7 . 1

If Y_1, Y_2, and Y_3 are the (random) results of a sample of three individuals from a population, define a sample mean estimator. If, in a particular sample, the values 106.8, 102.0, and 105.0 are obtained, what is the resulting estimate?

Solution

The estimator

$$\overline{Y} = \frac{Y_1 + Y_2 + Y_3}{3}$$

can be interpreted as the process "take a sample of three values and average them." In the particular sample, $y_1 = 106.8$, $y_2 = 102.0$, and $y_3 = 105.0$ yield $\overline{y} = 104.6$ as an estimate of the population mean from this particular sample.   ■

The first property that we want an estimator (and its sampling distribution) to have is the capability of estimating the population parameter correctly on the average. For example, it seems wrong to use the sample 90th percentile to estimate the median (50th percentile) of a population as opposed to using the sample median. Although it is conceivable that, in a particular sample, the 90th percentile is closer to the population median than is the sample median, generally the sample 90th percentile is too large; that is, the 90th percentile of the sample tends to overestimate the median of the population. We want to use an estimating statistic that does not systematically overestimate or underestimate the desired population parameter.

To state the definition, we need a bit of notation. We use the symbol $\hat{\theta}$ to mean an estimator and the symbol θ without a "hat" to mean a population quantity (parameter).

Definition 7.2   Unbiased Estimator

An estimator $\hat{\theta}$ that is a function of the sample data $Y_1, Y_2, \ldots, Y_n$ is called unbiased for the population parameter θ if its expected value equals θ; that is, $\hat{\theta}$ is an unbiased estimator of the parameter θ if $E(\hat{\theta}) = \theta$.   ■

An unbiased estimator is correct on the average. We can think of the expected value of $\hat{\theta}$ as the average of $\hat{\theta}$ values for all possible samples or, alternatively, as the long-run average of $\hat{\theta}$ values for repeated samples. The condition that the estimator $\hat{\theta}$ should be unbiased says that the *average* $\hat{\theta}$ value is exactly correct. It does not say that a *particular* $\hat{\theta}$ value is exactly correct. If the estimator is biased, the amount of bias is $\text{Bias}(\hat{\theta}) = E(\hat{\theta}) - \theta$.

E X A M P L E   7 . 2

Suppose that $Y_1, Y_2, \ldots, Y_n$ represent the values obtained by a simple random sample from a population having mean μ and variance σ^2. Verify that $\overline{Y}$, the sample mean, is an unbiased estimator of μ.

Solution

In Chapter 6, we showed that $E(\overline{Y}) = \mu$. Thus, by definition, the sample mean is an unbiased estimator of the population mean.   ■

The requirement that an estimator be unbiased is not very restrictive, and it does not rule out many potential estimators. Usually there are many unbiased estimators of any population parameter. For example, as noted before, when sampling from a normal population, the sample mean, median, and trimmed mean are all unbiased estimators of the population mean μ.

Lack of bias is not the only property that we want an estimator to possess. An estimator that is unbiased but grossly overestimates the parameter of interest half the time and grossly underestimates it the other half isn't a very good estimator. A second property, then, that we require of an estimator is that it have a sampling distribution with most of its probability concentrated near the parameter to be estimated. One measure of this concentration of the sampling distribution of an estimator is given by its standard error: The smaller the standard error, the more concentration of probability there is near the parameter of interest.

The standard error of an estimator is also related to the probable degree of error of an estimator: The smaller the standard error, the smaller the probable degree of error. Therefore we would like to find an unbiased estimator with the smallest possible standard error or, equivalently, the smallest probable error.

Definition 7.3   Efficient Estimator

An estimator is called *most efficient* for a particular problem if it has the smallest standard error of all possible unbiased estimators.   ■

The word *efficient* is used because the estimator makes the best possible use of the sample data in a given situation. According to standard statistical theory, a most efficient unbiased estimator is usually preferred to any other. Given some very specific assumptions, it is possible to find most efficient estimators. For example, if the population from which the sample measurements are drawn is normal, the sample mean has a smaller standard error than the sample median, any sample trimmed mean, or any other unbiased estimator. Therefore, if there is good reason to assume a normal population, the sample mean is the best estimator of the population mean.

EXAMPLE 7.3

A computer program draws 1000 samples, each of size 30, from a normally distributed population having mean 50 and standard deviation 10. For each sample, the mean, median, and trimmed mean (average of the middle 80% of the sample data) are computed. The average value and standard deviation of each set of estimates for the 1000 samples are as follows:

Statistic	Average Value	Standard Deviation
Mean	50.1254	1.8373
Median	50.1696	2.2607
Trimmed mean	50.1196	1.8947

Do the three statistics appear to be unbiased? Which one appears to be most efficient?

Solution

The average value of each estimator is (a simulation approximation to) its expected value. The average value of each estimator is very close to the population mean, 50, so all three estimators appear to be unbiased, at least in this situation. The standard deviation of each estimator is (a simulation approximation to) its standard error. The sample mean has the smallest standard error, so it seems to be most efficient in this situation.   ■

robust estimators

Unfortunately, efficiency claims are heavily dependent on assumptions. When the population distribution is not normal, the sample mean is not always most efficient. In particular, when the population distribution has heavy tails (is prone to having outliers), the sample mean is less efficient than a trimmed mean (although it still is unbiased). Heavy-tailed distributions tend to yield lots of extreme, "oddball" values that influence a mean more than a trimmed mean. A great deal of research is being conducted to find so-called **robust estimators**—that is, statistics that are nearly unbiased and nearly efficient for a wide variety of possible population distributions. There is not yet any general agreement on ideal robust estimators, but it's reasonable to assume that such methods will be used increasingly in the near future. We do not spend much time on these methods despite their potential usefulness. The formulas involved in robust estimation are more complicated than those we present, but the basic principles for using the formulas are the same.

EXAMPLE 7.4

A computer is programmed to draw 1000 samples, each of size 30, from an extremely heavy-tailed, outlier-prone population having mean 0 and standard deviation 9.95. Sample means, medians, and trimmed means are computed for each sample. The average values and standard deviations of the estimates are shown here:

Statistic	Average Value	Standard Deviation
Mean	.0228	1.8757
Median	.0148	.4510
Trimmed mean	.0081	.5667

What do these results indicate about the bias and efficiency of the three estimators when sampling from this population?

Solution

All three averages—approximations to the expected values—are close to zero, so all three estimators seem to be unbiased. In this case, the standard error of the median appears to be much smaller than the standard error of the mean and somewhat smaller than that of the trimmed mean. Thus, for this outlier-prone population, the sample median appears to be somewhat more efficient than the trimmed mean and much more efficient than the sample mean. ■

consistency

One additional criterion of a good estimator is **consistency**. If we're lucky enough to have a very, very large sample, our estimator should be guaranteed to be very close to the population (or process) parameter.

Definition 7.4 Consistent Estimator

An estimator is consistent if it approaches the parameter with probability 1 as the sample size goes to infinity. ■

For example, the sample mean $\overline{Y}$ from a random sample has expected value μ and a standard error that approaches zero as n goes to infinity. Therefore, as the sample size goes to infinity, $\overline{Y}$ will be as close as you want to μ; according to the definition, $\overline{Y}$ is consistent. (All the estimators discussed in this book are consistent as long as stated assumptions hold.)

An inconsistent estimator is rather clearly a bad one. It is not good to come up with an inaccurate estimate based on infinite data. Such a bad estimate could happen if the bias of an estimator didn't approach zero as n went to infinity. Using the sample 25th percentile to estimate the population median would yield an inconsistent estimator. Inconsistency would also result if the standard error of an estimator didn't go to zero as the sample size increased. Typically, an inconsistent estimator is the result of doing something foolish or, more likely, the failure of a key assumption.

EXAMPLE 7.5

In Section 4.7, we defined the (population) correlation of two random variables. This parameter can be estimated by sample data if the variables are measured accurately, without measurement error. However, if there is measurement error, the sample correlation approaches a number somewhere between zero and the population correlation (depending on the extent of the measurement error). What does this fact say about the sample correlation as an estimator?

Solution

When there is measurement error, the sample correlation is an inconsistent estimator of the true correlation because its bias doesn't disappear as the sample size gets large. ■

EXERCISES

7.1 A random sample of 20 vice presidents of Fortune 500 firms is taken. The amount each vice president paid in federal income taxes as a percentage of gross income is determined. The data are

16.0	18.1	18.6	20.2	21.7	22.4	22.4	23.1	23.2	23.5
24.1	24.3	24.7	25.2	25.9	26.3	27.9	28.0	30.4	33.7

    a Compute the sample mean and median.

    b Compute the 20% trimmed mean; that is, delete the lowest 10% and the highest 10% of the data and find the mean of the remainder.

7.2 Refer to the data of Exercise 7.1.

    a Construct a histogram using about 6 classes.

    b Use a computer package to obtain a normal probability plot.

    c Is there evidence of nonnormality in the data?

    d Which of the sample statistics computed in Exercise 7.1 would you select to estimate the population mean?

7.3 A Monte Carlo study involves 10,000 random samples of size 16 from a normal population with $\mu = 100$ and $\sigma = 20$. For each sample, the mean, the median, and the 20% trimmed mean are calculated, with the following results:

Estimator	Mean	Median	Trimmed Mean
Average	100.23	99.96	99.98
Variance	26.52	40.61	27.49

    a What does the study suggest about the bias of the three estimators in this situation?

    b Which of the three estimators appears most efficient?

7.4 A sample of 30 editions of a weekly newspaper reveals the following numbers of column-inches of classified advertising:

171	185	193	199	204	210	216	218	221	223
225	228	228	230	234	235	237	240	241	243
245	249	251	254	257	262	263	271	280	379

    a Compute the mean and median.

    b Compute the 20% trimmed mean, the average of the middle 80% of the values.

7.5 Refer to the data of Exercise 7.4.

    a Construct a stem-and-leaf display. What is the most conspicuous aspect of the display?

    b Do the data suggest that the mean is the most efficient estimator for this situation?

7.6 Boxplots of means, trimmed means (with the top 10% and bottom 10% of the data deleted), and medians for samples of size 10 from a Laplace (mildly outlier-prone) population are shown in Figure 7.1. The mean of this population is zero.

a Do the three estimators appear to be unbiased?

b Which estimator appears to be most efficient?

FIGURE 7.1 **Boxplots for Three Estimators**

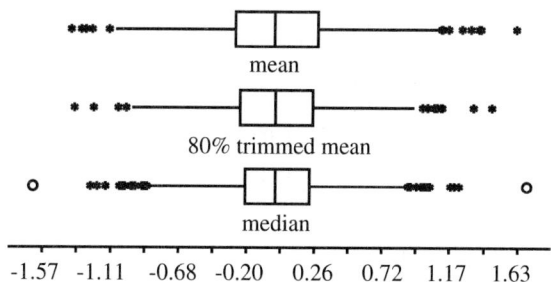

7.7 The averages and standard deviations for the three estimators in Exercise 7.6 are as follows:

Estimator	Average	Standard Deviation
Mean	.0100	.4366
Trimmed mean	.0040	.3899
Median	.0032	.3704

Are these results consistent with your answers to Exercise 7.6?

7.8 The operations manager for the automatic transmission department of an automobile maker obtains data on the operating pressure of a sample of 50 transmissions each week. One of the concerns is the mean for the entire weekly production, which is about 2200 transmissions. (Another concern is the variability around that mean.) Typically, the pressure for most transmissions is very slightly below or above the nominal level of 35 pounds per square inch. A few transmissions can have pressure readings quite far below or above the nominal level. One way to estimate the average for the entire production is to use the midrange of the sample data—the average of the largest and smallest of the 50 data values.

a From the (admittedly limited) information that you have, is there reason to believe that this method will systematically underestimate the mean? Systematically overestimate it? What technical statistical concept is in question here?

b Even if there is no systematic under- or overestimate, the midrange method may not be an effective use of the data. Explain why not. ■

7.2

Interval Estimation of a Mean, Known Standard Deviation

Any sample statistic we choose to use will vary from one sample to another. This fact is recognized in your daily newspaper, where the results of political polls indicate an allowance for sampling error. Whether we estimate using a mean, a median, a trimmed mean, a sample correlation, or whatever, the estimate will vary from one sample to another, and therefore from the true population or process value. In this section, we begin to consider how to allow for random error in estimating a population or process number.

The ideas discussed in the previous section dealt with point estimation—finding a best guess for a population parameter. Such point estimates are almost inevitably in error to some degree. Specification of a **probable range** for the parameter—a plus or minus range for error—is crucial in indicating the reliability of estimates. A statement like "the estimated response rate is 28%" is less useful than one like "the estimated response rate is 28% ± 2%." And "28% ± 2%" indicates a much more reliable estimate than "28% ± 15%." In this section, we use the idea of a sampling distribution to construct an **interval estimate** for a population mean. We discuss confidence intervals for proportions in the next section.

The idea is best introduced by an example. Suppose that a random sample of size 36 is to be taken and that the sampling distribution of $\overline{Y}$ is normal. (If the population can be assumed to be reasonably close to symmetric, the Central Limit Theorem should apply.) Somewhat artificially, we assume that the population standard deviation is known to be 18.0. The expected value of $\overline{Y}$ is the population mean μ, the parameter being estimated, and the standard error of $\overline{Y}$ is $\sigma_{\overline{Y}} = \sigma/\sqrt{n} = 18/\sqrt{36} = 3.0$. From the properties of a normal distribution, there is a 95% chance that $\overline{Y}$ is within 1.96 standard errors of μ (see Figure 7.2):

$$P[\mu - 1.96(3.0) \le \overline{Y} \le \mu + 1.96(3.0)] = .95$$

FIGURE 7.2 **Sampling Distribution of $\overline{Y}$**

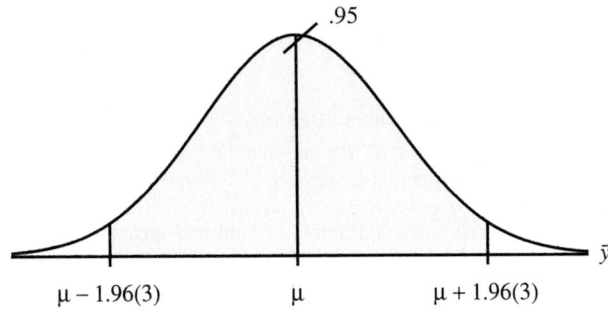

Look at it another way: Any time the observed sample mean $\overline{y}$ lies in the interval $\mu \pm 1.96(3)$, the interval $\overline{y} \pm 1.96(3)$ encloses μ. This is shown in Figure 7.3. Because there is a 95% chance that $\overline{Y}$ lies in the interval $\mu \pm 1.96(3)$, there is a 95% chance that the interval $\overline{Y} \pm 1.96(3)$ encloses μ. The interval $\overline{y} \pm 1.96(3)$ that we construct using the observed sample mean is called a **95% confidence interval for μ.**

We derive the general formula for a confidence interval for a population mean in the same way. The result is exactly correct only when the population distribution is normal and the population standard deviation is known. Because of the Central Limit Theorem, it provides an excellent approximation—for sample sizes of, say, 30 or more—when the population distribution is symmetric or only modestly skewed.

To state confidence intervals (and other statistical methods) generally, we need a bit of notation for probability table values. When we write z with a subscript, we mean "the z table value that cuts off a right-tail area specified by the subscript." Therefore, $z_{.025}$ means the z table (Appendix Table 3) value cutting off a right tail equal to .025. The area to the right of 0 is .5000, so the area between 0 and $z_{.025}$ must be $.5000 - .025 = .4750$. The required value is $z_{.025} = 1.96$. Similarly, $z_{.05} = 1.645$.

FIGURE 7.3 **Sampling Distribution of** $\overline{Y}$

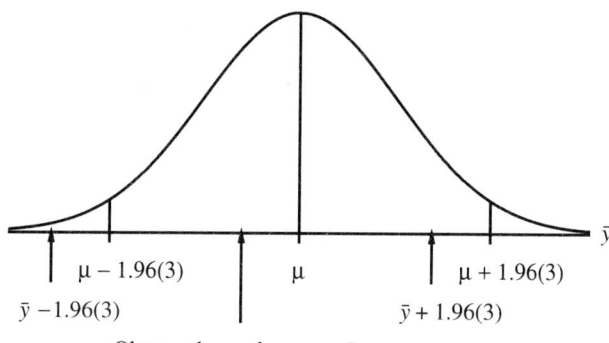

$$\mu - 1.96(3) \qquad \mu \qquad \mu + 1.96(3)$$

$$\overline{y} - 1.96(3) \qquad\qquad \overline{y} + 1.96(3)$$

Observed sample mean, $\overline{y}$

Definition 7.5   100(1 − α)% Confidence Interval for μ, with σ Known

Using the sample mean as an estimate of the population or process mean, allow for sampling error with a plus or minus term equal to a z table value times the standard error of the sample mean:

$$\overline{y} - z_{\alpha/2}\sigma_{\overline{Y}} \le \mu \le \overline{y} + z_{\alpha/2}\sigma_{\overline{Y}}$$

where $\sigma_{\overline{Y}} = \sigma/\sqrt{n}$ and $z_{\alpha/2}$ is the tabulated value cutting off a right-tail area of $\alpha/2$ in the standard normal (z) distribution.   ∎

EXAMPLE 7.6

An airline needs an estimate of the average number of passengers on a newly scheduled flight. Its experience is that data for the first month of flights are unreliable, but that thereafter the passenger load settles down. Therefore, the mean passenger load is calculated for the first 20 weekdays of the second month (regarded as a random sample of 20 days from a hypothetical population of weekdays) after initiation of this particular new flight. If the sample mean is 112.0 and the population standard deviation is assumed to be 25, find a 90% confidence interval for the true, long-run average number of passengers on this flight.

Solution

We assume that the hypothetical population of daily passenger loads for weekdays is not badly skewed. Then the sampling distribution of $\overline{Y}$ is approximately normal and the confidence interval results are approximately correct, even for a sample size of only 20 weekdays. For this example, $\overline{y} = 112.0$, $\sigma = 25$, and $\sigma_{\overline{Y}} = \sigma/\sqrt{20} = 5.59$. Then for a 90% confidence interval, we use $z_{.05} = 1.645$ in the formula to obtain

$$112 \pm 1.645(5.59) \quad \text{or} \quad 102.80 \text{ to } 121.20$$

We are 90% confident that the long-run mean μ lies in this interval.   ∎

This confidence interval states an explicit allowance for random sampling error. It does not, and cannot, allow for other kinds of error such as bias in selecting the data.

The "90%" in a 90% confidence interval refers to the *process* of constructing confidence intervals. Each particular confidence interval either does or does not include the true value of the parameter being estimated. We can't say that this particular estimate is correct to within the error. In the long run, 90% of the intervals so constructed include the population value. So, in the preceding example, we say that we have 90% confidence that $102.80 \le \mu \le 121.20$. This is shorthand for "the interval $102.80 \le \mu \le 121.20$ is the result of a process that in the long run has 90% probability of being correct."

E X A M P L E   7 . 7

A Monte Carlo study considers 5000 samples, each of size 40, from a near-normal population. For each sample, 90% and 95% confidence intervals for the population mean are calculated. A count is made of those samples for which the true mean falls below, within, and above the confidence interval:

	Below	Within	Above
90% interval	236	4513	251
95% interval	129	4753	118

What are the expected frequencies? Compare the theoretical (expected) and the observed frequencies.

Solution

The expected frequencies can be found by multiplying the theoretical probabilities by 5000:

	Below	Within	Above
90% interval	250	4500	250
95% interval	125	4750	125

The simulation frequencies are all quite close to the expected frequencies.   ■

The discussion in this section has included one rather unrealistic assumption—namely, that the population standard deviation is known. Usually both the mean and the standard deviation must be estimated from the sample. Because σ is estimated by the sample standard deviation s, the actual standard error of the mean $\sigma/\sqrt{n}$ is naturally estimated by $s/\sqrt{n}$. This estimation introduces another source of random error (s varies randomly, from sample to sample, around σ). The logically correct way to handle this problem is to use the t distribution introduced later in this chapter. If the sample size is quite large, say 100 or more, using the z confidence interval of this section with the sample standard deviation s substituted for the population standard deviation σ is a very good approximation. A better approximation uses the sample standard deviation and the t distribution, discussed later in this chapter.

E X A M P L E   7 . 8

Suppose that the airline in Example 7.6 takes a sample of 40 days and finds a sample mean of 112.0 and a sample standard deviation of 25. Find a 95% confidence interval for the true mean.

Solution

We do not know the correct population standard deviation σ and must estimate it by the sample standard deviation $s = 25$. For $\bar{y} = 112$, $s = 25$, and $n = 40$, $\sigma_{\bar{Y}} \approx 25/\sqrt{40} = 3.95$. Then, using $z_{.025} = 1.96$, the 95% confidence interval for μ is

$$112 \pm 1.96(3.95) \quad \text{or} \quad 104.26 \text{ to } 119.74$$

Because n is only 40, this confidence interval is not as appropriate as the correct t method introduced later in this chapter. ∎

EXERCISES

7.9 The data from Exercise 7.1, specifying how much a sample of 20 executives paid in federal income taxes as a percentage of gross income, are reproduced here:

16.0	18.1	18.6	20.2	21.7	22.4	22.4	23.1	23.2	23.5
24.1	24.3	24.7	25.2	25.9	26.3	27.9	28.0	30.4	33.7

Assume that the standard deviation for the underlying population is 4.0.

a Calculate a 95% confidence interval for the population mean.

b Calculate a 99% confidence interval for the population mean.

7.10 Give a careful verbal interpretation of the confidence interval in part a of Exercise 7.9.

7.11 From the appearance of the data in Exercise 7.9, is it reasonable to assume that the sampling distribution of the mean is nearly normal?

7.12 A business magazine samples 90 individuals responsible for economic forecasting for regional banks. The population is large enough that the with/without replacement distinction doesn't matter. Suppose that the sample of 90 forecasts yields an average prediction of a 2.7% growth in real disposable income. Assume that the population standard deviation is 0.4%. Calculate a 90% confidence interval for the population mean forecast.

7.13 In an audit of inventories, an internal auditor takes a sample of 36 items and determines the "shrinkage" (loss due to shoplifting or employee theft) for each item in percentage terms. The sample mean is 5.8% and the standard deviation is 4.2%. Calculate a 95% confidence interval for the true mean shrinkage.

7.14 Do you believe that the sampling distribution of $\bar{Y}$ in Exercise 7.13 would be approximately normal?

7.15 A chain of "quick lube" shops has a standard service for performing oil changes and basic checkups on automobiles. The chain has a standard that says that the average time per car for this service should be 12.5 minutes. There is considerable variability in times due to differences in layout of engines, degree of time pressure from other jobs, and many other sources. The standard deviation for the chain has been 2.4 minutes. The manager of one shop picked 48 random times (four per day for 12 days) and timed the next job after each random time. The data were analyzed using Minitab, which gave the following results:

```
MTB > zinterval 95% confidence assuming sigma = 2.4 for `timeused´

THE ASSUMED SIGMA =2.40
                 N      MEAN    STDEV   SE MEAN    95.0 PERCENT C.I.
timeused        48    13.104    2.417    0.346   ( 12.424,   13.784)
```

a Write out the 95% confidence interval for the mean. State what the 95% figure means.

b Does this interval indicate that the mean for this shop differs from the 12.5-minute standard?

7.16 Minitab also calculated a 90% confidence interval for the mean using the same data as in Exercise 7.15:

```
MTB > zinterval 90% confidence assuming sigma = 2.4 for `timeused´

THE ASSUMED SIGMA =2.40
                N      MEAN   STDEV   SE MEAN    90.0 PERCENT C.I.
timeused       48    13.104   2.417    0.346   ( 12.534,  13.675)
```

Does this interval indicate that the mean for this shop differs from the 12.5-minute standard? Why is the answer here different from the answer in part b of Exercise 7.15?

7.17 A boxplot of the data in Exercise 7.15 is shown in Figure 7.4.

a What form of nonnormality is indicated by the boxplot?

b Does this nonnormality invalidate the claimed confidence levels in Exercises 7.15 and 7.16?

FIGURE 7.4 **Boxplot of Job Time Data**

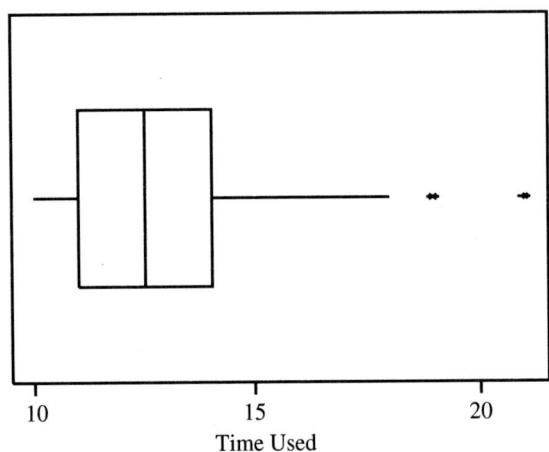

Time Used

Confidence Intervals for a Proportion

The proportion of successes—whether "success" means a likely voter favoring a particular candidate, a process yielding an unacceptable part, or a motel customer indicating a willingness to return on another trip—is another summary statistic from a random sample. It is therefore subject to random error just as any other summary number is. The confidence interval method in Section 7.2 can be adapted quite directly to give a confidence interval for a population proportion. Once again, we allow a plus or minus amount to deal with sampling error (but not with bias). The method is based on a normal approximation to the sampling distribution of a sample proportion. As such, it is an approximation, and some guidelines are needed for its use.

The sample proportion of successes, denoted $\hat{\pi}$, is just the number Y of successes divided by the sample size. If we think of a sample of 1s (successes) and 0s (failures), the $\hat{\pi}$ is the sample mean of these 1s and 0s. The **expected value and standard error of $\hat{\pi}$** are, respectively,

expected value and
standard error of $\hat{\pi}$

$$E(\hat{\pi}) = \pi \qquad \text{and} \qquad \sigma_{\hat{\pi}} = \sqrt{\pi(1-\pi)/n}$$

where π is the population proportion.

For sufficiently large n, $\hat{\pi}$ has an approximately normal distribution; so, for instance,

$$P\left(-1.96 \leq \frac{\hat{\pi} - \pi}{\sigma_{\hat{\pi}}} \leq 1.96\right) \approx .95$$

Equivalently,

$$P(\hat{\pi} - 1.96\sigma_{\hat{\pi}} \leq \pi \leq \hat{\pi} + 1.96\sigma_{\hat{\pi}}) \approx .95$$

This looks very much like a confidence interval formula, but there is the problem that the standard error $\sigma_{\hat{\pi}} = \sqrt{\pi(1-\pi)}/n$ involves the unknown population parameter π. Just as we can replace σ by s in $\sigma_{\overline{Y}}$ when n is large, so can we replace $\pi(1-\pi)$ by $\hat{\pi}(1-\hat{\pi})$ in $\sigma_{\hat{\pi}}$. This yields the following usable confidence interval formula for the population proportion:

Definition 7.6   100(1 − α)% Confidence Interval for a Proportion

$$\hat{\pi} - z_{\alpha/2}\sqrt{\frac{\hat{\pi}(1-\hat{\pi})}{n}} \leq \pi \leq \hat{\pi} + z_{\alpha/2}\sqrt{\frac{\hat{\pi}(1-\hat{\pi})}{n}} \qquad \blacksquare$$

This is the same "sample statistic ± table value times standard error" that occurs in the confidence interval for a mean. The sample mean $\overline{y}$ is replaced by the sample proportion $\hat{\pi}$. Similarly, $\sigma_{\overline{Y}}$ is replaced by $\sigma_{\hat{\pi}}$.

E X A M P L E   7 . 9

Suppose that in a sample of 2200 households with one or more television sets, 471 watch a particular network's show at a given time. Find a 95% confidence interval for the population proportion of households watching this show.

Solution

The sample proportion is $\hat{\pi} = 471/2200 = .214$, and $\sqrt{\hat{\pi}(1-\hat{\pi})/n} = .00874$. The z table value that cuts off a right-tail area of .025 is 1.96. The confidence interval is

$$.214 - 1.96(.00874) \leq \pi \leq .214 + 1.96(.00874)$$

or

$$.197 \leq \pi \leq .231$$

You might check the rankings of current television shows to see how much the difference between a 19.7% share and a 23.1% share would make in a show's ranking. $\blacksquare$

normal approximation to a binomial distribution

This confidence interval method is based on a **normal approximation to a binomial distribution** that is appropriate for sufficiently large n. The rule is that both $n\pi$ and $n(1-\pi)$ should be at least 5, but, because π is the unknown population proportion, the rule has to be based on $n\hat{\pi}$ and $n(1-\hat{\pi})$ instead. Usually a sample size that violates this rule (or even comes close) yields a confidence interval that is too wide to be informative. For example, if $n = 20$ and $\hat{\pi} = .20$, then $n\hat{\pi} = 4$ and the 95% confidence interval for π is $.025 \leq \pi \leq .375$. This confidence interval is practically useless; we know of few product managers who would consider "your product's market share is between 2.5% and 37.5%" to be very informative. However, even if a sample size satisfies the rule, we are not assured that the interval is informative. The rule judges only the adequacy of the sample size and the accuracy of the confidence interval based on the normal approximation. It is possible to use binomial probabilities to develop exact, if very wide, 90% or 95% confidence intervals.

Simply stating whether or not a result is a success is not very informative. Each trial of a binomial (yes/no) experiment yields very limited information. As a consequence, confidence intervals for modest samples in the hundreds tend to be very wide. Typically, actual measurements yield greater information per trial than simple yes/no categorization. However, sometimes all that can be measured is a yes or no value. In such a case, larger sample sizes are needed to get results that "feel" adequate for managerial purposes. In the next section, we'll consider how big a sample size must be to obtain a given degree of uncertainty.

EXERCISES

7.18 The sales manager for a hardware wholesaler finds that 229 of the previous 500 calls to hardware store owners resulted in new product placements. Assuming that the 500 calls represent a random sample, find a 95% confidence interval for the long-run proportion of new product placements.

7.19 Give a careful verbal interpretation of the confidence interval found in Exercise 7.18.

7.20 As part of a market research study, in a sample of 125, 84 individuals are aware of a certain product. Calculate a 90% confidence interval for the proportion of individuals in the population who are aware of the product.

7.21 Should the normal approximation underlying the confidence interval of Exercise 7.20 be adequate?

7.22 In a sample of 40 middle managers of a large firm, it is found that 8 are actively involved in local civic or charitable organizations. Calculate a 90% confidence interval for the proportion of all middle managers who are so involved. ∎

How Large a Sample Is Needed?

Information is expensive. Gathering it is costly in terms of salaries, expenses, and time (and profits) lost. Obviously, some information is crucial for making management decisions. So the question of how much information (how large a sample) to gather is basic. The confidence interval provides a convenient method for answering this question.

Suppose that an operations officer of a large multibranch bank is concerned about the daily average level of checks left at branches on weeknights. Each day, armored cars take each branch's receipts to a processing center, where checks are recorded and sent to a clearinghouse. The cars must visit some of the branches before the end of banking hours, so a substantial volume of checks can remain uncollected until the next day. The lost interest can be costly. For how many days must the volume of uncollected checks be calculated to get a reasonable idea of the true daily average?

There are two related aspects of the phrase "reasonable idea" to consider in the context of a confidence interval. First, what confidence level should be selected? Second, how wide a confidence interval can be tolerated? The confidence level is often set at 95% or 90%. In part, this is a primitive tribal custom, passed on by generations of statistics textbooks. In part, it's a decent translation of reasonable certainty. It's fairly easy to understand 90 (or 95) chances in 100, but hard to comprehend 999,999 chances in 1,000,000.

tolerable width

The **tolerable width** depends heavily on the context of the problem. Plus or minus $80,000 (or a width of $160,000) is moderately large for the nightly idle check volume of an entire bank, enormous for the nightly idle volume of one branch, and tiny for the average daily amount cleared by all U.S. banks. The tolerance must be determined by a manager who knows the situation.

When considering a confidence interval for a population mean μ, the plus or minus term of a confidence interval is $z_{\alpha/2}\sigma_{\bar{Y}}$, where $\sigma_{\bar{Y}} = \sigma/\sqrt{n}$. Three quantities determine the value of the plus or minus term: the desired confidence level (which determines the z table value used), the standard deviation σ, and the sample size (which together with σ determines the standard error $\sigma_{\bar{Y}}$). Usually a guess must be made about the size of the population standard deviation. (Sometimes an initial sample is taken to estimate the standard deviation; this estimate provides a basis for determining the additional sample size that is needed.) For a given tolerable width, once the confidence level is specified and an estimate of σ supplied, the required sample size can be calculated by trial and error or by a formula.

The trial-and-error approach can be illustrated with the idle check example. Suppose that a 95% confidence interval is desired with a width of no more that $5000 (a plus or minus range no greater than $2500) and that the long-run standard deviation is assumed to be $10,000. Suppose we first try $n = 16$. The confidence interval is $\bar{y} \pm 1.96(10,000/\sqrt{16})$ or $\bar{y} \pm 4900$. This interval is about twice as wide as desired; to halve the width of the confidence interval, we must quadruple the sample size because the sample size appears in the standard error formula as $\sqrt{n}$. With $n = 64$, the 95% confidence interval is $\bar{y} \pm 1.96(10,000/\sqrt{64})$ or $\bar{y} \pm 2450$, which is about what we want. Because the assumption that the standard deviation is $10,000 is just a guess, there's not much point in arguing over whether n should be 64 or 63 or 65; a "ballpark" value for n serves the purpose.

We can also calculate the required sample size directly. Set $z_{\alpha/2}\sigma/\sqrt{n}$ equal to the specified plus or minus tolerance E and solve for n.

Definition 7.7 Sample Size for Interval of Given Width for μ

The sample size required to obtain a $100(1 - \alpha)\%$ confidence interval for a population mean μ of the form $\bar{y} \pm E$, where $E = z_{\alpha/2}\sigma/\sqrt{n}$, is

$$n = \frac{z_{\alpha/2}^2 \sigma^2}{E^2}$$

The width of the confidence interval is $2E$. ■

E X A M P L E   7 . 1 0

Union officials are concerned about reports of inferior wages being paid to employees of a company under its jurisdiction. How large a sample is needed to obtain a 90% confidence interval for the population mean hourly wage μ with width equal to $1.00? Assume that $\sigma = \$4.00$.

Solution

The desired width is $2E = 1.00$ (so $E = .50$) and $\sigma = 4.00$. Substituting into the sample size formula with $z_{\alpha/2} = 1.645$, we obtain

$$n = \frac{(1.645)^2(4^2)}{(.5)^2} \approx 173 \quad ■$$

EXAMPLE 7.11

How large a sample is needed to obtain a 95% confidence interval for μ with a width of two-tenths of a (population) standard deviation?

Solution

The desired width $2E = .2\sigma$, so $E = .1\sigma$. Therefore

$$n = \frac{(1.96)^2\sigma^2}{(.1\sigma)^2} = \frac{(1.96)^2}{(.1)^2} \approx 384 \quad \blacksquare$$

Determining sample size for a confidence interval for a proportion is a similar process. The corresponding equation is

$$n = \frac{z_{\alpha/2}^2 \hat{\pi}(1 - \hat{\pi})}{E^2}$$

The only problem is that the sample size depends on $\hat{\pi}$. Until the sample size is determined and the sample taken, we do not know $\hat{\pi}$. There are several possible solutions to our problem. We can substitute $\hat{\pi} = .5$ into the sample size formula, which results in a conservative sample size that is usually larger than is actually required. If $\hat{\pi} = .5$ is not reasonable in the problem context (such as the market share of a new product in a fragmented market, where a .10 share would be excellent), choose a $\hat{\pi}$ value that is plausible, perhaps shading toward .5. Thus, if a reasonable guess for the proportion is somewhere between .05 and .15, use $\hat{\pi} = .15$, the reasonable value closest to .5. Another possibility is to substitute a value of $\hat{\pi}$ obtained from either a previous study or a pilot study. The sample size calculation for estimating a binomial proportion is given next.

Definition 7.8 Sample Size for Interval of Given Width for π

The sample size required to obtain a $100(1 - \alpha)\%$ confidence interval for π of the form $\hat{\pi} \pm E$, where

$$E = z_{\alpha/2}\sqrt{\frac{\hat{\pi}(1 - \hat{\pi})}{n}}$$

is

$$n = \frac{z_{\alpha/2}^2 \hat{\pi}(1 - \hat{\pi})}{E^2}$$

Note: Use $\hat{\pi} = .5$ or the closest plausible value to .5 for a conservative (large) sample size or use the value of $\hat{\pi}$ from a previous (or pilot) study. $\blacksquare$

EXAMPLE 7.12

A direct-mail sales company must determine its credit policies quite carefully. Suppose the firm suspects that advertisements in a certain magazine have led to an excessively high rate of write-offs (accounts regarded as uncollectible). The firm wants to establish a 90% confidence interval for this magazine's write-off proportion that is accurate to $\pm.02$.

a   How many accounts must be sampled to guarantee this goal?

b   If this many accounts are sampled and 10% of the sampled accounts are determined to be write-offs, what is the resulting 90% confidence interval?

Solution

a The sample size formula is

$$n = \frac{z_{\alpha/2}^2 \hat{\pi}(1 - \hat{\pi})}{E^2}$$

Using the conservative estimate $\hat{\pi} = .5$ and substituting $E = .02$ with $z_{\alpha/2} = 1.645$, the required sample size is

$$n = \frac{(1.645)^2(.5)^2}{(.02)^2} \approx 1691$$

b If a sample of 1691 accounts shows 169 (essentially 10%) write-offs, the 90% confidence interval for the true write-off proportion is

$$.10 \pm 1.645\sqrt{(.10)(.90)/1691} = .10 \pm .012$$

The conservative nature of the confidence interval that results from a sample size determined by setting $\hat{\pi} = .5$ in the formula is indicated here. The actual confidence interval has $E = .012$, whereas the target was $E = .02$. Had the firm been willing to make an initial guess that $\hat{\pi}$ would be about .10, it could have used a smaller sample size:

$$n = \frac{(1.645)^2(.1)(.9)}{(.02)^2} = 609 \qquad \blacksquare$$

As Example 7.12 indicates, basing a sample size determination on the assumption that $\hat{\pi}$ is .5 can be excessively conservative. Whenever there is information to suggest that the sample proportion differs from .5, the substitution $\hat{\pi} = .5$ results in a large (conservative) sample size. The corresponding confidence interval has a smaller width than the target width.

EXERCISES

7.23 **a** Refer to Example 7.10, where σ was assumed to be $4.00. How large a sample is needed to obtain a 90% confidence interval with $0.50? With width $0.25? With width $0.125?

b In general, how much must one increase a sample size to cut the width of a confidence interval in half (using a specific confidence level)?

7.24 How large a sample is needed to obtain a 95% confidence interval with a width of three-tenths of a standard deviation? Four-tenths?

7.25 An automobile insurance firm wants to find the average amount per claim for auto body repairs. Its summary records combine amounts for body repair with all other amounts, so a sample of individual claims must be taken. A 95% confidence interval with a width no greater than $50 is wanted. A "horseback guess" says that the standard deviation is about $400. How large a sample is needed?

7.26 Suppose that the guess of the standard deviation in Exercise 7.25 is somewhere between $300 and $450.

a Compute the required sample sizes for $\sigma = 300$ and for $\sigma = 450$.

b What would happen to the width of the confidence interval if the n corresponding to $\sigma = 450$ was used but in fact the standard deviation came out $300?

7.27 Do you think that the sample size used in Exercise 7.25 would be adequate to assume that $\overline{Y}$ had approximately a normal sampling distribution?

7.28 A manufacturer of boxes of candy is concerned about the proportion of imperfect boxes—those containing cracked, broken, or otherwise unappetizing candies.

a How large a sample is needed to get a 95% confidence interval for this proportion with a width no greater than .02? Use the conservative substitution.

b How does the answer to part a change if we assume that the proportion of imperfect boxes is at least .005 and no more than .08? ■

The t Distribution

The confidence interval procedure for a population mean μ presented in Section 7.2 is based on the assumption that either σ, the standard deviation in the entire population, is known (even though the population mean isn't known and is being estimated) or that there is a large enough number of measurements (for example, 100 or more) so that the sample standard deviation s can replace σ in the standard error for $\bar{y}$, $\sigma/\sqrt{n}$. Sometimes it is impossible or uneconomical to obtain a large sample when making an inference about a population mean. For example, in a study of rush-hour traffic patterns around a bridge on Friday evenings, it would take more than six months to generate 30 observations on the total Friday evening rush-hour traffic volume. This may be too long before corrective remedies need to be proposed.

Thus far, the confidence interval has been based on the z statistic

$$\frac{\bar{Y} - \mu}{\sigma/\sqrt{n}}$$

When the population standard deviation σ is unknown (and it usually is unknown), it must be replaced by s, the sample standard deviation. This yields a summary statistic denoted as t:

$$t = \frac{\bar{Y} - \mu}{s/\sqrt{n}}$$

The theoretical distribution of this statistic was first investigated by W. S. Gosset in the 1900s. Gosset was employed by the Guinness brewery, which didn't allow him to publish his results under his own name. So he published his results under the pseudonym "Student." The statistic and its distribution have become known as *Student's t*.

When we substitute the sample standard deviation s for the population standard deviation σ, we introduce a second source of variability. Now, as we go from sample to sample, not only the sample mean will vary, but also the sample standard deviation. Thus, the variance of the t statistic will be larger, reflecting the extra variability. We can summarize the properties of a t distribution by comparing it to a standard normal (z) distribution.

Definition 7.9   Properties of Student's t Distribution

1   The t distribution, like the z distribution, is symmetric about the mean $\mu = 0$.

2   The t distribution is more variable than the z distribution (see Figure 7.5).

3   There are many different t distributions. We specify a particular one by its "degrees of freedom," d.f. If a random sample is taken from a normal population, then the statistic

$$t = \frac{\bar{Y} - \mu}{s/\sqrt{n}}$$

has a t distribution with d.f. $= n - 1$.

4   As n increases (or equivalently as d.f. increases), the distribution of t approaches the distribution of z.

FIGURE 7.5 **A *t* Distribution with a Normal Distribution Superimposed**

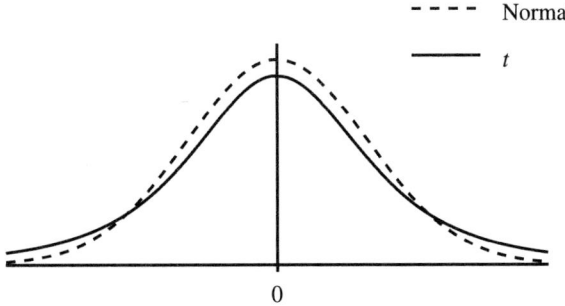

degrees of freedom

A general definition of the term **degrees of freedom** requires n-dimensional geometry and an understanding of linear algebra. We don't go into such detail; rather, we try to give an intuitive idea of what the term means. The term d.f. refers to the estimated standard deviation; it is used to indicate the number of pieces of information available for that estimate. The standard deviation is based on n deviations from the mean; but the deviations must sum to 0, so only $n - 1$ deviations are free to vary. The last (nth) deviation is determined by the other $n - 1$ and conveys no new information. Therefore, the t statistic is said to have $n - 1$ degrees of freedom.

Although a mathematical formula can be given for the probability density function of the t distribution, we don't need it in this book. There are tables to evaluate t probabilities, and most statistical computer packages can do the same. In Excel, the TDIST function calculates the cumulative probability up to a specified value for t, assuming a specified number of degrees of freedom. The "inverse" problem, finding the value of t corresponding to a specified cumulative probability with a specified number of degrees of freedom, is handled by the TINV function.

If a computer program isn't available, tables can be used. Because of the symmetry of t, only upper-tail percentage points (probabilities or areas) of the distribution of t have been tabulated. These appear in Appendix Table 4. The degrees of freedom (d.f.) are listed along the left-hand column of the page. An entry in the table specifies a value of t—say, t_a—such that an area a lies to its *right* (see Figure 7.6). Note that this table is the inverse of Appendix Table 3; now we enter a probability and find a value, rather than entering a value and finding a probability.

Various values of a appear across the top of the page. Thus, for example, with d.f. = 7, the value of t with an area .05 to its right is 1.895 (found in the $a = .05$ column and d.f. = 7 row).

FIGURE 7.6 **Illustration of Area Tabulated in Appendix Table 4 for the *t* Distribution**

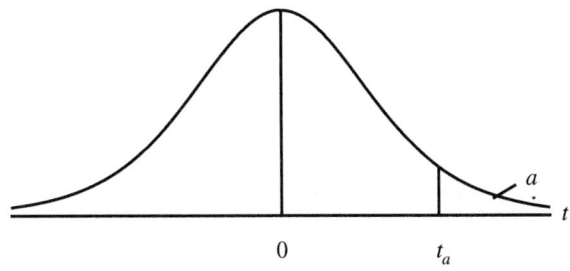

EXAMPLE 7.13

If a random sample of size $n = 15$ is taken from a normally distributed population, use the t table to find

$$P\left(\frac{\overline{Y} - \mu}{s/\sqrt{n}} > 2.145\right)$$

and

$$P\left(-2.145 \leq \frac{\overline{Y} - \mu}{s/\sqrt{n}} \leq 2.145\right)$$

Compare your result to the following Minitab output:

```
MTB > CDF 2.145;
SUBC> t 14.

            Cumulative Distribution Function

            Student's t distribution with 14 d.f.

          X       P( X <= x)
      2.1450        0.9750


MTB > InvCDF .9750;
SUBC> t 14.

            Inverse Cumulative Distribution Function

            Student's t distribution with 14 d.f.

    P( X <= x)           X
      0.9750          2.1448
```

Solution

We must use the t table, Appendix Table 4, with $n - 1 = 14$ d.f. The table indicates values that cut off specific right-tail areas. In particular, $P(t_{14 \text{ d.f.}} > 2.145)$ is shown to be .025, so

$$P\left(\frac{\overline{Y} - \mu}{s/\sqrt{n}} > 2.145\right) = .025$$

(see Figure 7.7). The t distribution is symmetric around zero, so the left-tail area $P(t_{14 \text{ d.f.}} < -2.145) = .025$ also. The remaining area after both tails are cut off is .95, so

$$P\left(-2.145 \leq \frac{\overline{Y} - \mu}{s/\sqrt{n}} \leq 2.145\right) = .95$$

The first part of the Minitab output specified the value 2.145, and finds the cumulative probability (cdf) up to 2.145 as .975. Therefore, the probability that t will be greater than 2.145 is the complement, $1 - .975 = .025$. The second part of the Minitab output reverses the procedure. In this "inverse" procedure, we state the desired probability as .975 and the program returns the table value 2.1448 (2.145 rounded to three decimal places).

FIGURE 7.7   *t* Distribution with 14 d.f.

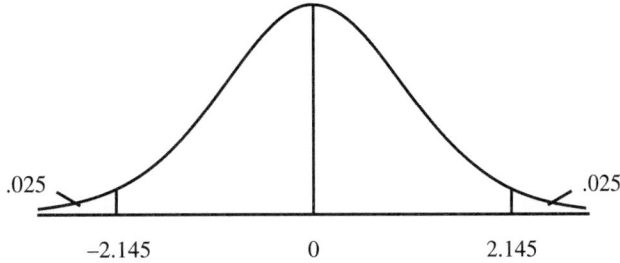

An examination of the *t* table indicates the effect of changing from

$$z = \frac{\overline{Y} - \mu}{\sigma/\sqrt{n}}$$

to

$$t = \frac{\overline{Y} - \mu}{s/\sqrt{n}}$$

For very small *n*, *t* table values are quite large. For d.f. = 2, the right-tail area of .025 is cut off at 4.303, as compared to the *z* table value 1.96. As the d.f. increases, the *t* table values for a given tail area decrease. At the bottom line, which has infinite degrees of freedom, the *t* table contains the normal distribution (*z*) values.

This phenomenon can be explained by considering how the *t* distribution arises. We get a *t* statistic by replacing the true standard deviation σ by the sample standard deviation *s*, thus introducing an additional source of random variation. When *n* is small, the value of *s* can vary widely from the value of σ, and the *t* distribution must have quite a large variance. As *n* gets larger, there is less random variation of *s* from σ, and the *t* distribution's variance gets smaller. As *n* approaches infinity, *s* approaches σ and the only important source of randomness is $\overline{Y}$; the *z* distribution accounts for the variation of $\overline{Y}$ around μ.

When we first discussed replacing σ by *s*, we followed a rule that we could use the *z* tables if *n* was greater than or equal to 100. The *t* table values for large d.f. are fairly close to normal table values except for very small tail areas. But there's no need to preserve this rule any longer. We might as well use the *t* tables routinely for all *t* statistics. If the actual d.f. is not shown in the table, a conservative approach is to use the next lower d.f. that appears in the table.

EXERCISES

7.29 A random sample of size 4 is to be taken from a normal population with mean $\mu = 100$. Let

$$t = \frac{\overline{Y} - 100}{s/\sqrt{4}}$$

Evaluate the following probabilities using Appendix Table 4 or a computer package:

a $P(t > 1.638)$ **b** $P(t > 5.841)$

c $P(t < -2.353)$ **d** $P(-2.353 < t < 2.353)$

e $P(|t| > 3.182)$ **f** $P(|t| > 4.541)$

Draw pictures.

7.30 Suppose that the t statistic in Exercise 7.29 is mistakenly assumed to have a normal (z) distribution. Evaluate $P(t > 1.638)$ and $P(|t| > 1.638)$ under this erroneous assumption. Does this assumption cause an overstatement or an understatement of the probabilities?

7.31 A Monte Carlo study is made by taking 1100 samples, each of size 4, from the normal population of Exercise 7.29. The t statistic is defined in that exercise. The results of the study are summarized as follows:

Event	Frequency
$t < -2.353$	44
$-2.353 < t < -1.638$	59
$-1.638 < t < 1.638$	896
$1.638 < t < 2.353$	47
$t > 2.353$	54

a What are the theoretical relative frequencies?

b Is there any evidence of a major, systematic departure from these theoretical relative frequencies? ■

7.6 Confidence Intervals with the t Distribution

The mathematical development of the previous section has led to inference procedures for a mean that can be used in the (typical) case where the population standard deviation is not known. This section is devoted to confidence intervals.

Remember that a confidence interval is designed to allow for some degree of sampling (random) error in estimating a population quantity. Remember also that a confidence interval does *not* allow for systematic biases in data collection. The z confidence interval for a population mean is calculated as the sample mean plus or minus a z table value times the true standard error, $\sigma/\sqrt{n}$. The changes in the confidence interval procedure when σ is unknown are easy enough. Replace the unknown σ by s to get an estimated standard error $s/\sqrt{n}$; use t tables instead of z tables.

EXAMPLE 7.14

Calculate a 95% confidence interval for the population mean if a sample of size $n = 25$ from a nearly normal population yields a sample mean of 96.2; assume that the population standard deviation is 15.0. Recalculate the interval assuming that the population standard deviation is unknown and that the sample standard deviation is 16.2.

Solution

We can use the procedures of Section 7.2 for the first problem:

$$\bar{y} - z_{\alpha/2}\frac{\sigma}{\sqrt{n}} \leq \mu \leq \bar{y} + z_{\alpha/2}\frac{\sigma}{\sqrt{n}}$$

$$96.2 - 1.96\frac{(15.0)}{\sqrt{25}} \leq \mu \leq 96.2 + 1.96\frac{(15.0)}{\sqrt{25}}$$

$$90.32 \leq \mu \leq 102.08$$

In the second problem, we need the t table value for $n - 1 = 24$ d.f. This value must cut off combined left- and right-tail areas of .05 so the desired right-tail area is .025. The t table value is 2.064. Replace $\sigma = 15.0$ by $s = 16.2$ and $z_{.025} = 1.96$ by $t_{.025} = 2.064$.

$$96.2 - 2.064\frac{(16.2)}{\sqrt{25}} \le \mu \le 96.2 + 2.064\frac{(16.2)}{\sqrt{25}}$$

$$89.51 \le \mu \le 102.89$$

This interval is wider than the previous one because $t_{.025} > z_{.025}$ and also because in this case $s = 16.2$ happens to be greater than the assumed $\sigma = 15.0$. ∎

The general t confidence interval for μ based on a t distribution with d.f. $= n - 1$ is shown here.

Definition 7.10   100$(1 - \alpha)$% Confidence Interval for μ, σ Unknown

$$\bar{y} - t_{\alpha/2}\frac{s}{\sqrt{n}} \le \mu \le \bar{y} + t_{\alpha/2}\frac{s}{\sqrt{n}}$$

where $t_{\alpha/2}$ is the tabulated t value cutting off a right-tail area of $\alpha/2$, with $n - 1$ d.f.   ∎

---

small-sample confidence interval

This formula is often called a **small-sample confidence interval** for the mean, but it is valid for *any* sample size. For a large sample size, the difference between using t tables and z tables is negligible, so the importance of the t versus z distinction is greatest for small sample sizes. The assumption of a normal population is most crucial for small sample sizes, where the Central Limit Theorem has relatively little effect. Even with a larger sample, a confidence interval based on a mean may be inefficient (unnecessarily wide).

E X A M P L E   7 . 1 5

An airline has four ticket-counter positions at a particular airport. In an attempt to reduce waiting lines for customers, the airline introduces the "snake system." Under this system, all customers enter a single waiting line that winds back and forth in front of the counter. A customer who reaches the front of the line proceeds to the first free position.

Each weekday for three weeks, the airline customer-relations manager charts the waiting time in minutes for the first customer entering after 4 P.M. One observation is excluded because of an unusual condition: The airport was fogged in, and many flight plans had to be changed. The data are

4.3   5.2   2.1   6.2   5.8   4.7   3.8   9.3   5.0   4.1   6.0   8.7   0.5   4.9

Find a 95% confidence interval for the long-run mean waiting time on weekdays under normal conditions.

Solution

First calculate $n = 14$, $\bar{y} = 5.043$, and $s = 2.266$. The t table value (13 d.f., one-tail area .025) is 2.160. The interval is

$$5.043 - 2.160\frac{(2.266)}{\sqrt{14}} \le \mu \le 5.043 + 2.160\frac{(2.266)}{\sqrt{14}}$$

or

$$3.735 \le \mu \le 6.351$$

It would be better to report this, rounded off to roughly the accuracy of the data, as $3.7 \le \mu \le 6.4$. ∎

A confidence interval is a useful way to present information to managers. Most people are familiar with the idea that political polls have an "allowance for error" of about 3 percentage points. Confidence intervals simply express that allowance for error (although, once again, they don't allow for bias). There are many other confidence intervals for other population quantities. Many, but not all, of them have the same "estimate plus or minus table value times standard error" form. The t table is often, but not always, the useful table in these confidence intervals.

One of the important uses of confidence intervals is determining the sample size required to yield a desired degree of statistical accuracy. Accuracy is defined by the level of confidence and the width of the interval. Recall that when we assume σ is known and specify the degree of confidence $100(1 - \alpha)\%$ and the desired confidence interval width $2E$, we find the desired sample size by solving the equation

$$\frac{z_{\alpha/2}\sigma}{\sqrt{n}} = E$$

sample size required for estimating μ

for n. Now we would like to find n by solving $t_{\alpha/2}s/\sqrt{n} = E$, but there are two difficulties. First, s is not known until the sample is taken and, second, we do not have the d.f. for $t_{\alpha/2}$ until n is specified. The first problem can be handled either by using a rough, ballpark guess for s or by specifying the desired width as some fraction of a standard deviation. (An error in estimating a mean to within .01 standard deviation would be dwarfed by the variation of individual values from the mean, whereas an error of 1.00 standard deviation would be pretty substantial.) The second problem can be solved by making a preliminary assumption that n is large enough that z can be substituted for t. If the resulting n turns out to be too small, trial and error (in the direction of increasing n a little bit) usually gets an answer quickly.

E X A M P L E   7 . 1 6

Suppose that a 95% confidence interval with a plus or minus tolerance of half a standard deviation is desired. What sample size is needed?

Solution

E is to be $.5s$. For the moment, assume that we can use the z table value 1.96 as an approximation to $t_{.025}$. Solving the equation

$$\frac{1.96s}{\sqrt{n}} = .5s$$

for n, we get

$$n = \frac{(1.96s)^2}{(.5s)^2} = 15.4$$

For $n = 16$ (15 d.f.) we would use $t_{.025} = 2.131$ instead of 1.96 and get an actual value of E equal to

$$\frac{2.131s}{\sqrt{16}} \approx .533(s)$$

which is a bit too large an error. We need to increase n a little bit. Try $n = 18$ (17 d.f.); $t_{.025} = 2.110$, and

$$\frac{2.110s}{\sqrt{18}} \approx .497(s)$$

so $n = 18$ will do.   ■

EXERCISES

7.32 A manufacturer of cookies and crackers does a small survey of the age at sale of one of its brands. A random sample of 23 retail markets in a particular region is chosen. In each store, the number of days since manufacture of the frontmost box of crackers is determined by a date code on the box. The data (age in days, arranged from lowest to highest) are

27	34	36	36	38	39	39	39	40	40	42	45
47	51	52	57	63	71	75	84	96	110	147	

Output from Excel follows. A boxplot is shown in Figure 7.8.

```
DESCRIPTIVE STATISTICS

VARIABLE    LO 99% CI      MEAN   UP 99% CI        SD
DAYS           39.841    56.869      73.898    28.972
```

FIGURE 7.8 **Boxplot for Cracker Age Data**

a Locate the 99% confidence interval for the true mean age.

b Is there any indication of a nonnormal population?

c Do you think that the manufacturer would find the interval narrow enough to be useful?

7.33 Suppose that the manufacturer in Exercise 7.32 wants to obtain a 90% confidence interval with a width of no more than 6 days. Assuming that the sample standard deviation does not change, how large a sample is needed?

7.34 A consumer group wants to estimate the average delivered price of a certain model of refrigerator in the New York metropolitan area. Prices are determined by comparison shoppers at 14 randomly selected stores in the area. The following Minitab output was obtained:

```
MTB > print 'price'

price
   341   347   319   331   326   298   335   351   316   307   335
   320   329   346

MTB > tinterval 95% confidence for 'price'

               N      MEAN    STDEV   SE MEAN    95.0 PERCENT C.I.
price         14    328.64    15.49      4.14   ( 319.70,  337.59)

MTB > stem and leaf of 'price'

Stem-and-leaf of price       N  = 14
Leaf Unit = 1.0

         1    29 8
         2    30 7
         4    31 69
         7    32 069
         7    33 155
         4    34 167
         1    35 1
```

Locate the 95% confidence interval for the true mean.

7.35 In the previous exercise, is there a clear indication that the underlying population of prices does not have a normal distribution?

7.36 An electric utility routinely tracks usage of electricity monthly. The data, expressed in monthly relative change form, were analyzed by JMP, with results shown in Figure 7.9.

    a Is there a consistent upward or downward trend in the output?

    b What does the output indicate about the monthly relative change?

FIGURE 7.9 **Time Plot for Electricity Usage**

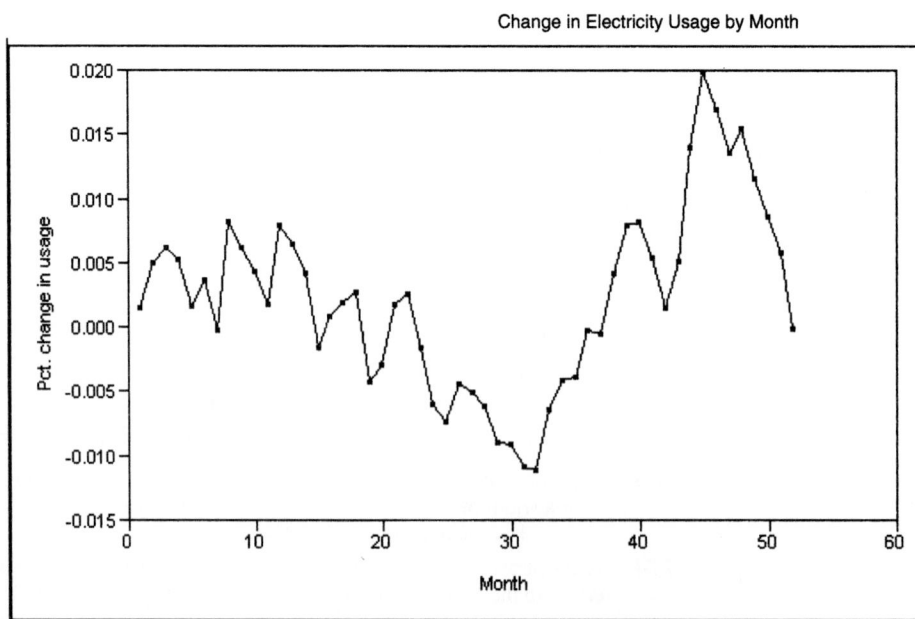

7.37 Changes in electricity usage tend to be cyclical, with periods of many months of above-average growth followed by periods of many months of below-average growth. Why is this a problem for the interpretation of the confidence interval in the preceding output?

7.38 The electric utility's strategic plan assumed a growth of .0015 per month (0.15% or roughly 1.8% per year). What does the output in Figure 7.10 indicate about this plan?

FIGURE 7.10   **Summary of Electricity Usage Data**

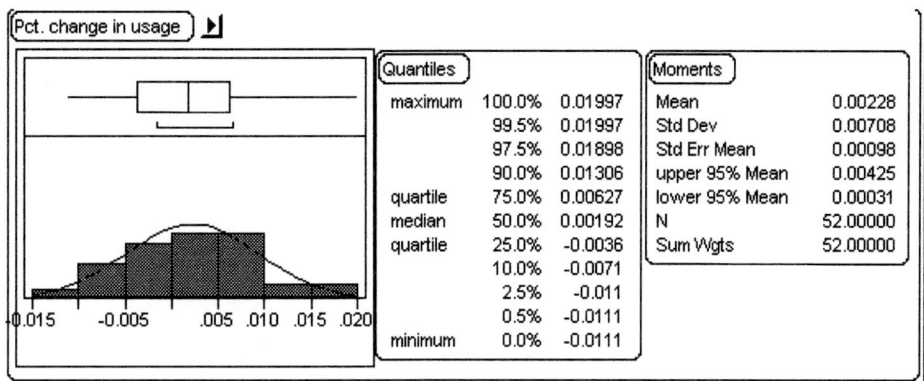

Quantiles			Moments	
maximum	100.0%	0.01997	Mean	0.00228
	99.5%	0.01997	Std Dev	0.00708
	97.5%	0.01898	Std Err Mean	0.00098
	90.0%	0.01306	upper 95% Mean	0.00425
quartile	75.0%	0.00627	lower 95% Mean	0.00031
median	50.0%	0.00192	N	52.00000
quartile	25.0%	-0.0036	Sum Wgts	52.00000
	10.0%	-0.0071		
	2.5%	-0.011		
	0.5%	-0.0111		
minimum	0.0%	-0.0111		

7.39 A random sample of 20 taste testers rate the quality of a proposed new product on a 0–100 scale. The ordered scores are

16	20	31	50	50	50	51	53	53	55
57	59	60	60	61	65	67	67	81	92

Statistix output follows. A boxplot is shown in Figure 7.11.

```
DESCRIPTIVE STATISTICS

                SCORES
N                   20
LO 95% CI       46.611
MEAN            54.900
UP 95% CI       63.188
SD              17.710
```

a Locate the 95% confidence interval for the population mean score. Were t tables or z tables used?

b Is there any reason to think that the use of a mean-based confidence interval is a poor idea?

7.40 A furniture mover calculates the actual weight of a shipment as a proportion of estimated weight for a sample of 31 recent jobs. The sample mean is 1.13 and the sample standard deviation is .16.

a Calculate a 95% confidence interval for the population mean using t tables.

b Assume that the population standard deviation is .16. Calculate a 95% confidence interval for the population mean using z tables.

c Are the intervals calculated in parts a and b of roughly similar size?

7.41 When the data underlying Exercise 7.40 are plotted, the plot shows a strong skewness to the right. Does this indicate that the nominal 95% confidence level may be in error?

FIGURE 7.11   **Boxplot for Taste Test Data**

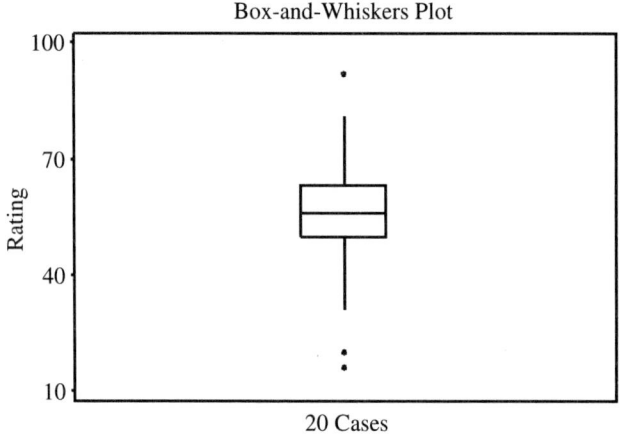

Box-and-Whiskers Plot

20 Cases

■

Assumptions for Interval Estimation

7.7

Any statistical method involves assumptions. Some assumptions are general and apply to a wide variety of methods; others are specific to a particular method. We'll have a lot to say about assumptions in future chapters. Because interval estimation of a single parameter (whether it be a mean, a proportion, or a median) is a relatively simple concept, we can deal with the issues of assumptions and assumption violation most clearly in this context.

First, we should emphasize that the methods in this chapter apply only to random samples. The allowance for error inherent in confidence intervals is only an allowance for *random* error; no allowance is made for any biases in data collection. If the data underlying a confidence interval have been collected in a lazy, convenient sample, the confidence interval is very likely to be wrong simply because of the biases in data collection. There are no known methods to compensate for the biases in badly chosen samples.

Within the context of legitimate random samples, some specific assumptions can be problematic. One key assumption is independence within samples. All the methods described in this chapter assume that the observations are independent of each other. Not all random sampling methods yield independent observations. For example, suppose a real estate assessor chooses 22 city blocks of homes to evaluate from the tax lists of a city, and then assesses the market value of all homes in each block. Assuming that the assessor does, in fact, choose the blocks randomly, there is no systematic bias in favor of low-value homes or high-value homes. But there is a dependence problem. Given the well-established tendency of high-value homes to cluster together (and low-value homes to occur in bunches), if one home in the sample has higher than average values, so do adjacent homes. The assessment may involve, say, 300 homes; however, the method does not give 300 separate, independent measurements of home values. In fact, the data arising from the assessor's evaluations would be more appropriately evaluated by what are known as cluster-sampling methods.

time-series data   The most common problems with the assumption of independence occur in **time-series data**—data collected in a well-defined chronological order. Suppose, for example, that we measure the dollar volume of back orders for a particular manufacturer on 20 consecutive Friday afternoons. It's reasonable to suppose that a high back-order volume on one Friday is likely to be followed by high back-order volumes on succeeding Fridays, and the same for low volumes. The standard error formulas that we use in confidence intervals depend very heavily on the assumption of independence of observations. When there is dependence, the standard error formulas may underestimate the actual uncertainty in an estimate. Even for modest dependencies, the degree of underestimation may be serious.

In effect, dependence means that we don't have as much information as the value of n indicates. Consider the extreme dependence that would arise in a sample of 25 observations if the first observation were genuinely random, but every succeeding observation had to equal the first one. The confidence interval formula would be based on a sample of 25, but in fact we'd only have a sample of 1.

Whenever the data are taken in time order, it's a good idea to plot the observations against time. If the observations are really independent, there should be no pattern in the plot; the data should look random. Any clear pattern—cycles or trends—in this plot is reason for concern about independence. For example, look for a pattern in the Minitab plot of weekly worker absences in Figure 7.12. There is a clear up-down-up cyclic pattern in the data. We wouldn't be at all happy with an assumption of independence.

FIGURE 7.12   **Plot of Absences by Week**

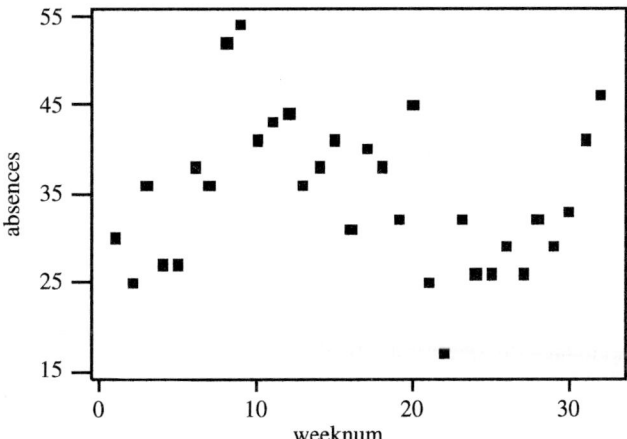

Beyond the assumption of independence, methods for means involve an assumption that the underlying population is normally distributed. *In practice, no population is exactly normal.* When we use t distribution methods for a mean, we are assuming that the underlying population is normal, and this assumption is guaranteed to be more or less wrong.

There are two types of issues to consider when populations are assumed to be nonnormal. First, what kind of nonnormality is assumed and, second, what possible effects do these specific forms of nonnormality have on the t distribution procedures? The most important deviations from normality are skewed distributions and heavy-tailed distributions. (Heavy-tailed distributions show up in otherwise roughly symmetric data due to outliers.)

In order to evaluate the effect of nonnormality as exhibited by skewness or heavy tails, we consider whether the t distribution procedures are still approximately correct for these forms of nonnormality and whether there are other more efficient procedures. Even if a confidence interval for μ based on t gives nearly correct results for, say, a heavy-tailed population distribution, there may be a more efficient procedure (which gives a smaller confidence interval width) based on a median, for example.

The question of approximate correctness of t procedures has been studied for quite a long time. The general conclusion of these studies is that the probabilities specified by the t procedures, particularly the confidence level, are fairly accurate even when the population distribution is heavy-tailed (or light-tailed). In contrast, skewness, particularly with small sample sizes, can have some effect on these probabilities, particularly in one-tailed procedures. A t distribution is symmetric, of course. When the population distribution is skewed, the actual sampling distribution of a t statistic is skewed. The skewness decreases as the sample size increases, but there is no magic sample size that completely deskews the actual sampling distribution.

The second question, that of the efficiency of t procedures, has only recently been studied seriously. There has been a near-unanimous conclusion from these studies: When the population distribution is symmetric but heavy-tailed, various **robust procedures** are more efficient than the standard t procedures. Virtually all robust procedures eliminate or give low weight to the few largest and smallest observations in the sample. The ordinary sample mean gives equal weight to all observations and is sensitive to extreme sample values. Therefore, when the population distribution is heavy-tailed, robust procedures tend to give more accurate estimates and have smaller standard errors than the ordinary sample mean.

Unfortunately, less work has been done on the effectiveness of these robust procedures when the population distribution is skewed. A 20% trimmed mean, which averages the middle 80% of the data values, is unquestionably a biased estimator of the population mean when the population is skewed. Whether this bias is compensated for by a lower standard error is an open mathematical and conceptual question. However, it would be worrisome to have an estimator with a small standard error that always overestimated the population parameter.

So what is a nonexpert manager to do? First of all, *look at the data*. One of the serious dangers of using available statistical software is that statistical analyses may be done, untouched by human minds. A simple histogram of the data, or some other plotting device, reveals any gross skewness or extreme outliers. If there's no blatant nonnormality, the nominal t distribution probabilities should be reasonably correct and the t procedure should be reasonably efficient. If the data values are obviously skewed or heavy-tailed, the t distribution probabilities and the efficiency of the t procedure are highly suspect. Whenever possible, you should try something else in these situations.

E X A M P L E   7 . 1 7

A supermarket chain is considering reformulating its house brand of diet cola. Marketing managers for the store arrange for a sample of diet cola buyers to taste-test the new formulation. Each panelist was actually given three diet colas to taste. The first was identified as the current brand; this was the reference standard, assigned a rating of 50. The other two colas were the reformulation and a competitor brand. Each panelist assigned a preference rating to the other two colas, on a 0–100 scale. Higher scores indicated greater preference. The marketing manager took the data for the reformulation and analyzed it using Minitab. The "tinterval" in the following output is the t confidence interval for the mean. The "sinterval" is a confidence interval for the population median, obtained by a method we haven't discussed. What data problem is shown in Figure 7.13? How is this problem reflected in the confidence intervals? Is there a concern about dependence in the data?

robust procedures

FIGURE 7.13 **Normal Plot for Cola Taste Data**

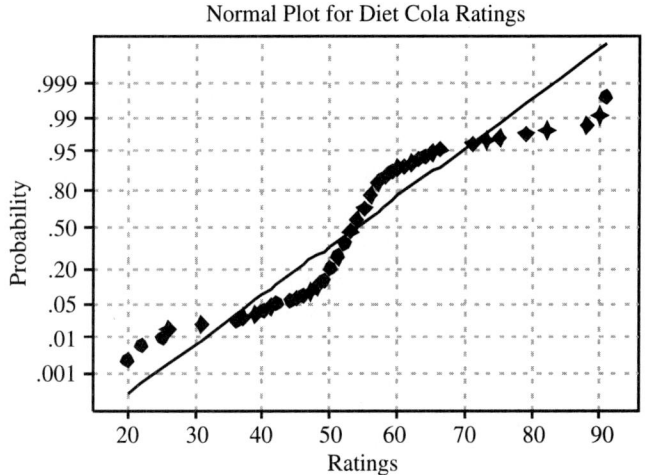

Average: 53.5019
Std Dev: 8.41794
N of data: 263

Anderson-Darling Normality Test
A-Squared: 16.564
p-value: 0.000

```
MTB > tinterval 'Ratings'

Confidence Intervals

Variable     N      Mean    StDev  SE Mean      95.0 % C.I.
Ratings     263    53.502   8.418   0.519   ( 52.480,  54.524)

MTB > sinterval 'Ratings'

Sign Confidence Interval

Sign confidence interval for median

                            ACHIEVED
             N    MEDIAN   CONFIDENCE   CONFIDENCE INTERVAL   POSITION
Ratings     263    53.00     0.9357     ( 53.00,   54.00)       117
                              0.9500     ( 53.00,   54.00)       NLI
                              0.9515     ( 53.00,   54.00)       116
```

Solution

The normal plot has data on the horizontal axis and theoretical values on the vertical axis. There is a clear S shape in the plot, indicating that the data are outlier-prone (heavy-tailed). The sample size of 263 is certainly large enough that there is no need to worry about the correctness of the claimed 95% confidence. Outlierish data tend to make mean-based methods inefficient. In this case, the confidence interval for the mean is more than twice as wide as any of the intervals for the median.

There shouldn't be a problem of dependence in the data if the study is done sensibly. The data are cross-sectional, not time series. About the only reason we can think of for dependence is if the raters could influence each other's decisions. As long as the raters were working separately, we do not believe that dependence is a problem. ∎

Summing Up

H ere are some basic principles for estimating population or process quantities based on sample data:

1 Plot the data first, before doing arithmetic. Histograms, stem-and-leaf displays, boxplots, and normal probability plots are all useful in indicating the shape of the sample data (and therefore roughly indicating the shape of the population).

2 Methods based on sample means are best suited to data that are at least roughly normally distributed. Severe skewness can make normal and *t* distributions poor approximations, especially for small sample sizes. Outliers make sample means an inefficient way to use the data.

3 A confidence interval provides an indication of how accurately the sample statistic estimates a population or process parameter. It allows for random sampling error, but not for systematic bias.

4 In most practical situations, a population standard deviation is not known, so *t* distribution methods should be applied.

5 A confidence interval for a proportion based on a normal approximation is almost identical to a *t* confidence interval for a mean of a set of 1s and 0s.

6 The assumption of statistical independence is important for the correctness of confidence interval methods (and indeed of most other statistical methods). Dependence among measurements can reduce the effective sample size, thus making confidence intervals too optimistic (too narrow).

In addition, you may want to reread the summary of key ideas at the beginning of the chapter.

E X A M P L E   7 . 1 8

Health insurance claims for a small business association (SBA) are processed by a benefits corporation (BC), a third-party administrative agent. Health insurance policies are very complicated; determining whether or not a particular charge is covered by a particular policy is a difficult task, often undertaken by an underpaid, undertrained clerk. In 1995, an audit was proposed to determine whether BC performed the required processing procedures to ensure that claims paid were in compliance with the SBA health plan. A study was designed to determine the extent of BC's compliance with the required procedures to ensure the propriety of claims payment and to determine the extent of the dollar value error in the subpopulation of claim files processed erroneously by BC. The data to be collected in the audit would indicate whether or not any claim in a claim file contained a compliance deviation (error) and the actual dollar value error. A random sample of 90 claim files was selected. Of the 90 claim files, 51 were found to be in compliance deviation. JMP IN output from the data is shown in Figure 7.14. What do the results of the audit indicate about the proportion of erroneous accounts and about the average dollar amount of error per erroneous account?

Solution

There are two separate issues to consider: the proportion of errors and the dollar average of those errors. First, consider the question of the proportion of errors. The relevant output

FIGURE 7.14 **Output for Claims Data**

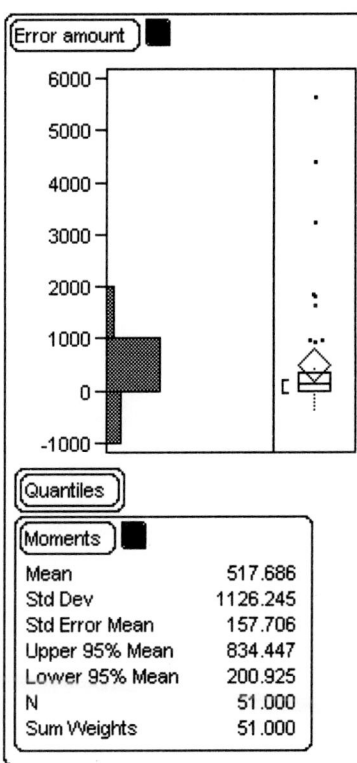

refers to the "Error?" variable, which equals 1 for all the erroneous accounts, 0 for all the others. This output shows a sample mean of 0.56667, which is simply the proportion 51/90 of erroneous accounts. A 95% confidence interval is shown by the "Lower 95% Mean" and "Upper 95% Mean" entries as 0.462 to 0.671, respectively. This interval is calculated using t distribution tables rather than z tables; we could calculate the z interval by hand, getting

$$0.56667 \pm 1.96\sqrt{\frac{(0.56667)(1 - 0.56667)}{90}}$$

which comes to $0.464 \leq \pi \leq 0.669$. The two methods give essentially identical answers. Somewhere between 46% and 67% of the accounts have errors.

The second issue is the average dollar amount of error. For this question, we turn to the "Error amount" portion of the output. The first step is to check a plot of the data. There is fairly severe skewness, especially evident in the boxplot, and some major outliers. The confidence interval indicates that, within the subpopulation of erroneous accounts, the mean error amount is between $201 and $834. This is a very wide range, partly because of the relatively small sample size, but also because of the very high variability in the amounts. In addition, the severe skewness means that the claimed 95% confidence may be in error. All in all, this audit didn't yield very satisfactory results. ∎

SUPPLEMENTARY EXERCISES

7.42 A random sample of the year-end statements of 22 small businesses (under $500,000 in yearly sales) in a city shows that the sample mean of gross margin on sales is 5.2% and the standard deviation is 3.3%. Use these results to calculate a 90% confidence interval for the population mean, where the population is (the gross margin of) the several thousand small businesses in the city.

7.43 Refer to Exercise 7.42. Obviously the gross margin of a functioning business can't be negative. The Empirical Rule for 2 standard deviations would indicate that a substantial fraction of the businesses have negative gross margins.

  a Is it likely that the sample data would appear nearly normal?

  b What does your answer to part a indicate about the confidence interval calculated in Exercise 7.42?

7.44 A chain of shoe stores sets a budgeted sales figure for each store. Data are collected on the actual sales of a sample of stores as a fraction of the budgeted sales. The Minitab output shown in Figure 7.15 is obtained.

  a Locate the sample mean and median.

  b Which of these values should be the better estimate of the population mean?

FIGURE 7.15 **Minitab Output for Sales Data**

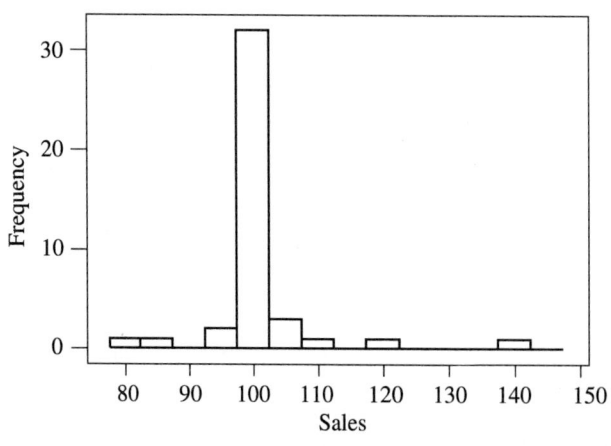

Variable	N	Mean	Median	TrMean	StDev	SEMean
sales	42	100.71	100.10	100.09	8.61	1.33

Variable	Min	Max	Q1	Q3
sales	80.50	142.30	98.60	101.22

7.45 A normal plot for the data of Exercise 7.44 is shown in Figure 7.16.

  a What does the shape of the normal plot indicate about the shape of the sample data?

  b Does the normal plot confirm your answer to part b of Exercise 7.44?

7.46 A sales representative for a coffee producer measures the fraction of shelf space for all coffees devoted to the producer's brands. The following results are obtained:

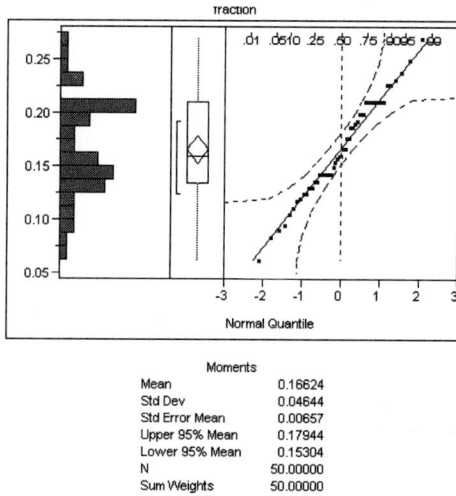

Fraction

Moments	
Mean	0.16624
Std Dev	0.04644
Std Error Mean	0.00657
Upper 95% Mean	0.17944
Lower 95% Mean	0.15304
N	50.00000
Sum Weights	50.00000

Is there any reason to think that the sample mean is an inefficient estimator of the population mean?

7.47 A normal plot of the data in Exercise 7.46 is shown in the output. Does the shape of the normal plot confirm your answer to Exercise 7.46?

7.48 A research project for an insurance company wishes to investigate the mean value of the personal property held by urban apartment renters. A previous study suggested that the population standard deviation should be roughly $10,000. A 95% confidence interval with a width of $1000 (a plus or minus of $500) is desired. How large a sample must be taken to obtain such a confidence interval?

7.49 It could be argued that the data of Exercise 7.48 would be quite skewed, with a few individuals having very large personal property values. Therefore (the argument goes) the confidence interval would be completely invalid. Is the argument correct?

7.50 Many individuals over the age of 40 develop an intolerance for milk and milk-based products. A dairy has developed a line of lactose-free products that are more tolerated by such individuals. To assess the potential market for these products, the dairy commissions a market research study of individuals over age 40 in its sales area. A random sample of 250 individuals shows that 86 of them suffer from milk intolerance. Calculate a 90% confidence interval for the population proportion that suffers milk intolerance based on the sample results.

FIGURE 7.16   **Shelf Space Data Analysis**

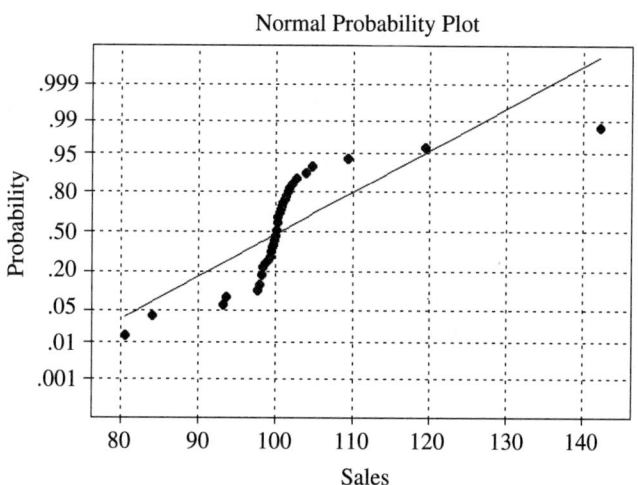

7.51 A follow-up study to the survey of Exercise 7.50 is planned. A 90% confidence interval is to be constructed. What sample size is needed to estimate the population proportion with an error of no more than .02, under the following conditions:

a Assume that the sample proportion is approximately the same as that found in Exercise 7.50.

b Now assume that the population proportion may be anything.

7.52 A manufacturer of computer chips tracked the cost per wafer (a wafer contains a fairly large number of individual chips) for producing a new kind of chip. The cost was obtained weekly and analyzed using JMP. The results are shown in Figures 7.17 and 7.18. What is the most evident feature of the time plot?

FIGURE 7.17 **Time Plot of Chip Cost Data**

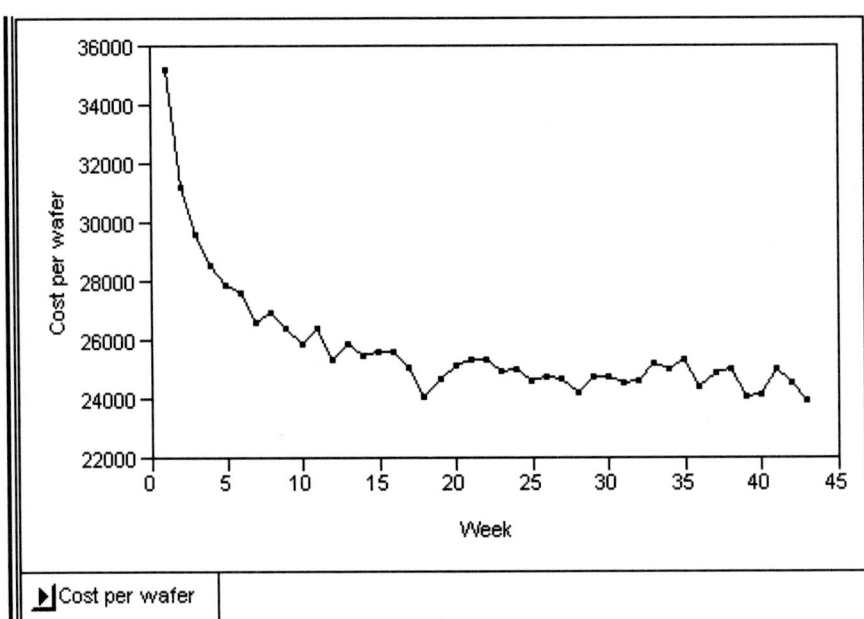

FIGURE 7.18 **Summary of Chip Cost Data**

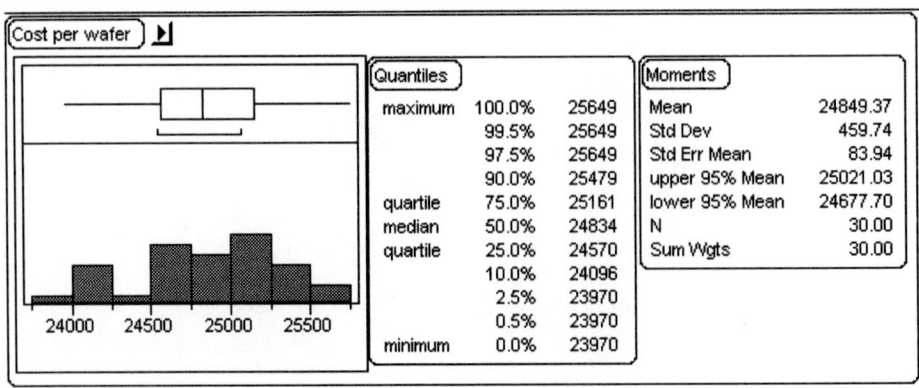

7.53 Refer to Exercise 7.52. The chip cost data were analyzed by omitting the first 13 weeks of data. Taking the output at face value, what does it reveal about the cost per wafer?

7.54 Is there an evident problem with using the output of the previous question?

7.55 Shortly before April 15 of a particular year, a team of sociologists conduct a survey to study their theory that tax cheaters tend to allay their guilt by holding certain beliefs. A total of 500 adults are interviewed and asked under what situations they think cheating on an income tax return is justified. The responses include these:

56% agree that "other people don't report all their income."

50% agree that "the government is often careless with tax dollars."

46% agree that "cheating can be overlooked if one is generally law abiding."

Assuming that the data are a simple random sample of the population of taxpayers (or non-taxpayers), calculate 95% confidence intervals for the population proportion that agrees with each statement.

7.56 An editorial writer, commenting on the study of Exercise 7.55, claims that the opinion of 500 individuals out of the total number of taxpayers in the United States is virtually worthless; these might be the "cheatingest" 500 people in the entire country. Criticize this editorial stand.

7.57 The caffeine content (in milligrams) of a random sample of 50 cups of black coffee dispensed by a new machine is measured. The mean and standard deviation are 100 milligrams and 7.1 milligrams, respectively. Construct a 98% confidence interval for the true (population) mean caffeine content per cup dispensed by the machine.

7.58 The machine in Exercise 7.57 is capable of dispensing 3000 cups per day. The caffeine content varies because of variation in caffeine content of the ground coffee beans and because of variation in brewing time.

a Is the study in Exercise 7.57 questionable because such a small fraction of the machine's output is analyzed?

b The 50 cups sampled are taken consecutively from the machine. Does this make the study questionable?

7.59 A random sample of 100 scores was obtained. Minitab output is shown here:

```
MTB > print 'values'

values
 40  42  45  47  48  48  49  49  50  51  51  52  53
 54  55  55  55  55  56  56  56  56  56  56  57  57
 57  57  58  58  58  58  58  59  59  59  59  59  59
 60  60  60  60  60  60  60  60  60  61  61  61  61
 61  62  62  62  62  63  63  63  64  64  64  65  65
 65  65  65  66  66  66  66  66  67  67  67  67  67
 67  67  68  68  68  68  69  69  69  69  70  70  72
 72  72  73  73  74  76  79  81  81

MTB > describe 'values'

                   N     MEAN   MEDIAN   TRMEAN    STDEV   SEMEAN
values           100   61.460   61.000   61.478    7.845    0.784

                 MIN      MAX       Q1       Q3
values        40.000   81.000   57.000   67.000

MTB > tinterval with 95% confidence for 'values'

                   N     MEAN    STDEV   SE MEAN    95.0 PERCENT C.I.
values           100   61.460    7.845    0.784   ( 59.903, 63.017)

MTB > stem and leaf of 'values'
```

```
Stem-and-leaf of values    N = 100
Leaf Unit = 1.0

    2     4 02
    8     4 578899
   14     5 011234
   39     5 555566666677778888899999
  (24)    6 000000000111112222333444
   37     6 55555666667777777788889999
   12     7 00222334
    4     7 69
    2     8 11
```

a What is the general shape of the data?

b Should a 95% confidence interval based on the sample mean be wider or narrower than a 95% confidence interval using a robust method?

7.60 A normal plot of the data in Exercise 7.59, done using Minitab, is shown in Figure 7.19. Does the plot confirm your judgment made in part a of Exercise 7.59?

7.61 The police department of a medium-sized city recorded the response time to nonemergency crime calls, usually ones involving burglary or car theft. The times in minutes for 29 calls recorded during one week were thought of as a random sample from the ongoing process. The output from Minitab is shown here:

```
MTB > print 'resptime'

resptime
    4   25   18   25   15   11   11   19   36   29   13   21   12
   12   26   16   19   12   21   12   12   18   11   19   16   24
   14   23   17

MTB > describe 'resptime'

                 N     MEAN   MEDIAN   TRMEAN   STDEV   SEMEAN
resptime        29    18.31    18.00    17.93    6.29     1.17

               MIN      MAX      Q1       Q3
resptime     11.00    36.00   12.00    23.50

MTB > zinterval with 90% confidence sigma = 6.0 data 'resptime'

THE ASSUMED SIGMA =6.00

                 N     MEAN    STDEV   SE MEAN   90.0 PERCENT C.I.
resptime        29    18.31    6.29      1.11   (  16.48,   20.14)

MTB > tinterval with 90% confidence data 'resptime'

                 N     MEAN    STDEV   SE MEAN   90.0 PERCENT C.I.
resptime        29    18.31    6.29      1.17   (  16.32,   20.30)
```

a Locate a 90% confidence interval for the process (long-run) mean time, assuming that the long-run process standard deviation is 6.0 minutes.

b Locate the confidence interval done without assuming that the long-run standard deviation is known.

c Why did the second interval come out wider than the first?

7.62 The data of Exercise 7.61 were plotted in a histogram (Figure 7.20). Does it appear that the distribution of response times is approximately normal?

7.63 A state fish hatchery raises trout for stocking streams and lakes. The size of the fish at release time can be controlled to a fair degree by varying the rate of feeding. The target is a mean of 10 ounces; if the fish are too small, those who catch the fish aren't happy, but if the fish are too large, those who buy the feed aren't happy. A sample of 61 fish is weighed at release time. The weights, to the nearest tenth of an ounce, are as follows:

	A	B	C	D	E	F	G	H	I	J
4	9.3	11.7	11	9.8	10.1	8.9	8.7	9.5	10.8	8.7
5	7.6	10	8.8	9.3	9.2	8.1	9.9	9.4	8.3	10.3
6	9.8	9.5	9.8	9	10.7	9.3	9.6	10.4	9.4	9.8
7	9.8	9.2	11	10.2	9.1	11	9.4	9.7	12.1	9.8
8	7.1	8.3	10.3	10.6	10.1	10.2	8.8	9.3	10.3	10.7
9	10.8	7.5	9	10.1	9.2	9.7	10.4	9.1	9.7	10.7
10	10.6									
11										
12										
13		Weights								
14	N	61								
15	Mean	9.680328								
16	St. Dev	0.95983								
17	SE Mean	0.123								

FIGURE 7.19 **Normal Plot**

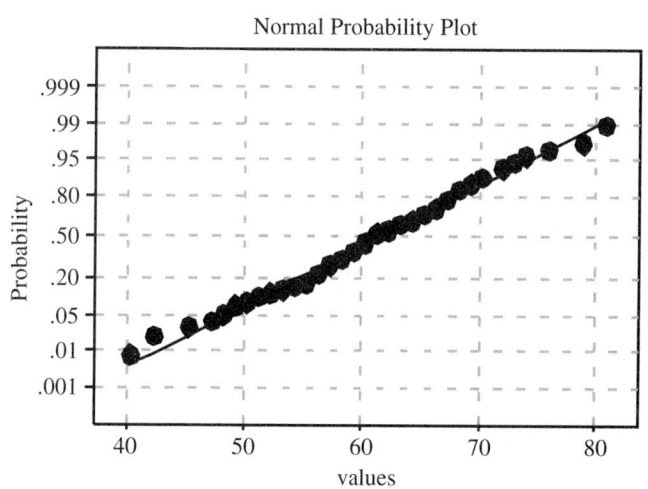

Average: 61.46
Std Dev: 7.84499
N of data: 100

Anderson-Darling Normality Test
A-Squared: 0.391
p-value: 0.374

FIGURE 7.20 **Histogram for Response Times**

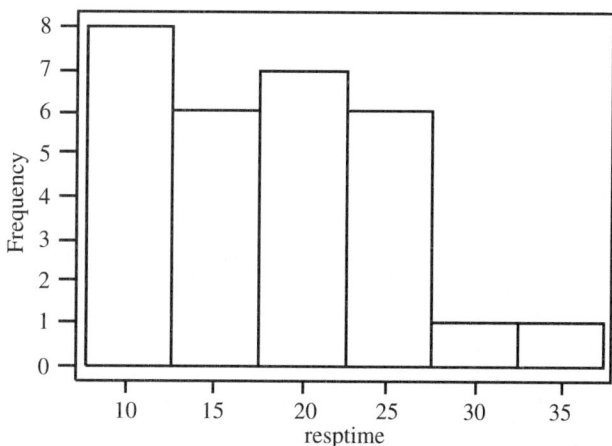

a Calculate a 95% confidence interval for the mean weight of the entire group of many, many thousands of fish. Should the indicated standard deviation be regarded as a population or a sample standard deviation?

b Does the confidence interval indicate that the hatchery is clearly not meeting its 10-ounce goal?

7.64 Obtain a stem-and-leaf display of the data of Exercise 7.63. Does the plot indicate that the distribution of weights is roughly normal? If not, would that invalidate the confidence interval that we calculated in Exercise 7.63?

7.65 The data for Exercise 7.63 were obtained by dividing the fish randomly into batches intended for different destinations. Then some fish within each batch were taken out (as randomly as possible). One might suspect that larger fish would be netted first and put into the first few batches. A plot of fish weights against batch numbers is shown in Figure 7.21. Is there a clear indication that the weights are decreasing as batch number increases?

FIGURE 7.21 **Plot of Fish Weights by Batch**

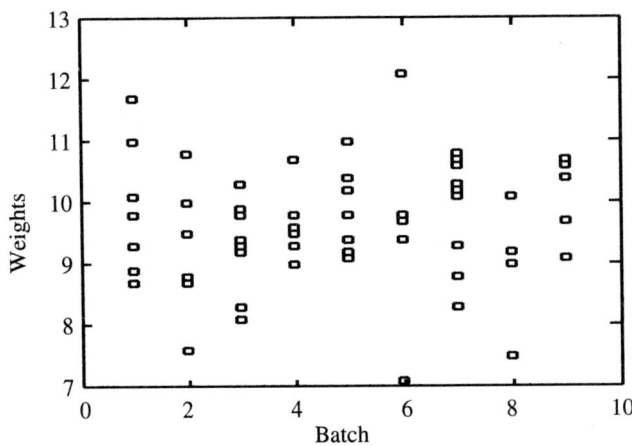

7.66 A manufacturer of mesh screening tries to limit the number of defects per thousand feet to no more than 5. The defects usually are broken wires in the mesh or "blobs" of paint. Each day, 24 sample sections of wire, each 500 feet long, are inspected for defects. The following data and Statistix output are of defects found in the sampled sections:

| 3 | 4 | 3 | 0 | 6 | 1 | 0 | 2 | 1 | 3 | 4 | 4 | 3 | 6 |
| 4 | 4 | 3 | 4 | 5 | 2 | 1 | 0 | 5 | 2 | | | | |

DESCRIPTIVE STATISTICS

VARIABLE	LO 99% CI	MEAN	UP 99% CI	SD	MEDIAN
DEFECTS	1.8899	2.9166	3.9433	1.7916	3.0000

a Locate a 99% confidence interval for the mean number of defects in the entire day's production of many thousands of 500-foot sections.

b According to the manufacturer's goal, what should the mean number of defects in 500-foot sections equal? Does the confidence interval indicate that this value is not plausible?

7.67 The data of Exercise 7.66 were collected by visual inspection of the screen for defects. Suppose that the inspection on this particular day was not as thorough as it should have been. What bias should this introduce? Should the confidence interval be too low or too high as a result?

7.68 **a** In Exercise 7.67 the mean-minus-2-standard-deviations value is a negative number of defects. What does this fact suggest about the shape of the data?

b Statistix produced the following stem-and-leaf display. Does the picture confirm your answer in part a?

```
STEM AND LEAF PLOT OF DEFECTS

    LEAF DIGIT UNIT = 0.1
    1  2  REPRESENTS 1.2

         STEM  LEAVES
      3   0   000
      6   1   000
      9   2   000
     (5)  3   00000
     10   4   000000
      4   5   00
      2   6   00
```

7.69 An automobile rental firm buys new cars and uses them for about 6 months, then resells them at auction. In effect, the firm is in the used-car futures business. Therefore, the firm wants accurate estimates of the future value of its current fleet of cars. A consultant proposes a new method of estimating future value. This method is tried on a sample of cars. The estimates are made initially, the cars are used in the business, and then the actual auction price for each car is obtained. The data are the ratio of actual to estimated values for each of 121 cars that had not been damaged during rental use. The computer output is shown here:

```
MTB > print 'ratioAE'

RatioAE
0.96872  1.02149  1.01100  1.03069  1.01039  1.03266  0.98667
1.01080  0.96833  1.01814  0.98233  0.98950  1.00423  0.96911
0.94118  0.97219  1.00409  1.00595  0.98702  0.97397  1.01228
1.02320  0.97978  0.89570  1.02869  0.99189  1.00378  0.96988
1.04872  1.01224  0.95713  0.96719  1.07646  1.00463  0.96637
0.96125  0.95879  0.98965  0.97314  1.02847  1.01319  0.96875
0.99000  0.99463  1.07783  0.98070  0.95106  1.04667  0.98620
0.96406  0.96311  1.01996  0.98937  0.99123  1.00000  1.04423
0.99622  1.06927  0.92623  1.03237  0.99904  1.05807  0.99028
0.96011  1.03959  0.94857  0.98135  0.93376  1.00000  1.01877
1.00280  1.02494  0.98779  0.96610  0.94118  0.99445  1.02761
1.00183  1.04700  0.99011  1.04338  1.06329  0.96900  0.96613
1.01532  0.99293  1.01865  1.06040  1.03927  0.96418  0.99283
1.00563  1.05370  0.99537  1.00424  1.00686  1.05361  0.97479
0.98227  0.97611  1.00074  1.08310  1.01981  1.03604  1.01578
1.00000  1.00579  0.95124  0.99522  0.96184  0.98585  0.98786
0.95688  1.02029  0.99295  1.00000  1.00435  1.01088  1.02974
1.07150  1.01643

MTB > tinterval for 'RatioAE'

              N     MEAN    STDEV   SE MEAN   95.0 PERCENT C.I.
RatioAE    121   0.99984  0.03404  0.00309  ( 0.99371, 1.00597)
```

a Locate the value of the 95% confidence interval for the mean, based on *t* methods.

b Can the interval be interpreted to mean that the actual price is between 99.371% and 100.597% of estimate for 95% of the cars?

7.70 The data for Exercise 7.69 were plotted in Figure 7.22. Any evidence of nonnormality?

7.71 A restaurant tried to increase business on Monday nights, traditionally the slowest night of the week, by featuring a special $1.00 "Oh, Go Ahead!" dessert menu. The number of diners on each of 12 Mondays was recorded while the special menu was in effect. The data were:

119   139   112   126   121   128   108   63   118   105   131   142

FIGURE 7.22 **Boxplot of Ratio of Actual Price to Estimate**

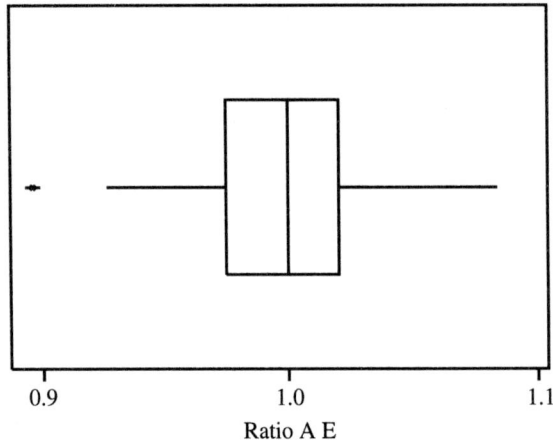

0.9   1.0   1.1

Ratio A E

with mean 117.67 and standard deviation 20.65. Systat computed summary figures as follows:

```
                    DINERS

N OF CASES              12
MEAN                117.667
STANDARD DEV         20.646
STD. ERROR            5.960
```

a Calculate a 95% confidence interval for the long-run mean number of diners.

b Before the special menu, the restaurant averaged 105.2 diners per Monday night. Is it reasonable to interpret the confidence interval from part a as indicating that the special menu did not increase the average number of diners?

7.72 A retail lumberyard routinely inspects incoming shipments of lumber from suppliers. For select grade 8-foot 2-by-4 pine shipments, the lumberyard supervisor chooses one gross (144 boards) randomly from a shipment of several tens of thousands of boards. In the sample, 18 boards are not salable as select grade.

a Calculate a 95% confidence interval for the proportion of boards in the entire shipment that is not salable as select grade.

b If 20% or more of the shipment is not salable as select grade lumber, the shipment is unprofitable. Does the confidence interval indicate that there is reason for concern about possible unprofitability of this shipment?

7.73 **a** The lumberyard in Exercise 7.72 must decide how many boards per shipment will be inspected. What sample size is needed to obtain a 95% confidence interval for the proportion of unsalable boards with a width of .04? Assume that somewhere between 10% and 20% of a shipment is unsalable.

b In this situation, would it be sensible to calculate a sample size based on the worst-case assumption that 50% of the shipment is unsalable?

7.74 **a** The sample in Exercise 7.72 is always obtained from the pallet at the right rear of the truckload shipment. A pallet contains 4 gross (576 boards), so the lumberyard selects the 144 gross to sample by rotation—the first shipment, sample upper left; next shipment, sample upper right; and so on. Why isn't this a random sample of the boards? Wouldn't an unethical supplier take advantage of this process?

b Do you think it would be feasible to take a simple random sample in this situation? How would you sample to make it more diffcult for an unethical supplier to cheat? Of course, there is no single correct answer here.

7.75 An electrical utility offers reduced rates to homeowners who have installed "peak hours" meters. These meters effectively shut off high-consumption electrical appliances (primarily dishwashers and clothes dryers) during the peak electrical usage hours between 3 P.M. and 9 P.M. daily. The utility wants to inspect a sample of these meters to determine the proportion that is not working, either because they were bypassed or because of equipment failure. There are 45,300 meters in use and the utility isn't about to inspect them all.

    a The utility wants a 90% confidence interval for the proportion with a width of no more than .04. How many meters must be sampled if one makes no particular assumption about the correct proportion?

    b How many meters must be sampled if the utility assumes that the true population proportion is between .05 and .15?

    c Does the assumption in part b lead to a substantial reduction in the required sample size?

7.76 The electrical utility in Exercise 7.75 samples 640 meters and finds that 61 are not working, 28 because of bypass and 33 because of equipment failure. Calculate 90% confidence intervals for the population proportions of bypassed meters, equipment failure meters, and nonworking meters.

7.77 The sample in Exercise 7.76 was obtained by randomly selecting 16 of the 1062 service sectors in the utility's area and inspecting all the meters in each selected sector. Each sector contains 30 to 50 meters. Why isn't this procedure a simple random sample?

7.78 Many newspapers, when reporting results of political polls, say that "with 95% confidence, the results are in error by no more than $\pm$ 3 percentage points." The typical sample size is about 1500. The allowance for error is intended to cover both sampling variability and the effect of small biases.

    a Assume that the poll (sample) indicates that just about 50% of likely voters favor a particular candidate. How large a $\pm$ term is required for a 95% confidence interval for the population proportion?

    b Would the $\pm$ term be much different if 40% of likely voters in the sample favored the candidate?

    c Why is the quoted $\pm$ .03 larger than the $\pm$ term you calculated in part a?

7.79 Consider political polls again, as in Exercise 7.78. When there are many political candidates, as in the early stages of a presidential primary, a particular candidate may be favored by only 2% of the poll participants. Given the quoted $\pm$ 3 percentage points, the standard joke is that such a candidate may have a negative preference. What $\pm$ term should apply, with 95% confidence, if a candidate is favored by 30 of 1500 likely voters in a sample?

7.80 The marketing division of an automobile manufacturer wants to estimate customer satisfaction with a particular new-car dealer, six months after purchase of a car. The marketing managers don't want to use mail surveys because they believe that nonresponse would lead to major biases. Sampling by telephone is feasible because customers' phone numbers are on warranty records. One key question would be: "Would you recommend this dealer to your friends and neighbors?" The marketing managers want to estimate the proportion of all customers that would answer yes, based on a telephone sample.

    a How large a sample must be taken to obtain a 90% confidence interval for this proportion with a width of .10 (a $\pm$ term of .05)? Use the conservative, worst-case estimate.

    b Would doubling the sample size cut the width to .05?

7.81   **a** By using the worst-case estimate in Exercise 7.80, what are you assuming about customer satisfaction with the dealer? Do you think this would be a sensible assumption in practice?

    b How would the required sample size in part a of Exercise 7.80 change if you assumed that the yes proportion would be somewhere between .80 and .95?

7.82 A sample of 215 urban residents between the ages of 22 and 35 kept diaries for a month, recording all expenses on entertainment. The total expenditure for each individual, expressed as a percentage of monthly take-home income, is stored in column 1 of the EX0782.DAT file on the data disk. (The number of the individual is stored in column 2.) Load the data into a computer program that is available to you.

    a Obtain the mean and standard deviation of the expenditure sample.

b Calculate (either by computer or by hand) a 95% confidence interval for the population mean.

c Interpret the confidence interval carefully.

7.83 **a** Obtain a stem-and-leaf display or a boxplot of the expenditure data from Exercise 7.82.

b On the basis of this plot of the data, is there reason to be concerned that the claimed 95% confidence level in Exercise 7.82 is incorrect?

7.84 An office equipment dealer provides service for leased copiers. All calls for service are logged with the time of request and the time of completion of service. The elapsed times (in minutes) between request and completion for the most recent 61 calls are stored in column 1 of the EX0784.DAT file on the data disk; column 2 contains the call number, in order from 1 to 61. Load the data into a computer program.

a Obtain the mean and standard deviation of the elapsed time data.

b Calculate, by the program or by hand, a 90% confidence interval for the long-run process mean.

7.85 **a** Obtain a normal plot of the elapsed time data for Exercise 7.84. (If the program won't provide that, get a stem-and-leaf display instead.) Does it appear that the data are roughly normally distributed?

b Have the program plot the elapsed time data against the call number. (The call numbers are the time order of the requests.) Is there an indication of a pattern in this plot? If so, what is indicated about the assumption of independent observations?

7.86 An investment banking firm was considering two spreadsheet programs for possible use in its analyses. A sample of 20 typical analysis problems was carried out using both programs on the firm's standard personal computer. The time in minutes needed to load the data, program the spreadsheet calculations, carry them out, and print the results was recorded for each problem and each program. The data for spreadsheet A are stored in column 1 of the EX0786.DAT file on the data disk; the corresponding data for spreadsheet B are stored in column 2. Each row of the data corresponds to one of the 20 problems. Load the data into a computer program.

a Have the program compute the differences of the 20 scores.

b Obtain a 95% confidence interval for the mean of the differences.

c Does this confidence interval clearly indicate that either spreadsheet program is better (requires less time on average)?

7.87 **a** Obtain a boxplot of the difference data in Exercise 7.86. Are there any outliers?

b Does it appear that the differences are seriously skewed?

7.88 A leading manufacturer of packaged cereals regularly introduces new brands or new versions of existing brands. There is unavoidable uncertainty about how successful a new item will be. Despite extensive market research, about 80% of all new items introduced fail to win adequate market share. However, the company is compelled to keep sending out new items, so that its competitors can't erode its market share so easily.

After a new product's initial introduction, the company must forecast its sales for about 3 months in advance. The purchasing group prefers to contract for ingredients (largely wheat, corn, or oats, but also a number of special–purpose flours and flavorings) rather than buy ingredients on the spot market; contracts usually provide substantial cost savings. Packaging materials, particularly the actual cereal boxes, are best produced in large runs; therefore, reasonable estimates of future demand can save some money. Production planning requires an estimate of demand. There are methods for adjusting production runs short-term, but they tend to result in idle lines or bottlenecks.

The company's standard practice has been to obtain actual sales data for months 1 and 2 after introduction of a new item, and to apply the percentage growth rate (month 2 as a percentage of month 1) as a forecast. The marketing staff has proposed using a model based on product life cycle ideas instead. As a test, historical data for 38 previous new product introductions were used to forecast demand using both methods. The results were compared to the actual demand.

You have been asked to use the data and preliminary analysis shown next to recommend which method to use. In particular, the new products manager is concerned whether either method seems consistently too optimistic or too pessimistic, which method seems to be more accurate most of the time, and any indication that one method or the other is liable to give wildly poor estimates.

```
MTB > name c4 ´diff1´ c5 ´diff2´ c6 ´ratio1´ c7 ´ratio2´
MTB > let c4=c1-c2
MTB > let c5=c1-c3
MTB > let c6=c1/c2
MTB > let c7=c1/c3
MTB > describe c4-c5
```

	N	MEAN	MEDIAN	TRMEAN	STDEV	SEMEAN
diff1	38	-3027	-1681	-2614	4105	666
diff2	38	278	352	373	2028	329

	MIN	MAX	Q1	Q3
diff1	-18566	3223	-4021	-765
diff2	-6466	4478	-672	1185

```
MTB > describe c6-c7
```

	N	MEAN	MEDIAN	TRMEAN	STDEV	SEMEAN
ratio1	38	0.8446	0.7924	0.8288	0.1609	0.0261
ratio2	38	1.0584	1.0437	1.0536	0.1570	0.0255

	MIN	MAX	Q1	Q3
ratio1	0.6234	1.3766	0.7482	0.9170
ratio2	0.8262	1.3766	0.9383	1.2021

```
MTB > boxplot c4
MTB > boxplot c5
MTB > boxplot c6
MTB > boxplot c7
```

FIGURE 7.23   **Boxplots for Cereal Sales Predictions**

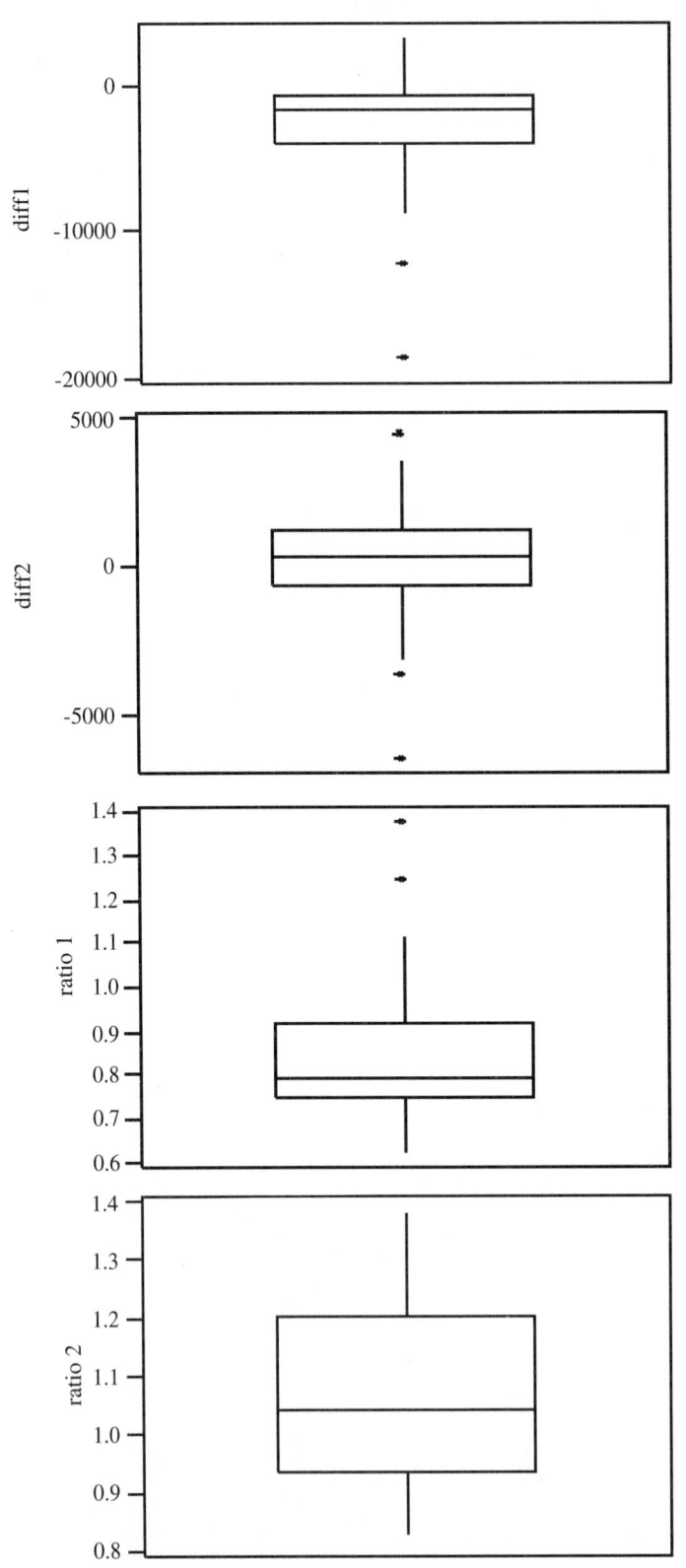

Interval Estimation

The benefits manager of a large university was asked to evaluate the costs of a proposed flexible benefits system. Under such a plan, individuals choose a "basket" of benefits best suited to their needs. The most important choices, in terms of cost to the university, are amount of life insurance, amount of medical insurance, and amount of retirement contribution. The benefits manager needed information about the average amounts of each of these choices to assess the university's cost per employee. Each employee would pay part of the cost (above a university-paid minimum), but the university's cost would also increase somewhat with increased benefits.

The manager did not want to survey the entire faculty and staff of the university. First, there were about 17,000 eligible employees, so such a survey would be too large a task. Second, the "flex" plan had not yet been approved, so there was a real danger that a campuswide survey could be interpreted as a promise that the plan would be available soon. The manager chose to take a sample of eligible employees from the current benefits file. Each employee was interviewed in person, partly to explain the choices and partly to stress the tentative nature of the plan. Data were obtained for 61 employees. The yearly costs, in current dollars, of each employee's choices were calculated. They are the following:

Empl	Life	Medical	Retiremt	Empl	Life	Medical	Retiremt
1	759	1184	915	32	585	740	646
2	424	239	538	33	472	847	637
3	157	630	639	34	535	1287	783
4	616	868	862	35	174	465	481
5	655	867	752	36	751	1143	794
6	559	945	613	37	579	751	700
7	651	1248	722	38	666	1098	770
8	519	648	750	39	596	729	571
9	358	361	670	40	251	1024	690
10	456	581	502	41	341	862	409
11	97	391	590	42	77	398	718
12	478	837	788	43	225	388	387
13	129	395	546	44	590	1262	851
14	661	535	633	45	330	609	742
15	245	472	597	46	736	1194	667
16	602	492	767	47	601	713	715
17	557	382	706	48	555	921	778
18	245	672	602	49	775	644	519
19	331	245	546	50	745	1183	868
20	545	1126	690	51	630	670	715
21	395	605	748	52	169	790	730
22	577	435	701	53	521	701	688
23	345	645	683	54	647	839	683
24	367	365	540	55	543	529	676
25	189	181	655	56	699	598	613
26	716	775	717	57	602	825	759
27	238	572	507	58	493	1120	882
28	867	776	799	59	731	481	761
29	475	1123	646	60	267	390	624
30	369	921	857	61	689	1179	629
31	245	881	724				

The benefits manager wants to know a reasonable range for the average cost to the university of each type of contribution, as well as the average total cost per employee. In addition, the manager's boss wants an idea of how large a survey must be done to estimate total cost per employee to within plus or minus $50. They have asked you to work with the available data and to send them a brief memo answering their questions. Both of them studied statistics some time ago, but they've forgotten most of the concepts, so your report will have to explain any technical terms. ■

Astrologer Jones has a bent
For forecasting trouble's descent.
His prophecies dire
Say "Flood, storm, and fire"
With confidence seven percent.

Hypothesis Testing

Hypothesis testing, or significance testing, is a method for checking whether an apparent result from a sample could possibly be due to randomness. It serves to check on how strong the evidence is. Are sample data reflecting a real change or effect rather than a random fluke? This is a legitimate and useful task, but you shouldn't read more into the results than can be justified. The results of a test indicate how good the evidence is, not how important the result is. The key ideas include the following:

1   A research hypothesis typically states that there is a real change, a real difference, or a real effect in the underlying population or process. The opposite, null hypothesis states that there is no real change, difference, or effect.

2   The basic strategy of hypothesis testing is to try to support a research hypothesis by showing that the sample results are highly unlikely assuming the null hypothesis, and more likely assuming the research hypothesis.

3   The strategy can be implemented in equivalent ways by creating a formal rejection region, by obtaining a p-value, or by seeing whether the null hypothesis value falls within a confidence interval.

4   There are risks of both false positive (Type I) and false negative (Type II) errors. The basic strategy controls the probability α of a false positive error in setting up a rejection region, as a comparison standard for a p-value, or in setting a confidence level. The β probability of a false negative error depends on the choice of α, the sample size, and the hypothesized value of a mean or other parameter within the research hypothesis.

5   Tests of a mean usually are based on the t distribution unless somehow the population or process standard deviation is known.

6   Tests of a proportion can be done by using a normal (z) approximation to binomial probabilities or by using a t test with data 1s for successes and 0s for failures.

Very often sample data will suggest that something relevant is happening in the underlying population or process. A sample of potential customers may show that a higher proportion prefer a new brand to the existing one. A sampling of telephone response time by reservation clerks may show an increase in mean customer waiting time. A sample of crankshafts produced with a new alloy composition may show a decrease in the standard deviation of metal hardness. In each case, the data are only from a limited sample and therefore they are subject to some degree of random variation.

The question is whether the apparent effect or result in the sample is an indication of something happening in the underlying population (or process) or is possibly a mere fluke—a result of random variation alone. Statistical hypothesis testing is a means of assessing whether apparent results in a sample conclusively indicate that something is really happening. This chapter is devoted to the basic concepts of hypothesis testing.

Hypothesis testing involves quite a few new concepts and definitions, plus a number of formulas for carrying out computations. While working on these, try not to lose sight of the basic idea. Sample data are subject to random variation, so apparent results from the sample may be misleading. How conclusive is the evidence that sample results indicate a real, more-than-random effect in the underlying population or process?

There are almost always several ways to carry out a hypothesis test. We'll describe them all in this chapter. One can carry out a formal test using a five-step procedure described in this chapter, or one can compute a p-value to do the test, or one can use a confidence interval as a hypothesis test. These methods are equivalent; they will all lead to the same conclusion. The formal, five-step method is easiest to grasp initially, the p-value method is commonly used by computer packages, and the confidence interval approach is easy to interpret (and hard to misinterpret). They are all useful, equivalent ways to solve the problem. ■

A Test for a Mean, Known Standard Deviation

W e'll start to explain basic hypothesis-testing concepts in the context of a statistical test for a single population mean. Many other statistical tests are discussed later in this chapter and beyond, but a test for a single mean is very simple. In addition, to keep things simple, we'll make the assumption—which is *not* usually valid in practice—that the population standard deviation is known.

As usual, we work by example. A manufacturer of frozen dinners must spend money every time it changes from one product to another on its production line, to clean out leftovers from the previously produced dinner and to set up production for the next one. Past practice has been to minimize this cost by scheduling very long production runs of a single product, but this practice led to large inventories, slow response to changing tastes, and frozen dinners being sold many weeks after they were produced. A worker team has suggested an alternate changeover procedure that it hopes will reduce the changeover cost. The current procedure requires an average of 16.2 worker-hours, with a standard deviation of 2.40 hours per changeover. The manufacturer decides to test the new procedure on the next 16 changeovers, which can be regarded as a random sample. How should the results of this test be used to see whether there is evidence that the new procedure really reduces changeover cost?

research hypothesis

We can formulate this problem in terms of a statistical test about the population mean cost μ for all changeovers. There is a **research hypothesis**, also called an *alternative hypothesis*, that the long-run mean changeover time μ is less than 16.2 worker-hours. This is a statement about the long-run population or process mean—*not* merely a statement about the mean in the sample of 16 changeovers. We write the research hypothesis as H_a; this notation comes from the name, alternative hypothesis. Here H_a: $\mu < 16.2$ worker-hours.

null hypothesis

The **null hypothesis**, denoted H_0, is the denial of the research hypothesis H_a. As the name suggests, the null hypothesis often has a negative quality. For the changeover time example, the corresponding null hypothesis is H_0: $\mu \geq 16.2$ worker-hours. The primary concern is with the boundary value of the null hypothesis, so in this case we will take H_0: $\mu = 16.2$. (If we have clear evidence that the mean is less than 16.2, we have even clearer evidence that it is less than 16.3 or 17.1 or some other number larger than 16.2.) We denote the boundary value of the hypothesized mean by μ_0; here $\mu_0 = 16.2$.

one-sided/two-sided research hypothesis

The research hypothesis may be either **one-sided** (directional) or **two-sided** (nondirectional). In the example, we specify a particular direction for H_a relative to H_0—H_a: $\mu < 16.2$ is a one-sided hypothesis. In contrast, had we specified H_a: $\mu \neq 16.2$, we would have had a two-sided, nondirectional research hypothesis. The purpose of the study determines the choice of one-sided or two-sided research hypotheses. In comparing the new changeover process to the old one, we want to see if the new process is better, so we use a one-sided research hypothesis. If we were comparing two versions of a new process, we would want to test whether either version is clearly superior to the other and would use a two-sided, nondirectional research hypothesis.

basic strategy

The **basic strategy** in hypothesis testing is to attempt to support the research hypothesis by "contradicting" the null hypothesis. The null hypothesis is "contradicted" if the sample data are highly unlikely given H_0 and more likely given H_a. Thus, to support H_a: $\mu < 16.2$, we would need to find that the sample results are highly improbable assuming that H_0: $\mu = 16.2$ is true.

test statistic

The data must be summarized in a **test statistic** (T.S.). We calculate this statistic to see if it is reasonably compatible with the null hypothesis. When we are testing a population mean, the most plausible test statistic is the sample mean changeover time $\overline{Y}$

of the 16 trials. Sample means much less than μ_0 are likely under H_0 and relatively more likely if H_a: $\mu < 16.2$ is true. Therefore, the rejection region is "reject H_0 if $\overline{Y}$ is smaller than could reasonably occur by chance."

To repeat, the basic logic is as follows:

1   Assume that H_0: $\mu = 16.2$ is true.

2   Calculate the value of the T.S.: $\overline{Y}$ = mean of the sample of 16 trials.

3   If this value is highly unlikely (which, in this case, means clearly smaller than 16.2), reject H_0 and support H_a.

It's necessary in hypothesis testing to draw the line between values of the test statistic that are relatively likely given the null hypothesis and values that are relatively unlikely. At what value of the test statistic do we start to say that the data support the research hypothesis? Knowledge of the sampling distribution of the test statistic is used to answer this question. Values of the test statistic that are sufficiently unlikely given the null hypoth-

rejection region

esis (as determined by the sampling distribution) form a **rejection region** (R.R.) for the statistical test.

Specification of a rejection region must recognize the possibility of error. Suppose that, for a sample of 16 trials, we set the rejection region at $\overline{Y} < 10.0$ worker-hours. Even if the null hypothesis H_0: $\mu = 16.2$ is true, there is a small probability of observing $\overline{Y} < 10.0$. If such a situation were to occur, the manufacturer would erroneously think that the new process was superior to the old one. This error—rejecting a null hypothesis that is, in fact,

Type I error

true—is called a **Type I error**. In establishing a rejection region, an investigator must specify the maximum tolerable probability of a Type I error; this maximum probability is denoted by α.

To determine the exact rejection region, we need to know the sampling distribution of $\overline{Y}$. Recall from Chapter 6 that if the population distribution of weights is normal with mean μ and standard deviation σ, then the sampling distribution of the sample mean is also normal with expected value equal to the population mean weight ($\mu_{\overline{Y}} = \mu$) and with standard error equal to $\sigma_{\overline{Y}} = \sigma/\sqrt{n}$.

Even if the population distribution is mildly nonnormal, the Central Limit Theorem helps to make this distribution a good approximation. For the changeover time problem, $\sigma = 2.40$ (assuming that the new procedure has the same standard deviation as the current one), $n = 16$, and the crucial value for μ is the boundary null hypothesis value $\mu_0 = 16.2$. Thus, if the null hypothesis is true, the sample mean $\overline{Y}$ is normally distributed with $\mu = 16.2$ and standard error $\sigma_{\overline{Y}} = 2.40/\sqrt{16} = 0.60$. We can use this information about the sampling distribution of the test statistic $\overline{Y}$ to determine a rejection region.

Remember that we want to reject H_0 if the value of the test statistic is highly unlikely assuming that H_0 is true, and more likely assuming that H_a is true. In this example, H_a specifies that the population mean is less than the null hypothesis mean. If so, only sample means clearly lower than 16.2 should lead us to reject H_0. In this case, we should use a one-tailed rejection region. The entire rejection region for testing H_0: $\mu = 16.2$ against H_a: $\mu < 16.2$ is in the lower tail of the distribution of $\overline{Y}$. In particular, from our knowledge of the properties of a normal distribution, we know that the boundary of the rejection region is located at a distance of 1.645 standard errors ($1.645\sigma_{\overline{Y}}$) below $\mu = 16.2$ if α is taken to be .05 (see Figure 8.1).

z statistic

To determine whether or not to reject the null hypothesis, we can also compute the number of standard errors $\overline{Y}$ lies below $\mu = 16.2$. This is done by computing a z **statistic** for the sample mean $\overline{Y}$:

$$z = \frac{\overline{Y} - \mu_0}{\sigma/\sqrt{n}} = \frac{\overline{Y} - 16.2}{0.60}$$

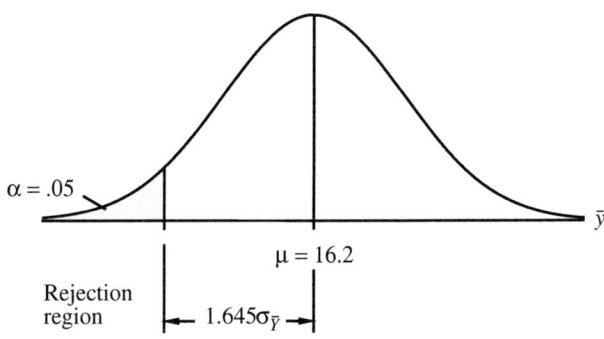

This suggests two ways to state the rejection region for a statistical test about μ. First, in terms of the test statistic $\bar{Y}$, the rejection region is

rejection region using $\bar{Y}$

R.R.: For $\alpha = .05$, reject H_0: $\mu = 16.2$ if the observed value of $\bar{Y}$ is more than $1.645\sigma_{\bar{Y}}$ below $\mu = 16.2$ (see Figure 8.1).

An equivalent way to state the rejection region is in terms of the test statistic $z = (\bar{Y} - \mu_0)/\sigma_{\bar{Y}}$, also called the z statistic:

rejection region using z

R.R.: For $\alpha = .05$, reject H_0: $\mu = 16.2$ if the computed value of z is less than -1.645 (see Figure 8.2).

Because the latter approach is shorter, simpler, and used by virtually all statistical computer programs, we use it throughout this text.

FIGURE 8.2 Rejection Region for the Test Statistic z ($\alpha = .05$, one-tailed)

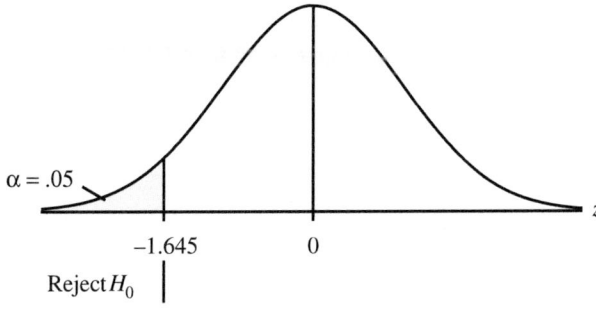

Finally, suppose that the sample mean changeover time for a sample of $n = 16$ trials is $\bar{y} = 14.4$ worker-hours. What can the manufacturer conclude concerning the population mean time? The z statistic

$$z = \frac{14.4 - 16.2}{2.40/\sqrt{16}} = -3.00$$

indicates that the sample mean lies 3 standard errors below the hypothesized mean $\mu = 16.2$. Because the computed value of the z statistic lies in the rejection region well beyond the critical value -1.645, the manufacturer can reject the null hypothesis and claim that the new process leads to lower changeover times. A five-step summary list displays the full process.

Definition 8.1   Summary of One-Tailed Test of μ, σ Known

$$H_0: \mu = \mu_0 \ (\mu_0 = 16.2 \text{ worker-hours})$$

$$H_a: \mu < \mu_0$$

T.S.: $z = \dfrac{\bar{y} - \mu_0}{\sigma_{\bar{Y}}}, \quad \sigma_{\bar{Y}} = \dfrac{\sigma}{\sqrt{n}}$

R.R.: For $\alpha = .05$, reject H_0 if $z < -1.645$.

Conclusion: $z = \dfrac{14.4 - 16.2}{2.40/\sqrt{16}} = -3.00; \text{ reject } H_0$

Note: For $H_0: \mu = \mu_0$ and $H_a: \mu > \mu_0$, the R.R. for $\alpha = .05$ is $z > 1.645$. ∎

We have noted that the boundary value of the null hypothesis is the important value. In the changeover time example, suppose we had taken some other value within H_0 as our hypothesized mean, such as $\mu = 16.3$ worker-hours. The resulting z statistic would fall even farther into the rejection region:

$$z = \frac{14.4 - 16.3}{2.40/\sqrt{16}} = -3.17$$

If the test statistic based on the boundary value leads to rejection of H_0, a test statistic based on any other value in H_0 also leads to rejection of H_0. Hereafter, we only worry about the critical boundary value.

This test procedure for μ can easily be modified to handle other research hypotheses. For example, if a cereal company wants to establish beyond a reasonable doubt that the true mean weight of its nominal 16-ounce packages is in fact more than 16 ounces, it could start with the one-sided research hypothesis $H_a: \mu > 16$. Large values of $\bar{Y}$ would then indicate rejection of the null hypothesis $H_0: \mu = 16$. In particular, for $\alpha = .05$, the rejection region would be values of $\bar{Y}$ more than $1.645\sigma_{\bar{Y}}$ *above* $\mu_0 = 16$, or equivalently, values of $z > 1.645$ (see Figure 8.3).

E X A M P L E   8 . 1

A researcher claims that the amount of time urban preschool children ages 3–5 watch television per week has a mean of 22.6 hours and a standard deviation of 6.1 hours. A market research firm believes that the claimed mean is too low. The television-watching habits of a random sample of 60 urban preschool children are measured, with a parent of each child keeping a daily log of television watching. If the mean weekly amount of time spent watching television is 25.2 hours and if the population standard deviation σ is assumed to be 6.1 hours, should the researcher's claim be rejected at an α value of .01?

Solution

The marketing firm's research hypothesis is that 22.6 is too small a value for the population mean. Thus, the research hypothesis of interest is $H_a: \mu > 22.6$, and the null hypothesis is $H_0: \mu = 22.6$. We summarize the elements of the statistical test for $\alpha = .01$ as follows:

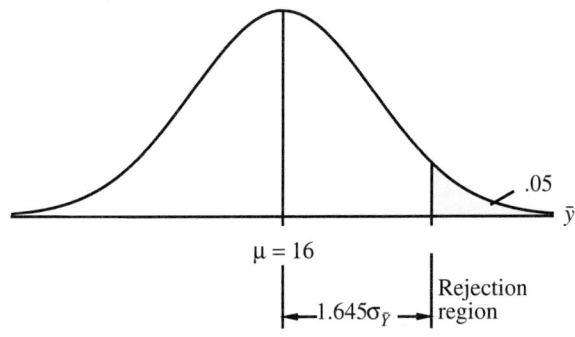

H_0: $\mu = 22.6$

H_a: $\mu > 22.6$

T.S.: $z = \dfrac{\bar{y} - \mu_0}{\sigma_{\bar{Y}}} = \dfrac{25.2 - 22.6}{6.1/\sqrt{60}} = 3.30$

R.R.: For $\alpha = .01$, reject H_0 if $z > 2.33$.

Conclusion: Because $z = 3.30$ is well within the rejection region, we reject H_0: $\mu = 22.6$, which was the researcher's claim. ■

A two-tailed test for the research hypothesis H_a: $\mu \neq \mu_0$ follows directly from our discussion of one-tailed tests. For example, the manager of a cereal company that is concerned about possible overfilling or underfilling might well take as a research hypothesis that $\mu \neq 16$. Both large and small values of $\bar{Y}$ would indicate rejection of H_0: $\mu = 16$. If we split the rejection region evenly in the tails, the rejection region for $\alpha = .05$ is as shown in Figure 8.4.

The summary chart for the z test can be written to cover all three forms for the research hypothesis. Recall that z_α is the z value that cuts off an area a in the right-hand tail of the z curve; thus $z_{.05} = 1.645$ and $z_{.025} = 1.96$. For a two-tailed test and a given α, the desired cutoff points are $z_{\alpha/2}$. For $\alpha = .05$, we use $z_{.025} = 1.96$ and $-z_{.025} = -1.96$. The first four steps of the statistical test for μ (σ known) are shown here. These steps formulate

FIGURE 8.4 **Rejection Region for H_0: $\mu = 16$, with $\overline{Y}$ as Test Statistic**

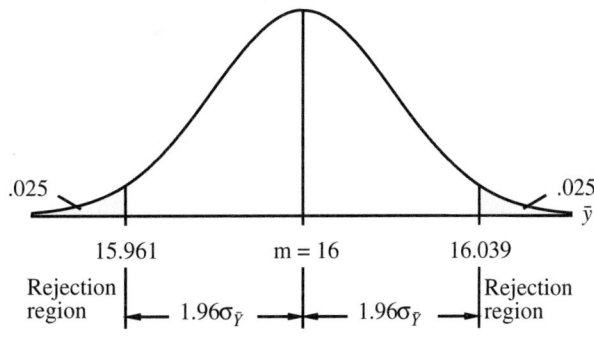

the problem and establish the rejection region; the last step simply involves drawing a conclusion based on the computed value of the z test statistic. If the computed z value falls within the rejection region, we reject the null hypothesis in favor of the research hypothesis. If the z value does not fall within the rejection region, we don't have enough evidence to support our research hypothesis.

Definition 8.2 Summary for z Test, with σ Known

$$H_0: \mu = \mu_0$$

$$H_a: 1.\ \mu > \mu_0$$

$$2.\ \mu < \mu_0$$

$$3.\ \mu \neq \mu_0$$

$$\text{T.S.: } z = \frac{\overline{Y} - \mu_0}{\sigma/\sqrt{n}}$$

R.R.: For the probability of a Type I error α, reject H_0 if

1. $z > z_\alpha$

2. $z < -z_\alpha$

3. $z > z_{\alpha/2}$ or $z < -z_{\alpha/2}$ ■

E X A M P L E   8 . 2

Refer to the television-watching data of Example 8.1. Test the research hypothesis H_a: $\mu \neq 22.6$ using $\alpha = .01$.

Solution

The five steps of the solution are summarized here:

$$H_0: \mu = 22.6$$

$$H_a: \mu \neq 22.6$$

$$\text{T.S.: } z = \frac{\overline{y} - \mu_0}{\sigma_{\overline{Y}}} = 3.30$$

R.R.: For $\alpha = .01$, reject H_0 if $z > 2.58$ or if $z < -2.58$.

Conclusion: Because the computed value of z (3.30) falls within the rejection region, we reject H_0: $\mu = 22.6$. Practically speaking, because the sample mean is greater than 22.6 and because we reject H_0: $\mu = 22.6$, we can safely conclude that $\mu > 22.6$.   ■

The examples in this section are unrealistic in that we assumed a population standard deviation was known. In the changeover-time example, we had to assume that the new procedure had exactly the same standard deviation as the current one. Population parameters such as the standard deviation usually have unknown values. We managed the problem of unknown standard deviations in Chapter 7 by using the t distribution. Hypothesis-testing methods using the t distribution are discussed in Section 8.4. It is convenient to use z tests in our examples for a bit longer, only to avoid minor complications. Recall that for large samples, the difference between t and z tables is minor.

Type II Error, β Probability, and Power of a Test

Type II error

U p to this point, we have been concerned about only one kind of error in hypothesis testing: a Type I error, which rejects the null hypothesis when it is true. In the changeover-time example of the previous section, a Type I error would be a claim that the new process is better than the old one, when, in fact, it is the same (or worse). But there is a second possibility for error in hypothesis testing. This error, a **Type II error**, is the failure to reject the null hypothesis when the research hypothesis is true. In the changeover-time example, a Type II error would be a claim that the new process is the same (or worse) than the old one, when, in fact, it is better. This error would lead the manufacturer to overlook a chance to improve operations; often a Type II error is a missed opportunity.

When the null hypothesis is negative, as it often is, a Type I error can be called a *false positive* error; by coming to the erroneous conclusion that a positive hypothesis H_a is true, we commit a false positive, Type I error. Similarly, a Type II error can be called a *false negative* error—an erroneous conclusion that a negative hypothesis H_0 is true.

E X A M P L E   8 . 3

A private-label bottler of soft drinks asks each of 100 members of a tasting panel (who are regarded as a sample from millions of potential customers) to rate each of two possible formulations of a cola drink on a 100-point scale; higher scores are desirable. Formulation G is less expensive and will be used unless there is clear evidence that formulation R is preferred. From the data, the bottler obtains the difference (R - G) in ratings for each panelist. State the null hypothesis that the two formulations are equally good on average and an appropriate research hypothesis, based on the difference data. What are the consequences of false positive and false negative errors?

Solution

If the two formulations are equally preferred, the mean of the differences will be 0. Therefore we take H_0: $\mu = 0$. The bottler wants to see if there is evidence that R is preferred, in which case the average difference will be positive; H_a: $\mu > 0$. A false positive error would be to conclude that R is preferred even though in fact it is not. If this error happens, the bottler will waste money by using a more expensive formulation when the market can't detect the difference. A false negative (Type II) error would be to conclude that the two formulations are equally preferred, even though in fact R is preferred. If a false negative error occurs, the bottler will use the less expensive G formulation even though the market would prefer R. ∎

The two types of errors may be understood in the context of control charts. A false positive, Type I, error corresponds to saying that the process is out of control when in fact it's fine. In effect, this error is a false alarm. A false negative, Type II, error corresponds to saying that the process is in control when in fact there's a problem. In effect, this error is failure to sound an alarm when we should. By setting control limits at 3 standard errors from the nominal value, we guarantee a low "false alarm" rate at any given time but leave open the probability that we will not detect a problem quickly.

power

The probability that a Type II error will be committed, given that the research hypothesis is true, is denoted by β. The quantity $1 - \beta$ is called the **power** of the test; power is the probability that the test will support the research hypothesis given that it is in fact true. The possible outcomes of a statistical test and the associated probabilities are summarized in Table 8.1.

TABLE 8 . 1 **Possible Outcomes and Probabilities for a Hypothesis Test**

	Condition	
Conclusion	H_0 **Is True**	H_a **Is True**
Accept H_0	Correct conclusion probability $1 - \alpha$	Type II error probability β
Reject H_0	Type I error probability α	Correct conclusion probability $1 - \beta$ ($=$ power)

E X A M P L E   8 . 4

Refer to Example 8.3. Under certain conditions, the power of the test is .60. What does this mean?

Solution

Power refers to the probability that a research hypothesis will be correctly supported. The sentence thus means that if the research hypothesis is true, there is a 60% chance that the test will discover that fact. ■

One problem with calculating β is that H_a usually doesn't specify one particular value for the population parameter. To calculate the risk of a Type II error (the probability of incorrectly accepting H_0), we must assume a hypothetical value for μ under H_a. The value of β depends on the assumed value of μ in H_a. Specifically, in the changeover-time example of the previous section (H_0: $\mu = 16.2$, $\alpha = .05$, with $\sigma = 2.40$ and $n = 16$), what if $\mu = 14.6$? This means that the new process, in the long run (not just in the short-run sample), would result in about a 10% decrease in the average number of worker-hours per changeover. What is the probability that the manager will retain the null hypothesis that the new process is no better than the old?

We will work through the logic of the calculation of β, then present a shortcut computation. The calculation is easier to understand if the rejection region is stated in terms of the sample mean $\bar{y}$ rather than the z statistic. The rejection region is $z < -1.645$, corresponding to a one-tailed α of .05; we therefore reject H_0: $\mu = 16.2$ for values of $\bar{y}$ at 1.645 standard errors below $\mu = 16.2$. That is, we reject H_0 if $\bar{y} < 16.2 - 1.645(2.40)/\sqrt{16} = 15.213$. If the true mean is $\mu = 14.6$, the probability β that the sample mean does *not* fall within the rejection region is

$$\beta = P(\bar{Y} \geq 15.213 | \mu = 14.6) = P\left(\frac{\bar{Y} - 14.6}{2.40/\sqrt{16}} \geq \frac{15.213 - 14.6}{2.40/\sqrt{16}}\right)$$

$$= P(z \geq 1.02) \approx .15$$

The calculation is illustrated in Figure 8.5. Such calculations can be carried out for any test situation, and they can be summarized in a general formula. If μ_0 is the boundary

β for a one-tailed test

FIGURE 8.5 **Calculation of β for One-Tailed z Test**

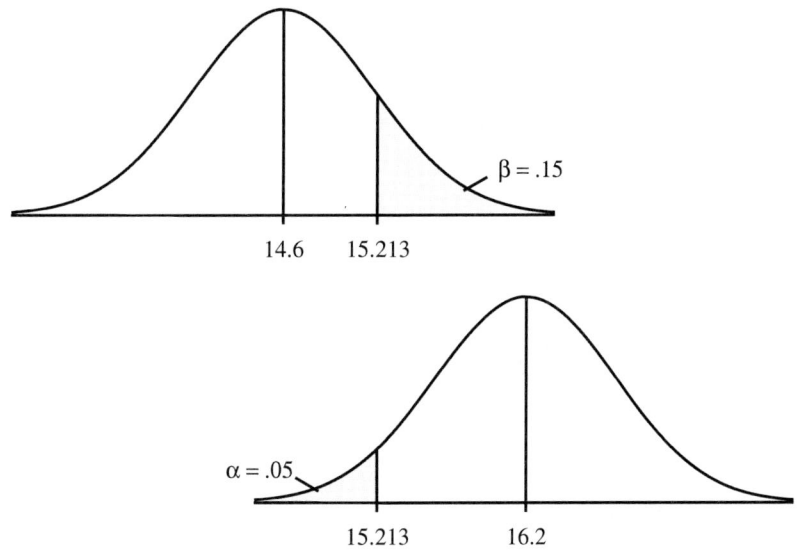

value of μ under H_0 and μ_a is the selected research hypothesis mean, for a one-tailed test,

$$\beta = P\left(z \geq -z_\alpha + \frac{|\mu_a - \mu_0|}{\sigma/\sqrt{n}}\right)$$

In our changeover-time example, $-z_\alpha = -z_{.05} = -1.645$, whereas

$$\frac{|\mu_a - \mu_0|}{\sigma/\sqrt{n}} = \frac{|14.6 - 16.2|}{2.40/\sqrt{16}} = \frac{1.6}{.60} = 2.667$$

(Recall that "| |" indicates absolute value, or magnitude of a number without regard to sign.) Hence

$$\beta = P(z \geq -1.645 + 2.667) = P(z \geq 1.022) \approx .15$$

Therefore, the manufacturer has a moderately small probability ($\beta = .15$) of failing to reject H_0 if the long-run improvement is about 10%. In other words, with this test procedure, there is a fairly high power ($1 - \beta \approx .85$) for detecting a 10% improvement if it exists.

A similar calculation can be made for a two-tailed test. The only change is that z_α is replaced by $z_{\alpha/2}$. For $\alpha = .05$, replace 1.645 by 1.96.

Definition 8.3   Calculation of β for a z Test

One-tailed test: $\beta = P\left(z \geq -z_\alpha + \frac{|\mu_a - \mu_0|}{\sigma/\sqrt{n}}\right)$

Two-tailed test: Replace $-z_\alpha$ in the one-tailed test by $-z_{\alpha/2}$. ■

The numerical value of β depends on the value chosen for μ_a, the hypothesized value within the research hypothesis. One can calculate β for different values of μ_a and draw a curve with β on the vertical axis and μ_a on the horizontal axis. This curve will indicate how likely we are to get a false negative conclusion, depending on "how true" the research hypothesis is.

EXAMPLE 8.5

In Example 8.1, we planned to carry out a test of the research hypothesis that mean television-watching time per week was greater than 22.6 hours. The assumed standard deviation was 6.1, the sample size was 60, and α was .01. Suppose that the mean for the entire population (not merely the sample of 60) is 25.0. Find the probability that the research hypothesis will *not* be supported.

Solution

First, the research hypothesis is one-sided. The probability that the research hypothesis will not be supported, assuming a true mean of 25.0, is the probability that H_0 is retained, assuming that H_a is true. That is the β probability. Because $\alpha = .01$, the required z table value cuts off a right tail equal to .01; that value is $z_{.01} = 2.33$. We take $\mu_a = 25.0$, $\mu_0 = 22.6$, $\sigma = 6.1$, and $n = 60$. Using the shortcut calculation,

$$\beta = P\left(z \geq -2.33 + \frac{|25.0 - 22.6|}{6.1/\sqrt{60}}\right)$$

$$= P(z \geq .72) = .2358 \quad \blacksquare$$

EXERCISES

8.1 The manager of a health maintenance organization has set as a target that the mean waiting time of nonemergency patients not exceed 30 minutes. In spot checks, the manager finds the waiting times for 22 patients; the patients are selected randomly on different days. Assume that the population standard deviation of waiting times is 10 minutes.

    a What is the relevant parameter to be tested?

    b Formulate null and research hypotheses.

    c State the test statistic and the rejection region corresponding to $\alpha = .05$.

8.2 Suppose that the mean waiting time for the 22 patients in Exercise 8.1 is 38.1 minutes. Can H_0 be rejected?

8.3 For the test procedure of Exercise 8.2, find the probability that H_0 will not be rejected, assuming a true mean waiting time of 34 minutes. Do the same for other values of μ, and sketch a β curve.

8.4 We stated in Exercise 8.1 that the 22 patients were selected on different days. Why would one not want to select 22 patients on one randomly chosen day?

8.5 A radio station wants to control the time allotted to unpaid public service commercials. If there are too many such commercials, the station loses revenue; if there are too few, the station loses points with the Federal Communications Commission. The target figure is an average of 1.5 commercial minutes per hour. A sample of 18 hours gives the following times (in minutes) allotted to public service commercials:

.0	.0	.0	.0	.0	.0	.5	.5	.5	1.0	1.5	1.5
1.5	2.0	2.0	2.5	3.0	6.5	(mean = 1.278)					

Assume that the population standard deviation is 1.60. State all parts of a z test of H_0: $\mu = 1.5$. Should H_a be one- or two-tailed? Use $\alpha = .05$.

8.6 Refer to Exercise 8.5. Calculate β probabilities for $\mu = 1.0, 1.2, 1.4, 1.6, 1.8,$ and 2.0. Sketch a β curve.

8.7 The theory underlying the test in Exercise 8.5 assumes that $\overline{Y}$ has an approximately normal distribution. From the appearance of the data, do you believe that the approximation is a good one for this problem?   ■

The *p*-Value for a Hypothesis Test

In the hypothesis-testing problems we've considered so far, we always come to a reject/don't reject decision, without regard to the conclusiveness of the decision. In practice, this is often an oversimplification. Evidently, the farther the value of the test statistic extends into the rejection region, the more conclusive is the rejection of the null hypothesis. How can we measure the weight of the sample evidence for rejecting a null hypothesis in favor of a research hypothesis?

The weight of evidence, or conclusiveness index, for rejecting a null hypothesis is called the **p-value** or attained significance level. *The p-value is the probability (assuming H_0) of a test statistic value equal to or more extreme than the actually observed value.* Recall the basic strategy of hypothesis testing. We hope to support the research hypothesis and reject the null hypothesis, by showing that the data are highly unlikely assuming that H_0 is true. As the test statistic gets farther into the rejection region, the data become more unlikely assuming H_0, the weight of the evidence for rejecting the null hypothesis becomes more conclusive, and the p-value becomes smaller. The farther within the rejection region the test statistic falls, the smaller the p-value is, and the stronger the evidence we have to reject the null hypothesis and support the research hypothesis.

Very small p-values are strong, conclusive evidence for rejecting the null hypothesis. This is because a small p-value indicates that the actually observed data are very unlikely, assuming that the null hypothesis is true. Although no null hypothesis can ever be absolutely disproven, a very small p-value leads to its rejection and to support of the research hypothesis beyond a reasonable doubt.

The computation of p-values is straightforward for a z test. In Section 8.1, we discussed a test of H_0: $\mu = 16.2$ versus H_a: $\mu < 16.2$ with $\sigma = 2.40$ and $n = 16$. The sample mean was $\bar{y} = 14.4$, leading to a z statistic of

$$z = \frac{14.4 - 16.2}{2.40/\sqrt{16}} = -3.00$$

The p-value is the probability of at least as extreme a value as $z = -3.00$; in this case, "more extreme" means less than (more negative than) -3.00. The one-tailed p-value is $P(z \leq -3.00) = .5 - .4987 = .0013$. See Figure 8.6.

Figure 8.6 looks very much like the calculation of a rejection region, but the calculation of a p-value goes in the opposite direction. To find a rejection region, we specify α and look up the appropriate z value. To find a p-value, we specify a z value—namely, the observed z test statistic—and look up the appropriate tail probability. Note also that α is

FIGURE 8.6 **One-Tailed *p*-Value**

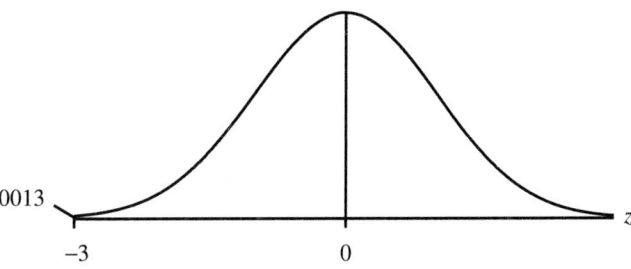

a long-run probability (of a false positive error), whereas a p-value is a property of one particular sample. If we redid a hypothesis test using a new sample, α would not change, but we would get a different value for the test statistic, and a different p-value.

For a two-tailed test, such as that for H_0: $\mu = 16.2$, H_a: $\mu \neq 16.2$ in the preceding example, the p-value, $P(z \leq -3.00 \text{ or } z \geq 3.00|\mu = 16) = .0026$, is twice the one-tailed p-value, by symmetry. See Figure 8.7.

FIGURE 8.7   **Two-Tailed p-Value**

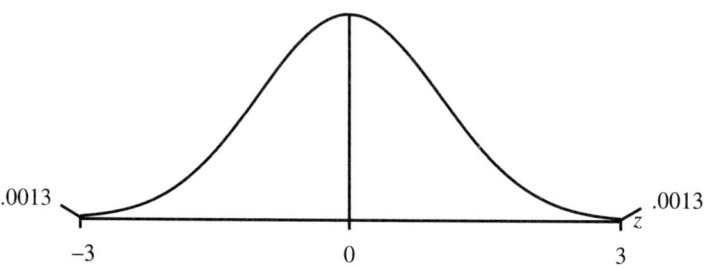

In general, the computation of p-values based on the z statistic proceeds as follows.

Definition 8.4 p-Value for a z Test

The p-value is the probability, assuming that the null hypothesis is true, of obtaining a test statistic at least as extreme as the observed value.

1   If H_a: $\mu > \mu_0$, p-value $= P(z > z_{\text{actual}})$

2   If H_a: $\mu < \mu_0$, p-value $= P(z < z_{\text{actual}})$

3   If H_a: $\mu \neq \mu_0$, p-value $= 2P(z > |z_{\text{actual}}|)$ ■

Most computer programs automatically compute p-values. A very small p-value indicates that the null hypothesis may be rejected at any plausible α value; a large p-value, such as .4 or .6, indicates that the null hypothesis should not be rejected at plausible α values. A very general principle relates p-values to α; the principle is so general that it deserves to be called the Universal Rejection Region.

Definition 8.5   Universal Rejection Region

If α has been specified, reject the null hypothesis if and only if the p-value is less than the specified α.   ■

EXAMPLE 8.6

Many computer software programs for statistical analyses routinely compute p-values, usually in two-tailed form.

a   For the following Minitab output, find the appropriate one-tailed p-value.

b   Verify the p-value computation using z tables.

c   Can the null hypothesis be rejected at $\alpha = .05$?

```
MTB > ZTest 150.0 20.0 'Data';
SUBC>   Alternative 1.
```

```
Z-Test

Test of mu = 150.00 vs mu > 150.00
The assumed sigma = 20.0

Variable    N     Mean    StDev   SE Mean      Z    P-Value
Data        25   156.48   22.55     4.00     1.62    0.053



MTB > ZTest 150.0 20.0 'Data';
SUBC>   Alternative 0.

Z-Test

Test of mu = 150.00 vs mu not = 150.00
The assumed sigma = 20.0

Variable    N     Mean    StDev   SE Mean      Z    P-Value
Data        25   156.48   22.55     4.00     1.62    0.11
```

Solution

a   The first part of the output indicates a "Test of mu = 150.00 vs mu > 150.00." This is a one-sided research hypothesis and should indicate a one-tailed *p*-value. The *p*-value is shown as .053.

b   The *z* statistic is shown as 1.62. From the normal tables, the area to the right of 1.62 is $.5000 - .4474 = .0526$.

c   Because the *p*-value is not less than .05, we cannot reject H_0 at $\alpha = .05$, although we can come close. Note also that the test statistic, $z = 1.62$, is not greater than the z table value for $\alpha = .05$—namely, 1.645—although it also is close. Thus, we barely retain the null hypothesis; there is not quite enough evidence to support the research hypothesis.   ■

The *p*-value is sometimes called the attained significance level of a statistical test. The results of a statistical test are often summarized by stating that the result is **statistically significant** at the specified *p*-value. In the changeover-time example, $z = -3.00$ is statistically significant at $p = .0013$. The smaller the *p*-value, the more conclusive the rejection of the null hypothesis.

statistically significant

The phrase "statistically significant" is unfortunate. The word *significant* suggests "important," "interesting," and "large." Statistical significance does not necessarily imply importance, relevance, or practical significance. Statistical significance only implies that a null hypothesis can be rejected with a specified low risk of error. A better phrase would be "statistically detectable." To say that a difference is statistically significant or statistically detectable is to say that the observed result cannot reasonably be attributed to random variation alone.

The *p*-value is an indication of the amount of evidence supporting a research hypothesis. It is not a measure of how large the apparent deviation is from the null hypothesis. A test statistic and therefore a *p*-value are affected by two factors: the amount of deviation from the null hypothesis value and the sample size. The *z* statistic can be rewritten as

$$z = \frac{\bar{y} - \mu_0}{\sigma}\sqrt{n}$$

The first part of this expression is the deviation of the sample mean from the H_0 value expressed as a fraction of the standard deviation. The second part is a function only of the sample size. A large deviation of $\bar{y}$ from the null hypothesis, together with a modest n, will produce a fairly large z statistic and therefore a fairly small p-value. But so will a modest deviation and a large n. In either case, there will be fairly conclusive evidence to support a research hypothesis. That is the only role for a p-value.

One should recognize that rarely is any null hypothesis exactly true. For this reason, with a large enough sample size, almost any null hypothesis can be rejected. What does this mean? If the null hypothesis is rejected, it means that a difference has been established fairly conclusively, but no judgment has been made as to the importance or practical significance of the apparent difference.

Conversely, a sample result with associated p-value $> .05$ (and considered by some to indicate "not statistically significant") could—but may not—have been the result of random fluctuation; that is, even though the p-value is greater than .05, there still may be an underlying effect. The problem is that we have not established it beyond a reasonable doubt. A large p-value does not necessarily mean that nothing is happening; it means that we don't have enough evidence to say that the apparent change is more than random. All in all, you should be careful not to read too much into statistical significance. The p-value gives the weight of the sample evidence for rejection of the null hypothesis. A manager must still judge the practical significance of observed results that are declared statistically significant.

EXERCISES

8.8 A sales manager believes that a firm's sales representatives should spend about 40% of their working days traveling. If they are on the road for much less, new orders decline and the service and news-gathering functions of the representatives are not adequately met. If they travel much more than 40% of the time, expense accounts eat up any incremental profit. A study of the previous 5 months (110 working days) shows the following data (number of traveling days by each representative):

$$32 \quad 36 \quad 41 \quad 45 \quad 48 \quad 48 \quad 51 \quad 54 \quad 57 \quad 64$$
$$(\bar{y} = 47.6, s = 9.65, n = 10)$$

Minitab computer output for these data is as follows (based on an assumed population standard deviation of 10.0):

```
MTB > ztest of mean = 44 assuming sigma = 10 data in 'Data'

TEST OF MU = 44.00 VS MU N.E. 44.00
The assumed sigma = 10.0

               N     MEAN    STDEV   SE MEAN      Z    P VALUE
Data          10    47.60     9.65      3.16   1.14      0.26
```

a Identify the value of the z statistic.   **b** Identify the p-value.

c Is a one-tailed or a two-tailed p-value more appropriate for this problem?

8.9 The sales manager of Exercise 8.8 concludes that the discrepancy between the observed average of 47.6 and the desired average of 44.0 is not statistically significant and therefore the study proves that the travel days situation is under control.

a Do you agree that the result is not statistically significant (at the usual α levels)?

b Do you agree that the study proves that the travel days situation is under control?

8.10 The battery pack of a hand calculator is supposed to perform 20,000 calculations before needing recharging. The quality-control manager for the manufacturer is concerned that the pack may not be working for as long as the specifications state. A test of 114 battery packs gives an average of 19,695 calculations and a standard deviation of 1103.

a Formulate null and research hypotheses.

b Calculate the appropriate test statistic and *p*-value.

8.11 Is the result in Exercise 8.10 statistically significant at the usual α levels? Would you call the result practically significant? ■

Hypothesis Testing with the t Distribution

N ow we get rid of the usually false assumption that a population standard deviation is known in hypothesis testing. The changes we make will be technical; the basic ideas of hypothesis testing aren't affected. We still hope to support a research hypothesis by rejecting the null hypothesis. H_0 is still rejected if the data are highly unlikely given that hypothesis and relatively more likely given the research hypothesis. The *p*-value still measures the degree of evidence supporting the research hypothesis.

The modifications of normal (z) procedures to get t distribution confidence intervals also apply to hypothesis tests. Once again, we replace σ by s and use t tables instead of z tables. In this section, we summarize the procedure and take care of some other small differences in mechanics.

The basic procedure for any hypothesis-testing method requires formulating null and research hypotheses (H_0 and H_a), choosing a test statistic (T.S.), defining a rejection region (R.R.), calculating the T.S. value, and finally stating a conclusion. Here we are concerned with testing hypotheses about a population mean; we are still making the formal mathematical assumption that the population distribution is exactly normal.

Definition 8.6 t **Test of Hypotheses About** μ

$$H_0: \mu = \mu_0$$

$$H_a: 1.\ \mu > \mu_0$$

$$2.\ \mu < \mu_0$$

$$3.\ \mu \neq \mu_0$$

T.S.: $t = \dfrac{\bar{y} - \mu_0}{s/\sqrt{n}}$

R.R.: For a given probability α of a Type I error, reject H_0 if

$$1.\ t > t_\alpha$$

$$2.\ t < -t_\alpha$$

$$3.\ |t| \geq t_{\alpha/2}$$

where t_α cuts off a right-tail area of α in a t distribution with $n - 1$ d.f.   ■

E X A M P L E   8 . 7

An airline institutes a "snake system" waiting line at its counters to try to reduce the average waiting time. The mean waiting time under specific conditions with the previous system was 6.1 minutes. A sample of 14 waiting lines is taken; the times are measured at widely separated times to eliminate the possibility of dependent observations. The resulting sample mean is 5.043 and the standard deviation is 2.266. Test the null hypothesis of no change against an appropriate research hypothesis using $\alpha = .10$. Assume that the population of waiting times is approximately normal.

Solution

The population parameter of interest is μ, the long-run mean waiting time under normal conditions using the snake system. The research hypothesis is that the mean is lower than the previous mean, 6.1, so H_a: $\mu < 6.1$. We may take the null hypothesis to be H_0: $\mu = 6.1$ (no change). As usual, we need worry only about the boundary value of the null hypothesis.

$$H_0: \mu = 6.1$$

$$H_a: \mu < 6.1$$

$$\text{T.S.: } t = \frac{5.043 - 6.1}{2.266/\sqrt{14}} = -1.75$$

R.R.: For $\alpha = .10$ and d.f. $= 13$, reject H_0 for $t < -1.350$.

Because the observed value of t, -1.75, is less than -1.350, we reject H_0 and conclude that the apparent reduction in mean waiting time (from 6.1 to about 5 minutes) is not merely a random, statistical fluke. ∎

Earlier in this chapter we introduced the p-value as an index of the degree of support for a research hypothesis from a given data set. There we were able to use z tables to compute p-values. Now we must use t tables, which are much less extensive; for given degrees of freedom, a t table gives only a few values. Most computer packages will compute exact p-values for a t test, so the problem is not too serious.

p-value for a t test

E X A M P L E   8 . 8

The data for Example 8.6 were used to test H_a: $\mu > 150$ under the assumption that σ was somehow known to be 20.0. The following Minitab output carries out a t test for this research hypothesis without assuming that σ is known. Locate the p-value. What does it indicate?

```
MTB > TTest 150.0 'Data';
SUBC>   Alternative 1.


T-Test of the Mean


Test of mu = 150.00 vs mu > 150.00


Variable    N    Mean    StDev    SE Mean      T    P-Value
Data       25  156.48    22.55     4.51     1.44     0.082
```

Solution

The output indicates that a one-sided research hypothesis is being used. The p-value is shown as .082. That indicates that the evidence in support of the research hypothesis is modest at best. The difference between the sample mean and the null hypothesis value could possibly have arisen by chance. ∎

With tables, we can get only approximate p-values. The key to the approximation is the fact that the p-value is the smallest α value that allows rejection of the null hypothesis. Remember the Universal Rejection Region: Reject the null hypothesis if and only if the p-value is less than α. If the null hypothesis can be rejected at a particular α level, the p-value must be less than that α. Therefore, we can often bracket the p-value between two numbers. All that is needed is to locate the actually observed t statistic between two t table values. The bounds on the p-value can be read directly.

E X A M P L E   8 . 9

Find the bounds on the p-value in Example 8.7.

Solution

In Example 8.7, we found that we could reject H_0 at $\alpha = .10$ because $t = -1.75$ was below $-t_{.10, 13 \text{ d.f.}} = -1.350$. Therefore, $p < .10$. When we try $\alpha = .05$, we find that we cannot quite reject H_0; the tabulated t value is $-t_{.05, 13 \text{ d.f.}} = -1.771$. Therefore, $p > .05$. We can summarize the approximate p-value as $.05 < p < .10$. ∎

E X A M P L E   8 . 1 0

An insurance adjuster in a small city uses two different garages to handle repairs to foreign cars damaged in collisions. To test whether the garages are competitive in cost, the adjuster obtains estimates from both garages for repair cost on each of 15 such cars. The data are shown in the table. Test the null hypothesis that the mean difference is zero against an appropriate research hypothesis. What can be said about a p-value?

Repair Estimates (in Hundreds of Dollars)

Car	1	2	3	4	5	6	7
Garage 1	7.6	10.2	9.5	1.3	3.0	6.3	5.3
Garage 2	7.3	9.1	8.4	1.5	2.7	5.8	4.9
Difference, d	.3	1.1	1.1	−.2	.3	.5	.4

Repair Estimates (in Hundreds of Dollars)

Car	8	9	10	11	12	13	14	15
Garage 1	6.2	2.2	4.8	11.3	12.1	6.9	7.6	8.4
Garage 2	5.3	2.0	4.2	11.0	11.0	6.1	6.7	7.5
Difference, d	.9	.2	.6	.3	1.1	.8	.9	.9

Solution

The null hypothesis is that the true mean difference $\mu_d = 0$. As no particular direction has been specified for the research hypothesis, take H_a: $\mu_d \neq 0$. We base the test on the differences (which are designated by d rather than y here). The test statistic is

$$t = \frac{\bar{d} - 0}{s_d / \sqrt{n}}$$

and is based on $n - 1 = 14$ d.f. Routine calculations give $\bar{d} = .613$ and $s_d = .394$, so

$$t = \frac{.613 - 0}{.394/\sqrt{15}} = 6.03$$

The largest tabled t value for 14 d.f. is 2.977, corresponding to a one-tailed area of .005. Thus, even for a (two-tailed) α of .01, H_0 could easily be rejected. The p-value must be less than .01; in fact, we suspect that the p-value is much smaller than .01. Formally, we conclude that the two garages have different average estimates. Practically, it is clear that garage 1 has higher average estimates than garage 2. ∎

Evaluation of β and power is a bit more difficult for t tests than for z tests. The method for calculating β stated in Section 8.2 is strictly valid only for z tests, but it can be used as an approximation for t tests. Because a t statistic is more variable than a z statistic, the formula tends to underestimate β and therefore to overestimate power. The easiest way to use the method is to specify a value for

$$\frac{\mu_a - \mu_0}{\sigma}$$

and a value for α. For example, suppose that a t test is run using $n = 25$ and $\alpha = .05$ (two-tailed) and that we hypothesize that the true population mean is .8 standard deviation above the null hypothesis mean:

$$\frac{\mu_a - \mu_0}{\sigma} = .8$$

Then,

$$\beta \approx P\left(z > -z_{\alpha/2} + \frac{|\mu_a - \mu_0|}{\sigma/\sqrt{n}}\right)$$

$$= P\left(z > -1.96 + \frac{.8}{1/\sqrt{25}}\right)$$

$$= P(z > 2.04) = .0207$$

It follows that power is approximately $1 - .0207 = .9793$ under these conditions. As we indicated, the calculation underestimates β and overestimates power. Thus, the power is not quite as good as the calculation indicates.

E X A M P L E   8 . 1 1

In a computer simulation, 1000 samples of size 30 are drawn from a normal population having mean 55 and standard deviation 10. The null hypothesis that the population mean is 50 is tested, based on each sample. For a test of H_a: $\mu > 50$, using $\alpha = .10$, the null hypothesis is rejected 919 times out of the 1000 samples. What probability is being approximated by the fraction 919/1000? How close is this approximation to the theoretical probability calculated by formula?

Solution

In this simulation, the null hypothesis is false; μ is 55, not 50. The fraction 919/1000 approximates the probability that the test will reject the null hypothesis when it is false; by definition, that probability is $1 - \beta$, the power of the test. We can calculate the theoretical β by formula. For a one-tailed test with $\alpha = .10$, the required table value is $z_{.10} = 1.28$: $\mu_0 = 50$, $\mu_a = 55$, $\sigma = 10$, and $n = 30$. Therefore

$$\beta = P\left(z > -1.28 + \frac{|55 - 50|}{10/\sqrt{30}}\right) = P(z > 1.46)$$

$$= .0721$$

So power $= 1 - .0721 = .9279$. The simulation value, .919, is quite close to the calculated power. ∎

E X E R C I S E S

8.12 A dealer in recycled paper places empty trailers at various sites; these are gradually filled by individuals who bring in old newspapers and the like. The trailers are picked up (and replaced by empties) on several schedules. One such schedule involves a pickup every second week. This schedule is desirable if the average amount of recycled paper is more than 1600 cubic feet per two-week period. The dealer's records for 18 two-week periods show the following volumes (in cubic feet) at a particular site:

1660	1820	1590	1440	1730	1680	1750	1720	1900
1570	1700	1900	1800	1770	2010	1580	1620	1690

$(\bar{y} = 1718.3, s = 137.8)$

Assume that these figures represent the results of a random sample. Do they support the research hypothesis that $\mu > 1600$ using $\alpha = .10$? Write out all parts of the hypothesis-testing procedure.

8.13 Place an upper bound on the p-value of Exercise 8.12. That is, state "p-value less than number." Would you say that $\mu > 1600$ is strongly supported?

8.14 A federal regulatory agency is investigating an advertised claim that a certain device can increase the gasoline mileage of cars. Seven such devices are purchased and installed in seven cars belonging to the agency. Gasoline mileage for each of the cars under standard conditions is recorded both before and after installation.

	Car						
	1	**2**	**3**	**4**	**5**	**6**	**7**
Mpg Before	19.1	19.9	17.6	20.2	23.5	26.8	21.7
Mpg After	20.0	23.7	18.7	22.3	23.8	19.2	24.6
Change	.9	3.8	1.1	2.1	.3	−7.6	2.9

The Stata package gave the following results:

```
. summarize

Variable |    Obs      Mean    Std. Dev.      Min       Max
---------+-----------------------------------------------------
  Before |      7   21.25714   3.080507      17.6      26.8
   After |      7   21.75714   2.42546       18.7      24.6
  Change |      7         .5   3.772267      -7.6       3.8

. ttest Change=0

Variable |    Obs      Mean    Std. Dev.
---------+-------------------------------
  Change |      7         .5   3.772267

        Ho:  mean = 0
                 t = 0.35 with 6 d.f.
           Pr > |t| = 0.7378

. ci Change, level(90)
```

```
Variable |   Obs   Mean   Std. Err.      [90% Conf. Interval]
---------+-----------------------------------------------------------------
  Change |    7    .5    1.425783       -2.270553    3.270553
```

a Formulate appropriate null and research hypotheses.

b Is the advertised claim supported at $\alpha = .05$? What is the two-tailed p-value? How could we find a one-tailed p-value?

8.15 Use the output of Exercise 8.14 to find a 90% confidence interval for the mean change. On the basis of this interval, can one reject the hypothesis of no mean change?

8.16 Would you say that the agency of Exercises 8.14 and 8.15 has conclusively established that the device has no effect on the average mileage of cars? What does the width of the interval in Exercise 8.15 have to do with your answer?

8.17 A small manufacturer has a choice between shipping via the postal service and shipping via a private shipper. As a test, 10 destinations are chosen and packages are shipped to each by both routes. The delivery times in days are as follows:

	Destination									
	1	**2**	**3**	**4**	**5**	**6**	**7**	**8**	**9**	**10**
Postal Service	3	4	5	4	8	9	7	10	9	9
Private Shipper	2	2	3	5	4	6	9	6	7	6
Difference	1	2	2	−1	4	3	−2	4	2	3

Stata output:

```
. ttest Postal=Private

Variable |    Obs     Mean    Std. Dev.
---------+------------------------------
  Postal |     10      6.8    2.573368
 Private |     10        5    2.260777
---------+------------------------------
   diff. |     10      1.8    1.988858

      Ho:  diff = 0  (paired data)
             t = 2.86 with 9 d.f.
        Pr > |t| = 0.0187
```

a Locate the mean and standard deviation of the differences.

b Test the null hypothesis of no mean difference in delivery times against the research hypothesis that the private shipper has a shorter average delivery time. Use $\alpha = .01$. Note that the p-value shown in the output is two-tailed. ∎

8.5

Assumptions for *t* Tests

Like any other statistical procedures, hypothesis tests rely on assumptions. The assumptions underlying t tests are exactly the same as those underlying t confidence intervals. In fact, in the next section we will show that hypothesis tests and confidence intervals are equivalent.

Hypothesis tests allow for random variation but not for bias. A bias in selecting the sample may cause either kind of error: false positive or false negative. It is always worth considering how the data were obtained to see if there are serious, evident biases.

In addition, the t test of a mean, and most other statistical tests, assume that the measurements in the sample are statistically independent. The most likely source of dependence arises in time-series data, where values of a variable are measured at successive times. If there are carryover effects from one time to the next, the values will be dependent. Just as in the confidence interval case, statistical dependence causes a change in the "effective n." Positive correlation of successive values means that the effective sample size is less than it appears. This fact makes the apparent result of the test too strong, too conclusive. The stated p-value will be less than it should be. When the data arise from a time series, it's always useful to plot the data in time order, looking for cycles and trends.

We discussed the effect of population nonnormality on t confidence intervals in Section 7.7. The same conclusions apply to t tests. If the underlying population is skewed and the sample size is fairly small, the claimed α and p-value probabilities may be in error. This is particularly a problem for one-tailed probabilities. If there is skewness, typically one tail is too large but the other is too small; when the probabilities are combined in a two-tailed test, the effect of skewness tends to cancel out. The nominal α value and p-value are reasonably accurate if the population is symmetric but heavy- or light-tailed relative to the normal distribution. In this case, a t test may be inefficient. Inefficiency, in hypothesis-testing terms, means that some other test—such as a median test—has better power at the same α level. We illustrate these effects of nonnormality with computer simulation studies.

EXAMPLE 8.12

A simulation study takes 1000 samples of size 30 from a Laplace population, a symmetric, moderately outlier-prone population. The population mean is 50 and the population standard deviation is 10. For $\alpha = .025$, the null hypothesis H_0: $\mu = 50$ is rejected in favor of H_a: $\mu > 50$ 28 times; similarly, for $\alpha = .025$, the null hypothesis H_0: $\mu = 50$ is rejected in favor of H_a: $\mu < 50$ 24 times.

Which hypothesis is true in the simulation? Does the outlier-proneness of the Laplace population have a serious effect?

Solution

Here H_0 is $\mu = 50$, and indeed the population mean is 50. The null hypothesis is true, so rejecting it constitutes a false positive (Type I) error. Therefore, fractions such as 28/1000 are approximating α, the probability of a Type I error; the fractions are approximations because they are based on 1000 samples, not an infinite number. The fractions 28/1000 and 24/1000 are very close to the nominal α value, .025. ∎

EXAMPLE 8.13

Another simulation study involves samples of size 30 from a Laplace population. In this study, the mean is 55, so H_0: $\mu = 50$ is false. A t test and also a sign test (a test for the median, which is also 55 by the symmetry of the Laplace population) were performed for each sample. Using $\alpha = .05$, H_a: $\mu > 50$ was supported in 831 of the samples and H_a: median > 50 was supported (by the sign test) in 905 of the samples. Which test appears to have better power?

Solution

Recall that power is the probability that the null hypothesis will be rejected, assuming that it is false. The sign test rejects the (false) null hypothesis more frequently than does the t test. Therefore, the sign test appears generally more powerful for this moderately outlier-prone population. ∎

Testing a Proportion: Normal Approximation

Thus far in this chapter, we have concentrated on testing hypotheses about means. We can equally well test hypotheses about proportions. Recall that defining successes to be 1s and failures to be 0s allows us to regard a proportion as a mean. In this section, we will sketch how such tests are done.

For example, suppose we wish to compare two versions of a product. We ask a panel of 100 customers (which we hope is an unbiased random sample of potential customers) to choose between a new version of the product and the existing version. We will adopt the new product only if there is clear evidence that more than half the customers prefer it. Thus, we take the null hypothesis as $H_0: \pi = .50$ and the research hypothesis as $H_a: \pi > .50$. Hence we want a one-tailed test. If n is large and π is not too close to 0 or 1, the z statistic for the standardized binomial random variable Y,

$$z = \frac{Y - n\pi}{\sqrt{n\pi(1 - \pi)}}$$

is approximately standard (tabled) normal. This z can be used as the test statistic instead of Y, the number of successes; the relevant value for π is the (boundary) null hypothesis value, $\pi_0 = .50$. As with a statistical test for μ, the one-tailed rejection region for $\alpha = .05$ is $z > 1.645$. In fact, 68 of the 100 panelists preferred the new version. The observed y value of 68 corresponds to a z score of 3.6:

$$z = \frac{y - n\pi_0}{\sqrt{n\pi_0(1 - \pi_0)}} = \frac{68 - 50}{\sqrt{100(.5)(.5)}} = 3.6$$

Hence, we reject $H_0: \pi = .05$ for $\alpha = .05$ (and in fact for $\alpha = .01$). The approximate procedure for testing a population proportion using a z statistic is summarized next.

Definition 8.7   Test of a Population Proportion, Normal Approximation

$H_0: \pi = \pi_0$

$H_a: 1. \pi > \pi_0$

$\quad\ 2. \pi < \pi_0$

$\quad\ 3. \pi \neq \pi_0$

T.S.: $z = \dfrac{y - n\pi_0}{\sqrt{n\pi_0(1 - \pi_0)}}$

R.R.: For the probability of a Type I error α, reject H_0 if

$\quad 1. z > z_\alpha$

$\quad 2. z < -z_\alpha$

$\quad 3. z > z_{\alpha/2} \quad$ or $\quad z < -z_{\alpha/2}$

Note: π_0 is the (boundary) null hypothesis value of the population proportion π. ■

There's another way to write the test statistic z. If $\hat{\pi}$ is the sample proportion (so $\hat{\pi} = Y/n$), then z can be written

$$z = \frac{\hat{\pi} - \pi_0}{\sqrt{\pi_0(1 - \pi_0)/n}}$$

For the product-comparison example, $\hat{\pi} = 68/100 = .68$ and again $z = 3.6$. The two forms of z are algebraically equal, so they always give the same answer.

Most computer packages do not include this test. However, by coding successes as 1s and failures as 0s, we can approximate this test. This trick works exactly if the package includes a z test. Specify σ as $\sqrt{(\pi_0)(1 - \pi_0)}$. If the package includes a one-sample t test, the result will be slightly different, but often close enough. For example, in the product-comparison example, we input as data 68 1s and 32 0s in a column labeled "Yes_No." We obtained the following Minitab results; note that we specified σ as $\sqrt{(\pi_0)(1 - \pi_0)} = \sqrt{(.5)(1 - .5)} = .5$:

```
MTB > ZTest .5 .5 'Yes_No';
SUBC>   Alternative 0.


Z-Test


Test of mu = 0.5000 vs mu not = 0.5000
The assumed sigma = 0.500


Variable     N     Mean    StDev   SE Mean      Z    P-Value
Yes_No     100   0.6800   0.4688   0.0500    3.60    0.0003


MTB > TTest 0.5 'Yes_No';
SUBC>   Alternative 0.


T-Test of the Mean


Test of mu = 0.5000 vs mu not = 0.5000


Variable     N     Mean    StDev   SE Mean      T    P-Value
Yes_No     100   0.6800   0.4688   0.0469    3.84    0.0002
```

The results of the ZTest procedure are exactly what we obtained by hand. The results of the TTest procedure are not quite the same, basically because that procedure used a sample standard deviation instead of $\sqrt{(\pi_0)(1 - \pi_0)}$. The conclusion is the same, however: The research hypothesis of a difference in preferences is strongly supported, with a very low p-value. Though the t test based on 1s and 0s is not exactly the same as the z test, usually the results are so similar that we needn't worry too much about the difference.

We said that the z test for π is approximate and works best if n is large and π_0 is not too near 0 or 1. A natural next question is: When can we use it? There are several rules to answer the question; none of them should be considered sacred. Our sense of the many studies that have been done is this: If either $n\pi_0$ or $n(1 - \pi_0)$ is less than about 2, treat the results of a z test very skeptically. If $n\pi_0$ and $n(1 - \pi_0)$ are at least 5, the z test should be reasonably accurate. For the same sample size, tests based on extreme values of π_0 (for example, .001) are less accurate than tests for values of π_0, such as .05 or .10. For example, a test of H_0: $\pi = .0001$ with $n\pi_0 = 1.2$ is much more suspect than one for H_0: $\pi = .10$ with $n\pi_0 = 50$. If the issue becomes crucial, it's best to interpret the results skeptically.

sample-size requirement

EXERCISES

8.18 A market research firm interviewed a large number of potential automobile buyers by phone. One of the several questions asked was whether the customer would prefer a passenger side airbag or a $300 discount on the price of the car. In the following Minitab output, the variable PrefBag is 1 for customers indicating a preference for the airbag, 0 for customers indicating a preference for the discount:

```
MTB > ZTest .50 .50 'PrefBag'

Z-Test

Test of mu = 0.5000 vs mu not = 0.5000
The assumed sigma = 0.500

Variable     N      Mean    StDev   SE Mean      Z    P-Value
PrefBag    1586    0.5340   0.4990   0.0126    2.71    0.0068

MTB > TTest .50 'PrefBag'

T-Test of the Mean

Test of mu = 0.5000 vs mu not = 0.5000

Variable     N      Mean    StDev   SE Mean      T    P-Value
PrefBag    1586    0.5340   0.4990   0.0125    2.72    0.0067
```

a Formulate the null hypothesis that customers are equally divided in preferring the airbag or the discount.

b Before taking such a survey, would you use a one-sided or two-sided research hypothesis? Which was used in the output?

c Is there a statistically significant difference in preference in the data, using $\alpha = .01$?

8.19 Can the market researcher claim there is a dramatic preference for airbags because the p-value is so low in Exercise 8.18?

8.20 In Exercise 8.18, should the normal approximation used to compute the p-value be reasonably accurate?

8.21 A team of builders has surveyed buyers of their new homes for years. Consistently, only 41% of the buyers have indicated they were "quite satisfied" or "very satisfied" with the construction quality of their homes. The builders have adopted a revised quality inspection system to try to improve customer satisfaction. They have surveyed 104 buyers since then; these buyers seem representative, with no systematic changes from past purchasers. Of the 104 buyers, 51 indicated they were quite or very satisfied.

a Formulate the null hypothesis that there has been no real change in customer satisfaction from the past rate.

b Before taking such a survey, would you use a one-sided or two-sided research hypothesis?

c Calculate a z statistic for testing the null hypothesis.

d Show that the null hypothesis cannot be rejected, using $\alpha = .05$.

8.22 Can the builders in Exercise 8.21 interpret the results as showing that the new inspection system has proven *not* to increase satisfaction?

8.23 In Exercise 8.21, is the normal approximation reasonably accurate?

8.24 A bakery produces bread for specialty stores. It wants to provide enough bread to meet the demand, but not so much that it has lots of unsold bread. Balancing the costs of lost sales and unsold bread, the bakery wants 10% of stores to be sold out each day. The bakery's delivery people reported on one particular day that 27 of 137 stores were sold out. Coding the sold-out stores as 1 and the others as 0, the bakery owner obtained the following Statistix output:

```
DESCRIPTIVE STATISTICS

VARIABLE       N    LO 95% CI     MEAN   UP 95% CI       SD
SOLDOUT      137    0.1296      0.1970    0.2645      0.3992
```

a Is there a statistically detectable deviation from the desired 10% sold-out rate? Use $\alpha = .05$.

b Find a two-tailed p-value.

8.25 The delivery people reported that several stores in one area had had unusually high demand because of a rumor of heavy snow. Show that this fact violates an assumption underlying the test. ■

8.7 Hypothesis Tests and Confidence Intervals

We now have two forms of inference: confidence intervals and hypothesis tests. Both can be performed on the same data. How are they related? For the changeover-time example we used in previous sections, a 95% confidence interval for the true mean time is $\bar{y} \pm 1.96\sigma_{\bar{Y}}$; the sample mean was $\bar{y} = 14.4$, with $\sigma = 2.40$ and $n = 16$. Substituting $\bar{y} = 14.4$, $n = 16$, and $\sigma = 2.40$, we have

$$14.4 - 1.96\frac{(2.40)}{\sqrt{16}} \leq \mu \leq 14.4 + 1.96\frac{(2.40)}{\sqrt{16}} \quad \text{or} \quad 13.22 \leq \mu \leq 15.58$$

In our statistical test of H_0: $\mu < 16.2$, the boundary value $\mu_0 = 16.2$ does not fall within the 95% confidence interval, so it seems plausible to reject H_0. The probability of a Type I error for a statistical test based on a 95% confidence interval is just $\alpha = .05$.

Definition 8.8   Use of Confidence Interval for Testing

In general, a particular null hypothesis value—say, θ_0—of any population parameter θ may be rejected with the probability of a Type I error α if and only if θ_0 does not fall in a $(1 - \alpha) \times 100\%$ confidence interval for θ.   ■

For example, because the 95% confidence interval $13.22 \leq \mu \leq 15.58$ does not include $\mu_0 = 16.2$, we can reject H_0: $\mu = 16.2$, based on $\alpha = .05$. In fact, this is a general method for constructing confidence intervals; a 95% confidence interval can be defined as the set of nonrejectable ($\alpha = .05$) null hypothesis values. In a two-tailed test, a particular μ value is not rejected using $\alpha = .05$ if the z statistic lies in the interval

$$-1.96 \leq \frac{\bar{y} - \mu}{\sigma/\sqrt{n}} \leq 1.96$$

A little algebra shows that this is equivalent to

$$\bar{y} - 1.96\frac{\sigma}{\sqrt{n}} \leq \mu \leq \bar{y} + 1.96\frac{\sigma}{\sqrt{n}}$$

which is the 95% confidence interval for μ. In this sense, confidence intervals and hypothesis tests give equivalent results.

The usual confidence interval is two-sided. As in the preceding, such confidence intervals correspond to two-tailed tests. There is such a thing as a one-sided confidence interval. The nonrejection region for a left-tailed test at $\alpha = .05$ is

$$\frac{\bar{y} - \mu}{\sigma/\sqrt{n}} \geq 1.645$$

When solved for μ, this is

$$\mu \leq \bar{y} + 1.645\frac{\sigma}{\sqrt{n}}$$

one-sided confidence interval

which is a **one-sided confidence interval**. In the changeover-time example, this becomes $\mu \leq 15.39$; because the boundary value $\mu_0 = 16.2$ does not fall within this interval, H_0: $\mu = 16.2$ may be rejected using $\alpha = .05$, one-tailed. For the remainder of this text, we use two-sided confidence intervals, which can be used to test two-sided research hypotheses.

EXAMPLE 8.14

For the television-watching data of Example 8.1, use a 99% confidence interval to test H_0: $\mu = 22.6$ versus H_a: $\mu \neq 22.6$ at $\alpha = .01$. Recall that the sample mean was 25.2 and the population standard deviation was assumed to be 6.1. The sample size is 60.

Solution

The two-sided research hypothesis implies that a two-sided confidence interval may be used to test the null hypothesis. In Example 8.1, $\bar{y} = 25.2$, σ is assumed to be 6.1, and $n = 50$. The 99% confidence interval is

$$25.2 - 2.576\frac{6.1}{\sqrt{60}} \leq \mu \leq 25.2 + 2.576\frac{6.1}{\sqrt{60}} \quad \text{or} \quad 23.2 \leq \mu \leq 27.2$$

Because the value of μ under H_0, 22.6, does not fall within the interval, we reject H_0 using $\alpha = .01$. Of course, the same conclusion was obtained in Example 8.1. ■

confidence interval and β

When the null hypothesis is not rejected, confidence intervals are useful in giving a crude measure of the risk of a Type II error. Roughly speaking, a wide 95% confidence interval indicates a high degree of uncertainty and therefore a high probability β of a Type II error. (Of course, 95% confidence fixes α at .05.) For example, if a seller of high-intensity lights for portable television cameras claims a mean life of 40 hours and a sample of 10 lights yields a 95% confidence interval of $28.0 \leq \mu \leq 44.0$, the seller's claim cannot be rejected using an $\alpha = .05$ level. Note, too, that the interval is very wide; the lower limit of 28.0 is 30% below the claimed value. If the difference between a mean life of 40 hours and, say, a mean life of 30 hours was crucial in deciding whether to buy, the buyer would not be comfortable in accepting $\mu = 40$. The probability of a Type II error corresponding to $\mu = 30$ would undoubtedly be quite large.

The equivalence of hypothesis tests and confidence intervals works for any sort of statistical test. Whether we're doing a z test of a mean, a z test of a proportion, a t test of a mean, or any of the other procedures we will discuss in later chapters, we can reject a null hypothesis at a specified α (and have a p-value $< \alpha$) if and only if a $100(1 - \alpha)\%$ confidence interval does not include the H_0 value. The five-step formal test method, the p-value method, and the confidence interval method are equivalent.

EXERCISES

8.26 In Chapter 2, we considered claims (in thousands of dollars) for automobile collision damage from a particular insurance company. A boxplot of data is shown in Figure 8.8. Data analysis using the Statistix package follows:

```
DESCRIPTIVE STATISTICS

VARIABLE        N    LO 95% CI    MEAN    UP 95% CI    SD
CLAIMSIZE      187     4.4152    5.1775    5.9398    5.2838
```

a The company's national mean claim size is 4.62 thousand dollars. The data come from a particular midwestern city. Does the confidence interval for the mean indicate that the city's mean claim size might be the same?

b One claims department staff member said that the deviation from 4.62 was not statistically significant, so the company could safely assume that the mean for this city was also 4.62. Is this a valid interpretation of the results?

8.27 The boxplot of claims in Figure 8.8 shows some skewness. Does that mean that the claimed probabilities for the test of the mean are wrong?

FIGURE 8.8   **Boxplot of Collision Claims Data**

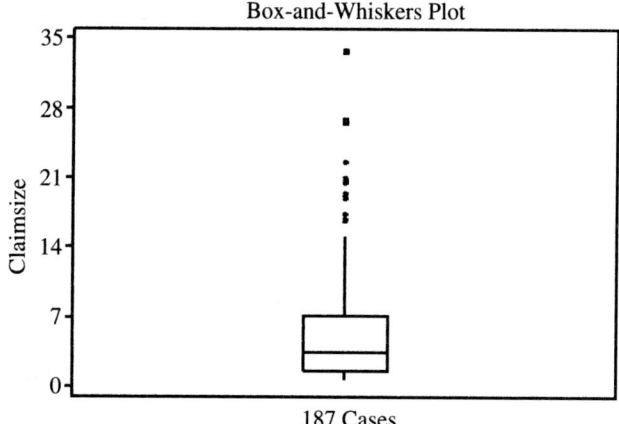

Box-and-Whiskers Plot

187 Cases

8.28   In Exercise 8.5, we tested the null hypothesis that the long-run mean number of public service commercials was 1.50. The test was based on a sample of 18 observations with a sample mean of 1.278; the assumed population standard deviation was 1.60. The null hypothesis was retained, using $\alpha = .05$.

    a   Calculate a 95% confidence interval for the population (long-run) mean. Because we're assuming that σ is known, use the z table.

    b   Show that this confidence interval is consistent with the conclusion of Exercise 8.5.

8.29   The null hypothesis in Exercise 8.8 that the mean number of travel days of a population of sales representatives was 44 was barely retained using $\alpha = .20$. The sample mean was 47.6, the sample size was 10, and the assumed σ was 10.0.

    a   Calculate an 80% confidence interval for the population mean; the required z_{10} value is 1.28.

    b   How does this confidence interval indicate that the null hypothesis must be retained?

    c   How does it indicate that H_0 is barely retained?

8.30   In Exercise 8.10, we tested a claim that the mean life of a battery for a calculator was 20,000 calculations. In a sample of 114 batteries, the mean was 19,695 and the standard deviation was 1103.

    a   Calculate a 99% confidence interval for the population mean lifetime.

    b   Show that the null hypothesis that the mean is 20,000 must be rejected at $\alpha = .01$.

    c   Would it be reasonable to say that, because H_0 is rejected so emphatically, the mean lifetime must be much lower than 20,000?

8.31   The main access road to a suburban shopping mall sometimes becomes severely congested. On weekdays, excluding holidays, the average number of vehicles that pass a counter going toward the mall between 9 A.M. and 7 P.M. is 11,260. The highway department tried to improve traffic flow by changing stoplight cycles and improving turn lanes. For the first five nonholiday weekdays after the changes, the volumes were 10,690, 11,452, 12,316, 12,297, and 12,647. The mean for this sample is 11,880.4 and the standard deviation is 798.68.

    a   Calculate a 95% confidence interval for the long-run (population) mean.

    b   Show that the null hypothesis that the mean is still 11,260 must be retained at $\alpha = .05$.

8.32   A local politician who reviewed the results of Exercise 8.31 said that the data proved there had been no improvement in traffic volume. Is this a reasonable interpretation of the confidence interval?

8.33   The data for Exercise 8.31 are listed in time order. Is there any suggestion of dependence or a trend over time?

8.34 Most lenders to individuals use some form of credit-scoring system to evaluate applicants for loans. One lender used such a system on a supposedly random sample of applicants drawn from a new direct-mail source. JMP output is shown in Figure 8.9. The lender regards any direct-mail source as desirable if the mean credit score is 82 (or perhaps even higher). What does the output (taken at face value, without regard to any criticisms of the study) indicate about the goal for this source?

FIGURE 8.9 **Output for Credit-Scoring Data**

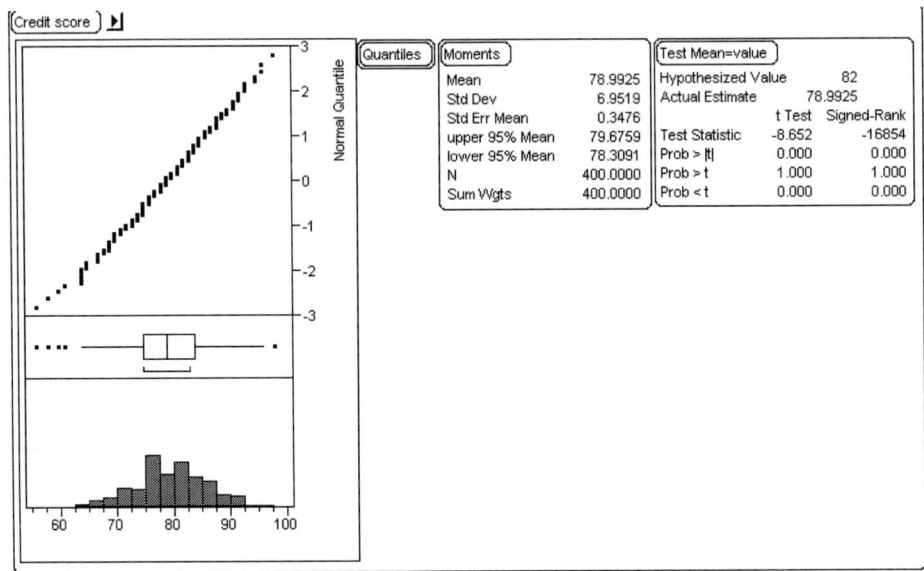

8.35 The manager who selected the sample said he had discarded obvious low and high scorers and replaced them with scorers nearer the average. What is the consequence of this action, as compared to truly random sampling?

8.36 A clothing manufacturer cuts fabric from bolts. In the process, a certain amount of cloth is wasted. Using standard methods, the wastage is 9.26%. The maker of a computer-controlled machine allowed the manufacturer to test the machine on a sample of 762 different cuts. In the sample, the mean wastage was 9.11% and the standard deviation was 1.07%.

    a Calculate a 99% confidence interval for the mean wastage using the computer-controlled machine.

    b Show that there has been a statistically detectable (significant) change in the mean, using $\alpha = .01$.

8.37 In Exercise 8.36, can the maker of the machine legitimately say that statistics show the machine makes a large improvement in wastage?

8.38 The data underlying Exercise 8.36 were skewed by a few cases with large wastage numbers. Does this fact invalidate the confidence interval and test in Exercise 8.36? ■

8.8

Summing Up

H ere are some suggestions for understanding statistical hypothesis-testing methods.

1 Any hypothesis test has a limited, though useful, purpose: to assess whether a deviation of a sample result from a theoretical population or process value might possibly have occurred by chance, merely by sampling variation.

2 The result of a hypothesis test can't tell you directly whether the deviation is large or small. The test is affected not only by the size of the deviation but also by the sample size.

3 A *p*-value is a convenient way to summarize a test, especially because it is so often reported by computer packages. A *p*-value is an index of how conclusive the evidence is of a real, more than random, deviation from the hypothetical value. Again, it is not a direct indication of how large that deviation is.

4 A confidence interval can indicate not only whether a deviation is statistically detectable (significant) but also how large the deviation might reasonably be. A confidence interval is often easier to interpret correctly than a hypothesis test.

5 The choice of test method is similar to the choice of an estimation method. Tests based on means are most effective when the underlying population or process generates approximately normally distributed data. Other methods are more powerful (have a higher probability of detecting a real change) for serious skewed or outlier-prone populations.

6 A result that is not statistically significant does *not* prove that the difference is 0. Such a result only says that the discrepancy *might* have occurred by chance. If the power of the test is low or the associated confidence interval is very wide, a nonsignificant result means very little.

In addition, you may want to reread the summary of key ideas at the beginning of the chapter.

EXAMPLE 8.15

Transportation companies are often involved in intermodal operations. Intermodal refers to freight that travels by rail in combination with some other form of transportation, instead of the traditional rail siding to rail siding mode. Units may be trucked by the shipper to the railroad terminal or loaded from a seafaring steamship. After the rail trip, the units are picked up from the rail destination or loaded onto a ship. A continuing concern of intermodal shippers has been delay in customer pickup. Customers often leave the shipment at the terminal and take advantage of storage space. This causes congestion at the facility as well as administrative overhead. Transportation companies usually charge customers for the storage time, but the bills are often disputed or ignored, and are therefore ineffective.

One particular transportation company recently implemented a new collection process in hopes of decreasing "dwell time." Dwell time is the amount of time the unit "dwells" (stays) and takes up space at the destination terminal while awaiting customer pickup. Under the old collection process, the population mean dwell time was 96 hours. After implementation of the new process, dwell time was tracked for all units that were grounded (unloaded from a rail car) during a specific, otherwise typical, one-week period. Data, regarded as a sample from the ongoing process, are analyzed in the JMP IN output shown in Figure 8.10.

Company managers want to know what the data indicate about whether there has been a decrease in average dwell time, and if so, by how much.

Solution

As always, we begin by examining plots of the data. The normal plot shows some curvature (along with some "wiggles"), indicating skewness. The skewness is confirmed by the boxplot, which also shows one modest outlier. Given a sample size of 141, the Central Limit Theorem effect should make the stated probabilities quite close to correct.

FIGURE 8.10   Ouput for Dwell Time Data

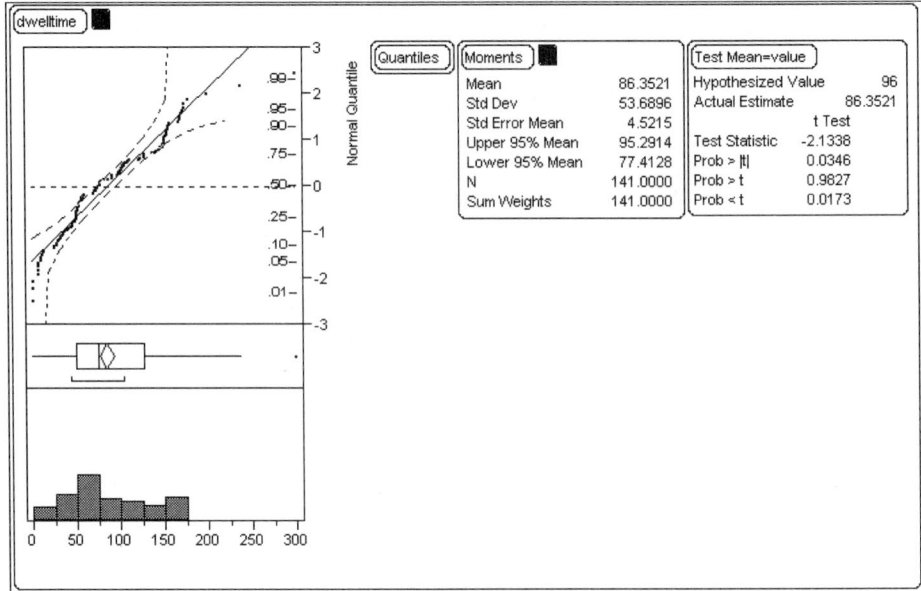

The "Test Mean=value" portion of the output carries out a *t* test. Because the managers are asking about a *decrease* in mean dwell time, we can report a one-tailed *p*-value, shown as 0.0173. Therefore, we have reasonably strong evidence that there has been at least some decrease in mean dwell time from 96 hours.

To assess how much the mean has decreased, we can use the 95% confidence interval shown in the output. It indicates that $77.4 \leq \mu \leq 95.3$. Therefore we can say that the mean may have decreased by as much as $96 - 77.4 = 18.6$ hours or by as little as $96 - 95.3 = 0.7$ hour. We would need more data to get a more accurate indication of how much the mean has decreased.   ■

SUPPLEMENTARY EXERCISES

8.39   EPA miles per gallon ratings are obtained for all models of cars sold in the United States. One of these figures purports to represent mileage in combined city–country driving. Suppose a consumer group test-drives 8 cars of a model with an EPA rating of 28.2 miles per gallon. If H_0 is $\mu = 28.2$, what argument would lead to a one-sided research hypothesis?

8.40   In Exercise 8.39, assume that the population standard deviation is 2.1 and the mean gas mileage for the 8 cars is 26.7. Can a two-sided research hypothesis be supported at $\alpha = .01$?

8.41   Find the *p*-value in Exercise 8.40.

8.42   An official of the consumer group interprets the result of Exercise 8.40 as being not statistically significant. The official concludes that it can reliably be assumed that the true mean is 28.2. Do you agree?

8.43   Compute a 99% confidence interval for the true mean mileage in Exercise 8.40. Use this interval to confirm the result of that exercise. What can we "reliably assume" about the true mean mileage?

8.44   In a nationwide opinion poll based on a random sample of 2417 people, one question is: "How do you rate the ethics of business executives of large companies?" A rating of 3 means "no better or worse than most people," a rating of 1 is "much better than most people," and 5 is "much worse than most people." The mean rating is 3.05 and the standard deviation is 0.62.

a   Calculate a 95% confidence interval for the population mean rating.

b Can H_0: $\mu = 3.00$ be rejected (against a two-sided alternative) at $\alpha = .05$?

8.45 A newspaper reporting on the poll of Exercise 8.44 reports that "respondents rated the ethics of big business significantly worse than average."

    a Is this statement true in the statistical sense?

    b Do you think it might mislead the general public?

8.46 What can be said about the *p*-value of Exercise 8.44?

8.47 In an exercise in the previous chapter, a police department obtained data on response times to nonemergency crime calls. The data and Minitab output are reproduced here:

```
resptime
  24   25   18   25   15   11   11   19   36   29   13   21   12
  12   26   16   19   12   21   12   12   18   11   19   16   24
  14   23   17
```

```
MTB > describe 'resptime'

                 N    MEAN   MEDIAN   TRMEAN   STDEV   SEMEAN
resptime        29   18.31    18.00    17.93    6.29     1.17

               MIN     MAX      Q1       Q3
resptime     11.00   36.00   12.00    23.50

MTB > ztest of mean 20 with sigma = 6 for 'resptime';
SUBC> alternative -1.

TEST OF MU = 20.00 VS MU L.T. 20.00
The assumed sigma = 6.00

                 N    MEAN   STDEV   SE MEAN       Z   P VALUE
resptime        29   18.31    6.29      1.11   -1.52     0.065
```

    a The department wants to have conclusive evidence that the mean is less than 20 minutes. Formulate this goal as a research hypothesis. What is the corresponding null hypothesis?

    b Assume that the distribution of response times is roughly normal and that the true (population or process) standard deviation is 6.0 minutes. What is the appropriate test statistic?

    c Write out the five parts of a formal hypothesis test using $\alpha = .05$. The preceding Minitab output may be helpful; the command "alternative -1" produces a test of the research hypothesis that the mean is less than the H_0 mean.

8.48 What is the *p*-value for the data in Exercise 8.47?

8.49 The data in Exercise 8.47 were plotted as a stem-and-leaf display. Is there a clear indication of a nonnormal distribution? If so, does this completely invalidate your answers in Exercise 8.47?

```
MTB > stem-and-leaf of 'resptime'

Stem-and-leaf of resptime   N = 29
Leaf Unit = 1.0

     3     1 111
     9     1 222223
    11     1 45
    14     1 667
    (5)    1 88999
    10     2 11
     8     2 3
     7     2 4455
     3     2 6
     2     2 9
     1     3
     1     3
     1     3
     1     3 6
```

8.50 In Exercise 8.47, we assumed a population standard deviation of 6.0 minutes. Test the research hypothesis that the population mean is less than 20 minutes, using $\alpha = .05$, without making this assumption. The following Minitab output may be of use:

```
MTB > ttest of mean 20 for 'resptime';
SUBC> alternative -1.

TEST OF MU = 20.00 VS MU L.T. 20.00

               N     MEAN   STDEV  SE MEAN      T   P VALUE
resptime      29    18.31    6.29    1.17    -1.45    0.080
```

8.51 In Exercise 7.63 in the previous chapter, a fish hatchery was concerned that the (population) mean weight of released fish might differ from 10.0 ounces. Differences in either direction were undesirable. The data are reproduced here:

9.3	11.7	11.0	9.8	10.1	8.9	8.7	9.5	10.8	8.7	7.6
10.0	8.8	9.3	9.2	8.1	9.9	9.4	8.3	10.3	9.8	9.5
9.8	9.0	10.7	9.3	9.6	10.4	9.4	9.8	9.8	9.2	11.0
10.2	9.1	11.0	9.4	9.7	12.1	9.8	7.1	8.3	10.3	10.6
10.1	10.2	8.8	9.3	10.3	10.7	10.8	7.5	9.0	10.1	9.2
9.7	10.4	9.1	9.7	10.7	10.6					

(mean = 9.6803, standard deviation = 0.95983)

a Formulate a research hypothesis and a null hypothesis.

b Assume that the population standard deviation is 1.0 ounce. Write a test statistic.

c Carry out the five parts of a statistical test with $\alpha = .10$. State the conclusion carefully.

8.52 State a p-value for Exercise 8.51. Should it be one-tailed or two-tailed?

8.53 In the previous chapter, we obtained the following Statistix output from a sample of 61 fish. Use these results to test the research hypothesis that the population mean weight is not equal to 10.0 ounces. Make no assumption about the population standard deviation.

```
DESCRIPTIVE STATISTICS

VARIABLE      N   LO 90% CI    MEAN   UP 90% CI      SD
WEIGHTS      61     9.4750   9.6803    9.8856    0.9598
```

8.54 What can be said about a two-tailed p-value in Exercise 8.53?

8.55 A consulting firm often submits health care management proposals for projects in competition with one particular firm of very similar capabilities. A relatively new vice president in charge of the health care division has submitted 16 proposals against the competitor. The firm has won contracts in only 5 of these cases, with the competitor winning the other 11. The president of the firm, noting this fact, concludes that the data prove that the vice president can't win half the time against the competitor.

a Formulate the null hypothesis that the firm will win half the time in the long run.

b Show that the research hypothesis that the firm will win less than half the time can't be supported at $\alpha = .05$.

c Does this fact prove that the firm will, in fact, win half the time?

8.56 In Exercise 8.55, will a normal approximation be reasonably accurate?

8.57 As cable television availability has increased, broadcast television networks and advertisers have become increasingly concerned with the amount of time that their target audiences spend watching conventional, broadcast television. A sampling of one particular target group recorded the hours of conventional TV watched in one week to the nearest half hour. A Minitab stem-and-leaf display is as follows:

```
MTB > stem-and-leaf of 'hrswatch'

Stem-and-leaf of hrswatch   N  = 44
Leaf Unit = 1.0
```

```
    2    2 23
    5    2 555
   15    2 6677777777
  (18)   2 888888888889999999
   11    3 000
    8    3 3
    7    3 4444
    3    3
    3    3 9
    2    4
    2    4 2
    1    4 4
```

Is it fair to say that the data appear close to normally distributed?

8.58 A normal probability plot of the data of Exercise 8.57 is shown in Figure 8.11. (Note that the data are on the horizonal axis and the theoretical, normal distribution scores are on the vertical axis, which is the reverse of some other normal plots shown in this text.) Would you judge that the data fell close to the indicated straight line? If not, what sort of nonnormality seems to be present?

F I G U R E 8 . 1 1   **Normal Plot for Hours Watched Data**

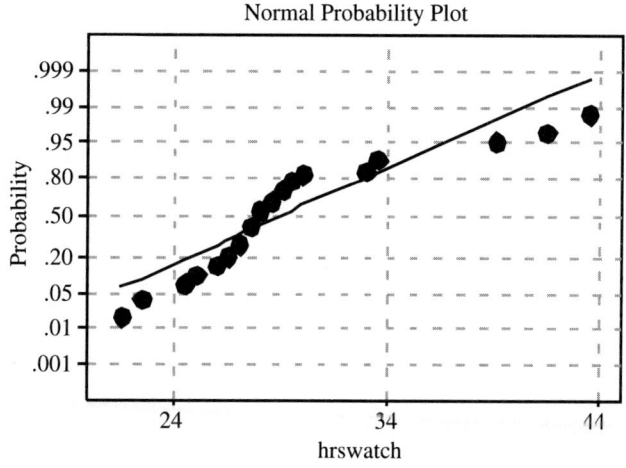

Average: 28.8977
Std Dev: 4.29518
N of data: 44

Anderson-Darling Normality Test
A-Squared: 2.987
p-value: 0.000

8.59 For the target population of Exercise 8.57, the mean (and median) hours watched was 30.4, according to a very extensive survey made 2 years previously. The data of Exercise 8.57 were analyzed by the Minitab package, with the following results:

```
MTB > tinterval 90% for 'hrswatch'

            N    MEAN   STDEV  SE MEAN   90.0 PERCENT C.I.
hrswatch   44  28.898   4.295   0.648   ( 27.809,  29.987)
```

a According to the confidence interval for the mean, is there conclusive evidence that the mean hours watched has changed since the previous survey?

b The plots of Exercises 8.57 and 8.58 indicate that the data are not normally distributed. Does this fact mean that the claimed confidence of the interval for the mean is seriously incorrect?

8.60 The Minitab output from Exercise 8.59 also included the result of a formal hypothesis test, as follows:

```
MTB > ttest of mean 30.4 for 'hrswatch'
TEST OF MU = 30.400 VS MU N.E. 30.400
```

	N	MEAN	STDEV	SE MEAN	T	P VALUE
hrswatch	44	28.898	4.295	0.648	-2.32	0.025

a According to the computed t statistic, can the null hypothesis be rejected using $\alpha = .10$ and a two-tailed test? The output indicated 43 d.f.

b Is your answer consistent with the answer to part a of Exercise 8.59?

c How is the p-value shown in the output? Does this p-value indicate that the null hypothesis should be rejected using $\alpha = .10$?

8.61 A mortgage service company processes a large volume of transactions every day. Because many of the transactions involve depositing funds, it's important for the company to complete processing and not leave unprocessed items for the following day. The operations manager has a target that processing will be complete in 96% of all workdays. Records for the last 212 days have been kept. In the following Minitab output, an AllDone value of 1 indicates complete processing and a 0 indicates that unprocessed items were left for the next day. Does the output indicate there has been a statistically significant departure from the 96% target, using reasonable α levels?

```
MTB > TTest .96 'AllDone'

Test of mu = 0.9600 vs mu not = 0.9600
```

Variable	N	Mean	StDev	SE Mean	T	P-Value
AllDone	212	0.9151	0.2794	0.0192	-2.34	0.020

8.62 Examination of the data in Exercise 8.61 shows that the incomplete-processing days occurred in "streaks." On one occasion, there was incomplete processing for 8 consecutive days; on others, 4 consecutive days. This fact suggests that one of the assumptions underlying hypothesis tests was violated. Which one? What is the consequence of the violation?

8.63 A package delivery service adopted a new dispatching system to try to reduce the total mileage required by its truck fleet to make deliveries. The new system would be worth the cost if it reduced the fleet mileage by more than 5% from its current level of 2420 miles per day (that is, if it decreased it to less than 2299 miles per day). The miles required for each of 49 days under a trial of the new system are recorded in column 1 of the EX0863.DAT file on the data disk; day number is recorded in column 2. Load the data into a computer package.

a Obtain the mean and standard deviation of the miles data.

b Using the computer package, if possible, test the research hypothesis that the long-run mean will be less than 2299. Obtain a p-value. (*Note:* Many packages will test a null hypothesis that a mean is 0. To convert the problem to that form, subtract 2299 from each observation.)

8.64 **a** Obtain a stem-and-leaf display of the miles data from Exercise 8.63. Is there reason to think there is a problem of nonnormality?

b The data are a time series. Obtain a plot of miles against day number. Is there evidence of a trend? Of cycles, indicating day-to-day dependence in the data?

8.65 An inexpensive restaurant featuring steak dinners makes most of its profits from side orders suggested to diners by the staff. As an experiment, the restaurant owner rewarded each server with 10% of the price of all side orders made through that server. After 10 days, the owner computed the side order volume per customer for each of 41 servers. The data are stored in column 1 of the EX0865.DAT file on the data disk; server number is stored in column 2. Load the data into a computer package.

a Obtain the mean and standard deviation of the volume data.

b The reward policy will be profitable if the mean volume is more than $2.40 per customer. Is there strong evidence in the data that the policy will, in fact, be profitable?

8.66   **a** Obtain a boxplot of the volume data of Exercise 8.65. Are there any outliers?

      b Obtain a normal plot of the data. What nonnormality, if any, appears to be present?

8.67   The human resources director for a large corporation tested an incentive policy to try to reduce the number of personal leave days taken by employees. A sample of 50 employees (out of several hundred in the company) was offered bonuses if the average number of leave days taken could be reduced from the current level of 5.7 per employee per year. After a year, the number of leave days was computed for each employee. The data are stored in column 1 of the EX0867.DAT file on the data disk. Employee ID number is in column 2. Load the data into whatever statistical computer package you can use.

      a Obtain the mean, median, and standard deviation of the leave-days data. What does this information suggest about the skewness of the data?

      b Get a stem-and-leaf display or histogram of the data. Does the plot confirm your impression about the skewness in the data?

8.68   **a** For Exercise 8.67, have the computer package test the null hypothesis that the mean leave days is still 5.7. You may have to subtract 5.7 from all the data to be able to test the hypothesis that the mean is 0.

      b Obtain a p-value for the test. Is it one-sided or two-sided in the computer output? Do you think a one-sided test or a two-sided test is more appropriated in this situation?

8.69   Builders of custom single homes must estimate construction costs (not including land costs) from plans provided by the customer, a designer, or an architect. The estimate is the basis of the builder's bid. If the estimate is too high, the customer is likely to find another builder. If it's too low, the builder has to pay for the extra cost out of pocket. The estimating process that the builder has used is extremely time-consuming, requiring many hours and much consulting of manuals.

      The builders hoped to use a simplified system in order to spend more time building and less time estimating. To test the simpler system, they estimated the cost of 10 "spec" houses. These are houses built without a particular customer having a contract and sold after they are finished. The builders recorded the estimates from the simplified system and the actual cost once each house was completed.

      The builders ask you to explain the results shown in the following computer output. They write: "We don't understand the analysis here. Our accountant calculated the ratio of the actual cost to the estimated cost. If the estimate was right on target, the ratio would be 1.00, of course. The accountant says that the p-value proves that the average ratio really is 1.00. But that doesn't seem right. Most of the estimates were too low, and some of them were off by quite a bit. It seems to us that the system didn't work well at all. What's going on?"

      Write them a brief, not too technical note, explaining what the results do (and don't) say.

```
MTB > print 'Estimate' 'Actual' 'Ratio'

ROW  Estimate  Actual    Ratio

 1    150500   151929   1.00950
 2    186200   152134   0.81705
 3    178300   215200   1.20695
 4    215200   238845   1.10987
 5    187000   194183   1.03841
 6    164500   176432   1.07253
 7    210000   236050   1.12405
 8    175000   184571   1.05469
 9    180200   190295   1.05602
10    169900   179289   1.05526

MTB > ttest of value 1.00 for 'Ratio'

TEST OF MU = 1.0000 VS MU N.E. 1.0000

               N     MEAN    STDEV   SE MEAN     T    P VALUE
Ratio         10    1.0544   0.1001  0.0316    1.72    0.12
```

Hypothesis Testing

A manufacturer of heavy-duty leaf springs for trucks begins by making basic castings. The most important factor in the quality of a casting is its length. Ideally, the casting should be 8.05 inches. (The basic casting is finished to a specification length of 8.00 inches.) There is substantial variation of casting lengths, even if the process is working properly, because of variation in outside temperature and humidity and variations in the quality of the steel raw material. Experience has indicated that the standard deviation of lengths of basic castings is about 0.180 inch, when the casting process is working well.

Systematic problems with the process tend to show up mostly in incorrect mean lengths rather than in increased variability. Therefore, the length of each casting is measured. After each set of 16 castings, the average length is found. If the mean for any sample of 16 castings is too far away from the desired mean,

8.05 inches, the casting process is halted and a lengthy (and moderately expensive) reset procedure is carried out to bring the process back to standard. One major problem is the definition of "too far away" from 8.05 inches. The casting process manager wants to establish limits of 7.915 inches and 8.185 inches, but the finishing process manager favors limits of 8.000 inches and 8.100 inches. Both of them agree with an official target that says that the long-run mean (over many thousands of castings) must be kept within the range of 7.95 to 8.15 inches; they disagree over the implications of this target for the samples of 16 castings.

Write a report to both managers and explain the implications of their choice of limits. Indicate what seem to be the important issues and what other facts may need to be found to come to a reasonable conclusion. Neither manager knows much statistical theory, so try to explain any technical ideas carefully. ■

Let's break out our finest old wine!
The goddess of data's benign.
The actual diff
Has come out signif
With p-value .049.

Oh woe for poor Horace P. Nunn
His research career's come undone.
Though test as he might
He can't get it right;
His p-value's .051.

R45 A larger computer software firm installs a new editor for use by a random sample of its programmers. After the programmers have learned to use the editor comfortably, the firm measures the number of lines of debugged code produced by each programmer. (The programming tasks are of comparable difficulty.) The data are

178	183	199	201	204	210	218	218	219	220	225	227	231
232	232	233	233	235	238	239	241	243	244	246	247	249
250	251	264	266	270	271	271	283	275	276	277	279	283
284	285	286	289	289	298	303	306	315	315	345		

For these data, the sample size is 50, the sample mean is 253.32, and the sample standard deviation is 36.1.

a The population standard deviation using the previous editor was 35.4. Assume that this population standard deviation applies to the new editor as well. Calculate a 99% confidence interval for the population mean using the new editor. Compare to the following Minitab results:

```
MTB > ZInterval 99.0 35.4 'CodeDone'.

Confidence Intervals

The assumed sigma = 35.4

Variable     N      Mean    StDev  SE Mean      99.0 % C.I.
CodeDone    50    253.32    36.09     5.01  (  240.42,  266.22)
```

b Is there clear evidence in the normal plot shown in Figure 8.12 that the sample mean is likely to be an inefficient estimator of the population mean?

R46 Refer to the confidence interval calculated in part a of the previous exercise. The population mean using the old editor was 230.2. Can we reject the null hypothesis that the mean for the new editor is 230.2, using $\alpha = .01$, based on the confidence interval?

FIGURE 8.12 **Normal Plot for Programmer Data**

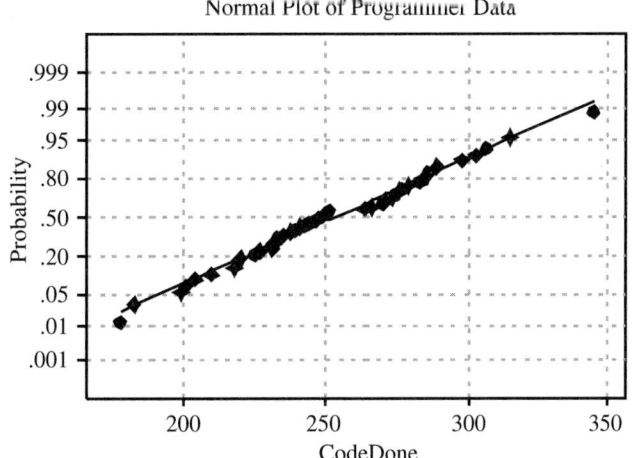

Average: 253.32
Std Dev: 36.0948
N of data: 50

Anderson-Darling Normality Test
A-Squared: 0.287
p-value: 0.606

R47 Carry out a formal hypothesis test of the null hypothesis that the population mean remains 230.2 against the research hypothesis that it is not equal to 230.2 for the data of the previous exercise. Use $\alpha = .01$ and assume that the population standard deviation is 35.4.

R48 For this hypothesis test, state a p-value. Compare it to the following Minitab results:

```
MTB > ZTest 230.2 35.4 'CodeDone';
SUBC>   Alternative 0.

Z-Test

Test of mu = 230.20 vs mu not = 230.20
The assumed sigma = 35.4

Variable    N     Mean   StDev  SE Mean       Z   P-Value
CodeDone   50   253.32   36.09     5.01    4.62    0.0000
```

R49 Redo the preceding exercises without making the assumption that the population standard deviation is 35.4. Compare your results to the following Minitab output. Do any of your conclusions change substantially?

```
MTB > TInterval 99.0 'CodeDone'.

Confidence Intervals

Variable    N    Mean  StDev  SE Mean      99.0 % C.I.
CodeDone   50  253.32  36.09     5.10  ( 239.64,  267.00)


MTB > TTest 230.2 'CodeDone';
SUBC>   Alternative 0.

T-Test of the Mean

Test of mu = 230.20 vs mu not = 230.20

Variable    N     Mean   StDev  SE Mean       T   P-Value
CodeDone   50   253.32   36.09     5.10    4.53    0.0000
```

R50 Minitab calculated a 99% confidence interval for the population median by a method not discussed in this book. On the basis of this interval, can one reject the null hypothesis that the population median is 230, using $\alpha = .01$?

```
MTB > Sinterval 99% 'CodeDone'

Sign confidence interval for median

                       ACHIEVED
            N  MEDIAN  CONFIDENCE   CONFIDENCE INTERVAL  POSITION
CodeDone   50   248.0     0.9847    (  233.0,   273.0)       17
                          0.9900    (  233.0,   273.9)      NLI
                          0.9934    (  233.0,   275.0)       16
```

R51 Which 99% confidence interval is wider, the t interval or the interval for the median? What does your answer suggest about the efficiency of the sample mean as compared to the sample median in this particular case?

R52 It is claimed that 45% of all walk-in customers at a particular real estate office eventually buy a home through that office. To test the claim, the realtors plan to regard the next 100 customers as a random sample. Set up a formal test of the research hypothesis that the population proportion is less than .45, using $\alpha = .05$.

R53 How does the rejection region in the previous exercise change if the maximum allowable α is set at .01?

R54 Suppose that the head of the real estate office in the previous exercise determines that 32 of the 100 walk-in customers eventually buy homes through the office. Does this fact support H_a if α is set at .05?

R55 Does the result in Exercise R54 lead to rejection of H_0 if α is set at .01? What does your answer indicate about the p-value for the data?

R56 A forester needs to test a new method for growing pine trees for lumber, one designed to minimize the loss to browsing deer. A 5-year trial is needed. A sample of 25 stands is to be planted and tended using the new method. The current yield has a mean of 272.6 and a standard deviation of 67.3, in appropriate units of measurement.

    a Formulate reasonable null and research hypotheses. In particular, should the research hypotheses be one-sided or two-sided?

    b Set up the first four parts of a formal test of the null hypothesis. Assume that the population standard deviation remains unchanged. The desired α value is .05.

R57 Suppose that the population mean yield under the new growing method is 305. Calculate the probability that the test will not reject the null hypothesis. What is the technical name for this probability?

R58 Assume that the population mean yield is 295 rather than the 305 assumed previously. Should the probability that the null hypothesis will not be rejected be larger or smaller than the probability calculated in the previous exercise?

R59 Assume that the experiment results in the following yield data:

135	185	231	247	262	285	300	304	310	312	313	319	322
322	324	328	335	362	366	368	370	384	384	385	401	

$(\bar{y} = 314.16, s = 64.0)$

The following Execustat output was obtained; note that it uses t, not z:

```
                  One Sample Analysis for Yield

Sample size = 25
Mean = 314.16
Variance = 4095.06
Std. deviation = 63.9926

95% confidence intervals
    Mean: (287.745,340.575)
    Variance: (2496.57,7934.23)
    Std. deviation: (49.9657,89.0743)

                  Hypothesis Test - Mean

Null hypothesis: mean = 272.6
Alternative: greater than

Computed t statistic = 3.24725
            P value = 0.0017

Stem-and-leaf display for Yield: unit = 10     1|2 represents 120

            LO|135,185

        3     2|3
        4     2|4
        5     2|6
        6     2|8
       12     3|001111
       (5)    3|22223
        8     3|
        8     3|6667
        4     3|888
        1     4|0
```

What is the conclusion of the t test? Is there clear evidence that the mean has increased?

R60 In the previous output, locate the probability that a sample mean is equal to or larger than 314.16, given a population mean of 272.6. What is the technical name for this probability?

R61 The Execustat output in Exercise R59 contains a stem-and-leaf plot of the yield data. Is there any reason to believe that the sample mean is not the best estimator of the population mean?

R62 A computer center that serves, among other clients, small savings and loan associations needs to know the proportion of jobs from these businesses that requires intervention by the computer operator. In a random sample of 133 such jobs, 22 require operator intervention. Calculate a 95% confidence interval for the population proportion of jobs requiring intervention.

R63 Suppose that the confidence interval in Exercise R62 is felt to be too wide. Calculate the sample size required to obtain a 95% confidence interval with a width of .06 (a plus or minus of .03) under each of two assumptions:

  a Assume that the sample proportion will continue to be roughly 22/133.

  b Assume that the sample proportion can take any value.

R64 A normal approximation is used in the confidence intervals of the preceding exercises. Can we be confident that the approximation is a good one?

R65 An auditor wishes to verify transaction records of a firm. The transactions are placed in random order. An auditor trainee keeps a cumulative total of the dollar amounts of the transactions; every time the total moves over a $100,000 increment (that is, when the total passes $100,000, $200,000, $300,000, and so on), the transaction is set aside for verification. Show that this process does not yield a random sample of the transactions.

R66 The process of the previous exercise yields 241 transactions. The mean size of the transactions is $5381 and the standard deviation is $2271. The amounts, when plotted, show substantial right skewness.

  a Calculate a supposed 95% confidence interval for the population mean transaction size.

  b This interval is in fact quite likely *not* to include the actual mean transaction size of the population. Explain why.

R67 A chemical manufacturer doing a pilot study of yields obtains a sample of 26 small batches. The yields, expressed as percentages of the theoretical maximum, are

67.6 68.5 74.7 77.6 78.4 79.3 79.5 80.3 80.3 80.7 80.8 80.8 80.9
81.2 81.4 81.4 81.5 82.5 82.5 82.9 82.9 83.8 84.4 84.4 85.4 86.0
($\bar{y} = 80.37$, $s = 4.37$)

The following Statistix output was obtained:

DESCRIPTIVE STATISTICS

VARIABLE	N	LO 90% CI	MEAN	UP 90% CI	SD
YIELD	26	78.908	80.373	81.837	4.3705

State a 90% confidence interval for the population mean yield.

R68 Use the confidence interval in the previous exercise to test the null hypothesis that the population mean is 82.0 against a two-sided research hypothesis. What does the conclusion indicate about the *p*-value?

R69 The complete pilot study for the preceding exercises eventually involves a sample of 150 batches. Assuming that the population standard deviation is about 4.4 and that the population mean is 80.4, find the probability that H_0: population mean = 82.0 will be rejected. Assume an α of .05.

R70 The probability calculated in the preceding exercise is *not* a *p*-value. Explain why not. ■

9

Comparing Two Samples

This chapter applies the basic ideas of statistical inference—confidence intervals and hypothesis tests—to problems of comparison. The choice of method depends on the nature of the problem and the apparent shape of the data distribution. The key ideas are:

1   Samples may be paired or independent. In paired (matched) samples, each value in one sample is linked to a specific value in the other sample; in independent samples, there is no logical connection between items. Paired samples may be analyzed by considering the differences between paired values.

2   The most efficient, effective way to analyze data that appear nearly normally distributed is by t distribution methods. For paired samples, a test or confidence interval based on the single sample of differences may be used. For independent samples, either a pooled-variance procedure (which assumes equal population variances) or a separate-variance (t') method may be used. The two methods give substantially different answers only when the sample sizes are quite different; if the population variances are also different, the pooled-variance method is not reliable.

3   If the data in independent samples are severely skewed or outlier-prone, a rank-sum test is more efficient—better able to detect a real difference than a t method. The rank-sum method is based on ranking the data from smallest to largest and thus is less affected by skewness or outliers.

4   If the difference data from paired samples is outlier-prone, a signed-rank test is more effective than a t test. The signed-rank test, however, is not reliable if the underlying population is badly skewed.

5   Bias in gathering the data cannot be overcome with these (or any other) statistical procedures.

6   Dependence within samples can make any of these procedures erroneous. This problem is particularly likely with time-series data.

Comparing sets of data is basic to using statistics in management. To decide which of two formulations of a cereal to introduce, a market researcher needs to compare consumer reactions to the two. To decide which parts supplier will receive a contract, a manufacturer needs to compare the quality of samples of the suppliers' goods. To decide which of two telephone systems to purchase, an office manager needs to compare rates for calls to a sample of places. Until now we have discussed basic principles of statistical inference in the context of a single sample. The basic ideas of estimation, confidence intervals, and hypothesis tests have much wider applications. In this chapter, we extend them to deal with comparisons of two samples.

In this chapter we develop methods for comparison. The first section describes using confidence intervals and hypothesis tests for comparing two means from independent samples. Then we describe an alternative approach to inference based on ranking data from lowest to highest. Sections 9.3 and 9.4 describe methods for comparing two samples based on paired or matched individuals.

This chapter is an extension of the basic principles we discussed in the last two chapters. The formulas get a little longer, but the basic principles are those we've already described. All the methods discussed in this chapter are carried out by almost every statistical computer package. The key issues for a manager are what method to use and what the results mean. ∎

9.1   Comparing the Means of Two Populations

aking comparisons is a fundamental part of a manager's job. If we want to ask how much a market research panel likes a new product, we need to compare that product to another one. If we want to assess the effect of production speed on variability of the resulting products, we should compare two (or more) speeds. If we want to look at the effect of tax-auditing procedures for state income taxes, we can compare the results for states with two different auditing methods. Therefore, we begin by considering methods for comparing two samples.

independent vs. paired samples

A key distinction for comparing two samples is **independent vs. paired samples**. Two samples are paired if each data value in one sample is naturally linked to a specific data value in the other sample by the way the data are gathered. For example, if a panelist rates product A and product B, the A and B samples are paired by rater. If worker output is measured before and after a new computer program is installed, the before and after samples are paired by worker. If there is no pairing, the samples are independent. You can usually sense when samples are paired because it's natural to write down the paired measurements side by side in entering the data. With independent samples, there's no particular reason to write a value from one sample next to a particular value for the other. In this section and the next, we deal with independent samples.

The basic principles underlying the statistical methods for two-sample inferences are the same as those developed in the preceding chapters for single-sample inferences. For example, suppose a chain of coffeehouses is trying to decide which of two bakers should supply pastries to sell in the chain's outlets. The managers of the chain decide to test the sales appeal of both by putting pastries from baker 1 into some coffeehouses and those from baker 2 in others, randomly. They obtain total dollar sales over a 2-week period for each outlet. Boxplots of the sales data, shown in Figure 9.1, appear reasonably normal.

The following Execustat output indicates that there are two different confidence intervals for the difference in mean sales. The difference is whether or not the underlying population variances are assumed to be equal. Similarly, there are two different forms of the hypothesis test.

```
        Two Sample Analysis for Sales by Baker


                            1                 2

Sample size               14                23
Mean                      243               259.913      diff. = -16.913
Variance                  934.615           258.628      ratio = 3.61374
Std. deviation            30.5715           16.0819


95% confidence intervals
     mu1 - mu2: (-32.4496,-1.37651) assuming equal variances
     mu1 - mu2: (-35.5098,1.68376)  not assuming equal variances


              Hypothesis Test - Difference of Means


Null hypothesis: difference of means = 0
Alternative: not equal
Equal variances assumed: yes


Computed t statistic = -2.20998
           P value = 0.0337


              Hypothesis Test - Difference of Means


Null hypothesis: difference of means = 0
Alternative: not equal
```

FIGURE 9.1   **Pastry Sales for Two Bakers**

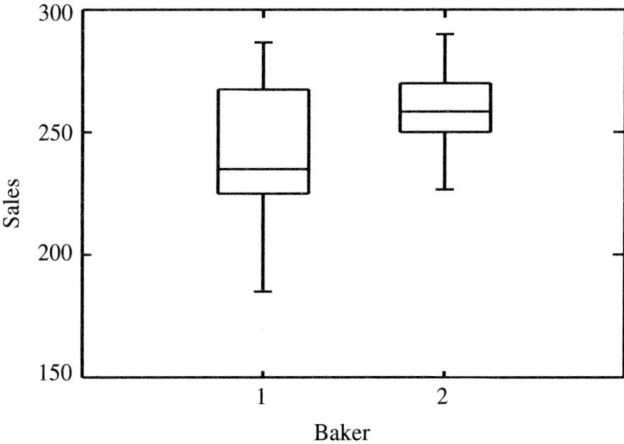

Equal variances assumed: no

Computed t statistic = -1.91499
            P value = 0.0720

The methods are based on assumptions much like those in the previous chapters. We assume that the samples are not biased, that the underlying populations are (more or less) normally distributed, and that the observations are all independent. Because each sample mean is an unbiased estimator of the corresponding population mean, $\overline{Y}_1 - \overline{Y}_2$ is

unbiased estimator of
$\mu_1 - \mu_2$

an **unbiased estimator of $\mu_1 - \mu_2$**:

$$E(\overline{Y}_1 - \overline{Y}_2) = E(\overline{Y}_1) - E(\overline{Y}_2) = \mu_1 - \mu_2$$

The key to inference problems related to $\mu_1 - \mu_2$ is that the variances (not the standard errors) of $\overline{Y}_1$ and $\overline{Y}_2$ can be added because the random variables $\overline{Y}_1$ and $\overline{Y}_2$ are independent.

Definition 9.1   Variance of $\overline{Y}_1 - \overline{Y}_2$; Independent Samples

$$\mathrm{Var}(\overline{Y}_1 - \overline{Y}_2) = \mathrm{Var}(\overline{Y}_1) + \mathrm{Var}(\overline{Y}_2) = \frac{\sigma_1^2}{n_1} + \frac{\sigma_2^2}{n_2} \quad \blacksquare$$

standard error of $\overline{Y}_1 - \overline{Y}_2$

The true **standard error of $\overline{Y}_1 - \overline{Y}_2$** is

$$\sigma_{\overline{Y}_1 - \overline{Y}_2} = \sqrt{\frac{\sigma_1^2}{n_1} + \frac{\sigma_2^2}{n_2}}$$

*assumption of equal
variances*

Technically, when the standard deviations are unknown, exact t inferences about $\mu_1 - \mu_2$ based on independent random samples require an additional assumption besides unbiased sampling, independence, and population normality. We also assume that the two unknown population variances are equal: $\sigma_1^2 = \sigma_2^2$. The common unknown variance is designated σ^2. The *sample* variances will not be equal, if only because of random variation. Given the assumption of equal population variances, we must combine the sample variances to estimate the common population variance. Then the confidence interval has the usual form: estimate plus or minus a table value times a standard error. Most computer packages will do the arithmetic.

Definition 9.2 Confidence Interval for $\mu_1 - \mu_2$, σ's Equal

$$\bar{y}_1 - \bar{y}_2 - t_{\alpha/2}s_p\sqrt{\frac{1}{n_1} + \frac{1}{n_2}} \le \mu_1 - \mu_2 \le \bar{y}_1 - \bar{y}_2 + t_{\alpha/2}s_p\sqrt{\frac{1}{n_1} + \frac{1}{n_2}}$$

where

$$s_p = \sqrt{\frac{(n_1 - 1)s_1^2 + (n_2 - 1)s_2^2}{n_1 + n_2 - 2}}$$

and

$$\text{d.f.} = n_1 + n_2 - 2$$

Note: This procedure can be used for all sample sizes. ■

pooled variance

The pooled standard deviation, s_p, in the confidence interval for $\mu_1 - \mu_2$ is an estimate of the common population standard deviation σ and is formed by combining information from the two independent samples. The two estimates s_1^2 and s_2^2 are weighted by their respective degrees of freedom to form the **pooled variance** s_p^2. For the special case in which the sample sizes are the same ($n_1 = n_2$), the formula for s_p^2 reduces to $s_p^2 = (s_1^2 + s_2^2)/2$, the average of the two sample variances. The degrees of freedom for s_p^2 combine the degrees of freedom for s_1^2 and s_2^2: d.f. $= (n_1 - 1) + (n_2 - 1) = n_1 + n_2 - 2$.

EXAMPLE 9.1

A taxicab company wants to test two programs for improving the gasoline mileage of its drivers. Under program A, drivers are assigned a target mileage and receive modest bonuses for better performance. Under program B, drivers are allowed a maximum monthly quota of gasoline; if it runs out, a driver has to pay for extra gasoline out of pocket. All taxis used are standard models and they are given standard maintenance. After three months, each driver's mileage per gallon is calculated. The data are as follows:

A:	15.9	17.5	19.1	16.9	18.3	17.3	17.0	16.2	16.8	17.1
B:	16.1	15.8	15.3	16.5	14.9	15.5	16.4	16.0	16.7	17.2

Excel output yielded the following results:

	A	B	C
1	t-Test: Two-Sample Assuming Equal Variances		
2			
3		A	B
4	Mean	17.21	16.04
5	Variance	0.8788	0.4804
6	Observations	10	10
7	Pooled Variance	0.6796	
8	Hypothesized Mean Difference	0	
9	df	18	
10	t Stat	3.1735	
11	P(T<=t) one-tail	0.0026	
12	t Critical one-tail	1.7341	
13	P(T<=t) two-tail	0.0053	
14	t Critical two-tail	2.1009	
15			
16	95% CI for MU1 - MU2:	(0.40, 1.94)	
17	POOLED STDEV =	0.824	

Locate the 95% confidence interval for the difference in mean gasoline mileage. Verify the calculation.

Solution

The confidence interval is shown as (0.40, 1.94).

Program	Mean	Variance	Standard Deviation	Sample Size
A	17.21	.8788	.9374	10
B	16.04	.4804	.6931	10

The required table value for a 95% confidence interval with $10 + 10 - 2 = 18$ d.f. is $t_{.025}$; from Appendix Table 4, $t_{.025} = 2.101$. The pooled sample variance is

$$s_p^2 = \frac{9(.8788) + 9(.4804)}{18} = .6796$$

so

$$s_p = \sqrt{.6796} = .8244$$

The confidence interval is

$$(17.21 - 16.04) - 2.101(.8244)\sqrt{\frac{1}{10} + \frac{1}{10}}$$

$$\leq \mu_A - \mu_B \leq (17.21 - 16.04) + 2.101(.8244)\sqrt{\frac{1}{10} + \frac{1}{10}}$$

or

$$.40 \leq \mu_A - \mu_B \leq 1.94 \quad \blacksquare$$

The corresponding t test for comparing μ_1 and μ_2 based on independent samples with the standard deviations unknown is summarized next.

Definition 9.3 Hypothesis Test for $\mu_1 - \mu_2$, σ's Equal

$$H_0: \quad \mu_1 - \mu_2 = D_0 (D_0 \text{ is specified; often } D_0 = 0)$$

H_a: 1. $\mu_1 - \mu_2 > D_0$

2. $\mu_1 - \mu_2 < D_0$

3. $\mu_1 - \mu_2 \neq D_0$

T.S.: $$t = \frac{(\bar{y}_1 - \bar{y}_2) - D_0}{s_p\sqrt{\frac{1}{n_1} + \frac{1}{n_2}}}$$

R.R.: 1. $t > t_\alpha$

2. $t < -t_\alpha$

3. $|t| > t_{\alpha/2}$

where t_a cuts off a right-tail area a for the t distribution with $n_1 + n_2 - 2$ d.f. *Note:* This method can be used for all sample sizes. $\quad \blacksquare$

EXAMPLE 9.2

Refer to Example 9.1 and the Excel output shown there. Verify the calculations to test the research hypothesis that program A yields a higher mean mileage than program B. Use $\alpha = .10$.

Solution

The output shows a t statistic equal to 3.17 and a two-tailed p-value of .0053. The one-tailed p-value should be about .0027; thus, the research hypothesis is supported.

$$H_0 : \mu_A - \mu_B = 0$$

$$H_a : \mu_A - \mu_B > 0$$

$$\text{T.S.} : t = \frac{(\bar{y}_A - \bar{y}_B) - 0}{s_p\sqrt{\dfrac{1}{n_1} + \dfrac{1}{n_2}}} = \frac{(17.21 - 16.04)}{.8244\sqrt{\dfrac{1}{10} + \dfrac{1}{10}}} = 3.17$$

R.R. :Reject H_0 if $t > t_{.10, 18 \text{ d.f.}} = 1.330$.

Conclusion :Because $t = 3.17 > 1.33$, the mean mileage under A is significantly greater than under B based on $\alpha = .10$. In fact, because H_0 can be rejected at $\alpha = .01 (t_{.01, 18} = 2.552)$, the p-value is less than .01. ■

The two-sample t test and confidence interval are based on several mathematical assumptions. Once again, these assumptions are not exactly satisfied in practice. We assume that the samples are taken without bias. Sometimes managers note that a bias in taking one sample is also present when taking the other sample, and so the biases cancel out. That's a legitimate hope, but it would certainly be better to take both samples without bias in the first place. Consider whether the biases built into gathering the data favor one situation over the other.

Assuming no serious bias, the most crucial assumption is the independence of the two samples, both within samples and between samples. Once again, dependence within samples will result in a smaller effective sample size than is indicated in the output.

Now we must also be concerned with dependence between the two samples. The assumption is that the two samples were taken completely at random. If this assumption is not valid, the procedures can be grossly erroneous. If the samples are taken randomly from different populations, and if there is no connection between the elements of one sample and those of the other, the **independence assumption** should be valid. But if the two measurements are taken on the same elements at different times or if there is any connection between elements of the samples, the two-sample t test is not appropriate, and other methods of analysis must be used. For example, if one sample represents measurements on product awareness for individuals before an advertising campaign and the second sample represents measurements of product awareness on these same individuals after advertising exposure, the two-sample t test is not appropriate. The paired-sample procedures of Sections 9.3 and 9.4 should be used to compare the difference in mean awareness before and after.

The assumption that both populations are normally distributed is less crucial because of the Central Limit Theorem. Even if the populations are not normal, the sampling distributions of $\bar{Y}_1$ and $\bar{Y}_2$ are approximately normal for modestly large sample sizes. Moderate population skewness is not a serious problem. If both populations are skewed in the same direction, the fact that we are dealing with a difference in means tends to make the sampling distribution of $\bar{Y}_1 - \bar{Y}_2$ more symmetric. In effect, the skewness will cancel when

independence assumption

normality assumption

we take the difference. Generally, if $n_1 + n_2$ is at least 30 or so, we are confident of the t probabilities. Of course, with small samples, confidence intervals are wide and β probabilities high. The point is that the t probabilities are reasonably accurate. A nonparametric alternative to the two-sample t test (called Wilcoxon's rank-sum test) that does not require normality of the two populations is discussed in Section 9.2.

equal variance assumption

The new assumption is that of equal population variances. However, even though two *population* variances are equal, the *sample* variances differ because of random variation. Many studies have been made about the effect of unequal population variances. The universal conclusion is that for *equal* sample sizes, even substantial differences in variances (such as $\sigma_1^2 = 3\sigma_2^2$) have remarkably little effect. The most dangerous situation for the accuracy of claimed probabilities is one in which a larger population variance is associated with a smaller sample size. If n_1 is only half the size of n_2 but σ_1^2 is, say, twice σ_2^2, the usual t probabilities may be seriously in error. The best cure for this problem is to take equal sample sizes.

When the sample variances (s_1^2 and s_2^2) suggest there may be a problem in assuming that the two population variances are equal, we can modify the usual t statistic to obtain an approximate t test or t confidence interval. Welch (1938) showed that the distribution of the statistic

$$t' = \frac{\bar{y}_1 - \bar{y}_2}{\sqrt{s_1^2/n_1 + s_2^2/n_2}}$$

can be approximated by a t distribution using approximate degrees of freedom.

Definition 9.4 t' Statistic; Independent Samples

1 $H_0 : \mu_1 = \mu_2 = 0$

2   The test statistic is

$$t' = \frac{\bar{y}_1 - \bar{y}_2}{\sqrt{(s_1^2/n_1) + (s_2^2/n_2)}}$$

3   The rejection region for t' can be obtained from Appendix Table 4 for

$$\text{d.f.} = \frac{(n_1 - 1)(n_2 - 1)}{(n_2 - 1)c^2 + (1 - c)^2(n_1 - 1)}$$

where

$$c = \frac{s_1^2/n_1}{s_1^2/n_1 + s_2^2/n_2}$$

Note: If d.f. is not an integer, round down to the nearest integer.   ■

separate variance t test
unequal variance t test

The test based on the t' statistic is sometimes referred to as the **separate variance t test** or the **unequal variance t test**. The statistic replaces each population variance (σ_1^2 and σ_2^2) with the separate sample variances s_1^2 and s_2^2.

E X A M P L E   9 . 3

A firm has a generous but rather complicated policy concerning end-of-year bonuses for its lower-level managerial personnel. The policy's key component is a subjective judgment of "contribution to corporate goals." A personnel officer takes samples of 24 female and 36 male managers to see if there is evidence of any differences in average bonuses, expressed as a percentage of yearly salary. The data are listed here:

Gender				Bonus Percentage					
F	9.2	7.7	11.9	6.2	9.0	8.4	6.9	7.6	7.4
	8.0	9.9	6.7	8.4	9.3	9.1	8.7	9.2	9.1
	8.4	9.6	7.7	9.0	9.0	8.4			
M	10.4	8.9	11.7	12.0	8.7	9.4	9.8	9.0	9.2
	9.7	9.1	8.8	7.9	9.9	10.0	10.1	9.0	11.4
	8.7	9.6	9.2	9.7	8.9	9.2	9.4	9.7	8.9
	9.3	10.4	11.9	9.0	12.0	9.6	9.2	9.9	9.0

The Excel spreadsheet program yields the following output:

```
t-Test: Two-Sample Assuming Equal Variances

                                 Female    Male
Mean                           8.533333  9.683333
Variance                       1.413623  1.007714
Observations                         24        36
Pooled Variance                1.168678
Hypothesized Mean Difference          0
df                                   58
t Stat                         -4.03675
P(T<=t) one-tail               8.04E-05
t Critical one-tail            1.671553
P(T<=t) two-tail               0.000161
t Critical two-tail            2.001716


t-Test: Two-Sample Assuming Unequal Variances

                                 Female    Male
Mean                           8.533333  9.683333
Variance                       1.413623  1.007714
Observations                         24        36
Hypothesized Mean Difference          0
df                                   44
t Stat                         -3.90126
P(T<=t) one-tail               0.000162
t Critical one-tail            1.68023
P(T<=t) two-tail               0.000324
t Critical two-tail            2.015367
```

a   Identify the value of the pooled-variance t statistic.

b   Identify the value of the t' statistic.

c   Use both statistics to test the research hypothesis of unequal means at $\alpha = .05$ and at $\alpha = .01$. Does the conclusion depend on which statistic is used?

Solution

a   The pooled-variance statistic is shown under "Assuming Equal Variances" as $t = -4.03675$.

b   The "Assuming Unequal Variances" t statistic is $t' = -3.90126$.

c   In both cases, the p-value is much smaller than α, so the null hypthesis is conclusively rejected.

Alternatively, we can construct a rejection region. The t statistic based on the pooled variance has d.f. $= 24 + 36 - 2 = 58$. For a two-sided H_a, we reject H_0 at $\alpha = .05$ if $|t| > t_{.025} \approx 2.00$ (as shown in the output); with $\alpha = .01$, reject if $|t| > t_{.005} \approx 2.66$. Because $|t| = 4.037$, we can easily reject H_0 even at $\alpha = .01$. For the t' statistic based on separate variances, the degrees of freedom can be computed using the formula

$$\text{d.f.} = \frac{(n_1 - 1)(n_2 - 1)}{(n_2 - 1)c^2 + (1 - c)^2(n_1 - 1)} \quad \text{with } c = \frac{s_1^2/n_1}{s_1^2/n_1 + s_2^2/n_2}$$

For these data,

$$c = \frac{1.4137/24}{1.4137/24 + 1.0076/36} = \frac{.0589}{.0589 + .0280} = .6778$$

and

$$c^2 = .4594 \quad (1 - c)^2 = .1038$$

Then

$$\text{d.f.} = \frac{23(35)}{35(.4594) + .1038(23)}$$
$$= \frac{805}{16.0790 + 2.3876}$$
$$= \frac{805}{18.4671} = 43.59$$

Rounding down to the nearest integer, d.f. $= 43$. (The output shows 44 d.f.; the difference isn't important.) For a two-sided research hypothesis and $\alpha = .05$, we reject H_0 if $|t'| > t_{.025,43} \approx 2.02$. For $\alpha = .01$, we reject H_0 if $|t'| > t_{.005,43} = 2.70$. Because $|t'| = 3.90$, we can easily reject H_0 even at $\alpha = .01$. The conclusions from the t and t' tests are essentially the same and the research hypothesis is quite conclusively supported. ∎

We have presented two slightly different approaches. We developed pooled-variance t methods based on an assumption of equal population variances, and we introduced the t' statistic for an approximate t when the variances are not equal. Confidence intervals and hypothesis tests based on these different procedures (t or t') need not give identical results. Standard computer packages often report the results of both the pooled-variance and separate-variance t tests. Which should a manager believe?

The choice depends on the evidence about underlying assumptions. If plots of each sample appear roughly normal, and if the sample variances are roughly equal, the pooled-variance t test should be valid and most efficient. If plots of each sample are normal but the sample variances are clearly different (especially if the sample sizes differ), the separate-variance t' test is more believable. If the sample sizes are equal, the pooled-variance and separate-variance t tests will usually give the same results; in fact, the test statistics are algebraically equal for equal sample sizes. But if the data in one or both samples are obviously nonnormal, the rank-sum approach discussed in the next section is preferred. As usual, a little thought and some careful looks at the data will let a manager make a reasonable choice.

E X A M P L E   9 . 4

A simulation study involves 1000 samples taken from each of two independent, normal populations. Both population means equal 50. The first population has $\sigma = 14.1421$; the second, $\sigma = 10$. The sample sizes are $n_1 = 10$ and $n_2 = 20$. At $\alpha = .10$, two-tailed, using the pooled-variance t test, H_0 is rejected 70 times, indicating that the first mean is higher, and an additional 71 times, indicating the second mean is higher. For the t' test, the corresponding numbers are 44 and 41. What do these results indicate about the choice of pooled-variance t versus t'?

Solution

One of the assumptions underlying the pooled-variance t test has been violated; the population variances aren't equal. In addition, the sample sizes aren't equal, and the larger sample size is associated with the smaller variance. The null hypothesis is true because the population means are equal. The pooled-variance t test rejects the null hypothesis more frequently than the nominal α value would indicate. For example, for a nominal $\alpha/2$ of .05, we would expect 50 and 50 rejections, but we get 70 and 71 rejections. The t' test rejects the null hypothesis just about as often as α indicates, or perhaps slightly less often. If anything, the t' method is conservative in making too few false positive errors. ∎

EXERCISES

9.1 A processor of recycled aluminum cans is concerned about the levels of impurities (principally other metals) contained in lots from two sources. Laboratory analysis of sample lots yields the following data (kilograms of impurities per hundred kilograms of product):

Source I: 3.8   3.5   4.1   2.5   3.6   4.3   2.1   2.9   3.2   3.7   2.8   2.7
                 (mean = 3.267, standard deviation = 0.676)

Source II: 1.8   2.2   1.3   5.1   4.0   4.7   3.3   4.3   4.2   2.5   5.4   4.6
                 (mean = 3.617, standard deviation = 1.365)

Excel output follows:

	A	B	C	D	E	F	G
1	t-Test: Two-Sample Assuming Equal Variances						
2							
3		*Source I*	*Source II*		95% CI:	(-1.16, 0.63)	
4	Mean	3.266667	3.616667				
5	Variance	0.45697	1.863333				
6	Observations	12	12				
7	Pooled Variance	1.160152					
8	Hypothesized Mean Difference	0					
9	df	22					
10	t Stat	-0.795951					
11	P(T<=t) one-tail	0.217283					
12	t Critical one-tail	1.717144					
13	P(T<=t) two-tail	0.434566					
14	t Critical two-tail	2.073875					
15							
16	t-Test: Two-Sample Assuming Unequal Variances						
17							
18		*Source I*	*Source II*		95% CI:	(-1.15, 0.62)	
19	Mean	3.266667	3.616667				
20	Variance	0.45697	1.863333				
21	Observations	12	12				
22	Hypothesized Mean Difference	0					
23	df	16					
24	t Stat	-0.795951					
25	P(T<=t) one-tail	0.218856					
26	t Critical one-tail	1.745884					
27	P(T<=t) two-tail	0.437711					
28	t Critical two-tail	2.119905					

a Locate a 95% confidence interval for the difference in mean impurity levels, assuming equal variances. Do the same without assuming equal variances. How much of a difference does it make which interval is used?

b Can the processor conclude, using $\alpha = .05$, that there is a nonzero difference in means?

9.2 Locate the *p*-value in Exercise 9.1, part b.

9.3 Examine the plots of the impurities data in Figure 9.2. Which of the assumptions (if any) of the *t* test seem suspect? Do you think there is serious reason to doubt the conclusion?

9.4 In a computer simulation study, 1000 samples are taken from each of two populations. Both populations are normal, and both populations have means equal to 50. The first population has a standard deviation of 20; the second has a standard deviation of 10. The first sample size is 5; the second sample size is 20. The null hypothesis of equal means is rejected at $\alpha = .05$ in 203 of the samples using the pooled-variance *t* test; this hypothesis is rejected, again at $\alpha = .05$, in 48 samples using the t' test.

a Would the pooled-variance *t* test or the t' test be better in this situation? What does "better" mean?

b Does the computer simulation result confirm your judgment in part a?

9.5 Company officials are concerned about the length of time a particular drug retains its potency. A random sample (sample 1) of 10 bottles of the product is drawn from current production and analyzed for potency. A second sample (sample 2) of 10 bottles is obtained, stored for one year, and then analyzed. The data are analyzed by a standard program package (Statistix). The relevant output follows:

```
Sample 1:   10.2    9.5    10.3    10.8    9.8    10.6    10.7    10.2    10.0    10.6
Sample 2:    9.8    9.6    10.1    10.2   10.1     9.7     9.5     9.6     9.8     9.9
```

TWO-SAMPLE T TESTS FOR POTENCY BY SAMPLE

		SAMPLE		
SAMPLE	MEAN	SIZE	S.D.	S.E.
1	10.370	10	0.3233	0.1022
2	9.8300	10	0.2406	0.0760

	T	DF	P
EQUAL VARIANCES	4.24	18	0.0005
UNEQUAL VARIANCES	4.24	16.6	0.0006

a Identify the sample means and standard deviations.

b Locate the value of the *t* statistic. Is the pooled-variance *t* statistic identified as "equal variances" or "unequal variances"?

FIGURE 9.2 **Boxplots for Impurities Data**

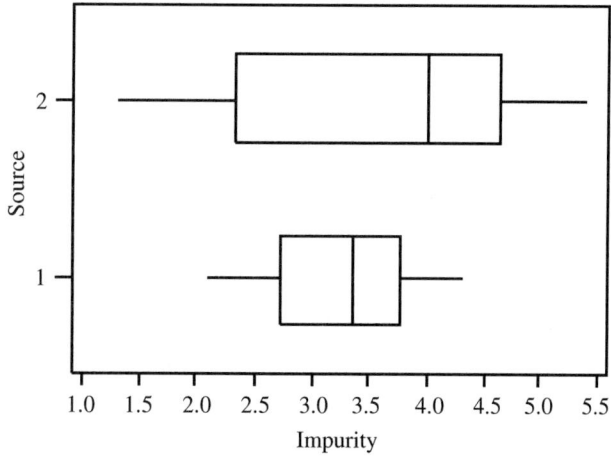

c Locate the value of the t' statistic.

d Why are these two statistics equal in this case?

e A plot of the data of the previous exercise is shown in Figure 9.3. Does it seem there are serious violations of the assumptions underlying the pooled-variance test?

f Locate the *p*-value for the pooled-variance *t* test in the output. Is it one-tailed or two-tailed?

g What conclusion would you reach concerning the possibility of a decrease in mean potency over one year?

9.6 To compare the performance of personal computer spreadsheet programs, teams of three students each choose whatever spreadsheet program they wish. Each team is given the same set of standard accounting and finance problems to solve. The time (in minutes) required for each team to solve the set of problems is recorded. The following data and Minitab output are obtained for the two most widely used programs.

Program	Time										$\bar{y}$	s	n
A	39	57	42	53	41	44	71	56	49	63	51.50	10.46	10
B	43	38	35	45	40	28	50	54	37	29			
	36	27	52	33	34	30					38.00	8.67	16

```
MTB > TwoT 99.0 'Time' 'Program';
SUBC>    Pooled.

TWOSAMPLE T FOR Time
Program  N     MEAN    STDEV   SE MEAN
1       10     51.5    10.5      3.3
2       16     38.00    8.67     2.2

99 PCT CI FOR MU 1 - MU 2: ( 2.9,  24.1)

TTEST MU 1 = MU 2 (VS NE): T= 3.57  P=0.0016  DF=  24

POOLED STDEV =       9.38

MTB > TwoT 99.0 'Time' 'Program'.

TWOSAMPLE T FOR Time
Program  N     MEAN    STDEV   SE MEAN
1       10     51.5    10.5      3.3
2       16     38.00    8.67     2.2
```

FIGURE 9.3 Boxplots for Drug Potency Data

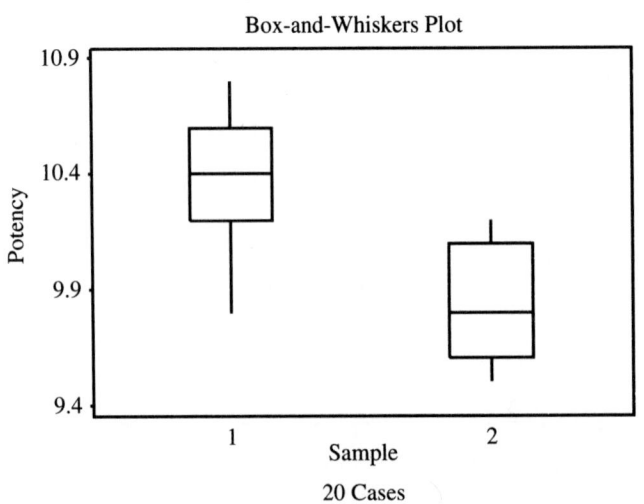

Box-and-Whiskers Plot

20 Cases

99 PCT CI FOR MU 1 - MU 2: (1.9, 25.1)

TTEST MU 1 = MU 2 (VS NE): T= 3.41 P=0.0036 DF= 16

  a Locate the pooled standard deviation.

  b Find a 99% confidence interval for the difference of population means, assuming equal variances.

  c According to this interval, can the null hypothesis of equal means be rejected at $\alpha = .01$?

9.7 Redo parts b and c of Exercise 9.6 using a separate-variance (t') method. Which method is more appropriate in this case? How critical is it which method is used?

9.8 A health organization wished to compare the billed cost of an operation to replace a cataract clouded eye with an artificial lens in uncomplicated cases. The data compared randomly assigned patients who were treated with an experimental method (1) with the standard method (2). JMP output from the data is shown in Figure 9.4. Is there evidence of a real difference in means?

9.9 Why would it be unwise to use the pooled-variance t method in the cataract operation data in Exercise 9.8?

FIGURE 9.4 **Cost of Two Types of Operation**

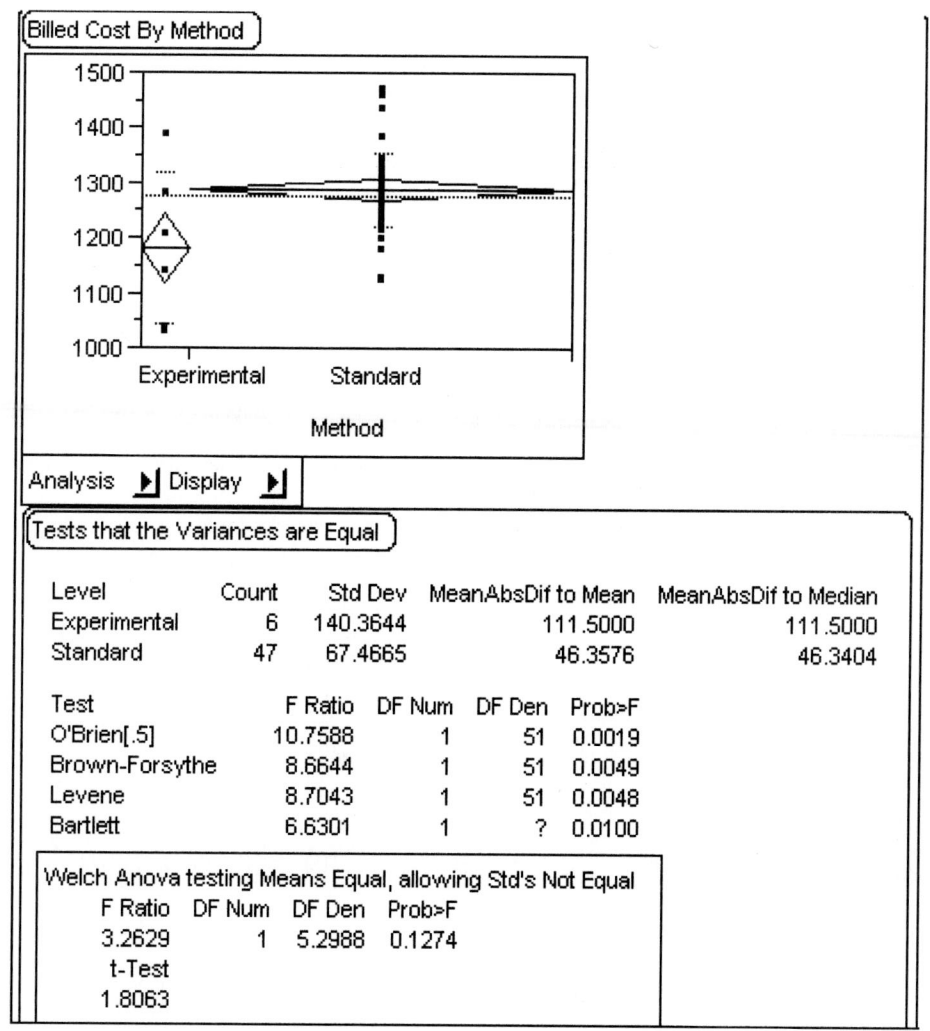

9.10 A manufacturer of modems uses microcomputer chips from two different sources. As part of quality-control testing, the manufacturer obtains data on the rate of defective chips per thousand for each lot of chips. The following results and Excel output are obtained; note that the rate is not necessarily an integer number because the lot sizes are not exactly 1000 chips per lot.

Source	Number of Defectives/1000									
I	9.8	9.9	10.2	10.5	10.7	10.8	11.7	13.9	19.2	27.6
II	10.6	11.0	11.5	11.8	11.9	12.7	14.2	16.8	21.7	29.9

	A	B	C
2	t-Test: Two-Sample Assuming Equal Variances		
3			
4			
5		Source I	Source II
6	Mean	13.43	15.21
7	Variance	32.92456	38.121
8	Observations	10	10
9	Pooled Variance	35.52278	
10	Hypothesized Mean Difference	0	
11	df	18	
12	t Stat	-0.66781	
13	P(T<=t) one-tail	0.256364	
14	t Critical one-tail	1.734063	
15	P(T<=t) two-tail	0.512728	
16	t critical two-tail	2.100924	
17			
18			
19	t-Test: Two-Sample Assuming Unequal Variances		
20			
21			
22		Source I	Source II
23	Mean	13.43	15.21
24	Variance	32.92456	38.121
25	Observations	10	10
26	Hypothesized Mean Difference	0	
27	df	18	
28	t Stat	-0.66781	
29	P(T<=t) one-tail	0.256364	
30	t Critical one-tail	1.734063	
31	P(T<=t) two tail	0.512728	
32	t Critical two-tail	2.100924	

    a What are the means and standard deviations for each source? Which source appears to be better?

    b Locate the pooled-variance t statistic for testing the null hypothesis of equal means.

    c Locate the t' statistic for testing the same hypothesis.

    d Explain why t and t' are equal for these data.

9.11   **a** Can the null hypothesis in Exercise 9.10 be rejected at $\alpha = .05$ in favor of a two-sided research hypothesis? Use the pooled-variance t statistic. State the p-value.

    b Locate the approximate d.f. for the t' statistic.

    c Based on this output, is there clear evidence that one source is better than the other? Explain your answer. ■

9.2

A Nonparametric Test: The Wilcoxon Rank-Sum Test

The two-sample t test we described in the previous section is based on several mathematical assumptions. In particular, we assume that both populations have normal distributions with equal variances. When the assumptions are not satisfied, the t test may still be valid, in the sense that the nominal probabilities are approximately correct, particularly if the sample sizes are large and equal. However, there is another hypothesis-testing method that requires weaker mathematical assumptions, is almost as powerful when the t assumptions are satisfied, and is more powerful in other situations. We describe this test, called the *Wilcoxon rank-sum test* or sometimes the Mann-Whitney test, in this section.

The mathematical assumption for this test is that independent random samples are taken from two populations; the null hypothesis is that the two population distributions are identical (but not necessarily normal). The Wilcoxon rank-sum test probabilities are exactly correct for any two populations with identical continuous distributions and are generally slightly conservative (committing slightly fewer false positive errors than the claimed α would indicate) for two populations with identical discrete distributions.

The test is based on the ranks of the sample data values. The rank of an individual observation is its position in the combined sample: Rank 1 indicates the smallest value, rank 2 indicates the next smallest value, and so on. As the term *rank-sum test* indicates, the Wilcoxon rank-sum test is based on the sum of the ranks in either sample. Under the null hypothesis of identical population distributions, the sum of the ranks in one sample is proportional to the sample size. If one population is shifted to the right of another—that is, if the first population tends to yield larger observations—the rank sum for the first sample tends to be large. Of course, a small rank sum for the first sample indicates that the first population is shifted to the left of the second. Define T to be the sum of the ranks in the first sample. Under the null hypothesis, the expected value and variance of T have been determined:

$$\mu_T = \frac{n_1(n_1 + n_2 + 1)}{2} \qquad \sigma_T^2 = \frac{n_1 n_2}{12}(n_1 + n_2 + 1)$$

If both n_1 and n_2 are 10 or larger, the sampling distribution of T is approximately normal. This allows use of a z statistic in testing the hypothesis of equal distributions.

(margin note: ranking sample data)

Definition 9.5   Wilcoxon Rank-Sum Test

H_0:   The two populations are identical.

H_a: 1. Population 1 is shifted to the right of population 2.

2. Population 1 is shifted to the left of population 2.

3. Population 1 is shifted to the right or left of population 2.

T.S.: $z = \dfrac{T - \mu_T}{\sigma_T}$

where T denotes the rank sum for sample 1

R.R. :   1. $z > z_\alpha$

2. $z < -z_\alpha$

3. $|z| > z_{\alpha/2}$

Note: The normal approximation is reasonably accurate if $n_1 \geq 10$ and $n_2 \geq 10$. Special tables are available for smaller values of n_1 and n_2 (for example, see Hollander & Wolfe, 1973).   ■

EXAMPLE 9.5

Perform a rank-sum test for Example 9.1. Compare to the following Minitab output:

```
MTB > Mann-Whitney 95.0 'Program1' 'Program2'.

Mann-Whitney Confidence Interval and Test

Program1   N =  10     Median =     17.050
Program2   N =  10     Median =     16.050
Point estimate for ETA1-ETA2 is      1.050
95.5 Percent C.I. for ETA1-ETA2 is (0.399,1.900)
W = 141.0
Test of ETA1 = ETA2  vs.  ETA1 not = ETA2 is significant at 0.0073
```

Solution

Minitab shows the rank sum as $W = 141.0$, and the p-value as 0.0073. To do the analysis by hand, the first step is to rank the observations. It helps in doing the ranking to order the values in each sample from lowest to highest.

Program A

Value:	15.9	16.2	16.8	16.9	17.0	17.1	17.3	17.5	18.3	19.1
Rank:	5	8	12	13	14	15	17	18	19	20

Program B

Value:	14.9	15.3	15.5	15.8	16.0	16.1	16.4	16.5	16.7	17.2
Rank:	1	2	3	4	6	7	9	10	11	16

The sum of the ranks in the A sample is

$$T = 5 + 8 + \cdots + 20 = 141$$

Under the null hypothesis

$$\mu_T = \frac{10(10 + 10 + 1)}{2} = 105$$

$$\sigma_T^2 = \frac{(10)(10)}{12}(10 + 10 + 1) = 175$$

$$\sigma_T = \sqrt{175} = 13.23$$

So

$$z = \frac{T - \mu_T}{\sigma_T}$$

$$= \frac{141 - 105}{13.23}$$

$$= 2.72$$

In Example 9.1, the research hypothesis H_a was that the mean for program A was larger than the mean for program B. The corresponding research hypothesis for the rank-sum test is that the program A distribution is shifted to the right of the program B distribution. This research hypothesis is supported and the null hypothesis is rejected if T (and therefore z) is too large to be attributed to chance. The one-tailed p-value for $z = 2.72$ is .0033, so the null hypothesis is rejected for $\alpha = .10, .05, .01,$ or even .005. The calculated *p*-value differs from the one shown in the output, which corrects for the fact that the rank sum is a discrete quantity that doesn't take on fractional values. Because $n_1 = n_2 = 10$, we are barely within the adequacy range of the normal approximation. It is conceivable that the real *p*-value is a bit larger than .0033, but still the null hypothesis should be rejected at any conventional α level. ■

EXAMPLE 9.6

Refer to the following Execustat computer output for Example 9.3:

```
                Hypothesis Test - Difference of Medians

Null hypothesis: difference = 0
Alternative: not equal
Average rank of 24 values in F = 20.0417
Average rank of 36 values in M = 37.4722


Computed z statistic = 3.80188 (continuity correction applied)
P value = 0.0001
```

a Identify the value of the rank-sum statistic.

b Find the test statistic for the null hypothesis of equal distribution of bonuses by gender.

c State an approximate two-tailed *p*-value for the test in part b.

d How does the conclusion of this test compare with that found in Example 9.3?

Solution

a The average of the ranks in the F sample is shown as 20.0417. If we wish, we can multiply by the sample size, 24, to find that the sum is 481.0.

b Because $n_1 = 24$ and $n_2 = 36$, a normal approximation should be quite good. The z statistic is shown as 3.80188.

c The *p*-value is shown as 0.0001.

d As in Example 9.3, we have conclusive support for the research hypothesis. ■

treatment of ties

    The theory behind the rank-sum test assumes that the population distributions are continuous, so there is zero probability that two observations are exactly equal. In practice, however, there are often ties—two or more equal observations. Each observation in a set of tied values is assigned the average of the ranks for the set. If two observations are tied for ranks 2 and 3, for example, each is given rank 2.5; the next larger value gets rank 4, and so on. There is a correction to the variance formula for the case of tied ranks (see Ott, 1984). The variance formula is generally conservative and usually very close, unless there are many, many ties.

    The Wilcoxon rank-sum test is a direct competitor of the two-sample *t* test. Both tests are sensitive to differences in location (mean or median) as opposed to dispersion or spread. Also, in most situations, the two tests give the same basic conclusion, so it doesn't matter which test is used. The rank-sum test requires fewer assumptions than the *t* test (in particular, it does not assume population normality), but it uses less information from the data; only ordering information is relevant to the rank-sum test.[1] When the assumptions underlying the t test are close to correct, the t test is better. Both theoretical results and simulations clearly indicate that a t test (using the pooled variance if the sample variances are roughly equal or if the sample sizes are roughly equal, but separate variances if both variances and sample sizes aren't equal) will have correct α values and optimal power for normal populations. For obviously nonnormal data, the rank-sum test has a more believable α value (especially for small samples) and it usually has better power.

E X A M P L E   9 . 7

To investigate the effect of skewness on the pooled-variance t test as well as the rank-sum test, 1000 samples are drawn from two squared-exponential populations; this type of population is extremely right-skewed. Both population means are 50; both standard deviations are 10. The sample sizes are 5 and 25, respectively. At a nominal $\alpha = .05$, one-tailed, the pooled-variance t test rejects the null hypothesis of equal means in favor of H_a: $\mu_1 > \mu_2$, 95 times. The rank-sum test rejects the null hypothesis of identical distributions in favor of H_a: first population tends to be larger than the second, 37 times. What do the results indicate about the effect of skewness on the two tests?

Solution

The null hypothesis is true in this simulation; both means are 50. The actual number of rejections of the null hypothesis by the t test is far from what is indicated by the nominal α value for one-tailed probabilities. The rank-sum test, which doesn't assume normal populations, appears to be rejecting the null hypothesis the correct number of times.   ■

E X A M P L E   9 . 8

A simulation study investigating the effect of outliers on the t and rank-sum tests involves independent samples from Laplace (mildly outlier-prone) populations. One part of the study has both population means equal; a second part involves different means. When the means (and variances) are equal, both the pooled-variance t and the rank-sum test reject the null hypothesis (at $\alpha = .05$, one-tailed) 47 times out of 1000. When the first mean is 50, the second mean is 60, and both standard deviations are 10, the pooled-variance t test rejects H_0: $\mu_1 = \mu_2$ 986 times, and the rank-sum test rejects it 998 times. What do these results indicate about the choice of the t or rank-sum test when the populations are outlier-prone?

Solution

The results for both tests when the null hypothesis is true indicate that the nominal α is (very close to) correct. The simulation obtained just about the expected number of false rejections. When the research hypothesis is true, as in the second part of the study, we want to reject the null hypothesis: The rank-sum test yields more rejections than does the t test. The rank-sum test is more powerful in this situation.   ■

---

[1] Therefore, the rank-sum test can be used when the observations are qualitative and ordinal, as when 1 = strongly opposed, 2 = opposed, 3 = neutral, and so on.

9.12 The Statistix computer package used in Exercise 9.5 also calculated rank sums. The relevant output follows:

```
RANK SUM TWO-SAMPLE (MANN-WHITNEY) TEST FOR POTENCY BY SAMPLE

    SAMPLE    RANK SUM    SIZE    U STAT    MEAN RANK

      1        146.00      10     91.000      14.6
      2        64.000      10     9.0000      6.4
    TOTAL      210.00      20


NORMAL APPROXIMATION WITH CONTINUITY CORRECTION    3.062
TWO-TAILED P-VALUE FOR NORMAL APPROXIMATION        0.0022
```

a Identify the rank sums.

b Locate the value of the z statistic.

c Formulate appropriate null and research hypotheses.

d Is H_a supported at $\alpha = .01$?

9.13 **a** Locate the p-value in the output of Exercise 9.12. Is it one-tailed or two-tailed? What p-value should be reported in Exercise 9.12?

b What conclusion would be reached in using the rank-sum test? How does it compare to the conclusion of the t test ($t = 4.24$, p-value .0005)? Does it matter much which test is used?

9.14 The data for Exercise 9.6 are reproduced here:

Program				Time							$\bar{y}$	s	n
A	39	57	42	53	41	44	71	56	49	63	51.50	10.46	10
B	43	38	35	45	40	28	50	54	37	29			
	36	27	52	33	31	30					38.00	8.67	16

```
MTB > TwoT 99.0 'Time' 'Program';
SUBC>    Pooled.

TWOSAMPLE T FOR Time
Program    N      MEAN     STDEV    SE MEAN
1         10      51.5     10.5       3.3
2         16      38.00    8.67       2.2

99 PCT CI FOR MU 1 - MU 2: ( 2.9,  24.1)

TTEST MU 1 = MU 2 (VS NE): T= 3.57  P=0.0016  DF=  24

POOLED STDEV =       9.38

MTB > Mann-Whitney 99.0 'ProgramA' 'ProgramB'

Mann-Whitney Confidence Interval and Test

ProgramA   N = 10     Median =      51.00
ProgramB   N = 16     Median =      36.50
Point estimate for ETA1-ETA2 is      13.00
99.1 Percent C.I. for ETA1-ETA2 is (2.00,26.00)
W = 191.0
Test of ETA1 = ETA2  vs.  ETA1 ~= ETA2 is significant at 0.0034
```

a Find the ranks of the combined data. It's much easier if you sort the data in each sample first.

b Verify that the sum of ranks in the first sample is 191.

c Is there a statistically significant difference ($\alpha = .01$) between programs according to the rank-sum test?

9.15   Do the data of Exercise 9.14 indicate that the rank-sum test is preferable to a t test? Explain, preferably with pictures.

9.16   The data of Exercise 9.10 are as follows:

Source	Number of Defectives/1000									
I	9.8	9.9	10.2	10.5	10.7	10.8	11.7	13.9	19.2	27.6
II	10.6	11.0	11.5	11.8	11.9	12.7	14.2	16.8	21.7	29.9

a Use a rank-sum test to test the null hypothesis that both sources have the same distribution of defectives per 1000. Use $\alpha = .05$ and a two-sided research hypothesis.

b Find the two-tailed p-value.

9.17   Is there reason to think that a rank-sum test is more appropriate than a t test for the data of Exercise 9.16?   ■

Paired-Sample Methods

The methods of the preceding two sections are appropriate for the analysis of two independent samples. We have emphasized that those methods are not appropriate for situations in which each measurement in one sample is matched or paired with a corresponding measurement in the other. In this section, we discuss methods for paired-sample data.

control of variability

The advantage of pairing observations is the **control of variability** that would otherwise obscure a real difference in means. For example, suppose that an office manager wants to test two new word processors to find which one yields greater average speed. One test procedure would be to assign 10 secretaries randomly to one model and another 10 secretaries to the other. This procedure would yield two independent samples. Another procedure would be to have 10 randomly chosen secretaries type on both models; the 10 typing speeds on each model would constitute paired or matched samples. Of course, there are large differences in speed among secretaries. These differences would cause large variability in the independent-samples experiment and would tend to conceal any real differences between the two models. In the paired-sample experiment, the manager can calculate the difference in the two models' speeds for the same secretaries; individual variability in speed cancels out of the difference. The individual variability factor does not cause random variability in the paired-sample experiment.

As indicated in the secretary example, statistical methods for working with paired samples are all based on the same idea. Calculate all differences of matched scores and apply single-sample methods to the resulting sample of differences. In particular, the t distribution methods for confidence intervals and hypothesis tests described in Chapters 7 and 8 may be used.

EXAMPLE 9.9

Insurance adjusters investigate the relative automobile repair costs at two garages. Each of 15 cars recently involved in accidents is taken to both garages 1 and 2 for separate estimates of repair costs. The resulting data are analyzed incorrectly as coming from two independent samples and correctly as coming from paired samples. Use the following computer printout to compare the resulting t statistic. What accounts for the difference in these statistics? (Costs are entered in hundreds of dollars.)

Two Sample Analysis for Estimate by Garage

	1	2	
Sample size	15	15	
Mean	7.68	6.636	diff. = 1.044
Variance	7.42453	9.29134	ratio = 0.79908
Std. deviation	2.7248	3.04817	

95% confidence intervals
    mu1 - mu2: (-1.1184,3.2064) assuming equal variances
    mu1 - mu2: (-1.11962,3.20762) not assuming equal variances
    variance ratio: (0.267848,2.38393)

Hypothesis Test - Difference of Means

Null hypothesis: difference of means = 0
Alternative: not equal
Equal variances assumed: yes

Computed t statistic = 0.988967
           P value = 0.3311

Hypothesis Test - Difference of Means

Null hypothesis: difference of means = 0
Alternative: not equal
Equal variances assumed: no

Computed t statistic = 0.988967
           P value = 0.3313

Paired Samples Comparison

	Garage1	Garage2	differences
Sample size	15	15	15
Mean	7.68	6.636	1.044
Variance	7.42453	9.29134	1.18263
Std. deviation	2.7248	3.04817	1.08749

95% confidence intervals for differences:
    Mean: (0.441769,1.64623)
    Variance: (0.633884,2.9519)
    Std. deviation: (0.796168,1.71811)

Hypothesis Test - Mean

Null hypothesis: mean = 0
Alternative: not equal

Computed t statistic = 3.71811
           P value = 0.0023

Solution

The pooled-sample and separate-sample (t') statistics are equal because $n_1 = n_2$; the value is only .989. The p-value is about .33, so there isn't enough evidence to say that the garages differ in their average estimates. The difference t statistic equals 3.72, and the p-value is .0023, statistically significant at all reasonable α levels. The reason for the difference in conclusions is that there is huge variability in the severity of damage to the 15 cars. This source of variability makes the standard error very large and therefore t_{pooled} and t' quite small. Because the difference t is based on differences between the two garages' estimates on the same cars, it is not affected by the variability among cars. ■

EXAMPLE 9.10

A tasting panel of 15 people is asked to rate two new kinds of tea on a scale ranging from 0 to 100; 25 means "I would try to finish it only to be polite," 50 means "I would drink it but not buy it," 75 means "It's about as good as any tea I know," and 100 means "It's superb; I would drink nothing else." (What 0 means is left to your imagination.) The ratings are as follows:

	Person							
	1	2	3	4	5	6	7	8
Tea S	85	40	75	81	42	50	60	15
Tea J	65	50	43	65	20	65	35	38
Difference	+20	−10	+32	+16	+22	−15	+25	−23

	Person						
	9	10	11	12	13	14	15
Tea S	65	40	60	40	65	75	80
Tea J	60	47	60	43	53	61	63
Difference	+5	−7	0	−3	+12	+14	+17

a Calculate a 95% confidence interval for the population difference in mean ratings.

b Test the null hypothesis of no difference against a two-sided alternative using $\alpha = .05$.

c What advantage does matching have in this situation?

Solution

a If we call the differences d_i, then $\bar{d} = 7.00$ and $s_d = 16.08$. Of course

$$\bar{d} = \frac{\sum d_i}{15} \quad \text{and} \quad s_d^2 = \frac{\sum(d_i - \bar{d})^2}{14}$$

The population mean of the differences is the same as the difference in means, so $\mu_d = \mu_S - \mu_J$. Because our calculations are based on 15 differences, there are 14 d.f., and the required t table value is 2.145. The confidence interval is

$$7.00 - 2.145\frac{16.08}{\sqrt{15}} \le \mu_S - \mu_J \le 7.00 + 2.145\frac{16.08}{\sqrt{15}}$$

or

$$-1.9 \le \mu_S - \mu_J \le 15.9$$

b Because the value 0 is included in this 95% confidence interval, it follows that $H_0: \mu_S - \mu_J = 0$ cannot be rejected at $\alpha = .05$ using a two-tailed test. The t statistic is

$$t = \frac{7.00 - 0}{16.08/\sqrt{15}} = 1.69$$

which has a two-tailed p-value a little larger than .10.

c Matching is somewhat useful in accounting for individual differences in taste. There is some tendency for those who give high scores to S to also give high scores to J, and for those who give low S scores to also give low J scores. Had we erroneously used the two-sample formula, we would have had a larger standard error

$$s_p\sqrt{\frac{1}{15} + \frac{1}{15}} = 6.21$$

rather than the correct standard error

$$s_d/\sqrt{15} = 4.15 \quad \blacksquare$$

The formal statement of these matched-pairs procedures merely requires replacing y's by d's in the one-sample t distribution procedures. These are summarized next.

Definition 9.6   Confidence Interval for μ_d, Matched Samples

$$\bar{d} - t_{\alpha/2}s_d/\sqrt{n} \leq \mu_d \leq \bar{d} + t_{\alpha/2}s_d/\sqrt{n}$$

where n is the number of pairs of observations (and therefore the number of differences) and $t_{\alpha/2}$ cuts off a right-tail area of $\alpha/2$ for the t distribution with $n - 1$ d.f. $\quad \blacksquare$

Definition 9.7   Hypothesis Test for Matched Samples

$$H_0: \quad \mu_d = D_0 (D_0 \text{ is specified; often } D_0 = 0)$$

$$H_a: \quad 1.\ \mu_d > D_0$$
$$2.\ \mu_d < D_0$$
$$3.\ \mu_d \neq D_0$$

$$\text{T.S.}: \quad t = \frac{\bar{d} - D_0}{s_d/\sqrt{n}}$$

$$\text{R.R.}: \quad 1.\ t > t_\alpha$$
$$2.\ t < -t_\alpha$$
$$3.\ |t| > t_{\alpha/2} \quad \blacksquare$$

Most computer packages will carry out these calculations. For example, the tea-tasting experiment data of Example 9.10 were analyzed using Minitab, with the following results:

```
MTB > name c3 'Diff'
MTB > let 'Diff' = 'TeaS' - 'TeaJ'
MTB > ttest of 'Diff'
```

T-Test of the Mean

Variable	N	Mean	StDev	SE Mean	T	P-Value
Diff	15	7.00	16.08	4.15	1.69	0.11

The results are the same as we calculated in the example.

9.4

The Signed-Rank Method

On the previous section, we considered a t test for paired samples. Like any t test, it is based on an assumption that the underlying population (or process) has something reasonably close to a normal distribution. But what if a histogram, stem-and-leaf display, or boxplot of the differences—which are the data we're analyzing—clearly indicates a nonnormal distribution? There are alternatives to the t test that are more effective in clear nonnormal cases. One could test the null hypothesis that the *median* difference is 0. In this context, a median test is usually called a **sign test**; it counts the number of successes (values above the hypothesized median, zero), which is the same as counting the number of plus signs in the data. The sign test or, equivalently, a median confidence interval, is often a good choice in the case of a highly skewed distribution, especially if the sample size is too small to place much reliance on the Central Limit Theorem.

sign test

Wilcoxon signed-rank test

An alternative test, designed for data that are basically symmetric but outlier-prone, is the **Wilcoxon signed-rank test**. The formal null hypothesis for this test is that the true distribution of differences is symmetric around a specified number D_0; almost always D_0 is taken to be zero. The test is primarily sensitive to the distribution being shifted to the right or left of D_0; one- or two-sided research hypotheses may be tested. Again the test works with differences (if D_0 is not zero, D_0 is subtracted from each difference). Discard all differences that are exactly zero and reduce n accordingly. Then the differences are ranked in order of absolute value, smallest to largest. The appropriate sign is attached to each rank. Define

$T_+ =$ the sum of the positive ranks; if there are no positive ranks, $T_+ = 0$

$T_- =$ the sum of the negative ranks; if there are no negative ranks, $T_- = 0$

and $n =$ the number of nonzero differences

The Wilcoxon signed-rank test is presented next.

Definition 9.8   Wilcoxon Signed-Rank Test

H_0:   The distribution of differences is symmetric around D_0 (usually D_0 is zero).

H_a: 1. The differences tend to be larger than D_0.

2. The differences tend to be smaller than D_0.

3. The differences tend to be shifted away from D_0.

T.S.:   1. $T = |T_-|$

2. $T = T_+$

3. $T =$ smaller of $|T_-|, T_+$

$(n \leq 50)$: For a specified value of α (one-tailed .05, .025, .01, or .005; two-tailed .10, .05, .02, .01) and fixed number of nonzero differences n, reject H_0 if the value of T is less than or equal to the appropriate entry in Appendix Table 7.
$(n > 50)$: Compute the test statistic

$$z = \frac{T - \frac{n(n+1)}{4}}{\sqrt{\frac{n(n+1)(2n+1)}{24}}}$$

For cases 1 and 2, reject H_0 if $z < -z_\alpha$; for case 3, reject H_0 if $z < -z_{\alpha/2}$. ■

E X A M P L E   9 . 1 1

Refer to the data of Example 9.10. Use the signed-rank test to test the null hypothesis of symmetry around $D_0 = 0$ against a two-sided alternative. Use $\alpha = .05$. Compare your results to the following Minitab output; the signed-rank test is called "WTest" in this output.

```
MTB > WTest of 'Diff'

Wilcoxon Signed Rank Test

  TEST OF MEDIAN = 0.000000 VERSUS MEDIAN N.E. 0.000000

             N FOR   WILCOXON            ESTIMATED
         N   TEST   STATISTIC  P-VALUE    MEDIAN
Diff    15    14      78.0     0.117      7.250
```

Solution

The differences and their signed ranks are as follows:

	Person									
	1	2	3	4	5	6	7	8	9	10
Difference	+20	−10	+32	+16	+22	−15	+25	−23	+5	−7
Signed rank	+10	−4	+14	+8	+11	−7	+13	−12	+2	−3

	Person				
	11	12	13	14	15
Difference	0	−3	+12	+14	+17
Signed rank	X	−1	+5	+6	+9

The 0 difference (person 11) is discarded, so $n = 14$.

$$T_+ = 10 + 14 + 8 + 11 + 13 + 2 + 5 + 6 + 9 = 78$$
$$T_- = -4 - 7 - 12 - 3 - 1 = -27$$

(A good check is that $T_+ - T_-$ must always equal $n(n + 1)/2$, which equals 105 here.) For a two-sided research hypothesis, $T = \{$smaller of $|-27|$ and $78\} = 27$. Note that the Minitab output selects the value 78 for the test statistic. As long as the program has tables that are consistent with the choice, it doesn't matter; if we know the sample size and the sum of the positive ranks, we also know the sum of the negative ranks, and can use either one.

Because $n = 14 < 50$, we find the $\alpha = .05$ (two-sided) entry in Appendix Table 7; it is 21. Because $T = 27 > 21$, we cannot reject H_0 at $\alpha = .05$. We cannot reject at $\alpha = .10$ either; the table value is 25. Although we do not need the large-sample ($n > 50$) approximation in this problem, it can be computed:

$$z = \frac{27 - (14)(15)/4}{\sqrt{\frac{(14)(15)(29)}{24}}} = -1.60$$

For $\alpha = .10$ (two-tailed), we reject if $z < -z_{.05} = -1.645$; if we had used the z approximation we would not have rejected H_0 at $\alpha = .10$. Note that the output shows a p-value slightly larger than .10, which is consistent with our calculations. However we carry out the test, we can't reject the null hypothesis, even at $\alpha = .10$. There isn't much evidence that customers can detect the difference in the two teas, based on our data. ■

EXAMPLE 9.12

Use the signed-rank information in the following computer printout for the data of Example 9.9 to test the research hypothesis that garage 1's estimates tend to be higher than garage 2's. How does the result of the signed-rank test compare with the result of the t test of Example 9.9?

```
                   Hypothesis Test - Mean


Null hypothesis: mean = 0
Alternative: not equal


Computed t statistic = 3.71811
          P value = 0.0023




              Hypothesis Test - Median (Ranks Method)


Sample median = 1.08
Null hypothesis: median = 0
Alternative: not equal
Average rank of 12 values above 0 = 9.25
Average rank of 3 values below 0 = 3
0 values equal to 0 ignored.


Computed z statistic = 2.86821 (continuity correction applied)
P value = 0.0041
```

Solution

The output shows the signed-rank results as a test of median (ranks method). The p-value is shown as .0041, compared to the p-value of .0023 shown for the t test. The t test is slightly more conclusive, but whichever test is used, there is fairly clear evidence that the first garage has higher estimates than the second. ■

The choice of the appropriate paired-sample test from this section follows the guidelines of Chapter 8. If the assumptions of the t test are satisfied—in particular, if the distribution of differences is roughly normal—the t test is more powerful. If the distribution of differences is grossly skewed, the nominal t and signed-rank probabilities may be misleading. If the distribution is roughly symmetric but has heavy tails (as indicated by the presence of outliers), the signed-rank test may be more powerful. Often, as in Examples 9.10 and 9.11, the tests yield essentially the same conclusion.

Unless there are very obvious features (such as severe skewness or major outliers) in the data, these three methods will often give very similar conclusions. With a computer package, it's not difficult to obtain tests or confidence intervals using all three methods. If the results are similar, you can report them with comfort. If the results are clearly different, you should be able to find the "data gremlin" that is causing the difference; in such a case, use the analysis that is least sensitive to the particular problem you found.

EXAMPLE 9.13

A normal probability plot of the differences for the tea-tasting example is shown in Figure 9.5. Does this plot indicate that the signed-rank test should definitely be used instead of the t test of differences?

Solution

The plot is pretty much a straight line. There is no evident reason to think that the differences are nonnormal and therefore no evident reason to prefer a signed-rank test.

FIGURE 9.5 **Normal Probability Plot—Tea-Tasting Experiment**

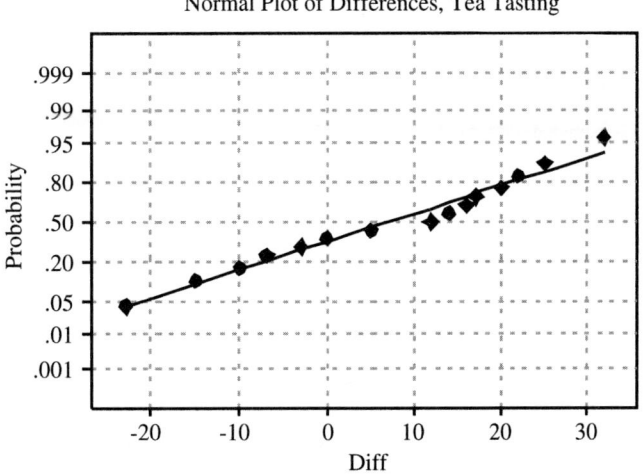

Normal Plot of Differences, Tea Tasting

EXERCISES

9.18 A manufacturer of an air compressor and tire pump wants to test two possible point-of-purchase displays. The product is sold through independent auto parts stores, which vary greatly in sales volume. A total of 30 stores agree to feature the display for one month. The stores are matched on the basis of annual sales volume. One of the two largest stores is randomly chosen to receive display A; the other receives B. The same thing is done for the third and fourth largest stores, and so on down to the two smallest. Sales for the 1-month period are recorded, along with Minitab output:

	Pairing														
Display	1	2	3	4	5	6	7	8	9	10	11	12	13	14	15
A	46	39	40	37	32	26	21	23	20	17	13	15	11	8	9
B	37	42	37	38	27	19	20	17	20	12	12	9	7	2	6
Difference	+9	−3	+3	−1	+5	+7	+1	+6	0	+5	+1	+6	+4	+6	+3

```
MTB > TInterval 90.0 'Diff'.

              N     MEAN    STDEV  SE MEAN    90.0 PERCENT C.I.
Diff         15    3.467    3.314   0.856   (  1.959,    4.974)

MTB > TTest 0.0 'Diff'

TEST OF MU = 0.000 VS MU N.E. 0.000

              N     MEAN    STDEV  SE MEAN       T    P VALUE
Diff         15    3.467    3.314   0.856     4.05     0.0012

MTB > WTest 0.0 'Diff'

TEST OF MEDIAN = 0.000000 VERSUS MEDIAN N.E. 0.000000

                  N FOR    WILCOXON            ESTIMATED
              N   TEST   STATISTIC  P-VALUE     MEDIAN
Diff         15    14       98.0     0.005      3.500
MTB > STest 0.0 'Diff'

SIGN TEST OF MEDIAN = 0.00000 VERSUS  N.E.  0.00000

              N  BELOW  EQUAL  ABOVE   P-VALUE    MEDIAN
Diff         15    2     1     12     0.0129     4.000
MTB > stem and leaf of 'Diff'

Stem-and-leaf of Diff     N = 15
Leaf Unit = 1.0


        1   -0 2
        2   -0 0
        5    0 011
        7    0 33
       (3)   0 455
        5    0 6667
        1    0 9
```

a Use a paired-sample *t* test to test the research hypothesis of unequal means. Use $\alpha = .10$.

b Locate the 90% confidence interval for the true mean difference. Show that it gives the same conclusion as the *t* test.

9.19 **a** The signed-rank test for the data of the previous exercise is shown as "WTest." Perform a two-tailed test of the null hypothesis that the median is 0, with $\alpha = .10$.

b How does the conclusion of this test compare with that of the *t* test?

c Does the stem-and-leaf display indicate that either test should not be believed?

9.20 Locate the *p*-values for the tests in the two preceding exercises.

9.21 Consider the situation of Exercise 9.18. An alternative approach would be to assign display A to 15 randomly chosen stores and display B to the rest. Assuming that the data were collected in that way, consider the following Minitab output.

```
MTB > Twosample of 'DisplayA' vs 'DisplayB'

TWOSAMPLE T FOR DisplayA VS DisplayB
              N    MEAN   STDEV   SE MEAN
DisplayA   15    23.8    12.3     3.2
DisplayB   15    20.3    13.0     3.4

95 PCT CI FOR MU DisplayA - MU DisplayB: ( -6.0,  13.0)

TTEST MU DisplayA = MU DisplayB (VS NE): T= 0.75  P=0.46  DF=  27
```

a Does the *t* test support the research hypothesis of unequal means at usual α values?

b Does there seem to be any advantage to the pairing process actually used?

9.22 Carry out a binomial (sign) test—called "STest" in the Minitab output—of the null hypothesis that the proportion of positive differences equals the proportion of negative differences. What was done about a zero difference?

9.23 A naive user of the Internet wanted to assess the performance of two "search engines" for finding sites on the World Wide Web. There were two candidate programs (engines), so the user tried out both on a sample of more or less typical search tasks. The programs were used in random order (sometimes engine 1 first; other times, engine 2). The important figure for ease of use was the total time required to complete a search, including both the input time and the actual computer usage. JMP output is shown in Figure 9.6.

FIGURE 9.6   **Comparison of Search Times**

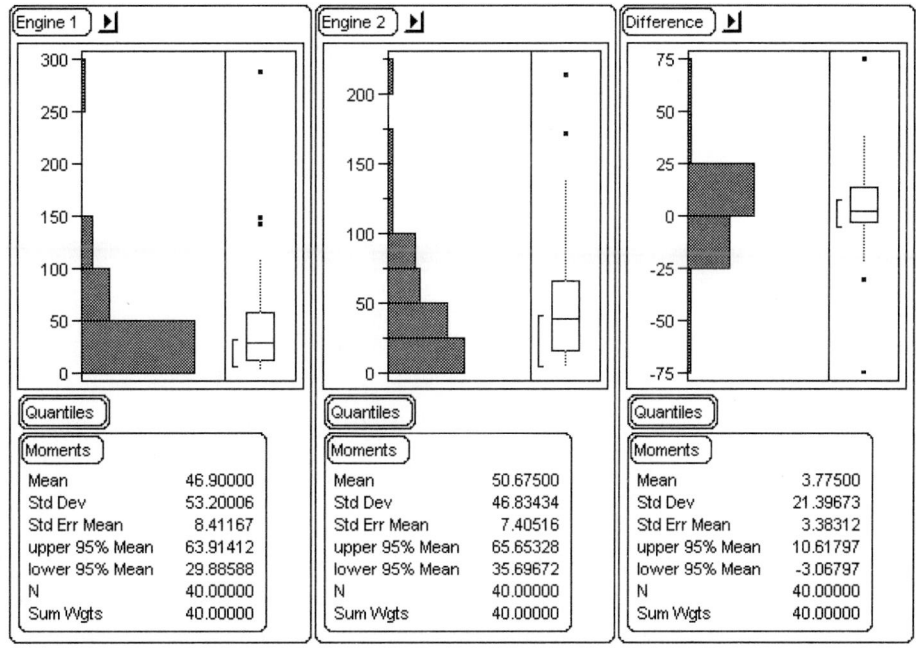

a Should the data be analyzed as independent or paired samples?

b Assuming (for better or for worse) that the paired-sample *t* test is used, what conclusion can be reached?

9.24 A maker of over-the-counter pain relief products feels ethically bound to put its products in child-resistant packages. However, many of its sales are to older people who might also have problems opening the packages. Two package designs were proposed. A sample of 40 older customers opened both packages; the time required (in seconds) was recorded. The data were input to the Systat computer package, with the following results:

```
PAIRED SAMPLES T-TEST ON PACKAGE1  VS PACKAGE2 WITH    40 CASES
MEAN DIFFERENCE =      -3.850
SD DIFFERENCE =     13.480
T =      -1.806 DF =   39 PROB =       0.079


SIGN TEST RESULTS

   COUNTS OF DIFFERENCES (ROW VARIABLE GREATER THAN COLUMN)

              PACKAGE1    PACKAGE2

PACKAGE1           0          10
PACKAGE2          30           0


   TWO-SIDED PROBABILITIES FOR EACH PAIR OF VARIABLES

              PACKAGE1    PACKAGE2

PACKAGE1        1.000
PACKAGE2        0.003       1.000


WILCOXON SIGNED RANKS TEST RESULTS

   COUNTS OF DIFFERENCES (ROW VARIABLE GREATER THAN COLUMN)

              PACKAGE1    PACKAGE2

PACKAGE1           0          10
PACKAGE2          30           0


   Z = (SUM OF SIGNED RANKS)/SQUARE ROOT(SUM OF SQUARED RANKS)

              PACKAGE1    PACKAGE2

PACKAGE1        0.000
PACKAGE2        2.704       0.000


     TWO-SIDED PROBABILITIES USING NORMAL APPROXIMATION

              PACKAGE1    PACKAGE2

PACKAGE1        1.000
PACKAGE2        0.007       1.000
```

Does the t test indicate a statistically detectable difference, say at $\alpha = .01$?

9.25 A normal probability plot of the data from Exercise 9.24 was created using Systat. The actual data are plotted on the horizontal axis and the normal scores on the vertical axis in Figure 9.7. Does this plot show that the data aren't normally distributed?

9.26 Systat also performed sign and signed-rank tests of the null hypothesis that the median difference is 0, using the data of Exercise 9.24. The tests were based on the differences, although the output may be unclear on that point.

a Does the sign test indicate that the null hypothesis should be rejected at $\alpha = .01$?

FIGURE 9.7   **Normal Plot of Delivery Time Differences**

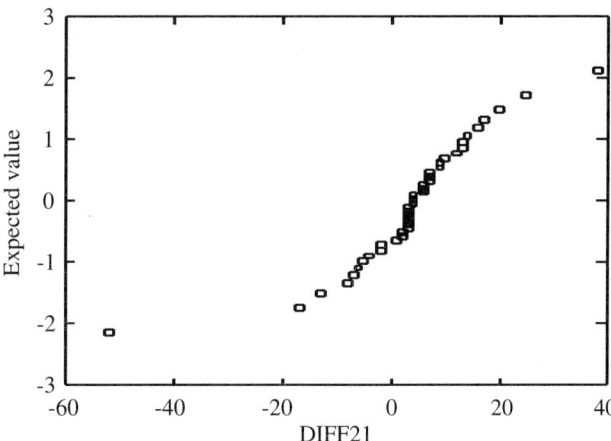

b Does the signed-rank test indicate that the null hypothesis should be rejected at $\alpha = .01$?

c How do the results of these tests compare to the results of the t test in Exercise 9.24? If there is a difference in the conclusion of the tests, what accounts for it? ∎

9.5   Summing Up

H ere are some suggestions for making comparisons between two samples.

1   As usual, consider possible biases in the sample. Equivalent biases may more or less cancel in making the comparison, but that's a risky assumption.

2   In analyzing the results, the first consideration is whether the samples are independent or paired. If there is a link between specific items in the two samples, they are paired.

3   For independent samples, plot the two samples separately. As usual, tests based on means (the pooled-variance t and the t' tests) are most effective for populations or processes that generate roughly normally distributed data. A rank-sum test is more powerful for highly skewed or outlier–prone data.

4   The choice between the pooled-variance t and the t' test depends on whether the sample sizes are roughly equal. If they aren't, the pooled-variance t method can give badly incorrect probability statements. If the sample sizes are balanced, the pooled-variance t method will give correct probabilities unless there is extreme skewness.

5   For paired samples, the relevant plot is a plot of differences. If the differences appear roughly normally distributed, it doesn't matter what the two samples look like.

6   Again, the t methods work best for roughly normally distributed data. The signed-rank approach works well for symmetric but outlier-prone differences, but can give incorrect probabilities if the differences are clearly skewed. In the skewed data case, a median (sign) procedure is the safest choice unless the sample size is large enough that the Central Limit Theorem effect can work.

In addition, you may want to reread the summary of key ideas at the beginning of the chapter.

EXAMPLE 9.14

Air quality specialists have developed a device that supposedly reduces air pollution through more vehicle engine combustion. In order to check this claim, a study was conducted. Sixteen cars were selected and measured for baseline readings of hydrocarbon (HC, measured in ppm) and carbon monoxide (CO). Three months later, each car was measured again for concentrations of HC and CO. The data are as follows:

Before		After	
HC	CO	HC	CO
040	0.36	030	0.21
120	0.42	105	0.44
051	2.61	049	2.21
240	0.63	221	0.65
210	0.85	150	0.70
058	0.28	050	0.25
304	0.53	250	0.39
161	0.25	175	0.42
037	0.41	024	0.35
125	0.66	131	0.72
428	0.93	404	0.81
401	0.61	385	0.40
287	0.22	301	0.29
322	0.71	330	0.73
144	1.16	125	10.1
098	0.13	085	0.09

Use the JMP IN output of Figure 9.8 to assess whether there is evidence of a reduction in HC and/or CO emissions, and if so, by how much.

Solution

First, note that this is a paired-sample situation. The same cars are measured before and after treatment. We begin, as usual, by examining plots of the data. The HC differences are roughly symmetric (although it's hard to say much with only 16 measurements) but the CO data are quite skewed.

To see if there is evidence of a reduction in emissions, we can use the "Test" portion of the output, which shows both t and signed-rank results. Note that the differences are calculated as before and after; because we're looking for a reduction in emissions, we hope that the average difference will be positive. For the CO data, the sample mean difference is actually negative, so there is no evidence of a reduction. For the HC data, the sample mean is positive, and the one-sided p-values for both t and signed-rank tests are quite small. Therefore, we have reasonably good evidence that there was a more than random reduction in HC emissions.

The 95% confidence interval for the HC differences indicates that if we treated the larger population of all similar cars, we would most likely obtain a mean reduction of somewhere between 2 and 24 ppm. Notice that most of the "before" HC emission values are in the hundreds; thus the mean change appears small. In summary, there is clear evidence of a small reduction in HC emissions, but no evidence of a reduction in CO emissions.

FIGURE 9.8 **Output for Emissions Data**

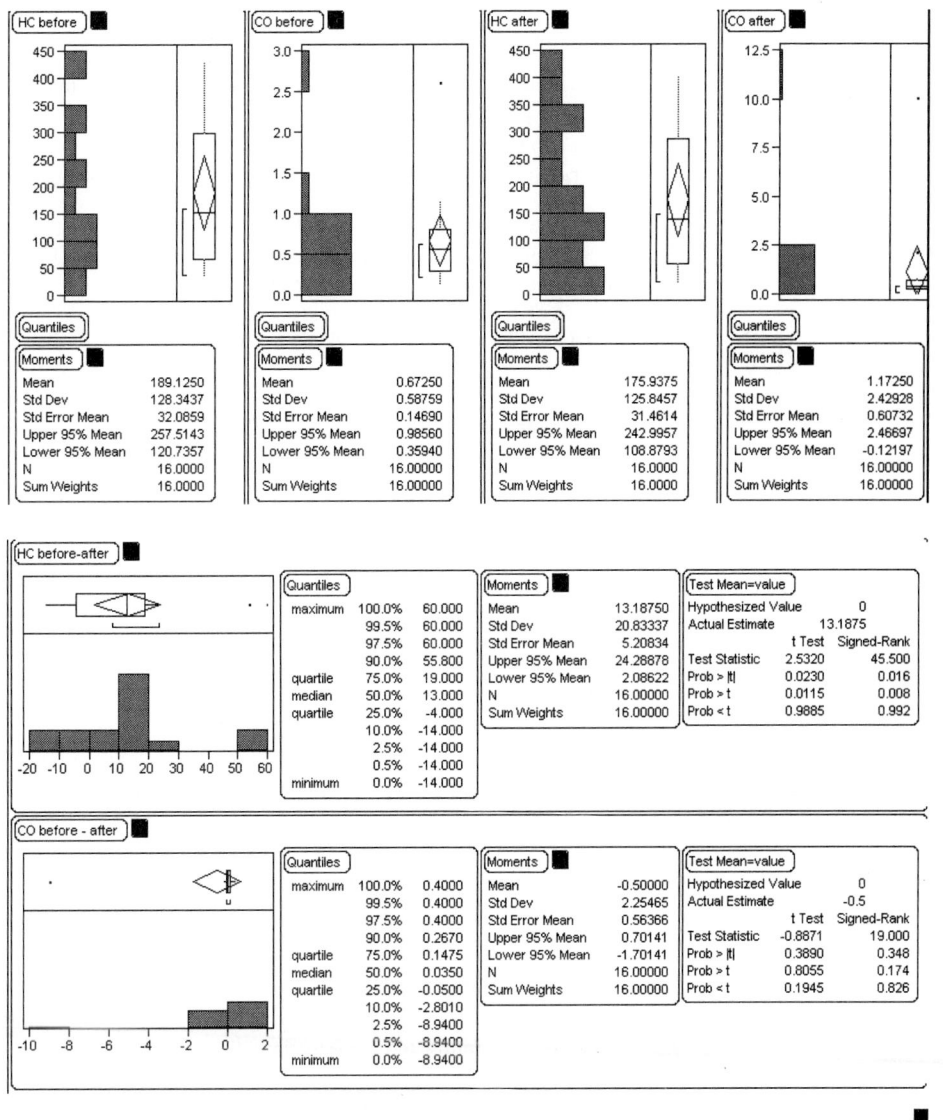

9.27 An auditor for a national bank credit card samples the accounts of two local banks that process cardholders' accounts. The results are

Bank	Accounts Audited	Accounts in Error	Mean Error	Standard Deviation
A	475	41	$41.27	$19.42
B	384	39	$60.38	$31.68

The mean and standard deviations are based on only those accounts that are in error.

a Calculate a 95% confidence interval for the difference in true error proportions.

b Can the research hypothesis of unequal proportions be supported using $\alpha = .05$?

9.28 Find the *p*-value for the test in Exercise 9.27.

9.29 Refer to the data of Exercise 9.27.

    a Calculate a 90% confidence interval for the difference in means.

    b Give a careful interpretation of this confidence interval. To what population(s) does it apply?

    c Test the research hypothesis of unequal means. Use $\alpha = .05$.

9.30 Find the *p*-value for the test of Exercise 9.29, part c.

9.31 A fruit grower plants 12 stands of each of two varieties of apple tree. At maturity, the following yields are observed (in bushels per 100 trees):

Variety R:	64.2	71.1	59.8	74.6	37.1	58.7	61.6	54.0	47.3	53.2	68.0	61.1
Variety K:	59.9	72.0	62.1	66.7	32.4	49.0	57.4	50.8	49.0	48.6	61.9	60.0

Assume that the 24 stands are randomly selected from the grower's available acreage and that the yields are listed in an arbitrary order. Minitab output follows:

```
MTB > TwoSample 95.0 'VarietyR' 'VarietyK';
SUBC>    Alternative 0;
SUBC>    Pooled.

TWOSAMPLE T FOR VarietyR VS VarietyK
             N     MEAN   STDEV   SE MEAN
VarietyR    12     59.2    10.4      3.0
VarietyK    12     55.8    10.5      3.0

95 PCT CI FOR MU VarietyR - MU VarietyK: ( -5.4,  12.2)

TTEST MU VarietyR = MU VarietyK (VS NE): T= 0.80  P=0.43  DF= 22

POOLED STDEV =      10.4
```

    a Use the *t* test to test the research hypothesis that the mean yield of variety R exceeds that of variety K. Use $\alpha = .10$.

    b Use an appropriate rank test for the same hypothesis. Again use $\alpha = .10$.

9.32 Histograms of the data of Exercise 9.31 are shown in Figure 9.9. Which of the tests in that exercise seems more appropriate? Does it matter (to the conclusion) which test is used?

9.33 Find *p*-values for the tests of Exercise 9.31.

9.34 Refer to the data of Exercise 9.31. Now assume that the grower plants the two varieties side by side on 12 plots and that the data are presented by plot number, as analyzed in the following Minitab output:

```
MTB > Let 'Diff' = 'VarietyR'- 'VarietyK'
MTB > TTest 0.0 'Diff';
SUBC>    Alternative 0.

TEST OF MU = 0.00 VS MU N.E. 0.00

              N     MEAN   STDEV   SE MEAN      T    P VALUE
Diff         12     3.41    3.74     1.08    3.15     0.0092

MTB > WTest 0.0 'Diff';
SUBC>    Alternative 0.

TEST OF MEDIAN = 0.000000 VERSUS MEDIAN N.E. 0.000000

                 N FOR   WILCOXON            ESTIMATED
            N    TEST   STATISTIC  P-VALUE    MEDIAN
Diff       12     12       70.0     0.017      3.700
```

FIGURE 9.9   **Histograms for Yield Data**

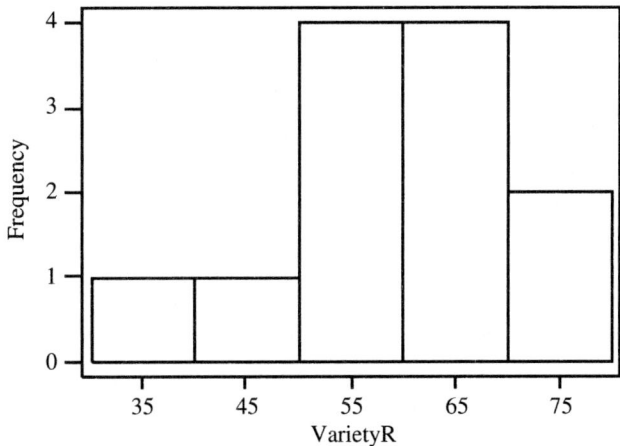

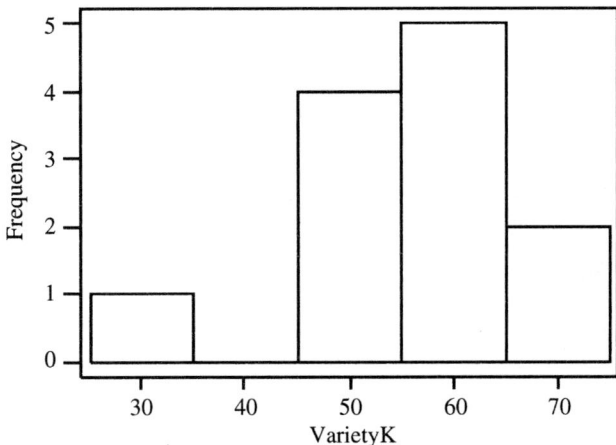

a Use a *t* test for the research hypothesis that the mean yield of variety R exceeds that of variety K. Use $\alpha = .10$.

b Use a rank test for this hypothesis, again using $\alpha = .10$.

9.35 Plot the relevant data for Exercise 9.34. Which of the tests in that exercise seems more appropriate? Does it matter (to the conclusion) which test is used?

9.36 Find *p*-values for the tests of Exercise 9.34.

9.37 Exercises 9.31 and 9.34 present two alternative experimental designs. What is the advantage of the design in Exercise 9.31? If this design is adopted, how would you select the plots to ensure that the yield ratings were reasonably valid for the grower's entire farm?

9.38 A coffee company wished to test its current method for grinding premium coffee against an experimental "coarse grind." The market research staff assembled 80 coffee drinkers as a test panel. Each panelist was present when pots of both grinds were brewed (because aroma during brewing was thought to be a cause of customer preference) and each tasted cups of coffee made from both grinds. The panelists evaluated taste and aroma on a 10-point scale, where 1 was worst and 10 was best.

a Why might the research staff want to make the study "blind," so that the panelists didn't know which coffee was which? How could blinding be arranged?

b Why might the staff want to present the coffees in random order? How could that be done?

9.39 The panelists' ratings in Exercise 9.38 were entered into Minitab and analyzed.

a Why should we regard the study as a paired-sample experiment?

b One part of the Minitab output is the following:

```
MTB > TInterval 95.0 'diff'.

              N     MEAN    STDEV   SE MEAN    95.0 PERCENT C.I.
diff         80    0.900    1.063    0.119   (  0.663,   1.137)
```

The differences were taken as "coarse"–"original." What does the interval indicate about the null hypothesis that $\mu_d = 0.00$?

c Calculate a 99% confidence interval for the mean difference. What does this interval indicate about the null hypothesis that $\mu_d = 0.00$?

9.40 Further output for Exercise 9.39, this time from Excel, is the following:

	A	B	C
1	t-Test: Paired Two Sample for Means		
2			
3			
4		Original	Coarse
5	Mean	4.7625	5.6625
6	Variance	2.208703	0.302373
7	Observations	80	80
8	Pearson Correlation	0.749864	
9	Hypothesized Mean Difference	0	
10	df	79	
11	t Stat	-7.57563	
12	P(T<=t) one-tail	2.91E-11	
13	t Critical one-tail	1.664371	
14	P(T<=t) two-tail	5.28E-11	
15	t Critical two-tail	1.990452	

Explain why the two-tailed p-value shown in the output is compatible with your answers in parts b and c of Exercise 9.39.

9.41 The data from Exercise 9.39 are also analyzed using a pooled-variance t method.

a Explain why this method should *not* be used in this situation.

b The Minitab results are as follows:

```
MTB > TwoSample 95.0 'original' 'coarse';
SUBC>    Pooled.

TWOSAMPLE T FOR original VS coarse
             N     MEAN    STDEV   SE MEAN
original    80     4.76     1.49     0.17
coarse      80     5.66     1.52     0.17

95 PCT CI FOR MU original - MU coarse: ( -1.37,  -0.43)

TTEST MU original = MU coarse (VS NE): T= -3.79  P=0.0002  DF= 158

POOLED STDEV =      1.50
```

What do the confidence interval and p-value in the output indicate about the null hypothesis of equal means?

c How does the width of this confidence interval compare to the width of the interval based on differences? What does the comparison indicate about the effectiveness of the pairing of observations?

9.42 A confidence interval and test based on the signed-rank method was also obtained for the data of Exercise 9.39.

```
MTB > WInterval 95.0 'diff'

                 ESTIMATED   ACHIEVED
              N    MEDIAN  CONFIDENCE  CONFIDENCE INTERVAL
diff         80     1.000       95.0  (   0.500,    1.000)
MTB > WTest 0.0 'diff'

TEST OF MEDIAN = 0.000000 VERSUS MEDIAN N.E. 0.000000

              N FOR   WILCOXON             ESTIMATED
          N   TEST   STATISTIC  P-VALUE     MEDIAN
diff     80     60     1669.5    0.000       1.000
```

Would you call these results substantially different from those we obtained in Exercises 9.39 and 9.40?

9.43 A stem-and-leaf display of the differences in Exercise 9.42 was obtained from Minitab:

```
MTB > stem and leaf of 'diff' data

Stem-and-leaf of diff      N = 80
Leaf Unit = 0.10


     1   -1 9
     7   -0 999999
    17   -0 0000000000
    27    0 0000000000
   (31)   1 0000000000000000000000000000000
    22    2 00000000000000000
     5    3 00000
```

Are the data so nonnormal that a *t* method should not be used?

9.44 Recently, a number of opticians established on-site laboratories for preparing prescription eyeglasses. These labs provide much more rapid service than conventional off-premises labs. Conventional opticians have questioned the accuracy of on-site labs. As a test, eyeglasses prescribed for nearsightedness were prepared by both types of labs. The glasses were evaluated by very accurate devices that determine the percentage deviation from the prescribed correction. A minus sign indicates that the actual correction is less than was prescribed; a plus sign, more than prescribed. The data were analyzed by Stata; source 1 is conventional labs, source 2 is on-site labs:

```
. ttest Discrep, by (Source)

  Variable |    Obs       Mean   Std. Dev.
  ---------+--------------------------------
        1 |     43  -.2446512   3.571654
        2 |     26      -.365   7.086478
  ---------+--------------------------------
  combined |     69       -.29   5.132753

        Ho:  mean(x) = mean(y)  (assuming equal variances)
                t = 0.09 with 67 d.f.
            Pr > |t| = 0.9256

. sdtest Discrep, by (Source)

  Variable |    Obs       Mean   Std. Dev.
  ---------+--------------------------------
        1 |     43  -.2446512   3.571654
        2 |     26      -.365   7.086478
  ---------+--------------------------------
  combined |     69          .   5.170577
```

$$\begin{aligned} \text{Ho:} \quad \text{sd}(x) &= \text{sd}(y) \\ F(25,42) &= 3.94 \\ \text{Pr} > F &= 0.0000 \end{aligned}$$

a Is there a statistically detectable (significant) difference of means, according to the output?

b Can the result be interpreted that there is no evidence of a difference between conventional and on-site labs?

9.45 **a** Use the computer output of Exercise 9.44 to test the null hypothesis of equal standard deviations, using a two-sided research hypothesis. Find bounds on the p-value. Note that we have not described this test, but the p-value may be interpreted as usual.

b What does the result of this test indicate about the relative quality of the two sources?

9.46 An accountant decides to test whether submitting federal income tax forms electronically will speed the delivery of refunds. The accountant submits one sample of forms electronically and sends another sample by mail. The number of business days until a refund is received is recorded in column 1 of the EX0946.DAT file on the data disk. Column 2 contains a code for the type of submission; a 1 indicates electronic submission, a 2 indicates mail submission. Load the data into the statistical computer package you use.

a Obtain means, standard deviations, and sample sizes for the two samples.

b Obtain separate plots of the two samples (histograms, stem-and-leaf displays, or normal plots, as you prefer).

c Based on this information, which of the several possible methods for comparing the average values in the samples seems most appropriate to you? Why?

d Carry out a formal test of the null hypothesis of equal means using the method you selected in part c. Locate the p-value.

9.47 **a** Obtain a 99% confidence interval for the difference of means in Exercise 9.46. Use the method you selected in that exercise.

b How does the interval confirm the result of the test in part d of Exercise 9.46?

9.48 A magazine conducted an experiment concerning investment advisers. The editors prepared 50 descriptions of the financial positions of hypothetical families with the husband earning a larger share of the income; they prepared an additional 50 descriptions that were identical, except that the wife earned the larger share of the income. Each description was sent to one of 100 advisers, who recommended a portfolio of investments. The editors calculated the previous year's yield on each investment. The yields are stored in the EX0948.DAT file on the data disk, with the husband-larger-income descriptions in column 1 and the matching wife-larger-income descriptions in column 2. Load the data into a statistical computer package that you can use.

a Explain why the data should *not* be analyzed using pooled-variance t methods.

b Have the package compute differences. Obtain a normal plot of the differences. Is there a clear indication of nonnormality?

c Obtain a t statistic for the null hypothesis that the mean of the differences is 0. Obtain a p-value.

d Should a one-sided or two-sided test be used here? (This question might just possibly provoke some gender-based disagreement.)

9.49 **a** Have the computer package perform a signed-rank test of the null hypothesis that the differences are symmetric around 0, using the difference data from Exercise 9.48. Which result is more conclusive, the signed-rank or the t test of Exercise 9.48?

b Using the same data, test the null hypothesis that the *median* difference is 0. Is this test more or less conclusive than the other two, or do they all give about the same conclusion?

9.50 **a** Ignore the fact that the pooled-variance t test isn't appropriate for the data of Exercise 9.48 and have the computer package use that method to test the null hypothesis of equal means. Locate the p-value.

b Is the pooled-variance t result more conclusive (that there is a detectable difference) than the t test on differences, or less so? What does the comparison of results indicate about the usefulness of matching descriptions.

9.51 A supermarket mailed coupons good for 25 cents off the price of cleaning products. At random, either product 1 or product 2 received the cents-off promotion. The supermarket wanted to find out which product would attract better-spending shoppers. The amount spent by each shopper who redeemed a coupon is recorded in column 1 of the EX0951.DAT file on the data disk; the product receiving the cents off for that coupon is shown in column 2. Load the data into your computer package.

   a Obtain histograms or stem-and-leaf displays of the purchase amounts separately for the two products. Do the plots appear roughly normal?

   b Obtain a 95% confidence interval for the difference of means using the pooled-variance t method. Also, obtain a similar interval using the separate-variance (t') method. For each interval, can we reject the null hypothesis of equal means using $\alpha = .05$?

   c Are the two intervals we obtained in part b essentially identical? If not, which one should be believed?

9.52 **a** Carry out formal t tests (both pooled variance and t') of the null hypothesis of equal means for the spending data of Exercise 9.51. Obtain two-tailed p-values for both tests.

   b Carry out a test of the null hypothesis of equal distributions using a rank-sum test. Again, obtain a two-tailed p-value.

   c Which of the three test results appears to be most conclusive? Can the p-value for this test be believed?

9.53 A university is negotiating a new contract with unionized staff members. One of the major issues in the negotiation is the structure of the benefits package. The largest component of this package is medical insurance, but there are other, substantial benefits as well. After considerable preliminary discussion, the union representatives have proposed a restructuring of the package. In return for union members accepting an increased deductible payment in the medical insurance plan, the representatives have proposed major increases in dental and tuition benefits, plus other small items.

   The university's human resources director is trying to estimate the cost of the proposed package as compared to the current one. The benefits that each staff member actually uses varies individually, so determining the cost requires analysis by hand. Rather than carrying out this analysis for every one of the several thousand unionized staff members, the director took a random sample of members. For each member, the director determined the cost in the past year of the current package and (a close approximation to) the cost of the proposal.

   The director asks you for help in analyzing the results, saying: "I'm not sure what's the best way to analyze the data. I got several different analyses from Minitab. They seem to give me very different answers, and I don't know which answers to believe. Plus, I've pretty much forgotten what the statistical terms mean, so I'd appreciate your explaining the results to me."

   Write the director a brief memo, indicating what the data say about the relative costs of the current and proposed packages. The data are in thousands of dollars per year. The output is shown here.

```
MTB > twosample t test of 'proposed' vs 'current'

TWOSAMPLE T FOR proposed VS current
             N      MEAN    STDEV   SE MEAN
proposed    100    13.18     6.72     0.67
current     100    12.57     6.29     0.63

95 PCT CI FOR MU proposed - MU current: ( -1.21,  2.43)

TTEST MU proposed = MU current (VS NE): T= 0.66  P=0.51  DF=  197

MTB > mann-whitney rank sum test of 'proposed' vs 'current'

Mann-Whitney Confidence Interval and Test

proposed   N = 100    Median =     11.142
current    N = 100    Median =     10.536
Point estimate for ETA1-ETA2 is      0.383
95.0 Percent C.I. for ETA1-ETA2 is (-0.894,1.714)
```

```
W = 10307.5
Test of ETA1 = ETA2  vs.  ETA1 ~= ETA2 is significant at 0.5300
The test is significant at 0.5300 (adjusted for ties)

Cannot reject at alpha = 0.05

MTB > let 'diff' = 'proposed' - 'current'
MTB > ttest of mean 0 using 'diff'

TEST OF MU = 0.000 VS MU N.E. 0.000

                N     MEAN    STDEV   SE MEAN        T    P VALUE
diff          100    0.611    1.427    0.143     4.28     0.0000

MTB > tinterval for 'diff'

                N     MEAN    STDEV  SE MEAN   95.0 PERCENT C.I.
diff          100    0.611    1.427    0.143  (  0.327,   0.894)

MTB > wtest (signed rank test) for 'diff'

TEST OF MEDIAN = 0.000000 VERSUS MEDIAN N.E. 0.000000

                    N FOR   WILCOXON           ESTIMATED
                N   TEST   STATISTIC  P-VALUE    MEDIAN
diff          100    100     3697.0    0.000     0.4798

MTB > stem-and-leaf of 'current'

Stem-and-leaf of current   N  = 100
Leaf Unit = 1.0

       4    0 5555
      20    0 66666667777777777
      39    0 88888888899999999999
     (15)   1 000000000001111
      46    1 22222222333333
      32    1 444455
      26    1 6666666777
      16    1 9
      15    2 0001
      11    2 233
       8    2 55
       6    2 667
       3    2
       3    3 0
       2    3 23

MTB > stem-and-leaf of 'proposed'

Stem-and-leaf of proposed  N  = 100
Leaf Unit = 1.0

       2    0 55
      15    0 6666677777777
      36    0 888888888889999999999
     (16)   1 0000000000011111
      48    1 222222222222333
      33    1 555555
      27    1 66777777
      19    1 899
      16    2 001
      13    2 233
```

```
10    2 55
 8    2 66
 6    2
 6    3 00111
 1    3

      HI  34,

MTB > stem-and-leaf of 'diff'

Stem-and-leaf of diff     N  = 100
Leaf Unit = 0.10

    1    -3 2
    2    -2 0
    5    -1 660
   34    -0 99998766654444433221100000000
  (36)    0 001111122233333445555666667778888899
   30     1 00012333555568
   16     2 012335799
    7     3 11112
    2     4
    2     5 8
    1     6 1
```

CASE STUDY

Comparing Two Samples

A maker of crackers and other snack food was market-testing two versions of a microwaved snack. A total of 200 adult volunteers were recruited at a suburban shopping mall one evening. Each person filled out a brief questionnaire concerning age, education, income, and similar facts. From these facts, each person received a Target Customer Score (TCS) based on how desirable the person would be as a customer. Then the questionnaires were sorted from lowest to highest TCS score. Customers with TCS scores 1, 4, 5, 8, 9, 12, and so on were assigned to Group K; TCS scores 2, 3, 6, 7, 10, 11, and so on went to Group S. (The letters meant nothing, deliberately.) Customers in both groups evaluated several other products and a number of possible television commercials. The important data were approval ratings of two versions (also labeled K and S) of the microwaved snack product. The ratings were based on a bidding system that the company believed gave accurate readings of actual preferences. The company thought that each additional bidding point, on average, would result in about three-tenths of a point of additional market share for the selected version of the product.

Group K

```
33  67  39  48  69  55  66  52  58  43  57  77  58
58  71  40  54  52  60  69  70  76  62  73  69  72
56  54  68  55  45  82  82  66  63  67  59  69  65
73  65  66  62  83  59  77  62  68  67  71  75  74
59  65  59  73  71  75  59  76  72  61  79  63  58
64  68  77  85  68  58  88  65  74  60  62  59  58
```

```
66  77  65  60  68  73  74  78  68  60  71  67  75
71  84  65  63  57  83  75  72  67
```

Group S

```
27  64  48  43  66  45  64  52  45  35  62  69  70
55  66  52  48  45  61  72  64  57  61  60  63  85
55  51  76  68  48  81  80  67  70  68  68  63  63
76  67  66  62  76  67  73  59  66  61  66  85  65
60  78  56  78  74  76  72  78  62  72  76  64  66
70  72  73  86  84  60  87  78  82  73  61  59  68
73  81  69  66  84  82  75  78  69  67  80  72  86
74  78  67  62  71  86  79  82  70
```

MTB > Describe 'Group K', 'Group S'

	N	MEAN	MEDIAN	TRMEAN	STDEV	SEMEAN
Group K	100	65.76	66.50	66.14	10.15	1.01
Group S	100	67.42	68.00	67.97	11.65	1.16

	MIN	MAX	Q1	Q3
Group K	33.00	88.00	59.00	73.00
Group S	27.00	87.00	61.25	76.00

The data, in order from lowest to highest TCS score, and some very preliminary analyses have been supplied to you. You have been selected as a consultant to determine whether the study has provided adequate information to decide which microwaved snack is better, and by how much. Perform whatever additional analyses you feel are necessary and prepare a consultant's report to the company. In your report, try to minimize the use of technical jargon. ■

A clever young student named Lee
Examined her data with glee.
The sample was small,
No skewness at all,
Which suited her test to a t.

Methods for Proportions

This chapter discusses standard methods for analyzing qualitative, categorical variables, where the data are simply counts or proportions of the number of items falling into various categories. The key ideas are:

1   The probability of a particular result may be compared for two samples. The procedure is essentially a t test or confidence interval based on data that are all 1 (when the result occurs) or 0 (when it doesn't).

2   If a set of theoretical probabilities is specified (separately from the sample data), the deviation of actually observed frequencies from these probabilities may be tested by a χ^2 goodness-of-fit test. One danger of this test is that a "good fit" conclusion may be wrongly taken as an indication that the theoretical probabilities are exactly correct.

3   A test of whether the data indicate a relation between two qualitative variables is based on a different χ^2 test, called a test of independence or of homogeneity. This test indicates only whether the apparent relation could reasonably have occurred by chance alone; it does not directly measure the strength of the relation.

4   The strength of a relation can be assessed by comparing percentages in different parts of a tabulation of the data, or by a measure λ of how well information about one variable can be used to predict the value of another.

5   An alternative form of expressing probabilities, the odds of an event, is a convenient way of assessing how a condition changes probabilities. The ratio of two odds is another way of assessing dependence between events.

6   All the probability statements, such as p-values and confidence levels, made in this chapter are approximations that work best for large samples. A conservative guideline for the use of these approximations requires that all expected frequencies be at least 5.

7   Because an individual observation of categories carries relatively little information, such as simply a 1 or 0, sample sizes often must be quite large to give a manager adequate tests or confidence intervals.

In the previous chapters, we concentrated largely on tests and confidence intervals for means. In this chapter, we consider procedures for proportions. The methods are based on the normal approximation to the binomial distribution, like the test in Section 8.6, so some consideration of required sample size is necessary. ∎

10.1   Two-Sample Procedures for Proportions

To begin, we consider comparing just two proportions. We assume that two *independent* random samples of sizes n_1 and n_2 are taken. The respective sample proportions are denoted as $\hat{\pi}_1$ and $\hat{\pi}_2$, and the (unknown) population proportions are called π_1 and π_2. Our goal is to make inferences about the difference, if any, in the population proportions. The natural estimator is the difference in sample proportions: $\hat{\pi}_1 - \hat{\pi}_2$. It is unbiased: $E(\hat{\pi}_1 - \hat{\pi}_2) = \pi_1 - \pi_2$. To calculate confidence intervals and perform hypothesis tests, we need a standard error formula. Recall from Chapter 7 that the variance of a sample

standard error of $\hat{\pi}_1 - \hat{\pi}_2$

proportion $\hat{\pi}$ is $\pi(1 - \pi)/n$. By the assumed independence of the two samples, we can add the variances of $\hat{\pi}_1$ and $\hat{\pi}_2$ to obtain

$$\text{Var}(\hat{\pi}_1 - \hat{\pi}_2) = \frac{\pi_1(1 - \pi_1)}{n_1} + \frac{\pi_2(1 - \pi_2)}{n_2}$$

$$\sigma_{\hat{\pi}_1 - \hat{\pi}_2} = \sqrt{\frac{\pi_1(1 - \pi_1)}{n_1} + \frac{\pi_2(1 - \pi_2)}{n_2}}$$

The confidence interval for $\hat{\pi}_1 - \hat{\pi}_2$ follows the familiar form: estimate plus or minus a table value times a standard error. The estimate is the difference of sample proportion of successes, $\hat{\pi}_1 - \hat{\pi}_2$, and $\sigma_{\hat{\theta}}$ is $\sigma_{\hat{\pi}_1 - \hat{\pi}_2}$. Because the standard error ($\sigma_{\hat{\pi}_1 - \hat{\pi}_2}$) depends on the unknown population proportions, π_1 and π_2, in practice we must substitute the sample proportions, $\hat{\pi}_1$ and $\hat{\pi}_2$, into the standard error formula. If both sample sizes are sufficiently large (say, at least 30), this substitution can be made without affecting the normal approximation.

Definition 10.1   100$(1 - \alpha)$% Confidence Interval for $\pi_1 - \pi_2$

$$(\hat{\pi}_1 - \hat{\pi}_2) - z_{\alpha/2}\sigma_{\hat{\pi}_1 - \hat{\pi}_2} \leq \pi_1 - \pi_2 \leq (\hat{\pi}_1 - \hat{\pi}_2) + z_{\alpha/2}\sigma_{\hat{\pi}_1 - \hat{\pi}_2}$$

where

$$\sigma_{\hat{\pi}_1 - \hat{\pi}_2} \approx \sqrt{\frac{\hat{\pi}_1(1 - \hat{\pi}_1)}{n_1} + \frac{\hat{\pi}_2(1 - \hat{\pi}_2)}{n_2}} \quad \blacksquare$$

EXAMPLE 10.1

A new product is test-marketed in the Grand Rapids, Michigan, and Wichita, Kansas, metropolitan areas. Advertising in the Grand Rapids area is based almost entirely on television commercials. In Wichita, a roughly equal dollar amount is spent on a balanced mix of television, radio, newspaper, and magazine ads. Two months after the ad campaign begins, surveys are taken to determine consumer awareness of the product.

	Grand Rapids	Wichita
Number interviewed	608	527
Number aware	392	413

Calculate a 95% confidence interval for the regional difference in the proportion of all consumers who are aware of the product.

Solution

The sample awareness proportion is higher in Wichita, so let's make Wichita region 1.

$$\hat{\pi}_1 = 413/527 = .784 \qquad \hat{\pi}_2 = 392/608 = .645$$

The estimated standard error is

$$\sqrt{\frac{(.784)(.216)}{527} + \frac{(.645)(.355)}{608}} = .0264$$

Therefore, the 95% confidence interval is

$$(.784 - .645) - 1.96(.0264) \leq \pi_1 - \pi_2 \leq (.784 - .645) + 1.96(.0264)$$

or

$$.087 \leq \pi_1 - \pi_2 \leq .191$$

which indicates that somewhere between 8.7% and 19.1% more Wichita consumers than Grand Rapids consumers are aware of the product. ∎

rule for sample sizes

This confidence interval method is based on the normal approximation to the binomial distribution. In Chapter 7 we indicated as a general rule that $n\hat{\pi}$ and $n(1 - \hat{\pi})$ should both be at least 5 to use this normal approximation. For this confidence interval to be used, the rule should hold for each sample. In practice, sample sizes that come even close to violating this rule aren't very useful because they lead to excessively wide confidence intervals. For instance, even though $n\hat{\pi}$ and $n(1 - \hat{\pi})$ are greater than 5 for both samples when $n_1 = 30$, $\hat{\pi}_1 = .20$ and $n_2 = 60$, $\hat{\pi}_2 = .10$, the 95% confidence interval is $-.06 \leq \pi_1 - \pi_2 < .26$; π_1 could be anything from 6 percentage points lower than π_2 to 26 percentage points higher.

The reason for confidence intervals that seem very wide and unhelpful is that each measurement conveys very little information. In effect, each measurement conveys only one "bit": a 1 for a success or a 0 for a failure. For example, surveys of the compensation of chief executive officers of companies often give a manager's age in years. If we replaced the actual age by a category such as "over 55 years old" versus "under 55," we definitely would have far less information. When there is little information per item, we need a large number of items to get an adequate total amount of information. Wherever possible, it is better to have a genuinely numerical measure of a result rather than mere categories. When numerical measurement isn't possible, relatively large sample sizes will be needed.

Hypothesis testing about the difference between two population proportions is based on the z statistic from a normal approximation. The typical null hypothesis is that there is no difference between the population proportions, though any specified value for $\pi_1 - \pi_2$ may be hypothesized. The procedure is very much like a t test of the difference of means, and is summarized next.

Definition 10.2   Hypothesis Test for $\pi_1 - \pi_2$

$$H_0: \quad \pi_1 - \pi_2 = D_0 \quad (D_0 \text{ is specified; often } D_0 = 0)$$

$$H_a: \quad 1. \ \pi_1 - \pi_2 > D_0$$

$$2. \ \pi_1 - \pi_2 < D_0$$

$$3. \ \pi_1 - \pi_2 \neq D_0$$

$$\text{T.S.:} \quad z = \frac{(\hat{\pi}_1 - \hat{\pi}_2) - D_0}{\sqrt{\dfrac{\hat{\pi}_1(1 - \hat{\pi}_1)}{n_1} + \dfrac{\hat{\pi}_2(1 - \hat{\pi}_2)}{n_2}}}$$

$$\text{R.R.:} \quad 1. \ z > z_\alpha$$

$$2. \ z < -z_\alpha$$

$$3. \ |z| > z_{\alpha/2}$$

Note: This test should be used only if $n_1\hat{\pi}_1$, $n_1(1 - \hat{\pi}_1)$, $n_2\hat{\pi}_2$, and $n_2(1 - \hat{\pi}_2)$ are all at least 5. ∎

E X A M P L E   1 0 . 2

Refer to Example 10.1. Test the hypothesis of equal population-awareness proportions against a two-sided alternative. State a p-value.

Solution

$\hat{\pi}_1 = .784$, $n_1 = 527$, $\hat{\pi}_2 = .645$, and $n_2 = 608$. The general rule for using a z test is amply met; the smallest of the four indicators is $n_1(1 - \hat{\pi}_1) = 114$.

$$z = \frac{(.784 - .645) - 0}{\sqrt{\frac{(.784)(.216)}{527} + \frac{(.645)(.355)}{608}}}$$

$$= \frac{.139}{.0264} = 5.26$$

A z value of 5.26 is far beyond the range of our z table. The p-value is some very small number. ∎

As in the one-sample situation, tests for a proportion can be approximated by t tests of means, using 1s and 0s for data. For example, the data of the previous examples, as a set of 392 1s and 216 0s for Grand Rapids and 413 1s and 114 0s for Wichita, yielded the following Minitab output:

```
MTB > TwoT of 'Aware' by 'City'


                Two
Sample T-Test and Confidence Interval


Twosample T for Aware
City    N     Mean    StDev   SE Mean
1      608    0.645   0.479   0.019
2      527    0.784   0.412   0.018


95% C.I. for mu 1 - mu 2: ( -0.191,  -0.087)
T-Test mu 1 = mu 2 (vs not =): T= -5.25  P=0.0000  DF=  1132
```

The confidence interval and test are very close to the results we obtained with hand calculation. For all practical purposes, the 1s and 0s method is as good as the hand calculation method.

EXERCISES

10.1 A consumer finance company considers its bad-debt experience for married and unmarried couples. A sample of 3200 loans yields the following data:

Status	Number of Loans	Bad Debts
Married	2128	102
Unmarried	1072	31

Calculate a 90% confidence interval for the true difference in proportions of bad debts.

10.2 Refer to the preceding exercise. Test the null hypothesis of equal proportions. Let H_a be two-sided. Use $\alpha = .10$.

10.3 Find p-values for the z statistic in Exercise 10.2.

10.4 In a survey, it is found that 1697 of 2961 urban area residents regularly watch a network television news program, whereas 674 of 983 rural or small-town residents are regular watchers.

a Calculate a 95% confidence interval for the difference in proportions.

b Test the research hypothesis that a higher percentage of rural (small-town) residents are regular watchers. Use $\alpha = .05$.

10.5 Find the *p*-value in Exercise 10.4. How conclusive is the evidence favoring the research hypothesis?

10.6 A retail computer dealer is trying to decide between two methods for servicing customers' equipment. The first method emphasizes preventive maintenance; the second emphasizes quick response to problems. Samples of customers are each served by one of the two methods. After six months, it is found that 171 of 200 customers served by the first method are very satisfied with the service, as compared to 153 of 200 customers served by the second method. Execustat output, based on 1s and 0s for data, follows:

```
Two Sample Analysis for satisfied by method


                          1              2

Sample size           200            200
Mean                    0.855          0.765      diff. = 0.09
Variance                0.124598       0.180678   ratio = 0.689612

Std. deviation          0.352984       0.425063

95% confidence intervals
    mu1 - mu2: (0.0131926,0.166807) assuming equal variances
    mu1 - mu2: (0.0131847,0.166815) not assuming equal variances

                Hypothesis Test - Difference of Means

Null hypothesis: difference of means = 0
Alternative: not equal
Equal variances assumed: no

Computed t statistic = 2.30362
            P value = 0.0218
```

Test the research hypothesis that the population proportions are different. Use $\alpha = .05$. State your conclusion carefully.

10.7 Locate a confidence interval for the difference of proportions in Exercise 10.6. Show that it reaches the same conclusion as the formal test about the research hypothesis.

10.8 The media selection manager for an advertising agency inserts the same advertisement for a client bank in two magazines. The ads are similarly placed in each magazine. One month later, a market research study finds that 226 of 473 readers of the first magazine are aware of the banking services offered in the ad, as are 165 of 439 readers of the second magazine (readers of both magazines are excluded). The following Minitab output was based on the appropriate number of 1s and 0s as data:

```
MTB > TwoT 'Aware?' 'Magazine'


            Two
Sample T-Test and Confidence Interval

Twosample T for Aware?
Magazine   N     Mean    StDev   SE Mean
1         473    0.478    0.500   0.023
2         439    0.376    0.485   0.023

95% C.I. for mu 1 - mu 2: ( 0.038,  0.166)
T-Test mu 1 = mu 2 (vs not =): T= 3.13  P=0.0018  DF=  908
```

a Calculate by hand a 95% confidence interval for the difference of proportions of readers who are aware of the advertised services. Compare your answer to the interval given by Minitab.

b Are the sample sizes adequate to use the normal approximation?

c Does the confidence interval indicate that there is a statistically significant difference using $\alpha = .05$?

10.9 Using the output of Exercise 10.8, perform a formal test of the null hypothesis of equal populations. Use $\alpha = .05$.

10.10 Samples of 30 electric motors for dot matrix printers are subjected to severe testing for reliability. Of the motors from supplier 1, 22 pass the test; of the motors from supplier 2, only 16 pass.

   a Show that the difference is not statistically significant at $\alpha = .05$ (two-tailed).

   b Can we claim to have shown that the two suppliers provide equally reliable motors?

10.11 Use the data of Exercise 10.10 to calculate a 95% confidence interval for the difference of proportions. Interpret the result carefully in terms of the relative reliability of the two suppliers. ■

10.2   Tests for Several Proportions

    In Chapter 8, we discussed hypothesis testing about a single proportion, often using an approximate z statistic. In this section, we'll extend the test to a single statistic for testing whether several deviations of sample data from theoretical proportions could plausibly have occurred by chance. The test uses a new distribution, the χ^2 (pronounced "ki square") distribution.

    The χ^2 distribution is not symmetric around 0, unlike the z and t distributions. A χ^2 statistic takes on only positive values. The distribution is right-skewed. Like the t distribution, it depends on degrees of freedom; unlike the t distribution, the degrees of freedom don't always depend on the sample size. The expected value of a χ^2 statistic happens to equal its degrees of freedom.

    Probabilities and values for a χ^2 distribution can be calculated by computer or looked up in tables. In most computer packages, a command such as CHISQDIST will give the cumulative probability up to a specified value for specified degrees of freedom; in Excel, the name is CHIDIST. The inverse problem, finding the value corresponding to specified cumulative probability and degrees of freedom, usually has INV in its name; in Excel, the name is CHIINV. Consult the package's help files for the exact name.

    The χ^2 table (Appendix Table 5) gives critical values that cut off a specified right-tail area a for given degrees of freedom (d.f.). In this respect, the χ^2 table is similar to the t table we used in the past few chapters. The χ^2 distribution is not symmetric; in this section we need only be concerned about values in the upper tail of the distribution, so the asymmetry won't be crucial.

goodness-of-fit test   The χ^2 **goodness-of-fit test** is used to test the hypothesis that several proportions have specified numerical values. For instance, suppose that a life insurance company has a mix of 40% whole life policies, 25% level term policies, 15% decreasing term policies, and 20% other types. A change in this mix could signal a need to change commission, reserve, or investment practices, but the company does not want to react to random short-term fluctuation. If the company does a study of the last 1200 policies issued (regarded as a random sample), the χ^2 goodness-of-fit test can be used to test the statistical significance of deviations from the historical percentages.

    In Chapter 8, we developed a test for a single binomial proportion; we often used a z approximation. We could run a separate test on the proportion for each policy type. The trouble with such a procedure is that although the Type I error is controlled at some level α for each test, the overall probability of error (incorrectly rejecting the null hypothesis in at least one test) may be much larger than α. If four separate tests are run at $\alpha = .05$, what is the probability of at least one Type I error? The tests are not independent. If one sample proportion is too high, the others tend to be too low because the sample proportions must add to 1. But there is no way to get an accurate assessment of the overall probability of error from combining several z tests. The goodness-of-fit method yields a combined test of all proportions with a specified overall α level.

multinomial sampling

The χ^2 procedure assumes **multinomial sampling**. This is the extension of binomial sampling to more than two categories. Now we have k categories, and in each of n independent trials, the probability of observing a member of category i is π_i. This probability is assumed to be constant over trials.

expected number

The procedure works by comparing the observed number in each category to the **expected number** in that category. If there are n items in a sample and the probability of any items falling in category i is π_i, then, by the binomial distribution, the expected number in category i is

$$E_i = n\pi_i$$

The test procedure is summarized next.

Definition 10.3 Goodness-of-Fit Test for Several Proportions

H_0: $\pi_i = \pi_{i,0}$ for categories $i = 1, \ldots, k$; $\pi_{i,0}$ are specified probabilities or proportions.

H_a: H_0 is not true.

T.S.: $\chi^2 = \sum_i \frac{(n_i - E_i)^2}{E_i}$, where n_i is the observed number in category i and $E_i = n\pi_{i,0}$ is the expected number under H_0.

R.R.: Reject H_0 if $\chi^2 > \chi^2_\alpha$, the right-tail α percentage point of a χ^2 distribution with d.f. $= k - 1$. Note that the d.f. depends on k, the number of categories, not on n, the number of observations. ■

E X A M P L E   1 0 . 3

Suppose that, in the insurance company illustration at the beginning of this section, the previous 1200 policies issued consist of 439 whole life policies, 323 level term policies, 197 decreasing term policies, and 241 others. Assess the statistical significance (at $\alpha = .10$) of any shift from the historical policy mix.

Solution

The following table summarizes the calculations:

Category, i	Whole Life	Level Term	Decreasing Term	Other	Total
Historical proportions, $\pi_{i,0}$	.40	.25	.15	.20	1.00
Observed number, n_i	439	323	197	241	1200
Expected number, $E_i = 1200\pi_{i,0}$	480	300	180	240	1200
$n_i - E_i$	−41	+23	+17	+1	0
$\frac{(n_i - E_i)^2}{E_i}$	3.502	1.763	1.606	.004	6.875

The number of categories is $k = 4$, so there are $k - 1 = 3$ d.f.; $\chi^2_{.10} = 6.25$ for 3 d.f. Because $\chi^2 = 6.875 > 6.25$, H_0 is rejected, and the shift from the historical mix is statistically significant at $\alpha = .10$. It appears that term policies are becoming more popular and whole life policies less so. (*Note:* The $\alpha = .05$ percentage point is 7.81. H_0 could not be rejected at $\alpha = .05$; therefore the p-value is somewhere between .05 and .10.) ■

Most statistical packages don't compute the goodness-of-fit test automatically because there isn't a convenient way to specify the hypothesized probabilities. A spreadsheet program will do the calculations. For example, Figure 10.1 shows the formulas for an Excel calculation of the previous example; Figure 10.2 shows the result.

FIGURE 10.1 **Excel Formulas for Goodness-of-Fit Test**

	A	B	C	D	E
1	HO probs.	Observed	Expected	(O-E)sq/E	p-value
2	0.4	439	=$A2*$B$7	=(($B2-$C2)^2)/$C2	=CHIDIST(D7,3)
3	0.25	323	=$A3*$B$7	=(($B3-$C3)^2)/$C3	
4	0.15	197	=$A4*$B$7	=(($B4-$C4)^2)/$C4	
5	0.2	241	=$A5*$B$7	=(($B5-$C5)^2)/$C5	
6					
7		=SUM(B2:B5)		=SUM(D2:D5)	

FIGURE 10.2 **Result of Goodness-of-Fit Test**

	A	B	C	D	E
1	HO probs.	Observed	Expected	(O-E)sq/E	p-value
2	0.4	439	480	3.502083	0.0760
3	0.25	323	300	1.763333	
4	0.15	197	180	1.605556	
5	0.2	241	240	0.004167	
6					
7		1200		6.8751	

multinomial assumptions

As with the binomial distribution, the key **multinomial assumptions** are independence of trials and constant probabilities over trials. Independence would be violated if several of the policies were sold to the same person or within the same family. Constant probability would be violated if the 1200 policies were sold over a long enough period that a time trend could matter. The most serious possible violation would occur if the policies were sold by relatively few agents and if there were major differences in product mix among agents.

The statistic for the χ^2 goodness-of-fit test is the sum of k terms, which is why d.f. depends on k, not n. There are $k - 1$ d.f. instead of k because the sum of the $n_i - E_i$ terms must always equal $n - n = 0$; $k - 1$ of these terms are free to vary, but the kth is determined by this requirement.

The mathematics underlying this test is based on an approximation that is a lineal descendant of the normal approximation to the binomial distribution. The quality of this approximation has been extensively studied. A fairly conservative general rule is that the approximation is adequate if all E_i are at least 5.0.

The goodness-of-fit test is used extensively to test the adequacy of various scientific theories. One problem of such applications is that the hypothesis of interest is formulated as the null hypothesis, not the research hypothesis. If a scientist has a pet theory and wants to show that it gives a good fit to the data, the scientist wants to accept the null hypothesis. But the potential error in accepting it is Type II, and β probabilities of Type II errors are hard to calculate. In general, the null hypothesis tends to be accepted (the β probability is high) if n is small or if there are many categories. Even if the general rule that all E_i are at

A "good fit" conclusion

least 5.0 is satisfied, the β risk can be large. **A "good fit" conclusion is always suspect.** Perhaps the best procedure for a manager is to look at deviations of sample proportions from theoretical proportions and to use the χ^2 test results as an indicator of the degree of potential random variation.

EXAMPLE 10.4

Suppose that in a test of a random walk theory of stock price changes, 125 security analysts are each asked to select four stocks listed on the New York Stock Exchange that are expected to outperform the Standard and Poor's Index over a 90-day period. According to one random walk theory of stock price changes, the analysts should do no better than coin flipping; the number of correct guesses by any particular analyst should follow a binomial distribution with $n = 4$ and probability of success .50. The data are

Number correct:	0	1	2	3	4
Frequency:	3	23	51	39	9

Test the random walk hypothesis at $\alpha = .05$ and at $\alpha = .10$.

Solution

The JMP IN package was used to carry out the calculations. The value of χ^2 and the p-value are shown several times in Figure 10.3. H_0 cannot be rejected at $\alpha = .05$ or even at $\alpha = .10$, and the data might be declared "a good fit" to the random walk theory. But the actual proportions of analysts who are correct for two, three, or four stocks are larger than those predicted by the theory. The result of the χ^2 test indicates that this fact could conceivably have been a collective lucky break for the analysts. We would say that such data would suggest, although by no means conclusively prove, that analysts can do somewhat better than the random walk theory would indicate.

FIGURE 10.3 **Goodness-of-Fit to Binomial Probabilities**

Number correct	H0 probs.	Observed	Expected	(O-E)sq/E	Chi-sq	p-value
0	0.0625	3	7.8125	2.9645	7.608	0.10704
1	0.25	23	31.25	2.178	7.608	0.10704
2	0.375	51	46.875	0.363	7.608	0.10704
3	0.25	39	31.25	1.922	7.608	0.10704
4	0.0625	9	7.8125	0.1805	7.608	0.10704

EXERCISES

10.12 The director of a data-processing center wants to test the Poisson distribution model for arrivals of jobs to a central computer. The mean arrival rate during the relevant period is 3.8 jobs per minute. Records are kept on the number of arrivals in each of 2000 1-minute periods. The results are

Arrivals:	0	1	2	3	4	5	6	7	8	9+
Frequency:	38	155	328	392	415	399	170	61	27	15

a Use Poisson tables ($\mu = 3.8$) to calculate probabilities for each category of number of arrivals.

b Calculate expected frequencies.

c Is the Poisson model a good fit to the data? Use $\alpha = .01$.

10.13 Can you detect any systematic discrepancy between the observed frequencies and the expected (Poisson model) frequencies in the data of Exercise 10.12?

10.14 A gift shop owner believes that 30% of the customers who enter the shop buy no items, 45% buy 1 item, and 25% buy 2 or more items. Observation of 25 customers yields the following data:

Number of purchases:	0	1	2+
Frequency:	10	6	9

a Calculate the expected frequencies, assuming that the owner's hypothesis is valid.

b Test the owner's hypothesis using $\alpha = .05$. Can the owner claim a good fit based on these data?

10.15 Suppose that the data in Exercise 10.14 are based on 250 customers, with respective frequencies 100, 60, and 90.

a Test the owner's hypothesis at $\alpha = .05$.

b Explain the discrepancy in the conclusion between this exercise and Exercise 10.14. ■

10.3 Chi-Square Tests for Count Data

I n Section 10.1, we showed a test for comparing two proportions. The data were simply counts of how many times we got a particular result in two samples. In this section, we extend that test. First, we present a single test statistic for testing whether several deviations of sample data from theoretical proportions could plausibly have occurred by chance.

When we first introduced probability ideas in Chapter 3, we started by using tables of frequencies (counts). At the time, we treated these counts as if they represented the whole population. In practice, we'll hardly ever know the complete population data; we'll usually have only a sample. When we have counts from a sample, they're usually arranged in **cross tabulations** or **contingency tables** such as those in Chapter 3. In this section, we'll describe one particular test that is often used for such tables, a chi-square test of independence.

In Chapter 3, we introduced the idea of independence. In particular we discussed the idea that **dependence** of variables means that one variable has some value for predicting the other. With sample data, there usually appears to be some degree of dependence. In this section, we develop a χ^2 test that assesses whether the perceived dependence in sample data may be a fluke—the result of random variability rather than real dependence.

First, the frequency data are to be arranged in a cross tabulation with r rows and c columns. The possible values of one variable determine the rows of the table, and the possible values of the other determine the columns. We denote the population proportion (or probability) falling in row i, column j as π_{ij}. The total proportion for row i is $\pi_{i.}$ and the total proportion for column j is $\pi_{.j}$. If the row and column proportions (probabilities) are independent, then $\pi_{ij} = \pi_{i.}\pi_{.j}$. For instance, suppose that a personnel manager for a large firm wants to assess the popularity of three alternative flexible time-scheduling (flextime) plans among clerical workers in four different offices. The following indicates a set of proportions (π_{ij}) that exhibit independence. The proportion of all clerical workers

cross tabulations
contingency tables

dependence

who favor plan 2 and work in office 1 is $\pi_{21} = .03$, the proportion of all workers favoring plan 2 is $\pi_{2.} = .30$, and the proportion working in office 1 is $\pi_{.1} = .10$. Independence holds for that cell because $\pi_{21} = .03 = (\pi_{2.})(\pi_{.1}) = (.30)(.10)$. Independence also holds for all other cells.

Favored Plan	Office				Total
	1	2	3	4	
1	.05	.20	.15	.10	.50
2	.03	.12	.09	.06	.30
3	.02	.08	.06	.04	.20
Total	.10	.40	.30	.20	

The null hypothesis for this χ^2 test is independence. The research hypothesis specifies only that there is some form of dependence—that is, that it is not true that $\pi_{ij} = \pi_{i.}\pi_{.j}$ in every cell of the table. The test statistic is once again the sum over all cells of

$$\text{(observed value} - \text{expected values)}^2/\text{expected value}$$

The computation of expected values E_{ij} under the null hypothesis is different for the independence test than for the goodness-of-fit test. The null hypothesis of independence does not specify numerical values for the row probabilities $\pi_{i.}$ and column probabilities $\pi_{.j}$, so these probabilities must be estimated by the row and column relative frequencies. If $n_{i.}$ is the actual frequency in row i, estimate $\pi_{i.}$ by $\hat{\pi}_{i.} = n_{i.}/n$; similarly $\hat{\pi}_{.j} = n_{.j}/n$. Assuming the null hypothesis of independence is true, it follows that $\hat{\pi}_{ij} = \hat{\pi}_{i.}\hat{\pi}_{.j} = (n_{i.}/n)(n_{.j}/n)$.

Definition 10.4   Estimated Expected Values $\hat{E}_{ij}$

Under the hypothesis of independence, the estimated expected value in row i, column j is

$$\hat{E}_{ij} = n\hat{\pi}_{ij} = n\frac{(n_{i.})}{n}\frac{(n_{.j})}{n} = \frac{(n_{i.})(n_{.j})}{n}$$

the row total multiplied by the column total divided by the grand total.   ■

E X A M P L E   1 0 . 5

Suppose that in the flexible time-scheduling illustration, a random sample of 216 workers yields the following frequencies:

Favored Plan	Office				Total
	1	2	3	4	
1	15	32	18	5	70
2	8	29	23	18	78
3	1	20	25	22	68
Total	24	81	66	45	216

Calculate a table of $\hat{E}_{ij}$ values.

Solution

For row 1, column 1 the estimated expected number is

$$\hat{E}_{11} \frac{(\text{row 1 total})(\text{column 1 total})}{\text{grand total}} = \frac{(70)(24)}{216} = 7.78$$

Similar calculations for all cells yield the following table.

Plan	Office 1	2	3	4	Total
1	7.78	26.25	21.39	14.58	70.00
2	8.67	29.25	23.83	16.25	78.00
3	7.56	25.50	20.78	14.17	68.01
Total	24.01	81.00	66.00	45.00	216.01

Note that the row and column totals in the $\hat{E}_{ij}$ table equal (except for round-off error) the corresponding totals in the observed (n_{ij}) table. ∎

Definition 10.5 χ^2 Test of Independence

H_0: The row and column variables are independent.

H_a: The row and column variables are dependent (associated).

T.S.: $\chi^2 = \sum_{i,j}(n_{ij} - \hat{E}_{ij})^2/\hat{E}_{ij}$

R.R.: Reject H_0 if $\chi^2 > \chi_\alpha^2$, where χ_α^2 cuts off area α in a χ^2 distribution with $(r-1)(c-1)$ d.f.; $r =$ number of rows, $c =$ number of columns.

The test statistic is sometimes called the Pearson χ^2 statistic. ∎

E X A M P L E   1 0 . 6

Carry out the χ^2 test of independence for the data of Example 10.5. First use $\alpha = .05$; then obtain a bound for the p-value.

Solution

The term for cell (1,1) is $(n_{11} - \hat{E}_{11})^2/\hat{E}_{11} = (15 - 7.78)^2/7.78 = 6.70$. Similar calculations are made for each cell. Substituting into the test statistic, we find $\chi^2 = 6.70 + \cdots + 4.33 = 27.12$. For $(3-1)(4-1) = 6$ d.f., the tabled χ^2 value (6 d.f., $\alpha = .05$) is 12.59. The observed χ^2 value of 27.12 far exceeds 12.59, so H_0 is rejected at $\alpha = .05$. In fact, 27.12 exceeds the tabled value even for $\alpha=.001$ (the smallest α in the table)—namely, 21.46. Therefore, H_0 is rejected even for $\alpha = .001$ and p-value $< .001$. ∎

d.f. for table

The degrees of freedom for the χ^2 test of independence relate to the number of cells in the two-way table that are free to vary while the marginal totals remain fixed. For example, in a 2×2 table (2 rows, 2 columns), only one cell entry is free to vary. Once that entry is fixed, we can determine the remaining cell entries by subtracting from the corresponding row or column total. In Table 10.1a, we have indicated some (arbitrary) totals. The cell indicated by * could take any value (within the limits implied by the totals), but then all remaining cells would be determined by the totals. Similarly, with a 2×3 table (2 rows, 3 columns), two of the cell entries, as indicated by *, are free to vary. Once these entries are set, the remaining cell entries are determined by subtracting from the appropriate row or column total (see Table 10.1b). In general, for a table with r rows and c columns, $(r-1)(c-1)$ of the cell entries are free to vary. This number represents the degrees of freedom for the χ^2 test of independence.

	Category B		Total			Category B			Total
Category A	*		16		Category A	*	*		51
			34						40
Total	21	29	50		Total	28	41	22	91

(a)   (b)

This χ^2 test of independence is also based on an approximation. A conservative rule is that each $\hat{E}_{ij}$ must be at least 5 to use the approximation comfortably. Standard practice if some $\hat{E}_{ij}$'s are too small is to lump together those rows (or columns) with small totals until the rule is satisfied.

likelihood ratio statistic

There is an alternative χ^2 statistic called the **likelihood ratio statistic** that is often shown in computer outputs. It is defined as

$$\text{likelihood ratio } \chi^2 = \sum_{ij} n_{ij} \ln(n_{ij}/(n_{i.} n_{.j}))$$

where $n_{i.}$ is the total frequency in row i, $n_{.j}$ is the total in column j, and ln is the natural logarithm (base $e = 2.71828$). Its value should also be compared to the χ^2 distribution with the same $(r-1)(c-1)$ d.f. Although it isn't at all obvious, this form of the χ^2 independence test is approximately equal to the Pearson form. There is some reason to believe that the Pearson χ^2 yields a better approximation to table values, so we prefer to rely on it rather than on the likelihood ratio form.

The only function of a χ^2 test of independence is to determine whether apparent dependence in sample data may be a fluke, plausibly a result of random variation. Rejection of the null hypothesis indicates only that the apparent association is not reasonably attributable to **strength of association** chance. It does not indicate anything about the **strength** or type **of association**.

The same χ^2 test statistic applies to a slightly different sampling procedure. An implicit assumption of our discussion surrounding the χ^2 test of independence is that the data result from a single random sample from the whole population. Often, separate random samples are taken from the subpopulations defined by the column (or row) variable. In the flextime example (Example 10.5), the data might well have resulted from separate samples (of respective sizes 24, 81, 66, and 45) from the four offices rather than from a single random sample of 216 workers. The null hypothesis of independence is then stated (in an equivalent form) as H_0: the conditional probability of row i given column j is the same for **test of homogeneity** all columns j. The test is called a **test of homogeneity** of distributions (that is, a test that the probabilities or proportions by column are equal). The mechanics and conclusions of the test are identical, so the distinction is minor.

E X A M P L E   1 0 . 7

A poll of attitudes toward five possible energy policies is taken. Random samples of 200 individuals from major oil-producing and natural gas-producing states, 200 from coal states, and 400 from other states are drawn. Each respondent indicates the most preferred alternative from among the following:

1   primarily emphasize conservation

2   primarily emphasize domestic oil and gas exploration

3 primarily emphasize investment in solar-related energy

4 primarily emphasize nuclear energy development and safety

5 primarily reduce environmental restrictions and emphasize coal-burning activities

The results are as follows:

Policy Choice	Oil/Gas States	Coal States	Other States	Total
1	50	59	161	270
2	88	20	40	148
3	56	52	188	296
4	4	3	5	12
5	2	66	6	74
Total	200	200	400	800

Execustat output also carries out the calculations. The second entry in each cell is a percentage in the column.

```
                              Crosstabulation
           OilGas      Coal      Other              Row
                                                    Total


   1           50        59        161              270
             25.0      29.5       40.3            33.75


   2           88        20         40              148
             44.0      10.0       10.0            18.50


   3           56        52        188              296
             28.0      26.0       47.0            37.00


   4            4         3          5               12
              2.0       1.5        1.3             1.50


   5            2        66          6               74
              1.0      33.0        1.5             9.25


Column        200       200        400              800
Total       25.00     25.00      50.00           100.00


              Summary Statistics for Crosstabulation

     Chi-square      D.F.           P Value


       289.22         8            0.0000


Warning: Some table cell counts < 5.
```

Conduct a χ^2 test of homogeneity of distributions for the three groups of states. Give the p-value for this test.

Solution

A test that the corresponding population distributions are different makes use of the following table of expected values:

Policy Choice	Oil/Gas States	Coal States	Other States
1	67.5	67.5	135
2	37	37	74
3	74	74	148
4	3	3	6
5	18.5	18.5	37

The table violates our general rule that all $\hat{E}_{ij}$'s be at least 5. There is no obvious choice for combining policy 4 with some other. Therefore, we leave the table as is, but we realize that the nominal χ^2 probabilities are slightly suspect. The test procedure is outlined here:

H_0: The column distributions are homogeneous.

H_a: The column distributions are not homogeneous.

T.S.: $\chi^2 = \sum (n_{ij} - \hat{E}_{ij})^2 / \hat{E}_{ij}$
$= (50 - 67.5)^2/67.5 + (88 - 37)^2/37 + \cdots + (6 - 37)^2/37$
$= 289.22$

R.R. and Conclusion: Because the tabled value of χ^2 for d.f. = 8 and $\alpha = .001$ is 26.12, p-value is $< .001$.

Even recognizing the limited accuracy of the χ^2 approximations, we can reject the hypothesis of homogeneity at some very small p-value. Percentage analysis, particularly of state type for a given policy choice, shows dramatic differences; for instance, 1% of those living in oil/gas states favor policy 5, compared to 33% of those in coal states who favor policy 5. ■

The χ^2 test described in this section has a limited but important purpose. This test only assesses whether the data indicate a statistically detectable (significant) relation among various categories. It doesn't measure how strong the apparent relation might be. A weak relation in a large data set may be detectable (significant); a strong relation in a small data set may be nonsignificant.

EXERCISES

10.16 A personnel director for a large, research-oriented firm categorizes colleges and universities as most desirable, good, adequate, and undesirable for purposes of hiring their graduates. Data are collected on 156 recent graduates, and each is rated by a supervisor.

School	Rating		
	Outstanding	Average	Poor
Most desirable	21	25	2
Good	20	36	10
Adequate	4	14	7
Undesirable	3	8	6

Output from the Execustat computer package follows:

```
                              Crosstabulation
               Outstanding   Average     Poor       Row
                                                     Total

Most desira        21          25          2          48
ble               43.8        52.1        4.2        30.77
Good               20          36         10          66
                  30.3        54.5       15.2        42.31


Adequate            4          14          7          25
                  16.0        56.0       28.0        16.03


Undesirable         3           8          6          17
                  17.6        47.1       35.3        10.90


     Column        48          83         25         156
     Total        30.77       53.21      16.03      100.00
```

Summary Statistics for Crosstabulation

```
   Chi-square     D.F.        P Value
     15.97          6          0.0139
```

Warning: Some table cell counts < 5.

a Locate the value of the χ^2 statistic.   **b** Locate the p-value.

c Can the director safely conclude that there is a relation between school type and rating?

d Is there any problem in using the χ^2 approximation?

10.17 Do the row percentages (the second entry in each cell of the output) reflect the existence of the relation we found in Exercise 10.16?

10.18 A study of potential age discrimination considers promotions among middle managers in a large company. The data are

	Age				
	Under 30	**30–39**	**40–49**	**50 and Over**	**Total**
Promoted	9	29	32	10	80
Not promoted	41	41	48	40	170
Total	50	70	80	50	

Minitab output follows:

```
MTB > Table 'promoted' 'agegroup';
SUBC>   Counts;
SUBC>   ColPercents;
SUBC>   ChiSquare.

  ROWS: promoted    COLUMNS: agegroup

            1       2       3       4      ALL

   1        9      29      32      10      80
         18.00   41.43   40.00   20.00   32.00
            9      29      32      10      80


   2       41      41      48      40     170
         82.00   58.57   60.00   80.00   68.00
           41      41      48      40     170
```

```
ALL      50      70      80      50     250
        100.00  100.00  100.00  100.00  100.00
         50      70      80      50     250

CHI-SQUARE =    13.025   WITH D.F. =    3

  CELL CONTENTS --
                    COUNT
                    % OF COL
                    COUNT
```

a Find the expected numbers under the hypothesis of independence.

b Justify the indicated degrees of freedom.

c Is there a statistically significant relation between age and promotions, using $\alpha = .05$?

10.19 Place bounds on the p-value in Exercise 10.18.

10.20 The data of Exercise 10.18 are combined as follows:

	Age		
	Up to 39	**40 and Over**	**Total**
Promoted	38	42	80
Not promoted	82	88	170
Total	120	130	

Minitab results:

```
MTB > Table 'promoted' 'combined';
SUBC>   Counts;
SUBC>   ColPercents;
SUBC>   ChiSquare.
  ROWS: promoted     COLUMNS: combined
             1        2      ALL

   1        38       42       80
          31.67    32.31    32.00
            38       42       80

   2        82       88      170
          68.33    67.69    68.00
            82       88      170

 ALL       120      130      250
          100.00   100.00   100.00
           120      130      250

CHI-SQUARE =    0.012   WITH D.F. =    1
```

a Can the hypothesis of independence be rejected using a reasonable α?

b What is the effect of combining age categories? Compare the answers to Exercise 10.18.

■

10.4 Measuring Strength of Relation

The χ^2 test we discussed in Section 10.3 has a built-in limitation. By design, the test only answers the question of whether there is a statistically detectable (significant) relation among the categories. It cannot answer the question of whether the relation is strong, interesting, or relevant. This is not a criticism of the test; no hypothesis test can answer these questions. In this section, we discuss methods for assessing the strength of relation shown in cross-tabulated data.

The simplest (and often the best) method for assessing the strength of a relation is simple percentage analysis. If there is no relation (that is, if complete independence holds), then percentages by row or by column show no relation. For example, suppose that a direct-mail company tests two different offers to see if the response rates differ. Their results are as shown here:

Offer	Response Yes	No	Total
A	40	160	200
B	80	320	400
Total	120	480	600

To check the relation, if any, we calculate percentages of response for each offer. We see that $(40/200) = .20$ (that is, 20%) respond to offer A and $(80/400) = .20$ respond to offer B. Because the percentages are exactly the same, there is no indication of relation. Alternatively, we note that one-third of the "yes" respondents and one-third of the "no" respondents were given offer A. Because these fractions are exactly the same, there is no indication of a statistical relation.

Of course, it is rare to have data that show absolutely no relation in the sample. More commonly, the percentages by row or by column differ, which suggest some relation. For example, a firm planning to market a cleaning product commissions a market research study of the leading current product. The variables of interest are the frequency of use and the rating of the leading product. The data are shown here:

Use	Rating Fair	Good	Excellent	Total
Rare	64	123	137	324
Occasional	131	256	129	516
Frequent	209	171	45	425
Total	404	550	311	1265

One natural analysis of the data takes the frequencies of use as givens and looks at the ratings as functions of use. The analysis essentially looks at conditional probabilities of the rating factor, given the use factor, but it recognizes that the data are only a sample, not the population. When use is rare, the best estimate is that $64/324 = .1975$ (or 19.75%) will rate the product as fair, that $123/324 = .3796$ will rate it good, and that $137/324 = .4228$ will rate it excellent. The corresponding proportions for occasional users are $131/516 = .2539$, $256/516 = .4961$, and $129/516 = .2500$. For frequent users, the proportions are .4918, .4024, and .1059. The proportions (or percentages, if one multiplies by 100) are quite different for the three use categories, which indicates that rating is related to use. Alternatively, we may calculate the use categories as percentages of the rating categories. In either case, there appears to be a relation. Because the proportions of ratings differ quite a bit as one varies use (or the proportions of use differ quite a bit as one varies rating), there is a suggestion that there is a fairly strong relation between use and rating.

Another way to analyze relations in data is to consider predictability. The stronger the relation exhibited in data, the better one can predict the value of one variable from the value of the other. We can imagine a situation where every rare user rated the product as excellent, every occasional user rated the product as good, and every frequent user rated the product fair. In such a case, there would be a perfect statistical relation; in terms of predictability, given the use, one could predict the rating exactly. Of course, in practice, prediction and relation are not perfect; we need a measure of strength of relation defined as degree of predictability.

We need to distinguish between a **dependent variable**—the variable one is trying to predict—and an **independent variable**—the variable one is using to make the prediction. If one is trying to predict Rating given Use, Use serves as the independent variable and Rating as the dependent variable. No cause-and-effect connotations are intended; the choice of independent and dependent variables is entirely up to the person who is analyzing the data.

The simplest prediction rule is to predict the most common value (the mode) of the dependent variable; this rule is the basis of the λ (lambda) predictability measure. In our use–rating example, when Use is rare, the most common Rating is excellent, with 137 responses; if one predicts excellent for every rare case, one makes $187 = 64 + 123 = 324 - 137$ prediction errors. Similarly for occasional use, a prediction of rating as good gives $260 = 131 + 129 = 516 - 25$ errors; given frequent use, a prediction of rating as fair gives $216 = 171 + 45 = 425 - 209$ errors. The total number of errors is $187 + 260 + 216 = 663$. By comparison, if use is not known, we would have to predict the most common rating—namely, good—and we would make $715 = 404 + 311 = 1265 - 550$ errors. Reasonably enough, we do better in predicting rating when we have information about use than when we have no information.

The λ measure indicates how much better we predict. When Use is the independent variable and Rating is the dependent variable, the difference in prediction errors is $715 - 663 = 52$; we take this difference as a fraction of the errors made not knowing the independent variable—namely, 715. If Use is the independent variable, then

$$\lambda = \frac{\text{errors with unknown independent variable} - \text{errors with known independent variable}}{\text{errors with unknown independent variable}}$$

$$= \frac{715 - 663}{715} = .073$$

The value of λ ranges between 0 and 1; $\lambda = 1$ indicates that, at least in the sample, the dependent variable is predicted perfectly given the independent variable. A value of $\lambda = 0$ occurs if there is independence in the data, or if the same value of the dependent variable is always predicted. To interpret other values of λ, note that it is a proportionate reduction in error (PRE) measure. The value $\lambda = .073$ that we found means that we make 7.3% fewer errors predicting rating given use than we would predicting rating without information about use. Values of λ above about .30 are rare in real data; thus, $\lambda = .073$ indicates a modest relation between rating and use. Note that the value of λ depends on which variable is taken as the dependent variable. For rating predicting use, $\lambda = .115$.

Definition 10.6 Calculation of λ

For every level of the independent variable (every row or every column), find the modal value of the dependent variable. If there are two or more modal values with equal frequency, choose one arbitrarily. Add the frequencies in all nonmodal cells to find K = number of prediction errors with known independent variable value.

Refer to the marginal (total) frequencies of the dependent variables. Add the frequencies in all nonmodal categories to find U = number of prediction errors with unknown independent variable values.

$$\lambda = (U - K)/U \quad \blacksquare$$

E X A M P L E   1 0 . 8

An internal survey of samples of clerical workers, supervisory personnel, and junior managers is taken to obtain opinions on a proposed flextime schedule. The following output (SAS) is obtained:

TABLE OF OPINION BY LEVEL

OPINION   LEVEL

```
FREQUENCY      |
  COL PCT      |         |         | junior|
               |clerical|  superv| manager|  TOTAL
---------------+--------+--------+--------+
strongly oppose |   5 |    8 |    9 |    22
               | 12.50 | 26.67 | 45.00 |
---------------+--------+--------+--------+
        oppose |    8 |   10 |    5 |    23
               | 20.00 | 33.33 | 25.00 |
---------------+--------+--------+--------+
         favor |   14 |    7 |    4 |    25
               | 35.00 | 23.33 | 20.00 |
---------------+--------+--------+--------+
strongly  favor |  13 |    5 |    2 |    20
               | 32.50 | 16.67 | 10.00 |
---------------+--------+--------+--------+
TOTAL             40      30      20
```

STATISTICS FOR TABLE OF OPINION BY LEVEL

STATISTIC	DF	VALUE	PROB
CHI-SQUARE	6	12.110	0.060

STATISTIC	VALUE	ASE
LAMBDA ASYMMETRIC C|R	0.120	0.106
LAMBDA ASYMMETRIC R|C	0.123	0.079

SAMPLE SIZE = 90
ASE IS THE ASYMPTOTIC STANDARD ERROR.
R|C MEANS ROW VARIABLE DEPENDENT ON COLUMN VARIABLE.

a   What does the χ^2 test indicate about the relation shown in the data?

b   What can you see by examining the column percentages?

c   Locate the value for λ with Opinion taken as the dependent variable. Interpret the number.

d   Verify the calculation of λ.

Solution

a   The χ^2 statistic is shown as CHI-SQUARE = 12.110 with 6 d.f. The p-value is shown as the PROB = .060. We cannot reject the null hypothesis of independence at $\alpha = .05$, but we can reject it at $\alpha = .10$. There is only limited evidence that the apparent relation is nonrandom; therefore, we should not place too much reliance on any apparent dependence.

b The clerical staff seems to be largely in favor (35%) or strongly in favor (32.5%). The junior managers are largely strongly opposed (45%) or opposed (25%), and the supervisors are more or less evenly spread out over various opinions. Again, the result of the χ^2 test indicates that we can't rely too heavily on this apparent relation; it could conceivably have arisen by sheer random variation.

c Here the row variable is the dependent variable. The statement that R|C MEANS ROW VARIABLE DEPENDENT ON COLUMN VARIABLE indicates that we want LAMBDA ASYMMETRIC R|C, which is .123.

d The predicted cells, with the column listed first, are (CLERICAL, FAVOR), (SUPERV, OPPOSE), (JUNIOR MANAGER, STRONGLY OPPOSE). Adding the frequencies in all other cells, we find $K = 5 + 8 + 13 + 8 + 7 + 5 + 5 + 4 + 2 = 57$. In the TOTAL column for OPINION, we find that the most frequent opinion is FAVOR. Adding the frequencies for the other categories, we find $U = 22 + 23 + 20 = 65$. Therefore

$$\lambda = \frac{65 - 57}{65} = .123 \quad \blacksquare$$

Percentage analyses and values of λ play a fundamentally different role than does the χ^2 test. The point of a χ^2 test is to see how much evidence there is that there *is* a relation, whatever the size may be. The point of percentage analyses and λ is to see *how strong* the relation appears to be, taking the data at face value. The two types of analyses are complementary.

10.5 Odds

Another way to analyze count data on qualitative variables is to use the concept of odds. This approach is widely used in biomedical studies and could be useful in some market research contexts as well. The basic definition of odds is the ratio of the probability that an event happens to the probability that it doesn't happen.

Definition 10.7 Odds of an Event

$$\text{odds of event } A = \frac{P(A)}{1 - P(A)} \quad \blacksquare$$

If an event has probability 2/3 of happening, the odds are $\frac{2/3}{1/3} = 2$. Usually this is reported as "the odds of the event happening are 2 to 1." If an event has probability .2, the odds are $\frac{.2}{.8} = .25$. Although this is usually reported as "the odds are 1 to 4 against this event happening," we often say ".25 to 1" instead. It's often easier to think about results if the odds are stated consistently as "something to 1."

Odds can be converted back to probabilities:

$$P(A) = \frac{\text{odds of event } A}{1 + \text{odds of event } A}$$

If the odds of a firm winning a bid are 1 to 4, which we'd express as .25 to 1, the probability of the firm winning the bid is .25/(1.25) = .20. "Even odds"—odds of 1 to 1—convert to a probability of $1/(1 + 1) = .50$. If the odds of an event A are very small, such as .01 to 1, odds are almost equal to probability: $P(A) = .01/(1.01) \approx .01$.

Odds are a convenient way to see how the occurrence of a condition changes the probability of an event. Recall from Chapter 3 that the conditional probability of an event A given another event B is

$$P(A|B) = P(A \text{ and } B)/P(B)$$

The odds favoring an event A given another event B turn out after a little algebra to be

$$\frac{P(A|B)}{P(\text{not } A|B)} = \frac{P(A)}{P(\text{not } A)} \frac{P(B|A)}{P(B|\text{not } A)}$$

The initial odds are multiplied by the *likelihood ratio*, the ratio of the probability of the conditioning event given A to its probability given not A. If B is more likely to happen when A is true than when it is not, the occurrence of B makes the odds favoring A go up.

EXAMPLE 10.9

In Chapter 3, we considered both a population in which 1 of every 1000 people carried the HIV virus and a test that yielded positive results for 95% of those who carry the virus and (false) positive results for 2% of those who do not carry it. If a randomly chosen person obtains a positive test result, should the odds that that person carries the HIV virus go up or go down? By how much?

Solution

We certainly would think that a positive test result would increase the odds of carrying the virus. It would be a strange test indeed if a positive result decreased the chance of having the disease! Take the event A to be "carries HIV" and the event B to be "positive test result."

Before the test is made, the odds of a randomly chosen person carrying HIV are

$$\frac{.001}{.999} \approx .001$$

The occurrence of a positive test result causes the odds to change to

$$\frac{P(\text{HIV}|\text{positive})}{P(\text{not HIV}|\text{positive})} = \frac{P(\text{HIV})}{P(\text{not HIV})} \frac{P(\text{positive}|\text{HIV})}{P(\text{positive}|\text{not HIV})} = \frac{.001}{.999} \frac{.95}{.02}$$

$$\approx (.001)(47.5) = .0475$$

The odds of carrying HIV do go up given a positive test result, from about .001 (to 1) to about .0475 (to 1). ■

odds ratio

A closely related idea, widely used in biomedical studies, is the **odds ratio**. As the name indicates, it is the ratio of the odds of an event (for example, contracting a certain form of cancer) for one group (for example, men) to the odds of the same event for another group (for example, women). The odds ratio is usually defined using conditional probabilities but can be stated equally well in terms of joint probabilities.

Definition 10.8   Odds Ratio of an Event for Two Groups

If A is any event with probabilities $P(A|\text{Group 1})$ and $P(A|\text{Group 2})$, the odds ratio is

$$\frac{P(A|\text{Group 1})/[1 - P(A|\text{Group 1})]}{P(A|\text{Group 2})/[1 - P(A|\text{Group 2})]} = \frac{P(A \text{ and Group 1})/[1 - P(A \text{ and Group 1})]}{P(A \text{ and Group 2})/[1 - P(A \text{ and Group 2})]}$$

The odds ratio equals 1 if the event A is statistically independent of group. ■

For example, suppose we have the following table of frequencies of purchase of a special suspension package for two brands of sports sedans:

	Yes	No	Total
Brand 1	250	750	1000
Brand 2	400	1600	2000
Total	650	2350	3000

We would estimate the conditional probabilities of purchasing or not purchasing the package, given the brand, as

	Yes	No	Total
Brand 1	.250	.750	1.000
Brand 2	.200	.800	1.000

The odds ratio is $\frac{.250/.750}{.200/.800} = 1.333$, indicating that the odds of purchasing the package are 33.3% higher for purchasers of brand 1 than for purchasers of brand 2. It does not appear that purchasing the package is independent of brand (although we will have to allow for the fact that we have limited sample data). We could equally well have calculated the odds ratio as $\frac{(250/3000)(750/3000)}{(400/3000)/(1600/3000)} = \frac{250/750}{400/1600} = 1.333$.

Inference about the odds ratio is usually done by way of the natural logarithm of the odds ratio. Recall that "ln" is the usual notation for the natural logarithm (base $e = 2.71828$) and that $\ln(1) = 0$. When the natural logarithm of the odds ratio is estimated from count data, it has approximately a normal distribution, with expected value the natural logarithm of the population odds ratio. Its standard error can be estimated by summing up 1/frequency for all four counts in a table, and then taking the square root. For the suspension package purchasing data, $\ln(\text{odds ratio}) = \ln(1.333) = 0.2874$; the estimated standard error is

$$\sqrt{1/250 + 1/750 + 1/400 + 1/1600} = 0.0920$$

With these results, we can compute a 95% confidence interval as

$$0.2874 - 1.96(0.0920) \leq \ln(\text{odds ratio}) \leq 0.2874 + 1.96(0.0920)$$

or

$$0.1071 \leq \ln(\text{odds ratio}) \leq 0.4677$$

We may convert this to a statement about the odds ratio by "unlogging"—exponentiating—the interval.

$$e^{0.1071} \leq \text{odds ratio} \leq e^{0.4677}$$

or

$$1.113 \leq \text{odds ratio} \leq 1.596$$

Because the interval does not include an odds ratio of 1.000 (or, equivalently, the interval for ln(odds ratio) does not include 0.000), we may conclude that there is a statistically detectable relation in the data.

10.6 Summing Up

Here are some notions about dealing with count data involving qualitative (categorical) variables.

1. A χ^2 goodness-of-fit test compares counts to theoretical probabilites that are specified outside the data. In contrast, a χ^2 independence test compares counts in one subset (one row, for example) to counts in other rows within the data. One way to decide which test is needed is to ask whether there is an externally stated set of theoretical probabilities. If so, the goodness-of-fit test is in order.

2. As is true of any significance test, the only purpose of a χ^2 test is to see whether differences in sample data might reasonably have arisen by chance alone. A test cannot tell you directly how large or important the difference is.

3. In particular, a statistically detectable (significant) χ^2 independence test does not necessarily mean a strong relation, nor does a nonsignificant goodness-of-fit test necessarily mean that the sample fractions are very close to the theoretical probabilities.

4. Looking thoughtfully at percentages is crucial in deciding whether the results show practical importance.

In addition, you may want to reread the summary of key ideas at the beginning of the chapter.

E X A M P L E 1 0 . 1 0

A total of 9035 granted mortgage loans were categorized by the institution granting the loan (banks, bank-owned mortgage companies, or independent mortgage companies), as well as by income level of the borrower. Analysts wanted to know if there was a statistical relation between loan-granting institution and income level of borrowers who were granted loans. The data are as follows:

	A	B	C	D	E
1		Banks	Bank	Mortgage	Total
2			Owned	Company	
3					
4					
5	<$21,000	943	166	151	1260
6	$21,000 to <$33,000	2186	503	711	3400
7	$33,000 to <$42,000	708	211	589	1508
8	$42,000 to <$50,000	424	150	397	971
9	$50,000+	948	239	709	1896
10					
11	Total	5209	1269	2557	9035

Based on the Excel results shown in Figure 10.4, do we see a clear indication of some degree of statistical relation? If so, does it appear to be a strong one?

Solution

First, note that the type of mortgage lender is a qualitative variable. Also, the amount of the mortgage has been categorized into five groups, so we should treat it as qualitative as well.

To test for the presence of a statistical relation, we use the χ^2 statistic shown in the Excel results. The p-value is tiny; remember that the "E-110" notation means "move the decimal point 110 places to the left." So the p-value is a point followed by 109 zeros followed by 3!! This is slightly more than adequate evidence that there is a relation.

The small p-value does *not* necessarily imply a strong relation; it could also be the result of a weak relation and large sample size. To assess the strength of the relation, look at the percentages for each loan size in the lower left corner of the output. There is a clear pattern. As the size of the loan increases, an increasing percentage of the loans is

FIGURE 10.4 **Excel Results for Mortgage Data**

	A	B	C	D	E	F	G	H	I	J	K
1		Banks	Bank	Mortgage	Total			Banks	Bank	Mortgage	Total
2			Owned	Company					Owned	Company	
3											
4											
5	<$21,000	943	166	151	1260		<$21,000	726.435	176.972	356.593	1260
6	$21,000 to <$33,000	2186	503	711	3400		$21,000 to <$33,000	1960.22	477.543	962.236	3400
7	$33,000 to <$42,000	708	211	589	1508		$33,000 to <$42,000	869.416	211.804	426.78	1508
8	$42,000 to <$50,000	424	150	397	971		$42,000 to <$50,000	559.816	136.381	274.803	971
9	$50,000+	948	239	709	1896		$50,000+	1093.11	266.3	536.588	1896
10											
11	Total	5209	1269	2557	9035						
12											
13	Chi-square statistic	534.48									
14	p-value	3.E-110									
15											
16		Banks	Bank	Mortgage	Total						
17			Owned	Company							
18	<$21,000	78.84	13.17	11.98	100						
19	$21,000 to <$33,000	64.29	14.79	20.91	100						
20	$33,000 to <$42,000	46.95	13.99	39.06	100						
21	$42,000 to <$50,000	43.67	15.45	40.89	100						
22	$50,000+	50.00	12.61	37.39	100						
23											
24	Total	57.65	14.05	28.3	100						

held by mortgage companies and a decreasing percentage by banks. This trend reverses itself slightly for amounts over $50,000, but it generally holds fairly well. The change in percentages is not enormous, however, so we wouldn't say that the relation was extremely strong.

Rather, it's a clear but modest relation. ■

EXERCISES

10.21 A speaker who advises managers on how to avoid being unionized claims that only 25% of industrial workers favor union membership, 40% are indifferent, and 35% are opposed. In addition, the adviser claims that these opinions are independent of actual union membership. A random sample of 600 industrial workers yields the following data:

	Favor	Indifferent	Opposed	Total
Members	140	42	18	200
Nonmembers	70	198	132	400
Total	210	240	150	600

a What part of the data is relevant to the 25%, 40%, 35% claim?

b Test this hypothesis using $\alpha = .01$.

10.22 What can be said about the p-value in Exercise 10.21?

10.23 Test the hypothesis of independence in the data of Exercise 10.21. How conclusively is it rejected?

10.24 Calculate (for the data of Exercise 10.21) percentages of workers in favor of unionization, indifferent to it, and opposed to it; do so separately for members and for nonmembers. Do the percentages suggest there is a strong relation between membership and opinion?

10.25 Three different television commercials are advertising an established product. The commercials are shown separately to theater panels of consumers; each consumer views only one of the possible commercials and then states an opinion of the product. Opinions range from 1 (very favorable) to 5 (very unfavorable). The data are

Commercial	Opinion					
	1	2	3	4	5	Total
A	32	87	91	46	44	300
B	53	141	76	20	10	300
C	41	93	67	36	63	300
Total	126	321	234	102	117	900

   a Calculate expected frequencies under the null hypothesis of independence.

   b How many degrees of freedom are available for testing this hypothesis?

   c Is there evidence that the opinion distributions are different for the various commercials? Use $\alpha = .01$.

10.26 State bounds on the p-value for Exercise 10.25.

10.27 In your judgment, is there a strong relation between type of commercial and opinion in the data of Exercise 10.25? Support your judgment with computations of percentages and a λ value.

10.28 A direct-mail retailer experimented with three different ways of incorporating order forms into its catalog. In type 1 catalogs, the form was at the end of the catalog; in type 2, it was in the middle; and in type 3, there were forms both in the middle and at the end. Each form was sent to a sample of 1000 potential customers, none of whom had previously bought from the retailer. A code on each form allowed the retailer to determine which type it was; the number of orders received on each type of form was recorded. Excel was used to calculate expected frequencies and the χ^2 statistic. Excel's CHITEST function gave the p-value. The results are shown in Figure 10.5.

   a What does the null hypothesis of statistical independence indicate about the three types of order forms?

   b Can this null hypothesis be retained at normal α levels?

10.29 Locate the value of λ for predicting RECEIVED knowing TYPE FORM. Does it capture the relation between the two variables?

10.30 A programming firm had developed a more elaborate, more complex version of its spreadsheet program. A "beta test" copy of the program was sent to a sample of users of the current program. From information supplied by the users, the firm rated the sophistication of each user; 1 indicated standard, basic applications of the program and 3 indicated the most complex applications. Each user indicated a preference between the current version and the test version, with 1 indicating a strong preference for the current version, 3 indicating no particular preference between the two versions, and 5 indicating a strong preference for the new version. The data were analyzed using JMP IN. Partial output is shown here.

```
SOPHIST By PREFER
Crosstabs
SOPHIST PREFER
Count   1       2       3       4       5       Row %
1       32      28      17      12      8       97
        32.99   28.87   17.53   12.37   8.25
2       10      24      16      6       4       60
        16.67   40.00   26.67   10.00   6.67
3       2       4       5       8       14      33
        6.06    12.12   15.15   24.24   42.42
        44      56      38      26      26      190


Tests
Source    DF      -LogLikelihood   RSquare (U)
Model     8       19.91046         0.1036
Error     180     172.23173
C Total   188     192.14219
Total Count       190


Test               ChiSquare    Prob>ChiSq
Likelihood Ratio   39.821       <.0001
Pearson            44.543       <.0001
```

FIGURE 10.5 **Results for Catalog Experiment**

	A	B	C	D	E	F	G	H
1	Observed			Received?			max. freq.	
2			No	Yes	Total			
3		1	944	56	1000		944	
4	Type form	2	961	39	1000		961	
5		3	915	85	1000		915	
6			2820	180	3000		2820	
7							lambda (column dep.)	
8	Expected						0	
9			No	Yes	Total			
10		1	940	60	1000			
11	Type form	2	940	60	1000			
12		3	940	60	1000			
13			2820	180	3000			
14								
15		chi sq.	19.18440					
16		p-value	0.00007					

a Do the ROW PERCENT entries suggest there is a relation between SOPHIST and PREFER? If the data showed no relation, what would be true of the ROW PERCENTS?

b Does the (PEARSON) CHI-SQUARE computation indicate there is a statistically detectable (significant) relation at usual values of α?

10.31 A chain of video rental stores did a survey (a more-or-less random sample) of its customers. The two responses of most interest to the store were customers' frequency of renting and customers' rating of the adequacy of the stores' selection. The responses are stored in the 10PT31.EXR file of the data disk, which you should load into the computer package you use. Column 1 contains codes for the frequency of renting, with code 1 indicating the lowest frequency and 4 the highest. Similarly, column 2 contains codes for rating the adequacy of selection, with code 1 begin the poorest rating and code 4 the best.

a Obtain the frequencies for each category of adequacy of selection rating.

b Test the null hypothesis that the categories are equally likely. (Many computer packages won't do a goodness-of-fit test easily, so you may have to do some hand computation.) Can the hypothesis be rejected at $\alpha = 10$? What about at $\alpha = .01$?

10.32 **a** Using the data of Exercise 10.31, test the null hypothesis that frequency and selection adequacy are statistically independent. What does the p-value indicate about this null hypothesis?

b Is there any reason to think that the expected frequencies are so low that the claimed p-value in part a is a poor approximation?

10.33 Using the data of Exercise 10.31, obtain percentages of customers in each adequacy rating; do so separately for each frequency code. Can you find any trend in the percentages as the frequency of renting increases?

10.34 The benefits manager for a major bank surveyed a sample of 353 employees (out of several thousand) to obtain their opinions of two alternative medical benefits plans. The variables of interest were: age (five categories, with 1 being a code for the youngest employees, 5 for the oldest); opinion (five categories, with 1 being most in favor of a health maintenance organization option, 5 being most in favor of a traditional fee-for-service option, and 3 being neutral); and a code for whether the employee has dependents covered by the plan (0 if not, 1 if so). The responses are listed (in order stated for columns 1–3) in the 10PT34.EXR file of the data disk. Load that file into your computer package.

a Obtain a table of frequencies for each combination of age and opinion codes. If the computer package will do so, obtain percentages in each opinion code for each age category. Are the opinion percentages similar for the various age codes?

b Have the computer package carry out a formal test of the null hypothesis that age and opinion are independent. Can the null hypothesis be rejected at $\alpha = .05$?

10.35 The benefits manager in Exercise 10.34 suspected that there might be an indirect relation between age and opinion: age might be related to whether dependents are covered, and whether dependents are covered might be related to opinion.

a Have the computer package test for dependence between age and dependents. Is the relation conclusively established?

b Do the same analysis for dependents and opinion.

c Have the computer package test for dependence between age and opinion. Have the computer package test separately for those employees with dependents covered and for those employees without dependents covered. In these tests, is there any evidence of a relation?

10.36 The president of a motel chain is preparing to make a decision among four ownership groups competing for a franchise to open a new motel in a fast-growing "edge city" (a suburban area that has a large concentration of offices and shopping areas). All four groups have operated other motels in the same geographical area, so the chain has information about consumer satisfaction for them all.

The president has requested that the most recent guest survey results for the four groups be compared. The two key areas of interest, as far as the president is concerned, are guests' ratings of building quality and of service quality. Both are rated on a 1 to 5 scale, with 1 denoting poor, 5 denoting excellent, and 3 denoting average, in the guests' opinions.

Of course, the president would prefer to grant the franchise to the ownership group that had achieved the best ratings. The financial arrangements negotiated with the groups were very similar, so much of the decision hinged on the ratings. The president realized that the survey covered only a small fraction of the people who had stayed at the various groups' motels in the recent past. However, the survey was the most unbiased information available about how the chain's customers perceived the four contending groups.

The president is not sure whether to emphasize the building ratings or the service ratings. In addition, there is a question whether to compare the entire range of ratings or to concentrate on the proportion of above average (4 and 5) ratings.

The president obtained the following Systat output, and asks you to explain what that output indicates about the relative standing of the four ownership groups. Write an explanation; the president has only a vague idea of what technical statistical terms mean, but does understand percentages quite well.

```
TABLE OF BUILDING    (ROWS) BY    OWNER    (COLUMNS)

FREQUENCIES

               1.000    2.000    3.000    4.000    TOTAL
           -------------------------------------------
   1.000 |    11        8        15        6  |      40
         |                                    |
   2.000 |    10        6        18        5  |      39
         |                                    |
   3.000 |    51       50        42       38  |     181
         |                                    |
   4.000 |    30       41        26       40  |     137
         |                                    |
   5.000 |    22       29        16       40  |     107
           -------------------------------------------
   TOTAL     124      134       117      129         504
```

TABLE OF BUILDING   (ROWS) BY   OWNER   (COLUMNS)

COLUMN PERCENTS

	1.000	2.000	3.000	4.000	TOTAL	N
1.000	8.87	5.97	12.82	4.65	7.94	40.00
2.000	8.06	4.48	15.38	3.88	7.74	39.00
3.000	41.13	37.31	35.90	29.46	35.91	181.00
4.000	24.19	30.60	22.22	31.01	27.18	137.00
5.000	17.74	21.64	13.68	31.01	21.23	107.00
TOTAL	100.00	100.00	100.00	100.00	100.00	
N	124	134	117	129	504	

TEST STATISTIC	VALUE	DF	PROB
PEARSON CHI-SQUARE	34.167	12	0.001
LIKELIHOOD RATIO CHI-SQUARE	32.737	12	0.001

TABLE OF SERVICE   (ROWS) BY   OWNER   (COLUMNS)

FREQUENCIES

	1.000	2.000	3.000	4.000	TOTAL
1.000	15	16	23	11	65
2.000	18	21	17	18	74
3.000	36	31	33	24	124
4.000	29	35	21	33	118
5.000	26	31	23	43	123
TOTAL	124	134	117	129	504

TABLE OF SERVICE   (ROWS) BY   OWNER   (COLUMNS)

COLUMN PERCENTS

	1.000	2.000	3.000	4.000	TOTAL	N
1.000	12.10	11.94	19.66	8.53	12.90	65.00
2.000	14.52	15.67	14.53	13.95	14.68	74.00
3.000	29.03	23.13	28.21	18.60	24.60	124.00
4.000	23.39	26.12	17.95	25.58	23.41	118.00
5.000	20.97	23.13	19.66	33.33	24.40	123.00
TOTAL	100.00	100.00	100.00	100.00	100.00	
N	124	134	117	129	504	

TEST STATISTIC	VALUE	DF	PROB
PEARSON CHI-SQUARE	18.117	12	0.112
LIKELIHOOD RATIO CHI-SQUARE	17.679	12	0.126

TABLE OF SERVICE   (ROWS) BY BUILDING   (COLUMNS)

FREQUENCIES

	1.000	2.000	3.000	4.000	5.000	TOTAL
1.000	32	15	17	1	0	65
2.000	5	11	48	10	0	74
3.000	3	12	65	36	8	124
4.000	0	1	37	55	25	118
5.000	0	0	14	35	74	123
TOTAL	40	39	181	137	107	504

TEST STATISTIC	VALUE	DF	PROB
PEARSON CHI-SQUARE	422.856	16	0.000
LIKELIHOOD RATIO CHI-SQUARE	391.617	16	0.000

Testing a Relation

In the Case Study for Chapter 4, a bank was considering three variables from a sample survey of 2150 customers as part of a plan to offer a debit card. The relevant variables were X = numbers of active credit cards held by a customer, Y = number of credit cards carrying unpaid balances, and Z = number of debit cards desired. The following frequencies were reported in the case for Chapter 4:

x:	0	0	0	1	1	1	1	1	1	2	2	2	2	2	2
y:	0	0	0	0	0	0	1	1	1	0	0	0	1	1	1
z:	0	1	2	0	1	2	0	1	2	0	1	2	0	1	2
Freq.:	98	45	10	125	110	28	171	203	38	96	87	18	150	228	66

x:	2	2	2	3	3	3	3	3	3	3	3	3	3	3	3
y:	2	2	2	0	0	0	1	1	1	2	2	2	3	3	3
z:	0	1	2	0	1	2	0	1	2	0	1	2	0	1	2
Freq.:	43	160	51	11	15	10	37	78	29	13	51	22	10	23	34

Recall that the product manager thought that customers with low values of X (of Y) would tend to have high values of Z. Construct cross-tabulations of X and Z and also of Y and Z. Supplement your analysis of the Chapter 4 case with appropriate tests of the hypothesis of no relation. What do the results of these tests indicate? In particular, do they generally support the product manager's belief? ■

A voyeurish sort was dejected,
His Peeping Tom tries all deflected.
"Whatever I try,
I find out that my
Observed is much less than Expected."

Analysis of Variance and Designed Experiments

This chapter introduces some of the basic ideas of designing and analyzing statistical experiments. Careful experimentation is one key to improving quality of goods and services. Analysis of variance (ANOVA) methods can deal with a wide variety of experimental situations. The key ideas are:

1   The first step in analyzing an experiment is to determine what the factors are (variables that are deliberately varied in carrying out the experiment) and what the response or dependent variable is.

2   The analysis of variance is based on taking apart the total sum of squared deviations from the grand mean. In a one-factor experiment, the total sum of squares is analyzed into sums of squares between groups (reflecting differences in mean values for the levels of the factor) and within groups (reflecting random variation or error).

3   An F test is an overall test to determine whether there is a more than random difference somewhere among the means.

4   If the underlying populations are highly skewed or outlier-prone, a Kruskal-Wallis rank test usually is more effective in detecting any real differences.

5   The Tukey method for comparing pairs of means controls the overall risk of false positive errors. Each pair of means is compared to a critical value determined by a table value times a standard error.

6   When there are two or more factors, there is the possibility of interaction. Interaction is an "it depends" concept. Two factors interact if the effect on the response variable of varying one factor depends on the level of the other factor.

7   Interaction can be detected graphically by using a profile (interaction) plot. Profiles that are nearly parallel indicate little interaction. Interaction can be detected numerically by comparing cell means to the results predicted by simply adding the effects of each factor. The ANOVA table for a two-factor experiment with multiple measurements in each cell includes sums of squares for each factor separately, for interaction, and for random error.

8   When interaction is large, the separate effect of one factor (averaged over levels of the other) is usually not very relevant. What is more interesting is finding the best combination of factor levels.

9   A randomized block experiment is an extension of the idea of paired samples. In such an experiment, the factor of interest is randomized within levels of another, nuisance factor, which is thought to affect the response. The purpose is to avoid confounding (mixing together) the effects of the two factors and to control for an important source of variability. When there is only one observation per cell, as is usually true in randomized block experiments, it isn't possible to separate interaction from random error.

10   Carefully designed experiments can evaluate the main effects of many factors at once; there is no need to examine every combination of factor levels. Designs such as orthogonal arrays and fractional factorials can help managers improve quality performance at low cost.

One of the most notable trends in management during the past decade has been the use of scientifically controlled, carefully designed experiments. Controlled experiments are especially useful to managers in the assessment of the likely effect of changes. To assess the probable results of a change in product, process, or policy, one can perform an experiment on carefully chosen samples, make the change, and measure the results. Well-designed experiments convert a discussion from speculative opinion to the assessment of actual data. That's an improvement.

This chapter is devoted to analysis of variance (ANOVA) methods that were specifically developed to analyze experimental data. These methods are also useful in certain nonexperimental situations. Typically, the data resulting from an experiment consist of multiple samples, so we must extend the two-sample methods from Chapter 9 to apply to many samples. In Section 11.1, we discuss ANOVA methods for one-factor experiments in which the multiple samples are obtained by changing the values of a single experimental variable. We explore a rank-based alternative method in Section 11.2. We list some more detailed methods for exploring specific parts of the data when we discuss the topic of multiple comparisons in Section 11.3. The recent realization of the value of experiments has led to much more interest in more complex multifactor experiments, which we discuss in the remaining sections of this chapter. ■

Testing the Equality of Several Population Means

factor
dependent variable

The simplest experiments vary only one variable and measure the results on another, response variable. The experimental variable, which often is qualitative, is called a **factor**. The response variable, which is quantitative, is called a **dependent variable**, or simply the response. For example, suppose that a manufacturing firm is considering possible policies for selecting supervisors for work areas. Three possible policies are A, to promote from within the work force using in-house training; B, to promote from within, using a local community college for supervisory training; and C, to hire only experienced supervisors from outside. The firm wants to see if the effectiveness rating varies by selection policy. The response of interest is the rating. The factor being varied is the selection policy.

This is not a true designed experiment. The firm has supervisors hired under each of the three conditions. Ideally, these supervisors would be assigned completely at random to work areas to avoid any biases caused by the assignment process. This is an idealization; without randomization, we may have to make an unverified assumption that there are no biases. Assume that no evident source of bias can be identified, so that we're willing to use the data, which are effectiveness ratings on the firm's standard 100-point scale. The data are

								Mean	Variance	n
Policy A	39	51	58	61	65	72	86	61.71	225.24	7
Policy B	22	38	43	47	49	54	72	46.43	232.95	7
Policy C	18	31	41	43	44	54	65	42.29	229.24	7

It appears that the policy A supervisors have substantially higher average ratings, but there is a great deal of variability within each group, and the sample sizes are very small. Is it plausible to assume that the apparent differences in average ratings are merely the result of random variation?

We might be tempted to run a two-sample t test on all pairs of means, using the methods of Chapter 9. Resist the temptation. If we ran many t tests, each at a given alpha level, we wouldn't know what the **overall risk** of a Type I (false positive) error is. Certainly, the more tests one runs, the greater the risk of a false positive conclusion somewhere among the tests. The analysis of variance (ANOVA) method leads to a single test statistic for comparing all the means, so the overall risk of a Type I error can be controlled. Therefore, ANOVA is preferable to multiple t tests.

The analysis of variance is based on "taking apart" the variability in the data into (1) a part attributable to variation between groups, and (2) a remaining part attributable to variation within groups. Variation is assessed by **sums of squares** (SS). The calculations can be done by almost any statistical package. For example, here is part of the output analyzing the ratings data, using the Statistix package:

overall risk

sums of squares

```
ONE-WAY AOV FOR RATING BY POLICY

SOURCE    DF     SS        MS         F       P

BETWEEN    2    1466.00   733.000    3.20   0.0648
WITHIN    18    4124.57   229.142
TOTAL     20    5590.57

                         SAMPLE    GROUP
         POLICY    MEAN    SIZE    STD DEV

         A        61.714    7      15.007
         B        46.428    7      15.262
         C        42.285    7      15.140
         TOTAL    50.142   21      15.137
```

To begin with, we (or the computer program) calculate the total sum of squares as the sum of squared deviations of individual values around the grand mean of all scores. For the example, we can calculate the grand mean by averaging all 21 values or by averaging the 3 group means:

$$\bar{y} = \frac{(39 + 51 + 58 + \cdots + 44 + 54 + 65)}{21}$$
$$= (61.71 + 46.43 + 42.29)/3 = 50.142$$

Then SS(Total) is by definition the sum of all squared deviations around this mean:

$$SS(\text{Total}) = (39 - 50.142)^2 + (51 - 50.142)^2 + (58 - 50.142)^2 + \cdots$$
$$+ (44 - 50.142)^2 + (54 - 50.142)^2 + (65 - 50.142)^2$$
$$= 5590.57$$

variability between groups   **Variability between groups** is denoted SS(Between) or SS(Factor). It is the sum of squared deviations of each group mean from the grand mean, multiplied by the sample size for the group:

$$SS(\text{Between}) = 7(61.71 - 50.142)^2 + 7(46.43 - 50.142)^2 + 7(42.29 - 50.142)^2$$
$$= 1466.00$$

If the means for the various groups (the various levels of the experimental factor) are nearly the same, little variability is attributed to the factor, and SS(Between) will be small. But if the means differ greatly, large variability will be attributed to the factor, and SS(Between) will be large.

variability within groups   To evaluate **variability within groups**, we look at deviations within each group from the mean *for that group*. The calculation can be done either from the raw data or from the group variances multiplied by the respective degrees of freedom:

$$SS(\text{Within}) = (39 - 61.714)^2 + (51 - 61.714)^2 + \cdots + (22 - 46.428)^2$$
$$+ (38 - 46.428)^2 + \cdots + (18 - 42.285)^2 + \cdots + (65 - 42.285)^2$$
$$= (7 - 1)225.24 + (7 - 1)232.95 + (7 - 1)229.24$$
$$= 4124.57$$

If all the data in each group are close together and therefore close to the group mean, the variances and SS(Within) will be small. If the data in each group vary considerably, the variances and SS(Within) will be large.

ANOVA calculations are based on the following notation; they can be done by most statistical packages. See Table 11.1.

$$y_{ij} = j\text{th sample measurement in group } i$$

$$i = 1, 2, \ldots, I \qquad j = 1, 2, \ldots, n_i$$

$$n_i = \text{sample size for group } i$$

$$\bar{y}_i = \text{sample mean for group } i$$

$$\bar{y} = \text{average of all the sample measurements}$$

$$n = \text{total sample size (For the above data, } n = n_1 + n_2 + \cdots + n_I.)$$

With this notation, it is possible to express the variability of the n sample measurements about $\bar{y}$ as

SS(Total)

$$\mathbf{SS(Total)} = \sum_{i,j}(y_{ij} - \bar{y})^2$$

and to partition this quantity into two components, SS(Between) and SS(Within).

$$\sum_{i,j}(y_{ij} - \bar{y})^2 = \sum_i n_i(\bar{y}_i - \bar{y})^2 + \sum_{i,j}(y_{ij} - \bar{y}_i)^2$$

$$\text{SS(Total)} = \text{SS(Between)} + \text{SS(Within)}$$

SS(Within)

SS(Between)

Because **SS(Within)** is based on deviations from specific group means, it is not affected by possible deviations of these sample means from each other; SS(Within) reflects only random variation within the samples. In contrast, SS(Between) is strongly affected by discrepancies among group means. If the true group means μ_i are equal, the sample means $\bar{y}_i$ are close to each other and therefore close to the grand mean $\bar{y}$, and SS(Between) tends to be small. But if the true group means are different, the sample means tend to be far apart and **SS(Between)** tends to be large. If SS(Between) is large relative to SS(Within), the null hypothesis that the true group means are equal should be rejected.

We make the following formal mathematical assumptions:

Definition 11.1   Assumptions for an ANOVA

1   The sample measurements $y_{i1}, y_{i2}, \ldots, y_{in_i}$ are selected from a normal population $(i = 1, 2, \ldots, I)$.

2   The samples are independent.

3   The unknown population mean and variance for the measurements from sample i are μ_i and σ^2, respectively.   ∎

These assumptions are direct extensions of those made for the pooled-variance t test in Chapter 9.

TABLE 11.1   **Notation for Sample Data in an ANOVA**

Group	Sample Data	Sample Mean	Unknown Group Mean
1	$y_{11}y_{12}\cdots y_{1n_1}$	$\bar{y}_1$	μ_1
2	$y_{21}y_{22}\cdots y_{2n_2}$	$\bar{y}_2$	μ_2
⋮	⋮ ⋮ ⋮	⋮	⋮
I	$y_{I1}y_{I2}\cdots y_{In_i}$	$\bar{y}_I$	μ_I

The degrees of freedom for SS(Within) can be found by realizing that there are $n_i - 1$ d.f. for squared deviations within group i and that d.f.'s can be added across the groups. Therefore, there are $(n_1 - 1) + (n_2 - 1) + \cdots + (n_I - 1) = n - I$ d.f. for SS(Within). The quantity SS(Between) $= \sum_i n_i (\bar{y}_i - \bar{y})^2$ has I terms, but because the constraint $\sum_i n_i (\bar{y}_i - \bar{y}) = 0$ determines one term (once the remaining $I - 1$ have been found), there are $I - 1$ d.f. for SS(Between). The term **mean square (MS)** is given to any sum of squares divided by its degrees of freedom.

With this terminology, the test statistic for our analysis of variance is

$$F = \frac{\text{MS(Between)}}{\text{MS(Within)}}$$

Large positive values of MS(Between) relative to MS(Within) indicate differences among the population means and lead to the rejection of the null hypothesis.

The F statistic has another tabulated distribution, found in Appendix Table 6 and in many computer packages. An F distribution is not symmetric around 0; an F statistic can't be negative. Instead, an F statistic is right-skewed. If the null hypothesis is true, the expected value of F is very close to 1.00.

Computer packages typically calculate cumulative probabilities using a function called FDIST or something similar; occasionally, as in Excel, the name is FISHER (for R. A. Fisher, a pioneering statistician who studied the mathematical properties of the F distribution). The inverse problem, finding the value corresponding to a specified cumulative probability, is usually indicated by INV. Check the package's help files. Alternatively, we can use Appendix Table 6.

The F distribution has two d.f. numbers, $I - 1$ for the numerator and $n - I$ for the denominator. For example, if we had $I = 3$ groups and a total of $n = 21$ measurements, we would have $3 - 1 = 2$ d.f. in the numerator (shown along the top of the table) and $21 - 3 = 18$ d.f. in the denominator (shown on the side of the F table). The table value corresponding to $\alpha = .05$ for these d.f. is 3.55. The tables are rather large; they are effectively built in to computer routines.

Definition 11.2 ANOVA for Testing the Equality of I Group Means

H_0: $\mu_1 = \mu_2 = \cdots = \mu_I$

H_a: Not all μ_i are equal.

T.S.: $F = \dfrac{\text{MS(Between)}}{\text{MS(Within)}} = \dfrac{\sum_i n_i (\bar{y}_i - \bar{y})^2 / (I - 1)}{\sum_{ij} (\bar{y}_{ij} - \bar{y}_i)^2 / (n - I)}$

R.R.: For a specified α, reject H_0 if $F > F_\alpha$,

where F_α cuts off a right-tail area of α

in the F distribution with $I - 1$ numerator and $n - I$ denominator d.f. ■

We calculated the necessary sums of squares for the supervisor-effectiveness data given near the beginning of this section. The results are usually organized in an ANOVA table, as shown here:

Source	SS	d.f.	MS	F
Between	1466.00	2	733.00	3.20
Within	4124.57	18	229.14	
Total	5590.57	20		

For a test at $\alpha = .05$, we compare the F value of 3.20 to the tabled .05 point (2 and 18 d.f.), namely 3.55. Because $3.20 < 3.55$, we would retain the null hypothesis. It is possible that the apparent differences among the sample means are the result of chance variation. It is also possible that they reflect real differences; we can't say which is the case.

E X A M P L E 1 1 . 1

Suppose that a drug company testing two new products against a currently used drug is concerned about the possible side effect of increased blood pressure. In a clinical trial of the drugs, 12 patients are tested under each drug, at standard dosages. Blood pressures are recorded initially and again 1 hour after a single dose of the assigned drug product. Blood pressure changes are as follows:

Drug	Blood Pressure Changes											
1	−10	−10	−8	−5	0	3	5	7	8	10	12	15
2	0	5	8	10	12	15	16	17	20	22	25	25
3	−5	−1	0	2	5	8	8	10	14	16	20	20

An ANOVA is performed on the data; Excel output is shown next. Identify the following: the sample means, the mean squares, MS(Between) and MS(Within); the value of the F statistic; and the p-value for $H_0 : \mu_A = \mu_B = \mu_C$.

	A	B	C	D	E	F	G
1	Anova: Single Factor						
2							
3							
4	SUMMARY						
5							
6	Groups	Count	Sum	Average	Variance		
7	Drug A	12	27	2.25	76.75		
8	Drug B	12	175	14.583	62.2652		
9	Drug C	12	97	8.083	68.2652		
10							
11							
12	ANOVA						
13							
14	Source of Variation	SS	df	MS	F	P-value	F crit
15	Between Groups	913.556	2	456.8	6.61	0.004	3.285
16	Within Groups	2280.08	33	69.1			
17	Total	3193.64	35				

Solution

The sample means are shown as Average; they are, respectively, 2.250, 14.583, and 8.083. The mean square for Drug in this case is MS(Between), namely, 456.8. MS(Within) is 69.1. F is 6.61, and the p-value is .004. Thus, the evidence for differences in mean blood pressure change with different drugs is quite conclusive. As yet, we can't formally say which specific drugs differ in their effect on blood pressure. ■

Like all statistical inference procedures, this F test is based on certain assumptions. These are the same assumptions that we made for the pooled-variance t test of the previous chapter. Besides the fundamental assumption that the data aren't biased, the three basic assumptions are population normality, equal group variances, and independence of observations. The **normality assumption** is perhaps the least crucial. The ANOVA test is a test

normality assumption

on means (despite its name); the Central Limit Theorem has its effect. If the populations are badly skewed and if the sample sizes are small (such as 10 each), the Central Limit Theorem effect doesn't take over and the nominal F probabilities may be in error. However, barring severe skewness and quite small samples, this shouldn't be a major problem. But if the population distributions are seriously skewed or roughly symmetric with heavy tails (as indicated by outliers in the sample data), the F probabilities will be reasonably accurate. Alternative procedures, however, may be more efficient (may make better use of the data). One particular alternative, the Kruskal-Wallis rank test, is discussed in the next section.

assumption of equal variances
balanced design

The assumption of equal true variances for each group is important if sample sizes are substantially different. Many studies have indicated that when all n_i's are equal, in what is called a **balanced design**, the effect of even grossly unequal variances is minimal. However, if the n_i's are substantially different—say, if the largest n_i is at least twice the smallest—then unequal variances can cause major distortions in the nominal F probabilities. The worst case is when large variances occur in groups with small sample sizes. The best way to avoid problems is to strive for equal n_i's.

independence assumption

Once again, violation of the **independence assumption** can cause a great deal of trouble. Dependence within the sample indicates that the effective n differs from the apparent sample size, just as was the case for t tests. (For example, suppose all the supervisors in policy A were in one department, all those in policy B were in another, and all those in policy C were in a third; also, suppose that the ratings largely reflected department performance, not individual work. Then the scores within each policy would be highly correlated, and we would basically have one rating within a policy, not the apparent seven.) When the data arise from a cross-sectional random sample taken at a specific time, independence should hold unless there is some other connection than the experimental factor among the scores. If the data arise by measurements taken repeatedly over time, there is a possibility of dependence from one measurement to the next. In such situations, nominal F probabilities are very suspect. Any procedure that assumes independence will be unbelievable when that assumption is wrong.

EXAMPLE 11.2

Refer to the data of Example 11.1 and the boxplots in Figure 11.1. Is there any indication of trouble because of violation of assumptions?

Solution

The data are cross-sectional and there is no indication of a connection among the ratings, so independence is not a problem. The data don't appear to be particularly skewed. The variances appear very similar, and the n's are equal. The F test was quite conclusive, and there's no reason to question its correctness. ■

Comparing Several Distributions by a Rank Test

In Section 11.1, we noted that one assumption underlying the ANOVA F test was that all populations were normal. If that assumption is incorrect, as evidenced by substantial skewness or outliers in the samples, the nominal probabilities given by the F table may be slightly in error. More importantly, the F test may not be the most effective way to analyze

FIGURE 11.1 **Boxplots for Blood Pressure Changes**

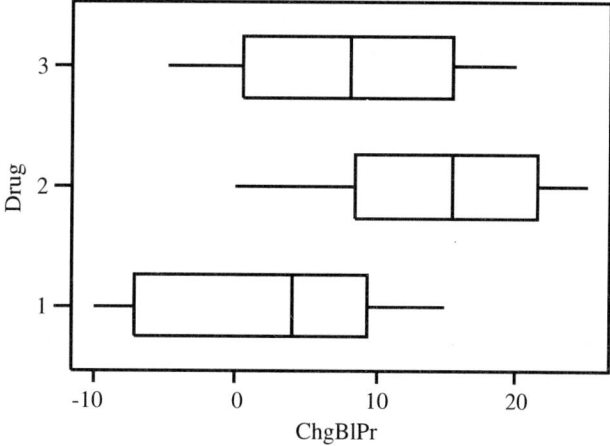

the data. In this section, we introduce the Kruskal-Wallis rank-sum test, which doesn't require the normal population assumption. This test is not terribly sensitive to the equal variance assumption, but it does depend heavily on the independence assumption.

The Kruskal-Wallis test is an extension of the Wilcoxon rank sum test we described in Chapter 9. The formal null hypothesis is that all the populations have the same distribution, not necessarily a normal distribution. The formal research hypothesis is that the populations differ in any way; the test is largely sensitive to differences of location (means or medians), rather than differences of variances.

To carry out the test, all the data values are combined and ranked from lowest to highest. In case of ties, average ranks are assigned, as in the Wilcoxon rank-sum test. The Kruskal-Wallis statistic may be thought of as

$$H = \frac{12}{n(n+1)} \text{SS(Between, ranks)}$$

where SS(Between, ranks) is the SS(Between) obtained for the rankings rather than the original data, and n is the combined sample size. Thus, if the average rank in every sample is equal, H will be 0, but if the average ranks differ greatly among samples (indicating a clear difference in locations), H will be large. Conventionally, the Kruskal-Wallis statistic is stated in terms of T_i, the sum of the ranks in group i, rather than in terms of the average rank. Of course, the average is simply the sum divided by the relevant sample size, so the test could be stated either way.

Definition 11.3 Kruskal-Wallis Test

H_0: The distributions are identical (effectively, have equal means).
H_a: The distributions differ in location.

T.S.: $H = \left\{ \frac{12}{n(n+1)} \sum_i \frac{T_i^2}{n_i} \right\} - 3(n+1)$

where n_i = sample size in sample i, $(i = 1, 2, \ldots, I)$, n = total sample size, and T_i = sum of combined-sample ranks for measurements in sample i.

R.R.: For specified α, reject H_0 if $H > \chi_\alpha^2$, where χ_α^2 cuts off a right-tail area α for the χ^2 distribution with $I - 1$ d.f. ■

EXAMPLE 11.3

Use the following Minitab output to perform a Kruskal-Wallis test for the data of Example 11.1. First use $\alpha = .05$; then find a p-value.

```
MTB > Kruskal-Wallis 'ChgBlPr' 'Drug'.

LEVEL    NOBS    MEDIAN    AVE. RANK    Z VALUE
  1       12      4.000      12.2       -2.55
  2       12     15.500      25.4        2.79
  3       12      8.000      17.9       -0.23
OVERALL   36                 18.5

H = 9.55  d.f. = 2  p = 0.009
```

Solution

The required χ^2 table value for $\alpha = .05$ and 2 d.f. is 5.99 from Appendix Table 5. The actual test statistic is 9.55, which is greater than 5.99, so we reject the null hypothesis that the three drugs have the same distribution of blood pressure changes.

The p-value is shown as .009, much smaller than $\alpha = .05$. This also indicates that we reject the null hypothesis. Note that this p-value is slightly less conclusive than that of the F test in the preceding section—namely, .004. The F test was slightly more effective in this case because the normality assumption underlying F appears to be good. ∎

EXERCISES

11.1 A test is made of five different incentive-pay schemes for piece-rate workers. Eight workers are assigned randomly to each plan. The total number of items produced by each worker over a 20-day period is recorded.

	Plan				
	A	**B**	**C**	**D**	**E**
Production	1106	1214	1010	1054	1210
	1203	1186	1069	1101	1193
	1064	1165	1047	1029	1169
	1119	1177	1120	1066	1223
	1087	1146	1084	1082	1161
	1106	1099	1062	1067	1200
	1101	1161	1051	1109	1189
	1049	1153	1029	1083	1197
Mean	1104.38	1162.62	1059.00	1073.88	1192.75
Variance	2136.55	1116.84	1137.71	662.41	409.93

```
MTB > oneway of 'productn' by 'plan'

ANALYSIS OF VARIANCE ON productn
SOURCE    DF      SS       MS      F       p
plan       4    105530    26382   24.14   0.000
ERROR     35     38244     1093
TOTAL     39    143774
```

```
                    INDIVIDUAL 95% CI'S FOR MEAN BASED ON POOLED STDEV
        LEVEL    N     MEAN    STDEV   ---+---------+---------+---------+---
          1      8   1104.4    46.2              (----*----)
          2      8   1162.6    33.4                           (----*---)
          3      8   1059.0    33.7   (----*----)
          4      8   1073.9    25.7       (----*----)
          5      8   1192.8    20.2                               (----*---)
                                       ---+---------+---------+---------+---
        POOLED STDEV =     33.1        1050      1100      1150      1200

        MTB > Kruskal-Wallis 'productn' by 'plan'.

        LEVEL   NOBS   MEDIAN  AVE. RANK   Z VALUE
          1      8      1104      18.7      -0.49
          2      8      1163      28.3       2.11
          3      8      1056       9.1      -3.09
          4      8      1074      12.3      -2.23
          5      8      1195      34.2       3.70
        OVERALL  40              20.5

        H = 26.37  d.f. = 4  p = 0.000
```

a Locate the grand mean.

b Locate SS(Between) and SS(Within).

c Explain the indicated degrees of freedom for these sums of squares.

11.2 Locate the ANOVA F test for the data of Exercise 11.1, and the p-value. What would you conclude?

11.3 Minitab constructed boxplots of the data of Exercise 11.1 by plan, as shown in Figure 11.2. Do there appear to be any blatant violations of assumptions?

FIGURE 11.2 **Boxplots for Production Data**

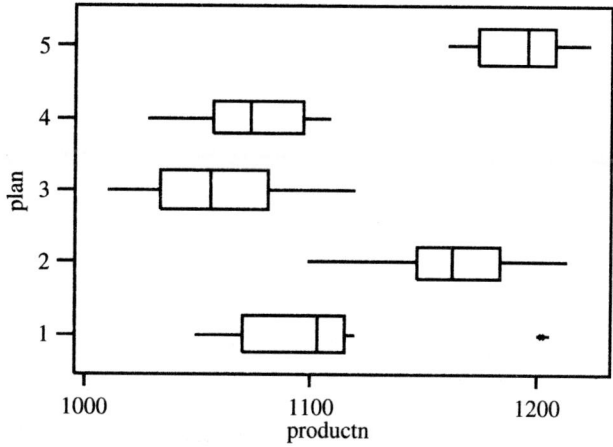

11.4 Locate the Kruskal-Wallis test in the output of Exercise 11.1. Find the p-value.

11.5 How do the results of the F test and Kruskal-Wallis test on the data of Exercise 11.1 compare? Does it matter much which test is used?

11.6 A supermarket experimented with three different staffing policies to try to determine when to open new cash registers or add more staff in service areas (such as the deli section). The time of most concern is weekdays between 5 and 6 P.M., when the store is crowded with impatient shoppers. The manager of the store was told to vary the three different staffing policies in a random way. A hired shopper came in each weekday shortly after 5 P.M. and measured the waiting time (in minutes) needed to obtained a standard set of items. The data and output from Statistix are as follows:

CASE	POLICY	WAIT			
1	1.0000	6.5000	19	1.0000	8.3000
2	1.0000	5.4000	20	2.0000	2.4000
3	2.0000	6.5000	21	2.0000	1.0000
4	1.0000	4.4000	22	2.0000	3.4000
5	3.0000	3.4000	23	1.0000	5.1000
6	3.0000	3.2000	24	3.0000	4.3000
7	2.0000	1.6000	25	2.0000	1.3000
8	3.0000	7.4000	26	1.0000	11.600
9	3.0000	9.6000	27	1.0000	7.5000
10	3.0000	2.8000	28	1.0000	6.6000
11	3.0000	15.500	29	3.0000	4.8000
12	1.0000	4.7000	30	2.0000	6.3000
13	2.0000	3.7000	31	1.0000	8.2000
14	1.0000	7.3000	32	1.0000	12.200
15	3.0000	6.6000	33	2.0000	0.5000
16	1.0000	8.5000	34	3.0000	17.900
17	1.0000	4.4000	35	1.0000	17.700
18	2.0000	0.9000	36	1.0000	8.7000

ONE-WAY AOV FOR WAIT BY POLICY

SOURCE	DF	SS	MS	F	P
BETWEEN	2	187.307	93.6535	6.47	0.0043
WITHIN	33	477.808	14.4790		
TOTAL	35	665.115			

POLICY	MEAN	SAMPLE SIZE	GROUP STD DEV
1	7.9437	16	3.4875
2	2.7600	10	2.1879
3	7.5500	10	5.2944
TOTAL	6.0845	36	3.8051

KRUSKAL-WALLIS ONE-WAY NONPARAMETRIC AOV FOR WAIT BY POLICY

POLICY	MEAN RANK	SAMPLE SIZE
1	24.0	16
2	8.1	10
3	20.1	10
TOTAL	17.4	36

KRUSKAL-WALLIS STATISTIC   14.5717
P-VALUE, USING CHI-SQUARED APPROXIMATION   0.0007

a Find mean and standard deviation of times for each policy. Find the grand mean.

b Locate d.f. and MS values, between and within groups.

c Find the F statistic for testing the null hypothesis of equal means.

d Can this null hypothesis be rejected at $\alpha = .01$?

e Locate the p-value.

11.7 a The Statistix package constructed stem-and-leaf displays of the waiting-time data in Exercise 11.6.

```
STEM AND LEAF PLOT OF WAIT FOR POLICY = 1

    LEAF DIGIT UNIT = 0.1
    1  2  REPRESENTS 1.2

            STEM  LEAVES
        3     4   447
        5     5   14
        7     6   56
       (2)    7   35
        7     8   2357
        3     9
              10
        3    11   6
        2    12   2
       HI   17.7


STEM AND LEAF PLOT OF WAIT FOR POLICY = 2

    LEAF DIGIT UNIT = 0.1
    1  2  REPRESENTS 1.2

            STEM  LEAVES
        2     0   59
        5     1   036
        5     2   4
        4     3   47
        2     4
        2     5
        2     6   35


STEM AND LEAF PLOT OF WAIT FOR POLICY = 3

    LEAF DIGIT UNIT = 1
    1  2  REPRESENTS 12.

            STEM  LEAVES
        3    +0T  233
        5    +0F  44
        5    +0S  67
        3    +0.  9
        2     1*
        2     1T
        2     1F  5
        1     1S  7
```

a Based on the data plots and on your own experience waiting in supermarkets, would it seem reasonable to you to assume normal populations?

b If the populations are, in fact, moderately nonnormal, does that mean that the conclusions of Exercise 11.6 are completely invalid?

11.8 **a** Plot the data of Exercise 11.6 against day number. Is there clear evidence of an upward or downward trend, or of a cyclic pattern?

b Suppose a cyclic pattern had been found, with high values usually followed by other high values, and lows usually followed by lows. Which assumption underlying analysis of variance would be called into question?

11.9 **a** A Kruskal-Wallis test is shown in the output for the waiting-time data of Exercise 11.6. According to the Kruskal-Wallis results, is there a statistically detectable (significant) difference in times among the groups?

b Is the result we found here greatly different from the result we found by an F test in Exercise 11.6?

11.10 A nationwide chain of automobile repair shops had a standard procedure for dealing with complaints of improper work. As part of a systematic practice of checking customer satisfaction, regional managers reviewed records of all complaints; one particular concern was the number of business days required before each complaint was resolved. A regional manager obtained samples of records from each of the districts in the region. Computer output of the results is shown here:

```
MTB > oneway of 'delay' by 'district'

ANALYSIS OF VARIANCE ON delay
SOURCE     DF      SS       MS       F      p
district    3    1774.5   591.5    7.52   0.000
ERROR      36    2831.3    78.6
TOTAL      39    4605.8
                                  INDIVIDUAL 95% CI'S FOR MEAN
                                  BASED ON POOLED STDEV
LEVEL      N     MEAN     STDEV   -+---------+---------+---------+-----
    1     10   38.000    9.933                        (------*-------)
    2     10   33.100    4.954                  (------*------)
    3     10   24.000    8.756       (------*------)
    4     10   21.600   10.710   (------*------)
                                  -+---------+---------+---------+-----
POOLED STDEV =   8.868           16.0      24.0      32.0      40.0
```

a Is the value of F statistically significant at $\alpha = .05$?

b What is the meaning of the indicated p-value?

11.11 According to the boxplots shown in Figure 11.3, is there strong evidence that the data are not coming from normal populations? If so, does that mean that the conclusions drawn in Exercise 11.10 are likely to be wrong?

11.12 A Kruskal-Wallis test of the delay time data for the repair chain was also performed in the following computer output:

```
MTB > Kruskal-Wallis 'delay' 'district'.

LEVEL    NOBS    MEDIAN   AVE. RANK   Z VALUE
    1     10     41.00      29.8       2.90
    2     10     34.50      25.6       1.61
    3     10     24.00      14.1      -2.00
    4     10     26.50      12.4      -2.51
OVERALL  40                 20.5

H = 16.01  d.f. = 3  p = 0.001
```

FIGURE 11.3 **Boxplots for Delay Data by District**

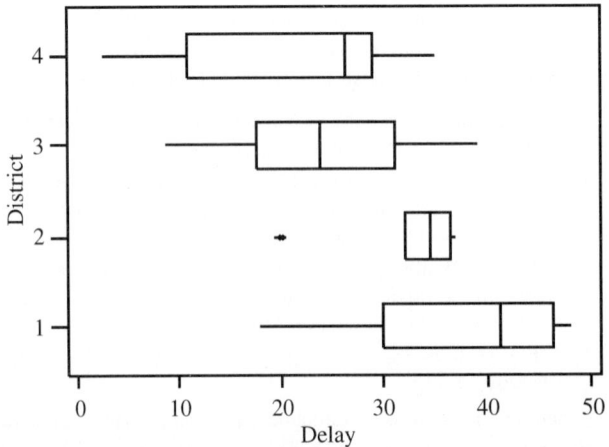

Is there a statistically significant difference among the four levels (which were the four districts in a particular region) using, say, $\alpha = .01$? Locate the p-value. Is there a radical difference between this p-value and the one from the F test of Exercise 11.11?

11.13 A manufacturer of wooden moldings takes "blanks" of pine wood and converts them to floor and ceiling decorative molding for sale in lumberyards. The important step in the manufacturing process involves a router, a tool for carving decorative shapes into wood. The router bit is a metal attachment that carries out this task. It is subject to wear just as any other manufacturing part. The wear, and the resulting production level, depends on the speed set for routing the wood. Too slow, and production quantities are too low; too fast, and the bit wears so fast that production time is lost changing bits. The manufacturer tested various speeds and measured the yield, in board feet per hour, of salable molding that resulted. The data were analyzed using JMP, with output shown in Figure 11.4.

a Which speed appears to be best, without doing any formal test?

b Is there any indication of a problem such as skewness, unequal variances, or outliers?

11.14 Additional JMP output, showing an ANOVA table, for the router yield data is shown in Figure 11.5. Is there a statistically significant difference somewhere among the 5 means at usual α levels?

FIGURE 11.4 **Plot of Router Yield Data**

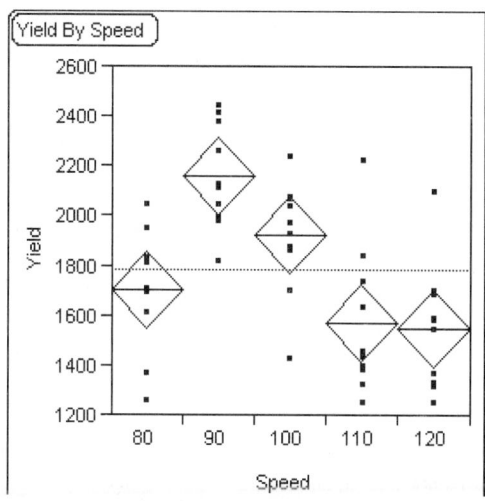

FIGURE 11.5 **ANOVA Table for Router Yield Data**

Analysis of Variance

Source	DF	Sum of Squares	Mean Square	F Ratio
Model	4	2686200.1	671550	11.0443
Error	45	2736226.1	60805	Prob>F
C Total	49	5422426.2		0.0000

Means for Oneway Anova

Level	Number	Mean	Std Error
80	10	1703.00	77.978
90	10	2162.80	77.978
100	10	1923.70	77.978
110	10	1572.40	77.978
120	10	1551.00	77.978

Std Error uses a pooled estimate of error variance

11.15 Still more JMP output, showing results of a Kruskal-Wallis test, is shown in Figure 11.6.

  a According to this test, is there a statistically significant difference in yield distribution among the 5 speeds?

  b How important is it to the conclusion whether an F test or a Kruskal-Wallis test is used?

11.16 A direct-mail retailer used three different ways of incorporating an order form into the catalog. A relevant question for the retailer is the dollar amount of each order using the different forms. The total sale and type of form were recorded for each order received ; the data were analyzed by Excel. Here are some of the results:

	A	B	C	D	E	F	G	H
1								
2	Anova: Single Factor							
3								
4								
5	SUMMARY							
6		Groups	Count	Sum	Average	Variance		
7		FormType1	56	3562.16	63.61	3328.67		
8		FormType2	39	2068.01	53.0259	4736.88		
9		FormType3	85	5570.39	65.534	3474.18		
10								
11								
12	ANOVA							
13		Source of Variation	SS	df	MS	F	P-value	F crit
14		Between Groups	4338.44	2	2169.22	0.586	0.5575	3.04701
15		Within Groups	654909	177	3700.05			
16								
17		Total	659247	179				

  a Are there statistically detectable differences among the means, using any reasonable alpha value?

  b How much evidence is there that the type of order form influences the amount of sale?

11.17 In the output of Exercise 11.16, the standard deviations (found by taking the square root of each variance) are about as big as the means, so a value that is 1 standard deviation below the mean would be essentially $0. The Empirical Rule indicates that a substantial proportion of individual scores should be even less than 1 standard deviation below the mean, but a negative order amount is impossible (the retailer fervently hopes).

  a What do these facts suggest about the shape of the data?

  b What assumption of analysis of variance seems likely to be violated in this situation?

11.18 Additional output for the data of Exercise 11.16 was obtained from Systat and showed a Kruskal-Wallis statistic equal to 3.12 and a p-value of 0.210. Does the Kruskal-Wallis result conclusively indicate that there is a difference in the average sale total for the three types of order forms?

FIGURE 11.6 **Kruskal-Wallis Test for Router Yield Data**

Wilcoxon / Kruskal-Wallis Tests (Rank Sums)

Level	Count	Score Sum	Score Mean	(Mean-Mean0)/Std0
80	10	220	22.0000	-0.837
90	10	418	41.8000	3.941
100	10	324	32.4000	1.661
110	10	168	16.8000	-2.098
120	10	145	14.5000	-2.656

1-way Test, Chi-Square Approximation

ChiSquare	DF	Prob>ChiSq
24.5760	4	0.0001

Specific Comparisons Among Means

The ANOVA F test and the Kruskal-Wallis test developed in this chapter test for an overall pattern of discrepancies among the group means. Rejection of the hypothesis that all population (group) means are equal does not indicate specifically which means are not equal. In this section, we outline one of many possible methods for assessing differences among specified means. Several other methods are available in standard computer packages. We state this method in terms of confidence intervals. As usual, we can use the resulting intervals to perform hypothesis tests.

One approach would be to use the t methods of Chapter 9 to construct t-type confidence intervals for all possible pairs of means. The objection to this is essentially the same as our objection to multiple t tests in the previous section. Although the confidence level for each interval separately may be 95%, there is no way to measure the overall confidence that all the intervals are correct. We use the Tukey method in this section to yield a desired overall confidence level.

The assumptions are the same as those underlying the F test. The data constitute independent random samples from I groups or subpopulations. The groups are labeled by the index i, where $i = 1, 2, \ldots, I$, and the sample size for group i is n_i. We assume that the population distribution in group i is normal with mean μ_i and variance σ^2. There is no subscript on σ^2 because we assume that the population variances for all groups are identical. The estimate $\hat{\sigma}^2$ is MS(Within), a generalization of the pooled variance we defined in Chapter 9.

Tukey method

The **Tukey method** is designed specifically to compare any two means—say, $\bar{y}_i$ and $\bar{y}_{i*}$. The underlying mathematical theory assumes that all sample sizes are equal: $n_1 = n_2 = \cdots = n_I$. The common sample size is usually denoted n. Note that here n means the individual sample size, *not* the overall sample size.

Definition 11.4   Confidence Intervals for Pairs of Means, Tukey Method

$$(\bar{y}_i - \bar{y}_{i*}) - q_\alpha(I, \mathrm{d.f.}_2)\sqrt{\mathrm{MS(Within)}/n} \le \mu_i - \mu_{i*}$$

$$\le (\bar{y}_i - \bar{y}_{i*}) + q_\alpha(I, \mathrm{d.f.}_2)\sqrt{\mathrm{MS(Within)}/n}$$

where n is the sample size for each sample, I is the number of samples, $\mathrm{d.f.}_2$ is the degrees of freedom for MS(Within), and $q_\alpha(I, \mathrm{d.f.}_2)$ is found in Appendix Table 8. There is $100(1 - \alpha)\%$ confidence that *all possible* intervals comparing two means are correct. ∎

EXAMPLE 11.4

Construct (overall) 95% confidence intervals for the differences in mean blood pressure increase for the data of Example 11.1.

Solution

The relevant summary statistics are

Drug i	1	2	3
$\bar{y}_i$	2.25	14.58	8.08
n_i	12	12	12

MS(Within) = 69.09

The desired $q_\alpha(I, \text{d.f.}_2)$ value has $\alpha = .05$, $I = 3$, and $\text{d.f.}_2 = 33$. There is no $\text{d.f.}_2 = 33$ entry in Appendix Table 8, so we use $\text{d.f.}_2 = 30$, $q_{.05}(3, 30) = 3.49$. It's clear from the table that $q_{.05}(3, 30)$ is just a little larger than the desired $q_{.05}(3, 33)$, so we err slightly on the conservative (wider interval) side. The desired 95% confidence intervals are

$$(2.25 - 14.58) - 3.49\sqrt{69.09/12} \le \mu_1 - \mu_2$$
$$\le (2.25 - 14.58) + 3.49\sqrt{69.09/12}$$

$$(14.58 - 8.08) - 3.49\sqrt{69.09/12} \le \mu_2 - \mu_3$$
$$\le (14.58 - 8.08) + 3.49\sqrt{69.09/12}$$

$$(2.25 - 8.08) - 3.49\sqrt{69.09/12} \le \mu_1 - \mu_3$$
$$\le (2.25 - 8.08) + 3.49\sqrt{69.09/12}$$

or

$$-20.70 \le \mu_1 - \mu_2 \le -3.96$$
$$-1.87 \le \mu_2 - \mu_3 \le 14.83$$
$$-14.20 \le \mu_1 - \mu_3 \le 2.54$$

Compare these results to the following Minitab output:

```
MTB > Oneway 'ChgBlPr' 'Drug';
SUBC>   Tukey 5.

Tukey's pairwise comparisons

    Family error rate = 0.0500
Individual error rate = 0.0196

Critical value = 3.47

Intervals for (column level mean) - (row level mean)

              1        2

  2    -20.660
         -4.007

  3    -14.160    -1.826
          2.493   14.826
```

Recall that confidence intervals may be used to conduct (two-sided) hypothesis tests. The natural null hypothesis, $H_0 : \mu_i - \mu_{i*} = 0$, is rejected if zero does not fall in the interval. The 95% confidence intervals indicate that at $\alpha = .05$, we can reject $\mu_1 - \mu_2 = 0$ but must retain $\mu_2 - \mu_3 = 0$ and $\mu_1 - \mu_3 = 0$. We conclude that the mean blood pressure increase under drug 2 is higher than under drug 1. Drug 3 is in the middle, and the difference of $\bar{y}_3$ from either $\bar{y}_1$ or $\bar{y}_2$ could be the result of random variation. ∎

The formal assumption in the Tukey method that $n_1 = n_2 = \cdots = n_I$ may be relaxed. A modification for unequal sample sizes, called the Tukey-Kramer method, is built into most computer programs that calculate Tukey tests or intervals.

E X E R C I S E S

11.19 Here is Minitab output for the data of Exercise 11.1, comparing production levels under five different plans:

```
MTB > Oneway 'productn' 'plan';
SUBC>    Tukey 5.

ANALYSIS OF VARIANCE ON productn
SOURCE     DF       SS       MS       F       p
plan        4   105530    26382   24.14   0.000
ERROR      35    38244     1093
TOTAL      39   143774
                                 INDIVIDUAL 95% CI'S FOR MEAN
                                 BASED ON POOLED STDEV
 LEVEL    N     MEAN    STDEV  ---+---------+---------+---------+---
     1    8   1104.4     46.2           (----*----)
     2    8   1162.6     33.4                      (----*---)
     3    8   1059.0     33.7  (----*----)
     4    8   1073.9     25.7      (----*----)
     5    8   1192.8     20.2                          (----*---)
                                 ---+---------+---------+---------+---
POOLED STDEV =    33.1          1050      1100      1150      1200

Tukey's pairwise comparisons

    Family error rate = 0.0500

Intervals for (column level mean) - (row level mean)

              1        2        3        4

    2     -105.8
          -10.7

    3       -2.2     56.1
           92.9    151.2

    4      -17.1     41.2    -62.4
           78.1    136.3     32.7

    5     -135.9    -77.7   -181.3   -166.4
          -40.8     17.4    -86.2    -71.3
```

a Write out overall 95% confidence intervals for all possible differences of means.

b Which differences can be declared significant at $\alpha = .05$?

11.20 The means, standard deviations, sample sizes, and MS(Within) for the supermarket waiting times in Exercise 11.6 are shown here:

$$\text{MS(Within)} = 14.479, \text{ with 33 d.f.}$$

Policy	n	Mean	St. Dev.
1	16	7.944	3.487
2	10	2.760	2.188
3	10	7.550	5.294

```
TUKEY (HSD) PAIRWISE COMPARISONS OF MEANS OF WAIT BY POLICY

                     HOMOGENEOUS
       POLICY   MEAN  GROUPS

         1     7.9437   I
         3     7.5500   I
         2     2.7600   .. I

THERE ARE 2 GROUPS IN WHICH THE MEANS ARE
NOT SIGNIFICANTLY DIFFERENT FROM ONE ANOTHER.

CRITICAL Q VALUE 3.471   REJECTION LEVEL 0.050
STANDARD ERRORS AND CRITICAL VALUES OF DIFFERENCES
VARY BETWEEN COMPARISONS BECAUSE OF UNEQUAL SAMPLE SIZES.
```

Which means, if any, are detectably (significantly) different?

11.21 The data in Exercise 11.6 were collected by asking the store manager to specify a policy for the day haphazardly. What would be a better way to obtain the data?

11.22 The relevant computer output for the delay time data for Exercise 11.10 is reproduced here:

```
MTB > Oneway 'delay' 'district';
SUBC>   Tukey 5.

ANALYSIS OF VARIANCE ON delay
SOURCE    DF      SS      MS      F      p
district   3   1774.5   591.5   7.52   0.000
ERROR     36   2831.3    78.6
TOTAL     39   4605.8
                                INDIVIDUAL 95% CI'S FOR MEAN
                                BASED ON POOLED STDEV
 LEVEL    N    MEAN    STDEV  -+---------+---------+---------+-----
   1     10   38.000   9.933                     (------*-------)
   2     10   33.100   4.954                  (------*------)
   3     10   24.000   8.756        (------*------)
   4     10   21.600  10.710    (------*------)
                                -+---------+---------+---------+-----
POOLED STDEV =    8.868        16.0      24.0      32.0      40.0

Tukey's pairwise comparisons

    Family error rate = 0.0500

Critical value = 3.81

Intervals for (column level mean) - (row level mean)

                1        2        3

      2      -5.78
             15.58

      3       3.32    -1.58
             24.68    19.78

      4       5.72     0.82    -8.28
             27.08    22.18    13.08
```

Locate the 95% confidence intervals for pairwise differences.

11.23 Calculate 99% (rather than 95%) Tukey confidence intervals for the differences of all pairs of means in Exercise 11.22. Do the results indicate that any of the pairs are significantly different? ■

Two-Factor Experiments

Until now, we have considered only single-factor experiments, in which one variable is manipulated. Often managers can learn more with more complex experiments. It is perfectly possible to vary several experimental factors in the same experiment. In this section, we describe the basic ideas and computations that arise when two factors are being varied. In this context, we will describe a fundamental statistical idea: interaction.

For example, a clothing contractor who supplies military uniforms must cut fabric for coats, shirts, and pants (in many different sizes) from layers of fabric. The fabric is expensive, so wastage has a big effect on profitability. The contractor has a choice among three computer-aided cutting machines, A, B, and C. Rather than guessing which machine will give the least wastage, the contractor can experiment by having each machine cut several lots for coats, several more for shirts, and several more for pants. This experiment has two factors: the machine and the type of garment. One possible set of mean wastage percentages is shown in the next table.

| | Factor 2 (Type of Garment) | | | |
Factor 1 (Machine)	Coats	Shirts	Pants	Average
A	7.6	9.1	7.3	8.0
B	6.5	8.0	6.2	6.9
C	5.1	6.6	4.8	5.5
Average	6.4	7.9	6.1	6.8

In this table, there's a consistent pattern. Machine A is consistently 1.1 percentage points higher (poorer) in wastage than machine B, whether we consider coats, shirts, or pants. In turn, machine B is consistently 1.4 percentage points higher than machine C. The consistency goes in the other direction, too; shirts have a 1.5 percentage point higher wastage than coats and a 1.8 percentage point higher wastage than pants, consistently, in all three machines.

Alternatively, the means might look like the following table:

| | Factor 2 (Type of Garment) | | | |
Factor 1 (Machine)	Coats	Shirts	Pants	Average
A	5.1	11.1	7.8	8.0
B	8.1	8.5	4.1	6.9
C	6.0	4.1	6.4	5.5
Average	6.4	7.9	6.1	6.8

interaction

In this second table, the averages across rows or down columns are exactly the same as in the first table, but the pattern is *not* consistent. For example, machine A is 3.0 percentage points lower than B for coats, but 2.6 points *higher* for shirts, and 3.7 points higher for pants. The second table shows an **interaction** between machine and garment type factors; there is no such interaction in the first table.

Interaction can be described in several equivalent ways. Two experimental factors interact in their effect on a response variable if the effect of changing one factor depends on the level of the other factor. In the second table, changing from machine A to machine B increases the wastage by 3.0 points for coats, decreases it 2.6 points for shirts, and decreases it 3.7 points for pants. Which machine is better? It depends on what type of garment we're cutting. This "it depends" answer is characteristic of interaction. What type of garment has the lowest wastage in the second table? It depends on which machine we're using.

Another way to say the same thing is that, when interaction is present, differences for one factor themselves differ as we change the other factor. The difference between A and B changes as we change type of garment in the second table.

A more mathematical description of interaction depends on the idea of effect of a factor. The (main) **effect** of one level of a factor is the difference between its mean response and the grand mean. In either of the preceding tables, the effect of machine A is $8.0 - 6.8 = 1.2$, the effect of B is $6.9 - 6.8 = 0.1$, and the effect of C is $5.5 - 6.8 = -1.3$. (In passing, note that the effects must sum to 0 because they are deviations from a mean. With three levels of a factor, only two of the effects are free to vary, so there are 2 degrees of freedom, as we saw in Section 11.1.) Similarly, the garment type effects are -0.4 for coats, 1.1 for shirts, and -0.7 for pants.

Effects are used to define models for cell means, where a cell is a particular combination of a row and a column (just as in spreadsheet computer programs). The **additive model** is

$$\text{cell mean} = \text{grand mean} + \text{row effect} + \text{column effect}$$

For example, for machine A working on coats, the additive model would predict a mean of $6.8 + (1.2) + (-0.4) = 7.6$; for machine C working on pants, the model would predict a mean of $6.8 + (-1.3) + (-0.7) = 4.8$. These predictions for the additive model are exactly correct for the first table. *When there is no interaction, the additive model is exactly correct. When there is interaction, effects are not additive, and the additive model is incorrect.* Another way to define interaction is that there is a "combination effect" for the levels of the two factors that cannot be predicted by adding the separate effects of the levels. For example, in the second table, adding the effects of machine A and of coats to the grand mean yields a predicted mean of 7.6; but this particular combination actually yields a mean of 5.1, which is substantially lower than we would predict from the separate effects of machine A and of coats.

EXAMPLE 11.5

A drug company tests the average decrease in blood pressure for both female and male patients. A table of means, based on sufficiently large samples that we can ignore sampling error, is shown here.

Drug	Gender		
	Female	Male	Average
A	10.8	12.8	11.8
B	9.8	10.4	10.1
C	8.2	9.2	8.7
Average	9.6	10.8	10.2

a Is there some degree of interaction between the drug and gender factors?

b Construct a table of predicted means using the additive model. Does a comparison of actual means with additive model values indicate the presence of interaction here?

Solution

a There are several ways to check for interaction. We could compare drug A to drug B; the difference is $10.8 - 9.8 = 1.0$ for females and $12.8 - 10.4 = 2.4$ for males. The difference between mean blood pressure decreases for drugs A and B depends on the gender of the patient, so there is interaction. Also, the $B - C$ difference is 1.6 for

effect

additive model

females and 1.2 for males, so again interaction is shown. In this case, the interaction is not extremely large. Drug A shows the highest decrease in blood pressure for both females and males, drug C the lowest for both.

b It's convenient to put the effects (mean − grand mean) in the rows and columns of the table. For example, the effect for drug A is $11.8 − 10.2 = 1.6$; the effect for females is $9.6 − 10.2 = −0.6$. Then we can fill in the cells for an additive model. We show the computations for females; the ones for males are similar.

	Gender		
Drug	Female	Male	Average
A	$10.2 + 1.6 − 0.6 = 11.2$	12.4	(+1.6)
B	$10.2 − 0.1 − 0.6 = 9.5$	10.7	(−0.1)
C	$10.2 − 1.5 − 0.6 = 8.1$	9.3	(−1.5)
Effect	(−0.6)	(+0.6)	Grand mean 10.2

The results for the additive model do not equal the actual means, so again we see interaction. The actual mean for (A, Female) is 10.8; the additive model for this cell is 11.2, a slightly different number. Note that the additive model values are close to the actual means, though not identical; again, the interaction seems to be small. ■

profile plot

A very convenient check for interaction is a **profile plot**. Label the horizontal axis with levels of one factor—it doesn't matter which one—and the vertical axis for means. Plot each mean as a point, and connect the points corresponding to a level of the other factor. For example, Figure 11.7 shows profile plots for the two tables of wastage means for the military clothing contractor example at the beginning of this section. The first table showed no interaction at all. Notice that the profile lines are exactly parallel. When there's no interaction, the differences between means for levels of one factor are equal over all levels of the other factor; that's why the no-interaction profiles are parallel. The second table had large interaction, and the profile plot shows the interaction by definite nonparallel profiles.

E X A M P L E   1 1 . 6

In Example 11.5, we noted that the means exhibited interaction, but the interaction didn't seem large. Construct a profile plot. How does it display the small interaction?

Solution

Several computer packages can produce plots with labels on each point. The plot shown in Figure 11.8 is from Minitab, with the drugs identified as A, B, and C. Gender = 1 was (arbitrarily) taken as Female, 2 as Male. If you draw lines connecting the two A's, the two B's, and the two C's, you will see that they aren't parallel. Therefore, the profile plot shows interaction. They are not far from parallel though, which indicates that the interaction is small. ■

general model

A full model for a two-factor experiment allows for possible interaction of the factors. The **general model** is

individual score = grand mean + row factor effect

+ column factor effect + interaction + random error

FIGURE 11.7 **Profile Plots for Wastage Means: (a) No Interaction; (b) Interaction**

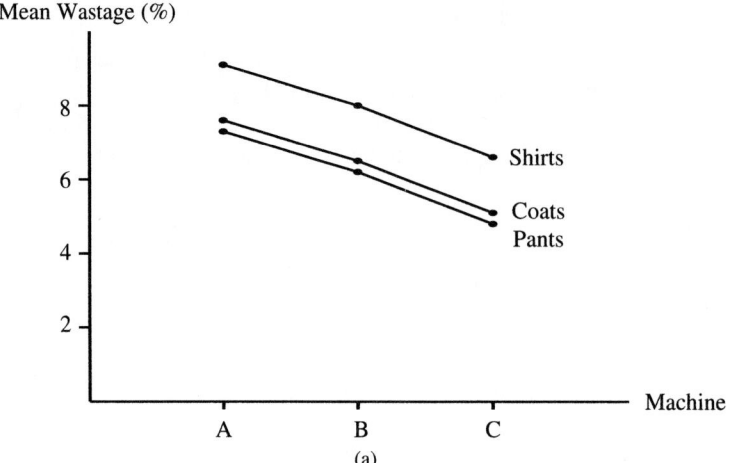

(a)

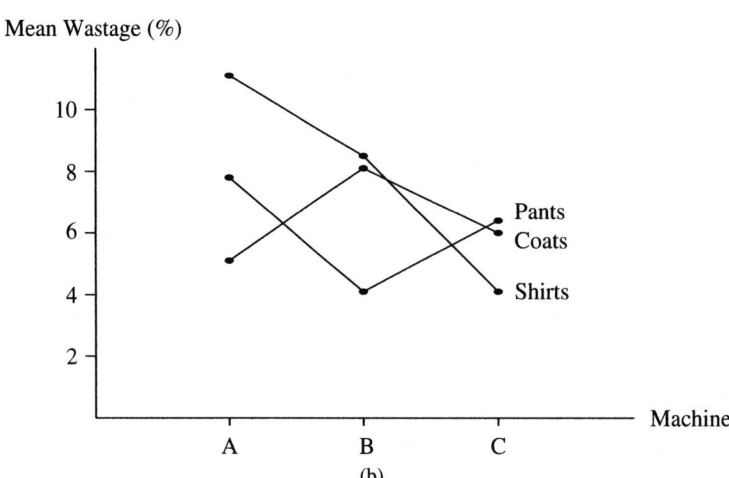

(b)

FIGURE 11.8 **Profile Plot for Blood Pressure Means**

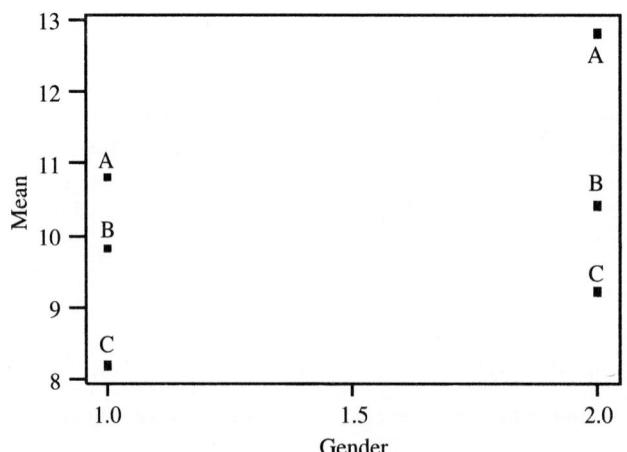

The additive model assumes that the interaction term is 0. An analysis of variance (ANOVA) for a two-factor experiment will take apart SS(Total), which is the total squared variation (of individual scores around the grand mean), into components that correspond to terms in the model:

$$SS(\text{Row effect}) + SS(\text{Column effect}) + SS(\text{Interaction}) + SS(\text{Error})$$

There's enough arithmetic involved to make a computer package very useful. We will discuss how to use computer output for two-factor experiments first, before we consider how the arithmetic is done.

One key to computer analysis is that most packages assume **balanced design**—equal numbers of observation in all cells. The analysis for unbalanced designs is possible but more subtle. Whenever possible, multiple-factor experiments should have balanced designs; we will assume balance throughout the rest of this section.

Virtually every computer package will produce an ANOVA table for a two-factor experiment. The table consists of sums of squares for rows, columns, interaction, and error—in that order, unless otherwise specified; the associated degrees of freedom (d.f.); and mean squares, defined as sums of squares divided by d.f. For example, consider an experiment to measure the heat loss through four different types of commercial thermal window glass. Five different levels of exterior temperature setting are used. Three panes of each type are tested at each temperature setting, and the heat loss is recorded for each pane. The data are shown here:

Exterior	Pane Type j			
Temperature i	A	B	C	D
60	3.2	7.5	10.3	12.4
	3.9	8.3	11.5	13.6
	4.3	8.0	10.9	12.9
50	5.7	10.6	12.9	15.0
	6.6	10.1	13.4	14.8
	6.1	9.7	13.0	15.5
40	7.5	11.0	13.4	15.5
	7.0	11.6	14.6	16.1
	6.5	10.7	14.0	16.2
30	8.0	12.0	14.6	17.5
	7.7	12.4	15.0	17.1
	8.2	11.7	15.3	16.4
20	10.1	13.6	17.1	18.8
	9.9	14.0	17.0	19.2
	10.0	14.5	16.8	18.8

The Minitab package produced the following ANOVA table:

```
SOURCE       DF    SS       MS
Temp          4  243.288   60.822
Panetype      3  689.244  229.748
INTERACTION  12    0.074    0.006
ERROR        40    7.353    0.184
TOTAL        59  939.960
```

A similar table could be obtained from most packages. The names for the sums of squares may vary; in particular, the error SS is sometimes called the within-cell SS or the residual SS. Interaction is often indicated by "multiplication" of factor names; for example, some packages might indicate the interaction of Temp and Panetype by Temp* Panetype or T*P. Don't treat this "multiplication" notation as literal multiplication; for our purposes, it's just conventional notation.

The first task in any two-factor experiment is to check for interaction. A profile plot is always a good idea; the profiles for the heat-loss data are very close to parallel, which indicates little or no interaction. The ANOVA tables allow for a formal F test of the null hypothesis of no interaction.

Definition 11.5   Test for Interaction

H_0: No interaction
H_a: There is interaction.
T.S.: $F = \text{MS(Interaction)}/\text{MS(Error)}$
R.R.: $F > F_\alpha$; the numerator d.f. are the indicated d.f. for interaction; the denominator d.f. are the error d.f.   ■

For the heat-loss data, the computer output yields $F = 0.006/0.184 = 0.03$, with 12 numerator d.f. and 40 denominator d.f. There's no need to even look this value up in the table; the expected value of an F statistic when H_0 is true is about 1.0, so $F = 0.03$ isn't even close to the expected value, let alone to the right-tail rejection region. (Note that all entries in the F table are greater than 1.0.) Thus we have no indication of more than random interaction, either by the formal F test or by the profile plot.

EXAMPLE 11.7

A consultant tested three different sets of materials for teaching basic statistical concepts. Three groups were the target audiences: college students, production workers, and staff managers. Randomly, 20 individuals from each group were taught with each set of materials. A score that measures ability to use statistical ideas in context was obtained for each individual. The data were analyzed using Systat and the following ANOVA table was obtained:

SOURCE	SUM-OF-SQUARES	DF	MEAN-SQUARE	F-RATIO	P
GROUP	195.300	2	97.650	0.992	0.373
MATERIAL	1435.633	2	717.817	7.291	0.001
GROUP*MATERIAL	6633.667	4	1658.417	16.845	0.000
ERROR	16835.200	171	98.451		

The means were condensed from (rather long) Systat output:

Group	Material A	B	C
Students	72.10	74.00	75.65
Workers	82.50	69.00	63.05
Managers	66.50	84.90	68.85

Is there evidence of interaction?

Solution

The F test for interaction, using the "multiplication" notation GROUP*MATERIAL, is shown as $F = 16.845$, with a p-value .000. Interaction is significant (detectable) at any reasonable alpha value. Just by looking at the means, we can see the interaction. As we go from A to B to C, the mean increases slightly for students, decreases sharply for workers, and first increases then decreases for managers. A profile plot would be thoroughly nonparallel. There is substantial, significant interaction. ∎

Further analysis of two-factor experiments usually depends on the result of the interaction check. If interaction is not close to significant (perhaps with a p-value around .25 or higher), or if the profile plots are close enough to parallel that we consider interaction to be negligible, we can assume the additive model

$$Y_{ijk} = \mu + \text{row effect} + \text{column effect} + \text{error}$$

main effects

with the interaction term set to 0. In this case the **main effects** for rows and columns become relevant. These are differences between row (or column) averages and the grand mean. Thus, if the means for all levels of the row factor are equal—and therefore are equal to the grand mean—the row effects are 0. To say that the row factor means differ is to say that there are nonzero row effects. The ANOVA table also yields an F test for row effects and for column effects. Technically, these tests are valid only for **fixed factors**, those for which the levels constitute the entire set of relevant levels. Most management experiments meet this condition; the exceptional **random factors**, in which the levels are only a sample of the relevant levels (like a sample of teachers leading classes, or a sample of possible orderings of a report), must be handled by more advanced methods.

fixed factors

random factors

Definition 11.6   Test for Row and Column Effects

H_0:   No row effects

H_a: There are row effects.

T.S.: $F = \text{MS(Row factor)}/\text{MS(Error)}$

R.R.:   Reject H_0 if $F > F_\alpha$, the tabled F value with numerator d.f. = d.f. for row factor and denominator d.f. = error d.f.

Note: To test column effects, replace "row" by "column."   ∎

In the example of four types of window panes, the relevant effect to test is Panetype; we don't need a statistical test to know that outside temperature has an effect on heat loss through windows. For Panetype, the output yields $F = 229.748/0.184$ with 3 and 40 d.f.; this is a huge number, far beyond all table values. Therefore we have conclusive evidence that there are real—more than random—differences in mean heat loss among types. Recall that in this example we found that there was no Temp–Panetype interaction. Therefore, we can also conclude that the pane type differences are consistent across different temperatures.

When there is significant interaction, or when the profile plots are substantially nonparallel (whether significant or not), then the tests for row and column effects often don't mean much. Interaction means that the effect of varying levels of the row factor depends on which column we're talking about; the overall average obscures this fact. Occasionally, the test makes sense. For example, suppose we had found interaction between outside temperature and type of pane in our heat-loss example, and suppose that the temperatures used were representative of the range of temperatures that the windows will actually be exposed to. We can't change window panes every time the outside temperature changes, so the pane that is best on average is the one to use, even if its relative effectiveness depends on the temperature. Usually, though, when there is interaction, the main effects (averages) aren't very relevant.

EXAMPLE 11.8

In Example 11.7, what do the F tests for main GROUP and MATERIAL effects tell us?

Solution

Not much. There is a large interaction. The materials that are most effective for one group are relatively ineffective for other groups. There is no need to use the same materials for all groups, so there's no reason to consider the overall average scores for each set of materials. Similarly, the performance of each group depends so heavily on the materials used that the average scores don't indicate much. ■

Even if interaction is present, Tukey comparisons of cell means are still possible and useful. In effect, we simply consider the IJ cell means as if they were means from a single factor.

Definition 11.7   Confidence Intervals for Cell Means, Tukey Method

Treat the cell means as means from a single-factor experiment and carry out the Tukey procedure. Formally,

$$(\bar{y}_{ij} - \bar{y}_{i*j*}) - q_\alpha(IJ, \text{d.f.}_2)\sqrt{\text{MS(Within)}/n} \le \mu_{ij} - \mu_{i*j*}$$
$$\le (\bar{y}_{ij} + \bar{y}_{i*j*}) - q_\alpha(IJ, \text{d.f.}_2)\sqrt{\text{MS(Within)}/n}$$

where IJ is the number of cells, $\text{d.f.}_2 = IJ(n-1)$ is the d.f. for MS(Within), $q_\alpha(IJ, \text{d.f.}_2)$ is given by Appendix Table 8, and $n =$ sample size per cell. n is the total sample size divided by the number of cells. ■

EXAMPLE 11.9

A state environmental agency tests two different methods of burning bituminous coal to generate electricity, in connection with four different "scrubbers" that will reduce the resulting air pollution. The primary concern is the emission of particulate matter. Four trials are run with each scrubber combined with each burning method. Particulate emission is measured for each trial. The data are:

Method	Scrubber			
	1	2	3	4
A	18.9	8.8	23.7	23.6
	16.1	16.5	15.9	22.1
	14.7	11.7	16.2	16.7
	16.9	13.0	18.0	18.9

Method	Scrubber 1	2	3	4
B	24.3	24.0	9.3	18.4
	21.1	27.1	12.1	8.6
	18.0	22.6	15.6	15.1
	16.2	23.1	12.4	9.9

A portion of computer output (Excel) is shown here. Notice that the programmer erroneously calculated the Total averages by adding the cell means; this leads to the interesting claim that the average of 16.65 and 19.9 is 36.55! The variance calculation (not shown here) is also wrong.

	A	B	C	D	E	F	G
1	Anova: Two-Factor With Replication						
2							
3	SUMMARY						
4	Scrubber1						
5		MethodA	MethodB	Total			
6	Count	4	4	8			
7	Average	16.65	19.9	36.55			
8							
9	Scrubber2						
10							
11	Count	4	4	8			
12	Average	12.5	24.2	36.7			
13							
14	Scrubber3						
15							
16	Count	4	4	8			
17	Average	18.45	12.35	30.8			
18							
19	Scrubber4						
20							
21	Count	4	4	8			
22	Average	20.325	13	33.325			
23							
24	Total						
25							
26	Count	16	16				
27	Average	67.925	69.45				
28							
29							
30	ANOVA						
31							
32	Source of Variation	SS	df	MS	F	P-Value	F crit
33							
34	Sample	48.03094	3	16.010	1.5945	0.2168	3.008786
35	Columns	1.162813	1	1.1628	0.1158	0.736585	4.259675
36	Interaction	475.4734	3	158.49	15.7848	7.01E-06	3.008786
37	Within	240.9775	24	10.041			
38							
39	Total	765.6447	31				

Construct a profile plot. Does it indicate that interaction is present? Does the ANOVA table confirm your answer?

Solution

A profile plot is shown in Figure 11.9. The profiles aren't close to parallel, indicating that interaction is present. The ANOVA table in the output shows the interaction SS to be more than half the total variation and much larger than the effect for Sample or Columns.

The output shows a large F value and a very small p-value, confirming that interaction is present.

FIGURE 11.9 **Profile Plot for Emission Means**

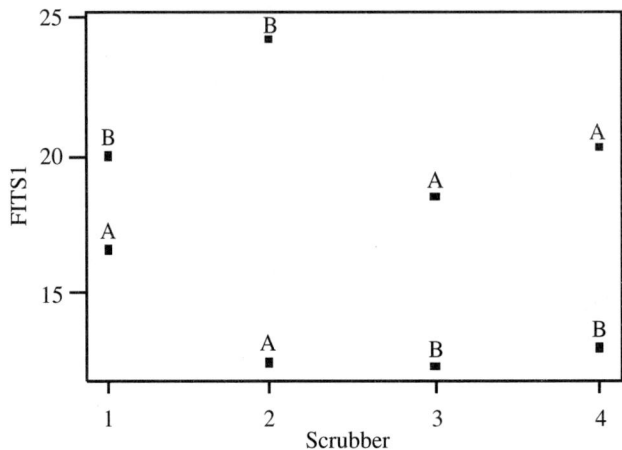

EXAMPLE 11.10

Because there is considerable interaction in the situation of Example 11.9, we would like to compare the performance of each method when mated with the best scrubber. Construct a 95% Tukey confidence interval for the difference in best scrubber performance for each method.

Solution

The best (lowest emission) scrubber for method A is scrubber 2, with $\bar{y}_{A2} = 12.500$. The best scrubber for method B is scrubber 3, with $\bar{y}_{B3} = 12.350$. Eight means are being compared: 2 methods times 4 scrubbers. For a 95% confidence interval with $IJ = 8$ means being compared, and error degrees of freedom d.f.$_2 = 24$, the value of $q_{.05}(8, 24)$ is 4.68. Substituting into the formula with $n = 4$ and MS(Within) = 10.0407, we have

$$(12.500 - 12.350) - 4.68\sqrt{10.0407/4} \leq \mu_{A2} - \mu_{B3}$$

$$\leq (12.500 - 12.350) + 4.68\sqrt{10.0407/4}$$

or

$$-7.265 \leq \mu_{A2} - \mu_{B3} \leq 7.565 \quad \blacksquare$$

When interaction is not substantial or significant, or when a manager is willing to ignore it and compare equally weighted means, the Tukey method still applies. Take the row means and allow for random error with the usual plus or minus a table value times a standard error. The notation is different, but the idea is exactly the same as in a one-factor study.

Definition 11.8   Confidence Intervals for Row Means, Tukey Method

Treat the row means as though they came from a single-factor study:

$$(\bar{y}_{i..} - \bar{y}_{i^*.}) - q_\alpha(I, \text{d.f.}_2)\sqrt{\text{MS(Error)}/nJ} \leq \mu_i - \mu_{i^*}$$

$$\leq (\bar{y}_{i..} - \bar{y}_{i^*.}) + q_\alpha(I, \text{d.f.}_2)\sqrt{\text{MS(Error)}/nJ}$$

Note that nJ is the number of observations per row mean; it can also be calculated as the total sample size divided by the number of rows. ∎

In this section, we have relied on computer output for ANOVA tables and the resulting inferences. This is the way we usually analyze two-factor experiments; occasionally, the work must be done by hand. Therefore, for the record, we present methods for computing the ANOVA table by hand. Skip to the end of the section unless you need this for reference.

The formulas for these sums of squares use the following notation:

y_{ijk} : kth observation at the ith level (row) of factor 1 and the jth level (column) of factor 2

$$i = 1, 2, \ldots, I$$

$$j = 1, 2, \ldots, J$$

$$k = 1, 2, \ldots, n$$

Note that n is the number of observations per cell, not the overall sample size.

$\bar{y}_{ij.}$:   sample mean response for the ith level of factor 1 and the jth level of factor 2

$$\bar{y}_{ij.} = \sum_k \frac{y_{ijk}}{n}$$

$\bar{y}_{i..}$:   sample mean response for the ith level of factor 1

$$\bar{y}_{i..} = \sum_{j,k} \frac{y_{ijk}}{nJ}$$

$\bar{y}_{.j.}$:   sample mean response for the jth level of factor 2

$$\bar{y}_{.j.} = \sum_{i,k} \frac{y_{ijk}}{nI}$$

$\bar{y}_{...}$:   grand mean for all sample observations

$$\bar{y}_{...} = \sum_{i,j,k} \frac{y_{ijk}}{nIJ}$$

two-factor sums of squares   With this notation, the sums of squares for a two-factor ANOVA are defined as follows:

$$\text{Factor 1: SS(Rows)} = nJ\sum_i (\bar{y}_{i..} - \bar{y}_{...})^2$$

$$\text{Factor 2: SS(Columns)} = nI\sum_j (\bar{y}_{.j.} - \bar{y}_{...})^2$$

$$\text{Interaction: SS(Interaction)} = n\sum_{i,j} (\bar{y}_{ij.} - \bar{y}_{i..} - \bar{y}_{.j.} + \bar{y}_{...})^2$$

$$\text{SS(Within)} = \sum_{i,j,k} (y_{ijk} - \bar{y}_{ij.})^2$$

EXAMPLE 11.11

Compute the sums of squares for an ANOVA of the heat-loss data.

Solution

The following table of means can be used to compute these sums of squares. Entries in the body of the table are the $\bar{y}_{ij.}$'s. Note that $n = 3$, $I = 5$, and $J = 4$.

Exterior			Pane Type j		
Temperature i	A	B	C	D	$\bar{y}_{i..}$
60	3.800	7.933	10.900	12.967	8.900
50	6.133	10.133	13.100	15.100	11.117
40	7.000	11.100	14.000	15.933	12.008
30	7.967	12.033	14.967	17.000	12.992
20	10.000	14.033	16.967	19.933	14.983
$\bar{y}_{.j.}$	6.980	11.047	13.987	15.987	$\bar{y}_{...} = 12.000$

Substituting (unrounded) means from this table, we find

$$SS(Rows) = (3)(4)[(-3.100)^2 + (-.883)^2 + (.008)^2 + (.992)^2 + (2.983)^2]$$

$$= 243.288$$

$$SS(Columns) = (3)(5)[(-5.020)^2 + (-.953)^2 + (1.987)^2 + (3.987)^2]$$

$$= 689.244$$

$$= 3[(-.080)^2 + (-.014)^2 + \cdots + (-.037)^2] = .074$$

$$SS(Interaction) = 3[(-.080)^2 + (-.014)^2 + \cdots + (.963)^2]$$

$$= .074$$

The within-cell sum of squares must be calculated from the original data. For this example,

$$SS(Within) = (3.2 - 3.800)^2 + (7.5 - 7.933)^2 + \cdots + (3.9 - 3.800)^2$$

$$+ (8.3 - 7.933)^2 + (4.3 - 3.800)^2 + (8.0 - 7.933)^2$$

$$+ \cdots + (18.8 - 18.933)^2 = 7.353 \quad \blacksquare$$

EXERCISES

11.24 Three products are tested in each of five geographic regions. A mean approval rating is found in each case. The sample sizes are large enough that the means can be regarded essentially as population means.

	Product		
Region	A	B	C
1	68	80	77
2	55	64	58
3	62	72	67
4	67	76	70
5	58	68	63

a Calculate the grand mean. Interpret this value.

b Calculate region effects and product effects.

c What does the difference in effects of products A and B represent?

11.25 Refer to the means of Exercise 11.24. Calculate a table of interaction effects.

11.26 Construct a profile plot for the means of Exercise 11.24. (Arbitrarily, put products along the horizontal axis.)

   a Is there interaction in the means?

   b Is any one product consistently superior over all regions?

11.27 An experiment on workfare programs is undertaken by a state welfare agency. Three plans are tested. Plan A requires that all physically able welfare recipients work at assigned jobs for minimum wages. Plan B allows recipients to select or reject jobs, and welfare benefits are reduced by $1 for every $2 earned. Plan C is a "control": Welfare officials visit plan C recipients as often as subjects in plans A and B and encourage job searching, but they offer no special job-taking incentives. Each plan is used with 20 families in each of four geographic areas of the state. For each family, the 1-year increase in income is found. The following means (in thousands of dollars) are observed:

		Area		
Plan	1	2	3	4
A	2.1	1.7	1.3	1.7
B	1.9	1.8	1.7	1.8
C	.8	.7	.6	.7

An ANOVA table follows:

Source	SS	d.f.	MS
Plan	59.20	2	29.60
Area	4.80	3	1.60
Interaction	2.40	6	.40
Error	273.60	228	1.20
	340.00	239	

   a Find the grand mean.   **b** Find the row and column effects.

11.28 Refer to Exercise 11.27. Calculate F tests for the effects of (a) plan, (b) area, and (c) interaction. Use $\alpha = .05$ in each case. State a conclusion for each test.

11.29 **a** Construct a profile plot for the data of Exercise 11.28. Arrange plans along the horizontal axis.

   b Does this plot suggest the possibility that interaction is present?

   c Does the F test of Exercise 11.28 indicate that interaction is present? Is that a conflict between the plot and the test? If so, what is a possible explanation?

11.30 Refer to the data of Exercise 11.28. Use a Tukey test with $\alpha = .05$ to see if any of the plan mean differences can be declared statistically significant.

11.31 A maker of packaged cake mixes wants consistently good results from its mixes, and therefore minimal variation in quality from one box to another. Standard procedure in testing any new mix is to prepare four versions of the mix. Six batches of each version are tested at each of three geographical altitudes. Typically, there is greater variability at higher altitudes. Most customers are at altitude 1, the lowest altitude, and most of the rest are at the middling altitude, 2. A standard measure of variability is computed for the cakes baked from each batch. The variability measure reflects differences in the height and texture among cakes, which is ideally very small. The data were analyzed by Minitab to obtain the following averages of the variation measure:

```
MTB > table by 'Altitude' and 'Mixture';
SUBC> means of 'Variatn'.

  ROWS: Altitude    COLUMNS: Mixture
```

```
                1        2        3        4       ALL

    1       64.667   59.233   54.083   66.317   61.075
    2       69.900   53.200   73.633   92.633   72.342
    3       36.967   90.450   88.233   94.700   77.588
  ALL       57.178   67.628   71.983   84.550   70.335

  CELL CONTENTS --
            Variatn:MEAN
```

a Would it be sensible to say that mixture 1, which has the lowest average score, appears to be the most desirable mixture?

b A profile plot of the mean variation score, constructed using Minitab, is shown in Figure 11.10. What does this plot say about your answer to part a?

FIGURE 11.10   **Profile Plot of Variation Score Means**

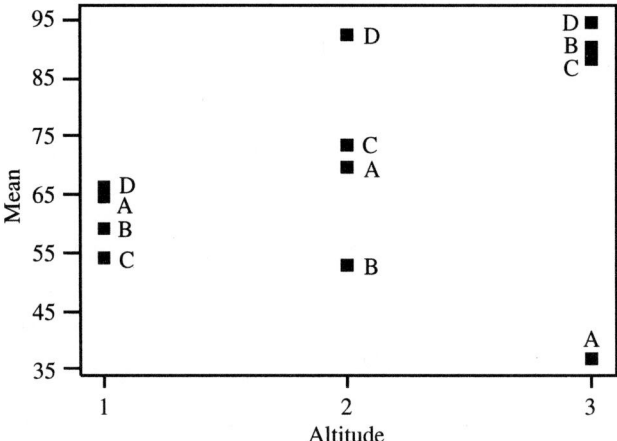

11.32   The data for Exercise 11.31 were also analyzed to yield an ANOVA table. The Minitab output is as follows:

```
MTB > Twoway 'Variatn' 'Altitude' 'Mixture';
SUBC>   Means 'Altitude' 'Mixture'.

ANALYSIS OF VARIANCE  Variatn

SOURCE         DF        SS       MS
Altitude        2      3417     1708
Mixture         3      6934     2311
INTERACTION     6     11667     1944
ERROR          60     20036      334
TOTAL          71     42054
```

a Show that there is a statistically detectable (significant) interaction at any reasonable α value.

b Explain what interaction means in this context. In particular, how does interaction relate to your answers to Exercise 11.31?

c How meaningful are the tests for the main effects in this case?

11.33   A supermarket chain wanted to select a new house brand of instant coffee. A taste test was arranged. Three different methods for preparing the coffee were used. Also, three different ages of coffee were tested. Age 1 was as fresh as the distribution system would allow, age 2 was the maximum age allowed for selling the coffee, and age 3 was basically, "What's this stuff in the back of the cupboard?" The chain manager obtained six jars of each method of coffee at each age and prepared coffee from every jar. A consensus rating was obtained for each jar from a tasting panel; the ideal rating was 100. Mean ratings were obtained from Systat output as follows:

		METHOD		
		1	2	3
	1	63.000	55.000	57.167
AGE	2	50.667	43.667	40.167
	3	46.333	37.000	27.667

a Which method seems to obtain the best ratings?

b Is there an evident effect of age? Does the pattern of changes in means make sense in this context?

c Are differences between methods reasonably consistent across different ages? What effect is being considered here?

11.34 The data underlying Exercise 11.33 were given to the Systat package, which yielded the following ANOVA output:

ANALYSIS OF VARIANCE

SOURCE	SUM-OF-SQUARES	DF	MEAN-SQUARE	F-RATIO	P
AGE	4215.593	2	2107.796	18.749	0.000
METHOD	1287.259	2	643.630	5.725	0.006
AGE*METHOD	306.519	4	76.630	0.682	0.608
ERROR	5059.000	45	112.422		

a Is there clear evidence that the effect of METHOD depends on which AGE is considered? That is, is there clear evidence of an interaction effect?

b What does the *p*-value for AGE indicate about the main effect of AGE?

c Is there conclusive evidence of a more than random difference of METHOD averages?

11.35 Use the means from Exercise 11.33 and the output from Exercise 11.34 to test for significant differences of all pairs of METHOD means. You'll need to compute METHOD means by hand from the cell means. Do the results indicate a clear choice of the method to adopt? ■

11.5

Randomized Block Designs

The ANOVA methods we discussed in this chapter extend the basic methods of comparing two means to the more general problem of comparing several means. We applied the procedure in two experimental settings—one-factor ANOVA, which we described in Section 11.1, and two-factor ANOVA, which we described in Section 11.4. In this section, we describe an experimental design that is a hybrid of these settings: the **randomized block design**.

randomized block design

A chain of personal computer stores wants to test three possible point-of-purchase displays of a new type of holder for computer disks. The chain managers propose to test-market the displays in three stores in each of three sales districts. One approach is to assign displays completely randomly to stores. The only factor is the type of display; the one-factor ANOVA methods of Section 11.1 can be used to analyze the resulting sales volume data. One problem with this approach is that there is a chance of obtaining an assignment such as the following:

	Products Displayed		
District 1:	A	A	A
District 2:	B	B	B
District 3:	C	C	C

This would be a disastrous assignment. Because all the displays of a given type are in one district, there is no way to tell whether differences in sales volume are due to differences in displays or to differences in districts; that is, with this assignment, effect of display and effect of district are **confounded**. But even if the assignment of displays to stores does not turn out to be confounded, there is another objection to a one-factor experiment. By not controlling for district, this design implies that any district-to-district differences are part of random error. If there are, in fact, large district-to-district differences, MS(Error) is large; by failing to control for district, this design leads to very wide confidence intervals and to tests with very poor power.

The one-factor experimental design can be modified to control for differences among districts. The chain's managers can restrict the random assignment of displays to stores by requiring that each display be used once in each district. One such randomization is shown here. Note that each display is placed in one (randomly chosen) store in each district.

	Products Displayed		
District 1:	A	C	B
District 2:	B	A	C
District 3:	A	B	C

This experimental setting is referred to as a randomized block design. Characteristically, one factor, called the **treatment factor**, is of primary interest; in this example, the treatment factor is type of display. In addition, another factor, called a **block factor**, is of less interest in itself but should be controlled to avoid confounding and to reduce random error. In this example, districts would be considered block factors. Randomized block methods can be thought of as extensions of the paired-sample methods of Chapter 9; had the chain been considering only displays A and B, the sales volume data could be regarded as paired by district. One reason for blocking is the same as the reason for pairing: to reduce the amount of random variation.

A randomized block is a two-factor (treatments and blocks) experiment with a one-factor focus; that is, the primary aim of the design is to compare means for the treatment factor. The block factor tends to be regarded as a "nuisance" factor; it is controlled, not so much to find out what its effects are as to avoid having those effects contaminate the analysis of the treatment factor.

There is another difference between a randomized block design and the two-factor designs we discussed in Section 11.4. There is typically only $n = 1$ observation per cell in a randomized block design. In the ANOVA table for a two-factor design, the d.f. for error is $IJ(n - 1)$; if we used two-factor methods for a randomized block design, we would have no d.f. for error, no MS(Error) number, and no way to do tests or confidence intervals. To avoid this problem, we assume there is no interaction between treatments and blocks; the degrees of freedom that would have been used up in estimating interaction become available, given the assumption of no interaction, for estimating error.

The model for a randomized block design is

$$Y_{ij} = \text{grand mean} + \text{treatment effect} + \text{block effect} + \text{error}$$

Note that, by assumption, there is no interaction term in the model.

The ANOVA computations (again, easily done by computer) for a randomized block design are similar to those for a two-factor ANOVA, with the exception that there is, by assumption, no SS(Interaction).

$$SS(\text{Treatment}) = J \sum (\bar{y}_{i.} - \bar{y}_{..})^2 \qquad \text{with d.f.} = I - 1$$

$$SS(\text{Block}) = I \sum (\bar{y}_{.j} - \bar{y}_{..})^2 \qquad \text{with d.f.} = J - 1$$

$$SS(\text{Error}) = \sum (y_{ij} - \bar{y}_{i.} - \bar{y}_{.j} + \bar{y}_{..})^2 \qquad \text{with d.f.} = (I - 1)(J - 1)$$

$$SS(\text{Total}) = \sum (y_{ij} - \bar{y}_{..})^2$$

$$= SS(\text{Treatment}) + SS(\text{Block}) + SS(\text{Error}) \qquad \text{with d.f.} = IJ - 1$$

In these formulas, $\bar{y}_{i.}$ is the mean for treatment i, $\bar{y}_{.j}$ is the mean for block j, and $\bar{y}_{..}$ is the grand mean; I is the number of treatments and J is the number of blocks. Usually, the easy way is to compute SS(Treatment), SS(Block), and SS(Total), and then find SS(Error) by subtraction. ■

Suppose that the sales volume data for the three different displays in three different districts are as follows:

	District			
Display	1	2	3	Average
A	86	97	96	93.0
B	55	82	79	72.0
C	60	88	77	75.0
Average	67.0	89.0	84.0	80.0

Then

$$SS(\text{Treatment}) = SS(\text{Display})$$
$$= 3[(93.0 - 80.0)^2 + (72.0 - 80.0)^2 + (75.0 - 80.0)^2]$$
$$= 774.0$$

$$SS(\text{Block}) = SS(\text{District})$$
$$= 3[(67.0 - 80.0)^2 + (89.0 - 80.0)^2 + (84.0 - 80.0)^2]$$
$$= 798.0$$

$$SS(\text{Total}) = (86 - 80.0)^2 + (97 - 80.0)^2 + \cdots + (77 - 80.0)^2$$
$$= 1684.0$$

$$SS(\text{Error}) = SS(\text{Total}) - SS(\text{Treatment}) - SS(\text{Block})$$
$$= 1684.0 - 774.0 - 798.0$$
$$= 112.0$$

The ANOVA table and F tests are completed just as in previous sections. The results for the sales volume data are as follows:

Source	SS	d.f.	MS	F
Treatment (display)	774.0	2	387.0	13.82
Block (district)	798.0	2	399.0	14.25
Error	112.0	4	28.0	
Total	1684.0	8		

The F statistics are obtained, as usual, by dividing the indicated MS by MS(Error); the degrees of freedom for the F statistic are those indicated by the ANOVA table. For the sales volume data, both F statistics have $\text{d.f.}_1 = 2$ and $\text{d.f.}_2 = 4$; for these d.f., $F_{.025} = 10.65$ and $F_{.01} = 18.00$. For the display factor, the F statistic falls between 10.65 and 18.00; the p-value is therefore between .025 and .01. Thus, the chain's managers have fairly conclusive evidence that there are real—more than random—differences in mean sales volume by type of display. The F test for the district factor also shows that there are differences in mean volume by district; the managers knew that very well already. Note that the block factor does indeed account for a large fraction of SS(Total); had the managers not adopted a randomized block design, the SS(Error) would have been much larger, possibly concealing the effect of the display factor.

The Tukey method for comparing pairs of means works the same way as for other designs. The role of MS(Within) is taken by MS(Error) and the d.f. are those for error. In a randomized block design, the sample size per mean, n, is equal to the number of blocks; however, it can also be calculated as the total number of observations divided by the number of treatments. For example, suppose that 4 levels of a treatment factor had been applied within each of 11 blocks; there would be a total of 44 observations (and 43 total d.f.). If an ANOVA table showed MS(Error) = 16.0 with 30 d.f., the Tukey plus or minus for $\alpha = .05$ (95% confidence) would be $q_{.05}$ $(I = 4, \text{d.f.} = 30)\sqrt{\text{MS(Error)}/n} = 3.85\sqrt{16.0/11} = 4.64$. The Tukey procedure is the same for randomized block designs as for other designs, given the proper interpretation of the various entries.

Most computer packages can compute the ANOVA table for a randomized block design.

EXERCISES

11.36 An information systems manager tests four database management systems for possible use. A key variable is speed of execution of programs. The manager chooses six representative tasks and writes programs within each management system. The following times and Statistix output are recorded:

	Task					
System	1	2	3	4	5	6
I	58	324	206	94	39	418
II	47	331	163	75	30	397
III	73	355	224	106	59	449
IV	38	297	188	72	25	366

```
ANALYSIS OF VARIANCE TABLE FOR TIME

SOURCE          DF      SS         MS        F        P

SYSTEM (A)       3    7505.50    2501.83    18.41   0.0000
TASK (B)         5    4.722E+05  94442.9   694.94   0.0000
A*B             15    2038.50    135.900

TOTAL           23    4.818E+05


TUKEY (HSD) PAIRWISE COMPARISONS OF MEANS OF TIME BY SYSTEM

                        HOMOGENEOUS
      SYSTEM    MEAN    GROUPS

         3     211.00   I
         1     189.83   .. I
         2     173.83   .. I I
         4     164.33   .... I
```

THERE ARE 3 GROUPS IN WHICH THE MEANS ARE
NOT SIGNIFICANTLY DIFFERENT FROM ONE ANOTHER.

```
CRITICAL Q VALUE                    4.077    REJECTION LEVEL    0.050
CRITICAL VALUE FOR COMPARISON      19.401
STANDARD ERROR FOR COMPARISON       6.7305

ERROR TERM USED: SYSTEM*TASK, 15 DF
```

a Locate means for each system. Find the grand mean.

b Is there a statistically detectable (significant) difference among system means? State the *p*-value.

11.37 Test all pairs of means for significant differences in Exercise 11.36 using $\alpha = .05$.

11.38 An experiment compares four different mixtures of the components of a rocket propellant; the mixtures contain differing proportions of oxidizer, fuel, and binder. To compare the mixtures, five different samples of propellant are prepared for each mixture. Each of five investigators is randomly assigned one sample of each of the four mixtures and is asked to measure the propellant thrust. The data are shown here:

| | *Investigator* | | | | |
Mixture	1	2	3	4	5
1	2340	2355	2362	2350	2348
2	2658	2650	2665	2640	2653
3	2449	2458	2432	2437	2445
4	2403	2410	2418	2397	2405

a Identify the blocks and treatments for this design.

b Why would one want to use this design, as opposed to assigning mixtures completely randomly to investigators?

11.39 **a** Refer to Exercise 11.38. Use the Excel output shown here to conduct an ANOVA. The row factor is investigator and the column factor is mixture. Use $\alpha = .05$.

b Which mixture appears to have the best (highest) mean? Is its mean significantly ($\alpha = .05$) higher than each of the other three means?

	A	B	C	D	E	F	G
1	Anova: Two-Factor Without Replication						
2							
3	SUMMARY						
4		Count	Sum	Average	Variance		
5	Investigator1	4	9850	2462.5	18983		
6	Investigator2	4	9873	2468.25	16452.25		
7	Investigator3	4	9877	2469.25	17944.92		
8	Investigator4	4	9824	2456	16311.33		
9	Investigator5	4	9851	2462.75	17670.92		
10							
11	Mixture1	5	11755	2351	67		
12	Mixture2	5	13266	2653.2	86.7		
13	Mixture3	5	12221	2444.2	103.7		
14	Mixture4	5	12033	2406.6	62.3		
15							
16	ANOVA						
17							
18	Source of Variation	SS	df	MS	F	P-value	F crit
19	Rows	452.5	4	113.125	1.643	0.2273	3.2592
20	Columns	261261	3	87086.98	1264.7	2.88E-15	3.4903
21	Error	826.3	12	68.85833			
22							
23	Total	262540	19				

11.40 Is there evidence of a significant investigator effect in the computer output of Exercise 11.39? What would such an effect indicate about the accuracy of the investigators?

11.41 A supermarket chain offered a private label product in competition with national labels. The package design had been a generic, boring one, and the product had not sold well at all. The chain decided to use an upgraded package design, but needed to choose among 3 alternative designs. As a test, the chain manager had substantial numbers of packages made up in each of the three designs. Each store in the chain offered each type of package for one day. The order was randomized so that a few stores sold design 1, then 2, then 3; others sold 3, then 1, then 2; and still others 2, then 1, then 3; and so on. The sales in each market each day were recorded. JMP results follow:

```
Response: Sales
Effect Test
Source    Nparm      DF    Sum of Squares  F Ratio   Prob>F
Design      2          2    1476.722       4.3055    0.0172
Store      35         35   26525.667       4.4192    0.0000

Least Squares Means
Level    Least Sq Mean      Std Error      Mean
1        79.38888889        2.182598123    79.3889
2        84.08333333        2.182598123    84.0833
3        75.02777778        2.182598123    75.0278
```

a Is there a clear indication that store makes a difference in sales? Defend your answer briefly.

b Is there a clear indication that design 2 is better than design 3? You will need to do some calculations by hand. MS(Error) = 171.49.

11.42 In the supermarket data, why was it important for each store to sell each design, rather than having some stores sell only design 1, others only design 2, and others only design 3?

11.43 In the supermarket data, why was it desirable to randomize the order in which the designs were sold?

11.44 As one part of a taste-testing experiment, three different formulations of a new frozen dinner product are tested. Samples of each formulation are given, in random order, to each of 12 testers. Each tester gives a score to each formulation. A Minitab analysis of the data is shown here:

```
MTB > Twoway 'Rating' 'form' 'person';
SUBC>    Additive.

ANALYSIS OF VARIANCE  Rating

SOURCE       DF      SS       MS
form          2     767.4    383.7
person       11    5301.2    481.9
ERROR        22    1532.6     69.7
TOTAL        35    7601.2

MTB > table by 'form';
SUBC> means of 'Rating'.

 ROWS: form

        Rating
         MEAN
   1    57.667
   2    46.917
   3    49.250
 ALL   51.278
```

a Perform an F test of the null hypothesis of equal score (Rating) means by formulation (form). State bounds on the p-value.

b Are there statistically significant ($\alpha = .01$) differences among taste-tester (person) means? What does the result of the test indicate about the people in the experiment?

11.45 **a** Calculate 95% confidence intervals for all pairwise differences of score means for the three formulations, using the results in Exercise 11.44. Note that each mean is an average of 12 scores.

b According to these intervals, which pairwise differences, if any, are statistically significant at $\alpha = .05$? ■

More Complex Experiments

Carefully designed experiments have become an important tool for managers in the past few years. Experiments have always been relevant in the context of the research and development laboratory; recently, they have also become important in market research and in quality control. The most important concepts of experimental design have already been introduced in this chapter. In this section, we elaborate on some of the basic ideas.

Perhaps the most widely known role for designed experiments is in quality control. The quality of a manufactured product is the result of a number of different factors, including the quality of the parts supplied, the design of the product, and the skill of the workers who assemble the product. One of the key findings from modern quality-control literature is that uncovering a quality problem by varying one factor at a time is not an effective approach. Instead, there should be carefully planned experiments that control all critical factors. For example, suppose that the quality of a video monitor is measured by an index that reflects the brightness of display, the size of flaws on the screen, and the appearance of the case. After some consideration, three key factors are isolated: which of three suppliers of the internal electronic "gun" is used, which of two types of glass is used for the screen, and which of four assembly teams puts together the product.

It would not be wise to have teams A and B always use glass 1 and teams C and D always use glass 2, with team A using guns from supplier 1, team B guns from supplier 2, and teams C and D guns from supplier 3. In this situation, one can't separate the effect of the supplier from the effect of the gun, and neither can be separated from the effect of the assembly team. Or suppose that only the source of the gun varies across assembly teams. If teams A and B consistently put out inferior products in such a situation, it can't be determined whether their work is poor or whether glass 1 is inferior. Instead, all teams should use all gun suppliers and all glass types. The most convenient and effective way to vary team, supplier, and glass type is in a balanced design.

factorial experiment

Measuring the quality index as a function of team, gun supplier, and glass type in a balanced design is a **factorial experiment** with three factors. The data can be analyzed in terms of main effects, two-way interactions (team by supplier, team by glass type, and supplier by glass type), and a three-way interaction. If a quality problem arises, the analysis will suggest the appropriate remedy. For example, if the mean for supplier 1 is consistently low, that supplier should bring up quality standards, but if there is a strong supplier-by-glass type interaction, the technical compatibility of the guns and glass type should be investigated. The computations required for a multifactor experiment are similar to those for a two-factor experiment, but they are tedious enough to be left to a computer. Analyses can be done by F tests and Tukey methods that are obvious extensions of those for two-factor studies. In particular, one should check for interactions before considering overall averages (main effects).

For example, suppose that samples of eight monitors each are taken from the production of each combination of team, supplier, and glass type, and that the following computer output is obtained:

```
THREE-WAY ANOVA FOR QUALITY CONTROL DATA

ANALYSIS OF VARIANCE PROCEDURE

DEPENDENT VARIABLE: QUALITY


SOURCE                DF    SUM OF SQUARES    MEAN SQUARE    F VALUE    PR > F
MODEL                 23    24557.95312500    1067.73709239   10.94    0.0001
ERROR                168    16398.62500000      97.61086310             ROOT MSE
CORRECTED TOTAL      191    40956.57812500                            9.87982101


SOURCE                DF         ANOVA SS    F VALUE    PR > F
TEAM                   3    1957.89062500       6.69    0.0003
SUPPLIER               2   20509.96875000     105.06    0.0001
TEAM*SUPPLIER          6     203.15625000       0.35    0.9109
TYPE                   1     435.00520833       4.46    0.0362
TEAM*TYPE              3     303.05729167       1.03    0.3786
SUPPLIER*TYPE          2     460.01041667       2.36    0.0979
TEAM*SUPPLIER*TYPE     6     688.86458333       1.18    0.3213


                              MEANS

                TEAM      N      QUALITY
                1        48    229.645833
                2        48    220.625000
                3        48    225.145833
                4        48    224.770833

              SUPPLIER    N      QUALITY
                1        64    231.953125
                2        64    210.437500
                3        64    232.750000

                TYPE      N      QUALITY
                1        96    223.541667
                2        96    226.552083
```

First, we look for interactions. SAS uses an asterisk to denote interactions; we see that TEAM*SUPPLIER, TEAM*TYPE, SUPPLIER*TYPE, and TEAM*SUPPLIER*TYPE all have p-values (shown as $PR > F$) that are relatively large. The only interaction that is even close to statistically significant is SUPPLIER*TYPE (p-value .0979).

Then, we look for main effects. There is a huge SUPPLIER effect; the SS for SUPPLIER is extremely large, the F value is enormous at 105.06, and the p-value ($PR > F$) is tiny at .0001. The computed MEANS clearly shows that SUPPLIER 2 has a very low quality average. There is also clear evidence of a significant effect of TEAM ($PR > F = 0.003$); the TEAM 1 mean is high and the TEAM 2 mean is low. There is a marginally significant ($PR > F = 0.0362$) TYPE effect; TYPE 2 has a slightly higher mean than TYPE 1. Tukey method tests could be performed for each main effect to verify that the apparent differences of means are statistically detectable.

Careful experimentation isn't easy. Everyone who is involved in the study must understand the importance of balanced design and of randomization. The effort required has a real payoff. A well-designed, well-executed experiment can reveal the important variables much more clearly than any other data-gathering method.

off-line quality control

Designed experiments are crucial for **off-line quality control**—the design of products and processes to achieve high effectiveness and, equally important, low variability. This approach was popularized in Japan by Taguchi (see Taguchi, 1980). Experts in the product or process of interest are asked to specify what factors would influence the quality of the result. These factors may be categorized as *control* factors (those that can be set as desired) and *noise* factors (those that are impossible or very expensive to control).

In a typical off-line quality-control experiment, there will be many, many factors. For example, Lin and Kacker (1986) discuss a study of how to solder circuit pack assemblies; there were 17 distinct factors, 7 having two levels and 10 having three levels. From a practical viewpoint, it is often impossible to study every possible combination of levels. In the soldering study, there would be $2^7 3^{10} = 7,558,272$ possible combinations of levels of the factors; at 1 hour per combination, 24 hours per day, 365.25 days per year, evaluating all possible combinations would take about 860 years! Therefore, most off-line quality experiments need a method that reduces the number of experimental runs while still preserving the essential balanced design property.

orthogonal array designs

Taguchi suggested **orthogonal array designs**. An example, OA_8 (which stands for orthogonal array with 8 rows), is shown in Table 11.2. These designs are "pairwise-balanced"; that is, within any two columns, all pairs of numbers occur exactly the same number of times. In OA_8, the pairs (1,1),(1,2),(2,1), and (2,2) appear exactly twice in any pair of columns. Each factor is assigned to a column; thus, a seven-factor experiment (each factor having two levels) could be handled using OA_8. It isn't necessary to use every column. If an experiment had six two-level factors, the OA_8 design could be used by omitting any one column. Notice that instead of $2^7 = 128$ runs, an OA_8 experiment requires only 8 runs. Shoemaker and Kacker (1988) discuss these designs and show several orthogonal arrays.

TABLE 11.2 **Orthogonal Array OA_8**

Row	Column 1	2	3	4	5	6	7
1	1	1	1	1	1	1	1
2	1	1	1	2	2	2	2
3	1	2	2	1	1	2	2
4	1	2	2	2	2	1	1
5	2	1	2	1	2	1	2
6	2	1	2	2	1	2	1
7	2	2	1	1	2	2	1
8	2	2	1	2	1	1	2

EXAMPLE 11.12

Another orthogonal array design, OA_9, is shown in Table 11.3. How many factors and levels does it accommodate? How many runs (rows) would be required to obtain all possible combinations of the levels? How does the pairwise-balanced property show in this design?

TABLE 11.3 Orthogonal Array OA_9

Row	Column 1	2	3	4
1	1	1	1	1
2	1	2	2	2
3	1	3	3	3
4	2	1	2	3
5	2	2	3	1
6	2	3	1	2
7	3	1	3	2
8	3	2	1	3
9	3	3	2	1

Solution

There are four columns, so a four-factor study could be handled by this design. Because the numbers 1, 2, and 3 appear in each column, all four factors could have three levels. Therefore, there are $3^4 = 81$ combinations of the levels of the four factors. The pairwise-balanced property is reflected by the fact that in any two columns, the pairs (1,1), (1,2), (1,3), (2,1), ..., (3,3) all appear exactly once. ■

These orthogonal array designs make it possible to perform experiments even when there are enormous numbers of factors. The cost is that it is difficult or impossible to discover interactions among factors. The whole point of orthogonal array designs is to avoid using all combinations of factor levels, but interaction is by definition the effect of specific combinations. Alternatively, we may see the problem by considering degrees of freedom (d.f.). In OA_8, only 8 measurements are taken on the response variable, which corresponds to the 8 rows; thus, there are $8 - 1 = 7$ total d.f. If all 7 columns are used for 7 two-level factors, 1 degree of freedom will be used to assess the effect of each factor. With all 7 d.f. used up, there is no available information about interaction.

EXAMPLE 11.13

In the OA_9 design, if all four columns are used for factors, will there be any information about interactions?

Solution

There are $9 - 1 = 8$ total d.f. Because each factor has three levels, the main effect of each factor accounts for 2 d.f. The main effects account for $4(2) = 8$ d.f., which leaves none for interaction. ■

fractional factorial designs

The most useful variety of orthogonal array designs is **fractional factorial designs**. Rather than having a full factorial experiment with all combinations of factor levels represented, these designs pick only a fraction of the combinations. The selected combinations are chosen so that some balance is preserved. The simplest example involves factors A, B, and C, each having levels 1 and 2. Table 11.4 shows the $2^3 = 8$ possible combinations of levels. The * denotes those combinations selected in a "1/2 replication" fractional factorial. This design can be displayed as an orthogonal array, OA_4, as shown in Table 11.5.

TABLE 11.4 **Fractional Factorial for Three Two-Level Factors**

	Factor $A = 1$			Factor $A = 2$	
	B			**B**	
	1	**2**		**1**	**2**
1	*		**1**		*
C			**C**		
2		*	**2**	*	

TABLE 11.5 **OA_4**

	Column		
Row	**1**	**2**	**3**
1	1	1	1
2	1	2	2
3	2	1	2
4	2	2	1

These fractional factorial designs often allow for at least some interactions to be estimated. A good description of fractional factorial designs is given in Box, Hunter, and Hunter (1978). Shoemaker and Kacker (1988) suggest that a good strategy is to have a fractional factorial design for the control factors and to have each row of this design tested with each combination of the noise factors. Thus, if there were 5 two-level control factors and 2 two-level noise factors, we could use an OA_8 design for the control factors (omitting two columns) with level 1 of both noise factors; then another OA_8 design with level 1 of noise factor A and level 2 of noise factor B; still another OA_8 with $A = 2$ and $B = 1$; and finally another OA_8 with $A = 2$ and $B = 2$. If there were many noise factors, we could have another orthogonal array design (preferably a fractional factorial) for the noise factors, and we could combine every row of the control OA with every row of the noise OA.

In off-line quality-control experiments, several dependent variables are usually measured for each run (row) of the experiment. For example, suppose that we were experimenting with a process that deposits a coating on silicon wafers. We could measure the coating thickness of each of several wafers during each run (row) of the experiment. One obvious measure of interest would be the deviation of the average thickness from the target value. Another important measure would be the variability in thickness from one wafer to another. Rather than using variance to measure variability, it's usually better to measure the logarithm of the variance to minimize the effect of occasional, very large outlying variances. Shoemaker and Kacker (1988) indicate that in their experience, a variability measure is usually more important because it's harder to control. They suggest finding combinations of some of the factors that minimize variability and using other factors to bring the mean close to the target.

Once the experiment is designed and the data collected, we can use many different computer programs to perform an analysis of variance (ANOVA). A difficulty is deciding which effects can be estimated from the data. One good approach is to count degrees of freedom (d.f.), as we did earlier in this section. The maximum d.f. available for estimating effects is the number of runs (rows) in the orthogonal array, less one. (If many observations of a response variable are made within each run, this information is useful for measuring random error and reducing standard errors, but the information does not add d.f. for measuring the effects of factors.) If, as we saw previously, these d.f. can be completely used up in estimating main effects, then no interactions can be estimated. If an interaction can't be estimated, the computer program should return an error message. Shoemaker and Kacker (1988) and the references cited therein discuss more sophisticated approaches.

EXAMPLE 11.14

Certain packaged cereals will settle in the box before reaching the customer. Although the box contains the advertised weight, it appears only partially filled; customers aren't happy when this happens. Engineers at the cereal plant identify four control factors: cut, the size of the bits of dough to be baked into the cereal; moisture, the wetness of the dough; temperature, the heat in the baking ovens; and speed, the rate at which a package-filling machine fills boxes. An experiment used columns 1, 2, 4, and 7 of OA_8 for these factors. Cartons from morning and afternoon runs for each row of the OA were selected, labeled to indicate the experimental conditions under which they were produced, and shipped by the usual process to a distant store. Each box in each carton was opened and the degree of settling, in inches, was carefully measured. The mean and variance of settling degree were calculated for each carton. The experimenters attempted to use Systat to perform an analysis of variance involving the main effects of all four factors and four interactions that they thought might be relevant. They obtained a message: ∗ ∗ ∗ERROR∗ ∗ ∗ A DESIGN MATRIX WAS SINGULAR. Why did they get that message?

Solution

In trying to evaluate four main effects of two-level factors and four interactions, they needed 8 d.f. But OA_8 has 8 rows and, therefore, only 7 available d.f. ∎

Shoemaker and Kacker also suggest that it's important to have a small follow-up experiment that uses the levels of the various factors that seem to be best. The reason for the follow-up experiment is that the factors may interact in ways that can't be analyzed by the experimental design, so the chosen levels of the factors may not give the predicted results.

EXAMPLE 11.15

The cereal engineers in Example 11.14 reanalyzed their data using Systat, omitting one of the interaction terms. They obtained the following output. What factors and/or interactions have a detectable influence on the logarithm of the variance (LOGVAR)? What has a detectable influence on the mean (MEANSET)? How should the engineers proceed to design a follow-up study?

```
DEP VAR: MEANSET   N:   16   MULTIPLE R:  .980   SQUARED MULTIPLE R:  .961
```

ANALYSIS OF VARIANCE

SOURCE	SUM-OF-SQUARES	DF	MEAN-SQUARE	F-RATIO	P
C	0.449	1	0.449	161.766	0.000
M	0.001	1	0.001	0.225	0.648
T	0.000	1	0.000	0.081	0.783
S	0.001	1	0.001	0.324	0.585
C*M	0.006	1	0.006	2.306	0.167
M*T	0.087	1	0.087	31.360	0.001
C*T	0.005	1	0.005	1.766	0.221
ERROR	0.022	8	0.003		

```
DEP VAR: LOGVAR    N:  16    MULTIPLE R:   .784    SQUARED MULTIPLE R:   .614

                        ANALYSIS OF VARIANCE

     SOURCE  SUM-OF-SQUARES   DF   MEAN-SQUARE    F-RATIO      P
        C          0.897       1      0.897        1.120     0.321
        M          1.673       1      1.673        2.089     0.186
        T          0.103       1      0.103        0.128     0.730
        S          6.143       1      6.143        7.670     0.024
      C*M          0.418       1      0.418        0.522     0.491
      M*T          0.947       1      0.947        1.183     0.309
      C*T          0.011       1      0.011        0.014     0.910

     ERROR         6.408       8      0.801
```

Solution

The rightmost column of the output is presumably the *p*-value corresponding to each *F* statistic. Only the S (speed) factor has a detectable effect on LOGVAR, with a *p*-value of .024. In the output for MEANSET, the *p*-values for C and M*T are very small, which indicates that cut and the moisture/temperature interaction have a detectable effect on mean settling. The engineers should select the speed setting that consistently gave lower variance, and the setting for cut and combination of settings for moisture and temperature that gave the most desirable (in this case, least) mean settling. These settings and perhaps other similar ones should be used in a follow-up study to verify that no neglected interactions cause trouble. ■

11.7

Summing Up

H ere are some points to consider when dealing with designed experiments.

1   Before running any analyses, think carefully about all the experimental factors that are being varied. Make sure that all of them are considered together in the analysis.

2   The various *F* tests are intended to see if the overall pattern of means is a statistically detectable (significant) result. It does not directly tell you which means differ, unless there are only two means and that's the only possible difference.

3   The Tukey procedure (along with other multiple comparison methods in some packages) is designed to make more specific comparisons of particular means.

4   When dealing with two or more factors, consider possible interactions first. When substantial interaction is present, the averages for any one factor usually aren't very interesting and conceal the essential story told by the data.

5   The idea of blocking is a direct extension of the idea of paired samples. The reason for blocking is to control a major source of variability. The typical randomized block experiment can be recognized by having only one observation per cell.

6   Designed experiments are particularly useful in quality improvement because it is possible (with effort) to vary a number of potentially important factors at the same time, rather than using a tedious and slow one-by-one process.

7 The key assumptions for analysis of variance are the same as those of the pooled-variance t method: no biases, independence, normality, and constant variance, basically in that order of importance.

In addition, you may want to reread the summary of key ideas at the beginning of the chapter.

E X A M P L E   1 1 . 1 6

Transportation companies are often involved in intermodal operations. Intermodal refers to freight that travels by rail in combination with some other form of transportation, instead of the traditional rail siding to rail siding mode. Units may be trucked by the shipper to the railroad terminal or loaded from a seafaring ship. After the intercity trip, the units are picked up from the rail destination or loaded to ship. A continuing concern has been delays in customer pickup. Customers often leave the shipment at the terminal and take advantage of storage space. This causes congestion at the facility as well as administrative overhead. Transportation companies usually charge customers for the storage time, but the bills are often disputed or ignored, and therefore are ineffective.

One particular transportation company recently implemented a new collection process in hopes of decreasing "dwell time." Dwell time is the amount of time the unit "dwells" and takes up space at the destination terminal while awaiting customer pickup. Under the old collection process, the population mean dwell time was 96 hours. After implementation of the new process, dwell time was tracked for all units that were grounded during one specific 1-week period. Data is given below.

dwell	cust	dwell	cust	dwell	cust	dwell	cust	dwell	cust	dwell	cust	dwell	cust
108.17	1	37.87	1	34.62	1	35.58	1	51.20	1	128.10	2	102.08	2
128.68	2	25.47	2	7.03	2	72.87	2	107.38	2	199.75	2	59.42	2
31.87	2	53.40	2	146.90	2	25.22	2	299.33	2	146.40	3	52.62	3
91.00	3	58.33	3	101.18	3	148.77	3	104.98	3	45.67	3	52.70	3
32.87	3	79.37	3	153.68	3	9.88	3	72.45	3	48.50	3	153.37	3
50.75	3	46.72	3	168.77	3	48.83	3	44.97	3	51.27	3	91.52	3
155.62	3	56.50	3	30.62	3	151.25	3	151.50	3	155.50	3	92.23	3
28.58	3	78.32	3	76.93	3	54.37	3	44.15	3	173.05	3	152.17	3
149.07	3	56.05	3	78.43	3	78.77	3	150.50	3	74.35	3	150.23	3
150.82	3	128.12	3	82.43	3	51.92	3	51.13	3	54.65	3	100.33	3
170.25	3	236.43	3	104.35	3	148.80	3	76.70	3	70.05	3	153.90	3
127.63	3	74.15	3	35.78	3	166.92	3	99.18	3	171.87	3	174.22	3
50.38	3	80.02	3	60.43	4	101.32	4	101.77	4	53.37	4	101.67	4
53.82	4	28.42	4	51.47	4	58.27	4	57.07	4	6.33	5	155.78	5
13.57	5	52.03	5	12.65	5	29.83	5	56.38	5	42.45	5	122.53	5
107.83	5	157.08	5	78.35	5	105.38	5	54.28	5	57.62	5	74.20	5
11.60	5	77.75	5	6.10	6	137.72	6	123.65	6	50.75	6	1.52	6
110.93	6	6.17	6	46.38	6	91.28	6	144.90	6	87.87	6	140.42	6
99.35	6	71.02	6	9.38	6	104.10	6	71.13	6	142.37	6	50.83	6
97.60	6	178.75	6	110.65	6	48.65	6	50.88	6	168.72	6	40.38	6

Company managers wanted to know if the data provide evidence of a decrease in dwell time. This problem was addressed in Chapter 8. The data here show the dwell time for each of 140 units as well as which of 6 customers the unit is associated with. The company also wanted to know if there were differences among the 6 customers with respect to the average dwell time.

Use the JMP IN output in Figure 11.11 to decide if there are any statistically detectable differences among means and, if so, which particular shippers differ from others in average dwell time.

Solution

The plot of the data shows a few long dwell times; note that customer 2 had one truck in storage for about 300 hours, almost 2 weeks. Thus, there is some indication of right skewness. However, the plot doesn't seem grossly unreasonable.

To test for differences among all means, we want the F test results. The p-value is shown as .0887, not very strong evidence at all that there is a real difference.

(A Kruskal-Wallis test, not shown in the output, has an even less conclusive p-value of .1327.) The apparent differences among customers might have arisen by chance.

To test the differences between specific pairs of customers, use the Tukey-Kramer results from the output. Because the F and Tukey procedures are not equivalent, they occasionally give different answers. The last line of the output indicates that "Positive

FIGURE 11.11 **Output for Dwell Time Data**

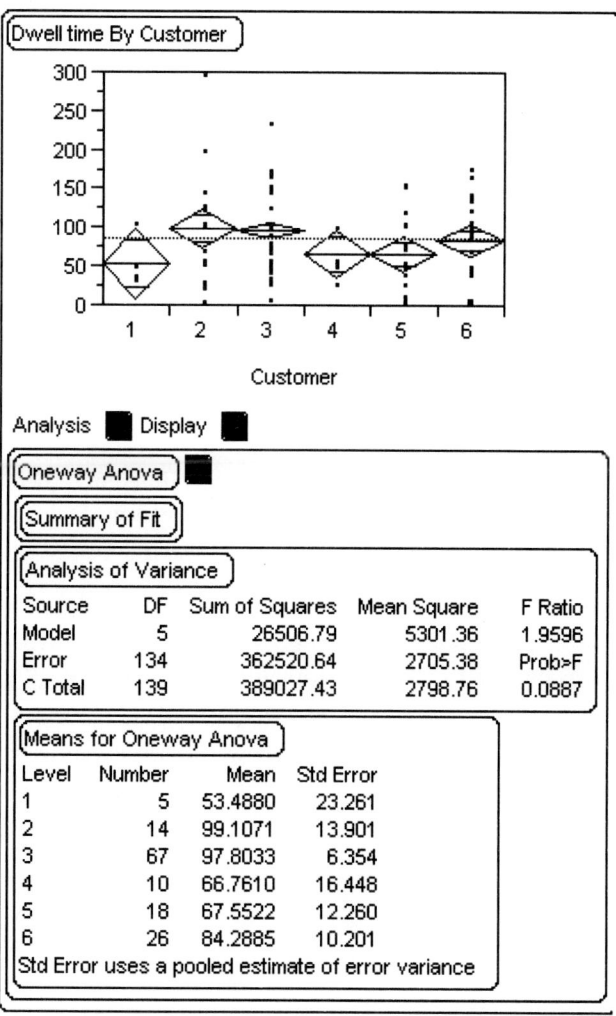

FIGURE 11.11 **(continued) Output for Dwell Time Data**

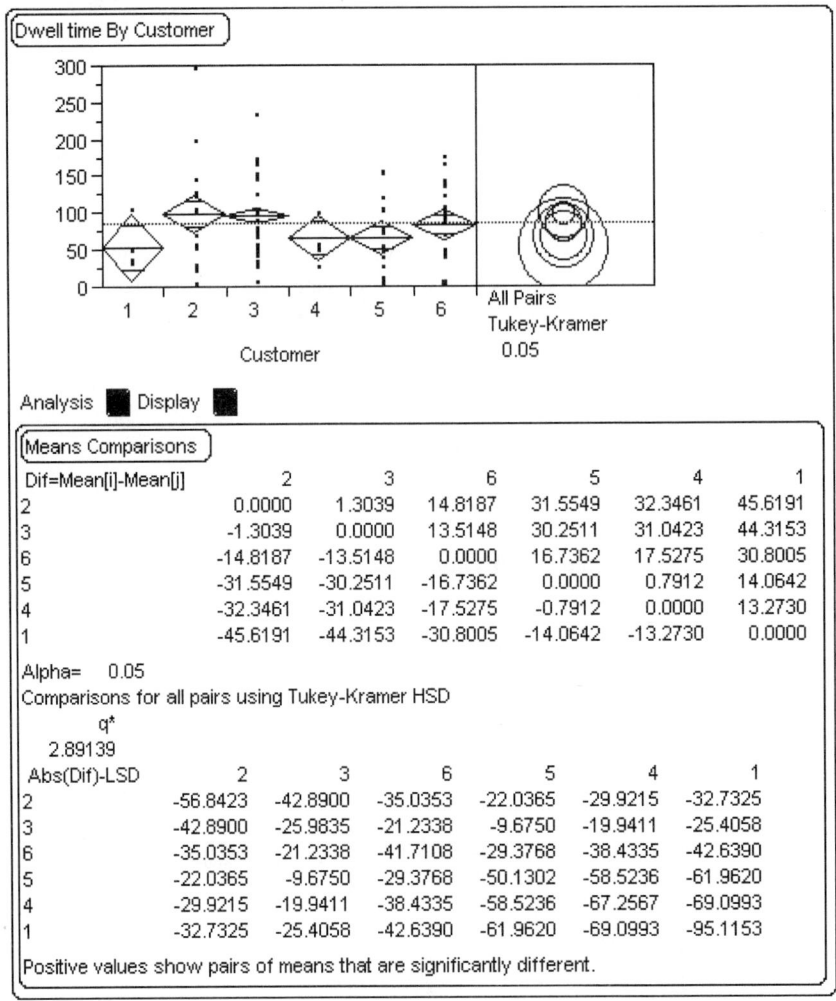

values show pairs of means that are significantly different." There are no positive values in the table, so there are no significant pairwise differences. In this situation, the F and Tukey results are the same. ∎

SUPPLEMENTARY EXERCISES

11.46 Three different designs of video recording equipment are subjected to accelerated use testing, and the times to failure (in hours) of each unit are recorded:

					Time					
Design A:	226	400	462	489	510	541	547	563	581	603
Design B:	329	366	409	451	465	490	517	546	577	615
Design C:	421	484	506	566	589	605	619	634	651	600

The data were analyzed using Excel and the following results were obtained:

	A	B	C	D	E	F	G
1	Anova: Single Factor						
2							
3							
4	SUMMARY						
5		Groups	Count	Sum	Average	Variance	
6		DesignA	10	4922	492.2	12351.3	
7		DesignB	10	4765	476.5	8360.06	
8		DesignC	10	5735	573.5	6258.94	
9							
10	ANOVA						
11							
12	Source of Variation	SS	df	MS	F	P-value	F crit
13	Between Groups	54217.3	2	27108.6	3.015	0.0658	3.354
14	Within Groups	242733	27	8990.1			
15							
16	Total	296950	29				

    a Locate means and variances for each design. Which design appears to be best?

    b Locate SS(Between) and SS(Within).

    c Explain why the d.f. shown are correct.

11.47 Refer to Exercise 11.46. Is the research hypothesis of unequal means supported?

11.48 Perform the Kruskal-Wallis test for the hypothesis of Exercise 11.46. Is the conclusion substantially different from that of Exercise 11.47?

11.49 Boxplots of the data in Exercise 11.46 are shown in Figure 11.12. Do there appear to be any major violations of ANOVA assumptions?

FIGURE 11.12   **Boxplots of Failure Time Data**

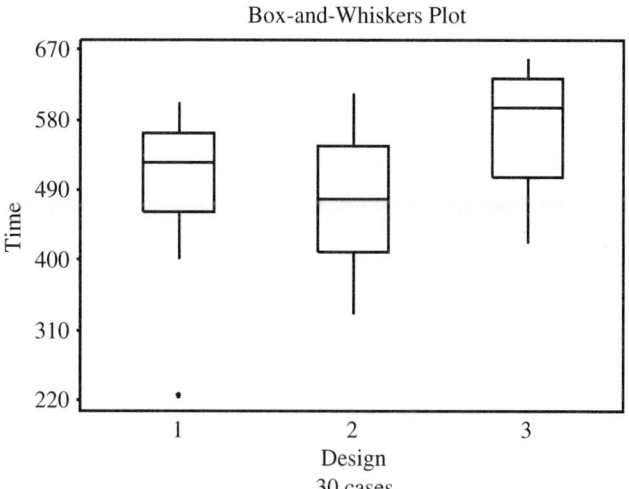

11.50 Use the Tukey procedure to calculate overall 95% confidence intervals for the pairwise differences among the means of Exercise 11.46.

11.51 In a study of the effects of television commercials on 7-year-old children, the attention span of children watching commercials for clothing, food products, and toys is measured. To reduce the effects of outliers, only the median attention span for each commercial is used.

Commercial	Median Attention Span (Seconds)										
Clothes	21	30	23	37	21	18	30	42	36		
Food	32	51	46	30	25	41	38	50	45	53	57	41
Toys	48	59	51	47	58	56	49	55	52	49	60	

Stata output is as follows:

```
. oneway Attspan Commtype, tabulate

            |        Summary of Attspan
   Commtype |      Mean   Std. Dev.       Freq.
------------+------------------------------------
      Duds  |  28.666667   8.4261498          9
      Foods |  42.416667   9.8392381         12
      Toys  |  53.090909   4.7000967         11
------------+------------------------------------
     Total  |  42.21875   12.453097         32


                  Analysis of Variance
  Source            SS          df      MS            F      Prob > F
----------------------------------------------------------------------
Between groups    2953.64299     2   1476.8215      23.10    0.0000
Within groups     1853.82576    29   63.9250261
----------------------------------------------------------------------
   Total          4807.46875    31   155.079637


. kwallis Attspan, by (Commtype)

Test: Equality of populations (Kruskal-Wallis Test)

  Commtype     _Obs    _RankSum
      1          9       60.00
      2         12      193.50
      3         11      274.50

chi-square =   18.843 with 2 d.f.
probability =   0.0001
```

a Locate the value of the F statistic for the null hypothesis of equal means.

b Can this hypothesis be rejected using $\alpha = .01$?

c Locate the p-value for this test.

11.52 **a** Find the value of the Kruskal-Wallis statistic in Exercise 11.51.

b Can the hypothesis of equal means (or more properly "locations") be rejected using $\alpha = .01$?

11.53 **a** Plot the data of Exercise 11.51.

b Do there appear to be serious violations of ANOVA assumptions?

c Does it matter much whether an F test or a Kruskal-Wallis test is used?

11.54 Use a statistical package to find 99% Tukey confidence intervals for differences in means for the data of Exercise 11.51. Are any differences significant at $\alpha = .01$?

11.55 A township manager had four appraisers estimate the fair market value of 12 houses. The estimates, in thousands of dollars, are

	Home											
Appraiser	1	2	3	4	5	6	7	8	9	10	11	12
A	86	76	93	110	73	55	96	74	96	140	88	72
B	81	75	95	105	70	53	91	75	95	120	75	68
C	90	76	96	108	78	63	99	77	99	135	94	75

Output from the Statistix package follows:

```
ANALYSIS OF VARIANCE TABLE FOR VALUE

SOURCE          DF      SS          MS          F       P

APPRAISR (A)     3    381.562     127.187     10.66   0.0000
HOME (B)        11   16086.0     1462.36     122.58   0.0000
A*B             33    393.687      11.9299


TOTAL           47   16861.3
GRAND AVERAGE    1    3.733E+05

TUKEY (HSD) PAIRWISE COMPARISONS OF MEANS OF VALUE BY APPRAISR

                        HOMOGENEOUS
APPRAISR    MEAN        GROUPS

   4       90.833       I
   3       90.083       I
   1       88.250       I
   2       83.583       .. I

CRITICAL Q VALUE                    3.826    REJECTION LEVEL    0.050
CRITICAL VALUE FOR COMPARISON       3.8151
STANDARD ERROR FOR COMPARISON       1.4100

ERROR TERM USED: APPRAISR*HOME, 33 DF
```

a How relevant is the null hypothesis of equality of house prices? Is this hypothesis rejected?

b Locate the value of the F statistic for testing the null hypothesis of the equality of appraiser effects.

c Can the null hypothesis be rejected at typical α levels? What is the indicated p-value?

11.56 Use the Tukey method to test ($\alpha = .05$) the significance of pairwise differences in appraiser effects for the data of Exercise 11.55.

11.57 The data of Exercise 11.55 were also analyzed incorrectly as a one-way ANOVA experiment, with the following output:

```
ONE-WAY AOV FOR VALUE BY APPRAISR

SOURCE    DF     SS          MS        F       P

BETWEEN    3    381.562     127.187   0.34   0.7968
WITHIN    44   16479.7     374.539
TOTAL     47   16861.3
```

a Would the null hypothesis of equal appraiser means be rejected at $\alpha = .05$?

b How important is it to control for the effect of house differences in Exercise 11.55?

11.58 A manufacturer of (snow) skis must bond the main assembly to the bottom of the ski (the part that makes contact with the snow). The bonding agent should be applied as uniformly as possible to obtain a good ski. Uniformity is indicated by low "wiggle" values. The manufacturer tested various temperatures for the application, bonding 20 skis at each of 5 temperatures. The data were analyzed using JMP, with results shown in Figure 11.13. Is there clear evidence that temperature makes a difference in the average "wiggle" value?

11.59 The bonding agents for the data for the ski manufacturer of the preceding exercise were obtained from two different suppliers. The data were reanalyzed, taking into account the supplier factor. The results are shown in Figure 11.14. Is there clear evidence that temperature matters? Supplier? The interaction between them?

11.60 A profile plot of the means for the ski bonding data is shown in Figure 11.15. Is there a clear indication that interaction is present? Is your answer consistent with the output shown in the previous exercise?

FIGURE 11.13 **Data for Ski Bonding**

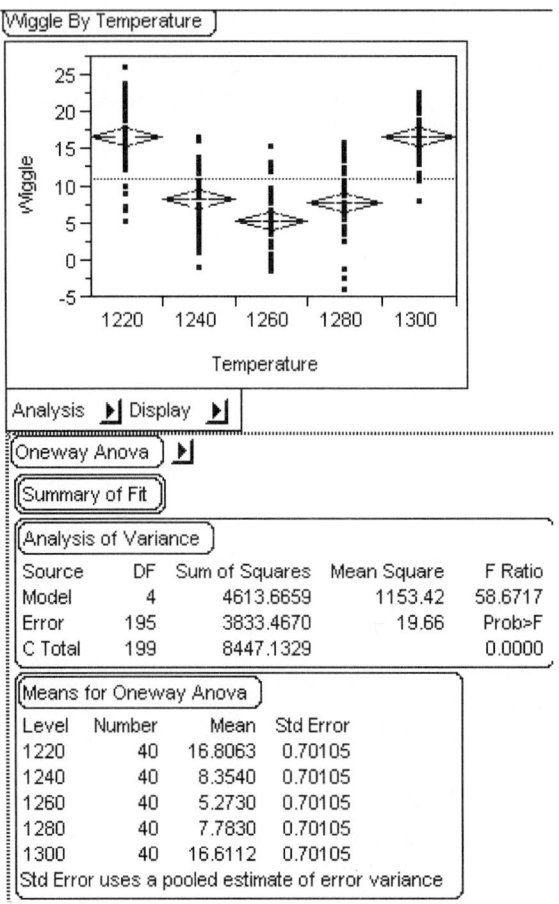

FIGURE 11.14 **Ski Bonding by Supplier**

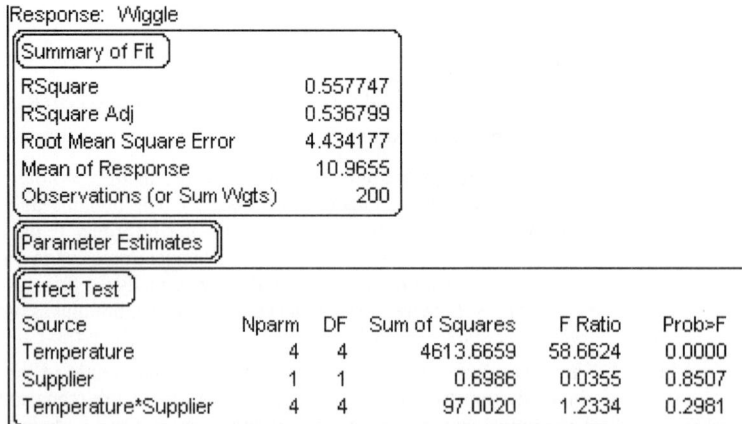

11.61 A paint manufacturer experimented with six possible formulations for a new economy-grade paint. Six samples of each formulation were tested in a high-stress laboratory environment. The time to paint failure was recorded for each sample. High scores are

FIGURE 11.15 **Profile Plot for Ski Bonding Data**

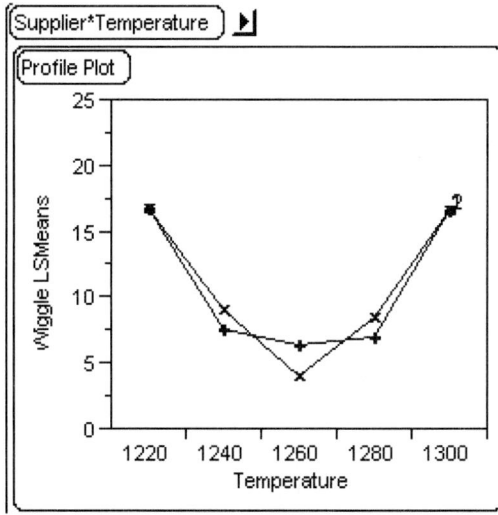

preferable and the company regarded 40 as a minimum acceptable score. The following results were obtained:

```
MTB > Table 'formuln';
SUBC>    Means 'failtime';
SUBC>    StDev 'failtime'.

 ROWS: formuln

     failtime failtime
        MEAN  STD DEV

   1   42.000   6.542
   2   51.833   7.139
   3   48.833   4.956
   4   45.000   4.733
   5   55.333   3.615
   6   49.500   5.167
 ALL   48.750   6.720


MTB > Oneway 'failtime' 'formuln';
SUBC>    Tukey 5.

ANALYSIS OF VARIANCE ON failtime
SOURCE     DF      SS       MS       F       p
formuln     5     678.2    135.6    4.51    0.003
ERROR      30     902.5     30.1
TOTAL      35    1580.7
                                  INDIVIDUAL 95% CI'S FOR MEAN
                                  BASED ON POOLED STDEV
  LEVEL     N     MEAN     STDEV  -------+---------+---------+---------
     1      6    42.000    6.542  (------*------)
     2      6    51.833    7.139                 (-----*------)
     3      6    48.833    4.956             (------*-----)
     4      6    45.000    4.733    (-----*------)
     5      6    55.333    3.615                    (-----*------)
     6      6    49.500    5.167              (------*-----)
                                  -------+---------+---------+---------
 POOLED STDEV =    5.485           42.0      49.0      56.0
```

```
Tukey's pairwise comparisons

    Family error rate = 0.0500

Critical value = 4.30

Intervals for (column level mean) - (row level mean)

              1        2        3        4        5

    2   -19.462
         -0.205

    3   -16.462   -6.628
          2.795   12.628

    4   -12.628   -2.795   -5.795
          6.628   16.462   13.462

    5   -22.962  -13.128  -16.128  -19.962
         -3.705    6.128    3.128   -0.705

    6   -17.128   -7.295  -10.295  -14.128   -3.795
          2.128   11.962    8.962    5.128   15.462
```

Is there a statistically detectable difference among means, using $\alpha = .05$? What is the *p*-value?

11.62 According to the Tukey method of paired comparisons, which pairs of means in Exercise 11.61 are detectably different, using $\alpha = .05$?

11.63 The 36 samples in Exercise 11.61 were collected and then tested in the lab in completely random order. Why is this method preferable to (for example) testing all of formulation 1 first, all of formulation 2 next, and so on?

11.64 The six paint formulations in Exercise 11.61 were, in fact, put together as all combinations of three bases and two coloring agents. If we wanted to separate the effect of different bases from the effect of different coloring agents, how should we reanalyze the data?

11.65 The data of Exercise 11.61 were treated as a two-factor ANOVA. The following computer output was obtained using Excel:

	A	B	C	D	E	F	G
1	Anova: Two-Factor With Replication						
2							
3	SUMMARY		color1	color2			
4		Base1					
5	Count		6	6			
6	Average		42	45			
7							
8		Base2					
9	Count		6	6			
10	Average		51.833	55.333			
11							
12		Base3					
13	Count		6	6			
14	Average		48.833	49.5			
15							
16							
17	ANOVA						
18							
19	Source of Variation	SS	df	MS	F	P-value	F crit
20	Sample	613.17	2	306.583	10.191	0.0004	3.31583
21	Columns	51.361	1	51.361	1.7073	0.2013	4.17089
22	Interaction	13.722	2	6.861	0.228	0.7974	3.31583
23	Within	902.5	30	30.083			
24							
25	Total	1580.75	35				

a Is there evidence of a statistically significant interaction between the factors?

b Show that the effect of coloring is not statistically significant at usual α levels, but the effect of base is statistically significant.

11.66 Use the Tukey method to construct 95% confidence intervals for all differences of base means, using the computer output in Exercise 11.65. Are any of the differences of means significant at $\alpha = .05$?

11.67 A manufacturer of laser printers is trying to improve the design of the toner cartridge, which determines much of the perceived quality of the printer output. In particular, the manufacturer wants to increase the life of the cartridge as measured by the number of thousands of pages printed satisfactorily. Four cartridge designs are tested. Sixteen cartridges of each design are tested and the number of thousands of pages produced is obtained for each cartridge. A computer analysis of the data yields the following output:

```
MTB > Oneway 'copies' 'design';
SUBC>    Tukey 5.

ANALYSIS OF VARIANCE ON copies
SOURCE     DF       SS       MS       F       p
design      3     7022     2341    17.08   0.000
ERROR      60     8222      137
TOTAL      63    15244
                                    INDIVIDUAL 95% CI'S FOR MEAN
                                    BASED ON POOLED STDEV
LEVEL      N      MEAN    STDEV   ----+---------+---------+---------+--
  1       16    123.31    12.40                 (----*----)
  2       16    109.44    12.59   (----*----)
  3       16    137.25    10.75                           (----*----)
  4       16    115.00    10.97       (----*----)
                                    ----+---------+---------+---------+--
POOLED STDEV =    11.71            108       120       132       144
```

Tukey's pairwise comparisons

Family error rate = 0.0500

Critical value = 3.74

Intervals for (column level mean) - (row level mean)

```
                1        2        3

     2        2.93
              24.82

     3      -24.88   -38.76
             -2.99   -16.87

     4       -2.63   -16.51    11.30
             19.26     5.38    33.20
```

MTB > Kruskal-Wallis 'copies' 'design'.

```
LEVEL    NOBS   MEDIAN   AVE. RANK   Z VALUE
  1       16    122.0      35.5       0.75
  2       16    107.0      18.4      -3.50
  3       16    138.5      51.2       4.63
  4       16    116.5      24.9      -1.88
OVERALL   64               32.5
```

H = 28.32   d.f. = 3   p = 0.000

According to the ANOVA table, is there a statistically significant difference somewhere among the means, using $\alpha = .05$?

11.68 According to the Kruskal-Wallis output shown in Exercise 11.67, is there a significant difference among the the average life of the cartridges? Again, use $\alpha = .05$. Does the result differ greatly from the result for the F test?

11.69 In the output for Exercise 11.67, which design seems to be best? (The first question is whether high or low scores are best.) Use the Tukey approach with $\alpha = .05$ to see if this design has a significantly better mean than each of the other designs.

11.70 As part of a market test of a new package design, a cereal manufacturer prepared boxes in each of two colors with each of two new type styles. Each color–type style combination was tested in 12 randomly assigned supermarkets in the test area. Sales of the cereal over a 3-day period were recorded. The data are recorded in the EX1170.DAT file on the data disk. Load the data into your computer program. Sales are shown in column 1, color code (1 or 2) in column 2, and type style code (1 or 2) in column 3.

   a Obtain mean sales for each combination of color code and type style code.

   b Does there appear to be a large interaction between color and type style, based on these means?

11.71 **a** Obtain an analysis of variance (ANOVA) table for the data of Exercise 11.70, with sales as the dependent variable. Is there a relatively large interaction sum of squares?

   b Are there statistically detectable (significant) effects of color and of type style? Obtain p-values if the program will do so; otherwise, try $\alpha = .05$ and $\alpha = .01$.

11.72 If the computer program will do so conveniently, obtain residuals (actual sales minus the mean for the color–type style combination) for the data of Exercise 11.70. Obtain a histogram, stem-and-leaf display, or normal plot of the residuals. Is there any evidence of serious nonnormality in the data?

11.73 A furniture store targeted eight zip codes for promotional activity. The store's records for the past 2 months showed all purchases by residents of each zip code. The data are stored in the EX1173.DAT file on the data disk, which should be read into your computer package. Sales amounts are stored in column 1 of the file, and numbers 1–8 for the eight zip codes are stored in column 2.

   a Obtain boxplots of the sales data separately for each zip code. Do these boxplots indicate that the data are roughly normally distributed within each zip code?

   b Obtain an ANOVA table for testing the null hypothesis of equal means. Can this hypothesis be rejected at conventional α values?

11.74 **a** Use the computer program to perform a Kruskal-Wallis test of the null hypothesis of equal distributions for the data of Exercise 11.73. Can the null hypothesis be rejected at conventional α values?

   b Do the F and Kruskal-Wallis tests give similar conclusions? If not, what explains the difference in results?

11.75 A company wanted to select a long-distance telephone service on the basis of lowest cost. A clerk took 50 calls at random from the list of those made by the company in the last 3 months and determined what each call would cost using each service. The results are in the EX1175.DAT file on the data disk. Cost of the calls is in column 1, call number is in column 2, and service company number is in column 3. Load the data into your statistical computer program.

   a Obtain an ANOVA table using call number and service number as factors.

   b Is there a statistically detectable (significant) effect of service number? If possible, obtain a p-value.

   c Explain why there shouldn't be an interaction term between the two factors in the ANOVA model.

11.76 If your computer program will do so conveniently, perform Tukey tests of significance for all pairwise differences among service company means in Exercise 11.75 using $\alpha = .05$. If the computer isn't programmed to do so, obtain the means for each service and do the tests by hand. Is there a clear-cut lowest cost service among the four?

11.77 **a** Reanalyze the data of Exercise 11.75, ignore the call number factor, and treat the service company number as the only factor. Obtain an ANOVA table.

b Does the error mean square for this analysis differ much from the error mean square in the two-factor analysis? If so, what does that fact say about the wisdom of blocking, using call numbers (as opposed to allocating 200 calls completely at random, 50 to each of the four service companies)?

11.78 **a** If possible, have the computer program find predicted values and residuals (actual − predicted) for the data of Exercise 11.75. Obtain a plot of residuals against predicted values. Does the variability around predicted values appear to be constant?

b Have the computer program calculate the logarithms, either natural (base e) or common (base 10), of the costs. Obtain a new ANOVA table and use the logarithm of cost as the dependent variable, with call number and service company number as factors. Is there a statistically detectable (significant) service company effect?

c Obtain a plot of residuals against predicted values for the logarithm model. Does the variability around predicted values appear constant?

11.79 A fast-food restaurant chain regularly introduces new products. Some are successes, others not. The chain introduced a lower-fat hamburger, which did not do well. Now the chain is considering whether to replace that burger with a "new, improved" burger. Three different versions of low-fat burger have been developed by the chain's test kitchen. The product manager for this product conducted a careful experiment to evaluate customer response to all three versions, and wants you to analyze the results.

The product manager's memo to you includes: "We put together a tasting panel of 192 people from our target market, which is adults over age 25. The panel looks to us to be a good cross section of that group; we didn't see any major imbalances. We asked them all to taste each of the three burgers and rate them on a 0 to 100 scale, where 0 is worst and 100 best.

"We've done this sort of testing before. A good product should average out to at least a 70 rating. A difference of 2 or 3 points makes quite a difference in sales, so we want to analyze the results carefully.

"I think the test was done pretty well. Everyone rated all three versions. The versions are called 1, 2, and 3 in the output, but for the test they were H217, H343, and H287; those numbers don't mean anything, but they don't give any cues to the tasters. We were a little worried that the order in which they ate the burgers would matter; maybe the third burger wouldn't taste as good—regardless of which it was. So we balanced that out. One set of 36 got the burgers in 1, 2, 3 order, another set of 36 got 2, 1, 3 order, and so on. In the output, WHEN-DONE indicates whether that taster tested that version first, second, or third. We didn't see any crazy ratings that were way out of line, so we think people took the tasting seriously.

"What I need from you is a reading on whether the results give a clear indication that one or another version is preferred on average. Some of the output says, I think, that there's a difference; other parts of the output say no. What's the right way to look at the numbers? Also, am I right that the WHENDONE issue didn't seem to matter much?

"I'm sorry now that I forgot most of the stat course I took. If you can explain the results without all the technical terms, I'd appreciate it."

```
Oneway ANOVA for RATING
```

Source of Variation	Sum of Squares	D.F.	Mean Square	F-Ratio	P Value
VERSION	155.861	2	77.9306	1.68058	0.1881
Error	13215.8	285	46.3712		
Total (corr.)	13371.7	287			

```
Table of Means
```

VERSION	Sample Size	Sample Mean	Standard Error	Estimated Effect
1	96	77.5417	0.695006	-0.423611
2	96	79	0.695006	1.03472
3	96	77.3542	0.695006	-0.611111
Overall	288	77.9653	0.401262	

Pairwise Differences - Comparison by 95% HSD Intervals

	Contrast	Difference	+-HSD	Significant
1	-2	-1.45833	2.32314	No
1	-3	0.1875	2.32314	No
2	-3	1.64583	2.32314	No

Twoway ANOVA for RATING

Source of Variation	Sum of Squares	D.F.	Mean Square	F-Ratio	P Value
VERSION	155.861	2	77.9306	4.7906	0.0093
RATER	10125	95	106.579	6.55168	0.0000
Error	3090.81	190	16.2674		
Total (corr.)	13371.7	287			

Pairwise Differences - Comparison by 95% HSD Intervals

	Contrast	Difference	+-HSD	Significant
1	-2	-1.45833	1.37597	Yes
1	-3	0.1875	1.37597	No
2	-3	1.64583	1.37597	Yes

Twoway ANOVA for RATING

Source of Variation	Sum of Squares	D.F.	Mean Square	F-Ratio	P Value
VERSION	155.861	2	77.9306	1.68257	0.1878
WHENDONE	24.9236	2	12.4618	0.269059	0.7643
Interaction	268.618	4	67.1545	1.44991	0.2177
Error	12922.2	279	46.3163		
Total (corr.)	13371.7	287			

Pairwise Differences - Comparison by 95% HSD Intervals

	Contrast	Difference	+-HSD	Significant
1	-2	-1.45833	2.32177	No
1	-3	0.1875	2.32177	No
2	-3	1.64583	2.32177	No

Designed Experiments

A large insurance company employs many clerical workers for routine computer-based tasks. The flow of tasks is enormous and never-ending, so worker efficiency is crucial to the company's smooth operation. The director of human resources feels that new working conditions could improve productivity by a few percentage points, more than enough to cover the cost of the changes. What isn't clear is *which* new conditions would have the best effect on productivity. An experiment was carried out to test the effects.

The director of human resources has written you a memo asking you to analyze the results. The relevant part of the memo says:

> We took three divisions: claims (1), data processing (2), and investments (3). The way it turned out, we could get 33 clerical people in each division to participate. We picked the people randomly from personnel lists and—even though there were a few refusals, so we had to pick other people—we think that the groups are reasonably representative. Then we had everybody draw numbers from a hat. Number 1 meant that the person went to a flextime schedule, 2 meant a 4-day

workweek, and 3 meant a regular week in an enhanced work environment. We ignored the data for the first 2 weeks while people were getting used to the new setup. Then we measured percentage efficiency gains for everybody over the next 4 weeks. The efficiency measures are good enough that we think they'll be accurate for our purposes. We think we did the study pretty well.

> We can't figure out the results. The averages for the three conditions are practically the same, so it seems as though the new conditions didn't make much difference. But I've got some supervisors who think that one or another of the new conditions is doing great things for efficiency, and other supervisors who think some condition is actually hurting efficiency. Are they nuts, or is there something in the results that we haven't noticed?

The data and means are reproduced here for you. Reanalyze the data—you might want to use a computer program—and see what you can find about average efficiency gains. Write a memo to the director and explain your findings. The director doesn't remember any statistical theory, so try to use ordinary language.

ROW	%Improve	dept	conditn	ROW	%Improve	dept	conditn	ROW	%Improve	dept	conditn
1	5.5	1	1	41	12.7	2	1	81	10.0	3	2
2	5.5	1	1	42	21.2	2	1	82	14.7	3	2
3	7.1	1	1	43	10.6	2	1	83	17.5	3	2
4	-2.1	1	1	44	16.6	2	1	84	17.2	3	2
5	4.2	1	1	45	-1.1	2	2	85	13.4	3	2
6	-0.9	1	1	46	-7.2	2	2	86	16.0	3	2
7	8.9	1	1	47	-5.9	2	2	87	17.5	3	2
8	3.5	1	1	48	-4.3	2	2	88	22.4	3	2
9	6.9	1	1	49	-2.1	2	2	89	6.7	3	3
10	3.3	1	1	50	-2.0	2	2	90	7.0	3	3
11	5.7	1	1	51	-4.0	2	2	91	8.4	3	3
12	-3.7	1	2	52	-5.1	2	2	92	11.1	3	3
13	8.1	1	2	53	-9.0	2	2	93	9.5	3	3
14	6.6	1	2	54	-6.2	2	2	94	10.7	3	3
15	5.3	1	2	55	-5.3	2	2	95	13.3	3	3
16	-0.1	1	2	56	-0.3	2	3	96	7.3	3	3
17	-0.6	1	2	57	4.1	2	3	97	10.0	3	3
18	6.3	1	2	58	1.4	2	3	98	8.4	3	3
19	0.9	1	2	59	4.0	2	3	99	10.8	3	3

20	5.7	1	2	60	4.5	2	3				
21	2.9	1	2	61	-2.3	2	3				
22	3.0	1	2	62	6.7	2	3				
23	5.3	1	3	63	4.4	2	3	ROWS: dept			
24	11.5	1	3	64	-1.6	2	3		%Improve		
25	5.9	1	3	65	1.5	2	3		MEAN		
26	5.2	1	3	66	2.0	2	3				
27	4.0	1	3	67	0.4	3	1	1	3.885		
28	-1.7	1	3	68	-3.0	3	1	2	4.788		
29	6.4	1	3	69	-7.2	3	1	3	6.867		
30	1.8	1	3	70	-6.8	3	1	ALL	5.180		
31	2.9	1	3	71	-4.2	3	1				
32	0.6	1	3	72	-8.2	3	1				
33	4.3	1	3	73	-5.0	3	1	ROWS: conditn			
34	19.5	2	1	74	-11.4	3	1				
35	17.9	2	1	75	-6.6	3	1		%Improve		
36	19.7	2	1	76	-5.9	3	1		MEAN		
37	17.5	2	1	77	-4.3	3	1				
38	16.4	2	1	78	21.5	3	2	1	5.188		
39	14.4	2	1	79	19.3	3	2	2	5.085		
40	19.3	2	1	80	16.1	3	2	3	5.267		
								ALL	5.180		■

A New Drug Alert has been sounded.
The medical world's been astounded.
The drug is amnesiac,
And quite aphrodisiac,
Thus treatment and sex are confounded.

A vain movie star name of Sprott
Change camera angles, he'd not.
The face of this actor
Was mostly Max Factor,
A terrible profile to plot.

The neighbors of Jeremy Mock
Put dynamite under his rock.
They lit it too fast,
And sure had a blast,
Creating a randomized block.

R71 A sample of 40 testers rates the thirst-quenching property of both an old formulation of a soft drink and a new formulation. The drinks are scored on a 0–100 scale. The results are

Formulation	Mean	Standard Deviation
Old	41.15	14.7
New	45.55	17.8

a Calculate a 95% confidence interval for the difference of the true (population) means using a pooled-variance procedure.

b Based on this interval, can the null hypothesis of equal means be rejected, using $\alpha = .05$?

c In fact, it's a very bad idea to use a pooled-variance procedure for these data. Why?

R72 The differences between ratings of the new formulation and the old one from Exercise R71 are shown here:

```
 4    3   -1    9   -4    7   -6    4   -2    7    2    4   14    1
 2   12   -7   11   12    9    4   10   -5   -7   -2   -3   10
-1   23    2    7    5   15    4    0    1    5   -4   16   15
```

Minitab output is as follows:

```
MTB > tinterval for 'Diffs'

Confidence Intervals
Variable    N    Mean   StDev  SE Mean      95.0 % C.I.
Diffs      40    4.40    7.05    1.11  (   2.15,    6.65)

MTB > stem-and-leaf for 'Diffs';
SUBC> trim.

Character Stem-and-Leaf Display

Stem-and-leaf of Diffs    N = 40
Leaf Unit = 1.0

     3    -0 776
     6    -0 544
     9    -0 322
    11    -0 11
    14     0 011
    18     0 2223
    (7)    0 4444455
    15     0 777
    12     0 99
    10     1 001
     7     1 22
     5     1 455
     2     1 6
     1   ' 1
     1     2
     1     2 3

MTB > ttest for mean 0 using 'Diffs'

T-Test of the Mean

Test of mu = 0.00 vs mu not = 0.00

Variable    N    Mean   StDev  SE Mean      T   P-Value
Diffs      40    4.40    7.05    1.11    3.95    0.0003
```

a Locate the 95% confidence interval for the population mean difference.

b Based on this interval, can the null hypothesis that the mean difference is zero be rejected using $\alpha = .05$?

c Show that the formal test and p-value give the same conclusion about the null hypothesis as the confidence interval.

d Is there any evidence of a serious violation of assumptions for this procedure?

R73 Minitab carried out a rank test for the differences data of Exercise R71 using $\alpha = .05$ (two-sided). Does this test lead to the same conclusion as the t test of that exercise?

```
MTB > wtest for median 0 using 'Diffs'

Wilcoxon Signed Rank Test

TEST OF MEDIAN = 0.000000 VERSUS MEDIAN N.E. 0.000000

              N FOR   WILCOXON              ESTIMATED
         N    TEST   STATISTIC  P-VALUE      MEDIAN
Diffs    40    39      628.5     0.001       4.000
```

R74 Compare the widths of the confidence intervals for independent and for paired samples. What do the relative sizes of the intervals indicate about the effect of having the same tasters rate both formulations (as opposed to having different tasters rating each formulation)?

R75 A large corporation has a pool of individuals responsible for most word-processing jobs. To help create a pleasant and productive atmosphere, the company plays taped music during the workday. Some individuals complain that the music occasionally becomes distracting. As an experiment, the company provides varying degrees of control over the music's volume (ranging from 1 = no control to 4 = complete control) to samples of size 16 each of word-processing operators. An efficiency score is obtained for each person.

Efficiency	Degree of Control			
	1	**2**	**3**	**4**
	42	55	63	66
	57	50	57	63
	37	65	24	64
	52	22	55	57
	58	65	64	64
	58	56	56	60
	56	63	61	62
	57	58	60	62
	41	65	63	58
	49	57	64	54
	53	52	67	65
	55	61	66	60
	53	64	66	63
	42	57	52	64
	48	65	47	49
	48	66	65	61
$\bar{y}$	50.38	57.56	58.13	60.75
s	6.80	10.76	10.71	4.45

Statistix output is as follows:

```
ONE-WAY AOV FOR EFFIC BY CONTROL

SOURCE    DF    SS        MS        F      P

BETWEEN    3    946.921   315.640   4.26   0.0087
WITHIN    60   4448.43     74.1406
TOTAL     63   5395.35
```

```
                   SAMPLE    GROUP
CONTROL    MEAN     SIZE    STD DEV
   1      50.375     16      6.8007
   2      57.562     16     10.763
   3      58.125     16     10.707
   4      60.750     16      4.4497
TOTAL     56.703     64      8.6105
```

TUKEY (HSD) PAIRWISE COMPARISONS OF MEANS OF EFFIC BY CONTROL

```
                   HOMOGENEOUS
CONTROL    MEAN     GROUPS
   4      60.750    I
   3      58.125    I I
   2      57.562    I I
   1      50.375    .. I
```

THERE ARE 2 GROUPS IN WHICH THE MEANS ARE
NOT SIGNIFICANTLY DIFFERENT FROM ONE ANOTHER.

```
CRITICAL Q VALUE                    4.600
REJECTION LEVEL                     0.010
CRITICAL VALUE FOR COMPARISON       9.9024
```

a Test the null hypothesis that the four population means are equal, using $\alpha = .01$. State the conclusion carefully.

b Place bounds on the p-value.

c Is there any indication that any of the formal mathematical assumptions have been violated? If so, do the violations make your answers to parts a and b seriously wrong?

R76 **a** Using the output of the previous exercise, calculate simultaneous 99% confidence intervals for the differences of all pairs of means.

b Which pairs of means, if any, are significantly different at $\alpha = .05$?

R77 Statistix also calculated the Kruskal-Wallis statistic for the efficiency and control data:

KRUSKAL-WALLIS ONE-WAY NONPARAMETRIC AOV FOR EFFIC BY CONTROL

```
           MEAN    SAMPLE
CONTROL    RANK     SIZE
   1      16.0      16
   2      36.2      16
   3      37.7      16
   4      40.1      16
TOTAL     32.5      64
```

```
KRUSKAL-WALLIS STATISTIC                        17.2438
P-VALUE, USING CHI-SQUARED APPROXIMATION         0.0006
```

a Can the null hypothesis that the four groups' distributions are equal be rejected at $\alpha = .01$?

b Does this test yield essentially the same conclusion as the F test?

R78 In the efficiency study, the participants who have some degree of control also rate that control as not useful, somewhat useful, or very useful. Statistix was used to analyze these results:

CHI-SQUARE TEST FOR HETEROGENEITY OR INDEPENDENCE

```
                             CONTROL
RATING              1          2          3

Not   OBSERVED      7          3          2        12
      EXPECTED      4.00       4.00       4.00
      CELL CHI-SQ   2.25       0.25       1.00
```

```
Somewhat    OBS           4        7        5        16
            EXPECTED     5.33     5.33     5.33
            CELL CHI-SQ  0.33     0.52     0.02

Very    OBSERVED          5        6        9        20
        EXPECTED         6.67     6.67     6.67
        CELL CHI-SQ      0.42     0.07     0.82

                         16       16       16       48

OVERALL CHI-SQUARE    5.67
P-VALUE               0.2248
DEGREES OF FREEDOM       4
```

CAUTION: 3 cell(s) have expected values less than 5.0

a Is there a statistically significant relation between rating and degree of control, using $\alpha = .05$?

b Locate the p-value for the test statistic used in part a.

c Is there any reason to be skeptical of the (approximate) p-value bounds?

R79 Do the frequencies of Exercise R78 indicate a moderately strong relation, whether or not the relation is statistically significant?

R80 One person interprets the results of the χ^2 test in Exercise R78 as proving that there is no relation between rating and degree of control. Is this interpretation appropriate?

R81 A real estate firm in the headquarters city of a large corporation is contracted to find housing and mortgages for the corporation's newly arriving managers. One concern is the length of mortgage contracts. Samples are taken of managers arriving by transfer from other corporation offices and of newly hired managers. The data are taken over a time when mortgage availability and terms are stable. The following lengths (in months) of mortgage contracts are obtained:

```
Transfers:  180   240   300   360   240   180   144   300   240   240   360   180   180
            300   240      (n = 15, ȳ = 245.6, s = 66.9)
New hires:  360   360   360   240   270   300   360   360   300   360   360   300   300
            240   300   360   360   360   360   360   300   300   360   240   360   360
            360   360   300   360   360   300      (n = 32, ȳ = 329.1, s = 41.4)
```

The following results were obtained from Excel:

	A	B	C
1	t-Test: Two-Sample Assuming Equal Variances		
2			
3			
4		Transfer	New Hire
5	Mean	245.6	329.1
6	Variance	4481.83	1712.00
7	Observations	15	32
8	Pooled Variance	2573.72	
9	Hypothesized Mean Difference	0	
10	df	45	
11	t Stat	-5.2575	
12	P(T<=t) one-tail	0.0000	
13	t Critical one-tail	1.6794	
14	P(T<=t) two-tail	0.0000	
15	t Critical two-tail	2.0141	

a According to the output, is there strong evidence of a real difference in means?

b Use pooled-variance methods to calculate a 95% confidence interval for the difference of population means. Based on this interval, can you conclude that there is a statistically significant difference?

R82 The use of pooled-variance methods in the mortgage–length data is a poor idea for (at least) two reasons. Why?

R83 Additional Excel output for the mortgage–length data of Exercise R81 follows:

	A	B	C
1	t-Test: Two-Sample Assuming Unequal Variances		
2			
3			
4		Transfer	New Hire
5	Mean	245.6	329.1
6	Variance	4481.8	1712.0
7	Observations	15	32
8	Hypothesized Mean Difference	0	
9	df	19	
10	t Stat	-4.4467	
11	P(T<=t) one-tail	0.0001	
12	t Critical one-tail	1.7291	
13	P(T<=t) two-tail	0.0003	
14	t Critical two-tail	2.093	

a According to this test, is there strong evidence of a real difference of means?

b Recalculate the confidence interval for the difference of means using a more appropriate method. Does the new interval lead to the same conclusion about the significance of the difference?

R84 When the mortgage–length data are ranked, the sum of the ranks in the transfers sample is 198.0. Test the null hypothesis that the distribution of mortgage lengths is the same in the transfers and new hires populations against a general research hypothesis. State a bound on the p-value.

R85 An income tax preparation service tests three computer programs designed to help its staff prepare state and federal tax returns. Random samples of 10 experienced and 10 inexperienced preparers are assigned to each of three programs. The time required to prepare a standard return is obtained for each of the 60 preparers. The following Minitab output was used to analyze the data:

```
MTB > table by 'Program' and 'Exper';
SUBC> means of 'TimeReq';
SUBC> stdevs of 'TimeReq'.

Tabulated Statistics

 ROWS: Program     COLUMNS: Exper

            0        1      ALL

   1    36.800   36.200   36.500
         2.700    8.094    5.880

   2    29.500   42.100   35.800
         2.550    5.896    7.831

   3    34.300   40.400   37.350
         2.584    5.680    5.314

 ALL   33.533   39.567   36.550
         3.980    6.892    6.355

   CELL CONTENTS --
         TimeReq:MEAN
                  STD DEV

MTB > Twoway ANOVA of 'TimeReq' by 'Program' 'Exper'
```

```
Two-way Analysis of Variance

Analysis of Variance for TimeReq
Source        DF      SS       MS
Program        2     24.1     12.1
Exper          1    546.0    546.0
Interaction    2    435.6    217.8
Error         54   1377.1     25.5
Total         59   2382.9
```

Is there a statistically significant difference among the program means using $\alpha = .05$?

R86   Which pairs of program means, if any, are significantly different, using $\alpha = .05$?

R87   Minitab was used to construct a profile plot, as shown in Figure 11.16, of the data from Exercise R85. Is there any reason to think that the overall program means might not be a good indication of the relative merits of the programs? It might be relevant to know that the service has relatively low turnover among its preparers; only about 15% of the preparers are inexperienced.

FIGURE 11.16   **Profile Plot for Tax Preparation Data**

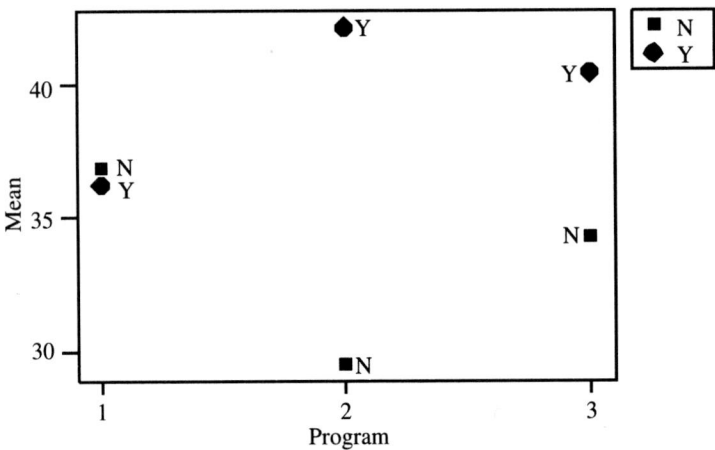

R88   Data are collected on the price-to-earnings ratio (P/E) of common stocks of companies in two industries, electric utilities and computer services. Basic financial concepts suggest that the mean P/E should be lower for utilities than for the computer service industry. Do the data support this hypothesis? The following Minitab output will be helpful:

```
MTB > TwoT 95.0 'P\E' 'Industry';
SUBC>    Alternative -1.

Two Sample T-Test and Confidence Interval

Twosample T for P\E
Industry   N     Mean     StDev    SE Mean
1          20    10.75    6.52     1.5
2          20    17.50    9.42     2.1

95% C.I. for mu 1 - mu 2: ( -12.0, -1.5)
T-Test mu 1 = mu 2 (vs <): T= -2.63  P=0.0064  DF=  33

MTB > TwoT 95.0 'P\E' 'Industry';
SUBC>    Alternative -1;
SUBC>    Pooled.
```

Two Sample T-Test and Confidence Interval

```
Twosample T for P\E
Industry    N     Mean    StDev   SE Mean
1          20    10.75    6.52      1.5
2          20    17.50    9.42      2.1


95% C.I. for mu 1 - mu 2: ( -11.9,  -1.6)
T-Test mu 1 = mu 2 (vs <): T= -2.63  P=0.0061  DF=  38
Both use Pooled StDev = 8.10
```

R89   Test the hypothesis about price–earnings ratios using the following Minitab rank-sum test. Interpret the *p*-value.

```
MTB > Mann-Whitney 95.0 'Utility' 'Computer';
SUBC>   Alternative -1.


Mann-Whitney Confidence Interval and Test


Utility   N = 20    Median =      9.000
Computer  N = 20    Median =     13.000
Point estimate for ETA1-ETA2 is     -5.000
95.0 Percent C.I. for ETA1-ETA2 is (-8.999,-2.001)
W = 291.0
Test of ETA1 = ETA2  vs.  ETA1 < ETA2 is significant at 0.0007 The test is
significant
at 0.0007 (adjusted for ties)
```

R90   From the appearance of the price–earnings data in Figure 11.17, is a *t* test or a rank test more appropriate? How much difference does the choice of test make in the conclusion?

FIGURE 11.17   **Boxplots for Price–Earnings Ratios**

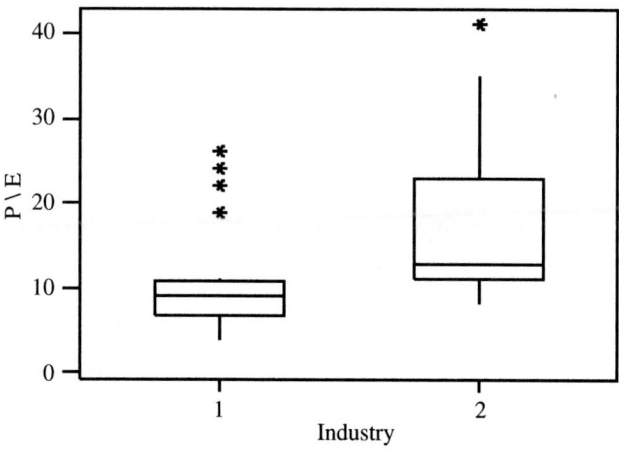

R91   The P/E ratios should be more variable in the computer services stocks than in the utilities. Without doing any formal test, do you feel this theory is supported by the data?

R92   What are the critical assumptions underlying your choice of method in analyzing the price–earnings ratio data? Do these assumptions appear reasonable?

R93   A package delivery company tests its current dispatching procedure against a computerized rule. One of the methods is selected randomly for use on a given day; a key customer records the service as excellent, good, fair, or poor for each day. The following Execustat output is obtained; the second entry in each cell is the percentage within the row:

Crosstabulation

	Excellent	Good	Fair	Poor	Row Total
Current	36	39	15	10	100
	36.0	39.0	15.0	10.0	
Computerized	48	42	8	2	100
	48.0	42.0	8.0	2.0	
Column Total	84	81	23	12	200
	42.00	40.50	11.50	6.00	

Summary Statistics for Crosstabulation

Chi-square	D.F.	P Value
9.29	3	0.0257

Warning: Some table cell counts < 5.

a Calculate a 95% confidence interval for the difference in proportions of excellent ratings between the current and computerized rules.

b Use this interval to test the null hypothesis of equal proportions. What conclusion can be reached?

R94 For the data in Exercise R93, perform a formal hypothesis test for the null hypothesis of equal proportions of excellent ratings. Assume that $\alpha = .05$.

R95 In gathering the service rating data of Exercise R93, it is noted that there may be carryover effects from one day to the next such that one poor day may tend to be followed by another poor day. If, in fact, there are carryover effects, does this violate any of the assumptions underlying the methods used in analyzing the data?

R96 Using the ratings data and Execustat output from Exercise R93, test the null hypothesis that the distribution of opinion is the same for the current rule as for the computerized rule. State the p-value.

R97 Other than the potential carryover problem noted in the previous exercises, are there any serious violations of assumptions for this test?

R98 A chain of restaurants makes much of its profit from "add-ons," items such as desserts or beverages ordered at extra cost by customers. Servers taking the orders are instructed to suggest such items to diners. At one restaurant in the chain, the manager took samples of orders taken by each of 7 servers to see if there were evident differences in the servers' success at obtaining add-on orders. The data were analyzed using JMP, with results shown in Figure 11.18.

FIGURE 11.18   Plot and ANOVA Table for Add-On Data

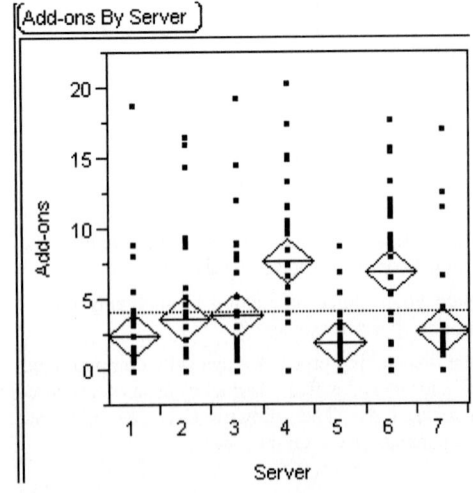

Analysis of Variance

Source	DF	Sum of Squares	Mean Square	F Ratio
Model	6	915.0728	152.512	7.3693
Error	203	4201.2162	20.696	Prob>F
C Total	209	5116.2891		0.0000

Means for Oneway Anova

Level	Number	Mean	Std Error
1	30	2.39667	0.83058
2	30	3.67167	0.83058
3	30	3.94167	0.83058
4	30	7.65333	0.83058
5	30	1.90000	0.83058
6	30	6.96167	0.83058
7	30	2.76333	0.83058

Std Error uses a pooled estimate of error variance

a Is there a statistically detectable difference among the servers in the mean add-on per order?

b Is any major violation of assumptions apparent in the data?

R99 JMP also performed Tukey comparisons of means for the data in Exercise R98, with results shown in Figure 11.19. The value 3.49816 shown along the diagonal of the second table in the figure is the plus or minus required for 95% confidence.

FIGURE 11.19 **Tukey Comparisons for Add-On Data**

```
Means Comparisons
Dif=Mean[i]-Mean[j]        4         6         3         2         7         1         5
4                     0.00000   0.69167   3.71167   3.98167   4.89000   5.25667   5.75333
6                    -0.69167   0.00000   3.02000   3.29000   4.19833   4.56500   5.06167
3                    -3.71167  -3.02000   0.00000   0.27000   1.17833   1.54500   2.04167
2                    -3.98167  -3.29000  -0.27000   0.00000   0.90833   1.27500   1.77167
7                    -4.89000  -4.19833  -1.17833  -0.90833   0.00000   0.36667   0.86333
1                    -5.25667  -4.56500  -1.54500  -1.27500  -0.36667   0.00000   0.49667
5                    -5.75333  -5.06167  -2.04167  -1.77167  -0.86333  -0.49667   0.00000

Alpha=    0.05
Comparisons for all pairs using Tukey-Kramer HSD
       q*
    2.97815
Abs(Dif)-LSD          4         6         3         2         7         1         5
4                 -3.49816  -2.80650   0.21350   0.48350   1.39184   1.75850   2.25517
6                 -2.80650  -3.49816  -0.47816  -0.20816   0.70017   1.06684   1.56350
3                  0.21350  -0.47816  -3.49816  -3.22816  -2.31983  -1.95316  -1.45650
2                  0.48350  -0.20816  -3.22816  -3.49816  -2.58983  -2.22316  -1.72650
7                  1.39184   0.70017  -2.31983  -2.58983  -3.49816  -3.13150  -2.63483
1                  1.75850   1.06684  -1.95316  -2.22316  -3.13150  -3.49816  -3.00150
5                  2.25517   1.56350  -1.45650  -1.72650  -2.63483  -3.00150  -3.49816
Positive values show pairs of means that are significantly different.
```

a Which pairs of means show a statistically detectable difference?

b Find a 95% confidence interval for the difference of means for servers 4 and 5. Does this interval confirm your judgment of whether these means are statistically significantly different?

R100 A Kruskal-Wallis test for the add-on data of Exercise R98, performed using JMP, is shown in Figure 11.20. Does this test give the same essential conclusion as the F test?

R101 A law firm tests two models of printers for use in its office. A random sample of 20 documents is chosen; each document is printed out by each printer. The time required (in seconds) is recorded. The data are as follows:

						Document					
	1	**2**	**3**	**4**	**5**	**6**	**7**	**8**	**9**	**10**	**11**
Printer A	24	40	16	28	28	43	18	25	19	17	17
Printer B	22	36	29	21	20	36	16	27	15	13	11
A − B	2	4	−13	7	8	7	2	−2	4	4	6

	12	**13**	**14**	**15**	**16**	**17**	**18**	**19**	**20**	$\bar{y}$	s
Printer A	21	37	25	43	22	38	30	32	41	28.20	9.32
Printer B	13	30	20	36	23	29	24	25	30	23.80	7.83
A − B	8	7	5	7	−1	9	6	7	11	4.40	5.21

FIGURE 11.20 **Kruskal-Wallis Test for Add-On Data**

```
Wilcoxon / Kruskal-Wallis Tests (Rank Sums)

Level   Count   Score Sum   Score Mean   (Mean-Mean0)/Std0
1        30       2495        83.167          -2.203
2        30       2907        96.900          -0.847
3        30      3134.5      104.483          -0.099
4        30      4292.5      143.083           3.708
5        30       2569        85.633          -1.959
6        30      4098.5      136.617           3.070
7        30      2658.5       88.617          -1.665

1-way Test, Chi-Square Approximation

ChiSquare    DF   Prob>ChiSq
 30.3480      6     0.0000
```

Systat output for the data is as follows:

```
PAIRED SAMPLES T-TEST ON   A  VS   B    WITH    20 CASES

MEAN DIFFERENCE =       4.400
SD DIFFERENCE =         5.205
T =       3.780 DF =   19 PROB =      0.001
```

a Is the paired-sample method an appropriate t test for the null hypothesis of equal means against a two-sided research hypothesis? What is the conclusion, using $\alpha = .05$.

b State the p-value for the test in part a. Can one safely come to a conclusion about the relative speed of the two printers?

R102 Use the following Systat signed-rank test output for the printer data in Exercise R101 to test the null hypothesis that the mean (or median) difference is zero. Does this test give the same conclusion as the t test?

```
WILCOXON SIGNED RANKS TEST RESULTS

COUNTS OF DIFFERENCES (ROW VARIABLE GREATER THAN COLUMN)

                          A         B

        A                 0        17
        B                 3         0


Z = (SUM OF SIGNED RANKS)/SQUARE ROOT(SUM OF SQUARED RANKS)

                     A          B

        A         0.000
        B        -3.032      0.000


TWO-SIDED PROBABILITIES USING NORMAL APPROXIMATION

                     A          B

        A         1.000
        B         0.002      1.000
```

R103 For Exercise R101, compare the standard deviation of the differences to the standard deviations in the printer A and B data. What does this comparison indicate about the desirability of printing out the same 20 documents on both printers rather than using one set of 20 documents for one printer and a different set for the other printer?

R104 As part of a performance review, junior managers are rated on a 50-point scale of managerial potential. The following results are obtained:

```
Anova: Single Factor

SUMMARY
     Groups     Count   Sum   Average  Variance
Business          12     254   21.167   68.152
Engineer           9     139   15.444   53.528
LibArts           18     493   27.389   66.369


ANOVA
Source of Variation   SS      df    MS      F     P-value  F crit
Between Groups      897.73     2  448.87  7.007  0.0027   3.259
Within Groups      2306.17    36   64.06


Total              3203.90    38
```

a Verify the computation of the sums of squares.

b Is there a statistically significant difference among the means, using $\alpha = .05$?

R105 Examination of the managerial potential data in Exercise R104 shows a definite right-skewness in all three samples. What does this fact indicate about the relative appropriateness of the F and Kruskal-Wallis tests for these data?

R106 The scale underlying the managerial potential data in Exercise R104 is interpreted such that a score under 20 indicates little potential, a score between 20 and 29 indicates some potential, and a score above 30 indicates high potential. Examination of the data gives the following frequencies:

	Potential			
	Little	**Some**	**High**	**Total**
Business	7	3	2	12
Engineering	8	0	1	9
Liberal Arts	2	9	7	18
Total	17	12	10	39

Test the null hypothesis that rated managerial potential is unrelated to type of education. Use $\alpha = .05$.

R107 A fast-food chain has a continuing problem of training new employees. The director of human resources carried out an experiment on the relative effectiveness of three forms of training. Method 1 was based on videotape, method 2 was a combination tape/manual approach, and method 3 was based on the current employee manual. The director classified employees as teenagers (coded age = 1) and adults (age = 2). Store managers assigned the first new employees hired in a season to training method 1, until there were 20 people in each age category in this method. The next set of new employees went to method 2, until there were 20 in each age in this method, and then similarly for method 3. The employees were rated after one month on the job, on a standard 100-point scale, where 60 is the minimum acceptable score. JMP output follows. The director has asked you to explain the results of the study clearly. What do the data indicate about the effects of training method and age? In addition, you should note any oddities in the data and make any suggestions about how to carry out a repetition of the same study.

```
Summary of Fit
RSquare                      0.175975
RSquare Adj                  0.139833
Root Mean Square Error       16.80676
Mean of Response             62.50833
Observations (or Sum Wgts)    120
```

```
Effect Test
Source          Nparm    DF    Sum of Squares  F Ratio    Prob>F
Training          2       2     2636.8667        4.6676    0.0113
Age               1       1     3979.0083       14.0866    0.0003
Training*Age      2       2      260.8667        0.4618    0.6313

Analysis of Variance
Source      DF    Sum of Squares  Mean Square    F Ratio
Model        5      6876.742       1375.35        4.8691
Error      114     32201.250        282.47        Prob>F
C Total    119     39077.992                      0.0004

Means for Training, then for Age
Least Squares Means
Level      Least Sq Mean      Std Error      Mean
1          60.92500000        2.657381725    60.9250
2          68.87500000        2.657381725    68.8750
3          57.72500000        2.657381725    57.7250

Least Squares Means
Level      Least Sq Mean      Std Error      Mean
1          56.75000000        2.169743093    56.7500
2          68.26666667        2.169743093    68.2667

Least Squares Means
Level      Least Sq Mean      Std Error
1,1        56.75000000        3.758105276
1,2        65.10000000        3.758105276
2,1        61.15000000        3.758105276
2,2        76.60000000        3.758105276
3,1        52.35000000        3.758105276
3,2        63.10000000        3.758105276
```

Linear Regression and Correlation Methods

This chapter introduces regression analysis. It is devoted to simple regression, using only one independent variable to predict a dependent variable. The basic questions involve the nature of the relation (linear or curved), the amount of variability around the predicted value, whether that variability is constant over the range of prediction, how useful the independent variable is in predicting the dependent variable, and how much to allow for sampling error. The key concepts of the chapter include:

1   The data should be plotted in a scatterplot. A smoother such as LOWESS or a spline curve is useful in deciding whether a relation is nearly linear or is clearly curved. Curved relations can often be made nearly linear by transforming either the independent variable or the dependent variable or both.

2   The coefficients of a linear regression are estimated by least squares, which minimizes the sum of squared residuals (actual values minus predicted). Because squared error is involved, this method is sensitive to outliers.

3   Observations that are extreme in the X (independent variable) direction have high leverage in fitting the line. If a high leverage point also falls well off the line, it has high influence, in that removing the observation substantially changes the fitted line. A high influence point should be omitted if it comes from a different population than the remainder. If it must be kept in the data, a method other than least squares should be used.

4   Variability around the line is measured by the standard deviation of the residuals. This standard deviation may be interpreted using the Empirical Rule. The standard deviation sometimes increases as the predicted value increases. In such a case, try transforming the dependent variable.

5   Hypothesis tests and confidence intervals for the slope of the line (and, less interestingly, the intercept) are based on the t distribution. If there is no relation, the slope is 0. The line is estimated most accurately if there is a wide range of variation in the X variable.

6   The fitted line may be used to forecast at a new x value, again using the t distribution. This forecasting is potentially inaccurate if the new x value is extrapolated far from the previous ones.

7   A standard method of measuring the strength of relation is the coefficient of determination, the square of the correlation. This measure is diminished by nonlinearity or by an artificially limited range of X variation.

One of the most important uses of statistics for managers is prediction. A manager may want to forecast the cost of a particular contracting job given the size of that job; to forecast the sales of a particular product given the current rate of growth of the gross national product; or to forecast the number of parts that will be produced given a certain size work force. The statistical method most widely used in making predictions is *regression analysis*.

In the regression approach, past data on the relevant variables are used to develop and evaluate a prediction equation. The variable that is being predicted by this equation is the dependent variable. A variable that is being used to make the prediction is an independent variable. In this chapter, we discuss regression methods involving a single independent variable. In Chapter 13, we extend these methods to multiple regression, the case of several independent variables.

A number of tasks can be accomplished in a regression study:

1   The data can be used to obtain a prediction equation.

2   The data can be used to estimate the amount of variability or uncertainty around the equation.

3   The data can be used to identify unusual points far from the predicted value, which may represent unusual problems or opportunities.

4   Because the data are only a sample, inferences can be made about the true (population) values for the regression quantities.

5   The prediction equation can be used to predict a reasonable range of values for future values of the dependent variable.

6   The data can be used to estimate the degree of correlation between dependent and independent variables, a measure that indicates how strong the relation is.

In this chapter, these tasks are carried out for the case of one independent variable.

As with any statistical method, regression analysis is based on a model that incorporates some assumptions. We begin in Section 12.1 by describing the simplest regression model and its assumptions. Methods for estimating both the prediction equation and the variability around it are given in Section 12.2. In that section, we consider how to identify and deal with outliers. We discuss basic inference methods for regression in Section 12.3. In Section 12.4, we deal with prediction of future values of the dependent variable. Section 12.5 contains methods for assessing correlation.   ■

12.1   The Linear Regression Model

Predicting future values of a variable is a crucial management activity. Financial officers must predict future cash flows, production managers must predict needs for raw materials, and human resource managers must predict future personnel needs. Explanation of past variation is also important. Explaining the past variation in number of clients of a social service agency can help a manager understand demand for the agency's services. Finding the variables that explain deviations from an automobile component's specifications can help to improve the quality of that component. The basic idea of regression analysis is to use data on a *quantitative* independent variable to predict or explain variation in a *quantitative* dependent variable.

prediction vs. explanation

We can distinguish between prediction (reference to future values) and explanation (reference to current or past values). Because of the virtues of hindsight, explanation is easier than prediction. However, it is often clearer to use the term *prediction* to include both cases. Therefore, in this book, we sometimes blur the distinction between prediction and explanation.

For prediction (or explanation) to make much sense, there must be some connection between the variable we're predicting (the dependent variable) and the variable we're using to make the prediction (the independent variable). No doubt, if you tried long enough, you could find 28 common stocks whose price changes over a year have been accurately predicted by the won–loss percentage of the 28 major league baseball teams on the fourth of July. But such a prediction is absurd because there is no connection between the two

unit of association

variables. Prediction requires a **unit of association**. There should be an entity that relates the two variables. With time-series data, the unit of association may be simply time. The variables may be measured at the same time period or, for genuine prediction, the independent variable may be measured at a time period before the dependent variable. For cross-sectional data, an economic or physical entity should connect the variables. If we're trying to predict the change in market share of various soft drinks, we should consider the promotional activity for those drinks, not the advertising for various brands of spaghetti sauce. The need for a unit of association seems obvious, but many predictions are made for situations in which no such unit is evident.

simple regression

In this chapter, we consider simple linear regression analysis, in which there is a single independent variable and the equation for predicting a dependent variable y is a linear function of a given independent variable x. Suppose, for example, that the director of a county highway department wants to predict the cost of a resurfacing contract that is up for bids. We could reasonably predict the costs to be a function of the road miles to be resurfaced. A reasonable first attempt is to use a linear production function. Let $y =$ total cost of a project in thousands of dollars, $x =$ number of miles to be resurfaced, and $\hat{y} =$ the predicted cost, also in thousands of dollars. A prediction equation $\hat{y} = 2.0 + 3.0x$ (for example) is a linear equation. The constant term, such as the 2.0, is the **intercept** term and is interpreted as the predicted value of y when $x = 0$. In the road resurfacing example, we may interpret the intercept as the fixed cost of beginning the project. The coefficient of x, such as the 3.0, is the **slope** of the line, the predicted change in y when there is a one-unit change in x. In the road resurfacing example, if two projects differed by 1 mile in length, we would predict that the longer project cost 3 (thousand dollars) more than the shorter one. In general, we write the prediction equation as

$$\hat{y} = \hat{\beta}_0 + \hat{\beta}_1 x$$

where $\hat{\beta}_0$ is the intercept and $\hat{\beta}_1$ is the slope. See Figure 12.1.

intercept

slope

FIGURE 12.1 **Linear Prediction Function**

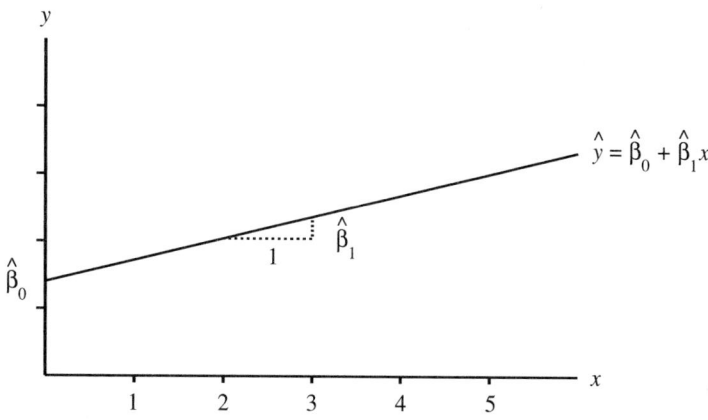

The basic idea of simple linear regression is to use data to fit a prediction line that relates a dependent variable y and a single independent variable x. The first assumption in simple regression is that the relation is, in fact, linear. According to the **assumption of linearity**, the slope of the equation does not change as x changes.[1] In the road resurfacing example, we would assume that there were no (substantial) economies or diseconomies from projects of longer mileage. There is little point in using simple linear regression unless the linearity assumption makes sense (at least roughly).

assumption of linearity

Linearity is not always a reasonable assumption, on its face. For example, if we tried to predict $y =$ number of drivers that are aware of a car dealer's midsummer sale, using $x =$ number of repetitions of the dealer's radio commercial, the assumption of linearity means that the first broadcast of the commercial leads to no greater an increase in aware drivers than the thousand-and-first. (You've heard commercials like that.) We strongly doubt that such an assumption is valid over a wide range of x values. It makes far more sense to us that the effect of repetition would diminish as the number of repetitions got larger, so a straight-line prediction wouldn't work well.

Assuming linearity, we would like to write y as a linear function of x: $y = \beta_0 + \beta_1 x$. However, according to such an equation, y is an exact linear function of x; no room is

[1] In terms of calculus, we assume the first derivative of the equation (of total cost with respect to mileage) to be constant.

random error term

left for the inevitable errors (deviation of actual y values from their predicted values). Therefore, corresponding to each y we introduce a **random error term** ϵ_i and assume the model

$$Y = \beta_0 + \beta_1 x + \epsilon$$

We assume the random variable Y to be made up of a predictable part (a linear function of x) and an unpredictable part (the random error ϵ_i). The coefficients β_0 and β_1 are interpreted as the true, underlying intercept and slope. The error term ϵ includes the effects of all other factors, known or unknown. In the road resurfacing project, unpredictable factors such as strikes, weather conditions, and equipment breakdowns would contribute to ϵ, as would factors such as hilliness or prepair condition of the road—factors that might have been used in prediction but were not. The combined effects of unpredictable and ignored factors yield the random error terms ϵ.

For example, one way to predict the gas mileage of various new cars (the dependent variable) based on their curb weight (the independent variable) would be to assign each car to a different driver, say, for a 1-month period. What unpredictable and ignored factors might contribute to prediction error? Unpredictable (random) factors in this study would include the driving habits and skills of the drivers, the type of driving done (city versus highway), and the number of stoplights encountered. Factors that would be ignored in a regression analysis of mileage and weight would include engine size and type of transmission (manual versus automatic).

In regression studies, the values of the independent variable (the x_i values) are usually taken as predetermined constants, so the only source of randomness is the ϵ_i terms. Although most economic and business applications have fixed x_i values, this is not always the case. For example, suppose that x_i is the score of an applicant on an aptitude test and Y_i is the productivity of the applicant. If the data are based on a random sample of applicants, X_i (as well as Y_i) is a random variable. The question of fixed versus random in regard to X is not crucial for regression studies. If the X_i's are random, we can simply regard all probability statements as conditional on the observed x_i's.

When we assume that the x_i's are constants, the only random portion of the model for Y_i is the random error term ϵ_i. We make the following formal assumptions.

Definition 12.1   Formal Assumptions of Regression Analysis

1   The relation is, in fact, linear, so that the errors all have expected value zero: $E(\epsilon_i) = 0$ for all i.

2   The errors all have the same variance: $\text{Var}(\epsilon_i) = \sigma_\epsilon^2$ for all i.

3   The errors are independent of each other.

4   The errors are all normally distributed; ϵ_i is normally distributed for all i.   ■

These assumptions are illustrated in Figure 12.2. The actual values of the dependent variable are distributed normally, with mean values falling on the regression line and the same standard deviation at all values of the independent variable. The only assumption not shown in the figure is independence from one measurement to another.

These are the formal assumptions, made in order to derive the significance tests and prediction methods that follow. We can begin to check these assumptions by looking at a **scatterplot** of the data. This is simply a plot of each (x, y) point, with the independent variable value on the horizontal axis, and the dependent variable value measured on the vertical axis. Look to see whether the points basically fall around a straight line or whether there is a definite curve in the pattern. Also look to see if there are any evident outliers falling far from the general pattern of the data. A scatterplot is shown in the top part of Figure 12.3.

scatterplot

FIGURE 12.2 Theoretical Distribution of Y in Regression

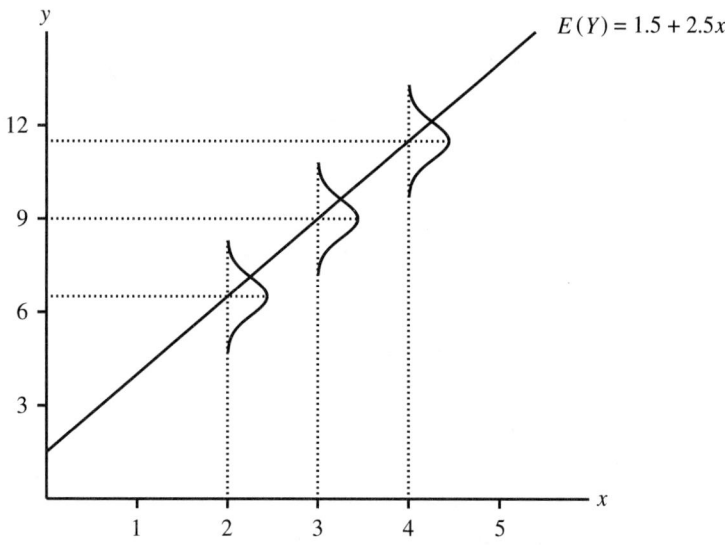

FIGURE 12.3 Scatterplot (a) and LOWESS Curve (b)

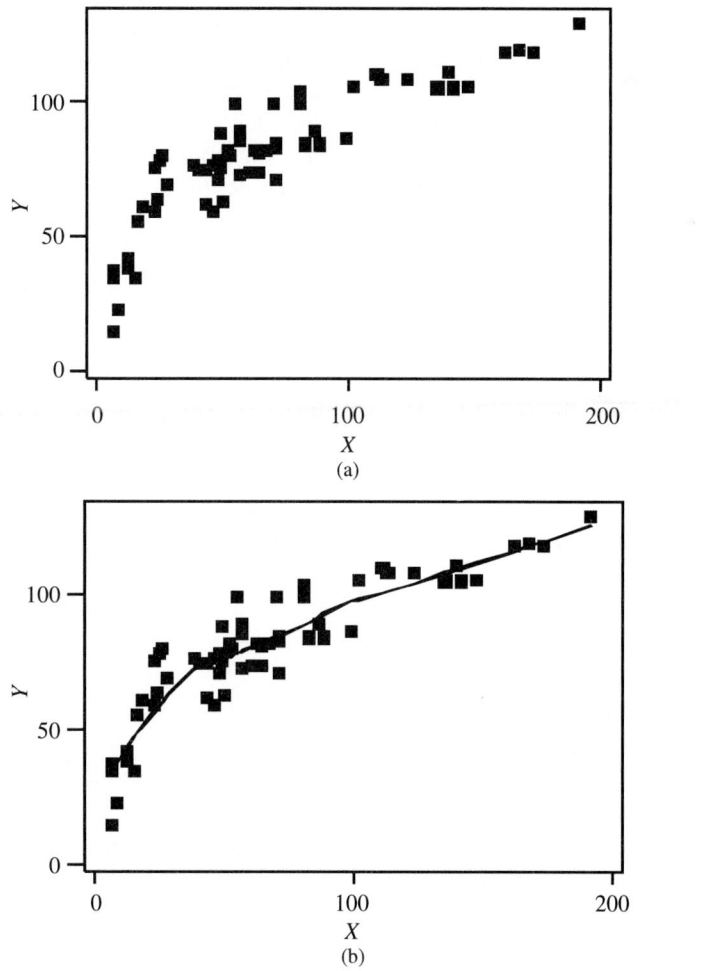

Recently, **smoothers** have been developed to sketch a curve through data without necessarily assuming any particular model. If such a smoother yields something close to a straight line, then linear regression is reasonable. One such method is called LOWESS (locally weighted scatterplot smoother). It is related to the smoothed histogram in Section 2.1. Roughly, a smoother takes a relatively narrow "slice" of data along the x axis, calculates a line that fits the data in that slice, moves the slice slightly along the x axis, recalculates the line, and so on. Then all the little lines are connected in a smooth curve. The width of the slice is called the *bandwidth*; this may often be controlled in the computer program that does the smoothing. The plain scatterplot (Figure 12.3a) is shown again (Figure 12.3b) with a LOWESS curve through it. The scatterplot shows a curved relation. The LOWESS curve confirms that impression.

Another type of scatterplot smoother is the **spline fit**. It can be understood as taking a narrow slice of data, fitting a curve (often a cubic equation) to the slice, moving to the next slice, fitting another curve, and so on. The curves are calculated in such a way as to form a connected, continuous curve.

Many economic relations are not linear. For example, any diminishing returns pattern will tend to yield a relation that increases, but at a decreasing rate. If the scatterplot does not appear linear, by itself or when fitted with a LOWESS curve, it can often be "straightened

out" by a **transformation** of either the independent variable or the dependent variable. A good statistical computer package or a spreadsheet program will compute such functions as the square root of each value of a variable. The transformed variable should be thought of as simply another variable.

For example, a large city dispatches crews each spring to patch potholes in its streets. Records are kept of the number of crews dispatched each day and the number of potholes filled that day. A scatterplot of the number of potholes patched and the number of crews and the same scatterplot with a LOWESS curve through it are shown in Figure 12.4. The relation is not linear. Even without the LOWESS curve, the decreasing slope is obvious. That's not surprising; as the city sends out more crews, they will be using less effective workers, the crews will have to travel farther to find holes, and so on. All these reasons suggest that diminishing returns will occur.

We can try several transformations of the independent variable to find a more linear scatterplot. Three common transformations are square root, natural logarithm, and inverse (one divided by the variable). We applied each of these transformations to the pothole repair data. The results are shown in Figure 12.5a–c, with LOWESS curves. The square root (a) and inverse transformations (c) didn't really give us a straight line. The natural logarithm (b) worked very well, however. Therefore, we would use LnCrew as our independent variable.

Finding a good transformation often requires trial and error. Following are some suggestions to try for transformations. Notice that there are *two* key features to look for in a scatterplot. First, is the relation nonlinear? Second, is there a pattern of increasing variability along the Y (vertical) axis? If there is, the assumption of constant variance is questionable. These suggestions don't cover all the possibilities, but do include the most common problems.

Definition 12.2   Choosing a Transformation

1   If the plot indicates a relation that is increasing but at a decreasing rate, and if variability around the curve is roughly constant, transform x using square root, logarithm, or inverse transformations.

2   If the plot indicates a relation that is increasing at an increasing rate, and if variability is roughly constant, try using both x and x^2 as predictors. Because this method uses two variables, the multiple regression methods of the next two chapters are needed.

3   If the plot indicates a relation that increases to a maximum and then decreases, and

---

FIGURE 12.4 **Scatterplots for Pothole Data**

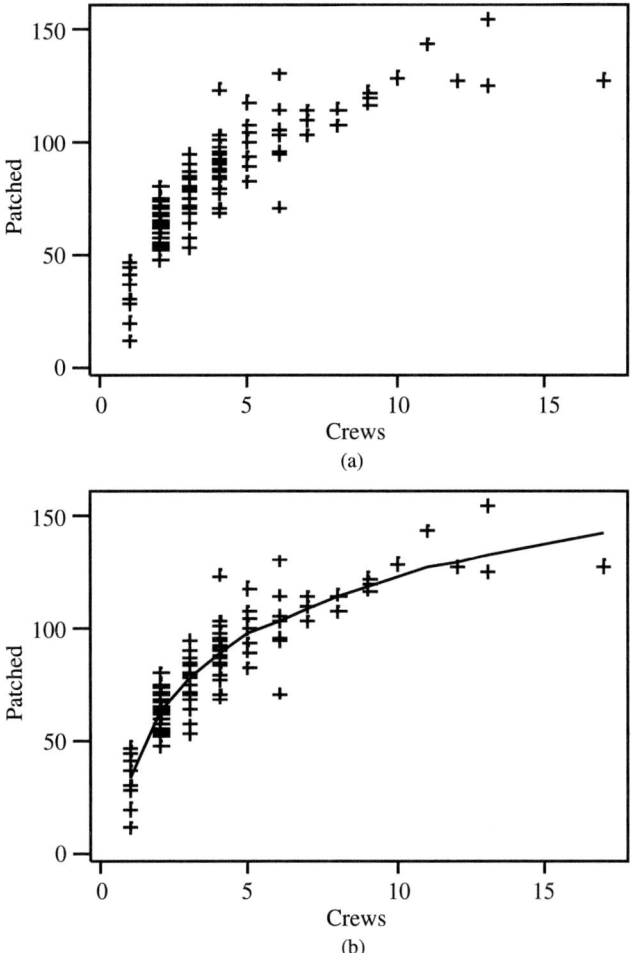

if variability around the curve is roughly constant, again try using both x and x^2 as predictors.

4 If the plot indicates a relation that is increasing at a decreasing rate, and if variability around the curve increases as the predicted y value increases, try using y^2 as the dependent variable.

5 If the plot indicates a relation that is increasing at an increasing rate, and if variability around the curve increases as the predicted y value increases, try using $\ln(y)$ as the dependent variable. It sometimes may also be helpful to use $\ln(x)$ as the independent variable. Recall that a change in a natural logarithm corresponds quite closely to a percentage change in the original variable. Thus the slope of a transformed variable can be interpreted quite well as a percentage change. ■

EXAMPLE 12.1

An airline has seen a very large increase in the number of free flights used by participants in its frequent flyer program. To try to predict the trend in these flights in the near future,

FIGURE 12.5 **Scatterplots with Transformed Predictor**

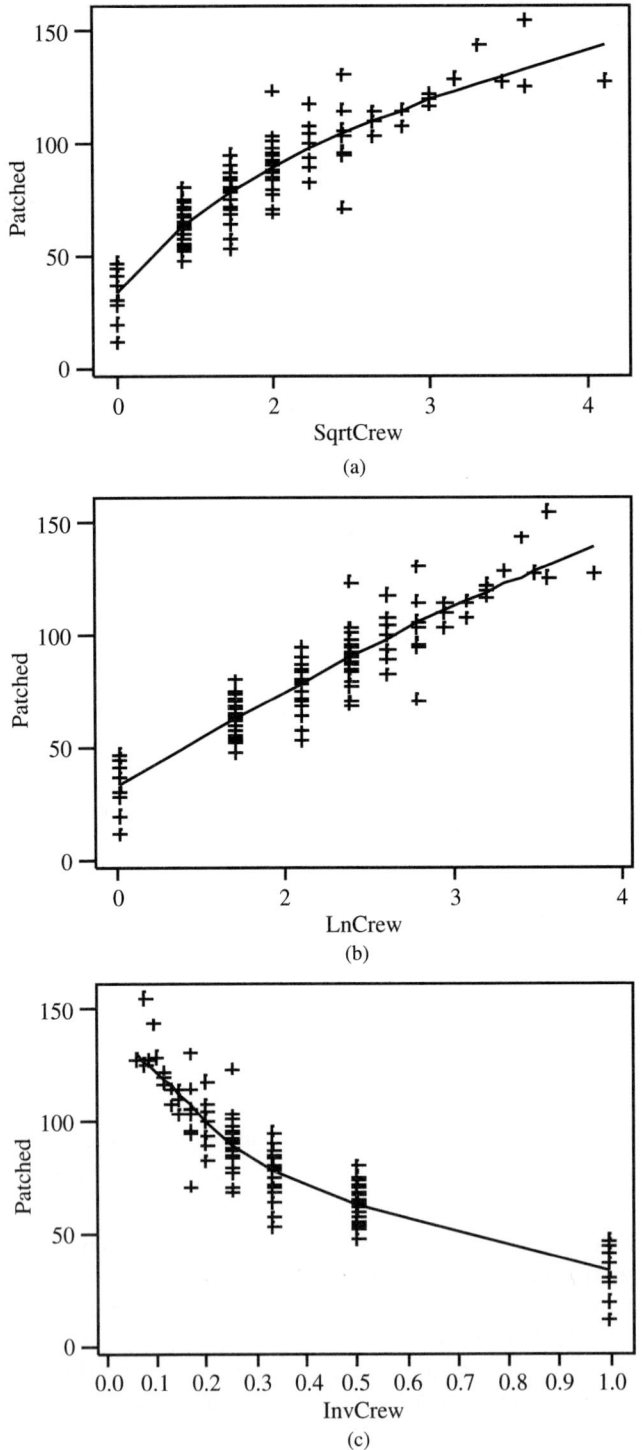

(a)

(b)

(c)

the director of the program assembled data for the last 72 months. The dependent variable *y* is the number of thousands of free flights; the independent variable *x* is month number. A scatterplot with a LOWESS smoother, done by Minitab, is shown in Figure 12.6. What transformation is suggested?

FIGURE 12.6 **Frequent Flyer Free Flights by Month**

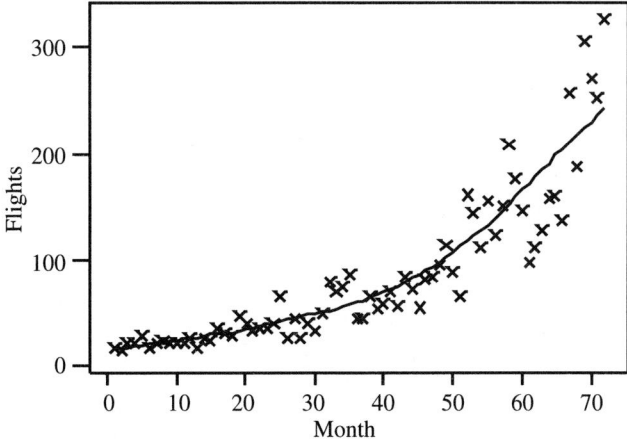

Solution

The pattern shows flights increasing at an increasing rate. The LOWESS curve is definitely turning upward. In addition, variation (up and down) around the curve is increasing. The points around the high end of the curve (on the right, in this case) scatter much more than the ones around the low end of the curve. The increasing variability suggests transforming the y variable. A natural logarithm (ln) transformation often works well. Minitab computed the logarithms and replotted the data, as shown in Figure 12.7. The pattern is much closer to a straight line, and the scatter around the line is much closer to constant.

FIGURE 12.7 **Result of Logarithm Transformation**

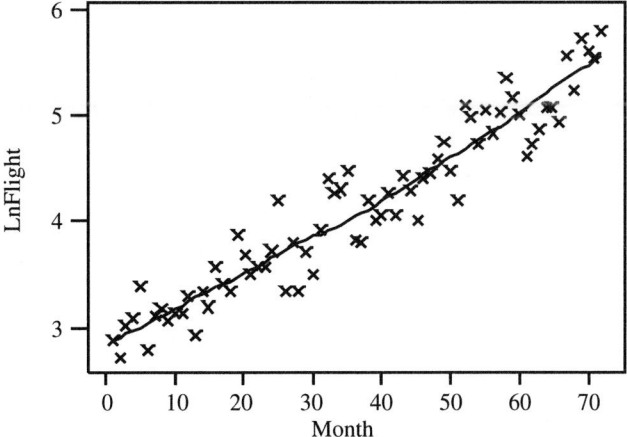

We have more to say about checking assumptions in Chapter 14. For a simple regression with a single predictor, careful checking of a scatterplot, ideally with a smooth curve fit through it, will help avoid serious blunders.

Once we have decided on any mathematical transformations, we must estimate the actual equation of the regression line. In practice, only sample data are available. The population intercept, slope, and error variance all have to be estimated from limited sample data. The assumptions we made in this section allow us to make inferences about the true parameter values from the sample data.

Estimating Model Parameters

The intercept β_0 and slope β_1 in the regression model

$$Y = \beta_0 + \beta_1 x + \epsilon$$

are population quantities. We must estimate these values from sample data. The error variance σ_ϵ^2 is another population parameter that must be estimated. The first regression problem is to obtain estimates of the slope, intercept, and variance; we discuss how to do so in this section.

The road resurfacing example of Section 12.1 is a convenient illustration. Suppose the following data for similar resurfacing projects in the recent past are available. Note that we do have a unit of association: The connection between a particular cost and mileage is that they're based on the same project.

Cost y_i (in thousands of dollars):	6.0	14.0	10.0	14.0	26.0
Mileage x_i (in miles):	1.0	3.0	4.0	5.0	7.0

A first step in examining the relation between y and x is to plot the data as a scatterplot. Remember that each point in such a plot represents the (x, y) coordinates of one data entry, as in Figure 12.8. The plot makes it clear that there is an imperfect but generally increasing relation between x and y. A straight-line relation appears plausible; there is no evident transformation with such limited data.

The regression analysis problem is to find the best straight-line prediction. The most common criterion for "best" is based on squared prediction error. We find the equation

FIGURE 12.8 **Scatterplot of Cost Versus Mileage**

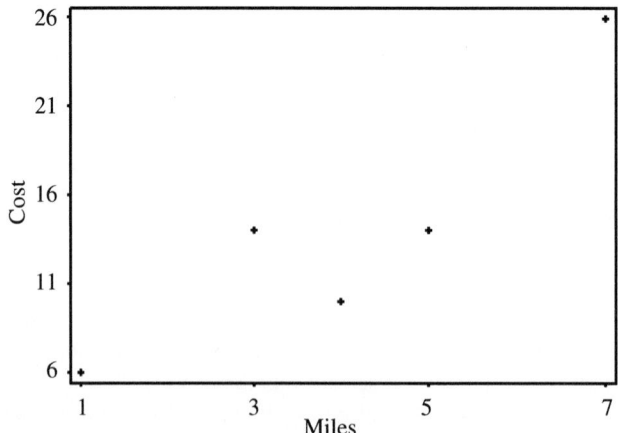

least-squares method

of the prediction line—that is, the slope $\hat{\beta}_1$ and intercept $\hat{\beta}_0$ that minimize the total squared prediction error. The method that accomplishes this goal is called the **least-squares method** because it chooses $\hat{\beta}_0$ and $\hat{\beta}_1$ to minimize the quantity

$$\sum_i (y_i - \hat{y}_i)^2 = \sum_i [y_i - (\hat{\beta}_0 + \hat{\beta}_1 x_i)]^2$$

The prediction errors are shown on the plot of Figure 12.9 as vertical deviations from the line. The deviations are taken as vertical distances because we're trying to predict y values, and errors should be taken in the y direction. For these data, the least-squares line can be shown to be $\hat{y} = 2.0 + 3.0x$; one of the deviations from it is indicated by the smaller brace. For comparison, the mean $\bar{y} = 14.0$ is also shown; deviation from the mean is indicated by the larger brace. The least-squares principle leads to some fairly long computations for the slope and intercept. Usually, these computations are done by computer.

FIGURE 12.9   **Deviations from the Least-Squares Line from the Mean**

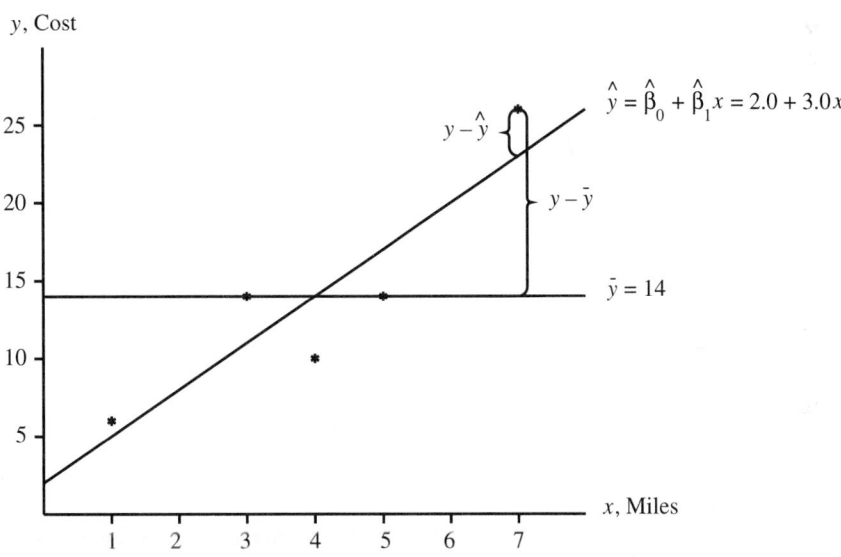

Definition 12.3   Least-Squares Estimates of Slope and Intercept

The least-squares estimates are obtained as follows:

$$\hat{\beta}_1 = \frac{S_{xy}}{S_{xx}} \qquad \text{and} \qquad \hat{\beta}_0 = \bar{y} - \hat{\beta}_1 \bar{x}$$

where

$$S_{xy} = \sum_i (x_i - \bar{x})(y_i - \bar{y})$$

and

$$S_{xx} = \sum_i (x_i - \bar{x})^2$$

Thus, S_{xy} is the sum of x deviations times y deviations and S_{xx} is the sum of x deviations times x deviations—that is, the sum of x deviations squared. ∎

For the road resurfacing data, $n = 5$ and

$$\sum x_i = 1.0 + \cdots + 7.0 = 20.0 \quad \text{so} \quad \bar{x} = \frac{20.0}{5} = 4.0$$

Similarly,

$$\sum y_i = 70.0, \quad \bar{y} = \frac{70.0}{5} = 14.0$$

Also,

$$S_{xx} = \sum (x_i - \bar{x})^2$$
$$= (1.0 - 4.0)^2 + \cdots + (7.0 - 4.0)^2$$
$$= 20.00$$

and

$$S_{xy} = \sum (x_i - \bar{x})(y_i - \bar{y})$$
$$= (1.0 - 4.0)(6.0 - 14.0) + \cdots + (7.0 - 4.0)(26.0 - 14.0)$$
$$= 60.0$$

So

$$\hat{\beta}_1 = \frac{60.0}{20.0} = 3.0$$

and

$$\hat{\beta}_0 = 14.0 - (3.0)(4.0) = 2.0$$

EXAMPLE 12.2

Data from a sample of 10 pharmacies are used to examine the relation between prescription sales volume and the percentage of prescription ingredients purchased directly from the supplier. The sample data are shown here:

Pharmacy	Sales Volume, y (in $1000)	% of Ingredients Purchased Directly, x
1	25	10
2	55	18
3	50	25
4	75	40
5	110	50
6	138	63
7	90	42
8	60	30
9	10	5
10	100	55

a Find the least-squares estimates for the regression line $\hat{y} = \hat{\beta}_0 + \hat{\beta}_1 x$.

b Predict sales volume for a pharmacy that purchases 15% of its prescription ingredients directly from the supplier.

c Plot the (x, y) data and the prediction equation $\hat{y} = \hat{\beta}_0 + \hat{\beta}_1 x$.

Solution

a The equation can be calculated by virtually any statistical computer package; for example, here is abbreviated Minitab output:

```
MTB > Regress 'Sales' on 1 variable 'Directly'

The regression equation is
Sales = 4.70 + 1.97 Directly


Predictor      Coef      Stdev     t-ratio      p
Constant      4.698      5.952       0.79      0.453
Directly     1.9705     0.1545      12.75      0.000
```

Just to see how the computer does the calculations, the least-squares estimates can be obtained from the following table:

	y	x	$y - \bar{y}$	$x - \bar{x}$	$(x - \bar{x})(y - \bar{y})$	$(x - \bar{x})^2$
	25	10	−46.3	−22.8	1101.94	566.44
	55	18	−16.3	−15.8	257.54	249.64
	50	25	−21.3	−8.8	187.44	77.44
	75	40	3.7	6.2	22.94	38.44
	110	50	38.7	16.2	626.94	262.44
	138	63	66.7	29.2	1947.64	852.64
	90	42	18.7	8.2	153.34	67.24
	60	30	−11.3	−3.8	42.94	14.44
	10	5	−61.3	−28.8	1765.44	829.44
	100	55	28.7	21.2	608.44	449.44
Totals	713	338	0	0	6714.60	3407.60
Means	71.3	33.8				

$$S_{xx} = \sum (x - \bar{x})^2 = 3407.6$$

$$S_{xy} = \sum (x - \bar{x})(y - \bar{y}) = 6714.6$$

Substituting into the formulas for $\hat{\beta}_0$ and $\hat{\beta}_1$,

$$\hat{\beta}_1 = \frac{S_{xy}}{S_{xx}} = \frac{6714.6}{3407.6} = 1.9704778 \qquad \text{rounded to 1.97}$$

$$\hat{\beta}_0 = \bar{y} - \hat{\beta}_1 \bar{x} = 71.3 - 1.9704778(33.8) = 4.6978519 \qquad \text{rounded to 4.70}$$

b When $x = 15\%$, the predicted sales volume is $\hat{y} = 4.70 + 1.97(15) = 34.25$ (that is, $34,250$).

c The (x, y) data and prediction equation are shown in Figure 12.10. ∎

E X A M P L E   1 2 . 3

Use the following Statistix output to identify the least-squares estimates for the road resurfacing data:

```
PREDICTOR
VARIABLES    COEFFICIENT    STD ERROR    STUDENT'S T      P

CONSTANT       2.00000       3.82970        0.52        0.6376
MILES          3.00000       0.85634        3.50        0.0394
```

FIGURE 12.10   **Sample Data and Least-Squares Prediction Equation**

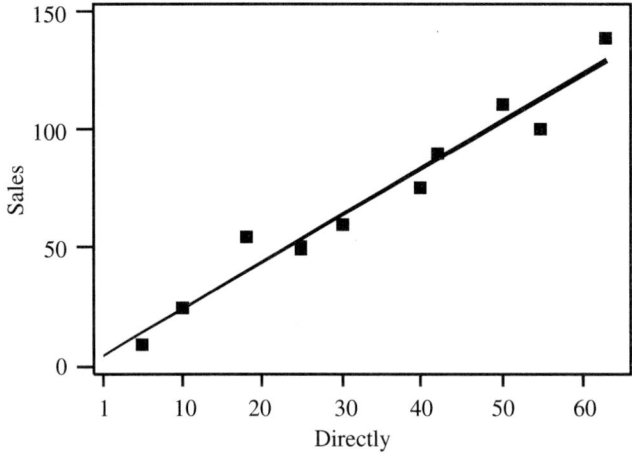

R-SQUARED	0.8036	RESID. MEAN SQUARE (MSE)	14.6666
ADJUSTED R-SQUARED	0.7381	STANDARD DEVIATION	3.82970

SOURCE	DF	SS	MS	F	P
REGRESSION	1	180.000	180.000	12.27	0.0394
RESIDUAL	3	44.0000	14.6666		
TOTAL	4	224.000			

Solution

The intercept is shown in the COEFFICIENT column as $\hat{\beta}_0 = 2.00000$. The slope (coefficient of $x =$ miles) is $\hat{\beta}_1 = 3.00000$.   ■

high leverage point

high influence point

    The estimate of the regression slope can potentially be greatly affected by **high leverage points**. These are points that have very high or very low values of the independent variable—outliers in the x direction. They carry great weight in the estimate of the slope. A high leverage point that also happens to correspond to a y outlier is a **high influence point**. It will alter the slope and twist the line badly.

    A point has high influence if omitting it from the data will cause the regression line to change substantially. To have high influence, a point must first have high leverage and, in addition, must fall outside the pattern of the remaining points. Consider the two scatterplots in Figure 12.11. In plot a, the point in the upper left corner is far to the left of the other points; it has a much lower x value and therefore has high leverage. If we drew a line through the other points, the line would fall far below this point, so the point is an outlier in the y direction as well. Therefore, it also has high influence. Including this point would change the slope of the line greatly. In contrast, in plot b, the y outlier point corresponds to an x value very near the mean, having low leverage. Including this point would pull the line upward, increasing the intercept, but it wouldn't increase or decrease the slope much at all. Therefore, it does not have great influence.

    A high leverage point indicates only a *potential* distortion of the equation. Whether or not including the point will "twist" the equation depends on its influence (whether or not

FIGURE 12.11 **(a) High Influence and (b) Low Influence Points**

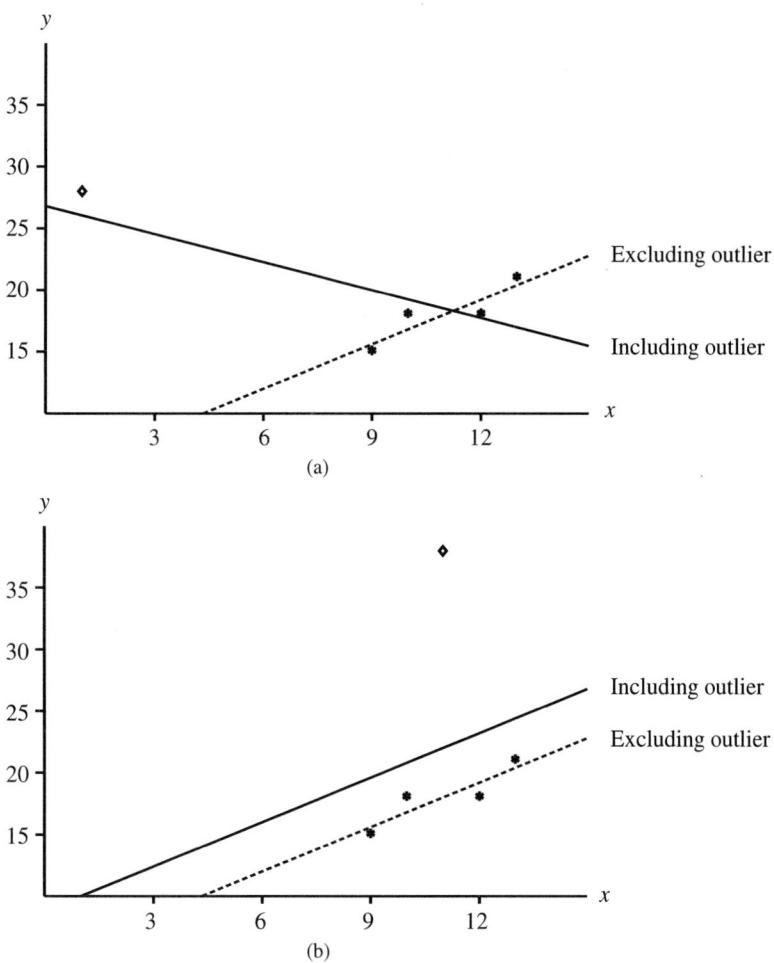

(a)

(b)

the point falls near the line through the remaining points). A point must have *both* high leverage and an outlying Y value to qualify as a high influence point.

Mathematically, the effect of a point's leverage can be seen in the S_{xy} term that enters into the slope calculation. One of the many ways this term can be written is

$$S_{xy} = \sum (x_i - \bar{x}) y_i$$

We can think of this equation as a weighted sum of y values. The weights are large positive or negative numbers when the x value is far from its mean and has high leverage. The weight is almost 0 when x is very close to its mean and has low leverage.

diagnostic measures

Most computer programs that perform regression analyses will calculate one or another of several **diagnostic measures** of leverage and influence. We won't try to summarize all of these measures. We only note that very large values of any of these measures correspond to very high leverage or influence points. The distinction between high leverage (X outlier) and high influence (X outlier and Y outlier) points is not universally agreed upon yet. Check the program's documentation to see what definition is being used.

The standard error of the slope $\hat{\beta}_1$ is calculated by all statistical packages. Typically, it is shown in output in a column to the right of the coefficient column. Like any standard error, it indicates how accurately one can estimate the correct population or process value.

The quality of estimation of $\hat{\beta}_1$ is influenced by two quantities: the error variance σ_ϵ^2 and the amount of variation in the independent variable S_{xx}:

$$\sigma_{\hat{\beta}_1} = \frac{\sigma_\epsilon}{\sqrt{S_{xx}}}$$

The greater the variability σ_ϵ of the y value for a given value of x, the larger $\sigma_{\hat{\beta}_1}$ is. Sensibly, if there is high variability around the regression line, it is difficult to estimate that line. Also, the smaller the variation in x values (as measured by S_{xx}), the larger $\sigma_{\hat{\beta}_1}$ is. The slope is the predicted change in Y per unit change in x; if x changes very little in the data, so that S_{xx} is small, it is difficult to estimate the rate of change in Y accurately. If the price of a brand of diet soda hasn't changed for years, it's obviously hard to estimate the change in quantity demanded when price changes.

The variance of the estimated intercept $\hat{\beta}_0$ is influenced by n, naturally, and also by the size of the square of the sample mean, $\bar{x}^2$, relative to S_{xx}. The intercept is the predicted y value when $x = 0$; if all the x_i are, for instance, large positive numbers, predicting Y at $x = 0$ is a huge extrapolation from the actual data. Such extrapolation magnifies small errors, and $\text{Var}(\hat{\beta}_0)$ is large. The ideal situation for estimating $\hat{\beta}_0$ is when $\bar{x} = 0$.

To this point, we have considered only the estimates of intercept and slope. We also have to estimate the true error variance σ_ϵ^2. We can think of this quantity as "variance around the line," or as the mean squared prediction error. The estimate of σ_ϵ^2 is based on the **residuals** $y_i - \hat{y}_i$, which are the prediction errors in the sample. The estimate of σ_ϵ^2 based on the sample data is the sum of squared residuals divided by $n - 2$, the degrees of freedom. The estimated variance is often shown in computer output as MS(Error) or MS(Residual). MS, recall, stands for "mean square" and is always a sum of squares divided by the appropriate degrees of freedom:

residuals

$$s_\epsilon^2 = \frac{\sum_i (y_i - \hat{y}_i)^2}{n - 2} = \frac{\text{SS(Residual)}}{n - 2}$$

In the computer output for Example 12.3, SS(Residual) is shown to be 44.0.

Just as we divide by $n - 1$ rather than by n in the ordinary sample variance S^2 (in Chapter 2), we divide by $n - 2$ in s_ϵ^2, the estimated variance around the line. To see why, suppose our sample size is $n = 2$. No matter how large or small σ_ϵ^2 may be, the estimated regression line goes exactly through the two points and the residuals are automatically zero. Thus, for $n = 2$, we simply don't have enough information to estimate σ_ϵ^2 at all. In our definition, s_ϵ^2 is undefined for $n = 2$, as it should be. Another argument for dividing by $n - 2$ is that

$$E(s_\epsilon^2) = \sigma_\epsilon^2$$

Dividing by $n - 2$ makes s_ϵ^2 an unbiased estimator of σ_ϵ^2. In the computer output of Example 12.3, $n - 2 = 5 - 2 = 3$ is shown as DF (degrees of freedom) for RESIDUAL and $s_\epsilon^2 = 14.6666$ is shown as MS for RESIDUAL.

The square root s_ϵ of the sample variance is called the **sample standard deviation around the regression line**, the **standard error of estimate**, or the **residual standard deviation**. Because s_ϵ estimates σ_ϵ, the standard deviation of Y_i, σ_ϵ estimates the standard deviation of the population of y values associated with a given value of the independent variable x. The Statistix output in Example 12.3 labels s_ϵ as STANDARD DEVIATION; it shows that s_ϵ, rounded off, is 3.830.

residual standard deviation

Like any other standard deviation, the residual standard deviation may be interpreted by the Empirical Rule. About 95% of the prediction errors will fall within ± 2 standard deviations of the mean error; the mean error is always 0 in the least-squares regression model. Therefore, a residual standard deviation of 3.830 means that about 95% of prediction errors will be less than $\pm 2(3.830) = 7.660$.

The estimates $\hat{\beta}_0, \hat{\beta}_1$ and s_ϵ are basic in regression analysis. They specify the regression line and the probable degree of error associated with y values for a given value of x. The next step is to use these sample estimates to make inferences about the true parameters.

EXAMPLE 12.4

The human resources director of a chain of fast-food restaurants studied the absentee rate of employees. Whenever employees called in sick, or simply didn't appear, the restaurant manager had to find replacements in a hurry, or else work short-handed. The director had data on the number of absences per 100 employees per week (y) and the average number of months' experience at the restaurant (x) for 10 restaurants in the chain. The director expected that longer-term employees would be more reliable and absent less often.

For the following data and Minitab output, do the following:

a   Examine the scatterplot and decide whether a straight line is a reasonable model.

b   Identify the least-squares estimates for β_0 and β_1 in the model $Y = \beta_0 + \beta_1 x + \epsilon$.

c   Predict y for $x = 19.5$.

d   Identify s_ϵ, the sample standard deviation about the regression line.

y:	31.5	33.1	27.4	24.5	27.0	27.8	23.3	24.7	16.9	18.1
x:	18.1	20.0	20.8	21.5	22.0	22.4	22.9	24.0	25.4	27.3

```
MTB > Regress 'y' on 1 predictor 'x'.

The regression equation is
y = 64.7 - 1.75 x

Predictor      Coef      Stdev    t-ratio       p
Constant     64.672      6.762       9.56   0.000
x           -1.7487     0.2995      -5.84   0.000

s = 2.388     R-sq = 81.0%    R-sq(adj) = 78.6%

Analysis of Variance

SOURCE      DF        SS         MS        F       p
Regression   1    194.45     194.45    34.10   0.000
Error        8     45.61       5.70
Total        9    240.06
```

Solution

a   A scatterplot drawn by the Statistix package is shown in Figure 12.12; the data appear to fall approximately along a downward-sloping line. There is no reason to use a more complicated model.

b   The output shows the coefficients twice, with differing numbers of digits. The intercept (constant) is 64.672 and the slope (coefficient of x) is -1.7487. Note that the negative slope corresponds to a downward-sloping line.

FIGURE 12.12   Scatterplot of Absences Versus Average Length of Employment

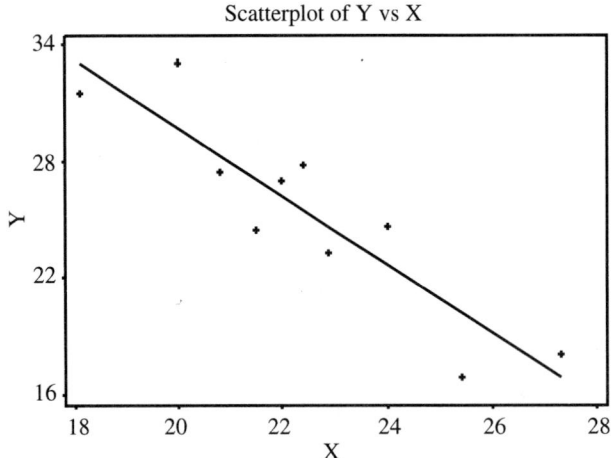
Scatterplot of Y vs X

c   The least-squares prediction value when $x = 19.5$ is

$$\hat{y} = 64.672 - 1.7487(19.5) = 30.57$$

d   The standard deviation around the line (the residual standard deviation) is shown as $s = 2.388$. Therefore, about 95% of the prediction errors should be less than $\pm 2(2.388) = 4.776$.   ■

EXERCISES

12.1   A regression study yielded the following data and the Statistix plots shown in Figure 12.13.

	x:	1	1	1	3	3	3
$x' = \log_{10}$	x:	.000	.000	.000	.477	.477	.477
	y:	13.5	15.4	16.1	18.3	19.9	20.9

	x:	5	5	5	7	7	7
$x' = \log_{10}$	x:	.699	.699	.699	.845	.845	.845
	y:	20.8	23.1	22.1	22.8	24.9	24.5

a   In the plot of y versus x, approximate the slope as the difference between predicted values for $x = 7$ and for $x = 1$ divided by the difference in x values—namely, 6.

b   In the plot of y versus x', approximate the slope of the prediction line.

c   Which plot appears more nearly linear to you?

12.2   Refer to the data of Exercise 12.1 and the following Minitab output:

```
MTB > Regress 'y' 1 'x'.

The regression equation is
y = 14.3 + 1.48 x

Predictor      Coef      Stdev    t-ratio       p
Constant    14.2917     0.7962      17.95   0.000
x            1.4750     0.1737       8.49   0.000

s = 1.346      R-sq = 87.8%     R-sq(adj) = 86.6%
```

FIGURE 12.13 Scatterplots Using Original and Transformed Scales

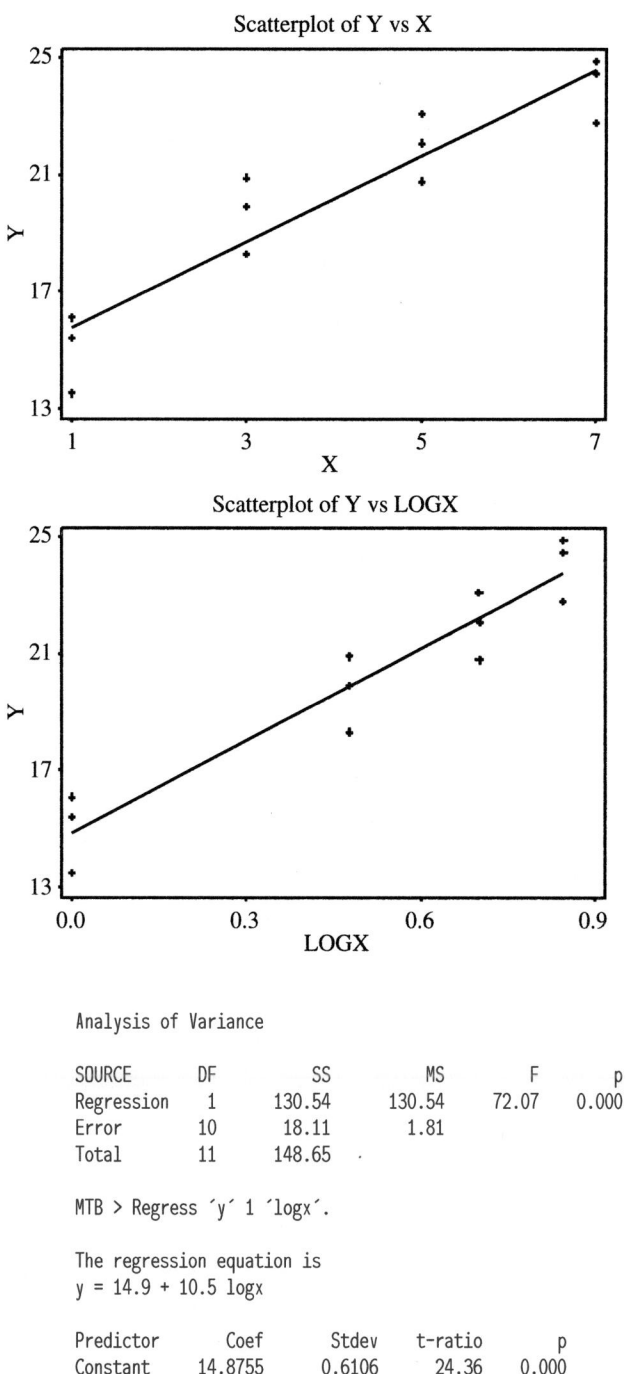

Scatterplot of Y vs X

Scatterplot of Y vs LOGX

```
Analysis of Variance

SOURCE       DF        SS        MS        F        p
Regression    1     130.54    130.54    72.07    0.000
Error        10      18.11      1.81
Total        11     148.65

MTB > Regress 'y' 1 'logx'.

The regression equation is
y = 14.9 + 10.5 logx

Predictor      Coef     Stdev    t-ratio       p
Constant    14.8755    0.6106     24.36    0.000
logx         10.522     1.021     10.30    0.000

s = 1.131      R-sq = 91.4%      R-sq(adj) = 90.5%

Analysis of Variance

SOURCE       DF        SS        MS         F        p
Regression    1     135.85    135.85    106.17    0.000
Error        10      12.80      1.28
Total        11     148.65
```

a Locate the least-squares equation $\hat{y} = \hat{\beta}_0 + \hat{\beta}_1 x$.

b Locate the residual standard deviation.

12.3 Refer to the output for the data in Exercise 12.2.

    a Find the least-squares equation $\hat{y} = \hat{\beta}_0 + \hat{\beta}_1 x'$.

    b What is the residual standard deviation?

12.4 Compare the residual standard deviations s_ϵ in the two preceding exercises. Which is smaller? Does this confirm your opinion about the choice of model based on the plots of Exercise 12.1?

12.5 A mail-order retailer spends considerable effort in "picking" orders—selecting the ordered items and assembling them for shipment. A small study took a sample of 100 orders. An experienced picker carried out the entire process. The time in minutes needed was recorded for each order. A scatterplot and spline fit, created using JMP, are shown in Figure 12.14. What sort of transformation is suggested by the plot?

FIGURE 12.14 **Scatterplot and Spline Fit for Order-Picking Data**

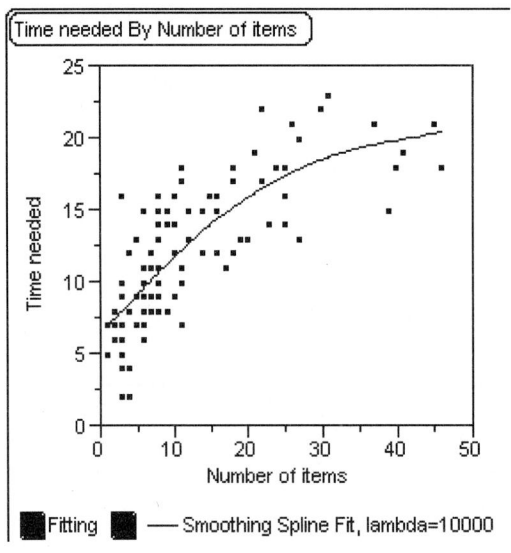

12.6 The order-picking time data in Exercise 12.5 were transformed by taking the square root of the number of items. A scatterplot of the result is shown in Figure 12.15 and regression results are shown in Figure 12.16.

    a Does the transformed scatterplot appear reasonably linear?

    b Write out the prediction equation based on the transformed data.

12.7 In the JMP output of Exercise 12.6, the residual standard deviation is called "Root Mean Square Error." Locate and interpret this number.

12.8 In the preceding exercises, why can the residual standard deviation for the transformed data be compared to the residual standard deviation for the original data?

12.9 As one part of a study of commercial bank branches, data are obtained on the number of independent businesses (x) located in sample zip code areas and the number of bank branches (y) located in these areas. The commercial centers of cities are excluded.

x:	92	116	124	210	216	267	306	378	415	502	615	703
y:	3	2	3	5	4	5	5	6	7	7	9	9

Output (StataQuest) for the analysis of the data is as follows:

FIGURE 12.15 **Scatterplot of Transformed Order-Picking Times**

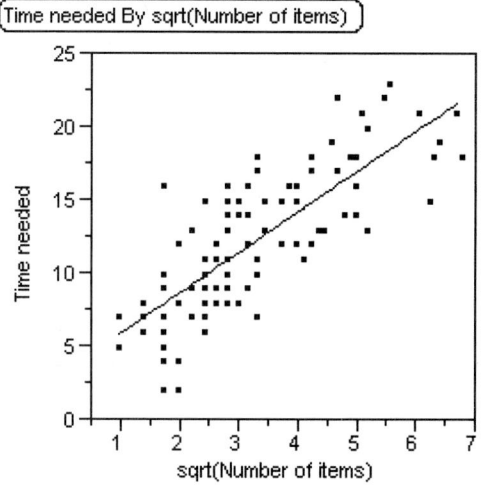

FIGURE 12.16 **Regression Results for Transformed Data**

Summary of Fit

RSquare	0.624567
RSquare Adj	0.620736
Root Mean Square Error	2.923232
Mean of Response	12.29
Observations (or Sum Wgts)	100

Analysis of Variance

Source	DF	Sum of Squares	Mean Square	F Ratio
Model	1	1393.1522	1393.15	163.0317
Error	98	837.4378	8.55	Prob>F
C Total	99	2230.5900		0.0000

Parameter Estimates

Term	Estimate	Std Error	t Ratio	Prob>|t|
Intercept	3.097869	0.776999	3.99	0.0001
sqrt(Number of items)	2.7633138	0.216418	12.77	0.0000

```
. regress Branches Business

    Source |       SS       df       MS              Number of obs =      12
-----------+------------------------------           F(  1,    10) =  172.60
     Model |  53.7996874     1  53.7996874           Prob > F      =  0.0000
  Residual |  3.11697922    10  .311697922           R-square      =  0.9452
-----------+------------------------------           Adj R-square  =  0.9398
     Total |  56.9166667    11  5.17424242           Root MSE      =  .5583
```

```
----------------------------------------------------------------
Branches |    Coef.  Std. Err.    t   P>|t|   [95% Conf. Interval]
---------+------------------------------------------------------
Business | .0111049  .0008453  13.138 0.000   .0092216   .0129883
   _cons | 1.766846  .3211751   5.501 0.000  1.051223   2.482469
----------------------------------------------------------------
```

  a Plot the data. Does a linear equation relating y to x appear plausible?

  b Locate the regression equation (with y as the dependent variable).

  c Locate the sample residual standard deviation s_ϵ.

12.10 Does it appear that variability of y increases with x in the data plot of Exercise 12.9? (This would violate the assumption of constant variance.)

12.11 A manufacturer of cases for sound equipment requires drilling holes for metal screws. The drill bits wear out and must be replaced. There is expense not only in the cost of the bits but also for lost production. Engineers varied the rotation speed of the drill and measured the lifetime Y (thousands of holes drilled) of four bits at each of five speeds X. The data were:

X:	60	60	60	60	80	80	80	80	100	100
Y:	4.6	3.8	4.9	4.5	4.7	5.8	5.5	5.4	5.0	4.5
X:	100	100	120	120	120	120	140	140	140	140
Y:	3.2	4.8	4.1	4.5	4.0	3.8	3.6	3.0	3.5	3.4

  a Create a scatterplot of the data. Does there appear to be a relation? Does it appear to be linear?

  b Is there any evident outlier? If so, does it have high influence?

12.12 The data of Exercise 12.11 were analyzed using Excel's regression function. The following output was obtained:

	A	B	C	D	E	F
1	SUMMARY OUTPUT					
2						
3	Regression Statistics					
4	Multiple R	0.6254				
5	R Square	0.3911				
6	Adjusted R Square	0.3573				
7	Standard Error	0.6324				
8	Observations	20				
9						
10						
11	ANOVA					
12		df	SS	MS	F	Significance F
13	Regression	1	4.624	4.624	11.563	0.0032
14	Residual	18	7.198	0.400		
15	Total	19	11.822			
16						
17						
18		Coefficient	Standard Error	t Stat	P-value	
19	Intercept	6.03	0.5195	11.606	8.617E-10	
20	Speed	-0.017	0.005	-3.400	3.188E-03	

  a Locate the intercept and slope of the least-squares regression line.

  b What does the sign of the slope indicate about the relation between speed and bit lifetime?

  c Locate the residual standard deviation. Interpret the resulting number.

12.13 Again refer to Exercise 12.11.

a Use the regression line of Exercise 12.12 to calculate predicted values for $x = 60, 80, 100, 120$, and 140.

b For which x values are most of the actual Y values larger than the predicted values? For which x values are most Y values lower than predicted? What does this pattern indicate about whether there is a linear relation?

12.14 A realtor studied the relation between $X =$ yearly income (in thousands of dollars per year) of home purchasers and $Y =$ sale price of the house (in thousands of dollars). Data were obtained from mortgage applications for 24 sales in the realtor's basic sales area in one season. Stata output was obtained, as shown after the data.

x:	25.0	28.5	29.2	30.0	31.0	31.5	31.9	32.0	33.0
y:	84.9	94.0	96.5	93.5	102.9	99.5	101.0	105.0	99.9
x:	33.5	34.0	35.9	36.0	39.0	39.0	40.5	40.9	42.5
y:	110.0	100.0	116.0	110.0	125.0	119.9	130.6	120.8	129.9
x:	44.0	45.0	50.0	54.6	65.0	70.0			
y:	135.5	140.0	150.7	170.0	110.0	185.0			

```
. regress Price Income

      Source |       SS       df       MS              Number of obs =      24
-------------+------------------------------           F(  1,    22) =   45.20
       Model |  9432.58336     1  9432.58336           Prob > F      =  0.0000
    Residual |   4590.6746    22  208.667027           R-square      =  0.6726
-------------+------------------------------           Adj R-square  =  0.6578
       Total |   14023.258    23  609.706868           Root MSE      =  14.445

-------------------------------------------------------------------------------
       Price |      Coef.   Std. Err.     t    P>|t|     [95% Conf. Interval]
-------------+-----------------------------------------------------------------
      Income |    1.80264   .2681147   6.723   0.000     1.246604     2.358676
       _cons |   47.15048   10.93417   4.312   0.000      24.4744     69.82657
-------------------------------------------------------------------------------

. drop in 23
(1 observation deleted)

. regress Price Income
      Source |       SS       df       MS              Number of obs =      23
-------------+------------------------------           F(  1,    21) =  512.02
       Model |  13407.5437     1  13407.5437           Prob > F      =  0.0000
    Residual |  549.902031    21  26.185811           R-square      =  0.9606
-------------+------------------------------           Adj R-square  =  0.9587
       Total |  13957.4457    22  634.429351           Root MSE      =  5.1172

-------------------------------------------------------------------------------
       Price |      Coef.   Std. Err.     t    P>|t|     [95% Conf. Interval]
-------------+-----------------------------------------------------------------
      Income |   2.461967    .108803  22.628   0.000     2.235699     2.688236
       _cons |  24.35755    4.286011   5.683   0.000      15.4443     33.27079
-------------------------------------------------------------------------------
```

a A scatterplot with a LOWESS smooth, drawn using Minitab, is shown in Figure 12.17. Does the relation appear to be basically linear?

b Are there any high leverage points? If so, which ones seem to have high influence?

12.15 For Exercise 12.14:

a Locate the least-squares regression equation for the data.

b Interpret the slope coefficient. Is the intercept meaningful?

c Find the residual standard deviation.

12.16 The output of Exercise 12.14 also contains a regression line when we omit the point with $X = 65.0$ and $Y = 110.0$. Does the slope change substantially? Why?

FIGURE 12.17 **Scatterplot with LOWESS Smooth**

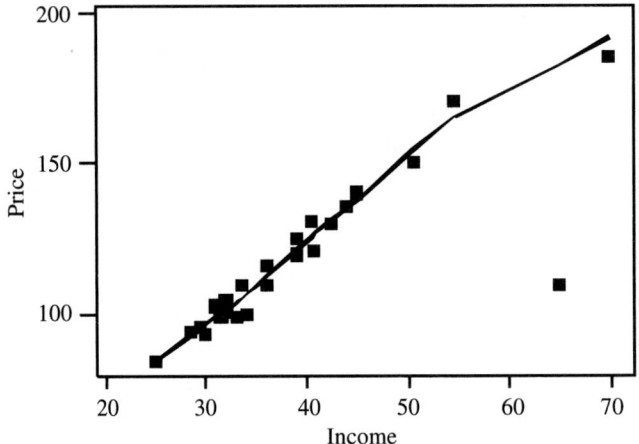

12.3

Inferences About Regression Parameters

t test for β_1

The slope, intercept, and residual standard deviation in a simple regression model are all estimates based on limited data. As with all other statistical quantities, they are affected by random error. In this section, we consider how to allow for that random error. The concepts of hypothesis tests and confidence intervals that we have applied to means and proportions apply equally well to regression summary figures.

The *t* distribution can be used to make significance tests and confidence intervals for the true slope and intercept. One natural null hypothesis is that the true slope β_1 equals 0. If this H_0 is true, a change in *x* yields no predicted change in *y*, and it follows that *x* has no value in predicting *y*. We know from the previous section that the sample slope $\hat{\beta}_1$ has the expected value β_1 and standard error

$$\sigma_{\hat{\beta}_1} = \sigma_\epsilon \sqrt{\frac{1}{S_{xx}}}$$

In practice, σ_ϵ is not known and must be estimated by s_ϵ, the residual standard deviation. In almost all regression analysis computer outputs, the estimated standard error is shown next to the coefficient. A test of this null hypothesis is given by the *t* statistic

$$t = \frac{\hat{\beta}_1 - \beta_1}{\text{estimated standard error}(\hat{\beta}_1)} = \frac{\hat{\beta}_1 - \beta_1}{s_\epsilon \sqrt{\frac{1}{S_{xx}}}}$$

The most common use of this statistic is in testing H_0: $\beta_1 = 0$, as in the following summary.

Definition 12.4 *t* Test of H_0: $\beta_1 = 0$

$$H_0: \quad \beta_1 = 0$$
$$H_a: \quad 1.\ \beta_1 > 0$$
$$2.\ \beta_1 < 0$$
$$3.\ \beta_1 \neq 0$$

$$\text{T.S.:} \quad t = \frac{\hat{\beta}_1 - 0}{s_\epsilon / \sqrt{S_{xx}}}$$

R.R.: For d.f. $= n - 2$ and Type I error α,
1. reject H_0 if $t > t_\alpha$
2. reject H_0 if $t < -t_\alpha$
3. reject H_0 if $|t| > t_{\alpha/2}$

All regression analysis outputs show this t value. ■

In most computer outputs, this test is indicated after the standard error and labeled as T TEST or T STATISTIC. Often, a p-value is also given, which eliminates the need for looking up the t value in a table.

E X A M P L E   1 2 . 5

Use the computer output of Example 12.3 (reproduced here) to locate the value of the t statistic for testing $H_0: \beta_1 = 0$ in the road resurfacing example. Give the observed level of significance for the test.

PREDICTOR VARIABLES	COEFFICIENT	STD ERROR	STUDENT'S T	P
CONSTANT	2.00000	3.82970	0.52	0.6376
MILES	3.00000	0.85634	3.50	0.0394

R-SQUARED	0.8036	RESID. MEAN SQUARE (MSE)	14.6666
ADJUSTED R-SQUARED	0.7381	STANDARD DEVIATION	3.82970

SOURCE	DF	SS	MS	F	P
REGRESSION	1	180.000	180.000	12.27	0.0394
RESIDUAL	3	44.0000	14.6666		
TOTAL	4	224.000			

Solution

It is clear from the output that the value of the test statistic in the column labeled STUDENT'S T is $t = 3.50$. The p-value for the two-tailed alternative $H_a: \beta_1 \neq 0$, labeled as P, is .0394. Because this value is fairly small, we can reject the hypothesis that mileage has no effect on predicting cost. ■

E X A M P L E   1 2 . 6

The following data show mean ages of executives of 15 firms in the food industry and the previous year's percentage increase in earnings per share of the firms. Use the Systat output shown to test the hypothesis that executive age has no predictive value for change in earnings. Should a one-sided or two-sided alternative be used?

Mean age	x:	38.2	40.0	42.5	43.4	44.6	44.9	45.0	45.4
Change, earnings per share	y:	8.9	13.0	4.7	-2.4	12.5	18.4	6.6	13.5
	x:	46.0	47.3	47.3	48.0	49.1	50.5	51.6	
	y:	8.5	15.3	18.9	6.0	10.4	15.9	17.1	

```
DEP VAR:  CHGEPS  N: 15  MULTIPLE R: 0.383  SQUARED MULTIPLE R: 0.147
STANDARD ERROR OF ESTIMATE: 5.634

        VARIABLE      COEFFICIENT   STD ERROR    STD COEF   T      P(2 TAIL)
        CONSTANT        -16.991       18.866       0.000  0.901     0.384
        MEANAGE           0.617        0.413       0.383  1.496     0.158

                         ANALYSIS OF VARIANCE

        SOURCE      SUM-OF-SQUARES   DF  MEAN-SQUARE    F-RATIO    P
        REGRESSION         71.055     1      71.055      2.239   0.158
        RESIDUAL          412.602    13      31.739
```

Solution

In the model $Y = \beta_0 + \beta_1 x + \epsilon$, the null hypothesis is $H_0: \beta_1 = 0$. The myth in American business is that younger managers tend to be more aggressive and harder driving, but it is also possible that the greater experience of the older executives leads to better decisions. Therefore, there is a good reason to choose a two-sided research hypothesis, $H_a: \beta_1 \neq 0$. The t statistic is shown in the output column marked T, reasonably enough. It shows $t = 1.496$, with a (two-sided) p-value of 0.158. There is not enough evidence to conclude that there is any relation between age and change in earnings.

In passing, note that the interpretation of $\hat{\beta}_0$ is rather interesting in this example; it would be the predicted change in earnings of a firm with mean age of its managers equal to 0. Hmm. ■

It is also possible to calculate a confidence interval for the true slope. This is an excellent way to communicate the likely degree of inaccuracy in the estimate of that slope. The confidence interval once again is simply the estimate plus or minus a t table value times the standard error.

Definition 12.5   Confidence Interval for Slope β_1

$$\hat{\beta}_1 - t_{\alpha/2} s_\epsilon \sqrt{\frac{1}{S_{xx}}} \leq \beta_1 \leq \hat{\beta}_1 + t_{\alpha/2} s_\epsilon \sqrt{\frac{1}{S_{xx}}}$$

The required degrees of freedom for the table value $t_{\alpha/2}$ is $n - 2$, the error d.f. ■

E X A M P L E   1 2 . 7

Compute a 95% confidence interval for the slope β_1 using the output from Example 12.3.

Solution

In the output, $\hat{\beta}_1 = 3.000$ and the estimated standard error of $\hat{\beta}_1$ is shown as .856, rounded off. Because n is 5, there are $5 - 2 = 3$ d.f. for error. The required table value for $\alpha/2 = .05/2 = .025$ is 3.182. The corresponding confidence interval for the true value of β_1 is then

$$3.00 \pm 3.182(.856) \qquad \text{or} \qquad .276 \text{ to } 5.724$$

The predicted cost per additional mile of resurfacing could be anywhere from \$276 to \$5724. The enormous width of this interval results largely from the small sample size. ■

There is an alternative test, an F test, for the null hypothesis of no predictive value. It was designed to test the null hypothesis that *all* predictors have no value in predicting y. This test gives the same result as a two-sided t test of H_0: $\beta_1 = 0$ in simple linear regression; to say that all predictors have no value is to say that the (only) slope is 0. The F test is summarized next.

Definition 12.6   **F Test for H_0: $\beta_1 = 0$**

$$H_0: \quad \beta_1 = 0$$
$$H_a: \quad \beta_1 \neq 0$$
$$\text{T.S.:} \quad F = \frac{\text{SS(Regression)}/1}{\text{SS(Residual)}/(n-2)} = \frac{\text{MS(Regression)}}{\text{MS(Residual)}}$$
R.R.:   With d.f.$_1 = 1$ and d.f.$_2 = n - 2$, reject H_0 if $F > F_\alpha$.

SS(Regression) is the sum of squared deviations of predicted y values from the y mean. SS(Regression)$= \sum(\hat{y}_i - \overline{y})^2$. SS(Residual) is the sum of squared deviations of actual y values from predicted y values. SS(Residual)$= \sum(y_i - \hat{y}_i)^2$. ■

Virtually all computer packages calculate this F statistic. In the road resurfacing example, the output shows $F = 12.27$ with a p-value of .0394. Again, the hypothesis of no predictive value can be rejected. It is always true for simple linear regression problems that $F = t^2$; in the example, $12.27 = (3.50)^2$, to within round-off error. The F and two-sided t tests are equivalent in simple linear regression; they serve different purposes in multiple regression.

E X A M P L E   1 2 . 8

For the output of Example 12.4, reproduced here, use the F test for H_0: $\beta_1 = 0$. Show that $t^2 = F$.

```
The regression equation is
y = 64.7 - 1.75 x

Predictor     Coef      Stdev    t-ratio       p
Constant    64.672      6.762       9.56    0.000
x          -1.7487     0.2995      -5.84    0.000

s = 2.388      R-sq = 81.0%     R-sq(adj) = 78.6%

Analysis of Variance

SOURCE       DF        SS        MS        F       p
Regression    1    194.45    194.45    34.10   0.000
Error         8     45.61      5.70
Total         9    240.06
```

Solution

The F statistic is shown in the output as 34.10, with a p-value of 0.000 (indicating that the actual p-value is something smaller than 0.0005). Note that the t statistic is -5.84, and that $t^2 = (-5.84)^2 = 34.11$, equal to F, to within round-off error. ∎

You should be able to work out comparable hypothesis-testing and confidence interval formulas for the intercept β_0 using the estimated standard error of $\hat{\beta}_0$ as

$$s_\epsilon \sqrt{\frac{1}{n} + \frac{\bar{x}^2}{S_{xx}}}$$

In practice, this parameter is of less interest than the slope. In particular, there is often no reason to hypothesize that the true intercept is zero (or any other particular value). Computer packages almost always test the null hypothesis of zero slope, but some don't bother with a test on the intercept term.

EXERCISES

12.17 Refer to the data of Exercise 12.9.

    a Calculate a 90% confidence interval for β_1.

    b What is the interpretation of $H_0: \beta_1 = 0$ in Exercise 12.9?

    c What is the natural research hypothesis H_a for that problem?

    d Do the data support H_a at $\alpha = .05$?

12.18 Find the p-value of the test of $H_0: \beta_1 = 0$ for the previous exercise.

12.19 A firm that prints automobile bumper stickers investigates the relation between the total direct cost of a lot of stickers and the number produced in the printing run. The data are analyzed by the Execustat computer package. The relevant output is as follows:

```
                Simple Regression Analysis

Linear model: TotalCost = 99.777 + 5.19179*Runsize

                    Table of Estimates

                            Standard        t          P
                 Estimate    Error       Value      Value

Intercept        99.777     2.8273       35.29      0.0000
Slope            5.19179    0.0586455    88.53      0.0000

R-squared = 99.64%
Correlation coeff. =  0.998
Standard error of estimation = 12.2065
Durbin-Watson statistic = 2.67999

                  Analysis of Variance

              Sum of                                    P
Source        Squares    D.F.   Mean Square   F-Ratio  Value

Model       1.16775e+006   1   1.16775e+006   7837.26  0.0000
Error       4171.98       28   148.999

Total (corr.) 1.17192e+006  29
```

a Plot the data. Do you detect any difficulties with using a linear regression model? Can you see any blatant violations of assumptions? The raw data are

Runsize:	2.6	5.0	10.0	2.0	.8	4.0	2.5	.6	.8	1.0	2.0	
Total cost:	230	341	629	187	159	327	206	124	155	147	209	

Runsize:	3.0	.4	.5	5.0	20.0	5.0	2.0	1.0	1.5	.5	1.0	1.0
Total cost:	247	135	125	366	1146	339	208	150	179	128	155	143

Runsize:	.6	2.0	1.5	3.0	6.5	2.2	1.0	
Total cost:	131	219	171	258	415	226	159	

b Write the estimated regression equation indicated in the output. Find the residual standard deviation.

c Calculate a 95% confidence interval for the true slope. What are the interpretations of the intercept and slope in this problem?

12.20 Refer to the computer output of Exercise 12.19.

a Locate the value of the t statistic for testing H_0: $\beta_1 = 0$.

b Locate the p-value for this test. Is the p-value one-tailed or two-tailed? If necessary, calculate the p-value for the appropriate number of tails.

12.21 Refer to the computer output of Exercise 12.19.

a Locate the value of the F statistic and the associated p-value.

b How do the p-values for this F test and the t test of Exercise 12.20 compare? Why should this relation hold? ■

12.4

Predicting New Y Values Using Regression

In all the regression analyses we've done so far, we have been summarizing and making inferences about relations in data that have already been observed. Thus we've been predicting the past. One of the most important uses of regression is trying to forecast the future. In the road resurfacing example, the county highway director wants to predict the cost of a new contract that is up for bids. In a regression predicting quantity sold given price, a manager will want to predict the demand at a new price. In this section, we discuss how to make such regression forecasts and how to determine the plus or minus probable error factor.

There are two possible interpretations of a Y prediction based on a given x. Suppose that the highway director substitutes $x = 6$ miles in the regression equation $\hat{y} = 2.0 + 3.0x$ and gets $\hat{y} = 20$. This can be interpreted as either

"The average cost $E(Y)$ of *all* resurfacing contracts for 6 miles of road will be $20,000."

or

"The cost Y of *this specific* resurfacing contract for 6 miles of road will be $20,000."

The best guess prediction in either case is 20, but the plus or minus factor differs. It's easier to predict an average value $E(Y)$ than an individual Y value, so the plus or minus factor should be less for predicting an average. We discuss the plus or minus range for predicting an average first, with the understanding that this is an intermediate step toward solving the specific-value problem.

In the mean-value forecasting problem, suppose that the value of the predictor x is known. Because the previous values of x have been designated $x_1, \ldots, x_n$, call the new value x_{n+1}. Then $\hat{y}_{n+1} = \beta_0 + \beta_1 x_{n+1}$ is used to predict $E(Y_{n+1})$. Because $\hat{\beta}_0$ and $\hat{\beta}_1$ are unbiased, $\hat{y}_{n+1}$ is an unbiased predictor of $E(Y_{n+1})$. The standard error of $\hat{y}_{n+1}$ can be shown to be

$$\sigma_\epsilon \sqrt{\frac{1}{n} + \frac{(x_{n+1} - \bar{x})^2}{S_{xx}}}$$

Here S_{xx} is the sum of squared deviations of the original n values of x_i; it can be found from most computer outputs as

$$\left(\frac{s_\epsilon}{\text{standard error}(\hat{\beta}_1)} \right)^2$$

Again, t tables with $n - 2$ d.f. (the error d.f.) must be used. The usual approach to forming a confidence interval—namely, estimate plus or minus t (standard error)—yields a confidence interval for $E(Y_{n+1})$. Some of the better statistical computer packages will calculate this confidence interval if a new x value is specified without specifying a corresponding y.

Definition 12.7   Confidence Interval for $E(Y_{n+1})$

$$\hat{y}_{n+1} - t_{\alpha/2} s_\epsilon \sqrt{\frac{1}{n} + \frac{(x_{n+1} - \bar{x})^2}{S_{xx}}} \le E(Y_{n+1})$$

$$\le \hat{y}_{n+1} + t_{\alpha/2} s_\epsilon \sqrt{\frac{1}{n} + \frac{(x_{n+1} - \bar{x})^2}{S_{xx}}}$$

where t_α cuts off area a in the right tail of the t distribution with $n - 2$ d.f. *Note:* S_{xx} may be calculated as

$$\left(\frac{s_\epsilon}{\text{standard error}(\hat{\beta}_1)} \right)^2 \qquad \blacksquare$$

For the resurfacing example, the computer output shows the estimated value of $E(Y_{n+1})$ to be 20 when $x = 6$. The corresponding 95% confidence interval on $E(Y_{n+1})$ is 12.29 to 27.71. The forecasting plus or minus term in the confidence interval for $E(Y_{n+1})$ depends on the sample size n and the standard deviation around the regression line, as one might expect. It also depends on the squared distance of x_{n+1} from $\bar{x}$ (the mean of the previous x_i values) relative to S_{xx}. As x_{n+1} gets farther from $\bar{x}$, the term

$$\frac{(x_{n+1} - \bar{x})^2}{S_{xx}}$$

gets larger. When x_{n+1} is far away from the other x values, so that this term is large, the prediction is a considerable extrapolation from the data. Small errors in estimating the regression line are magnified by the extrapolation. The term $(x_{n+1} - \bar{x})^2/S_{xx}$ could be called an **extrapolation penalty** because it increases with the degree of extrapolation.

extrapolation penalty

Extrapolation—predicting the results at independent variable values far from the data—is often tempting and always dangerous. Using it requires an assumption that the relation will continue to be linear, far beyond the data. By definition, you have no data to check this assumption. For example, a firm might find a negative correlation between the number of employees (ranging between 1200 and 1400) in a quarter and the profitability in that quarter; the fewer the employees, the greater the profit. It would be spectacularly risky to conclude from this fact that cutting the number of employees to 600 would vastly improve profitability. (Do you suppose we could have a negative number of employees?) Sooner or later, the declining number of employees must adversely affect the business so that profitability turns downward. The extrapolation penalty term actually understates the risk of extrapolation. It is based on the assumption of a linear relation, and that assumption gets very shaky for large extrapolations.

The confidence and prediction intervals also depend heavily on the assumption of constant variance. In some regression situations, the variability around the line increases as the predicted value increases, violating this assumption. In such a case, the confidence and prediction intervals will be too wide where there is relatively little variability and too narrow where there is relatively large variability. A scatterplot that shows a "fan" shape indicates nonconstant variance. In such a case, the confidence and prediction intervals are not very accurate.

E X A M P L E   1 2 . 9

For the data of Example 12.4, and the following Minitab output from that data, obtain a 95% confidence interval for $E(Y_{n+1})$ based on an assumed x_{n+1} of 22.4. Compare the width of the interval to one based on an assumed x_{n+1} of 30.4.

```
MTB > regress 'y' on 1 variable 'x';
SUBC> predict at 22.4;
SUBC> predict at 30.4.
```

```
The regression equation is
y = 64.7 - 1.75 x
```

Predictor	Coef	Stdev	t-ratio	p
Constant	64.672	6.762	9.56	0.000
x	-1.7487	0.2995	-5.84	0.000

```
s = 2.388     R-sq = 81.0%     R-sq(adj) = 78.6%
```

Analysis of Variance

SOURCE	DF	SS	MS	F	p
Regression	1	194.45	194.45	34.10	0.000
Error	8	45.61	5.70		
Total	9	240.06			

Fit	Stdev.Fit	95% C.I.	95% P.I.
25.500	0.755	(23.758, 27.242)	(19.723, 31.277)
11.510	2.500	(5.742, 17.278)	(3.535, 19.485) XX

```
X  denotes a row with X values away from the center
XX denotes a row with very extreme X values
```

Solution

For $x_{n+1} = 22.4$, the first of the two Fit entries shows a predicted value equal to 25.5. The confidence interval is shown as 23.758 to 27.242. For $x_{n+1} = 30.4$, the predicted value is 11.51, with a confidence interval of 5.742 to 17.278. The second interval has a width of about 11.5, much larger than the first interval's width of about 3.5. The value

$x_{n+1} = 30.4$ is far outside the range of x data; the extrapolation penalty makes the interval very wide. ∎

Usually, the more relevant forecasting problem is that of predicting an individual Y_{n+1} value rather than $E(Y_{n+1})$. In most computer packages, the interval for predicting an individual value is called a **prediction interval**. The same best guess $\hat{y}_{n+1}$ is used, but the forecasting plus or minus term is larger when predicting Y_{n+1} than $E(Y_{n+1})$. In fact, it can be shown that the plus or minus forecasting error using $\hat{y}_{n+1}$ to predict Y_{n+1} is as follows.

prediction interval

Definition 12.8   Prediction Interval for Y_{n+1}

$$\hat{y}_{n+1} - t_{\frac{\alpha}{2}} s_\epsilon \sqrt{1 + \frac{1}{n} + \frac{(x_{n+1} - \bar{x})^2}{S_{xx}}} \le Y_{n+1}$$

$$\le \hat{y}_{n+1} + t_{\frac{\alpha}{2}} s_\epsilon \sqrt{1 + \frac{1}{n} + \frac{(x_{n+1} - \bar{x})^2}{S_{xx}}}$$

where t_α cuts off area a in the right tail of the t distribution with $n - 2$ d.f. ∎

In the road resurfacing example, the corresponding 95% prediction limits for Y_{n+1} when $x = 6$ are 5.58 to 34.42, as shown in the following output. The 95% intervals for $E(Y_{n+1})$ and for Y_{n+1} are shown in Figure 12.18; the inner curves are for $E(Y_{n+1})$ and the outer ones for Y_{n+1}.

```
PREDICTOR
VARIABLES    COEFFICIENT    STD ERROR    STUDENT'S T      P
CONSTANT       2.00000       3.82970        0.52        0.6376
MILES          3.00000       0.85634        3.50        0.0394


R-SQUARED              0.8036    RESID. MEAN SQUARE (MSE)     14.6666
ADJUSTED R-SQUARED     0.7381    STANDARD DEVIATION            3.82970


SOURCE       DF      SS          MS         F       P


REGRESSION    1    180.000     180.000    12.27   0.0394
RESIDUAL      3     44.0000     14.6666
TOTAL         4    224.000


PREDICTED/FITTED VALUES OF COST


LOWER PREDICTED BOUND     5.5791    LOWER FITTED BOUND     12.291
PREDICTED VALUE          20.000     FITTED VALUE           20.000
UPPER PREDICTED BOUND    34.420     UPPER FITTED BOUND     27.708
SE (PREDICTED VALUE)      4.5313    SE (FITTED VALUE)       2.4221


PREDICTOR VALUES: MILES = 6.0000
```

The only difference between prediction of a mean $E(Y_{n+1})$ and prediction of an individual Y_{n+1} is the term $+1$ in the standard error formula. The presence of this extra term indicates that predictions of individual values are less accurate than predictions of means. The extrapolation penalty term still applies, as does the warning that it understates the risk of extrapolation. If n is large and the extrapolation term is small, the $+1$ term dominates

FIGURE 12.18 **Predicted Versus Observed Values with 95% Limits**

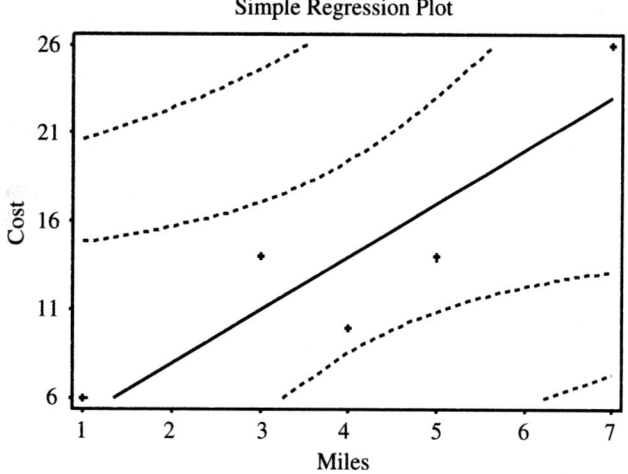

Simple Regression Plot

Cost = 2.0000 + 3.0000 * Miles   95% conf and pred intervals

the square root factor in the prediction interval. In such cases, the interval becomes approximately $\hat{y}_{n+1} - t_{\alpha/2}s_\epsilon \leq Y_{n+1} \leq \hat{y}_{n+1} + t_{\alpha/2}s_\epsilon$. Thus, for large n, roughly 68% of the residuals (forecast errors) are less than $\pm 1s_\epsilon$ and 95% less than $\pm 2s_\epsilon$. There isn't much point in devising rules for when to ignore the other terms in the square root factor. They are normally calculated in computer outputs and it does no harm to include them.

EXAMPLE 12.10

Using the output of Example 12.9 (reproduced here), find a 95% prediction interval for Y_{n+1} with $x_{n+1} = 22.4$, and find the interval with $x_{n+1} = 30.4$. Compare these to widths estimated by the $\pm 2s_\epsilon$ rules just discussed.

```
MTB > regress 'y' on 1 variable 'x';
SUBC> predict at 22.4;
SUBC> predict at 30.4.

The regression equation is
y = 64.7 - 1.75 x

Predictor      Coef      Stdev     t-ratio        p
Constant     64.672      6.762        9.56    0.000
x           -1.7487     0.2995       -5.84    0.000

s = 2.388      R-sq = 81.0%    R-sq(adj) = 78.6%

Analysis of Variance

SOURCE       DF        SS          MS         F       p
Regression    1     194.45      194.45     34.10    0.000
Error         8      45.61        5.70
Total         9     240.06
```

```
     Fit  Stdev.Fit        95% C.I.             95% P.I.
   25.500      0.755    ( 23.758, 27.242)  ( 19.723, 31.277)
   11.510      2.500    (  5.742, 17.278)  (  3.535, 19.485) XX
```

X denotes a row with X values away from the center
XX denotes a row with very extreme X values

Solution

As in Example 12.9, $\hat{y}_{n+1} = 25.5$ if $x_{n+1} = 22.4$. The prediction interval is shown as

$$19.72 \le Y_{n+1} \le 31.28$$

The $\pm 2s_\epsilon$ range is

$$25.5 - (2)(2.388) \le Y_{n+1} \le 25.5 + (2)(2.388) \qquad \text{or} \qquad 20.72 \le Y_{n+1} \le 30.28$$

The latter interval is a bit too narrow, mostly because the tabled t value with only 8 d.f. is quite a bit larger than 2.

For $x_{n+1} = 30.4$, $\hat{y}_{n+1} = 11.51$, the 95% prediction interval is

$$3.54 \le Y_{n+1} \le 19.48$$

The $\pm 2s_\epsilon$ range is

$$11.5 - (2)(2.388) \le Y_{n+1} \le 11.5 + (2)(2.388) \qquad \text{or} \qquad 6.72 \le Y_{n+1} \le 16.28$$

The latter is much too narrow. Not only is the tabled t value larger than 2, but also the large extrapolation penalty is not reflected. The output labels this prediction XX and notes that the x value used is far from the data. Be warned. ■

EXERCISES

12.22 Another part of the output of Exercise 12.19 is shown here.

Table of Predicted Values

Row	Runsize	Predicted TotalCost	95.00% Prediction Limits Lower	Upper	95.00% Confidence Limits Lower	Upper
1	2	203.613	178.169	229.057	198.902	208.323

a Predict the mean total direct cost for all bumper sticker orders with a print run of 2000 stickers (that is, with Runsize = 2.0).

b Locate a 95% confidence interval for this mean.

12.23 Does the prediction in Exercise 12.22 represent a major extrapolation?

12.24 Refer to Exercise 12.22.

a Predict the total direct cost for a particular bumper sticker order with a print run of 2000 stickers. Obtain a 95% prediction interval.

b Would an actual total direct cost of $250 be surprising for this order?

12.25 A heating contractor sends a repair person to homes in response to calls about heating problems. The contractor would like to have a way to estimate how long the customer will have to wait before the repair person can begin work. Data on the number of minutes of wait and the backlog of previous calls waiting for service were obtained. A scatterplot and regression analysis of the data, obtained from JMP, is shown in Figure 12.19.

FIGURE 12.19   **Analysis of Waiting Time Data**

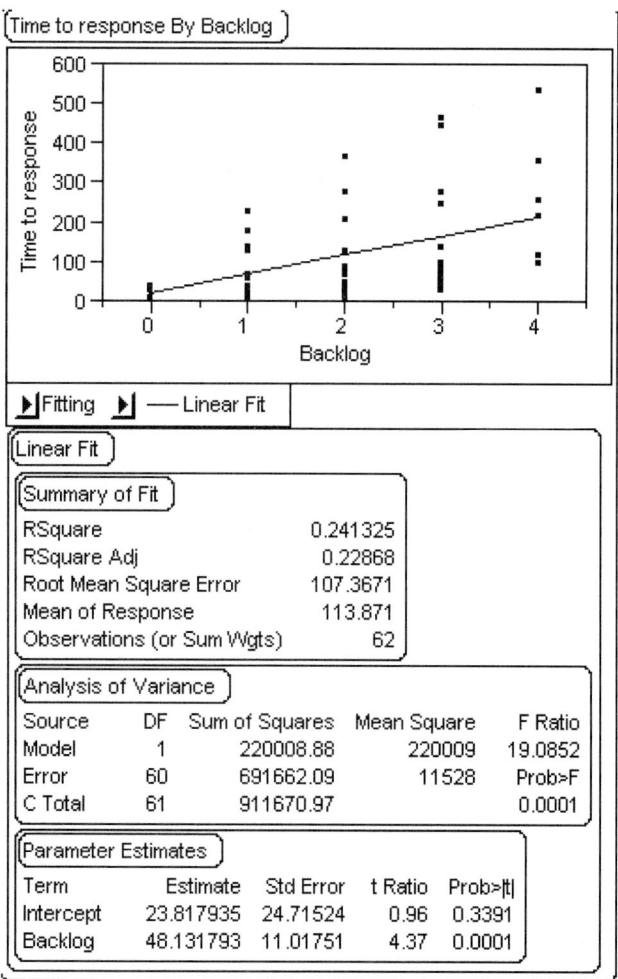

a   Calculate the predicted value and an approximate 95% prediction interval for the time to response of a call when the backlog is 6. Neglect the extrapolation penalty.

b   If we had calculated the extrapolation penalty, would it most likely be very small?

12.26   In the prediction interval of the previous exercise, is the calculated interval likely to be too narrow or too wide?

12.27   Here is some of the output of Exercise 12.25.

```
MTB > Regress 'y' 1 'x';
SUBC>   Predict 20.

The regression equation is
y = 14.3 + 1.48 x

Predictor      Coef     Stdev    t-ratio       p
Constant    14.2917    0.7962      17.95   0.000
x            1.4750    0.1737       8.49   0.000

s = 1.346     R-sq = 87.8%    R-sq(adj) = 86.6%
```

```
      Fit  Stdev.Fit        95% C.I.              95% P.I.
   43.792     2.807   ( 37.536,  50.047) ( 36.854,  50.729) XX
```

X denotes a row with X values away from the center
XX denotes a row with very extreme X values

```
MTB > Regress 'y' 1 'logx';
SUBC>   Predict 20.
```

The regression equation is
y = 14.9 + 10.5 logx

```
Predictor      Coef      Stdev    t-ratio       p
Constant    14.8755     0.6106      24.36   0.000
logx        10.522      1.021       10.30   0.000
```

s = 1.131   R-sq = 91.4%   R-sq(adj) = 90.5%

```
      Fit  Stdev.Fit        95% C.I.              95% P.I.
  225.311    19.910   ( 180.937, 269.684) ( 180.866, 269.756) XX
```

X denotes a row with X values away from the center
XX denotes a row with very extreme X values

a If the model with Y a linear function of x is adopted, what is the predicted Y when $x = 20$?

b If the model with Y a linear function of $x' = \log_{10} x$ is adopted, what is the predicted value of Y when $x = 20$?

c Which of the two predictions seems more reasonable (or perhaps less unreasonable)?

12.28 Give a 95% prediction interval for the prediction you selected in the preceding exercise. ■

12.5

Correlation

Once we've found the prediction line, we need to measure how well it predicts actual values. One way to do so is to look at the size of the residual standard deviation in the context of the problem. About 95% of the prediction errors will be within $\pm 2s_\epsilon$. For example, suppose we are trying to predict the yield of a chemical process, where yields range from 0.50 to 0.94. If a regression model had a residual standard deviation of 0.01, we could predict most yields within ± 0.02—fairly accurate in context. But if the residual standard deviation were 0.08, we could predict most yields within ± 0.16, which isn't very impressive given that the yield range is only $0.94 - 0.50 = 0.44$. But this approach requires that we know the context of the study well; an alternative, more general approach is based on the idea of correlation.

Suppose that we compare the squared prediction error for two prediction methods: one using the regression model, the other ignoring the model and always predicting the mean y value. In the road resurfacing example, if we are given the mileage values x_i, we could use the prediction equation $\hat{y}_i = 2.0 + 3.0x_i$ to predict costs. The deviations of actual values from predicted values, the residuals, measure prediction errors. These errors are summarized by the sum of squared residuals, SS(Residual) $= \sum(y_i - \hat{y}_i)^2$, which is 44 for these data. For comparison, if we were not given the x_i values, the best squared error predictor of y would be the mean value $\bar{y} = 14$, and the sum of squared prediction errors would, in this case, be $\sum_i (y_i - \bar{y}_i)^2 = $ SS(Total) $= 224$. The proportionate reduction in error would be

$$\frac{SS(\text{Total}) - SS(\text{Residual})}{SS(\text{Total})} = \frac{224 - 44}{224} = .804$$

In words, use of the regression model reduces squared prediction error by 80.4%, which indicates a fairly strong relation between the mileage to be resurfaced and the cost of resurfacing.

correlation coefficient

This proportionate reduction in error is closely related to the **correlation coefficient** of x and y. A *correlation measures the strength of the linear relation between x and y.* The stronger the correlation, the better x predicts y. The mathematical definition of the correlation coefficient, denoted r_{yx}, is

$$r_{yx} = \frac{S_{xy}}{\sqrt{S_{xx}S_{yy}}}$$

where S_{xy} and S_{xx} are defined as before and

$$S_{yy} = \sum_i (y_i - \bar{y})^2 = SS(\text{Total})$$

In the example,

$$r_{yx} = \frac{60}{\sqrt{(20)(224)}} = .896$$

Generally, the correlation r_{yx} is a positive number if y tends to increase as x increases; r_{yx} is negative if y tends to decrease as x increases; and r_{yx} is zero if there is either no relation between changes in x and changes in y, or there is a nonlinear relation such that patterns of increase and decrease in y (as x increases) cancel each other.

E X A M P L E 1 2 . 1 1

Consider the following data:

y:	25	41	47	59	54	56	49	43	30
x:	10	20	20	30	30	30	40	40	50

a Should the correlation be positive or negative?

b Calculate the correlation.

Solution

a Notice that as x increases from 10 to 50, y first increases and then decreases. Therefore, the correlation should be small. The y values don't decrease quite back to where they started, so the correlation should be positive.

b By easy calculation, the sample means are $\bar{x} = 30.0000$ and $\bar{y} = 44.8889$.

$$S_{xx} = (10 - 30.0000)^2 + \cdots + (50 - 30.0000)^2 = 1200$$

$$S_{yy} = (25 - 44.8889)^2 + \cdots + (30 - 44.8889)^2 = 1062.8889$$

$$S_{xy} = (10 - 30.0000)(25 - 44.8889) + \cdots + (50 - 30.0000)(30 - 44.8889) = 140$$

$$r_{yx} = \frac{140}{\sqrt{(1200)(1062.8889)}} = .1240$$

The correlation is indeed a small positive number. ∎

Correlation and regression predictability are closely related. The proportionate reduc-

coefficient of determination

tion in error for regression we defined earlier is called the **coefficient of determination**. The coefficient of determination is simply the square of the correlation coefficient,

$$r_{yx}^2 = \frac{\text{SS(Total)} - \text{SS(Residual)}}{\text{SS(Total)}}$$

which is the proportionate reduction in error. In the resurfacing example, $r_{yx} = .896$ and $r_{yx}^2 = .804$.

A correlation of zero indicates no predictive value in using the equation $y = \hat{\beta}_0 + \hat{\beta}_1 x$; that is, one can predict y as well without knowing x as one can knowing x. A correlation of 1 or -1 indicates perfect predictability—a 100% reduction in error attributable to knowledge of x. A correlation coefficient should routinely be interpreted in terms of its squared value, the coefficient of determination. Thus, a correlation of $-.3$, say, indicates only a 9% reduction in squared prediction error. Many books and most computer programs use the equation

$$\text{SS(Total)} = \text{SS(Residual)} + \text{SS(Regression)}$$

where

$$\text{SS(Regression)} = \sum_i (\hat{y}_i - \bar{y})^2$$

Because the equation can be expressed as $\text{SS(Residual)} = (1 - r_{yx}^2)\text{SS(Total)}$, it follows that $\text{SS(Regression)} = r_{yx}^2 \text{SS(Total)}$, which again says that regression on x explains a proportion r_{yx}^2 of the total squared error of y.

E X A M P L E   1 2 . 1 2

Find SS(Total), SS(Regression), and SS(Residual) for the data of Example 12.11.

Solution

SS(Total) $= S_{yy}$, which we computed to be 1062.8889 in Example 12.11. We also found that $r_{yx} = .1240$, so $r_{yx}^2 = (.1240)^2 = .0154$. Using the fact that SS(Regression) $= r_{yx}^2$ SS(Total), we have SS(Regression) $= (.0154)(1062.8889) = 16.3685$. Because SS(Residual) $=$ SS(Total) $-$ SS(Regression), SS(Residual) $= 1062.8889 - 16.3685 = 1046.5204$.

Note that SS(Regression) and r_{yx}^2 are very small. This suggests that x is not a good predictor of y. The reality, though, is that the relation between x and y is extremely nonlinear. A *linear* equation in x does not predict y very well, but a nonlinear equation would do far better. ∎

The sample correlation r_{yx} is the basis for estimation and significance testing of the population correlation ρ_{yx}. Statistical inferences are always based on assumptions. The assumptions of regression analysis—linear relation between x and y and constant variance around the regression line, in particular—are also assumed in correlation inference. In

assumptions for correlation inference

regression analysis, we regard the x values as predetermined constants. In correlation analysis, we regard the x values as randomly selected (and the regression inferences are conditional on the sampled x values). If the x's are not drawn randomly, it is possible that the correlation estimates are biased. In some texts, the additional assumption is made that the x values are drawn from a normal population. The inferences we make do not depend crucially on this normality assumption.

The most basic inference problem is potential bias in estimation of ρ_{yx}. A problem arises when the x values are predetermined, as often happens in regression analysis. The choice of x values can systematically increase or decrease the sample correlation. In general, a wide range of x values tends to increase the magnitude of the correlation coefficient and a small range to decrease it. This effect is shown in Figure 12.20. If all the points in this scatterplot are included, there is an obvious, strong correlation between x and y. But suppose we consider only x values in the range between the dashed vertical lines. By eliminating the outside parts of the scatter diagram, the sample correlation coefficient (and the coefficient of determination) are much smaller. Correlation coefficients can be affected by systematic choices of x values; the residual standard deviation is *not* affected systematically, although it may change randomly if part of the x range changes. Thus, it's a good idea to consider the residual standard deviation s_ϵ and the magnitude of the slope when you decide how well a linear regression line predicts y.

FIGURE 12.20 **Effect of Limited x Range on Sample Correlation Coefficient**

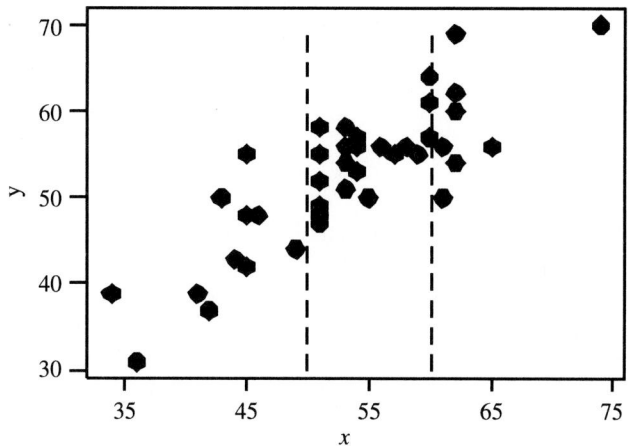

EXAMPLE 12.13

Suppose that a company has the following data on productivity y and aptitude test score x for 12 data-entry operators:

y:	41	39	47	51	43	40	57	46	50	59	61	52
x:	24	30	33	35	36	36	37	37	38	40	43	49

Is the correlation larger or smaller if we consider only the last 6 values?

Simple Regression Analysis

Linear model: y = 20.5394 + 0.775176*x

Table of Estimates

	Estimate	Standard Error	t Value	P Value
Intercept	20.5394	10.7251	1.92	0.0845
Slope	0.775176	0.289991	2.67	0.0234

```
R-squared = 41.68%
Correlation coeff. =  0.646
Standard error of estimation = 5.99236


File subset has been turned on, based on  x>=37.

                   Simple Regression Analysis

Linear model: y = 44.7439 + 0.231707*x

                       Table of Estimates

                            Standard          t           P
                Estimate      Error        Value       Value
Intercept       44.7439      24.8071        1.80       0.1456
Slope           0.231707     0.606677       0.38       0.7219


R-squared =  3.52%
Correlation coeff. =  0.188
Standard error of estimation = 6.34357
```

Solution

For all 12 observations, the output shows a correlation coefficient of .646; the residual standard deviation is labeled as the standard error of estimation, 5.992. For the 6 highest x scores, shown as the subset having x greater than or equal to 37, the correlation is .188 and the residual standard deviation is 6.344. In going from all 12 observations to the 6 observations with the highest x values, the correlation has decreased drastically, but the residual standard deviation has hardly changed at all. ∎

Just as it is possible to test the null hypothesis that a true slope is zero, we can also test H_0: $\rho_{yx} = 0$.

Definition 12.9   Test of H_0: Correlation = 0

$$H_0: \quad \rho_{yx} = 0$$
$$H_a: \quad 1.\ \rho_{yx} > 0$$
$$2.\ \rho_{yx} < 0$$
$$3.\ \rho_{yx} \neq 0$$

T.S.: $$t = r_{yx}\frac{\sqrt{n-2}}{\sqrt{1 - r_{yx}^2}}$$

R.R.: With $n - 2$ d.f. and Type I error probability α,
1. $t > t_\alpha$
2. $t < -t_\alpha$
3. $|t| > t_{\frac{\alpha}{2}}$ ∎

We tested the hypothesis that the true slope is zero (in predicting resurfacing cost from mileage) in Example 12.5; the resulting t statistic was 3.50. For those data, we can calculate r_{yx} as .896421 and r_{yx}^2 as .803571. Hence, the correlation t statistic is

$$\frac{.896\sqrt{3}}{\sqrt{1 - .803571}} = 3.50$$

In general, the t tests for a slope and for a correlation give identical results; it doesn't matter which form is used. It follows that the t test is valid for any choice of x values. The bias we mentioned previously does not affect the sign of the correlation.

E X A M P L E   1 2 . 1 4

Perform t tests for the null hypothesis of zero correlation and zero slope for the data of Example 12.13 (all observations). Use an appropriate one-sided alternative.

Solution

First, the appropriate H_a ought to be $\rho_{yx} > 0$ (and therefore $\beta_1 > 0$). It would be nice if an aptitude test had a positive correlation with the productivity score it was predicting! In Example 12.13, $n = 12$, $r_{yx} = .646$, and

$$t = \frac{.646\sqrt{12 - 2}}{\sqrt{1 - (.646)^2}} = 2.68$$

Because this value falls between the tabled t values for d.f. $= 10$, $\alpha = .025(2.228)$ and for d.f. $= 10$, $\alpha = .01(2.764)$, the p-value lies between .010 and .025. Hence, H_0 may be rejected.

The t statistic for testing the slope β_1 is shown in the output of Example 12.13 as 2.67, which equals (to within round-off error) the correlation t statistic, 2.68. ∎

The test for a correlation provides a neat illustration of the difference between statistical significance and statistical importance. Suppose that a psychologist has devised a skills test for production-line workers and tests it on a huge sample of 40,000. If the sample correlation between test score and actual productivity is .02, then

$$t = \frac{.02\sqrt{39,998}}{\sqrt{1 - (.02)^2}} = 4.0$$

We would reject the null hypothesis at any reasonable α level, so the correlation is "statistically significant." However, the test accounts for only $(.02)^2 = .0004$ of the squared error in skill scores, so it is *almost* worthless as a predictor. Remember, the rejection of the null hypothesis in a statistical test is the conclusion that the sample results cannot plausibly have occurred by chance if the null hypothesis is true. The test itself does not address the practical significance of the result. Clearly, for a sample size of 40,000, even a trivial sample correlation like .02 is not likely to occur by mere luck of the draw. There is no practically meaningful relationship between these test scores and productivity scores in this example.

E X E R C I S E S

12.29 The output of Exercise 12.9 is reproduced here. Calculate the correlation coefficient r_{yx} from the R-square (r_{yx}^2) value. Should its sign be positive or negative?

```
. regress Branches Business

  Source |       SS       df       MS              Number of obs =      12
---------+------------------------------          F( 1,    10) =  172.60
   Model |  53.7996874     1  53.7996874          Prob > F      =  0.0000
Residual |  3.11697922    10  .311697922          R-square      =  0.9452
---------+------------------------------          Adj R-square  =  0.9398
   Total |  56.9166667    11  5.17424242          Root MSE      =   .5583
------------------------------------------------------------------------
Branches |    Coef.  Std. Err.    t    P>|t|    [95% Conf. Interval]
---------+--------------------------------------------------------------
Business | .0111049  .0008453  13.138 0.000    .0092216     .0129883
   _cons | 1.766846  .3211751   5.501 0.000   1.051223     2.482469
------------------------------------------------------------------------
```

12.30 **a** For the data in Exercise 12.29, test the hypothesis of no true correlation between x and y. Use a one-sided H_a and $\alpha = .05$.

b Compare the result of this test to the t test of the slope found in the output.

12.31 Refer to the computer output of Exercise 12.19 (reproduced here).

```
                    Simple Regression Analysis
Linear model: TotalCost = 99.777 + 5.19179*Runsize


                          Table of Estimates


                                 Standard        t          P
                     Estimate      Error      Value      Value

Slope                5.19179     0.0586455    88.53     0.0000


R-squared = 99.64%
Correlation coeff. =  0.998
Standard error of estimation = 12.2065


                       Analysis of Variance


                        Sum of                                    P
Source                  Squares   D.F.   Mean Square  F-Ratio   Value

Model                 1.16775e+006    1  1.16775e+006  7837.26  0.0000
Error                 4171.98        28  148.999


Total (corr.)  1.17192e+006    29
```

a Locate r_{yx}^2. How is its very large value reflected in the Sum of Squares shown in the output?

b The estimated slope $\hat{\beta}_1$ is positive; what must be the sign of the sample correlation coefficient?

c Suppose that the study in Exercise 12.19 had been restricted to RUNSIZE values less than 1.8. Would you anticipate a larger or smaller r_{yx} value?

12.32 Suppose that an advertising campaign for a new product is conducted in 10 test cities. The intensity of the advertising X, measured as the number of exposures per evening of prime-time television, is varied across cities; the awareness percentage Y is found by survey after the ad campaign:

x:	4.0	4.5	5.0	5.5	6.0	6.5	7.0	7.5	8.0	8.5
y:	10.1	10.3	10.4	21.7	36.7	51.5	67.0	68.5	68.2	69.3

```
MTB > Correlation 'Intensty' 'Aware'.

Correlation of Intensty and Aware = 0.956
```

a Interpret the correlation coefficient r_{yx}.

b Plot the data. Does the relation appear linear to you? Does it appear to be generally increasing?

12.33 A survey of recent M.B.A. graduates of a business school obtained data on first-year salary and years of prior work experience. The following results were obtained by the Systat package:

CASE	EXPER	SALARY	CASE	EXPER	SALARY
1	8.000	53.900	27	7.000	51.700
2	5.000	52.500	28	9.000	56.200
3	5.000	49.000	29	6.000	48.900
4	11.000	65.100	30	6.000	51.900
5	4.000	51.600	31	4.000	36.100
6	3.000	52.700	32	6.000	53.500
7	3.000	44.500	33	5.000	50.400
8	3.000	40.100	34	1.000	38.700
9	0.000	41.100	35	13.000	60.100
10	13.000	66.900	36	1.000	38.900
11	14.000	37.900	37	6.000	48.400
12	10.000	53.500	38	2.000	50.600
13	2.000	38.300	39	4.000	41.800
14	2.000	37.200	40	1.000	44.400
15	5.000	51.300	41	5.000	46.600
16	13.000	64.700	42	1.000	43.900
17	1.000	45.300	43	4.000	45.000
18	5.000	47.000	44	1.000	37.900
19	1.000	43.800	45	2.000	44.600
20	5.000	47.400	46	7.000	46.900
21	5.000	40.200	47	5.000	47.600
22	7.000	52.800	48	1.000	43.200
23	4.000	40.700	49	1.000	41.600
24	3.000	47.300	50	0.000	39.200
25	3.000	43.700	51	1.000	41.700
26	7.000	61.800			

a By scanning the numbers, can you sense there is a relation? In particular, does it appear that those with less experience have smaller salaries?

b Can you notice any cases that seem to fall outside the pattern?

12.34 The data in Exercise 12.33 were plotted by Systat's "influence plot." This plot is a scatterplot, with each point identified as to how much its removal would change the correlation. The larger the point, the more its removal would change the correlation. The plot is shown in Figure 12.21. Does there appear to be an increasing pattern in the plot? Do any points clearly fall outside the basic pattern?

12.35 Systat computed a regression equation with Salary as the dependent variable. A portion of the output is shown here:

```
DEP VAR: SALARY  N: 51  MULTIPLE R: 0.703  SQUARED MULTIPLE R: 0.494
ADJUSTED SQUARED MULTIPLE R:.484  STANDARD ERROR OF ESTIMATE: 5.402
VARIABLE    COEFFICIENT   STD ERROR   STD COEF    T   P(2 TAIL)
CONSTANT       40.507       1.257      0.000   32.219   0.000
EXPER           1.470       0.213      0.703    6.916   0.000

                    ANALYSIS OF VARIANCE

SOURCE      SUM-OF-SQUARES   DF   MEAN-SQUARE   F-RATIO     P
REGRESSION      1395.959      1     1395.959     47.838   0.000
RESIDUAL        1429.868     49       29.181
```

a Write out the prediction equation. Interpret the coefficients. Is the constant term (intercept) meaningful in this context?

b Locate the residual standard deviation. What does the number mean?

c Is the apparent relation statistically detectable (significant)?

FIGURE 12.21 **Influence Plot for Salary Data**

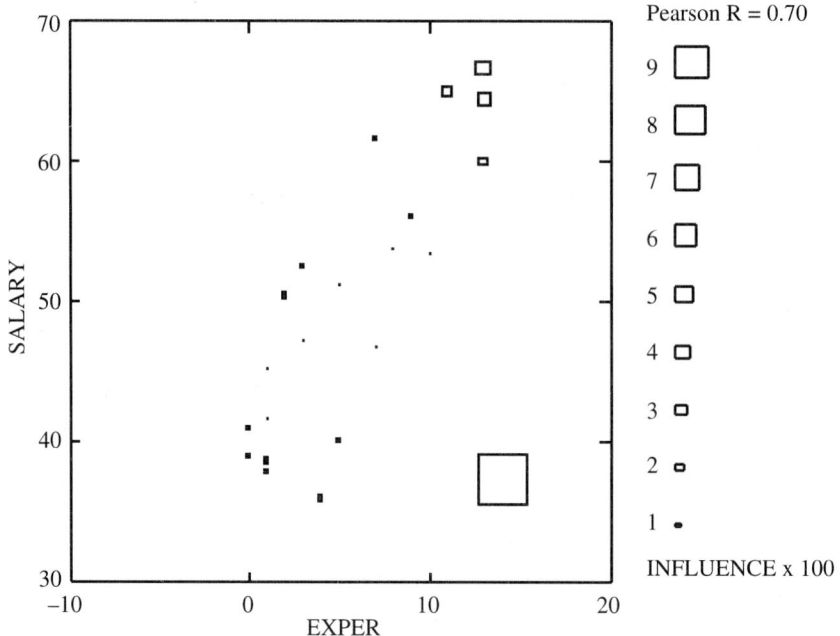

d How much of the variability in salaries is accounted for by variation in years of prior work experience?

12.36 The 11th person in the data of Exercise 12.33 went to work for a family business in return for a low salary but a large equity in the firm. This case (the high influence point in the influence plot) was removed from the data and the results reanalyzed by Systat. A portion of the output follows:

```
DEP VAR: SALARY  N: 50  MULTIPLE R: 0.842 SQUARED MULTIPLE R: 0.709
ADJUSTED SQUARED MULTIPLE R:.703  STANDARD ERROR OF ESTIMATE: 4.071

VARIABLE    COEFFICIENT   STD ERROR    STD COEF    T    P(2 TAIL)

CONSTANT      39.188       0.971        0.000   40.353    0.000
EXPER          1.863       0.172        0.842   10.812    0.000
```

a Should removing the high influence point in the plot increase or decrease the slope? Did it?

b In which direction (larger or smaller) should the removal of this point change the residual standard deviation? Did it? How large was the change?

c How should the removal of this point change the correlation? How large was this change? ■

<h2>12.6</h2>

Summing Up

H ere are some considerations when doing simple regression—trying to predict or explain variation in one variable based on values of one other variable:

1   Before you even think about doing calculations, plot the data. (Yes, we have suggested this step once or twice before.) A scatterplot can reveal nonlinear relations, increasing variability, or potentially influential points.

2   A scatterplot smoother such as LOWESS or a spline fit, if available on your computer package, can help in identifying curved relations. If there is a definite curve in the plot, consider a transformation such as a natural logarithm, square root, or inverse.

3   If the plot shows a pattern of increasing variability around a line or curve, try redefining the dependent variable, either by a transformation such as a logarithm, or as a ratio to some other variable.

4   If the plot shows an outlier, find the reason for that value. If it is a typographical error, fix it. If it is a point that doesn't belong with the others, delete it. If there is no apparent reason why the point is odd, do the analyses both with and without the point, to see what parts of the results can be trusted.

5   As always, statistical tests in regression only indicate whether an apparent relation could have resulted from sheer random variation. A low p-value does not necessarily mean a strong relation. Consideration of r^2 and the residual standard deviation will tell you more about how good the prediction is.

6   The residual standard deviation is a beast with many names. It may be called the standard error of estimation, the root mean square error, or something else. If in doubt, it can be calculated as the square root of the mean squared error value shown in the analysis of variance table.

7   In planning a regression study, it's desirable to have a wide range of variation in the independent variable. Having a large range of X values also helps avoid extrapolation troubles when using the model to predict Y at a new X value.

In addition, you may want to reread the summary of key ideas at the beginning of the chapter.

EXAMPLE 12.15

In the competitive clinical drug testing market, investments in advertising and client supplies are scrutinized for sales return value. In order to help management better understand the impact that expense variables (advertising and client supplies) have on gross sales, analysts at a pharmaceutical company conducted regression analyses. Data were collected on gross monthly sales, monthly advertising expenses (which included marketing and promotional expenses), and monthly client supply expenses (corporate expensed supplies that are given to clients to extract specimens from patients) for 36 consecutive months. Results from JMP IN are shown in Figure 12.22.

What do the results indicate about the effect on sales of advertising and of supply expenses? How accurately does either predictor estimate sales? Are there any assumption problems to worry about?

Solution

We can see from the scatterplots that supply expenses predict sales more accurately than does advertising; the points are much closer to the line in the supply expenses plot. From the Parameter Estimates portion of the output, we see that sales rise about 24.4 for each unit increase in supply expenses; a 95% confidence interval for that number will be roughly $24.4 \pm 2(2.42)$, or 19.6 to 29.2. Sales rise about 23.3 ($\pm 2(6.35)$) for each unit increase in advertising.

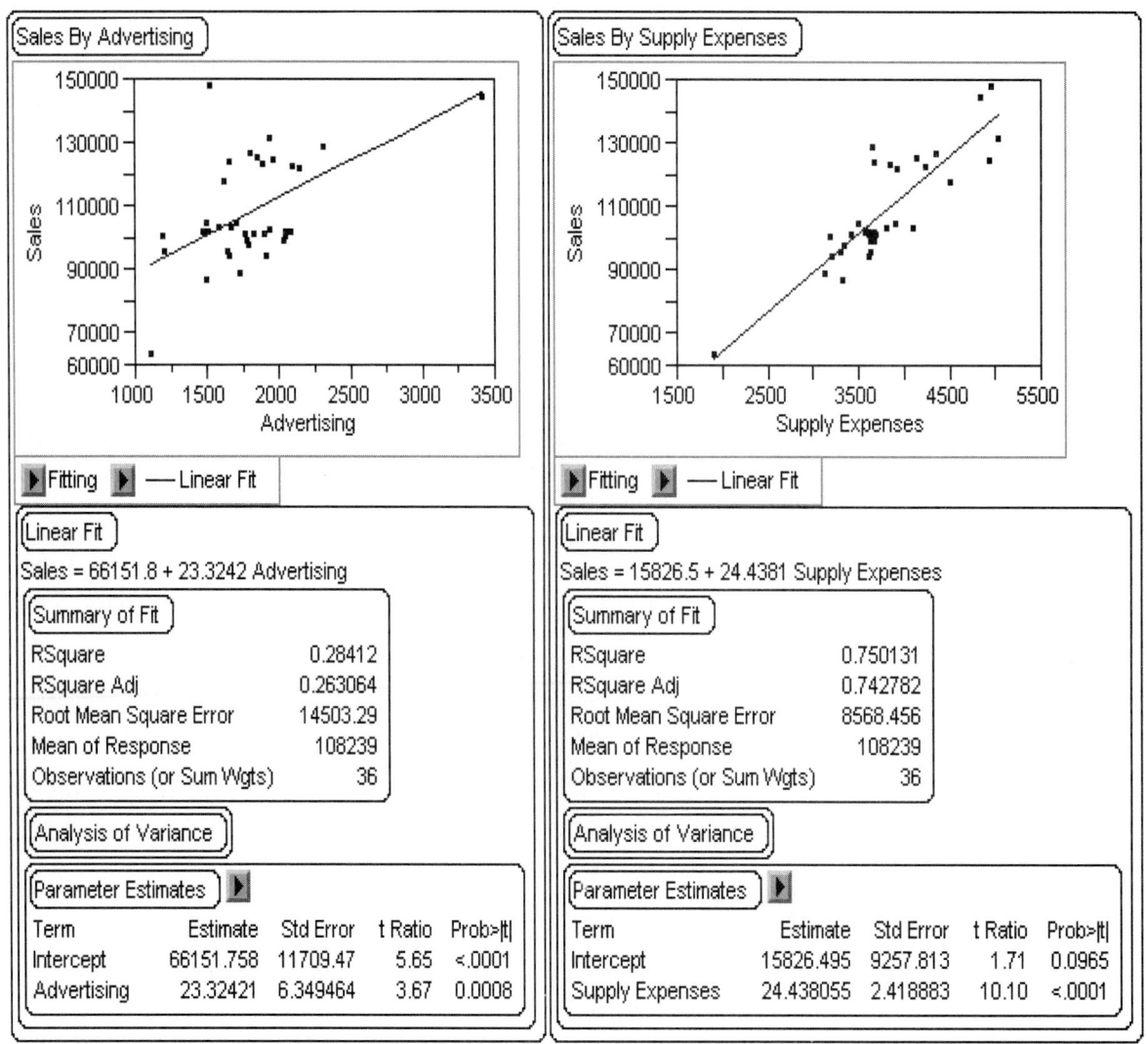

The residual standard deviation is shown as Root Mean Square Error. The output indicates that about 95% of the time we can predict sales to within $\pm2(14500)$ or ±29000 using advertising as our predictor, and to within $\pm2(8570)$ or ±17140 using supply expenses as the predictor. Again, the output indicates that the supply expenses variable is the better predictor.

The r^2 values, 0.28 for advertising and 0.75 for supply expenses, indicate how much of sales variability is accounted for by variation in each of the variables. Once more, the supply expenses variable is more effective in prediction.

The scatterplots don't indicate any wild violations of assumptions. There is one outlier at the top of the advertising plot and a higher leverage outlier at the bottom left. Perhaps there is a slightly increasing variability around the line in the supply expenses plot. None of these problems are severe enough to invalidate the main conclusion that supply expenses is the better predictor. ■

12.37 Consider the data shown here:

x:	10	12	14	15	18	19	23
y:	25	30	36	37	42	50	55

a Plot the data.

b Using the data, find the least-squares estimates for the model $Y_i = \beta_0 + \beta_1 x_i + \epsilon_i$.

c Predict Y when $x = 21$.

12.38 Refer to Exercise 12.37.

a Calculate s_ϵ, the residual standard deviation.

b Compute the residuals for these data. Do most lie within $\pm 2s_\epsilon$ of zero?

12.39 A government agency responsible for awarding contracts for much of its research work is under careful scrutiny by a number of private companies. One company examines the relationship between the amount of the contract ($\times\$10,000$) and the length of time between the submission of the contract proposal and contract approval:

Length (in months) y:	3	4	6	8	11	14	20
Size ($\times\$10,000$) x:	1	5	10	50	100	500	1000

A plot of y versus x is in Figure 12.23; Stata output follows:

```
. regress Length Size

    Source |       SS       df       MS              Number of obs =       7
-----------+------------------------------           F(  1,     5) =   33.78
     Model | 191.389193      1  191.389193           Prob > F      =  0.0021
  Residual | 28.3250928      5  5.66501856           R-square      =  0.8711
-----------+------------------------------           Adj R-square  =  0.8453
     Total | 219.714286      6  36.6190476           Root MSE      =  2.3801

------------------------------------------------------------------------------
    Length |      Coef.   Std. Err.       t     P>|t|     [95% Conf. Interval]
-----------+------------------------------------------------------------------
      Size |   .0148652   .0025575     5.812    0.002      .008291    .0214394
     _cons |   5.890659   1.086177     5.423    0.003     3.098553    8.682765
------------------------------------------------------------------------------
```

FIGURE 12.23   **Scatterplot of Length Versus Size**

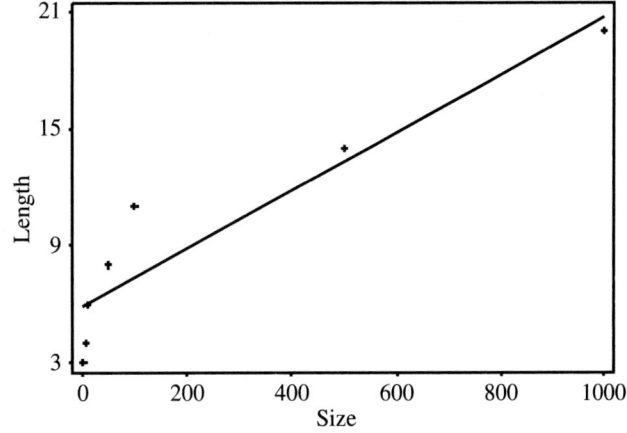

a What is the least-squares line?

b Conduct a test of the null hypothesis $H_0: \beta_1 = 0$. Give the p-value for your test assuming $H_a: \beta_1 > 0$.

12.40 Refer to the data of Exercise 12.39. A plot of Y versus the (natural) logarithm of x is shown in Figure 12.24, and more Stata output is given here:

```
. regress Length lnSize

    Source |       SS       df       MS              Number of obs =       7
-----------+------------------------------           F(  1,     5) =   49.20
     Model |  199.443893      1   199.443893         Prob > F      =  0.0009
  Residual |  20.2703932      5  4.05407863          R-square      =  0.9077
-----------+------------------------------           Adj R-square  =  0.8893
     Total |  219.714286      6  36.6190476          Root MSE      =  2.0135

------------------------------------------------------------------------------
    Length |     Coef.    Std. Err.      t     P>|t|     [95% Conf. Interval]
-----------+------------------------------------------------------------------
    lnSize |   2.307015   .3289169    7.014    0.000     1.461508    3.152523
     _cons |   1.007445   1.421494    0.709    0.510    -2.646622    4.661511
------------------------------------------------------------------------------
```

a What is the regression line using $\log x$ as the independent variable?

b Conduct a test of $H_0: \beta_1 = 0$, and give the level of significance for a one-sided alternative, $H_a: \beta_1 > 0$.

FIGURE 12.24 **Scatterplot of Length Versus Logarithm of Time**

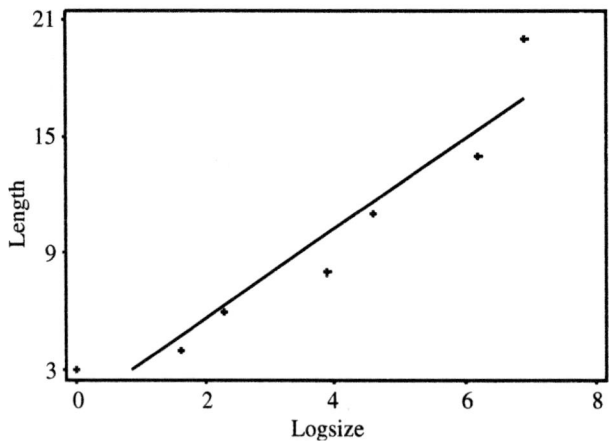

12.41 Use the results of Exercises 12.39 and 12.40 to determine which regression model provides the better fit. Give reasons for your choice.

12.42 Refer to the outputs of the previous two exercises.

a Give a 95% confidence interval for β_1, the slope of the linear regression line.

b Locate a 95% confidence interval for the slope in the logarithm model.

12.43 Use the model you prefer for the data of Exercise 12.40 to predict the length of time in months before approval of a $750,000 contract. Give a rough estimate of a 95% prediction interval.

12.44 An airline studying fuel usage by a certain type of aircraft obtains data on 100 flights. The air mileage x in hundreds of miles and the actual fuel use y in gallons are recorded. Statistix output follows and a plot is shown in Figure 12.25:

```
UNWEIGHTED LEAST SQUARES LINEAR REGRESSION OF GALLONS

PREDICTOR
VARIABLES     COEFFICIENT    STD ERROR     STUDENT'S T      P

CONSTANT        140.074       44.1293         3.17        0.0099
MILES           0.61896       0.04855        12.75        0.0000

R-SQUARED          0.9420    RESID. MEAN SQUARE (MSE)    1182.34
ADJUSTED R-SQUARED 0.9362    STANDARD DEVIATION          34.3852

SOURCE       DF      SS          MS         F        P

REGRESSION    1   1.921E+05   1.921E+05   162.48   0.0000
RESIDUAL     10   11823.4     1182.34
TOTAL        11   2.039E+05

PREDICTED/FITTED VALUES OF GALLONS

LOWER PREDICTED BOUND    678.33    LOWER FITTED BOUND    733.68
PREDICTED VALUE          759.03    FITTED VALUE          759.03
UPPER PREDICTED BOUND    839.73    UPPER FITTED BOUND    784.38
SE (PREDICTED VALUE)     36.218    SE (FITTED VALUE)     11.377

UNUSUALNESS (LEVERAGE)   0.1095
PERCENT COVERAGE         95.0
CORRESPONDING T          2.23

PREDICTOR VALUES: MILES = 1000.0
```

a Locate the regression equation.

b What are the sample correlation coefficient and coefficient of determination? Interpret these numbers.

c Is there any point in testing $H_0: \beta_1 = 0$?

FIGURE 12.25 **Scatterplot of Gallons Used Versus Miles**

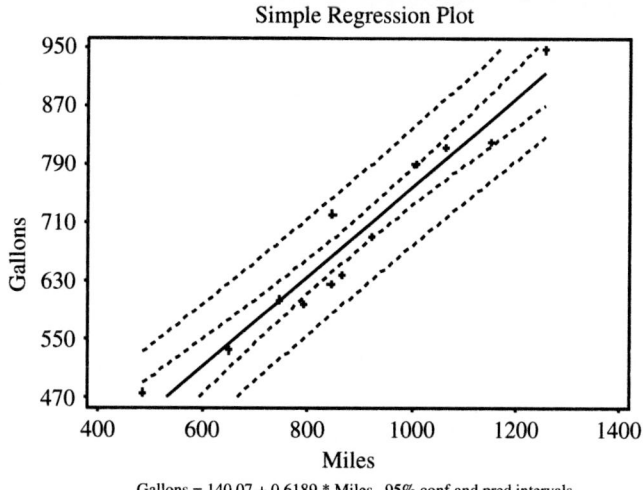

Gallons = 140.07 + 0.6189 * Miles   95% conf and pred intervals

12.45 Refer to the data and output of Exercise 12.44.

    a Predict the mean fuel usage of all 1000-mile flights. Give a 95% confidence interval.

    b Predict the fuel usage of a particular 1000-mile flight. Would a usage of 628 gallons be considered exceptionally low?

12.46 What is the interpretation of $\hat{\beta}_1$ in the situation of Exercise 12.44? Is there a sensible interpretation of $\hat{\beta}_0$?

12.47 A large suburban motel derives income from room rentals and purchases in its restaurant and lounge. It seems very likely that there should be a relation between room occupancy and restaurant/lounge sales, but the manager of the motel does not have a sense of how close that relation is. Data were collected for 36 nonholiday weekdays (Monday through Thursday nights) on the number of rooms occupied and the restaurant/lounge sales. A scatterplot of the data and regression results are shown in Figure 12.26.

    a According to the output, is there a statistically significant relation between rooms occupied and revenue?

FIGURE 12.26   **Scatterplot and Regression Analysis of Motel Data**

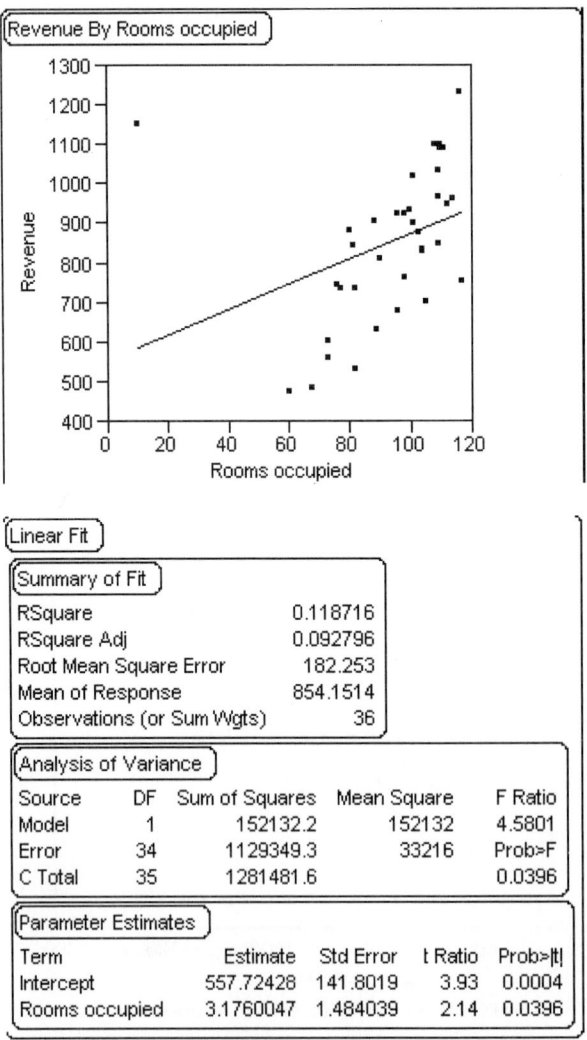

b If the point at the upper left of the scatterplot is deleted, will the slope be increased or decreased? Do you expect a substantial change?

12.48 One point in the hotel data was a data-entry error, with occupancy listed as 10 rather than 100. The error was corrected, leading to the output in Figure 12.27.

    a How has the slope changed as a result of the correction?

    b How has the intercept changed?

    c Did the outlier make the residual standard deviation (root mean square error) larger or smaller?

    d Did the outlier make the r^2 value larger or smaller?

FIGURE 12.27   **Results for Corrected Hotel Data**

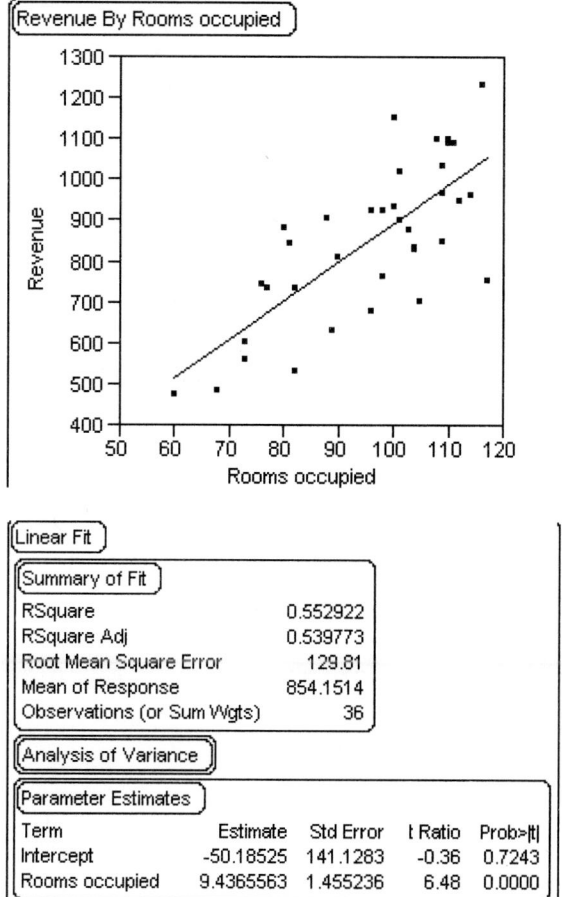

12.49 The management science staff of a grocery products manufacturer is developing a linear programming model for the production and distribution of its cereal products. The model requires transportation costs for a monstrous number of origins and destinations. It is impractical to do the detailed tariff analysis for every possible combination, so a sample of 50 routes is selected. For each route, the mileage x and shipping rate y (in dollars per 100 pounds) are found. A regression analysis is performed, yielding the scatterplot in Figure 12.28 and the following Excel output:

	A	B	C	D	E	F	G
1	SUMMARY OUTPUT						
2							
3	Regression Statistics						
4	Multiple R	0.9929					
5	R Square	0.9859					
6	Adjusted R Square	0.9856					
7	Standard Error	2.2021					
8	Observations	48					
9							
10							
11	ANOVA						
12		df	SS	MS	F	Significance F	
13	Regression	1	15558.63	15558.6	3208.47	0.00	
14	Residual	46	223.06	4.85			
15	Total	47	15781.7				
16							
17							
18		Coefficients	Standard Error	t Stat	P-value	Lower 95%	Upper 95%
19	Intercept	9.7709	0.4740	20.6122	0.0000	8.8167	10.7251
20	Mileage	0.0501	0.0009	56.6434	0.0000	0.0483	0.0519

FIGURE 12.28 **Scatterplot of Rate Versus Mileage**

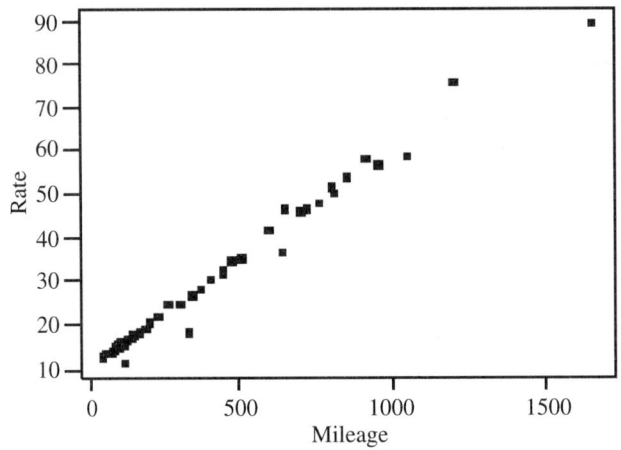

The data are as follows:

Mileage:	50	60	80	80	90	90	100	100	100	110	110	110
Rate:	12.7	13.0	13.7	14.1	14.6	14.1	15.6	14.9	14.5	15.3	15.5	15.9

Mileage:	120	120	120	120	130	130	140	150	170	190	200	230
Rate:	16.4	11.1	16.0	15.8	16.0	16.7	17.2	17.5	18.6	19.3	20.4	21.8

Mileage:	260	300	330	340	370	400	440	440	480	510	540	600
Rate:	24.7	24.7	18.0	27.1	28.2	30.6	31.8	32.4	34.5	35.0	36.3	41.4

Mileage:	650	700	720	760	800	810	850	920	960	1050	1200	1650
Rate:	46.4	45.8	46.6	48.0	51.7	50.2	53.6	57.9	56.1	58.7	75.8	89.0

a Write the regression equation and the residual standard deviation.

b Calculate a 90% confidence interval for the true slope.

12.50 In the plot of Exercise 12.49, do you see any problems with the data?

12.51   For Exercise 12.49, predict the shipping rate for a 340-mile route. Obtain a 95% prediction interval. How serious is the extrapolation problem in this exercise?

12.52   Suburban towns often spend a large fraction of their municipal budgets on public safety (police, fire, and ambulance) services. A taxpayers' group felt that very small towns were likely to spend large amounts per person just because they have such small financial bases. The group obtained data on the per capita expenditure for public saftey of 29 suburban towns in a metropolitan area, as well as the population of each town. The data were analyzed using the Minitab package. A regression model with dependent variable expendit and independent variable townpopn yields the following output:

```
MTB > regress 'expendit' 1 'townpopn'

The regression equation is
expendit = 119 +0.000532 townpopn


Predictor      Coef       Stdev     t-ratio       p
Constant      118.96       23.26       5.11     0.000
townpopn    0.0005324    0.0006181     0.86     0.397


s = 43.31      R-sq = 2.7%      R-sq(adj) = 0.0%

Analysis of Variance

SOURCE       DF          SS          MS        F       p
Regression    1         1392        1392     0.74    0.397
Error        27        50651        1876
Total        28        52043

Unusual Observations
Obs. townpopn    expendit       Fit  Stdev.Fit   Residual    St.Resid
  8    74151      334.00     158.43     25.32     175.57       5.00RX

R denotes an obs. with a large st. resid.
X denotes an obs. whose X value gives it large influence.
```

   a   If the taxpayers' group is correct, what sign should the slope of the regression model have?

   b   Does the slope in the output confirm the opinion of the group?

12.53   Minitab produced a scatterplot and LOWESS smooth of the data in Exercise 12.52, shown as Figure 12.29. Does this plot indicate that the regression line is misleading? Why?

FIGURE 12.29   **Scatterplot for Expenditure Data**

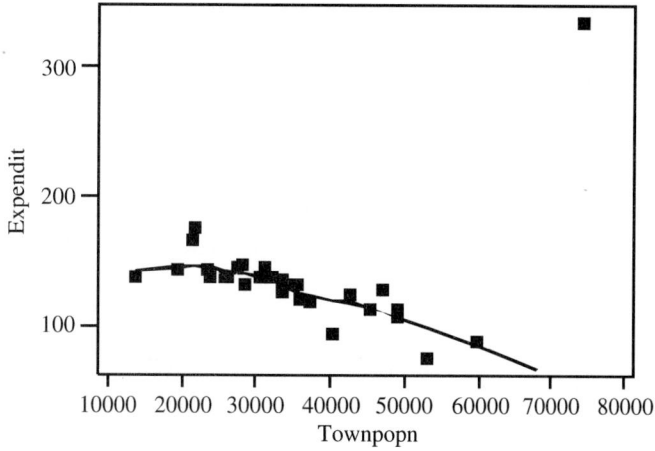

12.54 One town in the database of Exercise 12.52 is the home of an enormous regional shopping mall. A very large fraction of the town's expenditure on public safety is related to the mall; the mall management pays a yearly fee to the township that covers these expenditures. That town's data were removed from the database and the remaining data were reanalyzed by Minitab. A scatterplot is shown in Figure 12.30.

a Explain why removing this one point from the data changed the regression line so substantially.

b Does the revised regression line appear to conform to the opinion of the taxpayers' group in Exercise 12.52?

12.55 Regression output for the data of Exercise 12.52, excluding the one unusual town, is shown here. How has the slope changed from the one obtained previously?

```
MTB > regress 'expendit' 1 'townpopn'

The regression equation is
expendit = 184 - 0.00158 townpopn

Predictor       Coef       Stdev    t-ratio       p
Constant     184.240       7.481      24.63   0.000
townpopn   -0.0015766   0.0002099      -7.51   0.000

s = 12.14     R-sq = 68.5%     R-sq(adj) = 67.2%

Analysis of Variance

SOURCE        DF          SS          MS        F        p
Regression     1      8322.7      8322.7    56.43    0.000
Error         26      3834.5       147.5
Total         27     12157.2

Unusual Observations
Obs. townpopn   expendit       Fit  Stdev.Fit   Residual   St.Resid
   5    40307      96.00    120.69       2.66     -24.69     -2.08R
   6    13457     139.00    163.02       4.87     -24.02     -2.16R
  13    59779      89.00     89.99       5.89      -0.99     -0.09 X
  22    21701     176.00    150.03       3.44      25.97      2.23R
  27    53322      76.00    100.17       4.67     -24.17     -2.16R

R denotes an obs. with a large st. resid.
X denotes an obs. whose X value gives it large influence.
```

FIGURE 12.30   **Scatterplot with Unusual Town Data Removed**

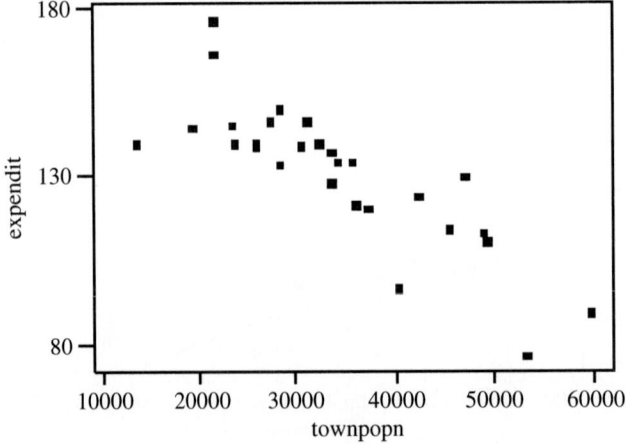

12.56 A realtor in a suburban area attempted to predict house prices solely on the basis of size. From a multiple listing service, the realtor obtained size in thousands of square feet and asking price in thousands of dollars. The information is stored in the EX1256.DAT file on the data disk, with price in column 1 and size in column 2. Have your statistical program read this file.

    a Obtain a plot of price against size. Does it appear there is an increasing relation?

    b Locate an apparent outlier in the data. Is it a high leverage point?

    c Obtain a regression equation and include the outlier in the data.

    d Delete the outlier and obtain a new regression equation. How much does the slope change without the outlier? Why?

    e Locate the residual standard deviations for the outlier-included and outlier-excluded models. Do they differ much? Why?

12.57 Obtain the outlier-excluded regression model for the data of Exercise 12.56.

    a Interpret the intercept (constant) term. How much meaning does this number have in this context?

    b What would it mean in this context if the slope were 0? Can the null hypothesis of zero slope be emphatically rejected?

    c Calculate a 95% confidence interval for the true population value of the slope. The computer output should give you the estimated slope and its standard error, but you'll probably have to do the rest of the calculations by hand.

12.58 **a** If possible, use your computer program to obtain a 95% prediction interval for the asking price of a home of 5000 square feet, based on the outlier-excluded data of Exercise 12.56. If you must do the computations by hand, obtain the mean and standard deviation of the size data from the computer, and find $S_{xx} = (n-1)s^2$ by hand. Would this be a wise prediction to make, based on the data?

    b Obtain a plot of the price against the size. Does the constant-variance assumption seem reasonable, or does variability increase as size increases?

    c What does your answer to part b say about the prediction interval obtained in part a?

12.59 A lawn care company tried to predict the demand for its service by zip code, using the housing density in the zip code area as a predictor. The owners obtained the number of houses and the geographic size of each zip code and calculated their sales per thousand homes and number of homes per acre. The data are stored in the EX1259.DAT file on the data disk. Sales data are in column 1 and density (homes/acre) are in column 2. Read the data into your computer package.

    a Obtain the correlation between two variables. What does its sign mean?

    b Obtain a prediction equation with sales as the dependent variable and density as the independent variable. Interpret the intercept (yes, we know the interpretation will be a bit strange) and the slope numbers.

    c Obtain a value for the residual standard deviation. What does this number indicate about the accuracy of prediction?

12.60 **a** Obtain a value of the t statistic for the regression model of Exercise 12.59. Is there conclusive evidence that density is a predictor of sales?

    b Calculate a 95% confidence interval for the true value of the slope. The package should have calculated the standard error for you.

12.61 Obtain a plot of the data of Exercise 12.59, with sales plotted against density. Does it appear that straight-line prediction makes sense?

12.62 Refer to Exercise 12.59. Have your computer program calculate a new variable as 1/density.

    a What is the interpretation of the new variable? In particular, if the new variable equals 0.50, what does that mean about the particular zip code area?

    b Plot sales against the new variable. Does a straight-line prediction look reasonable here?

    c Obtain the correlation of sales and the new variable. Compare its magnitude to the correlation obtained in Exercise 12.61 between sales and density. What explains the difference?

12.63 A manufacturer of paint used for marking road surfaces developed a new formulation that needs to be tested for durability. One question concerns the concentration of pigment in the paint. If the concentration is too low, the paint will fade quickly; if the concentration is too high, the paint will not adhere well to the road surface. The manufacturer applies paint at various concentrations to sample road surfaces and obtains a durability measurement for each sample. The data are stored in the EX1263.DAT file on the data disk, with durability in column 1 and concentration in column 2.

a Have your computer program calculate a regression equation with durability predicted by concentration. Interpret the slope coefficient.

b Find the coefficient of determination. What does it indicate about the predictive value of concentration?

12.64 In the regression model of Exercise 12.63, is the slope coefficient significantly different from 0 at $\alpha = .01$?

12.65 Obtain a plot of the data of Exercise 12.63, with durability on the vertical axis and concentration on the horizontal axis.

a What does this plot indicate about the wisdom of using straight-line prediction?

b What does this plot indicate about the correlation found in Exercise 12.63?

12.66 Previously, we considered a group of builders who were considering a method for estimating the cost of constructing custom houses. They have come back to you for additional advice.

Recall that the builders used the method to estimate the cost of 10 "spec" houses that were built without a commitment from a customer. The builders obtained the actual costs (exclusive of land costs) of completing each house, to compare with the estimated costs.

"We went back to our accountant, who did a regression analysis of the data and gave us these results. The accountant says that the estimates are quite accurate, with an 80% correlation and a very low p-value. We're still pretty skeptical of whether this new method gives us decent estimates. We only clear a profit of about 10 percent, so a few bad estimates would hurt us. Can you explain to us what this output says about the estimating method?"

Write a brief, not-too-technical explanation for them. Focus on the builder's question about the accuracy of the estimates. A plot is shown in Figure 12.31.

```
MTB > Regress 'Actual' on 1 variable 'Estimate'.
 The regression equation is
Actual = - 34739 + 1.25 Estimate

Predictor      Coef      Stdev     t-ratio      p
Constant     -34739      60147      -0.58    0.579
Estimate     1.2474     0.3293       3.79    0.005

s = 19313      R-sq = 64.2%     R-sq(adj) = 59.7%

Analysis of Variance

SOURCE       DF         SS           MS         F        p
Regression    1   5350811136   5350811136    14.35    0.005
Error         8   2983948032    372993504
Total         9   8334758912

Unusual Observations
Obs. Estimate  Actual     Fit  Stdev.Fit  Residual  St.Resid  2    186200   152134
     197531      6286  -45397              -2.49R

R denotes an obs. with a large st. resid.

MTB > Correlation 'Estimate' 'Actual'.

Correlation of Estimate and Actual = 0.801
```

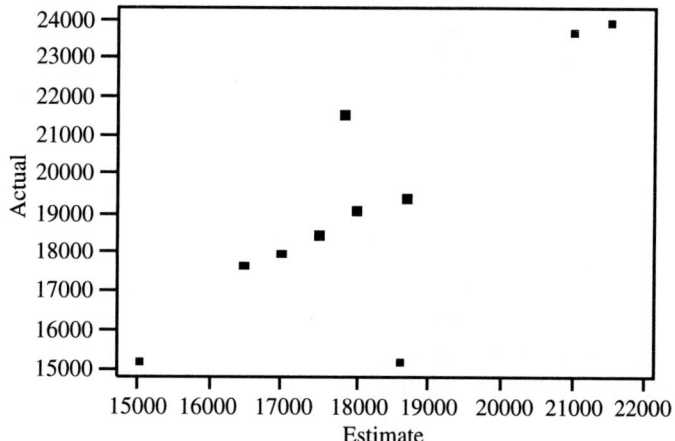

Regression and Correlation

In the Case Study for Chapter 7, the benefits manager of a large university obtained data from a sample of 61 employees on their intended use of a possible flexible benefits plan. Now the manager wants to analyze the data in more detail. In particular, the manager is interested in the relation between monthly life insurance cost and age of the employee. This relation is a matter of increasing concern because the age of the employee group has been rising and it will continue to rise. A work-study student took age and life insurance cost data from the sample and performed some basic Minitab analysis, as shown here:

employee	age	life	employee	age	life
1	52	759	32	47	585
2	28	424	33	32	472
3	42	157	34	65	535
4	51	616	35	22	174
5	42	655	36	52	751
6	44	559	37	39	579
7	46	651	38	43	666
8	49	519	39	35	596
9	51	358	40	61	251
10	25	456	41	51	341
11	33	97	42	27	77
12	59	478	43	28	225
13	35	129	44	51	590
14	44	661	45	53	330
15	30	245	46	47	736
16	37	602	47	50	601
17	32	557	48	40	555
18	41	215	49	40	775
19	29	331	50	52	745
20	48	545	51	46	630
21	61	395	52	58	139
22	38	577	53	44	521
23	32	345	54	55	647
24	33	367	55	29	543
25	24	189	56	44	699
26	43	716	57	53	602
27	43	238	58	54	493
28	50	867	59	45	731
29	55	475	60	38	267
30	56	369	61	49	689
31	68	245			

```
MTB > correlation of 'age' 'life'

Correlation of age and life = 0.271

MTB > regress 'life' on 1 variable 'age'

The regression equation is
life = 259 + 5.07 age
```

Predictor	Coef	Stdev	t-ratio	p
Constant	258.9	105.7	2.45	0.017
age	5.073	2.344	2.16	0.035

s = 195.3   R-sq = 7.4%   R-sq(adj) = 5.8%

Analysis of Variance

SOURCE	DF	SS	MS	F	p
Regression	1	178624	178624	4.68	0.035
Error	59	2250734	38148		
Total	60	2429357			

Unusual Observations

Obs.	age	life	Fit	Stdev.Fit	Residual	St.Resid
31	68.0	245.0	603.9	62.0	-358.9	-1.94 X
52	58.0	139.0	553.1	41.7	-414.1	-2.17R

R denotes an obs. with a large st. resid.
X denotes an obs. whose X value gives it large influence.

In a cover note to you accompanying the output, the benefits manager said, "I don't understand this very well. There doesn't seem to be a very good correlation, but the work-study student says it is significant. Can you explain what's going on in the output for me?" Explain what you think are the most important conclusions to be obtained from the output, in language the manager can understand. (A plot is shown in Figure 12.32.) You're welcome to suggest and carry out any further analysis that might help you interpret the data.

FIGURE 12.32   **Plot of Life Insurance Cost versus Employee Age**

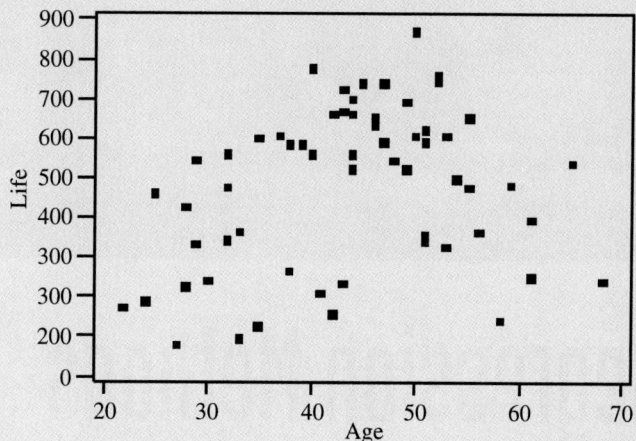

A stock-market guru named Wine
Cried "Check out these forecasts of mine!
I'll make you all rich
With never a hitch!"
His R-square was .009.

13

Multiple Regression Methods

This chapter introduces the technical aspects of multiple regression using several independent variables, possibly including nonlinear terms such as squared x values or products of two x values. The chapter is devoted to estimation, testing, and forecasting methods. The next chapter deals with constructing a multiple regression model and checking underlying assumptions. The key methods discussed in this chapter are the following:

1 The basic multiple regression model is a first-order model, containing each predictor but no nonlinear terms such as squared values. In this model, each slope should be interpreted as a partial slope, the predicted effect of a one-unit change in a variable, holding all other variables constant. The intercept is the predicted Y value when all predictors equal 0; this condition may not mean much in context.

2 The slopes in multiple regression do not generally equal the slopes in a series of simple regressions because of collinearity, correlation among the independent variables.

3 The overall strength of predictability is often measured by R^2, the coefficient of determination. It measures how much of the variation (squared error) in Y is accounted for or explained by variation in the independent variables. When there is substantial collinearity, it can be difficult to say which independent variables are responsible for most of R^2.

4 There are three distinct hypothesis tests on the slope coefficients in multiple regression. A test of the overall predictive value of *all* of the predictors together is done by an F test similar to that used

with the analysis of variance. A test of the value of *one* predictor, given all others, is based on a t statistic. A test of the value of *some*—a subset—of the predictors, given the remaining ones, is done by an incremental F test. The latter test may be based either on the increment to R^2 obtained by adding the subset of predictors to the others or on the increment to SS(Regression).

5 Forecasts using new x values in multiple regression are constructed in much the same way as in simple regression. It is important to consider whether the new x values are extrapolated far from the data, either individually or in combination.

Multiple regression uses many independent variables to predict or explain variation in a quantitative dependent variable. It's an extremely useful way to assess the explanatory value of many different, plausible predictors. In many management situations, there are several possible predictors of a result. We use multiple regression to try to sort out which of these plausible predictors really do explain variation in the dependent variable, and which others add little or no predictive value. It is probably the statistical technique most widely used by managers.

We devote two chapters to multiple regression. In this chapter, we develop the basic theoretical concepts, the assumptions, and the methods. We consider what the multiple regression model is and how it's interpreted, how the coefficients can be estimated from data, how inferences can be made from the limited database of the model, and how to use the model in forecasting new cases. Then, in Chapter 14, we'll describe how all the concepts fit together in developing a multiple regression study. ■

13.1

The Multiple Regression Model

E very manager faces situations in which changes or variations in something need to be understood and predicted and in which many plausible indicators point (in possibly conflicting ways) to the predicted changes. In every publicly held company, changes in the price of the company's common stock are of more than mild interest. There are both internal predictors of the price (such as earnings, growth rate, market share of primary products, and debt–equity ratio) and external predictors (such as interest rates, consumer confidence levels, and current unemployment). Variation in the cost of a print job depends on the number of pages, the number of graphic displays, the hours needed to set up, and the number of copies. Variation in the sales of a new product can be predicted by the size of the market, the rate of growth of that market, consumer satisfaction in tests of the product, and type of sales outlet for the product.

Multiple regression is a method for using data to sort out the predictive value of the competing predictors. Therefore, it is widely used by many types of managers.

Given the data, the first task in multiple regression is to specify a model, the mathematical form of the prediction equation. The simplest model takes each predictor, multiplies it by a numerical weight (coefficient), and adds the resulting quantities to an intercept term. For example, a multiple regression model for variation in price of a common stock over time might be

$$\text{price} = -12.72 + 5.21\,\text{earnings} + 3.34\,\text{growth} - 0.68\text{D/E}$$

where price = closing price of the stock at the end of each quarter; earnings = reported earnings per share in the quarter; growth = change in earnings from the same quarter of the previous year; and D/E = ratio of corporate debt to corporate equity. The intercept term, −12.72 in the example, is the predicted dependent variable value when all the independent variables equal 0. In many cases, the intercept has little meaning because the condition that all predictors are 0 is economically absurd. There can't be a stock with a price of −12.72 (even the ones we own), but the conditions of 0 earnings, 0 growth, and 0 debt-to-equity ratio are so far outside of reasonable economic values that we needn't worry about the impossible value.

The coefficients of the predictor variables are usually more relevant. They are the
partial slopes, which measure the predicted change in the dependent variable for a one-unit change in the independent variable, *holding other independent variables constant*. In the stock price equation, if we compare two quarters when the company had the same growth and debt–equity ratio, we'd predict that the price would be $5.21 higher for the quarter in which the earnings per share were $1 higher. Similarly, if we had two quarters when earnings and growth were the same, but D/E was 1.0 higher in quarter A than in quarter B, we would predict that the price would be 0.68 *lower* (because of the minus sign) in quarter A.

partial slopes

EXAMPLE 13.1

The manager of a copy center must estimate costs for jobs that differ in number of pages, number of copies, setup hours, and number of graphics. Data from past jobs were put into a computer multiple regression program and yielded a model:

$$\text{cost} = -160 + 7.43\,\text{pages} + 1.84\,\text{copies} + 4.44\,\text{setup} + 2.67\,\text{graphics}$$

Interpret each numerical value in the model.

Solution

The intercept, −160, refers to a job with no pages, no copies, no setup, and no graphics—in other words, to a nonjob! It is not interpretable. The partial slope for "pages," 7.43, is the predicted difference in cost between two jobs with the same number of copies, setup hours, and graphics, differing by one page. The partial slope for "copies," 1.84, is the predicted difference in cost between two jobs of equal number of pages, setup hours, and graphics, differing by one copy. Similar interpretations hold for the other slopes. Note that the total number of copied pages can be obtained by multiplying "pages" by "copies"; we'd expect such a product term to be a useful predictor. ■

Symbolically, we write the multiple regression model as

$$Y = \beta_0 + \beta_1 x_1 + \beta_2 x_2 + \cdots + \beta_k x_k + \epsilon$$

where Y is the dependent variable to be predicted, the x's are independent predictor values, and ϵ is the error term (in recognition of the fact that every prediction is in error to some degree). The intercept term is β_0; β_1 though β_k are the partial slopes. (For those who know some calculus, the partial slope β_j is exactly the partial derivative of predicted Y with respect to x_j.)

first-order model
The simplest regression model is called a **first-order model**. It contains each predictor by itself without mathematical transformations such as squared terms or logarithms. It doesn't combine predictors in such forms as product terms. A first-order model implicitly makes assumptions about the nature of the relation between Y and the predictors. First, it assumes that Y changes at a consistent rate as x_j changes, over the entire range of x_j—as opposed to, say, increasing at a decreasing rate or increasing to a maximum and then decreasing. In our first-order stock price model, we're implicitly assuming that, holding growth and D/E constant, an increase of \$1 in earnings leads to a \$5.21 increase in price per share, whether the earnings dollar is the first or the 379th. That may not be a good assumption; in the stock price case, it might well be that the price is very sensitive to changes in earnings on the low end of the scale but less sensitive when earnings start out very high.

interaction
A first-order model also assumes that there is no **interaction** among predictors. We encountered the idea of interaction in Chapter 10: The effect of changing one experimental factor depends on the level of another factor. Interaction in regression means the same thing. Two independent variables interact in their effect on the dependent variable if the predicted effect of a change in one predictor, holding the other constant, depends on *where* that other variable is held constant. In our stock price example, it wouldn't be surprising to have earnings and debt–equity ratio interact. At low D/E levels, higher earnings might have little effect; at high D/E levels, the leveraging effect might make stock prices very sensitive to changes in earnings. We will consider some methods for incorporating interaction into multiple regression in Chapter 14.

EXAMPLE 13.2

A brand manager for a new food product collected data on $Y =$ brand recognition (percent of potential consumers who can describe what the product is), $x_1 =$ length in seconds of an introductory TV commercial, and $x_2 =$ number of repetitions of the commercial over a 2-week period. What does the brand manager assume if a first-order model

$$Y = 0.31 + 0.042x_1 + 1.41x_2$$

is used to predict Y?

Solution

First, the manager assumes a straight-line, consistent rate of change. The manager assumes that a 1-second increase in length of the commercial will lead to a 0.042 percentage point increase in recognition, whether the increase is from, say, 10 to 11 seconds or from 59 to 60 seconds. Also, every additional repetition of the commercial is assumed to give a 1.41 percentage point increase in recognition, whether it is the second repetition or the twenty-second.

Second, there is a no-interaction assumption. The first-order model assumes that the effect of an additional repetition (that is, an increase in x_2) of a given length commercial (that is, holding x_1 constant) doesn't depend on *where* that length is held constant (at 10 seconds, 27 seconds, 60 seconds, whatever). ■

A first-order model is often a good starting point. In many managerial situations, there is no obvious reason to expect curvature or interaction. In such situations, a first-order model is a natural first try. In the next chapter, we'll have more to say about other, mathematically more complicated models. Until then, we simply note that a first-order multiple regression model is a useful possibility, but not the only one.

The error term ϵ plays exactly the same role in multiple regression as it does in simple linear regression. It includes all the effects of unpredictable and ignored factors. (The basic hope of multiple regression is to make the ϵ_i values small by including all or most of the relevant predictive factors.) The assumptions on the random error terms are identical to those stated in Chapter 12.

Definition 13.1 Assumptions for Multiple Regression

1 The mathematical form of relation is correct, so $E(\epsilon_i) = 0$ for all i.

2 $\text{Var}(\epsilon_i) = \sigma_\epsilon^2$ for all i.

3 The ϵ_i's are independent.

4 ϵ_i is normally distributed. ■

The effect of violations of these formal assumptions is discussed in Chapter 14.

We turn our attention now to the important problem of determining estimates for the coefficients (the intercept β_0 and the partial slopes $\beta_1, \ldots, \beta_k$) in the multiple regression model in order to obtain the multiple regression forecasting equation.

13.2 Estimating Multiple Regression Coefficients

T he first task of a multiple regression analysis is to estimate the intercept, the partial slopes, and the error variance. The basic principle is least-squares estimation, just as in simple linear regression. The arithmetic involved in multiple regression gets heavy very quickly, so the work is almost always done by a computer.

In simple linear regression, the least-squares principle leads to two equations that must be solved to obtain the estimated slope and intercept. In multiple regression, using k independent variables, there are $k + 1$ equations to solve for the intercept and the k partial slopes. If you recall the time and effort required to solve four equations in four unknowns by hand, you can appreciate why multiple regression is virtually always done by a computer package. There is a pattern to the equations for any number of independent variables that can be programmed. Therefore, a single program can handle any number of independent variables, up to the limits of computer storage.

Literally thousands of computer programs have been written to perform the calculations needed in multiple regression. The output of such programs typically has a list of variable names, together with the estimated partial slopes, labeled COEFFICIENTS (or ESTIMATES or PARAMETERS). The intercept term $\hat{\beta}_0$ is usually called INTERCEPT (or CONSTANT); sometimes it is shown along with the slopes but with no variable name.

EXAMPLE 13.3

The data for three variables (shown here) are analyzed with the Excel spreadsheet program. Identify the estimates of the partial slopes and the intercept.

y:	25	34	28	40	36	42	44	53	49
x_1:	−10	−10	−10	0	0	0	10	10	10
x_2:	−5	0	5	−5	0	5	−5	0	5

	Coefficients	Standard Error	t Stat	P-value
Intercept	39.0	1.256	31.055	7.4E-08
X1	0.983	0.154	6.393	0.0007
X2	0.333	0.308	1.084	0.3202

Solution

The intercept value 39.0 is labeled as such. The estimated partial slopes .983 and .333 are associated with x_1 and x_2, respectively. Most programs label the coefficients similarly, in a column. ∎

The coefficient of an independent variable x_j in a multiple regression equation does not, in general, equal the coefficient that would apply to that variable in a simple linear regression. In multiple regression, the coefficient refers to the effect of changing that x_j variable while other independent variables stay constant. In simple linear regression, all other potential independent variables are ignored. If other independent variables are correlated with x_j (and therefore don't tend to stay constant while x_j changes), simple linear regression with x_j as the only independent variable captures not only the direct effect of changing x_j but also the indirect effect of the associated changes in other x's. In multiple regression, by holding the other x's constant, we eliminate that indirect effect.

EXAMPLE 13.4

Compare the coefficients of x_1 in the multiple regression model and in the simple (one-predictor) regression model shown in the following StataQuest output. Explain why the two coefficients differ.

```
. regress y  x1 x2
```

y		Coef.	Std. Err.	t	P>|t|	[95% Conf. Interval]	
x1			1	1.870829	0.535	0.646	-7.049526	9.049526
x2			3	4.1833	0.717	0.548	-14.99929	20.99929
_cons			10	1.183216	8.452	0.014	4.909033	15.09097

```
. regress y  x1
```

```
        y |   Coef.   Std. Err.     t    P>|t|      [95% Conf. Interval]
----------+-----------------------------------------------------------------
       x1 |    2.2   .7659417    2.872   0.064     -.2375683    4.637568
    _cons |     10   1.083205    9.232   0.003      6.552758    13.44724
---------------------------------------------------------------------------

. correlate  y x1 x2

          |      y        x1       x2
----------+---------------------------
        y|  1.0000
       x1|  0.8563   1.0000
       x2|  0.8704   0.8944   1.0000
```

Solution

In the multiple regression model, the coefficient is shown as 1, but in the simple regression model, it's 2.2. The difference occurs because the two x's are correlated (correlation .8944 in the output). In the multiple regression model, we're thinking of varying x_1 while holding x_2 constant; in the simple regression model, we're thinking of varying x_1 and letting x_2 go wherever it goes. ∎

residual standard deviation

In addition to estimating the intercept and partial slopes, it is important to estimate the **residual standard deviation** s_ϵ, sometimes called the *standard error of estimate*. The residuals are defined as before, as the difference between the observed value and the predicted value of Y:

$$y_i - \hat{y}_i = y_i - (\hat{\beta}_0 + \hat{\beta}_1 x_{i1} + \hat{\beta}_2 x_{i2} + \cdots + \hat{\beta}_k x_{ik})$$

The sum of squared residuals, SS(Residual), also called SS(Error), is defined exactly as it sounds. Square the prediction errors and sum the squares:

$$SS(Residual) = \sum (y_i - \hat{y}_i)^2$$
$$= \sum [y_i - (\hat{\beta}_0 + \hat{\beta}_1 x_{i1} + \hat{\beta}_2 x_{i2} + \cdots + \hat{\beta}_k x_{ik})]^2$$

The d.f. for this sum of squares is $n - (k + 1)$. One d.f. is subtracted for the intercept and 1 d.f. is subtracted for each of the k partial slopes. The mean square residual, MS(Residual), also called MS(Error), is the residual sum of squares divided by $n - (k + 1)$. Finally, the residual standard deviation s_ϵ is the square root of MS(Residual).

The residual standard deviation may be called "std dev," "standard error of estimate," or "root MSE." If the output's not clear, you can take the square root of MS(Residual) by hand. As always, interpret the standard deviation by the Empirical Rule. About 95% of the prediction errors will be within ± 2 standard deviations of the mean (and the mean error is automatically zero):

$$s_\epsilon = \sqrt{MS(Residual)}$$
$$= \sqrt{\frac{SS(Residual)}{n - (k + 1)}}$$

E X A M P L E   1 3 . 5

Identify SS(Residual) and s_ϵ in the output shown here for the data of Example 13.3.

	A	B	C	D	E	F
1						
2	The regression equation is y= 39.0 + .983 x1 + .333 x2					
3						
4	Predictor	Coef	Stdev	t-ratio	p	
5						
6	Constant	39.000	1.256	31.05	0.000	
7	x1	0.9833	0.1538	6.39	0.001	
8	x2	0.3333	0.3076	1.08	0.320	
9						
10	s=3.768	R-sq= 87.5%	R-sq(adj)= 83.3%			
11						
12						
13	Analysis of Variance					
14						
15						
16	SOURCE	DF	SS	MS	F	P
17	Regression	2	596.83	298.420	21.02	0.002
18	Error	6	85.17	14.190		
19	Total	8	682.00			

Solution

In the section of the output labeled Analysis of Variance, SS(Residual) is shown as SS(Error) = 85.17, with 6 d.f. MS(Error) is 14.19. The residual standard deviation is indicated by $s = 3.768$. Note that $3.768 = \sqrt{14.19}$ to within round-off error. ∎

The residual standard deviation is crucial in determining the probable error of a prediction using the regression equation. The precise standard error to be used in forecasting an individual Y value is stated in Section 13.4. A rough approximation, ignoring extrapolation and d.f. effects, is that the probable error is $\pm 2s_\epsilon$. This approximation can be used as a rough indicator of the forecasting quality of a regression model.

E X A M P L E   1 3 . 6

The admissions office of a business school develops a regression model that uses aptitude test scores and class rank to predict the grade average (4.00 = straight A; 2.00 = C average, the minimum graduation average; 0.00 = straight F). The residual standard deviation is $s_\epsilon = .46$. Does this value suggest highly accurate prediction?

Solution

A measure of the probable error of prediction is $2s_\epsilon = .92$. For example, if a predicted average is 2.80, then an individual's grade is roughly between $2.80 - .92 = 1.88$ (not good enough to graduate) and $2.80 + .92 = 3.72$ (good enough to graduate magna cum laude)! This is *not* an accurate forecast. ∎

coefficient of determination

The **coefficient of determination**, R^2, is defined and interpreted very much like the r^2 value in Chapter 12. (The customary notation is R^2 for multiple regression and r^2 for simple linear regression.) As in Chapter 12, we define the coefficient of determination as the proportional reduction in the squared error of Y, which we obtain by knowing the values of $x_1, \ldots, x_k$. For example, if we have the multiple regression model with three x values, and $R^2_{y \cdot x_1 x_2 x_3} = .736$, then we can account for 73.6% of the variability of the y

values by variability in x_1, x_2, and x_3. Formally

$$R^2_{y \cdot x_1 \cdots x_k} = \frac{\text{SS(Total)} - \text{SS(Residual)}}{\text{SS(Total)}}$$

where

$$\text{SS(Total)} = \sum (y_i - \bar{y})^2$$

E X A M P L E 1 3 . 7

Locate the value of $R^2_{y \cdot x_1 x_2}$ in the computer output of Example 13.5.

Solution

We want R-sq $= 87.5\%$, not the one that is adj. Alternatively, SS(Total) $= 682.00$ and SS(Residual) $= 85.17$ are shown in the output, and we can compute $R^2_{y \cdot x_1 x_2} = (682.00 - 85.17)/682.00 = .875$. ∎

There is no general relation between the multiple R^2 from a multiple regression equation and the individual coefficients of determination $r^2_{yx_1}, r^2_{yx_2}, \ldots, r^2_{yx_k}$ other than that multiple R^2 must be at least as big as any of the individual r^2 values. If all the independent variables are themselves perfectly uncorrelated with each other, then multiple R^2 is just the sum of the individual r^2 values. Equivalently, if all the x's are uncorrelated with each other, SS(Regression) for the all-predictors model is equal to the sum of SS(Regression) values for simple regressions using one x at a time. If the x's are correlated, it is much more difficult to break apart the overall predictive value of $x_1, x_2, \ldots, x_k$ as measured by $R^2_{y \cdot x_1 \cdots x_k}$ into separate pieces that can be attributable to x_1 alone, to x_2 alone, $\ldots$, to x_k alone.

collinearity

When the independent variables are themselves correlated, **collinearity** (sometimes called *multicollinearity*) is present. In multiple regression, we are trying to separate out the predictive value of several predictors. When the predictors are highly correlated, this task is very difficult. For example, suppose that we try to explain variation in regional housing sales over time, using gross domestic product (GDP) and national disposable income (DI) as two of the predictors. DI has been almost exactly a fraction of GDP, so the correlation of these two predictors will be extremely high. Now, is variation in housing sales attributable more to variation in GDP or to variation in DI? Good luck taking those two apart! It's very likely that either predictor alone will explain variation in housing sales almost as well as both together.

Collinearity is usually present to some degree in a multiple regression study. It is a small problem for slightly correlated x's but a more severe one for highly correlated x's. Thus, if collinearity occurs in a regression study—and it usually does to some degree—it is not easy to break apart the overall $R^2_{y \cdot x_1 x_2 \cdots x_k}$ into separate components associated with each x variable. The correlated x's often account for overlapping pieces of the variability in y, so that often, but not inevitably,

$$R^2_{y \cdot x_1 x_2 \cdots x_k} < r^2_{yx1} + r^2_{yx2} + \cdots + r^2_{yxk}$$

sequential sums of squares

Many statistical computer programs will report **sequential sums of squares**. These SS are *incremental* contributions to SS(Regression) when the independent variables enter the regression model in the order you specify to the program. Sequential sums of squares depend heavily on the particular order in which the independent variables enter the model. Again, the trouble is collinearity. For example, if all variables in a regression study are strongly and positively correlated (as often happens in economic data), whichever independent variable happens to be entered first typically accounts for most of the explainable variation in Y and the remaining variables add little to the sequential SS. The explanatory power of any X given all the other X's (which is sometimes called the *unique predictive value* of that X) is small. When the data exhibit severe collinearity, separating out the predictive value of the various independent variables is very difficult indeed.

E X A M P L E   1 3 . 8

Interpret the sequential sums of squares in the following output for the data of Example 13.3. If x_2 and x_1 were used as predictors (in that order), would we obtain the same sequential sums of squares numbers?

```
MTB > Correlation 'y' 'x1' 'x2'.


            y        x1
x1        0.922
x2        0.156    0.000


MTB > Regress 'y' 2 'x1' 'x2'.


The regression equation is
y = 39.0 + 0.983 x1 + 0.333 x2


Predictor      Coef      Stdev    t-ratio        p
Constant     39.000      1.256      31.05    0.000
x1           0.9833     0.1538       6.39    0.001
x2           0.3333     0.3076       1.08    0.320


s = 3.768      R-sq = 87.5%     R-sq(adj) = 83.3%


Analysis of Variance


SOURCE       DF          SS         MS        F        p
Regression    2      596.83     298.42    21.02    0.002
Error         6       85.17      14.19
Total         8      682.00


SOURCE       DF      SEQ SS
x1            1      580.17
x2            1       16.67
```

Solution

The SEQ SS column shows that x_1 by itself accounts for 580.17 of the total variation in y and that adding x_2 after x_1 accounts for another 16.67 of the y variation. This example is a rarity in that the predictors are completely uncorrelated; in this unusual case, the order of adding predictors doesn't matter.

```
MTB > Regress 'y' 2 'x2' 'x1'.


The regression equation is
y = 39.0 + 0.333 x2 + 0.983 x1
```

```
Predictor       Coef      Stdev    t-ratio        p
Constant      39.000      1.256      31.05    0.000
x2            0.3333     0.3076       1.08    0.320
x1            0.9833     0.1538       6.39    0.001


s = 3.768      R-sq = 87.5%    R-sq(adj) = 83.3%

Analysis of Variance

SOURCE       DF         SS         MS        F        p
Regression    2     596.83     298.42    21.02    0.002
Error         6      85.17      14.19
Total         8     682.00

SOURCE       DF     SEQ SS
x2            1      16.67
x1            1     580.17
```

EXERCISES

13.1 A manufacturer of industrial chemicals investigates the effect on its sales of promotion activities (primarily direct contact and trade shows), direct development expenditures, and short-range research effort. Data are assembled for 24 quarters (6 years) and analyzed by the Stata multiple regression program, as shown here (in $100,000 per quarter):

```
. regress Sales Promo Devel Research

    Source |      SS      df      MS          Number of obs =      24
-----------+----------------------------      F( 3,   20) =   22.28
     Model | 43901.7677    3  14633.9226      Prob > F      = 0.0000
  Residual | 13136.2323   20  656.811614      R-square      = 0.7697
-----------+----------------------------      Adj R-square  = 0.7351
     Total |   57038.00   23  2479.91304      Root MSE      = 25.628


------------------------------------------------------------------------------
     Sales |     Coef.  Std. Err.     t    P>|t|   [95% Conf. Interval]
-----------+------------------------------------------------------------------
     Promo |  136.0983  28.10759   4.842   0.000    77.46689   194.7297
     Devel |  -61.17526 50.94102  -1.201   0.244  -167.4364    45.08585
  Research |  -43.69508 48.32298  -0.904   0.377  -144.495     57.10489
     _cons |  326.3893  241.6129   1.351   0.192  -177.6063    830.3849
------------------------------------------------------------------------------
```

   a Write the estimated regression equation.

   b Locate MS(Residual) and its square root, the residual standard deviation.

   c Locate SS(Residual) and the coefficient of determination, R^2.

13.2 State the interpretation of $\hat{\beta}_1$, the estimated coefficient of promotion expenses, of Exercise 13.1.

13.3 The following artificial data are designed to illustrate the effect of correlated and uncorrelated independent variables:

y:	17	21	26	22	27	25	28	34	29	37	38	38
x:	1	1	1	1	2	2	2	2	3	3	3	3
w:	1	2	3	4	1	2	3	4	1	2	3	4
v:	1	1	2	2	3	3	4	4	5	5	6	6

```
Regression Statistics
Multiple R              0.855984977
R Square                0.73271028
Adjusted R Square       0.705981308
Standard Error          3.78153408
Observations                   12

ANOVA
                df      SS      MS       F     Significance F
Regression       1     392     392   27.4126  0.0004
Residual        10     143    14.3
Total           11     535

              Coefficients    Standard Error    t Stat   P-value
Intercept         14.5           2.8882         5.0204   0.0005
X                    7           1.3370         5.2357   0.0004

Regression Statistics
Multiple R              0.94621726
R Square                0.895327103
Adjusted R Square       0.856074766
Standard Error          2.645751311
Observations                   12

ANOVA
                df      SS       MS        F     Significance F
Regression       3     479    159.667   22.8095  0.0003
Residual         8      56      7
Total           11     535

              Coefficients    Standard Error    t Stat   P-value
Intercept         10            5.7663         1.7342   0.1211
X                  5            6.8950         0.7252   0.4890
W                  2            1.5275         1.3093   0.2268
V                  1            3.4157         0.2928   0.7771

Correlations
             Y           X          W          V
Y            1
X          0.8560        1
W          0.4019      0.0000       1
V          0.9281      0.9562     0.2619       1
```

a Plot x versus w, x versus v, and w versus v.

b Which of these plots indicate zero correlations?

13.4 Use the Excel output for the data of Exercise 13.3.

    a For both models, write the least-squares prediction equation. Locate the residual standard deviation s_ϵ.

    b Show that the multiple R^2 is larger than the r^2 of simple regression. Is the residual standard deviation smaller?

13.5 A feeder airline transports passengers from small cities to a single larger "hub" airport. A regression study tried to predict the revenue generated by each of 22 small cities, based on the distance of each city (in miles) from the hub and on the population of the small cities. The correlations and scatterplots of Figure 13.1 were obtained.

    a Are the independent variables severely collinear?

    b Do the scatterplots indicate that there may be a problem with high leverage points?

13.6 The feeder airline data were used in a multiple regression analysis using JMP. Some of the results are shown in Figure 13.2.

FIGURE 13.1 **Correlations for Airline Data**

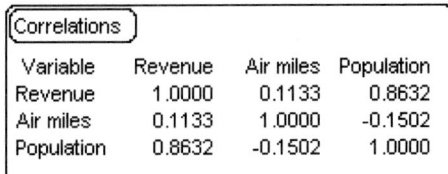

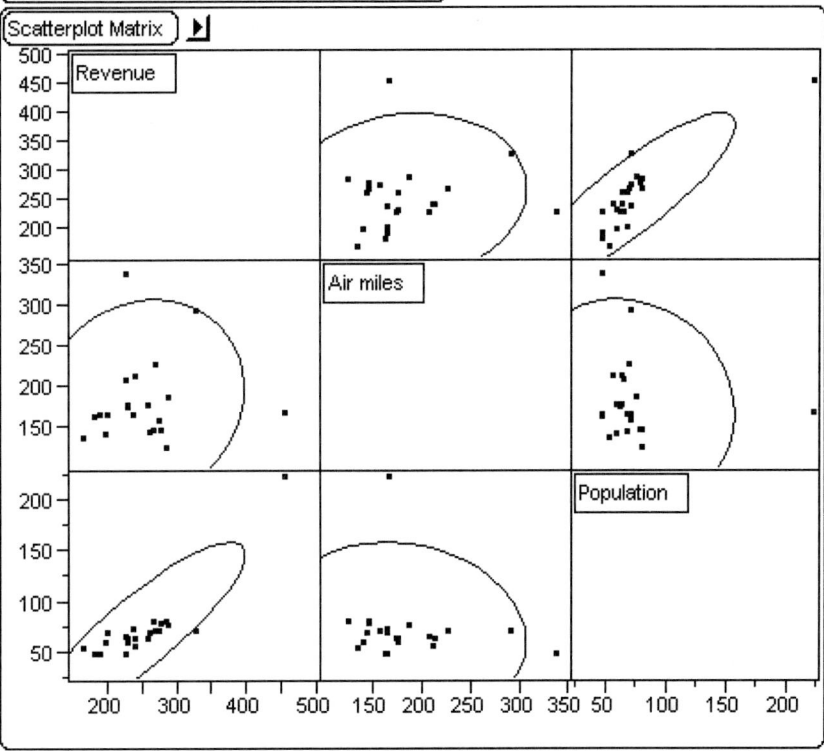

FIGURE 13.2 **Regression Results for Airline Data**

Response: Revenue

Summary of Fit

RSquare	0.805479
RSquare Adj	0.785003
Root Mean Square Error	27.7539
Mean of Response	252.5
Observations (or Sum Wgts)	22

Whole-Model Test

Analysis of Variance

Source	DF	Sum of Squares	Mean Square	F Ratio
Model	2	60602.202	30301.1	39.3378
Error	19	14635.298	770.3	Prob>F
C Total	21	75237.500		0.0000

Parameter Estimates

Term	Estimate	Std Error	t Ratio	Prob>|t|
Intercept	86.736862	27.74907	3.13	0.0056
Air miles	0.2922116	0.120336	2.43	0.0253
Population	1.5310653	0.174004	8.80	0.0000

a Without even considering the output, what sign (positive or negative) would you expect the slopes for air miles and population to have?

b Do the slopes in the output have the anticipated signs?

c State the meaning of the coefficient of air miles in the output.

13.7 In the feeder airline regression, what plus or minus should be allowed for 95% accuracy in predicting revenue for a typical route?

13.8 A chemical firm tests the yield that results from the presence of varying amounts of two catalysts. Yields are measured for five different amounts of catalyst 1 paired with four different amounts of catalyst 2. A second-order model is fit to approximate the anticipated nonlinear relation. The variables are y = yield, x_1 = amount of catalyst 1, x_2 = amount of catalyst 2, $x_3 = x_1^2$, $x_4 = x_1 x_2$, and $x_5 = x_2^2$. The data are analyzed by a standard computer package (Execustat). Selected output is as follows:

Correlation Analysis

	Cat1	Cat2	Yield
Cat1		0.0000	-0.7424
Cat2	0.0000		-0.1931
Yield	-0.7424	-0.1931	

The table shows estimated product-moment correlation

Multiple Regression Analysis

Dependent variable: Yield

Table of Estimates

	Estimate	Standard Error	t Value	P Value
Constant	50.0195	4.3905	11.39	0.0000
Cat1	6.64357	2.01212	3.30	0.0052
Cat2	7.3145	2.73977	2.67	0.0183
@Cat1Sq	-1.23143	0.301968	-4.08	0.0011
@Cat1Cat2	-0.7724	0.319573	-2.42	0.0299
@Cat2Sq	-1.1755	0.50529	-2.33	0.0355

R-squared = 86.24%
Adjusted R-squared = 81.33%
Standard error of estimation = 2.25973
Durbin-Watson statistic = 2.3601
Mean absolute error = 1.61843

Analysis of Variance

Source	Sum of Squares	D.F.	Mean Square	F-Ratio	P Value
Model	448.193	5	89.6386	17.55	0.0000
Error	71.489	14	5.10636		
Total (corr.)	519.682	19			

Conditional Sums of Squares

Source	Sum of Squares	D.F.	Mean Square	F-Ratio	P Value
Cat1	286.439	1	286.439	56.09	0.0000
Cat2	19.3688	1	19.3688	3.79	0.0718
@Cat1Sq	84.9193	1	84.9193	16.63	0.0011
@Cat1Cat2	29.8301	1	29.8301	5.84	0.0299
@Cat2Sq	27.636	1	27.636	5.41	0.0355
Model	448.193	5			

a Write the estimated regression equation.

b Locate SS(Residual) and the residual standard deviation.

13.9 Refer to Exercise 13.8.

a Find the R^2 value for predicting Yield using all 5 predictors.

b According to the conditional (sequential) sum of squares, how much of the variability is accounted for by Cat1 and Cat2, without the "@" terms? ∎

Inferences in Multiple Regression

The ideas of the preceding section involve point (best guess) estimation of the regression coefficients, the standard deviation s_ϵ, and the coefficient of determination R^2. Because these estimates are based on sample data, they will be in error to some extent, and a manager should allow for that error in interpreting the model. In this section we discuss tests about the partial slope parameters in a multiple regression model.

First, we present a test of an overall null hypothesis about the partial slopes $(\beta_1, \beta_2, \ldots, \beta_k)$ in the multiple regression model. According to this hypothesis, $H_0: \beta_1 = \beta_2 = \cdots = \beta_k = 0$, none of the variables included in the multiple regression has any predictive value at all. This is the "nullest" of null hypotheses; it says that all those carefully chosen predictors are absolutely useless. The research hypothesis is a very general one—namely, H_a: At least one $\beta_j \neq 0$. This merely says that there is some predictive value somewhere in the set of predictors.

The test statistic is the F statistic of Chapter 12. To state the test, we first define the sum of squares attributable to the regression of Y on the variables $x_1, x_2, \ldots, x_k$. We designate this sum of squares as SS(Regression); it is also called SS(Model) or the explained sum of squares. It is the sum of squared differences between predicted values and the mean y value.

Definition 13.2 SS(Regression)

$$SS(\text{Regression}) = \sum (\hat{y}_i - \overline{y})^2$$

$$SS(\text{Total}) = \sum (y_i - \overline{y})^2$$

$$= SS(\text{Regression}) + SS(\text{Residual}) \quad ∎$$

Unlike SS(Total) and SS(Residual), we don't interpret SS(Regression) in terms of prediction error. Rather, it measures the extent to which the predictions $\hat{y}_i$ vary as the x's vary. If SS(Regression) = 0, the predicted y values ($\hat{y}$) are all the same. In such a case, information about the x's is useless in predicting y. If SS(Regression) is large relative to SS(Residual), the indication is that there is real predictive value in the independent variables $x_1, x_2, \ldots, x_k$. We state the test statistic in terms of mean squares rather than sums of squares. As always, a mean square is a sum of squares divided by the appropriate d.f.

Definition 13.3 F Test of $H_0: \beta_1 = \beta_2 = \cdots = \beta_k = 0$

$H_0: \quad \beta_1 = \beta_2 = \cdots = \beta_k = 0$

$H_a: \quad$ At least one $\beta \neq 0$.

$$\text{T.S.:} \quad F = \frac{SS(\text{Regression})/k}{SS(\text{Residual})/[n - (k + 1)]} = \frac{MS(\text{Regression})}{MS(\text{Residual})}$$

R.R: With d.f.$_1 = k$ and d.f.$_2 = n - (k + 1)$, reject H_0 if $F > F_\alpha$. ∎

EXAMPLE 13.9

a   Locate SS(Regression) in the computer output of Example 13.8, reproduced here.

b   Locate the F statistic.

c   Can we safely conclude that the independent variables x_1 and x_2 together have at least some predictive power?

```
MTB > regress c1 on 2 vars c2 c3

The regression equation is
y = 39.0 + 0.983 x1 + 0.333 x2


Predictor      Coef      Stdev     t-ratio      p
Constant     39.000      1.256      31.05     0.000
x1           0.9833     0.1538       6.39     0.001
x2           0.3333     0.3076       1.08     0.320


s = 3.768      R-sq = 87.5%    R-sq(adj) = 83.3%

Analysis of Variance

SOURCE       DF        SS          MS        F        p
Regression    2      596.83      298.42    21.02    0.002
Error         6       85.17       14.19
Total         8      682.00
```

Solution

a   SS(Regression) is shown in the Analysis of Variance section of the output as 596.83.

b   The MS(Regression) and MS(Residual) values are also shown there. MS(Residual) is labeled as MS(Error), a common alternative name.

$$F = \frac{MS(\text{Regression})}{MS(\text{Residual})} = \frac{298.42}{14.19} = 21.02$$

c   For d.f.$_1 = 2$, d.f.$_2 = 6$, and $\alpha = .01$, the tabled F value is 10.92. Therefore, we have strong evidence (p-value well below .01—shown as .002) to reject the null hypothesis and conclude that the x's collectively have at least some predictive value. ∎

This F test may also be stated in terms of R^2. Recall that $R^2_{y \cdot x_1 \cdots x_k}$ measures the reduction in squared error for y attributed to knowledge of all the x predictors. Because the regression of y on the x's accounts for a proportion $R^2_{y \cdot x_1 \cdots x_k}$ of the total squared error in y,

$$SS(\text{Regression}) = R^2_{y \cdot x_1 \cdots x_k} SS(\text{Total})$$

The remaining fraction, $1 - R^2$, is incorporated in the residual squared error:

$$SS(\text{Residual}) = (1 - R^2_{y \cdot x_1 \cdots x_k}) SS(\text{Total})$$

F and R^2

The overall F test statistic can be rewritten as

$$F = \frac{MS(\text{Regression})}{MS(\text{Residual})} = \frac{R^2_{y \cdot x_1 \cdots x_k}/k}{(1 - R^2_{y \cdot x_1 \cdots x_k})/[n - (k+1)]}$$

This statistic is to be compared with tabulated F values for d.f.$_1 = k$ and d.f.$_2 = n - (k+1)$.

EXAMPLE 13.10

A large city bank studies the relation of average account size in each of its branches to per capita income in the corresponding zip code area, number of business accounts, and number of competitive bank branches. The data are analyzed by Statistix, as shown here:

CORRELATIONS (PEARSON)

	ACCTSIZE	BUSIN	COMPET
BUSIN	-0.6934		
COMPET	0.8196	-0.6527	
INCOME	0.4526	0.1492	0.5571

UNWEIGHTED LEAST SQUARES LINEAR REGRESSION OF ACCTSIZE

PREDICTOR VARIABLES	COEFFICIENT	STD ERROR	STUDENT'S T	P	VIF
CONSTANT	0.15085	0.73776	0.20	0.8404	
BUSIN	-0.00288	8.894E-04	-3.24	0.0048	5.2
COMPET	-0.00759	0.05810	-0.13	0.8975	7.4
INCOME	0.26528	0.10127	2.62	0.0179	4.3

R-SQUARED	0.7973	RESID. MEAN SQUARE (MSE)	0.03968
ADJUSTED R-SQUARED	0.7615	STANDARD DEVIATION	0.19920

SOURCE	DF	SS	MS	F	P
REGRESSION	3	2.65376	0.88458	22.29	0.0000
RESIDUAL	17	0.67461	0.03968		
TOTAL	20	3.32838			

a Identify the multiple regression prediction equation.

b Use the R^2 value shown to test $H_0: \beta_1 = \beta_2 = \beta_3 = 0$. (*Note: n = 21.*)

Solution

a From the output, the multiple regression forecasting equation is

$$\hat{y} = 0.15085 - 0.00288x_1 - 0.00759x_2 + 0.26528x_3$$

b The test procedure based on R^2 is

H_0: $\beta_1 = \beta_2 = \beta_3 = 0$

H_a: At least one β_j differs from zero.

$$\text{T.S.:} \quad F = \frac{R^2_{y \cdot x_1 x_2 x_3}/3}{(1 - R^2_{y \cdot x_1 x_2 x_3})/(21 - 4)}$$

$$= \frac{.7973/3}{.2027/17} = 22.29$$

R.R.: For d.f.$_1$ = 3 and d.f.$_2$ = 17, the critical .05 value of F is 3.20.

Because the computed F statistic, 22.29, is greater than 3.20, we reject H_0 and conclude that one or more of the x values has some predictive power. This also follows because the p-value, shown as .0000, is (much) less than .05. Note that the F value we compute is the same as that shown in the output. ∎

Rejection of the null hypothesis of this F test is not an overwhelmingly impressive conclusion. This rejection merely indicates that there is good evidence of *some* degree of predictive value *somewhere* among the independent variables. It does not give any direct indication of how strong the relation is, nor any indication of which individual independent variables are useful. The next task, therefore, is to make inferences about the individual partial slopes.

To make these inferences, we need the estimated standard error of each partial slope. As always, the standard error for any estimate based on sample data indicates how accurate that estimate should be. These standard errors are computed and shown by most regression computer programs. They depend on three things: the residual standard deviation, the amount of variation in the predictor variable, and the degree of correlation between that predictor and the others. The expression that we present for the standard error is useful in considering the effect of collinearity (correlated independent variables), but it is *not* a particularly good way to do the computation. Let a computer program do the arithmetic.

Definition 13.4   Estimated Standard Error of $\hat{\beta}_j$ in a Multiple Regression

$$s_{\hat{\beta}_j} = s_\epsilon \sqrt{\frac{1}{\sum(x_{ij} - \bar{x}_j)^2 (1 - R^2_{x_j \cdot x_1 \cdots x_{j-1} x_{j+1} \cdots x_k})}}$$

where $R^2_{x_j \cdot x_1 \cdots x_{j-1} x_{j+1} \cdots x_k}$ is the R^2 value obtained by letting x_j be the *dependent* variable in a multiple regression, with all other x's independent variables. Note that s_ϵ is the residual standard deviation for the multiple regression of y on $x_1, x_2, \ldots, x_k$. ∎

Just as in simple regression, the larger the residual standard deviation, the larger the uncertainty in estimating coefficients. Also, the less variability there is in the predictor, the larger is the standard error of the coefficient. The most important use of the formula for
effect of collinearity | estimated standard error is to illustrate the **effect of collinearity**. If the independent variable x_j is highly collinear with one or more other independent variables, $R^2_{x_j \cdot x_1 \cdots x_{j-1} x_{j+1} \cdots x_k}$ is by definition very large and $1 - R^2_{x_j \cdot x_1 \cdots x_{j-1} x_{j+1} \cdots x_k}$ is near zero. Division by a near-zero number yields a very large standard error. Thus, one important effect of severe collinearity is that it results in very large standard errors of partial slopes and therefore very inaccurate estimates of those slopes.

variance inflation factor | The term $1/(1 - R^2_{x_j \cdot x_1 \cdots x_{j-1} x_{j+1} \cdots x_k})$ is called the **variance inflation factor** (VIF). It measures how much the variance (square of the standard error) of a coefficient is increased because of collinearity. This factor is printed out by some computer packages and is helpful in assessing how serious the collinearity problem is. If the VIF is 1, there is no collinearity at all. If it is very large, such as 10 or more, collinearity is a serious problem.

A large standard error for any estimated partial slope indicates a large probable error for the estimate. The partial slope $\hat{\beta}_j$ of x_j estimates the effect of increasing x_j by one unit while all other x's remain constant. If x_j is highly collinear with other x's, when x_j increases, the other x's also vary rather than staying constant. Therefore, it is difficult to estimate β_j, and its probable error is large when x_j is severely collinear with other independent variables.

The standard error of each estimated partial slope $\hat{\beta}_j$ is used in a confidence interval and statistical test for β_j. The confidence interval follows the familiar format of estimate plus or minus (table value)(estimated standard error). The table value is the t table with the error d.f., $n - (k + 1)$.

Definition 13.5 Confidence Interval for β_j

$$\hat{\beta}_j - t_{\alpha/2}s_{\hat{\beta}_j} \leq \beta_j \leq \hat{\beta}_j + t_{\alpha/2}s_{\hat{\beta}_j}$$

where $t_{\alpha/2}$ cuts off area $\alpha/2$ in the tail of a t distribution with d.f. $= n - (k + 1)$, the error d.f. ∎

E X A M P L E   1 3 . 1 1

Calculate a 95% confidence interval for β_1 in the two-predictor model for the data of Example 13.4. Relevant output follows:

```
. regress y  x1 x2
```

y	Coef.	Std. Err.	t	P>|t|	[95% Conf. Interval]	
x1	1	1.870829	0.535	0.646	-7.049526	9.049526
x2	3	4.1833	0.717	0.548	-14.99929	20.99929
_cons	10	1.183216	8.452	0.014	4.909033	15.09097

Solution

$\hat{\beta}_1$ is 1.00 and the standard error is shown as 1.870829. The t value that cuts off an area of .025 in a t distribution with d.f. $= n - (k + 1) = 5 - (2 + 1) = 2$ is 4.303. The confidence interval is $1.00 - 4.303(1.870829) \leq \beta_1 \leq 1.00 + 4.303(1.870829)$, or $-7.050 \leq \beta_1 \leq 9.050$. The output shows this interval to more decimal places. ∎

E X A M P L E   1 3 . 1 2

Locate the estimated partial slope for x_2 and its standard error in the output of Example 13.9. Calculate a 90% confidence interval for β_2.

```
MTB > regress 'y' on 2 vars 'x1' 'x2'
```

The regression equation is
y = 39.0 + 0.983 x1 + 0.333 x2

Predictor	Coef	Stdev	t-ratio	p
Constant	39.000	1.256	31.05	0.000
x1	0.9833	0.1538	6.39	0.001
x2	0.3333	0.3076	1.08	0.320

Solution

$\hat{\beta}_2$ is .3333 with standard error (labeled Stdev) .3076. The tabled t value is 1.943 [tail area .05, $9 - (2 + 1) = 6$ d.f.]. The desired interval is $.3333 - 1.943(.3076) \leq \beta_2 \leq .3333 + 1.943(.3076)$, or $-.2644 \leq \beta_2 \leq .9310$. ∎

interpretation of
$H_0: \beta_j = 0$

last predictor in

The usual null hypothesis for inference about β_j is $H_0: \beta_j = 0$. This hypothesis does not assert that x_j has no predictive value by itself. It asserts that it has no *additional* predictive value over and above that contributed by the other independent variables; that is, if all other x's had already been used in a regression model and then x_j was added last, the prediction would not improve. We call $H_0: \beta_j = 0$, meaning that x_j has no additional predictive value, the **last predictor in**. The t test of this H_0 is summarized next.

Definition 13.6 Summary for Testing $H_0: \beta_j = 0$

$$H_0: \quad \beta_j = 0$$

$$H_a: \quad 1.\ \beta_j > 0$$
$$2.\ \beta_j < 0$$
$$3.\ \beta_j \neq 0$$

$$\text{T.S.:} \quad t = \hat{\beta}_j / s_{\hat{\beta}_j}$$

$$\text{R.R.:} \quad 1.\ t > t_\alpha$$
$$2.\ t < -t_\alpha$$
$$3.\ |t| > t_{\alpha/2}$$

where t_α cuts off a right-tail area a in the t distribution with d.f. $= n - (k + 1)$. This test statistic is shown by virtually all multiple regression programs. ∎

EXAMPLE 13.13

a   Use the information given in Example 13.11 to test $H_0: \beta_1 = 0$ at $\alpha = .05$. Use a two-sided alternative.

b   Is the conclusion of the test compatible with the confidence interval?

Solution

a   The test statistic for $H_0: \beta = 0$ versus $H_a: \beta_1 \neq 0$ is $t = \hat{\beta}_1 / s_{\hat{\beta}_1} = 1.00/1.871 = .535$. Because the .025 point for the t distribution with $5 - (2 + 1) = 2$ d.f. is 4.303, H_0 must be retained; x_1 has not been shown to have any additional predictive power in the presence of the other independent variable x_2.

b   The 95% confidence interval includes zero, which also indicates that $H_0: \beta_1 = 0$ must be retained at $\alpha = .05$, two-tailed. ∎

EXAMPLE 13.14

Locate the t statistic for testing $H_0: \beta_2 = 0$ in the output of Example 13.12. Can $H_a: \beta_2 > 0$ be supported at any of the usual α levels?

Solution

The t statistics are shown under the heading t–ratio. For x_2 the t statistic is 1.08. The t table value for 6 d.f. and $\alpha = .10$ is 1.440, so H_0 cannot be rejected even at $\alpha = .10$. Alternatively, the p-value is .320, larger than $\alpha = .10$, so again H_0 can't be rejected. ∎

The multiple regression F and t tests that we discuss in this chapter test different null hypotheses. It sometimes happens that the F test results in the rejection of $H_0: \beta_1 = \beta_2 = \cdots = \beta_k = 0$, while no t test of $H_0: \beta_j = 0$ is significant. In such a case, we can conclude that there is predictive value in the equation as a whole, but we cannot identify the specific variables that have predictive value. Remember that each t test is testing last-predictor-in value. Does this variable add predictive value, given all the other predictors, wherever they are listed? When two or more predictor variables are highly correlated among themselves, it often happens that no x_j can be shown to have significant "last-in" predictive value, even though the x's together have been shown to be useful. If we are trying to predict housing sales based on gross domestic product and disposable income, we probably can't prove that GDP adds value given DI, or that DI adds value given GDP. Whichever predictor we take last may not add more than random predictive value.

EXERCISES

13.10 Refer to the computer output of Exercise 13.1. Here it is again.

```
. regress Sales Promo Devel Research

    Source |       SS       df       MS              Number of obs =      24
-----------+------------------------------          F( 3,   20) =   22.28
     Model | 43901.7677     3  14633.9226            Prob > F      = 0.0000
  Residual | 13136.2323    20  656.811614            R-square      = 0.7697
-----------+------------------------------          Adj R-square  = 0.7351
     Total |    57038.00    23  2479.91304           Root MSE      = 25.628

------------------------------------------------------------------------------
     Sales |     Coef.  Std. Err.      t    P>|t|   [95% Conf. Interval]
-----------+------------------------------------------------------------------
     Promo |  136.0983  28.10759    4.842   0.000   77.46689    194.7297
     Devel | -61.17526  50.94102   -1.201   0.244  -167.4364    45.08585
  Research | -43.69508  48.32298   -0.904   0.377  -144.495     57.10489
     _cons |  326.3893  241.6129    1.351   0.192  -177.6063    830.3849
------------------------------------------------------------------------------
```

   a Locate the F statistic.

   b Can the hypothesis of no overall predictive value be rejected at $\alpha = .01$?

   c Locate the t statistic for the coefficient of promotion $\hat{\beta}_1$.

   d Test the research hypothesis that $\beta_1 \neq 0$. Use $\alpha = .05$.

   e State the conclusion of the test in part d.

13.11 Locate the p-value for the test of the previous exercise, part d. Is it one-tailed or two-tailed?

13.12 Summarize the results of the t tests in Exercise 13.10. What null hypotheses are being tested?

13.13 Here is Minitab output for the data of Exercise 13.3:

```
MTB > Regress 'Y' 3 'X' 'W' 'V'.

The regression equation is
Y = 10.0 + 5.00 X + 2.00 W + 1.00 V
```

```
Predictor      Coef     Stdev    t-ratio       p
Constant     10.000     5.766      1.73    0.121
X             5.000     6.895      0.73    0.489
W             2.000     1.528      1.31    0.227
V             1.000     3.416      0.29    0.777


s = 2.646     R-sq = 89.5%     R-sq(adj) = 85.6%
Analysis of Variance

SOURCE        DF        SS        MS        F        p
Regression     3     479.00    159.67    22.81    0.000
Error          8      56.00      7.00
Total         11     535.00


SOURCE        DF     SEQ SS
X              1     392.00
W              1      86.40
V              1       0.60
```

a Locate MS(Regression) and MS(Residual).

b What is the value of the F statistic?

c Determine the p-value for the F test.

d What conclusion can be established from the F test?

e Calculate a 95% confidence interval for the true coefficient of X.

13.14 In Exercise 13.6, we considered predicting revenue from each origin as a function of population and air miles to the hub airport. JMP output is shown again in Figure 13.3. Is there a clear indication that the two independent variables together have at least some value in predicting revenue?

13.15 In the feeder airline regression, is there strong evidence that each independent variable is adding predictive value, given the other?

13.16 Use the feeder airline output in Figure 13.3 to calculate 90% confidence intervals for the two partial slopes. The relevant degrees of freedom are those shown for Error in the output.

13.17 A metalworking firm conducts an energy study using multiple regression methods. The dependent variable is $Y =$ energy consumption cost per day (in thousands of dollars), and the independent variables are $x_1 =$ tons of metal processed in the day, $x_2 =$ average external temperature $-60°F$ (a union contract requires cooling of the plant whenever outside temperatures reach $60°$), $x_3 =$ rated wattage for machinery in use, and $x_4 = x_1 x_2$. The data are analyzed by Statistix. Selected output is shown here:

```
CORRELATIONS (PEARSON)

          ENERGY    METAL    METXTEMP    TEMP
METAL     0.6128
METXTEMP  0.4929   0.1094
TEMP      0.4007  -0.0606    0.9831
WATTS     0.5775   0.2239    0.3630    0.3529

UNWEIGHTED LEAST SQUARES LINEAR REGRESSION OF ENERGY

PREDICTOR
VARIABLES   COEFFICIENT   STD ERROR   STUDENT'S T      P      VIF

CONSTANT      7.20439     17.5322        0.41       0.6855
METAL         1.36291      0.92438       1.47       0.1559    8.8
TEMP          0.30588      1.62104       0.19       0.8522  250.0
WATTS         0.01024      0.00473       2.16       0.0427    1.5
METXTEMP     -0.00277      0.07722      -0.04       0.9717  246.4

R-SQUARED              0.6636    RESID. MEAN SQUARE (MSE)    6.51555
ADJUSTED R-SQUARED    0.5963    STANDARD DEVIATION          2.55255
```

FIGURE 13.3 **Regression Results for Airline Data**

Response: Revenue

Summary of Fit

RSquare	0.805479
RSquare Adj	0.785003
Root Mean Square Error	27.7539
Mean of Response	252.5
Observations (or Sum Wgts)	22

Whole-Model Test ▶

Analysis of Variance

Source	DF	Sum of Squares	Mean Square	F Ratio
Model	2	60602.202	30301.1	39.3378
Error	19	14635.298	770.3	Prob>F
C Total	21	75237.500		0.0000

Parameter Estimates

Term	Estimate	Std Error	t Ratio	Prob>|t|
Intercept	86.736862	27.74907	3.13	0.0056
Air miles	0.2922116	0.120336	2.43	0.0253
Population	1.5310653	0.174004	8.80	0.0000

SOURCE	DF	SS	MS	F	P
REGRESSION	4	257.048	64.2622	9.86	0.0001
RESIDUAL	20	130.311	6.51555		
TOTAL	24	387.360			

CASES INCLUDED 25   MISSING CASES 0

a Write the estimated model.

b Summarize the results of the various t tests.

c Calculate a 95% confidence interval for the coefficient of METXTEMP.

d What does the VIF column of the output indicate about collinearity problems? ■

13.4

F test for several β_j's

Testing a Subset of the Regression Coefficients

In the last section, we presented an F test for testing *all* the coefficients in a regression model and a t test for testing *one* coefficient. Another F test of the null hypothesis tests that *several* of the true coefficients are zero—that is, that several of the predictors have no value given the others. For example, if we try to predict the prevailing wage rate in various geographical areas for clerical workers based on the national minimum wage, national inflation rate, population density in the area, and median apartment rental price in the area, we might well want to test if the variables related to area (density and apartment price) added anything, given the national variables.

A null hypothesis for this situation would say that the true coefficients of density and apartment price were zero. According to this null hypothesis, these two independent variables together have no predictive value once minimum wage and inflation are included as predictors. The t test of the preceding section tests a single coefficient on a last-predictor-in basis. Now we are testing predictors on a last-two-predictors-in basis.

The idea is to compare the SS(Regression) or R^2 values when density and apartment price are excluded and when they are included in the prediction equation. When they are included, the R^2 is automatically at least as large as the R^2 when they are excluded because we can predict at least as well with more information as with less. Similarly, SS(Regression) will be larger for the complete model. The F test for this null hypothesis tests whether the gain is more than could be expected by chance alone. In general, let k be the total number of predictors, and let g be the number of predictors with coefficients not hypothesized to be zero ($g < k$). Then $k - g$ represents the number of predictors with coefficients that are hypothesized to be zero. The idea is to find SS(Regression) or R^2 values using all predictors (the **complete model**) and using only the g predictors that do not appear in the null hypothesis (the **reduced model**). Once these have been computed, the test proceeds as outlined next. The notation is easier if we assume that the reduced model contains $\beta_1, \beta_2, \ldots, \beta_g$, so that the variables in the null hypothesis are listed last.

Definition 13.7 *F* **Test of a Subset of Predictors**

$$H_0: \quad \beta_{g+1} = \beta_{g+2} = \cdots = \beta_k = 0$$

$$H_a: \quad H_0 \text{ is not true.}$$

$$\text{T.S.:} \quad F = \frac{(R^2_{\text{complete}} - R^2_{\text{reduced}})/(k-g)}{(1 - R^2_{\text{complete}})/[n - (k+1)]}$$

R.R.: $F > F_\alpha$, where F_α cuts off a right-tail of area α of the F distribution with $\text{d.f.}_1 = (k - g)$ and $\text{d.f.}_2 = [n - (k+1)]$.

Note: This test may also be performed with SS(Regression, complete) − SS(Regression, reduced) replacing $(R^2_{\text{complete}} - R^2_{\text{reduced}})$ and SS(Residual, complete) replacing $(1 - R^2_{\text{complete}})$. ■

E X A M P L E   1 3 . 1 5

A state fisheries commission wants to estimate the number of bass caught in a given lake during a season in order to restock the lake with the appropriate number of young fish. The commission could get a fairly accurate assessment of the seasonal catch by extensive "netting sweeps" of the lake before and after a season, but this technique is much too expensive to be done routinely. Therefore, the commission samples a number of lakes and records y, the seasonal catch (thousands of bass per square mile of lake area); x_1, the number of lakeshore residences per square mile of lake area; x_2, the size of the lake in square miles; $x_3 = 1$ if the lake has public access, 0 if not; and x_4, a structure index. (Structures are weed beds, sunken trees, drop-offs, and other living places for bass.) The data are

y	x_1	x_2	x_3	x_4
3.6	92.2	.21	0	81
.8	86.7	.30	0	26
2.5	80.2	.31	0	52
2.9	87.2	.40	0	64
1.4	64.9	.44	0	40
.9	90.1	.56	0	22
3.2	60.7	.78	0	80
2.7	50.9	1.21	0	60
2.2	86.1	.34	1	30
5.9	90.0	.40	1	90
3.3	80.4	.52	1	74
2.9	75.0	.66	1	50
3.6	70.0	.78	1	61
2.4	64.6	.91	1	40
.9	50.0	1.10	1	22
2.0	50.0	1.24	1	50
1.9	51.2	1.47	1	37
3.1	40.1	2.21	1	61
2.6	45.0	2.46	1	39
3.4	50.0	2.80	1	53

The commission is convinced that x_1 and x_2 are important variables in predicting y because they both reflect how intensively the lake has been fished. There is some question as to whether x_3 and x_4 are useful as additional predictor variables. Therefore, regression models (with all x's entering linearly) are run with and without x_3 and x_4. Relevant portions of the Minitab output follow:

```
MTB > regress 'catch' on 4 variables 'residenc' 'size' 'access' 'structur'
The regression equation is
catch = - 1.94 + 0.0193 residenc + 0.332 size + 0.836 access
              + 0.0477 structur


Predictor       Coef        Stdev      t-ratio        p
Constant      -1.9378      0.9081       -2.13      0.050
residenc      0.01929      0.01018       1.90      0.077
size           0.3323      0.2458        1.35      0.196
access         0.8355      0.2250        3.71      0.002
structur     0.047714    0.005056        9.44      0.000


s = 0.4336      R-sq = 88.2%      R-sq(adj) = 85.0%


Analysis of Variance


SOURCE        DF          SS          MS          F          p
Regression     4      21.0474      5.2619      27.98      0.000
Error         15       2.8206      0.1880
Total         19      23.8680


SOURCE        DF       SEQ SS
residenc       1       0.2780
size           1       1.5667
access         1       2.4579
structur       1      16.7448


MTB > regress 'catch' on 2 vars 'residenc' 'size'


The regression equation is
catch = - 0.11 + 0.0310 residenc + 0.679 size


Predictor       Coef        Stdev      t-ratio        p
Constant       -0.107       2.336       -0.05      0.964
residenc      0.03102      0.02650       1.17      0.258
size           0.6794      0.6178        1.10      0.287


s = 1.138      R-sq = 7.7%      R-sq(adj) = 0.0%


Analysis of Variance


SOURCE        DF          SS          MS          F          p
Regression     2       1.845       0.922       0.71      0.505
Error         17      22.023       1.295
Total         19      23.868
```

a   Write the complete and reduced models.

b Write the null hypothesis for testing that the omitted variables have no (incremental) predictive value.

c Perform an F test for this null hypothesis.

Solution

a The complete and reduced models are, respectively,

$$Y_i = \beta_0 + \beta_1 x_{i1} + \beta_2 x_{i2} + \beta_3 x_{i3} + \beta_4 x_{i4} + \epsilon_i$$

and

$$Y_i = \beta_0 + \beta_1 x_{i1} + \beta_2 x_{i2} + \epsilon_i$$

The corresponding multiple regression forecasting equations based on the sample data are

$$\text{Complete: } \hat{y} = -1.94 + .0193x_1 + .332x_2 + .836x_3 + .477x_4$$

$$\text{Reduced: } \hat{y} = -.11 + .0310x_1 + .679x_2$$

b The appropriate null hypothesis of no predictive power for x_3 and x_4 is $H_0: \beta_3 = \beta_4 = 0$

c The test statistic for the H_0 of part b makes use of $R^2_{\text{complete}} = .882$, $R^2_{\text{reduced}} = .077$, $k = 4$, $g = 2$, and $n = 20$:

$$\text{T.S.} : F = \frac{(R^2_{\text{complete}} - R^2_{\text{reduced}})/(4-2)}{[1 - R^2_{\text{complete}}/(20-5)]} = \frac{(.882 - .077)/2}{(1 - .882)/15} = 51.165$$

Alternatively, we can use the SS(Regression) values shown:

$$\text{T.S.} : F = \frac{[\text{SS(Regression, complete)} - \text{SS(Regression, reduced)}]/(4-2)}{\text{SS(Residual, complete)}/(20-5)}$$

$$= \frac{(21.0474 - 1.845)/2}{2.8206/15} = 51.059$$

which gives the same result except for round-off error. The tabled value $F_{.01}$ for 2 and 15 d.f. is 6.36. The actual value of 51.something is much larger than the tabled value, so we have conclusive evidence that the Access and Structur variables add predictive value. ■

EXERCISES

13.18 The output for Exercise 13.1 is shown here.

a Locate the R^2 value. Use it to confirm the calculation of the F statistic.

b Can we conclude that there is at least some more than random predictive value among the independent variables?

```
. regress Sales Promo Devel Research

    Source |       SS       df       MS              Number of obs =      24
-----------+------------------------------           F( 3,   20) =    22.28
     Model | 43901.7677        3  14633.9226         Prob > F      =  0.0000
  Residual | 13136.2323       20  656.811614         R-square      =  0.7697
-----------+------------------------------           Adj R-square  =  0.7351
     Total |   57038.00       23  2479.91304         Root MSE      =  25.628
```

```
-----------------------------------------------------------------
Sales |    Coef.   Std. Err.    t     P>|t|  [95% Conf. Interval]
---------+-------------------------------------------------------
   Promo |  136.0983  28.10759   4.842  0.000  77.46689   194.7297
   Devel |  -61.17526 50.94102  -1.201  0.244 -167.4364   45.08585
Research | -43.69508  48.32298  -0.904  0.377 -144.495    57.10489
   _cons |  326.3893  241.6129   1.351  0.192 -177.6063   830.3849
-----------------------------------------------------------------
```

13.19 Another regression analysis of the data of Exercise 13.18 used only development expenditures as an independent variable. The output is as follows:

```
. regress Sales Promo

  Source |     SS       df       MS          Number of obs =      24
---------+------------------------------      F( 1,    22) =   50.80
   Model | 39800.7248    1  39800.7248       Prob > F      =  0.0000
Residual | 17237.2752   22  783.512509       R-square      =  0.6978
---------+------------------------------      Adj R-square  =  0.6841
   Total |   57038.00   23  2479.91304       Root MSE      =  27.991

-----------------------------------------------------------------
Sales |    Coef.   Std. Err.    t     P>|t|  [95% Conf. Interval]
---------+-------------------------------------------------------
   Promo |  78.24931  10.97888   7.127  0.000  55.48051   101.0181
   _cons | -.6490769  44.58506  -0.015  0.989 -93.11283   91.81468
-----------------------------------------------------------------
```

a Locate R^2 for this reduced model. Use this value and the R^2 for the complete model to calculate an F statistic to test the null hypothesis that the other slopes are 0.

b Carry out the steps of an F test using $\alpha = .01$.

c Can we conclude that there is at least some more than random predictive value among the omitted independent variables?

13.20 Two models based on the data of Example (not Exercise) 13.10 were calculated, with the following results:

```
CORRELATIONS (PEARSON)

          ACCTSIZE   BUSIN    COMPET
BUSIN     -0.6934
COMPET     0.8196  -0.6527
INCOME     0.4526   0.1492   0.5571

CASES INCLUDED 21   MISSING CASES 0

(Model 1)
UNWEIGHTED LEAST SQUARES LINEAR REGRESSION OF ACCTSIZE

PREDICTOR
VARIABLES    COEFFICIENT   STD ERROR    STUDENT'S T      P       VIF

CONSTANT       0.15085      0.73776        0.20       0.8404
BUSIN         -0.00288     8.894E-04      -3.24       0.0048     5.2
COMPET        -0.00759      0.05810       -0.13       0.8975     7.4
INCOME         0.26528      0.10127        2.62       0.0179     4.3

R-SQUARED             0.7973    RESID. MEAN SQUARE (MSE)    0.03968
ADJUSTED R-SQUARED    0.7615    STANDARD DEVIATION          0.19920

SOURCE       DF       SS         MS         F        P

REGRESSION    3     2.65376    0.88458    22.29    0.0000
RESIDUAL     17     0.67461    0.03968
TOTAL        20     3.32838
```

```
(Model 2)
UNWEIGHTED LEAST SQUARES LINEAR REGRESSION OF ACCTSIZE

PREDICTOR
VARIABLES    COEFFICIENT    STD ERROR    STUDENT'S T      P

CONSTANT       0.12407       0.96768        0.13        0.8993
INCOME         0.20191       0.09125        2.21        0.0394

R-SQUARED              0.2049    RESID. MEAN SQUARE (MSE)    0.13928
ADJUSTED R-SQUARED     0.1630    STANDARD DEVIATION          0.37321

SOURCE        DF      SS           MS         F       P

REGRESSION     1    0.68192     0.68192     4.90    0.0394
RESIDUAL      19    2.64645     0.13928
TOTAL         20    3.32838

CASES INCLUDED 21   MISSING CASES 0
```

a Locate R^2 for the reduced model, with INCOME as the only predictor.

b Locate R^2 for the complete model.

c Calculate the F statistic based on the incremental R^2. State what null hypothesis is being tested, and state the conclusion.

13.21 Recalculate the F statistic in the previous exercise, based on the sums of squares shown in the output.

13.22 An automobile financing company uses a rather complex credit rating system for car loans. The questionnaire requires substantial time to fill out, taking sales staff time and risking alienating the customer. The company decides to see if three variables (Age, Monthly family income, and Debt payments as a fraction of income) will reproduce the credit score reasonably accurately. Data were obtained on a sample (with no evident biases) of 500 applications. The complicated rating score was calculated and served as the dependent variable in a multiple regression. Some results from JMP are shown in Figure 13.4.

a How much of the variation in ratings is accounted for by the three predictors?

b Use this number to verify the computation of the overall F statistic.

c Does the F test clearly show that the three independent variables have predictive value for the rating score?

13.23 The credit rating data were reanalyzed, using only the monthly income variable as a predictor. JMP results are shown in Figure 13.5.

a By how much has the regression sum of squares been reduced by eliminating age and debt percentage as predictors?

b Do these variables add statistically significant (at normal α levels) predictive value, once income is given?

13.24 The chemical data of Exercise 13.8 were analyzed both with and without squared and product terms. Here's the output, from Execustat:

Multiple Regression Analysis

Dependent variable: Yield

Table of Estimates

	Estimate	Standard Error	t Value	P Value
Constant	50.0195	4.3905	11.39	0.0000
Cat1	6.64357	2.01212	3.30	0.0052
Cat2	7.3145	2.73977	2.67	0.0183
@Cat1Sq	-1.23143	0.301968	-4.08	0.0011

FIGURE 13.4 **Regression Results for Credit Rating Data**

Response: Rating score

Summary of Fit

RSquare	0.979566
RSquare Adj	0.979443
Root Mean Square Error	2.023398
Mean of Response	65.044
Observations (or Sum Wgts)	500

Parameter Estimates

Term	Estimate	Std Error	t Ratio	Prob>|t|
Intercept	54.657197	0.634791	86.10	0.0000
Age	0.0056098	0.011586	0.48	0.6285
Monthly income	0.0100597	0.000157	64.13	0.0000
Debt fraction	-39.95239	0.883684	-45.21	0.0000

Effect Test

Source	Nparm	DF	Sum of Squares	F Ratio	Prob>F
Age	1	1	0.960	0.2344	0.6285
Monthly income	1	1	16835.195	4112.023	0.0000
Debt fraction	1	1	8368.627	2044.05	0.0000

Whole-Model Test ■

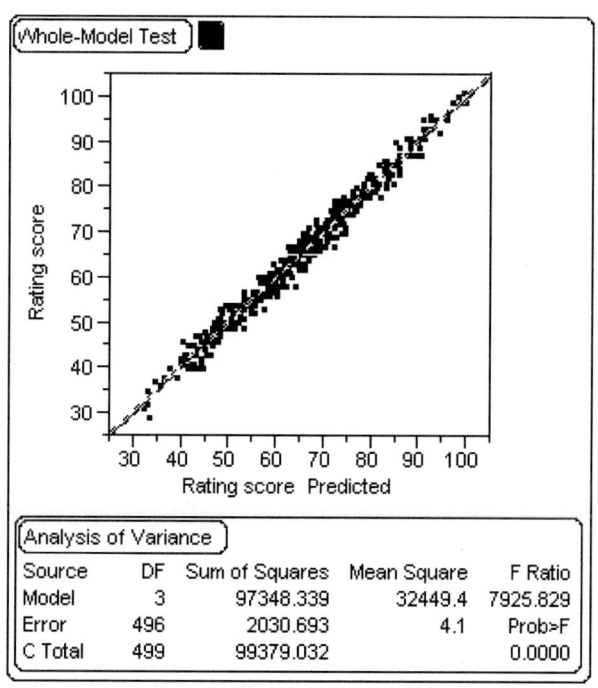

Analysis of Variance

Source	DF	Sum of Squares	Mean Square	F Ratio
Model	3	97348.339	32449.4	7925.829
Error	496	2030.693	4.1	Prob>F
C Total	499	99379.032		0.0000

```
        @Cat1Cat2      -0.7724     0.319573        -2.42     0.0299
        @Cat2Sq        -1.1755     0.50529         -2.33     0.0355

        R-squared = 86.24%
        Adjusted R-squared = 81.33%
        Standard error of estimation = 2.25973

                           Analysis of Variance

                    Sum of                                        P
        Source      Squares     D.F.    Mean Square    F-Ratio   Value
        Model       448.193      5       89.6386        17.55    0.0000
        Error        71.489     14        5.10636
```

FIGURE 13.5 **Regression Using Only Income Data**

Response: Rating score

Summary of Fit

RSquare	0.895261
RSquare Adj	0.895051
Root Mean Square Error	4.571792
Mean of Response	65.044
Observations (or Sum Wgts)	500

Lack of Fit

Parameter Estimates

Term	Estimate	Std Error	t Ratio	Prob>|t|
Intercept	30.152827	0.572537	52.67	0.0000
Monthly income	0.0135544	0.000208	65.24	0.0000

Total (corr.) 519.682   19

Conditional Sums of Squares

Source	Sum of Squares	D.F.	Mean Square	F-Ratio	P Value
Cat1	286.439	1	286.439	56.09	0.0000
Cat2	19.3688	1	19.3688	3.79	0.0718
@Cat1Sq	84.9193	1	84.9193	16.63	0.0011
@Cat1Cat2	29.8301	1	29.8301	5.84	0.0299
@Cat2Sq	27.636	1	27.636	5.41	0.0355
Model	448.193	5			

Multiple Regression Analysis

Dependent variable: Yield

Table of Estimates

	Estimate	Standard Error	t Value	P Value
Constant	70.31	2.57001	27.36	0.0000
Cat1	-2.676	0.560822	-4.77	0.0002
Cat2	-0.8802	0.70939	-1.24	0.2315

R-squared = 58.85%
Adjusted R-squared = 54.00%
Standard error of estimation = 3.54695

Analysis of Variance

Source	Sum of Squares	D.F.	Mean Square	F-Ratio	P Value
Model	305.808	2	152.904	12.15	0.0005
Error	213.874	17	12.5808		
Total (corr.)	519.682	19			

a Write the estimated complete model.

b Write the estimated reduced model.

c Locate the R^2 values for the complete and reduced models.

d Is there convincing evidence that the addition of the second-order terms improves the predictive ability of the model? ■

Forecasting Using Multiple Regression

O ne of the major uses for multiple regression models is in forecasting a y value given certain values of the independent x variables. The best guess forecast is easy; just substitute the assumed x values into the estimated regression equation. In this section, we discuss the relevant standard errors.

As in simple regression, the forecast of y for given x values can be interpreted two ways. The resulting value can, first, be thought of as the best guess for $E(Y)$, the long-run average y value that results from averaging infinitely many observations of y when the x's have the specified values. The alternative, and usually more interesting, interpretation is that this is the predicted y value for *one* individual case having the given x values. The standard errors for both interpretations require matrix algebra ideas that aren't required for this text.

Computer programs typically give a standard error for an individual y forecast. Athough this information can also be used to find a standard error for estimating $E(Y)$, the individual y forecast is usually more relevant. In most computer outputs, a forecast interval for the mean value is called a *confidence interval*; a forecast interval for an individual value is called a *prediction interval*. The appropriate plus or minus term for forecasting can be found by multiplying the standard error by a tabled t value with d.f. $= n - (k + 1)$. In fact, many computer programs give the plus or minus term directly. As a rough approximation, we can use $\pm 2s_\epsilon$ as an allowance for forecast error of an individual prediction.

E X A M P L E   1 3 . 1 6

An advertising manager for a manufacturer of prepared cereals wants to develop an equation to predict sales (s) based on advertising expenditures for children's television (c), daytime television (d), and newspapers (n). Data were collected monthly for the previous 30 months (and divided by a price index to control for inflation). A multiple regression is fit, yielding the following computer output:

```
MTB > regress c1 3 c2-c4;
SUBC> predict at 31 5 12.


The regression equation is
s = 0.053 + 0.00562 c + 0.0184 d - 0.00600 n


Predictor       Coef       Stdev     t-ratio        p
Constant      0.0526      0.1374        0.38    0.705
c          0.005618    0.002930        1.92    0.066
d           0.01841     0.01211        1.52    0.141
n          -0.005996    0.004362       -1.37    0.181


s = 0.04736     R-sq = 30.8%     R-sq(adj) = 22.9%
```

```
Analysis of Variance

SOURCE       DF        SS          MS          F        p
Regression    3    0.026003    0.008668      3.86    0.021
Error        26    0.058317    0.002243
Total        29    0.084320


SOURCE       DF      SEQ SS
c             1     0.000330
d             1     0.021434
n             1     0.004238


    Fit   Stdev.Fit        95% C.I.          95% P.I.
 0.24686    0.01998   (0.20579,0.28794)  (0.14118,0.35255)
```

a   Write the regression equation.

b   Locate the predicted y value ($\hat{y}$) when $c = 31$, $d = 5$, and $n = 12$. Locate the lower and upper limits for a 95% confidence interval for $E(Y)$ and the upper and lower 95% prediction limits for an individual Y value.

Solution

a   The column labeled Coef yields the equation

$$\hat{y} = .0526 + .005618c + .01841d - .005996n$$

b   The predicted y value is shown as Fit. As can be verified by substituting $c = 31$, $d = 5$, and $n = 12$ into the equation, the predicted y is 0.24686. The 95% confidence limits for the mean $E(Y)$ are shown in the 95% C.I. part of the output as 0.20579 to 0.28794, whereas the wider prediction limits for an individual y value are 0.14118 to 0.35255.   ∎

extrapolation in multiple regression

   The notion of extrapolation is more subtle in multiple regression than in simple linear regression. In simple regression, extrapolation occurred when we tried to predict Y using an x value that was well beyond the range of the data. In multiple regression, we must be concerned not only about the range of each individual predictor but also about the set of values of several predictors together. It might well be reasonable to use multiple regression to predict the salary of a 30-year-old middle manager or the salary of a middle manager with 25 years of experience, but it would *not* be reasonable to use regression to predict the salary of a 30-year-old middle manager with 25 years of experience! Extrapolation depends not only on the range of each separate x_j predictor used to develop the regression equation but also on the correlations among the x_j values. In the salary prediction example, obviously age and experience will be positively correlated, so the combination of a low age and high amount of experience wouldn't occur in the data. When making forecasts using multiple regression, we must consider not only whether each independent variable value is reasonable by itself, but also whether the chosen combination of predictor values is reasonable.

E X A M P L E   1 3 . 1 7

The state fisheries commission hoped to use the data of Example 13.15 to predict the catch at a lake with 8 residences per square mile, size .7 square mile, 1 public access, and structure index 55, and also for another lake with values 55, 1.0, 1, and 40. The following Minitab output was obtained:

```
MTB > regress 'catch' on 4 variables 'residenc' 'size' 'access' 'structur';
SUBC> predict at 8 .7 1 55;
SUBC> predict at 55 1.0 1 40.


The regression equation is
catch = - 1.94 + 0.0193 residenc + 0.332 size + 0.836 access
        + 0.0477 structur
```

Predictor	Coef	Stdev	t-ratio	p
Constant	-1.9378	0.9081	-2.13	0.050
residenc	0.01929	0.01018	1.90	0.077
size	0.3323	0.2458	1.35	0.196
access	0.8355	0.2250	3.71	0.002
structur	0.047714	0.005056	9.44	0.000

```
s = 0.4336    R-sq = 88.2%    R-sq(adj) = 85.0%
```

Fit	Stdev.Fit	95% C.I.	95% P.I.	
1.9090	0.6812	(0.4567, 3.3613)	(0.1874, 3.6306)	XX
2.1998	0.1850	(1.8054, 2.5941)	(1.1947, 3.2049)	

```
X  denotes a row with X values away from the center
XX denotes a row with very extreme X values
```

Locate the 95% prediction intervals for the two lakes. Why is the first interval so much wider than the second?

Solution

The prediction intervals are the respective 95% P.I. values, 0.1874 to 3.6306 for the first lake and 1.1947 to 3.2049 for the second. The first interval carries a warning that the X values are "very extreme." If we check back with the data, we find that no lake was even close to 8 residences per square mile. Thus, the prediction is a severe extrapolation, which makes the interval very wide. In this case, the problem is with one predictor; the remaining x values are well within the range of the data. ∎

EXERCISES

13.25 A prediction was made based on the data of Exercise 13.3. Recall that x varied from 1 to 3, w from 1 to 4, and v from 1 to 6. Here is relevant Minitab output:

```
MTB > Correlation 'y' 'x' 'w' 'v'.
```

	y	x	w
x	0.856		
w	0.402	0.000	
v	0.928	0.956	0.262

```
MTB > Regress 'y' 3 'x' 'w' 'v';
SUBC>    Predict at x 3 w 1 v 6.
```

```
The regression equation is
y = 10.0 + 5.00 x + 2.00 w + 1.00 v

s = 2.646      R-sq = 89.5%    R-sq(adj) = 85.6%

   Fit  Stdev.Fit       95% C.I.            95% P.I.
 33.000     4.077   ( 23.595,  42.405) ( 21.788,  44.212) XX

X  denotes a row with X values away from the center
XX denotes a row with very extreme X values
```

Locate the 95% prediction interval. Explain why Minitab gave the "very extreme X values" warning.

13.26 Refer to the chemical firm data of Exercise 13.8. Predicted yields for $x_1 = 3.5$ and $x_2 = 0.35$ (observation 21) and also for $x_1 = 3.5$ and $x_2 = 2.5$ (observation 22) are calculated based on models with and without second-order terms. Execustat output follows:

```
                 Multiple Regression Analysis

Dependent variable: Yield

                    Table of Estimates

                                 Standard        t        P
                    Estimate       Error      Value    Value
   Constant        50.0195       4.3905       11.39   0.0000
   Cat1             6.64357      2.01212       3.30   0.0052
   Cat2             7.3145       2.73977       2.67   0.0183
   @Cat1Sq         -1.23143      0.301968     -4.08   0.0011
   @Cat1Cat2       -0.7724       0.319573     -2.42   0.0299
   @Cat2Sq         -1.1755       0.50529      -2.33   0.0355

R-squared = 86.24%
Adjusted R-squared = 81.33%
Standard error of estimation = 2.25973


           Table of Predicted Values (Missing Data Only)

                        95.00%               95.00%
            Predicted  Prediction Limits   Confidence Limits
   Row        Yield   Lower      Upper     Lower      Upper

   21        59.926   54.7081   65.1439   57.993    61.8589
   22        62.3679  57.0829   67.6529   60.2605   64.4753


                 Multiple Regression Analysis

Dependent variable: Yield

                    Table of Estimates

                                 Standard        t        P
                    Estimate       Error      Value    Value

   Constant        70.31         2.57001      27.36   0.0000
   Cat1            -2.676        0.560822     -4.77   0.0002
   Cat2            -0.8802       0.70939      -1.24   0.2315

R-squared = 58.85%
Adjusted R-squared = 54.00%
Standard error of estimation = 3.54695
```

Table of Predicted Values (Missing Data Only)

| | | 95.00% Prediction Limits | | 95.00% Confidence Limits | |
Row	Predicted Yield	Lower	Upper	Lower	Upper
21	57.8633	50.028	65.6986	55.5416	60.185
22	58.7435	51.0525	66.4345	56.9687	60.5183

a Locate the 95% limits for individual prediction in the model $\hat{y} = 50.0195 + 6.6436x_1 + 7.3145x_2 - 1.2314x_1^2 - 0.7724x_1x_2 - 1.1755x_2^2$.

b Locate the 95% limits for individual prediction in the model $\hat{y} = 70.3100 - 2.6760x_1 - 0.8802x_2$.

c Are the limits for the model of part a much tighter than those for the model of part b? ■

13.6 Summing Up

H ere are some reminders about multiple regression concepts:

1 Regression coefficients in a first-order model (one not containing transformed values, such as squares of a variable or product terms) should be interpreted as partial slopes—the predicted change in a dependent variable when an independent variable is increased by one unit, while other variables are held constant.

2 Correlations are important, not only between an independent variable and the dependent variable, but also between independent variables. Collinearity—correlation between independent variables—implies that regression coefficients will change as variables are added to or deleted from a regression model.

3 The effectiveness of a regression model can be indicated not only by the R^2 value but also by the residual standard deviation. It's often helpful to use that standard deviation to see roughly how much of a plus or minus must be allowed around a prediction.

4 As always, the various statistical tests in a regression model only indicate how strong the evidence is that the apparent pattern is more than random. They don't directly indicate how good a predictive model is. In particular, a large overall F statistic may merely indicate a weak prediction in a large sample.

5 A t test in a multiple regression assesses whether that independent variable adds predictive value as the last predictor included in the model. It is quite possible that several variables may not add a statistically detectable amount of predicted value when each is added last; yet, deleting all of them from the model causes a serious drop in predictive value. Especially when there is severe collinearity, being added second to last is quite different from being added last.

6 The variance inflation factor (VIF) is a useful indicator of the overall impact of collinearity in estimating the coefficient of an independent variable. The higher the VIF number, the more serious the impact of collinearity on the accuracy of a slope estimate.

7 Extrapolation in multiple regression can be subtle. A new set of X values may not be unreasonable when considered one by one, but the combination of values may be far outside the range of previous data.

In addition, you may want to reread the summary of key ideas at the beginning of the chapter.

13.27 A study of demand for imported subcompact cars incorporates data from 12 metropolitan areas. The variables are

Demand: Imported subcompact car sales as a percentage of total sales
Educ: Average number of years of schooling completed by adults
Income: Per capita income
Popn: Area population
Famsize: Average size of intact families

Minitab output is as follows:

```
MTB > Regress 'Demand' 4 'Educ' 'Income' 'Popn' 'Famsize'.

The regression equation is
Demand = - 1.3 + 5.55 Educ + 0.89 Income + 1.92 Popn - 11.4 Famsize

Predictor      Coef      Stdev     t-ratio      p
Constant      -1.32      57.98      -0.02      0.982
Educ           5.550      2.702      2.05       0.079
Income         0.885      1.308      0.68       0.520
Popn           1.925      1.371      1.40       0.203
Famsize      -11.389      6.669      -1.71      0.131

s = 2.686      R-sq = 96.2%      R-sq(adj) = 94.1%

Analysis of Variance

SOURCE          DF        SS         MS        F         p
Regression      4      1295.70     323.93     44.89     0.000
Error           7        50.51       7.22
Total          11      1346.22

SOURCE          DF      SEQ SS
Educ            1      1239.95
Income          1        32.85
Popn            1         1.86
Famsize         1        21.04

Unusual Observations
Obs.    Educ     Demand      Fit  Stdev.Fit  Residual  St.Resid
  9      9.3     13.100    9.760     2.149     3.340     2.07R

R denotes an obs. with a large st. resid.
```

a Write the regression equation. Place the standard error of each coefficient below the coefficient, perhaps in parentheses.

b Locate R^2 and the residual standard deviation.

c The Unusual Observations entry in the output indicates that observation 9 had a value 2.07 standard deviations away from the predicted Fit value. Does this indicate that observation 9 is a very serious outlier?

13.28 Summarize the conclusions of the F test and the various t tests in the output of Exercise 13.27.

13.29 Another analysis of the data of Exercise 13.27 uses only Educ and Famsize to predict Demand. The output is as follows:

```
MTB > Regress 'Demand' 2 'Educ'  'Famsize'.

The regression equation is
Demand = - 19.2 + 7.79 Educ - 9.46 Famsize
```

```
Predictor      Coef     Stdev    t-ratio      p
Constant     -19.17     45.87     -0.42    0.686
Educ           7.793     2.490      3.13    0.012
Famsize       -9.464     5.207     -1.82    0.103

s = 2.939      R-sq = 94.2%    R-sq(adj) = 92.9%

Analysis of Variance

SOURCE        DF        SS         MS        F        p
Regression     2    1268.48     634.24    73.43    0.000
Error          9      77.73       8.64
Total         11    1346.22
```

a Locate the R^2 value for this reduced model.

b Test the null hypothesis that the true coefficients of Income and Popn are zero. Use $\alpha = .05$. What is the conclusion?

13.30 One of the functions of bank branch offices is to arrange profitable loans to small businesses and individuals. As part of a study of the effectiveness of branch managers, a bank collected data from a sample of branches on current total loan volumes (the dependent variable), the total deposits held in accounts opened at that branch, the number of such accounts, the average number of daily transactions, and the number of employees at the branch. Correlations and a scatterplot matrix are shown in Figure 13.6.

FIGURE 13.6 **Correlations and Scatterplot Matrix for Bank Branch Data**

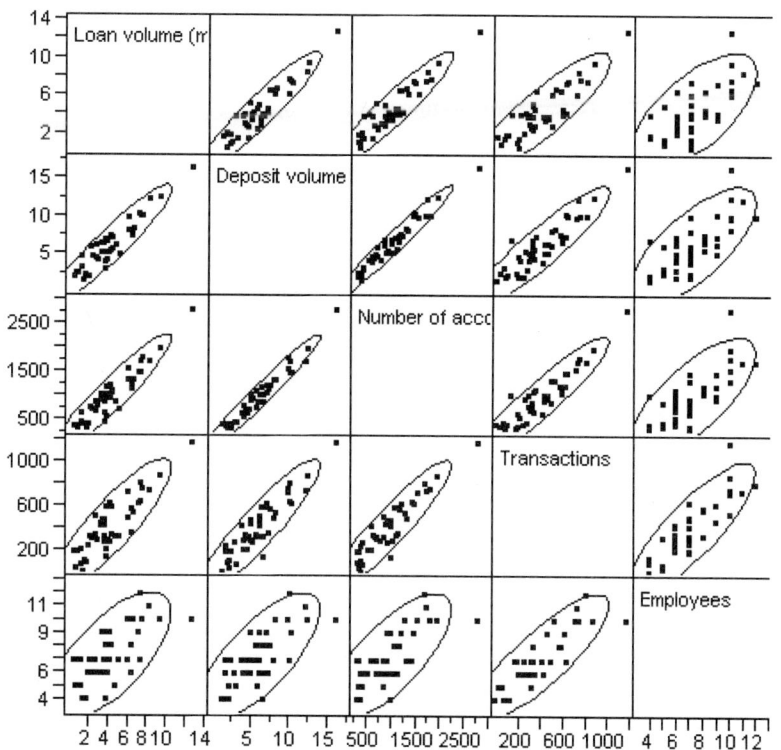

Correlations					
Variable	Loan volume (millions)	Deposit volume (millions)	Number of accounts	Transactions	Employees
Loan volume (millions)	1.0000	0.9369	0.9403	0.8766	0.6810
Deposit volume (millions)	0.9369	1.0000	0.9755	0.9144	0.7377
Number of accounts	0.9403	0.9755	1.0000	0.9299	0.7487
Transactions	0.8766	0.9144	0.9299	1.0000	0.8463
Employees	0.6810	0.7377	0.7487	0.8463	1.0000

a Which independent variable is the best predictor of loan volume?

b Is there a substantial collinearity problem?

c Do any points seem extremely influential?

13.31 A regression model was created for the bank branch office data using JMP. Some of the results are shown in Figure 13.7.

a Use the R^2 value shown to compute an overall F statistic. Is there clear evidence that there is predictive value in the model, using $\alpha = .01$?

b Which individual predictors have been shown to have "last-in" predictive value, again using $\alpha = .01$?

c Explain the apparent contradiction between your answers to the first two parts.

13.32 Another multiple regression model used only deposit volume and number of accounts as independent variables, with results as shown in Figure 13.8.

a Does omitting the transactions and employees variables seriously reduce R^2?

b Use the R^2 values to test the null hypothesis that the coefficients of transactions and employees are 0. What is your conclusion?

13.33 The manager of documentation for a computer software firm wants to forecast the time required to document moderate-size computer programs. Records are available for 26 programs. The variables are $y =$ number of writer-days needed, $x_1 =$ number of subprograms, $x_2 =$ average number of lines per subprogram, $x_3 = x_1 x_2$, $x_4 = x_2^2$, and $x_5 = x_1 x_2^2$. A portion of the output from a regression analysis of the data is shown here:

Multiple Regression Analysis

Dependent variable: Y

Table of Estimates

	Estimate	Standard Error	t Value	P Value
Constant	-16.8198	11.631	-1.45	0.1636
X1	1.47019	0.365944	4.02	0.0007
X2	0.994778	0.611441	1.63	0.1194
@X1X2	-0.0240071	0.0237565	-1.01	0.3243
@X2Sq	-0.01031	0.007374	-1.40	0.1774
@X1X2Sq	0.000249574	0.000351779	0.71	0.4862

R-squared = 91.72%

FIGURE 13.7 **Regression Results for Bank Branch Data**

Response: Loan volume (millions)

Summary of Fit

RSquare	0.894477
RSquare Adj	0.883369
Root Mean Square Error	0.870612
Mean of Response	4.383395
Observations (or Sum Wgts)	43

Parameter Estimates

Term	Estimate	Std Error	t Ratio	Prob>|t|
Intercept	0.2284381	0.6752	0.34	0.7370
Deposit volume (millions)	0.3222099	0.191048	1.69	0.0999
Number of accounts	0.0025812	0.001314	1.96	0.0569
Transactions	0.0010058	0.001878	0.54	0.5954
Employees	-0.119898	0.130721	-0.92	0.3648

FIGURE 13.8 **Regression with Two Predictors for Bank Branch Data**

Response: Loan volume (millions)

```
Summary of Fit
RSquare                        0.892138
RSquare Adj                    0.886744
Root Mean Square Error         0.857923
Mean of Response               4.383395
Observations (or Sum Wgts)           43
```

```
Parameter Estimates
```

Term	Estimate	Std Error	t Ratio	Prob>|t|
Intercept	-0.324812	0.290321	-1.12	0.2699
Deposit volume (millions)	0.3227636	0.187509	1.72	0.0929
Number of accounts	0.002684	0.001166	2.30	0.0266

```
Adjusted R-squared = 89.65%
Standard error of estimation = 3.39011
Durbin-Watson statistic = 2.12676
Mean absolute error = 2.4127
```

Analysis of Variance

Source	Sum of Squares	D.F.	Mean Square	F-Ratio	P Value
Model	2546.03	5	509.205	44.31	0.0000
Error	229.857	20	11.4929		
Total (corr.)	2775.88	25			

a Write the multiple regression model and locate the residual standard deviation.

b Does x_3 have a statistically significant predictive value as "last predictor in"?

13.34 The model $Y = \beta_0 + \beta_1 x_1 + \beta_2 x_2 + \epsilon$ is fit to the data of Exercise 13.33. Selected output is shown here:

Multiple Regression Analysis

Dependent variable: Y

Table of Estimates

	Estimate	Standard Error	t Value	P Value
Constant	0.840085	3.43375	0.24	0.8089
X1	1.01583	0.0792925	12.81	0.0000
X2	0.0558262	0.0515066	1.08	0.2897

```
R-squared = 90.64%
Adjusted R-squared = 89.83%
Standard error of estimation = 3.36066
Durbin-Watson statistic = 2.2053
Mean absolute error = 2.57584
```

Analysis of Variance

Source	Sum of Squares	D.F.	Mean Square	F-Ratio	P Value
Model	2516.12	2	1258.06	111.39	0.0000
Error	259.763	23	11.294		
Total (corr.)	2775.88	25			

a Write the complete and reduced-form estimated models.

b Is the improvement in R^2 obtained by adding x_3, x_4, and x_5 statistically significant at $\alpha = .05$? Approximately what is the p-value for this test?

13.35 A chain of small convenience food stores performs a regression analysis to explain variation in sales volume among 16 stores. The variables in the study are

Sales: Average daily sales volume of a store, in thousands of dollars
Size: Floor space in thousands of square feet
Parking: Number of free parking spaces adjacent to the store
Income: Estimated per household income of the zip code area of the store

Output from a regression program (StataQuest) is shown here:

```
. regress Sales  Size Parking Income

  Source |     SS        df        MS            Number of obs =      16
---------+-------------------------------        F(  3,     12) =   15.16
   Model | 27.1296056     3  9.04320188          Prob > F      =  0.0002
Residual |  7.15923792   12   .59660316          R-square      =  0.7912
---------+-------------------------------        Adj R-square  =  0.7390
   Total | 34.2888436    15  2.2859229           Root MSE      =  .7724


   Sales |    Coef.   Std. Err.    t      P>|t|    [95% Conf. Interval]
---------+-----------------------------------------------------------------
    Size | 2.547936  1.200827   2.122   0.055    -.0684405    5.164313
 Parking |  .2202793  .1553877  1.418   0.182    -.1182814     .5588401
  Income |  .5893221  .1780576  3.310   0.006     .2013679     .9772763
   _cons |  .872716  1.945615   0.449   0.662    -3.366415    5.111847
```

```
. correlate  Sales Size Parking Income
(obs=16)

         |   Sales    Size  Parking  Income
---------+------------------------------------
   Sales |  1.0000
    Size |  0.7415  1.0000
 Parking |  0.6568  0.6565  1.0000
  Income |  0.7148  0.4033  0.3241  1.0000
```

a Write the regression equation. Indicate the standard errors of the coefficients.

b Carefully interpret each coefficient.

c Locate R^2 and the residual standard deviation.

d Is there a severe collinearity problem in this study?

13.36 Summarize the results of the F and t tests for the output of Exercise 13.35.

13.37 A producer of various feed additives for cattle conducts a study of the number of days of feedlot time required to bring beef cattle to market weight. Eighteen steers of essentially identical age and weight are purchased and brought to a feedlot. Each steer is fed a diet with a specific combination of protein content, antibiotic concentration, and percentage of feed supplement. The data are

STEER:	1	2	3	4	5	6	7	8	9
PROTEIN:	10	10	10	10	10	10	15	15	15
ANTIBIO:	1	1	1	2	2	2	1	1	1
SUPPLEM:	3	5	7	3	5	7	3	5	7
TIME:	88	82	81	82	83	75	80	80	75

STEER:	10	11	12	13	14	15	16	17	18
PROTEIN:	15	15	15	20	20	20	20	20	20
ANTIBIO:	2	2	2	1	1	1	2	2	2
SUPPLEM:	3	5	7	3	5	7	3	5	7
TIME:	77	76	72	79	74	75	74	70	69

Computer output from a Systat regression analysis follows:

CORRELATIONS (PEARSON)

```
             TIME      PROTEIN   ANTIBIO
PROTEIN   -0.7111
ANTIBIO   -0.4180     0.0000
SUPPLEM   -0.4693     0.0000    -0.0000
```

CASES INCLUDED 18   MISSING CASES 0

UNWEIGHTED LEAST SQUARES LINEAR REGRESSION OF TIME

```
PREDICTOR
VARIABLES    COEFFICIENT    STD ERROR    STUDENT'S T      P        VIF

CONSTANT       102.708       2.31037       44.46       0.0000
PROTEIN        -0.83333      0.09870       -8.44       0.0000     1.0
ANTIBIO        -4.00000      0.80589       -4.96       0.0002     1.0
SUPPLEM        -1.37500      0.24675       -5.57       0.0001     1.0

R-SQUARED           0.9007    RESID. MEAN SQUARE (MSE)    2.92261
ADJUSTED R-SQUARED  0.8794    STANDARD DEVIATION          1.70956

SOURCE       DF     SS         MS        F       P

REGRESSION    3   371.083    123.694    42.32   0.0000
RESIDUAL     14    40.9166     2.92261
TOTAL        17   412.000
```

PREDICTED/FITTED VALUES OF TIME

```
LOWER PREDICTED BOUND     73.566     LOWER FITTED BOUND      76.469
PREDICTED VALUE           77.333     FITTED VALUE            77.333
UPPER PREDICTED BOUND     81.100     UPPER FITTED BOUND      78.197
SE (PREDICTED VALUE)       1.7564    SE (FITTED VALUE)        0.4029

UNUSUALNESS (LEVERAGE)     0.0556
PERCENT COVERAGE          95.0
CORRESPONDING T            2.14
```

PREDICTOR VALUES: PROTEIN = 15.000, ANTIBIO = 1.5000, SUPPLEM = 5.0000

a Write the regression equation.

b Find the standard deviation.

c Find the R^2 value.

d How much of a collinearity problem is there with these data?

13.38 Refer to Exercise 13.37.

a Predict the feedlot time required for a steer fed 15% protein, 1.5% antibiotic concentration, and 5% supplement.

b Do these values of the independent variables represent a major extrapolation from the data?

c Give a 95% confidence interval for the mean time predicted in part a.

13.39 The data of Exercise 13.37 are also analyzed by a regression model using only protein content as an independent variable, with the following output:

```
UNWEIGHTED LEAST SQUARES LINEAR REGRESSION OF TIME

PREDICTOR
VARIABLES     COEFFICIENT    STD ERROR     STUDENT'S T      P

CONSTANT       89.8333        3.20219       28.05         0.0000
PROTEIN        -0.83333       0.20598       -4.05         0.0009

R-SQUARED            0.5057    RESID. MEAN SQUARE (MSE)    12.7291
ADJUSTED R-SQUARED   0.4748    STANDARD DEVIATION          3.56779

SOURCE        DF      SS          MS        F       P

REGRESSION     1    208.333    208.333    16.37    0.0009
RESIDUAL      16    203.666     12.7291
TOTAL         17    412.000
```

a Write the regression equation.   **b** Find the R^2 value.

c Test the null hypothesis that the coefficients of ANTIBIO and SUPPLEM are zero at $\alpha = .05$.

13.40 A sex discrimination suit alleges that a small college discriminated against women faculty in terms of salaries. A regression study considers the following variables:

Salary:	Base salary per year (thousands of dollars)
Senior:	Seniority at the college (in years)
Sex:	1 for men, 0 for women
RankD1:	1 for full professors, 0 for others
RankD2:	1 for associate professors, 0 for others
RankD3:	1 for assistant professors, 0 for others
Doct:	1 for holders of doctorate, 0 for others

Note that lecturers and instructors have value 0 for all 3 RankD variables. Computer output (Excel) from the study is shown here:

	A	B	C	D	E	F
1						
2	Regression Statistics					
3						
4	Multiple R	0.9716				
5	R Square	0.944				
6	Adjusted R Square	0.9294				
7	Standard Error	2.3375				
8	Observations	30				
9						
10						
11	ANOVA					
12		df	SS	MS	F	Significance F
13	Regression	6	2119.347	353.225	64.646	0.000
14	Residual	23	125.672	5.464		
15	Total	29	2245.019			
16						
17						
18		Coefficients	Standard Error	t Stat	P-value	
19	Intercept	18.6784	1.3788	13.5470	0.0000	
20	Senior	0.5420	0.0762	7.1176	0.0000	
21	Sex	1.2074	0.0649	1.1339	0.2685	
22	RankD1	8.7779	1.9380	4.5293	0.0002	
23	RankdD2	4.4211	1.7797	2.4842	0.0207	
24	RankD3	2.7165	1.4239	1.9079	0.0690	
25	Doct	0.9225	1.2589	0.7328	0.4711	

a Write the regression equation.

b What is the interpretation of the coefficient of Sex?

c What is the interpretation of the coefficient of RankD1?

13.41 Refer to Exercise 13.40.

a Test the hypothesis that the true coefficient of Sex is positive. Use $\alpha = .05$.

b What does the conclusion of this test indicate about allegations of discrimination?

13.42 **a** Locate the value of the F statistic in Exercise 13.40.

b What null hypothesis is being tested by this statistic?

c Is this null hypothesis rejected at $\alpha = .01$? How plausible is this null hypothesis?

13.43 Another regression model of the data of Exercise 13.40 omits Sex and Doct from the list of independent variables. The output is as follows:

Regression Statistics

Multiple R	0.9697
R Square	0.9403
Adjusted R Square	0.9307
Standard Error	2.3160
Observations	30

ANOVA

	df	SS	MS	F	Significance F
Regression	4	2110.925	527.731	98.389	0.0000
Residual	25	134.093	5.364		
Total	29	2245.019			

	Coefficients	Standard Error	t Stat	P-value
Intercept	19.7113	1.0776	18.2913	0.0000
Senior	0.5572	0.0744	7.4893	0.0000
RankD1	9.2414	1.8214	5.0738	0.0000
RankD2	5.1050	1.5875	3.2158	0.0036
RankD3	3.2243	1.3204	2.4418	0.0220

a Locate R^2 for this reduced model.

b Test the null hypothesis that the true coefficients of Sex and Doct are zero. Use $\alpha = .01$.

13.44 A survey of information systems managers was used to predict the yearly salary of beginning programmer/analysts in a metropolitan area. Managers specified their standard salary for a beginning programmer/analyst, the number of employees in the firm's information processing staff, the firm's gross profit margin in cents per dollar of sales, and the firm's information processing cost as a percentage of total administrative costs. The data are stored in the EX1344.DAT file on the data disk, with salary in column 1, number of employees in column 2, profit margin in column 3, and information processing cost in column 4.

a Obtain a multiple regression equation with salary as the dependent variable and the other three variables as predictors. Interpret each of the (partial) slope coefficients.

b Is there conclusive evidence that the three predictors together have at least some value in predicting salary? Locate a p-value for the appropriate test.

c Which of the independent variables, if any, have statistically detectable ($\alpha = .05$) predictive value as the last predictor in the equation?

13.45 **a** Locate the coefficient of determination (R^2) for the regression model in Exercise 13.44.

b Obtain another regression model with number of employees as the only independent variable. Find the coefficient of determination for this model.

c By hand, test the null hypothesis that adding profit margin and information processing cost does not yield any additional predictive value, given the information about number of employees. Use $\alpha = .10$. What can you conclude from this test?

13.46 Obtain correlations for all pairs of predictor variables in Exercise 13.44. Does there seem to be a major collinearity problem in the data?

13.47 A government agency pays research contractors a fee to cover overhead costs, over and above the direct costs of a research project. Although the overhead cost varies considerably among contracts, it is usually a substantial share of the total contract cost. An agency task force obtained data on overhead cost as a fraction of direct costs, number of employees of the contractor, size of contract as a percentage of the contractor's yearly income, and personnel costs as a percentage of direct cost. These four variables are stored (in the order given) in the EX1347.DAT file on the data disk.

a Obtain correlations of all pairs of variables. Is there a severe collinearity problem with the data?

b Plot overhead cost against each of the other variables. Locate a possible high influence outlier.

c Obtain a regression equation (Overhead cost as dependent variable) using all the data including any potential outlier.

d Delete the potential outlier and get a revised regression equation. How much did the slopes change?

13.48 Consider the outlier-deleted regression model of Exercise 13.47.

a Locate the F statistic. What null hypothesis is being tested? What can we conclude based on the F statistic?

b Locate the t statistic for each independent variable. What conclusions can we reach based on the t tests?

13.49 Use the outlier-deleted data of Exercise 13.47 to predict overhead cost of a contract when the contractor has 500 employees, the contract is 2.50% of the contractor's income, and personnel cost is 55% of the direct cost. Obtain a 95% prediction interval. Would an overhead cost equal to 88.9% of direct cost be unreasonable in this situation?

13.50 The owner of a rapidly growing computer store tried to explain the increase in biweekly sales of computer software, using four explanatory variables: Number of titles displayed, Display footage, Current customer base of IBM-compatible computers, and Current customer base of Apple-compatible computers. The data are stored in time-series order in the EX1350.DAT file of the data disk, with sales in column 1, titles in 2, footage in 3, IBM base in 4, and Apple base in 5.

a Before doing the calculations, consider the economics of the situation and state what sign you would expect for each of the partial slopes.

b Obtain a multiple regression equation with sales as the dependent variable and all other variables as independent. Does each partial slope have the sign you expected in part a?

c Calculate a 95% confidence interval for the coefficient of the Titles variable. The computer output should contain the calculated standard error for this coefficient. Does the interval include 0 as a plausible value?

13.51 a In the regression model of Exercise 13.50, can the null hypothesis that none of the variables has predictive value be rejected at normal α levels?

b According to t tests, which predictors, if any, add statistically detectable predictive value ($\alpha = .05$) given all the others?

13.52 Obtain correlation coefficients for all pairs of variables from the data of Exercise 13.50. How severe is the collinearity problem in the data?

13.53 Compare the coefficient of determination (R^2) for the regression model of Exercise 13.50 to the square of the correlation between sales and titles in Exercise 13.52. Compute the incremental F statistic for testing the null hypothesis that footage, IBM base, and Apple base add no predictive value given titles. Can this hypothesis be rejected at $\alpha = .01$?

13.54 The market research manager of a catalog clothing supplier has begun an investigation of what factors determine the typical order size the supplier receives from customers. From the sales records stored on the company's computer, the manager obtained average order size data for 180 zip code areas. A part-time intern looked up the latest census information on per capita income, average years of formal education, and median price of an existing house in each of these zip code areas. (The intern couldn't find house price data for two zip codes, and entered 0 for those areas.) The manager also was curious whether climate had any bearing on order size, and included data on the average daily high temperature in winter and in summer.

The market research manager has asked for your help in analyzing the data. The output provided is only intended as a first try. The manager would like to know whether there was any evidence that the temperature variables mattered much, and also which of the other variables seemed useful. There is some question about whether putting in 0 for the missing house price data was the right thing to do, or if that might distort the results. Please provide a basic, not too technical explanation of the results in this output and any other analyses you choose to perform.

```
MTB > name c1 'AvgOrder' c2 'Income' c3 'Educn' &
CONT> c4 'HousePr' c5 'WintTemp' c6 'SummTemp'
MTB > correlations of c1-c6
```

	AvgOrder	Income	Educn	HousePr	WintTemp
Income	0.205				
Educn	0.171	0.913			
HousePr	0.269	0.616	0.561		
WintTemp	-0.134	-0.098	0.014	0.066	
SummTemp	-0.068	-0.115	0.005	0.018	0.481

```
MTB > regress c1 on 5 variables in c2-c6
```

The regression equation is
AvgOrder = 36.2 + 0.078 Income − 0.019 Educn
  + 0.0605 HousePr − 0.223 WintTemp + 0.006 SummTemp

Predictor	Coef	Stdev	t-ratio	p
Constant	36.18	12.37	2.92	0.004
Income	0.0780	0.4190	0.19	0.853
Educn	-0.0189	0.5180	-0.04	0.971
HousePr	0.06049	0.02161	2.80	0.006
WintTemp	-0.2231	0.1259	-1.77	0.078
SummTemp	0.0063	0.1646	0.04	0.969

s = 4.747   R-sq = 9.6%   R-sq(adj) = 7.0%

Analysis of Variance

SOURCE	DF	SS	MS	F	p
Regression	5	417.63	83.53	3.71	0.003
Error	174	3920.31	22.53		
Total	179	4337.94			

SOURCE	DF	SEQ SS
Income	1	182.94
Educn	1	7.18
HousePr	1	142.63
WintTemp	1	84.84
SummTemp	1	0.03

Unusual Observations

Obs.	Income	AvgOrder	Fit	Stdev.Fit	Residual	St.Resid
25	17.1	23.570	36.555	0.632	-12.985	-2.76R
78	11.9	24.990	34.950	0.793	-9.960	-2.13R
83	13.4	36.750	29.136	2.610	7.614	1.92X
87	14.3	45.970	35.918	0.463	10.052	2.13R
111	11.1	21.720	33.570	0.802	-11.850	-2.53R
113	10.4	43.500	33.469	0.817	10.031	2.15R
143	16.1	20.350	27.915	3.000	-7.565	-2.06RX
149	13.2	44.970	35.369	0.604	9.601	2.04R
169	13.5	44.650	34.361	0.660	10.289	2.19R
180	13.7	23.050	34.929	0.469	-11.879	-2.51R

R denotes an obs. with a large st. resid.
X denotes an obs. whose X value gives it large influence.

∎

Multiple Regression

Engineers for a manufacturer of power tools for home use were trying to design an electric drill that didn't heat up under strenuous use. The three key design factors were insulation thickness, quality of the wire used in the motor, and size of the vents in the body of the drill. The engineers had learned a little about off-line quality control, so they designed an experiment that varied these design factors. They created 10 drills using each combination of the three design factors, split them into two lots, and tested the lots under two (supposedly equivalent) "torture tests." The temperature of each drill was measured at the end of each test; for each lot, the mean temperature and the logarithm of the variance of temperatures were computed. The engineers wanted to minimize both the mean and the logarithm of the variance.

The engineers have asked you to analyze the resulting data. They present you with the following data and explain that they included squared terms to try to capture any curves in the relation. Average temperature is avtem, logarithm of variance is logv, insulation thickness is IT, quality of wire is QW, vent size is VS, and the "2" variables are the respective squared terms. The squared terms are of the form

$$(\text{predictor} - \text{mean of predictor})^2$$

They have asked you to try to figure out which of the predictors seem to affect the mean (and by how much), which affect the variance, which squared terms seem to matter, and, finally, whether the lot number (corresponding to the type of test) is relevant. They don't know any statistical jargon, so please write your report without it.

avtem	logv	IT	QW	VS	I2	Q2	V2	Lot	avtem	logv	IT	QW	VS	I2	Q2	V2	Lot
185	3.6	2	6	10	4	1	1	1	168	3.4	4	7	11	0	0	0	2
176	3.7	2	6	10	4	1	1	2	160	2.9	4	7	12	0	0	1	1
177	3.6	2	6	11	4	1	0	1	154	3.1	4	7	12	0	0	1	2
184	3.7	2	6	11	4	1	0	2	169	2.8	4	8	10	0	1	1	1
178	3.6	2	6	12	4	1	1	1	156	2.9	4	8	10	0	1	1	2
169	3.4	2	6	12	4	1	1	2	168	2.7	4	8	11	0	1	0	1
185	3.2	2	7	10	4	0	1	1	161	2.7	4	8	11	0	1	0	2
184	3.2	2	7	10	4	0	1	2	156	2.6	4	8	12	0	1	1	1
180	3.2	2	7	11	4	0	0	1	158	2.7	4	8	12	0	1	1	2
184	3.5	2	7	11	4	0	0	2	164	3.7	5	6	10	1	1	1	1
179	3.0	2	7	12	4	0	1	1	163	3.7	5	6	10	1	1	1	2
173	3.2	2	7	12	4	0	1	2	161	3.7	5	6	11	1	1	0	1
179	2.9	2	8	10	4	1	1	1	158	3.4	5	6	11	1	1	0	2
185	2.7	2	8	10	4	1	1	2	154	3.4	5	6	12	1	1	1	1
180	2.8	2	8	11	4	1	0	1	162	3.7	5	6	12	1	1	1	2
180	2.7	2	8	11	4	1	0	2	163	2.8	5	7	10	1	0	1	1
169	2.9	2	8	12	4	1	1	1	166	3.0	5	7	10	1	0	1	2
177	2.8	2	8	12	4	1	1	2	159	3.3	5	7	11	1	0	0	1
172	3.6	3	6	10	1	1	1	1	156	3.3	5	7	11	1	0	0	2
171	3.9	3	6	10	1	1	1	2	152	3.3	5	7	12	1	0	1	1
172	3.8	3	6	11	1	1	0	1	150	3.3	5	7	12	1	0	1	2
167	3.6	3	6	11	1	1	0	2	165	2.9	5	8	10	1	1	1	1
165	3.3	3	6	12	1	1	1	1	156	2.7	5	8	10	1	1	1	2
159	3.4	3	6	12	1	1	1	2	155	2.8	5	8	11	1	1	0	1
169	3.0	3	7	10	1	0	1	1	155	3.2	5	8	11	1	1	0	2

174	3.3	3	7	10	1	0	1	2	149	2.6	5	8	12	1	1	1	1
163	3.3	3	7	11	1	0	0	1	152	2.9	5	8	12	1	1	1	2
170	3.3	3	7	11	1	0	0	2	165	3.4	6	6	10	4	1	1	1
169	3.2	3	7	12	1	0	1	1	160	3.7	6	6	10	4	1	1	2
163	3.2	3	7	12	1	0	1	2	157	3.7	6	6	11	4	1	0	1
178	2.7	3	8	10	1	1	1	1	149	3.7	6	6	11	4	1	0	2
165	2.7	3	8	10	1	1	1	2	149	3.8	6	6	12	4	1	1	1
167	2.8	3	8	11	1	1	0	1	145	3.7	6	6	12	4	1	1	2
171	2.8	3	8	11	1	1	0	2	154	3.4	6	7	10	4	0	1	1
166	2.9	3	8	12	1	1	1	1	153	3.2	6	7	10	4	0	1	2
166	2.7	3	8	12	1	1	1	2	150	3.0	6	7	11	4	0	0	1
161	3.7	4	6	10	0	1	1	1	156	3.1	6	7	11	4	0	0	2
162	3.7	4	6	10	0	1	1	2	146	3.2	6	7	12	4	0	1	1
169	3.4	4	6	11	0	1	0	1	153	3.3	6	7	12	4	0	1	2
162	3.7	4	6	11	0	1	0	2	161	2.8	6	8	10	4	1	1	1
159	3.5	4	6	12	0	1	1	1	160	2.9	6	8	10	4	1	1	2
168	3.4	4	6	12	0	1	1	2	156	2.9	6	8	11	4	1	0	1
169	3.1	4	7	10	0	0	1	1	150	2.7	6	8	11	4	1	0	2
165	3.2	4	7	10	0	0	1	2	149	2.9	6	8	12	4	1	1	1
163	3.2	4	7	11	0	0	0	1	151	2.8	6	8	12	4	1	1	2

■

The business school students confess
Their stat training's really a mess.
When faced with a bunch
Of data to crunch
An MBA tends to regress.

A

Some Multiple Regression Theory

In this section, we use matrix notation to sketch some of the mathematics underlying multiple regression. The focus is on how multiple regression calculations are actually done, whether by hand or by computer. We do not prove most of the results; proofs are available in many specialized texts, such as Draper and Smith (1981).

The starting point for the use of matrix notation is the multiple regression model itself. Recall that a model relating a response Y to a set of independent variables of the form

$$Y = \beta_0 + \beta_1 x_1 + \beta_2 x_2 + \cdots + \beta_k x_k + \epsilon$$

is called the *general linear model*. The least-squares estimates $\hat{\beta}_0, \hat{\beta}_1, \ldots, \hat{\beta}_k$ of the intercept and partial slopes in the general linear model can be obtained using matrices.

Let the $n \times 1$ matrix $\mathbf{Y}$

$$
\mathbf{Y} = \begin{bmatrix} y_1 \\ y_2 \\ \vdots \\ y_n \end{bmatrix}
$$

be the matrix of observations, and let the $n \times (k+1)$ matrix $\mathbf{X}$

$$
\mathbf{X} = \begin{bmatrix} 1 & x_{11} & \cdots & x_{1k} \\ 1 & x_{21} & \cdots & x_{2k} \\ \vdots & \vdots & & \vdots \\ 1 & x_{n1} & \cdots & x_{nk} \end{bmatrix}
$$

be a matrix of settings for the independent variables augmented with a column of 1s. The first row of $\mathbf{X}$ contains a 1 and the settings for the k independent variables for the first observation. Row 2 contains a 1 and corresponding settings on the independent variables for y_2. Similarly, the other rows contain settings for the remaining observations.

Next we turn to the least-squares estimates $\hat{\beta}_0, \hat{\beta}_1, \ldots, \hat{\beta}_k$ of the intercept and partial slopes in the multiple regression model. Recall that the least-squares principle involves choosing the estimates to minimize the sum of squared residuals. Those familiar with the calculus will see that the solution can be found by differentiating SS(Residual) with respect to $\hat{\beta}_j (j = 0, \ldots, k)$ and setting the result to zero. The resulting normal equations, in matrix notation, are

$$
(\mathbf{X}'\mathbf{X})\hat{\beta} = \mathbf{X}'\mathbf{Y}
$$

where

$$
\hat{\beta} = \begin{bmatrix} \hat{\beta}_0 \\ \hat{\beta}_1 \\ \vdots \\ \hat{\beta}_k \end{bmatrix}
$$

is the desired vector of estimated coefficients. Provided that the matrix $\mathbf{X}'\mathbf{X}$ has an inverse (it does as long as no x_j is perfectly collinear with other x's), the solution is

$$
\hat{\beta} = (\mathbf{X}'\mathbf{X})^{-1}\mathbf{X}'\mathbf{Y}
$$

E X A M P L E 1 3 . 1 8

Suppose that in a given experimental situation,

$$
\mathbf{Y} = \begin{bmatrix} 25 \\ 19 \\ 33 \\ 23 \end{bmatrix} \quad \text{and} \quad \mathbf{X} = \begin{bmatrix} 1 & -2 & 5 \\ 1 & -2 & -5 \\ 1 & 2 & 5 \\ 1 & 2 & -5 \end{bmatrix}
$$

Obtain the least-squares estimates for the prediction equation

$$
\hat{y} = \hat{\beta}_0 + \hat{\beta}_1 x_1 + \hat{\beta}_2 x_2
$$

Solution

For these data,

$$\mathbf{X'X} = \begin{bmatrix} 4 & 0 & 0 \\ 0 & 16 & 0 \\ 0 & 0 & 100 \end{bmatrix}$$

$$\mathbf{X'Y} = \begin{bmatrix} 100 \\ 24 \\ 80 \end{bmatrix}$$

The $\mathbf{X'X}$ matrix is a diagonal one, so inverting the matrix is easy. The solution is

$$\hat{\beta} = (\mathbf{X'X})^{-1}\mathbf{X'Y}$$

$$= \begin{bmatrix} .25 & 0 & 0 \\ 0 & .625 & 0 \\ 0 & 0 & .01 \end{bmatrix} \begin{bmatrix} 100 \\ 24 \\ 80 \end{bmatrix} = \begin{bmatrix} 25 \\ 1.5 \\ 0.8 \end{bmatrix}$$

and the prediction equation is

$$\hat{y} = 25 + 1.5x_1 + .8x_2 \quad \blacksquare$$

The hard part of the arithmetic in multiple regression is computing the inverse of $\mathbf{X'X}$. For the most realistic multiple regression problems, this task takes hours by hand and fractions of a second by computer. This is the major reason why most multiple regression problems are done with computer software.

Once the inverse of the $\mathbf{X'X}$ matrix is found and the $\hat{\beta}$ vector is calculated, the next task is to compute the residual standard deviation. The hard work is to compute $SS(Residual) = \sum(y_i - \hat{y}_i)^2$. The shortcut formula given in Section 13.2 can be written as $SS(Residual) = \mathbf{Y'Y} - \hat{\beta}'(\mathbf{X'Y})$.

E X A M P L E   1 3 . 1 9

Compute SS(Residual) for the data of Example 13.18.

Solution

$\hat{\beta}$ and $\mathbf{X'Y}$ were calculated to be

$$\begin{bmatrix} 25 \\ 1.5 \\ 0.8 \end{bmatrix} \quad \text{and} \quad \begin{bmatrix} 100 \\ 24 \\ 80 \end{bmatrix}$$

respectively, and

$$\mathbf{Y'Y} = [\,25 \quad 19 \quad 33 \quad 23\,] \begin{bmatrix} 25 \\ 19 \\ 33 \\ 23 \end{bmatrix} = 2604$$

The shortcut formula yields

$$SS(\text{Residual}) = 2604 - [\,25 \quad 1.5 \quad 0.8\,] \begin{bmatrix} 100 \\ 24 \\ 80 \end{bmatrix} = 4 \quad \blacksquare$$

Similar calculations yield SS(Regression) and SS(Total). Although the formulas for these sums can be expressed artificially in pure matrix notation, they can be expressed more easily in mixed matrix and algebraic notation:

$$SS(\text{Regression}) = \hat{\beta}'(\mathbf{X'Y}) - \frac{(\sum y_i)^2}{n}$$

$$SS(\text{Total}) = \mathbf{Y'Y} - \frac{(\sum y_i)^2}{n}$$

EXAMPLE 13.20

Calculate SS(Regression) and SS(Total) for the data of Example 13.18.

Solution

$\sum y_i = 100$ and $n = 4$. The relevant matrix calculations were performed in the previous example.

$$SS(\text{Regression}) = 2600 - \frac{(100)^2}{4} = 100$$

$$SS(\text{Total}) = 2604 - \frac{(100)^2}{4} = 104$$

Note that SS(Total) $= 104 = 100 + 4 = $ SS(Regression) + SS(Residual). $\quad \blacksquare$

These sum-of-squares calculations are necessary for making inferences based on R^2 using F tests. For inferences about individual coefficients using t tests, the estimated standard errors of the coefficients are necessary. In Section 13.3 we presented a conceptually useful but computationally cumbersome formula for these estimated standard errors. A much easier way of computing them involves only the standard deviation s_ϵ and the main diagonal elements of the $(\mathbf{X'X})^{-1}$ matrix.

Definition 13.8   Estimated Standard Error of $\hat{\beta}_j$

$$s_{\hat{\beta}_j} = s_\epsilon \sqrt{v_{jj}}$$

where s_ϵ is the standard deviation from the regression equation and v_{jj} is the entry in row $j + 1$, column $j + 1$ of $(\mathbf{X'X})^{-1}$:

$$(\mathbf{X'X})^{-1} = \begin{bmatrix} v_{00} & & & \\ & v_{11} & & \\ & & \ddots & \\ & & & v_{kk} \end{bmatrix}$$

Because the $(\mathbf{X'X})^{-1}$ matrix must be computed to obtain the $\hat{\beta}_j'$s, it is easy to get the estimated standard errors. $\quad \blacksquare$

Constructing a Multiple Regression Model

This chapter describes the typical steps to take in constructing a multiple regression model. The important steps in this procedure are initial selection of possible predictors, creating nonlinear terms, selecting among the predictors, checking critical assumptions, and possibly validating the model using new or reserved data. The key ideas for this procedure are:

1   Predictor variables should be selected based on the management situation. Each predictor should be correlated with the dependent variable, but not severely collinear with other predictors.

2   Collinearity—correlated independent variables—means that coefficients are sensitive to which variables are included in the model. In addition, the explanatory power of a variable depends strongly on the order in which predictors are listed in the model.

3   Categorical (qualitative) predictors may be incorporated into the model by using dummy variables. Each dummy variable equals 1 if a specified category holds, 0 if not. Use one fewer dummy variable than there are categories. The "undummied" category serves as a baseline standard against which we compare the effect of other categories.

4   Combination—interaction effects ("it depends")—may be incorporated by using product terms. When product terms involve dummy variables times a quantitative variable, the coefficients of the product terms are differences in slopes as compared to the slope for the baseline category; the coefficients of the dummy variables themselves are differences in intercepts as compared to the baseline category.

5   In a time-series regression, independent variables may be lagged by one or more time periods. Using lagged variables is a necessity if the model is to be used for forecasting, and it may improve predictive value in general. Lagged variables may be treated like any other predictors, but using too many lags will often result in severe collinearity.

6   Predictors may be selected for inclusion or exclusion by a stepwise method, using either forward selection or backward elimination. This method tends to overstate the predictive value of the resulting model, and it may be inaccurate because it capitalizes on random variation in correlations. A check on the reasonableness of the chosen model can be done using the C_p statistic; a reasonable model should have $C_p \approx p$, the number of coefficients (including the intercept) in the chosen model.

7   Assumption checking is based on plots of residuals—actual values minus predicted values. A plot of residuals against an independent variable may reveal a nonlinear relation. A smoother such as LOWESS helps to see any nonlinearity. If there is nonlinearity, try transforming that independent variable or the dependent variable.

8   A plot of residuals against predicted values may reveal increasing variability. If it does, try transforming Y or using weighted least squares.

9   In time-series data, a plot of residuals against period number may reveal that the errors are autocorrelated, one with the next. A value of the Durbin-Watson statistic much below 2.0 also indicates autocorrelation. This violation of the independence assumption results in some overstatement of the predictive value of the model and severe overstatement of the accuracy of estimation of the coefficients. Confidence intervals and tests are much too optimistic in the presence of autocorrelation. If autocorrelation is present, try using differences of all variables.

10   Because the many steps in model building may capitalize on random error, it is useful to validate the selected model using new data. If the average error is near 0 and the residual standard deviation increases only slightly, the model should be reasonable.

This chapter presents some suggestions for actually creating a useful multiple regression model. It is, we hope, a practical chapter that builds on and extends the material of Chapter 13.

A typical multiple regression study passes through at least four steps.

1　Select potentially useful predictor (independent) variables. Qualitative variables can be incorporated by the "dummy variable" device that is discussed in Section 14.2. Additional variables may be created (in time-series data) by lagging independent variables; this process is discussed in Section 14.3. Interaction may be captured by using products of independent variables.

2　Tentatively select plausible forms for the multiple regression model. This step may require transformation or combination of either the dependent variable or the independent variables; this process is discussed in Section 14.4.

3　Select a particular model that is appropriate and useful for the given situation; this usually requires fitting several candidate models. The step may be done simply by comparing the results of several models or, more elaborately, by the process of stepwise regression, which is discussed in Section 14.5.

4　Check the selected model for potential violations of assumptions. At this step, the residuals (actual y values minus predicted y values) are examined for evidence of severe nonnormality, nonlinearity, or nonconstant variance; this is discussed in Section 14.6. If, in addition, the multiple regression model involves time-series data, the residuals are also checked for nonindependence (autocorrelation); this is discussed in Section 14.7.

With luck, a satisfactory multiple regression model can be found in one pass through this four-step process. Usually, several passes are necessary.

Ideally, we should add a fifth step before the model is put into use. This step is to check the results of the model on new data, which we discuss in Section 14.8. Such a check confirms that the selected model has the indicated predictive value and that it is not merely an artifact of too much "data massaging."

Obviously, a great deal of calculating is required in the process of selecting a model, and access to statistical software programs is a practical necessity. This chapter follows the basic steps in constructing a model; it should be of considerable practical use.　∎

14.1　Selecting Possible Independent Variables [Step 1]

Perhaps the most critical decision in constructing a multiple regression model is the initial selection of independent variables. In later sections of this chapter, we consider many methods for refining a multiple regression analysis, but first we must make a decision about which independent (x) variables to consider for inclusion—and, hence, which data to gather. If we don't have useful data, we're unlikely to come up with a useful predictive model.

Although initially it may appear that an optimum strategy might be to construct a monstrous multiple regression model with very many variables, such models are difficult to interpret and are much more costly from a data-gathering and analysis time standpoint. How can a manager make a reasonable selection of initial variables to include in a regression analysis?

selection of the
independent variables

Knowledge of the problem area is critically important in the initial selection of data. First, identify the dependent variable to be studied. Individuals who have had experience with this variable by observing it, trying to predict it, and trying to explain changes in it often have remarkably good insight as to what factors (independent variables) affect it. As a consequence, the first step involves consulting those who have the most experience with the dependent variable of interest. For example, suppose that the problem is to forecast the next quarter's sales volume of an inexpensive brand of computer printer for each of 40 districts. The dependent variable Y is then district sales volume. Certain independent variables, such as the advertising budget in each district and the number of sales outlets, are obvious candidates. A good district sales manager undoubtedly could suggest others.

collinearity

A major consideration in selecting predictor variables is the problem of **collinearity**—that is, severely correlated independent variables (we discussed them in Sections 13.2 and 13.3). A partial slope in multiple regression estimates the predictive effect of changing one independent variable while holding all others constant. But when some or all of the predictors vary together, it can be almost impossible to separate out the predictive effects of each one. A common result when predictors are highly correlated is that the overall F test is highly significant, but none of the individual t tests comes close to significance. The significant F result indicates only that there is detectable predictive value somewhere among the independent variables; the nonsignificant t values indicate that we can't detect *additional* predictive value for any variable, given all the others. The reason is that highly correlated predictors are surrogates for each other; any of them individually may be useful, but adding others will not be. When seriously collinear independent variables are all used in a multiple regression model, it can be virtually impossible to decide which predictors are in fact related to the dependent variable.

correlation matrix

There are several ways to assess the amount of collinearity in a set of independent variables. The simplest method is to look at a (Pearson) **correlation matrix**, which can be produced by almost all computer packages. The higher these correlations, the more severe the collinearity problem is. In most situations, any correlation over .9 or so definitely indicates a serious problem.

scatterplot matrix

Some computer packages can produce a **scatterplot matrix**, a set of scatterplots for each pair of variables. Collinearity appears in such a matrix as a close linear relation between two of the *independent* variables. For example, a sample of automotive writers rated a new compact car on 0 to 100 scales for performance, comfort, appearance, and overall quality. The promotion manager doing the study wanted to know which variables best predicted the writers' rating of overall quality. A Minitab scatterplot matrix is shown in Figure 14.1. There are clear linear relations among the performance, comfort, and appearance ratings, indicating substantial collinearity. The following matrix of correlations confirms that fact:

```
MTB > correlations c1-c4
          Correlations (Pearson)

          overall  perform  comfort
perform   0.698
comfort   0.769    0.801
appear    0.630    0.479    0.693
```

FIGURE 14.1 **Scatterplot Matrix for Auto Writers Data**

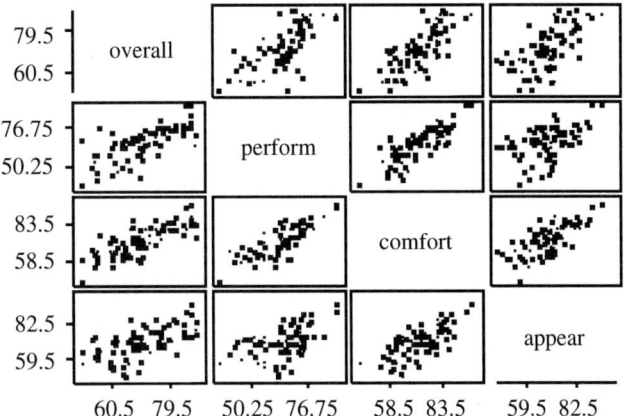

A scatterplot matrix can also be useful in detecting nonlinear relations or outliers. The matrix contains scatterplots of the dependent variable against each independent variable separately. Sometimes a curve or a serious outlier will be clear in the matrix. Other times, the effect of other independent variables may conceal a problem. The analysis of residuals, discussed later in this chapter, is another good way to look for assumption violations.

The correlation matrix and scatterplot matrix may not reveal the full extent of a collinearity problem. Sometimes two predictors together predict a third all too well, even though either of the two by itself shows a more modest correlation with the third one. (Direct labor hours and indirect labor hours together predict total labor hours remarkably well, even if either one predicts the total imperfectly.) A number of more sophisticated ways of diagnosing collinearity are built into various computer packages. One such diagnostic is the variance inflation factor (VIF) that we discussed in Chapter 13. It is $1/(1 - R^2)$, where this R^2 refers to how much of the variation in one *independent* variable is explained by the others. The VIF takes into account all relations among predictors, so it is more complete than simple correlations. The books by Cook and Weisberg (1982) and by Belsley, Kuh, and Welsch (1980) define several diagnostic measures for collinearity. The manuals for most statistical computer programs will indicate which of these can be computed and what the results indicate.

EXAMPLE 14.1

A supermarket chain staged a promotion for a superpremium brand of ice cream. Data on actual sales of the brand for the weekend of the promotion were obtained from scanner data gathered at the checkout stands. Three explanatory variables being considered were the size of the store (in thousands of square feet), the number of customers processed in the store (in hundreds), and the average size of purchase (also obtained from scanner data). A scatterplot matrix is shown in Figure 14.2. What does it indicate about collinearity? Does it show any other problems?

Solution

Look at the six scatterplots in the upper right of the matrix. There is a clear increasing relation, but not extremely strong, between SqFeet, the size of the store, and NumCusts, the number of customers. There is little correlation between either of these independent variables and AvgSize of purchase. Thus there is a modest collinearity problem. There is no indication of a serious nonlinearity problem in the matrix. However, there is an outlier. In the plot of Sales against SqFeet, one store has the largest size but nearly the smallest sales. This outlier has fairly high leverage; it is extreme on two of the independent variables (size and number of customers). It may well have substantial influence as well, because it falls well off the line for predicting sales from either of these predictors. Further checking showed that the ice cream display case at store 41 had lost power during the weekend, forcing the store manager to remove all the ice cream from the case. The store was omitted from the regression analysis. ■

One of the best ways to avoid collinearity problems is to choose predictor variables intelligently, right at the beginning of a regression study. Try to find independent variables that should correlate decently with the dependent variable but do not have obvious correlations with each other. If possible, try to find independent variables that reflect various components of the dependent variable. For example, suppose we want to predict the sales of inexpensive printers for personal computers in each of 40 sales districts. Total sales are made up of several sectors of buyers. We might identify the important sectors as college students, home users, small businesses, and computer network workstations. Therefore,

FIGURE 14.2 **Scatterplot Matrix for Ice Cream Data**

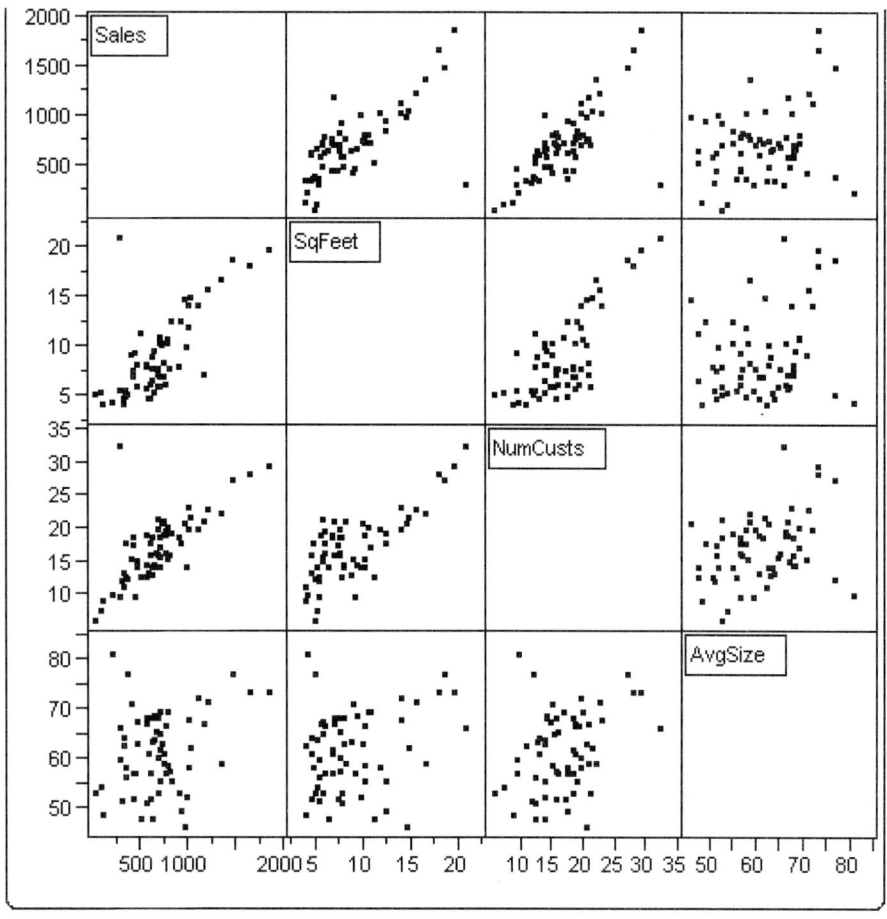

we might well try number of college freshmen, household income, small business starts, and new network installations as independent variables. Each one makes sense as a predictor of printer sales, and there is no screamingly obvious correlation among the predictors. People who are knowledgeable about the variable you want to predict can often identify components and suggest reasonable predictors for the different components.

EXAMPLE 14.2

A firm that sells and services minicomputers is concerned about the volume of service calls. The firm maintains several district service branches within each sales region, and computer owners requiring service call the nearest branch. The branches are staffed by technicians trained at the main office. The key problem is whether technicians should be assigned to main office duty or to service branches; assignment decisions have to be made monthly. The required number of service branch technicians grows in almost exact proportion to the number of service calls. Discussion with the service manager indicates that the key variables in determining the volume of service calls seem to be the number of computers in use, the number of new installations, whether or not a model change has been introduced recently, and the average temperature. (High temperatures, or possibly the associated high humidity, lead to more frequent computer troubles, especially in imperfectly air conditioned offices.) Which of these variables can be expected to correlate with the others?

Solution

It is hard to imagine why temperature should be correlated with any of the other variables. There should be some correlation between number of computers in use and number of new installations, if only because every new installation is a computer in use. Unless the firm has been growing at an increasing rate, we wouldn't expect a severe correlation (we would, however, like to see the data). The correlation of model change to number in use and new installations isn't at all obvious; surely data should be collected and correlations analyzed. ■

14.2 Using Qualitative Predictors: Dummy Variables [Step 1]

dummy variable

One special type of independent variable that could be included in the multiple regression model is the **dummy**, or *indicator*, **variable**. Such variables are used to represent qualitative (categorical) variables such as geographic region, type of incentive plan, or "protected-class" membership in a discrimination suit. The simplest dummy variable situation occurs when the qualitative variable has only two categories, such as female–male or protected–not protected; then the dummy variable is defined by assigning one category of the qualitative variable the value 1 and the other the value 0. For example, suppose that y is the total production cost (in dollars) of a print run, x_1 is the number of items printed (in thousands of items), and x_2 is a dummy variable that equals 1 when the run is on a rush basis and 0 when it is on a regular basis. Assume that the multiple regression prediction equation is

$$\hat{y} = 86.2 + 5.1x_1 + 20.5x_2$$

The coefficient $\hat{\beta}_2 = 20.5$ of x_2 may be interpreted as the estimated difference in cost between a rush job ($x_2 = 1$) and a regular job ($x_2 = 0$) for any specified run size (x_1). By substituting $x_2 = 1$ into the multiple regression prediction equation, we get an equation relating y to x_1 for rush jobs. The corresponding equation relating y to x_1 for regular jobs is obtained by substituting $x_2 = 0$.

Rush jobs: $\hat{y} = 86.2 + 5.1x_1 + 20.5(1) = 106.7 + 5.1x_1$

Regular jobs: $\hat{y} = 86.2 + 5.1x_1 + 20.5(0) = 86.2 + 5.1x_1$

Note that the two prediction equations (corresponding to $x_2 = 0$ or $x_2 = 1$) are parallel lines with different intercepts. These equations are shown in Figure 14.3.

If a qualitative variable can take on more than two levels, definition of the dummy variable is a bit more complicated. We do not want to code residence as $0 =$ urban, $1 =$ suburban, and $2 =$ rural and then use the resulting x in a regression. A one-unit increase in this x could mean either a change from urban to suburban or a change from suburban to rural. There is no reason to assume that the two possible changes would predict the same change in any y; the coefficient of such a variable wouldn't mean much. Instead, we could use two dummy variables to define residence: Define $x_1 = 1$ if residence = suburban and $x_1 = 0$ otherwise, and define $x_2 = 1$ if residence = rural and $x_2 = 0$ otherwise. If both

FIGURE 14.3   **Effect of a Two-Value Dummy Variable**

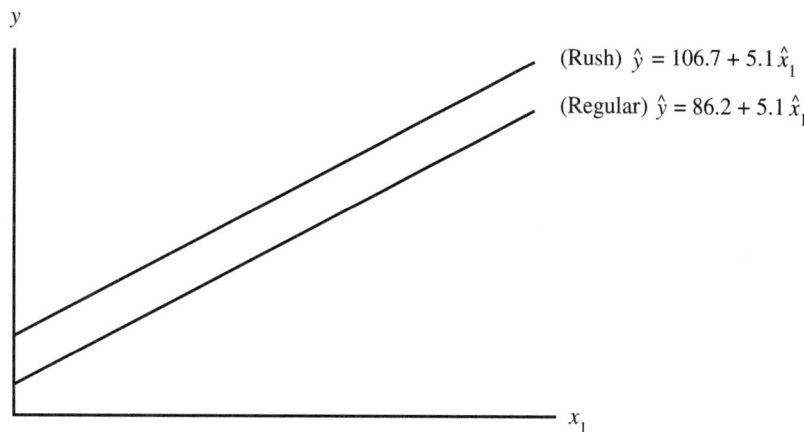

x_1 and x_2 are zero, it follows by elimination that residence = urban. In general, with this scheme, a qualitative variable with k categories can be coded using $k - 1$ dummy variables. If all $k - 1$ dummies are zero for an observation, the observation must fall into the kth category.

interpreting coefficients   The interpretation of regression coefficients in the prediction equation requires some thought. Suppose that x_1 and x_2 are the dummy variables for the qualitative variable residence, x_3 is education in years, and y is income in thousands of dollars. An appropriate multiple regression model is

$$Y = \beta_0 + \beta_1 x_1 + \beta_2 x_2 + \beta_3 x_3 + \epsilon$$

where

$$x_1 = \begin{cases} 1 & \text{if suburban} \\ 0 & \text{otherwise} \end{cases} \qquad x_2 = \begin{cases} 1 & \text{if rural} \\ 0 & \text{otherwise} \end{cases}$$

The interpretations assigned to the β's for the dummy variables x_1 and x_2 can be seen by examining the corresponding expectations $E(Y)$:

For urban residence $(x_1 = x_2 = 0)$: $E(Y) = \beta_0 + \beta_3 x_3$

For suburban residence $(x_1 = 1, x_2 = 0)$: $E(Y) = \beta_0 + \beta_1 + \beta_3 x_3$

For rural residence $(x_1 = 0, x_2 = 1)$: $E(Y) = \beta_0 + \beta_2 + \beta_3 x_3$

It follows that the coefficient for the "suburban" dummy is the difference in expected income between suburban and urban residents for a fixed number of years of education x_3. Similarly, the coefficient for the "rural" dummy is the difference in expected income between rural and urban residents for a fixed number of years of education x_3. It follows, too, that the difference between the coefficients of the dummy variables is the difference in expected income between rural and suburban residents at a fixed education level.

Knowing the interpretations of the coefficients, one can make sense of a least-squares prediction equation. Suppose that the least-squares prediction equation based on sample data is

$$\hat{y} = 3.05 + 5.91 x_1 - 1.84 x_2 + .12 x_3$$

The coefficient of x_1, the "suburban" dummy, is the estimated difference in incomes (in thousands of dollars) for suburban residents when compared to urban residents with the same years of education. Similarly, the coefficient of x_2, the "rural" dummy, is the predicted difference in average income between rural and urban residents with the same education. With years of education x_3 fixed, the regression equation tells us that suburban residents average $5910 higher income than urban residents, whereas rural residents average $1840 lower than urban residents. The "undummied" category (urban residents in the example) serves as the comparison standard. A comparison of rural and suburban residents can be made by comparing each to an urban resident. For education held constant, a suburban resident is predicted to earn $5.91 - (-1.84) = 7.75$ thousand dollars more than a rural resident.

Some computer packages, notably SAS and JMP, use a different system for dummy variables. Consult a package's manual or help files to make sure you understand the system being used.

Dummy variables are often used in product terms—typically, a dummy variable multiplied by another independent variable. We will return to this topic when we consider nonlinear models later in this chapter.

EXAMPLE 14.3

A regression model relates $Y =$ a person's percentage salary increase to seniority in years, gender, and location of the workplace (urban, suburban, or rural). The prediction equation is

$$\hat{y} = 1.31 + 0.09x_1 - 0.43x_2 + 1.02x_3 - 0.66x_4$$

where $x_1 =$ seniority in years,

$$x_2 = \begin{cases} 1 & \text{if female} \\ 0 & \text{otherwise} \end{cases} \qquad x_3 = \begin{cases} 1 & \text{if suburban} \\ 0 & \text{otherwise} \end{cases} \qquad x_4 = \begin{cases} 1 & \text{if rural} \\ 0 & \text{otherwise} \end{cases}$$

Interpret the coefficients in the general linear model.

Solution

Because there are several dummy variables and one quantitative independent variable, the easiest way to interpret the coefficients is to obtain expected values $E(Y)$ for each combination of settings of the dummy variables. These expected values are as follows:

	Urban ($x_3 = 0, x_4 = 0$)	Suburban ($x_3 = 1, x_4 = 0$)	Rural ($x_3 = 0, x_4 = 1$)
Male $\hat{y} = 1.31 + 0.09x_1$ ($x_2 = 0$)		$\hat{y} = 1.31 + 0.09x_1 + 1.02$	$\hat{y} = 1.31 + 0.09x_1 - 0.66$
Female $\hat{y} = 1.31 + 0.09x_1 - 0.43$ ($x_2 = 1$)		$\hat{y} = 1.31 + 0.09x_1 - 0.43 + 1.02$	$\hat{y} = 1.31 + 0.09x_1 - 0.43 - 0.66$

From this table, it is clear that $\hat{\beta}_2 = -.043$ is the difference in mean salary increase $E(Y)$ between females and males, for a given level of seniority (x_1) and location of residence. For example, at a given level of x_1 in an urban district, the difference in mean salary increases between females and males is

$$(\hat{\beta}_0 + \hat{\beta}_1 x_1 + \hat{\beta}_2) - (\hat{\beta}_0 + \hat{\beta}_1 x_1) = \hat{\beta}_2 = -.043$$

This result also applies for any other fixed geographic location. Similarly, $\hat{\beta}_3$ is the difference in mean salary increase between suburban and urban residences for females (or males) at a given seniority level, and $\hat{\beta}_4$ is the difference in mean salary increase in the rural and urban districts for females (or males) at a given seniority level. ■

EXAMPLE 14.4

The minicomputer firm of Example 14.2 is concerned with recent model changes as a source of service calls. The firm feels that most of the effects of model changes occur in the first two months. After that time, minor manufacturing changes eliminate any blatant problems. Discuss how dummy variables can be used in a regression model (based on monthly data) to treat the issue of model change.

Solution

There are three possibilities in any given month: model has changed that month, model changed the previous month, or neither of these. Two dummies are needed, and one way to define them is

$$x_1 = \begin{cases} 1 & \text{if model has changed this month} \\ 0 & \text{if not} \end{cases}$$

$$x_2 = \begin{cases} 1 & \text{if model changed the previous month} \\ 0 & \text{if not} \end{cases}$$

A problem with this approach is that it does not reflect the *number* of new installations in the model change months. ■

14.3 Lagged Predictor Variables (Step 1)

lagged variables

I n many time-series regression problems, the independent variables in the equation should be **lagged**. A regional sales manager may try to forecast monthly sales (s) given the number of initial calls (c) and the number of sales presentations (p) by salespeople. For many types of products, the calls and presentations will result in sales some months later, rather than immediately. The sales manager does not want an equation of the form

$$\hat{s}_t = \hat{\beta}_0 + \hat{\beta}_1 c_t + \hat{\beta}_2 p_t$$

but rather an equation something like

$$\hat{s}_t = \hat{\beta}_0 + \hat{\beta}_1 c_{t-2} + \hat{\beta}_2 p_{t-1}$$

In this example, initial calls are lagged two months behind sales, and presentations one month behind. The implicit idea is that initial calls in one month tend to generate presentations the next month, which in turn tend to generate sales a month later.

Lagging variables is often necessary when regression is to be used for forecasting. A sales forecasting equation like

$$\hat{s}_t = \hat{\beta}_0 + \hat{\beta}_1 c_t + \hat{\beta}_2 p_t$$

is most likely useless because the values of c_t and p_t are not known when the forecast has to be made. To make regression useful in forecasting, the predictor variables must be lagged at least far enough that their values can be known at forecast time.

The major problem with lagging variables is deciding the number of periods to lag. Should the sales manager lag the presentation variable by one month, two months, or what? It's tempting to include many lags in a single regression equation, such as

$$\hat{s}_t = \hat{\beta}_0 + \hat{\beta}_1 c_{t-1} + \hat{\beta}_2 c_{t-2} + \hat{\beta}_3 c_{t-3} + \hat{\beta}_4 c_{t-4} + \hat{\beta}_5 c_{t-5}$$
$$+ \hat{\beta}_6 p_{t-1} + \hat{\beta}_7 p_{t-2} + \hat{\beta}_8 p_{t-3} + \hat{\beta}_9 p_{t-4} + \hat{\beta}_{10} p_{t-5}$$

There are two problems with this strategy, however. First, the number of independent variables is large. Because one must have more observations than variables in a regression (the d.f. for error is number of observations − number of predictors − 1), this strategy requires a lot of data. Second, the lagged variables are likely to be severely correlated.

Econometricians have proposed several other strategies for deciding on lags (see Johnston, 1977, or any other econometrics text.). These strategies typically involve rather severe assumptions that are difficult to verify. If one has no inkling of plausible lag structures, these methods are worth a try.

Often it's possible to find reasonable lags by thoughtful trial and error. The sales manager may well try lagging presentations by one month in one regression equation, and by both one and two in a second. If the second equation doesn't forecast much better than the first, and if most sales result within a month or so of presentations, there is no reason to try further lags. Knowledge of the basic process involved is almost always useful in choosing lags.

E X A M P L E   1 4 . 5

An automobile dealer offers a 12-month or 12,000-mile warranty on new cars and a 3-month or 3000-mile warranty on used cars. As a consequence, the dealer's repair department handles a certain number of warranty-covered repair jobs each month. Data are collected on y_t, the number of warranty repair jobs in month t; x_{t1}, the number of new car sales in month t; and x_{t2}, the number of used car sales in month t. The data are analyzed by two regression models:

$$Y_t = \beta_0 + \beta_1 x_{t1} + \beta_2 x_{t2} + \epsilon_t$$

$$Y_t = \beta_0 + \beta_1 x_{t1} + \beta_2 x_{t-1,1} + \beta_3 x_{t-2,1} + \beta_4 x_{t2} + \beta_5 x_{t-1,2} + \beta_6 x_{t-2,2} + \epsilon_t$$

Computer output from Stata is as follows:

. regress Repairs NewCars UsedCars

```
    Source |       SS       df       MS              Number of obs =      34
-----------+------------------------------           F( 2,    31) =    9.61
     Model |  514.49951      2  257.249755           Prob > F      =  0.0006
  Residual |  829.735784    31  26.7656704           R-square      =  0.3827
-----------+------------------------------           Adj R-square  =  0.3429
     Total |  1344.23529    33  40.7344029           Root MSE      =  5.1736
```

```
-----------------------------------------------------------------------------
   Repairs |    Coef.   Std. Err.     t    P>|t|    [95% Conf. Interval]
-----------+-----------------------------------------------------------------
   NewCars |  .3115306   .1411587   2.207  0.035    .0236356    .5994257
  UsedCars |  .1714632   .1857211   0.923  0.363   -.2073175    .5502439
     _cons |  .3260345   6.535169   0.050  0.961  -13.00253    13.6546
-----------------------------------------------------------------------------
```

. regress Repairs NewCars NewLag1 NewLag2 UsedCars UsedLag1 UsedLag2

```
    Source |       SS       df       MS              Number of obs =      34
-----------+------------------------------           F( 6,    27) =   22.09
     Model |  1116.72055     6  186.120092           Prob > F `    =  0.0000
  Residual |  227.514744    27  8.426472             R-square      =  0.8307
-----------+------------------------------           Adj R-square  =  0.7931
     Total |  1344.23529    33  40.7344029           Root MSE      =  2.9028
```

```
Repairs |    Coef.   Std. Err.    t    P>|t|    [95% Conf. Interval]
--------+-------------------------------------------------------------
NewCars |  .1764289   .0872763   2.021  0.053   -.0026473    .355505
NewLag1 |  .1405518   .0918728   1.530  0.138   -.0479557    .3290593
NewLag2 |  .1229747   .089702    1.371  0.182   -.0610785    .3070279
UsedCars|  .2643788   .1081735   2.444  0.021    .0424251    .4863325
UsedLag1| -.0030381   .106016   -0.029  0.977   -.2205649    .2144888
UsedLag2|  .2590071   .1241269   2.087  0.046    .0043197    .5136945
  _cons | -25.05221   5.775626  -4.338  0.000  -36.90282   -13.2016
--------------------------------------------------------------------
```

a Write the regression equation for the nonlagged model, together with the residual standard deviation and R^2 values.

b Do the same for the lagged model.

c Is there reason to believe that the lagged variables are useful in prediction?

Solution

a For this model, the regression equation is

$$\hat{y}_t = .33 + .312x_{i1} + .171x_{i2}$$

The corresponding values of s_ϵ and R^2 are

$$s_\epsilon = 5.174 \quad \text{and} \quad R^2 = .383$$

b The regression equation for the second model is

$$\hat{y}_t = -25.1 + .176x_{t1} + .141x_{t-1,1} + .123x_{t-2,1} + .264x_{t2}$$
$$- .003x_{t-1,2} + .259x_{t-2,2}$$

The values of s_ϵ and R^2 are

$$s_\epsilon = 2.903 \quad \text{and} \quad R^2 = .831$$

c The inclusion of lagged variables has helped in the prediction of y. The value of R^2 has been increased considerably, and s_ϵ is much smaller. We could carry out the incremental F test of Chapter 12, but the result is clear. ∎

E X A M P L E   1 4 . 6

In Example 14.2, introduction of a new model affected service calls for two months. What lags should be used in a (monthly) database?

Solution

New installations reflect only the current month. To capture the 2-month effect, the new-installations variable should also be lagged by a month. As a check on the belief that the new-model effect lasts only two months, it wouldn't be totally inappropriate to lag new installations by another month as well. ∎

14.1 A city probation office tries to use various reported crime rates to forecast the volume of new cases. The total number of nonviolent crimes reported in the city is determined for 12 quarters, as is the volume of new cases. The data are

Quarter, t:	1	2	3	4	5	6	7	8	9	10	11	12
Crimes (thousands), x_t:	6.4	5.6	5.8	6.6	7.0	6.7	6.5	7.1	7.2	6.9	6.8	6.7
New cases (hundreds), y_t:	13.1	13.5	12.7	12.9	14.3	14.8	14.4	13.9	15.0	15.5	15.1	14.6

Output from Stata follows:

```
. correlate Crimes Newcases
(obs=12)

         |  Crimes Newcases
---------+------------------
  Crimes|  1.0000
Newcases|  0.6347   1.0000

. generate LagCrime = Crimes[_n-1]
(1 missing value generated)

. correlate LagCrime Newcases
(obs=11)

         | LagCrime Newcases
---------+------------------
LagCrime|  1.0000
Newcases|  0.9742   1.0000

. regress Newcases LagCrime

    Source |       SS       df       MS              Number of obs =      11
---------+------------------------------            F(  1,     9) =  167.37
     Model |  7.78846402     1  7.78846402           Prob > F      =  0.0000
  Residual |  .418811627     9  .046534625           R-square      =  0.9490
---------+------------------------------            Adj R-square  =  0.9433
     Total |  8.20727564    10  .820727564           Root MSE      =  .21572

------------------------------------------------------------------------------
  Newcases |     Coef.   Std. Err.      t    P>|t|   [95% Conf. Interval]
---------+--------------------------------------------------------------------
  LagCrime |  1.73077   .1337832    12.937  0.000   1.428131    2.033408
     _cons |  2.822375  .8853612     3.188  0.011   .8195487    4.825201
------------------------------------------------------------------------------
```

a Locate the correlation between x_t and y_t.

b Locate the lag 1 correlation—the correlation between x_{t-1} and y_t. Note that the effective sample size is 11, not 12.

c Which of the correlations is stronger? Does this result seem sensible?

14.2 Refer to the output of Exercise 14.1.

a Locate the regression equation $\hat{y}_t = \hat{\beta}_0 + \hat{\beta}_1 x_{t-1}$.

b Find the residual standard deviation.

14.3 Refer to Exercise 14.1. What would happen if you tried to calculate lag 10 and lag 11 correlations? (What sample size would you have?)

14.4 A textbook publisher begins a sales forecasting system. The chief editors for each of three divisions forecast first-year sales for all new books published in a certain year. These forecasts are later compared to actual sales. Computer output (Excel) from a regression study follows:

	A	B	C	D	E	F	G
1							
2	Regression Statistics						
3							
4	Multiple R	0.9613					
5	R Square	0.9240					
6	Adjusted R Square	0.9156					
7	Standard Error	1.6506					
8	Observations	31					
9							
10							
11	ANOVA						
12		df	SS	MS	F	Significance F	
13	Regression	3	894.745	298.248	109.468	3.178E-15	
14	Residual	27	73.562	2.725			
15	Total	30	968.307				
16							
17							
18		Coefficients	Standard Error	t Stat	P-value	Lower 95%	Upper 95%
19	Intercept	-1.8631	1.0017	-1.8599	0.0738	-3.9184	0.1923
20	Forecast	1.3542	0.0829	16.3292	0.0000	1.184	1.5243
21	Div2	-4.0066	0.7068	-5.6688	0.0000	-5.4567	-2.5564
22	Div3	0.9158	0.7302	1.2541	0.2205	-0.5825	2.4141

a Identify the dummy variables.

b What is the interpretation of the coefficients of these dummy variables?

c Do the t statistics suggest that the dummy variables separately have some predictive value?

14.5 For the data of Exercise 14.4, what additional computer output would you need to test the null hypothesis that the dummy variables collectively have no predictive value once the forecast value has been included in the regression equation?

14.6 Refer to Exercise 14.4.

a What null hypothesis is being tested by the F statistic? What does this hypothesis say about the forecasting system?

b Can this null hypothesis be rejected at $\alpha = .01$? Locate the p-value.

14.7 Refer to Exercise 14.4.

a If the forecast sales had been exactly correct on the average within each division, what would the regression equation be? In particular, what would the coefficient of forecast equal?

b Locate a 95% confidence interval for the forecast coefficient. Does it include the value you specified in part a? ■

14.4

Nonlinearity and Interaction (Step 2)

residual plots

In Section 14.1, we pointed out that use of a first-order regression model (one containing only linear terms in the x's) assumes linearity in each variable separately and also assumes that there are no interactions among the independent variables. In this section, we discuss how to modify a first-order model to handle curved relations and also interactions.

In some situations, it is evident in advance that a model that is linear in all the independent variables will be inadequate. A regression model that predicts y, a taste-test preference score for a lime drink, as a linear function of x_1, lime concentration, and x_2, sweetness, is very dubious. Assuming both coefficients are positive, say, that would mean that the ideal drink would have the maximum concentration of lime flavor and maximum sweetness. (Syrup?) If, however, the range of variation in the independent variables is not large, a linear relation may be a good approximation *over that range*.

In other cases, scatterplots of the data may reveal nonlinearities. In linear regression, the ordinary plot of y versus x is adequate. In multiple regression, the effect of variation in other x's can obscure the nonlinearity. For this reason, a standard strategy is to fit a first-order model and then plot the residuals from this model against each independent variable. If a more appropriate model should contain, for instance, a term in x_1^2, then the plot of residuals against x_1 shows a nonlinear pattern. Because the use of a first-order model removes the linear effect of the other independent variables, nonlinearities often show up more clearly in these residual plots.

For example, in a regression analysis with three independent variables, a Minitab plot of Y against $X1$ is shown in Figure 14.4. The pattern of relation isn't too easy to see. A multiple regression run (with all three independent variables) yielded residuals, which are plotted against $X1$ in Figure 14.5. Now the curve pattern is easier to see. Also, it appears

F I G U R E 1 4 . 4 **Plot of *Y* Against *X*1**

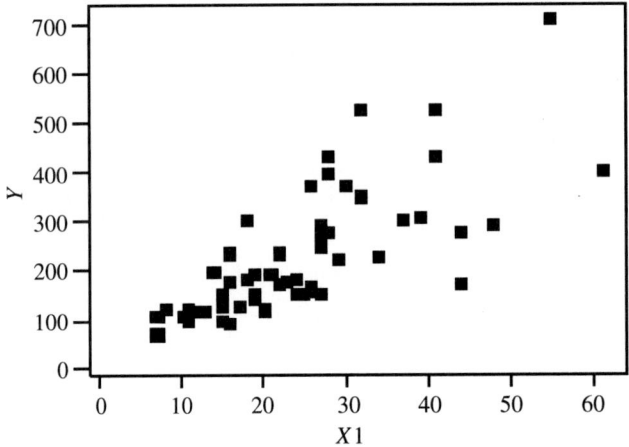

F I G U R E 1 4 . 5 **Plot of Residuals Against *X*1**

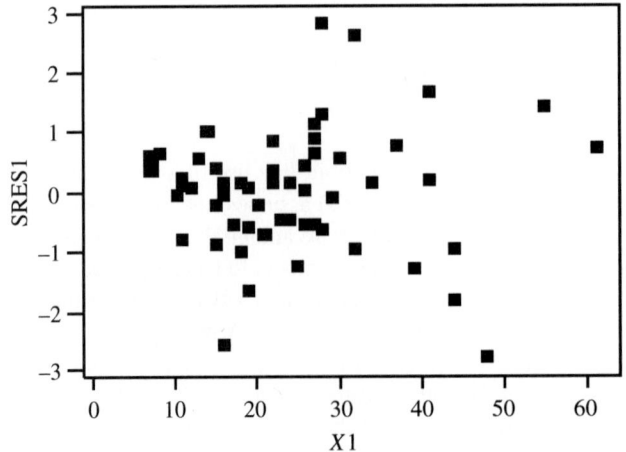

that variability in the residuals may be increasing as $X1$ increases. The up-and-down variation in Figure 14.5 is larger on the right side of the plot.

Once potential nonlinearity has been discovered, we can deal with it either by transforming existing variables or by adding additional, higher-order terms such as x^2 in the x's. Often we use both of these strategies. Transformations may be suggested either by the nature of the problem or by the look of the data. Recall that we discussed transformations in Section 12.1 while looking at scatterplots of the data. The same principles work when examining residual plots. Some packages will fit a LOWESS or spline curve smoother to residuals plots. If a curve is evident in plotting residuals against an x variable (either by eye or using a smoother), transform that x or the dependent variable, or both. If the residual plot looks like a parabola, try adding an x^2 term to the model. If the residual plot has an "elbow," with a clear curve followed by a straighter part, try replacing x by its square root, its logarithm, or its inverse. (When in doubt, it's often helpful to go back to the original scatterplot.) If several residual plots show both curvature and increasing variability from one side to the other, try replacing y by its logarithm.

Figure 14.4 seems to show both an "elbow" pattern and increasing variability. We transformed all the independent variables to natural logarithms, and recalculated the regression. A plot of the residuals from this regression against the logarithm of $X1$ is shown in Figure 14.6. Now the pattern appears quite random, indicating that we succeeded in removing the nonlinearity (and the increasing variability).

FIGURE 14.6 **Plot of Residuals Against ln(X1), Logarithmic Model**

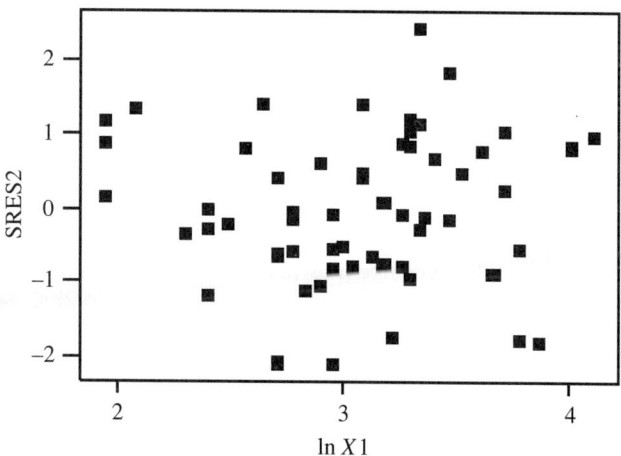

Some of the output from the original and logarithmic models is shown in the following output. Note that the R^2 and residual standard deviation values have changed. The standard deviation has changed greatly. When we transform the dependent variable Y, the results before and after transformation can't be compared directly. The dependent variable scales change, so the summary statistics refer to completely different scales.

```
MTB > Regress 'Y' 3 'X1' 'X2' 'X3'

Regression Analysis

The regression equation is
Y = - 32.3 + 3.06 X1 + 5.22 X2 + 2.98 X3
```

```
Predictor      Coef      Stdev    t-ratio       p
Constant     -32.28      17.34     -1.86    0.068
X1            3.0646     0.8538     3.59    0.001
X2            5.2171     0.9513     5.48    0.000
X3            2.9844     0.5515     5.41    0.000


s = 53.30      R-sq = 83.8%      R-sq(adj) = 82.9%


MTB > name c11 'lnY' c12 'lnX1' c13 'lnX2' c14 'lnX3'
MTB > let c11=loge('Y')
MTB > let c12=loge('X1')
MTB > let c13=loge('X2')
MTB > let c14=loge('X3')


MTB > Regress 'lnY' 3 'lnX1' 'lnX2' 'lnX3'


Regression Analysis


The regression equation is
lnY = 2.09 + 0.357 lnX1 + 0.450 lnX2 + 0.257 lnX3


Predictor      Coef      Stdev    t-ratio       p
Constant     2.0870     0.1859     11.23    0.000
lnX1         0.35709    0.08994     3.97    0.000
lnX2         0.4499     0.1042      4.32    0.000
lnX3         0.25673    0.06096     4.21    0.000


s = 0.2087     R-sq = 85.2%      R-sq(adj) = 84.3%
```

With economic variables and time-series data, growth often occurs at a roughly constant percentage rather than at an absolute rate. For instance, total sales of a large company may grow at the rate of 8% per year, as opposed to $8 million per year. Of course, if initial sales are $100 million, 8% growth in the first year is the same as $8 million growth. But in later years, constant percentage growth and constant additive growth differ. The following table shows the total sales for a company over a 5-year period, based on each of the two types of growth:

	Year					
	0	**1**	**2**	**3**	**4**	**5**
8% growth	100.0	108.0	116.6	126.0	136.0	146.9
$8 million growth	100.0	108.0	116.0	124.0	132.0	140.0

Most basic finance books show that if a quantity y grows at a rate r per unit time (continuously compounded), the value of y at time t is

$$y_t = y_0 e^{rt}$$

where y_0 is the initial value. This relation may be converted into a linear relation between Y_t and t by a **logarithmic transformation**:

logarithmic transformation

$$\log y_t = (\log y_0) + rt$$

The simple linear regression methods of Chapter 13 can be used to fit data for this regression model with $\beta_0 = \log y_0$ and $\beta_1 = r$. When y is an economic variable such as total sales, the logarithmic transformation is often used in a multiple regression model:

$$\log Y_i = \beta_0 + \beta_1 x_{i1} + \beta_2 x_{i2} + \cdots + \beta_k x_{ik} + \epsilon_i$$

The Cobb-Douglas production function is another standard example of a nonlinear model that can be transformed into a regression equation:

$$y = cl^\alpha k^\beta$$

where y is production, l is labor input, k is capital input, and α and β are unknown constants. Again, to transform the dependent variable, we take logarithms to obtain

$$\log y = (\log c) + \alpha(\log l) + \beta(\log k)$$
$$= \beta_0 + \beta_1(\log l) + \beta_2(\log k)$$

This suggests that a regression of log production on log labor and log capital is linear.

EXAMPLE 14.7

An important economic concept is the *price elasticity of demand*, defined as the negative of the percentage change in quantity demanded per percentage change in price. It can be shown that a price elasticity of 1 means that a (small) price change yields no change in total revenue. An inelastic demand (elasticity less than 1) means that a small price increase yields an increase in revenue; elastic demand is the opposite.

Data are obtained on y, daily demand for lettuce (in heads sold per hundred customers) for varying levels of price x (dollars per head). As much as possible, other conditions that might affect demand are held constant: All participating stores are located in middle-class suburbs, no competitors are running sales on lettuce, and so on. The data are

x:	.79	.79	.84	.84	.89	.89	.94	.94	.99	.99
y:	40.2	37.1	37.4	34.9	32.8	35.5	30.6	34.2	31.2	29.8
xy:	31.758	29.309	31.416	29.316	29.192	31.595	28.764	32.148	30.888	29.502

a What economic quantity does xy represent?

b Does there appear to be any trend in xy values as x increases?

c If xy is constant, what is true of $\log x + \log y$?

d If a product has price elasticity equal to 1, what does the regression equation of $\log y$ versus $\log x$ look like?

Solution

a The term xy is price per head times heads per hundred customers. Therefore it represents revenue per hundred customers.

b No trend is apparent in a plot of the data. Revenue, xy, appears constant.

c Because $\log xy = \log$ constant $= \log x + \log y$, $\log x + \log y$ should be constant.

d A price elasticity of 1 means that $\log y = $ constant $- \log x$. The regression equation with $\log y$ as dependent variable and $\log x$ as independent value should have a slope nearly equal to -1 (plus or minus random error). Thus, a regression model in $\log y$ and $\log x$ is useful in elasticity studies. ∎

A logarithmic transformation is only one possibility. It is, however, a particularly useful one, because logarithms convert a multiplicative relation to an additive one. A natural logarithm (base $e = 2.7182818$), often denoted $\ln(y)$, is especially useful, because the results are approximately interpretable as percentage changes. For example, if a prediction of high school teachers' salaries yields predicted ln(salary) = constant + .042(years experience) + other terms, then an additional year's experience, other terms held constant, predicts (about) a 4.2 *percent* increase in salary. This guideline isn't perfect, but it is very close for values less than 0.2 or so.

Another transformation that is sometimes useful is an inverse transformation, $1/y$. If, for instance, y is speed in meters per second, then $1/y$ is time required in seconds per meter. This transformation works well with very severe curvature; a logarithm works well with moderate curvature. Try them both; it's easy with a computer package. Another transformation that is particularly useful when a dependent variable increases to a maximum, then decreases, is a quadratic, x^2 term. In this transformation, do not replace x by x^2; use them both as predictors. The same use of both x and x^2 works well if a dependent variable decreases to a minimum, then increases. A fairly extensive discussion of possible transformations is found in Tukey (1977).

EXAMPLE 14.8

For the service call situation of Example 14.2, the effect of temperature may not be linear. A regression model is calculated using the independent variables indicated in that example. Residuals are plotted against average temperature, as shown in Figure 14.7. A LOWESS smooth is also shown in the figure. Does this plot suggest that a quadratic term would be a useful predictor?

FIGURE 14.7 **Residual Plot for Minicomputer Data**

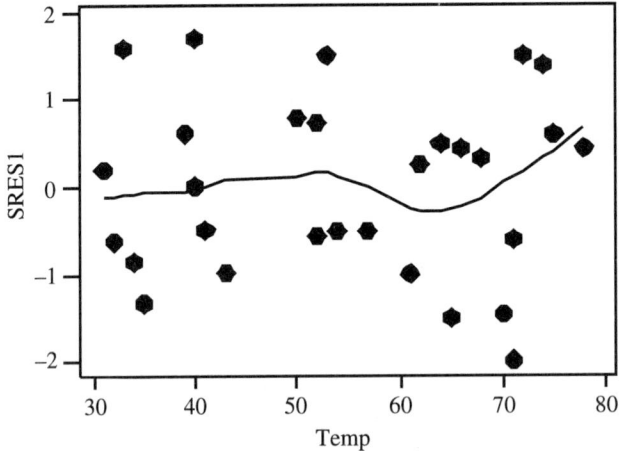

Solution

There is certainly nothing blatant here. The LOWESS curve does not look at all like a parabola, which is the shape for a quadratic term. What curve there is seems to be caused by a few points at the right. We wouldn't expect any additional value to speak of using a quadratic term. ∎

Interactions among variables can sometimes be detected in scatterplots of the original data or in residual plots. If x_1 and x_2 interact in determining y, three variables are involved;

unfortunately, three-dimensional plots are hard to draw. Common sense is one approach to determine whether interactions are present. For the special case in which one of the independent variables is a qualitative variable represented by one or more dummy variables, interaction may be detected in the original plot or by plotting residuals (from a first-order model) against the other independent variables. The better statistical packages will allow you to identify each point by a value of a third variable.

For example, a department store is considering sending mail-order catalogs to cities in its region that are too small to support a branch store. As a test, it sends catalogs to a sample of zip (mail) code areas. A market research firm, using census data, has classified zip codes into a number of types, depending on income, education, and lifestyle. The store selects three upscale (maybe even "yupscale") types and selects 15 areas of each type. They record the resulting sales volume (in thousands of dollars), along with the population (in thousands) of each selected area. A Minitab plot of sales against population, identified by the three types of areas, is shown in Figure 14.8.

FIGURE 14.8 **Plot of Sales Volume Against Population, by Region**

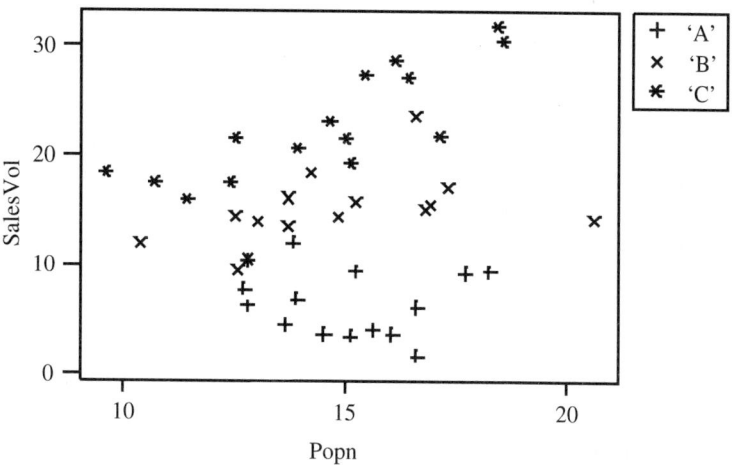

Think of drawing separate lines through each type of symbol. A line through the asterisks (shown in the legend at the upper right of the figure as type C) would clearly go up as population increases. A line through the plus signs (zip code type A) would be flat or maybe even would decrease. The third line, for type B, would be flat or increase slowly. The first-order, no-interaction model implies that these lines should be parallel. Because the separate lines are not close to parallel, the possibility of interaction should be considered. Exactly the same idea works for residual plots. Plot residuals against a quantitative variable. Identify each point in the plot by the value of a qualitative variable. Draw separate lines through each set of symbols. If these lines clearly aren't parallel, interaction is present.

E X A M P L E   1 4 . 9

In Example 14.2 we noted that the new-model dummy variables did not reflect the number of new installations in new-model months. Data for 29 months are collected on the following variables:

Variable	Description
7	Total number of service calls in the month
1	Number of minicomputers in use, beginning of month
2	Number of new installations this month
3	Number of new installations, previous month
4	1 if model change in this month, 0 if not
5	1 if model change in previous month, 0 if not
6	Average temperature this month

A first-order model is fit to the data. Plots of residuals against NewInst and LagNewIn are shown in Figure 14.9. To see if the effect of this month's installation depends on whether there was a model change this month, we plot residuals against NewInst and identify the cases where NewModel = 1 by a different symbol. Similarly, to see if the effect of installations in the previous month depends on whether there was a model change last month, we plot residuals against LagNewIn and identify the cases where LagNewMo = 1 specially. Is there evidence that interaction terms should be used?

Solution

There is some indication of interaction. Only four points correspond to new-model introductions, so the pattern isn't obvious. It appears that these four points slope upward in

FIGURE 14.9 **Plots for Possible Interaction**

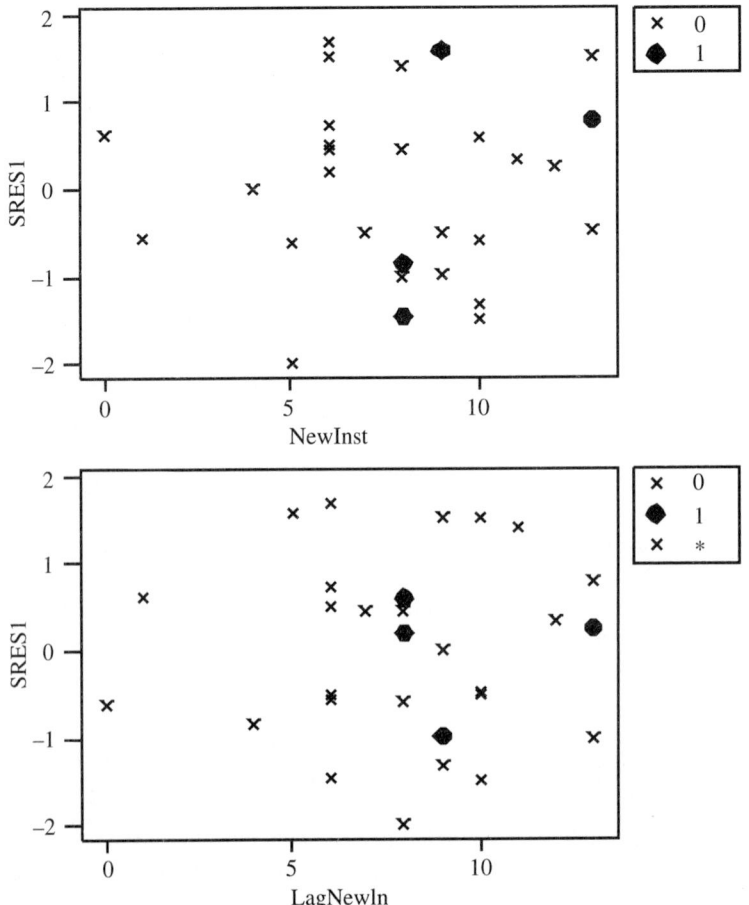

the plot of residuals against NewInst. If there were no interaction, the four points should appear random. The theoretical reasoning behind the idea is strong enough, and the plot suggestive enough, that we may well want to test for interaction. ■

Interaction terms may also be added to the multiple regression model to cure some forms of nonlinearity. Unfortunately, multiple regression was not designed to capture interaction effects. The experimental design, ANOVA approach (where every possible value of one predictor is combined with each possible value of every other predictor) yields a much more easily intelligible treatment of this form of nonlinearity. In practice, however, it may not be possible to plan the neatly balanced data-gathering schemes of the ANOVA approach. In such situations, the regression approach may be modified to yield some information about interaction effects.

cross-product terms   One device is to include **cross-product terms**. This method is often used to test interaction of a qualitative variable and a quantitative one in predicting the dependent variable. In the example of the department store testing types of zip code areas, there seemed to be an interaction of type of area with population in predicting sales volume. We used Minitab to create dummy variables for types B and C, and then created new, cross-product variables, by multiplying each dummy by population. The following results were obtained; the product terms are DumB_Pop and DumC_Pop:

```
MTB > Indicator of 'ZIPType' put in c6-c8
MTB > name c6 'DummyA' c7 'DummyB' c8 'DummyC'
MTB > let c9=c7*c3
MTB > let c10=c8*c3
MTB > name c9 'DumB_Pop' c10 'DumC_Pop'
MTB > Regress 'SalesVol' 5 'Popn' 'DummyB' 'DummyC' 'DumB_Pop' 'DumC_Pop';
SUBC> Constant.

Regression Analysis

The regression equation is
SalesVol = 9.60 - 0.199 Popn - 3.42 DummyB - 9.45 DummyC + 0.794 DumB_Pop
+ 1.77 DumC_Pop
```

A model involving dummy variables and product terms can be understood by plugging in appropriate 1s and 0s. In the department store example, the equations for the three types of zip codes are

Type A (both dummy variables equal 0):

$$\text{SalesVol} = 9.60 - 0.199\text{Popn} - 3.42(0) - 9.45(0) + 0.794(0)\text{Popn} + 1.77(0)\text{Popn}$$
$$= 9.60 - 0.199\text{Popn}$$

Type B (DummyB equal 1, DummyC equal 0):

$$\text{SalesVol} = 9.60 - 0.199\text{Popn} - 3.42(1) - 9.45(0) + 0.794(1)\text{Popn} + 1.77(0)\text{Popn}$$
$$= 6.18 + 0.595\text{Popn}$$

Type C (DummyB equal 0, DummyC equal 1):

$$\text{SalesVol} = 9.60 - 0.199\text{Popn} - 3.42(0) - 9.45(1) + 0.794(0)\text{Popn} + 1.77(1)\text{Popn}$$
$$= 0.15 + 1.571\text{Popn}$$

The coefficients of the dummy variables change the intercept. For type B, the intercept decreased from 9.60 to 6.18 exactly because the coefficient of DummyB was -3.42. The coefficients of the product terms change the slope. For type B, the slope for Popn increased from -0.199 to 0.595 exactly because the coefficient of DumB_Pop was 0.794.

If there is no interaction at all, the lines will be parallel and have the same slopes. Therefore, the product terms (which control the change in slope) will have 0 coefficients. If the coefficients of these product terms are very small compared to the coefficient of the quantitative predictor, the slopes will be nearly parallel, and interaction will be small. In our department store example, the coefficients of the product terms are quite large compared to the coefficient of Popn. Therefore, we have an indication of substantial interaction, just as we saw in looking at the scatterplot.

We can test product terms to see if the apparent nonzero value could reasonably have occurred by sheer randomness. If there is only one product term of interest, the t test shown on most outputs will indicate whether the coefficient is statistically detectable (significant). If there are several product terms, the incremental F test is useful. Take the complete model as including the product terms, and the reduced model as excluding them. Test the difference in R^2 values, or equivalently the difference in SS(Regression) values, to see if we can reject the null hypothesis that the true coefficients are all 0. Although we don't show it here, the product terms in the department store zip code–type example yielded a very large, statistically significant value. Therefore, there is strong evidence that the apparent interaction is real, not just a fluke.

Product terms can also be used with two quantitative variables. A sales forecasting equation such as

$$\hat{y} = .40 + .04c + .01d + .005cd$$

allows for a certain type of interaction between d and c. If $c = 200$, the predicted change in y per unit change in d is $.01 + .005(200)$. If $c = 500$, the predicted change in sales y per unit change in d is $.01 + .005(500)$. In general, if

$$\hat{y} = \hat{\beta}_0 + \hat{\beta}_1 c + \hat{\beta}_2 d + \hat{\beta}_3 cd$$

the predicted change in y per unit change in d is $\hat{\beta}_2 + \hat{\beta}_3 c$ for a given value of c. Thus, the effect of a change in d depends in a certain way on the level of c. This is one form of interaction, though by no means the only one. A cross-product term such as cd may be treated as just another predictor variable. Its coefficient may be tested for statistical significance by a t test, and its predictive value may be assessed by the increase in squared correlation. Therefore, this approach to the problem of interaction can be done routinely within the ordinary regression structure.

Note that interaction is *not* the same concept as collinearity. Collinearity refers to the degree of (linear) correlation between independent variables and says nothing about the dependent variable; interaction refers to an "it depends" combination effect of independent variables on the dependent variable.

E X A M P L E   1 4 . 1 0

Salary data for 427 teachers are examined for a seniority and unionization study. Product terms are created: $x_6 = x_1 x_2$ and $x_7 = x_1 x_3$. A summary computer output is shown for the model $Y = \beta_0 + \beta_1 x_1 + \beta_2 x_2 + \cdots + \beta_7 x_7 + \epsilon$. Test the hypotheses that x_6 and x_7 have no incremental predictive value.

VARIABLE	COEFF	ST.ERROR	T-STATISTIC
INTERCEPT	10.243	------	------
X1	2.070	7.912	0.262
X2	2.963	0.031	16.065
X3	1.475	0.203	7.249

X4	1.932	0.396	5.590
X5	0.808	0.301	2.686
X6	0.177	0.032	5.554
X7	0.093	0.011	8.183

Solution

It would be better to test both values using an incremental F test. That way, we would see if adding the variables together improved prediction by a detectable amount. However, the output doesn't give us the required information, so we'll have to settle for the second best method: using two t tests. For these data, $n = 427$. The d.f. for the t test is $427 - (7 + 1) = 419$, so the relevant t table is effectively the normal table. The t statistics for x_6 and x_7 fall far beyond normal table values. Therefore, we may conclude that some degree of interaction between x_1 and x_2 and between x_1 and x_3 has been shown. ■

Insertion of cross-product terms into the regression equation is sometimes thought to be the only way to handle interaction in regression. Certainly this approach does not handle all possible kinds of interaction, but it does provide a useful approximation to solving the problem of interaction within regression. A manager who believes that interaction effects are crucial in predicting a dependent variable may well spend the extra money to gather data in the neatly balanced form of ANOVA methods.

Finally, thoughtful consideration of underlying economic relations may suggest other combinations of variables to address questions of nonlinearity. For example, suppose that a regression study is made of the total yearly expenditures of cities (y) on water supply systems. Natural independent variables are x_1, the population size; x_2, the total water consumption; and x_3, the number of miles of water lines (of course, there are other possibilities). A regression analysis based on these variables would be bedeviled by collinearity; every other variable would be strongly correlated with city size. A better analysis would take the dependent variable as y/x_1, the per capita expenditure. Natural independent variables would be x_2/x_1, x_3/x_1, and perhaps x_1 itself.

EXAMPLE 14.11

The data of Example 14.9 indicated (to no one's surprise) that variable 7, the number of service calls, increases as variable 1, the number of minicomputers in use, increases. What would be the interpretation of a new variable, defined as variable 7 divided by variable 1? Why might the new variable be an appropriate dependent variable?

Solution

The new variable represents the number of service calls per computer. For a growing business such as the minicomputer firm, defining the variables as fractions of the number of computers in use might well reduce collinearity. ■

EXAMPLE 14.12

A manufacturer of feed for chickens faces a great deal of month-to-month variability in sales. A regression study attempts to forecast monthly sales volumes. The feed is used largely for chickens aged 20–50 days, so the number of chicken starts in the previous month is expected to be a critical predictor variable. Monthly data on starts are available. In addition, feed sales are expected to be quite sensitive to price. The prices of the manufacturer's feed and the primary competitor's feed, as well as the wholesale price of chickens, are very plausible predictor variables.

The working group charged with performing the regression study argues over the form of the regression equation. The following suggestions are made for models:

1 A linear (first-order) model in starts, price, competitor's price, and chicken price

2 A first-order model in starts, difference in price (between manufacturer and competitor), and chicken price

3 A first-order model in starts and the price difference as a fraction of chicken price

Write the three suggested models. Is there a simple relation between one model and any other?

Solution

Let

$$y = \text{monthly sales of the manufacturer's feed}$$

$$x_1 = \text{starts in the previous month}$$

$$x_2 = \text{current price of the manufacturer's feed}$$

$$x_3 = \text{current price of competitor's feed}$$

$$x_4 = \text{current price of chickens}$$

Model 1 is a first-order model in these variables:

$$Y = \beta_0 + \beta_1 x_1 + \beta_2 x_2 + \beta_3 x_3 + \beta_4 x_4 + \epsilon$$

Model 2 involves x_2 and x_3 only through their difference:

$$Y = \beta_0^* + \beta_1^* x_1 + \beta_2^* (x_2 - x_3) + \beta_3^* x_4 + \epsilon$$

Model 3 involves the difference as a fraction of chicken price x_4:

$$Y = \beta_0^{**} + \beta_1^{**} x_1 + \beta_2^{**} (x_2 - x_3)/x_4$$

Model 2 is equal to model 1 if $\beta_2^* = \beta_2$ and $-\beta_2^* = \beta_3$.

Model 3 is not a first-order model in $x_1, \ldots, x_4$, so there is no simple relation between it and the others. ∎

EXERCISES

14.8 A consultant who specializes in corporate gifts to charities, schools, cultural institutions, and the like is often asked to suggest an appropriate dollar amount. The consultant undertakes a regression study to try to predict the amount contributed by corporations to colleges and universities and is able to obtain information on the contributions of 38 companies. Financial information about these companies is available from their annual reports. Other information is obtained from such sources as business magazines. From experience, the consultant believes that the level of contributions is affected by the profitability of a firm, the size of the firm, whether the firm is in a high-education industry (such as data processing, electronics, or chemicals), the educational level of the firm's executives, and whether the firm matches the contributions of employees. Profitability can be measured by pre-tax or post-tax income, size by number of employees or gross sales, and educational level by average number of years of education or by percentage of executives holding advanced degrees.

a Would you expect pre-tax and post-tax income to be highly correlated? How about number of employees and gross sales?

b Discuss how to define profitability, size, and educational level so that the correlations among these variables are not automatically huge.

14.9 The consultant of Exercise 14.8 proposes to define an industry-type variable as follows:

$$\text{Industry} = \begin{cases} 3 & \text{if firm is primarily in the electronics industry} \\ 2 & \text{if firm is primarily in the data-processing industry} \\ 1 & \text{if firm is primarily in the chemical industry} \\ 0 & \text{otherwise} \end{cases}$$

a Explain why this is not a good idea.

b Suggest an alternative approach for indicating these industries.

c How could the factor of whether the firm matches employee contributions be incorporated into a regression model?

14.10 The consultant of Exercise 14.8 collects data on the following variables:

CONTRIB:	Millions of dollars contributed
INCOME:	Pre-tax income, in millions of dollars
SIZE:	Number of employees, in thousands
DPDUMMY:	1 if firm is primarily in the data-processing industry 0 if not
ELDUMMY:	1 if firm is primarily in the electronics industry 0 if not
CHDUMMY:	1 if firm is primarily in the chemical industry 0 if not
EDLEVEL:	Proportion of executives holding advanced degrees
MATCHING:	1 if firm matches employee contributions 0 if not

a Does it seem like a good idea to take CONTRIB as the dependent variable, with all other variables as independent variables? In particular, why would this method invite collinearity troubles?

b What does the variable CONTRIB/INCOME represent?

14.11 Refer to Exercise 14.10. The consultant suspects that the effect of SIZE on CONTRIB/INCOME differs greatly among firms in the data-processing, electronics, chemical, and other industries. How can the regression model be modified to test this suspicion?

14.12 Refer to Exercise 14.10. The consultant suspects that the effect of increasing EDLEVEL is itself increasing; that is, all else being equal, there is little difference in CONTRIB/INCOME for firms with EDLEVEL = .2 versus .3, more for firms with EDLEVEL = .4 versus .5, and still more for firms with EDLEVEL = .6 versus .7.

a How can a regression model be formulated to test this suspicion?

b If the consultant's suspicion is correct, and if the residuals from a first-order regression model are scatterplotted against EDLEVEL, what pattern of residuals would you expect to see?

14.13 A supermarket chain analyzed data on sales of a particular brand of snack cracker at 104 stores in the chain for a certain 1-week period. The analyst tried to predict sales based on the total sales of all brands in the snack cracker category, the price charged for the particular brand in question, and whether or not there was a promotion for a competing brand at a given store (promotion = 1 if there was such a promotion, 0 if not). (There were no promotions for the brand in question.) A portion of the JMP multiple regression output is shown in Figure 14.10.

a Interpret the coefficient of the promotion variable.

b Should a promotion by a competing product increase or decrease sales of the brand in question? According to the coefficient, does it?

c Is the coefficient significantly different from 0 at usual α values?

FIGURE 14.10 Regression Results for Snack Cracker Data

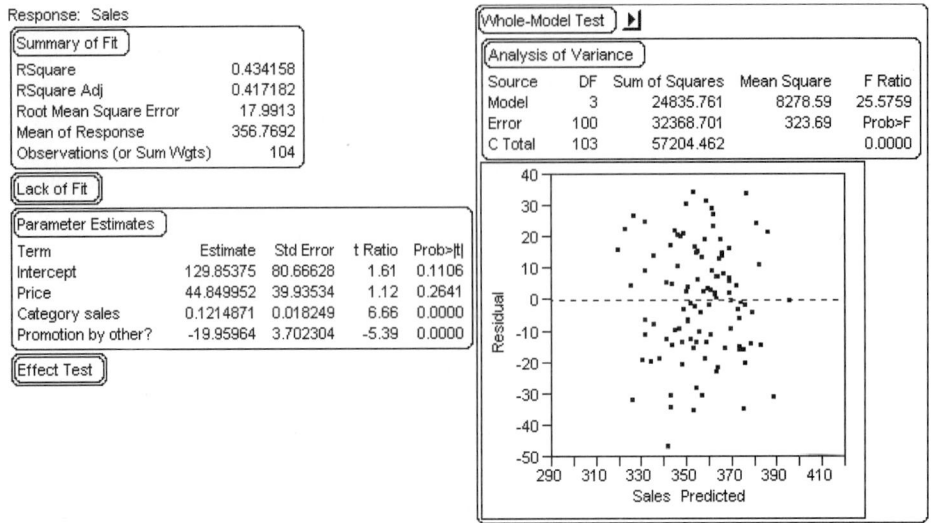

14.14 In the previous question, how accurately can sales be predicted for one particular week, with 95% confidence?

14.15 An additional regression model for the snack cracker data is run, incorporating products of the promotion variable with price and with category sales. The output for this model is given in Figure 14.11. What effect do the product term coefficients have in predicting sales when there is a promotion by a competing brand? In particular, do these coefficients affect the intercept of the model or the slopes?

FIGURE 14.11 Snack Cracker Regression with Product Terms

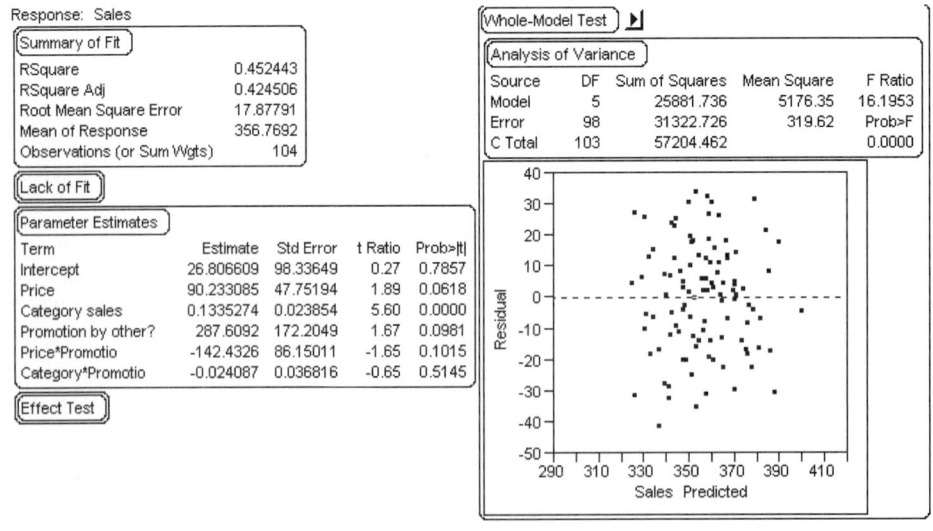

14.16 A company that has developed a plastic film for use in wrapping food (such as crackers and cookies) has a problem with film stiffness. To be useful with modern packaging machines, stiffness (as given by an accepted measure) must be high. Stiffness is thought to be the result of certain variables of the production process. A regression study attempts to predict film stiffness for various combinations of these variables. A total of 32 pilot plant runs is made. Data are recorded on the following variables:

STIFF:	Stiffness	REPEL:	Percentage of recycled
MELT:	Melt temperature (^oF)		pelletized material used
CHILL:	Chill temperature (^oF)	SPEED:	Line production speed
			(feet per minute)
		KNIFE:	Setting of vacuum knife

There is considerable uncertainty among the firm's chemical engineers as to the mathematical form of the relation among these variables. The following output is obtained for a first-order model:

```
PEARSON CORRELATION MATRIX

            CHILL      KNIFE      MELT      REPEL      SPEED      CHILL
            1.000
    KNIFE  -0.000      1.000
    MELT   -0.000      0.000     1.000
    REPEL   0.000      0.000     0.000     1.000
    SPEED   0.000     -0.000    -0.000    -0.000      1.000
    STIFF   0.138     -0.308     0.059    -0.886      0.030

NUMBER OF OBSERVATIONS:   32
```

a How much collinearity is present in these data?

b The 32 observations involved one measurement of each combination of MELT = 510, 530, 550, 570 with CHILL = 70, 80, 90, 100, and REPEL = 20, 30. How much correlation should there be between MELT and CHILL and between MELT and REPEL?

14.17 A first-order model is fit to the data of Exercise 14.16. The following (Systat) output is obtained and plotted in Figure 14.12. Is there any evidence, by eye, of nonlinearity? RESSTIFF is the name of the residuals.

```
DEP VAR:  STIFF  N: 32  MULTIPLE R: 0.951  SQUARED MULTIPLE R: 0.904
ADJUSTED SQUARED MULTIPLE R: .885  STANDARD ERROR OF ESTIMATE: 3.571
VARIABLE   COEFFICIENT  STD ERROR  STD COEF TOLERANCE      T   P(2 TAIL)
CONSTANT     170.962     20.509     0.000      .        8.336  0.000
MELT           0.028      0.028     0.059     1.000     0.974  0.339
CHILL          0.128      0.056     0.138     1.000     2.250  0.033
REPEL         -1.838      0.126    -0.886     1.000   -14.556  0.000
SPEED          0.007      0.014     0.030     1.000     0.487  0.630
KNIFE         -0.319      0.063    -0.308     1.000    -5.050  0.000

                    ANALYSIS OF VARIANCE

SOURCE      SUM-OF-SQUARES  DF  MEAN-SQUARE   F-RATIO    P
REGRESSION     3106.400      5    621.280     48.732   0.000
RESIDUAL        331.475     26     12.749
```

14.18 In an attempt to detect nonlinearity in the data of Exercise 14.16, a second-order model (containing squared MELT and CHILL terms) is run, and the following output is obtained:

```
DEP VAR:  STIFF  N: 32  MULTIPLE R: 0.956  SQUARED MULTIPLE R: 0.914
ADJUSTED SQUARED MULTIPLE R: .889  STANDARD ERROR OF ESTIMATE: 3.513
VARIABLE    COEFFICIENT  STD ERROR  STD COEF TOLERANCE      T   P(2 TAIL)
CONSTANT     -308.000    459.031     0.000      .       -0.671  0.509
MELT            1.377      1.677     2.972     0.000     0.821  0.420
CHILL           3.634      2.362     3.920     0.001     1.539  0.137
REPEL          -1.838      0.124    -0.886     1.000   -14.793  0.000
SPEED          -0.034      0.031    -0.148     0.200    -1.107  0.279
KNIFE          -0.319      0.062    -0.308     1.000    -5.132  0.000
MELT*MELT      -0.001      0.002    -2.913     0.000    -0.805  0.429
CHILL*CHILL    -0.021      0.014    -3.787     0.001    -1.485  0.151
```

FIGURE 14.12 **Residual Plots for Film Data**

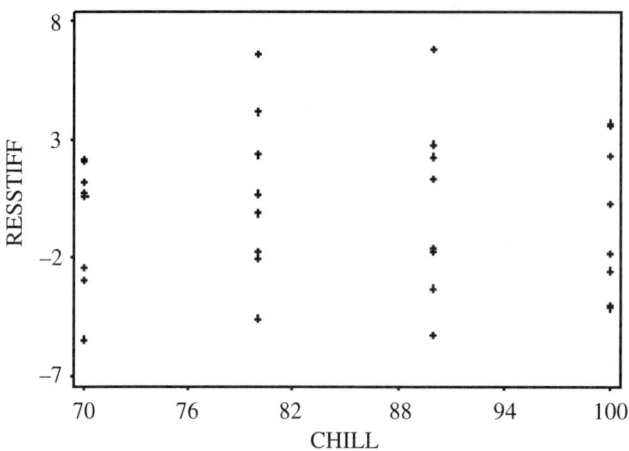

Scatterplot of RESSTIFF vs CHILL

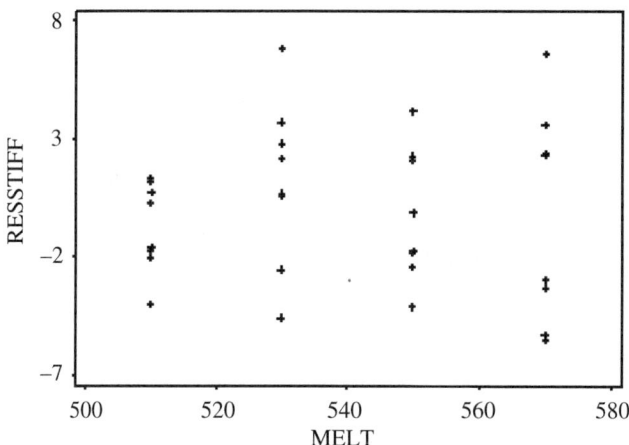

Scatterplot of RESSTIFF vs MELT

ANALYSIS OF VARIANCE

SOURCE	SUM-OF-SQUARES	DF	MEAN-SQUARE	F-RATIO	P
REGRESSION	3141.625	7	448.804	36.359	0.000
RESIDUAL	296.250	24	12.344		

a How much larger is the R^2 for this model than the R^2 for the first-order model of Exercise 14.17?

b Use the F test for complete and reduced models to test the null hypothesis that the addition of the squared terms yields no additional predictive value. Use $\alpha = .05$.

c Do the t statistics indicate that either squared term is a statistically significant ($\alpha = .05$) predictor as last predictor in? ■

14.5

Choosing Among Regression Models [Step 3]

In the previous sections of this chapter, we suggested many reasons to include variables in a regression study. The variables may be defined directly or they may be defined by using dummy variables, lagged variables, transformed variables, interaction cross-product variables, or some other combination. Most of these suggestions involve adding more independent variables to the study. A manager who begins a regression study may well suffer from the "kitchen sink syndrome" and try to throw every possible variable into a regression model. Some sensible guidelines are needed for selecting the independent variables, from all candidates, to be used in the final regression model.

Stepwise regression is a rather mechanical and mindless device for computerized selection of the "best" independent variables. There are several types of stepwise regression procedures; we concentrate on the simplest one: **forward selection**.

Forward-selection stepwise regression selects independent variables for inclusion in a regression model one at a time. The first variable included is the one that has the highest r^2 value for predicting y; assume that this variable is called x_1. The second variable included is the one that, when combined with x_1, yields the highest R^2 value; call the second variable x_2. If there is any degree of collinearity among the x's, x_2 may not have the second-largest r^2_{xy} value. In fact $R^2_{y \cdot x_1 x_2}$ may not even have the highest R^2 value of any two-x regression model.

The third variable included by forward selection yields the highest R^2 value when combined with x_1 and x_2. The process continues in this same manner. Obviously, a considerable amount of computation is necessary. That is why we would never attempt stepwise regression without access to a computer.

When should the selection process stop? There are several criteria, depending in part on which stepwise computer program is used. A common one uses the t test (or $F = t^2$) for the statistical significance of a single regression coefficient. When a variable is selected for possible inclusion, a t test is performed on the coefficient. If the null hypothesis, $H_0: \beta_j = 0$, can be rejected at an α level specified by the user, the variable x_j is included and stepwise selection continues. If the null hypothesis is retained, the variable is not included and selection stops. To avoid stopping too early, a relatively large α such as .10 or .20 is typically used. Of course, it is also possible to force the procedure to include all variables, one at a time, if the α value is very large.

E X A M P L E   1 4 . 1 3

A forward-selection stepwise regression analysis is performed for the data of Example 14.9 (first-order model). The variables are as indicated in that example, and the row labeled R-squared gives the value at each step of R^2. Thus, InUse explains .4943 of the variation in ServCalls, NewInst an additional .3278 (for a total of .8221), and so on.

```
                 Stepwise selection for ServCalls


Method: forward
F-to-enter: 1
F-to-remove: 1


Step: 1
R-squared: 0.4943      Adjusted: 0.4756      MSE: 1543.99     d.f.: 27
In Model        Coeff.    F-Remove
InUse          -1.07138     26.39


Step: 2
R-squared: 0.8221      Adjusted: 0.8084      MSE: 563.954     d.f.: 26
In Model        Coeff.    F-Remove
InUse          -1.54041    115.87
NewInst       -10.1549      47.92
```

14.5   *Choosing Among Regression Models (Step 3)*   633

Step: 3
R-squared: 0.8813   Adjusted: 0.8670   MSE: 391.545   d.f.: 25

In Model	Coeff.	F-Remove
InUse	-1.53332	165.31
NewInst	-9.6603	61.65
ModelChg	-37.8768	12.45

Step: 4
R-squared: 0.9054   Adjusted: 0.8896   MSE: 324.894   d.f.: 24

In Model	Coeff.	F-Remove
InUse	-1.49705	186.52
NewInst	-8.97428	60.43
ModelChg	-42.551	18.25
LagModChg	-25.0816	6.13

Step: 5
R-squared: 0.9378   Adjusted: 0.9243   MSE: 222.8   d.f.: 23

In Model	Coeff.	F-Remove
InUse	-1.42918	236.85
NewInst	-7.80816	59.35
ModelChg	-50.8661	35.07
LagModChg	-30.1589	12.54
Temp	-0.704675	12.00

Table of Estimates

	Estimate	Standard Error	t Value	P Value
Constant	-94.5833	24.7778	-3.82	0.0009
InUse	1.42918	0.0928645	15.39	0.0000
NewInst	7.80816	1.01358	7.70	0.0000
ModelChg	50.8661	8.58987	5.92	0.0000
LagModChg	30.1589	8.51705	3.54	0.0017
Temp	0.704675	0.203443	3.46	0.0021

a   Which variables are not statistically significant at $\alpha = .10$ as last predictor in?

b   How much higher an R^2 value does the 5-variable model have than the model with only InUse and NewInst?

Solution

a   The indicated p-values are all less than .10, so every variable is declared statistically significant.

b   The 5-variable R^2 is .9378 as compared to the R^2 of .8221 given by the 2-variable model. The F statistic for incremental R^2 could be computed; it is large.   ■

backward elimination

There are many variations in stepwise procedures. Variables may be successively removed from the model in **backward elimination**. This process begins with all variables included in the model. Then, one at a time, variables that offer very little predictive value are deleted. In addition, forward or backward selection can be modified to use various checkup procedures for retesting variables already included in, or excluded from, the model. For example, in forward selection, a variable included at one step can be found at a later step to be of little use; a checkup procedure allows later elimination of the variable. There are sophisticated stepwise procedures that incorporate these and other checks. In fact, some packages will compute regression models based on all possible subsets of independent variables.

Stepwise regression can be helpful in suggesting reasonable models. Like any other statistical method, however, it requires thinking and judgment for proper use.

stepwise bias

One technical problem is that stepwise regression introduces biases. Because stepwise regression selects variables to yield a large R^2 value, the resulting R^2 may well be an overestimation of the actual predictive value of the variables in the model. The magnitudes of the resulting coefficients and of the t and F tests also tend to be too large.

In addition, stepwise regression involves decisions that are based on differences of R^2 values. These differences contain an element of random error, which can be quite large. For example, suppose that in a forward selection based on 28 y values, the correlation between y and the first selected variable x_1 is $r_{yx_1} = .6$ (hence, $r_{yx_1}^2 = .36$). A 95% confidence interval on $r_{yx_1}^2$, calculated by a method not shown in this text, ranges from .09 to .64. Because of this large sampling variation, one variable could be selected over another for inclusion in the regression model, even though the selected variable has less actual predictive value than others not selected.

Stepwise methods usually involve some form of hypothesis test to select among models. An alternative approach to model selection is based on the C_p statistic of Mallows (1973). If a model contains p coefficients—typically, one intercept and $p - 1$ slopes corresponding to $p - 1$ independent variables—then

$$C_p = \frac{\text{SS(Residual, } p \text{ coefficients)}}{\text{MS(Residual, all coefficients)}} - (n - 2p)$$

$$= \frac{(n - p)\,\text{MS(Residual, } p \text{ coefficients)}}{\text{MS(Residual, all coefficients)}} - (n - 2p)$$

where the last step follows because the d.f. for MS(Residual, p coefficients) is $n - (k + 1) = n - (p - 1 + 1) = n - p$. If the p coefficient model contains all the useful predictors, MS(Residual, p coefficients) is essentially the same as MS(Residual, all coefficients). In this case, C_p roughly equals $(n - p) - (n - 2p) = p$. But if the p coefficient model is inadequate, C_p is substantially larger than p. One plausible model-selection strategy is to select the regression model with the fewest independent variables having C_p approximately equal to p.

E X A M P L E   1 4 . 1 4

Assume that data are collected for 20 independent pharmacies in an attempt to predict prescription volume (sales per month). The independent variables are total floor space, percentage of floor space allocated to the prescription department, number of available parking spaces, whether the pharmacy is in a shopping center, and per capita income for the surrounding community. The data and selected Statistix output are shown next, using a "best subsets" method that locates the best six models for each number of variables. What does the C_p statistic suggest as the most reasonable model?

BEST SUBSET REGRESSION MODELS FOR VOLUME

UNFORCED INDEPENDENT VARIABLES: (A)FLOOR_SP (B)INCOME (C)PARKING
(D)PRESC_RX (E)SHOPCNTR
6 "BEST" MODELS FROM EACH SUBSET SIZE LISTED.

P	CP	ADJUSTED R SQUARE	R SQUARE	RESID SS	MODEL VARIABLES
1	28.7	0.0000	0.0000	750.550	INTERCEPT ONLY
2	10.2	0.4082	0.4393	420.809	D
2	23.8	0.1007	0.1480	639.476	B
2	28.8	-0.0122	0.0411	719.737	E
2	29.1	-0.0202	0.0335	725.382	A
2	30.5	-0.0505	0.0048	746.944	C
3	1.6	0.6263	0.6657	250.936	A D
3	2.5	0.6055	0.6471	264.895	D E
3	7.1	0.4943	0.5475	339.632	B D
3	7.9	0.4763	0.5314	351.689	C D
3	9.5	0.4364	0.4958	378.451	B E
3	20.7	0.1691	0.2565	558.006	A E
4	2.4	0.6327	0.6907	232.126	A D E
4	3.0	0.6193	0.6794	240.601	A C D
4	3.6	0.6039	0.6664	250.374	A B D
4	3.7	0.5993	0.6626	253.242	C D E
4	4.5	0.5809	0.6471	264.857	B D E
4	6.6	0.5279	0.6024	298.394	B C D
5	4.1	0.6184	0.6987	226.111	A C D E
5	4.3	0.6115	0.6933	230.218	A B D E
5	4.9	0.5954	0.6806	239.736	A B C D
5	5.7	0.5731	0.6630	252.928	B C D E
5	13.3	0.3683	0.5013	374.307	A B C E
6	6.0	0.5930	0.7001	225.109	A B C D E

Solution

Note that for k variables in the model, $p = k + 1$; there are k slopes and one intercept. For the 1-variable models, no C_p is close to $p = 2$. The model using FLOOR_SP and PRESC_RX (shown as variables A and D) has $C_p = 1.6$, actually below p. On the C_p criterion, this model appears to be a good one. Note also that the R^2 value for this model is almost as large as the R^2 value for the model involving all variables. ∎

E X A M P L E   1 4 . 1 5

Statistix also performed a stepwise regression for the data of Example 14.14. Did the stepwise procedure identify the same model as the "best subsets" procedure?

```
STEPWISE REGRESSION OF VOLUME
UNFORCED VARIABLES: FLOOR_SP INCOME PARKING PRESC_RX SHOPCNTR
  F TO ENTER  1.00  F TO EXIT   1.00
```

STEP	VARIABLE	COEFFICIENT	T	R SQ	MSE
1	CONSTANT	17.1500	12.20	0.0000	39.5026
2	CONSTANT	25.9813	10.04	0.4393	23.3783
	PRESC_RX	-0.32055	-3.76		

3	CONSTANT	48.2908	7.01	0.6657	14.7609
	FLOOR_SP	-0.00384	-3.39		
	PRESC_RX	-0.58189	-5.67		
4	CONSTANT	42.8270	5.13	0.6907	14.5079
	FLOOR_SP	-0.00247	-1.50		
	PRESC_RX	-0.52941	-4.74		
	SHOPCNTR	-3.03834	-1.14		

Solution

The stepwise procedure added SHOPCNTR as a third predictor, with only a modest increment to R^2 and very little change to MSE. The T value, -1.14, for this variable indicates there is little evidence that it adds any real predictive value; we would omit it. Effectively, the two procedures have given the same solution. ■

Mallows (1973) points out the C_p statistic is as susceptible to random variation as any other statistic; it is not an infallible guide. No statistical method is. In selecting a regression model, a manager should use experience and judgment as well as statistical results. If one model involves reasonable relations and variables, yet does somewhat less well than another, less plausible model on a purely statistical basis, a manager might well choose the first model anyway.

E X E R C I S E S

14.19 A forward-selection stepwise regression is run using a first-order model for the data of Exercise 14.16. The following output is obtained:

```
PEARSON CORRELATION MATRIX

              CHILL     KNIFE      MELT     REPEL     SPEED
    CHILL     1.000
    KNIFE    -0.000     1.000
     MELT    -0.000     0.000     1.000
    REPEL     0.000     0.000     0.000     1.000
    SPEED     0.000    -0.000    -0.000    -0.000     1.000
    STIFF     0.138    -0.308     0.059    -0.886     0.030

MINIMUM TOLERANCE FOR ENTRY INTO MODEL =    .010000

STEP #    1 R=  .886 RSQUARE=   .786
TERM ENTERED: REPEL

VARIABLE      COEFFICIENT  STD ERROR  STD COEF  TOLERANCE    F     'P'
 1 CONSTANT
 4 REPEL           -1.838    -0.175    -0.886   .1E+01  109.988   0.000

STEP #    2 R=  .938 RSQUARE=   .880
TERM ENTERED: KNIFE

VARIABLE      COEFFICIENT  STD ERROR  STD COEF  TOLERANCE    F     'P'
 1 CONSTANT
 4 REPEL           -1.838    -0.133    -0.886   .1E+01  190.301   0.000
 6 KNIFE           -0.319    -0.067    -0.308   .1E+01   22.906   0.000

STEP #    3 R=  .948 RSQUARE=   .899
TERM ENTERED: CHILL
```

VARIABLE	COEFFICIENT	STD ERROR	STD COEF	TOLERANCE	F	'P'
1 CONSTANT						
3 CHILL	0.128	0.056	0.138	.1E+01	5.253	0.030
4 REPEL	-1.838	-0.124	-0.886	.1E+01	218.210	0.000
6 KNIFE	-0.319	-0.062	-0.308	.1E+01	26.265	0.000

STEP #   4 R= .950 RSQUARE=   .903
TERM ENTERED: MELT

VARIABLE	COEFFICIENT	STD ERROR	STD COEF	TOLERANCE	F	'P'
1 CONSTANT						
2 MELT	0.028	0.028	0.059	.1E+01	0.977	0.332
3 CHILL	0.128	0.056	0.138	.1E+01	5.249	0.030
4 REPEL	-1.838	-0.124	-0.886	.1E+01	218.028	0.000
6 KNIFE	-0.319	-0.062	-0.308	.1E+01	26.243	0.000

a List the order in which the independent variables enter the regression model.

b List the independent variables from largest (in absolute value) to smallest correlation with STIFF.

c Compare the ordering of the variables given by the two lists.

14.20 Refer to Exercise 14.19. Use the F test for complete and reduced models, described in Section 13.4, to test the hypothesis that the last two variables entered in the stepwise regression have no predictive value.

14.21 The consultant of Exercise 14.10 runs a regression model with CONTRIB/INCOME as the dependent variable.

```
MTB > regress c9 on 7 vars in 'Income'-'Matching'
```

```
The regression equation is
Cont/Inc = 0.0211 -0.000093 Income + 0.00153 Size + 0.00168 DPDummy
           + 0.00713 ELDummy + 0.00281 CHDummy - 0.0144 EdLevel
           + 0.00138 Matching
```

Predictor	Coef	Stdev	t-ratio	p
Constant	0.021085	0.003497	6.03	0.000
Income	-0.0000933	0.0001033	-0.90	0.372
Size	0.0015301	0.0006699	2.28	0.028
DPDummy	0.001684	0.004720	0.36	0.723
ELDummy	0.007132	0.006355	1.12	0.269
CHDummy	0.002808	0.003810	0.74	0.466
EdLevel	-0.01436	0.01597	-0.90	0.374
Matching	0.001381	0.002092	0.66	0.513

```
s = 0.006057    R-sq = 21.3%    R-sq(adj) = 6.8%
```

Analysis of Variance

SOURCE	DF	SS	MS	F	p
Regression	7	0.00037698	0.00005385	1.47	0.208
Error	38	0.00139418	0.00003669		
Total	45	0.00177115			

a Can the hypothesis that none of the independent variables has predictive value be rejected (using reasonable α values)?

b Which variables have been shown to have statistically significant (say, $\alpha = .05$) predictive value as last predictor in?

14.22 A simpler regression model than that of Exercise 14.21 is obtained by regressing the dependent variable on the independent variables DPDummy, ELDummy, EdLevel, and Matching. The following output is obtained:

```
MTB > regress c9 on 4 vars 'DPDummy' 'ELDummy' 'EdLevel' 'Matching'
```

```
The regression equation is
```

```
Cont/Inc = 0.0202 - 0.00378 DPDummy - 0.00099 ELDummy
            + 0.0097 EdLevel + 0.00197 Matching

Predictor      Coef      Stdev    t-ratio      p
Constant    0.020233   0.002304      8.78   0.000
DPDummy    -0.003775   0.003912     -0.97   0.340
ELDummy    -0.000995   0.005131     -0.19   0.847
EdLevel     0.00969    0.01276       0.76   0.452
Matching    0.001974   0.001995      0.99   0.328

s = 0.006343    R-sq = 6.9%     R-sq(adj) = 0.0%

Analysis of Variance

SOURCE       DF        SS          MS         F       p
Regression    4  0.00012167  0.00003042    0.76   0.560
Error        41  0.00164949  0.00004023
Total        45  0.00177115
```

a What is the increment to R^2 for the model of Exercise 14.21, as opposed to the model considered here?

b Is this increment statistically significant by an F test, at $\alpha = .05$?

c Compute C_p for this model, treating the previous model as the "all coefficients" model. Which of the two models do you think is more sensible, given the information you have? ■

Residuals Analysis (Step 4)

 nce independent variables, including any polynomial or cross-product terms, have been defined and a tentative model selected, the next step in a careful regression analysis is to check for any gross violations of assumptions. The method for this check is analysis of the residuals from the model.

standardized residuals

Recall that residuals are differences between actual Y values and predicted values using the regression model. In plotting residuals, we often use **standardized residuals**. A standardized residual is expressed in standard deviation units, so a standardized residual of -3.00 means that the point is 3 standard deviations from the regression line. Often, subtracting out the predictive part of the data reveals other structure more clearly. In particular, plotting the residuals from a first-order (linear terms only) model against each independent variable often reveals further structure in the data that can be used to improve the regression model.

One possibility is nonlinearity. We discussed nonlinearity and transformations earlier in the chapter. A noticeable curve in the residuals reflects a curved relation in the data, indicating that a different mathematical form for the regression equation would improve the predictive value of the model. A plot of residuals against each independent variable X often reveals this problem. A scatterplot smoother, such as LOWESS, can be useful in looking for curves in residual plots. For example, Figure 14.13 shows a scatterplot of Y against X_2 and a residual plot against X_2. We think that the curved relation is more evident in the residual plot. The LOWESS curve helps considerably in both plots.

When nonlinearity is found, try transforming either independent or dependent variables. One standard method for doing this is to use (natural) logarithms of all variables except dummy variables. Such a model essentially estimates *percentage* changes in the dependent variable for a small percentage change in an independent variable, other

FIGURE 14.13   *Y* **and Residual Plots Showing Curvature**

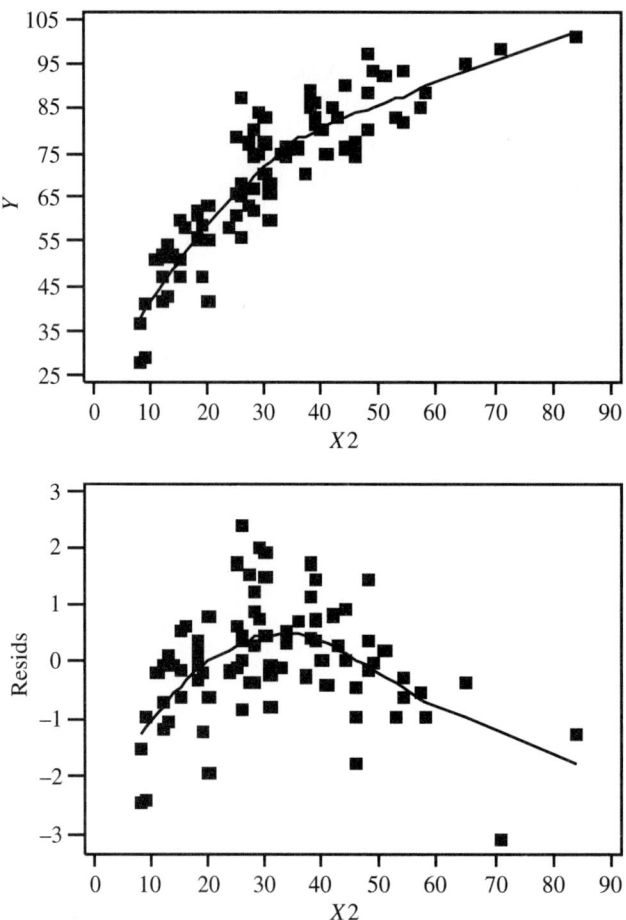

independent variables held constant. Other useful transformations are logarithms of one or more independent variables only, square roots of independent variables, or inverses of the dependent variable or an independent variable. With a good computer package, a number of these transformations can be tested easily.

skewness

    A simple histogram of the residuals reveals severe **skewness** or wild outliers. Skewness is not a terribly serious problem for sample sizes of, say, 30 or more. The Central Limit Theorem effect works for normal distribution methods for inferences about means, even if the population distribution is not normal. A more complicated version of the theorem allows us to make inferences about the coefficients and correlations if the distribution of errors isn't normal. In particular, the *t* and *F* tests of Chapter 12 are valid to a good approximation for even modestly large sample sizes. The guidelines given in discussing inferences about means also apply in regression.

    Nonnormality arising from skewness may have some effect when predicting individual *y* values. Because the prediction is about one particular *y* value, there is no averaging involved, and the Central Limit Theorem doesn't apply. If serious skewness is detected in a histogram of residuals, the "95%" of a 95% prediction interval must be taken with a grain of salt.

    An outlier is a data point that falls far away from the rest of the data. Recall from Chapter 13 that we must be concerned with the leverage (*x* outlier) and influence (both *x* and *y* outlier) properties of a point. A high influence point may seriously distort the regression equation. In addition, some outliers may signal a need for management action. If a regression analysis indicates that the price of a particular parcel of land is very much lower than predicted, that parcel may be an excellent purchase. (It may also be useless— the land may be under water. Regression analysis can't cover everything.) A sales office that has far better results than a regression model predicts may have employees who are doing outstanding work that can be copied. Conversely, a sales office that has far poorer results than the model predicts may have problems. Sometimes it is possible to isolate the reason for the outlier; other times it is not. An outlier may arise because of an error in recording the data or in entering it into a computer, or because the observation is obtained under different conditions from the other observations. If such a reason can be found, the data entry can be corrected or the point omitted from the analysis. If there is no identifiable reason to correct or omit the point, run the regression both with and without it to see which results are sensitive to that point. No matter what the source or reason for outliers, if they go undetected they can cause serious distortions in a regression equation.

E X A M P L E   1 4 . 1 6

Suppose the data for a regression study are as follows:

x:	10	13	16	18	20	22	24	27	30
y:	31	35	42	45	51	53	59	31	70

Draw a scatterplot of the data, identify the outlier, and fit a simple regression model with and without the outlier point.

Solution

A scatterplot of the data (Figure 14.14) shows that any line with slope about 2 and intercept about 10 fits all the data points fairly well, except for the *x* = 27, *y* = 31 point. If that point is included, the least-squares equation is

$$\hat{y} = 19.94 + 1.32x$$

FIGURE 14.14   **Effect of an Outlier**

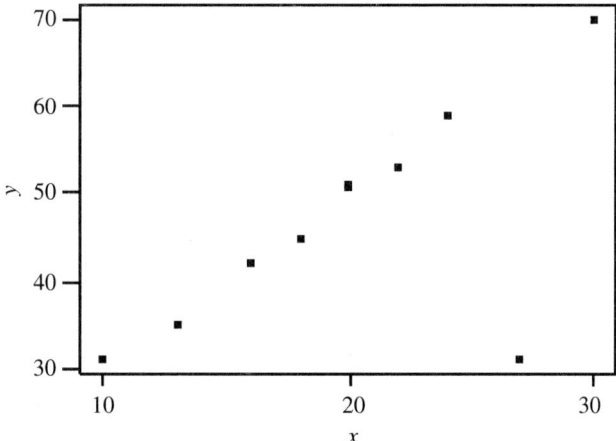

If it is excluded, the equation is

$$\hat{y} = 9.93 + 2.00x$$

The scatterplot shows clearly that the observation (27,31) is a high influence outlier and that the regression equation is distorted by inclusion of this point. ∎

Outliers cause particularly serious distortions because regression is based on minimizing total squared error. Rather than fitting a line with many small errors and one or two large ones (which yield huge squared errors), the least-squares method accepts numerous moderate errors to avoid large ones. The effect is to twist the line in the direction of the outlier.

The first problem with outliers is detection. In simple linear regression, a scatterplot of y versus x reveals outliers very clearly. In multiple regression, because it is not possible to plot all variables at once, scatterplots of y against each x separately are sometimes helpful. However, examination of the residuals (prediction errors) often provides more information regarding outliers than the separate scatterplots. A large residual suggests that the data point may be an outlier, but the fact that the regression line is twisted toward outliers (as indicated in the sample linear regression situation) sometimes causes an outlier to have a modest residual; residuals for perfectly legitimate data points are larger.

EXAMPLE 14.17

Use the following computer output and the residual $(y - \hat{y})$ for each observation to identify potential outliers for the data of Example 14.16:

ROW	y	Predictd	Residual
1	31	33.1381	-2.1381
2	35	37.0966	-2.0966
3	42	41.0552	0.9448
4	45	43.6943	1.3057
5	51	46.3333	4.6667
6	53	48.9724	4.0276
7	59	51.6114	7.3886
8	31	55.5700	-24.5700
9	70	59.5286	10.4714

Solution

From the output, the residual for the data point $x = 27$, $y = 31$ is $31 - 55.57 = -24.57$. The next largest residual is 10.47 for the data point $x = 30$, $y = 70$. Most other residuals are quite a bit smaller. Note that the outlier data point $x = 27$, $y = 31$ twists the least-squares line down, making larger residuals for the data points near $x = 27$. ∎

jackknife method

Another approach to detecting outliers is the **jackknife method**. This involves calculating a series of regression equations, each time excluding one data point. When an outlier is excluded, coefficients in the regression equation change substantially. In principle, one could try excluding two or three points at a time, but the number of equations to calculate and examine would become prohibitive. The one-at-a-time jackknife method may not always catch multiple outliers, but often it does.

In practice, it may be necessary to consider a combination of techniques for examining the sample data for outliers. First, simple x, y scatterplots may suggest that certain observations are outliers. An examination of the residuals may (or may not) confirm this suspicion. If neither the scatterplots nor residuals suggest the existence of one or more outliers, one can probably end the search. However, identification of possible outliers could require additional work with jackknife techniques to isolate specific outliers.

If you detect outliers, what should you do with them? Of course, recording or transcribing errors should simply be corrected. Sometimes an outlier obviously comes from a different population than the other data points. For example, a Fortune 500 conglomerate firm doesn't belong in a study of small manufacturers. In such situations, the outliers can reasonably be omitted from the data. Unless a compelling reason can be found, throwing out a data point seems like cheating. **Robust regression** methods retain possible outliers and try to minimize distortions caused by them. One such method minimizes the sum of absolute (rather than squared) deviations. These methods should be used if outliers cannot be justifiably excluded from the data.

robust regression

E X A M P L E   1 4 . 1 8

Apply a jackknife procedure, eliminating one data point at a time, to the data of Example 14.16. Examine the estimated slopes and intercepts to locate possible outliers.

Solution

We ran repeated regression analyses by computer, each time omitting one of the points. The estimated slopes and intercepts are listed next. Note that the last two data points appear to be outliers because omitting them caused a large change in the equation.

Data Point Excluded	Slope	Intercept
10,31	1.21286	22.47672
13,35	1.26116	21.42333
16,42	1.33281	19.55234
18,45	1.32834	19.60120
20,51	1.31953	19.35947
22,53	1.29235	19.97601
24,59	1.21563	21.04531
27,31	2.00354	9.93239
30,70	.79712	28.42905

Thus, while the scatterplot of Figure 14.14 identified one potential outlier (the point 27, 31), an examination of the residuals as well as the jackknife procedure detects a second potential outlier (the point 30, 70). An examination of residuals from the regression omitting the point 27, 31 indicates that the point 30, 70 is not in fact an outlier. ∎

constant variance

Another formal assumption of regression analysis is that the (true, population) error variance σ_ϵ^2 is constant, regardless of the values of the x predictors. This assumption may also be violated in practice. In particular, it often occurs that combinations of x values leading to large predicted values of y also lead to relatively large variance around the predicted value. We here consider the consequences, detection, and possible cure of the problem of nonconstant error variance.

When the variance around the prediction equation is not constant, there are two basic consequences: (1) Ordinary least-squares regression does not give the most accurate possible estimate of the regression equation and (2) the plus or minus error of prediction given in Chapters 12 and 13 may be seriously in error.

The estimation problem is less serious. If the error variance is not constant, the usual least-squares estimates are still valid in the sense of being unbiased. Furthermore, various studies have indicated that the F and t statistic may be slightly biased but still give about the same conclusions. The issue here is one of "opportunity cost"; if **heteroscedasticity** (nonconstant variance) is recognized, it is possible to improve the estimation of the regression equation and the various related statistics. The technique of **weighted least squares** yields somewhat more accurate estimates of the regression coefficients than does ordinary least-squares regression (more accurate estimates have smaller standard errors). The same technique makes the F and t statistics more powerful for testing the appropriate null hypotheses. Weighted least squares, in the presence of heteroscedasticity around the equation, makes more efficient use of the data.

The more serious problem arises in making forecasts. The best guess forecast based on ordinary least-squares regression is still unbiased, but (given nonconstant error variance) the usual plus or minus formulas can be badly wrong. If the forecast y value falls in a high-variance zone, the theoretical plus or minus term may be much too small.

Probably the best way to detect heteroscedasticity is by eye and by data plot. The most useful is actual y versus predicted y, or residual $y - \hat{y}$ versus predicted y. Most standard statistical computer programs can calculate predicted, actual, and residual values. Some have commands that produce the desired plots. In such plots, look for evidence that the variability of actual y values (or of residuals) increases as predicted y increases. There are several statistical significance tests for the research hypothesis of nonconstant variance, such as regressing the absolute value of the residuals against predicted values from the original regression. These generally tend to confirm the evidence of the "eyeball test."

heteroscedasticity

weighted least squares

EXAMPLE 14.19

A very crude model for predicting the price of common stocks might take price per share (y) as a linear function of the previous year's earnings per share (x_1), change in earnings per share (x_2), and asset value per share (x_3). A scatterplot of residuals versus predicted y values for a regression study of 26 stocks is shown in Figure 14.15. Is there evidence of a problem of heteroscedasticity?

FIGURE 14.15   **Residuals Versus Predicted Values**

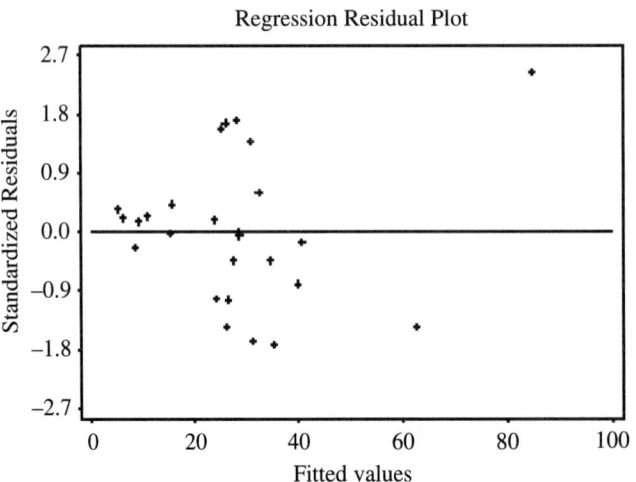

Solution

In the plot of residuals versus predicted values, there is a general tendency for the magnitude of the residuals to increase as $\hat{y}$ increases. All residuals on the left are small, but "the plot thickens" as we move to the right. Therefore, there seems to be a problem of nonconstant variance. ∎

Once we detect the problem of nonconstant variance, there are two basic cures. One is weighted least squares. The other, which often turns out to be equivalent to weighted least squares, is appropriate reexpression of the dependent variable, often by logarithmic transformation or by restating it as a ratio. For example, one may try to predict the number of airline tickets sold for a particular airport from the population of the relevant metropolitan area, the average disposable income in the area, the number of Fortune 500 companies in the area, and so on. Almost certainly, there will be larger variance in number of tickets sold at larger airports. If the dependent variable is redefined as number of tickets sold per capita, the problem of heteroscedasticity may well disappear. A little thought in defining the regression equation often goes a long way.

EXAMPLE 14.20

The dependent variable in Example 14.19 is redefined to be price per share divided by earnings per share (the P/E ratio). The Statistix output follows and the revised model is plotted in Figure 14.16.

```
UNWEIGHTED LEAST SQUARES LINEAR REGRESSION OF PERATIO


PREDICTOR
VARIABLES     COEFFICIENT   STD ERROR   STUDENT'S T     P      VIF
CONSTANT         7.37264     0.39670       18.58     0.0000
CHGEARN         -0.45916     1.85963       -0.25     0.8072    4.3
ASSETVAL         0.00891     0.02395        0.37     0.7132    4.3
```

FIGURE 14.16 **Residuals Versus Predicted Values**

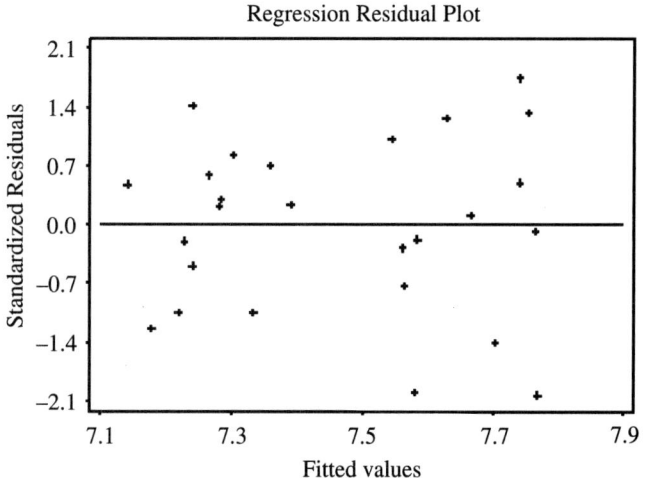

| R-SQUARED | 0.0071 | RESID. MEAN SQUARE (MSE) | 0.91988 |
| ADJUSTED R-SQUARED | -0.0792 | STANDARD DEVIATION | 0.95910 |

SOURCE	DF	SS	MS	F	P
REGRESSION	2	0.15206	0.07603	0.08	0.9209
RESIDUAL	23	21.1573	0.91988		
TOTAL	25	21.3094			

a   Identify the estimated coefficients in the revised model.

b   Does there appear to be a problem of nonconstant variance with the revised model?

c   Use the revised model to predict the price of a stock with earnings 3.00, change in earnings .27, and assets 14.25.

Solution

a $\hat{\beta}_0 = 7.37264$, $\hat{\beta}_1 = -.45916$ and $\hat{\beta}_2 = .00891$

b   The residual plot is much better for the revised model.

c   Substituting CHGEARN = .27, and ASSETVAL = 14.25 into the ratio model, we have $\hat{y} = 7.37264 - .45916(.27) + .00891(14.25) = 7.3756$. This is the predicted value of price–earnings; multiply by earnings (3.00) and obtain a predicted price $= 22.13$.   ■

EXAMPLE 14.21

A first-order model is developed for predicting feed sales using the independent variables defined in Example 14.12. A plot of residuals versus predicted values is shown in Figure 14.17. Is there evidence of nonconstant variance?

Solution

There appears to be some increase in variability as the predicted values increase. Most of the large errors are on the right side of the plot, corresponding to larger predicted values.

FIGURE 14.17   **Standardized Residuals Versus Predicted Values**

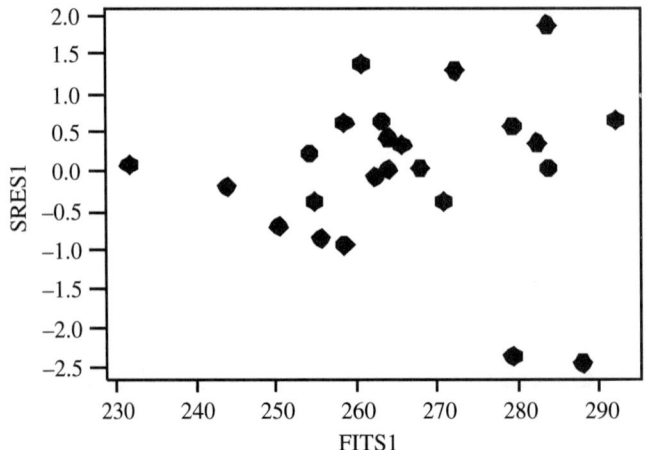

Autocorrelation [Step 4]

 ne of the crucial assumptions of regression analysis is that the error terms ϵ_i, which might be called the "true residuals," are independent. Much of the statistical theory of regression depends heavily on this assumption. In practice the assumption may be wrong. Time-series data, where the data points are measured at successive times, often shown more-or-less cyclic behavior. If such behavior is shown by a dependent variable y, and if no x variable matches the apparent cycles, the sample residuals show evidence of dependence. This problem, which is largely restricted to time-series data, is called **autocorrelation**.

autocorrelation

Autocorrelation occurs when there is a carryover from one observation to the next. If one y value is higher than predicted, the next one also tends to be higher than predicted. Similarly, if one y is lower than predicted, the next one also tends to be lower. Thus, autocorrelation appears as a pattern in which positive residuals tend to be followed by other positive ones, negative residuals by more negative ones. In such a pattern, each residual is positively correlated with the succeeding one. If the errors were independent, there would be no pattern—simply random variation—in the residuals. In a plot of residuals versus time, autocorrelation yields a "snakelike" pattern that looks somewhat cyclical.

Note that autocorrelation is a different idea from collinearity. Collinearity is correlation among independent *variables*; autocorrelation is correlation of successive *residuals*.

effects of autocorrelation

What are the **effects of autocorrelation** on the results we obtain in regression? First, the least-squares prediction equation provides too good a fit to the sample data; that is, the least-squares line is closer to the y values than is the true regression line. Because of this, the residuals (the observed errors, $y - \hat{y}$) are smaller than the true errors (the ϵ's) and the residual standard deviation s_ϵ provides an underestimate of the population standard deviation σ_ϵ. Positive correlation of residuals leads to "delusions of predictability." We think that we can predict more accurately than we actually can.

Furthermore, when autocorrelation is present, the effective sample size is smaller than the number of measurements. Because there is a carryover from one residual to the next, a measurement reflects partly the previous measurement and only partly new information. Therefore, there is not as much information in the data as the apparent sample size indicates. At the extreme, where the errors are perfectly correlated, we would really have *one* observation on the errors, not the apparent sample size n. With a smaller "effective n," standard errors are underestimated, often quite badly. Therefore, when there is positive autocorrelation, confidence intervals will be too narrow. All F and t tests will be more significant (for example, have smaller p-values) than they really should be. Autocorrelation leads to "delusions of significance." We think that estimates are more accurate and tests more conclusive than they actually are.

Finally, if the residual standard deviation is somewhat too small in the presence of autocorrelation, the coefficient of determination is somewhat too large—another case of "delusions of predictability."

In practice, the detection of autocorrelation is based on the residuals because the true errors (the ϵ's) are unknown. If a plot of the residuals versus time shows a cyclic, nonrandom pattern, it is likely that the true errors are dependent, and hence that autocorrelation is present.

E X A M P L E   1 4 . 2 2

Suppose that the data for a simple regression study of y = sales of a new product and x = week number are as follows:

y:	6.1	6.0	5.9	6.3	6.8	6.8	7.0	7.1	7.0	6.7	6.8	7.0	7.2	7.4	7.6
x:	1	2	3	4	5	6	7	8	9	10	11	12	13	14	15

Calculate and graph the least-squares regression line on a scatterplot of the data. Does there seem to be an autocorrelation problem?

Solution

First, notice that we have time-series data, so autocorrelation is a reasonable possibility. The regression line is $\hat{y} = 5.98 + .10x$. It is shown on a scatterplot of the data in Figure 14.18. The cyclic pattern (several negative residuals followed by several positive residuals and so on) clearly indicates that autocorrelation is present.

FIGURE 14.18 **Correlated Residuals**

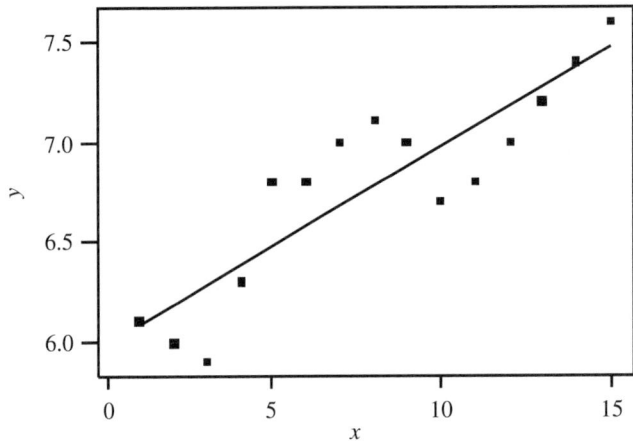

Durbin-Watson statistic

A formal check for autocorrelation uses the **Durbin-Watson statistic**, which is calculated by virtually all regression programs. This statistic is based on the idea that, given (positive) autocorrelation, any one residual tends to be close to the following residual; a large positive residual tends to be followed by another large positive one, and so on. Therefore the squared differences of successive residuals tend to be smaller under positive autocorrelation than they are when independent. The Durbin-Watson statistic is

$$d = \frac{\sum_{t=1}^{n-1}(\hat{\epsilon}_{t+1} - \hat{\epsilon}_t)^2}{\sum_{t=1}^{n}\hat{\epsilon}_t^2}$$

where $\hat{\epsilon}_t$ is the residual at time t. If the true errors are in fact independent, the expected value of d is about 2.0. Positive autocorrelation tends to make $\hat{\epsilon}_{t+1}$ close to $\hat{\epsilon}_t$ and therefore to make d less than 2.0. Tables for a formal hypothesis test based on d are available (see Johnston, 1977). In practice, though, we would hope to accept the null hypothesis of zero autocorrelation. Because accepting any null hypothesis leads to the nasty question of Type II errors, we prefer to use the Durbin-Watson statistic as an index rather than as a formal test. Any value of d less than 1.5 or 1.6 leads us to suspect autocorrelation.

EXAMPLE 14.23

Calculate (just this once) the Durbin-Watson statistic for the data of Example 14.22. Does it indicate an autocorrelation problem?

Solution

x_t	y_t	$\hat{y}_t = 5.98 + .10x_t$	$\hat{\epsilon}_t = y_t - \hat{y}_t$	$\hat{\epsilon}_{t+1} - \hat{\epsilon}_t$	$(\hat{\epsilon}_{t+1} - \hat{\epsilon}_t)^2$	$\hat{\epsilon}^2$
1	6.1	6.08	+.02	−.20	.04	.0004
2	6.0	6.18	−.18	.20	.04	.0324
3	5.9	6.28	−.38	+.30	.09	.1444
4	6.3	6.38	−.08	+.40	.16	.0064
5	6.8	6.48	+.32	−.10	.01	.1024
6	6.8	6.58	+.22	+.10	.01	.0484
7	7.0	6.68	+.32	.00	.00	.1024
8	7.1	6.78	+.32	−.20	.04	.1024
9	7.0	6.88	+.12	−.40	.16	.0144
10	6.7	6.98	−.28	.00	.00	.0784
11	6.8	7.08	−.28	+.10	.01	.0784
12	7.0	7.18	−.18	+.10	.01	.0324
13	7.2	7.28	−.08	+.10	.01	.0064
14	7.4	7.38	+.02	+.10	.01	.0004
15	7.6	7.48	+.12	—	—	.0144
					.59	.764

The Durbin-Watson statistic $d = .59/.764 = .772$. This value is far below the ideal value of 2.0 and the cutoff of 1.5. Autocorrelation is clearly a problem. ∎

EXAMPLE 14.24

Data for 24 months for the feed manufacturer of Example 14.12 are shown here STARTS is the number of starts in the previous month, RELPRI is the manufacturer's feed price in the month (relative to an index), CHICKP is the monthly average price of chickens, COMPPR is the chief competitor's price (also relative to an index), and SALES is monthly feed sales by the manufacturer.

Month	Starts	Relpri	Chickp	Comppr	Sales
1	6.96	16.21	0.493	15.99	231
2	7.20	16.19	0.517	16.31	264
3	6.68	16.06	0.462	16.26	259
4	7.01	15.97	0.490	16.12	258
5	7.47	16.31	0.536	16.41	265
6	7.68	16.58	0.594	16.49	255
7	7.65	16.97	0.570	17.00	241
8	7.49	17.21	0.538	17.01	233
9	7.38	17.08	0.499	16.96	244
10	7.46	17.00	0.486	17.21	268
11	7.58	17.15	0.525	17.47	277
12	7.56	17.31	0.490	17.22	260

13	7.60	17.08	0.473	17.11	266
14	7.31	17.11	0.431	17.01	277
15	7.04	16.97	0.456	16.99	275
16	7.03	16.90	0.464	17.16	278
17	7.36	16.84	0.477	17.24	295
18	7.53	17.17	0.509	17.38	277
19	7.68	17.52	0.492	17.46	264
20	7.73	17.67	0.474	17.81	284
21	7.51	17.65	0.510	17.70	267
22	7.84	17.34	0.495	17.47	291
23	7.67	17.59	0.501	17.50	263
24	7.70	17.52	0.423	17.63	279

A first-order model is run with independent variables STARTS, RELPRI, CHICKP, and COMPPR (using Minitab). The following selected output is obtained. Is there evidence of autocorrelation?

```
The regression equation is
Sales = 181 + 24.3 Starts - 66.8 Relpri - 204 Chickp + 66.9 Comppr
```

```
Predictor      Coef      Stdev    t-ratio       p
Constant     181.01      73.04       2.48   0.023
Starts        24.29      11.32       2.14   0.045
Relpri       -66.85      11.75      -5.69   0.000
Chickp      -203.80      61.16      -3.33   0.003
Comppr        66.91      11.23       5.96   0.000
```

```
s = 8.391     R-sq = 78.6%    R-sq(adj) = 74.1%
```

```
Analysis of Variance
```

```
SOURCE        DF        SS        MS        F        p
Regression     4    4918.2    1229.5    17.46    0.000
Error         19    1337.8      70.4
Total         23    6256.0
```

```
Durbin-Watson statistic = 1.45
```

Solution

There is some suggestion of autocorrelation. The Durbin-Watson statistic is 1.45 and Figure 14.19 may show some cyclic behavior. In a previous example, we had also seen an indication of nonconstant variance, so this model seems to have several assumption problems. ■

EXAMPLE 14.25

In an attempt to solve the problem of nonconstant variance detected in Example 14.21, a revised model is run. The dependent variable is SHARE = SALES/STARTS. The independent variables are RELPRI and RELDIF = (RELPRI − COMPPR)/CHICKP. Selected output follows, and the residuals are plotted in Figure 14.20. Is there evidence of an autocorrelation problem?

FIGURE 14.19 **Sequence Plot of Standardized Residuals**

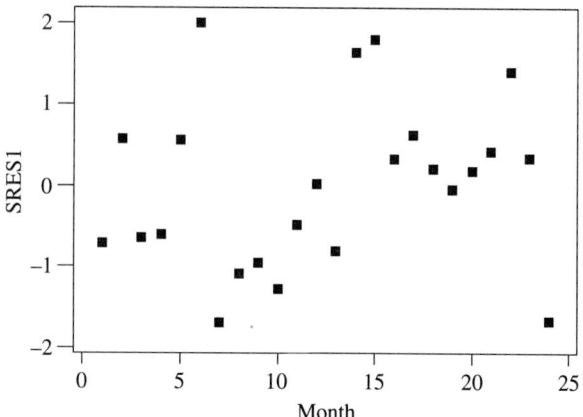

FIGURE 14.20 **Sequence Plot of Standardized Residuals**

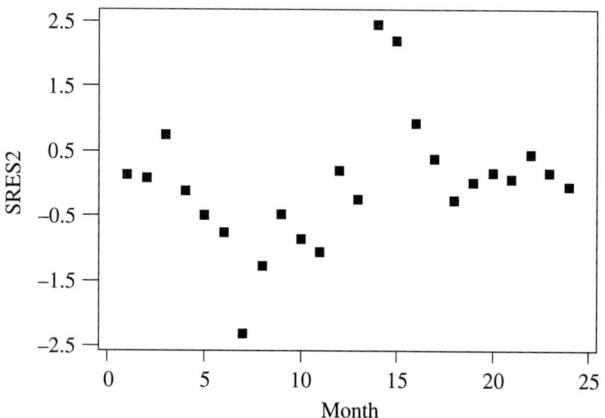

```
The regression equation is
Share = 39.7 - 0.269 Relpri - 5.20 Reldif


Predictor      Coef      Stdev    t-ratio       p
Constant      39.69      12.01       3.31   0.003
Relpri      -0.2692     0.7061      -0.38   0.707
Reldif       -5.196      1.094      -4.75   0.000


s = 1.718       R-sq = 52.7%     R-sq(adj) = 48.2%

Analysis of Variance

SOURCE       DF         SS         MS       F       p
Regression    2     69.004     34.502   11.70   0.000
Error        21     61.951      2.950
Total        23    130.955


Durbin-Watson statistic = 0.78
```

Solution

The Durbin-Watson statistic is 0.78, and the sequence plot of residuals clearly suggests autocorrelation. There is a up-down-up pattern to the residuals. ∎

If autocorrelation is suspected, either because of a plot of residuals versus time or because of a Durbin-Watson statistic less than about 1.5 or 1.6, what should be done about the regression model? Ideally, we can find another predictor that accounts for the "snakelike" behavior of the data; we would try to find a predictor whose cycles matched the cycles of the residuals. One good thing to try is some macroeconomic variable such as disposable income or consumer confidence. If we found such a predictor, we would improve the predictive value of the model, as well as solve an assumption problem. Failing that, we could adopt an autocorrelation model for the error terms. One simple error model is the **first-order autoregressive model**

first-order autoregressive model

$$\epsilon_t = u_t + \rho u_{t-1}$$

where the u_t values are independent and ρ is a model parameter; $\rho > 0$ yields positive autocorrelation. If this model is correct and if (miraculously) ρ is known, then it can be proven that

$$Y_t - \rho Y_{t-1} = \beta_0(1 - \rho) + \beta_1(x_{t1} - \rho x_{t-1,1})$$
$$+ \cdots + \beta_k(x_{tk} - \rho x_{t-1,k}) + (\epsilon_t - \rho \epsilon_{t-1})$$

is a model satisfying the assumption of independent error. In practice, the problem is to estimate the unknown error parameter ρ.

use of differences

A quick approach to the problem is to assume $\rho = 1$. This leads to a regression of the differences $y_t - y_{t-1}$ on the differences $x_{t1} - x_{t-11}, \ldots, x_{tk} - x_{t-1,k}$. Often, using differences eliminates any autocorrelation problems. This method also tends to reduce collinearity, which is often a major problem with time-series data.

Cochrane-Orcutt method

Regression of differences is a crude approach because it assumes that the autocorrelation parameter ρ equals 1. A more sophisticated approach is the **Cochrane-Orcutt method**. In this method, we begin with a raw data regression, estimate $\hat{\rho}$, calculate all differences $y_t - \hat{\rho}y_{t-1}$ and $x_t - \hat{\rho}x_{t-1}$, regress using these differences, reestimate $\hat{\rho}$, and so on to convergence. This is a technical chore for a special computer program, so we only mention the possibility. Alternatively, it is possible to search for the least-squares value of $\hat{\rho}$. For details, consult a time-series specialist.

EXAMPLE 14.26

Differences of the variables of Example 14.25 are calculated and a regression run. Selected Minitab output is shown here. Note that although there were 24 observations initially, we now have 23 first differences.

```
The regression equation is
DShare = 0.239 - 3.43 DRelpr - 2.89 DReldf


23 cases used 1 cases contain missing values


Predictor      Coef     Stdev   t-ratio      p
Constant     0.2388    0.2940      0.81   0.426
DRelpr       -3.429     1.633     -2.10   0.049
DReldf      -2.8934    0.8211     -3.52   0.002
```

s = 1.310   R-sq = 64.1%   R-sq(adj) = 60.5%

Analysis of Variance

SOURCE	DF	SS	MS	F	p
Regression	2	61.225	30.613	17.85	0.000
Error	20	34.302	1.715		
Total	22	95.527			

Durbin-Watson statistic = 2.20

The variables are DSHARE, DRELPR, and DRELDF, where the initial D in the variable names indicates that the quantities are differences. Is there evidence of an autocorrelation problem or a problem of nonconstant variance? See Figure 14.21.

Solution

The Durbin-Watson statistic is 2.20 and the sequence plot of residuals (Figure 14.21a) shows no particular pattern. If anything, the differencing method has produced overkill;

FIGURE 14.21 **(a) Sequence Plot of Standardized Residuals; (b) Plot of Standardized Residuals Versus Predicted Values**

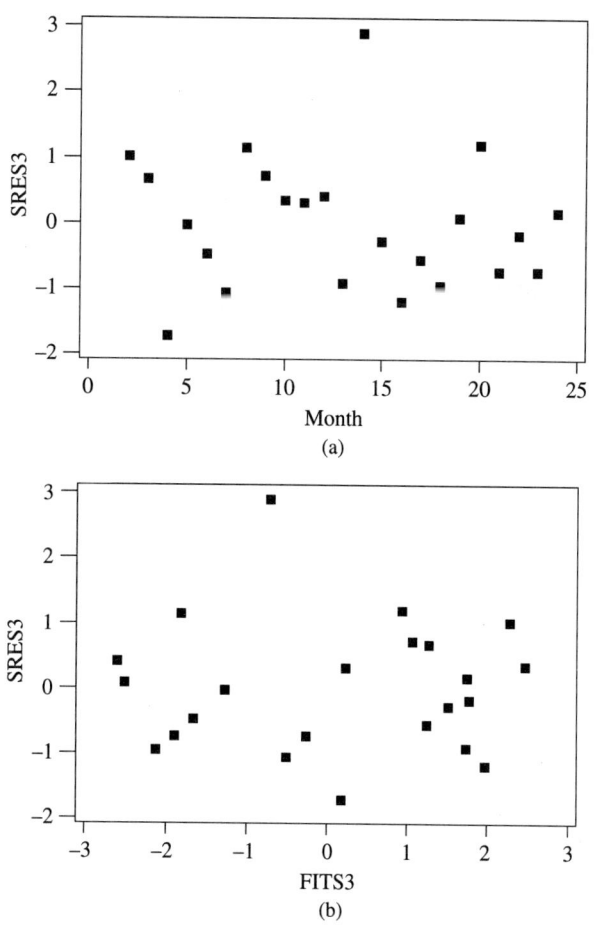

positive autocorrelation has been converted to apparent negative autocorrelation. Negative autocorrelation at least yields conservative results. A Cochrane-Orcutt or search method might make more efficient use of the data. The plot of residuals against predicted values shows no pattern, so there is no reason to think that nonconstant variance is a problem. ■

E X E R C I S E S

14.23   Residual plots for the regression model of Exercise 14.22 are shown in Figure 14.22.

   a Is there any strong suggestion of nonlinearity?

   b Is there any strong suggestion of nonconstant variance?

F I G U R E 1 4 . 2 2   **Residual Plot for Contributions Data**

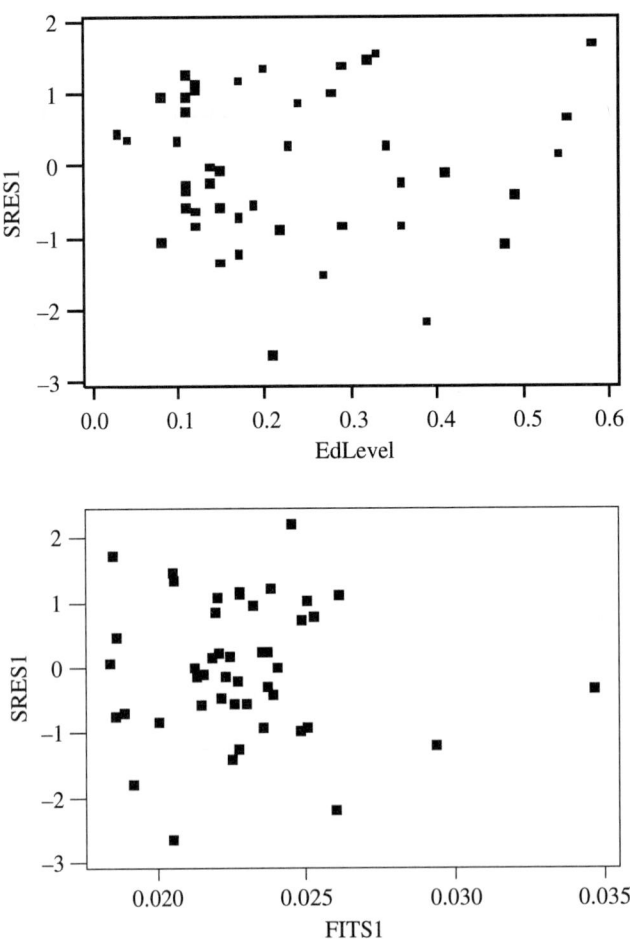

14.24   The district sales office for a particular automobile manufacturer is interested in predicting the sales of the "top of the line" luxury car in the district. It is obvious that sales are affected by the rated gasoline mileage of the car and by the car loan interest rate charged by the company's financing agency. It also seems plausible that sales are affected by gasoline prices and by the price of the car. Data are collected for 48 months; the last 6 months are reserved for model validation (to be discussed in Section 14.8). The variables are:

MILAGE: Rated gas mileage of the car
GASPRI: Average price per gallon (in cents) in the district
PREGAS: Average gas price in the previous month
INTRAT: Interest rate (percent per year)
CARPRI: Sticker price divided by the consumer price index

A first-order model is fit. Selected output follows. Figure 14.23 shows the sequence plot of residuals.

```
MTB > regress c1 on 5 vars c2-c6;
SUBC> dw.

The regression equation is
Sales = 5760 + 231 Mileage - 8.49 GasPri - 14.5 PreGas - 252 IntRate - 56.4 CarPrice

Predictor      Coef     Stdev    t-ratio      p
Constant       5760      2098      2.75     0.009
Mileage      230.79     53.91      4.28     0.000
GasPri       -8.493     1.701     -4.99     0.000
PreGas      -14.538     1.637     -8.88     0.000
IntRate     -251.70     94.15     -2.67     0.011
CarPrice     -56.44     42.27     -1.34     0.190

s = 47.54     R-sq = 87.2%    R-sq(adj) = 85.4%

Analysis of Variance

SOURCE       DF        SS        MS        F        p
Regression    5     554702    110940    49.08    0.000
Error        36     81373      2260
Total        41    636076

Durbin-Watson statistic = 0.80
```

a In the estimated regression model, what do the positive and negative signs indicate about the effect of each independent variable?

b Locate the residual standard deviation.

FIGURE 14.23   **Sequence Plot of Residuals for Car Sales**

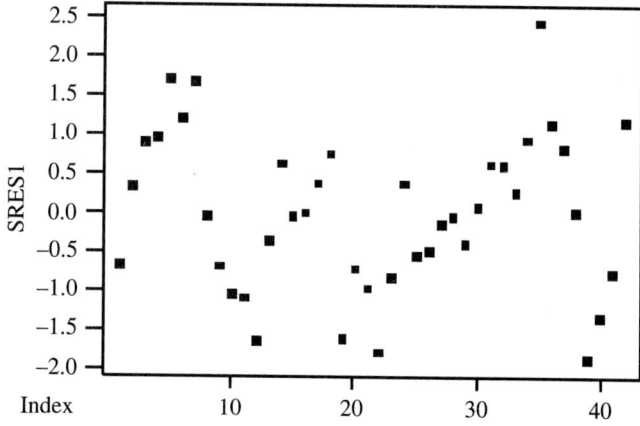

14.25 Refer to the output for the model for Exercise 14.24 and to Figure 14.23.

    a Does the Durbin-Watson statistic indicate that there is a problem of (positive) autocorrelation?

    b Does the sequence plot of residuals indicate that autocorrelation is a problem?

14.26 The auto sales forecasting model of Exercise 14.24 is modified in two ways. First, the gas price variables are divided by the mileage figure to yield rated gas price per mile driven. The current month's price per mile is called PRIMIL and the previous month's is LAGPRM. Second, differences of the variables SALES, PRIMIL, LAGPRM, INTRAT, and CARPRI are calculated; the names are prefaced by a D. A regression model based on these differences is fit, with the following results. The sequence plot of residuals is shown in Figure 14.24.

```
The regression equation is
CSales = - 0.66 - 89.7 CPriMil - 222 CLagPrM - 110 CIntRat + 5.9 CCarPri

41 cases used 1 cases contain missing values

Predictor     Coef     Stdev    t-ratio      p
Constant    -0.662     6.603     -0.10    0.921
CPriMil     -89.66     16.95     -5.29    0.000
CLagPrM    -221.95     15.78    -14.06    0.000
CIntRat    -109.50     85.13     -1.29    0.207
CCarPri       5.89     39.18      0.15    0.881

s = 37.34      R-sq = 86.0%     R-sq(adj) = 84.5%

Analysis of Variance

SOURCE        DF        SS        MS        F        p
Regression     4    309524     77381    55.50    0.000
Error         36     50191      1394
Total         40    359715

Durbin-Watson statistic = 1.89
```

    a In the regression equation, have any signs changed compared to the original model? How different are the coefficients?

    b Locate the residual standard deviation.

    c Is the residual standard deviation larger for the difference model than for the original? Why would this be a common result?

FIGURE 14.24 **Sequence Plot of Residuals; Modified Car Sales Model**

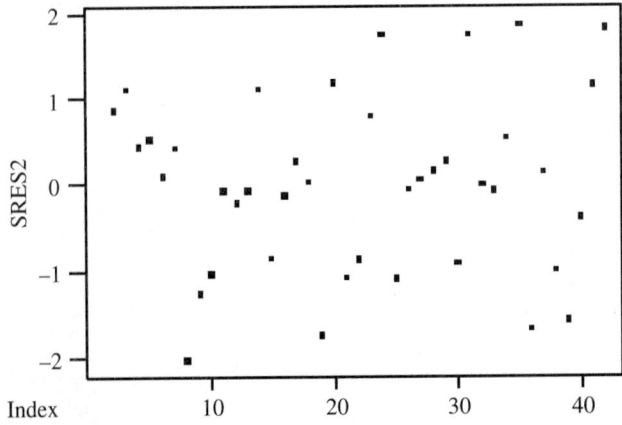

14.27 Previously we considered sales of a certain snack cracker. We developed a model that did not include product terms because there was little evidence that such terms improved the prediction. As one more check on the adequacy of the model, we plotted residuals against the quantitative predictors, price and sales, in the category. The results are shown in Figure 14.25.

FIGURE 14.25 **Residual Plots for Snack Cracker Data**

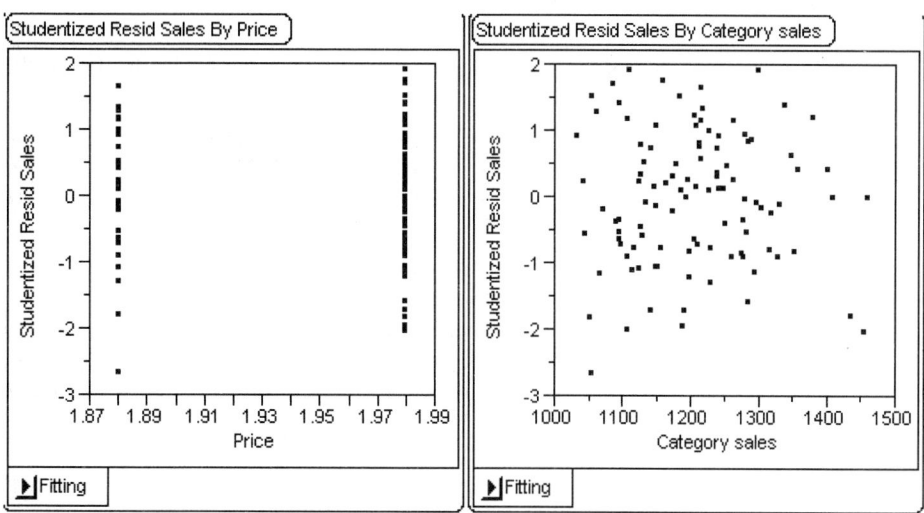

a Is there any clear indication of nonlinearity in the plots?

b Are there any outliers, whether or not they have high leverage? ■

14.8

Model Validation

In this computer era, data can be "massaged" repeatedly at little cost. Regressions can be run with every conceivable combination of variables, transformations, and lags. It isn't unusual to have a hundred different regression equations run to try to predict a variable y. The statistical theory of regression analysis implicitly assumes that the choice of predictors x and dependent variable y has been made, once and for all, and that a single regression equation is found. The gap between theory and practice is wide.

The practice of calculating many regression equations and selecting the best one often leads to overoptimism. The apparent predictability decreases when the equation is used with new data—for two reasons. First, any regression equation is based on predicting the past; the equation is chosen to yield the best fit to available data. If the underlying economic structure changes, the predictive value of the model will decrease. Second, when one selects the best of many equations, one runs a risk of "capitalizing on chance." Even purely random phenomena can be explained after the fact by some combination of variables, if you search long enough.

A good practical approach to selecting an appropriate prediction equation is to validate the chosen regression equation with new data. In a time-series study, we can withhold the most recent data from the original regression study. Then we can use the chosen regression equation to predict recent values. The resulting standard deviation gives a good indication of the future predictive value of the equation. We can use the same procedure with cross-section data. Select some subset of observations (perhaps 10% or 20%) at random, withhold them from the original study, and use them for validation. The chosen regression typically does not perform quite as well in the validation study. If it still works reasonably well, that's good grounds for believing that it will be useful in practice.

EXAMPLE 14.27

An additional 12 months' data are collected for the feed manufacturer of Example 14.12. The difference model of Example 14.26 is used with these data. The results are as follows:

	Actual CSHARE	Predicted CSHARE	Error
	.6243	1.4735	−.8492
	2.7931	1.7694	1.0237
	−1.4616	−1.6785	.2169
	−2.1039	−.4668	−1.6371
	1.0487	.2520	.7967
	3.4225	1.3979	2.0246
	.8994	1.9018	−1.0024
	−1.1583	−.7206	−.4377
	1.2767	.4526	.8241
	4.0023	4.2146	−.2123
	−2.9046	−3.9520	1.0474
	−.8726	−.5465	−.3261
Mean	.4638	.3414	.1224
Standard deviation	2.2153	2.0665	1.0520

a   Is there any flagrant bias in the predictions?

b   Is the error standard deviation grossly different?

Solution

a   There's no obvious systematic error. The mean error is small (.1224) relative to the size of the actual values and to the error standard deviation. Exactly half of the errors are positive.

b   The error standard deviation (1.0520) is slightly smaller, in fact, than 1.310.   ■

14.9

Summing Up

H ere are some suggestions for the process of constructing a multiple regression model:

1   The most important step in obtaining a useful regression model is the choice of dependent and independent variables. Knowledge of the situation and any theoretical reasoning that's available should be used in selecting variables.

2   Possible lags in time-series data and possible interactions should be identified by whatever knowledge and theory are available. The analyst must identify these

possibilities to be able to test them; no computer package we know of can do so automatically.

3 In selecting independent variables, try to avoid obvious collinearity. Very little can be gained by having independent variables that are nearly the same.

4 Before starting the analysis, it's a useful practice to set aside a small fraction of the data for validating the final model.

5 A scatterplot matrix and a table of correlations are a good way to start the data analysis. They will indicate which predictors seem most effective, which X's are collinear, and possibly the presence of outliers.

6 The goal of regression modeling is to obtain a relatively simple equation that captures almost all of the predictive ability in the data. Try to eliminate variables that add little to the overall value of the model.

7 Residual plots and (for time series) the Durbin-Watson statistic should be checked routinely for assumption violations.

8 If data are available for validation, check to see if the average error in the validation sample is near 0 and if the standard deviation of the validation errors is reasonably close to the residual standard deviation of the model.

In addition, you may want to reread the summary of key ideas at the beginning of the chapter.

EXAMPLE 14.28

A sample of 70 communities was selected from the Philadelphia area in an attempt to predict the average price of houses. Data collected included: PRICE: average house price; CNTY: county (1 = Montgomery, 2 = Delaware, 3 = Bucks, 4 = Chester, 5 = Philadelphia); CRIME: crime rate per 1000 residents; MILES: miles to Center City (Philadelphia's downtown area); POPCHG: population change 1990–1994.

The data source is "Where Should I Live?" *Philadelphia* magazine, April 1996.

JMP IN regression results are shown in Figure 14.26. What do the results indicate about the effect of the various predictors on house prices? Are there any indications of serious violations of assumptions? If so, what modifications to the analysis would you propose?

Solution

As usual, it pays to look at data plots before worrying about calculated values. The plot of residuals against predicted prices shows a fan shape—increasing variability as the predicted values increase. This seems almost inevitable. Our predictions will not be in error by $100,000 for houses that are priced at $50,000, but they might well be in error that much for very expensive areas. To deal with this problem, we transformed the dependent variable scale to the natural logarithm of price. Recall that changes in the natural logarithm of a quantity are roughly equal to percentage changes in the original quantity. Output for the log-price analysis is shown in Figure 14.27.

The output for the log-price analysis seems to indicate that only the dummy variables for the various counties have statistically detectable predictive value. However, the residual plots against the quantitative independent variables show one extremely odd point, with a crime rate far higher than any other. This point is 0 miles from Center City, and therefore must be Center City itself.

FIGURE 14.26 **Output for House Price Regression**

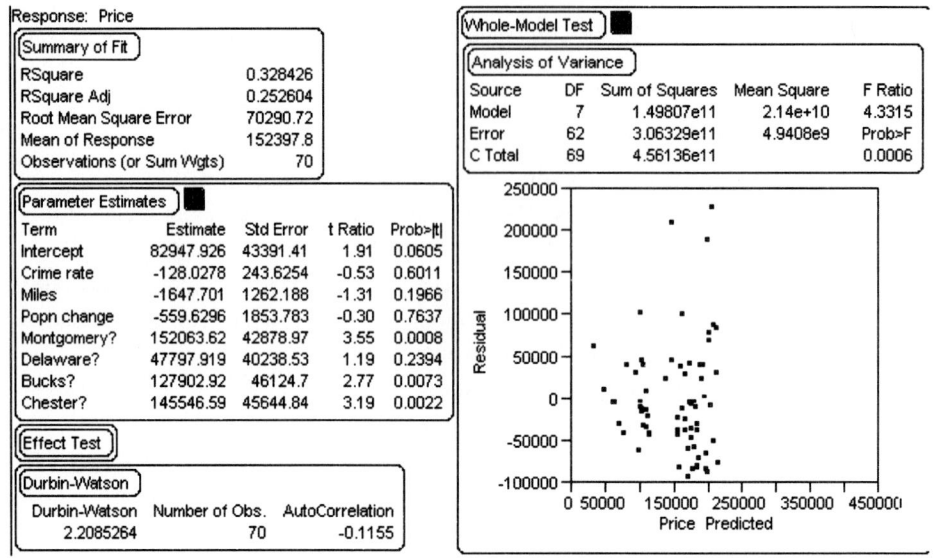

FIGURE 14.27 **Output for Logarithm of Price Regression**

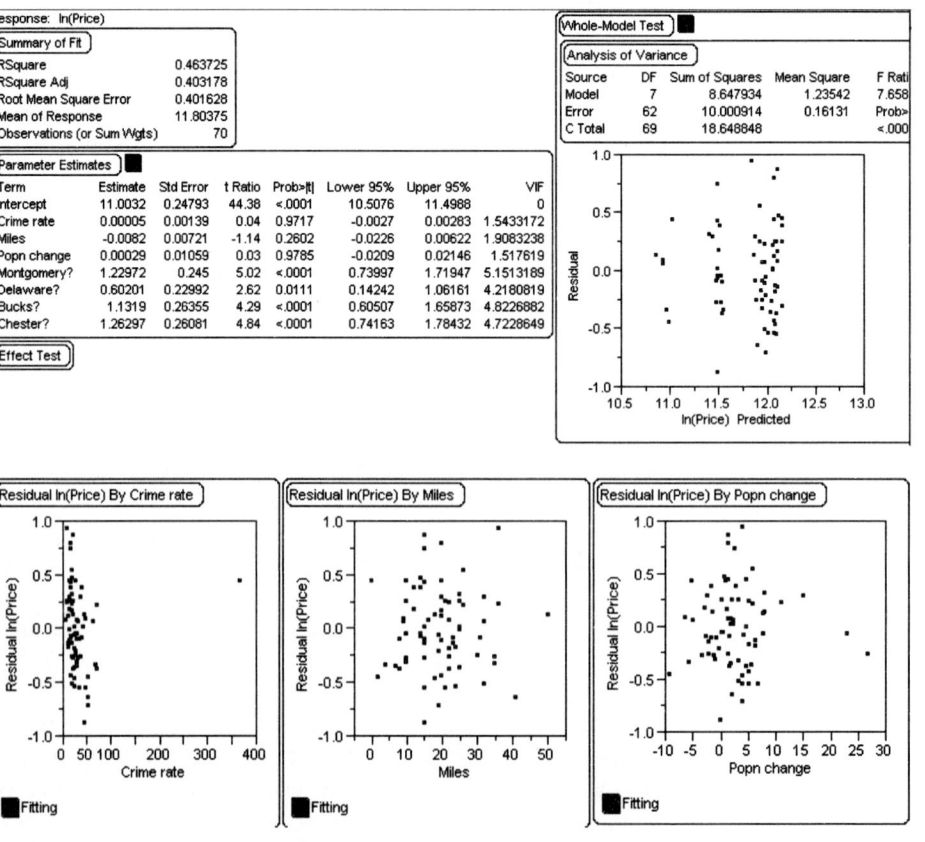

The crime rate per thousand residents is not very meaningful for this area, which has relatively few residents but a very large number of people employed there. Therefore, we felt justified in excluding this case as not belonging with the remaining data. The revised output is shown in Figure 14.28.

FIGURE 14.28   **Output for Logarithm of Price Regression, Excluding Center City**

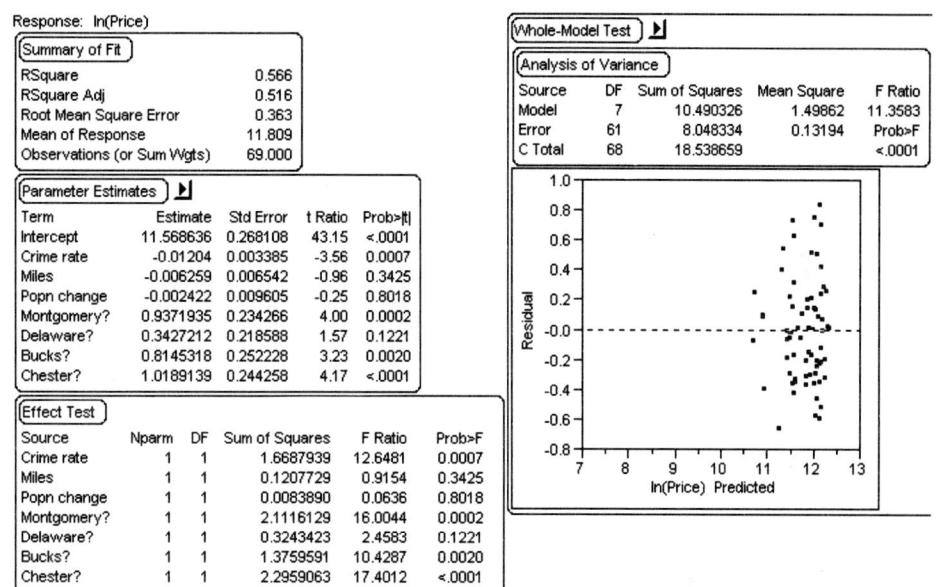

Response: ln(Price)

Summary of Fit

RSquare	0.566
RSquare Adj	0.516
Root Mean Square Error	0.363
Mean of Response	11.809
Observations (or Sum Wgts)	69.000

Parameter Estimates

Term	Estimate	Std Error	t Ratio	Prob>|t|
Intercept	11.568636	0.268108	43.15	<.0001
Crime rate	-0.01204	0.003385	-3.56	0.0007
Miles	-0.006259	0.006542	-0.96	0.3425
Popn change	-0.002422	0.009605	-0.25	0.8018
Montgomery?	0.9371935	0.234266	4.00	0.0002
Delaware?	0.3427212	0.218588	1.57	0.1221
Bucks?	0.8145318	0.252228	3.23	0.0020
Chester?	1.0189139	0.244258	4.17	<.0001

Effect Test

Source	Nparm	DF	Sum of Squares	F Ratio	Prob>F
Crime rate	1	1	1.6687939	12.6481	0.0007
Miles	1	1	0.1207729	0.9154	0.3425
Popn change	1	1	0.0083890	0.0636	0.8018
Montgomery?	1	1	2.1116129	16.0044	0.0002
Delaware?	1	1	0.3243423	2.4583	0.1221
Bucks?	1	1	1.3759591	10.4287	0.0020
Chester?	1	1	2.2959063	17.4012	<.0001

Whole-Model Test

Analysis of Variance

Source	DF	Sum of Squares	Mean Square	F Ratio
Model	7	10.490326	1.49862	11.3583
Error	61	8.048334	0.13194	Prob>F
C Total	68	18.538659		<.0001

In this output, the crime rate is clearly negatively related to log-price. In addition, the dummy variables for Montgomery, Bucks, and Chester counties are clearly positive; because Philadelphia county is the "undummied" county, all the other counties are being compared to it. Miles and population change don't have a detectable relation to log-price, once county and crime rate are given.

The model is not a very effective predictor. Although the R^2 of 0.566 may seem decent, the residual standard deviation (Root Mean Square Error) of 0.36 means that a 95% prediction interval will be roughly ±0.72, roughly 72% below or above the predicted value! The variables chosen are far too simple to give an accurate prediction of price.

The residual plots for the outlier-deleted model don't show any evident curves or outliers. The Durbin-Watson statistic is basically irrelevant here because the data are cross-sectional, not time-series. There is still some suggestion of nonconstant variance, but the variance around the model is so large in any case that it hardly matters whether it's constant or not!   ■

SUPPLEMENTARY   EXERCISES

14.28   A copy center wants to be able to tell customers how long a wait will be required before a job is ready. In the past, the receiving clerk has made a wild guess based on experience (or, all too often, lack of experience). Estimates of waiting time that are much too long are wasteful, in that the customer can't pick up the job even though it's ready. Estimates that are much too short result in customers returning to the center before the job is done and standing around waiting, unhappily. The center manager decides to try a regression model to predict the wait (in minutes). Data from 200 recent jobs include the waiting time in minutes, the number of jobs waiting in line ahead of the submitted jobs, the average number of pages of the waiting jobs, the type of job (regular, odd size, or color), and the type of service purchased (regular or rush). The manager suspected that color and odd size jobs, which used special copying machines, were not as severely affected by the number of waiting jobs. There was considerable question as to whether rush jobs were really processed more rapidly.

To begin the analysis, the manager used JMP to obtain plots of waiting time against number waiting and average pages. The JMP grouping variable feature provided separate regression lines for the three types of jobs. Plots are shown in Figure 14.29.

a Do these plots suggest that the average waiting time differs for the three types of jobs?

b Do these plots suggest that the effect on waiting time of number waiting and of average pages depends on the type of job?

FIGURE 14.29   **Waiting Times for Three Types of Jobs**

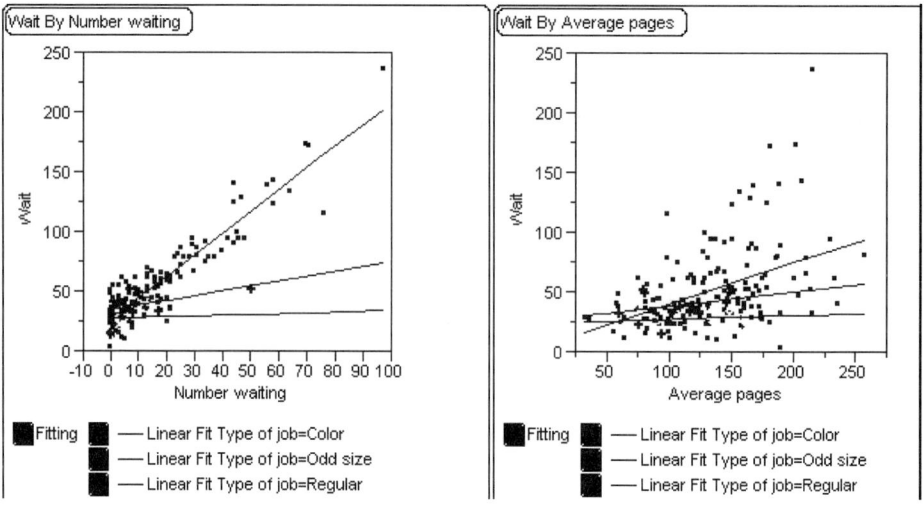

14.29 The manager obtained similar plots for regular vs. rush service, as shown in Figure 14.30.

a Do these plots suggest that the average waiting time differs for the two types of service?

b Do these plots suggest that the effect on waiting time of number waiting and of average pages depends on the type of service?

14.30 The copy center manager obtained a multiple regression model to predict waiting time based on four independent variables: number waiting, average pages, job type, and service type, along with products of the quantitative variables with the qualitative ones. (To produce the indicated results in JMP, job type and service type were declared to be ordinal. It is permissible to lie to a computer program to achieve desired results.) The output included the results shown in Figure 14.31.

a What does the sign of the coefficient of the odd size variable (which equals 1 for odd size jobs and 0 for all others) indicate about the intercept term for odd size jobs?

b What does the coefficient of the odd size*number waiting product indicate about the slope for odd size jobs?

c What does the sign of the coefficient of the rush variable (which equals 1 for rush jobs and 0 for all others) indicate about the intercept term for rush jobs?

d What does the coefficient of the rush*number waiting product indicate about the slope for rush jobs?

FIGURE 14.30 **Waiting Times for Two Types of Service**

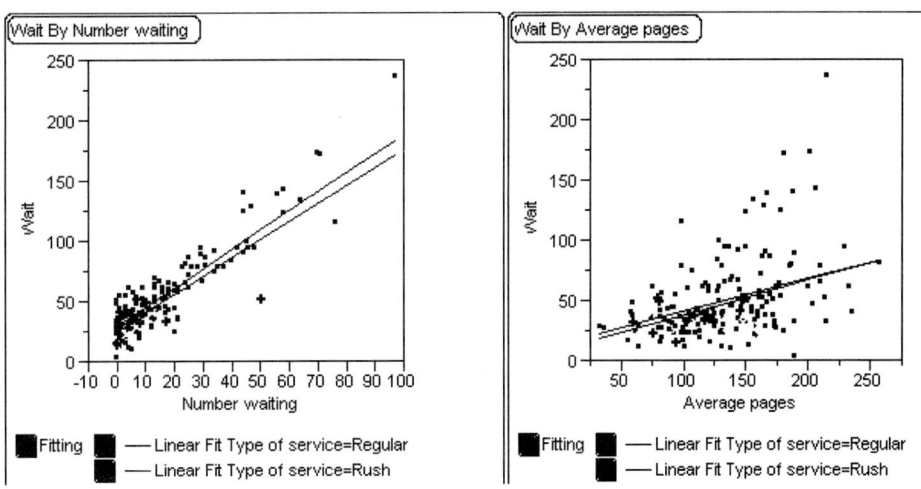

FIGURE 14.31 **Regression Results Including Product Terms**

Response: Wait

Summary of Fit

RSquare	0.873206
RSquare Adj	0.867895
Root Mean Square Error	11.66544
Mean of Response	48.7
Observations (or Sum Wgts)	200

Lack of Fit

Parameter Estimates

Term	Estimate	Std Error	t Ratio	Prob>|t|
Intercept	12.253918	4.327461	2.83	0.0051
Number waiting	0.0291797	0.133647	0.22	0.8274
Average pages	0.1087247	0.02081	5.22	0.0000
Job type[Odd siz]	10.306992	5.796198	1.78	0.0770
Job type[Regular]	-10.39532	4.928828	-2.11	0.0362
Service [Rush]	4.8798029	2.606219	1.87	0.0627
Number w*Job type[Odd siz]	0.4366076	0.293463	1.49	0.1385
Number w*Job type[Regular]	1.28538	0.268197	4.79	0.0000
Number w*Service [Rush]	-0.159613	0.129321	-1.23	0.2186

Effect Test

Source	Nparm	DF	Sum of Squares	F Ratio	Prob>F
Number waiting	1	1	6.487	0.0477	0.8274
Average pages	1	1	3714.550	27.2963	0.0000
Job type	2	2	607.892	2.2335	0.1099
Service type	1	1	477.073	3.5058	0.0627
Number waiting*Job type	2	2	21580.648	79.2925	0.0000
Number waiting*Service type	1	1	207.300	1.5233	0.2186

14.31 The Effect Test portion of the output in Figure 14.31 performs a partial F test for the indicated variable. According to this output, which interaction is statistically detectable at the usual α levels?

14.32 The copy center manager ran another regression model, omitting all product terms, with results shown in Figure 14.32. Is there a statistically significant effect of these product terms?

FIGURE 14.32 **Regression Results Excluding Product Terms**

Response: Wait

Summary of Fit

RSquare	0.767889
RSquare Adj	0.761907
Root Mean Square Error	15.66084
Mean of Response	48.7
Observations (or Sum Wgts)	200

Lack of Fit

Parameter Estimates

Term	Estimate	Std Error	t Ratio	Prob>|t|
Intercept	-13.6621	5.031367	-2.72	0.0072
Number waiting	1.4470954	0.067122	21.56	0.0000
Average pages	0.1251723	0.027788	4.50	0.0000
Job type[Odd siz]	24.229664	6.233513	3.89	0.0001
Job type[Regular]	3.4508982	5.447254	0.63	0.5271
Service [Rush]	3.5110227	2.643057	1.33	0.1856

Effect Test

Source	Nparm	DF	Sum of Squares	F Ratio	Prob>F
Number waiting	1	1	113998.33	464.8022	0.0000
Average pages	1	1	4976.70	20.2913	0.0000
Job type	2	2	15920.18	32.4555	0.0000
Service type	1	1	432.80	1.7646	0.1856

14.33 The manager tried one more regression model, incorporating only dummy variables for job type and only product terms involving job type. The results are shown in Figure 14.33.

a Compared to the original model, does omission of the terms involving rush jobs cause a significant decrease in ability to predict waiting times?

b What does this finding indicate about the effectiveness of rush service?

14.34 A plot of residuals against predicted values (for the model including job type and its product terms) is shown in Figure 14.34. Is there any indication of a problem with the constant variance assumption?

14.35 Plots of residuals against the quantitative variables are shown in Figure 14.35. Is there any indication of a problem of nonlinearity? A problem with high leverage points?

14.36 One variable that the copy center manager might have tried in a model is the product of number of jobs waiting times average pages per waiting job. Rather than an interaction term, how else can this variable be interpreted? That is, if the variable comes out to equal 6000 for a particular job, it means 6000 what?

FIGURE 14.33 **Regression Results Including Job Type and Interaction**

Response: Wait

```
Summary of Fit
RSquare                          0.870879
RSquare Adj                      0.866865
Root Mean Square Error           11.71086
Mean of Response                 48.7
Observations (or Sum Wgts)       200
```

```
Lack of Fit
```

```
Parameter Estimates
Term                          Estimate    Std Error   t Ratio   Prob>|t|
Intercept                    13.125009    4.31664      3.04     0.0027
Number waiting                0.0098111   0.133698     0.07     0.9416
Average pages                 0.1084258   0.02089      5.19     0.0000
Job type[Odd siz]             9.956289    5.815614     1.71     0.0885
Job type[Regular]            -9.764233    4.936428    -1.98     0.0494
Number w*Job type[Odd siz]    0.4491455   0.294477     1.53     0.1288
Number w*Job type[Regular]    1.2611036   0.268255     4.70     0.0000
```

FIGURE 14.34 **Residuals Versus Predicted Values**

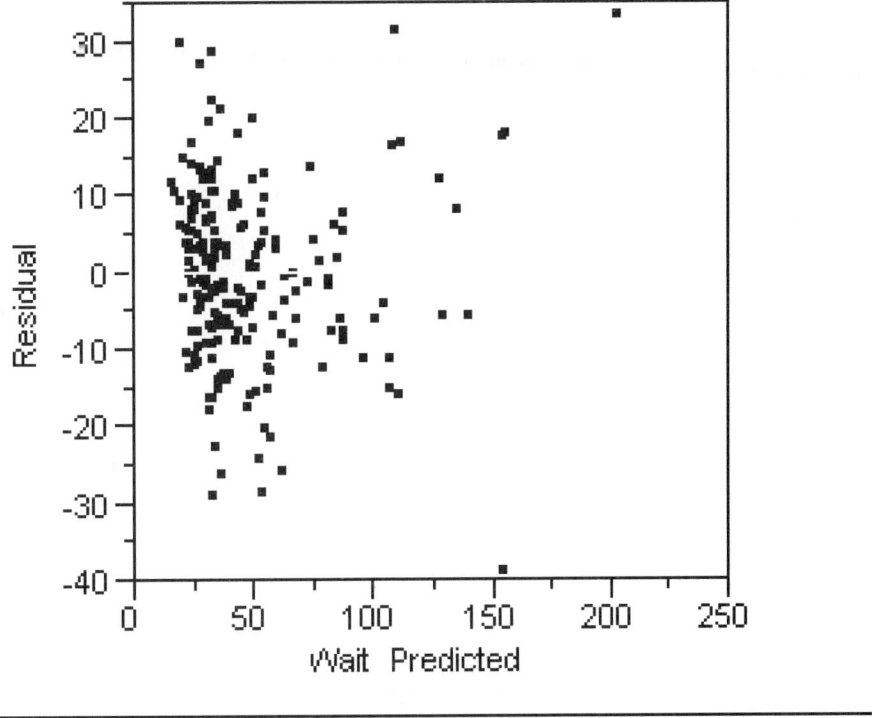

FIGURE 14.35   Residuals Versus Independent Variables

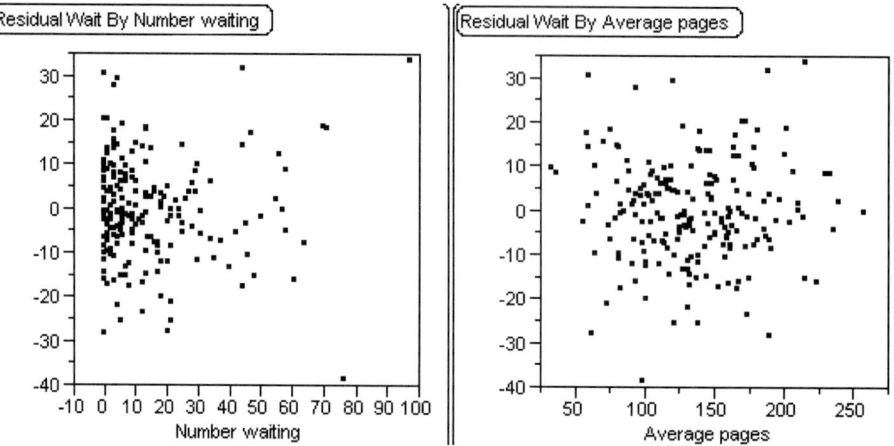

14.37   A firm that manufactures and sells moderately sophisticated desktop publishing equipment budgets a certain dollar amount for postsale support activities. This support is provided by field representatives who train users initially and by home office representatives who answer questions by telephone. Individuals shuttle between home office representative and field representative positions frequently, so it is not very meaningful to separate the positions in the budget. A regression study is made in an attempt to forecast the required support budget.

Analysis of the support requirements suggests that the training aspect of postsales support typically involves users who have installed the equipment in the current and preceding months. For the next four months, there is substantial call-back support as users forget aspects of training or add new equipment operators. After that period, support activity is mostly troubleshooting and new application work. Therefore, the installation data to be used as independent variables are broken down as

1   Number of installations in budget month (known in previous month)

2   Number of installations in previous month

3   Number of installations in preceding four months.

These data are collected separately for the two levels of sophistication (*A* and *B*) of equipment (the *A* class requires more sophisticated training). Thus, six independent variables are entered.

There is some question as to whether support costs increase in proportion to the number of installations. One opinion holds that the cost per installation decreases as installations increase because of improved users' manuals and more efficient training methods.

a   Identify any lagged variables.

b   Does the description of the situation indicate that any severe interaction can be expected?

c   Is there any indication of possible need for nonlinear terms in a regression model?

14.38   The firm of Exercise 14.37 collects data on the budgeted number of representatives (*y*) and the six independent variables described in that exercise. Data are available for 36 months; the most recent 6 months' data are reserved for validation. A first-order regression model is fit to the remaining 30 months' data. A plot of the residuals against time is shown in Figure 14.36.

a   Is there any indication of possible outliers?

b   Is there any indication of autocorrelation?

14.39   Investigation of the data of Exercise 14.38 shows that the support budget in months 16 and 17 was cut back drastically in a spasm of cost cutting. This action led to many user complaints, so the attempt was abandoned. The budget numbers of those months

FIGURE 14.36 Residuals Versus Time: Support Staff Data

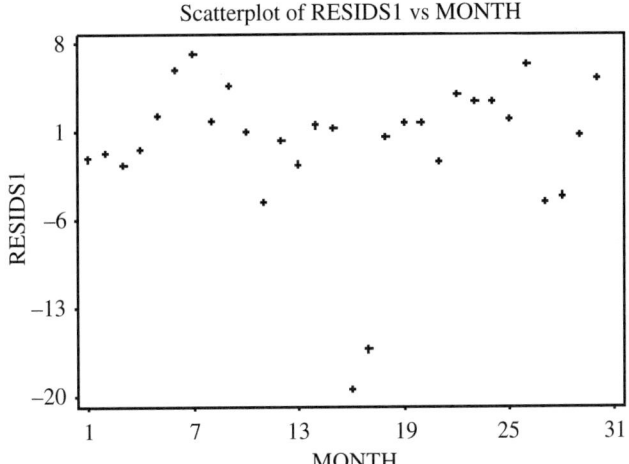

are changed in the database to the figures that had been planned before the cost-cutting attempt. A first-order model yields the plots of residuals versus predicted values shown in Figure 14.37. Is there any indication of possible heteroscedasticity (nonconstant variance)?

FIGURE 14.37 Residuals Versus Predicted Values: Corrected Support Staff Data

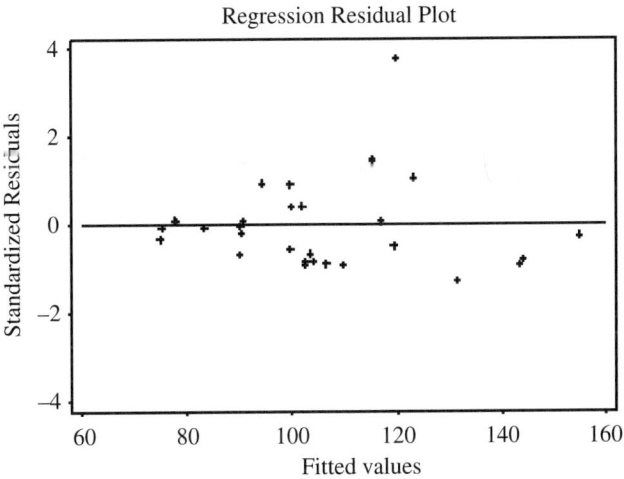

14.40 The square of the current month's installations (both *A* and *B* types) are added as independent variables. A stepwise (forward-selection) regression analysis yields the following Statistix output:

```
STEPWISE REGRESSION OF SUPP
UNFORCED VARIABLES:
 ACURR APREV APREC4 BCURR BPREV BPREC4 ACURRSQ BCURRSQ
  F TO ENTER  0.01
  F TO EXIT   0.01

STEP   VARIABLE    COEFFICIENT     T      R SQ      MSE
```

1	CONSTANT	105.233	27.97	0.0000	424.736
2	CONSTANT	63.5126	11.44	0.7015	131.326
	BCURRSQ	0.05965	8.11		
3	CONSTANT	63.6034	14.97	0.8314	76.9141
	ACURRSQ	0.06804	4.56		
	BCURRSQ	0.04008	5.66		
4	CONSTANT	40.0984	7.41	0.9180	38.8692
	BPREV	1.30231	5.24		
	ACURRSQ	0.06545	6.17		
	BCURRSQ	0.02676	4.75		
5	CONSTANT	39.3880	8.74	0.9454	26.8985
	APREV	0.90824	3.55		
	BPREV	0.95421	4.17		
	ACURRSQ	0.06031	6.74		
	BCURRSQ	0.02528	5.37		
6	CONSTANT	25.2298	5.15	0.9682	16.3279
	APREV	0.91929	4.61		
	BPREV	0.64736	3.35		
	BPREC4	0.26302	4.15		
	ACURRSQ	0.05073	6.91		
	BCURRSQ	0.02239	6.00		
7	CONSTANT	-13.8234	-1.05	0.9777	11.9351
	APREV	0.95721	5.60		
	BCURR	3.04413	3.14		
	BPREV	0.63056	3.82		
	BPREC4	0.26180	4.83		
	ACURRSQ	0.05398	8.48		
	BCURRSQ	-0.03533	-1.89		
8	CONSTANT	-19.5963	-1.52	0.9807	10.7909
	ACURR	1.30234	1.85		
	APREV	0.97530	5.98		
	BCURR	2.71988	2.90		
	BPREV	0.62197	3.96		
	BPREC4	0.28031	5.34		
	ACURRSQ	0.00656	0.25		
	BCURRSQ	-0.02890	-1.60		
9	CONSTANT	-12.6291	-1.00	0.9837	9.53711
	ACURR	1.37211	2.08		
	APREV	0.98643	6.43		
	APREC4	0.14845	1.97		
	BCURR	2.26441	2.48		
	BPREV	0.57312	3.83		
	BPREC4	0.20580	3.31		
	ACURRSQ	0.00578	0.23		
	BCURRSQ	-0.02072	-1.18		

RESULTING STEPWISE MODEL

VARIABLE	COEFFICIENT	STD ERROR	STUDENT'S T	P	VIF
CONSTANT	-12.6291	12.6088	-1.00	0.3279	
ACURR	1.37211	0.66119	2.08	0.0504	31.5
APREV	0.98643	0.15330	6.43	0.0000	1.6
APREC4	0.14845	0.07524	1.97	0.0618	2.5
BCURR	2.26441	0.91287	2.48	0.0217	74.9
BPREV	0.57312	0.14981	3.83	0.0010	2.1

BPREC4	0.20580	0.06217	3.31	0.0033	3.3
ACURRSQ	0.00578	0.02470	0.23	0.8171	35.0
BCURRSQ	-0.02072	0.01751	-1.18	0.2500	78.1

CASES INCLUDED	30	R SQUARED	0.9837	MSE	9.53711
MISSING CASES	0	ADJ R SQ	0.9775	SD	3.08822

   a List the sequence in which the variables are added.

   b How much of an increment to R^2 is obtained by inclusion of the last four variables?

14.41 Additional output from the regression analysis of Exercise 14.40, for the model with all variables included, yields the scatterplots shown in Figure 14.38.

   a Is there evidence of serious autocorrelation?

   b Is there evidence of nonconstant variance?

14.42 Differences for all variables in the data of Exercise 14.40 are calculated, and a stepwise (forward-selection) regression is run. The output follows. Is the sequence in which the variables are added similar to that found in Exercise 14.40?

FIGURE 14.38   **Residual Plots for Change in Support Staff: (a) Residuals and Predicted Values; (b) Residuals and Time**

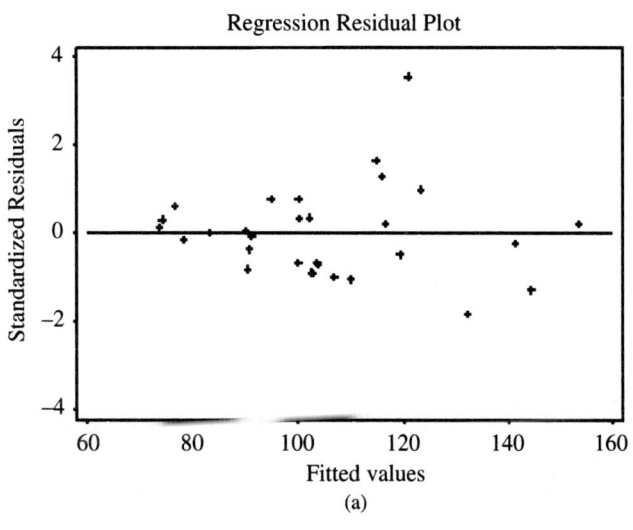

(a)

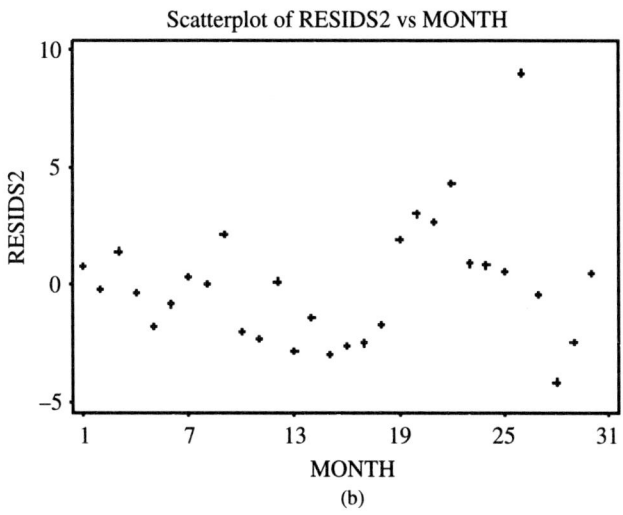

(b)

```
STEPWISE REGRESSION OF DSUPP
UNFORCED VARIABLES:
DACURR DAPREV DAPREC4 DBCURR DBPREV DBPREC4 DACURRSQ DBCURRSQ

  F TO ENTER  0.01
  F TO EXIT   0.01

STEP   VARIABLE   COEFFICIENT     T      R SQ      MSE

  1    CONSTANT     2.72413      1.25   0.0000   136.992

  2    CONSTANT     2.27188      1.40   0.4641   76.1399
       DACURR       1.45725      4.84
  3    CONSTANT     1.45106      1.27   0.7469   37.3414
       DACURR       1.91995      8.43
       DAPREV       1.22746      5.39

  4    CONSTANT     1.05831      1.52   0.9109   13.6636
       DACURR       1.59627     10.94
       DAPREV       1.14780      8.30
       DBCURR       0.86542      6.79

  5    CONSTANT     0.92078      1.46   0.9299   11.2027
       DACURR       1.52622     11.31
       DAPREV       0.99661      7.19
       DBCURR       0.94125      7.89
       DBPREV       0.35455      2.55

  6    CONSTANT     0.90897      1.47   0.9361   10.6551
       DACURR       1.54022     11.68
       DAPREV       0.98946      7.32
       DBCURR       1.87895      2.94
       DBPREV       0.37912      2.77
       DBCURRSQ    -0.01742     -1.49

  7    CONSTANT     0.69131      1.09   0.9403   10.4170
       DACURR       1.58961     11.65
       DAPREV       1.06396      7.26
       DAPREC4      0.13021      1.24
       DBCURR       1.91662      3.03
       DBPREV       0.34610      2.51
       DBCURRSQ    -0.01813     -1.57

  8    CONSTANT     0.67815      1.05   0.9408   10.8151
       DACURR       1.36966      2.62
       DAPREV       1.06324      7.12
       DAPREC4      0.12356      1.14
       DBCURR       1.95046      3.01
       DBPREV       0.35789      2.50
       DACURRSQ     0.00843      0.44
       DBCURRSQ    -0.01881     -1.59

  9    CONSTANT     0.52063      0.68   0.9413   11.2594
       DACURR       1.33473      2.47
       DAPREV       1.06333      6.97
       DAPREC4      0.11933      1.07
       DBCURR       2.02548      2.95
       DBPREV       0.39634      2.29
       DBPREC4      0.05833      0.41
       DACURRSQ     0.00966      0.48
       DBCURRSQ    -0.02003     -1.61

RESULTING STEPWISE MODEL
```

VARIABLE	COEFFICIENT	STD ERROR	STUDENT'S T	P	VIF
CONSTANT	0.52063	0.76264	0.68	0.5026	
DACURR	1.33473	0.54032	2.47	0.0226	21.7
DAPREV	1.06333	0.15247	6.97	0.0000	1.7
APREC4	0.11933	0.11117	1.07	0.2959	1.3
DBCURR	2.02548	0.68588	2.95	0.0079	39.4
DBPREV	0.39634	0.17293	2.29	0.0329	2.0
DBPREC4	0.05833	0.14092	0.41	0.6833	1.5
DACURRSQ	0.00966	0.01994	0.48	0.6333	21.4
DBCURRSQ	-0.02003	0.01246	-1.61	0.1236	38.8

```
CASES INCLUDED   29    R SQUARED  0.9413     MSE  11.2594
MISSING CASES     1    ADJ R SQ   0.9178     SD    3.35551
```

14.43 Additional output from the all-variables model of Exercise 14.42 is shown in Figure 14.39.

  a Is there an autocorrelation problem with the differenced data?

  b Is there evidence of heteroscedasticity?

FIGURE 14.39 **Residual Plots for Change in Support Staff Data: (a) Residuals and Predicted Values; (b) Residuals and Time**

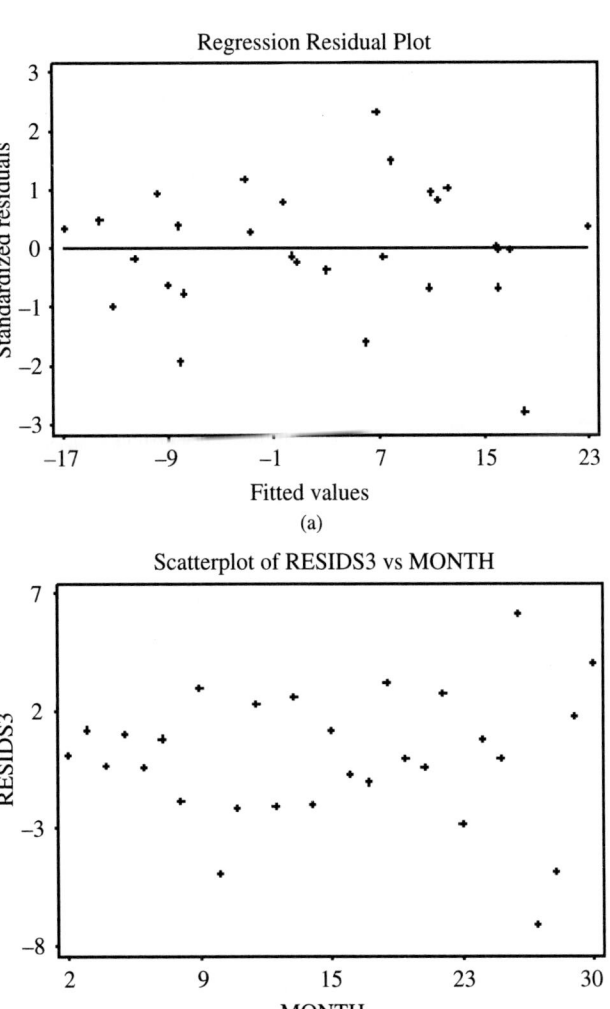

14.44 Consider the output from the regression study of Exercise 14.42.

    a Write out the final regression model.

    b Can the null hypothesis that all partial slopes are zero be rejected at reasonable α levels?

    c Which variables have coefficients that differ significantly (at $\alpha = .05$) from zero as last predictor in?

    d Identify and interpret the R^2 value.

    e Identify the residual standard deviation.

14.45 In Exercise 14.38 the most recent six months' data were reserved for validation. These values, in difference form, are shown here along with the predicted values given by the model of Exercise 14.42.

ACURR	APREV	APREC4	BCURR	BPREV	BPREC4	ACURRSQ	BCURRSQ	Actual Support	Predicted Support
−2	−3	9	5	3	1	−80	−135	2	5.78
5	−2	3	−6	5	1	215	−80	−3	−.97
−4	5	−1	4	−6	3	−176	215	5	2.99
−4	−4	−7	−6	4	8	−144	−176	−5	−9.94
14	−4	−4	7	−6	6	644	−144	17	15.29
−2	14	−5	4	7	−3	−116	644	11	12.78

    a Calculate the residuals and their standard deviation.

    b Is this residual standard deviation much larger than the one found in Exercise 14.42?

    c Previous forecasts of the budget were often in error by as much as ± 20 units. Does it appear that the regression model will be useful in predicting the budget figure?

14.46 A wholesale hardware company fills orders at a large warehouse. The volume of orders fluctuates substantially from day to day, and the company has a policy of filling each order on the day of receipt. Orders are phoned or mailed, and they are received by 10 A.M. The warehouse supervisor estimates the total time required for each order and assigns the required number of workers to fill the order. Excess workers, if any, are assigned to other tasks and cannot be recalled until the next day. The supervisor's estimates of time per order are often quite erroneous, so sometimes workers are idle and other times substantial overtime must be paid. A regression study is attempted to improve the prediction of required time per order. The minicomputer used for order processing and inventory control can easily calculate predicted times once a model is determined.

Items in the order are classified as frequently, moderately, or rarely ordered. The rarely ordered items are stored in the most distant parts of the warehouse and therefore require more time to obtain. Both the number of items ordered in each category and the average size per item are thought to influence the order-filling time. Most items ordered are in carton units, and less-than-carton items (which are mostly rarely ordered) are filled as "loose-box" items. Certain orders require special packing to protect fragile items. The supervisor assigns each such order to either packing station A or B. All items are assembled at a central station and placed on skids. A forklift is used to move the skids from the assembly station to delivery trucks.

A sample of 50 orders is selected; care is taken to include relatively extreme types of orders (small and large, mostly loose-box and mostly carton, mostly frequent and mostly rare). Values for each of the following variables are recorded:

TIME:	Time (in worker-minutes) needed to fill order
NUMFREQ:	Number of frequently ordered items in the order
NUMMOD:	Number of moderately ordered items in the order
NUMRARE:	Number of rarely ordered items in the order
NUMLOOSE:	Number of loose-box items
AVSZCAR:	Average size of carton items (cartons/item)
AVSZLB:	Average size of loose-box items (pieces/item)
SPECIALS:	0 if no special packing need
	1 if special packing done at station A
	2 if special packing done at station B
SKIDS:	Number of skids needed

The supervisor thinks that the most important predictor variables are the NUM ones because much of the order-filling time is taken up by workers moving to the appropriate locations. However, this travel time is not likely to be directly proportional to the number of items because a worker can combine items found in the same general area of the warehouse. The order size of each item is also relevant because some time is used in taking each item from the shelf. This time is expected to be in proportion to AVSZ. The time spent moving skids is expected to be in proportion to SKIDS. The only other major time factor is assembly-station time, which is expected to depend on a combination of NUM and AVSZ variables.

a Explain why the SPECIALS variable should be recoded as two variables:

SPECIALA	=	1 if special packing done at station A, 0 if not
SPECIALB	=	1 if special packing done at station B, 0 if not

b Explain the interpretation of the coefficients of these two variables.

c According to the information given by the supervisor, which independent variables might be transformed?

d Is there any indication that interaction terms might be useful?

14.47 The data for the study of Exercise 14.46 are shown here. A first-order model is fit, and the Minitab output and scatterplots shown in Figure 14.40 are obtained.

time	NumFreq	NumMod	NumRare	NumLoose	AvSzCar	AvSzLB	SpecialA	SpecialB	Skids
27	16	6	3	4	1.6	3.5	1	0	2
57	70	25	2	2	3.2	2.7	0	0	18
39	25	6	8	4	2.4	3.3	0	0	8
20	10	2	1	1	6.2	4.0	0	0	4
55	50	30	6	7	2.6	3.0	0	0	12
95	85	43	16	10	4.7	6.2	0	1	25
19	12	3	1	1	2.4	3.0	0	0	3
35	10	12	13	3	5.0	6.0	0	0	5
61	87	12	4	6	3.0	4.0	1	0	16
44	50	22	8	2	4.0	1.5	0	0	9
23	12	8	8	2	1.4	3.5	0	0	2
47	27	6	12	14	1.6	7.2	0	0	4
53	64	8	1	2	3.0	2.5	0	0	14
70	71	34	7	10	2.1	4.6	0	0	16
32	25	1	2	2	2.8	5.0	0	0	10

FIGURE 14.40 **Scatterplot for Order-Filling Data**

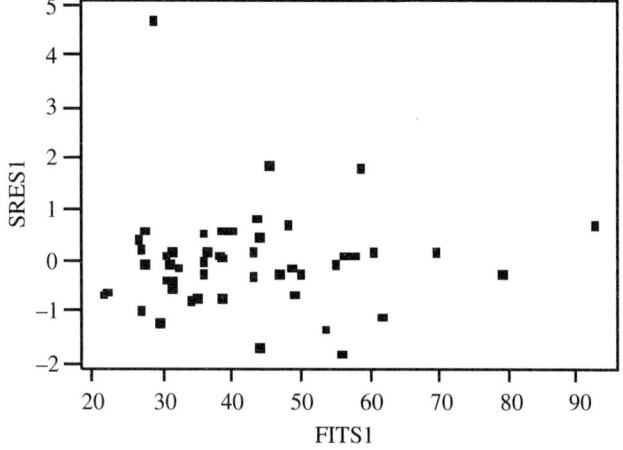

39	16	10	3	8	2.0	4.7	1	0	6
32	25	12	4	2	1.8	6.0	0	0	4
30	40	6	1	1	2.6	3.0	0	0	7
38	72	21	8	3	2.0	2.7	0	0	6
78	64	37	21	6	3.0	4.3	0	1	20
30	23	6	2	1	4.2	2.0	0	0	6
38	35	13	7	1	1.4	8.0	0	0	5
25	16	4	2	4	1.6	9.3	0	0	3
47	19	17	10	6	3.2	2.7	1	0	8
42	31	12	16	3	1.4	2.3	0	1	4
46	46	8	11	2	4.0	2.5	0	0	13
48	12	6	1	5	2.0	6.2	0	0	3
28	16	4	4	2	6.1	1.5	0	0	5
28	37	8	2	1	2.2	2.0	1	0	3
32	21	9	6	4	1.8	6.5	0	0	3
51	58	4	3	6	4.0	8.3	0	0	11
48	24	15	1	8	3.0	9.1	0	1	10
49	36	12	9	2	4.0	6.0	0	0	15
42	51	18	3	5	1.8	2.8	0	0	8
58	77	30	15	12	1.2	1.2	1	0	6
37	24	6	2	2	4.0	6.0	0	0	10
37	16	8	5	1	6.0	10.0	0	0	9
46	36	12	4	6	2.6	5.1	0	1	8
58	74	15	16	4	1.8	1.5	0	0	13
49	51	10	3	8	3.7	4.5	0	0	16
41	24	6	8	3	4.1	3.3	1	0	9
31	36	8	1	1	2.7	5.0	0	0	6
31	21	4	5	6	1.6	1.3	0	0	3
49	42	10	2	2	4.0	8.5	0	1	18
29	16	3	4	2	2.7	3.5	0	0	7
29	28	15	2	1	3.0	6.0	0	0	5
66	73	18	15	5	1.9	4.2	0	0	12
31	15	8	8	6	1.2	2.3	0	0	4
36	23	4	10	4	1.5	2.8	0	0	6
36	44	9	2	1	4.0	5.0	1	0	10

The regression equation is

time = 12.6 + 0.139 NumFreq + 0.234 NumMod + 0.542 NumRare + 1.17 NumLoose
       - 0.216 AvSzCar + 0.498 AvSzLB + 0.70 SpecialA + 1.82 SpecialB
       + 1.35 Skids

Predictor	Coef	Stdev	t-ratio	p
Constant	12.584	2.695	4.67	0.000
NumFreq	0.13947	0.05319	2.62	0.012
NumMod	0.2344	0.1086	2.16	0.037
NumRare	0.5424	0.1551	3.50	0.001
NumLoose	1.1713	0.2539	4.61	0.000
AvSzCar	-0.2162	0.6220	-0.35	0.730
AvSzLB	0.4975	0.3188	1.56	0.126
SpecialA	0.701	1.784	0.39	0.696
SpecialB	1.820	2.301	0.79	0.434
Skids	1.3513	0.2312	5.85	0.000

s = 4.341   R-sq = 93.2%   R-sq(adj) = 91.6%

Analysis of Variance

SOURCE	DF	SS	MS	F	p
Regression	9	10273.4	1141.5	60.58	0.000
Error	40	753.7	18.8		
Total	49	11027.1			

Durbin-Watson statistic = 2.13

a Is there any indication of outliers?

b Is there any indication of nonconstant variance?

c Is there any indication of autocorrelation? Would autocorrelation be expected in this study?

14.48 It was discovered that observation 27 of the data in Exercise 14.46 was taken during a brief strike. The order was filled by the president and vice president of the firm, who couldn't find most of the items. This observation is deleted from the data set. Regression runs are made using logarithms of the NumFreq, NumMod, and NumRare variables and using the square roots of these variables. The resulting residual standard deviations and R^2 values are

	Logarithms	Square Roots
s_ϵ	3.4804	3.0561
R^2	.9570	.9669

Which transformation appears more effective?

14.49 A forward-selection stepwise regression is run on the data resulting from Exercise 14.46. The square root transformation is used. The following output is obtained:

```
MTB > Stepwise 'time' 'NumLoose' 'AvSzCar' 'AvSzLB' 'SpecialA' 'SpecialB' &
MTB >      'Skids' 'sqrtNFrq' 'sqrtNMod' 'sqrtNRar';
SUBC>   FEnter 4.0;
SUBC>   FRemove 4.0.

 Stepwise regression of   time   on  9 predictors, with N =   49

      STEP      1       2       3       4       5
 CONSTANT   20.913  15.387   8.691   5.818   1.803

 Skids       2.43    2.17    1.75    1.80    1.55
 T-RATIO    10.96   13.71   12.35   15.22   12.58

 NumLoose            1.93    1.45    1.23    1.19
 T-RATIO             7.21    6.53    6.45    7.09

 sqrtNMod                    3.77    2.74    1.85
 T-RATIO                     5.79    4.67    3.24

 sqrtNRar                            2.89    3.00
 T-RATIO                             4.58    5.39

 sqrtNFrq                                    1.53
 T-RATIO                                     3.71

 S           8.11    5.62    4.30    3.58    3.15
 R-SQ       71.88   86.80   92.44   94.88   96.12
```

a How much does inclusion of the last variable increase R^2?

b Test the null hypothesis that the last two variables have no incremental predictive value.

14.50 The dependent variable in Exercise 14.49 is redefined to be the time *per item*—that is,

$$\frac{\text{TIME}}{\text{NUMFREQ} + \text{NUMMOD} + \text{NUMRARE}}$$

All independent variables (including the dummy variables) are divided by (NUMFREQ + NUMMOD + NUMRARE). The following output results from a regression run on the transformed data:

```
The regression equation is
TimePer = 0.0244 + 1.80 SqtNFPer + 1.63 SqtNMPer + 2.73 SqtNRPer
            + 1.15 NumLPer + 0.360 ASzCrPer + 0.210 ASzLBPer + 1.88 SpecAPer
            + 2.92 SpecBPer + 1.29 SkidsPer
```

Predictor	Coef	Stdev	t-ratio	p
Constant	0.02436	0.04060	0.60	0.552
SqtNFPer	1.8013	0.3227	5.58	0.000
SqtNMPer	1.6311	0.5503	2.96	0.005
SqtNRPer	2.7348	0.4012	6.82	0.000
NumLPer	1.1491	0.1345	8.55	0.000
ASzCrPer	0.3600	0.1633	2.20	0.033
ASzLBPer	0.2104	0.1279	1.64	0.108
SpecAPer	1.8752	0.8549	2.19	0.034
SpecBPer	2.925	1.411	2.07	0.045
SkidsPer	1.2882	0.1234	10.44	0.000

s = 0.04922   R-sq = 97.1%   R-sq(adj) = 96.4%

Analysis of Variance

SOURCE	DF	SS	MS	F	p
Regression	9	3.16378	0.35153	145.13	0.000
Error	39	0.09446	0.00242		
Total	48	3.25825			

Durbin-Watson statistic = 2.09

a Write the regression model and the residual standard deviation.

b Do the residual plots in Figures 14.41–14.44 show any violation of assumptions?

14.51 A validation study of the model obtained in Exercise 14.50 is based on an additional 10 orders. The results are as follows:

Actual Time	Time per Item	Regression Forecast	Superintendent's Forecast
36	.6316	.6691	.7895
24	1.0000	.9057	.8333
26	.7647	.8482	.7692
42	.7925	.6558	.9434
34	.5667	.5608	.8333
31	.9688	.9021	.7813
27	.8182	.9247	.9091
32	.6531	7567	.8163
34	.8293	.9272	.7317
38	.7451	.7479	.7843

a Compute the standard deviation of the regression prediction errors and the standard deviation of the superintendent's prediction errors.

b Has the regression standard deviation increased from the standard deviation shown in Exercise 14.50?

c Does the result of this study suggest that the regression model will yield better forecasts than the superintendent's forecasts?

14.52 An airline that is the major carrier at its airport hub analyzed its sales of full-fare seats on flights to various other cities. These sales are the most profitable for the airline, so it would like to reserve adequate space; full-fare passengers almost always reserve seats in the last few days before the flight. In addition, any exceptionally low sales figures may indicate a problem in scheduling or in operations at the destination city. For each of the airline's 315 weekly flights, the full-fare demand, averaged over 10 weeks, was determined; this demand included any requests for seats that couldn't be accommodated. In addition, the day of the flight (Sunday = 1 through Saturday = 7), the scheduled departure time (in military time, so 1700 = 5:00 P.M., for example), the airline's share of the gates at the destination airport, and the per capita income of the destination metropolitan area were recorded. The data are in the EX1452.DAT file of the data disk. Column 1 contains demand, column 2 has the day code, column 3 lists the departure time, column 4 is a dummy variable indicating the

FIGURE 14.41 **Residuals for Order-Filling Data**

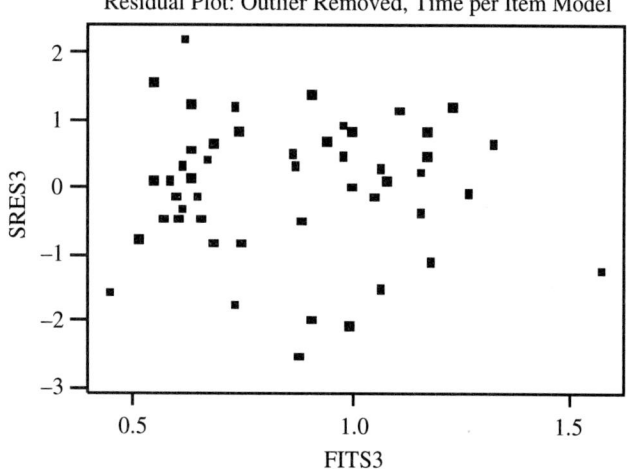

peak travel times (portions of Sunday afternoon, Monday morning, and Friday afternoon), column 5 contains the gate share, and column 6 has income.

a Explain why it would not make sense to include day and departure time as independent variables in a first-order model for predicting demand.

b Obtain a first-order regression equation using the peak-time dummy variable, gate share, and income as independent variables.

c Have the computer program create two new variables by multiplying the dummy variable by gate share and by income. Obtain a regression equation including the previous three independent variables plus the two new ones.

d Test the null hypothesis that the new product variables add no predictive value, given the previous three variables. Can this hypothesis be rejected at $\alpha = .05$? What does this test indicate about interaction in the data?

14.53 Obtain residuals from the regression equation without product terms found in Exercise 14.52.

a Plot the residuals against predicted values. Is there a clear indication that variability increases as the predicted value increases?

b Plot the residuals against gate share and against income. Is there a clear reason to incorporate nonlinear terms in these variables?

FIGURE 14.42   **Residuals for Order-Filling Data**

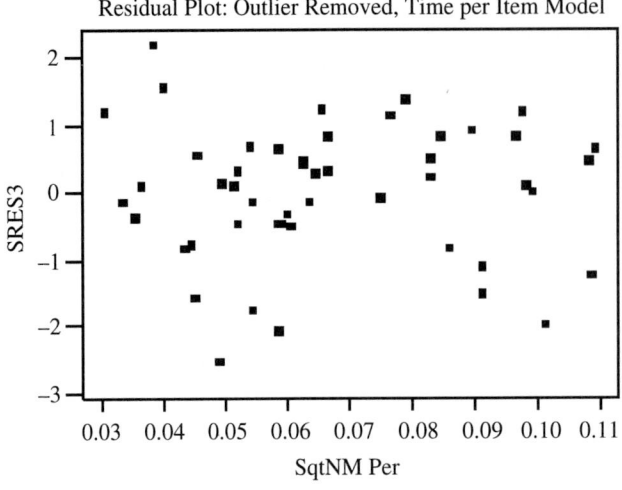

Residual Plot: Outlier Removed, Time per Item Model

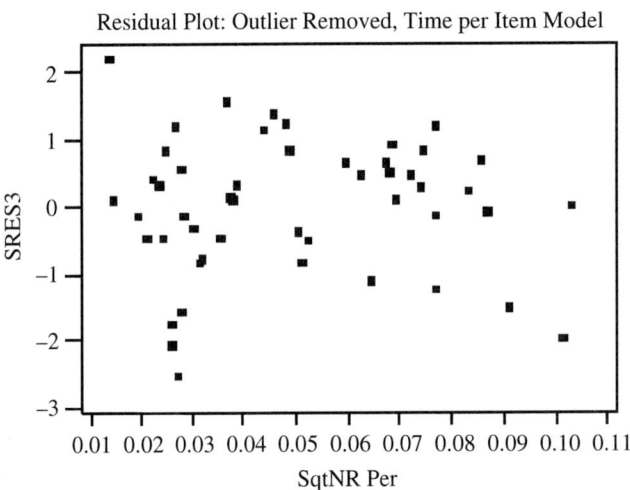

Residual Plot: Outlier Removed, Time per Item Model

   c Plot the residuals against the dummy variable. Does this plot reveal anything?

14.54 The data in Exercise 14.52 are time-series data in the sense that they are entered in the time order of the flights.

   a Plot the residuals calculated in Exercise 14.53 against observation number (time). Is there any evidence of a roughly cyclic pattern, which indicates autocorrelation?

   b Obtain the Durbin-Watson statistic for the model without product terms. Does this statistic indicate that there is a serious autocorrelation problem?

14.55 An auto supply store had 60 months of data on variables that were thought to be relevant to sales. The data, stored in the EX1455.DAT file of the data disk, include monthly sales in thousands of dollars (column 1), average daily low temperature in degrees Fahrenheit (column 2), advertising expenditure for the month in thousands of dollars (column 3), used car sales in the previous month (column 4), and month number (column 5).

   a Identify any variables that are already in lagged form.

   b Obtain a regression equation using temperature, current month's advertising, previous month's used car sales, and month number as the independent variables.

   c Have your computer program create a 1-month lagged variable for advertising expense. Use this lagged variable in place of the current month's advertising and obtain a new

FIGURE 14.43   **Residuals for Order-Filling Data**

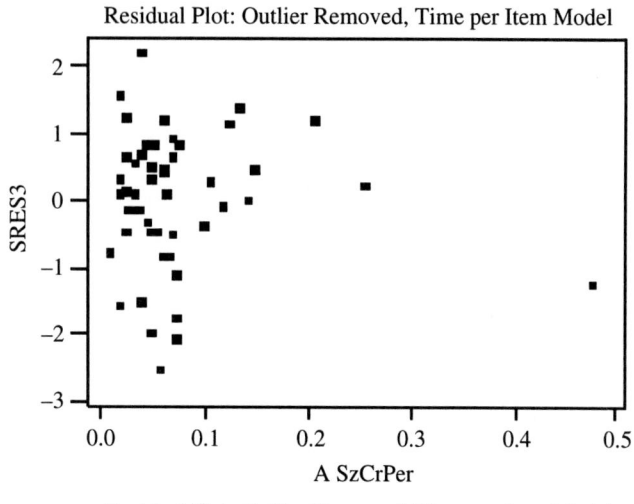

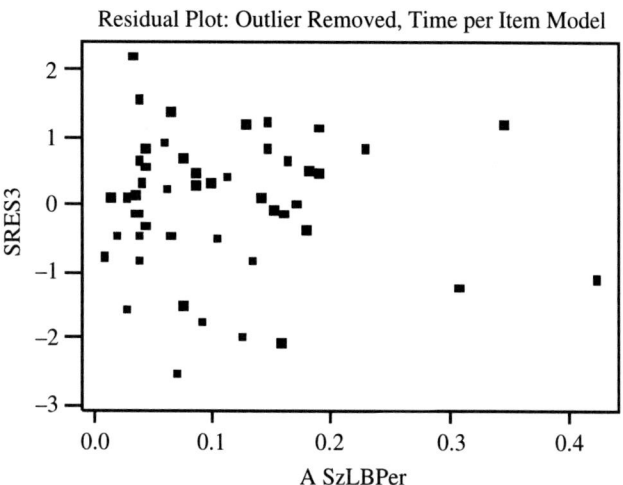

FIGURE 14.44   **Residuals for Order-Filling Data**

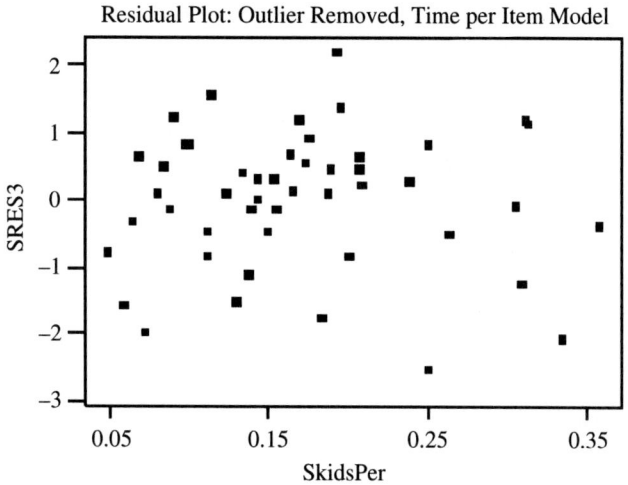

regression equation. Does this new model have a small residual standard deviation (and therefore a smaller mean square error) than the model in part b?

14.56   Consider the regression model using temperature, previous month's advertising previous month's used car sales, and month number, as in part b of Exercise 14.55.

   a Obtain correlations; is there a major collinearity problem?

   b Test to see if the four predictors together have at least some predictive value. Locate a *p*-value.

   c Test to see if each predictor adds statistically detectable predictive value, given the others. Locate *p*-values.

14.57   Obtain residuals for the model of Exercise 14.56.

   a Plot to see if there is evidence of nonconstant variance.

   b Plot to see if there is evidence of nonlinearity.

   c Plot to see if there is evidence of autocorrelation.

   d Obtain the Durbin-Watson statistic. What does it tell you?

14.58   Based on the results you obtained in the last three exercises, determine what changes, if any, you want to make in the regression model. Carry out these changes and see if the resulting regression model is more satisfactory.

14.59   A construction firm wanted to use regression methods to estimate the amount of concrete block foundation that could be constructed in a day, using various combinations of workers and delivery vehicles. Data on a sample of recent projects are included in the EX1458.DAT file on the data disk. The variables are: completion rate—the number of square feet of foundation wall constructed in a day (column 1), number of skilled workers (column 2); number of helpers (column 3), and number of delivery vehicles (column 4).

   a Obtain correlations. Is there an obvious collinearity problem?

   b Should any variables be replaced by dummy variables? Would it make sense to have lagged variables?

   c Obtain a first-order regression model to predict completion rate and use the other variables as they are. Locate the coefficient of determination.

14.60   Obtain residuals from the regression model of Exercise 14.59.

   a Plot the residuals against the predicted values. Is there a "fan" shape characteristic of increasing variability? Is there any other evident problem?

   b Plot the residuals against each of the predictors. Is there any evidence of a high influence outlier? Is there any other evident problem?

   c Why wouldn't the Durbin-Watson statistic be of much relevance in the problem?

14.61   Have your computer program calculate logarithms (natural, base *e*, if that's convenient) of all the variables from Exercise 14.59.

   a Obtain a regression equation using the logarithm of completion as the dependent variable and the other logarithm variables as independent variables.

   b Obtain residuals for this model and plot them against each independent variable. Is there an evident curve in any of the plots?

   c Convert the logarithmic model back to a model in the origin variables. Remember that the logarithm of a product is the sum of the logarithms of each component, and that the logarithm of a variable raised to a power is the power times the logarithm of the variable.

14.62   The managers of a cancer treatment center must forecast new arrivals to their outpatient clinic. New arrivals require different facilities from ongoing patients—for intake interviews, careful monitoring of initial treatments for side effects, and the inevitable paperwork. Demand must be met immediately; cancer patients obviously can't be "put on hold" until facilities open up. An unusually heavy arrival load strains both the clinic's physical facilities and its professional staff. The managers have some flexibility in scheduling physicians, nursing staff, and medical assistants, but must set the schedule at least a week in advance, preferably two weeks.

Most patients come to the outpatient clinic after inpatient treatment in a hospital, either the center's own or one of its affiliated hospitals. Hospital treatment is intense but typically fairly brief. Most patients stay in a hospital for about two weeks although some stay longer. Also, some patients come to the clinic from locations other than the center's hospital or the affiliates.

The center's management information system has tracked the number of inpatient arrivals for each 2-week period for the last several years. In addition, the center managers have assembled a "census" of the number of cancer patients in the center's hospital and in the affiliates, also for each 2-week period. The data were input into Minitab and some very preliminary analyses were done.

The managers have asked you to perform a more thorough analysis of the data. They are particularly interested in whether there is a noticeable time trend in admissions, whether the current patient counts or patient counts from preceding periods are better predictors, whether the center's own hospital sends it more patients than the affiliates do, and whether there are any noticeable jumps or dips in the number of new arrivals around the end of the calendar year and the beginning of the new year. (Periods 1, 27, 53, 79, and 105 are the first periods of calendar years.) Carry out the analysis and report to the managers. They are familiar with regression ideas.

period	census	affils	admits
1	59	119	78
2	55	120	72
3	58	118	73
4	63	118	69
5	55	120	77
6	60	127	67
7	56	114	76
8	51	121	70
9	50	127	71
10	56	122	62
11	59	128	72
12	63	119	71
13	60	121	73
14	55	119	71
15	42	122	70
16	54	121	66
17	52	117	66
18	45	115	70
19	55	135	58
20	53	133	73
21	54	137	71
22	55	118	74
23	52	123	72
24	50	124	67
25	50	125	66
26	51	119	65
27	51	121	67
28	49	126	66
29	54	131	66
30	62	126	71
31	58	135	75
32	57	137	77
33	62	135	78
34	49	114	76
35	58	122	68
36	58	122	71
37	50	125	73
38	51	120	69
39	53	116	66
40	53	127	65
41	54	135	71
42	54	126	70

43	50	116	72
44	51	130	65
45	46	116	67
46	52	115	64
47	61	115	66
48	57	112	69
49	61	120	64
50	56	113	75
51	51	127	69
52	53	145	67
53	55	148	78
54	47	141	80
55	52	138	73
56	54	121	75
57	56	117	70
58	61	115	67
59	58	119	71
60	55	115	69
61	55	109	68
62	58	119	65
63	51	122	70
64	43	132	65
65	46	144	67
66	45	147	75
67	53	144	72
68	48	134	78
69	58	126	74
70	56	113	70
71	57	123	65
72	50	124	70
73	54	136	64
74	55	129	74
75	57	115	71
76	59	123	69
77	63	120	73
78	63	127	75
79	58	135	76
80	57	132	76
81	54	116	76
82	54	110	74
83	47	112	68
84	45	125	65
85	54	129	68
86	46	127	69
87	45	131	72
88	61	127	67
89	68	142	75
90	66	137	82
91	68	118	81
92	66	126	79
93	67	103	81
94	59	102	74
95	54	121	63
96	53	127	67
97	51	133	70
98	47	134	65
99	55	124	73
100	55	131	75
101	52	133	74
102	51	127	79
103	69	136	71
104	67	132	75
105	67	132	83

```
        106    61    118    80
        107    59    125    72
        108    63    118    73
        109    54    117    71
        110    62    121    70


MTB > correlations of 'period' 'census' 'affils' 'admits'


         period   census   affils
census   0.205
affils   0.110   -0.107
admits   0.237    0.354    0.102


MTB > regress 'admits' on 3 predictors 'period' 'census' 'affils';
SUBC> dw.

The regression equation is
admits = 46.7 + 0.0233 period + 0.275 census + 0.0635 affils


Predictor      Coef       Stdev    t-ratio        p
Constant     46.680       7.525       6.20    0.000
period      0.02334     0.01375       1.70    0.092
census      0.27535     0.07500       3.67    0.000
affils      0.06352     0.04735       1.34    0.183


s = 4.439      R-sq = 16.8%    R-sq(adj) = 14.4%

Analysis of Variance

SOURCE       DF           SS         MS        F        p
Regression    3       421.18     140.39     7.12    0.000
Error       106      2089.08      19.71
Total       109      2510.26


SOURCE       DF      SEQ SS
period        1      141.00
census        1      244.72
affils        1       35.46


Unusual Observations
Obs.   period   admits      Fit   Stdev.Fit   Residual   St.Resid
  19       19   58.000   70.843       0.857    -12.843     -2.95R
  54       54   80.000   69.838       1.013     10.162      2.35R


R denotes an obs. with a large st. resid.

Durbin-Watson statistic = 1.72
```

CASE STUDY

Building a Regression Model

The marketing managers of an office products company have some difficulty in evaluating the field sales representatives' performance. The representatives travel among the outlets that carry the company's products, create displays, try to increase volume, introduce new products, and discover any problems that the outlets are having with the company's products. The job involves a great deal of travel time. The marketing managers believe that one important factor in the representatives' performance is the degree of motivation to spend a great deal of time on the road. Other variables also have an effect. Some sales districts have more potential than others, either because of differences in population or differences in the number of retail outlets. Large districts are difficult because of the extra travel time.

One important variable is compensation. Some of the representatives are paid a salary plus a commission on sales; others work solely for a larger commission on sales. The marketing managers suspect there is a difference in effectiveness between the two groups, although some managers argue that the important factor is the combination of commission status and number of outlets. In particular, they suspect that commission-only representatives with many outlets to cover are highly productive. Also, the managers suspect that

profit may be inflated for representatives with many outlets; they would prefer measuring profit per outlet.

Data are collected on 51 representatives. The data include DISTRICT number, PROFIT (net profit margin for all orders placed through the representative—the dependent variable of interest), AREA (of the district in thousands of square miles), POPN (millions of people in the district), OUTLETS (number of outlets in the district), and COMMIS, which is 1 for full-commission representatives and 0 for partially salaried representatives.

Use the following data to perform a multiple regression analysis. Find out if the variables suspected by the managers as having an effect on PROFIT actually do have an effect; in particular, try to discover if there is a combination effect of COMMIS and OUTLETS. Consider whether PROFIT itself or PROFIT divided by OUTLETS works better as a dependent variable. Omit variables that show little predictive value. Locate and, if possible, correct any serious violations of assumptions. Write a brief report to the marketing managers and explain your findings; the managers are not familiar with the technical language of statistics, although they do have an idea what a standard deviation is.

DIST	PROFIT	AREA	POPN	OUTLETS	COMMIS
1	1011	16.96	3.881	213	1
2	1318	7.31	3.141	158	1
3	1556	7.81	3.766	203	1
4	1521	7.31	4.587	170	1
5	979	19.84	3.648	142	1
6	1290	12.37	3.456	159	1
7	1596	6.15	3.695	178	1
8	1155	14.21	3.609	182	1
9	1412	7.45	3.801	181	1
10	1194	14.43	3.322	148	1
11	1054	6.12	5.124	227	0
12	1157	11.71	4.158	139	1
13	1001	9.36	3.887	179	0
14	831	19.14	2.230	124	1
15	857	11.75	4.468	205	0
16	188	40.34	.297	85	1
17	1030	7.16	4.224	211	0
18	1331	9.37	3.427	145	1

19	643	7.62	4.031	205	1
20	992	27.54	2.370	166	1
21	795	15.97	3.903	149	1
22	1340	12.97	3.423	186	1
23	689	17.36	2.390	141	0
24	1726	6.24	4.947	223	1
25	1056	11.20	4.166	176	0
26	989	18.09	4.063	187	1
27	895	13.32	3.105	131	1
28	1028	14.97	4.116	170	0
29	771	21.92	1.510	144	1
30	484	34.91	.741	126	1
31	917	8.46	5.260	234	0
32	1786	7.52	5.744	210	0
33	1063	14.43	2.703	141	1
34	1001	15.37	3.583	158	0
35	1052	11.20	4.469	167	1
36	1610	7.20	4.951	174	1
37	1486	13.49	3.474	211	1
38	1576	6.56	4.637	172	1
39	1665	9.35	3.900	185	1
40	878	11.12	3.766	166	0
41	849	10.58	3.876	189	0
42	775	17.82	2.753	164	0
43	1012	10.03	4.449	193	0
44	1436	10.01	4.680	157	1
45	798	10.70	4.806	200	0
46	519	24.38	2.367	142	0
47	1701	6.57	5.563	199	0
48	1387	6.64	4.357	166	1
49	1717	9.24	4.670	221	1
50	1032	11.62	3.993	180	0
51	973	12.85	3.923	193	0

Two foolish young sisters named Minnier
Had contests to see who was skinnier.
By starving with verve,
They lost every curve,
And wound up completely collinear.

REVIEW EXERCISES—CHAPTERS 12–14

R105   A contractor bids on many small jobs. The current process of preparing bids is expensive and time consuming. An attempt is made to predict y, the total direct cost of a job, based on x, the direct labor hours required. Data are collected on 26 jobs:

x:	214	228	235	239	247	248	278	289	291
y:	7444	7223	10,509	8931	9674	8084	11,784	10,067	11,344
x:	298	306	314	319	333	353	364	464	495
y:	7355	14,946	15,088	7409	15,475	11,524	13,209	16,012	22,570
x:	505	607	625	651	738	771	796	840	
y:	26,285	18,427	22,892	20,689	33,636	28,465	22,018	29,744	

The following regression output was obtained using Systat:

```
DEP VAR:  COST   N: 25  MULTIPLE R: 0.898  SQUARED MULTIPLE R: 0.807
ADJ. SQUARED MULTIPLE R: .799   STANDARD ERROR OF ESTIMATE: 3462.090


VARIABLE   COEFFICIENT  STD ERROR   STD COEF  TOLERANCE   T    P(2 TAIL)


CONSTANT    1160.693    1676.508     0.000       .       0.692   0.496
LABOR         34.562       3.524     0.898     1.000     9.807   0.000

                     ANALYSIS OF VARIANCE

SOURCE       SUM-OF-SQUARES  DF  MEAN-SQUARE    F-RATIO      P

REGRESSION    .115279E+10     1  .115279E+10    96.177     0.000
RESIDUAL      .275680E+09    23  .119861E+08
```

a Write out the least-squares regression equation.

b What is the economic interpretation of the slope coefficient?

c What is the economic interpretation of the intercept coefficient?

d Locate the residual standard deviation. Interpret its numerical value using the Empirical Rule.

R106 Locate the correlation between x and y for the data of the preceding exercise. Interpret the resulting number.

R107 Refer again to the regression of total cost on direct labor hours in Exercise R105.

a Locate the estimated standard error of the slope.

b Find a 95% confidence interval for the true value of the slope.

R108 In the regression of cost on labor hours in Exercise R107, is the null hypothesis that the slope is zero economically plausible? Can this hypothesis be rejected conclusively by the data?

R109 **a** The contractor of Exercise R105 has a new job with $x = 890$ hours. Calculate the predicted y value for the actual cost.

b The contractor has another new job with $x = 436$ hours. Calculate the predicted y value for the actual cost.

c Which of the predictions calculated in parts a and b should be more accurate? Why?

R110 A plot of the residuals from the regression analysis of the data of Exercise R105 shows that residuals corresponding to small x values are small positive or negative numbers, but that several of the residuals corresponding to large x values are relatively large in magnitude. What regression assumption is called into question by this finding? What are the consequences for the interpretation of the output?

R111 A bank that offers charge cards to customers studies the yearly purchase amount on the card as related to the age, income, and years of education of the cardholder, and whether the cardholder owns or rents a home. The following Minitab output is obtained; the variables are self-explanatory, except for owner, which equals 1 if the cardholder owns a home and 0 if the cardholder rents a home:

```
MTB > correlations of c1-c5

Correlations
(Pearson)

            purch     age    income   owner
age         0.932
income      0.928   0.837
```

```
owner    0.462    0.212    0.686
educn    0.222    0.057    0.310    0.476

MTB > Regress 'purch' 4 'age' 'income' 'owner' 'educn';
SUBC>   SResiduals 'SRES1';
SUBC>   Fits 'FITS1';
SUBC>   Constant;
SUBC>   VIF;
SUBC>   DW.

Regression Analysis

The regression equation is
purch = - 0.744 + 0.0329 age + 0.00900 income + 0.115 owner + 0.00818 educn

Predictor      Coef      Stdev    t-ratio       p       VIF
Constant    -0.74439    0.06978    -10.67    0.000
age          0.032896   0.003809     8.64    0.000     20.4
income       0.008999   0.005075     1.77    0.078     36.7
owner        0.11502    0.04982      2.31    0.022     11.4
educn        0.008176   0.003611     2.26    0.025      1.3

s = 0.09263    R-sq = 94.6%    R-sq(adj) = 94.4%

Analysis of Variance

SOURCE        DF         SS         MS        F         p
Regression     4     23.1295     5.7824    673.85    0.000
Error        155      1.3301     0.0086
Total        159     24.4596

SOURCE        DF     SEQ SS
age            1     21.2586
income         1      1.7745
owner          1      0.0524
educn          1      0.0440
```

a Locate the least-squares regression equation.

b Explain what each slope coefficient means.

c How meaningful is the intercept term?

R112 Refer to the Minitab output of Exercise R111.

a What would the hypothesis that all slopes are zero mean about predictability in this context?

b Show that this null hypothesis may be rejected emphatically.

c What do the various t statistics indicate about the incremental predictive value of the variables?

R113 In Exercise R111, is there evidence of collinearity in the Minitab output?

R114 A stepwise regression of the purchase amount data of Exercise R111 was conducted using Minitab, yielding the following output:

```
MTB > Stepwise 'purch' 'age' 'income' 'owner' 'educn';
SUBC>   FEnter 0.01;
SUBC>   FRemove 0.01.

Stepwise Regression

 Response is  purch   on  4 predictors, with N =  160

     Step       1        2        3        4
Constant    -0.5865  -0.5672  -0.6789  -0.7444
```

age	0.04201	0.03937	0.03947	0.03290
T-Ratio	32.39	44.58	45.34	8.64
owner		0.218	0.198	0.115
T-Ratio		14.13	11.47	2.31
educn			0.0088	0.0082
T-Ratio			2.44	2.26
income				0.0090
T-Ratio				1.77
S	0.142	0.0947	0.0933	0.0926
R-Sq	86.91	94.24	94.45	94.56

a Is the order in which the predictors enter the model the same as that indicated by the correlations of the predictors with purch?

b Do the coefficients change a great deal as new predictors are entered?

c Based on the stepwise output, what predictors would you use?

d Calculate the C_p statistic for this model (relative to the all-predictors model). Does the value of this statistic indicate that your choice of predictors is sensible?

R115 Additional predictor variables for the purchase amount problem of Exercise R111 are created by multiplying owner by each of the other independent variables. Minitab output follows; the product terms are indicated as a product of X variables:

```
The regression equation is
purch = - 0.916 + 0.0272 age + 0.0204 income + 0.247 owner + 0.00536 educn
              + 0.00043 X1X3 - 0.0066 X2X3 + 0.00510 X3X4
```

Predictor	Coef	Stdev	t-ratio	p	VIF
Constant	-0.9156	0.1332	-6.87	0.000	
age	0.027249	0.005535	4.92	0.000	43.4
income	0.020373	0.008714	2.34	0.021	109.3
owner	0.2468	0.2083	1.18	0.238	201.7
educn	0.005361	0.005250	1.02	0.309	2.8
X1X3	0.000432	0.009902	0.04	0.965	1036.1
X2X3	-0.00656	0.01312	-0.50	0.618	2180.8
X3X4	0.005105	0.007254	0.70	0.483	52.7

```
s = 0.09217     R-sq = 94.7%     R-sq(adj) = 94.5%
```

Analysis of Variance

SOURCE	DF	SS	MS	F	p
Regression	7	23.1682	3.3097	389.56	0.000
Error	152	1.2914	0.0085		
Total	159	24.4596			

SOURCE	DF	SEQ SS
age	1	21.2586
income	1	1.7745
owner	1	0.0524
educn	1	0.0440
X1X3	1	0.0327
X2X3	1	0.0018
X3X4	1	0.0042

a What is the reason for introducing the product terms X1X3, X2X3, X3X4?

b Test the null hypothesis that the coefficients of all the product terms are zero.

R116 Residuals for the product terms model in Exercise R115 are plotted against predicted values, as shown in Figure 14.45. Are there any obvious violations of regression assumptions?

FIGURE 14.45 **Residuals Versus Predicted Values for Purchase Data**

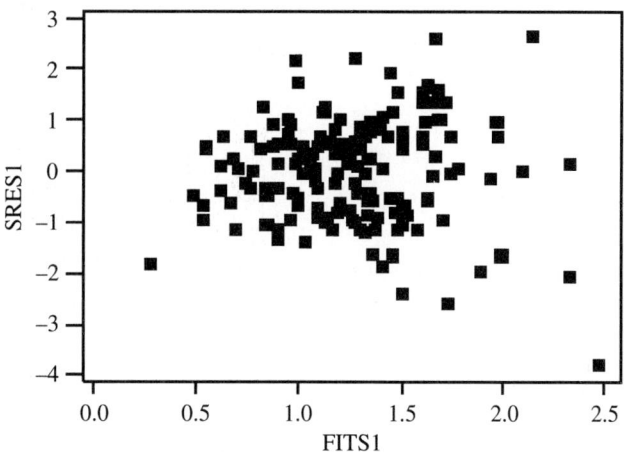

R117 Another regression model for the purchase amount data of Exercise R111 is attempted using the natural logarithm of income, rather than income itself, as an independent variable. The following output is from Minitab:

```
Regression Analysis

The regression equation is
purch = - 3.38 + 0.0247 age + 0.913 loginc + 0.0118 owner + 0.00784 educn

Predictor      Coef      Stdev     t-ratio      p       VIF
Constant    -3.3834     0.6754      -5.01     0.000
age          0.024719   0.003765     6.57     0.000     21.5
loginc       0.9134     0.2273       4.02     0.000     38.7
owner        0.01183    0.04916      0.24     0.810     12.0
educn        0.007844   0.003462     2.27     0.025      1.3

s = 0.08904    R-sq = 95.0%    R-sq(adj) = 94.8%

Analysis of Variance

SOURCE        DF       SS         MS        F        p
Regression     4    23.2306     5.8076    732.46    0.000
Error        155     1.2290     0.0079
Total        159    24.4596

SOURCE        DF     SEQ SS
age            1    21.2586
loginc         1     1.9296
owner          1     0.0016
educn          1     0.0407
```

a As compared to the original model, has predictive value improved?

b As compared to the original model, is the incremental predictive value of the loginc variable greater?

c Is the loginc variable more statistically significant than the income variable in the original model?

R118 A regression model is constructed to predict the spread between interest rates of government bonds (risk-free) and corporate bonds rated BAA (somewhat risky). The independent variables are a privately constructed leading economic indicator (LEADING), a measure of the relative supply of corporate and governmental bonds in a given month

(SUPPLY), the actual rate of government bonds in that month (RATE), and the month number (MONTH). Minitab output follows. A scatterplot matrix is shown in Figure 14.46. Is there evidence of collinearity in the data? Of a nonlinear relation? Of outliers?

```
MTB > Correlation C1-C5.
```

Correlations (Pearson)

	SPREAD	LEADING	SUPPLY	RATE
LEADING	-0.850			
SUPPLY	0.676	-0.227		
RATE	0.872	-0.982	0.259	
MONTH	-0.862	0.997	-0.244	-0.986

FIGURE 14.46 **Scatterplot Matrix for Bond Spread Data**

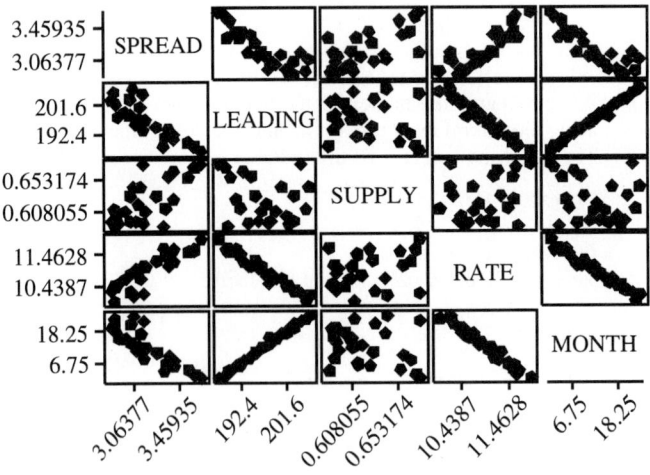

R119 A regression model is constructed using the bond spread data from the previous exercise, omitting MONTH. Minitab output is as follows:

Regression Analysis

The regression equation is
SPREAD = - 0.01 - 0.00827 LEADING + 3.75 SUPPLY + 0.227 RATE

Predictor	Coef	Stdev	t-ratio	p	VIF
Constant	-0.014	2.156	-0.01	0.995	
LEADING	-0.008265	0.007200	-1.15	0.265	28.5
SUPPLY	3.7541	0.2566	14.63	0.000	1.1
RATE	0.22700	0.07024	3.23	0.004	28.9

s = 0.03594   R-sq = 98.0%   R-sq(adj) = 97.7%

Analysis of Variance

SOURCE	DF	SS	MS	F	p
Regression	3	1.24510	0.41503	321.31	0.000
Error	20	0.02583	0.00129		
Total	23	1.27093			

```
SOURCE    DF    SEQ SS
LEADING   1     0.91916
SUPPLY    1     0.31245
RATE      1     0.01349
```

Durbin-Watson statistic = 0.81

a Show that the null hypothesis that all slopes are zero can be rejected at any reasonable level of significance.

b Do all the *t* tests of individual slopes lead to rejection of the null hypothesis?

R120 Locate the residual standard deviation in the bond spread regression output of Exercise R118. What does it indicate about the predictive value of the equation? (The SPREAD variable has a standard deviation of about 0.2.)

R121 The residuals for the bond spread model of Exercise R118 are plotted against time in Figure 14.47.

a Does there appear to be a violation of regression assumptions?

b Show that the regression output indicates a violation.

c What are the consequences of this violation?

FIGURE 14.47   **Residuals Versus Time, Bond Spread Data**

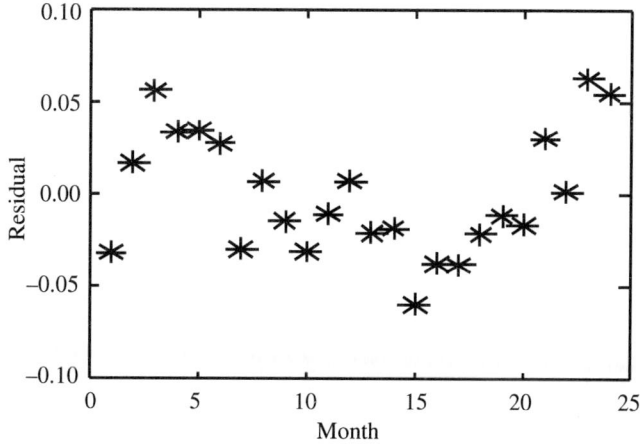

R122 The bond spread data of Exercise R118 are converted to differences and the model is recalculated. Minitab output is as follows:

Regression Analysis

The regression equation is
DSPREAD = 0.00404 - 0.0106 DLEADING + 3.35 DSUPPLY + 0.214 DRATE

23 cases used 1 cases contain missing values

```
Predictor    Coef       Stdev      t-ratio    p        VIF
Constant     0.004045   0.009158   0.44       0.664
DLEADING     -0.010622  0.008162   -1.30      0.209    1.1
DSUPPLY      3.3516     0.1314     25.51      0.000    1.1
DRATE        0.21391    0.03623    5.90       0.000    1.0
```

s = 0.02592   R-sq = 97.6%   R-sq(adj) = 97.3%

```
Analysis of Variance

SOURCE       DF        SS        MS         F       p
Regression    3    0.52522   0.17507   260.67   0.000
Error        19    0.01276   0.00067
Total        22    0.53798

SOURCE       DF     SEQ SS
DLEADING      1    0.03546
DSUPPLY       1    0.46635
DRATE         1    0.02341

Durbin-Watson statistic = 2.00
```

a How much have the coefficients changed as compared to those in the original model?

b Have the results of F and t tests changed, as compared to the previous results? If so, which set of tests is more believable?

c Has working with differences cured the violation of assumptions found previously?

R123 The residuals from the difference model of Exercise R122 are plotted against month number in Figure 14.48. Is there a clear pattern in this plot? Should there be, given the Durbin-Watson results?

FIGURE 14.48 **Residuals Versus Time—Difference Model**

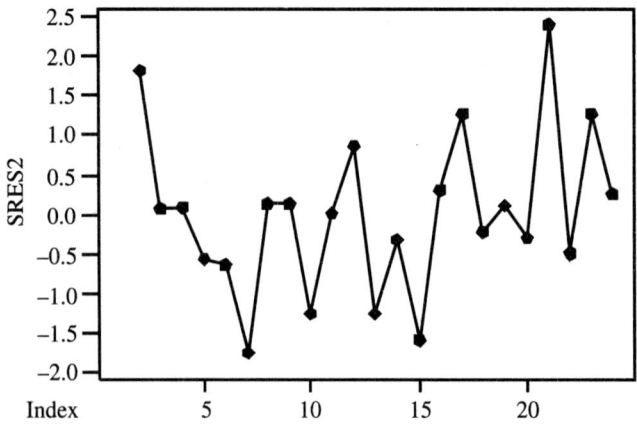

R124 Correlations for the difference data of Exercise R122 are shown in the following output. Has differencing decreased collinearity?

```
MTB > Correlation 'DSPREAD' 'DLEADING' 'DSUPPLY' 'DRATE'.

Correlations (Pearson)

           DSPREAD DLEADING  DSUPPLY
DLEADING   0.257
DSUPPLY    0.965    0.293
DRATE      0.344    0.129    0.146
```

R125 Estimating the construction cost of a new house is a very time-consuming task for builders. A builder planning a large suburban development was considering a large number of different plans, and did not want to invest the time to estimate the cost of every one of the plans in detail. From past designs, with prices updated to reflect current markets, the builder had actual costs for 34 different new houses. A regression analysis was performed with

$$Y = \text{actual cost (\$000)}$$

$$X_1 = \text{square feet of floor space}$$

$$X_2 = \text{square feet of wall area}$$

$$X_3 = \text{square feet of window area}$$

$$X_4 = \text{square feet of garage area}$$

$$X_5 = \text{type of foundation (slab, partial, or full basement)}$$

Which of the independent variables must be replaced by dummy variables?

R126 The JMP statistical package was used to perform a multiple regression analysis of the builder's cost estimation model of Exercise R125. By declaring X_5 to be an ordinal variable, the analyst caused creation of indicator (1/0) variables for partial and slab basements. The model also incorporated product terms of these indicator variables with the floor space and wall area variables. The results of this analysis are shown in Figure 14.49.

FIGURE 14.49 **Cost Estimation Model Including Product Terms**

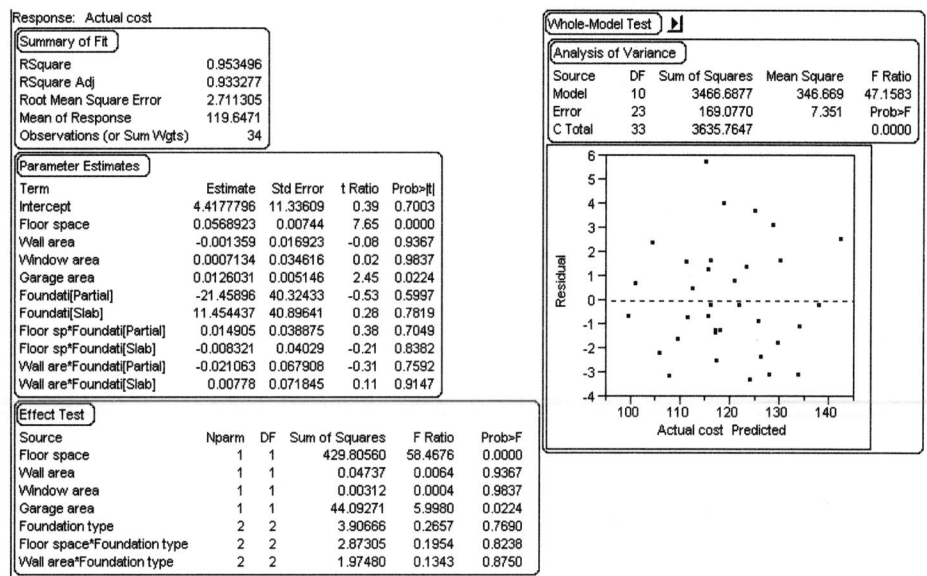

a How much of the variation in actual cost is accounted for by variation in all the predictors?

b Use this value to carry out (by hand) an *F* test of the null hypothesis that all true slopes are 0.

c Even though you may not be an expert in housing matters, does this null hypothesis make much sense to you? Is it rejected by the model?

d Which individual coefficients are statistically significant at the usual α levels?

R127 The analyst of the house construction data of Exercise R125 tried another multiple regression model, omitting the product terms. Some results are shown in Figure 14.50.

a Has the omission of product terms led to a statistically detectable ($\alpha = .05$) decrease in the explanatory value of the model?

FIGURE 14.50 Cost Estimation Model Excluding Product Terms

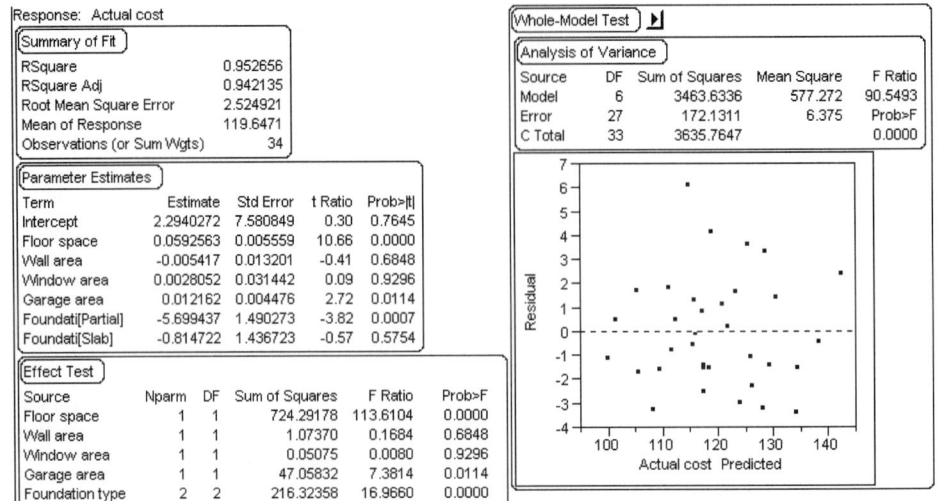

b What does the conclusion of this test indicate about the effect of floor space, wall area, and foundation type on the actual cost of the house?

R128 Residuals from the no-interaction model are plotted against predicted values in Figure 14.51. Is there any suggestion of violation of regression assumptions? If so, which assumption appears most suspect?

FIGURE 14.51 Residuals Versus Predicted Values

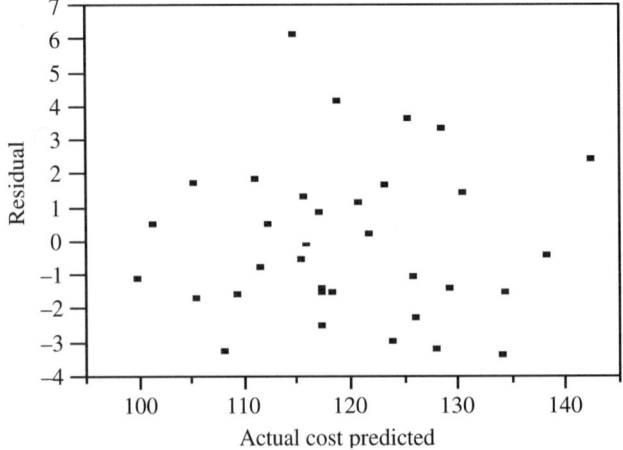

R129 Residuals from the no-interaction model are plotted against the quantitative independent variables in Figure 14.52. Is there any suggestion of violation of regression assumptions? If so, which assumption appears most suspect?

R130 An oil company does a small study of the sale of kerosene at its service stations. The dependent variable is monthly sales (thousands of gallons) of kerosene. The independent variables are monthly sales of gasoline (thousands of gallons), average income in the census tract where the station is located, and a rough index of the amount of traffic passed

FIGURE 14.52 Residuals Versus Independent Variables

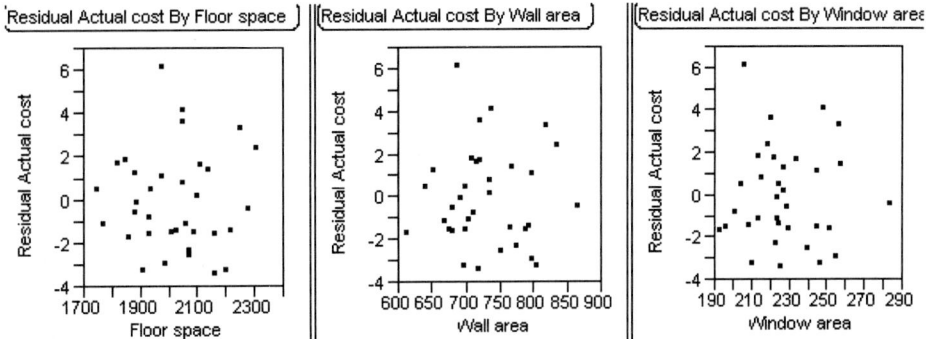

the station. The sample is of 21 company stations in a particular month. The data were analyzed using Excel.

```
Correlations
          Kero    Gas     Avginc  Traffic
Kero      1.0000
Gas       0.7559  1.0000
Avginc    0.3736  0.5321  1.0000
Traffic   0.5601  0.5659  0.3768  1.0000


Regression Statistics
Multiple R          0.7745
R Square            0.5999
Adjusted R Square   0.5293
Standard Error      4.3406
Observations           21

ANOVA
              df        SS         MS        F      Significance F
Regression     3     480.172   160.057    8.495      0.001
Residual      17     320.295    18.841
Total         20     800.467

              Coefficients  Standard Erro   t Stat    P-value
Intercept       -3.333        8.682        -0.384     0.706
Gas              0.079        0.024         3.294     0.004
Avginc          -0.132        0.392        -0.336     0.741
Traffic          7.861        7.304         1.076     0.297
```

a Locate the least-squares regression equation. Interpret each of the slopes.

b Negative sales are impossible; should we be concerned about a negative intercept?

R131 Refer to the Excel output of the kerosene sales model of Exercise R130.

a Locate SS(Regression).

b Do the results of t tests also suggest deleting one or more independent variables from the model?

R132 **a** Does the Excel output for the kerosene sales data of Exercise R130 indicate a serious collinearity problem?

b Would one expect autocorrelation in this study?

R133 A plot of residuals versus predicted values of the data from Exercise R130 is shown in Figure 14.53. Is there evidence of nonconstant variance? Are there any potentially serious outliers?

R134 It is discovered that station number 9 in the kerosene sales data of Exercise R130 has a rather large contract to supply kerosene to a group of stores. No other station known to

FIGURE 14.53   Residuals Versus Predicted for Kerosene Sales Data

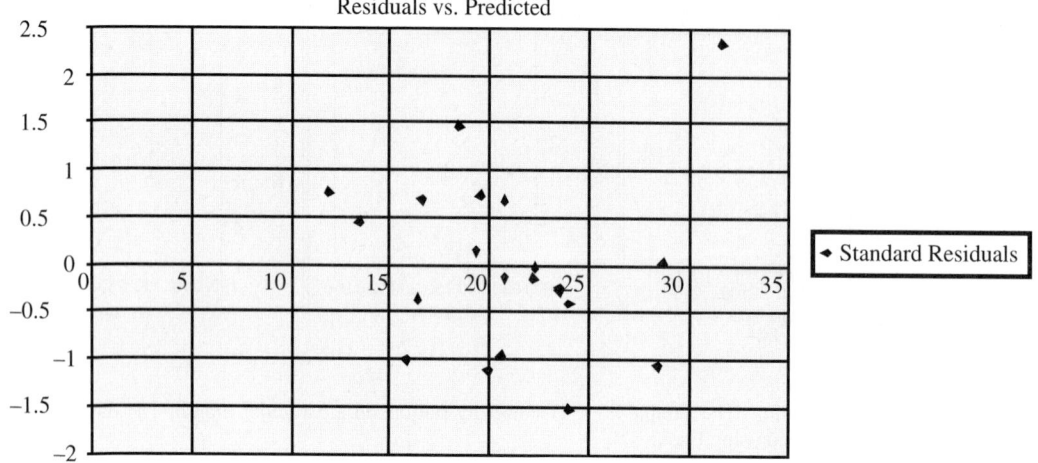

the company has a similar contract. Therefore station 9 is deleted from the sample and the regression is recalculated. The variables are given an N- (no contracts) prefix. Output is as follows:

```
Regression Statistics
Multiple R          0.7165
R Square            0.5134
Adjusted R Sq       0.4221
Standard Error      3.2585
Observations          20
```

ANOVA

	df	SS	MS	F	Significance F
Regression	3	179.2128	59.7376	5.6260	0.0079
Residual	16	169.8892	10.6181		
Total	19	349.1020			

	Coefficients	Standard Error	t Stat	P-value
Intercept	7.8171	7.1591	1.0919	0.2910
NGas	0.0640	0.0185	3.4512	0.0033
NAvginc	-0.2793	0.2972	-0.9395	0.3614
NTraffic	2.9033	5.6394	0.5148	0.6137

a Have the regression slopes changed because of the omission of station 9?

b How has the residual standard deviation changed?

c How has the coefficient of determination changed?

R135 The kerosene sales data of Exercise R130, omitting station 9, were also modeled using only NGas as a predictor, yielding the following Excel output:

```
Regression Statistics
Multiple R          0.7587
R Square            0.5756
Adjusted R Sq       0.5520
Standard Error      4.2417
Observations          20
```

ANOVA

	df	SS	MS	F	Significance F
Regression	1	439.2271	439.2271	24.4122	0.0001
Residual	18	323.8584	17.9921		
Total	19	763.0855			

Test the null hypothesis that the coefficients of NAVGINC and NTRAFF are both zero. Can this hypothesis be rejected at the usual α values?

R136 Data are collected on the yield of a chemical under various combinations of temperature and pressure. The data were as follows:

TEMP	PRES	YIELD	TEMP	PRES	YIELD	TEMP	PRES	YIELD
2200	3.8	75.50	2250	3.8	76.80	2300	3.8	78.50
2200	4.2	77.90	2250	4.2	79.20	2300	4.2	80.20
2200	3.8	75.90	2250	3.8	76.00	2300	3.8	78.80
2200	4.2	77.90	2250	4.2	78.90	2300	4.2	80.20

a A plot of Temp vs. Pres is shown in Figure 14.54. What must the value of $r_{TEMP.PRES}$ be?

b How severe is the collinearity problem for these data?

R137 A regression model is fit to the yield data of Exercise R136. Minitab output is as follows:

```
Regression Analysis
The regression equation is
yield = - 2.41 + 0.0262 temp + 5.33 pres

Predictor     Coef      Stdev     t-ratio     p        VIF
Constant    -2.412      6.915      -0.35     0.735
temp        0.026250  0.002889     9.09      0.000     1.0
pres        5.3333      0.5897      9.04      0.000     1.0

s = 0.4085     R-sq = 94.8%     R-sq(adj) = 93.7%

Analysis of Variance

SOURCE        DF        SS        MS        F        p
Regression     2      27.435    13.717    82.19    0.000
Error          9       1.502     0.167
Total         11      28.937

SOURCE        DF      SEQ SS
temp           1      13.781
pres           1      13.653

Durbin-Watson statistic = 2.28
```

FIGURE 14.54   **Plot of Temperature and Pressure for Yield Data**

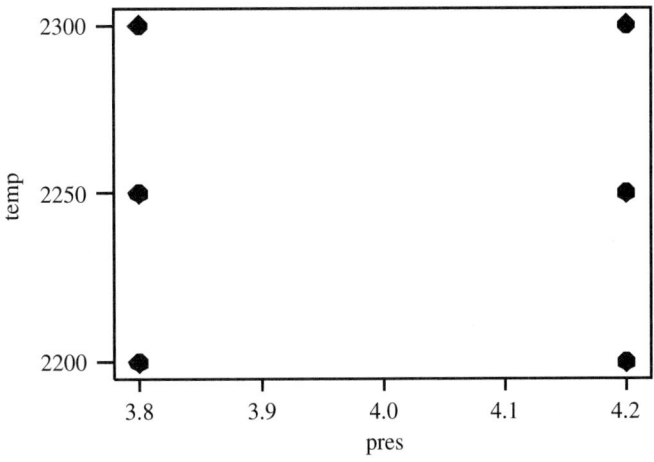

a Locate the prediction equation.

b Roughly, what is the width of a 95% prediction interval for a value of YIELD? Assume that any extrapolation penalty can be neglected.

R138 Summarize the results of overall F and t tests for the yield data of Exercise R136. What do the results indicate about the predictive value of TEMP and PRES?

R139 A residual plot against values of TEMP for the yield model of Exercise R136 is shown in Figure 14.55. Does this plot show any evidence of a problem?

FIGURE 14.55 **Residuals Versus Temperature—Yield Data**

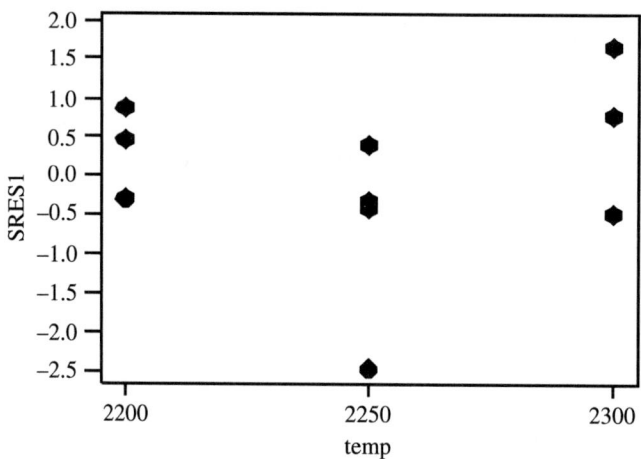

R140 Based on the residual plot in the preceding exercise, a new variable, TEMPSQ = $(TEMP - 2250)^2$, is created. A new regression analysis is performed.

```
Regression Analysis

The regression equation is
yield = - 2.67 + 0.0262 temp + 5.33 pres +0.000155 tempsq

Predictor        Coef        Stdev     t-ratio      p      VIF
Constant       -2.671        6.283       -0.43    0.682
temp         0.026250     0.002624       10.00    0.000     1.0
pres           5.3333       0.5356        9.96    0.000     1.0
tempsq     0.00015500   0.00009090        1.71    0.127     1.0

s = 0.3711     R-sq = 96.2%     R-sq(adj) = 94.8%

Analysis of Variance

SOURCE       DF          SS          MS        F        p
Regression    3     27.8350      9.2783    67.38    0.000
Error         8      1.1017      0.1377
Total        11     28.9366

SOURCE       DF      SEQ SS
temp          1     13.7812
pres          1     13.6533
tempsq        1      0.4004
```

a Have the coefficients of temp and pres changed much?

b Does adding tempsq greatly improve the prediction of YIELD? Indicate the parts of the output that support your judgment.

c Is there reason to be concerned about autocorrelation in this study?

R141 A store manager for a supermarket chain does a regression study of the weekly sales of the store and the volume of promotional activity (advertising and coupons) the previous week. The resulting data were analyzed using Statistix:

```
PREDICTOR
VARIABLES    COEFFICIENT   STD ERROR    STUDENT'S T       P

CONSTANT      -7.79036      24.9502        -0.31       0.7578
PROMO          5.31293       0.63818        8.33       0.0000

R-SQUARED            0.7591    RESID. MEAN SQUARE (MSE)    168.055
ADJUSTED R-SQUARED   0.7481    STANDARD DEVIATION           12.9636

SOURCE       DF      SS           MS         F        P

REGRESSION    1    11647.2     11647.2     69.31    0.0000
RESIDUAL     22     3697.21      168.055
TOTAL        23    15344.5

DURBIN-WATSON TEST FOR AUTOCORRELATION

DURBIN-WATSON STATISTIC  0.4331
```

a Is there evidence of a statistically significant predictive value of PROMO for predicting SALES?

b How much of the variability (squared error) of SALES is accounted for by PROMO?

R142 The Statistix output for the sales and promotion model in Exercise R141 indicates that there is a serious violation of at least one assumption. What is it, how do you know that this violation has occurred, and what are the consequences of the violation on your answers in the previous exercise?

R143 Differences are calculated for the sales and promotion data of the previous exercises, and a new regression equation is found.

```
PREDICTOR
VARIABLES    COEFFICIENT   STD ERROR    STUDENT'S T       P

CONSTANT      -1.69565       1.73655       -0.98       0.3400
DPROMO         5.01872       0.27638       18.16       0.0000

R-SQUARED            0.9401    RESID. MEAN SQUARE (MSE)    69.3595
ADJUSTED R-SQUARED   0.9373    STANDARD DEVIATION           8.32824

SOURCE       DF      SS           MS         F        P

REGRESSION    1    22870.3     22870.3    329.74    0.0000
RESIDUAL     21     1456.55      69.3595
TOTAL        22    24326.8

DURBIN-WATSON TEST FOR AUTOCORRELATION

DURBIN-WATSON STATISTIC  1.4314
```

a Is there a statistically significant predictive value of DPROMO for predicting DSALES?

b How much of the variability of DSALES is accounted for by variation in DPROMO?

c How do your answers here compare to the answers for the undifferenced model?

R144 Did the use of differences in Exercise R143 reduce the violation of assumptions in the original model?

R145 In a paper mill, a liquid slurry of wood fibers is forced through a screen. The yield of fibers is known to increase as the difference in pressure between the two sides of the screen increases. Data are collected and a regression equation found. A residual plot with a LOWESS smooth is shown in Figure 14.56.

FIGURE 14.56 **Residual Plot with LOWESS Smooth for Paper Mill Data**

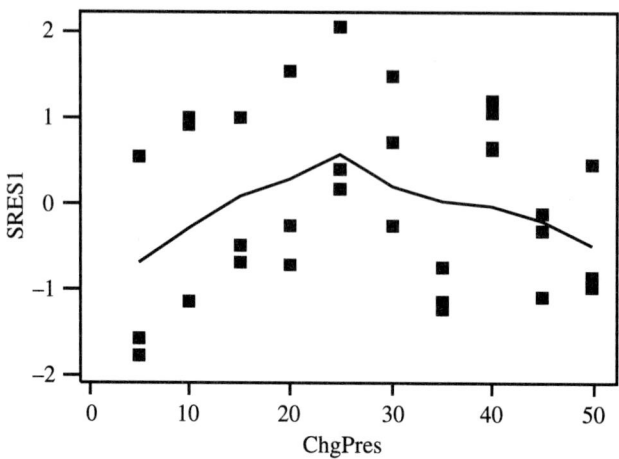

```
Regression Analysis

The regression equation is
Yield = 60.8 + 0.630 ChgPres

Predictor       Coef      Stdev     t-ratio       p
Constant      60.7844    0.9604      63.29     0.000
ChgPres       0.63002    0.03096     20.35     0.000

s = 2.435      R-sq = 93.7%      R-sq(adj) = 93.4%

Analysis of Variance

SOURCE       DF        SS        MS        F        p
Regression    1      2456.0    2456.0    414.23   0.000
Error        28       166.0       5.9
Total        29      2622.0
```

a What should the null hypothesis that the true slope is zero mean in this situation?

b Show that this hypothesis can be conclusively rejected.

R146 Locate and interpret the residual standard deviation in the output of Exercise R145.

R147 Consider the scatterplot and LOWESS smooth in Figure 14.56 for the paper mill data.

a Is there an indication that a nonlinear equation may give a better fit to the data?

b Are there any severe outliers?

R148 The square root of the pressure change is calculated for the data of Exercise R145 and a new regression is calculated. Has the square root transformation improved the fit of the model?

```
Regression Analysis

The regression equation is
Yield = 47.8 + 6.04 SqrtPres
```

```
Predictor      Coef      Stdev    t-ratio      p
Constant     47.752      1.463      32.64    0.000
SqrtPres     6.0426      0.2790     21.66    0.000

s = 2.297     R-sq = 94.4%     R-sq(adj) = 94.2%

Analysis of Variance

SOURCE        DF        SS         MS       F        p
Regression     1      2474.3     2474.3   469.10   0.000
Error         28       147.7        5.3
Total         29      2622.0
```

■

Time-Series Analysis

This chapter deals with time-series data—data collected on one or more variables over time. We begin our consideration of such data with a discussion of index numbers; these numbers are the result of attempts to summarize complicated patterns of price or quantity movement. The key ideas are the following:

1 The special price-level problem of economic time series can be partially remedied by the use of price indices. The construction of price indices involves a choice of quantity weights. Because such choices are not logically inevitable, they are another source of variability and uncertainty in time-series analysis.

2 The analysis of time-series data requires sophisticated approaches, and a number of methods have been proposed. The classic trend-cycle-season-irregularity approach is useful in isolating trends and correcting for seasonal factors, but it is less successful in dealing with cyclic behaviors. Various smoothing techniques, including moving-average, running-median, and various types of exponential smoothing methods, are useful in generating forecasts once the time series has been purged of trend and seasonal factors.

3 The ARIMA approach is an alternative forecasting scheme that involves explicit models for the evolution of a time series. This style of time-series analysis raises an interesting question about cycles. Though no explicit cycle feature appears in any ARIMA model, data that apparently follow a cyclic pattern can fit such models very well.

he part of statistical analysis of great relevance to managers is analysis of time-series data collected on the same variable for many time periods. From macroeconomic data such as disposable income to microeconomic data such as weekly sales of one particular product at one particular store, time-series data are basic data for managers. In Chapter 14 we discussed how we can apply multiple regression methods to time-series data. The emphasis there was on the special problems that such data presented, particularly the problem of autocorrelated errors.

If time-series data present problems, they also present opportunities. One of the very best predictors of the future behavior of a variable is its past behavior. Intelligent analysis of time-series data can often yield insights that help in understanding and predicting the future values of the series. In this chapter we discuss some useful ways of looking at time-series data.

The behavior of a time series is considered in isolation. We don't look at prediction of one time series by other series, as we did in regression. Instead, we use past values of a time series to predict future values of the same series. One major virtue of this approach is that the data requirements are minimal. As long as a series has been defined consistently over time (as, unfortunately, many series aren't), there's no need to bring together many different sets of data. Therefore, the methods described in this chapter are useful in situations such as inventory control, where many forecasts must be made and the value of a little extra accuracy is not huge.

One part of time-series analysis is the construction of index numbers to reflect changes in prices over time. We briefly discuss methods for constructing and using such indices in Section 15.1. In Section 15.2, we turn to the classic breakdown of time series into trend, seasonal, cyclic, and irregular components. In Section 15.3, we discuss smoothing methods that can be used as simple forecasting methods and also as methods for clearing up the effect of irregular, random movements of the series. The ARIMA (AutoRegressive Integrated Moving Average) methods of Section 15.4 are potentially very valuable, both in the context of a single series and as a way to combine concepts of regression and time series. ■

Index Numbers

I ndex numbers are among the best known results of statistical reasoning. The value of the Dow Jones Industrial Index is reported daily by newspapers and broadcasts. Many news radio stations interrupt their regular broadcasts to give the monthly Consumer Price Index as soon as it is released. Many cost-of-living adjustments are based on such indices, as are Social Security payments. In this section, we discuss some basic steps in index number construction, with primary emphasis on price indices.

There are essentially two types of indices: price indices and quantity indices. A price index measures the change in the prices of a group of items over time; a quantity index measures the change in the amount of a group of goods or services produced over time. Stock market indices such as the Dow Jones Industrial Average or the Standard and Poor's 500 are price indices; production indices for automobiles, steel, and the like are quantity indices.

A price index is useful in its own right as an indicator of the general level of prices. Also, measurements of general economic activity such as the gross domestic product (GDP) are divided by a price index to separate the effect of price changes from actual changes in activity. If all prices change by a constant percentage, any price index serves these functions; the interpretation of a price index gets more delicate when prices vary differently.

Once again we work by example. Suppose that we want to construct a simple index for the price of entertainment. The following price data are available in an Excel spreadsheet:

Item	1994 price	1995 price	1996 price
Color TV	400.00	440.00	420.00
Movie ticket	5.00	5.50	6.00
Baseball ticket	10.00	11.00	12.00
Compact disc	15.00	16.50	12.00
Total	430.00	473.00	450.00

There is no problem when comparing 1994 and 1995 entertainment prices. Every price shown increased by 10% from 1994 to 1995. No matter how any reasonable entertainment index is calculated, if 1994 is taken as the base year, with an index value of 100, the 1995 index value must be 110, a 10% increase.

There is a more interesting problem when comparing 1996 to 1994 prices because the price changes are not consistent. Color televisions are up 5% (1996 over 1994), movie tickets are up 20%, baseball tickets are up 20%, and compact discs are down 20%. An index must weight these changes somehow, to give an idea of the overall change in entertainment prices.

One (poor) solution to the weighting problem is to take the ratio of the total prices in 1996 to total prices in 1994. Conventionally, this ratio is multiplied by 100 so that we state the index in percentage terms. This index value is

$$\frac{450.00}{430.00} \times 100 = 104.65$$

which indicates a 4.65% rise in prices from 1994 to 1996. This is an example of a simple aggregate index. A formal definition follows.

Definition 15.1 Simple Aggregate Price Index

A simple aggregate price index for year k, denoted I_k, is the ratio of a sum of prices in year k to the sum of prices in the base year (year 0), expressed as a percentage:

$$I_k = \frac{\sum p_{ki}}{\sum p_{0i}} \times 100$$

where p_{ki} and p_{0i} are the prices of item i in year k and year 0, respectively. ∎

The Dow Jones Industrial Index began as a simple aggregate index of the prices of 30 blue chip stocks. Because modifications have been made to the DJI over the years to deal with such issues as stock splits, the index is no longer recognizable as a simple aggregate. Indeed, the DJI is quite difficult to interpret in any technical way. Perhaps it has retained its popularity because it is based on only 30 stocks and therefore varies more widely and dramatically than other, wider indices.

EXAMPLE 15.1

Closing 1994 and 1995 stock prices for a group of nonprescription drug wholesalers are shown here. Construct a simple aggregate price index for 1995 using 1994 as the base year.

Wholesaler	Closing Stock Price	
	1994	**1995**
Begley	$15\frac{1}{2}$	$16\frac{1}{4}$
Bindley	$9\frac{7}{8}$	19
Durr-Fillauer	$10\frac{1}{4}$	$15\frac{1}{4}$
Ketchum	$15\frac{1}{4}$	$20\frac{1}{4}$
Med. Shoppe	19	24

Solution

$$I_{1995} = \frac{16\frac{1}{4} + 19 + 15\frac{1}{4} + 20\frac{1}{4} + 24}{15\frac{1}{2} + 9\frac{7}{8} + 10\frac{1}{4} + 15\frac{1}{4} + 19} = 1.356$$

A stockholder owning one share of each wholesaler would have seen a 35.6% increase in the price of the portfolio. ∎

The obvious objection to a simple aggregate index is that it does not reflect the amounts of various goods that are actually purchased (or in the case of a stock price index, the number of shares of stock that are held). Our entertainment price index implicitly assumes that the relevant consumer buys as many color televisions as movie tickets. For most purposes, it is more reasonable to weight each price by an appropriate quantity to form a weighted aggregate index.

Definition 15.2 Weighted Aggregate Price Index

A weighted aggregate price index for year k is the ratio of a weighted sum of prices in year k to a weighted sum of prices in the base year 0 expressed as a percentage. The weights q_i are appropriately chosen quantities of each item:

$$I_k = \frac{\sum p_{ki} q_i}{\sum p_{0i} q_i} \times 100$$ ∎

EXAMPLE 15.2

In constructing an entertainment index using the data in this section, assume that a representative family buys one new color television set every eight years, 10 movie tickets and 4 baseball tickets per year, and 20 compact discs per year. Calculate the weighted aggregate price index values for 1995 and 1996.

Solution

The appropriate quantities can all be translated into amounts per year. For television sets, the quantity is $1/8 = .125$ per year; for movie and baseball tickets, 10 and 4 per year; and for compact discs, 20 per year. Computations from an Excel spreadsheet give the total cost in each year:

Item	Weights	94 cost	95 cost	96 cost
TV	0.125	50	55	52.5
Movie ticket	10	50	55	60
Baseball ticket	4	40	44	48
Compact disc	20	300	330	240
Total		440	484	400.5
Index			1.100	0.910

For example, the 1994 cost of compact discs is $20(\$15.00) = 300.00$. The price index value for 1995 is

$$I_{1995} = \frac{484}{440} \times 100 = 110.0$$

The price index value for 1996 is

$$I_{1996} = \frac{400.5}{440} = 91.0$$

The 1995 index value reflects the uniform 10% price increase. No matter what weights we used, we would get an index value of 110 for that year. The 1996 index value (91.0) is substantially lower than the simple aggregate value (104.65) found previously. The basic reason is that the price of compact discs decreased over that time. This price receives much more weight in the weighted aggregate index than it does in the simple aggregate index; the larger increases receive relatively less weight. ∎

choice of weights

The major difficulty in defining a weighted aggregate index is, of course, the specification of appropriate items and the weights attached to the items. The Bureau of Labor Statistics, in preparing the Consumer Price Index, selected about 300 carefully defined items. The quantities q_i are obtained by a sample of wage earners and their families. The selection of items and quantities inevitably becomes less appropriate as time goes by. Thus, almost any index must be revised periodically.

In a sense, the whole exercise of fixed-quantity weights in price indices is a denial of elementary economics. In fact, many economists believe that the Consumer Price Index has overstated the rate of inflation. When a particular commodity becomes more expensive, we buy less of it. When a new product of superior quality appears on the market, we change our purchasing behavior. However, if product quality declines, we may receive less utility for a given expenditure. Ideally, a price index would not be so closely tied to specific products but rather would reflect the cost of obtaining certain goals. Instead of basing a food price index on the price of so much steak, so much bread, and so many apples, we would prefer a food price index based on the total cost of a diet meeting specified nutrition and taste standards. The difficulties involved in pinning down such elusive goals, however, are formidable. At least the current fixed-quantity approach to price indices provides an objective, if somewhat arbitrary, standard. As we noted earlier in this section, the choice of weights matters only to the extent that price changes differ among products. All in all, we suggest that price indices should be treated like any other statistical quantities—as estimates that are subject to error.

EXERCISES

15.1 Data for a price index based on eight commodities are collected over a 3-year period, yielding the following results:

	Commodity							
	1	**2**	**3**	**4**	**5**	**6**	**7**	**8**
Price								
Year 1	6.00	7.25	6.60	10.50	4.60	12.50	25.00	300.00
Year 2	6.58	7.80	7.25	11.58	5.05	13.75	27.48	329.50
Year 3	7.25	8.59	7.99	12.75	5.50	15.10	30.21	362.45
Quantity								
Per Year	6.25	4.00	2.50	1.00	.80	.25	.10	.01

a Compute simple aggregate price indices for years 2 and 3, using year 1 as the base period. A spreadsheet would be very convenient for this and the following exercises.

b Compute weighted aggregate price indices for years 2 and 3, using year 1 as the base period.

15.2 A computing industry analyst gathered data on the cost and quantity sold of computing devices for a 4-year period. The data are collected in six major categories, from personal computers on up to mainframes, as follows:

	Category					
	A	**B**	**C**	**D**	**E**	**F**
Year 1						
Price	20.00	50.68	989	35,416	195,626	651,928
Quantity	2,060,000	121,200	86,104	82,147	21,047	1306
Year 2						
Price	18.64	48.21	1021	37,215	206,114	721,200
Quantity	2,547,000	142,900	89,216	81,021	21,926	1339
Year 3						
Price	16.93	47.03	1096	40,462	215,963	790,087
Quantity	2,997,000	163,800	95,114	76,050	20,875	1575
Year 4						
Price	16.61	46.89	1129	41,943	229,120	864,326
Quantity	3,451,000	177,500	94,397	71,194	19,975	1498

The following Excel spreadsheet shows the total expenditure when each year's prices are combined with each year's quantities. For example, the total expenditure for year 1 quantities at year 4 prices is shown in the upper-right corner as 9,533,701,101.

Total expenditure		Price			
		Year 1	Year 2	Year 3	Year 4
Quantity					
	Year 1	8010575814	8469222799	9036004617	9533701101
	Year 2	8178083800	8645593704	9219024966	9729012552
	Year 3	7966175280	8429592772	8992437418	9498803058
	Year 4	7577295231	8016539012	8548624046	9030079288

a Compute simple aggregate price indices for years 2, 3, and 4, using year 1 as the base period.

b Compute weighted aggregate price indices for these years, using year 1 quantities as weights. (Base-year weights define Laspeyres indices.)

c Compute weighted aggregate price indices for these years, using the quantities for each year as weights for that year. (Current-year weights define Paasche indices.)

15.3 Refer to the price indices you computed in Exercise 15.2.

a Is there a serious difference between the unweighted, simple aggregate index and the index that is weighted by yearly quantities? Why?

b Is there a serious difference between the year-1 weighted index and the year-4 weighted index? Why?

15.4 A manufacturer of small electric appliances uses mostly stainless steel sheets, copper wire, a plastic substance, and glass. As a part of its pricing policy, the company routinely calculates a raw material cost index. Price data (P) for the previous five years and utilization data (Q), in units used by that manufacturer, are shown in the following Excel output. The column at the right is the result of multiplying the first-year quantities by each year's prices and summing.

Year	Steel P	Copper P	Plastic P	Glass P	sum(Q1*P)
1	280	450	24	48	3705240
2	306	430	38	51	3811500
3	327	492	36	53	4194960
4	360	582	39	54	4781700
5	396	573	44	56	4938780
Total	1669	2527	181	262	

Year	Q	Q	Q	Q
1	220	30	40	21
2	244	34	43	24
3	256	36	45	25
4	280	38	49	30
5	308	44	52	35
	1308	182	229	135

a Compute simple aggregate price index values for years 2–5, using year 1 as the base period.

b Compute weighted aggregate price indices (using year-1 quantity weights) for these years.

c Explain any major discrepancies you find between the two sets of values. ∎

15.2

The Classic Trend, Cyclic, and Seasonal Approach

O ne way to examine a time series is to break it into components. A standard approach is to find components corresponding to a long-term trend, any cyclic behavior, seasonal behavior, and a residual, irregular part. For example, the Bureau of Labor Statistics of the United States government publishes typical prices for gasoline for each month. Here are the data, beginning with 1986:

```
Area : U.S. City Average
Item : Gasoline, unleaded regular (cost per gallon/3.8 liters)
```

Year	Jan	Feb	Mar	Apr	May	Jun	Jul	Aug	Sep	Oct	Nov	Dec
1986	1.194	1.120	0.981	0.888	0.923	0.955	0.890	0.843	0.860	0.831	0.821	0.823
1987	0.862	0.905	0.912	0.934	0.941	0.958	0.971	0.995	0.990	0.976	0.976	0.961
1988	0.933	0.913	0.904	0.930	0.955	0.955	0.967	0.987	0.974	0.957	0.949	0.930
1989	0.918	0.926	0.940	1.065	1.119	1.114	1.092	1.057	1.029	1.027	0.999	0.980
1990	1.042	1.037	1.023	1.044	1.061	1.088	1.084	1.190	1.294	1.378	1.377	1.354
1991	1.247	1.143	1.082	1.104	1.156	1.160	1.127	1.140	1.143	1.122	1.134	1.123
1992	1.073	1.054	1.058	1.079	1.136	1.179	1.174	1.158	1.158	1.154	1.159	1.136
1993	1.117	1.108	1.098	1.112	1.129	1.130	1.109	1.097	1.085	1.127	1.113	1.070
1994	1.043	1.051	1.045	1.064	1.080	1.106	1.136	1.182	1.177	1.152	1.163	1.143
1995	1.129	1.120	1.115	1.140	1.200	1.226	1.195	1.164	1.148	1.127	1.101	1.101
1996	1.129	1.124	1.162	1.251								

What can we see from the plot in Figure 15.1? First, there is a clear upward trend. Second, there appear to be some cycles. It may not be clear from the graph, but gasoline prices are thought to be seasonal, with prices higher in the summer months. Finally, there is an irregular, random component; even if we could determine the trend, cycles, and seasonal behavior exactly, we still couldn't predict gas prices perfectly.

FIGURE 15.1   **Gasoline Price Data**

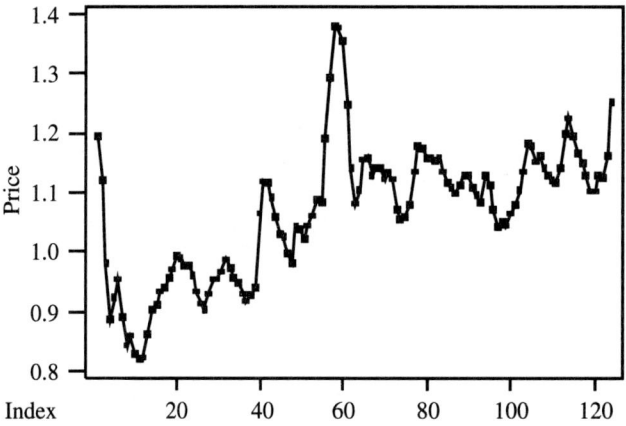

EXAMPLE 15.3

Monthly data on the number of paid admissions (in thousands) to a new indoor sports and entertainment arena for 72 months are given next and plotted in Figure 15.2. Identify any apparent trend and any seasonal and cyclic effects.

J	F	M	A	M	J	J	A	S	O	N	D
89	101	116	111	94	59	44	44	73	78	99	93
96	110	118	116	107	69	52	54	85	92	113	109
120	136	155	155	129	98	69	78	116	143	154	166
183	199	227	219	198	148	94	108	160	201	215	246
242	264	359	308	265	193	150	146	243	260	332	293
323	377	470	422	345	239	176	182	288	342	380	379

FIGURE 15.2 **Admissions to Arena**

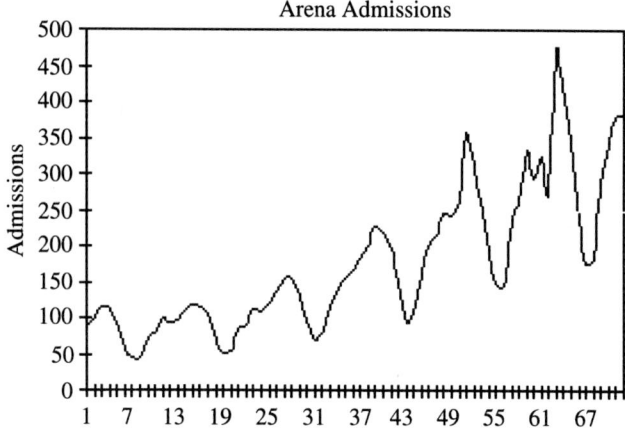

Arena Admissions

Solution

The upward trend in admissions is obvious in the figure. The trend may not be linear, however. Rather, it may be S-shaped, involving initial slow growth, a period of more rapid growth, and then a tapering off. (One consideration suggests that the trend cannot increase forever. Paid admissions to the arena are limited by the available number of dates and seats.) There is a strong seasonal effect; admissions drop dramatically in the summer months. If there's any cyclic component, it's not apparent in the figure. ∎

One typical approach to the analysis of a time series is to remove the trend first, then the seasonal effects. The hope is that this procedure will bring out any longer-term cycles more clearly. The key decision that must be made in removing a trend is the specification of the mathematical form of a trend equation. Denote the values of the time-series variable as y_t, where t runs from time 1 to some time T. Several mathematical forms for trends are widely used:

$$\text{Linear:} \quad Y_t = \beta_0 + \beta_1 t + \epsilon_t$$

$$\text{Exponential:} \quad Y_t = \beta_0 e^{\beta_1 t} \epsilon_t$$

$$\text{Logistic:} \quad Y_t = \frac{\beta_0}{1 + \beta_1 e^{\beta_2 t}} \epsilon_t$$

$$\text{Gompertz:} \quad Y_t = \beta_0 e^{\beta_1 e^{\beta_2 t}} \epsilon_t$$

linear trend

The **linear trend** equation is the simplest. The coefficient β_1 represents the average increase in y per unit time. This increase is measured in absolute terms (such as dollars) rather than in percentage terms. A linear trend equation should be used when there is no evident curvature in the plot of y_t against t. A standard way to estimate the intercept and slope is by least squares, as in simple linear regression, with t as the independent variable.

EXAMPLE 15.4

A linear trend was fit to the gasoline price data shown previously in this section. The following Minitab output is obtained, along with the plot in Figure 15.3. Does a linear trend appear reasonable? Write the estimated trend equation. Interpret the slope.

```
MTB > %Trend 'Price'.
Executing from file: Trend.MAC

Trend Analysis

Fitted Trend Equation

Yt = 0.9359 + 2.11E-03*t

Accuracy Measures
MAPE:       5.41474
MAD:        0.0582676
MSD:        0.00688385
```

FIGURE 15.3   **Trend Line for Gasoline Price Data**

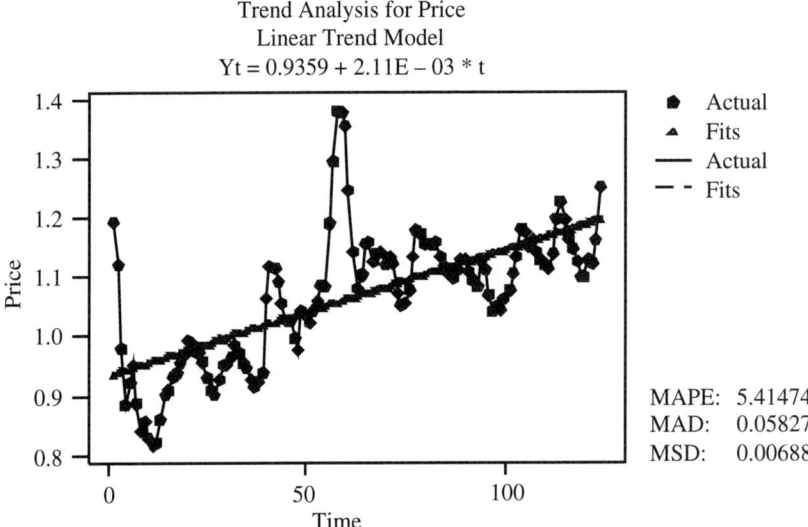

Solution

There is no evident curve in the plot, so a linear trend seems sensible. The trend equation is shown as $Y_t = 0.9359 + 0.00211t$, where t is the time period in months. (Remember that the E notation indicates how many places to move the decimal. So $2.11E - 03 = 2.11$ times $10^{-3} = 0.00211$.) The slope indicates that, over time, gas prices are increasing at 0.00211 dollars per month (which is about 2.5 cents per year).   ∎

exponential trend

We use the **exponential trend** equation when the trend reflects a roughly constant *percentage* growth; e^{β_1} is the percentage growth rate per time, whereas β_0 is the value of the trend at time $t = 0$. For instance, if at time 0 the trend value is 250, and the trend reflects an 8% growth rate per year, the trend equation is

$$\hat{y}_t = 250(1.08)^t$$

Because $e^{.077} = 1.08$ or, equivalently, $\log_e 1.08 = .077$, the trend equation can be rewritten as

$$\hat{y}_t = 250e^{.077t}$$

The exponential trend equation should be used if a plot of the logarithm of y_t against t appears roughly linear. If

$$Y_t = \beta_0 e^{\beta_1 t} \epsilon_t$$

then

$$\log Y_t = (\log \beta_0) + \beta_1 t + \log \epsilon_t$$

We can estimate the coefficients ($\log \beta_0$) and β_1 by regressing $\log y_t$ against $x_t = t$.

E X A M P L E   1 5 . 5

An exponential trend is fit to the gasoline price data. The output shown here results from a least-squares fit of $\log Y_t$ to t.

```
MTB > %Trend 'Price';
SUBC>   Growth.
Executing from file: Trend.MAC


Trend Analysis


Fitted Trend Equation


Yt = 0.93323*(1.00206**t)


Accuracy Measures


MAPE:      5.40736
MAD:       0.0585264
MSD:       0.00705154
```

a Write the estimated trend equation and identify the monthly percentage increase in sales.

b Does a linear trend or an exponential trend appear more appropriate?

Solution

a The prediction equation is shown as $0.93323(1.00206)^t$. The estimated change in ridership is 1.00206, a .00206% per month increase. Because the typical price is around a dollar, the percentage increase per month is about the same as the dollar increase per month.

b The choice between linear and exponential trend equations is not obvious. The plot of the data and the trend equations suggest that a linear trend fits the data as well as anything. ∎

It is risky to assume that exponential growth will continue indefinitely. The sales history of a product may reveal a consistent 15% growth rate in unit sales per year, but sooner or later the sales must approach some saturation level and the percentage growth must slow down. An old saying is "No tree grows to heaven."

logistic and Gompertz trends

The **logistic** and **Gompertz trend** equations yield very similar S-shaped trends. Fitting either logistic or Gompertz trend equations is a bit harder than fitting linear or exponential trends. It is not possible to transform either S-shaped curve into a regression model. More complicated numerical methods are available for fitting such equations.

One issue that arises in fitting a trend is what to use as the starting point. Naturally, we want to include the most recent values of the time series, but how far back should we go? There is usually no obvious right place. Starting the series at a high point in a cycle will make the trend somewhat lower; starting it at a low point will make the trend steeper. College professors discussing salaries like to start the series at a time when salaries were relatively high, so they can argue that salaries have not increased rapidly enough; college presidents like to start the series at a time when salaries were relatively low, so they can argue that salaries have increased quite nicely.

E X A M P L E 1 5 . 6

In the gasoline price time series, the lowest price occurred at month 11 of 1985. Starting the series at that month leads to the following linear trend equation. How does the coefficient of time change from the original trend line?

```
MTB > %Trend 'Price'.

Trend Analysis

Fitted Trend Equation

Yt = 0.955156 + 2.14E-03*t
```

Solution

The coefficient of time is 0.00214, slightly higher than the original slope, 0.00211. ∎

The trend, cyclic, seasonal, and irregular aspects of a time series can be combined in either of two ways. The **multiplicative model** is

$$y_t = T_t C_t S_t I_t$$

where T_t, C_t, S_t, and I_t are the trend, cyclic, seasonal, and irregular components at time t. This model can be understood in terms of percentage changes. For instance, a seasonal index for a particular month equal to 1.08 means that the series tends to be 8% above the value predicted by trend and cycle alone. (By definition, the irregular component is unpredictable.) The **additive model** is

$$y_t = T_t + C_t + S_t + I_t$$

This model can be understood in absolute units as opposed to percentages. For instance, a seasonal index for daily water consumption in a city might have a value of 8 million gallons per day for August. That means that the water consumption series for August would tend to be 8 million gallons above what was predicted by trend and cycle. A multiplicative model may be converted to an additive one by taking logarithms (to any base):

$$\log y_t = \log T_t + \log C_t + \log S_t + \log I_t$$

An additive model is very convenient when the trend equation is linear; a multiplicative model is convenient for an exponential trend. (Recall that we estimated an exponential trend by regressing the logarithm of y_t on t.) For most economic series, percentage changes tend to be more stable, and the multiplicative model is more commonly used.

Once a trend equation has been estimated, the influence of trend can be removed from the data, yielding a **detrended time series**. For the multiplicative model, divide the actual y_t by the trend value:

$$\frac{y_t}{T_t} = \frac{T_t C_t S_t I_t}{T_t} = C_t S_t I_t$$

to get an equation that contains no trend. If $y_t / T_t = 1.052$, for example, then the actual y_t is 5.2% above trend. For the additive model, subtract the trend value from y_t:

$$y_t - T_t = T_t + C_t + S_t + I_t - T_t = C_t + S_t + I_t$$

If $y_t - T_t = 620$, then y_t is 620 units above trend.

Next, the detrended values can be used to construct a **seasonal index**. Several methods can be used. The simplest method involves an additive model. To construct a seasonal index value for, say, October, simply average all the available detrended October values. For instance, if 60 months of data are available, and the five October detrended values are .982, .965, .961, .976, and .966, the seasonal index is the mean, .970. The same method could perhaps be used in a multiplicative model. Alternatively, because the multiplicative model is additive in logarithms, we can average the logarithms of detrended values, and then take the antilogarithm to obtain the index. The logarithms (base 10) of the five October detrended values are $-.0078885$, $-.0154727$, $-.0172766$, $-.0105502$, and $-.0150229$, which have a mean of $-.0132422$. Take the antilogarithm by calculating $10^{-.0132422} =$ .970. The two methods do not yield identical answers (in this case, the difference is in the fifth decimal place), but if the detrended values are not too variable, as is the case here, the difference is small. The interpretations of the additive and multiplicative seasonal indices are very different. The additive index of .970 means that October values tend to be .970 unit above the trend; the multiplicative index of .970 means that October values tend to be 97.0% of the trend.

For the gasoline data shown at the beginning of this section, the detrended values are shown in the following output:

```
Jan     Feb    Mar    Apr    May    Jun    Jul    Aug    Sep    Oct    Nov    Dec
 0.256   0.180  0.039 -0.056 -0.023  0.006 -0.061 -0.110 -0.095 -0.126 -0.138 -0.138
-0.101  -0.060 -0.055 -0.036 -0.031 -0.016 -0.005  0.017  0.010 -0.006 -0.008 -0.025
-0.056  -0.078 -0.089 -0.065 -0.042 -0.044 -0.034 -0.016 -0.031 -0.050 -0.061 -0.082
-0.096  -0.090 -0.078  0.045  0.097  0.090  0.066  0.028 -0.002 -0.006 -0.036 -0.057
 0.003  -0.004 -0.020 -0.001  0.014  0.038  0.032  0.136  0.238  0.320  0.317  0.292
 0.183   0.077  0.013  0.033  0.083  0.085  0.050  0.061  0.062  0.039  0.049  0.035
-0.017  -0.038 -0.036 -0.017  0.038  0.079  0.072  0.054  0.052  0.045  0.048  0.023
 0.002  -0.009 -0.021 -0.009  0.006  0.005 -0.019 -0.033 -0.047 -0.007 -0.023 -0.068
-0.097  -0.091 -0.099 -0.082 -0.069 -0.045 -0.017  0.027  0.020 -0.007  0.002 -0.020
-0.036  -0.048 -0.055 -0.032  0.026  0.050  0.017 -0.016 -0.034 -0.057 -0.085 -0.088
-0.062  -0.069 -0.033  0.054    *      *      *      *      *      *      *      *
```

To compute a seasonal index, we simply average the values for each period, obtaining

```
Index     Month
-0.00189  1
-0.02090  2
-0.03946  3
-0.01511  4
```

0.00987	5
0.02486	6
0.01016	7
0.01485	8
0.01725	9
0.01444	10
0.00644	11
-0.01277	12

Thus, price in month 1 tends to be 0.00189 dollars per gallon (0.189 cents per gallon) below the trend. Notice that in periods 6 through 10, the summer periods, prices tend to be substantially higher.

We can apply this procedure repeatedly. As new data come in, we can recompute seasonal indices to bring them up to date. Alternative methods of dealing with seasonal patterns, based on the ARIMA models of Section 15.4, are also commonly used.

deseasonalized data Once seasonal indices have been calculated, detrended data can be **deseasonalized**. Simply divide by the index value (in the multiplicative model) or subtract the index value (in the additive model). One limitation of this approach is that the seasonal index values are obtained from the entire series, rather than only from the series before the given time. We could, of course, recalculate trend and seasonal values each time period and deseasonalize using the updated seasonal indices. Another way to deseasonalize data each period is based on the ARIMA methods of Section 15.4.

cyclic patterns Detrended, seasonally adjusted values are useful in attempting to identify **cyclic patterns**. Only cyclic and irregular (random) components remain in such values. Even so, identification of cyclic patterns is a tricky business. The basic problem is identifying the peak-to-peak or trough-to-trough length (called the *period*) of a supposed cycle. Seasonal patterns don't present any such problem. By definition, seasonal cycles have a 1-year period. But identifying longer-term cyclic behavior is difficult. What do you do with data that appear to encompass $3\frac{1}{2}$ cycles, with peak-to-peak distances of $2\frac{1}{12}$ years, $3\frac{7}{12}$ years, and $4\frac{10}{12}$ years? One simple-minded idea is to take the mean distance ($3\frac{1}{2}$ years) as the apparent period of the cycle. But there is no guarantee that this is a very accurate estimate.

EXAMPLE 15.7

The detrended, deseasonalized gasoline price data were plotted using Minitab, as shown in Figure 15.4. Is there a regular cycle?

Solution

We certainly can't see cycles. The evident feature is the high price at the beginning and the "spike" in the middle of the series. ∎

spectral analysis A much more sophisticated version of time-series analysis, **spectral analysis**, is related to the idea of cyclic behavior. The sophisticated mathematics of spectral analysis, called *Fourier analysis*, is borrowed from physics and electrical engineering. The idea can be stated, without too much distortion, in terms of regression. A sine curve is a cyclic pattern, as shown in Figure 15.5; any period may be specified for a sine curve.

If several sine curves with different periods are specified and weights are assigned to each curve, very complicated cyclic patterns can be reconstructed as weighted sums of sine curves. Spectral analysis can be regarded as the result of regressing a (detrended

FIGURE 15.4 **Detrended, Deseasonalized Gasoline Prices**

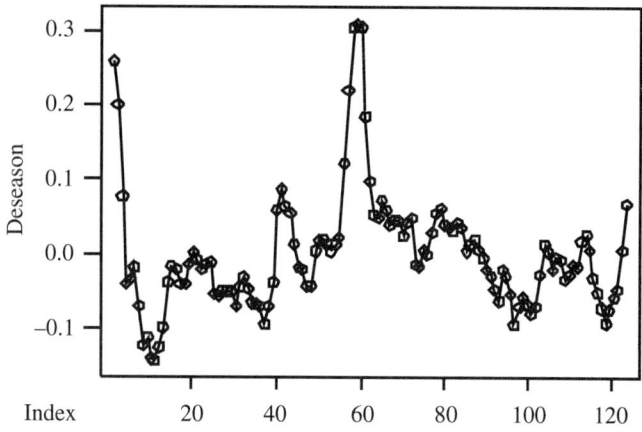

FIGURE 15.5 **Sine Wave**

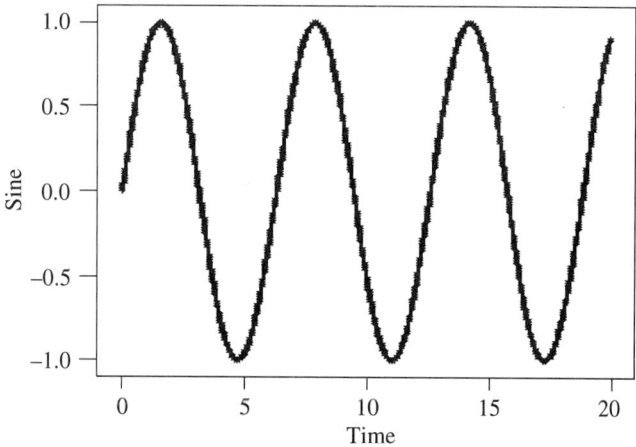

spectrum

or seasonally adjusted) time series on all possible sine curves. The **spectrum** of the time series indicates how much of the variation in y_t is explained by the sine curve having each possible period. If y_t shows a very strong cyclic pattern with a given period, spectral analysis shows that a sine curve with that period explains much of the variation in y_t, and the spectrum has a sharp peak corresponding to that period. Estimating the spectrum of a time series is not a job for amateurs. For our purposes, it is enough to say that spectral analysis is an available method for analyzing cyclic data.

EXERCISES

15.5 A supplier of high-quality audio equipment for automobiles accumulates monthly sales data on speakers and receiver-amplifier units for 5 years. The data (in thousands of units per month) are shown here:

Year	J	F	M	A	M	J	J	A	S	O	N	D
1	101.9	93.0	93.5	93.9	104.9	94.6	105.9	116.7	128.4	118.2	107.3	108.6
2	109.0	98.4	99.1	110.7	100.2	112.1	123.8	135.8	124.8	114.1	114.9	112.9
3	115.5	104.5	105.1	105.4	117.5	106.4	118.6	130.9	143.7	132.2	120.8	121.3
4	122.0	110.4	110.8	111.2	124.4	112.4	124.9	138.0	151.5	139.5	127.7	128.0
5	128.1	115.8	116.0	117.2	130.7	117.5	131.8	145.5	159.3	146.5	134.0	134.2

A plot of the sales data is shown in Figure 15.6. Do you see any overall trend in the data? Do there seem to be any cyclic or seasonal effects?

FIGURE 15.6   **Audio Sales Data**

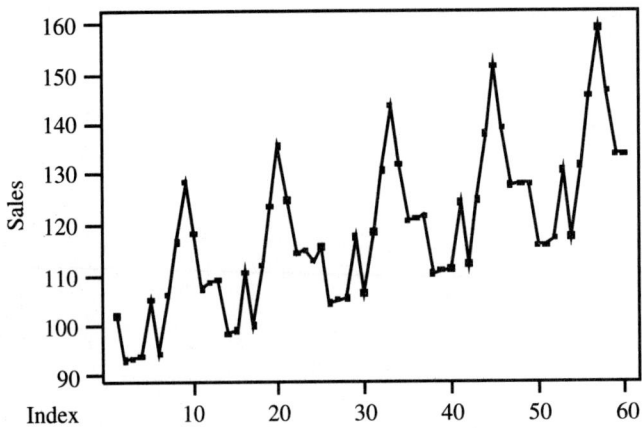

15.6 Minitab was used to fit a linear trend equation to the data of Exercise 15.5. The Period variable ranges from month 1 to month 60.

```
MTB > regress 'Sales' 1 'Period'
Regression Analysis

The regression equation is
Sales = 101 + 0.596 Period

Predictor      Coef      Stdev    t-ratio       p
Constant    100.513      2.855      35.21   0.000
Period      0.59629    0.08139       7.33   0.000

s = 10.92      R-sq = 48.1%    R-sq(adj) = 47.2%
```

What is the interpretation of the coefficient of Period?

15.7 The data of Exercise 15.5 are detrended by subtracting the trend equation values of Exercise 15.6, with the following results:

```
Jan    Feb    Mar    Apr    May    Jun   Jul   Aug   Sep   Oct   Nov   Dec
0.79  -8.71  -8.80  -9.00   1.41  -9.49  1.21 11.42 22.52 11.72  0.23  0.93
0.74 -10.46 -10.36   0.65 -10.45   0.85 11.96 23.36 11.76  0.47  0.67 -1.92
0.08 -11.52 -11.51 -11.81  -0.31 -12.00 -0.40 11.31 23.51 11.41 -0.58 -0.68
-0.58 -12.77 -12.97 -13.16  -0.56 -13.16 -1.25 11.25 24.15 11.56 -0.84 -1.14
-1.63 -14.53 -14.92 -14.32  -1.42 -15.21 -1.51 11.60 24.80 11.40 -1.69 -2.09
```

Are some months consistently below trend or consistently above trend? What does this imply about seasonal effects?

15.8 A simple seasonal index is constructed by averaging the detrended values of Exercise 15.7. The index values are

J	F	M	A	M	J	J	A	S	O	N	D
−0.12	−11.60	−11.71	−9.53	−2.27	−9.80	2.00	13.79	21.35	9.31	−0.44	−0.98

    a Construct detrended, deseasonalized data for January of year 5.

    b Construct forecast values for year 6 by calculating the trend values and then adding the seasonal factor.

15.9 A plot of the detrended, seasonally adjusted data from Exercise 15.5 is shown in Figure 15.7. Is there any visual evidence of a cyclic pattern?

FIGURE 15.7 **Detrended, Deseasonalized Audio Sales Data**

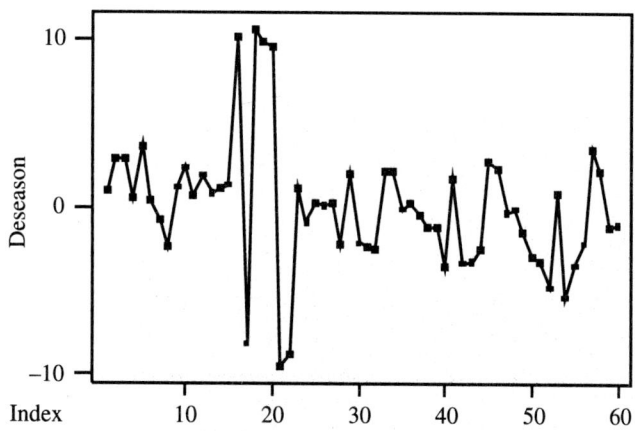

15.10 A machine tool firm that produces a variety of products for manufacturers has quarterly records of total activity for the previous 8 years. The data reflect activity rather than price, so inflation is irrelevant. The data are

	Quarter			
Year	1	2	3	4
1	97.2	100.2	102.8	102.6
2	106.1	107.8	110.5	110.6
3	116.5	117.3	119.9	119.3
4	126.1	125.7	128.3	132.1
5	133.2	133.8	141.1	142.1
6	144.2	146.1	151.6	154.0
7	155.8	158.6	165.8	167.0
8	171.1	172.6	176.5	179.7

    a A plot of the data against time (quarters 1–32) is shown in Figure 15.8. Does there appear to be a clear trend? If so, what form of trend equation would you suggest?

    b Can you detect cyclic or seasonal features?

15.11 The JMP computer package was used to fit an exponential trend to the data of Exercise 15.10. The following output summarizes a regression of the natural logarithm of the activity measure by period number, which is quarter 1 through quarter 32:

FIGURE 15.8 **Machine Tool Activity Data**

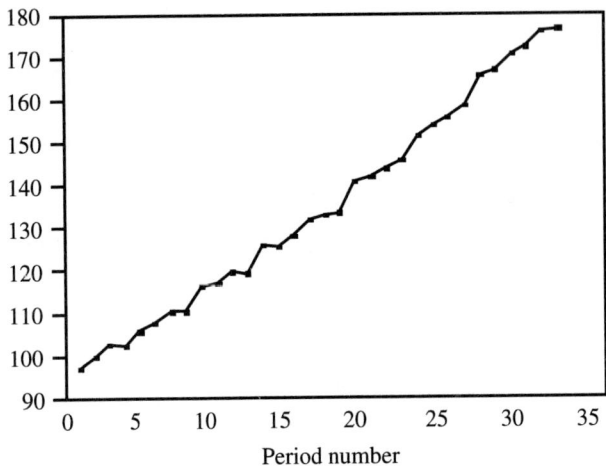

```
                    ln(Activity) By Period number

        Linear Fit
        Summary of Fit
        Rsquare                        0.997236
        RSquare Adj                    0.997144

        Root Mean Square Error         0.009879
        Mean of Response               4.887889
        Observations (or Sum Wgts)          32

                       Parameter Estimates
        Term          Estimate    Std Error    t Ratio    Prob>|t|
        Intercept     4.5632159   0.003576     1276       0.0000
        Period number 0.0196772   0.000189     104.03     0.0000
```

What is the interpretation of the coefficient of Period number?

15.12 Detrended values for the data of Exercise 15.10 are calculated by dividing by trend values, using the trend equation of Exercise 15.11. The detrended values are

| | *Quarter* | | | |
Year	1	2	3	4
1	.9939	1.0046	1.0106	.9890
2	1.0028	.9990	1.0041	.9854
3	1.0177	1.0048	1.0070	.9825
4	1.0182	.9952	.9960	1.0055
5	.9941	.9792	1.0125	.9998
6	.9948	.9882	1.0055	1.0015
7	.9935	.9916	1.0165	1.0038
8	1.0084	.9974	1.0001	.9984

A plot of the detrended values against time (quarters 1–32) is shown in Figure 15.9. Can you detect possible seasonal or cyclic effects?

15.13 Use the trend equation of Exercise 15.11 to forecast activity for quarters 33–36. How much compensation for seasonal effects is needed?

FIGURE 15.9 **Detrended Values Versus Time**

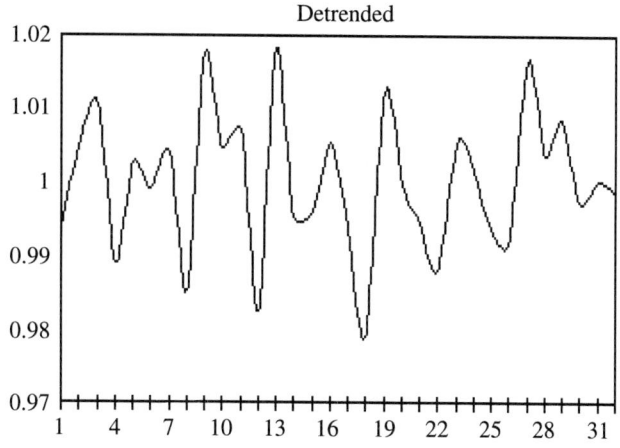

smoothing

Smoothing Methods

The classic approach described in the previous section does not lead directly to forecasts, though forecasts can be derived as a by-product. An alternative approach to time-series analysis is **smoothing**, which attempts to get rid of the irregular, random component of the series but does not concern itself with details of trends, seasons, and cycles.

Basic smoothing methods yield forecasts that are, in one sense or another, averages of past values. If the data show a pronounced trend, these forecasts tend to lag behind the trend. In addition, these methods usually ignore seasonal factors. We first discuss smoothing methods for no-trend, no-seasonal data.

moving averages

One of the most widely used smoothing methods is **moving averages**—averaging the M most recent values to forecast the next value.

EXAMPLE 15.8

One of the key elements of the budget of a small town television station is the monthly advertising-time sales. In the previous 36 months, monthly sales (measured in minutes per day) of paid, local advertising have been the following:

Month:	1	2	3	4	5	6	7	8	9	10	11	12
Sales:	86	80	85	93	96	102	97	89	96	87	82	81

Month:	13	14	15	16	17	18	19	20	21	22	23	24
Sales:	87	89	97	88	95	87	81	79	82	85	96	93

Month:	25	26	27	28	29	30	31	32	33	34	35	36
Sales:	99	103	96	85	78	83	90	96	85	82	89	96

Construct 3-month and 5-month moving-average forecasts.

Solution

The first 3-month moving average is $(86 + 80 + 85)/3 = 83.6667$, shown as 83.7 in the following table. The first 5-month moving average is $(86 + 80 + 85 + 93 + 96)/5 = 88.0$, as shown.

3-month moving average:

—	—	83.7	86.0	91.3	97.0	98.3	96.0	94.0	90.7	88.3	93.3
83.3	85.7	91.0	91.3	93.3	90.0	87.7	82.3	80.7	82.0	87.7	91.3
96.0	98.3	99.3	94.7	86.3	82.0	83.7	89.7	90.3	87.7	85.3	89.0

5-month moving average:

—	—	—	—	88.0	91.2	94.6	95.4	96.0	94.2	90.2	87.0
86.6	85.2	87.2	88.4	91.2	91.2	89.6	86.0	84.8	82.8	84.6	87.0
91.0	95.2	97.4	95.2	92.2	89.0	86.4	86.4	86.4	87.2	88.4	89.6 ∎

running median

A variation on the idea of moving-average smoothing is the method of moving (or running) medians. The **running-median** smoothing method involves calculating the median instead of the mean of the M most recent values of the time series. Because a median is not affected by extreme values, as a mean is, running-median forecasts are unaffected by the occasional fluke value, whether that value is extremely large or extremely small.

EXAMPLE 15.9

Calculate 3-month and 5-month running medians for the data of Example 15.8. How do these forecasts compare with the moving-average forecasts of that example?

Solution

The first 3-month running median is median $(86, 80, 85) = 85$. The first 5-month running median is median $(86, 80, 85, 93, 96) = 86$. The series of running medians is shown here.

3-month running median:

—	—	85	85	93	96	97	97	96	89	87	82	82
87	89	89	95	88	87	81	81	81	81	82	85	93
96	99	99	96	85	83	83	90	90	85	85	89	

5-month running median:

—	—	—	—	86	93	96	96	96	96	89	87
87	87	87	88	89	89	88	87	82	82	82	85
93	96	96	96	96	85	85	85	85	85	89	89 ∎

choice of time periods

How many time periods should be used in a moving average or running median? An extremely large value of M (the number of periods) causes the forecast to change very slowly, and such forecasts are not effective in picking up short-term variations. An extremely small value for M causes the forecasts to be very "jittery." In the extreme case of $M = 1$, the forecast for the next period is simply the current value. This forecast incorporates all the random, irregular features of the time series. If the series moves in fairly smooth waves with modest randomness, a small number of periods (such as 3) is desirable. If the series exhibits a great deal of randomness around a vaguely cyclic pattern, greater averaging (such as 5 or 7 periods) is preferred. Comparison of the past forecasting performance of several possible values of M often clarifies the choice.

statistically stationary
series

Moving averages and running medians are intended for **statistically stationary series**—ones that do not have a trend in means or standard deviations. (This is the same idea as processes in statistical control, from Chapter 2.) When there is a trend, moving averages or running medians will trail behind the trend. Three-month moving averages for the gas price data trail the actual values, as shown in Figure 15.10. The trailing is particularly clear when there is a succession of several months of increasing or decreasing prices.

FIGURE 15.10 **Moving Averages for Gas Price Data**

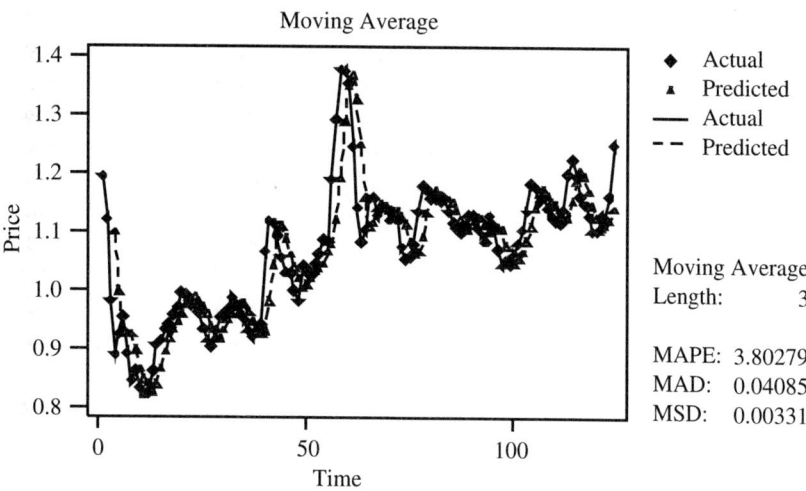

The moving-average and running-median smoothing methods are open to criticism on the grounds that they give the same weight to relatively old values as to the most recent values. The forecasts tend to be somewhat slow in responding to short-run trends or cycles. An alternative method, **exponential smoothing**, gives higher weight to the most recent values and often can be more effective in reacting to shifts or cycles in the series.

exponential smoothing

The exponential smoothing forecast $\hat{y}_{t+1}$ of the actual value y_{t+1} is defined as

$$\hat{y}_{t+1} = \alpha y_t + \alpha(1 - \alpha)y_{t-1} + \alpha(1 - \alpha)^2 y_{t-2} + \cdots$$

smoothing constant

The number α (no relation to α, the probability of Type I error) lies between 0 and 1 and is called the **smoothing constant**; an appropriate choice of α will be discussed shortly. For example, suppose that α is chosen to be .6. Then

$$\hat{y}_{t+1} = .6y_t + .24y_{t-1} + .096y_{t-2} + .0384y_{t-3} + \cdots$$

The most recent value of the time series is given the heaviest weight, and the weights given to previous values drop off rapidly. In fact, the weights α, $\alpha(1 - \alpha)$, $\alpha(1 - \alpha)^2$, $\alpha(1 - \alpha)^3$, ... decrease exponentially to zero. Hence the name *exponential smoothing*.

An alternative way of finding exponentially smoothed forecasts is easier computationally and also helps to indicate the effect of various choices of the smoothing constant α. This method has the form

$$\hat{y}_{t+1} = \alpha y_t + (1 - \alpha)\hat{y}_t$$

The next forecast value is the weighted average of the current actual value and the current forecast value. To use this formula in computation, an initial (time 1) forecast must be chosen; the effect of the initial forecast dies out quite rapidly. One good choice is $\hat{y}_1 = y_1$. Then

$$\hat{y}_2 = \alpha y_1 + (1-\alpha)\hat{y}_1 = y_1$$

$$\hat{y}_3 = \alpha y_2 + (1-\alpha)\hat{y}_2 = \alpha y_2 + (1-\alpha)y_1$$

$$\hat{y}_4 = \alpha y_3 + (1-\alpha)\hat{y}_3 = \alpha y_3 + \alpha(1-\alpha)y_2 + (1-\alpha)^2 y_1$$

$$\hat{y}_5 = \alpha y_4 + (1-\alpha)\hat{y}_4 = \alpha(1-\alpha)y_3 + \alpha(1-\alpha)^2 y_2 + (1-\alpha)^3 y_1$$

and so on.

With this choice of $\hat{y}_1$, the forecasts rapidly approach the infinite series value

$$\hat{y}_{t+1} = \alpha y_t + \alpha(1-\alpha)y_{t-1} + \alpha(1-\alpha)^2 y_{t-2} + \cdots$$

EXAMPLE 15.10

Compute the exponentially smoothed forecast values for the gas price data using $\alpha = .4$ and $\alpha = .8$. Plot the observed time series and the smoothed time series.

Solution

The exponentially smoothed values, calculated by Minitab, are plotted with the original time series in Figure 15.11. ■

choice of α

The **choice of α** is important in exponential smoothing. A large value of α, such as .8, makes the next forecast value very sensitive to the current value. Therefore, the forecast picks up shifts or short-run trends in the series quite quickly, at the cost of being very sensitive to random fluctuations in the series. A small value of α, such as .2, makes the forecast less affected by random fluctuations, but also less effective in picking up shifts or trends. One fairly simple way to select α is to try various α's on historical data; that is, select the α that minimizes average absolute or average squared error in the data.

Moving averages, running medians, and exponential smoothing all use averages (in one sense or another) of past values to forecast future values. If there is a clear upward (or downward) trend in the data, averages of past values will lag behind the trend, producing a clear bias in the forecasts. The method of **double exponential smoothing** is a way to overcome this problem. Double exponential smoothing not only takes a weighted average of the most recent value and the most recent forecast value, it also takes a weighted average of the most recent *change* and the most recent forecast *change*. There are two common versions of double exponential smoothing. Brown's method uses the same weighting constant for values and for changes; Holt's method uses different values and therefore is more general.

double exponential
smoothing

Neither method for double exponential smoothing is intended to deal with seasonal factors.

When there are both trend and seasonal features in the data, the Holt–Winters **triple exponential smoothing** method can be used. As the name suggests, this method uses three weighted averages: the most recent value averaged with the most recent forecast, the most recent change averaged with the most recent forecast change, and the most recent seasonal value averaged with the most recent forecast seasonal value. The equation gets complicated, so we won't present it here. This method is implemented in several standard computer packages.

triple exponential
smoothing

FIGURE 15.11 **Exponentially Smoothed Gas Price Data**

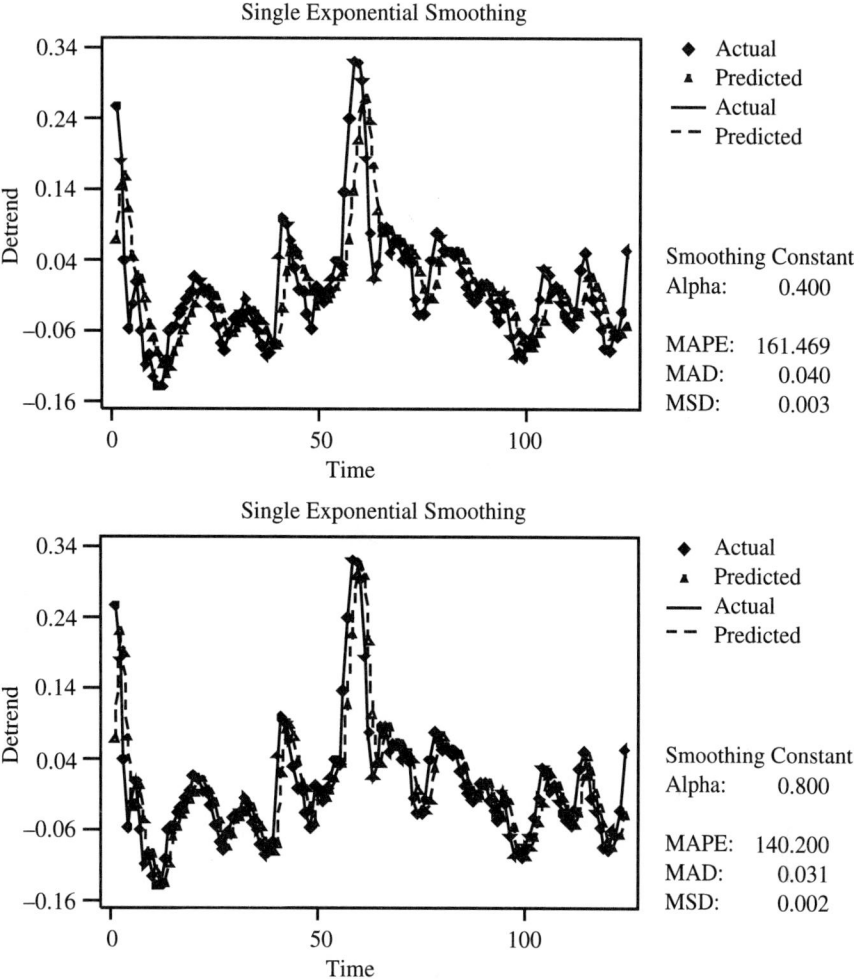

EXAMPLE 15.11

Locate the coefficients of double exponential smoothing in the following Minitab output for the gas price data:

```
MTB > %DES 'Price';
SUBC>   Weight 0.4 0.4;
SUBC>   Smoothed 'SMOO1';
SUBC>   Level 'LEVE1';
SUBC>   Trend 'TREN1'.
Executing from file: MTBWIN\MACROS\DES.MAC

Double Exponential Smoothing

Data     Price
Length   124.000
```

NMissing 0

Smoothing Constants
Alpha (level): 0.4
Gamma (trend): 0.4

Accuracy Measures
MAPE: 4.79856
MAD: 0.05159
MSD: 0.00494

Solution

The values are both shown as 0.4. Note that the program automatically stores the smoothed values. ∎

EXERCISES

15.14 As part of an inventory management method, the monthly demands for various products are recorded and used for future forecasting. The demands for the previous 24 months of one particular product are

Month:	1	2	3	4	5	6	7	8	9	10	11	12
Demand:	89	97	101	168	120	107	100	96	89	97	143	105

Month:	13	14	15	16	17	18	19	20	21	22	23	24
Demand:	96	84	93	110	125	110	93	95	89	93	105	110

  a Calculate 3-month and 5-month moving averages.

  b Plot the original time series, together with the 3-month and 5-month moving averages.

  c Calculate the average squared error for the 3-month moving average used as a forecast of the next month's demand. Do the same for the 5-month moving average.

15.15 Refer to Exercise 15.14.

  a Calculate 3-month and 5-month running medians.

  b Plot the original, 3-month, and 5-month smoothed data.

  c Calculate the average squared error for the 3-month running median used as a forecast of the next month's demand. Do the same for the 5-month moving average.

15.16 **a** Calculate exponentially smoothed forecasts of the demands in Exercise 15.14. Use a smoothing constant of .8.

  b Compute the average squared error for this forecast.

15.17 Compare the average squared error for the forecasts generated in Exercises 15.14–15.16. On the basis of this criterion, which forecast appears to be preferred?

15.18 A large supermarket tries to forecast volume (total number of transactions) to assist in its short-term staffing decisions. Of particular interest are the weekday evening (Monday–Thursday, 5 P.M.–11 P.M.) volumes, which fluctuate because of competitors' actions, weather, and many unknown factors. The average weekday evening volume is collected for 40 weeks. These volumes and 3- and 5-week moving averages are shown here:

Data:

40.2	43.1	44.2	43.6	45.1	47.3	45.9	46.3	45.7	43.9
44.1	43.8	43.1	41.5	42.1	41.6	40.8	42.4	44.5	46.9

Data:

49.4	50.0	51.6	52.3	51.8	53.1	51.9	48.7	49.2	47.1
45.2	41.1	43.8	46.0	41.7	39.4	41.2	43.1	42.5	44.9

3-week moving average:

—	—	42.5	43.6	44.3	45.3	46.1	46.5	46.0	45.3
44.6	43.9	43.7	42.8	42.2	41.7	41.5	41.6	42.6	44.6
46.9	48.8	50.3	51.3	51.9	52.4	52.3	51.2	49.9	48.3
47.2	44.5	43.4	43.6	43.8	42.4	40.8	41.2	42.3	43.5

5-week moving average:

—	—	—	—	43.2	44.7	45.2	45.6	46.1	45.8
45.2	44.8	44.1	43.3	42.9	42.4	41.8	41.7	42.3	43.2
44.8	46.6	48.5	50.0	51.0	51.8	52.1	51.6	50.9	50.0
48.4	46.3	45.3	44.6	43.6	42.4	42.4	42.3	41.6	42.2

a Plot the actual data and the moving averages on the same graph.

b Which moving average appears to track the actual values better?

15.19 The data of Exercise 15.18 lead to the following 3- and 5-week running medians:

3-week running median:

—	—	43.1	43.6	44.2	45.1	45.9	46.3	45.9	45.7
44.1	43.9	43.8	43.1	42.1	41.6	41.6	41.6	42.4	44.5
46.9	49.4	50.0	51.6	51.8	52.3	51.9	51.9	49.2	48.7
47.1	45.2	43.8	43.8	43.8	41.7	41.2	41.2	42.5	43.1

5-week running median:

—	—	—	—	43.6	44.2	45.1	45.9	45.9	45.9
45.7	44.1	43.9	43.8	43.1	42.1	41.6	41.6	41.6	42.1
42.4	44.5	46.9	49.4	50.0	51.6	51.8	51.9	51.9	51.8
44.2	48.7	47.1	45.2	45.2	43.8	41.7	41.7	41.7	42.5

a Plot the actual data and running medians on the same graph.

b Which running median seems to give better forecasts?

15.20 The average squared error and average absolute error for the forecasts of Exercises 15.18 and 15.19 are as follows:

	Mean Squared Error	Mean Absolute Error
3-Week Moving Average	.626	.604
5-Week Moving Average	2.183	1.166
3-Week Running Median	.608	.438
5-Week Running Median	2.420	1.154

Does the same forecast method appear to be best on each criterion?

15.21 An evening newspaper records the number of pages of display (unclassified) advertisements over a 70-month period. Monthly averages are computed. The data, plus exponentially smoothed forecasts, are shown here:

Sales:

69.2	67.2	68.0	70.5	73.4	65.2	68.7	72.5	74.1	76.9
70.0	73.2	78.0	75.6	74.9	72.2	70.9	74.3	69.1	63.5
66.7	68.0	64.7	68.9	69.0	69.7	71.3	74.5	70.8	75.6
74.8	73.5	72.8	69.9	71.5	70.4	68.5	67.1	63.5	66.8
67.9	69.0	68.3	71.1	73.2	72.9	74.6	76.1	75.3	77.9
78.3	75.4	72.9	73.6	71.5	69.9	67.3	69.3	67.2	67.4
63.8	64.7	65.8	68.0	67.2	68.7	70.2	72.5	73.6	71.7

Exponential smoothing, $\alpha = .2$:

—	69.20	68.88	68.70	69.06	69.93	68.98	68.93	69.64	70.53
71.81	71.45	71.80	73.04	73.55	73.82	73.50	72.98	73.24	72.41
70.63	69.84	69.48	68.52	68.60	68.68	68.88	69.37	70.39	70.47
71.50	72.16	72.43	72.50	71.98	71.89	71.59	70.97	70.20	68.86
68.45	68.34	68.47	68.44	68.97	69.81	70.43	71.27	72.23	72.85
73.86	74.75	74.88	74.48	74.30	73.74	72.98	71.84	71.33	70.51
69.88	68.67	67.87	67.46	67.57	67.49	67.74	68.23	69.08	69.99

Exponential smoothing, $\alpha = .8$:

—	69.20	67.92	67.98	70.00	72.72	66.70	68.30	71.66	73.61
76.24	71.25	72.81	76.96	75.87	75.09	72.78	71.28	73.70	70.02
64.80	66.32	67.66	65.29	68.18	68.84	69.53	70.95	73.79	71.40
74.76	74.79	73.76	72.99	70.52	71.30	70.58	68.92	67.46	64.29
66.30	67.58	68.72	68.38	70.56	72.67	72.85	74.25	75.73	75.39
77.40	78.12	75.94	73.51	73.58	71.92	70.30	67.90	69.02	67.56
67.43	64.53	64.67	65.57	67.51	67.26	68.41	69.84	71.97	73.27

a Plot the actual data. Is there a pronounced trend?

b Plot the exponentially smoothed forecasts for $\alpha = .2$ and $\alpha = .8$.

c Which forecast method seems to overrespond to random variation?

15.22 The mean squared error and mean absolute error for the most recent two years of data in Exercise 15.21 are calculated for each exponentially smoothed forecast:

	Mean Squared Error	Mean Absolute Error
$\alpha = .2$	11.735	2.852
$\alpha = .8$	7.224	2.221

Which α value seems better? ■

The ARIMA Approach

B oth the classic analysis (which takes into account the trend, seasonal, and cyclic components of time-series data) and the smoothing methods of the previous section have the problem that they don't reflect any theoretical structure. Instead, they are rough-and-ready methods for cleaning up time-series data without much regard to the process that generated the data in the first place. In this section, we sketch some of the basic ideas behind what is known as the ARIMA (AutoRegressive Integrated Moving Average) approach to the analysis of time-series data.

autoregressive model

The simplest ARIMA model is the **autoregressive model**. The idea of an autoregressive model is to use the past values of a time series as independent variables in predicting future values. The simplest autoregressive model is a first-order model, designated AR(1):

$$Y_t = \phi_0 + \phi_1 Y_{t-1} + \epsilon_t$$

The *order* of an ARIMA model refers to the maximum time lag used, not to the maximum power of a variable, as in regression analysis. In this model, we assume that only the most recent y value is a useful predictor. The ϵ_t term, which reflects only pure random error, is assumed to have mean zero, constant variance, no autocorrelation, and a normal distribution, just as in regression. The ϵ_t process is sometimes called **white noise**.

white noise

As stated, the autoregressive model does not contain a trend. ARIMA models were originally designed for **stationary time series**—ones with no trend, constant variability, and stable correlations over time. In particular, the series should be detrended. If the time series shows only a linear trend, taking (first) differences $y_t - y_{t-1}$ often yields an approximately stationary series. For an exponential trend, differences in logarithms of y values will serve.

EXAMPLE 15.12

The gasoline price data introduced in Section 15.2 had a moderate upward trend. Minitab was used to calculate month-to-month price differences; these differences, plotted in time order, are shown in Figure 15.12. Does the series of differences appear stationary?

FIGURE 15.12   **Changes in Gasoline Prices**

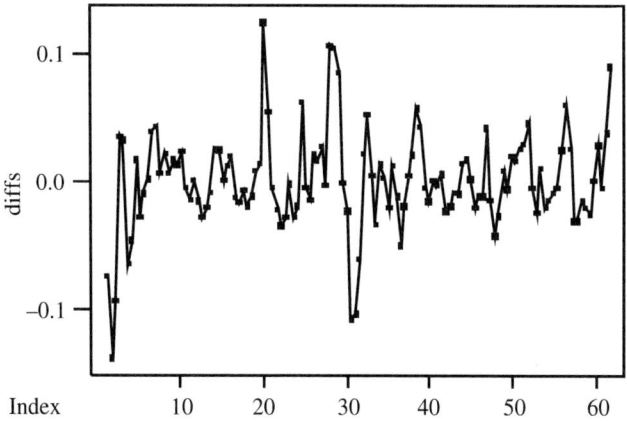

Solution

There is no apparent long-term trend in the data, though there are short periods of increases or of decreases. There is no indication of increasing variability. The data appear reasonably stationary.   ■

Autoregressive models often yield data with a distinct cyclic pattern, despite the lack of any cyclic function (such as a sine curve) in the model. Earlier in this chapter we noted that trying to determine the period of a particular type of cycle might not be fruitful, and that an alternative strategy is to seek models that tend to produce roughly cyclic behavior. ARIMA models provide one very rich class of possible models. An important part of the ARIMA method is the **correlogram**. This is a plot (against time) of the **autocorrelation coefficients** of a time series y_t. Autocorrelation coefficients are almost, but not quite, the same as ordinary correlations of the time series with the same series lagged by a number (j) of periods. For example, we might take the following series and lag it one period, as indicated:

Time, t:	1	2	3	4	5	6	7	8	9
Series, y_t:	86	81	82	85	90	93	89	86	—
Lagged series, y_{t-1}:	—	86	81	82	85	90	93	89	86

Omitting times 1 and 9 (because one series or the other does not have a value there), we can compute the correlation of y_t and y_{t-j} using the sample correlation definition of Chapter 12. The autocorrelation coefficient r_j of y_t and a variable y_{t-j} is only slightly different than the sample correlation between y_t and y_{t-j}. The lag j autocorrelation is

$$r_j = \frac{\sum_{t=j+1}^{T} (y_t - \bar{y})(y_{t-j} - \bar{y})}{\sum_{t=1}^{T} (y_t - \bar{y})^2}$$

where T is the number of periods of data available and

$$\bar{y} = \frac{\sum_{t=1}^{T} y_t}{T}$$

You should be able to verify that $\bar{y} = 86.5$ for the data shown in this paragraph and that the lag 1 autocorrelation is

$$r_1 = \frac{(81 - 86.5)(86 - 86.5) + \cdots + (86 - 86.5)(89 - 86.5)}{(86 - 86.5)^2 + \cdots + (86 - 86.5)^2} = .5855$$

(The ordinary correlation is .5867.) Although shortcut formulas can be used, the calculation of autocorrelations is almost always done by computer.

The correlogram is simply a scatterplot of lags versus autocorrelations r_j.

E X A M P L E   1 5 . 1 3

The autocorrelations [up to a maximum lag of 10 for the (difference)] data of Example 15.12 are shown in Figure 15.13. Identify the lag 1 and lag 2 autocorrelations.

Solution

The correlogram shows that the lag 1 autocorrelation is near 0.5 and the lag 2 value is near 0. More exact values are shown at the bottom of the output (along with other information that we don't as yet need). ∎

The sample correlogram in Figure 15.12 should be compared to a theoretical correlogram. For any particular ARIMA model, theoretical autocorrelation coefficients ρ_j can be derived [derivations are given in Nelson (1977) and Box and Jenkins (1970)]. For the first-order autoregressive model $Y_t = \phi_0 + \phi_1 Y_{t-1} + \epsilon_t$, it can be proved that these theoretical autocorrelation coefficients are given by the geometric series

$$\rho_j = \phi_1^j \qquad j = 1, 2, \ldots$$

Other ARIMA models yield different theoretical autocorrelations.

E X A M P L E   1 5 . 1 4

Calculate the theoretical autocorrelations, for lags up to 10, for an AR(1) model with $\phi_1 = .80$. Do these autocorrelations resemble those we found in Example 15.13?

FIGURE 15.13 **Sample Autocorrelation of Gasoline Price Changes**

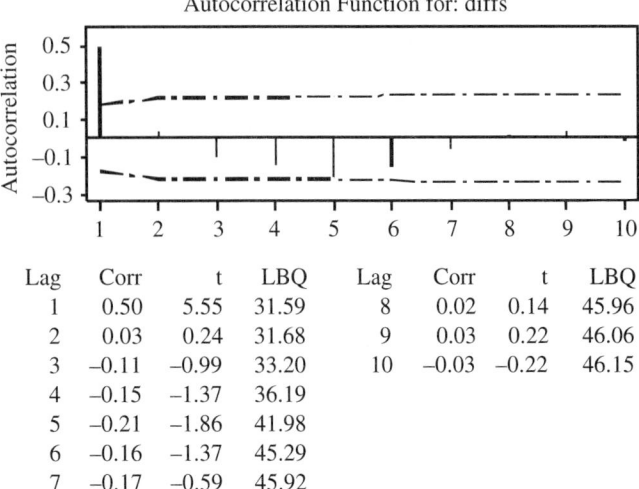

Lag	Corr	t	LBQ	Lag	Corr	t	LBQ
1	0.50	5.55	31.59	8	0.02	0.14	45.96
2	0.03	0.24	31.68	9	0.03	0.22	46.06
3	-0.11	-0.99	33.20	10	-0.03	-0.22	46.15
4	-0.15	-1.37	36.19				
5	-0.21	-1.86	41.98				
6	-0.16	-1.37	45.29				
7	-0.17	-0.59	45.92				

Solution

The theoretical autocorrelations are just successive powers of .80:

lag j:	1	2	3	4	5	6	7	8	9	10
ρ_j:	.8000	.6400	.5120	.4096	.3277	.2621	.2097	.1678	.1342	.1074

These values of ρ_j are plotted in Figure 15.14. Note how the theoretical autocorrelations for an AR(1) model with $\phi_1 > 0$ gradually decay toward zero. Although we never know the actual value of ϕ_1 (or, equivalently, the ρ_j's), the sample autocorrelations for an AR(1) model should possess a pattern similar to that for the ρ_j's.

FIGURE 15.14 **Theoretical Autocorrelations for an AR(1) Model, $\phi_1 = .80$**

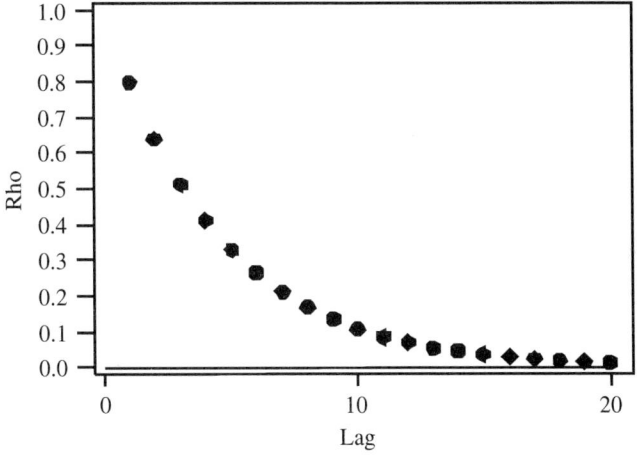

The theoretical autocorrelations for an AR(1) model with $\phi_1 < 0$ also decay toward zero, but the sign of ρ_j alternates from positive to negative (see Figure 15.15).

FIGURE 15.15 **Theoretical Autocorrelations for an AR(1) Model, $\phi_1 = -.80$**

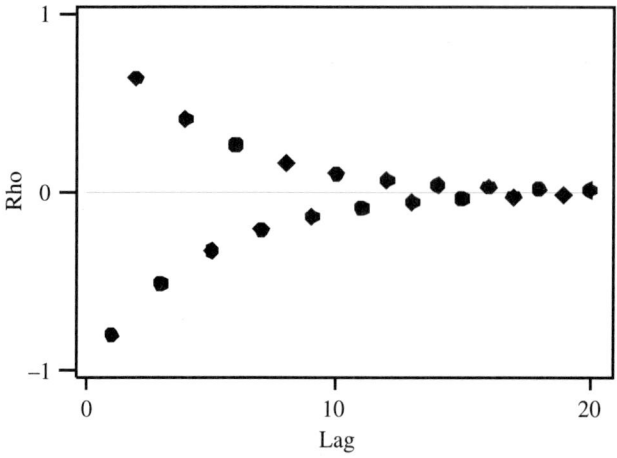

There are many other ARIMA models. The autoregressive idea can be extended to higher-order (longer lags) models. The pth-order autoregressive model AR(p) is

higher-order autoregressive models

$$Y_t = \phi_0 + \phi_1 Y_{t-1} + \cdots + \phi_p Y_{t-p} + \epsilon_t$$

where the errors ϵ_t are assumed to satisfy the white noise assumptions.

moving-average model

There is also a different type of model, called a **moving-average model**.[1] The first-order moving-average model MA(1) is

$$Y_t = \theta_0 + \epsilon_t - \theta_1 \epsilon_{t-1}$$

where the ϵ's are assumed to be white noise.[2]

We can see the difference between autoregressive and moving-average models when we consider the effect of past ϵ values on current y values. Think of the ϵ values as random shocks input to an economic system, and y values as the output of the system. By appropriate substitutions (for Y_{t-1}, then Y_{t-2}, and so on) in a first-order autoregressive model, the weight given the lag j shock is seen to be ϕ_1^j. Assuming that $|\phi_j| < 1$, it follows that the weights of long-ago shocks decline steadily. In contrast, the first-order moving-average model gives a weight of $-\theta_1$ to ϵ_{t-1} and no weight at all to shocks with longer lags. In a pure moving-average model, the effect of a shock persists for a specified number of time periods, and then disappears suddenly. In a pure autoregressive mode, the effect of a shock declines gradually.

A moving-average model may be appropriate for a machine shop, where ϵ_t represents a sudden burst of new orders and Y_t represents production. If all orders are filled in either the current month or the next month, the effect of 2-month-old orders on production is zero. An autoregressive model may be appropriate for a model of sales of a certain kind of four-wheel-drive car. A positive ϵ shock may represent an upsurge in interest in such cars. We may reasonably assume such a shock to signal a longer-term increase in sales,

[1] The phrase *moving average* is used in a different sense in ARIMA models than in smoothing models.

[2] The minus sign on θ_1 is conventional, allowing for a convenient "backshift" notation. See Box and Jenkins (1970).

but the effect should gradually decline because of such factors as new competitors and new technology.

The theoretical correlogram of a moving-average model reflects the difference between moving-average and autoregressive models. The general qth-order moving-average model, MA(q), is

$$Y_t = \theta_0 + \epsilon_t - \theta_1 \epsilon_{t-1} - \cdots - \theta_{t-q} \epsilon_q$$

We assume the effect of a shock ϵ to persist up to lag q, then suddenly drop to zero. The theoretical autocorrelation reflects the drop-to-zero pattern. For the first-order moving-average model, $y_t = \theta_0 + \epsilon_t - \theta_1 \epsilon_{t-1}$, the theoretical autocorrelations are

$$\rho_j = \begin{cases} 1 & \text{for } j = 0 \\ \dfrac{-\theta_1}{1 + \theta_1^2} & \text{for } j = 1 \\ 0, & \text{for } j \geq 2 \end{cases}$$

Thus, the correlogram for a MA(1) model has a single spike; all autocorrelations beyond $j = 1$ are zero, as shown in Figure 15.16. Note the difference between the correlograms for AR(1) and MA(1) models. The theoretical correlogram for a pure moving-average process MA(q) tapers off gradually for $j < q$, then suddenly drops to zero for $j > q$. The sample correlogram of a pure moving-average process behaves similarly, but with a degree of random error. For any sample autocorrelations, $1/\sqrt{T}$ provides a rough approximation for the standard error of the sample autocorrelation (assuming the true autocorrelation is zero), where T is the number of observations. A sample correlogram that suddenly drops to within $\pm 1/\sqrt{T}$ of zero is a good candidate for a pure moving-average model.

FIGURE 15.16 **Correlogram for an MA(1) Model with $\theta_1 = -.80$**

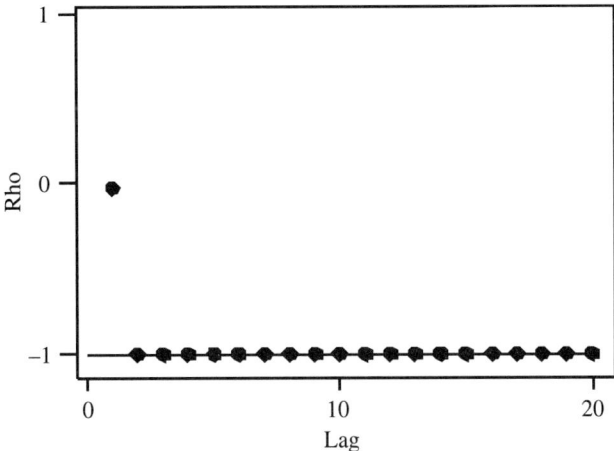

EXAMPLE 15.15

The sample correlogram for the differences of gasoline prices was shown in Figure 15.13. Does that correlogram indicate that an autoregressive model or a moving-average model is the better choice?

Solution

Notice that the first autocorrelation coefficient is clearly positive, but the second one is very near 0. All the remaining coefficients are within the dashed lines, indicating 2 standard errors around 0. Thus, there is little evidence of any nonzero autocorrelation beyond lag 1. This is an example of the "spike and drop to 0" pattern of a moving-average process. ∎

general model

Autoregressive and moving-average models may be combined. The general autoregressive–moving-average model ARIMA (p, q) is written

$$Y_t = \phi_0 + \phi_1 Y_{t-1} + \phi_2 Y_{t-2} + \cdots + \phi_p Y_{t-p} + \epsilon_t - \theta_1 \epsilon_{t-1}$$
$$- \theta_2 \epsilon_{t-2} - \cdots - \theta_q \epsilon_{t-q}$$

If the lags p and q are large, very complex models can result. The usual strategy is to try to find a simple model (with very small p and q lags) that fits the data adequately and approximates the autocorrelations of the series. There are several strategies for identifying such models. One is based on an examination of the estimated correlogram. As we have seen, the theoretical correlogram for a pure autoregressive process tapers gradually to zero as the lag increases, whereas the theoretical correlogram of a pure moving-average process drops suddenly to zero. A combination autoregressive and moving-average process exhibits a combination of these phenomena in its correlogram: The correlogram tapers off, then drops sharply, then tapers off again. The lag just before the drop-off is a good candidate for the maximum lag q of the moving-average part. The maximum lag for the autoregressive component is harder to identify in the correlogram. Other ARIMA methods, such as partial autocorrelation, are needed for precise identification of reasonable ARIMA models. Box and Jenkins (1970) and Nelson (1977) contain good tips on the difficult task of model identification.

Once the maximum lags for an ARIMA model have been specified, the next task is to estimate the ϕ or θ model parameters. The basic idea is to search for the **least-squares fit**. The process of finding the least-squares estimates is complex, especially if there is a moving-average component in the model. Any of the standard ARIMA computer programs estimates the model parameters.

least-squares fit

EXAMPLE 15.16

A time series contains the following data for a 40-month period:

134.59	97.60	74.03	55.75	84.24	126.61	141.67	128.72	146.22	157.66
158.57	157.85	154.02	113.37	109.29	160.06	177.27	161.21	123.35	124.43
170.74	175.41	201.49	227.60	233.43	239.80	184.09	133.22	119.65	123.52
139.92	175.82	166.81	163.33	122.41	111.96	151.67	160.21	180.46	188.86

The following autocorrelations are obtained:

Lag:	1	2	3	4	5	6	7	8	9	10
Correlation:	.767	.382	.093	−.040	−.014	.022	.035	.035	−.019	−.050

Plot the correlogram. What ARIMA models are indicated?

Solution

See Figure 15.17. Only the first two (possibly three) autocorrelations differ from zero by any substantial amount. Given the steep drop to zero, you might try a moving average

FIGURE 15.17 **Correlogram**

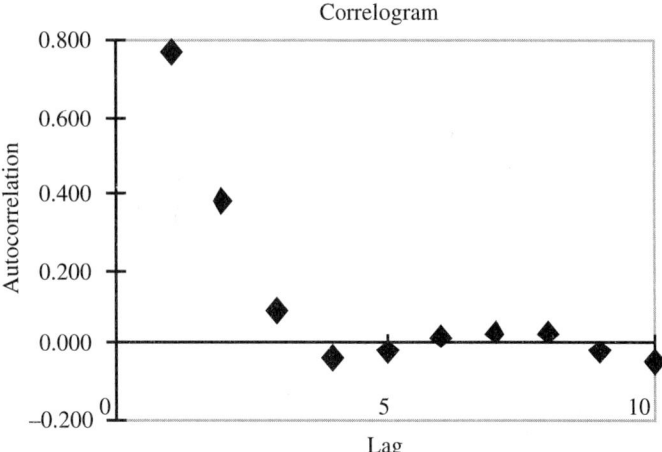

of two or three terms. Perhaps you can try a first-order (or at most a second-order) autoregressive term, given that there is some suggestion of a decay toward zero in the correlogram. ∎

EXAMPLE 15.17

ARIMA models with $q = 1$ were estimated for $p = 1$ and 2 for the data of Example 15.16. The respective average squared errors were 432.95 and 424.65. Does the more complex model with $p = 2$ do much better?

Solution

The average squared error for the more complicated model is only very slightly (about 2%) smaller, which hardly seems to be very useful. ∎

ARIMA seasonal models

In our discussion of ARIMA models, we have indicated how trends can be removed by differencing (of logs, if necessary) and how such models can capture apparent cyclic effects. We haven't said anything about seasonal effects; ARIMA models can be extended to capture seasonal effects, too. In fact, one of the most popular deseasonalizing methods used by U.S. government agencies, the X-11 procedure of the Census Bureau, is closely related to ARIMA methods (see Pierce, 1980). We do not go into detail here except to note that the basic idea is to include autoregressive and moving-average terms with lag 4 for quarterly data, lag 12 for monthly data, and so on. The Nelson (1977) and Box and Jenkins (1970) texts contain full discussions.

ARIMA forecasting

Once a model has been adopted and the coefficients estimated, an ARIMA model can be used for forecasting. For the first-order autoregressive model, the one-period-ahead forecast is $\hat{y}_{t+1} = \hat{\phi}_0 + \hat{\phi}_1 y_t$; the two-period-ahead forecast is

$$\hat{y}_{t+2} = \hat{\phi}_0 + \hat{\phi}_1 y_{t+1}$$

but y_{t+1} is not yet known and must be replaced by $\hat{y}_{t+1}$ (at the cost of additional random error). This process can be continued for forecasts of any period ahead; the obvious extension works for any higher-order autoregressive model. Moving-average models are trickier to use for forecasting. In the first-order moving-average model,

$$y_{t+1} = \hat{\theta}_0 - \hat{\theta}_1 \epsilon_t$$

but ϵ_t is the unknown true error at time t and must itself be estimated. Estimation of error terms in moving-average (or general ARIMA) models is done by a rather elaborate computerized method involving (among other things) backward forecasting. Any good ARIMA program can handle the technical problems. One good approach to checking ARIMA models uses the concept of validation, discussed in Chapter 14: Fit the model based on, say, the first 80% of the data, and then generate forecasts of the remaining data. Although more sophisticated model-selection methods are available, this approach should detect any gross deviations from a model.

EXAMPLE 15.18

An ARIMA model with $p = 1$ and $q = 1$ is fit to the first 32 periods of the data of Example 15.16, as is an ARIMA model with $p = 1$ and $q = 2$. Forecasts are generated for periods 33–40, with the following results:

Actual	ARIMA(1,1)	Error	ARIMA(1,2)	Error
166.81	188.55	−21.74	191.71	−24.90
163.33	175.40	−12.07	180.67	−17.34
122.41	166.94	−44.53	165.43	−43.02
111.96	161.51	−49.55	154.83	−42.87
151.67	158.02	−6.35	149.84	1.83
160.21	155.78	4.43	148.59	11.62
180.46	154.33	26.13	149.00	31.46
188.86	153.41	35.45	149.79	39.07
Mean		−8.53		−5.52
Standard deviation		30.41		31.67

Is there compelling evidence in favor of the more complicated ARIMA(1, 2) model?

Solution

Neither model seems to grossly over- or underestimate the data in the validation sample. Both commit some rather large errors. Although the average error for the ARIMA(1, 2) model is slightly better than that for the ARIMA(1, 1) model, the standard deviation is higher. We don't feel compelled to use the more complicated model. ∎

The ARIMA approach to time-series data is attractive in many ways. The general ARIMA structure is rich and allows for a wide variety of autocorrelation patterns. Many kinds of cyclic and seasonal patterns can be captured by ARIMA models. Yet it is important for a manager to realize that these models aren't magic. A typical ARIMA model used in forecasting a time series is based entirely on the past history of the series itself, and it doesn't allow for any predictive value of other variables. The virtue of such an approach is that it requires only readily available data—only the past history of the series. The weakness of the approach is that it doesn't take advantage of the predictive value of other, related series.

The ARIMA approach is a useful technique, and it can be applied within a regression context. It is not a cure-all, however.

15.23 Examination of the sales records of a firm for 60 months yields the following data on monthly sales of a standard product:

90.8	94.8	100.1	104.8	112.2	121.9	124.6	137.5	156.0	165.3	173.7	182.4
178.7	174.0	175.4	173.3	175.7	176.0	179.7	178.2	186.4	195.7	204.9	214.3
222.5	227.3	222.6	219.8	220.5	220.4	228.3	227.2	228.3	235.7	241.2	248.8
257.3	267.4	276.9	288.8	299.6	315.8	322.8	332.2	347.0	357.7	363.2	366.7
371.9	373.7	371.8	371.4	359.7	355.4	348.4	342.6	337.7	329.8	327.7	324.5

a Plot the data against time. Is there an evident trend?

b The month-to-month changes in sales are

3.9	5.3	4.7	7.4	9.7	2.7	12.9	18.5	9.3	8.4	8.7	−3.7
−4.7	1.4	−2.1	2.4	.3	3.7	−1.5	8.2	9.2	9.1	9.4	8.2
4.8	−4.7	−2.8	.7	.1	7.9	−1.1	1.1	7.4	5.5	7.6	8.5
1.10	9.5	11.9	10.8	16.2	7.0	9.4	14.8	10.7	5.5	3.5	5.2
1.8	−1.9	−.4	−11.7	−4.3	−7.0	−5.8	−4.9	−7.9	−2.1	−3.2	

Plot change against time. Is there an evident linear trend in the changes? Does there appear to be some cyclic behavior?

15.24 Autocorrelations are calculated for the change data of Exercise 15.23. The results are

Lag:	1	2	3	4	5	6
Correlation:	.693	.581	.490	.285	.154	.049

Lag:	7	8	9	10	11	12
Correlation:	−.042	−.208	−.232	−.250	−.284	−.231

a Verify the calculation of the lag 1 correlation.

b Plot the correlations against lag numbers. Is there any lag at which the lag correlations drop off suddenly?

15.25 A first-order autoregressive model is fit to the change data of Exercise 15.23. The estimated autoregressive model is

$$\hat{y}_t = 1.093 + .709 y_{t-1}$$

The predicted values are

3.8	3.9	4.9	4.4	6.3	7.9	3.1	10.2	14.2	7.7	7.0	7.3
−1.6	−2.2	2.1	−.4	2.8	1.3	3.7	.0	6.9	7.7	7.6	7.8
6.9	4.5	−2.2	−.9	1.6	1.1	6.6	.3	1.9	6.3	5.0	6.5
7.1	8.2	7.9	9.5	8.8	12.6	6.0	7.7	11.6	8.7	5.0	3.6
4.8	2.4	−.3	.8	−7.2	−1.9	−3.9	−3.0	−2.4	−4.5	−.4	

with a mean squared error of 21.67. Plot predicted and actual change values over time. Does it appear that the model yields useful forecasts of changes in sales?

15.26 The estimated lag correlations for the model of Exercise 15.25 are

Lag:	1	2	3	4	5	6
Correlation:	.690	.556	.472	.260	.121	.023

Lag:	7	8	9	10	11	12
Correlation:	−.094	−.229	−.258	−.265	−.289	−.240

How do the estimated lag correlations based on the model compare to the computed lag correlations of Exercise 15.24?

15.27 A manufacturer of novelty items produces (among other items) pennants for sports teams. Weekly production figures include both long-term runs, which are items that sell fairly steadily with slow fluctuation, and short-term runs, which are items that sell in sudden 1- or 2-week bursts. Data are collected on weekly production for the preceding 156 weeks. There is virtually no trend in the data. Lag correlations are as follows:

Lag:	1	2	3	4	5	6	7	8	9	10
Correlation:	.748	.541	.314	.133	.004	.021	.108	.165	.195	.181

a Plot these correlations against lag number. Is there any lag at which correlations drop off suddenly?

b What autoregressive and moving-average terms would you suggest for inclusion in a ARIMA model for these data?

15.28 The data of Exercise 15.27 are fitted to three possible ARIMA models: ARIMA(1, 1), ARIMA(1, 2), and ARIMA(2, 1) (see Figure 15.18). Do the more complicated models—ARIMA(1, 2) and ARIMA(2, 1)—yield obviously better correlograms than the ARIMA(1, 1) model?

FIGURE 15.18 **ARIMA Models for Sports Items Sales**

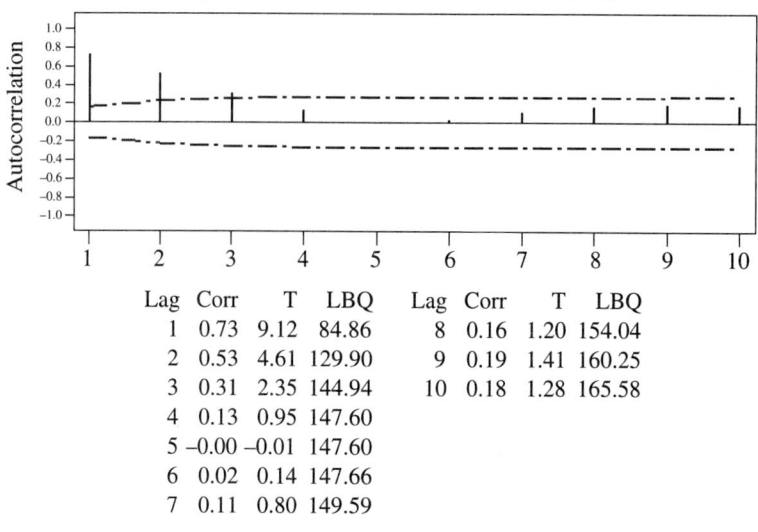

Autocorrelation Function for ARIMA 1,1

Lag	Corr	T	LBQ	Lag	Corr	T	LBQ
1	0.73	9.12	84.86	8	0.16	1.20	154.04
2	0.53	4.61	129.90	9	0.19	1.41	160.25
3	0.31	2.35	144.94	10	0.18	1.28	165.58
4	0.13	0.95	147.60				
5	-0.00	-0.01	147.60				
6	0.02	0.14	147.66				
7	0.11	0.80	149.59				

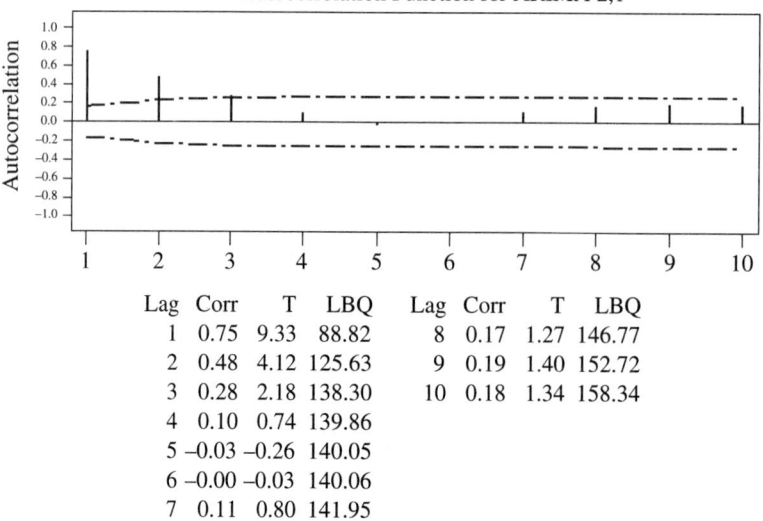

Autocorrelation Function for ARIMA 2,1

Lag	Corr	T	LBQ	Lag	Corr	T	LBQ
1	0.75	9.33	88.82	8	0.17	1.27	146.77
2	0.48	4.12	125.63	9	0.19	1.40	152.72
3	0.28	2.18	138.30	10	0.18	1.34	158.34
4	0.10	0.74	139.86				
5	-0.03	-0.26	140.05				
6	-0.00	-0.03	140.06				
7	0.11	0.80	141.95				

FIGURE 15.18 **(continued) ARIMA Models for Sports Items Sales**

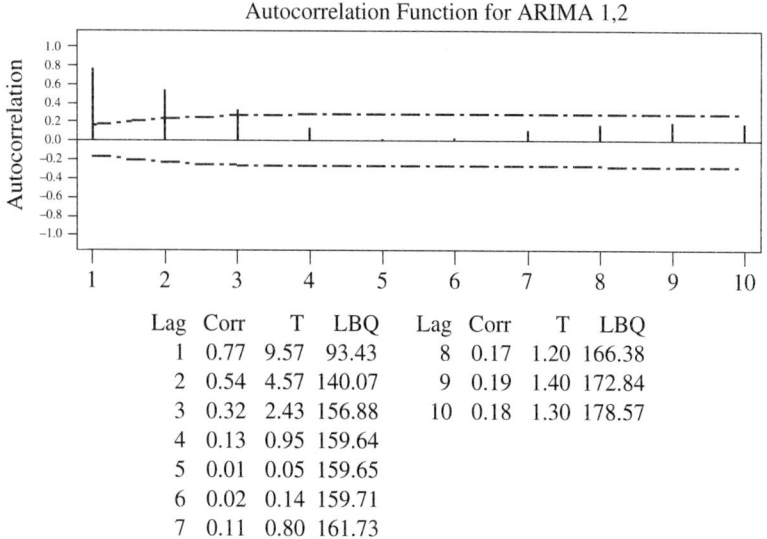

Autocorrelation Function for ARIMA 1,2

Lag	Corr	T	LBQ	Lag	Corr	T	LBQ
1	0.77	9.57	93.43	8	0.17	1.20	166.38
2	0.54	4.57	140.07	9	0.19	1.40	172.84
3	0.32	2.43	156.88	10	0.18	1.30	178.57
4	0.13	0.95	159.64				
5	0.01	0.05	159.65				
6	0.02	0.14	159.71				
7	0.11	0.80	161.73				

15.29 The sum of squared errors for the three models of Exercise 15.28 are as follows:

Model:	ARIMA(1,1)	ARIMA(1,2)	ARIMA(2,1)
SSE:	20231729	19808219	20213048

Is there any evidence to indicate that the more complicated models fit much better?   ■

15.5

Summing Up

H ere are some ideas to remember in analyzing time-series data.

1 Index numbers are used to make data comparable over time. Most indices use fixed weights, which may cause them to be somewhat misleading. The problem arises when some prices (in a price index) change in a sharply different way from other prices.

2 The basic idea of time-series methods is to use the past behavior of a series to predict its future behavior. These methods do not use other variables as predictors, as does regression. Therefore, these methods have minimal data needs but may not give highly accurate predictions.

3 Trend and seasonal components of a series can be based on either additive or multiplicative models. Use a multiplicative model to deal with percentage changes and an additive model for numerical changes.

4 Obtain a plot of the data to get an indication of whether a linear, exponential, or S-shaped trend is most reasonable. The plot will also indicate whether there is a seasonal pattern and any outliers.

5 Seasonal indices should be based on detrended data. A seasonal index should be added to the trend (for an additive model) or multiplied by the trend (for a multiplicative model).

6   Smoothing a series, whether by moving averages, running medians, or some type of exponential smoothing, is a simple way to obtain forecasts. These methods usually work best on detrended and deseasonalized time series unless they specifically incorporate means for dealing with trends or seasonality.

7   ARIMA models offer a way to build some theoretical structure into a time-series analysis. A correlogram (plot of autocorrelation coefficients) is a good way to get an idea of what ARIMA models should be tried. The amount of forecast error made by the model is a way to select among models.

In addition, you may want to reread the summary of key ideas at the beginning of the chapter.

EXAMPLE 15.19

Hydroelectric energy is electricity generated by falling water, usually a dammed-up river. Energy output depends both on available water flow and on electric demand. Because the variable cost of generating electricity this way is very low, it is normally used as much as water flow will allow. Monthly energy output at the RJ&R hydroelectric substation is available for a period of five consecutive years.

Output from the "decomposition" macro of Minitab is shown in Figure 15.19. This macro calculated a multiplicative model for trend and seasonal factors, and stored the residuals (actual − model). The autocorrelation function for the residuals is also shown in Figure 15.19.

What does the output indicate about the long-term trend and the degree of seasonal fluctuation? Does the autocorrelation function indicate there is a pattern in the residuals that an ARIMA model might capture?

A model for the residuals with one autoregressive term had a mean squared error (MSE) of 371,000, a model with one moving-average term had a MSE of 389,000, and a model with autoregressive, moving-average, and seasonal terms had a MSE of 377,000. Which model is preferred?

FIGURE 15.19   Decomposition Results for Hydroelectric Data

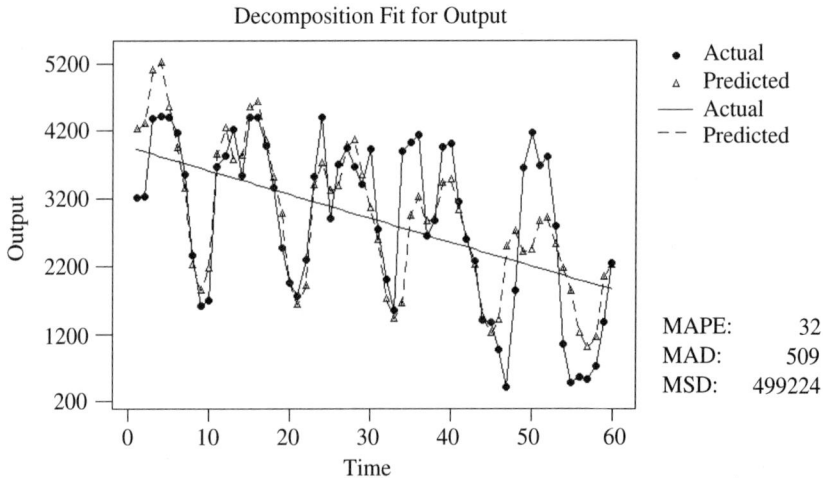

FIGURE 15.19 **(continued) Decomposition Results for Hydroelectric Data**

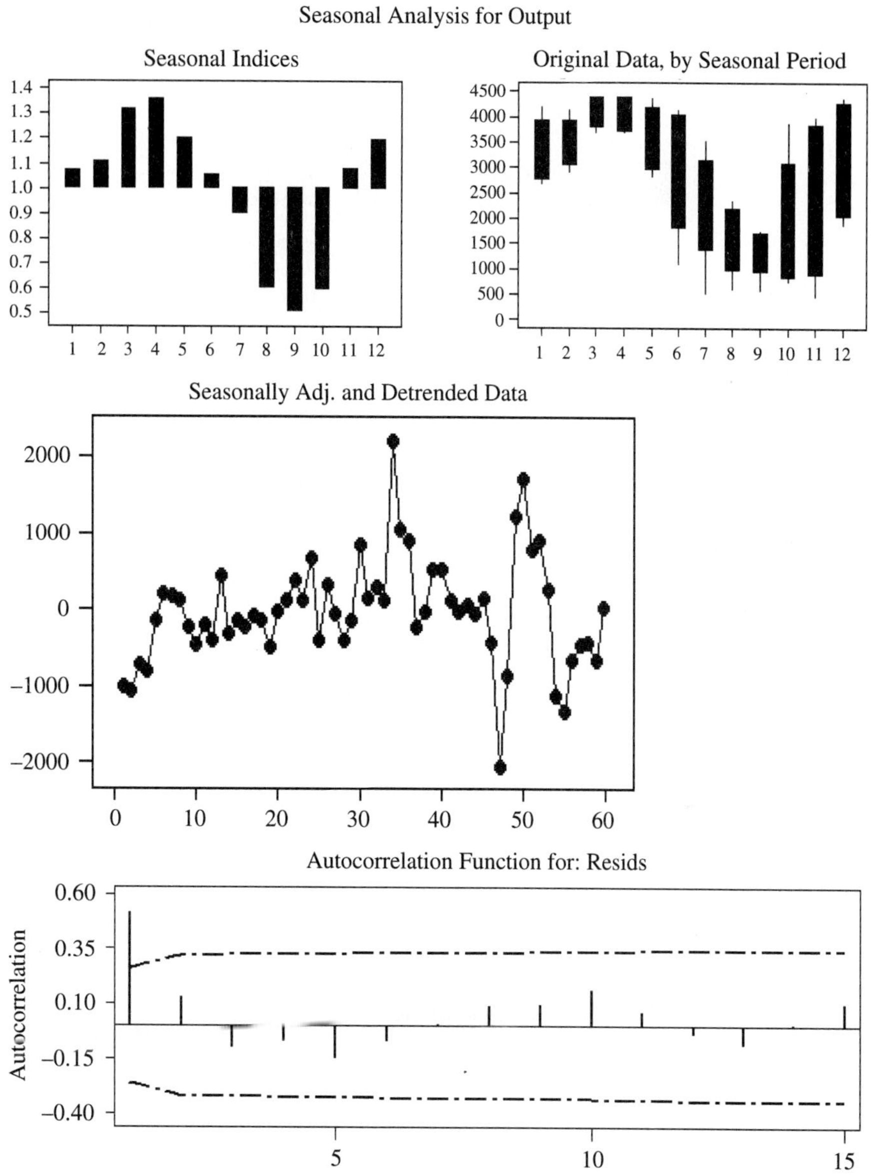

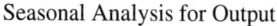

Solution

There is an evident downward trend; the output shows the trend equation, but even a casual look at the points shows that output is decreasing. There are clear seasonal variations. Output is higher in the low-numbered months (spring, when water flow is typically highest). The graph of seasonal factors shows that some are nearly 1.5 (months with output 50% above trend) and other seasonal factors are almost as low as 0.5 (months 50% below trend).

The autocorrelation function (correlogram) shows a moderately large lag 1 autocorrelation of about 0.5. The remaining autocorrelations are small. Thus, there is some pattern remaining in the residuals, but not a great deal. It isn't evident from the correlogram whether a moving-average model or an autoregressive model is better.

The calculated mean squared error values rule out the more complicated model with autoregressive, moving-average, and seasonal terms; this model is more complex than the autoregressive model and has a higher error. The autoregressive model has a slightly lower MSE than the moving-average model and therefore is slightly preferable. ∎

EXERCISES

15.30 A manufacturer of snack foods compiles dollar-volume sales monthly for four years. Because prices have changed substantially, the firm uses a price index to deflate the dollar figures. The results are shown here (sales in thousands of dollars per month):

Year 1	J	F	M	A	M	J	J	A	S	O	N	D
Sales	421.9	447.0	439.3	479.3	478.5	481.2	506.8	477.5	480.5	502.5	527.9	521.8
Deflated Sales	413.7	440.4	429.1	465.4	454.9	466.3	486.9	457.9	455.1	477.3	4898.1	487.7
Index	102.0	101.5	102.4	103.0	105.2	103.2	104.1	104.3	105.6	105.3	106.0	107.0

Year 2												
Sales	526.3	527.7	543.3	519.5	579.3	570.1	570.7	603.1	609.8	600.7	637.1	655.8
Deflated Sales	492.4	491.8	503.6	481.1	525.7	520.2	515.6	538.5	545.0	530.7	555.5	568.3
Index	106.9	107.3	107.9	108.0	110.2	109.6	110.7	112.0	111.9	113.2	114.7	115.4

Year 3												
Sales	632.6	631.8	661.8	670.5	677.2	701.4	711.1	700.3	712.2	750.9	729.7	764.2
Deflated Sales	548.7	544.4	560.9	563.5	565.8	583.6	592.1	582.2	586.7	609.5	588.0	608.0
Index	115.3	116.0	118.0	119.0	119.7	120.2	120.1	120.3	121.4	123.2	124.1	125.7

Year 4												
Sales	738.8	784.8	780.8	795.9	832.9	828.4	845.0	874.8	885.6	884.5	884.5	895.4
Deflated Sales	586.4	620.4	615.3	612.3	634.9	630.5	637.8	658.3	662.9	660.6	653.3	652.2
Index	126.0	126.5	126.9	130.0	131.2	131.4	132.5	132.9	133.6	133.9	135.4	137.3

a Plot the dollar-volume sales figures over time (months 1–48). What sort of trend equation seems appropriate?

b Plot the deflated sales figures over time. What sort of trend equation seems appropriate for these deflated values?

c Can you explain the discrepancy in the trends of parts a and b?

15.31 **a** Calculate a linear trend equation for the deflated sales values of Exercise 15.30. You will want to use a computer.

b Plot the trend line on the same plot as the deflated sales values. Does there appear to be any seasonal or cyclic fluctuation around the trend?

15.32 The deflated sales figures of Exercise 15.30 are divided by the trend values obtained in Exercise 15.31 to obtain the following detrended values:

Year 1:	.95	1.00	.97	1.04	1.00	1.02	1.05	.98	.96	1.00	1.03	1.00
Year 2:	1.00	.99	1.00	.95	1.03	1.01	.99	1.02	1.02	.99	1.03	1.04
Year 3:	.99	.98	1.00	1.00	.99	1.01	1.02	.99	.99	1.02	.98	1.00
Year 4:	.96	1.01	.99	.98	1.01	.99	1.00	1.02	1.02	1.0	.99	.98

a Calculate a seasonal index by averaging the values for each month separately.

b Calculate detrended, deseasonalized values for the last six months of year 4.

15.33 An intercity transportation company maintains quarterly records on the number of riders on its "milk-run" (short distance, many stops) bus routes. The data (in thousands of riders per quarter) are

Year	Quarter 1	2	3	4
1	3.83	4.61	5.68	3.90
2	4.17	4.92	6.29	4.18
3	4.63	5.45	6.79	4.55
4	4.95	5.92	7.32	4.98
5	5.41	6.55	7.94	5.41
6	6.16	6.98	8.71	6.06
7	6.45	7.63	9.55	6.43
8	6.75	8.38	10.67	7.04

a Plot the data (ridership vs. quarters 1–32).

b What sort of trend equation seems appropriate?

15.34 Fit an exponential trend curve to the data of Exercise 15.33. A computer is needed.

15.35 The following detrended values are calculated by dividing the data of Exercise 15.33 by trend values (from the equation obtained in Exercise 15.34):

Year	Quarter 1	2	3	4
1	.891	1.050	1.266	.851
2	.891	1.028	1.287	.837
3	.907	1.045	1.275	.836
4	.890	1.042	1.261	.840
5	.893	1.058	1.255	.837
6	.933	1.034	1.263	.860
7	.896	1.038	1.271	.838
8	.861	1.044	1.303	.840

a Does there appear to be a strong seasonal component in the data?

b Calculate seasonal indices for each quarter by simple averaging.

15.36 **a** Calculate exponentially smoothed forecasts of the detrended values of Exercise 15.35. Use $\alpha = .5$.

b Do these forecasts work well for quarter 3 in various systems? Can you think of an explanation?

15.37 **a** Calculate fifth-quarter moving averages for the data of Exercise 15.35.

b Calculate fifth-quarter running medians for these data.

c Would these figures, used as forecasts, do well for quarter 3?

d What further step would you suggest for improving moving-average or running-median forecasting for this situation?

15.38 A food service company provides vending machines for a growing number of companies in a metropolitan area. Data have been collected for the past seven years on the quarterly prices of the major lines of the business—sandwiches, hot meals, beverages, and desserts. In addition, total dollar-sales data are available. The data on prices are as follows:

Year 1	Quarter 1	2	3	4
Sandwiches	.62	.62	.65	.66
Hot Meals	.80	.83	.86	.88
Beverages	.20	.20	.20	.20
Desserts	.35	.35	.36	.38

Year 2

Sandwiches	.65	.68	.69	.71
Hot Meals	.88	.91	.93	.99
Beverages	.20	.20	.21	.23
Desserts	.38	.38	.39	.41

Year 3

Sandwiches	.73	.75	.78	.80
Hot Meals	1.01	1.04	1.07	1.11
Beverages	.23	.25	.25	.26
Desserts	.41	.42	.45	.45

Year 4

Sandwiches	.82	.85	.85	.87
Hot Meals	1.14	1.19	1.20	1.22
Beverages	.30	.30	.30	.32
Desserts	.45	.47	.48	.50

Year 5

Sandwiches	.90	.94	.97	1.00
Hot Meals	1.26	1.32	1.35	1.40
Beverages	.32	.35	.35	.37
Desserts	.50	.51	.53	.56

Year 6

Sandwiches	1.02	1.05	1.08	1.10
Hot Meals	1.43	1.47	1.53	1.55
Beverages	.37	.38	.39	.39
Desserts	.57	.58	.61	.63

Year 7

Sandwiches	1.12	1.15	1.20	1.23
Hot Meals	1.56	1.61	1.70	1.74
Beverages	.40	.40	.41	.41
Desserts	.65	.66	.69	.71

The data on total sales (in thousands of dollars per quarter) are

	Quarter			
Year	1	2	3	4
1	138.93	143.60	150.47	155.77
2	158.00	164.89	171.77	184.48
3	189.45	198.38	209.69	220.37
4	231.40	244.36	249.67	260.99
5	271.25	289.20	300.49	316.63
6	327.25	340.49	357.53	367.32
7	376.85	389.49	411.34	422.54

a Assume that the relative quantity weights are sandwiches, .30; hot meals, .28; beverages, .26; and desserts, .16. Calculate price indices for the fourth quarter in years 1 to 7.

b Recalculate the price indices using the relative quantity weights sandwiches, .25; hot meals, .35; beverages, .28; and desserts, .12.

c How much difference does it make which set of weights is used? Why?

15.39 The total-sales data of Exercise 15.38 are deflated by a price index based on the quantity weights shown in part a. The deflated values are

Year	Quarter 1	Quarter 2	Quarter 3	Quarter 4
1	138.93	141.48	143.17	144.76
2	147.52	149.63	152.41	155.42
3	156.82	158.96	162.05	165.69
4	168.29	171.36	173.98	176.94
5	179.40	182.70	185.03	187.46
6	190.38	192.91	195.27	197.38
7	199.29	201.08	202.73	203.63

a Plot the values. What form of trend equation seems appropriate?

b Calculate a linear trend equation.

15.40 Differences of successive quarterly values for the data of Exercise 15.39 are calculated. The following lag correlations are computed for these differences:

Lag:	0	1	2	3	4	5	6
Correlation:	1.000	.318	.152	.170	.127	.050	.148
Lag:	7	8	9	10	11	12	
Correlation:	−.058	−.198	−.160	−.140	−.123	−.307	

a Plot the correlations against lag number.

b Is there any visually obvious place where the lag correlations fall off sharply?

c What ARIMA model would you fit to the difference data?

15.41 Autoregressive models of order $p = 1$ and $p = 2$ are fit to the data of Exercise 15.40. The following results are obtained:

Parameter	AR(1)Model Estimate	AR(1)Model Standard Error
Autoregressive Lag 1	.409	.211
Constant	1.401	—
Residual Standard Deviation	.602	(25 d.f.)
Sum of Squared Residuals	9.076	

Parameter	AR(2) Model Estimate	AR(2) Model Standard Error
Autoregressive Lag 1	.378	.222
Autoregressive Lag 2	.108	.228
Constant	1.205	—
Residual Standard Deviation	.612	(24 d.f)
Sum of Squared Residuals	9.000	

a Write the respective models.

b Does the more complicated AR(2) model have a dramatically smaller average squared error?

c Which of the two models would you use?

15.42 A motel along a major highway just outside a small city caters to vacation travelers and business customers. It's been established for many years, as have its major competitors. The motel has data on the average number of daily room rentals each week, out of a capacity of 241 rooms. The occupancy data for three years (156 weeks) is in the EX1542.DAT file on the data disk, with occupancy in column 1 and week number in column 2.

a Would you expect to see a strong trend in this situation? Plot occupancy against week number; by eye, is there an evident trend?

b Use a regression program to calculate a trend equation. Assume a linear, rather than an exponential trend. Does the magnitude of the slope indicate that there is a substantial trend?

c Have the computer program calculate predicted values based on the trend equation and subtract these from actual values to obtain residuals. (Many computer packages calculate studentized residuals when asked directly for residuals; the two-step procedure of calculating predicted values, then differences, ensures that we get unstudentized residuals, as desired.)

d The last week of each year (weeks 52, 104, and 156) attracts holiday travelers, but few business travelers. Find the average value of these three residuals. What does this average indicate about the seasonal pattern for the end of the year?

15.43 **a** Use a computer package to calculate autocorrelation coefficients for lags of 1, 2, 3, up to about 10 weeks, based on the residuals from Exercise 15.42. Obtain a plot of the correlations against lag number.

b In your judgment, is there a lag number at which the autocorrelations drop off suddenly to near 0? What does your answer indicate about the kind of ARIMA model that should be fit?

15.44 **a** Use an ARIMA computer program to fit a first-order autoregressive model to the residuals from Exercise 15.42. Locate the average squared error of the model.

b Do the same for a first-order moving-average model.

c Which of the two models appears to fit the data better? Is there a clear choice between the two?

15.45 Local television channels rely heavily on their early-evening news broadcasts for advertising revenue. The ratings for these broadcasts are critical in determining the advertising rates they can charge. The EX1545.DAT file contains ratings (in column 1) of one such broadcast, as well as week number (in column 2), from week 1 to week 104.

a Plot ratings against week number. Is there evidence of a trend?

b Use a regression program to fit a linear trend of ratings against week number. What does the sign of the trend equation indicate about how well the broadcast is doing?

c What does the magnitude of the slope indicate about the extent of the trend? Note that multiplying the slope by 52 gives the predicted change in ratings over a 1-year period.

15.46 Obtain predicted values for the trend equation in Exercise 15.45. Subtract these from the actual values to obtain residuals. You might expect the "dog days of summer" (roughly weeks 30 through 34 and 82 through 87) to give lower ratings if many people are on vacation. Alternatively, people might have more time and actually watch the news more. Average the residuals for these weeks. What does the average value indicate about a seasonal effect of these weeks?

15.47 **a** Calculate autocorrelation coefficients for lags 1, 2, 3, up to 10 or so weeks for the data in Exercise 15.42. Obtain a plot of autocorrelation against lag numbers.

b In your opinion, is there a lag at which the autocorrelations drop suddenly to 0?

c Fit autoregressive models of orders 1, 2, and 3. Do the more complex AR models fit the data conspicuously better than the first-order AR model?

15.48 Electrical utilities must gear their capacity planning to peak demand periods. Data on peak demands each week for 260 weeks for one such utility are stored in column 1 of the EX1548.DAT file on the data disk; week number is in column 2.

a Plot the demands against week number. Is there evidence of a trend?

b Fit a linear trend to the demand data, using a regression program. Obtain predicted values and residual (actual − predicted) values. If there is a general pattern that the residuals at both ends of the data have one sign and the residuals in the middle have the opposite sign, there is reason to think that a curved trend equation would work better. In your opinion, is this pattern in fact the case?

c Have a computer program calculate the logarithms of the peak demands. Fit a linear trend corresponding to an exponential trend in the original data to the logarithms.

Obtain residuals from this trend equation. Is there a pattern of "same signs at the ends, opposite sign in the middle" evident in these residuals?

15.49   **a** Would you expect to see seasonal patterns in peak demand for electricity? From what you know generally, at what times would you expect to see the highest demands?

   b The week numbers in the data begin with week 1 at the beginning of January. Define the week numbers that you would expect to have the highest demands. Find the average of the residuals (from the logarithmic model of Exercise 15.48, part c). Does this average confirm your opinion about the demands in these weeks?

15.50   Use the residuals from the logarithmic model of Exercise 15.48, part c. If a program is available to you that fits ARIMA models with a seasonal component, obtain models with a first-order autoregressive term only and with a first-order moving-average term only (plus seasonal components). Which model seems to fit better?

15.51   A company that manufacturers fasteners supplies a wide variety of nuts and bolts, sheet metal screws, and wood screws. Their customers are home supply centers and hardware wholesalers in the eastern part of the United States. Production methods are well established, and there are several competent competitors for the company's business. Market size and market shares are quite stable. One key to profitability is control over inventory levels.

The company's product line includes several hundred different items, considering the different sizes, types, and finishes they sell.

The company needs to forecast demand for all these items to do an efficient job of producing or acquiring products. Inventory carrying costs are substantial, and the clerical and handling costs of maintaining the inventory also are large. The company has used rather simple forecasting methods, typically assuming that next week's demand will approximately equal current week's demand. The process hasn't been satisfactory, leading to many crisis situations where shipments must be made on an emergency basis and other situations where unsold inventory builds up.

The president wants to try fairly simple statistical methods to obtain forecasts. The company's information system has kept track of the number of cases shipped weekly for about four years, so a fair amount of data is available. The president tried out some time-series methods found in Minitab, which the company had used for other purposes.

"This is what I got for product WFSB615, which is flat head slotted wood screws, brass finish, size 6 by 1.5. That's a typical product; the demand rises and falls quite a bit over time. Can you tell me which of these methods seems to be the best, and roughly how good the forecasts ought to be, looking ahead one or two weeks? Also, if you have any other suggestions for methods, please let me know. If we find something halfway decent, we plan to use it for most of our items."

In the output, AR 1 identifies the coefficient of an autoregressive term lagging the series 1 week; MA 1, a moving-average term, also multiplying the previous week's term; and SAR 52, a seasonal autoregressive term with a 52-week lag. Use the output to respond to the president's requests. You may be able to use other methods not in the output as well, if you have access to an appropriate computer program.

```
MTB > ACF (autocorrelations) 12 lags of 'Shipped'.

ACF of Shipped

          -1.0 -0.8 -0.6 -0.4 -0.2  0.0  0.2  0.4  0.6  0.8  1.0
          +----+----+----+----+----+----+----+----+----+----+
  1  0.576                              XXXXXXXXXXXXXXX
  2  0.281                              XXXXXXXX
  3  0.094                              XXX
  4 -0.116                           XXXX
  5 -0.153                          XXXXX
  6 -0.087                           XXX
  7 -0.003                             X
  8  0.067                             XXX
  9  0.047                             XX
 10  0.031                             XX
 11 -0.029                            XX
 12 -0.068                           XXX
```

```
MTB > ARIMA 1 autoreg 0 diffs 1 moving avg 1 0 0 52 'Shipped';
SUBC>   Constant.

Final Estimates of Parameters
Type      Estimate    St. Dev.   t-ratio
AR   1     0.4955      0.1044      4.75
SAR 52     0.0267      0.0802      0.33
MA   1    -0.1228      0.1199     -1.02
Constant 161.376       1.132     142.59
Mean     328.672       2.305

No. of obs.:  209
Residuals:   SS = 43522.4  (backforecasts excluded)
             MS =   212.3  DF = 205

Modified Box-Pierce (Ljung-Box) chisquare statistic
Lag              12          24          36          48
Chisquare   13.6(DF= 9)  30.0(DF=21)  42.4(DF=33)  57.8(DF=45)

MTB > ARIMA 1 0 0 1 0 0 52 'Shipped';
SUBC>   Constant.

Final Estimates of Parameters
Type      Estimate    St. Dev.   t-ratio
AR   1     0.5769      0.0570     10.13
SAR 52     0.0367      0.0797      0.46
Constant 133.950       1.008     132.88
Mean     328.687       2.474

No. of obs.:  209
Residuals:   SS = 43742.2  (backforecasts excluded)
             MS =   212.3  DF = 206

Modified Box-Pierce (Ljung-Box) chisquare statistic
Lag              12          24          36          48
Chisquare   15.8(DF=10)  31.6(DF=22)  43.1(DF=34)  56.9(DF=46)

MTB > ARIMA 1 0 1 0 0 0 52 'Shipped';
SUBC>   Constant.

Final Estimates of Parameters
Type      Estimate    St. Dev.   t-ratio
AR   1     0.4923      0.1043      4.72
MA   1    -0.1269      0.1192     -1.07
Constant 166.846       1.133     147.22
Mean     328.650       2.232

No. of obs.:  209
Residuals:   SS = 43542.9  (backforecasts excluded)
             MS =   211.4  DF = 206

Modified Box-Pierce (Ljung-Box) chisquare statistic
Lag              12          24          36          48
Chisquare   13.1(DF=10)  29.4(DF=22)  41.3(DF=34)  56.4(DF=46)
```

Time Series

A production manager for a packaged cereal manufacturer has asked you for help in scheduling production of one of its established cereals. The product is a mature one, with reasonably consistent sales from year to year. As a mature product, it is usually promoted through local stores' coupons and point-of-sale displays; the national advertising budget is negligible.

Production is scheduled based on periods of five working days each. Holidays aren't counted in the periods. The product isn't produced on weekends because the overtime cost would be excessive. Actual production of the cereal is done, whenever possible, in a single run per 5-day period. Multiple runs are undesirable because the production line is used for several products and must be thoroughly cleaned each time a product change occurs. The manager tries to keep a low level of inventory, both to save inventory cost and to make sure that fresh product is shipped. The manager's basic problem is to determine the amount to produce per period in order to match outgoing shipments.

The manager has written the following to you:

> We'd like to use our shipment data as the basis for forecasting outgoing shipments for the next period; the next two periods would be even better. We've tried to use information about promos and coupons to guess the demand, but there are so many deals—and you never can tell how well they'll work—so that hasn't worked at all.
>
> There seem to be surges and slow spells in our shipments. We ought to be able to use the pattern to get decent forecasts. I'm sending you two years' worth of shipment data, which is basically all we have because

they gave us some new shipping territory. The data are all measured in equivalent cases shipped; an equivalent case is like twelve 16-ounce boxes with 192 ounces of cereal in one box or another. I don't have any problem with the different box sizes; I can change sizes on the packing line in three minutes flat. Can you give me some way to predict the overall demand for the next period or two?

The data are shown here for 100 periods. See what forecasting you can do using the data; you'll probably want to use a computer program. Any of the standard smoothing or modeling methods could be used. The production manager has computer facilities available. Write a report to the manager with your recommendations. Remember that the production manager is a production manager—not a statistician; explain any technical ideas clearly in English.

```
MTB > print 'Shipped'

Shipped
 12412 10695 10784 12702 12025 12469 13365 13416
 13978 12264 13178 10078  9312  9980 11072 11149
  9634 11156  9561  9045 12018 11334 10298 10384
 11426 10138  9613 11430 10587 12001 10938 10964
  8943 10858 11879 10647 11491 10585 12146 13114
 11145 13016 12839 12726 14868 13192 12752 14178
 14484 14657 12641 14914 14410 13737 15278 14062
 11844 10167  8904 10023  9924 11389 12680 12139
 11392 11715 12223 10110  9249 13526 15046 12976
 10988 11032 11163 10869  9224  9094 10927 10363
 11098 10893 14124 15378 15142 16080 12376 13017
 11398 12839 14637 12689 12364 11969 12689 15353
 12292 11075  8948  9919
```

My car isn't very impressive;
My budget woes sure are repressive.
'Cause I can't pay the loan
On the clunker I own,
My process is autoregressive.

16

Some Alternative Sampling Methods

Many sampling situations are more complex than simple random sampling. This chapter considers some of them. The major ideas are:

1. The simplest type of sampling procedure is simple random sampling. We obtain a simple random sample of n elements if each sample of size n from the N elements in the population has the same probability of being selected. For estimating a population mean μ or total τ, we use the sample mean $\overline{y}$ or sample total $N\overline{y}$, respectively. The procedure for estimating a population proportion can be thought of as a variation on estimating a population mean. By assigning a 1 to each element with the characteristic of interest and a 0 to all others, the population and sample proportions π and $\hat{\pi}$ are also the population and sample mean μ and $\overline{y}$, respectively.

2. The second sampling procedure is stratified random sampling. We obtain a stratified random sample by separating the population of elements into groups (strata) such that each element belongs to one and only one stratum. A simple random sample is then selected from each of the strata.

3. Stratified random sampling has three major advantages over simple random sampling. First, the variances of estimation procedures for μ and τ are usually reduced because the variance of observations within each stratum is usually smaller than the overall population variance. Second, the cost of collecting observations is often reduced when the population of elements is separated into smaller groups. And finally, separate estimates of parameters in each stratum can also be computed from the same sample data.

4. The next sampling procedure is cluster sampling. In this procedure, the elements of the population are separated into groups called *clusters*, and the experimenter selects a simple random sample of clusters. An observation is obtained from each element in the sampled clusters. Cluster sampling may provide more information per unit cost than simple random sampling or stratified random sampling either when a list of the elements in the population is not available or when the cost of obtaining observations increases as the distance between elements increases.

5. We discuss sample size considerations for estimating μ, τ, and π under simple random sampling, stratified random sampling, and cluster sampling in Section 16.4. For each design, we present a formula for computing the sample size necessary to achieve a 95% confidence interval of a specified width. These formulas require information from a preliminary sample or guessed values for sample variances.

We discussed the basic idea of random sampling in Chapter 6. There we defined a **simple random sample**: A set of n observations chosen from a population of size N in such a way that all possible samples of size n have an equal chance of being selected. The calculations (particularly those for standard errors) of later chapters were based on an assumption of simple random sampling. There are other ways of choosing random samples, and in this chapter we discuss a few of them. The chapter serves as an introduction to a broad area of statistical methods called **sample survey design**.

Why should a manager bother with fancy sample survey designs? The purpose of selecting a sample is to obtain the most accurate information possible for a given expenditure (of both time and money). Accuracy is measured by amount of bias, which ideally is zero, and by probable sampling variability, as summarized by a standard error. In some situations, it may be possible to break the population down into subpopulations, called **strata**, that have relatively small within-strata variability. Then **stratified sampling** can yield better accuracy for a given sample size. Stratified sampling is the subject of Section 16.2. In other situations, simple random sampling is too expensive; for example, if we tried to interview a simple random sample of 1000 adult Americans, the travel costs for interviewers would be horrendous. An alternative sampling procedure is to select 50 zip code areas randomly and then interview 20 randomly selected individuals in each area. This procedure is an example of two-stage **cluster sampling**; we discuss cluster sampling in Section 16.3. The advantage of cluster sampling is that the cost per observation can be much lower than the cost of simple random sampling. These sampling methods (and some other slightly more complex ones) can be useful in getting good information economically.

One obvious area of application of sample survey design is in market research. Another rapidly growing area of application is in accounting, particularly auditing. We can expect the use of these methods to grow even more in the future.

Some of these methods are not routinely handled in statistical computer packages. Therefore, we must spend a bit of effort on understanding how the calculations are done. Nonetheless, the more important ideas involve the various types and benefits of sampling. ■

Taking a Simple Random Sample

Selecting a good simple random sample takes planning and effort. A sloppy sample can reflect several potential biases. Because most good approaches to sampling involve simple random sampling (from the whole population or from strata or of clusters), it is worthwhile to consider some pitfalls to avoid in sampling.

target population
sampling frame

One kind of potential bias arises in selecting the entities (people, accounts, or whatever) to be sampled. Survey statisticians distinguish the **target population** (the set of entities that ideally should be sampled) from the **sampling frame** (the set of entities that actually can be sampled). In a study of consumer satisfaction with the service departments of new-car dealers, the target population is, say, all private purchasers of new cars within the past two years. The sampling frame may well be the set of all purchasers for whom dealers have current addresses. Purchasers who have moved (without forwarding addresses) are part of the target population, but because they cannot be sampled, they are not part of the sampling frame. Naturally, the best possible situation is that the target population and sampling frame be identical. This is often possible in auditing situations, but it is very difficult to achieve in sampling human populations. When the target population and sampling frame differ, a manager must usually assume that those entities that cannot be sampled have the same characteristics as those that can. If the assumption is false, one

selection bias

kind of **selection bias** occurs.

EXAMPLE 16.1

A chain of paint and wallpaper stores in a midsize city is considering strategies for pricing its house brand of interior paints. A critical element of this strategy is consumer perception of the quality of its paints. A survey is planned of current homeowners in the city. A list of those who paid real estate taxes the previous year is used to select a sample of 200 homeowners. Identify the target population and the sampling frame. Are there any major selection biases?

Solution

The target population presumably is all current homeowners in the city, but ideally it is the persons in each home who decide on paint purchases. The sampling frame is all homeowners who paid real estate taxes the previous year. A minor selection bias is the omission of homeowners who paid no taxes; this is minor because it seems plausible that their homes would be neglected and poor candidates for painting. A more serious bias is the omission of those who purchased homes in the current year. These people are likely to be major paint purchasers and quite possibly less familiar with local (as opposed to national) paint brands. ■

A subtle form of selection bias can occur if members of the sampling frame have unequal probabilities of being sampled. We would not be very impressed by a study of consumer satisfaction with new-car dealers' service departments that proceeded by taking a random sample of service orders and interviewing the car owners. People who were happy with the service would bring their cars back several times and therefore would have a high probability of being sampled. Conversely, people who didn't like the service would have a low selection probability. This kind of bias is called a **size bias** because it often reflects the size or number of transactions of an individual in the sampling frame.

size bias

E X A M P L E   1 6 . 2

A brokerage firm anticipates an increase in the margin requirements for purchasers of common stock and wishes to estimate what fraction of its customers would have been affected by such an increase during the past year. A clerk randomly samples 1000 purchases of common stocks during the year and determines the fraction of these purchases that would have been affected. Identify a size bias.

Solution

The target population is customers, not purchases. The sampling procedure is biased toward those customers who purchased stock frequently during the past year. ■

nonresponse bias

A different kind of bias can arise even though no selection biases are present. That is, once selected, individuals in a sample may not give accurate responses. At the extreme, many individuals may not respond at all. As many as 80% or even more of individuals contacted by mail surveys do not respond; a 30% nonresponse rate in telephone surveys is considered much better than average. In any competent survey, a follow-up mechanism is provided to give some indication as to whether (first-round) nonrespondents differ from respondents, but this device has only limited value. The problem of nonresponse is perhaps the most serious limitation of the usefulness of surveys of human populations. A great deal of ingenuity has been expended to minimize nonresponse rates because this is a crucial part of any survey design.

sensitive-question bias

In addition, those who do respond may not respond accurately. Questions can be ambiguous or "loaded" to favor a certain answer. In some situations, certain answers may be more socially acceptable or polite than others. Pretesting usually reveals any serious defects in questions. You can use the randomized-response technique we will discuss in Section 16.5 to deal with sensitive questions.

This litany of potential problems doesn't mean that surveys are impossible, but it does mean they must be done carefully.

Assuming that a survey design has removed potential biases, the remaining source of error is "luck of the draw": pure random variability. Here is where the standard error formulas of statistical theory are useful. In the next several sections we set out standard errors for various types of survey design. The aim of a survey typically is estimation (rather than hypothesis testing). The desired population parameter may be the population mean μ, the population proportion π, or the total value in the population, which we denote by τ. Because the population mean is the total divided by the population size N (that is, $\mu = \tau/N$), it follows that $\tau = N\mu$. If the sample mean $\bar{y}$ is used to estimate μ, a natural estimate of the population total τ is $N\bar{y}$.

We developed confidence interval methods for a mean in Chapter 7. We found that t tables should be used for small samples. In most sample surveys, sample sizes are large enough that normal tables may be used. Remember that the normal table "magic number" for 95% confidence intervals is 1.96.

Definition 16.1   Estimation of μ and τ Using Simple Random Sampling

Estimate

of μ: $\bar{y}$

of τ: $N\bar{y}$

95% Confidence interval

for μ: $\bar{y} \pm 1.96\hat{\sigma}_{\bar{Y}}$

for τ: $N\bar{y} \pm 1.96N\hat{\sigma}_{\bar{Y}}$

where

$$\hat{\sigma}_{\bar{Y}} = \sqrt{\frac{s^2}{n}\left(\frac{N-n}{N-1}\right)} \quad \blacksquare$$

---

finite population correction factor

The quantity $(N - n)/(N - 1)$, called a **finite population correction factor**, accounts for the fact that there is slightly more information in a sample of 50 from a population of 1000 than in a sample of 50 from a population of 10,000. Perhaps surprisingly, though, there isn't all that much more information; the absolute sample size primarily determines sample accuracy. The fraction of the population that's being sampled is far less important.

E X A M P L E   1 6 . 3

An industrial firm is concerned about the time per week spent by employees on certain trivial tasks. The time log sheets of a simple random sample of 50 employees in one week show that the average amount of time spent on these tasks is 10.31 hours with a sample variance of 2.25. If the corporation employs 750 people, estimate the total number of hours lost per week on these trivial tasks. Give a 95% confidence interval for τ.

Solution

We are told that the population consists of $N = 750$ employees, from which a random sample of $n = 50$ time log sheets is obtained. The mean amount of work lost for the sampled employees is 10.31. An estimate of the total amount of time lost per week is

$$N\bar{y} = 750(10.31) = 7732.5 \text{ hours}$$

The 95% confidence interval for τ is

$$N\bar{y} \pm 1.96N\hat{\sigma}_{\bar{Y}}$$

where

$$\hat{\sigma}_{\bar{Y}} = \sqrt{\frac{s^2}{n}\left(\frac{N-n}{N-1}\right)}$$

Substituting into the formula for $\hat{\sigma}_{\bar{Y}}$, we obtain

$$\hat{\sigma}_{\bar{Y}} = \sqrt{\frac{2.25}{50}\left(\frac{750-50}{750-1}\right)} = .205$$

The corresponding 95% confidence interval for τ, the total number of hours lost per week on these trivial tasks for the 750 employees, is

$$7732.5 \pm 1.96(750)(.205)$$

or

$$7732.5 \pm 301.4$$

Thus we are 95% confident that the time lost per week is between 7431.1 and 8033.9 hours. This is a staggering amount— approximately 26% of the scheduled work hours. ∎

Rather than estimating a population mean or total, sample surveys are frequently conducted to estimate the proportion of experimental units in a population that possesses a specified characteristic. For example, suppose we are interested in determining a television program's rating by estimating the proportion of families in a given district who watch the program during a given week. Let $y_i = 0$ if the ith family in a simple random sample of n does not possess the characteristic of interest (did not watch the show) and $y_i = 1$ if the ith family does possess the characteristic of interest. Then the proportion of elements in the sample possessing the specified characteristic also is the sample mean of the y_i's. With this fact in mind, $\hat{\pi}$ is actually $\bar{y}$, and π can be thought of as the mean for the entire population of 0s and 1s. Thus formulas developed for estimating μ can also be used for estimating π. These formulas are a bit simpler when expressed in terms of proportions.

Definition 16.2   Estimation of π Using Simple Random Sampling

Point estimate of π: $\qquad\qquad \hat{\pi} = \frac{y}{n}$

95% Confidence interval for π: $\qquad \hat{\pi} \pm z_{\alpha/2}\hat{\sigma}_{\hat{\pi}}$

where

$$\hat{\sigma}_{\hat{\pi}} = \sqrt{\frac{\hat{\pi}(1 - \hat{\pi})}{n}\left(\frac{N - n}{N - 1}\right)} \qquad ∎$$

E X A M P L E   1 6 . 4

A business manager in charge of a large-volume product is concerned about the proportion of customers with delinquent accounts and the proportion of customers with a balance due exceeding $500. An internal audit is made of a random sample of 120 accounts from a total of 2280 accounts. From this sample, 17 are found to be delinquent and 64 have balances due in excess of $500. Use these data to give a 95% confidence interval for

a   The proportion of delinquent accounts

b   The proportion of accounts with balances in excess of $500

Solution

a   The point estimate of the proportion of customers with delinquent accounts is $17/120 = .14$. The 95% confidence interval for π is

$$.14 \pm 1.96\sqrt{\frac{.14(.86)}{120}\left(\frac{2280 - 120}{2280 - 1}\right)}$$

or

$$.14 \pm .060$$

We are 95% confident that the actual proportion of delinquent accounts is between .080 and .200.

b In a similar way, the point estimate of the proportion of accounts with balances in excess of $500 is $64/120 = .53$. The corresponding approximate 95% confidence interval for π is

$$.53 \pm 1.96 \sqrt{\frac{.53(.47)}{120}\left(\frac{2280-120}{2280-1}\right)}$$

or

$$.53 \pm .087$$

We are 95% confident that the actual proportion of accounts with balances in excess of $500 is between .443 and .617. ■

The concepts presented in this section are essentially a review of ideas from Chapters 6–8. The procedures of the next sections extend these ideas to more complicated sample survey designs. Although the formulas become more complicated, the essential idea of estimate plus or minus 1.96 standard errors for 95% confidence still holds.

EXERCISES

16.1 Refer to Example 16.1. Suppose that the paint store chain conducts a telephone survey based on random selection of telephone numbers. (Business phones can be excluded.) Identify the sampling frame and any major selection biases.

16.2 A state commission investigates problems of wheelchair-bound people in obtaining access to public transit and to state offices. A survey is planned in which 150 wheelchair-bound people each keep a diary recording all instances of inaccessibility. The 150 people are selected from the membership list of a statewide association for handicapped persons. Identify the target population, the sampling frame, and possible selection bias.

16.3 Assume that the survey of the previous exercise can be regarded as a simple random sample. Suppose that 66 of the 150 persons report encountering an inaccessible public building. Give a 95% confidence interval for the population proportion.

16.4 An organization that specializes in arranging rentals and trades of vacation homes wishes to survey the condominium apartments on a certain large island off the Florida coast. Interviewers are instructed to call on randomly chosen apartments during the month of March between 10 A.M. and noon. Follow-up calls are made between 3 P.M. and 5 P.M. the next day, and then again between 7 P.M. and 9 P.M. the following day. Apartment owners are interviewed to determine their interest in renting out their apartments during specified times. What biases could be present in this study?

16.5 Assume that the survey conducted in Exercise 16.4 can be regarded as a simple random sample. Suppose that, of 221 apartment owners who respond, 83 are willing to rent their apartments. The mean availability of the 83 apartments is 4.2 weeks and the standard deviation is 2.8 weeks.

a Find a 95% confidence interval for the population proportion of rentable apartments.

b Find a 95% confidence interval for the true mean availability of rentable apartments.

16.6 In an audit of sales for a certain store, an accounting clerk is told to keep a running total of sales accounts. Every sale that takes the total into the next $10,000 interval is selected for examination. For example, a sale that took the total from $29,972 to $30,041 would be selected. The sales are assumed to be in random order for all practical purposes. Does this procedure yield a practically unbiased simple random sample of all sales?

16.7 Suppose that the sample of Exercise 16.6 yields 267 sales with a mean amount of $112.24 and a standard deviation of $91.49. Calculate a 95% confidence interval for the true mean sale amount, assuming that the sample constitutes a simple random sample.

16.8 Did you identify any bias in Exercise 16.6? What effect do you think it has on the confidence interval of Exercise 16.7? ■

Stratified Random Sampling

Stratification offers an alternative to simple random sampling and, in many instances, increases the accuracy of information available for estimating μ or τ.

Definition 16.3   Stratified Random Sample

A stratified random sample is a sample obtained by dividing the population of experimental units into nonoverlapping groups, called *strata*. A simple random sample is selected from each stratum. ■

The first step in selecting a stratified random sample is to clearly specify the strata, making certain that each experimental unit can be classified into only one stratum. For example, in a local election survey, we may wish to stratify registered voters according to one of five voting precincts. If precinct boundary lines are clearly defined and the voter registration lists are up to date, there should be no problem in placing registered voters into the appropriate precincts (strata). After the experimental units are divided into strata, we select a simple random sample of unit from each stratum.

Before presenting the formulas for the estimates of μ (or π) and τ, we need the following notation:

I: Number of strata

N_i: Number of elements in stratum i $(i = 1, 2, \ldots, I)$

n_i: Sample size in stratum i

N: Total population size, $N = \sum_i N_i$

n: Total sample size, $n = \sum_i n_i$

$\bar{y}_i$:   Sample mean in stratum i

s_i^2 Sample variance in stratum i

The estimation procedures for μ and τ given next are based on weighting the strata means in proportion to the strata sizes. It makes sense that large strata should be given more weight in the estimates.

Definition 16.4   Estimation of μ and τ Using Stratified Random Sampling

Point estimate

of μ: $\bar{y}_{ST} = \dfrac{\sum_i N_i \bar{y}_i}{N}$

of τ: $N\bar{y}_{ST}$

95% Confidence interval

for μ: $\bar{y}_{ST} \pm z_{\alpha/2}\hat{\sigma}_{\bar{Y}_{ST}}$

for τ: $N\bar{y}_{ST} \pm z_{\alpha/2}N\hat{\sigma}_{\bar{Y}_{ST}}$

---

where

$$\hat{\sigma}_{\bar{Y}_{ST}} = \frac{1}{N}\sqrt{\sum N_i^2 \left(\frac{N_i - n_i}{N_i - 1}\right) \frac{s_i^2}{n_i}} \quad \blacksquare$$

In order to use stratified sampling methods, we must know (fairly accurately) the relative proportions (N_i/N) of the various subpopulations. The estimate of the population mean weights the strata means by these proportions. If the strata means are quite different, the choice of weights will have considerable effect; however, if the means are similar, then the weights will not matter much. The actual magnitudes (N_i) of the subpopulations are less crucial. The estimate of the mean depends only on the relative proportions (and the strata means). The standard error expression can be rewritten algebraically to show that it depends only on the relative proportions N_i/N and the finite population correction factor $(N_i - n_i)/(N_i - 1)$. As usual, the correction factor has very little effect if the population sizes are large compared to the sample sizes. As long as the relative proportions of the strata are correct, changing the magnitudes of the N_i and N won't matter much.

EXAMPLE 16.5

A wholesale food distributor in a large metropolitan area would like to know if demand is great enough to justify adding a new product to the stock. To aid in making the decision, the wholesaler plans to add this product to a sample of the stores serviced to estimate average monthly sales. Because only four large chains are serviced in the metropolitan area, it is administratively convenient to stratify the stores, with each chain serving as a stratum. There are 24 stores in stratum 1, 36 in stratum 2, 30 in stratum 3, and 30 in stratum 4. The wholesaler decides there is enough money to obtain data in a total of 20 retail stores. If we allocate the total sample size among the strata, with each sample size proportional to the stratum size, we obtain sample sizes of 4, 6, 5, and 5 for the four chains, respectively. Thus, the product is introduced into 4 stores chosen at random from chain 1, 6 stores from chain 2, and 5 stores each from chains 3 and 4. The sales (in hundreds of dollars, after a 1-month trial period) are tabulated next. Estimate the average sales for the month and give a 95% confidence interval for μ.

	Stratum (Chain)			
	1	2	3	4
	89	91	108	102
	80	99	96	120
	92	93	100	104
	100	105	93	101
		111	93	123
		101		
Sample Mean	89	100	98	110
Sample Variance	78.67	55.60	39.50	112.50

Solution

The point estimate of μ, the average monthly sales for all stores across the four chains, is

$$\bar{y}_{ST} = \frac{\sum_i N_i \bar{y}_i}{N} = \frac{24(89) + 36(100) + 30(98) + 30(110)}{120} = 99.8$$

The 95% confidence interval for μ is

$$\bar{y}_{ST} \pm 1.96 \hat{\sigma}_{\bar{Y}_{ST}}$$

where

$$\hat{\sigma}_{\bar{Y}_{ST}} = \frac{1}{N} \sqrt{\sum_i N_i^2 \left(\frac{N_i - n_i}{N_i - 1} \right) \left(\frac{s_i^2}{n_i} \right)}$$

$$= \frac{1}{120} \left[(24)^2 \left(\frac{24 - 4}{24 - 1} \right) \frac{78.67}{4} + (36)^2 \left(\frac{36 - 6}{36 - 1} \right) \frac{55.60}{6} \right.$$

$$\left. + (30)^2 \left(\frac{30 - 5}{30 - 1} \right) \frac{39.50}{5} + (30)^2 \left(\frac{30 - 5}{30 - 1} \right) \frac{112.5}{5} \right]^{1/2}$$

$$= \frac{1}{120} \sqrt{43731.0} = 1.74$$

The corresponding confidence interval is

$$99.8 \pm 1.96(1.74) \quad \text{or} \quad 99.8 \pm 3.41$$

We are 95% confident that the average monthly sales for these 120 stores are in the interval 96.39 to 103.21 (thousand dollars). ∎

Most statistical packages do not have a direct command to calculate results for stratified sampling. However, some packages have macros—programmed routines included in the package—that do the work. For example, here is a macro from Minitab (version 10) and the result of analyzing the data in the preceding example. It assumes that the data are in one column and the strata numbers in another.

```
MACRO
STRATSAM Data Strata
#Generate means and variances by strata
MCOLUMN Data Strata StrMeans StrVars StrNums BigNs Smallns
MCONSTANT YBarStr SEStr TotBigN
Stats Data;
  by Strata;
  GValues StrNums;
  N Smallns;
  Mean StrMeans;
  Variance StrVars.
Print StrNums StrMeans StrVars
Note Enter list of population sizes by stratum
Note When done, enter    End
Set BigNs;
  File 'TERMINAL'.
Let TotBigN=sum(BigNs)
Let YBarStr=sum(StrMeans*BigNs/TotBigN)
Let SEStr&
=sqrt(sum(((BigNs/TotBigN)**2)*(StrVars/Smallns)*((BigNs&
-Smallns)/(BigNs-1))))
Print YBarStr SEStr
ENDMACRO

MTB > %STRATSAM 'Sales' 'Chain'
```

```
Executing from file: STRATSAM.MAC

Data Display

  Row  StrNums  StrMeans   StrVars

   1      1        89      78.667
   2      2       100      55.600
   3      3        98      39.500
   4      4       110     112.500


Enter list of population sizes by stratum
When done, enter    End
DATA> 24 36 30 30
DATA> End

Data Display

YBarStr   99.8000
SEStr      1.74265
```

Alternatively, one can obtain means and variances (or standard deviations) for each stratum by almost any package, and then use a spreadsheet program to do the calculations of the stratified sample mean and standard error.

The standard error of $\bar{y}_{ST}$ depends on the estimated variances s_i^2 in the various strata, whereas the standard error of $\bar{y}$ based on simple random sampling depends on s^2, which estimates the overall population variance. If there is relatively little variability in each stratum as compared to the overall population variability, stratification yields a smaller standard error and hence more accurate estimation than does simple random sampling. In the language of Chapter 11, it is desirable to have relatively low **variability within strata** as compared to the **variability between strata**. In other words, it is desirable to divide the population into relatively homogeneous (low-variability) strata.

variability within and between strata

EXAMPLE 16.6

Refer to Example 16.5 and assume that the tabulated data were obtained from a simple random sample of stores. Compute a 95% confidence interval for μ and compare it to the one obtained in Example 16.5 using stratified random sampling.

Solution

One can easily verify that the sample mean and variance for the $n = 20$ observations are $\bar{y} = 99.8$ and $s^2 = 111.85$ with $N = 120$. The 95% confidence interval for μ is

$$99.8 \pm 1.96\hat{\sigma}_{\bar{Y}}$$

where

$$\hat{\sigma}_{\bar{Y}} = \sqrt{\frac{s^2}{n}\left(\frac{N-n}{N-1}\right)} = \sqrt{\frac{111.85}{20}\left(\frac{120-20}{119}\right)} = 2.17$$

so the 95% confidence interval for μ using simple random sampling is

$$99.8 \pm 1.96(2.17) \quad \text{or} \quad 99.8 \pm 4.25$$

Note that this interval is wider than that for stratified random sampling. This will not always be so; but when stratification produces smaller, homogeneous groups, stratified random sampling is an improvement over simple random sampling. ■

The mathematics behind the formulas for stratified random sampling follows from the formulas for linear combinations of independent random variables (see Appendix 4A). The point estimate $\bar{y}_{ST}$ is a weighted average of the strata means $\bar{y}_i$; the weights are the strata sizes N_i. Thus

$$\sigma^2_{\bar{Y}_{ST}} = \text{Var}\left(\sum_i \frac{N_i}{N} \bar{Y}_i\right) = \sum_i \frac{N_i^2}{N^2} \sigma^2_{\bar{Y}_i}$$

Because a simple random sample is taken within each stratum,

$$\sigma^2_{\bar{Y}_i} = \frac{\sigma_i^2}{n_i}\left(\frac{N_i - n_i}{N_i - 1}\right)$$

The standard error formula for $\bar{y}_{ST}$ follows by estimating each true stratum variance σ_i^2 by the sample variance s_i^2.

Stratified sampling can also be used to estimate a population proportion π. For example, suppose that the personnel department of a large corporation is interested in estimating the proportion of all vested employees who participate in a company-run stock savings program. If the divisions of the corporation represent strata and a simple random sample of n_i employee records is obtained from stratum $i(i = 1, \ldots, I)$, then a point estimate and approximate confidence interval can be obtained using the following formulas.

Definition 16.5 Estimation of π Using Stratified Random Sampling

Point estimate: $\hat{\pi}_{ST} = \frac{1}{N}\sum N_i \hat{\pi}_i$

95% Confidence interval: $\hat{\pi}_{ST} \pm z_{\alpha/2}\hat{\sigma}_{\hat{\pi}_{ST}}$

where

$$\hat{\sigma}_{\hat{\pi}_{ST}} = \frac{1}{N}\sqrt{\sum_i N_i^2\left(\frac{N_i - n_i}{N_i - 1}\right)\frac{\hat{\pi}(1 - \hat{\pi}_i)}{n_i}}$$ ■

E X A M P L E   1 6 . 7

The sample data for the survey of vested employees is shown for each of the three divisions of the corporation. Use these data to estimate π, the proportion of all vested employees who participate in the company-run stock program.

Stratum (Division)	Number N_i of Vested Employees	Sample Size n_i	Number Who Participate
1	450	45	12
2	300	30	15
3	760	76	30

Solution

The point estimate of π is

$$\hat{\pi}_{ST} = \frac{1}{N}\sum_i N_i \hat{\pi}_i = \frac{1}{1510}[450(.2667) + 300(.5000) + 760(.3947)] = .3775$$

The 95% confidence interval for π can be found after we compute $\hat{\sigma}_{\hat{\pi}_{ST}}$:

$$\hat{\sigma}_{\pi_{ST}} = \frac{1}{N}\sqrt{\sum_i N_i^2 \left(\frac{N_i - n_i}{N_i - 1}\right) \frac{\hat{\pi}_i(1 - \hat{\pi}_i)}{n_i}}$$

$$= \frac{1}{1510}\left[(450)^2 \left(\frac{450 - 45}{450 - 1}\right) \frac{(.2667)(.7333)}{45} + (300)^2 \left(\frac{300 - 30}{300 - 1}\right) \frac{(.5)(.5)}{30}\right.$$

$$\left. + (760)^2 \left(\frac{760 - 76}{760 - 1}\right) \frac{(.3947)(.6053)}{76}\right]^{1/2}$$

$$= \frac{1}{1510}\sqrt{3106.67} = .0369$$

The corresponding 95% confidence interval for π is

$$.3775 \pm 1.96(.0369) \quad \text{or} \quad .3775 \pm .0723$$

The actual proportion of vested employees in the corporation who participate in the stock program is estimated to be in the interval .305–.450.

A Statistix data set with the calculations done using that package's transformation feature gets the same results:

```
Divn  Popn  ni  Partic   Fracn   PihatSt   SEStr
  1    450  45     12  0.26667  0.37748  0.03692
  2    300  30     15  0.50000  0.37748  0.03692
  3    760  76     30  0.39474  0.37748  0.03692
```

■

advantages of stratified random sampling

There are several reasons why stratified random sampling often results in an increase in information for a given cost. First, the data often are more homogeneous within each stratum than in the population as a whole. Taking advantage of the reduced variability within each stratum, we obtain estimates that have smaller confidence intervals than comparable estimates from a simple random sample of the same size. Second, the cost of conducting a stratified random sample tends to be less than that for a simple random sample. The elements in each stratum are usually located within a smaller geographic area, and separate teams of interviewers can be sent to the strata for collection of the sample data. Third, separate estimates of population parameters for each stratum can be obtained without additional sampling.

EXERCISES

16.9 A group of college students conducts a survey to determine the average number of college hours (credits) an undergraduate student must earn for various majors to obtain a bachelor's degree from a large university. To do this, the departments of the university are stratified by colleges. Use the following sample data to estimate μ, the average number of credit hours required for a bachelor's degree. Construct a 95% confidence interval. You may wish to use a computer package to obtain means and standard deviations.

College	Number of Departments	Sample Data
Architecture and Fine Arts	7	192, 199, 188, 191
Arts and Sciences	40	186, 195, 186, 189, 186, 192, 193, 195, 200, 183, 187, 192
Business Administration	6	193, 186, 180, 182
Education	8	197, 198, 188, 196
Engineering	20	202, 203, 213, 202, 204, 206, 210, 206

16.10 Refer to Example 16.5. Use the sales data from all 20 stores as a single random sample. Estimate the mean sales with a 95% confidence interval. Compare your results to those of Example 16.5. Does it appear that stratification has helped?

16.11 A study of television viewing habits stratifies people in a metropolitan area by gender and age. Random samples are chosen within strata, and the sampled individuals record one week's prime-time viewing in diaries. The results were analyzed using JMP, with the following results:

Gender	Age	Popn Size	SampleSize	Mean	StDev.	Stratified Mean	Stratified Std. Error
F	18-34	312000	127	10.4	4.2	10.52071	0.14835
M	18-34	317000	129	11.2	3.8		
F	35-49	285000	116	9.8	3.9		
M	35-49	279000	114	10.3	4.1		
F	50-64	248000	101	10.6	4.5		
M	50-64	221000	90	11	4.8		
F	65+	189000	77	10.1	4.4		
M	65+	114000	46	10.9	3.9		

a Calculate a 95% confidence interval for the overall mean viewing time.

b Calculate a 95% confidence interval for the mean viewing times of all people age 65 and over. Note that only the last two strata are relevant.

16.12 Recalculate a 95% confidence interval for the overall mean viewing time in Exercise 16.11, assuming that the eight strata represent equal proportions of the population. Is there a substantial shift in the interval? Explain why.

16.13 In a study of the 1899 largest nonfinancial corporations, a sample of 250 firms is chosen and the number of firms that value inventory on the LIFO principle is determined. The sample is stratified into five major industries. The results were analyzed using an Excel worksheet, as follows:

	C	D	E	F	G	H
5	Industry type	No. Firms	Sample size	LIFO firms	Fraction	PiHatStr
6	A	425	66	16	0.242424	0.19773
7	B	489	61	10	0.163934	SEStr
8	C	441	55	9	0.163636	0.02342
9	D	379	47	11	0.234043	
10	E	165	21	4	0.190476	

Calculate a 95% confidence interval for the overall proportion of firms using LIFO.

16.14 Refer to the data of Exercise 16.13. Calculate a 95% confidence interval assuming (incorrectly) that the data resulted from a simple random sample of 250 of 1899 firms, of which 50 use LIFO. Do the point estimate and confidence interval differ substantially from those found in Exercise 16.13? Can you explain why? ■

Cluster Sampling

When units to be sampled are grouped together, possibly geographically, a third type of sampling, *cluster sampling*, can often give more information for a given cost than simple or stratified random sampling. In cluster sampling, just as in stratified sampling, we think of the individual units as being divided into groups. One difference is that stratification is based on a characteristic of interest such as gender, age, or educational level, whereas clusters are based on physical nearness in space or time. Another difference is that we sample units in all strata, but only in some clusters. In other words, we sample *some* units in *all* subsets when doing stratified sampling, but *all* units in *some* subsets when doing cluster sampling.

A **one-stage cluster sample** is obtained by taking a simple random sample of clusters and then observing all the units in the sampled clusters. For example, a suburban town council considering a major house reassessment project might divide the town into blocks, choose a random sample of blocks, and send an assessor to value each house on the sampled blocks. In this way, the assessor can spend more time assessing and less time running around town, which wouldn't be the case for a simple random sample of individual houses scattered throughout the town.

In general, the **advantage of cluster sampling** increases as units become more separated and the cost of proceeding from one unit to another increases. The limitation of cluster sampling is that one tends to get less information per unit sampled because the units within a cluster tend to be similar. For example, in our assessment example, houses in a block tend to be similarly valued. Once an assessor finds, for example, that one house in a block is valued at 180% of the old assessment, it's very likely that all the other houses will have similar values, so the extra information from the other houses won't tell us much. In contrast to stratified sampling, we would like to have little variability among clusters and high variability within clusters; unfortunately, clusters tend to be rather homogeneous in practice.

If a cluster sample is taken, the point estimates of a mean or a proportion are, in effect, the sample mean or sample proportion. The standard error for cluster sampling is somewhat more complicated than for simple random sampling. It must reflect the possible relation among units in a single cluster. The notation is as follows:

N: Number of clusters

n: Number of clusters selected in a simple random sample

m_i: : Number of elements in cluster i ($i = 1, 2, \ldots, N$)

$\overline{m}$: Average cluster size for the sampled clusters, $\overline{m} = \sum_i m_i / n$

M: Number of elements in the population, $M = \sum_i m_i$

$\overline{M}$: Average cluster size for the population, $\overline{M} = M/N$; if $\overline{M}$ is unknown,

it may be estimated by $\overline{m}$

T_i: Total for all observations in the ith cluster

The estimation procedures for μ and τ are presented next.

Definition 16.6   Estimation of μ and τ Using Cluster Sampling

Estimate

of μ: $\overline{y}_c = \dfrac{\sum T_i}{\sum m_i}$

of τ: $M\overline{y}_c$

95% Confidence interval

for μ: $\overline{y}_c \pm z_{\alpha/2}\hat{\sigma}_{\overline{Y}_c}$

for τ: $M\overline{y}_c \pm z_{\alpha/2}M\hat{\sigma}_{\overline{Y}_c}$

where

$$\hat{\sigma}_{\overline{Y}_c} = \sqrt{\left(\frac{N-n}{nN\overline{M}^2}\right)\frac{\sum_i (T_i - \overline{y}_c m_i)^2}{n-1}} \quad \blacksquare$$

EXAMPLE 16.8

Interviews are conducted in each of 25 blocks sampled from a set of 415 blocks in a city. The data on yearly housing expenditures are presented next. Use the data to estimate the average yearly expenditure in the city using a 95% confidence interval.

Cluster i	Number of Homes m_i	Total Expenditure per Cluster T_i
1	8	$96,000
2	12	121,000
3	4	42,000
4	5	65,000
5	6	52,000
6	6	40,000
7	7	75,000
8	5	65,000
9	8	45,000
10	3	50,000
11	2	85,000
12	6	43,000
13	5	54,000
14	10	49,000
15	9	53,000
16	3	50,000
17	6	32,000
18	5	22,000
19	5	45,000
20	4	37,000
21	6	51,000
22	8	30,000
23	7	39,000
24	3	47,000
25	8	41,000
	$\sum_i m_i = 151$	$\sum_i T_i = \$1,329,000$

Solution

The best estimate of the population mean μ is

$$\bar{y}_c = \frac{\sum_i T_i}{\sum_i m_i} = \frac{\$1,329,000}{151} = \$8801$$

To calculate the confidence interval, we must compute

$$\sum_i (T_i - \bar{y}_c m_i)^2 = \sum_i T_i^2 - 2\bar{y}_c \sum_i T_i m_i + \bar{y}_c^2 \sum_i m_i^2$$

Thus we have

$$\sum_i T_i^2 = T_1^2 + T_2^2 + \cdots + T_{25}^2$$

$$= (96,000)^2 + (121,000)^2 + \cdots + (41,000)^2 = 82,039,000,000$$

$$\sum_i m_i^2 = m_1^2 + m_2^2 + \cdots + m_{25}^2 = (8)^2 + (12)^2 + \cdots + (8)^2 = 1047$$

$$\sum_i T_i m_i = T_1 m_1 + T_2 m_2 + \cdots + T_{25} m_{25}$$
$$= (96,000)(8) + (121,000)(12) + \cdots + (41,000)(8)$$
$$= 8,403,000$$

and hence

$$\sum_i (T_i - \bar{y}_c m_i)^2 = 82,039,000,000 - 2(8801)(8,403,000) + (8801)^2(1047)$$
$$= 15,227,502,247$$

Because M is not known, the $\overline{M}$ appearing in the formula for standard error must be estimated by $\overline{m}$, where

$$\overline{m} = \frac{\sum_i m_i}{n} = \frac{151}{25} = 6.04$$

Then

$$\left(\frac{N-n}{Nn\overline{M}^2}\right)\left(\frac{\sum_i (T_i - \bar{y}_c m_i)^2}{n-1}\right) = \left(\frac{415-25}{(415)(25)(6.04)^2}\right)\left(\frac{15,227,502,247}{24}\right)$$
$$= 653,785$$

and the approximate 95% confidence interval is

$$8801 \pm 1.96\sqrt{653,785} \quad \text{or} \quad 8801 \pm 1584.8$$

We are 95% confident that the mean expenditure in the city lies between \$7216.20 and \$10,385.80. Although the width of this confidence interval is rather large, it can be reduced by sampling more clusters, thereby increasing the sample size. ■

As with stratified sampling, most statistical computer packages do not have a direct command for calculating mean and standard error for cluster sampling. Some provide a macro for doing the calculations. For example, here is a Minitab macro called CLUSSAM2 that takes cluster numbers, totals, and sizes as inputs, and yields the results found in the previous example.

```
MACRO
ClusSam2 ClusNum ClusTots Clusn
#Estimate mean and standard error from cluster sampling
#Inputs are cluster number, total, and number in cluster
MCONSTANT YBarClus SEClus ClusPopn ClusTot PopKnown BigM MBar MCOLUMN ClusNum ClusTots
Clusn ReadIn
Note How many clusters are there in the whole population?
Set ReadIn;
  File 'TERMINAL';
  NObs = 1.
Let ClusPopn = ReadIn
Note Is the total population size known? Enter Y or N.
YESNO PopKnown
IF PopKnown=1
  Note Enter total population size.
  Set ReadIn;
    File 'TERMINAL';
    Nobs = 1.
  Let BigM = ReadIn
```

```
      Let MBar = BigM/ClusPopn
    ELSE
      Let MBar = (sum(Clusn)/Count(ClusNum))
    ENDIF
    Let YBarClus = sum(ClusTots)/sum(Clusn)
    Let SEClus = sqrt((((ClusPopn - Count(ClusNum))/(Count(ClusNum)*&
    ClusPopn*MBar**2))*sum((ClusTots - YBarClus*Clusn)**2)/(Count&   (ClusNum)-1))  Print
    YBarClus SEClus
    ENDMACRO


    MTB > %CLUSSAM2 'Cluster' 'TotalExp' 'NumHomes'
    Executing from file: C:\MTBWIN\MACROS\CLUSSAM2.MAC
    How many clusters are there in the whole population?
    DATA> 415
    Is the total population size known? Enter Y or N.
    N


    Data Display


    YBarClus 8801.32
    SEClus   808.570
```

Another Minitab macro, called CLUSSAM, takes the original data and cluster numbers as inputs, obtains the totals and sizes, and carries out the same calculations.

The calculations can be carried out using a spreadsheet. You may wish to input cluster means instead of cluster totals; the totals can be calculated simply by multiplying each mean by the corresponding cluster size.

The number of clusters in the entire population, N, is not too crucial in these cluster-sampling calculations. This number does not affect the calculation of the cluster-sampling mean at all, and only enters the standard error calculation by way of a finite population correction factor $(N - n)/N$. This factor will be near 1 if the number of clusters in the population, N, is large compared to n, the number of clusters sampled.

If we incorrectly used too large a value for N, the only effect would be to increase the standard error slightly and make the confidence interval slightly wider than absolutely necessary. Usually, the effect of using too large an N value is negligible.

A much more serious error would be to treat a cluster sample as if it were a simple random sample. Measurements taken within a single cluster often are highly correlated. For example, suppose we send an assessor to place values on homes in new suburban developments. To avoid wasting a great amount of time traveling from one home to another, we would most likely select a sample of developments at random and have the assessor evaluate all the homes in the sampled developments. Homes in a particular development usually have very similar values; the value of one home will be an excellent predictor of the values of other homes in the same development. This statistical dependence from one measurement means that incorrectly regarding a cluster-sampling method as simple random sampling leads to a very substantial underestimate of the correct standard error and therefore leads to a falsely narrow confidence interval.

A population proportion can also be estimated using cluster sampling. For example, in a survey of rank and file workers, the leaders of a labor union may be interested in the proportion of members who favor a proposed new benefits package. If the locals of the labor union represent the clusters and a simple random sample of clusters is selected, we can estimate the population proportion π in the following way. Let a_i denote the number of laborers in cluster i who favor the new benefits package ($i = 1, 2, \ldots, n$) and let m_i denote the number of members of the local in the ith cluster. Then an estimate of π is given by

$$\hat{\pi}_c = \frac{\sum_i a_i}{\sum_i m_i}$$

The details are given next.

Definition 16.7   Estimation of π Using Cluster Sampling

Point estimate:
$$\hat{\pi}_c = \frac{\sum_i a_i}{\sum_i m_i}$$

95% Confidence interval:
$$\hat{\pi}_c \pm z_{\alpha/2}\hat{\sigma}_{\hat{\pi}_c}$$

where

$$\hat{\sigma}_{\hat{\pi}_c} = \sqrt{\left(\frac{N-n}{nN\overline{M}^2}\right)\frac{\sum(a_i - \hat{\pi}_c m_i)^2}{n-1}}$$

Note: n should be 20 or more unless all the cluster sizes are approximately the same. ■

E X A M P L E   1 6 . 9

Suppose that a random sample of 25 local unions is selected from the total of 520 possible clusters. The sample data from the 25 clusters are shown in the following table. Use these data to construct an approximate 95% confidence interval for π.

Cluster	Number of Members m_i	Number Favoring a_i	Cluster	Number of Members m_i	Number Favoring a_i
1	65	30	14	115	60
2	78	35	15	150	92
3	80	49	16	43	31
4	40	16	17	67	17
5	50	32	18	39	24
6	100	51	19	26	14
7	120	75	20	98	56
8	75	40	21	106	52
9	80	39	22	112	76
10	85	52	23	59	33
11	90	55	24	71	47
12	73	19	25	82	55
13	61	34			

Solution

For these data, you should verify that

$$\sum m_i = 1965 \quad \sum m_i^2 = 174{,}499 \quad \overline{m} = 78.60$$

$$\sum a_i = 1084 \quad \sum a_i^2 = 56{,}424 \quad \sum a_i m_i = 97{,}669$$

The estimate of π, the proportion of all union members favoring the new benefits package, is

$$\hat{\pi}_c = \frac{\sum a_i}{\sum m_i} = \frac{1084}{1965} = .55$$

To calculate $\hat{\sigma}_{\hat{\pi}_c}$ we need

$$\sum(a_i - \hat{\pi}_c m_i)^2 = \sum a_i^2 - 2\hat{\pi}_c \sum a_i m_i + \hat{\pi}_c^2 \sum m_i^2$$

$$= 56,424 - 2(.55)(97,669) + (.55)^2(174,499)$$
$$= 1774.05$$

Because we do not know the exact number of union members M, we can use $\overline{m}$ for $\overline{M}$ in the formula for $\hat{\sigma}_{\hat{\pi}_c}$:

$$\hat{\sigma}_{\hat{\pi}_c} = \sqrt{\left(\frac{N-n}{nN\overline{M}^2}\right)\frac{\sum_i(a_i - \hat{\pi}_c m_i)^2}{n-1}}$$

$$= \sqrt{\left(\frac{520-25}{25(520)(78.60)^2}\right)\frac{1774.05}{24}} = .021$$

Hence the approximate 95% confidence interval for π is

$$.55 \pm 1.96(.021) \quad \text{or} \quad .55 \pm .041$$

We are 95% confident that the actual proportion of union members favoring the new benefits package is between .509 and .591. It appears that a majority favors the package. ∎

The standard error and confidence interval for a proportion using cluster sampling are exactly what one would get using a confidence interval for a mean of a set of 1s (for successes) and 0s (for failures). The a_i are, in effect, the total of the 1s and 0s for the clusters. Therefore, a computer program or macro that does cluster-sampling analyses for a mean can also be used for a proportion.

For example, here is the result of Minitab's CLUSSAM2 macro for the preceding example:

```
MTB > %CLUSSAM2 'Cluster' 'Favoring' 'Members'
Executing from file: CLUSSAM2.MAC
How many clusters are there in the whole population?
DATA> 520
Is the total population size known? Enter Y or N.
n

Data Display

YBarClus 0.551654
SEClus   0.0213136
```

We pointed out earlier that the total population size (number of clusters that might be sampled) has little effect on cluster-sampling calculations. To illustrate the point, we "accidentally on purpose" entered a population size of 52000. Notice that the miscalculated standard error is just a tiny bit too large.

```
How many clusters are there in the whole population?
DATA> 52000
Is the total population size known? Enter Y or N.
n

Data Display

YBarClus 0.551654
SEClus   0.0218399
```

16.15 A utility that supplies natural gas to a suburban area needs to estimate the average R value of insulation in the attic area of homes in its service area. A random sample of 18 of 19,790 blocks is selected from the area, and the R value is found for each house in the selected blocks. The data are as follows:

Block:	1	2	3	4	5	6	7	8	9
Mean:	10.1	12.5	14.0	13.5	9.3	8.0	7.0	9.0	11.2
Number of houses:	20	16	10	8	14	16	22	15	12

Block:	10	11	12	13	14	15	16	17	18
Mean:	12.0	15.0	10.2	16.0	12.0	8.2	10.0	14.2	9.0
Number of houses:	10	7	14	6	12	22	16	10	21

Relevant summary figures are

$$\sum T_i = 2610.8, \quad \sum m_i = 251, \quad \sum T_i m_i = 38{,}556.6,$$

$$\sum T_i^2 = 395{,}206.4, \quad \sum m_i^2 = 3931$$

a Calculate a 95% confidence interval for the true mean R level.

b Why might this form of sampling be adopted in preference to a simple random sample of houses?

16.16 Suppose that the data of Exercise 16.15 are wrongly assumed to have arisen from a simple random sample.

a Calculate a 95% confidence interval for the population mean. The sample mean and variance of the R values for the 251 houses included are 10.40 and 29.97, respectively.

b How does the width of this interval compare to that of the interval in Exercise 16.15? What is the explanation for the difference?

16.17 A package delivery service's operations manager wanted to estimate the time that drivers spent at each delivery office, as opposed to time spent driving between offices. If the time spent in offices was a large fraction of the total time spent in making deliveries, that would indicate that productivity could be improved by improving the procedures used at offices. To estimate the average time spent, the manager selected 24 of the 217 delivery routes, and obtained the total time spent in offices and the number of office deliveries on each route. Summary numbers were recorded in Excel as follows:

	D	E	F
1	Sampled Routes	Total of times	Total of stops
2	24	5616	587
3	Popn. of routes	Average no. of stops	
4	217	24.458	
5	Mean	Std. Error	
6	9.567	0.016	

The following Excel formulas were used to compute the cluster-sampling mean and standard error:

	D	E	F
1	Sampled routes	Total of times	Total of stops
2	=COUNT(A2:A25)	=SUM(B2:B25)	=SUM(C2:C25)
3	Popn of routes	Average no. of stops	
4	217	=$F$2/$D$2	
5	Mean	Std.error	
6	=E2/F2	=SQRT(($D$4-$D$2)/($D$2*$D$4*$E$4^2)	
		*SUM((B2:B25-$D$6*C2:C25)^2)/($D$2-1))	

a Locate the mean and standard error.

b Calculate a 95% confidence interval for the mean time over all routes and offices.

c The times were measured in minutes. Would you think that the accuracy of this interval would be good enough for the manager's purposes?

16.18 In the previous exercise, would it matter much to the resulting mean and standard error if there were a total of 267 routes rather than 217?

16.19 A state agricultural agency is charged with estimating the likely yield of wheat from farms in the state. Rather than have the (notoriously busy and optimistic) farmers submit guesses, the agency uses its own personnel, who are trained to make reasonably unbiased estimates. Given limited personnel, the agency must base their estimates on a sample. To minimize travel time, the agency decides to inspect all the farms in selected areas. The relevant wheat-growing area is divided into 412 sections, and a random sample of 20 sections is chosen. Agency personnel estimated yields for each farm in the selected sections. The data were summarized and entered into the JMP statistical package, with the following results; the column headed Deviation is $T_i - \bar{y}_c m_i$.

Total Yield	Number of Farms	Mean	Deviation	Std. Error
710	6	114.4785	23.12883	3.855842
1260	12	114.4785	-113.742	3.855842
750	8	114.4785	-165.828	3.855842
350	5	114.4785	-222.393	3.855842
250	3	114.4785	-93.4356	3.855842
1220	12	114.4785	-153.742	3.855842
420	4	114.4785	-37.9141	3.855842
2250	19	114.4785	74.90798	3.855842
1200	10	114.4785	55.21472	3.855842
670	5	114.4785	97.60736	3.855842
1100	8	114.4785	184.1718	3.855842
770	6	114.4785	83.12883	3.855842
1900	15	114.4785	182.8221	3.855842
810	7	114.4785	8.650307	3.855842
620	6	114.4785	-66.8712	3.855842
870	10	114.4785	-274.785	3.855842
850	8	114.4785	-65.8282	3.855842
520	4	114.4785	62.08589	3.855842
1120	8	114.4785	204.1718	3.855842
1020	7	114.4785	218.6503	3.855842

The mean, deviation, and standard error columns were created by JMP "formulas."

a Identify the clusters in this sampling study.

b Locate the cluster sampling mean and standard error.

c Calculate a 95% confidence interval for the true mean yield in the entire state.

16.20 A lumber company must estimate the number of board-feet of lumber available in harvest-age trees. The company owns 1200 10-acre stands of trees, from which 60 stands are selected at random. Inspectors assess the usable board-feet per tree in each stand. Summary figures are as follows:

$$\sum T_i = 4{,}735{,}000, \quad \sum m_i = 47{,}200, \quad \sum T_i m_i = 3{,}806{,}930{,}000,$$

$$\sum T_i^2 = 380{,}989{,}000{,}000, \quad \sum m_i^2 = 38{,}074{,}000$$

a Calculate $\bar{y}_c$.

b Calculate a 95% confidence interval for the mean number of board-feet per tree.

16.21 A chain of retail stores is considering discontinuing advertising mailings to its inactive accounts (those with less than $25 purchased in the past six months). There are 97 stores in the chain with an average of 1827 accounts per store. It is not possible to process the records of all stores, so a random sample of 20 stores is chosen. Analysis of the records of these stores yields the following data:

	Store									
	1	**2**	**3**	**4**	**5**	**6**	**7**	**8**	**9**	**10**
Number of Accounts	2020	1659	1854	1371	2530	1614	1901	2301	1745	1299
Total Purchases ($000)	186	153	162	114	259	158	224	261	189	117
Number of Inactive Accounts	429	371	403	327	580	312	365	417	357	226

	Store									
	11	**12**	**13**	**14**	**15**	**16**	**17**	**18**	**19**	**20**
Number of Accounts	1884	1901	1624	1346	1403	2119	1946	1784	1974	1838
Total Purchases ($000)	219	198	1446	132	265	243	216	168	199	174
Number of Inactive Accounts	394	373	327	301	415	401	373	361	411	216

a Calculate $\bar{y}_c$ for purchase amounts.

b Calculate a 95% confidence interval for the true mean sales per account in the past six months.

c Calculate a 95% confidence interval for the proportion of inactive accounts. ■

16.4

Selecting the Sample Size

S o far, we have assumed that the sample size of a survey is known. Of course, the selection of a sample size is one of the most important parts of a sample survey design. We discussed the issue of sample size determination for simple random sampling in Section 8.3. Now we extend the discussion to cover stratified and cluster sampling.

The width of a 95% confidence interval is a useful measure of the probable accuracy of a sample estimator. Because sample information is costly, the aim is to find the smallest sample size that yields a 95% (or whatever level is desired) confidence interval of a specified width, using a particular sample survey design.[1] In general, the width of

---

[1] If several designs are available, with possibly differing costs per observation, you can compute the costs and the required sample sizes and select the least expensive design.

a confidence interval depends not only on the design and sample size but also on one or more unknown variances. These variances may be estimated either in a preliminary study or by a manager's "horseback guess." Then we can find the desired sample size by trial and error or by formula.

Formulas for the sample size are usually stated in terms of the desired **half-width** E of a confidence interval. An interval of the form point estimate $\pm E$ has width $2E$ and therefore half-width E. Sample sizes needed to yield a desired half-width are shown next. In the case of stratified sampling, it is assumed that the overall sample size is allocated among strata in proportion to strata sizes, so n_i, the sample size for stratum i, equals nN_i/N. If some other allocation is chosen, the formula is a first approximation. Trial and error can be used to find a more exact value of n.

Definition 16.8   Sample Sizes for Estimating μ

Simple random sampling:

$$n = \frac{Ns^2}{(N-1)\dfrac{E^2}{z_{\alpha/2}^2} + s^2}$$

where s^2 is an estimate of the overall population variance.

Stratified random sampling:

$$n = \frac{\sum_i N_i s_i^2}{(N-1)\dfrac{E^2}{z_{\alpha/2}^2} + \dfrac{1}{N}\sum_i N_i s_i^2}$$

where s_i^2 is an estimate of the variance in stratum i.

Cluster sampling:

$$n = \frac{Ns_c^2}{(N-1)\dfrac{E^2\overline{M}^2}{z_{\alpha/2}^2} + s_c^2}$$

where s_c^2 is an estimate of the variance of cluster totals. If the estimate is based on a preliminary sample of n' clusters,

$$s_c^2 = \frac{\sum(T_i - \bar{y}_c m_i)^2}{n' - 1} \qquad \blacksquare$$

E X A M P L E   1 6 . 1 0

Use the data of Example 16.8 as preliminary information in a pilot study to calculate the sample size required to obtain a 95% confidence interval of width \$500 with cluster sampling.

Solution

From Example 16.8, we have $\sum(T_i - \bar{y}_c m_i)^2 = 15,227,502,247$; $N = 415$ and $\bar{m} = 6.04$. Therefore

$$s_c^2 = \frac{\sum(T_i - \bar{y}_c m_i)^2}{n' - 1} = \frac{15,227,502,247}{24} = 634,479,260.3$$

If the desired width is 500, $E = 250$. Substituting into the formula for n with $\overline{M}$

approximated by $\overline{m}$, we obtain

$$n = \frac{415(634, 479, 260.3)}{\dfrac{414(250)^2(6.04)^2}{(1.96)^2} + 634, 479, 260.3} = 302$$

A cluster sample of size 302 is needed to obtain a 95% confidence interval for μ with width $500 (that is, $\pm\$250$). ∎

In the same way, we can calculate approximate sample sizes for estimating either τ or π for each of the three sample survey designs, as shown in the following.

Definition 16.9   Approximate Sample Size for Estimating τ

Simple random sampling:

$$n = \frac{Ns^2}{\dfrac{(N-1)E^2}{z_{\alpha/2}^2 N^2} + s^2}$$

Stratified random sampling:

$$n = \frac{\displaystyle\sum_i N_i s_i^2}{\dfrac{(N-1)E^2}{z_{\alpha/2}^2 N^2} + \dfrac{1}{N}\sum N_i s_i^2}$$

Cluster sampling:

$$n = \frac{Ns_c^2}{\dfrac{(N-1)E^2}{z_{\alpha/2}^2 N^2} + s_c^2}$$

where $s_c^2 = [\sum_i (y_i - \bar{y}_c m_i)^2]/(n'-1)$ from a preliminary sample of n' clusters. ∎

Definition 16.10   Approximate Sample Size for Estimating π

Simple random sampling:

$$n = \frac{N\hat{\pi}(1-\hat{\pi})}{\dfrac{(N-1)E^2}{z_{\alpha/2}^2} + \hat{\pi}(1-\hat{\pi})}$$

where $\hat{\pi}$ is the estimated proportion from a preliminary sample or is a guessed value.

Stratified random sampling:

$$n = \frac{\displaystyle\sum_i N_i \hat{\pi}(1-\hat{\pi}_i)}{\dfrac{(N-1)E^2}{z_{\alpha/2}^2} + \dfrac{1}{N}\sum_i N_i \hat{\pi}_i(1-\hat{\pi}_i)}$$

where $\hat{\pi}_i$ is the estimated proportion obtained from a preliminary sample from the ith stratum.

Cluster sampling:

$$n = \frac{Ns_c^2}{\dfrac{(N-1)E^2\overline{M}^2}{z_{\alpha/2}^2} + s_c^2}$$

where $s_c^2 = [\sum_i (a_i - \hat{\pi}_c m_i)^2]/(n'-1)$ is from a preliminary sample of n' clusters.

Note: If no preliminary information is available and it is difficult to guess π_i, substitute $\hat{\pi}_i = .5$ to obtain a conservative sample size (one that is likely to be larger than needed). ■

E X A M P L E   1 6 . 1 1

The manager for a chain of department stores wants to conduct an in-house survey to estimate the proportion of accounts that has been delinquent by one month or more at least once in the previous calendar year. The chain consists of five stores. To reduce the cost of sampling, it is decided to use a stratified random sample, with the stores serving as strata. Use the information shown here to determine the sample size (and allocation) necessary to achieve a 95% confidence interval for π with a width of .02.

Stratum	Stratum Size N_i	Extimate of π_i from Previous Year
1	1000	.22
2	2500	.35
3	3200	.24
4	1700	.30
5	4100	.15

Solution

The formula for n is

$$n = \frac{\sum_i N_i \hat{\pi}_i (1 - \hat{\pi}_i)}{\dfrac{(N-1)E^2}{z_{\alpha/2}^2} + \dfrac{1}{N}\sum_i N_i \hat{\pi}_i (1 - \hat{\pi}_i)}$$

We'll use the previous year's estimates for the $\hat{\pi}_i$'s in the formula and set the interval half-width E equal to .01. Then

$$\sum_i N_i \hat{\pi}_i (1 - \hat{\pi}_i) = 1000(.22)(.78) + 2500(.35)(.65) + \cdots + 4100(.15)(.85)$$

$$= 2203.78$$

The required sample size is

$$n = \frac{2203.78}{12,499\dfrac{(.01)^2}{(1.96)^2} + \dfrac{2203.78}{12,500}} = \frac{2203.78}{.5017} \approx 4393$$

The required total sample size is approximately 4393. The allocation of this sample size to the strata utilizes the formula $n_i = n(N_i/N)$. Thus

$$n_i = 4393 \left(\frac{1000}{12,500} \right) \approx 351$$

$$n_2 = 4393 \left(\frac{2500}{12,500} \right) \approx 879$$

$$n_3 = 4393 \left(\frac{3200}{12,500} \right) \approx 1125$$

$$n_4 = 4393 \left(\frac{1700}{12,500} \right) \approx 597$$

$$n_5 = 4393 \left(\frac{4100}{12,500} \right) = 1441 \quad \blacksquare$$

EXERCISES

16.22 In planning a stratified sample, a manager guesses that all strata variances equal approximately 40. Each of the 10 strata is made up of 1000 individuals, and equal sample sizes are to be taken in all strata. How large a sample is required to estimate the population mean to within $\pm.5$ unit with 95% confidence?

16.23 The variance for the overall population of Exercise 16.22 is guessed as approximately 80.

    a If a simple random sample is taken, how large a sample is required to estimate the mean to within $\pm.5$ unit with 95% confidence?

    b Is there any major advantage to stratification in this situation? Why?

16.24 A population is divided into 3000 clusters, with an average cluster size of 40. The variance of total cluster scores s_c^2 is estimated to be roughly 20,000. How many clusters must be sampled to yield a 95% confidence interval for the population mean with a half-width of 4?

16.25 Refer to Exercise 16.15. How many blocks have to be sampled to yield a 90% confidence interval with a half-width of 2.0?

16.26 The utility company of Exercise 16.15 also wants to estimate the proportion of homes with insulation that meets minimum government standards. A (very) preliminary sample of five blocks is taken. If the number of houses per block is 20, 15, 16, 18, and 22, and the number of houses per block with at least the minimum insulation is 3, 6, 4, 3, and 5, respectively, how many additional blocks must be sampled to estimate this proportion to within $\pm.2$ with 95% confidence? $\blacksquare$

16.5   Other Sampling Techniques

The sample survey designs that we have discussed in this chapter are among the most widely used designs in business surveys. There are, however, many extensions to these designs, as well as other sampling techniques. We discuss a few of these very briefly.

Systematic sampling

Systematic sampling is a useful alternative to simple random sampling that is easier to use and hence less subject to interviewer errors. To select a systematic sample, we imagine the elements of the population numbered from 1 to N. A random selection of one element is made from the first k elements of the population. Every kth element of the population is selected thereafter. This is called a 1-in-k systematic sample. For example, suppose a manager wants to sample $n = 200$ of a total of $N = 1000$ invoices to determine the proportion of invoices with one or more errors. A 1-in-5 systematic sample gives the desired sample size and is easy to obtain. Imagine that the invoices are numbered from 1 to 1000.

To obtain a 1-in-5 systematic sample, we make a random selection of one invoice from the first five. Suppose number 2 is selected. Then we take every fifth invoice from there on. The 200 invoices to be included in the sample are invoices numbered 2, 7, 12, 17, ..., 997. The formulas for point estimates of μ, τ, and π and the corresponding 95% confidence intervals are the same as those for simple random sampling.

If systematic sampling is easier to use and the formulas are the same as for simple random sampling, why would we ever use simple random sampling? Sometimes the elements of the population, when ordered, have inherent cycles. For example, sales volumes for grocery stores tend to have weekly cycles, with greater sales volumes toward the end of the week. Similarly, retail sales of over-the-counter cough syrups and other cold preparations have cyclic sales patterns over the year, as do prices on agricultural commodities. If a systematic sample is used and the sampling pattern corresponds to the inherent cycle, a bias is introduced; the population parameter of interest is either consistently overestimated or underestimated. Systematic sampling should also be avoided if the manager has no information about the population size N, because it is then impossible to determine the sampling rate (value of k) to achieve the desired sample size. For further details, see Scheaffer, Mendenhall, and Ott (1986).

Recall that, with cluster sampling, the elements of the population are arranged in naturally occurring groups (clusters), and a simple random sample of clusters is selected. Each element in the selected clusters is surveyed. Sometimes, however, the cluster sizes are too large to make it feasible to sample all elements in the selected clusters. In these situations, we could employ **two-stage cluster sampling**. First we obtain a simple random sample of clusters; then we select a simple random sample of elements from the selected clusters. Pollsters in national surveys often use two-stage cluster sampling. For example, a national public opinion survey on the mood of the nation could be done using geographic areas (such as counties) as clusters and then taking a simple random sample of elements within the sampled clusters.

two-stage cluster sampling

There are obvious extensions to two-stage clustering. In the previous example, we could use multistage cluster sampling by first obtaining a simple random sample of states, then a simple random sample of counties within the sampled states, then a simple random sample of voting districts within the selected counties, and finally a simple random sample of people within the selected voting districts. By subdividing the population a number of times, it is possible to use well-defined sampling units at each stage, and the final stage (for example, voting district) has a readily available list of elements (frame) from which to draw the simple random sample of opinions. For further details on multistage cluster sampling, see Cochran (1977), Kish (1965), and Scheaffer, Mendenhall, and Ott (1986).

randomized-response technique

The **randomized-response technique** was developed by Warner (1965) to improve the response rate of individuals surveyed about sensitive or embarrassing questions. Direct questions about involvement with such activities as shoplifting, abortion, tax evasion, drug usage, and sexual harassment, for example, are often difficult to respond to truthfully.

We illustrate the randomized-response technique for the situation in which a yes or no answer is required. Extensions to this original work are discussed in Greenberg et al. (1971). The randomized-response technique involves pairing the sensitive question with an innocuous question. For example, in a survey of factory supervisors, those surveyed could be asked to answer yes or no to one of the two questions:

(sensitive) A: Have you been involved in sexual harassment of employees of the opposite sex?

(nonsensitive) B: Is your birthday in January, February, or March?

The particular question given to an interviewee is unknown to the interviewer. Typically, a box containing a certain number of red and white balls is presented to the interviewee. The interviewee selects one of the balls without revealing the color to the interviewer. If the ball selected is red, the interviewee answers yes or no to the A question. Otherwise, the interviewee answers yes or no to the B question.

The interesting result is that, without knowing which question individuals answer, but knowing the proportion of red balls in the box and the proportion of yes responses (to either question) in the sample, it is possible to estimate π, the proportion of persons who have been involved with sexual harassment. The randomized response technique is described in greater detail in Warner (1965) and Greenberg et al. (1971).

Summing Up

In this chapter, we have presented several sampling approaches: simple random sampling, stratified sampling, one-stage and two-stage cluster sampling, and systematic sampling. What are the considerations when deciding which sampling method to use?

What methods are feasible? There must be a method to ensure (nearly) unbiased sampling. Haphazard, unplanned sampling is almost worthless. A good sampling frame of individual units or of clusters is highly desirable. With a table of random numbers (or computer-generated random numbers), one can guarantee legitimate random sampling. If an explicit sampling frame can't be constructed, a method that clearly guarantees randomness and avoids bias should be used. One-in-k systematic sampling is such a method—*provided* that one can safely assume there are no cycles in the units that might match the cycle of sampling. Random sampling can be done at random times; there are watches available that beep at random times. An important question about any sampling method is: Will particular types of units systematically, predictably be overrepresented or underrepresented? If there are, the method is biased and undesirable.

When there are several feasible methods, the decision can be based on efficiency. If the units can be grouped according to a basis of interest such as age or educational level, stratified sampling of the groups should be considered. This method will be particularly advantageous if the groups (strata) are relatively homogeneous, with little variability within strata. If the units can be divided into subsets that are easily sampled together—whether because they are geographically close together, in the same computer subfile, or for some other reason—then cluster sampling may allow for a larger sample at lower cost. If measuring every unit in a cluster is not desirable because the clusters are too big or because the units in a cluster are so similar as to be uninformative, two-stage cluster sampling might well be useful. It can be tempting to define a very elaborate, multistage sampling scheme involving layers of stratification and clusterings—just remember that the old acronym K.I.S.S. (Keep It Simple, Stupid) applies to sampling methods, too.

Before the measurements are actually made on sampled units, it's crucial to be sure of what is being measured. If a questionnaire is being used, it should be pretested for clarity and lack of ambiguity. If sensitive questions are involved, the randomized-response technique may be helpful. If financial data from many companies are being collected, it's important that the accounting ground rules be the same for all companies. A little anticipation can save a great deal of grief.

However the sample is finally conducted, as long as it's conducted thoughtfully, the important payoff is that sampling allows managers to get useful information, at a reasonable cost, that otherwise would be prohibitively difficult to obtain.

EXERCISES

16.27 A publisher of college dictionaries surveys bookstores in the neighborhoods of various colleges and universities to determine the average number of dictionaries displayed on shelves. To do this, the publisher selects 12 colleges and universities at random from a list of all accredited institutions of higher education. Every bookstore on or near these 12 campuses is visited and the number of dictionaries on display is counted.

a Identify the sample survey method used. Is it a stratified sample or a cluster sample?

b Why might this method be preferred to a simple random sample of bookstores?

16.28 The survey of Exercise 16.27 yields the following data:

School	Number of Stores	Number of Dictionaries
1	2	4, 6
2	6	8, 3, 4, 5, 2, 5
3	3	5, 7, 2
4	1	6
5	2	4, 8
6	4	3, 2, 5, 2
7	3	4, 7, 3
8	1	5
9	2	6, 3
10	4	4, 4, 2, 6
11	3	3, 2, 3
12	2	5, 5

a Calculate a 95% confidence interval for the true mean number of displayed dictionaries.

b What is the 95% confidence interval if the data are assumed (incorrectly) to be the result of a simple random sample?

c How large a sample of universities is required to estimate the mean within $\pm.1$ with 95% confidence?

16.29 An "inner-ring" suburb of a large eastern United States city was considering a program to replace dangerous sidewalk squares in its residential neighborhoods at a cost to both the township government and the homeowners. To get an idea of the extent of the problem, the township manager selected 10 city blocks randomly from among the 8774 blocks in the township. A township employee counted the number of dangerous squares in front of each house on the selected blocks. The results were analyzed using the Minitab CLUSSAM macro, with the following results:

```
MTB > %CLUSSAM 'BadSqs' 'Block'
Executing from file: CLUSSAM.MAC

Data Display

Row  ClusNum  ClusTots  Clusn

  1      1       15       12
  2      2       35       24
  3      3       17       18
  4      4       22       16
  5      5       29       20
  6      6       17       14
  7      7       20       17
  8      8       14       13
  9      9       19       16
 10     10       17       16

How many clusters are there in the whole population?
DATA> 8774
Is the total population size known? Enter Y or N.
n

Data Display

YBarClus  1.23494
SEClus    0.0612418
```

a In this sampling procedure, what are the clusters?

b Calculate a 95% confidence interval for the mean number of bad sidewalk squares per house in the entire suburb.

c Write a one-paragraph summary of the results to the township manager, using nontechnical language.

16.30 In the output of the previous exercise, the macro requested the number of clusters in the whole population. If the number entered had been 18,774 instead of 8774, how large a change would you expect in the resulting mean and standard error?

16.31 An auto parts firm wants to estimate the average time required to fill its orders. The orders are classified into four types:

A: single item, off the shelf

B: single item, production required

C: multiple item, off the shelf

D: multiple item, production required

Random samples of 30 orders of each of the four types are selected, and times are determined.

a Identify the type of sample survey design.

b Why might this kind of design be preferable to a simple random sample of 120 orders?

16.32 Suppose that the orders of the previous exercise are numbered (without regard to type) from 0001 to 8260, and suppose that you have a table of 4-digit random numbers. How would you go about actually drawing the sample? You can expect to get some numbers larger than 8260 and some repetitions. It is very unlikely that the first 120 orders selected would contain exactly 30 of each type.

16.33 Suppose that the survey of Exercise 16.31 yields the following results (times in days):

Type	Mean	Standard Deviation
A	3.21	.82
B	7.39	2.14
C	4.65	1.05
D	9.27	3.65

Assume that the four types of orders are equally represented in the population of all orders. Calculate a 95% confidence interval for the true mean time.

16.34 Assume that the population of orders in Exercise 16.33 consists of 2216 *A*'s, 2715 *B*'s, 1874 *C*'s, and 1455 *D*'s.

a Recalculate the 95% confidence interval.

b How sensitive is the interval to assumptions about the number of each type of order?

16.35 Assume that the population of orders is as given in Exercise 16.34. How large a sample is needed to estimate the mean time within ±.3 day with 95% confidence? How should the sample be allocated among the four types?

16.36 A survey of university students in a large, multicampus state system obtained simple random samples separately for students in each of the four years of an undergraduate program. As one question in a much larger survey, the students were asked whether they agreed or disagreed with the statement "I expect to change my career completely at least once in my working life." The answers were analyzed using Excel, with the following results:

	A	B	C	D	E	F
1	College class	Total in popn.	Sample size	Number agreeing	Fraction	PiHatStr
2	Fr.	54000	422	361	0.8555	0.8241
3	Soph.	51000	405	337	0.8321	SEStr
4	Jr.	49000	389	302	0.7763	0.0094
5	Sr.	48000	392	325	0.8291	v

a Find a 95% confidence interval for the true proportion agreeing.

b If the population totals had each been 50,000, would you expect the confidence interval to change substantially? Why?

16.37 Assume that a follow-up survey of students in the system in Exercise 16.36 is to be done the next year. A half-width of .04 for a 95% confidence interval is desired, the sample will be allocated equally over the four classes, and the proportion agreeing should not change greatly. What sample size is needed?

16.38 An executive recruiting firm (popularly known as a "headhunter") performs searches for educational institutions, government agencies, private industry, and nonprofit organizations. The firm sampled its records of recent searches and found the time in weeks needed for searches in the four areas. The data were analyzed using Minitab.

```
MTB > %StratSam ´srchtime´ ´industry´
Executing from file: StratSam.MAC

Data Display

  Row  StrNums  StrMeans   StrVars

    1        1   34.6250   267.850
    2        2   23.8500   212.661
    3        3   27.9667   181.137
    4        4   40.6875   634.896


Enter list of population sizes by stratum
When done, enter     End
DATA> 300 600 600 300
DATA> end


Data Display

YBarStr   29.8243
SEStr     1.80859
```

Calculate a 95% confidence interval for the population mean.

16.39 The population sizes entered into Minitab in the previous exercise were very rough approximations of the numbers expected by the firm in the next year. To see if these numbers had much impact on the result, the analyst also entered a different set of population sizes.

```
Enter list of population sizes by stratum
When done, enter     End
DATA> 600 300 300 600
DATA> end


Data Display

YBarStr   33.7403
SEStr     2.55737
```

Did the change affect the point estimate of the mean? If so, why?

16.40 A large hospital surveys its accounts for the past year to see what proportion of accounts was not settled within 60 days. The accounts are stratified by size, and random samples are taken of all accounts. The following data are obtained:

Stratum	Account Size	Total Number of Accounts	Number of Accounts Sampled	Number of Accounts Not Settled in 60 Days
A	Under $100	8251	41	5
B	100–499	2917	29	6
C	500–999	843	42	8
D	1000–2499	487	49	15
E	2500 or over	202	40	23

Calculate a 95% confidence interval for the true proportion of accounts not settled in 60 days.

16.41 The formula for required stratified sample size given in Section 16.2 is based on the assumption that the sample size is allocated among strata in proportion to the relative sizes of the strata. This assumption does not hold for Exercise 16.40.

    a Use the formula to calculate the sample size required to give the half-width that was actually obtained in Exercise 16.40.

    b How much difference in required sample size is caused by the difference in allocation?

16.42 A regional bank did a test of the profitability of putting automatic teller machines into three types of locations: supermarkets, shopping malls, and rest areas along interstate highways. The bank placed ATMs in 20 markets, 20 malls, and 10 rest areas for a month; the locations were effectively random samples from 400 markets, 400 malls, and 200 rest areas that the bank could service. The weekly fee income from each machine was determined. The results were analyzed by JMP.

Location	Popn Size	Sample Size	Mean	Std. Dev.	Str Mean	Str Std. Error
Markets	400	20	164.3055	69.1035	182.4312	9.159808
Malls	400	20	246.531	71.0777		
Rest Areas	200	10	90.483	48.6178		

    a Calculate a 95% confidence interval for the population mean.

    b Calculate a 95% confidence interval for the total income, assuming 1000 ATMs.

16.43 In the preceding exercise, would the confidence interval for the mean change greatly if the population sizes were 800, 800, and 400? Why?

16.44 A business that sells to suburban governments wanted to estimate the proportion of such governments that uses a full-time manager to run day-to-day operations. To get the information required calls to each government, which took time. To keep from spending too long on the task, the president of the business took a sample of 20 standard metropolitan statistical areas (SMSAs) from the largest 200 areas. For each sampled SMSA, the president determined TOT, the total number of suburban governments, and M, the number of governments that use a full-time manager. The data were analyzed using the Statistix package. Using the transformation feature of that package, the president computed the cluster-sampling proportion (labeled CLUSMEAN) and (after intermediate steps) the cluster-sampling standard error (CLUSSE). Here is the output:

MA	TOT	M	CLUSMEAN	DEVIATN	VARDEV	CLUSSE
1	12	8	0.54838	1.41935	6.68262	0.03634
2	17	8	0.54838	-1.32258	6.68262	0.03634
3	32	19	0.54838	1.45161	6.68262	0.03634
4	11	6	0.54838	-0.03225	6.68262	0.03634
5	20	12	0.54838	1.03225	6.68262	0.03634
6	10	5	0.54838	-0.48387	6.68262	0.03634
7	14	9	0.54838	1.32258	6.68262	0.03634
8	20	10	0.54838	-0.96774	6.68262	0.03634
9	14	11	0.54838	3.32258	6.68262	0.03634
10	11	7	0.54838	0.96774	6.68262	0.03634
11	18	16	0.54838	6.12903	6.68262	0.03634
12	18	11	0.54838	1.12903	6.68262	0.03634
13	10	5	0.54838	-0.48387	6.68262	0.03634
14	11	8	0.54838	1.96774	6.68262	0.03634
15	14	5	0.54838	-2.67741	6.68262	0.03634
16	14	3	0.54838	-4.67741	6.68262	0.03634
17	19	5	0.54838	-5.41935	6.68262	0.03634
18	13	6	0.54838	-1.12903	6.68262	0.03634
19	20	11	0.54838	0.03225	6.68262	0.03634
20	12	5	0.54838	-1.58064	6.68262	0.03634

    Is this procedure really a cluster-sampling method? Assuming that it is, what are the clusters? What does the output indicate about a confidence interval for the true proportion?

16.45 A problem for the study in the preceding exercise is that a few SMSAs do not have suburban governments because the central city is permitted to annex adjacent areas as they develop. These SMSAs were not considered part of the relevant population, but it wasn't known how many such areas there were. How critical is it to the calculations whether N is taken to be 200 or some smaller number such as 180 or 190?

16.46 A city agency buys streetlight bulbs from four different suppliers. The contract specifications require that no more than 30% of the bulbs should function for less than 5000 hours. The agency took samples of bulbs from each supplier, installed them, and measured the lifetime of each bulb. The data (both mean life and percentage of bulbs lasting less than 5000 hours) were analyzed using Minitab. The measured hours were labeled "bulblife"; each bulb that lasted less than 5000 hours was a 1 in the lowqual variable, with the remaining bulbs 0 in this variable.

```
MTB > %Stratsam 'bulblife' 'supplier'
Executing from file: Stratsam.MAC

Data Display

   Row   StrNums   StrMeans    StrVars

    1       1        9059      30640626
    2       2        9871      44164708
    3       3        9091      31735776
    4       4       10344      51274812


Enter list of population sizes by stratum
When done, enter     End
DATA> 80000 80000 80000 80000
DATA> end

Data Display

YBarStr  9591.25
SEStr     313.868


MTB > %StratSam 'lowqual' 'supplier'
Executing from file: StratSam.MAC

Data Display

   Row   StrNums   StrMeans    StrVars

    1       1        0.29      0.207980
    2       2        0.22      0.173333
    3       3        0.25      0.189394
    4       4        0.22      0.173333


Enter list of population sizes by stratum
When done, enter     End
DATA> 80000 80000 80000 80000
DATA> end

Data Display

YBarStr  0.245000
SEStr    0.0215511
```

a Calculate a 95% confidence interval for the mean bulblife.

b Calculate a 95% confidence interval for the proportion of low-quality bulbs.

16.47 In the preceding exercise, if the population sizes for suppliers 1 and 2 had been 90,000 and the population sizes for suppliers 3 and 4 had been 70,000, should there be much change in either confidence interval? Why or why not?

16.48 A bakery in a large city was considering marketing a pastry through convenience stores—those that open early in the morning and sell (among other things) coffee to automobile commuters. One question that concerned the bakery president was how many competitive products were in such stores. There were far too many such stores in the bakery's service region to check every one. A summer intern (a relative of the president's) was assigned to take a sample. The intern divided the service area into 140 squares, each 2 miles square, and selected 12 of them at random. For each selected square, the intern drove to each convenience store and counted the number of competitive brands on the shelf. Two squares had no convenience stores in them. The intern entered the data into Minitab and analyzed them three ways: as a simple random sample, as a stratified sample with each square as a stratum, and as a cluster sample. Here is the Minitab output:

```
MTB > tinterval 'Stock'

Confidence Intervals


Variable     N     Mean    StDev  SE Mean      95.0 % C.I.
Stock       36    4.639    1.659    0.276  (   4.078,    5.200)

MTB > %STRATSAM 'Stock' 'Section'
Executing from file: F:\MTBWIN\MACROS\STRATSAM.MAC

Data Display

 Row  StrNums  StrMeans    StrVars

   1        1   5.75000    0.91667
   2        2   2.66667    0.33333
   3        3   6.00000    2.00000
   4        4   8.00000          *
   5        5   7.00000    0.00000
   6        6   3.71429    0.23810
   7        7   7.00000    0.00000
   8        8   4.00000    0.50000
   9        9   3.00000    1.00000
  10       10   3.75000    0.25000


Enter list of population sizes by stratum
When done, enter    End
DATA> 4 3 5 1 2 7 2 5 3 4
DATA> end
MTB > -Smallns)/(BigNs-1))))
                J
*** Values out of bounds during operation at J
    Missing returned 1 times on line 3

Data Display

YBarStr  4.63889
SEStr    0

MTB > %CLUSSAM 'Stock' 'Section'
Executing from file: CLUSSAM.MAC

Data Display

 Row  ClusNum  ClusTots  Clusn

   1        1        23      4
   2        2         8      3
   3        3        30      5
   4        4         8      1
   5        5        14      2
   6        6        26      7
```

7	7	14	2
8	8	20	5
9	9	9	3
10	10	15	4

```
How many clusters are there in the whole population?
DATA> 140
Is the total population size known? Enter Y or N.
n

Data Display

YBarClus 4.63889
SEClus    0.442432
```

At this point, the intern was stumped. Should the procedure be regarded as a simple random sample, a stratified sample (despite the troubling error message), or a cluster sample? What is the most appropriate confidence interval to report back to the president? Write a brief memo describing your opinion. ■

CASE STUDY

Sampling Methods

A motel chain recently introduced a special club for high-usage customers, mostly those who use the chain frequently on business trips. The club offers various "perks" for its members; the chain hopes to make up the cost by increased usage and by expenditures of club members in motel restaurants and lounges. Club members make reservations through a centralized system, so the chain can determine usage directly. However, restaurant and lounge expenditures aren't available centrally, and the totals they report aren't really useful because they combine club members and non-members.

To get an indication of the average restaurant/lounge expenditure per club member and the proportion of club members who used the restaurant or lounge at all, the chain picked 30 of its 612 motels. Each motel determined how many club members stayed at the motel during a specified week, how many used the motel's restaurant and lounge facilities, and the total dollar restaurant/lounge expenditure of club members at the motel during that week. The chain's records showed that there had been 61,518 club members staying at some motel in the chain during that week—an average of 100.52 per motel.

The data have been provided to you with a request that you give the chain's director of promotions estimates of the chainwide proportion of users and average expenditure per user. The director vaguely remembers what a confidence interval is, but will need clear explanations of any technical terms in your report.

In addition, the director is considering a longer-range study. The chain divides its motels into urban, small-city, and roadside units. The director has speculated that restaurant use by club members varies

greatly among the three types of motels. You have been invited to make suggestions about how to obtain data to check this speculation.

motel	totalnum	numused	total$
541	82	65	1789.66
603	136	103	2992.73
118	90	70	2115.65
285	77	48	1629.12
378	121	98	4477.40
116	88	68	2387.59
233	144	115	2638.08
322	111	96	1872.58
528	92	80	2520.17
245	94	71	1764.60
384	79	62	1922.76
383	108	81	3211.59
69	93	77	2231.67
181	85	66	2007.10
508	152	122	4651.71
78	108	80	2110.06
184	91	74	2437.86
202	88	62	1910.82
244	94	77	2474.85
144	113	90	4593.19
502	88	66	1158.76
172	84	62	2449.39
342	121	95	2198.28
547	106	88	2358.49
320	97	71	2830.13
40	79	55	970.76
610	133	111	2967.30
536	87	70	2409.40
391	94	71	1380.08
70	90	60	2318.05

A hopeful young chef name of Hampel
Invited friends in for a sample.
But after one taste,
They fled in great haste.
With Hampel, a sample was ample.

17

Data Management and Report Preparation

In the past chapters we've discussed particular statistical methods, how those methods are applied to specific data sets, and how findings from statistical analyses in the form of computer output are interpreted. We have not concentrated on the processing steps that one follows between the time the data are received and the time they are available in computer-readable form for analysis, nor have we discussed the form and content of the report that summarizes the results of a statistical analysis. In this chapter, we consider the data-processing steps and statistical report writing. This chapter is not a complete manual with all the tools required; rather, it is an overview—what a manager should know about these steps. As an example, the chapter reflects standard procedures in the pharmaceutical industry, which is highly regulated. Procedures differ somewhat in other industries. ■

17.1

Preparing Data for Statistical Analysis

 e begin with a discussion of the steps involved in processing data from a study. In practice, these steps may consume 75% of the total effort from the receipt of the raw data to the presentation of results from the analysis. What are these steps, why are they so important, and why are they so time-consuming?

To answer these questions, let's list the major data-processing steps in the cycle, which begin with receipt of the data and end when the statistical analysis begins. Then we'll discuss each step separately.

Definition 17.1   Steps in Preparing Data for Analysis

1   Receiving the raw data source

2   Creating the database from the raw data source

3   Editing the database

4   Correcting and clarifying the raw data source

5   Finalizing the database

6   Creating data files from the database   ■

1. Receiving the raw data source. For each study that is to be summarized and analyzed, the data arrive in some form, which we'll refer to as the **raw data source**. For a clinical trial, the raw data source is usually case report forms, sheets of $8\frac{1}{2}'' \times 11''$ paper that have been used to record study data for each patient entered into the study. For other types of studies, the raw data source may be sheets of paper from a laboratory notebook, a magnetic tape (or any other form of machine-readable data), hand tabulations, and so on.

It is important to retain the raw data source because it is the beginning of the **data trail**, which leads from the raw data to the conclusions drawn from a study. Many consulting operations involved with the analysis and summarization of many different studies keep a log that contains vital information related to the study and raw data source. General information contained in a study log is shown next.

Definition 17.2   Log for Study Data

1   Data received, and from whom

2   Study investigator

3   Statistician (and others) assigned

4   Brief description of study

5   Treatments (compounds, preparations, and so on) studied

6   Raw data source

7   Response(s) measured

8   Reference number for study

9   Estimated (actual) completion date

10   Other pertinent information   ■

Later, when the study has been analyzed and results have been communicated, additional information can be added to the log on how the study results were communicated, where these results are recorded, what data files have been saved, and where these files are stored.

2. Creating the database from the raw data source. For most studies that are scheduled for a statistical analysis, a machine-readable database is created. The steps taken to create the database and the eventual form of the database vary from one operation to another, depending on the software systems to be used in the statistical analysis. However, we can give a few guidelines based on the form of the entry system.

When the data are to be *key-entered* at a terminal, the raw data are first checked for legibility. Any illegible numbers or letters or other problems should be brought to the attention of the study coordinator. Then a coding guide that assigns column numbers and variable names to the data is filled out. Certain codes for missing values (for example, those not available) are also defined here. Also, it is helpful to give a brief description of each variable. The data file keyed in at the terminal is referred to as the **machine-readable database**. A listing of the contents of the database should be obtained and checked carefully against the raw data source. Any errors should be corrected at the terminal and verified against an updated listing.

Sometimes data are received in machine-readable form. In these situations, the magnetic tape or disk file is considered to be the database. You must, however, have a coding guide to "read" the database. Using the coding guide, obtain a listing of the contents of the database and check it *carefully* to see that all numbers and characters look reasonable and that proper formats were used to create the file. Any problems that arise must be resolved before proceeding further.

Some data sets are so small that it is not necessary to create a machine-readable data file from the raw data source. Instead, calculations can be performed by hand or the data entered into an electronic calculator. In these situations, check any calculations to see that they make sense. Don't believe everything you see; redoing the calculations is not a bad idea.

3. Editing the database. The types of edits done and the completeness of the editing process really depend on the type of study and how concerned you are about the accuracy and completeness of the data prior to analysis. For example, in using SAS files it is wise to examine the minimum, maximum, and frequency distribution for each variable to make certain nothing looks unreasonable.

Certain other checks should be made. Plot the data and look for problems. Also, certain **logic checks** should be done, depending on the structure of the data. If, for example, data are recorded for patients during several different visits, then the data recorded for visit 2 can't be earlier than the data for visit 1; similarly, if a patient is lost to follow-up after visit 2, we can't have any data for that patient at later visits.

For small data sets, we can do these data edits by hand, but for large data sets the job may be too time-consuming and tedious. If machine editing is required, look for a software system that allows the user to specify certain data edits. Even so, for more complicated edits and logic checks, it may be necessary to have a customized edit program written in order to machine edit the data. This programming chore can be a time-consuming step; plan for this well in advance of receipt of the data.

4. Correcting and clarifying the raw data source. Questions frequently arise concerning the legibility or accuracy of the raw data during any one of the steps from the receipt of the raw data to the communication of the results from the statistical analysis. We have found it helpful to keep a list of these problems or discrepancies in order to define the data trail for a study. If a correction (or clarification) is required to the raw data source, this should be indicated on the form and the appropriate change made to the raw data source. If no correction is required, this should be indicated on the form as well. Keep in mind that the machine-readable database should be changed to reflect any changes made to the raw data source.

5. Finalizing the database. You may have been led to believe that all data for a study arrive at one time. This, of course, is not always the case. For example, with a marketing survey, different geographic locations may be surveyed at different times, and hence those responsible for data processing do not receive all the data at one time. All these subsets of data, however, must be processed through the cycles required to create, edit, and correct the database. Eventually, the study is declared complete and the data is processed into the database. At this time, the database should be reviewed again and final corrections made before beginning the analysis. This is because, for large data sets, the analysis and summarization chores take considerable staff and computer time. It's better to agree on a final database analysis than to have to repeat all analyses on a changed database at a later date.

6. Creating data files from the database. Generally, one or two sets of data files are created from the machine-readable database. The first set, referred to as **original files**, reflects the basic structure of the database. A listing of the files is checked against the database listing to verify that the variables have been read with correct formats and missing value codes have been retained. For some studies, the original files are actually used for editing the database.

A second set of data files, called **work files**, may be created from the original files. Work files are designed to facilitate the analysis. They may require restructuring of the original files, a selection of important variables, or the creation or addition of new variables by insertion, computation, or transformation. A listing of the work files is checked against that of the original files to ensure proper restructuring and variable selection. Computed and transformed variables are checked by hand calculations to verify the program code.

logic checks

original files

work files

If original and work files are SAS data sets, you should utilize the documentation features provided by SAS. At the time an SAS data set is created, a descriptive label for the data set of up to 40 characters should be assigned. The label can be stored with the data set, imprinted wherever the contents procedure is used to print the data set's contents. All variables can be given descriptive names, up to 8 characters in length, which are meaningful to those involved in the project. In addition, variable labels up to 40 characters in length can be used to provide additional information. Title statements can be included in the SAS code to identify the project and describe each job. For each file, a listing (proc print) and a dictionary (proc contents) can be retained.

For files created from the database using other software packages, use the labeling and documentation features available in the computer program.

Even if appropriate statistical methods are applied to data, the conclusions drawn from the study are only as good as the data on which they are based. So you be the judge. The amount of time spent on these data-processing chores before analysis really depends on the nature of the study, the quality of the raw data source, and how confident you want to be about the completeness and accuracy of the data.

17.2 Guidelines for a Statistical Analysis and Report

In this section, we briefly discuss a few guidelines for performing a statistical analysis and list some important elements of a statistical report used to communicate results. The statistical analysis of a large study can usually be broken down into three types of analyses: (1) preliminary analyses, (2) primary analyses, and (3) backup analyses.

preliminary analyses

The **preliminary analyses**, which are often descriptive or graphic, familiarize the statistician with the data and provide a foundation for all subsequent analyses. These analyses may include frequency distributions, histograms, descriptive statistics, an examination of comparability of the treatment groups, correlations, or univariate and bivariate plots.

primary analyses
backup analyses

Primary analyses address the objectives of the study and the analyses on which conclusions are drawn. **Backup analyses** include alternate methods for examining the data that confirm the results of the primary analyses; they may also include new statistical methods that are not as readily accepted as the more standard methods. Several guidelines for analyses follow.

Definition 17.3   Preliminary, Primary, and Backup Analyses

1 Analyses should be performed with software that has been extensively tested.

2 Computer output should be labeled to reflect which study is analyzed, what subjects (animals, patients, and so on) are used in the analysis, and a brief description of the analysis preferred. For example, TITLE statements in SAS are very helpful.

3 Variable labels and value labels (for example, $0 =$ none, $1 =$ mild) should appear on the output.

4 A list of the data used in each analysis should be provided.

5 The output for all analyses should be checked *carefully*. Did the job run successfully? Are the sample sizes, means, and degrees of freedom correct? Other checks may be necessary as well.

6 All preliminary, primary, and backup analyses that provide the informational base from which study conclusions are drawn should be saved.   ■

After the statistical analysis is completed, conclusions must be drawn and the results communicated to the intended audience. Sometimes it is necessary to communicate these results as a formal written statistical report. A general outline for a statistical report that we have found useful and informative follows.

Definition 17.4   General Outline for a Statistical Report

1   Summary

2   Introduction

3   Experimental design and study procedures

4   Descriptive statistics

5   Statistical methodology

6   Results and conclusions

7   Discussion

8   Data listings   ■

17.3   Documentation and Storage of Results

The final part of this cycle of data processing, analysis, and summarization concerns the documentation and storage of results. For formal statistical analyses that are subject to careful scrutiny by others, it is important to provide detailed documentation for all data processing and the statistical analyses so the data trail is clear and the database or work files readily accessible. Then the reviewer can follow what has been done, redo it, or extend the analyses. The elements of a documentation and storage file depend on the particular setting in which you work. The contents for a general documentation storage file are as follows.

Definition 17.5   Study Documentation and Storage File

1   Statistical report

2   Study description

3   Random code (used to assign subjects to treatment groups)

4   Important correspondence

5   File creation information

6   Preliminary, primary, and backup analyses

7   Raw data source

8   A data management sheet, which includes the log, as well as information on the storage of the data files   ■

Summary

We hope the information presented in this chapter has opened your eyes and broadened your perspective on data processing and statistical analysis. Most textbooks assume that the data are ready for analysis when received or displayed. In practice, however, much work is required to prepare the data for analysis and to write a report. The material presented here gives the flavor of what is being done in the pharmaceutical industry. Because many other businesses or experimental settings are less highly regulated, it may be possible to relax some of these steps. The important point is that you should actively consider whether these steps are required for a study; don't just ignore them.

Besides discussing the steps required to prepare data for analysis, we have presented a few guidelines for a statistical analysis, a general outline for a statistical report, and the contents of a documentation and storage system. Remember, these are only examples of what can be done. Other variations are certainly reasonable and appropriate.

References

Belsley, D. A., Kuh, E., and Welsch, R. E. (1980). *Regression Diagnostics: Identifying Influential Data and Sources of Collinearity*. New York: Wiley.

Box, G. E. P., Hunter, W. G., and Hunter, J. S. (1978). *Statistics for Experimenters: An Introduction to Design, Data Analysis, and Model Building*. New York: Wiley.

Box, G. E. P., and Jenkins, G. (1970). *Time Series Analysis: Forecasting and Control*. San Francisco: Holden-Day.

Cochran, W. G. (1977). *Sampling Techniques*, 3rd ed. New York: Wiley.

Cook, R. D., and Weisberg, S. (1982). *Residuals and Influence in Regression*. New York: Chapman and Hall.

Deming, W. E. (1986). *Out of the Crisis*. Cambridge, MA: MIT Center for Advanced Engineering Study.

Draper, N. R., and Smith, H. (1981). *Applied Regression Analysis*, 2nd ed. New York: Wiley.

Greenberg, B. G., Kuebler, R. R., Abernathy, J. R., and Horovitz, D. G. (1971). "Applications of Randomized Response Techniques in Obtaining Quantitative Data." *Journal of the American Statistical Association 66:* 245–250.

Hollander, M., and Wolfe, D. (1973). *Nonparametric Statistical Methods*. New York: Wiley.

Johnston, J. (1984). *Econometric Methods*, 3rd ed. New York: McGraw-Hill.

Kish, L. (1965). *Survey Sampling*. New York: Wiley.

Mallows, C. L. (1973). "Some Comments on C_p." *Technometrics 15:* 661–675.

Nelson, C. R. (1977). *Applied Time Series Analysis for Managerial Forecasting*. San Francisco: Holden-Day.

Ott, L. (1993). *An Introduction to Statistics and Data Analysis*, 4th ed. Pacific Grove, CA: Duxbury Press.

Ott, L., Larson, R. F., Rexroat, C., and Mendenhall, W. (1987). *Statistics: A Tool for the Social Sciences*, 5th ed. Pacific Grove, CA: Duxbury Press.

Phadke, M. S. (1986). "Design Optimization Case Studies." *AT&T Technical Journal 65 (2):* 39–50.

Pierce, D. A. (1980). "A Survey of Recent Developments in Seasonal Adjustment." *The American Statistician 34:* 125–134.

Pignatiello, J. J., and Ramberg, J. S. (1985). "Discussion." *Journal of Quality Technology 17:* 198–206.

Schaeffer, R. L., Mendenhall, W., and Ott, L. (1996). *Elementary Survey Sampling*, 4th ed. Boston: PWS-Kent.

Shoemaker, A. C., and Kacker, R. N. (1988). "A Methodology for Planning Experiments in Robust Product and Process Design." *Quality and Reliability Engineering International 4:* 95–103.

Taguchi, G. (1980). *Introduction to Off-Line Quality Control*. Tokyo: Japanese Standards Association.

Tukey, J. W. (1977). *Exploratory Data Analysis*. Reading, MA: Addison-Wesley.

Walton, M. (1986). *The Deming Management Method*. New York: Dodd, Mead.

Warner, S. L. (1965). "Randomized Response: A Survey Technique for Eliminating Evasive Answer Bias." *Journal of the American Statistical Association 60:* 63–69.

Welch, B. L. (1938). "The Significance of the Differences Between Two Means When the Population Variances Are Unequal." *Biometrika 29:* 350–362.

Appendix

TABLE 1 Binomial probabilities (*n* between 2 and 6)

n = 2

$y \downarrow$	.05	.10	.15	.20	.25	.30	.35	.40	.45	.50	
0	.9025	.8100	.7225	.6400	.5625	.4900	.4225	.3600	.3025	.2500	2
1	.0950	.1800	.2550	.3200	.3750	.4200	.4550	.4800	.4950	.5000	1
2	.0025	.0100	.0225	.0400	.0625	.0900	.1225	.1600	.2025	.2500	0
	.95	.90	.85	.80	.75	.70	.65	.60	.55	.50	$y \uparrow$

n = 3

$y \downarrow$	.05	.10	.15	.20	.25	.30	.35	.40	.45	.50	
0	.8574	.7290	.6141	.5120	.4219	.3430	.2746	.2160	.1664	.1250	3
1	.1354	.2430	.3251	.3840	.4219	.4410	.4436	.4320	.4084	.3750	2
2	.0071	.0270	.0574	.0960	.1406	.1890	.2389	.2880	.3341	.3750	1
3	.0001	.0010	.0034	.0080	.0156	.0270	.0429	.0640	.0911	.1250	0
	.95	.90	.85	.80	.75	.70	.65	.60	.55	.50	$y \uparrow$

n = 4

$y \downarrow$	.05	.10	.15	.20	.25	.30	.35	.40	.45	.50	
0	.8145	.6561	.5220	.4096	.3164	.2401	.1785	.1296	.0915	.0625	4
1	.1715	.2916	.3685	.4096	.4219	.4116	.3845	.3456	.2995	.2500	3
2	.0135	.0486	.0975	.1536	.2109	.2646	.3105	.3456	.3675	.3750	2
3	.0005	.0036	.0115	.0256	.0469	.0756	.1115	.1536	.2005	.2500	1
4	.0000	.0001	.0005	.0016	.0039	.0081	.0150	.0256	.0410	.0625	0
	.95	.90	.85	.80	.75	.70	.65	.60	.55	.50	$y \uparrow$

n = 5

$y \downarrow$	.05	.10	.15	.20	.25	.30	.35	.40	.45	.50	
0	.7738	.5905	.4437	.3277	.2373	.1681	.1160	.0778	.0503	.0313	5
1	.2036	.3281	.3915	.4096	.3955	.3602	.3124	.2592	.2059	.1563	4
2	.0214	.0729	.1382	.2048	.2637	.3087	.3364	.3456	.3369	.3125	3
3	.0011	.0081	.0244	.0512	.0879	.1323	.1811	.2304	.2757	.3125	2
4	.0000	.0005	.0022	.0064	.0146	.0284	.0488	.0768	.1128	.1563	1
5	.0000	.0000	.0001	.0003	.0010	.0024	.0053	.0102	.0185	.0313	0
	.95	.90	.85	.80	.75	.70	.65	.60	.55	.50	$y \uparrow$

n = 6

$y \downarrow$	.05	.10	.15	.20	.25	.30	.35	.40	.45	.50	
0	.7351	.5314	.3771	.2621	.1780	.1176	.0754	.0467	.0277	.0156	6
1	.2321	.3543	.3993	.3932	.3560	.3025	.2437	.1866	.1359	.0938	5
2	.0305	.0984	.1762	.2458	.2966	.3241	.3280	.3110	.2780	.2344	4
3	.0021	.0146	.0415	.0819	.1318	.1852	.2355	.2765	.3032	.3125	3
4	.0001	.0012	.0055	.0154	.0330	.0595	.0951	.1382	.1861	.2344	2
5	.0000	.0001	.0004	.0015	.0044	.0102	.0205	.0369	.0609	.0938	1
6	.0000	.0000	.0000	.0001	.0002	.0007	.0018	.0041	.0083	.0156	0
	.95	.90	.85	.80	.75	.70	.65	.60	.55	.50	$y \uparrow$

$n = 7$ π

$y\downarrow$	.05	.10	.15	.20	.25	.30	.35	.40	.45	.50	
0	.6983	.4783	.3206	.2097	.1335	.0824	.0490	.0280	.0152	.0078	7
1	.2573	.3720	.3960	.3670	.3115	.2471	.1848	.1306	.0872	.0547	6
2	.0406	.1240	.2097	.2753	.3115	.3177	.2985	.2613	.2140	.1641	5
3	.0036	.0230	.0617	.1147	.1730	.2269	.2679	.2903	.2918	.2734	4
4	.0002	.0026	.0109	.0287	.0577	.0972	.1442	.1935	.2388	.2734	3
5	.0000	.0002	.0012	.0043	.0115	.0250	.0466	.0774	.1172	.1641	2
6	.0000	.0000	.0001	.0004	.0013	.0036	.0084	.0172	.0320	.0547	1
7	.0000	.0000	.0000	.0000	.0001	.0002	.0006	.0016	.0037	.0078	0
	.95	.90	.85	.80	.75	.70	.65	.60	.55	.50	$y\uparrow$

$n = 8$ π

$y\downarrow$	.05	.10	.15	.20	.25	.30	.35	.40	.45	.50	
0	.6634	.4305	.2725	.1678	.1001	.0576	.0319	.0168	.0084	.0039	8
1	.2793	.3826	.3847	.3355	.2670	.1977	.1373	.0896	.0548	.0313	7
2	.0515	.1488	.2376	.2936	.3115	.2965	.2587	.2090	.1569	.1094	6
3	.0054	.0331	.0839	.1468	.2076	.2541	.2786	.2787	.2568	.2188	5
4	.0004	.0046	.0185	.0459	.0865	.1361	.1875	.2322	.2627	.2734	4
5	.0000	.0004	.0026	.0092	.0231	.0467	.0808	.1239	.1719	.2188	3
6	.0000	.0000	.0002	.0011	.0038	.0100	.0217	.0413	.0703	.1094	2
7	.0000	.0000	.0000	.0001	.0004	.0012	.0033	.0079	.0164	.0313	1
8	.0000	.0000	.0000	.0000	.0000	.0001	.0002	.0007	.0017	.0039	0
	.95	.90	.85	.80	.75	.70	.65	.60	.55	.50	$y\uparrow$

$n = 9$ π

$y\downarrow$	.05	.10	.15	.20	.25	.30	.35	.40	.45	.50	
0	.6302	.3874	.2316	.1342	.0751	.0404	.0207	.0101	.0046	.0020	9
1	.2985	.3874	.3679	.3020	.2253	.1556	.1004	.0605	.0339	.0176	8
2	.0629	.1722	.2597	.3020	.3003	.2668	.2162	.1612	.1110	.0703	7
3	.0077	.0446	.1069	.1762	.2336	.2668	.2716	.2508	.2119	.1641	6
4	.0006	.0074	.0283	.0661	.1168	.1715	.2194	.2508	.2600	.2461	5
5	.0000	.0008	.0050	.0165	.0389	.0735	.1181	.1672	.2128	.2461	4
6	.0000	.0001	.0006	.0028	.0087	.0210	.0424	.0743	.1160	.1641	3
7	.0000	.0000	.0000	.0003	.0012	.0039	.0098	.0212	.0407	.0703	2
8	.0000	.0000	.0000	.0000	.0001	.0004	.0013	.0035	.0083	.0176	1
9	.0000	.0000	.0000	.0000	.0000	.0000	.0001	.0003	.0008	.0020	0
	.95	.90	.85	.80	.75	.70	.65	.60	.55	.50	$y\uparrow$

$n = 10$ π

$y\downarrow$	.05	.10	.15	.20	.25	.30	.35	.40	.45	.50	
0	.5987	.3487	.1969	.1074	.0563	.0282	.0135	.0060	.0025	.0010	10
1	.3151	.3874	.3474	.2684	.1877	.1211	.0725	.0403	.0207	.0098	9
2	.0746	.1937	.2759	.3020	.2816	.2335	.1757	.1209	.0763	.0439	8
3	.0105	.0574	.1298	.2013	.2503	.2668	.2522	.2150	.1665	.1172	7
4	.0010	.0112	.0401	.0881	.1460	.2001	.2377	.2508	.2384	.2051	6
5	.0001	.0015	.0085	.0264	.0584	.1029	.1536	.2007	.2340	.2461	5
6	.0000	.0001	.0012	.0055	.0162	.0368	.0689	.1115	.1596	.2051	4
7	.0000	.0000	.0001	.0008	.0031	.0090	.0212	.0425	.0746	.1172	3
8	.0000	.0000	.0000	.0001	.0004	.0014	.0043	.0106	.0229	.0439	2
9	.0000	.0000	.0000	.0000	.0000	.0001	.0005	.0016	.0042	.0098	1
10	.0000	.0000	.0000	.0000	.0000	.0000	.0000	.0001	.0003	.0010	0
	.95	.90	.85	.80	.75	.70	.65	.60	.55	.50	$y\uparrow$

TABLE 1 (continued) Binomial probabilities (*n* between 12 and 16)

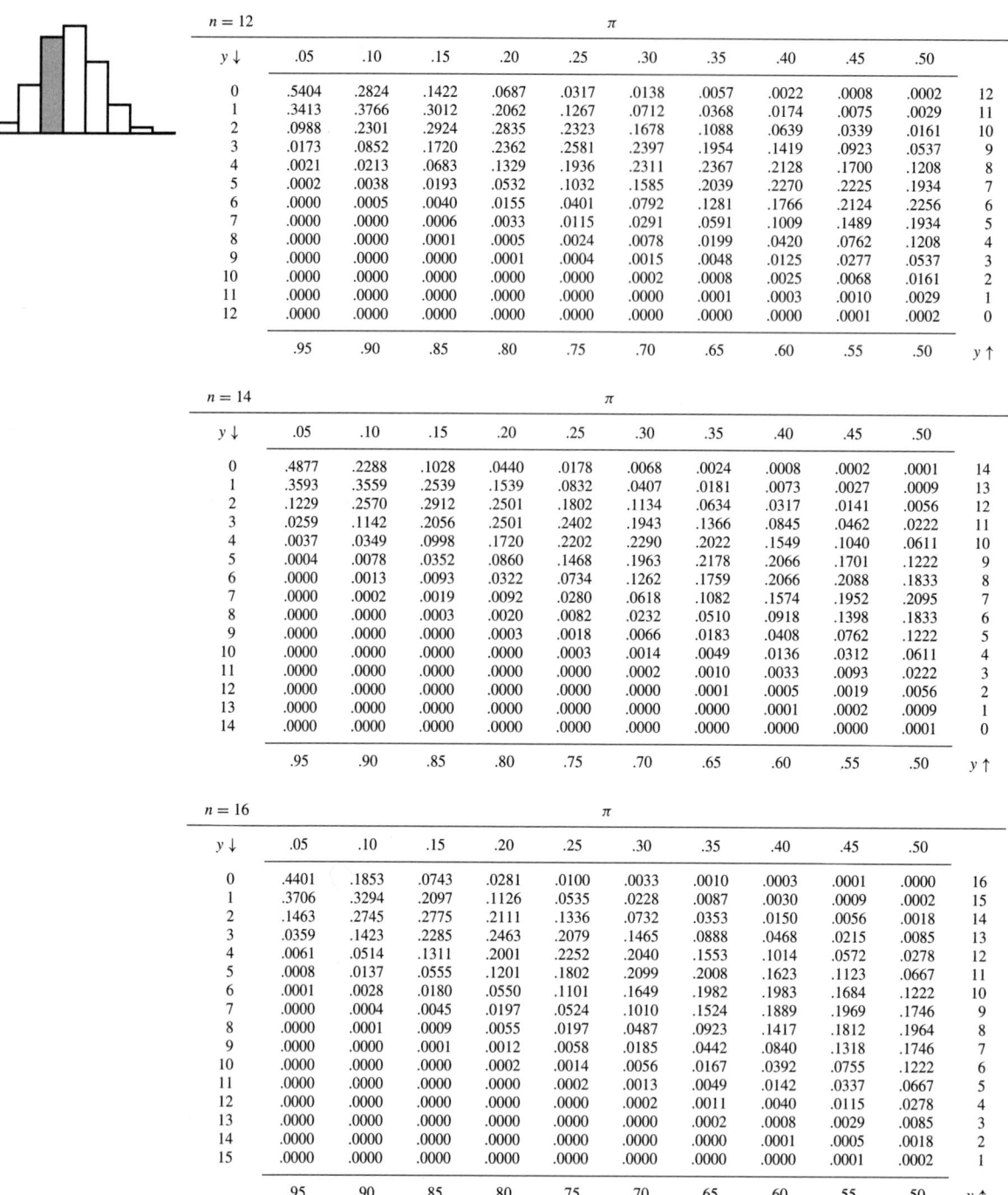

n = 12   π

y ↓	.05	.10	.15	.20	.25	.30	.35	.40	.45	.50	
0	.5404	.2824	.1422	.0687	.0317	.0138	.0057	.0022	.0008	.0002	12
1	.3413	.3766	.3012	.2062	.1267	.0712	.0368	.0174	.0075	.0029	11
2	.0988	.2301	.2924	.2835	.2323	.1678	.1088	.0639	.0339	.0161	10
3	.0173	.0852	.1720	.2362	.2581	.2397	.1954	.1419	.0923	.0537	9
4	.0021	.0213	.0683	.1329	.1936	.2311	.2367	.2128	.1700	.1208	8
5	.0002	.0038	.0193	.0532	.1032	.1585	.2039	.2270	.2225	.1934	7
6	.0000	.0005	.0040	.0155	.0401	.0792	.1281	.1766	.2124	.2256	6
7	.0000	.0000	.0006	.0033	.0115	.0291	.0591	.1009	.1489	.1934	5
8	.0000	.0000	.0001	.0005	.0024	.0078	.0199	.0420	.0762	.1208	4
9	.0000	.0000	.0000	.0001	.0004	.0015	.0048	.0125	.0277	.0537	3
10	.0000	.0000	.0000	.0000	.0000	.0002	.0008	.0025	.0068	.0161	2
11	.0000	.0000	.0000	.0000	.0000	.0000	.0001	.0003	.0010	.0029	1
12	.0000	.0000	.0000	.0000	.0000	.0000	.0000	.0000	.0001	.0002	0
	.95	.90	.85	.80	.75	.70	.65	.60	.55	.50	y ↑

n = 14   π

y ↓	.05	.10	.15	.20	.25	.30	.35	.40	.45	.50	
0	.4877	.2288	.1028	.0440	.0178	.0068	.0024	.0008	.0002	.0001	14
1	.3593	.3559	.2539	.1539	.0832	.0407	.0181	.0073	.0027	.0009	13
2	.1229	.2570	.2912	.2501	.1802	.1134	.0634	.0317	.0141	.0056	12
3	.0259	.1142	.2056	.2501	.2402	.1943	.1366	.0845	.0462	.0222	11
4	.0037	.0349	.0998	.1720	.2202	.2290	.2022	.1549	.1040	.0611	10
5	.0004	.0078	.0352	.0860	.1468	.1963	.2178	.2066	.1701	.1222	9
6	.0000	.0013	.0093	.0322	.0734	.1262	.1759	.2066	.2088	.1833	8
7	.0000	.0002	.0019	.0092	.0280	.0618	.1082	.1574	.1952	.2095	7
8	.0000	.0000	.0003	.0020	.0082	.0232	.0510	.0918	.1398	.1833	6
9	.0000	.0000	.0000	.0003	.0018	.0066	.0183	.0408	.0762	.1222	5
10	.0000	.0000	.0000	.0000	.0003	.0014	.0049	.0136	.0312	.0611	4
11	.0000	.0000	.0000	.0000	.0000	.0002	.0010	.0033	.0093	.0222	3
12	.0000	.0000	.0000	.0000	.0000	.0000	.0001	.0005	.0019	.0056	2
13	.0000	.0000	.0000	.0000	.0000	.0000	.0000	.0001	.0002	.0009	1
14	.0000	.0000	.0000	.0000	.0000	.0000	.0000	.0000	.0000	.0001	0
	.95	.90	.85	.80	.75	.70	.65	.60	.55	.50	y ↑

n = 16   π

y ↓	.05	.10	.15	.20	.25	.30	.35	.40	.45	.50	
0	.4401	.1853	.0743	.0281	.0100	.0033	.0010	.0003	.0001	.0000	16
1	.3706	.3294	.2097	.1126	.0535	.0228	.0087	.0030	.0009	.0002	15
2	.1463	.2745	.2775	.2111	.1336	.0732	.0353	.0150	.0056	.0018	14
3	.0359	.1423	.2285	.2463	.2079	.1465	.0888	.0468	.0215	.0085	13
4	.0061	.0514	.1311	.2001	.2252	.2040	.1553	.1014	.0572	.0278	12
5	.0008	.0137	.0555	.1201	.1802	.2099	.2008	.1623	.1123	.0667	11
6	.0001	.0028	.0180	.0550	.1101	.1649	.1982	.1983	.1684	.1222	10
7	.0000	.0004	.0045	.0197	.0524	.1010	.1524	.1889	.1969	.1746	9
8	.0000	.0001	.0009	.0055	.0197	.0487	.0923	.1417	.1812	.1964	8
9	.0000	.0000	.0001	.0012	.0058	.0185	.0442	.0840	.1318	.1746	7
10	.0000	.0000	.0000	.0002	.0014	.0056	.0167	.0392	.0755	.1222	6
11	.0000	.0000	.0000	.0000	.0002	.0013	.0049	.0142	.0337	.0667	5
12	.0000	.0000	.0000	.0000	.0000	.0002	.0011	.0040	.0115	.0278	4
13	.0000	.0000	.0000	.0000	.0000	.0000	.0002	.0008	.0029	.0085	3
14	.0000	.0000	.0000	.0000	.0000	.0000	.0000	.0001	.0005	.0018	2
15	.0000	.0000	.0000	.0000	.0000	.0000	.0000	.0000	.0001	.0002	1
	.95	.90	.85	.80	.75	.70	.65	.60	.55	.50	y ↑

TABLE 1 (continued) Binomial probabilities ($n = 18$ and 20)

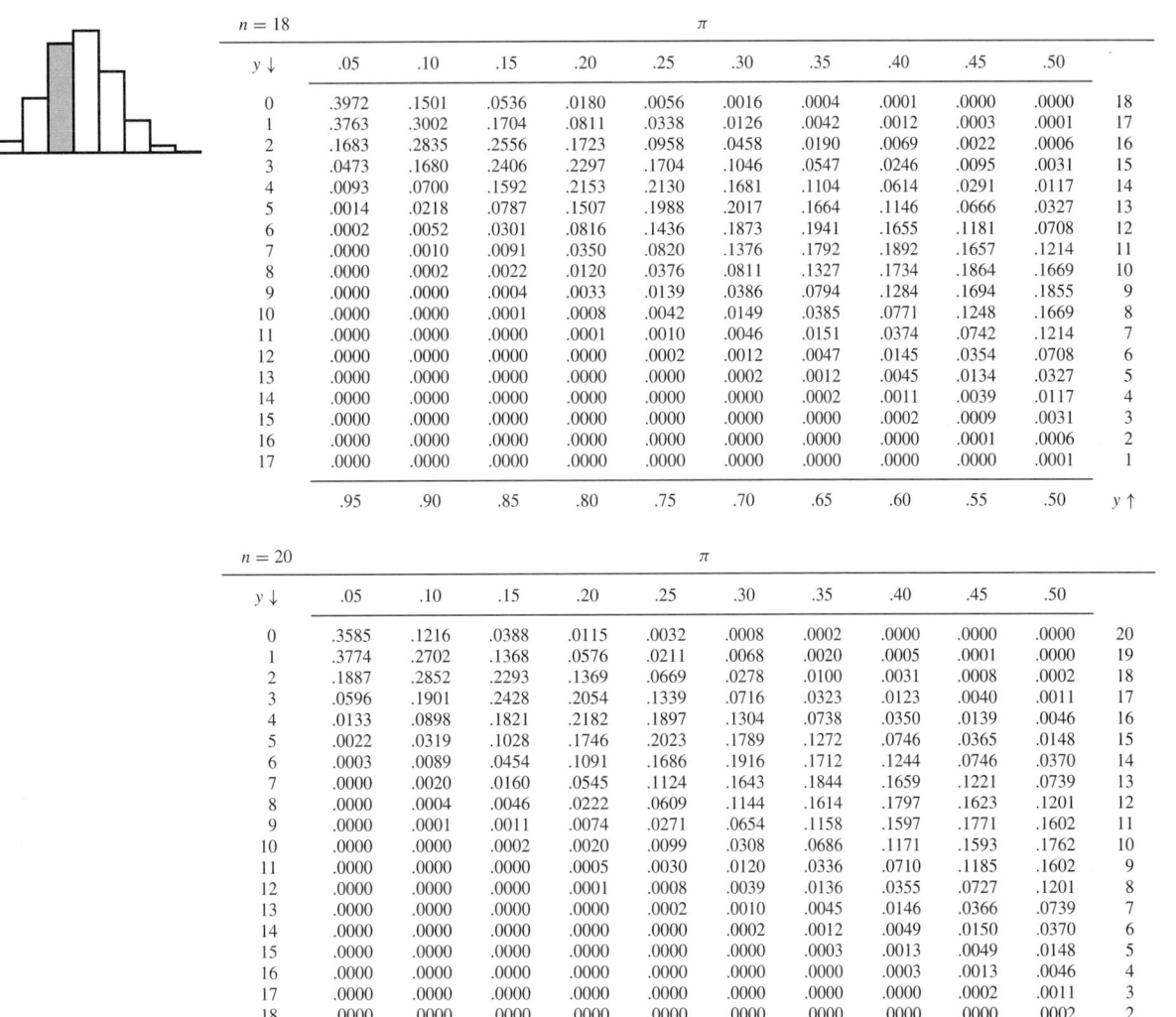

$n = 18$ π

$y\downarrow$	.05	.10	.15	.20	.25	.30	.35	.40	.45	.50	
0	.3972	.1501	.0536	.0180	.0056	.0016	.0004	.0001	.0000	.0000	18
1	.3763	.3002	.1704	.0811	.0338	.0126	.0042	.0012	.0003	.0001	17
2	.1683	.2835	.2556	.1723	.0958	.0458	.0190	.0069	.0022	.0006	16
3	.0473	.1680	.2406	.2297	.1704	.1046	.0547	.0246	.0095	.0031	15
4	.0093	.0700	.1592	.2153	.2130	.1681	.1104	.0614	.0291	.0117	14
5	.0014	.0218	.0787	.1507	.1988	.2017	.1664	.1146	.0666	.0327	13
6	.0002	.0052	.0301	.0816	.1436	.1873	.1941	.1655	.1181	.0708	12
7	.0000	.0010	.0091	.0350	.0820	.1376	.1792	.1892	.1657	.1214	11
8	.0000	.0002	.0022	.0120	.0376	.0811	.1327	.1734	.1864	.1669	10
9	.0000	.0000	.0004	.0033	.0139	.0386	.0794	.1284	.1694	.1855	9
10	.0000	.0000	.0001	.0008	.0042	.0149	.0385	.0771	.1248	.1669	8
11	.0000	.0000	.0000	.0001	.0010	.0046	.0151	.0374	.0742	.1214	7
12	.0000	.0000	.0000	.0000	.0002	.0012	.0047	.0145	.0354	.0708	6
13	.0000	.0000	.0000	.0000	.0000	.0002	.0012	.0045	.0134	.0327	5
14	.0000	.0000	.0000	.0000	.0000	.0000	.0002	.0011	.0039	.0117	4
15	.0000	.0000	.0000	.0000	.0000	.0000	.0000	.0002	.0009	.0031	3
16	.0000	.0000	.0000	.0000	.0000	.0000	.0000	.0000	.0001	.0006	2
17	.0000	.0000	.0000	.0000	.0000	.0000	.0000	.0000	.0000	.0001	1
	.95	.90	.85	.80	.75	.70	.65	.60	.55	.50	$y\uparrow$

$n = 20$ π

$y\downarrow$	.05	.10	.15	.20	.25	.30	.35	.40	.45	.50	
0	.3585	.1216	.0388	.0115	.0032	.0008	.0002	.0000	.0000	.0000	20
1	.3774	.2702	.1368	.0576	.0211	.0068	.0020	.0005	.0001	.0000	19
2	.1887	.2852	.2293	.1369	.0669	.0278	.0100	.0031	.0008	.0002	18
3	.0596	.1901	.2428	.2054	.1339	.0716	.0323	.0123	.0040	.0011	17
4	.0133	.0898	.1821	.2182	.1897	.1304	.0738	.0350	.0139	.0046	16
5	.0022	.0319	.1028	.1746	.2023	.1789	.1272	.0746	.0365	.0148	15
6	.0003	.0089	.0454	.1091	.1686	.1916	.1712	.1244	.0746	.0370	14
7	.0000	.0020	.0160	.0545	.1124	.1643	.1844	.1659	.1221	.0739	13
8	.0000	.0004	.0046	.0222	.0609	.1144	.1614	.1797	.1623	.1201	12
9	.0000	.0001	.0011	.0074	.0271	.0654	.1158	.1597	.1771	.1602	11
10	.0000	.0000	.0002	.0020	.0099	.0308	.0686	.1171	.1593	.1762	10
11	.0000	.0000	.0000	.0005	.0030	.0120	.0336	.0710	.1185	.1602	9
12	.0000	.0000	.0000	.0001	.0008	.0039	.0136	.0355	.0727	.1201	8
13	.0000	.0000	.0000	.0000	.0002	.0010	.0045	.0146	.0366	.0739	7
14	.0000	.0000	.0000	.0000	.0000	.0002	.0012	.0049	.0150	.0370	6
15	.0000	.0000	.0000	.0000	.0000	.0000	.0003	.0013	.0049	.0148	5
16	.0000	.0000	.0000	.0000	.0000	.0000	.0000	.0003	.0013	.0046	4
17	.0000	.0000	.0000	.0000	.0000	.0000	.0000	.0000	.0002	.0011	3
18	.0000	.0000	.0000	.0000	.0000	.0000	.0000	.0000	.0000	.0002	2
	.95	.90	.85	.80	.75	.70	.65	.60	.55	.50	$y\uparrow$

TABLE 1 (continued) Binomial probabilities (*n* = 50)

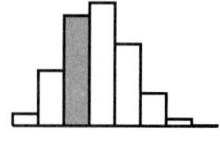

n = 50						π					
y ↓	.05	.10	.15	.20	.25	.30	.35	.40	.45	.50	
0	.0769	.0052	.0003	.0000	.0000	.0000	.0000	.0000	.0000	.0000	50
1	.2025	.0286	.0026	.0002	.0000	.0000	.0000	.0000	.0000	.0000	49
2	.2611	.0779	.0113	.0011	.0001	.0000	.0000	.0000	.0000	.0000	48
3	.2199	.1386	.0319	.0044	.0004	.0000	.0000	.0000	.0000	.0000	47
4	.1360	.1809	.0661	.0128	.0016	.0001	.0000	.0000	.0000	.0000	46
5	.0658	.1849	.1072	.0295	.0049	.0006	.0000	.0000	.0000	.0000	45
6	.0260	.1541	.1419	.0554	.0123	.0018	.0002	.0000	.0000	.0000	44
7	.0086	.1076	.1575	.0870	.0259	.0048	.0006	.0000	.0000	.0000	43
8	.0024	.0643	.1493	.1169	.0463	.0110	.0017	.0002	.0000	.0000	42
9	.0006	.0333	.1230	.1364	.0721	.0220	.0042	.0005	.0000	.0000	41
10	.0001	.0152	.0890	.1398	.0985	.0386	.0093	.0014	.0001	.0000	40
11	.0000	.0061	.0571	.1271	.1194	.0602	.0182	.0035	.0004	.0000	39
12	.0000	.0022	.0328	.1033	.1294	.0838	.0319	.0076	.0011	.0001	38
13	.0000	.0007	.0169	.0755	.1261	.1050	.0502	.0147	.0027	.0003	37
14	.0000	.0002	.0079	.0499	.1110	.1189	.0714	.0260	.0059	.0008	36
15	.0000	.0001	.0033	.0299	.0888	.1223	.0923	.0415	.0116	.0020	35
16	.0000	.0000	.0013	.0164	.0648	.1147	.1088	.0606	.0207	.0044	34
17	.0000	.0000	.0005	.0082	.0432	.0983	.1171	.0808	.0339	.0087	33
18	.0000	.0000	.0001	.0037	.0264	.0772	.1156	.0987	.0508	.0160	32
19	.0000	.0000	.0000	.0016	.0148	.0558	.1048	.1109	.0700	.0270	31
20	.0000	.0000	.0000	.0006	.0077	.0370	.0875	.1146	.0888	.0419	30
21	.0000	.0000	.0000	.0002	.0036	.0227	.0673	.1091	.1038	.0598	29
22	.0000	.0000	.0000	.0001	.0016	.0128	.0478	.0959	.1119	.0788	28
23	.0000	.0000	.0000	.0000	.0006	.0067	.0313	.0778	.1115	.0960	27
24	.0000	.0000	.0000	.0000	.0002	.0032	.0190	.0584	.1026	.1080	26
25	.0000	.0000	.0000	.0000	.0001	.0014	.0106	.0405	.0873	.1123	25
26	.0000	.0000	.0000	.0000	.0000	.0006	.0055	.0259	.0687	.1080	24
27	.0000	.0000	.0000	.0000	.0000	.0002	.0026	.0154	.0500	.0960	23
28	.0000	.0000	.0000	.0000	.0000	.0001	.0012	.0084	.0336	.0788	22
29	.0000	.0000	.0000	.0000	.0000	.0000	.0005	.0043	.0208	.0598	21
30	.0000	.0000	.0000	.0000	.0000	.0000	.0002	.0020	.0119	.0419	20
31	.0000	.0000	.0000	.0000	.0000	.0000	.0001	.0009	.0063	.0270	19
32	.0000	.0000	.0000	.0000	.0000	.0000	.0000	.0003	.0031	.0160	18
33	.0000	.0000	.0000	.0000	.0000	.0000	.0000	.0001	.0014	.0087	17
34	.0000	.0000	.0000	.0000	.0000	.0000	.0000	.0000	.0006	.0044	16
35	.0000	.0000	.0000	.0000	.0000	.0000	.0000	.0000	.0002	.0020	15
36	.0000	.0000	.0000	.0000	.0000	.0000	.0000	.0000	.0001	.0008	14
37	.0000	.0000	.0000	.0000	.0000	.0000	.0000	.0000	.0000	.0003	13
38	.0000	.0000	.0000	.0000	.0000	.0000	.0000	.0000	.0000	.0001	12
	.95	.90	.85	.80	.75	.70	.65	.60	.55	.50	*y* ↑

y ↓	.05	.10	.15	.20	.25	.30	.35	.40	.45	.50	
0	.0059	.0000	.0000	.0000	.0000	.0000	.0000	.0000	.0000	.0000	100
1	.0312	.0003	.0000	.0000	.0000	.0000	.0000	.0000	.0000	.0000	99
2	.0812	.0016	.0000	.0000	.0000	.0000	.0000	.0000	.0000	.0000	98
3	.1396	.0059	.0001	.0000	.0000	.0000	.0000	.0000	.0000	.0000	97
4	.1781	.0159	.0003	.0000	.0000	.0000	.0000	.0000	.0000	.0000	96
5	.1800	.0339	.0011	.0000	.0000	.0000	.0000	.0000	.0000	.0000	95
6	.1500	.0596	.0031	.0001	.0000	.0000	.0000	.0000	.0000	.0000	94
7	.1060	.0889	.0075	.0002	.0000	.0000	.0000	.0000	.0000	.0000	93
8	.0649	.1148	.0153	.0006	.0000	.0000	.0000	.0000	.0000	.0000	92
9	.0349	.1304	.0276	.0015	.0000	.0000	.0000	.0000	.0000	.0000	91
10	.0167	.1319	.0444	.0034	.0001	.0000	.0000	.0000	.0000	.0000	90
11	.0072	.1199	.0640	.0069	.0003	.0000	.0000	.0000	.0000	.0000	89
12	.0028	.0988	.0838	.0128	.0006	.0000	.0000	.0000	.0000	.0000	88
13	.0010	.0743	.1001	.0216	.0014	.0000	.0000	.0000	.0000	.0000	87
14	.0003	.0513	.1098	.0335	.0030	.0001	.0000	.0000	.0000	.0000	86
15	.0001	.0327	.1111	.0481	.0057	.0002	.0000	.0000	.0000	.0000	85
16	.0000	.0193	.1041	.0638	.0100	.0006	.0000	.0000	.0000	.0000	84
17	.0000	.0106	.0908	.0789	.0165	.0012	.0000	.0000	.0000	.0000	83
18	.0000	.0054	.0739	.0909	.0254	.0024	.0001	.0000	.0000	.0000	82
19	.0000	.0026	.0563	.0981	.0365	.0044	.0002	.0000	.0000	.0000	81
20	.0000	.0012	.0402	.0993	.0493	.0076	.0004	.0000	.0000	.0000	80
21	.0000	.0005	.0270	.0946	.0626	.0124	.0009	.0000	.0000	.0000	79
22	.0000	.0002	.0171	.0849	.0749	.0190	.0017	.0001	.0000	.0000	78
23	.0000	.0001	.0103	.0720	.0847	.0277	.0032	.0001	.0000	.0000	77
24	.0000	.0000	.0058	.0577	.0906	.0380	.0055	.0003	.0000	.0000	76
25	.0000	.0000	.0031	.0439	.0918	.0496	.0090	.0006	.0000	.0000	75
26	.0000	.0000	.0016	.0316	.0883	.0613	.0140	.0012	.0000	.0000	74
27	.0000	.0000	.0008	.0217	.0806	.0720	.0207	.0022	.0001	.0000	73
28	.0000	.0000	.0004	.0141	.0701	.0804	.0290	.0038	.0002	.0000	72
29	.0000	.0000	.0002	.0088	.0580	.0856	.0388	.0063	.0004	.0000	71
30	.0000	.0000	.0001	.0052	.0458	.0868	.0494	.0100	.0008	.0000	70
31	.0000	.0000	.0000	.0029	.0344	.0840	.0601	.0151	.0014	.0001	69
32	.0000	.0000	.0000	.0016	.0248	.0776	.0698	.0217	.0025	.0001	68
33	.0000	.0000	.0000	.0008	.0170	.0685	.0774	.0297	.0043	.0002	67
34	.0000	.0000	.0000	.0004	.0112	.0579	.0821	.0391	.0069	.0005	66
35	.0000	.0000	.0000	.0002	.0070	.0468	.0834	.0491	.0106	.0009	65
36	.0000	.0000	.0000	.0001	.0042	.0362	.0811	.0591	.0157	.0016	64
37	.0000	.0000	.0000	.0000	.0024	.0268	.0755	.0682	.0222	.0027	63
38	.0000	.0000	.0000	.0000	.0013	.0191	.0674	.0754	.0301	.0045	62
39	.0000	.0000	.0000	.0000	.0007	.0130	.0577	.0799	.0391	.0071	61
40	.0000	.0000	.0000	.0000	.0004	.0085	.0474	.0812	.0488	.0108	60
41	.0000	.0000	.0000	.0000	.0002	.0053	.0373	.0792	.0584	.0159	59
42	.0000	.0000	.0000	.0000	.0001	.0032	.0282	.0742	.0672	.0223	58
43	.0000	.0000	.0000	.0000	.0000	.0019	.0205	.0667	.0741	.0301	57
44	.0000	.0000	.0000	.0000	.0000	.0010	.0143	.0576	.0786	.0390	56
45	.0000	.0000	.0000	.0000	.0000	.0005	.0096	.0478	.0800	.0485	55
46	.0000	.0000	.0000	.0000	.0000	.0003	.0062	.0381	.0782	.0580	54
47	.0000	.0000	.0000	.0000	.0000	.0001	.0038	.0292	.0736	.0666	53
48	.0000	.0000	.0000	.0000	.0000	.0001	.0023	.0215	.0665	.0735	52
49	.0000	.0000	.0000	.0000	.0000	.0000	.0013	.0152	.0577	.0780	51
50	.0000	.0000	.0000	.0000	.0000	.0000	.0007	.0103	.0482	.0796	50
51	.0000	.0000	.0000	.0000	.0000	.0000	.0004	.0068	.0386	.0780	49
52	.0000	.0000	.0000	.0000	.0000	.0000	.0002	.0042	.0298	.0735	48
53	.0000	.0000	.0000	.0000	.0000	.0000	.0001	.0026	.0221	.0666	47
54	.0000	.0000	.0000	.0000	.0000	.0000	.0000	.0015	.0157	.0580	46
55	.0000	.0000	.0000	.0000	.0000	.0000	.0000	.0008	.0108	.0485	45
56	.0000	.0000	.0000	.0000	.0000	.0000	.0000	.0004	.0071	.0390	44
57	.0000	.0000	.0000	.0000	.0000	.0000	.0000	.0002	.0045	.0301	43
58	.0000	.0000	.0000	.0000	.0000	.0000	.0000	.0001	.0027	.0223	42
59	.0000	.0000	.0000	.0000	.0000	.0000	.0000	.0001	.0016	.0159	41
60	.0000	.0000	.0000	.0000	.0000	.0000	.0000	.0000	.0009	.0108	40
61	.0000	.0000	.0000	.0000	.0000	.0000	.0000	.0000	.0005	.0071	39
62	.0000	.0000	.0000	.0000	.0000	.0000	.0000	.0000	.0002	.0045	38
63	.0000	.0000	.0000	.0000	.0000	.0000	.0000	.0000	.0001	.0027	37
64	.0000	.0000	.0000	.0000	.0000	.0000	.0000	.0000	.0001	.0016	36
65	.0000	.0000	.0000	.0000	.0000	.0000	.0000	.0000	.0000	.0009	35
66	.0000	.0000	.0000	.0000	.0000	.0000	.0000	.0000	.0000	.0005	34
67	.0000	.0000	.0000	.0000	.0000	.0000	.0000	.0000	.0000	.0002	33
68	.0000	.0000	.0000	.0000	.0000	.0000	.0000	.0000	.0000	.0001	32
69	.0000	.0000	.0000	.0000	.0000	.0000	.0000	.0000	.0000	.0001	31
	.95	.90	.85	.80	.75	.70	.65	.60	.55	.50	y ↑

Source: Computed by D. K. Hildebrand.

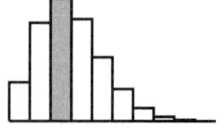

T A B L E 2 Poisson probabilities (μ between .1 and 5.0)

y	.1	.2	.3	.4	.5	.6	.7	.8	.9	1.0
0	.9048	.8187	.7408	.6703	.6065	.5488	.4966	.4493	.4066	.3679
1	.0905	.1637	.2222	.2681	.3033	.3293	.3476	.3595	.3659	.3679
2	.0045	.0164	.0333	.0536	.0758	.0988	.1217	.1438	.1647	.1839
3	.0002	.0011	.0033	.0072	.0126	.0198	.0284	.0383	.0494	.0613
4	.0000	.0001	.0003	.0007	.0016	.0030	.0050	.0077	.0111	.0153
5	.0000	.0000	.0000	.0001	.0002	.0004	.0007	.0012	.0020	.0031
6	.0000	.0000	.0000	.0000	.0000	.0000	.0001	.0002	.0003	.0005

y	1.1	1.2	1.3	1.4	1.5	1.6	1.7	1.8	1.9	2.0
0	.3329	.3012	.2725	.2466	.2231	.2019	.1827	.1653	.1496	.1353
1	.3662	.3614	.3543	.3452	.3347	.3230	.3106	.2975	.2842	.2707
2	.2014	.2169	.2303	.2417	.2510	.2584	.2640	.2678	.2700	.2707
3	.0738	.0867	.0998	.1128	.1255	.1378	.1496	.1607	.1710	.1804
4	.0203	.0260	.0324	.0395	.0471	.0551	.0636	.0723	.0812	.0902
5	.0045	.0062	.0084	.0111	.0141	.0176	.0216	.0260	.0309	.0361
6	.0008	.0012	.0018	.0026	.0035	.0047	.0061	.0078	.0098	.0120
7	.0001	.0002	.0003	.0005	.0008	.0011	.0015	.0020	.0027	.0034
8	.0000	.0000	.0001	.0001	.0001	.0002	.0003	.0005	.0006	.0009

y	2.1	2.2	2.3	2.4	2.5	2.6	2.7	2.8	2.9	3.0
0	.1225	.1108	.1003	.0907	.0821	.0743	.0672	.0608	.0550	.0498
1	.2572	.2438	.2306	.2177	.2052	.1931	.1815	.1703	.1596	.1494
2	.2700	.2681	.2652	.2613	.2565	.2510	.2450	.2384	.2314	.2240
3	.1890	.1966	.2033	.2090	.2138	.2176	.2205	.2225	.2237	.2240
4	.0992	.1082	.1169	.1254	.1336	.1414	.1488	.1557	.1622	.1680
5	.0417	.0476	.0538	.0602	.0668	.0735	.0804	.0872	.0940	.1008
6	.0146	.0174	.0206	.0241	.0278	.0319	.0362	.0407	.0455	.0504
7	.0044	.0055	.0068	.0083	.0099	.0118	.0139	.0163	.0188	.0216
8	.0011	.0015	.0019	.0025	.0031	.0038	.0047	.0057	.0068	.0081
9	.0003	.0004	.0005	.0007	.0009	.0011	.0014	.0018	.0022	.0027
10	.0001	.0001	.0001	.0002	.0002	.0003	.0004	.0005	.0006	.0008
11	.0000	.0000	.0000	.0000	.0000	.0001	.0001	.0001	.0002	.0002

y	3.1	3.2	3.3	3.4	3.5	3.6	3.7	3.8	3.9	4.0
0	.0450	.0408	.0369	.0334	.0302	.0273	.0247	.0224	.0202	.0183
1	.1397	.1304	.1217	.1135	.1057	.0984	.0915	.0850	.0789	.0733
2	.2165	.2087	.2008	.1929	.1850	.1771	.1692	.1615	.1539	.1465
3	.2237	.2226	.2209	.2186	.2158	.2125	.2087	.2046	.2001	.1954
4	.1733	.1781	.1823	.1858	.1888	.1912	.1931	.1944	.1951	.1954
5	.1075	.1140	.1203	.1264	.1322	.1377	.1429	.1477	.1522	.1563
6	.0555	.0608	.0662	.0716	.0771	.0826	.0881	.0936	.0989	.1042
7	.0246	.0278	.0312	.0348	.0385	.0425	.0466	.0508	.0551	.0595
8	.0095	.0111	.0129	.0148	.0169	.0191	.0215	.0241	.0269	.0298
9	.0033	.0040	.0047	.0056	.0066	.0076	.0089	.0102	.0116	.0132
10	.0010	.0013	.0016	.0019	.0023	.0028	.0033	.0039	.0045	.0053
11	.0003	.0004	.0005	.0006	.0007	.0009	.0011	.0013	.0016	.0019
12	.0001	.0001	.0001	.0002	.0002	.0003	.0003	.0004	.0005	.0006
13	.0000	.0000	.0000	.0000	.0001	.0001	.0001	.0001	.0002	.0002

y	4.1	4.2	4.3	4.4	4.5	4.6	4.7	4.8	4.9	5.0
0	.0166	.0150	.0136	.0123	.0111	.0101	.0091	.0082	.0074	.0067
1	.0679	.0630	.0583	.0540	.0500	.0462	.0427	.0395	.0365	.0337
2	.1393	.1323	.1254	.1188	.1125	.1063	.1005	.0948	.0894	.0842
3	.1904	.1852	.1798	.1743	.1687	.1631	.1574	.1517	.1460	.1404
4	.1951	.1944	.1933	.1917	.1898	.1875	.1849	.1820	.1789	.1755
5	.1600	.1633	.1662	.1687	.1708	.1725	.1738	.1747	.1753	.1755
6	.1093	.1143	.1191	.1237	.1281	.1323	.1362	.1398	.1432	.1462
7	.0640	.0686	.0732	.0778	.0824	.0869	.0914	.0959	.1002	.1044
8	.0328	.0360	.0393	.0428	.0463	.0500	.0537	.0575	.0614	.0653
9	.0150	.0168	.0188	.0209	.0232	.0255	.0281	.0307	.0334	.0363
10	.0061	.0071	.0081	.0092	.0104	.0118	.0132	.0147	.0164	.0181
11	.0023	.0027	.0032	.0037	.0043	.0049	.0056	.0064	.0073	.0082
12	.0008	.0009	.0011	.0013	.0016	.0019	.0022	.0026	.0030	.0034
13	.0002	.0003	.0004	.0005	.0006	.0007	.0008	.0009	.0011	.0013
14	.0001	.0001	.0001	.0001	.0002	.0002	.0003	.0003	.0004	.0005
15	.0000	.0000	.0000	.0000	.0001	.0001	.0001	.0001	.0001	.0002

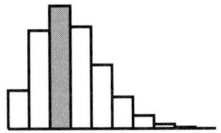

y	μ 5.5	6.0	6.5	7.0	7.5	8.0	8.5	9.0	9.5	10.0
0	.0041	.0025	.0015	.0009	.0006	.0003	.0002	.0001	.0001	.0000
1	.0225	.0149	.0098	.0064	.0041	.0027	.0017	.0011	.0007	.0005
2	.0618	.0446	.0318	.0223	.0156	.0107	.0074	.0050	.0034	.0023
3	.1133	.0892	.0688	.0521	.0389	.0286	.0208	.0150	.0107	.0076
4	.1558	.1339	.1118	.0912	.0729	.0573	.0443	.0337	.0254	.0189
5	.1714	.1606	.1454	.1277	.1094	.0916	.0752	.0607	.0483	.0378
6	.1571	.1606	.1575	.1490	.1367	.1221	.1066	.0911	.0764	.0631
7	.1234	.1377	.1462	.1490	.1465	.1396	.1294	.1171	.1037	.0901
8	.0849	.1033	.1188	.1304	.1373	.1396	.1375	.1318	.1232	.1126
9	.0519	.0688	.0858	.1014	.1144	.1241	.1299	.1318	.1300	.1251
10	.0285	.0413	.0558	.0710	.0858	.0993	.1104	.1186	.1235	.1251
11	.0143	.0225	.0330	.0452	.0585	.0722	.0853	.0970	.1067	.1137
12	.0065	.0113	.0179	.0263	.0366	.0481	.0604	.0728	.0844	.0948
13	.0028	.0052	.0089	.0142	.0211	.0296	.0395	.0504	.0617	.0729
14	.0011	.0022	.0041	.0071	.0113	.0169	.0240	.0324	.0419	.0521
15	.0004	.0009	.0018	.0033	.0057	.0090	.0136	.0194	.0265	.0347
16	.0001	.0003	.0007	.0014	.0026	.0045	.0072	.0109	.0157	.0217
17	.0000	.0001	.0003	.0006	.0012	.0021	.0036	.0058	.0088	.0128
18	.0000	.0000	.0001	.0002	.0005	.0009	.0017	.0029	.0046	.0071
19	.0000	.0000	.0000	.0001	.0002	.0004	.0008	.0014	.0023	.0037
20	.0000	.0000	.0000	.0000	.0001	.0002	.0003	.0006	.0011	.0019
21	.0000	.0000	.0000	.0000	.0000	.0001	.0001	.0003	.0005	.0009
22	.0000	.0000	.0000	.0000	.0000	.0000	.0001	.0001	.0002	.0004
23	.0000	.0000	.0000	.0000	.0000	.0000	.0000	.0000	.0001	.0002

y	μ 11.0	12.0	13.0	14.0	15.0	16.0	17.0	18.0	19.0	20.0
0	.0000	.0000	.0000	.0000	.0000	.0000	.0000	.0000	.0000	.0000
1	.0002	.0001	.0000	.0000	.0000	.0000	.0000	.0000	.0000	.0000
2	.0010	.0004	.0002	.0001	.0000	.0000	.0000	.0000	.0000	.0000
3	.0037	.0018	.0008	.0004	.0002	.0001	.0000	.0000	.0000	.0000
4	.0102	.0053	.0027	.0013	.0006	.0003	.0001	.0001	.0000	.0000
5	.0224	.0127	.0070	.0037	.0019	.0010	.0005	.0002	.0001	.0001
6	.0411	.0255	.0152	.0087	.0048	.0026	.0014	.0007	.0004	.0002
7	.0646	.0437	.0281	.0174	.0104	.0060	.0034	.0019	.0010	.0005
8	.0888	.0655	.0457	.0304	.0194	.0120	.0072	.0042	.0024	.0013
9	.1085	.0874	.0661	.0473	.0324	.0213	.0135	.0083	.0050	.0029
10	.1194	.1048	.0859	.0663	.0486	.0341	.0230	.0150	.0095	.0058
11	.1194	.1144	.1015	.0844	.0663	.0496	.0355	.0245	.0164	.0106
12	.1094	.1144	.1099	.0984	.0829	.0661	.0504	.0368	.0259	.0176
13	.0926	.1056	.1099	.1060	.0956	.0814	.0658	.0509	.0378	.0271
14	.0728	.0905	.1021	.1060	.1024	.0930	.0800	.0655	.0514	.0387
15	.0534	.0724	.0885	.0989	.1024	.0992	.0906	.0786	.0650	.0516
16	.0367	.0543	.0719	.0866	.0960	.0992	.0963	.0884	.0772	.0646
17	.0237	.0383	.0550	.0713	.0847	.0934	.0963	.0936	.0863	.0760
18	.0145	.0255	.0397	.0554	.0706	.0830	.0909	.0936	.0911	.0844
19	.0084	.0161	.0272	.0409	.0557	.0699	.0814	.0887	.0911	.0888
20	.0046	.0097	.0177	.0286	.0418	.0559	.0692	.0798	.0866	.0888
21	.0024	.0055	.0109	.0191	.0299	.0426	.0560	.0684	.0783	.0846
22	.0012	.0030	.0065	.0121	.0204	.0310	.0433	.0560	.0676	.0769
23	.0006	.0016	.0037	.0074	.0133	.0216	.0320	.0438	.0559	.0669
24	.0003	.0008	.0020	.0043	.0083	.0144	.0226	.0328	.0442	.0557
25	.0001	.0004	.0010	.0024	.0050	.0092	.0154	.0237	.0336	.0446
26	.0000	.0002	.0005	.0013	.0029	.0057	.0101	.0164	.0246	.0343
27	.0000	.0001	.0002	.0007	.0016	.0034	.0063	.0109	.0173	.0254
28	.0000	.0000	.0001	.0003	.0009	.0019	.0038	.0070	.0117	.0181
29	.0000	.0000	.0001	.0002	.0004	.0011	.0023	.0044	.0077	.0125
30	.0000	.0000	.0000	.0001	.0002	.0006	.0013	.0026	.0049	.0083
31	.0000	.0000	.0000	.0000	.0001	.0003	.0007	.0015	.0030	.0054
32	.0000	.0000	.0000	.0000	.0001	.0001	.0004	.0009	.0018	.0034
33	.0000	.0000	.0000	.0000	.0000	.0001	.0002	.0005	.0010	.0020

Source: Computed by D. K. Hildebrand.

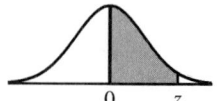

z	.00	.01	.02	.03	.04	.05	.06	.07	.08	.09
0.00	.0000	.0040	.0080	.0120	.0160	.0199	.0239	.0279	.0319	.0359
0.10	.0398	.0438	.0478	.0517	.0557	.0596	.0636	.0675	.0714	.0753
0.20	.0793	.0832	.0871	.0910	.0948	.0987	.1026	.1064	.1103	.1141
0.30	.1179	.1217	.1255	.1293	.1331	.1368	.1406	.1443	.1480	.1517
0.40	.1554	.1591	.1628	.1664	.1700	.1736	.1772	.1808	.1844	.1879
0.50	.1915	.1950	.1985	.2019	.2054	.2088	.2123	.2157	.2190	.2224
0.60	.2257	.2291	.2324	.2357	.2389	.2422	.2454	.2486	.2517	.2549
0.70	.2580	.2611	.2642	.2673	.2704	.2734	.2764	.2794	.2823	.2852
0.80	.2881	.2910	.2939	.2967	.2995	.3023	.3051	.3078	.3106	.3133
0.90	.3159	.3186	.3212	.3238	.3264	.3289	.3315	.3340	.3365	.3389
1.00	.3413	.3438	.3461	.3485	.3508	.3531	.3554	.3577	.3599	.3621
1.10	.3643	.3665	.3686	.3708	.3729	.3749	.3770	.3790	.3810	.3830
1.20	.3849	.3869	.3888	.3907	.3925	.3944	.3962	.3980	.3997	.4015
1.30	.4032	.4049	.4066	.4082	.4099	.4115	.4131	.4147	.4162	.4177
1.40	.4192	.4207	.4222	.4236	.4251	.4265	.4279	.4292	.4306	.4319
1.50	.4332	.4345	.4357	.4370	.4382	.4394	.4406	.4418	.4429	.4441
1.60	.4452	.4463	.4474	.4484	.4495	.4505	.4515	.4525	.4535	.4545
1.70	.4554	.4564	.4573	.4582	.4591	.4599	.4608	.4616	.4625	.4633
1.80	.4641	.4649	.4656	.4664	.4671	.4678	.4686	.4693	.4699	.4706
1.90	.4713	.4719	.4726	.4732	.4738	.4744	.4750	.4756	.4761	.4767
2.00	.4772	.4778	.4783	.4788	.4793	.4798	.4803	.4808	.4812	.4817
2.10	.4821	.4826	.4830	.4834	.4838	.4842	.4846	.4850	.4854	.4857
2.20	.4861	.4864	.4868	.4871	.4875	.4878	.4881	.4884	.4887	.4890
2.30	.4893	.4896	.4898	.4901	.4904	.4906	.4909	.4911	.4913	.4916
2.40	.4918	.4920	.4922	.4925	.4927	.4929	.4931	.4932	.4934	.4936
2.50	.4938	.4940	.4941	.4943	.4945	.4946	.4948	.4949	.4951	.4952
2.60	.4953	.4955	.4956	.4957	.4959	.4960	.4961	.4962	.4963	.4964
2.70	.4965	.4966	.4967	.4968	.4969	.4970	.4971	.4972	.4973	.4974
2.80	.4974	.4975	.4976	.4977	.4977	.4978	.4979	.4979	.4980	.4981
2.90	.4981	.4982	.4982	.4983	.4984	.4984	.4985	.4985	.4986	.4986
3.00	.4987	.4987	.4987	.4988	.4988	.4989	.4989	.4989	.4990	.4990

z	area
3.50	.49976737
4.00	.49996833
4.50	.49999660
5.00	.49999971

Source: Computed by P. J. Hildebrand.

TABLE 4 **Percentage points of the *t*-distribution**

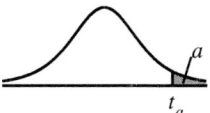

df	$a = .1$	$a = .05$	$a = .025$	$a = .01$	$a = .005$	$a = .001$
1	3.078	6.314	12.706	31.821	63.657	318.309
2	1.886	2.920	4.303	6.965	9.925	22.327
3	1.638	2.353	3.182	4.541	5.841	10.215
4	1.533	2.132	2.776	3.747	4.604	7.173
5	1.476	2.015	2.571	3.365	4.032	5.893
6	1.440	1.943	2.447	3.143	3.707	5.208
7	1.415	1.895	2.365	2.998	3.499	4.785
8	1.397	1.860	2.306	2.896	3.355	4.501
9	1.383	1.833	2.262	2.821	3.250	4.297
10	1.372	1.812	2.228	2.764	3.169	4.144
11	1.363	1.796	2.201	2.718	3.106	4.025
12	1.356	1.782	2.179	2.681	3.055	3.930
13	1.350	1.771	2.160	2.650	3.012	3.852
14	1.345	1.761	2.145	2.624	2.977	3.787
15	1.341	1.753	2.131	2.602	2.947	3.733
16	1.337	1.746	2.120	2.583	2.921	3.686
17	1.333	1.740	2.110	2.567	2.898	3.646
18	1.330	1.734	2.101	2.552	2.878	3.610
19	1.328	1.729	2.093	2.539	2.861	3.579
20	1.325	1.725	2.086	2.528	2.845	3.552
21	1.323	1.721	2.080	2.518	2.831	3.527
22	1.321	1.717	2.074	2.508	2.819	3.505
23	1.319	1.714	2.069	2.500	2.807	3.485
24	1.318	1.711	2.064	2.492	2.797	3.467
25	1.316	1.708	2.060	2.485	2.787	3.450
26	1.315	1.706	2.056	2.479	2.779	3.435
27	1.314	1.703	2.052	2.473	2.771	3.421
28	1.313	1.701	2.048	2.467	2.763	3.408
29	1.311	1.699	2.045	2.462	2.756	3.396
30	1.310	1.697	2.042	2.457	2.750	3.385
40	1.303	1.684	2.021	2.423	2.704	3.307
60	1.296	1.671	2.000	2.390	2.660	3.232
120	1.289	1.658	1.980	2.358	2.617	3.160
240	1.285	1.651	1.970	2.342	2.596	3.125
∞	1.282	1.645	1.960	2.326	2.576	3.090

Source: Computed by P. J. Hildebrand.

T A B L E 5   Percentage points of the chi-square distribution ($a > .5$)

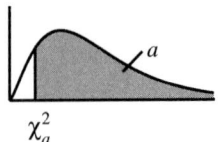

χ^2_a

df	$a = .999$	$a = .995$	$a = .99$	$a = .975$	$a = .95$	$a = .9$
1	.000002	.000039	.000157	.000982	.003932	.01579
2	.002001	.01003	.02010	.05064	.1026	.2107
3	.02430	.07172	.1148	.2158	.3518	.5844
4	.09080	.2070	.2971	.4844	.7107	1.064
5	.2102	.4117	.5543	.8312	1.145	1.610
6	.3811	.6757	.8721	1.237	1.635	2.204
7	.5985	.9893	1.239	1.690	2.167	2.833
8	.8571	1.344	1.646	2.180	2.733	3.490
9	1.152	1.735	2.088	2.700	3.325	4.168
10	1.479	2.156	2.558	3.247	3.940	4.865
11	1.834	2.603	3.053	3.816	4.575	5.578
12	2.214	3.074	3.571	4.404	5.226	6.304
13	2.617	3.565	4.107	5.009	5.892	7.042
14	3.041	4.075	4.660	5.629	6.571	7.790
15	3.483	4.601	5.229	6.262	7.261	8.547
16	3.942	5.142	5.812	6.908	7.962	9.312
17	4.416	5.697	6.408	7.564	8.672	10.09
18	4.905	6.265	7.015	8.231	9.390	10.86
19	5.407	6.844	7.633	8.907	10.12	11.65
20	5.921	7.434	8.260	9.591	10.85	12.44
21	6.447	8.034	8.897	10.28	11.59	13.24
22	6.983	8.643	9.542	10.98	12.34	14.04
23	7.529	9.260	10.20	11.69	13.09	14.85
24	8.085	9.886	10.86	12.40	13.85	15.66
25	8.649	10.52	11.52	13.12	14.61	16.47
26	9.222	11.16	12.20	13.84	15.38	17.29
27	9.803	11.81	12.88	14.57	16.15	18.11
28	10.39	12.46	13.56	15.31	16.93	18.94
29	10.99	13.12	14.26	16.05	17.71	19.77
30	11.59	13.79	14.95	16.79	18.49	20.60
40	17.92	20.71	22.16	24.43	26.51	29.05
50	24.67	27.99	29.71	32.36	34.76	37.69
60	31.74	35.53	37.48	40.48	43.19	46.46
70	39.04	43.28	45.44	48.76	51.74	55.33
80	46.52	51.17	53.54	57.15	60.39	64.28
90	54.16	59.20	61.75	65.65	69.13	73.29
100	61.92	67.33	70.06	74.22	77.93	82.36
120	77.76	83.85	86.92	91.57	95.70	100.62
240	177.95	187.32	191.99	198.98	205.14	212.39

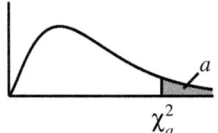

$$\chi_a^2$$

$a = .1$	$a = .05$	$a = .025$	$a = .01$	$a = .005$	$a = .001$	df
2.706	3.841	5.024	6.635	7.879	10.83	1
4.605	5.991	7.378	9.210	10.60	13.82	2
6.251	7.815	9.348	11.34	12.84	16.27	3
7.779	9.488	11.14	13.28	14.86	18.47	4
9.236	11.07	12.83	15.09	16.75	20.52	5
10.64	12.59	14.45	16.81	18.55	22.46	6
12.02	14.07	16.01	18.48	20.28	24.32	7
13.36	15.51	17.53	20.09	21.95	26.12	8
14.68	16.92	19.02	21.67	23.59	27.88	9
15.99	18.31	20.48	23.21	25.19	29.59	10
17.28	19.68	21.92	24.72	26.76	31.27	11
18.55	21.03	23.34	26.22	28.30	32.91	12
19.81	22.36	24.74	27.69	29.82	34.53	13
21.06	23.68	26.12	29.14	31.32	36.12	14
22.31	25.00	27.49	30.58	32.80	37.70	15
23.54	26.30	28.85	32.00	34.27	39.25	16
24.77	27.59	30.19	33.41	35.72	40.79	17
25.99	28.87	31.53	34.81	37.16	42.31	18
27.20	30.14	32.85	36.19	38.58	43.82	19
28.41	31.41	34.17	37.57	40.00	45.31	20
29.62	32.67	35.48	38.93	41.40	46.80	21
30.81	33.92	36.78	40.29	42.80	48.27	22
32.01	35.17	38.08	41.64	44.18	49.73	23
33.20	36.42	39.36	42.98	45.56	51.18	24
34.38	37.65	40.65	44.31	46.93	52.62	25
35.56	38.89	41.92	45.64	48.29	54.05	26
36.74	40.11	43.19	46.96	49.65	55.48	27
37.92	41.34	44.46	48.28	50.99	56.89	28
39.09	42.56	45.72	49.59	52.34	58.30	29
40.26	43.77	46.98	50.89	53.67	59.70	30
51.81	55.76	59.34	63.69	66.77	73.40	40
63.17	67.50	71.42	76.15	79.49	86.66	50
74.40	79.08	83.30	88.38	91.95	99.61	60
85.53	90.53	95.02	100.43	104.21	112.32	70
96.58	101.88	106.63	112.33	116.32	124.84	80
107.57	113.15	118.14	124.12	128.30	137.21	90
118.50	124.34	129.56	135.81	140.17	149.45	100
140.23	146.57	152.21	158.95	163.65	173.62	120
268.47	277.14	284.80	293.89	300.18	313.44	240

Source: Computed by P. J. Hildebrand

TABLE 6   Percentage points of the *F*-distribution (df$_2$ between 1 and 6)

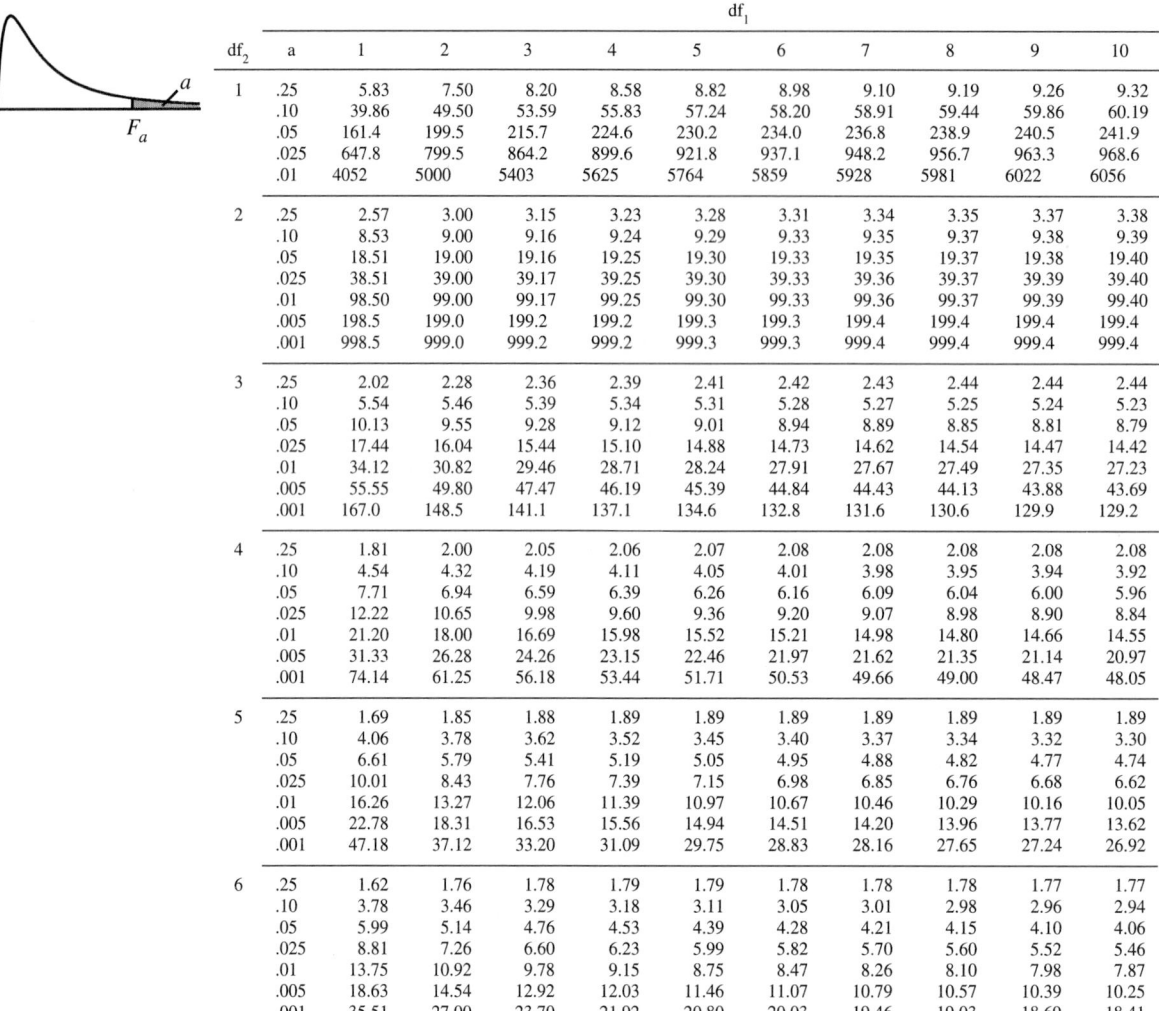

df$_2$	a	1	2	3	4	5	6	7	8	9	10
1	.25	5.83	7.50	8.20	8.58	8.82	8.98	9.10	9.19	9.26	9.32
	.10	39.86	49.50	53.59	55.83	57.24	58.20	58.91	59.44	59.86	60.19
	.05	161.4	199.5	215.7	224.6	230.2	234.0	236.8	238.9	240.5	241.9
	.025	647.8	799.5	864.2	899.6	921.8	937.1	948.2	956.7	963.3	968.6
	.01	4052	5000	5403	5625	5764	5859	5928	5981	6022	6056
2	.25	2.57	3.00	3.15	3.23	3.28	3.31	3.34	3.35	3.37	3.38
	.10	8.53	9.00	9.16	9.24	9.29	9.33	9.35	9.37	9.38	9.39
	.05	18.51	19.00	19.16	19.25	19.30	19.33	19.35	19.37	19.38	19.40
	.025	38.51	39.00	39.17	39.25	39.30	39.33	39.36	39.37	39.39	39.40
	.01	98.50	99.00	99.17	99.25	99.30	99.33	99.36	99.37	99.39	99.40
	.005	198.5	199.0	199.2	199.2	199.3	199.3	199.4	199.4	199.4	199.4
	.001	998.5	999.0	999.2	999.2	999.3	999.3	999.4	999.4	999.4	999.4
3	.25	2.02	2.28	2.36	2.39	2.41	2.42	2.43	2.44	2.44	2.44
	.10	5.54	5.46	5.39	5.34	5.31	5.28	5.27	5.25	5.24	5.23
	.05	10.13	9.55	9.28	9.12	9.01	8.94	8.89	8.85	8.81	8.79
	.025	17.44	16.04	15.44	15.10	14.88	14.73	14.62	14.54	14.47	14.42
	.01	34.12	30.82	29.46	28.71	28.24	27.91	27.67	27.49	27.35	27.23
	.005	55.55	49.80	47.47	46.19	45.39	44.84	44.43	44.13	43.88	43.69
	.001	167.0	148.5	141.1	137.1	134.6	132.8	131.6	130.6	129.9	129.2
4	.25	1.81	2.00	2.05	2.06	2.07	2.08	2.08	2.08	2.08	2.08
	.10	4.54	4.32	4.19	4.11	4.05	4.01	3.98	3.95	3.94	3.92
	.05	7.71	6.94	6.59	6.39	6.26	6.16	6.09	6.04	6.00	5.96
	.025	12.22	10.65	9.98	9.60	9.36	9.20	9.07	8.98	8.90	8.84
	.01	21.20	18.00	16.69	15.98	15.52	15.21	14.98	14.80	14.66	14.55
	.005	31.33	26.28	24.26	23.15	22.46	21.97	21.62	21.35	21.14	20.97
	.001	74.14	61.25	56.18	53.44	51.71	50.53	49.66	49.00	48.47	48.05
5	.25	1.69	1.85	1.88	1.89	1.89	1.89	1.89	1.89	1.89	1.89
	.10	4.06	3.78	3.62	3.52	3.45	3.40	3.37	3.34	3.32	3.30
	.05	6.61	5.79	5.41	5.19	5.05	4.95	4.88	4.82	4.77	4.74
	.025	10.01	8.43	7.76	7.39	7.15	6.98	6.85	6.76	6.68	6.62
	.01	16.26	13.27	12.06	11.39	10.97	10.67	10.46	10.29	10.16	10.05
	.005	22.78	18.31	16.53	15.56	14.94	14.51	14.20	13.96	13.77	13.62
	.001	47.18	37.12	33.20	31.09	29.75	28.83	28.16	27.65	27.24	26.92
6	.25	1.62	1.76	1.78	1.79	1.79	1.78	1.78	1.78	1.77	1.77
	.10	3.78	3.46	3.29	3.18	3.11	3.05	3.01	2.98	2.96	2.94
	.05	5.99	5.14	4.76	4.53	4.39	4.28	4.21	4.15	4.10	4.06
	.025	8.81	7.26	6.60	6.23	5.99	5.82	5.70	5.60	5.52	5.46
	.01	13.75	10.92	9.78	9.15	8.75	8.47	8.26	8.10	7.98	7.87
	.005	18.63	14.54	12.92	12.03	11.46	11.07	10.79	10.57	10.39	10.25
	.001	35.51	27.00	23.70	21.92	20.80	20.03	19.46	19.03	18.69	18.41

12	15	20	24	30	40	60	120	240	∞	a	df$_2$
9.41	9.49	9.58	9.63	9.67	9.71	9.76	9.80	9.83	9.85	.25	1
60.71	61.22	61.74	62.00	62.26	62.53	62.79	63.06	63.19	63.33	.10	
243.9	245.9	248.0	249.1	250.1	251.1	252.2	253.3	253.8	254.3	.05	
976.7	984.9	993.1	997.2	1001	1006	1010	1014	1016	1018	.025	
6106	6157	6209	6235	6261	6287	6313	6339	6353	6366	.01	
3.39	3.41	3.43	3.43	3.44	3.45	3.46	3.47	3.47	3.48	.25	2
9.41	9.42	9.44	9.45	9.46	9.47	9.47	9.48	9.49	9.49	.10	
19.41	19.43	19.45	19.45	19.46	19.47	19.49	19.49	19.49	19.50	.05	
39.41	39.43	39.45	39.46	39.46	39.47	39.48	39.49	39.49	39.50	.025	
99.42	99.43	99.45	99.46	99.47	99.47	99.48	99.49	99.49	99.50	.01	
199.4	199.4	199.4	199.5	199.5	199.5	199.5	199.5	199.5	199.5	.005	
999.4	999.4	999.4	999.5	999.5	999.5	999.5	999.5	999.5	999.5	.001	
2.45	2.46	2.46	2.46	2.47	2.47	2.47	2.47	2.47	2.47	.25	3
5.22	5.20	5.18	5.18	5.17	5.16	5.15	5.14	5.14	5.13	.10	
8.74	8.70	8.66	8.64	8.62	8.59	8.57	8.55	8.54	8.53	.05	
14.34	14.25	14.17	14.12	14.08	14.04	13.99	13.95	13.92	13.90	.025	
27.05	26.87	26.69	26.60	26.50	26.41	26.32	26.22	26.17	26.13	.01	
43.39	43.08	42.78	42.62	42.47	42.31	42.15	41.99	41.91	41.83	.005	
128.3	127.4	126.4	125.9	125.4	125.0	124.5	124.0	123.7	123.5	.001	
2.08	2.08	2.08	2.08	2.08	2.08	2.08	2.08	2.08	2.08	.25	4
3.90	3.87	3.84	3.83	3.82	3.80	3.79	3.78	3.77	3.76	.10	
5.91	5.86	5.80	5.77	5.75	5.72	5.69	5.66	5.64	5.63	.05	
8.75	8.66	8.56	8.51	8.46	8.41	8.36	8.31	8.28	8.26	.025	
14.37	14.20	14.02	13.93	13.84	13.75	13.65	13.56	13.51	13.46	.01	
20.70	20.44	20.17	20.03	19.89	19.75	19.61	19.47	19.40	19.32	.005	
47.41	46.76	46.10	45.77	45.43	45.09	44.75	44.40	44.23	44.05	.001	
1.89	1.89	1.88	1.88	1.88	1.88	1.87	1.87	1.87	1.87	.25	5
3.27	3.24	3.21	3.19	3.17	3.16	3.14	3.12	3.11	3.10	.10	
4.68	4.62	4.56	4.53	4.50	4.46	4.43	4.40	4.38	4.36	.05	
6.52	6.43	6.33	6.28	6.23	6.18	6.12	6.07	6.04	6.02	.025	
9.89	9.72	9.55	9.47	9.38	9.29	9.20	9.11	9.07	9.02	.01	
13.38	13.15	12.90	12.78	12.66	12.53	12.40	12.27	12.21	12.14	.005	
26.42	25.91	25.39	25.13	24.87	24.60	24.33	24.06	23.92	23.79	.001	
1.77	1.76	1.76	1.75	1.75	1.75	1.74	1.74	1.74	1.74	.25	6
2.90	2.87	2.84	2.82	2.80	2.78	2.76	2.74	2.73	2.72	.10	
4.00	3.94	3.87	3.84	3.81	3.77	3.74	3.70	3.69	3.67	.05	
5.37	5.27	5.17	5.12	5.07	5.01	4.96	4.90	4.88	4.85	.025	
7.72	7.56	7.40	7.31	7.23	7.14	7.06	6.97	6.92	6.88	.01	
10.03	9.81	9.59	9.47	9.36	9.24	9.12	9.00	8.94	8.88	.005	
17.99	17.56	17.12	16.90	16.67	16.44	16.21	15.98	15.86	15.75	.001	

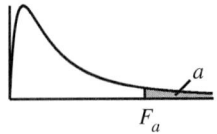

		df$_1$									
df$_2$	a	1	2	3	4	5	6	7	8	9	10
7	.25	1.57	1.70	1.72	1.72	1.71	1.71	1.70	1.70	1.69	1.69
	.10	3.59	3.26	3.07	2.96	2.88	2.83	2.78	2.75	2.72	2.70
	.05	5.59	4.74	4.35	4.12	3.97	3.87	3.79	3.73	3.68	3.64
	.025	8.07	6.54	5.89	5.52	5.29	5.12	4.99	4.90	4.82	4.76
	.01	12.25	9.55	8.45	7.85	7.46	7.19	6.99	6.84	6.72	6.62
	.005	16.24	12.40	10.88	10.05	9.52	9.16	8.89	8.68	8.51	8.38
	.001	29.25	21.69	18.77	17.20	16.21	15.52	15.02	14.63	14.33	14.08
8	.25	1.54	1.66	1.67	1.66	1.66	1.65	1.64	1.64	1.63	1.63
	.10	3.46	3.11	2.92	2.81	2.73	2.67	2.62	2.59	2.56	2.54
	.05	5.32	4.46	4.07	3.84	3.69	3.58	3.50	3.44	3.39	3.35
	.025	7.57	6.06	5.42	5.05	4.82	4.65	4.53	4.43	4.36	4.30
	.01	11.26	8.65	7.59	7.01	6.63	6.37	6.18	6.03	5.91	5.81
	.005	14.69	11.04	9.60	8.81	8.30	7.95	7.69	7.50	7.34	7.21
	.001	25.41	18.49	15.83	14.39	13.48	12.86	12.40	12.05	11.77	11.54
9	.25	1.51	1.62	1.63	1.63	1.62	1.61	1.60	1.60	1.59	1.59
	.10	3.36	3.01	2.81	2.69	2.61	2.55	2.51	2.47	2.44	2.42
	.05	5.12	4.26	3.86	3.63	3.48	3.37	3.29	3.23	3.18	3.14
	.025	7.21	5.71	5.08	4.72	4.48	4.32	4.20	4.10	4.03	3.96
	.01	10.56	8.02	6.99	6.42	6.06	5.80	5.61	5.47	5.35	5.26
	.005	13.61	10.11	8.72	7.96	7.47	7.13	6.88	6.69	6.54	6.42
	.001	22.86	16.39	13.90	12.56	11.71	11.13	10.70	10.37	10.11	9.89
10	.25	1.49	1.60	1.60	1.59	1.59	1.58	1.57	1.56	1.56	1.55
	.10	3.29	2.92	2.73	2.61	2.52	2.46	2.41	2.38	2.35	2.32
	.05	4.96	4.10	3.71	3.48	3.33	3.22	3.14	3.07	3.02	2.98
	.025	6.94	5.46	4.83	4.47	4.24	4.07	3.95	3.85	3.78	3.72
	.01	10.04	7.56	6.55	5.99	5.64	5.39	5.20	5.06	4.94	4.85
	.005	12.83	9.43	8.08	7.34	6.87	6.54	6.30	6.12	5.97	5.85
	.001	21.04	14.91	12.55	11.28	10.48	9.93	9.52	9.20	8.96	8.75
11	.25	1.47	1.58	1.58	1.57	1.56	1.55	1.54	1.53	1.53	1.52
	.10	3.23	2.86	2.66	2.54	2.45	2.39	2.34	2.30	2.27	2.25
	.05	4.84	3.98	3.59	3.36	3.20	3.09	3.01	2.95	2.90	2.85
	.025	6.72	5.26	4.63	4.28	4.04	3.88	3.76	3.66	3.59	3.53
	.01	9.65	7.21	6.22	5.67	5.32	5.07	4.89	4.74	4.63	4.54
	.005	12.23	8.91	7.60	6.88	6.42	6.10	5.86	5.68	5.54	5.42
	.001	19.69	13.81	11.56	10.35	9.58	9.05	8.66	8.35	8.12	7.92
12	.25	1.46	1.56	1.56	1.55	1.54	1.53	1.52	1.51	1.51	1.50
	.10	3.18	2.81	2.61	2.48	2.39	2.33	2.28	2.24	2.21	2.19
	.05	4.75	3.89	3.49	3.26	3.11	3.00	2.91	2.85	2.80	2.75
	.025	6.55	5.10	4.47	4.12	3.89	3.73	3.61	3.51	3.44	3.37
	.01	9.33	6.93	5.95	5.41	5.06	4.82	4.64	4.50	4.39	4.30
	.005	11.75	8.51	7.23	6.52	6.07	5.76	5.52	5.35	5.20	5.09
	.001	18.64	12.97	10.80	9.63	8.89	8.38	8.00	7.71	7.48	7.29

					df_1						
12	15	20	24	30	40	60	120	240	∞	a	df_2
1.68	1.68	1.67	1.67	1.66	1.66	1.65	1.65	1.65	1.65	.25	7
2.67	2.63	2.59	2.58	2.56	2.54	2.51	2.49	2.48	2.47	.10	
3.57	3.51	3.44	3.41	3.38	3.34	3.30	3.27	3.25	3.23	.05	
4.67	4.57	4.47	4.41	4.36	4.31	4.25	4.20	4.17	4.14	.025	
6.47	6.31	6.16	6.07	5.99	5.91	5.82	5.74	5.69	5.65	.01	
8.18	7.97	7.75	7.64	7.53	7.42	7.31	7.19	7.13	7.08	.005	
13.71	13.32	12.93	12.73	12.53	12.33	12.12	11.91	11.80	11.70	.001	
1.62	1.62	1.61	1.60	1.60	1.59	1.59	1.58	1.58	1.58	.25	8
2.50	2.46	2.42	2.40	2.38	2.36	2.34	2.32	2.30	2.29	.10	
3.28	3.22	3.15	3.12	3.08	3.04	3.01	2.97	2.95	2.93	.05	
4.20	4.10	4.00	3.95	3.89	3.84	3.78	3.73	3.70	3.67	.025	
5.67	5.52	5.36	5.28	5.20	5.12	5.03	4.95	4.90	4.86	.01	
7.01	6.81	6.61	6.50	6.40	6.29	6.18	6.06	6.01	5.95	.005	
11.19	10.84	10.48	10.30	10.11	9.92	9.73	9.53	9.43	9.33	.001	
1.58	1.57	1.56	1.56	1.55	1.54	1.54	1.53	1.53	1.53	.25	9
2.38	2.34	2.30	2.28	2.25	2.23	2.21	2.18	2.17	2.16	.10	
3.07	3.01	2.94	2.90	2.86	2.83	2.79	2.75	2.73	2.71	.05	
3.87	3.77	3.67	3.61	3.56	3.51	3.45	3.39	3.36	3.33	.025	
5.11	4.96	4.81	4.73	4.65	4.57	4.48	4.40	4.35	4.31	.01	
6.23	6.03	5.83	5.73	5.62	5.52	5.41	5.30	5.24	5.19	.005	
9.57	9.24	8.90	8.72	8.55	8.37	8.19	8.00	7.91	7.81	.001	
1.54	1.53	1.52	1.52	1.51	1.51	1.50	1.49	1.49	1.48	.25	10
2.28	2.24	2.20	2.18	2.16	2.13	2.11	2.08	2.07	2.06	.10	
2.91	2.85	2.77	2.74	2.70	2.66	2.62	2.58	2.56	2.54	.05	
3.62	3.52	3.42	3.37	3.31	3.26	3.20	3.14	3.11	3.08	.025	
4.71	4.56	4.41	4.33	4.25	4.17	4.08	4.00	3.95	3.91	.01	
5.66	5.47	5.27	5.17	5.07	4.97	4.86	4.75	4.69	4.64	.005	
8.45	8.13	7.80	7.64	7.47	7.30	7.12	6.94	6.85	6.76	.001	
1.51	1.50	1.49	1.49	1.48	1.47	1.47	1.46	1.45	1.45	.25	11
2.21	2.17	2.12	2.10	2.08	2.05	2.03	2.00	1.99	1.97	.10	
2.79	2.72	2.65	2.61	2.57	2.53	2.49	2.45	2.43	2.40	.05	
3.43	3.33	3.23	3.17	3.12	3.06	3.00	2.94	2.91	2.88	.025	
4.40	4.25	4.10	4.02	3.94	3.86	3.78	3.69	3.65	3.60	.01	
5.24	5.05	4.86	4.76	4.65	4.55	4.45	4.34	4.28	4.23	.005	
7.63	7.32	7.01	6.85	6.68	6.52	6.35	6.18	6.09	6.00	.001	
1.49	1.48	1.47	1.46	1.45	1.45	1.44	1.43	1.43	1.42	.25	12
2.15	2.10	2.06	2.04	2.01	1.99	1.96	1.93	1.92	1.90	.10	
2.69	2.62	2.54	2.51	2.47	2.43	2.38	2.34	2.32	2.30	.05	
3.28	3.18	3.07	3.02	2.96	2.91	2.85	2.79	2.76	2.72	.025	
4.16	4.01	3.86	3.78	3.70	3.62	3.54	3.45	3.41	3.36	.01	
4.91	4.72	4.53	4.43	4.33	4.23	4.12	4.01	3.96	3.90	.005	
7.00	6.71	6.40	6.25	6.09	5.93	5.76	5.59	5.51	5.42	.001	

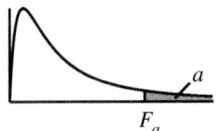

df$_2$	a	1	2	3	4	5	6	7	8	9	10
13	.25	1.45	1.55	1.55	1.53	1.52	1.51	1.50	1.49	1.49	1.48
	.10	3.14	2.76	2.56	2.43	2.35	2.28	2.23	2.20	2.16	2.14
	.05	4.67	3.81	3.41	3.18	3.03	2.92	2.83	2.77	2.71	2.67
	.025	6.41	4.97	4.35	4.00	3.77	3.60	3.48	3.39	3.31	3.25
	.01	9.07	6.70	5.74	5.21	4.86	4.62	4.44	4.30	4.19	4.10
	.005	11.37	8.19	6.93	6.23	5.79	5.48	5.25	5.08	4.94	4.82
	.001	17.82	12.31	10.21	9.07	8.35	7.86	7.49	7.21	6.98	6.80
14	.25	1.44	1.53	1.53	1.52	1.51	1.50	1.49	1.48	1.47	1.46
	.10	3.10	2.73	2.52	2.39	2.31	2.24	2.19	2.15	2.12	2.10
	.05	4.60	3.74	3.34	3.11	2.96	2.85	2.76	2.70	2.65	2.60
	.025	6.30	4.86	4.24	3.89	3.66	3.50	3.38	3.29	3.21	3.15
	.01	8.86	6.51	5.56	5.04	4.69	4.46	4.28	4.14	4.03	3.94
	.005	11.06	7.92	6.68	6.00	5.56	5.26	5.03	4.86	4.72	4.60
	.001	17.14	11.78	9.73	8.62	7.92	7.44	7.08	6.80	6.58	6.40
15	.25	1.43	1.52	1.52	1.51	1.49	1.48	1.47	1.46	1.46	1.45
	.10	3.07	2.70	2.49	2.36	2.27	2.21	2.16	2.12	2.09	2.06
	.05	4.54	3.68	3.29	3.06	2.90	2.79	2.71	2.64	2.59	2.54
	.025	6.20	4.77	4.15	3.80	3.58	3.41	3.29	3.20	3.12	3.06
	.01	8.68	6.36	5.42	4.89	4.56	4.32	4.14	4.00	3.89	3.80
	.005	10.80	7.70	6.48	5.80	5.37	5.07	4.85	4.67	4.54	4.42
	.001	16.59	11.34	9.34	8.25	7.57	7.09	6.74	6.47	6.26	6.08
16	.25	1.42	1.51	1.51	1.50	1.48	1.47	1.46	1.45	1.44	1.44
	.10	3.05	2.67	2.46	2.33	2.24	2.18	2.13	2.09	2.06	2.03
	.05	4.49	3.63	3.24	3.01	2.85	2.74	2.66	2.59	2.54	2.49
	.025	6.12	4.69	4.08	3.73	3.50	3.34	3.22	3.12	3.05	2.99
	.01	8.53	6.23	5.29	4.77	4.44	4.20	4.03	3.89	3.78	3.69
	.005	10.58	7.51	6.30	5.64	5.21	4.91	4.69	4.52	4.38	4.27
	.001	16.12	10.97	9.01	7.94	7.27	6.80	6.46	6.19	5.98	5.81
17	.25	1.42	1.51	1.50	1.49	1.47	1.46	1.45	1.44	1.43	1.43
	.10	3.03	2.64	2.44	2.31	2.22	2.15	2.10	2.06	2.03	2.00
	.05	4.45	3.59	3.20	2.96	2.81	2.70	2.61	2.55	2.49	2.45
	.025	6.04	4.62	4.01	3.66	3.44	3.28	3.16	3.06	2.98	2.92
	.01	8.40	6.11	5.18	4.67	4.34	4.10	3.93	3.79	3.68	3.59
	.005	10.38	7.35	6.16	5.50	5.07	4.78	4.56	4.39	4.25	4.14
	.001	15.72	10.66	8.73	7.68	7.02	6.56	6.22	5.96	5.75	5.58
18	.25	1.41	1.50	1.49	1.48	1.46	1.45	1.44	1.43	1.42	1.42
	.10	3.01	2.62	2.42	2.29	2.20	2.13	2.08	2.04	2.00	1.98
	.05	4.41	3.55	3.16	2.93	2.77	2.66	2.58	2.51	2.46	2.41
	.025	5.98	4.56	3.95	3.61	3.38	3.22	3.10	3.01	2.93	2.87
	.01	8.29	6.01	5.09	4.58	4.25	4.01	3.84	3.71	3.60	3.51
	.005	10.22	7.21	6.03	5.37	4.96	4.66	4.44	4.28	4.14	4.03
	.001	15.38	10.39	8.49	7.46	6.81	6.35	6.02	5.76	5.56	5.39

12	15	20	24	30	40	60	120	240	∞	a	df$_2$
1.47	1.46	1.45	1.44	1.43	1.42	1.42	1.41	1.40	1.40	.25	13
2.10	2.05	2.01	1.98	1.96	1.93	1.90	1.88	1.86	1.85	.10	
2.60	2.53	2.46	2.42	2.38	2.34	2.30	2.25	2.23	2.21	.05	
3.15	3.05	2.95	2.89	2.84	2.78	2.72	2.66	2.63	2.60	.025	
3.96	3.82	3.66	3.59	3.51	3.43	3.34	3.25	3.21	3.17	.01	
4.64	4.46	4.27	4.17	4.07	3.97	3.87	3.76	3.70	3.65	.005	
6.52	6.23	5.93	5.78	5.63	5.47	5.30	5.14	5.05	4.97	.001	
1.45	1.44	1.43	1.42	1.41	1.41	1.40	1.39	1.38	1.38	.25	14
2.05	2.01	1.96	1.94	1.91	1.89	1.86	1.83	1.81	1.80	.10	
2.53	2.46	2.39	2.35	2.31	2.27	2.22	2.18	2.15	2.13	.05	
3.05	2.95	2.84	2.79	2.73	2.67	2.61	2.55	2.52	2.49	.025	
3.80	3.66	3.51	3.43	3.35	3.27	3.18	3.09	3.05	3.00	.01	
4.43	4.25	4.06	3.96	3.86	3.76	3.66	3.55	3.49	3.44	.005	
6.13	5.85	5.56	5.41	5.25	5.10	4.94	4.77	4.69	4.60	.001	
1.44	1.43	1.41	1.41	1.40	1.39	1.38	1.37	1.36	1.36	.25	15
2.02	1.97	1.92	1.90	1.87	1.85	1.82	1.79	1.77	1.76	.10	
2.48	2.40	2.33	2.29	2.25	2.20	2.16	2.11	2.09	2.07	.05	
2.96	2.86	2.76	2.70	2.64	2.59	2.52	2.46	2.43	2.40	.025	
3.67	3.52	3.37	3.29	3.21	3.13	3.05	2.96	2.91	2.87	.01	
4.25	4.07	3.88	3.79	3.69	3.58	3.48	3.37	3.32	3.26	.005	
5.81	5.54	5.25	5.10	4.95	4.80	4.64	4.47	4.39	4.31	.001	
1.43	1.41	1.40	1.39	1.38	1.37	1.36	1.35	1.35	1.34	.25	16
1.99	1.94	1.89	1.87	1.84	1.81	1.78	1.75	1.73	1.72	.10	
2.42	2.35	2.28	2.24	2.19	2.15	2.11	2.06	2.03	2.01	.05	
2.89	2.79	2.68	2.63	2.57	2.51	2.45	2.38	2.35	2.32	.025	
3.55	3.41	3.26	3.18	3.10	3.02	2.93	2.84	2.80	2.75	.01	
4.10	3.92	3.73	3.64	3.54	3.44	3.33	3.22	3.17	3.11	.005	
5.55	5.27	4.99	4.85	4.70	4.54	4.39	4.23	4.14	4.06	.001	
1.41	1.40	1.39	1.38	1.37	1.36	1.35	1.34	1.33	1.33	.25	17
1.96	1.91	1.86	1.84	1.81	1.78	1.75	1.72	1.70	1.69	.10	
2.38	2.31	2.23	2.19	2.15	2.10	2.06	2.01	1.99	1.96	.05	
2.82	2.72	2.62	2.56	2.50	2.44	2.38	2.32	2.28	2.25	.025	
3.46	3.31	3.16	3.08	3.00	2.92	2.83	2.75	2.70	2.65	.01	
3.97	3.79	3.61	3.51	3.41	3.31	3.21	3.10	3.04	2.98	.005	
5.32	5.05	4.78	4.63	4.48	4.33	4.18	4.02	3.93	3.85	.001	
1.40	1.39	1.38	1.37	1.36	1.35	1.34	1.33	1.32	1.32	.25	18
1.93	1.89	1.84	1.81	1.78	1.75	1.72	1.69	1.67	1.66	.10	
2.34	2.27	2.19	2.15	2.11	2.06	2.02	1.97	1.94	1.92	.05	
2.77	2.67	2.56	2.50	2.44	2.38	2.32	2.26	2.22	2.19	.025	
3.37	3.23	3.08	3.00	2.92	2.84	2.75	2.66	2.61	2.57	.01	
3.86	3.68	3.50	3.40	3.30	3.20	3.10	2.99	2.93	2.87	.005	
5.13	4.87	4.59	4.45	4.30	4.15	4.00	3.84	3.75	3.67	.001	

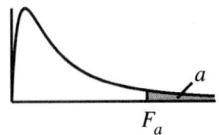

F_a

df_2	a	1	2	3	4	5	6	7	8	9	10
							df_1				
19	.25	1.41	1.49	1.49	1.47	1.46	1.44	1.43	1.42	1.41	1.41
	.10	2.99	2.61	2.40	2.27	2.18	2.11	2.06	2.02	1.98	1.96
	.05	4.38	3.52	3.13	2.90	2.74	2.63	2.54	2.48	2.42	2.38
	.025	5.92	4.51	3.90	3.56	3.33	3.17	3.05	2.96	2.88	2.82
	.01	8.18	5.93	5.01	4.50	4.17	3.94	3.77	3.63	3.52	3.43
	.005	10.07	7.09	5.92	5.27	4.85	4.56	4.34	4.18	4.04	3.93
	.001	15.08	10.16	8.28	7.27	6.62	6.18	5.85	5.59	5.39	5.22
20	.25	1.40	1.49	1.48	1.47	1.45	1.44	1.43	1.42	1.41	1.40
	.10	2.97	2.59	2.38	2.25	2.16	2.09	2.04	2.00	1.96	1.94
	.05	4.35	3.49	3.10	2.87	2.71	2.60	2.51	2.45	2.39	2.35
	.025	5.87	4.46	3.86	3.51	3.29	3.13	3.01	2.91	2.84	2.77
	.01	8.10	5.85	4.94	4.43	4.10	3.87	3.70	3.56	3.46	3.37
	.005	9.94	6.99	5.82	5.17	4.76	4.47	4.26	4.09	3.96	3.85
	.001	14.82	9.95	8.10	7.10	6.46	6.02	5.69	5.44	5.24	5.08
21	.25	1.40	1.48	1.48	1.46	1.44	1.43	1.42	1.41	1.40	1.39
	.10	2.96	2.57	2.36	2.23	2.14	2.08	2.02	1.98	1.95	1.92
	.05	4.32	3.47	3.07	2.84	2.68	2.57	2.49	2.42	2.37	2.32
	.025	5.83	4.42	3.82	3.48	3.25	3.09	2.97	2.87	2.80	2.73
	.01	8.02	5.78	4.87	4.37	4.04	3.81	3.64	3.51	3.40	3.31
	.005	9.83	6.89	5.73	5.09	4.68	4.39	4.18	4.01	3.88	3.77
	.001	14.59	9.77	7.94	6.95	6.32	5.88	5.56	5.31	5.11	4.95
22	.25	1.40	1.48	1.47	1.45	1.44	1.42	1.41	1.40	1.39	1.39
	.10	2.95	2.56	2.35	2.22	2.13	2.06	2.01	1.97	1.93	1.90
	.05	4.30	3.44	3.05	2.82	2.66	2.55	2.46	2.40	2.34	2.30
	.025	5.79	4.38	3.78	3.44	3.22	3.05	2.93	2.84	2.76	2.70
	.01	7.95	5.72	4.82	4.31	3.99	3.76	3.59	3.45	3.35	3.26
	.005	9.73	6.81	5.65	5.02	4.61	4.32	4.11	3.94	3.81	3.70
	.001	14.38	9.61	7.80	6.81	6.19	5.76	5.44	5.19	4.99	4.83
23	.25	1.39	1.47	1.47	1.45	1.43	1.42	1.41	1.40	1.39	1.38
	.10	2.94	2.55	2.34	2.21	2.11	2.05	1.99	1.95	1.92	1.89
	.05	4.28	3.42	3.03	2.80	2.64	2.53	2.44	2.37	2.32	2.27
	.025	5.75	4.35	3.75	3.41	3.18	3.02	2.90	2.81	2.73	2.67
	.01	7.88	5.66	4.76	4.26	3.94	3.71	3.54	3.41	3.30	3.21
	.005	9.63	6.73	5.58	4.95	4.54	4.26	4.05	3.88	3.75	3.64
	.001	14.20	9.47	7.67	6.70	6.08	5.65	5.33	5.09	4.89	4.73
24	.25	1.39	1.47	1.46	1.44	1.43	1.41	1.40	1.39	1.38	1.38
	.10	2.93	2.54	2.33	2.19	2.10	2.04	1.98	1.94	1.91	1.88
	.05	4.26	3.40	3.01	2.78	2.62	2.51	2.42	2.36	2.30	2.25
	.025	5.72	4.32	3.72	3.38	3.15	2.99	2.87	2.78	2.70	2.64
	.01	7.82	5.61	4.72	4.22	3.90	3.67	3.50	3.36	3.26	3.17
	.005	9.55	6.66	5.52	4.89	4.49	4.20	3.99	3.83	3.69	3.59
	.001	14.03	9.34	7.55	6.59	5.98	5.55	5.23	4.99	4.80	4.64

12	15	20	24	30	40	60	120	240	∞	a	df$_2$
1.40	1.38	1.37	1.36	1.35	1.34	1.33	1.32	1.31	1.30	.25	19
1.91	1.86	1.81	1.79	1.76	1.73	1.70	1.67	1.65	1.63	.10	
2.31	2.23	2.16	2.11	2.07	2.03	1.98	1.93	1.90	1.88	.05	
2.72	2.62	2.51	2.45	2.39	2.33	2.27	2.20	2.17	2.13	.025	
3.30	3.15	3.00	2.92	2.84	2.76	2.67	2.58	2.54	2.49	.01	
3.76	3.59	3.40	3.31	3.21	3.11	3.00	2.89	2.83	2.78	.005	
4.97	4.70	4.43	4.29	4.14	3.99	3.84	3.68	3.60	3.51	.001	
1.39	1.37	1.36	1.35	1.34	1.33	1.32	1.31	1.30	1.29	.25	20
1.89	1.84	1.79	1.77	1.74	1.71	1.68	1.64	1.63	1.61	.10	
2.28	2.20	2.12	2.08	2.04	1.99	1.95	1.90	1.87	1.84	.05	
2.68	2.57	2.46	2.41	2.35	2.29	2.22	2.16	2.12	2.09	.025	
3.23	3.09	2.94	2.86	2.78	2.69	2.61	2.52	2.47	2.42	.01	
3.68	3.50	3.32	3.22	3.12	3.02	2.92	2.81	2.75	2.69	.005	
4.82	4.56	4.29	4.15	4.00	3.86	3.70	3.54	3.46	3.38	.001	
1.38	1.37	1.35	1.34	1.33	1.32	1.31	1.30	1.29	1.28	.25	21
1.87	1.83	1.78	1.75	1.72	1.69	1.66	1.62	1.60	1.59	.10	
2.25	2.18	2.10	2.05	2.01	1.96	1.92	1.87	1.84	1.81	.05	
2.64	2.53	2.42	2.37	2.31	2.25	2.18	2.11	2.08	2.04	.025	
3.17	3.03	2.88	2.80	2.72	2.64	2.55	2.46	2.41	2.36	.01	
3.60	3.43	3.24	3.15	3.05	2.95	2.84	2.73	2.67	2.61	.005	
4.70	4.44	4.17	4.03	3.88	3.74	3.58	3.42	3.34	3.26	.001	
1.37	1.36	1.34	1.33	1.32	1.31	1.30	1.29	1.28	1.28	.25	22
1.86	1.81	1.76	1.73	1.70	1.67	1.64	1.60	1.59	1.57	.10	
2.23	2.15	2.07	2.03	1.98	1.94	1.89	1.84	1.81	1.78	.05	
2.60	2.50	2.39	2.33	2.27	2.21	2.14	2.08	2.04	2.00	.025	
3.12	2.98	2.83	2.75	2.67	2.58	2.50	2.40	2.35	2.31	.01	
3.54	3.36	3.18	3.08	2.98	2.88	2.77	2.66	2.60	2.55	.005	
4.58	4.33	4.06	3.92	3.78	3.63	3.48	3.32	3.23	3.15	.001	
1.37	1.35	1.34	1.33	1.32	1.31	1.30	1.28	1.28	1.27	.25	23
1.84	1.80	1.74	1.72	1.69	1.66	1.62	1.59	1.57	1.55	.10	
2.20	2.13	2.05	2.01	1.96	1.91	1.86	1.81	1.79	1.76	.05	
2.57	2.47	2.36	2.30	2.24	2.18	2.11	2.04	2.01	1.97	.025	
3.07	2.93	2.78	2.70	2.62	2.54	2.45	2.35	2.31	2.26	.01	
3.47	3.30	3.12	3.02	2.92	2.82	2.71	2.60	2.54	2.48	.005	
4.48	4.23	3.96	3.82	3.68	3.53	3.38	3.22	3.14	3.05	.001	
1.36	1.35	1.33	1.32	1.31	1.30	1.29	1.28	1.27	1.26	.25	24
1.83	1.78	1.73	1.70	1.67	1.64	1.61	1.57	1.55	1.53	.10	
2.18	2.11	2.03	1.98	1.94	1.89	1.84	1.79	1.76	1.73	.05	
2.54	2.44	2.33	2.27	2.21	2.15	2.08	2.01	1.97	1.94	.025	
3.03	2.89	2.74	2.66	2.58	2.49	2.40	2.31	2.26	2.21	.01	
3.42	3.25	3.06	2.97	2.87	2.77	2.66	2.55	2.49	2.43	.005	
4.39	4.14	3.87	3.74	3.59	3.45	3.29	3.14	3.05	2.97	.001	

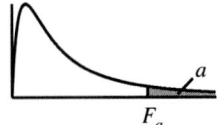

F_a

df$_2$	a	1	2	3	4	5	6	7	8	9	10
25	.25	1.39	1.47	1.46	1.44	1.42	1.41	1.40	1.39	1.38	1.37
	.10	2.92	2.53	2.32	2.18	2.09	2.02	1.97	1.93	1.89	1.87
	.05	4.24	3.39	2.99	2.76	2.60	2.49	2.40	2.34	2.28	2.24
	.025	5.69	4.29	3.69	3.35	3.13	2.97	2.85	2.75	2.68	2.61
	.01	7.77	5.57	4.68	4.18	3.85	3.63	3.46	3.32	3.22	3.13
	.005	9.48	6.60	5.46	4.84	4.43	4.15	3.94	3.78	3.64	3.54
	.001	13.88	9.22	7.45	6.49	5.89	5.46	5.15	4.91	4.71	4.56
26	.25	1.38	1.46	1.45	1.44	1.42	1.41	1.39	1.38	1.37	1.37
	.10	2.91	2.52	2.31	2.17	2.08	2.01	1.96	1.92	1.88	1.86
	.05	4.23	3.37	2.98	2.74	2.59	2.47	2.39	2.32	2.27	2.22
	.025	5.66	4.27	3.67	3.33	3.10	2.94	2.82	2.73	2.65	2.59
	.01	7.72	5.53	4.64	4.14	3.82	3.59	3.42	3.29	3.18	3.09
	.005	9.41	6.54	5.41	4.79	4.38	4.10	3.89	3.73	3.60	3.49
	.001	13.74	9.12	7.36	6.41	5.80	5.38	5.07	4.83	4.64	4.48
27	.25	1.38	1.46	1.45	1.43	1.42	1.40	1.39	1.38	1.37	1.36
	.10	2.90	2.51	2.30	2.17	2.07	2.00	1.95	1.91	1.87	1.85
	.05	4.21	3.35	2.96	2.73	2.57	2.46	2.37	2.31	2.25	2.20
	.025	5.63	4.24	3.65	3.31	3.08	2.92	2.80	2.71	2.63	2.57
	.01	7.68	5.49	4.60	4.11	3.78	3.56	3.39	3.26	3.15	3.06
	.005	9.34	6.49	5.36	4.74	4.34	4.06	3.85	3.69	3.56	3.45
	.001	13.61	9.02	7.27	6.33	5.73	5.31	5.00	4.76	4.57	4.41
28	.25	1.38	1.46	1.45	1.43	1.41	1.40	1.39	1.38	1.37	1.36
	.10	2.89	2.50	2.29	2.16	2.06	2.00	1.94	1.90	1.87	1.84
	.05	4.20	3.34	2.95	2.71	2.56	2.45	2.36	2.29	2.24	2.19
	.025	5.61	4.22	3.63	3.29	3.06	2.90	2.78	2.69	2.61	2.55
	.01	7.64	5.45	4.57	4.07	3.75	3.53	3.36	3.23	3.12	3.03
	.005	9.28	6.44	5.32	4.70	4.30	4.02	3.81	3.65	3.52	3.41
	.001	13.50	8.93	7.19	6.25	5.66	5.24	4.93	4.69	4.50	4.35
29	.25	1.38	1.45	1.45	1.43	1.41	1.40	1.38	1.37	1.36	1.35
	.10	2.89	2.50	2.28	2.15	2.06	1.99	1.93	1.89	1.86	1.83
	.05	4.18	3.33	2.93	2.70	2.55	2.43	2.35	2.28	2.22	2.18
	.025	5.59	4.20	3.61	3.27	3.04	2.88	2.76	2.67	2.59	2.53
	.01	7.60	5.42	4.54	4.04	3.73	3.50	3.33	3.20	3.09	3.00
	.005	9.23	6.40	5.28	4.66	4.26	3.98	3.77	3.61	3.48	3.38
	.001	13.39	8.85	7.12	6.19	5.59	5.18	4.87	4.64	4.45	4.29
30	.25	1.38	1.45	1.44	1.42	1.41	1.39	1.38	1.37	1.36	1.35
	.10	2.88	2.49	2.28	2.14	2.05	1.98	1.93	1.88	1.85	1.82
	.05	4.17	3.32	2.92	2.69	2.53	2.42	2.33	2.27	2.21	2.16
	.025	5.57	4.18	3.59	3.25	3.03	2.87	2.75	2.65	2.57	2.51
	.01	7.56	5.39	4.51	4.02	3.70	3.47	3.30	3.17	3.07	2.98
	.005	9.18	6.35	5.24	4.62	4.23	3.95	3.74	3.58	3.45	3.34
	.001	13.29	8.77	7.05	6.12	5.53	5.12	4.82	4.58	4.39	4.24

12	15	20	24	30	40	60	120	240	∞	a	df_2
											df_1
1.36	1.34	1.33	1.32	1.31	1.29	1.28	1.27	1.26	1.25	.25	25
1.82	1.77	1.72	1.69	1.66	1.63	1.59	1.56	1.54	1.52	.10	
2.16	2.09	2.01	1.96	1.92	1.87	1.82	1.77	1.74	1.71	.05	
2.51	2.41	2.30	2.24	2.18	2.12	2.05	1.98	1.94	1.91	.025	
2.99	2.85	2.70	2.62	2.54	2.45	2.36	2.27	2.22	2.17	.01	
3.37	3.20	3.01	2.92	2.82	2.72	2.61	2.50	2.44	2.38	.005	
4.31	4.06	3.79	3.66	3.52	3.37	3.22	3.06	2.98	2.89	.001	
1.35	1.34	1.32	1.31	1.30	1.29	1.28	1.26	1.26	1.25	.25	26
1.81	1.76	1.71	1.68	1.65	1.61	1.58	1.54	1.52	1.50	.10	
2.15	2.07	1.99	1.95	1.90	1.85	1.80	1.75	1.72	1.69	.05	
2.49	2.39	2.28	2.22	2.16	2.09	2.03	1.95	1.92	1.88	.025	
2.96	2.81	2.66	2.58	2.50	2.42	2.33	2.23	2.18	2.13	.01	
3.33	3.15	2.97	2.87	2.77	2.67	2.56	2.45	2.39	2.33	.005	
4.24	3.99	3.72	3.59	3.44	3.30	3.15	2.99	2.90	2.82	.001	
1.35	1.33	1.32	1.31	1.30	1.28	1.27	1.26	1.25	1.24	.25	27
1.80	1.75	1.70	1.67	1.64	1.60	1.57	1.53	1.51	1.49	.10	
2.13	2.06	1.97	1.93	1.88	1.84	1.73	1.70	1.67		.05	
2.47	2.36	2.25	2.19	2.13	2.07	2.00	1.93	1.89	1.85	.025	
2.93	2.78	2.63	2.55	2.47	2.38	2.29	2.20	2.15	2.10	.01	
3.28	3.11	2.93	2.83	2.73	2.63	2.52	2.41	2.35	2.29	.005	
4.17	3.92	3.66	3.52	3.38	3.23	3.08	2.92	2.84	2.75	.001	
1.34	1.33	1.31	1.30	1.29	1.28	1.27	1.25	1.24	1.24	.25	28
1.79	1.74	1.69	1.66	1.63	1.59	1.56	1.52	1.50	1.48	.10	
2.12	2.04	1.96	1.91	1.87	1.82	1.77	1.71	1.68	1.65	.05	
2.45	2.34	2.23	2.17	2.11	2.05	1.98	1.91	1.87	1.83	.025	
2.90	2.75	2.60	2.52	2.44	2.35	2.26	2.17	2.12	2.06	.01	
3.25	3.07	2.89	2.79	2.69	2.59	2.48	2.37	2.31	2.25	.005	
4.11	3.86	3.60	3.46	3.32	3.18	3.02	2.86	2.78	2.69	.001	
1.34	1.32	1.31	1.30	1.29	1.27	1.26	1.25	1.24	1.23	.25	29
1.78	1.73	1.68	1.65	1.62	1.58	1.55	1.51	1.49	1.47	.10	
2.10	2.03	1.94	1.90	1.85	1.81	1.70	1.67	1.64	1.65	.05	
2.43	2.32	2.21	2.15	2.09	2.03	1.96	1.89	1.85	1.81	.025	
2.87	2.73	2.57	2.49	2.41	2.33	2.23	2.14	2.09	2.03	.01	
3.21	3.04	2.86	2.76	2.66	2.56	2.45	2.33	2.27	2.21	.005	
4.05	3.80	3.54	3.41	3.27	3.12	2.97	2.81	2.73	2.64	.001	
1.34	1.32	1.30	1.29	1.28	1.27	1.26	1.24	1.23	1.23	.25	30
1.77	1.72	1.67	1.64	1.61	1.57	1.54	1.50	1.48	1.46	.10	
2.09	2.01	1.93	1.89	1.84	1.79	1.74	1.68	1.65	1.62	.05	
2.41	2.31	2.20	2.14	2.07	2.01	1.94	1.87	1.83	1.79	.025	
2.84	2.70	2.55	2.47	2.39	2.30	2.21	2.11	2.06	2.01	.01	
3.18	3.01	2.82	2.73	2.63	2.52	2.42	2.30	2.24	2.18	.005	
4.00	3.75	3.49	3.36	3.22	3.07	2.92	2.76	2.68	2.59	.001	

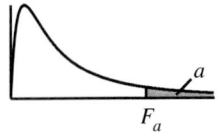

| | | | | | | df$_1$ | | | | | |
df$_2$	*a*	1	2	3	4	5	6	7	8	9	10
40	.25	1.36	1.44	1.42	1.40	1.39	1.37	1.36	1.35	1.34	1.33
	.10	2.84	2.44	2.23	2.09	2.00	1.93	1.87	1.83	1.79	1.76
	.05	4.08	3.23	2.84	2.61	2.45	2.34	2.25	2.18	2.12	2.08
	.025	5.42	4.05	3.46	3.13	2.90	2.74	2.62	2.53	2.45	2.39
	.01	7.31	5.18	4.31	3.83	3.51	3.29	3.12	2.99	2.89	2.80
	.005	8.83	6.07	4.98	4.37	3.99	3.71	3.51	3.35	3.22	3.12
	.001	12.61	8.25	6.59	5.70	5.13	4.73	4.44	4.21	4.02	3.87
60	.25	1.35	1.42	1.41	1.38	1.37	1.35	1.33	1.32	1.31	1.30
	.10	2.79	2.39	2.18	2.04	1.95	1.87	1.82	1.77	1.74	1.71
	.05	4.00	3.15	2.76	2.53	2.37	2.25	2.17	2.10	2.04	1.99
	.025	5.29	3.93	3.34	3.01	2.79	2.63	2.51	2.41	2.33	2.27
	.01	7.08	4.98	4.13	3.65	3.34	3.12	2.95	2.82	2.72	2.63
	.005	8.49	5.79	4.73	4.14	3.76	3.49	3.29	3.13	3.01	2.90
	.001	11.97	7.77	6.17	5.31	4.76	4.37	4.09	3.86	3.69	3.54
90	.25	1.34	1.41	1.39	1.37	1.35	1.33	1.32	1.31	1.30	1.29
	.10	2.76	2.36	2.15	2.01	1.91	1.84	1.78	1.74	1.70	1.67
	.05	3.95	3.10	2.71	2.47	2.32	2.20	2.11	2.04	1.99	1.94
	.025	5.20	3.84	3.26	2.93	2.71	2.55	2.43	2.34	2.26	2.19
	.01	6.93	4.85	4.01	3.53	3.23	3.01	2.84	2.72	2.61	2.52
	.005	8.28	5.62	4.57	3.99	3.62	3.35	3.15	3.00	2.87	2.77
	.001	11.57	7.47	5.91	5.06	4.53	4.15	3.87	3.65	3.48	3.34
120	.25	1.34	1.40	1.39	1.37	1.35	1.33	1.31	1.30	1.29	1.28
	.10	2.75	2.35	2.13	1.99	1.90	1.82	1.77	1.72	1.68	1.65
	.05	3.92	3.07	2.68	2.45	2.29	2.18	2.09	2.02	1.96	1.91
	.025	5.15	3.80	3.23	2.89	2.67	2.52	2.39	2.30	2.22	2.16
	.01	6.85	4.79	3.95	3.48	3.17	2.96	2.79	2.66	2.56	2.47
	.005	8.18	5.54	4.50	3.92	3.55	3.28	3.09	2.93	2.81	2.71
	.001	11.38	7.32	5.78	4.95	4.42	4.04	3.77	3.55	3.38	3.24
240	.25	1.33	1.39	1.38	1.36	1.34	1.32	1.30	1.29	1.27	1.27
	.10	2.73	2.32	2.10	1.97	1.87	1.80	1.74	1.70	1.65	1.63
	.05	3.88	3.03	2.64	2.41	2.25	2.14	2.04	1.98	1.92	1.87
	.025	5.09	3.75	3.17	2.84	2.62	2.46	2.34	2.25	2.17	2.10
	.01	6.74	4.69	3.86	3.40	3.09	2.88	2.71	2.59	2.48	2.40
	.005	8.03	5.42	4.38	3.82	3.45	3.19	2.99	2.84	2.71	2.61
	.001	11.10	7.11	5.60	4.78	4.25	3.89	3.62	3.41	3.24	3.09
∞	.25	1.32	1.39	1.37	1.35	1.33	1.31	1.29	1.28	1.27	1.25
	.10	2.71	2.30	2.08	1.94	1.85	1.77	1.72	1.67	1.63	1.60
	.05	3.84	3.00	2.60	2.37	2.21	2.10	2.01	1.94	1.88	1.83
	.025	5.02	3.69	3.12	2.79	2.57	2.41	2.29	2.19	2.11	2.05
	.01	6.63	4.61	3.78	3.32	3.02	2.80	2.64	2.51	2.41	2.32
	.005	7.88	5.30	4.28	3.72	3.35	3.09	2.90	2.74	2.62	2.52
	.001	10.83	6.91	5.42	4.62	4.10	3.74	3.47	3.27	3.10	2.96

df$_1$											
12	15	20	24	30	40	60	120	240	∞	a	df$_2$
1.31	1.30	1.28	1.26	1.25	1.24	1.22	1.21	1.20	1.19	.25	40
1.71	1.66	1.61	1.57	1.54	1.51	1.47	1.42	1.40	1.38	.10	
2.00	1.92	1.84	1.79	1.74	1.69	1.64	1.58	1.54	1.51	.05	
2.29	2.18	2.07	2.01	1.94	1.88	1.80	1.72	1.68	1.64	.025	
2.66	2.52	2.37	2.29	2.20	2.11	2.02	1.92	1.86	1.80	.01	
2.95	2.78	2.60	2.50	2.40	2.30	2.18	2.06	2.00	1.93	.005	
3.64	3.40	3.14	3.01	2.87	2.73	2.57	2.41	2.32	2.23	.001	
1.29	1.27	1.25	1.24	1.22	1.21	1.19	1.17	1.16	1.15	.25	60
1.66	1.60	1.54	1.51	1.48	1.44	1.40	1.35	1.32	1.29	.10	
1.92	1.84	1.75	1.70	1.65	1.59	1.53	1.47	1.43	1.39	.05	
2.17	2.06	1.94	1.88	1.82	1.74	1.67	1.58	1.53	1.48	.025	
2.50	2.35	2.20	2.12	2.03	1.94	1.84	1.73	1.67	1.60	.01	
2.74	2.57	2.39	2.29	2.19	2.08	1.96	1.83	1.76	1.69	.005	
3.32	3.08	2.83	2.69	2.55	2.41	2.25	2.08	1.99	1.89	.001	
1.27	1.25	1.23	1.22	1.20	1.19	1.17	1.15	1.13	1.12	.25	90
1.62	1.56	1.50	1.47	1.43	1.39	1.35	1.29	1.26	1.23	.10	
1.86	1.78	1.69	1.64	1.59	1.53	1.46	1.39	1.35	1.30	.05	
2.09	1.98	1.86	1.80	1.73	1.66	1.58	1.48	1.43	1.37	.025	
2.39	2.24	2.09	2.00	1.92	1.82	1.72	1.60	1.53	1.46	.01	
2.61	2.44	2.25	2.15	2.05	1.94	1.82	1.68	1.61	1.52	.005	
3.11	2.88	2.63	2.50	2.36	2.21	2.05	1.87	1.77	1.66	.001	
1.26	1.24	1.22	1.21	1.19	1.18	1.16	1.13	1.12	1.10	.25	120
1.60	1.55	1.48	1.45	1.41	1.37	1.32	1.26	1.23	1.19	.10	
1.83	1.75	1.66	1.61	1.55	1.50	1.43	1.35	1.31	1.25	.05	
2.05	1.94	1.82	1.76	1.69	1.61	1.53	1.43	1.38	1.31	.025	
2.34	2.19	2.03	1.95	1.86	1.76	1.66	1.53	1.46	1.38	.01	
2.54	2.37	2.19	2.09	1.98	1.87	1.75	1.61	1.52	1.43	.005	
3.02	2.78	2.53	2.40	2.26	2.11	1.95	1.77	1.66	1.54	.001	
1.25	1.23	1.21	1.19	1.18	1.16	1.14	1.11	1.09	1.07	.25	240
1.57	1.52	1.45	1.42	1.38	1.33	1.28	1.22	1.18	1.13	.10	
1.79	1.71	1.61	1.56	1.51	1.44	1.37	1.29	1.24	1.17	.05	
2.00	1.89	1.77	1.70	1.63	1.55	1.46	1.35	1.29	1.21	.025	
2.26	2.11	1.96	1.87	1.78	1.68	1.57	1.43	1.35	1.25	.01	
2.45	2.28	2.09	1.99	1.89	1.77	1.64	1.49	1.40	1.28	.005	
2.88	2.65	2.40	2.26	2.12	1.97	1.80	1.61	1.49	1.35	.001	
1.24	1.22	1.19	1.18	1.16	1.14	1.12	1.08	1.06	1.00	.25	∞
1.55	1.49	1.42	1.38	1.34	1.30	1.24	1.17	1.12	1.00	.10	
1.75	1.67	1.57	1.52	1.46	1.39	1.32	1.22	1.15	1.00	.05	
1.94	1.83	1.71	1.64	1.57	1.48	1.39	1.27	1.19	1.00	.025	
2.18	2.04	1.88	1.79	1.70	1.59	1.47	1.32	1.22	1.00	.01	
2.36	2.19	2.00	1.90	1.79	1.67	1.53	1.36	1.25	1.00	.005	
2.74	2.51	2.27	2.13	1.99	1.84	1.66	1.45	1.31	1.00	.001	

Source: Computed by P. J. Hildebrand.

TABLE 7 Critical values for the Wilcoxon signed rank test ($n - 5(1)54$)

One-sided	Two-sided	$n = 5$	$n = 6$	$n = 7$	$n = 8$	$n = 9$	$n = 10$	$n = 11$	$n = 12$	$n = 13$	$n = 14$
$p = .1$	$p = .2$	2	3	5	8	10	14	17	21	26	31
$p = .05$	$p = .1$	0	2	3	5	8	10	13	17	21	25
$p = .025$	$p = .05$		0	2	3	5	8	10	13	17	21
$p = .01$	$p = .02$			0	1	3	5	7	9	12	15
$p = .005$	$p = .01$				0	1	3	5	7	9	12
$p = .0025$	$p = .005$					0	1	3	5	7	9
$p = .001$	$p = .002$						0	1	2	4	6

One-sided	Two-sided	$n = 15$	$n = 16$	$n = 17$	$n = 18$	$n = 19$	$n = 20$	$n = 21$	$n = 22$	$n = 23$	$n = 24$
$p = .1$	$p = .2$	36	42	48	55	62	69	77	86	94	104
$p = .05$	$p = .1$	30	35	41	47	53	60	67	75	83	91
$p = .025$	$p = .05$	25	29	34	40	46	52	58	65	73	81
$p = .01$	$p = .02$	19	23	27	32	37	43	49	55	62	69
$p = .005$	$p = .01$	15	19	23	27	32	37	42	48	54	61
$p = .0025$	$p = .005$	12	15	19	23	27	32	37	42	48	54
$p = .001$	$p = .002$	8	11	14	18	21	26	30	35	40	45

One-sided	Two-sided	$n = 25$	$n = 26$	$n = 27$	$n = 28$	$n = 29$	$n = 30$	$n = 31$	$n = 32$	$n = 33$	$n = 34$
$p = .1$	$p = .2$	113	124	134	145	157	169	181	194	207	221
$p = .05$	$p = .1$	100	110	119	130	140	151	163	175	187	200
$p = .025$	$p = .05$	89	98	107	116	126	137	147	159	170	182
$p = .01$	$p = .02$	76	84	92	101	110	120	130	140	151	162
$p = .005$	$p = .01$	68	75	83	91	100	109	118	128	138	148
$p = .0025$	$p = .005$	60	67	74	82	90	98	107	116	126	136
$p = .001$	$p = .002$	51	58	64	71	79	86	94	103	112	121

One-sided	Two-sided	$n = 35$	$n = 36$	$n = 37$	$n = 38$	$n = 39$	$n = 40$	$n = 41$	$n = 42$	$n = 43$	$n = 44$
$p = .1$	$p = .2$	235	250	265	281	297	313	330	348	365	384
$p = .05$	$p = .1$	213	227	241	256	271	286	302	319	336	353
$p = .025$	$p = .05$	195	208	221	235	249	264	279	294	310	327
$p = .01$	$p = .02$	173	185	198	211	224	238	252	266	281	296
$p = .005$	$p = .01$	159	171	182	194	207	220	233	247	261	276
$p = .0025$	$p = .005$	146	157	168	180	192	204	217	230	244	258
$p = .001$	$p = .002$	131	141	151	162	173	185	197	209	222	235

One-sided	Two-sided	$n = 45$	$n = 46$	$n = 47$	$n = 48$	$n = 49$	$n = 50$	$n = 51$	$n = 52$	$n = 53$	$n = 54$
$p = .1$	$p = .2$	402	422	441	462	482	503	525	547	569	592
$p = .05$	$p = .1$	371	389	407	426	446	466	486	507	529	550
$p = .025$	$p = .05$	343	361	378	396	415	434	453	473	494	514
$p = .01$	$p = .02$	312	328	345	362	379	397	416	434	454	473
$p = .005$	$p = .01$	219	307	322	389	355	373	390	408	427	445
$p = .0025$	$p = .005$	272	287	302	318	334	350	367	384	402	420
$p = .001$	$p = .002$	249	263	277	292	307	323	339	355	372	389

Source: Computed by P. J. Hildebrand.

TABLE 8 **Percentage points of the studentized range**

Error d.f.	α	t = number of treatment means									
		2	3	4	5	6	7	8	9	10	11
5	.05	3.64	4.60	5.22	5.67	6.03	6.33	6.58	6.80	6.99	7.17
	.01	5.70	6.98	7.80	8.42	8.91	9.32	9.67	9.97	10.24	10.48
6	.05	3.46	4.34	4.90	5.30	5.63	5.90	6.12	6.32	6.49	6.65
	.01	5.24	6.33	7.03	7.56	7.97	8.32	8.61	8.87	9.10	9.30
7	.05	3.34	4.16	4.68	5.06	5.36	5.61	5.82	6.00	6.16	6.30
	.01	4.95	5.92	6.54	7.01	7.37	7.68	7.94	8.17	8.37	8.55
8	.05	3.26	4.04	4.53	4.89	5.17	5.40	5.60	5.77	5.92	6.05
	.01	4.75	5.64	6.20	6.62	6.96	7.24	7.47	7.68	7.86	8.03
9	.05	3.20	3.95	4.41	4.76	5.02	5.24	5.43	5.59	5.74	5.87
	.01	4.60	5.43	5.96	6.35	6.66	6.91	7.13	7.33	7.49	7.65
10	.05	3.15	3.88	4.33	4.65	4.91	5.12	5.30	5.46	5.60	5.72
	.01	4.48	5.27	5.77	6.14	6.43	6.67	6.87	7.05	7.21	7.36
11	.05	3.11	3.82	4.26	4.57	4.82	5.03	5.30	5.35	5.49	5.61
	.01	4.39	5.15	5.62	5.97	6.25	6.48	6.67	6.84	6.99	7.13
12	.05	3.08	3.77	4.20	4.52	4.75	4.95	5.12	5.27	5.39	5.51
	.01	4.32	5.05	5.50	5.84	6.10	6.32	6.51	6.67	6.81	6.94
13	.05	3.06	3.73	4.15	4.45	4.69	4.88	5.05	5.19	5.32	5.43
	.01	4.26	4.96	5.40	5.73	5.98	6.19	6.37	6.53	6.67	6.79
14	.05	3.03	3.70	4.11	4.41	4.64	4.83	4.99	5.13	5.25	5.36
	.01	4.21	4.89	5.32	5.63	5.88	6.08	6.26	6.41	6.54	6.66
15	.05	3.01	3.67	4.08	4.37	4.59	4.78	4.94	5.08	5.20	5.31
	.01	4.17	4.84	5.25	5.56	5.80	5.99	6.16	6.31	6.44	6.55
16	.05	3.00	3.65	4.05	4.33	4.56	4.74	4.90	5.03	5.15	5.26
	.01	4.13	4.79	5.19	5.49	5.72	5.92	6.08	6.22	6.35	6.46
17	.05	2.98	3.63	4.02	4.30	4.52	4.70	4.86	4.99	5.11	5.21
	.01	4.10	4.74	5.14	5.43	5.66	5.85	6.01	6.15	6.27	6.38
18	.05	2.97	3.61	4.00	4.28	4.49	4.67	4.82	4.96	5.07	5.17
	.01	4.07	4.70	5.09	5.38	5.60	5.79	5.94	6.08	6.20	6.31
19	.05	2.96	3.59	3.98	4.25	4.47	4.65	4.79	4.92	5.04	5.14
	.01	4.05	4.67	5.05	5.33	5.55	5.73	5.89	6.02	6.14	6.25
20	.05	2.95	3.58	3.96	4.23	4.45	4.62	4.77	4.90	5.01	5.11
	.01	4.02	4.64	5.02	5.29	5.51	5.69	5.84	5.97	6.09	6.19
24	.05	2.92	3.53	3.90	4.17	4.37	4.54	4.68	4.81	3.92	5.01
	.01	3.96	4.55	4.91	5.17	5.37	5.54	5.69	5.81	5.92	6.02
30	.05	2.89	3.49	3.85	4.10	4.30	4.46	4.60	4.72	4.82	4.92
	.01	3.89	4.45	4.80	5.05	5.24	5.40	5.54	5.65	5.76	5.85
40	.05	2.86	3.44	3.79	4.04	4.23	4.39	4.52	4.63	4.73	4.82
	.01	3.82	4.37	4.70	4.93	5.11	5.26	5.39	5.50	5.60	5.69
60	.05	2.83	3.40	3.74	3.98	4.16	4.31	4.44	4.55	4.65	4.73
	.01	3.76	4.28	4.59	4.82	4.99	5.13	5.25	5.36	5.45	5.53
120	.05	2.80	3.36	3.68	3.92	4.10	4.24	4.36	4.47	4.56	4.64
	.01	3.70	4.20	4.50	4.71	4.87	5.01	5.12	5.21	5.30	5.37
∞	.05	2.77	3.31	3.63	3.86	4.03	4.17	4.29	4.39	4.47	4.55
	.01	3.64	4.12	4.40	4.60	4.76	4.88	4.99	5.08	5.16	5.23

Source: This table is abridged from E. S. Pearson and H. O. Hartley, eds., *Biometrika Tables for Statisticians*, Vol. 1, 2nd ed. (New York: Cambridge University Press, 1958), Table 29. Reproduced with the kind permission of the editors and the trustees of *Biometrika*.

TABLE 8 (continued) Percentage points of the studentized range

t = number of treatment means

12	13	14	15	16	17	18	19	20	α	Error d.f.
7.32	7.47	7.60	7.72	7.83	7.93	8.03	8.12	8.21	.05	5
10.70	10.89	11.08	11.24	11.40	11.55	11.68	11.81	11.93	.01	
6.79	6.92	7.03	7.14	7.24	7.34	7.43	7.51	7.59	.05	6
9.48	9.65	9.81	9.95	10.08	10.21	10.32	10.43	10.54	.01	
6.43	6.55	6.66	6.76	6.85	6.94	7.02	7.10	7.17	.05	7
8.71	8.86	9.00	9.12	9.24	9.35	9.46	9.55	9.65	.01	
6.18	6.29	6.39	6.48	6.57	6.65	6.73	6.80	6.87	.05	8
8.18	8.31	8.44	8.55	8.66	8.76	8.85	8.94	9.03	.01	
5.98	6.09	6.19	6.28	6.36	6.44	6.51	6.58	6.64	.05	9
7.78	7.91	8.03	8.13	8.23	8.33	8.41	8.49	8.57	.01	
5.83	5.93	6.03	6.11	6.19	6.27	6.34	6.40	6.47	.05	10
7.49	7.60	7.71	7.81	7.91	7.99	8.08	8.15	8.23	.01	
5.71	5.81	5.90	5.98	6.06	6.13	6.20	6.27	6.33	.05	11
7.25	7.36	7.46	7.56	7.65	7.73	7.81	7.88	7.95	.01	
5.61	5.71	5.80	5.88	5.95	6.02	6.09	6.15	6.21	.05	12
7.06	7.17	7.26	7.36	7.44	7.52	7.59	7.66	7.73	.01	
5.53	5.63	5.71	5.79	5.86	5.93	5.99	6.05	6.11	.05	13
6.90	7.01	7.10	7.19	7.27	7.35	7.42	7.48	7.55	.01	
5.46	5.55	5.64	5.71	5.79	5.85	5.91	5.97	6.03	.05	14
6.77	6.87	6.96	7.05	7.13	7.20	7.27	7.33	7.39	.01	
5.40	5.49	5.57	5.65	5.72	5.78	5.85	5.90	5.96	.05	15
6.66	6.76	6.84	6.93	7.00	7.07	7.14	7.20	7.26	.01	
5.35	5.44	5.52	5.59	5.66	5.73	5.79	5.84	5.90	.05	16
6.56	6.66	6.74	6.82	6.90	6.97	7.03	7.09	7.15	.01	
5.31	5.39	5.47	5.54	5.61	5.67	5.73	5.79	5.84	.05	17
6.48	6.57	6.66	6.73	6.81	6.87	6.94	7.00	7.05	.01	
5.27	5.35	5.43	5.50	5.57	5.63	5.69	5.74	5.79	.05	18
6.41	6.50	6.58	6.65	6.73	6.79	6.85	6.91	6.97	.01	
5.23	5.31	5.39	5.46	5.53	5.59	5.65	5.70	5.75	.05	19
6.34	6.43	6.51	6.58	6.65	6.72	6.78	6.84	6.89	.01	
5.20	5.28	5.36	5.43	5.49	5.55	5.61	5.66	5.71	.05	20
6.28	6.37	6.45	6.52	6.59	6.65	6.71	6.77	6.82	.01	
5.10	5.18	5.25	5.32	5.38	5.44	5.49	5.55	5.59	.05	24
6.11	6.19	6.26	6.33	6.39	6.45	6.51	6.56	6.61	.01	
5.00	5.08	5.15	5.21	5.27	5.33	5.38	5.43	5.47	.05	30
5.93	6.01	6.08	6.14	6.20	6.26	6.31	6.36	6.41	.01	
4.90	4.98	5.04	5.11	5.16	5.22	5.27	5.31	5.36	.05	40
5.76	5.83	5.90	5.96	6.02	6.07	6.12	6.16	6.21	.01	
4.81	4.88	4.94	5.00	5.06	5.11	5.15	5.20	5.24	.05	60
5.60	5.67	5.73	5.78	5.84	5.89	5.93	5.97	6.01	.01	
4.71	4.78	4.84	4.90	4.95	5.00	5.04	5.09	5.13	.05	120
5.44	5.50	5.56	5.61	5.66	5.71	5.75	5.79	5.83	.01	
4.62	4.68	4.74	4.80	4.85	4.89	4.93	4.97	5.01	.05	∞
5.29	5.35	5.40	5.45	5.49	5.54	5.57	5.61	5.65	.01	

TABLE 9 Random numbers

Line/Col.	(1)	(2)	(3)	(4)	(5)	(6)	(7)	(8)	(9)	(10)	(11)	(12)	(13)	(14)
1	10480	15011	01536	02011	81647	91646	69179	14194	62590	36207	20969	99570	91291	90700
2	22368	46573	25595	85393	30995	89198	27982	53402	93965	34095	52666	19174	39615	99505
3	24130	48360	22527	97265	76393	64809	15179	24830	49340	32081	30680	19655	63348	58629
4	42167	93093	06243	61680	07856	16376	39440	53537	71341	57004	00849	74917	97758	16379
5	37570	39975	81837	16656	06121	91782	60468	81305	49684	60672	14110	06927	01263	54613
6	77921	06907	11008	42751	27756	53498	18602	70659	90655	15053	21916	81825	44394	42880
7	99562	72905	56420	69994	98872	31016	71194	18738	44013	48840	63213	21069	10634	12952
8	96301	91977	05463	07972	18876	20922	94595	56869	69014	60045	18425	84903	42508	32307
9	89579	14342	63661	10281	17453	18103	57740	84378	25331	12566	58678	44947	05585	56941
10	85475	36857	53342	53988	53060	59533	38867	62300	08158	17983	16439	11458	18593	64952
11	28918	69578	88231	33276	70997	79936	56865	05859	90106	31595	01547	85590	91610	78188
12	63553	40961	48235	03427	49626	69445	18663	72695	52180	20847	12234	90511	33703	90322
13	09429	93969	52636	92737	88974	33488	36320	17617	30015	08272	84115	27156	30613	74952
14	10365	61129	87529	85689	48237	52267	67689	93394	01511	26358	85104	20285	29975	89868
15	07119	97336	71048	08178	77233	13916	47564	81056	97735	85977	29372	74461	28551	90707
16	51085	12765	51821	51259	77452	16308	60756	92144	49442	53900	70960	63990	75601	40719
17	02368	21382	52404	60268	89368	19885	55322	44819	01188	65255	64835	44919	05944	55157
18	01011	54092	33362	94904	31273	04146	18594	29852	71585	85030	51132	01915	92747	64951
19	52162	53916	46369	58586	23216	14513	83149	98736	23495	64350	94738	17752	35156	35749
20	07056	97628	33787	09998	42698	06691	76988	13602	51851	46104	88916	19509	25625	58104
21	48663	91245	85828	14346	09172	30168	90229	04734	59193	22178	30421	61666	99904	32812
22	54164	58492	22421	74103	47070	25306	76468	26384	58151	06646	21524	15227	96909	44592
23	32639	32363	05597	24200	13363	38005	94342	28728	35806	06912	17012	64161	18296	22851
24	29334	27001	87637	87308	58731	00256	45834	15398	46557	41135	10367	07684	36188	18510
25	02488	33062	28834	07351	19731	92420	60952	61280	50001	67658	32586	86679	50720	94953

Source: Abridged with permission from William H. Beyer, ed. (1968), *Handbook of Tables for Probability and Statistics*, 2nd ed. Boca Raton, FL: The Chemical Rubber Co. Copyright CRC Press, Inc.

Answers to Selected Exercises

Chapter 2

2.2   **a** About 845, some variability, little skew   **b** Almost no skewness

2.3   Different width and midpoints; same shape

2.6   **a** Right skew   **b** Histogram is also right skewed.

2.10 Definite right skewness

2.13 **a** Sample 1: 10, sample 2: 12   **b** Sample 1: 4.16, sample 2: 2.92
          c Sample 1 seems to have more variability.

2.16 Variation in operator skill and experience, in nature of calls, many other possibilities

2.17 **a** 760 through 828
          b 85% rather than 68%; outliers or skewness may have inflated the standard deviation.

2.18 Outliers, including one extreme one, made the standard deviation large.

2.19 **a** Increase the mean, decrease the standard deviation.
          b Small increase in mean, large decrease in standard deviation.

2.27 **a** Means too small and decreasing gradually
          b Ranges well within limits, with little trend

2.28 Heating system drifting to lower temperatures

2.29 **a** Upward curve   **b** Isolated point at lower left

2.31 Nearly straight line indicates nearly normal distribution.

2.36 **a** One possible result, using a class width of 5, is based on the following table.

Class	Midpoint	Frequency
7.5–12.4	10	10
12.5–17.4	15	0
17.5–22.4	20	5
22.5–27.4	25	0
27.5–32.4	30	10

The data are symmetric and trimodal (three–peaked).
          b Mean and median are both 20, by symmetry.
          c $s = 9.18$

d 9 of 25 points, or 36%. Differs from 68% (Empirical Rule) because data are not single-peaked.

e 100%, compared to Empirical Rule 95%. Again, the data aren't mound-shaped.

2.42 Means larger in the last five days

2.43 In days 54 through 58

2.44 **a** 0.60 to 2.40   **b** Days 54 through 58

2.45 Also days 54 through 58

2.53 Absolutely nothing; qualitative variable

2.54 **a** Codes 6, 7, and 9   **b** Pay

2.55 Pay, clearly

2.61 **a** About 50 or 60, we'd guess   **b** About 1.0, we'd guess

2.62 **a** Skew makes it hard to guess MINPERBID; perhaps 50? BIDPERHR: A bit above 1.0, not 2.

b No. BIDPERHR is much less skewed.

2.63 **a** 62.462 and 1.432

b No; 60/62.462 is less than 1.0, but the mean is 1.432.

Chapter 3

3.3 **a** $P(C) = 541/723$ **b** $P(\text{Serious}) = 453/723$

c $P(\text{Dealer not fully reimbursed}) = 22/723$

3.4 **a** $P(\text{Engine}|C) = 106/541$

b

		Engine	Transm.	Exhaust	Fit/finish	Other
Given brand	C	.196	.390	.124	.246	.044
	G	.115	.632	.088	.132	.033

(Problem area across Engine, Transm., Exhaust, Fit/finish, Other)

The probabilities are not similar.

3.5 **a** $P(\text{more than one problem}) = 92/609$

b $P(\text{more than one problem}|C) = 71/453$

3.6

		1	2	3
Given brand	C	.843	.119	.038
	G	.865	.103	.032

(Number of problems: 1, 2, 3)

The probabilities are nearly identical.

3.7 No; depends on how many sold.

3.16 $P(\text{No substitute needed}) = (.6)(.6)(.5) = .18$

3.17 No, the reasons for absences (illness, bad weather) are common to all the schools.

3.21 Independence seems plausible. Form of order should not affect the chance of a return.

3.22 $P(\text{at least one run of 8 or more}) \approx .192$

3.23 With great difficulty!

3.27 **a** $P(\text{first-time bidder and satisfactory}) = .06$ by table or tree.

b $P(\text{satisfactory}) = .84$

c $P(\text{first-time bidder}|\text{satisfactory}) = .071$

3.32 $P(\text{has disease}|\text{positive}) \approx 3/100 = .03$

3.33 $P(\text{has disease}|\text{positive}) = .045$

3.35 **a** $P(\text{MBA or undergrad degree}) = .45$ **b** $P(\text{neither}) = .55$

3.36 $P(\text{exactly one degree}) = .37$

3.46 **a** $P(F_1 \cap F_2) = .25$ **b** $P(F_1 \cap F_2) = .25$

 c Independence of F_1 and $F2$, reasonable for different customers, not for same customer

3.47 **a** $P(F_1 \cap F_2) = .45$ **b** $P(\text{not } F_1 \cap \text{not } F_2) = .45$

 c $P(\text{exactly one}) = .10$

3.48 $P(F_1|F_2) = .90$

3.55 $P(\text{equipment works}) \approx .610$

3.56 $P(\text{equipment works}) = .605$

3.57 $P(\text{equipment works}) \approx .604$, similar

Review Exercises—Chapters 2–3

R3 $P(\text{decrease}|\text{not correct}) = .160$

R4 **a** mean 1.794, standard deviation 1.333. Empirical Rule doesn't work, because of skewness.

 b Hi outliers in each variable except TypeBank (qualitative)

R7 **a** mean 2.31, standard deviation 1.38 **b** Meaningless; qualitative variable

R8 Means: 32,938, 40,977, and 8,038; medians 21,200, 36,000, and 5,000; standard deviations 21,561, 26,433, and 6.256. The mean difference is the difference of means. No simple relation for medians or standard deviations.

R9 Mean is clearly larger than median; right skew.

R10 $P(\text{bottom } 1/3 \cap \text{not canceled}) = .075$

R11 Not independent; independence would mean chance of cancellation is not affected by ratings.

R12 **a** $P(\text{excellent} \cap \text{definite}) = .0432$

 b Independence; unreasonable. Probability is too low.

R19 **a** Separately, right skewed. Together, bimodal.

 b means: 11.250, 12.972, and 32.138; medians: 10.75, 12.25, and 31. Each mean larger than median; right skew.

R21 **a** No obvious trend **b** No trend

 c Yes, except for one mean

R22 Special cause, no real improvement

Chapter 4

4.6 **a** The probability histogram has a mode at $y = 2$ and a long right tail.

 b $P(Y \le 2) = .500$ **c** $P(Y \ge 7) = .130$ **d** $P(1 \le Y \le 5) = .71$

4.7

y	0	1	2	3	4	5	6	7	8	9	10
$F_Y(y)$	.10	.25	.50	.64	.73	.81	.87	.92	.96	.985	1.00

 The probabilities are the same as found in Exercise 4.4.

4.13 a

y	$f_Y(y)$
0	0
.25	.2801
.50	.4629
.75	.5625
1.00	.5926
1.25	.5671
1.50	.5000
1.75	.4051
2.00	.2963
2.25	.1875
2.50	.0926
2.75	.0255
3.00	0

Mode near 1.00, right skewed

b $P(Y \le 1.50) = .6875;\ P(Y \ge 2.00) = .1111,\ P(1.00 \le Y \le 2.50) = .5764$

c $F_Y(y) = \frac{4}{27}\left(\frac{9y^2}{2} - \frac{6y^3}{3} + \frac{y^4}{4}\right)$

4.14   Mode = 1.000

4.20 a $P(2 < Y < 4) = .1094$, including or excluding 2.0000 and 4.0000.

b $P(0.5 < Y < 1.5) = P(1 < Y < 1.5) = .7037$

4.21 a $F_Y(y) = 1 - 1/y^3,\ y > 1$ **b** $y = 4.642$

4.22 a The histogram has a peak at y = 3 and a long tail to the right.

b $E(Y) = 4.32$

c The expected value is the balance point of the histogram. The right skew pulls it well above the mode, 3.

4.23 a $\sigma_Y = 2.2798$ **b** $\sigma_Y = \sqrt{23.86 - (4.32)^2} = 2.2798$

4.24 $P(2.04 \le Y \le 6.60) = .63$, differing from .68 because of skewness and discreteness of the histogram

4.27 a $\mu_Y = 3.97$ **b** $\text{Var}(Y) = 7.0891$

c $\text{Var}(Y) = 22.85 - (3.97)^2 = 7.0891$

4.28 $P(-1.35 \le Y \le 9.29) = .97$

4.37 a

y	0	1	2	3
$P_Y(y)$	.343	.441	.189	.027

b Same probability; independence. They seem reasonable.

4.38 $\mu_Y = 0.90,\ \text{Var}(Y) = 0.63$

4.39   Same expected value, higher variance

4.40 a $\mu_Y = 1.5$, the long-run average Y value   **b** $\sigma_Y = 0.866$

4.41 a The density is extremely right-skewed.

b No, by skewness. $P(0.634 < Y < 2.366) = P(1 < Y < 2.366) = .924$, far from .68.

4.45 a $\mu_Y = 9.40$ **b** $\sigma_Y^2 = 11.643,\ \sigma_Y = 3.412$

4.46 a $P(X = 1, Y = 2) = P_{XY}(1, 2) = .055$ **b** $P(X \le 1, Y \le 2) = .21$

c

x	1	2	3	4
$P_X(x)$	.23	.27	.27	.23

y	1	2	3	4
$P_Y(y)$	.23	.27	.27	.23

d Not independent

4.47 Plug in x and y values. $P_X(x) = .005(30 + 20x - 4x^2)$

4.56 **a** $\mu_x = \mu_Y = 2$, by symmetry.   **b** $\sigma_X = 1.353, \sigma_Y = 1.285$

4.57 **a** $\text{Cov}(X, Y) = -0.70$

    b $\rho_{XY} = -0.403$. Inverse relation, not independent.

4.58

x	0	1	2	3	4
$E(Y\|X = x)$	2.778	2.359	2.000	1.641	1.222

The conditional expected value decreases as x increases.

4.59 **a**

t	0	1	2	3	4	5	6	7	8
$P_T(t)$	.010	.035	.090	.205	.320	.205	.090	.035	.010

    b $\mu_T = 4, \sigma_T^2 = 2.08$

    c $\mu_T = 2 + 2, \sigma_T^2 = (1.353)^2 + (1.285)^2 + 2(-0.70)$

4.62 **a** Expected return = 1650, variance = 1,650,000

    b Variance (1 and 4) = 1,440,000; variance (1 and 3) = 1,020,000, smaller because of smaller covariance

4.67 **a** Density is left-skewed.   **b** $P(.7 < Y < .9) = .4655$

    c $P(Y > .8) = .3446$

4.68 $\mu_Y = 0.7143, \sigma_Y = 0.1597$

4.71 **a** No; correlation is not 0.   **b** Very weak correlation

4.75 **a**

y	0	1	2	3
$P_Y(y)$	.080	.314	.414	.192

    b $P(Y \geq 2) = .606$

    c

y	0	1	2	3
$F_Y(y)$	.080	.394	.808	1.000

4.76 $\mu_Y = 1.718, \sigma_Y = .8640$

4.77 **a**

x	0	100	150	200	250	300	350	450
$P_X(x)$	.080	.020	.070	.224	.030	.096	.288	.192

    b $\mu_X = 280.8, \sigma_X = 128.69$

4.81 **a** Density is left-skewed.   **b** Mode at $y = .90$

    c $P(Y > .90) = .3516; P(Y < .85) = .3705$

4.82 **a** $\mu_Y = 0.8636$ **b** $\sigma_Y = 0.0716$

    c $P(Y < 0.649) = .0084$

4.88 **a** $P(X > .8) = .3446$ **b** $P(X < .5) = .1094$

4.89 $P(Y < .9 | Y > .8) = .6685$

4.97 **a** $P(.6 < Y < .8) = .3657$ **b** $\mu_Y = 0.80, \sigma_Y = 0.1206$

4.98 Mode at 0.875, larger than the mean, indicating left-skewness

4.101 **a** $x = 1$ (if first card is a National League player), 2, 3, ...

     b $P(X = 1) = .5$ **c** AL first, then NL   **d** $P(X = x) = (.5)^x$

4.102 $E(X) = 2$

4.103 Similar results; the mean is 1.94, compared to 2.

Chapter 5

5.3 $\binom{8}{4} = 70$ subsets

5.4 $\binom{4}{3}\binom{4}{1} = 16$ choices

5.5 **a** $P_Y(3) = .2013$ **b** $P_Y(2) = .3456$ **c** $P_Y(12) = .2040$

5.7 **a** $P(Y \geq 4) = .9840$ **b** $P(Y > 4) = .9490$

     c $P(Y \leq 10) = .8723$ **d** $P(Y > 16) = .0000$

5.8 $P(Y \leq 16) = .9840, P(Y < 16) = .9490$, same as previous exercise.

5.12 **a** Independence is questionable.   **b** $P(Y \geq 85) = .9601$

5.13 $\mu_Y = 90, \sigma_Y = 3$

5.16 **a** $P(Y \leq 25) \approx .023$ **b** $\mu_Y \approx 35.685, \sigma_Y \approx 5.264$

5.17 $P(Y \leq 25) = .023, \mu_Y = 36.0, \sigma_Y = 5.433$

5.19 **a**   **b** Slightly right-skewed

y	$P_Y(y)$
0	4/35
1	18/35
2	12/35
3	1/35

5.20 $\mu_Y = 1.2857, \sigma_Y = 0.6999$

5.23 **a** $P_Y(4) = 1/70$ **b**

y	$P_Y(y)$
0	1/70
1	16/70
2	36/70
3	16/70
4	1/70

5.29 **a** $P(Y \leq 10) = .7060$ **b** $P(Y \geq 7) = .7933$

     c $P(7 \leq Y \leq 11) = .5963$

5.30 $\mu_Y = 9.0, \sigma_Y = 3.0$

5.31 Multi-home fires, higher rate in winter?

5.38 **a** $P(300 < Y \leq 1300) = .1$ **b** $\sigma_Y^2 = 8,333,333.3$

5.42 **a** $P(Y > 1) = e^{(-.8)(1)} = .4493$ **b** $P(Y > 2) = e^{(-.8)(2)} = .2019$

5.43 The probabilities are the same; two ways of describing the same events.

5.46 **a** $P(20 < Y < 60) = .3834$ **b** $\sigma_Y = 40$

5.47 Expected rate not constant over time

5.52 **a** $k = 2.33$ **b** $k = 2.33$ **c** $-k = -2.33$

     d $k = 1.00$ **e** $k = 2.00$ **f** $k = -1.645$

5.53 Same probabilities, to more decimal places

5.54   **a** $(130 - 100)/15 = 2$ **b** $Z \geq -1.17$

        c $P(Y \leq 130) = .9772, P(Y \geq 82.5) = .8790$

        d $P(Y > 106) = .3446, P(Y < 94) = .3446, P(94 \leq Y \leq 104) = .3108$

        e $P(Y \leq 70) = .0228, P(Y \geq 130) = .0228, P(70 < Y < 130) = .9544$

5.58   **a** $P(Y > 5.40) = .2266$ **b** $P(4.70 < Y < 5.50) = .6826$

        c $P(Y > 3.90) = .9987$

5.61   **a** Binomial; $P(Y \leq 1) = .2794$ **b** $P(Y \geq 4) = .2396$

5.62   **a** $\binom{30}{14} = \frac{30!}{(14!)(16!)}$ **b** $\binom{6}{5}\binom{24}{9}$ **c** $P(Y \geq 5) = .059$

5.63   **a** $P(Y = 1) = .3614, P(Y \leq 1) = .6626$ **b** $E(Y) = 1.2, \sigma_Y = 1.095$

5.64   **a** $P(Y \leq 72.8) = .6915, P(71.2 \leq Y \leq 72.8) = .3830$

        b $P(Y \geq 74.0) = .1056$ **c** 75.7 cases

5.65   **a** $P(Y > 73.0) = .2659$, "splitting the difference" of table values

        b $P(3 \text{ successes}) = .055$

5.68   **a** $P(Y < 8) = .8666$ **b** Possible dependence (noisy lines or the like)

5.69 $P(Y < 8) = .2203$

5.75   P(at least one) = .3935.

5.81   **a** $E(Y) = 3.5$ **b** $P(Y \geq 4) = .4634$

        c Nonclumping and independence; independence wrong if a fire causes greater care.

Chapter 6

6.2   Selection bias

6.5   Biased in favor of those holding many seats

6.7 $\mu_Y = 7, \sigma_Y = 3.5496, \mu_{\bar{Y}} = 7, \sigma_{\bar{Y}} = 1.2550 = 3.5496/\sqrt{8}$

6.10   **a** $E(\bar{Y}) = 327, \sigma_{\bar{Y}} = 10.75$

        b, c $P(3150 \leq Y \leq 3390) = P(315 \leq \bar{Y} \leq 339) = .7372$

6.11 $k \approx 21$

6.16   **a** $P(Y > 170) = .1469$ **b** $P(\bar{Y} > 155 \text{ or } \bar{Y} < 135) = .1413$

6.17   **a** Left skewed   **b** No; Central Limit Theorem helps for sample mean.

6.20   **a** $P(Y > 80) = .2743$ **b** $P(\bar{Y} > 80) = .0287$

6.21   No; n isn't big enough for Central Limit Theorem to work well.

6.22   **a** Slight left skew   **b** Slight left skew (upward curve)

6.23   Strong right skew

6.24   Nearly normal or slight right skew

6.27   Not normal; right skewed

6.28   **a** Not normal; right skewed

        b No; as n increased, curve didn't approach normal.

6.29   **a** 20% or 10 beads   **b** Unbiased sampling

6.30   Small bias against red

6.35   **a** $E(\bar{Y}) = 2.13$ **b** $\sigma_{\bar{Y}} = 0.083$

6.36 Random sampling, including independence; bias could affect either, but dependence would affect $\sigma_{\bar{Y}}$.

6.37 Normal, by Central Limit Theorem

6.45 **a** .8224, .8202, .7808, respectively
 b Not good for $n = 2$ and 4, better for $n = 8$
 c .9224, .9024, .9334, respectively; fairly close to .95

6.46 **a** Data right skewed
 b mean $= 3.623$, standard deviation $= 2.904$. If data are regarded as a sample, divide by $n - 1$, not by n, with tiny effect.
 c Result varies randomly.
 d Much closer to normal, by Central Limit Theorem

6.47 Approximate standard error of the mean, should be about 0.65.

Review Exercises—Chapters 4–6

R26 **a**

x	0	1	2	3	4	5	6	7	8	9	10
$P_X(x)$	1/66	2/66	3/66	4/66	5/66	6/66	7/66	8/66	9/66	10/66	11/66

 b $E(X) = 6.667$, $\sigma_X = 2.687$ **c** $P(X \geq 3) = 60/66 = .909$

R27 **a** $E(\bar{X}) = 6.667$, $\text{Var}(\bar{X}) = 1.806$
 b Random sampling, specifically independence

R28 $P(\bar{Y} > 7) = .0401$, good approximation by Central Limit Theorem

R37 $P(Y \leq 3) = .0281$

R38 Same probability of success for each (random) customer, independence, fixed number of customers

R43 Poisson $P(Y \geq 10) = .2833$

R44 No "clumps" of special handling orders, no dependence. Seems sensible to us.

Chapter 7

7.3 **a** Unbiased   **b** Sample mean

7.4 **a** Mean 236.4, median 234.5   **b** 233.875; 20% trimmed mean

7.5 **a** One outlier   **b** No; the outlier distorts the mean.

7.9 **a** $22.23 \leq \mu \leq 25.74$ **b** $21.68 \leq \mu \leq 26.29$

7.10 The interval is the result of a process that is correct 95% of the time.

7.11 Yes; data are near normal, so sampling distribution will be, too.

7.13 $4.43 \leq \mu \leq 7.17$

7.14 Not too good, because of skewness and modest n

7.20 $.60 \leq \pi \leq .74$

7.21 Yes; $n\pi$ and $n(1 - \pi)$ are both large.

7.24 $n = 171$; $n = 96$

7.28 **a** $n = 9604$ **b** $n = 2827$

7.31 **a** .05, .05, .80, .05, .05   **b** Quite close

7.32 **a** $39.841 \leq \mu \leq 73.898$ **b** Right skewed
 c Interval is very wide and unhelpful.

7.33 $n = 252$

7.40 **a** $1.071 \le \mu \le 1.189$ **b** $1.074 \le \mu \le 1.186$ **c** Almost identical

7.41 Slightly suspect for this n

7.42 $3.99 \le \mu \le 6.41$

7.43 **a** Right skewed **b** Claimed 90% may be wrong.

7.55 $.516 \le \pi \le .604, .456 \le \pi \le .544, .416 \le \pi \le .504$, respectively

7.56 Confidence interval allows for sampling error. Bias is a valid concern.

7.59 **a** Normally distributed
b Narrower; mean is most efficient for normally distributed populations.

7.60 Yes; plot is nearly a straight line.

7.66 **a** $1.89 \le \mu \le 3.94$
b A mean of 2.5 per 500 feet is included. The goal *might* be being met.

7.67 Undercount; too low

7.68 **a** Skewed right **b** Not obvious

7.69 **a** $0.99371 \le \mu \le 1.00597$
b No; the 95% refers to the chance that the true *mean* is included, not to individual values.

7.70 No indication of nonnormality

7.75 **a** $n = 1692$ **b** $n = 863$
c The required n is just about cut in half.

7.76 $.030 \le \pi \le .057, .037 \le \pi \le .066, .076 \le \pi \le .114$, respectively

7.77 All *combinations* of meters don't have the same probability of being sampled; meters in the same sector are either not sampled or all sampled.

7.80 **a** $n = 271$ **b** No; would have to quadruple n

7.81 **a** That only half its customers were satisfied! **b** $n = 174$

7.82 **a** mean 5.52, standard deviation 2.60 **b** $5.174 \le \mu \le 5.873$
c Long run, 95% of such intervals will be correct.

7.83 **a** Right skewed, with outliers **b** No, by Central Limit Theorem

Chapter 8

8.1 **a** The mean waiting time for the whole population of such patients
b $H_0 : \mu \le 30, H_a : \mu > 30$ **c** $z = \frac{\bar{Y}-30}{10/\sqrt{22}} > 1.645$

8.2 $z = 3.7992$; reject H_0

8.3 For $\mu_a = 34, \beta = .4086$

8.4 Violates independence assumption

8.10 **a** $H_0 : \mu \ge 20,000, H_a : \mu < 20,000$ **b** $z = -2.95; p = .0016$

8.11 Statistically significant, but small change

8.12 $t = 3.64 > 1.333$; support H_a.

8.13 $p < .005$; quite strongly supported

8.17 **a** $\bar{d} = 1.8, s_d = 1.988858$ **b** One-tailed $p = .00935$; support H_a.

8.18   **a** $H_0 : \pi = .50$ **b** Two-sided ("mu not = 0.5000")

   c Yes; $p < \alpha$.

8.19   No; p is an index of evidence, not importance.

8.20   Yes; expected frequencies far larger than 5.

8.26   **a** Retain $H_0 : \mu = 4.62$; it's included in the interval.

   b Not significant, but that doesn't prove it's exactly 4.62.

8.27   No, using Central Limit Theorem

8.31   **a** $10,888.9 \le \mu \le 12,871.9$

   b The value 11,260 is well within the interval.

8.32   No; the interval is very wide.

8.33   Yes; increasing trend

8.39   Consumers would be misled only if ratings were too high.

8.40 $z = -2.02$; retain null hypothesis.

8.41 $p = .0434$, two-tailed

8.42   No; retain that value, but that doesn't prove it's true. There's not enough evidence to reject it. In fact, we would reject that value at $\alpha = .05$.

8.43 $24.8 \le \mu \le 28.6$; retain $\mu = 28.2$, but we can only reliably assume that the mean is somewhere in this range.

8.47   **a** $H_a : \mu < 20$; $H_0 : \mu = 20$ or $H_0 : \mu \ge 20$

   b z test, if σ is known

   c $z = -1.52$ which is not less than -1.645; retain null hypothesis.

8.48 $p = .065$

8.49   Right skewed; small n. Probabilities may be incorrect.

8.50 t test also retains H_0.

8.55   **a** $H_0 : \pi = .50$

   b $z = -1.50$ which is not smaller than (more negative than) -1.645

   c No; we have not proved that the null hypothesis is true.

8.56   Yes; expected numbers of wins and losses are each 8, given H_0.

8.67   **a** mean 5.04, median 4, standard deviation 4.02; right skewed data.

   b Right skewed, in any plot

8.68   **a** $t = -1.16$; retain null hypothesis   **b** One-tailed p-value = .126

Review Exercises—Chapters 7–8

R45   **a** $240.4 \le \mu \le 266.2$ **b** No; the plot is a line.

R46   Yes; not included in interval

R47 $z = 4.62 > 2.58$; reject null hypothesis.

R48 $p = .0000$ to four decimal places

R49 $239.6 \le \mu \le 267.0$; p-value .0000; reject null hypothesis.

R50   Yes; not in interval

R51   Median interval is wider, so mean is more efficient. Data are normally distributed.

R62 $.102 \le \pi \le .229$

R63   **a** $n = 590$ **b** $n = 1068$

R64   Yes; expected frequencies are much larger than needed for this purpose.

R65   Biased in favor of large accounts

R66   **a** $5,093 \leq \mu \leq 5,669$

     b Biased sample; skewness is not crucial by Central Limit Theorem.

Chapter 9

9.1   **a** $-1.16 \leq \mu_1 - \mu_2 \leq 0.63$ for the equal–variance analysis, $-1.15 \leq \mu_1 - \mu_2 \leq 0.62$ for the unequal–variance case. Negligible difference

     b No; 0 is contained in the 95% confidence interval.

9.2 $p = .55$ (pooled variance) or $p = .54(t')$

9.3   Equal variance assumption is suspect, but it doesn't matter here.

9.4   **a** Unequal variances and sample sizes; t' should be better in that the claimed α probability should be more accurate.

     b Yes; the frequency for t_{pooled} is seriously wrong.

9.6   **a** POOLED STDEV $= 9.38$ **b** $2.9 \leq \mu_A - \mu_B \leq 24.1$

     c Yes; 0.0 is not in the interval.

9.7 $1.9 \leq \mu_A - \mu_B \leq 25.1$; continue to reject the null hypothesis. t' is slightly preferable with unequal sample sizes and slightly unequal standard deviations; not critical.

9.16 **a** $z = -1.66$; retain null hypothesis.   **b** $p = .0970$

9.17 Yes; data (and presumably populations) are right skewed.

9.18 **a** $t = 4.05, p = .0012 < \alpha$; support the research hypothesis.

     b $1.959 \leq \mu_{\text{diff}} \leq 4.974$; 0 not included

9.19 **a** Test statistic $= 98.0$; $p = .005$; reject H_0.

     b Slightly less conclusive, but both reject H_0

     c Slight left-skewness, but not severe

9.20 $p = .0012(t), p = .005$ (signed rank)

9.21 **a** $t = 0.75, p = .46$; can't come close to rejecting H_0.

     b Yes; tests are much more conclusive.

9.22 $p = .0129 < \alpha = .10$; reject null hypothesis. Omit the 0 difference from the data.

9.31 **a** $t = 0.80, p = .43$ (but two-tailed); can't support H_a

     b Sum of ranks in first sample $= 162$, $z = 0.69$; can't support H_a

9.32 Little evidence; doesn't matter

9.33 For t, the one-tailed $p = .215$; for $z, p = .2451$.

9.34 **a** $t = 3.15$; support research hypothesis

     b $p < .10$ whether one- or two-tailed; support H_a.

9.35 Differences heavy-tailed, suggesting signed rank. Same conclusion either way.

9.36 One-tailed $p = .0046$ $(t), = .0085$ (signed rank)

9.37 Controls for variability **among** plots. Choose plots for full variety of conditions.

9.44 **a** $p = .9256$; not detectable

     b No evidence that *means* differ, but other characteristics still may.

9.45 **a** $p < .00005$ **b** Source 1 is definitely lower in variability.

9.51 **a** Plots slightly right-skewed

b 95% confidence intervals
mu1 - mu2: (-11.3385,-0.567797) assuming equal variances
mu1 - mu2: (-11.3501,-0.556203) not assuming equal variances
In each case, reject the null hypothesis.

c Virtually identical

9.52 **a** $p = .031$ for both tests   **b** $p = .0242$

c Rank sum slightly more conclusive, all believable

Chapter 10

10.4 **a** $.0785 \leq \pi_1 - \pi_2 \leq .1467$ **b** One-tailed test; $z = 6.47$, reject H_0.

10.5 $p \approx .0000$

10.6 $t = 2.30, p = .0218$; support the research hypothesis. We have reasonably strong evidence of a real difference in population proportions.

10.7 $.013 \leq \pi_1 - \pi_2 \leq .167$ does not include .000.

10.10 **a** $z = 1.64$; retain null hypothesis.   **b** Not proved!

10.11 $-.039 \leq \pi_1 - \pi_2 \leq .439$; we are reasonably sure that supplier 1 produces somewhere between 3.9% fewer and 43.9% more passing motors.(!)

10.14 **a** 7.50, 11.25, and 6.25, respectively   **b** $\chi^2 = 4.493$; "good fit" but small n

10.15 **a** $\chi^2 = 44.93$; "bad fit" with bigger n

b Larger n and lower probability of a false negative error

10.18 **a**

	Age				Total
	Under 30	**30-39**	**40-49**	**50 or Over**	
Promoted	16.0	22.4	25.6	16.0	80
Not promoted	34.0	47.6	54.4	34.0	170
Total	50	70	80	50	

b $(r - 1)(c - 1) = 3$

c $\chi^2 = 13.025 > 7.81$; there is evidence of a relation.

10.19 $.001 < p < .005$

10.20 **a** No; χ^2 is very small.

b Combining categories hid the relation.

10.25 $\chi^2 = 72.521 > 20.09$; clear evidence of some relation

10.26 $p < .001$

Chapter 11

11.6 **a** Shown in the output under MEAN and GROUP STD DEV

b Shown under ONE-WAY AOV; df = 2, 33; MS = 93.6535, 14.4790

c $F = 6.47$

d $F >$ table value, 5.3xx; reject H_0

e $p = .0043 < .01$; reject H_0

11.7 **a** Right skew, not normal

b Not too badly, by Central Limit Theorem

11.8 **a** By hand or computer, no evident trend or cycles

b Independence

11.9 **a** Yes; $p = .0007$ **b** Even more conclusive

11.16 **a** No; F is much less than tabled values.
       b Virtually no such evidence

11.17 **a** Right skew   **b** Normality assumption

11.18 Still not conclusive, though better

11.20 Mean for policy 2 differs from means for policies 1 and 3.

11.21 Potential for bias; use a random mechanism.

11.27 **a** Grand mean = 1.4
       b Row effects = .3, .4, -.7 respectively; column effects = .2, 0, -.2, 0 respectively

11.28 $F = 24.67, 1.60, 0.33$ respectively. Only the Plan effect is significant.

11.29 **a** For area 1, plan A has highest mean, then B, then C. For other areas, B highest, then A, then C.
       b Some interaction; profiles aren't parallel.
       c Test says the interaction could have occurred by random variation.

11.30 Plans A and C are significantly different, as are plans B and C. A and B are not.

11.31 **a** No; mixture 1 has a much higher score than mixture 3 at low altitudes, where most people live.
       b Major interaction

11.32 **a** $F = 5.82, p < .001$; significant even for $\alpha = .001$
       b The relative quality of mixtures depends on the altitude.
       c Not very meaningful at all

11.38 **a** Treatments: mixtures. Blocks: investigators.
       b Control for variation among investigators

11.39 **a** Investigator effect not significant; mixture effect highly significant with tiny p-value.
       b Mixture 2 appears to be best (highest); it is clearly different than any other mean, by Tukey's method.

11.40 Not significant. If present, it would indicate systematic differences among investigators, hence some lack of accuracy.

11.51 **a** $F = 23.10$
       b Yes; $F > 5.42$
       c $p = .0000$ (less than .00005)

11.52 **a** chi-square = 18.843   **b** Yes; $p = .0001 < .01$.

11.53 **a** No obvious skewness, no outliers
       b Slight problem of unequal variability (and unequal n's); but the result is very clear.
       c No; same, clear result

11.54 Use a computer package, because of unbalanced sample sizes.

11.55 **a** Irrelevant; we know they differ. $F = 122.58, p < .00005$
       b $F = 10.66$ **c** Yes; $p < .00005$

11.56 The mean for appraiser 2 differs significantly from each of the other means. There are no other significant differences.

11.57 **a** Not close; $F = 0.34; p = .7968$
       b Crucial to control for variation in home prices, which would otherwise mask the appraiser differences

11.67 Yes; $F = 17.08, p = .000 (< .0005)$

11.68 Same result; $H = 28.32$; $p = .000(< .0005)$

11.69 Design 3 appears highest, and is significantly different from each of the other means.

11.73 **a** Right skewness, with several outliers   **b** $F = 1.849, p = .085$

11.74 **a** $H = 15.080, p = .035$

  b Kruskal-Wallis is more conclusive, because less sensitive to skewness and outliers.

Review Exercises—Chapters 9–11

R71 **a** $-11.70 \le \mu_1 - \mu_2 \le 2.90$ **b** No; 0 is included in the interval.

  c Samples are paired by tester, not independent.

R72 **a** $2.15 \le \mu_d \le 6.65$ **b** Yes; 0 is not included in the interval.

  c $t = 3.95 >$ table value $2.0xx$, $p = .0003$ **d** No evident violation

R73 Yes; $p = .001$

R74 Similar; t slightly more conclusive

R75 Pairing helped greatly, by controlling for rater variability.

R85 $F = 0.47 < 3.2$; not close to significant.

R86 $-3.15 \le \mu_1 - \mu_2 \le 4.55$, etc.; no significant differences

R87 Serious interaction; program 1 seems best for experienced preparers.

R93 **a** $-.256 \le \pi_1 - \pi_2 \le .016$ **b** Retain H_0

R94 $z = -1.73$; retain H_0

R95 Violates independence assumption

R96 $\chi^2 = 9.29, p = .0257$

R97 No other evident violations

Chapter 12

12.1 **a** slope $\approx (25 - 16)/6 = 1.5$ **b** slope $\approx (24 - 15)/0.9 = 10$

  c vs. x'

12.2 **a** $\hat{y} = 14.3 + 1.48x$ **b** $s = 1.346$

12.3 **a** $\hat{y} = 14.9 + 10.5\log x$ **b** $s = 1.131$

12.4 Smaller in the logx model, indicating that model fits better

12.14 **a** Linear with slight bend at the high end

  b Two highest-income points have high leverage; outlier from line has high influence.

12.15 **a** $\hat{y} = 47.15048 + 1.80264x$

  b Comparing two purchasers, the one with one thousand dollars per year higher income is predicted to spend 1.80 thousand dollars more on a house. The intercept isn't meaningful; 0 income is not within the data.

  c $s = 14.445$

12.16 Large change; the omitted point was a high-influence outlier.

12.19 **a** Relation linear, one extreme observation, no violations evident

  b $\hat{y} = 99.777 + 51.9179x$; $s_\epsilon = 12.2065$

  c $50.695 \le \beta_1 \le 53.141$

12.20 **a** $t = 88.53$

  b $p = .0000(< .00005)$, two-tailed. One-tailed will also be .0000.

12.21 **a** $F = 7837.26, p = .0000$

 b Identical, because $F = t^2$ in simple regression

12.22 **a** $\hat{y} = 203.613$ **b** $198.902 \le E(Y_{n+1}) \le 208.323$

12.23 No; 2.0 is close to the average of the x data.

12.24 **a** $178.169 \le Y_{n+1} \le 229.057$ **b** Yes; 250 is far above the interval.

12.29 $r_{yx} = .9722$

12.30 **a** $t = 13.138 > 1.812$; reject H_0 **b** Identical

12.32 **a** Variation in intensity accounts for $r_{yx}^2 = (.954)^2 = .914$, or 91.4% of the variation in awareness.

 b Increasing but not linear

12.37 **a** Increasing, linear plot **b** $\hat{y} = 2.0252 + 2.3498x$

 c $\hat{y} = 51.37$

12.38 **a** $s_\epsilon = 1.9583$ **b** All within $\pm 2s_\epsilon$

12.44 **a** Predicted Gallons = 140.074 + 0.61896 Miles

 b $r_{yx}^2 = .9420$, so $r_{yx} = .9706$; 94.2% reduction in prediction error by using Miles

 c No; longer flights obviously take more fuel.

12.45 **a** $\hat{y} = 759.03$; $733.68 \le E(Y_{n+1}) \le 784.38$

 b $678.33 \le Y_{n+1} \le 839.73$; 628 is not in this interval and is exceptionally low.

12.46 $\hat{\beta}_1$ is the usage per mile; $\hat{\beta}_0$ is the initial usage for taking off.

12.52 **a** Negative slope **b** No; slope is positive

12.53 One very high-influence outlier twists the line.

12.54 **a** The point had very high influence. **b** Yes; slope is now negative.

12.55 Changed sign, larger in magnitude

12.59 **a** $r_{yx} = -.7707$

 b $\hat{y} = 141.525 - 12.8926x$. The intercept is the predicted sales for a ZIP code with 0 density (no homes)! An area with 1 extra home per acre is predicted to have sales that are 12.8926 lower.

 c $s_\epsilon = 21.74$; about 95% of ZIP codes will be predicted within ± 43.5.

12.60 **a** $t = -6.63$; highly conclusive **b** $-16.87 \le \beta_1 \le -8.92$

12.61 Evident curve in the plot

12.62 **a** Typical lot size **b** Much nearer to linear **c** $r_{yx} = .9517$

Chapter 13

13.8 **a** $\hat{y} = 50.0195 + 6.64357\text{Cat1} + 7.3145\text{Cat2} - 1.23143\text{Cat1Sq} - .7724\text{Cat1Cat2} - 1.1755\text{Cat2Sq}$

 b SS(Residual) $= 71.489$, $s_\epsilon = 2.25973$

13.9 **a** $R^2 = .8624$

 b SS(Model) would be 305.8078; R^2 would be .5885.

13.10 **a** $F = 22.28$

 b $F > 4.94$, or $p = .0000$; reject H_0

 c $t = 4.842$

 d $p = .000$; support the research hypothesis.

 e Conclude that Promo has additional predictive value, given the other variables.

13.11 As before, $p = .000$, two-tailed

13.12 Only Promo has been shown to have "last predictor in" predictive value.

13.20 **a** $R^2_{y \cdot x_3} = .2049$ **b** $R^2_{y \cdot x_1 x_2 x_3} = .7973$

c $F = 24.84$; reject H_0 that BUSIN and COMPET have no additional predictive value, once INCOME is used.

13.21 $F = \dfrac{(2.65376 - 0.68192)/(3-1)}{0.67461/17} = 24.84$

13.25 $21.788 \leq Y_{n+1} \leq 44.212$. Predicting when w is low but v is high violates the strong positive correlation between them, hence the extrapolation warning.

13.33 **a** $\hat{y} = -16.8198 + 1.47019X1 + 0.994778X2 - 0.0240071X1X2 - 0.01031X2SQ + .000249574X1X2SQ$; $s_\epsilon = 3.39011$

b $t = -1.01$, $p = .3243$; not significant

13.34 **a** Complete model as in 13.33a, reduced model: $\hat{y} = .840085 + 1.01583X1 + .0558262X2$

b Incremental $F = 0.867$, $p > .25$

13.40 **a** $\hat{y} = 18.6784 + .5420\text{Senior} + 1.2074\text{Sex} + 8.7779\text{RankD1} + 4.4211\text{RankD2} + 2.7165\text{RankD3} + 0.9225\text{Doct}$

b All else equal, a male (Sex = 1) is predicted to have a salary 1.2074 thousand dollars higher than a female (Sex = 0).

c All else equal, a full professor (RankD1 = 1) is predicted to have a salary 1.2074 thousand dollars higher than a lecturer (all Rank variables = 0).

13.41 **a** $t = 1.1339$, $p = .1342$ (one-tailed); not significant

b Not proved, *if* men and women have the same seniority, rank, and doctorate levels

13.42 **a** $F = 64.646$

b Implausible; it says that none of the predictors matters to salary.

c $F > 3.71$; $p \approx 0$; reject the implausible hypothesis.

13.43 **a** $R^2 = .9403$ **b** $F = 0.760$; retain the null hypothesis.

13.44 **a** Predicted Salary $= 25.5378 + 0.00389372\text{Employees} + 0.0957243\text{Margin} + 0.216348\text{IPCost}$

b $F = 13.10$, $p \approx 0$. Yes, conclusive

c All of them

13.45 **a** $R^2 = .3842$ **b** $R^2 = .0358$

c $F = 17.82$; strong evidence that these predictors do add predictive value

13.46 Not bad; largest correlation of x values is .5315.

Chapter 14

14.4 **a** Div2 and Div3; we need two dummies to identify the three divisions.

b -4.0066 is the difference in expected sales between division 1 and division 2 for a fixed forecast. 0.9158 is the difference in expected sales between division 1 and division 3 for a fixed forecast.

c $t = 5.67$ for division 2; $t = 1.25$ for division 3. Division 2 dummy has been shown to have predictive value.

14.5 We need regression done without the dummy variables, for a reduced model.

14.6 **a** Forecast value and division are useless predictors.

b $F = 109.468$; $p = 14$ zeros after the decimal. Reject H_0.

14.7 **a** Should be Actual $= 0.0000 + 1.0000$ Forecast. Slope should equal 1.0000.

b $1.18 \leq \beta_1 \leq 1.52$ doesn't include 1.0000.

14.16 **a** No collinearity at all

       b None; the values are completely balanced.

14.17 Nothing severe; perhaps slight nonlinearity vs. CHILL

14.18 **a** By .01 (.914 vs. .904)

       b $F = 1.427$; retain the null hypothesis.

       c No; both p−values are greater than .05.

14.19 **a** REPEL, KNIFE, CHILL, MELT

       b REPEL, KNIFE, CHILL, MELT, SPEED

       c Same

14.20 $F = 3.113 < 3.35$; retain H_0

14.24 **a** As Mileage increases, all else equal, Sales tend to increase. An increase in any of the other variables (holding the remaining ones constant) predicts a decrease in Sales.

       b $s_\epsilon = 47.54$

14.25 **a** Yes; the statistic equals 0.80, much lower than 1.50.

       b Yes; there is a clear cyclic pattern.

14.26 **a** The coefficient of interest rate is still negative but smaller in magnitude. The coefficient of car price became positive but small. (Note that autocorrelation disappeared.)

       b $s_\epsilon = 37.34$

       c It actually decreased. Often it will increase because autocorrelation biases s_ϵ to be too low.

14.37 **a** Installations in previous month, and installations in 4 preceding months

       b No indication of an "it depends" situation

       c Yes; support costs may increase at a decreasing rate as installations increase.

14.38 **a** Yes, large negative ones at months 16 and 17

       b Yes, especially in the early months

14.39 Yes, there is some degree of fan shape.

14.40 **a** BCURRSQ, ACURRSQ, BPREV, APREV, BPREC4, BCURR, ACURR, APREC4

       b .0383 = .9837 - .9454

14.41 **a** Yes; there's a cyclic pattern in the sequence plot.

       b Yes; in the plot vs. fitted values, the plot thickens to the right.

14.42 No. Now it is DACURR, DAPREV, DBCURR, DBPREV, DBCURRSQ, DAPREC4, DACURRSQ, DBPREC4.

14.43 **a** No; no evident cycles in the sequence plot

       b No severe fan shape in the plot vs. fitted values

14.44 **a** $\hat{y} = .52063 + 1.33473(\text{DACURR}) + 1.06333(\text{DAPREV}) + .119333(\text{DAPREC4}) + 2.02548(\text{DBCURR}) + .39634(\text{DBPREV}) + .05833(\text{DBPREC4}) + .00966(\text{DACURRSQ}) - .02003(\text{DBCURRSQ})$

       b $F = 40.09 >$ all table F values with 8 and 20 df. Reject H_0 at all tabled α values.

       c DACURR, DAPREV, DBCURR, and DBPREV

       d $R^2 = .9413$; 94.13% of the variation in changes in support (DSUPP) is accounted for by variation in the eight predictors.

       e SD = 3.35551

14.45 **a** Standard deviation 3.25   **b** A bit smaller

       c Yes; most errors will be predicted with an error less than 7.

14.59 **a** Serious collinearity; all X correlations are bigger than .8.

       b All variables are quantitative; no dummies are needed. The data aren't a time series, so lags are not useful.

    c $\hat{y} = 18.402 + 4.248$ skilled $+ 2.493$ helpers $+ 6.644$ vehicles; $R^2 = .838$.

14.60   **a** Slight fan shape, no other problems.

    b At least one high-leverage, high-influence outlier. There is a suggestion of a curved relation.

    c Data aren't a time series.

14.61   **a** The regression equation predicts the natural logarithm of 'sqft' as $3.013 + 0.390$ log(skilled) $+ 0.206$ log(helpers) $+ 0.252$ log(vehicles).

    b No evident curves

    c Predicted sqft $= e^{3.013}$(skilled)$^{.390}$(helpers)$^{.206}$(vehicles)$^{.252}$

Review Exercises—Chapters 12–14

R105   **a** $\hat{y} = 1,160.693 + 34.562x$

    b Variable direct cost per additional direct labor hour

    c Fixed cost, but an extrapolation

    d $s_\epsilon = 3462.090$

R106 $r_{yx} = .898$; $r^2 = .807$ indicates that variation in labor hours accounts for 80.7% of variation in cost.

R107   **a** STD. ERROR $= 3.524$ **b** $27.19 \leq \beta_1 \leq 41.74$

R108   No; surely labor hours affect cost. Rejct H_0; $t = 9.807$

R109   **a** $\hat{y} = 1,160.693 + 34.562(890) = 31,921$

    b $\hat{y} = 1,160.693 + 34.562(436) = 16,230$

    c The 436 prediction; 890 is an extrapolation.

R110   The constant-variance assumption is shaky. Prediction intervals will be wrong. Tests and intervals may be slightly off.

R118   Severe collinearity among LEADING, RATE, and MONTH. No evident nonlinearity or outliers.

R119   **a** $F = 321.31$, $p = .000 (< .0005)$

    b Reject H_0 for SUPPLY and RATE ($p < .01$) but retain for LEADING (p large).

R120 $s_\epsilon = 0.03594$ is much lower than the SPREAD standard deviation, indicating good predictive value.

R121   **a** Cyclic plot indicates autocorrelation.

    b Durbin-Watson statistic is 0.81, much less than 1.50, indicating autocorrelation.

    c Overoptimism of tests and about predictability

R122   **a** Coefficients changed little.

    b Tests similar; more believable in this model

    c Yes; Durbin-Watson $= 2.00$, the ideal value. Also, the VIF numbers are much smaller, indicating elimination of the collinearity problem.

R123   No evident cycles and no autocorrelation, agreeing with the Durbin-Watson results.

R124   Correlations among independent variables are much lower, confirming the VIF results.

R145   **a** No (linear) relation, contradicting the exercise statement

    b $t = 20.35$, $p = .000$

R146 $s = 2.435$; about 95% of the prediction errors will be within 4.870 in magnitude.

R147   **a** Yes; there's a clear curve in the plot and LOWESS.

    b Nothing far from the pattern

R148   Modestly; R^2 is larger, s_ϵ smaller.

Chapter 15

15.2   **a** $I_2 = 109.2, I_3 = 118.5, I_4 = 128.6$
         b $I_2 = 105.7, I_3 = 112.8, I_4 = 119.0$
         c $I_2 = 107.9, I_3 = 112.3, I_4 = 112.7$

15.3   **a**   Weighted index is consistently lower; largest-quantity categories decreased in price.
         b   Year 4 puts heavier weight on decreasing-price categories.

15.5   Upward trend is clear. Sales peak each September.

15.6   On average, sales are increasing by 0.596 thousand units per month.

15.7   August through October are consistently above trend; February, March, and (usually) April are below. Strong seasonal pattern.

15.8   **a** $101.9 - [100.513 + 0.59629(49)] - (-0.120)$
         b   For example, January's forecast is $100.513 + 0.59629(61) + (-0.120)$

15.9   No obvious cycles

15.18   **b**   The 3-week moving average appears better.

15.19   **b**   The 3-week running median appears better.

15.20   The 3-week running median, on both criteria

15.27   **a**   No sudden dropoffs
         b   Autoregressive with at most one moving average

15.28   The correlograms are nearly identical.

15.29   The sums of squares are nearly identical.

15.38   **a** $I_1 = 107.6, I_2 = 118.8, I_3 = 133.3, I_4 = 147.8, I_5 = 169.5, I_6 = 186.5, I_7 = 207.9$
         b $I_1 = 107.8, I_2 = 119.6, I_3 = 134.2, I_4 = 148.9, I_5 = 170.9, I_6 = 188.0, I_7 = 209.5$
         c   Results are very similar; prices have been increasing similarly.

15.39   **a**   A linear trend   **b**   trend $= 135.204 + 2.559\,t$

15.40   **b**   No; the correlations decrease smoothly.
         c   Autoregressive with 1 or 2 terms

15.41   **a** $\hat{y}_t = 1.401 + .409 y_{t-1},\ \hat{y}_t = 1.205 + .378 y_{t-1} + .108 y_{t-2}$
         b   No; similar results   **c**   AR[1] seems adequate.

15.45   **a**   Slightly decreasing, if any
         b   Slope $= 0.00813$ per week; losing ratings
         c   Losing about $0.00813(52) = 0.4$ ratings points per year

15.46   Mean $= 0.6837$; slightly higher than trend

15.47   **b**   No; they decrease smoothly.   **c**   Similar results for all three

Chapter 16

16.2   Target: all wheelchair-bound people in the state. Frame: Members of the association. Bias: nonmembers excluded.

16.3 $.36 \leq \pi \leq .52$

16.6   Biased in favor of large sales

16.7 $101.27 \leq \mu \leq 123.21$

16.8   Size bias makes confidence interval too high (and possibly too wide).

16.11   **a** $10.23 \leq \mu \leq 10.81$ **b** $9.66 \leq \mu \leq 11.14$

16.12 $10.23 \leq \mu \leq 10.85$; very similar, because strata quite similar

16.17　**a**　mean = 9.567, standard error = 0.340
　　　　b　$8.90 \leq \mu \leq 10.23$　　　　　**c**　Helpful, but still wide

16.18　Total population of clusters has little effect.

16.19　**a**　Sections
　　　　b　mean = 114.4785, standard error = 3.855842
　　　　c　$106.92 \leq \mu \leq 122.04$

16.22　$n = 602$, so 61 per stratum

16.23　**a**　$n = 1135$
　　　　b　Yes, because the within-strata variance is smaller than the overall variance.

16.27　**a**　Cluster sampling　　　　　　　**b**　Save travel time

16.28　**a**　$3.79 \leq \mu \leq 4.87$　　　**b**　$3.73 \leq \mu \leq 4.93$　　　**c**　$n \approx 366$

16.31　**a**　Stratified by type　　　　　**b**　Lower variability within type

16.32　Discard numbers over 8260 and any repetitions; continue until samples of 30 in all types.

16.33　$5.736 \leq \mu \leq 6.524$

16.38　$26.28 \leq \mu \leq 33.37$

16.39　Yes, because the relative weights for the strata changed.

16.42　**a**　$164.48 \leq \mu \leq 200.38$　　　　**b**　$164,480 \leq \tau \leq 200,380$

16.43　No. The relative strata weights don't change and the absolute population size makes little difference.　　■

Index